Lecture Notes in Computer Sc

T0238685

Commenced Publication in 1973
Founding and Former Series Editors:
Gerhard Goos, Juris Hartmanis, and Jan van Leeuw

Advanced Research in Computing and Software Science
Subline of Lectures Notes in Computer Science

Erika Ábrahám   Klaus Havelund (Eds.)

Tools and Algorithms for the Construction and Analysis of Systems

20th International Conference, TACAS 2014
Held as Part of the European Joint Conferences
on Theory and Practice of Software, ETAPS 2014
Grenoble, France, April 5-13, 2014
Proceedings

 Springer

Volume Editors

Erika Ábrahám
RWTH Aachen University
Aachen, Germany
E-mail: abraham@cs.rwth-aachen.de

Klaus Havelund
Jet Propulsion Laboratory
California Institute of Technology
Pasadena, CA, USA
E-mail: klaus.havelund@jpl.nasa.gov

ISSN 0302-9743   e-ISSN 1611-3349
ISBN 978-3-642-54861-1   e-ISBN 978-3-642-54862-8
DOI 10.1007/978-3-642-54862-8
Springer Heidelberg New York Dordrecht London

Library of Congress Control Number: 2014934147

LNCS Sublibrary: SL 1 – Theoretical Computer Science and General Issues

Typesetting: Camera-ready by author, data conversion by Scientific Publishing Services, Chennai, India

Printed on acid-free paper

Springer is part of Springer Science+Business Media (www.springer.com)

Foreword

ETAPS 2014 was the 17th instance of the European Joint Conferences on Theory and Practice of Software. ETAPS is an annual federated conference that was established in 1998, and this year consisted of six constituting conferences (CC, ESOP, FASE, FoSSaCS, TACAS, and POST) including eight invited speakers and two tutorial speakers. Before and after the main conference, numerous satellite workshops took place and attracted many researchers from all over the globe.

ETAPS is a confederation of several conferences, each with its own Program Committee (PC) and its own Steering Committee (if any). The conferences cover various aspects of software systems, ranging from theoretical foundations to programming language developments, compiler advancements, analysis tools, formal approaches to software engineering, and security. Organizing these conferences in a coherent, highly synchronized conference program, enables the participation in an exciting event, having the possibility to meet many researchers working in different directions in the field, and to easily attend the talks of different conferences.

The six main conferences together received 606 submissions this year, 155 of which were accepted (including 12 tool demonstration papers), yielding an overall acceptance rate of 25.6%. I thank all authors for their interest in ETAPS, all reviewers for the peer reviewing process, the PC members for their involvement, and in particular the PC co-chairs for running this entire intensive process. Last but not least, my congratulations to all authors of the accepted papers!

ETAPS 2014 was greatly enriched by the invited talks of Geoffrey Smith (Florida International University, USA) and John Launchbury (Galois, USA), both unifying speakers, and the conference-specific invited speakers (CC) Benoît Dupont de Dinechin (Kalray, France), (ESOP) Maurice Herlihy (Brown University, USA), (FASE) Christel Baier (Technical University of Dresden, Germany), (FoSSaCS) Petr Jančar (Technical University of Ostrava, Czech Republic), (POST) David Mazières (Stanford University, USA), and finally (TACAS) Orna Kupferman (Hebrew University Jerusalem, Israel). Invited tutorials were provided by Bernd Finkbeiner (Saarland University, Germany) and Andy Gordon (Microsoft Research, Cambridge, UK). My sincere thanks to all these speakers for their great contributions.

For the first time in its history, ETAPS returned to a city where it had been organized before: Grenoble, France. ETAPS 2014 was organized by the Université Joseph Fourier in cooperation with the following associations and societies: ETAPS e.V., EATCS (European Association for Theoretical Computer Science), EAPLS (European Association for Programming Languages and Systems), and EASST (European Association of Software Science and Technology). It had support from the following sponsors: CNRS, Inria, Grenoble INP, PERSYVAL-Lab, Université Joseph Fourier, and Springer-Verlag.

The organization team comprised:

General Chair: Saddek Bensalem
Conferences Chair: Alain Girault and Yassine Lakhnech
Workshops Chair: Axel Legay
Publicity Chair: Yliès Falcone
Treasurer: Nicolas Halbwachs
Webmaster: Marius Bozga

The overall planning for ETAPS is the responsibility of the Steering Committee (SC). The ETAPS SC consists of an executive board (EB) and representatives of the individual ETAPS conferences, as well as representatives of EATCS, EAPLS, and EASST. The Executive Board comprises Gilles Barthe (satellite events, Madrid), Holger Hermanns (Saarbrücken), Joost-Pieter Katoen (chair, Aachen and Twente), Gerald Lüttgen (treasurer, Bamberg), and Tarmo Uustalu (publicity, Tallinn). Other current SC members are: Martín Abadi (Santa Cruz and Mountain View), Erika Ábrahám (Aachen), Roberto Amadio (Paris), Christel Baier (Dresden), Saddek Bensalem (Grenoble), Giuseppe Castagna (Paris), Albert Cohen (Paris), Alexander Egyed (Linz), Riccardo Focardi (Venice), Björn Franke (Edinburgh), Stefania Gnesi (Pisa), Klaus Havelund (Pasadena), Reiko Heckel (Leicester), Paul Klint (Amsterdam), Jens Knoop (Vienna), Steve Kremer (Nancy), Pasquale Malacaria (London), Tiziana Margaria (Potsdam), Fabio Martinelli (Pisa), Andrew Myers (Boston), Anca Muscholl (Bordeaux), Catuscia Palamidessi (Palaiseau), Andrew Pitts (Cambridge), Arend Rensink (Twente), Don Sanella (Edinburgh), Vladimiro Sassone (Southampton), Ina Schäfer (Braunschweig), Zhong Shao (New Haven), Gabriele Taentzer (Marburg), Cesare Tinelli (Iowa), Jan Vitek (West Lafayette), and Lenore Zuck (Chicago).

I sincerely thank all ETAPS SC members for all their hard work in making the 17th ETAPS a success. Moreover, thanks to all speakers, attendants, organizers of the satellite workshops, and Springer for their support. Finally, many thanks to Saddek Bensalem and his local organization team for all their efforts enabling ETAPS to return to the French Alps in Grenoble!

January 2014   Joost-Pieter Katoen

Preface

This volume contains the proceedings of TACAS 2014: the 20th International Conference on Tools and Algorithms for the Construction and Analysis of Systems. TACAS 2014 took place during April 7–11, 2014, in Grenoble, France. It was part of ETAPS 2014: the 17th European Joint Conferences on Theory and Practice of Software.

TACAS is a forum for researchers, developers, and users interested in rigorously based tools and algorithms for the construction and analysis of systems. The research areas covered by TACAS include, but are not limited to, formal methods, software and hardware specification and verification, static analysis, dynamic analysis, model checking, theorem proving, decision procedures, real-time, hybrid and stochastic systems, communication protocols, programming languages, and software engineering. TACAS provides a venue where common problems, heuristics, algorithms, data structures, and methodologies in these areas can be discussed and explored.

TACAS 2014 solicited four kinds of papers, including three types of full-length papers (15 pages), as well as short tool demonstration papers (6 pages):

- Research papers – papers describing novel research.
- Case study papers – papers reporting on case studies (preferably in a "real life" setting), describing methodologies and approaches used.
- Regular tool papers – papers describing a tool, and focusing on engineering aspects of the tool, including, e.g., software architecture, data structures, and algorithms.
- Tool demonstration papers – papers focusing on the usage aspects of tools.

This year TACAS attracted a total of 161 paper submissions, divided into 117 research papers, 11 case study papers, 18 regular tool papers, and 15 tool demonstration papers. Each submission was refereed by at least three reviewers. Papers by PC members were refereed by four reviewers. 42 papers were accepted for presentation at the conference: 26 research papers, 3 case study papers, 6 regular tool papers, and 7 tool demonstration papers. This yields an overall acceptance rate of 26.1 %. The acceptance rate for full papers (research + case study + regular tool) was 24.0 %.

TACAS 2014 also hosted the Competition on Software Verification again, in its third edition. This volume includes an overview of the competition results, and short papers describing 11 of the 15 tools that participated in the competition. These papers were reviewed by a separate Program Committee, and each included paper was refereed by at least four reviewers. The competition was organized by Dirk Beyer, the Competition Chair. A session in the TACAS program was reserved for presenting the results (by the Chair) and the participating verifiers (by the developer teams).

In addition to refereed contributions, the program included an invited talk by Orna Kupferman. TACAS took place in an exciting and vibrant scientific atmosphere, jointly with five other sister conferences (CC, ESOP, FASE, FoSSaCS, and POST), with related scientific fields of interest, their invited speakers, and the ETAPS unifying speakers Geoffrey Smith and John Launchbury.

We would like to thank all of the authors who submitted papers to TACAS 2014, the Program Committee members, and additional reviewers, without whom TACAS would not be a success. Nikolaj Bjørner provided invaluable help as TACAS Tool Chair, and Dirk Beyer as the Chair of the Competition on Software Verification. We thank the competition teams for participating and show-casing their tools to the TACAS community. We benefited greatly from the EasyChair conference management system, which we used to handle the submission, review, discussion, and proceedings preparation processes. Finally, we would like to thank the TACAS Steering Committee, the ETAPS Steering Committee, and the ETAPS Organizing Committee chaired by Saddek Bensalem.

January 2014   Erika Ábrahám
                                                                         Klaus Havelund

Organization

Steering Committee

Rance Cleaveland	University of Maryland, USA
Holger Hermanns	Saarland University, Germany
Kim Guldstrand Larsen	Aalborg University, Denmark
Bernhard Steffen	TU Dortmund, Germany
Lenore Zuck	University of Illinois at Chicago, USA

Program Committee

Erika Ábrahám	RWTH Aachen University, Germany (Co-chair)
Christel Baier	Technische Universität Dresden, Germany
Saddek Bensalem	Verimag/UJF, France
Nathalie Bertrand	Inria/IRISA, France
Armin Biere	Johannes Kepler University, Austria
Nikolaj Bjørner	Microsoft Research, USA (Tool Chair)
Alessandro Cimatti	Fondazione Bruno Kessler, Italy
Rance Cleaveland	University of Maryland, USA
Cindy Eisner	IBM Research - Haifa, Israel
Martin Fränzle	Carl von Ossietzky University Oldenburg, Germany
Patrice Godefroid	Microsoft Research, Redmond, USA
Susanne Graf	Verimag, France
Orna Grumberg	Technion, Israel
Klaus Havelund	NASA/JPL, USA (Co-chair)
Boudewijn Haverkort	University of Twente, The Netherlands
Gerard Holzmann	NASA/JPL, USA
Barbara Jobstmann	Verimag/CNRS, France and EPFL, Switzerland
Joost-Pieter Katoen	RWTH Aachen University, Germany and University of Twente, The Netherlands
Kim Guldstrand Larsen	Aalborg University, Denmark
Roland Meyer	TU Kaiserslautern, Germany
Corina Pasareanu	NASA Ames Research Center, USA
Doron Peled	Bar Ilan University, Israel
Paul Pettersson	Mälardalen University, Sweden
Nir Piterman	University of Leicester, UK
Jaco van de Pol	University of Twente, The Netherlands
Sriram Sankaranarayanan	University of Colorado Boulder, USA
Natasha Sharygina	Università della Svizzera Italiana, Switzerland

Scott Smolka	Stony Brook University, USA
Bernhard Steffen	TU Dortmund, Germany
Mariëlle Stoelinga	University of Twente, The Netherlands
Cesare Tinelli	The University of Iowa, USA
Frits Vaandrager	Radboud University Nijmegen, The Netherlands
Willem Visser	University of Stellenbosch, South Africa
Ralf Wimmer	University of Freiburg, Germany
Lenore Zuck	University of Illinois at Chicago, USA

Program Committee for SV-COMP 2014

Aws Albarghouthi	University of Toronto, Canada
Dirk Beyer	University of Passau, Germany (Competition Chair)
Lucas Cordeiro	Federal University of Amazonas, Brazil
Stephan Falke	Karlsruhe Institute of Technology, Germany
Bernd Fischer	Stellenbosch University, South Africa
Arie Gurfinkel	SEI, USA
Matthias Heizmann	University of Freiburg, Germany
Stefan Löwe	University of Passau, Germany
Petr Muller	Brno University of Technology, Czech Republic
Vadim Mutilin	Russian Academy of Sciences, Russia
Alexander Nutz	University of Freiburg, Germany
Gennaro Parlato	University of Southampton, UK
Corneliu Popeea	TU Munich, Germany
Jiri Slaby	Masaryk University at Brno, Czech Republic
Michael Tautschnig	Queen Mary University of London, UK
Tomáš Vojnar	Brno University of Technology, Czech Republic

Additional Reviewers

Aarts, Fides	Badouel, Eric	Corbineau, Pierre
Abd Elkader, Karam	Balasubramanian,	Corzilius, Florian
Afzal, Wasif	Daniel	Csallner, Christoph
Alberti, Francesco	Bernardo, Marco	D'Ippolito, Nicolas
Aleksandrowicz, Gadi	Bollig, Benedikt	Dalsgaard, Andreas
Alt, Leonardo	Bortolussi, Luca	Engelbredt
Andres, Miguel	Bouajjani, Ahmed	Dang, Thao
Arbel, Eli	Bozga, Marius	David, Alexandre
Arenas, Puri	Bozzano, Marco	de Paula, Flavio M.
Aştefănoaei, Lacramioara	Bradley, Aaron	de Ruiter, Joeri
Aucher, Guillaume	Bruintjes, Harold	Defrancisco, Richard
Bacci, Giorgio	Chakraborty, Souymodip	Dehnert, Christian
Bacci, Giovanni	Chen, Xin	Derevenetc, Egor

Doganay, Kivanc
Dubslaff, Clemens
Dutertre, Bruno
Eggers, Andreas
Ellen, Christian
Enea, Constantin
Enoiu, Eduard Paul
Estievenart, Morgane
Fabre, Eric
Fedyukovich, Grigory
Feiten, Linus
Ferrere, Thomas
Filieri, Antonio
Fournier, Paulin
Frehse, Goran
Frias, Marcelo
Fu, Hongfei
Gao, Yang
Gario, Marco
Giesl, Jürgen
Girard, Antoine
Goessler, Gregor
Gopalakrishnan, Ganesh
Gretz, Friedrich
Griggio, Alberto
Groote, Jan Friso
Guck, Dennis
Haddad, Serge
Hahn, Ernst Moritz
Hatvani, Leo
Helouet, Loic
Herbreteau, Frederic
Hommersom, Arjen
Howar, Falk
Hyvärinen, Antti
Höfner, Peter
Hölzenspies, Philip
Isberner, Malte
Ivrii, Alexander
Jacobs, Bart
Jacobs, Swen
Jansen, Christina
Jansen, David
Jansen, David N.
Jansen, Nils

Johnsen, Andreas
Jéron, Thierry
Kant, Gijs
Klüppelholz, Sascha
Kneuss, Etienne
Komuravelli, Anvesh
Kordy, Barbara
Kuncak, Viktor
Kupferschmid, Stefan
Laarman, Alfons
Lafourcade, Pascal
Lamprecht, Anna-Lena
Leucker, Martin
Löding, Christof
Luckow, Kasper
Mahdi, Ahmed
Majumdar, Rupak
Maler, Oded
Marin, Paolo
Marinescu, Raluca
McMillan, Kenneth
Meller, Yael
Menet, Quentin
Micheli, Andrea
Monniaux, David
Mooij, Arjan
Mostowski, Wojciech
Mousavi, Mohammad
    Reza
Mover, Sergio
Naujokat, Stefan
Nellen, Johanna
Neubauer, Johannes
Nevo, Ziv
Nguyen, Viet Yen
Noll, Thomas
Olesen, Mads Chr.
Parker, David
Payet, Etienne
Pidan, Dmitry
Poplavko, Peter
Poulsen, Danny Bøgsted
Prochnow, Steffen
Puch, Stefan
Quilbeuf, Jean

Ranise, Silvio
Reimer, Sven
Remke, Anne
Rojas, Jose
Rollini, Simone Fulvio
Roveri, Marco
Rozier, Kristin Yvonne
Ruah, Sitvanit
Rungta, Neha
Rydhof Hansen, Rene
Rüthing, Oliver
Sadre, Ramin
Sanchez, Cesar
Sangnier, Arnaud
Sankur, Ocan
Sauer, Matthias
Scheibler, Karsten
Schivo, Stefano
Schupp, Stefan
Schwabe, Peter
Seidl, Martina
Shacham, Ohad
Sharma, Arpit
She, Zhikun
Sheinvald, Sarai
Shoham, Sharon
Sosnovich, Adi
Sproston, Jeremy
Srba, Jiri
Srivathsan, Balaguru
Steffen, Martin
Sticksel, Christoph
Suryadevara, Jagadish
Swaminathan, Mani
Sznajder, Nathalie
Te Brinke, Steven
Timmer, Judith
Timmer, Mark
Tkachuk, Oksana
Tonetta, Stefano
Trivedi, Ashutosh
Tzoref-Brill, Rachel
van den Broek, Pim
van der Pol, Kevin
Verriet, Jacques

Vizel, Yakir
Volpato, Michele
von Essen, Christian
von Styp, Sabrina
Weissenbacher, Georg
Widmer, Gerhard

Windmüller, Stephan
Xue, Bingtian
Yan, Rongjie
Yang, Junxing
Yorav, Karen
Zalinescu, Eugen

Zarzani, Niko
Zimmermann, Martin
Zuliani, Paolo

Additional Reviewers for SV-COMP 2014

Andrianov, Pavel
Dudka, Kamil

Inverso, Omar
Mandrykin, Mikhail

Peringer, Petr
Tomasco, Ermenegildo

Table of Contents

Modeling and Model Checking Discrete Systems

Timed and Hybrid Systems

Monitoring, Fault Detection and Identification

Competition on Software Verification

Specifying and Checking Linear Time Properties

Synthesis and Learning

Quantum and Probabilistic Systems

Tool Demonstrations

Case Studies

Variations on Safety

Orna Kupferman

Hebrew University, School of Engineering and Computer Science, Jerusalem 91904, Israel
orna@cs.huji.ac.il

Abstract. Of special interest in formal verification are *safety* properties, which assert that the system always stays within some allowed region, in which nothing "bad" happens. Equivalently, a property is a safety property if every violation of it occurs after a finite execution of the system. Thus, a computation violates the property if it has a "bad prefix", all whose extensions violate the property. The theoretical properties of safety properties as well as their practical advantages with respect to general properties have been widely studied. The paper surveys several extensions and variations of safety. We start with *bounded* and *checkable* properties – fragments of safety properties that enable an even simpler reasoning. We proceed to a *reactive* setting, where safety properties require the system to stay in a region of states that is both allowed and from which the environment cannot force it out. Finally, we describe a probability-based approach for defining different levels of safety.

1 Introduction

Today's rapid development of complex and safety-critical systems requires reliable verification methods. In formal verification, we verify that a system meets a desired property by checking that a mathematical model of the system meets a formal specification that describes the property. Of special interest are properties asserting that the observed behavior of the system always stays within some allowed region, in which nothing "bad" happens. For example, we may want to assert that every message sent is acknowledged in the next cycle. Such properties of systems are called *safety properties*. Intuitively, a property ψ is a safety property if every violation of ψ occurs after a finite execution of the system. In our example, if in a computation of the system a message is sent without being acknowledged in the next cycle, this occurs after some finite execution of the system. Also, once this violation occurs, there is no way to "fix" the computation.

In order to formally define what safety properties are, we refer to computations of a nonterminating system as infinite words over an alphabet Σ. Consider a language L of infinite words over Σ. A finite word x over Σ is a *bad prefix* for L iff for all infinite words y over Σ, the concatenation $x \cdot y$ of x and y is not in L. Thus, a bad prefix for L is a finite word that cannot be extended to an infinite word in L. A language L is a *safety language* if every word not in L has a finite bad prefix. For example, if $\Sigma = \{0, 1\}$, then $L = \{0^\omega, 1^\omega\}$ is a safety language. Indeed, every word not in L contains either the sequence 01 or the sequence 10, and a prefix that ends in one of these sequences cannot be extended to a word in L. [1].

---

[1] The definition of safety we consider here is given in [1,2], it coincides with the definition of limit closure defined in [12], and is different from the definition in [26], which also refers to the property being closed under stuttering.

E. Ábrahám and K. Havelund (Eds.): TACAS 2014, LNCS 8413, pp. 1–14, 2014.

The interest in safety started with the quest for natural classes of specifications. The theoretical aspects of safety have been extensively studied [2,28,29,33]. With the growing success and use of formal verification, safety has turned out to be interesting also from a practical point of view [14,20,23]. Indeed, the ability to reason about finite prefixes significantly simplifies both enumerative and symbolic algorithms. In the first, safety circumvents the need to reason about complex ω-regular acceptance conditions. For example, methods for temporal synthesis, program repair, or parametric reasoning are much simpler for safety properties [18,32]. In the second, it circumvents the need to reason about cycles, which is significant in both BDD-based and SAT-based methods [5,6]. In addition to a rich literature on safety, researchers have studied additional classes, such as liveness and co-safety properties [2,28].

The paper surveys several extensions and variations of safety. We start with *bounded* and *checkable* properties – fragments of safety properties that enable an even simpler reasoning. We proceed to a *reactive* setting, where safety properties require the system to stay in a region of states that is both allowed and from which the environment cannot force it out. Finally, we describe a probability-based approach for defining different levels of safety. The survey is based on the papers [24], with Moshe Y. Vardi, [21], with Yoad Lustig and Moshe Y. Vardi, [25], with Sigal Weiner, and [10], with Shoham Ben-David.

2   Preliminaries

Safety and Co-Safety Languages. Given an alphabet Σ, a *word over* Σ is a (possibly infinite) sequence $w = \sigma_0 \cdot \sigma_1 \cdots$ of letters in Σ. Consider a language $L \subseteq \Sigma^\omega$ of infinite words. A finite word $x \in \Sigma^*$ is a *bad prefix* for L iff for all $y \in \Sigma^\omega$, we have $x \cdot y \notin L$. Thus, a bad prefix is a finite word that cannot be extended to an infinite word in L. Note that if x is a bad prefix, then all the finite extensions of x are also bad prefixes. A language L is a *safety* language iff every infinite word $w \notin L$ has a finite bad prefix. For a safety language L, we denote by *bad-pref*(L) the set of all bad prefixes for L.

For a language $L \subseteq \Sigma^\omega$, we use *comp*$(L)$ to denote the complement of L; i.e., *comp*$(L) = \Sigma^\omega \setminus L$. A language $L \subseteq \Sigma^\omega$ is a *co-safety* language iff *comp*(L) is a safety language. (The term used in [28] is *guarantee* language.) Equivalently, L is co-safety iff every infinite word $w \in L$ has a *good prefix* $x \in \Sigma^*$: for all $y \in \Sigma^\omega$, we have $x \cdot y \in L$. For a co-safety language L, we denote by *good-pref*(L) the set of good prefixes for L. Note that for a safety language L, we have that *good-pref*$(comp(L)) = bad$-*pref*(L).

Word Automata. A *nondeterministic Büchi word automaton* (NBW, for short) is $\mathcal{A} = \langle \Sigma, Q, \delta, Q_0, F \rangle$, where Σ is the input alphabet, Q is a finite set of states, $\delta : Q \times \Sigma \to 2^Q$ is a transition function, $Q_0 \subseteq Q$ is a set of initial states, and $F \subseteq Q$ is a set of accepting states. If $|Q_0| = 1$ and δ is such that for every $q \in Q$ and $\sigma \in \Sigma$, we have that $|\delta(q,\sigma)| \leq 1$, then $\mathcal{A}$ is a *deterministic* Büchi word automaton (DBW, for short).

Given an input word $w = \sigma_0 \cdot \sigma_1 \cdots$ in Σ^ω, a *run* of $\mathcal{A}$ on w is a sequence $r_0, r_1, \ldots$ of states in Q such that $r_0 \in Q_0$ and for every $i \geq 0$, we have $r_{i+1} \in \delta(r_i, \sigma_i)$. For a run r, let *inf*(r) denote the set of states that r visits infinitely often. That is,

$inf(r) = \{q \in Q \ : \ r_i = q \text{ for infinitely many } i \geq 0\}$. As Q is finite, it is guaranteed that $inf(r) \neq \emptyset$. The run r is *accepting* iff $inf(r) \cap F \neq \emptyset$. That is, iff there exists a state in F that r visits infinitely often. A run that is not accepting is *rejecting*. When $\alpha = Q$, we say that $\mathcal{A}$ is a *looping* automaton. We use NLW and DLW to denote non-deterministic and deterministic lopping automata. An NBW $\mathcal{A}$ accepts an input word w iff there exists an accepting run of $\mathcal{A}$ on w. The *language* of an NBW $\mathcal{A}$, denoted $\mathcal{L}(\mathcal{A})$, is the set of words that $\mathcal{A}$ accepts. We assume that a given NBW $\mathcal{A}$ has no empty states, except maybe the initial state (that is, at least one word is accepted from each state – otherwise we can remove the state).

Linear Temporal Logic. The logic *LTL* is a linear temporal logic. Formulas of LTL are constructed from a set AP of atomic propositions using the usual Boolean operators and the temporal operators G ("always"), F ("eventually"), X ("next time"), and U ("until"). Formulas of LTL describe computations of systems over AP. For example, the LTL formula $G(req \rightarrow Fack)$ describes computations in which every position in which req holds is eventually followed by a position in which ack holds. Thus, each LTL formula ψ corresponds to a language, denoted $||\psi||$, of words in $(2^{AP})^\omega$ that satisfy it. For the detailed syntax and semantics of LTL, see [30]. The *model-checking problem* for LTL is to determine, given an LTL formula ψ and a system M, whether all the computations of M satisfy ψ.

General methods for LTL model checking are based on translation of LTL formulas to nondeterministic Büchi word automata. By [36], given an LTL formula ψ, one can construct an NBW $\mathcal{A}_\psi$ over the alphabet 2^{AP} that accepts exactly all the computations that satisfy ψ. The size of $\mathcal{A}_\psi$ is, in the worst case, exponential in the length of ψ.

Given a system M and an LTL formula ψ, model checking of M with respect to ψ is reduced to checking the emptiness of the product of M and $\mathcal{A}_{\neg\psi}$ [36]. This check can be performed on-the-fly and symbolically [7,35], and the complexity of model checking that follows is PSPACE, with a matching lower bound [34].

It is shown in [2,33,22] that when ψ is a safety formula, we can assume that all the states in $\mathcal{A}_\psi$ are accepting. Indeed, $\mathcal{A}_\psi$ accepts exactly all words all of whose prefixes have at least one extension accepted by $\mathcal{A}_\psi$, which is what we get if we define all the states of $\mathcal{A}_\psi$ to be accepting. Thus, safety properties can be recognized by NLWs. Since every NLW can be determined to an equivalent DLW by applying the subset construction, all safety formulas can be translated to DLWs.

3 Interesting Fragments

In this section we discuss two interesting fragments of safety properties: *clopen* (a.k.a. bounded) properties, which are useful in bounded model checking, and *checkable* properties, which are useful in real-time monitoring.

3.1 Clopen Properties

Bounded model checking methodologies check the correctness of a system with respect to a given specification by examining computations of a bounded length. Results from set-theoretic topology imply that sets in Σ^ω that are both open and closed (*clopen sets*) are bounded: membership in a clopen set can be determined by examining a bounded number of letters in Σ.

In [24] we studied safety properties from a topological point of view. We showed that clopen sets correspond to properties that are both safety and co-safety, and show that when clopen specifications are given by automata or LTL formulas, we can point to a bound and translate the specification to bounded formalisms such as bounded LTL and cycle-free automata.

Topology. Consider a set X and a distance function $d : X \times X \to \mathbb{R}$ between the elements of X. For an element $x \in X$ and $\gamma \geq 0$, let $K(x, \gamma)$ be the set of elements x' such that $d(x, x') \leq \gamma$. Consider a set $S \subseteq X$. An element $x \in S$ is called an *interior element* of S if there is $\gamma > 0$ such that $K(x, \gamma) \subseteq S$. The set S is *open* if all the elements in S are interior. A set S is *closed* if $X \setminus S$ is open. So, a set S is open if every element in S has a nonempty "neighborhood" contained in S, and a set S is closed if every element not in S has a nonempty neighborhood whose intersection with S is empty. A set that is both open and close is called a *clopen* set.

A *Cantor space* consists of $X = D^\omega$, for some finite set D, and d defined by $d(w, w') = \frac{1}{2^n}$, where n is the first position where w and w' differ. Thus, elements of X can be viewed as infinite words over D and two words are close to each other if they have a long common prefix. If $w = w'$, then $d(w, w') = 0$. It is known that clopen sets in Cantor space are *bounded*, where a set S is bounded if it is of the form $W \cdot D^\omega$ for some finite set $W \subseteq D^*$. Hence, clopen sets in our Cantor space correspond exactly to bounded properties: each clopen language $L \subseteq \Sigma^\omega$ has a bound $k \geq 0$ such that membership in L can be determined by the prefixes of length k of words in Σ^ω.

It is not hard to see that a language $L \subseteq \Sigma^\omega$ is co-safety iff L is an open set in our Cantor space [27,17]. To see this, consider a word w in a co-safety language L, and let x be a good prefix of w. All the words w' with $d(w, w') \leq \frac{1}{2^{|x|}}$ have x as their prefix, so they all belong to L. For the second direction, consider a word w in an open set L, and let $\gamma > 0$ be such that $K(w, \gamma) \subseteq L$. The prefix of w of length $\lfloor \log \frac{1}{\gamma} \rfloor$ is a good prefix for L. It follows that the clopen sets in Σ^ω are exactly these properties that are both safety and co-safety!

Bounding Clopen Properties. Our goal in this section is to identify a bound for a clopen property given by an automaton. Consider a clopen language $L \subseteq \Sigma^\omega$. For a finite word $x \in \Sigma^*$, we say that x is *undetermined* with respect to L if there are $y \in \Sigma^\omega$ and $z \in \Sigma^\omega$ such that $x \cdot y \in L$ and $x \cdot z \notin L$. As shown in [24], every word in Σ^ω has only finitely many prefixes that are undetermined with respect to L. It follows that L is *bounded*: there are only finitely many words in Σ^* that are undetermined with respect to L. For an integer k, we say that L is *bounded by k* if all the words $x \in \Sigma^*$ such that $|x| \geq k$ are determined with respect to L. Moreover, since L is bounded, then a minimal DLW that recognizes L must be cycle free. Indeed, otherwise we can pump a cycle to infinitely many undetermined prefixes. Let $diameter(L)$ be the diameter of the minimal DLW for L.

Lemma 1. *A clopen ω-regular language $L \subseteq \Sigma^\omega$ is bounded by $diameter(L)$.*

Proof: Let $\mathcal{A}$ be the minimal deterministic looping automaton for L. Consider a word $x \in \Sigma^*$ with $|x| \geq diameter(L)$. Since $\mathcal{A}$ is cycle free, its run on x either reaches an accepting sink, in which case x is a good prefix, or it does not reach an accepting sink, in which case, by the definition of $diameter(\mathcal{A})$, we cannot extend x to a word accepted by $\mathcal{A}$, thus x is a bad prefix. $\qquad\square$

For a language L, the *in index* of L, denoted $inindex(L)$, is the minimal number of states that an NBW recognizing L has. Similarly, the *out index* of L, denoted $outindex(L)$, is the minimal number of states that an NBW recognizing $comp(L)$ has.

Lemma 2. *A clopen ω-regular language $L \subseteq \Sigma^\omega$ is bounded by $inindex(L) \cdot outindex(L)$.*

Proof: Assume by way of contradiction that there is a word $x \in \Sigma^*$ such that $|x| \geq inindex(L) \cdot outindex(L)$ and x is undetermined with respect to L. Thus, there are suffixes y and z such that $x \cdot y \in L$ and $x \cdot z \notin L$. Let $\mathcal{A}_1$ and $\mathcal{A}_2$ be nondeterministic looping automata such that $\mathcal{L}(\mathcal{A}_1) = L$, $\mathcal{L}(\mathcal{A}_2) = comp(L)$, and $\mathcal{A}_1$ and $\mathcal{A}_2$ have $inindex(L)$ and $outindex(L)$ states, respectively. Consider two accepting runs r_1 and r_2 of $\mathcal{A}_1$ and $\mathcal{A}_2$ on $x \cdot y$ and $x \cdot z$, respectively. Since $|x| \geq inindex(L) \cdot outindex(L)$, there are two prefixes $x[1, \ldots, i]$ and $x[1, \ldots, j]$ of x such that $i < j$ and both runs repeat their state after these two prefixes; i.e., $r_1(i) = r_1(j)$ and $r_2(i) = r_2(j)$. Consider the word $x' = x[1, \ldots, i] \cdot x[i+1, \ldots, j]^\omega$. Since $\mathcal{A}_1$ is a looping automaton, the run r_1 induces an accepting run r_1' of $\mathcal{A}_1$ on x'. Formally, for all $l \leq i$ we have $r_1'(l) = r_1(l)$ and for all $l > i$, we have $r_1'(l) = r_1(i + ((l - i)\bmod(j - i)))$. Similarly, the run r_2 induces an accepting run of $\mathcal{A}_2$ on x'. It follows that x' is accepted by both $\mathcal{A}_1$ and $\mathcal{A}_2$, contradicting the fact that $\mathcal{L}(\mathcal{A}_2) = comp(\mathcal{L}(\mathcal{A}_1))$. $\qquad\square$

3.2 Checkable Properties

For an integer $k \geq 1$, a language $L \subseteq \Sigma^\omega$ is *k-checkable* if there is a language $R \subseteq \Sigma^k$ (of "allowed subwords") such that a word w belongs to L iff all the subwords of w of length k belong to R. A property is locally checkable if its language is k-checkable for some k. Locally checkable properties, which are a special case of safety properties, are common in the specification of systems. In particular, one can often bound an eventuality constraint in a property by a fixed time frame, which results in a checkable property.

The practical importance of locally checkable properties lies in the low memory demand for their run-time verification. Indeed, k-checkable properties can be verified with a bounded memory – one that has access only to the last k-computation cycles. Run-time verification of a property amounts to executing a monitor together with the system allowing the detection of errors in run time [20,3,9]. Run-time monitors for checkable specifications have low memory demand. Furthermore, in the case of general ω-regular properties, when several properties are checked, we need a monitor for each property, and since the properties are independent of each other, so are the state spaces of the monitors. Thus, the memory demand (as well as the resources needed to maintain the memory) grow linearly with the number of properties monitored. Such a memory demand is a real problem in practice. In contrast, as shown in [21], a monitor for a k-checkable property needs only a record of the last k computation cycles. Furthermore, even if a large number of k-checkable properties are monitored, the monitors can share their memory, resulting in memory demand of $|\Sigma|^k$, which is independant of the number of properties monitored.

As in the case of clopen properties, our goal is to identify a bound for a checkable property given by an automaton. We first need some notations. For a word $w \in \Sigma^\omega$ and $k \geq 0$, we denote by $sub(w,k)$ the set of finite subwords of w of length k, formally, $sub(w,k) = \{y \in \Sigma^* : |y| = k$ and there exist $x \in \Sigma^*$ and $z \in \Sigma^\omega$ such that $w = xyz\}$. A language $L \subseteq \Sigma^\omega$ is k-checkable if there exists a finite language $R \subseteq \Sigma^k$ such that $w \in L$ iff all the k-long subwords of w are in R. That is, $L = \{w \in \Sigma^\omega : sub(w,k) \subseteq R\}$. A language $L \subseteq \Sigma^\omega$ is k-co-checkable if there exists a finite language $R \subseteq \Sigma^k$ such that $w \in L$ iff there exists a k-long subword of w that is in R. That is, $L = \{w \in \Sigma^\omega : sub(w,k) \cap R \neq \emptyset\}$. A language is checkable (co-checkable) if it is k-checkable (k-co-checkable, respectively) for some k. We refer to k as the width of L. It is easy to to see that all checkable languages are safety, and similarly for co-checkable and co-safety. In particular, L is a checkable language induced by R iff $comp(L)$ is co-checkable and induced by $comp(L)$.

In order to demonstrate the the subtlety of the width question, consider the following example.

Example 1. Let $\Sigma = \{0,1,2\}$. The DBW $\mathcal{A}$ below recognizes the language L of all the words that contain 10, 120 or 220 as subwords. Note that L is the 3-co-checkable language L co-induced by $R = \{010, 110, 210, 100, 101, 102, 120, 220\}$. Indeed, a word w is in L iff $sub(w,3) \cap R \neq \emptyset$.

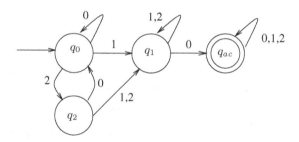

At first sight, it seems that the same considerations applied in Lemma 1 can be used in order to prove that the width of a checkable language is bounded by the diameter of the smallest DBW recognizing the language. Indeed, it appears that in an accepting run, the traversal through the minimal good prefix should not contain a cycle. This impression, however, is misleading, as demonstrated in the DBW $\mathcal{A}$ from Example 1, where a traversal through the subword 120 contains a cycle, and similarly for 010. The diameter of the DBW $\mathcal{A}$ is 3, so it does not constitute a counterexample to the conjecture that the diameter bounds the width, but the problem remains open in [21], and the tightest bound proven there depends on the size of $\mathcal{A}$ and not only on its diameter, and is even not linear. Intuitively, it follows form an upper-bound on the size of a DBW that recognizes minimal bad prefixes of L. Formally, we have the following.

Theorem 1. *If a checkable (or co-checkable) language L is recognized by a DBW with n states, then the width of L is bounded by $O(n^2)$.*

As noted above, the bound in Theorem 1 is not tight and the best known lower bound is only the diameter of a DBW for L. For the nondeterministic setting the bound is tighter:

Theorem 2. *If a checkable language L is recognized by an NBW with n states, then the width of L is bounded by $2^{O(n)}$. Also, There exist an NBW $\mathcal{A}$ with $O(n)$ states such that $L(\mathcal{A})$ is k-checkable but not $(k-1)$-checkable, for $k = (n+1)2^n + 2$.*

4 Safety in a Reactive Setting

Recall that safety is defined with respect to languages over an alphabet Σ. Typically, $\Sigma = 2^{AP}$, where AP is the set of the system's atomic propositions. Thus, the definition and studies of safety treat all the atomic propositions as equal and do not distinguish between input and output signals. As such, they are suited for closed systems – ones that do not maintain an interaction with their environment. In open (also called *reactive*) systems [19,31], the system interacts with the environment, and a correct system should satisfy the specification with respect to all environments. A good way to think about the open setting is to consider the situation as a game between the system and the environment. The interaction between the players in this game generates a computation, and the goal of the system is that only computations that satisfy the specification will be generated.

Technically, one has to partition the set AP of atomic propositions to a set I of input signals, which the environment controls, and a set O of output signals, which the system controls. An open system is then an I/O-*transducer* – a deterministic automaton over the alphabet 2^I in which each state is labeled by an output in 2^O. Given a sequence of assignments to the input signals (each assignment is a letter in 2^I), the run of the transducer on it induces a sequence of assignments to the output signals (that is, letters in 2^O). Together these sequences form a computation, and the transducer *realizes* a specification ψ if all its computations satisfy ψ [31].

The transition from the closed to the open setting modifies the questions we typically ask about systems. Most notably, the *synthesis* challenge, of generating a system that satisfies the specification, corresponds to the satisfiability problem in the closed setting and to the realizability problem in the open setting. As another example, the equivalence problem between LTL specifications is different in the closed and open settings [16]. That is, two specifications may not be equivalent when compared with respect to arbitrary systems on $I \cup O$, but be *open equivalent*; that is, equivalent when compared with respect to I/O-transducers. To see this, note for example that a satisfiable yet non-realizable specification is equivalent to false in the open but not in the closed setting.

As mentioned above, the classical definition of safety does not distinguish between input and output signals. The definition can still be applied to open systems, as a special case of closed systems with $\Sigma = 2^{I \cup O}$. In [11], Ehlers and Finkbeiner introduced *reactive safety* – a definition of safety for the setting of open systems. Essentially, reactive safety properties require the system to stay in a region of states that is both allowed and from which the environment cannot force it out. The definition in [11] is by means of sets of trees with directions in 2^I and labels in 2^O. The use of trees naturally locate reactive safety between linear and branching safety. In [25], we suggested an equivalent yet differently presented definition, which explicitly use realizability, and study the theoretical aspects of receive safety and other reactive fragments of specifications. In this section, we review the definition and results from [25].

4.1 Definitions

We model open systems by *transducers*. Let I and O be finite sets of input and output signals, respectively. Given $x = i_0 \cdot i_1 \cdot i_2 \cdots \in (2^I)^\omega$ and $y = o_0 \cdot o_1 \cdot o_2 \cdots \in (2^O)^\omega$, we denote their composition by $x \oplus y = (i_0, o_0) \cdot (i_1, o_1) \cdot (i_2, o_2) \cdots \in (2^{I \cup O})^\omega$. An I/O-transducer is a tuple $\mathcal{T} = \langle I, O, S, s_0, \eta, L \rangle$, where S is a set of states, $s_0 \in S$ is an initial state, $\eta : S \times 2^I \to S$ is a transition function, and $L : S \to 2^O$ is a labeling function. The *run* of $\mathcal{T}$ on a (finite or infinite) input sequence $x = i_0 \cdot i_1 \cdot i_2 \cdots$, with $i_j \in 2^I$, is the sequence $s_0, s_1, s_2, \ldots$ of states such that $s_{j+1} = \eta(s_j, i_{j+1})$ for all $j \geq 0$. The *computation* of $\mathcal{T}$ on x is then $x \oplus y$, for $y = L(s_0) \cdot L(s_1) \cdot L(s_2) \cdots$ Note that $\mathcal{T}$ is responsive and deterministic (that is, it suggests exactly one successor state for each input letter), and thus $\mathcal{T}$ has a single run, generating a single computation, on each input sequence. We extend η to finite words over 2^I in the expected way. In particular, $\eta(s_0, x)$, for $x \in (2^I)^*$ is the $|x|$-th state in the run on x. A transducer $\mathcal{T}$ induces a *strategy* $f : (2^I)^* \to 2^O$ such that for all $x \in (2^I)^*$, we have that $f(x) = L(\eta(s_0, x))$. Given an LTL formula ψ over $I \cup O$, we say that ψ is I/O-*realizable* if there is a finite-state I/O-transducer $\mathcal{T}$ such that all the computations of $\mathcal{T}$ satisfy ψ [31]. We then say that $\mathcal{T}$ realizes ψ. When it is clear from the context, we refer to I/O-realizability as *realizability*, or talk about realizability of languages over the alphabet $2^{I \cup O}$.

Since the realizability problem corresponds to deciding a game between the system and the environment, and the game is determined [15], realizability is determined too, in the sense that either there is an I/O-transducer that realizes ψ (that is, the system wins) or there is an O/I-transducer that realizes $\neg \psi$ (that is, the environment wins). Note that in an O/I-transducer the system and the environment "switch roles" and the system is the one that provides the inputs to the transducer. A technical detail is that in order for the setting of O/I-realizability to be dual to the one in I/O-realizability we need, in addition to switching the roles and negating the specification, to switch the player that moves first and consider transducers in which the environment initiates the interaction and moves first. Since we are not going to delve into constructions, we ignore this point, which is easy to handle.

Let I and O be sets of input and output signals, respectively. Consider a language $L \subseteq (2^{I \cup O})^\omega$. For a finite word $u \in (2^{I \cup O})^*$, let $L^u = \{s : u \cdot s \in L\}$ be the set of all infinite words s such that $u \cdot s \in L$. Thus, if L describes a set of allowed computations, then L^u describes the set of allowed suffixes of computations starting with u.

We say that a finite word $u \in (2^{I \cup O})^*$ is a *system bad prefix* for L iff L^u is not realizable. Thus, a system bad prefix is a finite word u such that after traversing u, the system does not have a strategy to ensure that the interaction with the environment would generate a computation in L. We use $sbp(L)$ to denote the set of system bad prefixes for L. Note that by determinacy of games, whenever L^u is not realizable by the system, then its complement is realizable by the environment. Thus, once a bad prefix has been generated, the environment has a strategy to ensure that the entire generated behavior is not in L.

A language $L \subseteq (2^{I \cup O})^\omega$ is a *reactive safety language* if every word not in L has a system bad prefix. Below are two examples, demonstrating that a reactive safety language need not be safe. Note that the other direction does hold: Let L be a safe language. Consider a word $w \notin L$ and a bad prefix $u \in (2^{I \cup O})^*$ of w. Since u is a bad prefix, the set L^u is empty, and is therefore unrealizable, so u is also a system bad prefix. Thus, every word not in L has a system bad prefix, implying that L is reactively safe.

Example 2. Let $I = \{fix\}$, $O = \{err\}$, $\psi = G(err \rightarrow F fix)$, and $L = \|\psi\|$. Note that ψ is realizable using the system strategy "never err". Also, L is clearly not safe, as every prefix can be extended to one that satisfies ψ. On the other hand, L is reactively safe. Indeed, every word not in L must have a prefix u that ends with $\{err\}$. Since $L^u = \|F fix\|$, which is not realizable, we have that u is a system bad prefix and L is reactively safe.

Example 3. Let $I = \{fix\}$, $O = \{err\}$, $\psi = G\neg err \vee FG fix$, and $L = \|\psi\|$. Note that ψ is realizable using the system strategy "never err". Also, L is clearly not safe. We show L is reactively safe. Consider a word $w \notin L$. Since w does not satisfy $G\neg err$, there must be a prefix u of w such that u contains a position satisfying err. Since words with prefix u do not satisfy $G\neg err$, we have that $L^u = \|FG fix\|$, which is not realizable. Thus, u is a system bad prefix and L is reactively safe.

4.2 Properties of Reactive Safety

In the closed settings, the set $bad\text{-}pref(L)$ is closed under finite extensions for all languages $L \subseteq \Sigma^\omega$. That is, for every finite word $u \in bad\text{-}pref(L)$ and finite extension $v \in \Sigma^*$, we have that $u \cdot v \in bad\text{-}pref(L)$. This is not the case in the reactive setting:

Theorem 3. *System bad prefixes are not closed under finite extension.*

Proof: Let $I = \{fix\}$, $O = \{err\}$, and $\psi = G(err \rightarrow X fix) \wedge FG\neg err$. Thus, ψ states that every error the system makes is fixed by the environment in the following step, and that there is a finite number of errors. Let $L = \|\psi\|$. Clearly, ψ is realizable, as the strategy "never err" is a winning strategy for the system. Also, L is reactively safe, as a word $w \notin L$ must have a prefix u that ends in a position satisfying err, and u is a system bad prefix. We show that $sbp(L)$ is not closed under finite extensions. To see this, consider the word $w = (\{err, fix\} \cdot \{fix\})^\omega$. That is, the system makes an error on every odd position, and the environment always fixes errors. Since there are infinitely many errors in w, it does not satisfy ψ. The prefix $u = \{err, fix\}$ of w is a system bad prefix. Indeed, an environment strategy that starts with $\neg fix$ is a winning strategy. On the other hand, u's extension $v = \{err, fix\} \cdot \{fix\}$ is not a system bad prefix. Indeed, L^v is realizable using the winning system strategy "never err". $\square$

Recall that reasoning about safety properties is easier than reasoning about general properties. In particular, rather than working with automata on infinite words, one can model check safety properties using automata (on finite words) for bad prefixes. The question is whether and how we can take advantage of reactive safety when the specification is not safe (but is reactively safe). In [11], the authors answered this question to the positive and described a transition from reactively safe to safe formulas. The translation is by means of nodes in the tree in which a violation starts. The translation from [25] we are going to describe here uses realizability explicitly, which we find simpler.

For a language $L \subseteq (2^{I \cup O})^\omega$, we define $close(L) = L \cap \{w : w$ has no system bad prefix for $L\}$. Equivalently, $close(L) = L \setminus \{w : w$ has a system bad prefix for $L\}$. Intuitively, we obtain $close(L)$ by defining all the finite extensions of $sbp(L)$ as bad prefixes. It is thus easy to see that $sbp(L) \subseteq bad\text{-}pref(close(L))$.

As an example, consider again the specification $\psi = G(err \to X fix) \wedge FG\neg err$, with $I = \{fix\}$, $O = \{err\}$. An infinite word contains a system bad prefix for ψ iff it has a position that satisfies err. Accordingly, $close(\psi) = G\neg err$. As another example, let us add to O the signal ack, and let $\psi = G(err \to X(fix \wedge Fack))$, with $I = \{fix\}$, $O = \{err, ack\}$. Again, ψ is reactively safe and an infinite word contains a system bad prefix for ψ iff it has a position that satisfies err. Accordingly, $close(\psi) = G\neg err$.

Our definition of $close(L)$ is sound, in the following sense:

Theorem 4. *A language $L \subseteq (2^{I \cup O})^\omega$ is reactively safe iff $close(L)$ is safe.*

While L and $close(L)$ are not equivalent, they are *open equivalent* [16]. Formally, we have the following.

Theorem 5. *For every language $L \subseteq (2^{I \cup O})^\omega$ and I/O-transducer $\mathcal{T}$, we have that $\mathcal{T}$ realizes L iff $\mathcal{T}$ realizes $close(L)$.*

It is shown in [11] that given an LTL formula ψ, it is possible to construct a deterministic looping word automaton for $close(\psi)$ with doubly-exponential number of states. In fact, as suggested in [23], it is then possible to generate also a deterministic automaton for the bad prefixes of $close(\psi)$. Note that when L is not realizable, we have that $\epsilon \in sbp(L)$, implying that $close(L) = \emptyset$. It follows that we cannot expect to construct small automata for $close(L)$, even nondeterministic ones, as the realizability problem for LTL can be reduced to easy questions about them.

Theorem 5 implies that a reactive safety language L is open equivalent to a safe language, namely $close(L)$. Conversely, open equivalence to a safe language implies reactive safety. This follows from the fact that if L and L' are open-equivalent languages, then a prefix x is a minimal system bad prefix in L iff x is a minimal system bad prefix in L'. We can thus conclude with the following.

Theorem 6. *A language L is reactively safe iff L is open equivalent to a safe language.*

In the setting of open systems, dualization of specifications is more involved, as one has not only to complement the language but to also dualizes the roles of the system and the environment. Accordingly, we actually have four fragments of languages that are induced by dualization of the reactive safety definition. We define them by means of bad and good prefixes.

Consider a language $L \subseteq (2^{I \cup O})^\omega$ and a prefix $u \in (2^{I \cup O})^*$. We say that:

– u is a *system bad prefix* if L^u is not I/O-realizable.
– u is a *system good prefix* if L^u is I/O-realizable.
– u is an *environment bad prefix* if L^u is not O/I-realizable.
– u is an *environment good prefix* if L^u is O/I-realizable.

Now, a language $L \subseteq (2^{I \cup O})^\omega$ is a *system (environment) safety language* if every word not in L has a system (environment, respectively) bad prefix. The language L is a *system (environment) co-safety language* if every word in L has a system (environment, respectively) good prefix. System safety and environment co-safety dualize each other: For every language $L \subseteq (2^{I \cup O})^\omega$, we have that L is system safe iff $comp(L)$ is environment co-safe.

Since each language L^u is either I/O-realizable or not I/O-realizable, and the same for O/I-realizability, all finite words are determined, in the following sense.

Theorem 7. *Consider a language $L \subseteq (2^{I \cup O})^\omega$. All finite words in $(2^{I \cup O})^*$ are determined with respect to L. That is, every prefix is either system good or system bad, and either environment good or environment bad, with respect to L.*

Note that while every prefix is determined, a word may have both system bad and system good prefixes, and similarly for the environment, which is not the case in the setting of closed systems. For example, recall the language $L = \|G(err \to X\mathit{fix}) \wedge FG \neg err\|$, for $I = \{\mathit{fix}\}$ and $O = \{err\}$. As noted above, the word $(\{err, \mathit{fix}\} \cdot \{\mathit{fix}\})^\omega$ has both a system bad prefix $\{err, \mathit{fix}\}$, and a system good prefix $\{err, \mathit{fix}\} \cdot \{\mathit{fix}\}$.

In Section 3.1 we showed that in the closed setting, the intersection of safe and co-safe properties induces the fragment of *bounded* properties. It is shown in [25] that boundedness in the open setting is more involved, as a computation may have both infinitely many good and infinitely many bad prefixes. It is still possible, however, to define reactive bounded properties and use their appealing practical advantages.

5   A Spectrum between Safety and Co-safety

Safety is a binary notion. A property may or may not satisfy the definition of safety. In this section we describe a probability-based approach for defining different levels of safety. The origin of the definition is a study of *vacuity* in model checking [4,23]. Vacuity detection is a method for finding errors in the model-checking process when the specification is found to hold in the model. Most vacuity algorithms are based on checking the effect of applying mutations on the specification. It has been recognized that vacuity results differ in their significance. While in many cases vacuity results are valued as highly informative, there are also cases in which the results are viewed as meaningless by users. In [10], we suggested a method for an automatic ranking of vacuity results according to their level of importance. Our method is based on the *probability* of the mutated specification to hold in a random computation. For example, two natural mutations of the specification $G(req \to F\,ready)$ are $G(\neg req)$, obtained by mutating the subformula *ready* to **false**, and $GF\,ready$, obtained by mutating the subformula *req* to **true**. It is agreed that vacuity information about satisfying the first mutation is more alarming than information about satisfying the second. The framework in [10] formally explains this, as the probability of $G(\neg req)$ to hold in a random computation is 0, whereas the probability of $GF\,ready$ is 1. In this section we suggest to use probability also for defining levels of safety.

5.1 The Probabilistic Setting

Given a set S of elements, a *probability distribution* on S is a function $\mu : S \to [0,1]$ such that $\Sigma_{s \in S}\, \mu(s) = 1$. Consider an alphabet Σ. A random word over Σ is a word in which for all indices i, the i-th letter is drown uniformly at random. In particular, when $\Sigma = 2^{AP}$, then a random computation π is such that for each atomic proposition q and for each position in π, the probability of q to hold in the position is $\frac{1}{2}$. An equivalent definition of this probabilistic model is by means of the probabilistic labeled structure $\mathcal{U}_\Sigma$, which generates computations in a uniform distribution. Formally, $\mathcal{U}_\Sigma$ is a clique with $|\Sigma|$ states in which a state $\sigma \in \Sigma$ is labeled σ, is initial with probability $\frac{1}{|\Sigma|}$, and the probability to move from a state σ to a state σ' is $\frac{1}{|\Sigma|}$.

We define the probability of a language $\mathcal{L} \subseteq \Sigma^\omega$, denoted $Pr(\mathcal{L})$, as the probability of the event $\{\pi : \pi$ is a path in $\mathcal{U}_\Sigma$ that is labeled by a word in $\mathcal{L}\}$. Accordingly, for an LTL formula φ, we define $Pr(\varphi)$ as the probability of the event $\{\pi : \pi$ is a path in $\mathcal{U}_{2^{AP}}$ that satisfies $\varphi\}$. For example, the probabilities of Xp, Gp, and Fp are $\frac{1}{2}, 0$, and 1, respectively. Using $\mathcal{U}_\Sigma$ we can reduce the problem of finding $Pr(\varphi)$ to φ's model checking. Results on probabilistic LTL model checking [8] then imply that the problem of finding the probability of LTL formulas is PSPACE-complete.

First-order logic respects a 0/1-law: the probability of a formula to be satisfied in a random model is either 0 or 1 [13]. It is easy to see that a 0/1-law does not hold for LTL. For example, for an atomic proposition p, we have that $Pr(p) = \frac{1}{2}$. Back to our safety story, it is not hard to see that $Pr(G\xi)$, for a formula ξ with $Pr(\xi) \neq 1$, is 0. Dually, $Pr(F\xi)$, for a formula ξ with $Pr(\xi) \neq 0$ is 1. Can we relate this to the fact that Gp is a safety property whereas Fp is a co-safety property? Or perhaps it has to do with Fp being a liveness property?[2] This is not clear, as, for example, the probability of clopen formulas depends on finitely many events and can vary between 0 to 1. As another example, consider the two possible semantics of the Until temporal operator. For the standard, strong, Until, which is not a safe, we have $Pr(pUq) = \frac{2}{3}$. By changing the semantics of the Until to a weak one, we get the safety formula pWq, with $pWq = pUq \vee Gp$. Still, $Pr(pWq) = Pr(pUq)$. Thus, the standard probabilistic setting does not suggest a clear relation between probability and different levels of safety.

We argue that we can still use the probabilistic approach in order to measure safety. The definition of $Pr(\varphi)$ in [10] assumes that the probability of an atomic proposition to hold in each position is $\frac{1}{2}$. This corresponds to computations in an infinite-state system and is the standard approach taken in studies of 0/1-laws. Alternatively, one can also study the probability of formulas to hold in computations of finite-state systems. Formally, for an integer $l \geq 1$, let $Pr_l(\varphi)$ denote the probability that φ holds in a random cycle of length l. Here too, the probability of each atomic proposition to hold in a state is $\frac{1}{2}$, yet we have only l states to fix an assignment to. So, for example, while $Pr(Gp) = 0$,

---

[2] A language L is a liveness language if $L = \Sigma^* \cdot L$ [1].

we have that $Pr_1(Gp) = \frac{1}{2}$, $Pr_2(Gp) = \frac{1}{4}$, and in general $Pr_j(Gp) = \frac{1}{2^j}$. Indeed, an l-cycle satisfies Gp iff all its states satisfy p.

There are several interesting issues in the finite-state approach. First, it may seem obvious that the bigger l is, the closer $Pr_l(\varphi)$ gets to $Pr(\varphi)$. This is, however, not so simple. For example, issues like cycles in φ can cause $Pr_l(\varphi)$ to be non-monotonic. For example, when φ requires p to hold in exactly all even positions, then $Pr_1(\varphi) = 0, Pr_2(\varphi) = \frac{1}{4}, Pr_3(\varphi) = 0, Pr_4(\varphi) = \frac{1}{16}$, and so on.

Assume now that we have cleaned the cycle-based issue (for example by restricting attention to formulas without Xs, or by restricting attention to cycles of "the right" length). Can we characterize safety properties by means of the asymptotic behavior of $Pr_l(\varphi)$? Can we define different levels of safety according to the rate the probability decreases or increases? For example, clearly $Pr_l(Gp)$ tends to 0 as l increases, whereas $Pr_l(Fp)$ tends to 1. Also, now, for a given l, we have that $Pr_l(pWq) > Pr_l(pUq)$. In addition, for a clopen property φ, we have that $Pr_l(\varphi)$ stablizes once l is bigger than the bound of φ. Still, the picture is not clean. For example, FGp is a liveness formula, but $Pr_l(FGp)$ decreases as l increases. Finding a characterization of properties that is based on the analysis of Pr_l is an interesting question, and our initial research suggests a connection between the level of safety of φ and the behavior of $Pr_l(\varphi)$.

References

1. Alpern, B., Schneider, F.B.: Defining liveness. IPL 21, 181–185 (1985)
2. Alpern, B., Schneider, F.B.: Recognizing safety and liveness. Distributed Computing 2, 117–126 (1987)
3. Barringer, H., Goldberg, A., Havelund, K., Sen, K.: Rule-based runtime verification. In: Steffen, B., Levi, G. (eds.) VMCAI 2004. LNCS, vol. 2937, pp. 44–57. Springer, Heidelberg (2004)
4. Beer, I., Ben-David, S., Eisner, C., Rodeh, Y.: Efficient detection of vacuity in ACTL formulas. In: Grumberg, O. (ed.) CAV 1997. LNCS, vol. 1254, pp. 279–290. Springer, Heidelberg (1997)
5. Biere, A., Cimatti, A., Clarke, E., Zhu, Y.: Symbolic model checking without BDDs. In: Cleaveland, W.R. (ed.) TACAS 1999. LNCS, vol. 1579, pp. 193–207. Springer, Heidelberg (1999)
6. Bloem, R., Gabow, H.N., Somenzi, F.: An algorithm for strongly connected component analysis in $n \log n$ symbolic steps. In: Johnson, S.D., Hunt Jr., W.A. (eds.) FMCAD 2000. LNCS, vol. 1954, pp. 37–54. Springer, Heidelberg (2000)
7. Courcoubetis, C., Vardi, M.Y., Wolper, P., Yannakakis, M.: Memory efficient algorithms for the verification of temporal properties. FMSD 1, 275–288 (1992)
8. Courcoubetis, C., Yannakakis, M.: The complexity of probabilistic verification. J. ACM 42, 857–907 (1995)
9. d'Amorim, M., Roşu, G.: Efficient monitoring of omega-languages. In: Etessami, K., Rajamani, S.K. (eds.) CAV 2005. LNCS, vol. 3576, pp. 364–378. Springer, Heidelberg (2005)
10. Ben-David, S., Kupferman, O.: A framework for ranking vacuity results. In: Van Hung, D., Ogawa, M. (eds.) ATVA 2013. LNCS, vol. 8172, pp. 148–162. Springer, Heidelberg (2013)
11. Ehlers, R., Finkbeiner, B.: Reactive safety. In: Proc. 2nd GANDALF. Electronic Proceedings in TCS, vol. 54, pp. 178–191 (2011)
12. Emerson, E.A.: Alternative semantics for temporal logics. TCS 26, 121–130 (1983)
13. Fagin, R.: Probabilities in finite models. Journal of Symb. Logic 41(1), 50–58 (1976)

14. Filiot, E., Jin, N., Raskin, J.-F.: An antichain algorithm for LTL realizability. In: Bouajjani, A., Maler, O. (eds.) CAV 2009. LNCS, vol. 5643, pp. 263–277. Springer, Heidelberg (2009)

15. Gale, D., Stewart, F.M.: Infinite games of perfect information. Ann. Math. Studies 28, 245–266 (1953)

16. Greimel, K., Bloem, R., Jobstmann, B., Vardi, M.: Open implication. In: Aceto, L., Damgård, I., Goldberg, L.A., Halldórsson, M.M., Ingólfsdóttir, A., Walukiewicz, I. (eds.) ICALP 2008, Part II. LNCS, vol. 5126, pp. 361–372. Springer, Heidelberg (2008)

17. Gumm, H.P.: Another glance at the Alpern-Schneider characterization of safety and liveness in concurrent executions. IPL 47, 291–294 (1993)

18. Harel, D., Katz, G., Marron, A., Weiss, G.: Non-intrusive repair of reactive programs. In: ICECCS, pp. 3–12 (2012)

19. Harel, D., Pnueli, A.: On the development of reactive systems. In: Logics and Models of Concurrent Systems, NATO ASI, vol. F-13, pp. 477–498. Springer (1985)

20. Havelund, K., Roşu, G.: Synthesizing monitors for safety properties. In: Katoen, J.-P., Stevens, P. (eds.) TACAS 2002. LNCS, vol. 2280, pp. 342–356. Springer, Heidelberg (2002)

21. Kupferman, O., Lustig, Y., Vardi, M.Y.: On locally checkable properties. In: Hermann, M., Voronkov, A. (eds.) LPAR 2006. LNCS (LNAI), vol. 4246, pp. 302–316. Springer, Heidelberg (2006)

22. Kupferman, O., Vardi, M.Y.: Model checking of safety properties. In: Halbwachs, N., Peled, D.A. (eds.) CAV 1999. LNCS, vol. 1633, pp. 172–183. Springer, Heidelberg (1999)

23. Kupferman, O., Vardi, M.Y.: Model checking of safety properties. FMSD 19(3), 291–314 (2001)

24. Kupferman, O., Vardi, M.Y.: On bounded specifications. In: Nieuwenhuis, R., Voronkov, A. (eds.) LPAR 2001. LNCS (LNAI), vol. 2250, pp. 24–38. Springer, Heidelberg (2001)

25. Kupferman, O., Weiner, S.: Environment-friendly safety. In: Biere, A., Nahir, A., Vos, T. (eds.) HVC 2012. LNCS, vol. 7857, pp. 227–242. Springer, Heidelberg (2013)

26. Lamport, L.: Logical foundation. In: Alford, M.W., Hommel, G., Schneider, F.B., Ansart, J.P., Lamport, L., Mullery, G.P., Zhou, T.H. (eds.) Distributed Systems. LNCS, vol. 190, pp. 19–30. Springer, Heidelberg (1985)

27. Manna, Z., Pnueli, A.: he anchored version of the temporal framework. In: de Bakker, J.W., de Roever, W.-P., Rozenberg, G. (eds.) Linear Time, Branching Time and Partial Order in Logics and Models for Concurrency. LNCS, vol. 354, pp. 201–284. Springer, Heidelberg (1989)

28. Manna, Z., Pnueli, A.: The Temporal Logic of Reactive and Concurrent Systems: Specification. Springer (1992)

29. Manna, Z., Pnueli, A.: The Temporal Logic of Reactive and Concurrent Systems: Safety. Springer (1995)

30. Pnueli, A.: The temporal semantics of concurrent programs. TCS 13, 45–60 (1981)

31. Pnueli, A., Rosner, R.: On the synthesis of a reactive module. In: Proc. 16th POPL, pp. 179–190 (1989)

32. Pnueli, A., Shahar, E.: Liveness and acceleration in parameterized verification. In: Emerson, E.A., Sistla, A.P. (eds.) CAV 2000. LNCS, vol. 1855, pp. 328–343. Springer, Heidelberg (2000)

33. Sistla, A.P.: Safety, liveness and fairness in temporal logic. Formal Aspects of Computing 6, 495–511 (1994)

34. Sistla, A.P., Clarke, E.M.: The complexity of propositional linear temporal logic. Journal of the ACM 32, 733–749 (1985)

35. Touati, H.J., Brayton, R.K., Kurshan, R.: Testing language containment for ω-automata using BDD's. I & C 118(1), 101–109 (1995)

36. Vardi, M.Y., Wolper, P.: Reasoning about infinite computations. I & C 115(1), 1–37 (1994)

Decision Procedures for Flat Array Properties*

Francesco Alberti[1], Silvio Ghilardi[2], and Natasha Sharygina[1]

[1] University of Lugano, Lugano, Switzerland
[2] Università degli Studi di Milano, Milan, Italy

Abstract. We present new decidability results for quantified fragments of theories of arrays. Our decision procedures are fully declarative, parametric in the theories of indexes and elements and orthogonal with respect to known results. We also discuss applications to the analysis of programs handling arrays.

1 Introduction

Decision procedures constitute, nowadays, one of the fundamental components of tools and algorithms developed for the formal analysis of systems. Results about the decidability of fragments of (first-order) theories representing the semantics of real system operations deeply influenced, in the last decade, many research areas, from verification to synthesis. In particular, the demand for procedures dealing with quantified fragments of such theories fast increased. Quantified formulas arise from several static analysis and verification tasks, like modeling properties of the heap, asserting frame axioms, checking user-defined assertions in the code and reasoning about parameterized systems.

In this paper we are interested in studying the decidability of quantified fragments of theories of arrays. Quantification is required over the indexes of the arrays in order to express significant properties like "the array has been initialized to 0" or "there exist two different positions of the array containing an element c", for example. From a logical point of view, array variables are interpreted as functions. However, adding free function symbols to a theory T (with the goal of modeling array variables) may yield to undecidable extensions of widely used theories like Presburger arithmetic [17]. It is, therefore, mandatory to identify fragments of the quantified theory of arrays which are on one side still decidable and on the other side sufficiently expressive. In this paper, we show that by combining restrictions on quantifier prefixes with 'flatness' limitations on dereferencing (only positions named by variables are allowed in dereferencing), one can restore decidability. We call the fragments so obtained *Flat Array Properties*; such fragments are orthogonal to the fragments already proven decidable in the literature [8, 15, 16] (we shall defer the technical comparison with these contributions to Section 5). Here we explain the *modularity* character of our

---

* The work of the first author was supported by Swiss National Science Foundation under grant no. P1TIP2_152261.

E. Ábrahám and K. Havelund (Eds.): TACAS 2014, LNCS 8413, pp. 15–30, 2014.

results and their *applications* to concrete decision problems for array programs annotated with assertions or postconditions.

We examine Flat Array Properties in two different settings. In one case, we consider Flat Array Properties over the theory of arrays generated by adding free function symbols to a given theory T modeling both indexes and elements of the arrays. In the other one, we take into account Flat Array Properties over a theory of arrays built by connecting two theories T_I and T_E describing the structure of indexes and elements. Our decidability results are fully declarative and parametric in the theories T, T_I, T_E. For both settings, we provide sufficient conditions on T and T_I, T_E for achieving the decidability of Flat Array Properties. Such hypotheses are widely met by theories of interest in practice, like Presburger arithmetic. We also provide suitable decision procedures for Flat Array Properties of both settings. Such procedures reduce the decidability of Flat Array Properties to the decidability of T-formulæ in one case and T_I- and T_E-formulæ in the other case.

We further show, as an application of our decidability results, that the safety of an interesting class of programs handling arrays or strings of unknown length is decidable. We call this class of programs simple$_A^0$-*programs* : this class covers non-recursive programs implementing for instance searching, copying, comparing, initializing, replacing and testing functions. The method we use for showing these safety results is similar to a classical method adopted in the model-checking literature for programs manipulating integer variables (see for instance [7,9,12]): we first assume flatness conditions on the control flow graph of the program and then we assume that transitions labeling cycles are "acceleratable". However, since we are dealing with array manipulating programs, acceleration requires specific results that we borrow from [3]. The key point is that the shape of most accelerated transitions from [3] matches the definition of our Flat Array Properties (in fact, Flat Array Properties were designed precisely in order to encompass such accelerated transitions for arrays).

From the practical point of view, we tested the effectiveness of state of the art SMT-solvers in checking the satisfiability of some Flat Array Properties arising from the verification of simple$_A^0$-programs. Results show that such tools fail or timeout on some Flat Array Properties. The implementation of our decision procedures, once instantiated with the theories of interests for practical applications, will likely lead, therefore, to further improvements in the areas of practical solutions for the rigorous analysis of software and hardware systems.

Plan of the Paper. The paper starts by recalling in Section 2 required background notions. Section 3 is dedicated to the definition of Flat Array Properties. Section 3.1 introduces a decision procedure for Flat Array Properties in the case of a mono-sorted theory $\text{ARR}^1(T)$ generated by adding free function symbols to a theory T. Section 3.2 discusses a decision procedure for Flat Array Properties in the case of the multi-sorted array theory $\text{ARR}^2(T_I, T_E)$ built over two theories T_I and T_E for the indexes and elements (we supply also full lower and upper complexity bounds for the case in which T_I and T_E are both Presburger arithmetic). In Section 4 we recall and adapt required notions from [3], define the class of flat^0-programs and establish the requirements for achieving the decidability of reachability analysis on some flat^0-programs. Such requirements are instantiated in Section 4.1 in the case of simple$^0_\mathcal{A}$-programs, array programs with flat control-flow graph admitting definable accelerations for every loop. In Section 4.2 we position the fragment of Flat Array Properties with respect to the actual practical capabilities of state-of-the-art SMT-solvers. Section 5 compares our results with the state of the art, in particular with the approaches of [8,15].

2 Background

We use lower-case latin letters $x, i, c, d, e, \ldots$ for variables; for tuples of variables we use bold face letters like $\mathbf{x}, \mathbf{i}, \mathbf{c}, \mathbf{d}, \mathbf{e} \ldots$. The n-th component of a tuple $\mathbf{c}$ is indicated with c_n and $| - |$ may indicate tuples length (so that we have $\mathbf{c} = c_1, \ldots, c_{|\mathbf{c}|}$). Occasionally, we may use free variables and free constants interchangeably. For terms, we use letters $t, u, \ldots$, with the same conventions as above; $\mathbf{t}, \mathbf{u}$ are used for tuples of terms (however, tuples of variables are assumed to be distinct, whereas the same is not assumed for tuples of terms - this is useful for substitutions notation, see below). When we use $\mathbf{u} = \mathbf{v}$, we assume that two tuples have equal length, say n (i.e. $n := |\mathbf{u}| = |\mathbf{v}|$) and that $\mathbf{u} = \mathbf{v}$ abbreviates the formula $\bigwedge_{i=1}^{n} u_i = v_i$.

With $E(\mathbf{x})$ we denote that the syntactic expression (term, formula, tuple of terms or of formulæ) E contains at most the free variables *taken from* the tuple $\mathbf{x}$. We use lower-case Greek letters $\phi, \varphi, \psi, \ldots$ for **quantifier-free** formulæ and $\alpha, \beta, \ldots$ for arbitrary formulæ. The notation $\phi(\mathbf{t})$ identifies a quantifier-free formula ϕ obtained from $\phi(\mathbf{x})$ by substituting the tuple of variables $\mathbf{x}$ with the tuple of terms $\mathbf{t}$.

A *prenex formula* is a formula of the form $Q_1 x_1 \ldots Q_n x_n \varphi(x_1, \ldots, x_n)$, where $Q_i \in \{\exists, \forall\}$ and $x_1, \ldots, x_n$ are pairwise different variables. $Q_1 x_1 \cdots Q_n x_n$ is the *prefix* of the formula. Let R be a regular expression over the alphabet $\{\exists, \forall\}$. The R-class of formulæ comprises all and only those prenex formulæ whose prefix generates a string $Q_1 \cdots Q_n$ matched by R.

According to the SMT-LIB standard [22], a theory T is a pair $(\Sigma, \mathcal{C})$, where Σ is a signature and $\mathcal{C}$ is a class of Σ-structures; the structures in $\mathcal{C}$ are called the models of T. Given a Σ-structure $\mathcal{M}$, we denote by $S^\mathcal{M}, f^\mathcal{M}, P^\mathcal{M}, \ldots$ the interpretation in $\mathcal{M}$ of the sort S, the function symbol f, the predicate symbol P, etc. A Σ-formula α is T-satisfiable if there exists a Σ-structure $\mathcal{M}$ in $\mathcal{C}$ such that α is true in $\mathcal{M}$ under a suitable assignment to the free variables of α (in symbols, $\mathcal{M} \models \alpha$); it is T-valid (in symbols, $T \models \alpha$) if its negation is T-unsatisfiable. Two formulæ α_1 and α_2 are T-equivalent if $\alpha_1 \leftrightarrow \alpha_2$ is T-valid; α_1 T-entails α_2 (in symbols, $\alpha_1 \models_T \alpha_2$) iff $\alpha_1 \rightarrow \alpha_2$ is T-valid. The satisfiability modulo the theory T $(SMT(T))$ problem amounts to establishing the T-satisfiability of quantifier-free Σ-formulæ. **All theories T we consider in this paper have decidable $SMT(T)$-problem** (we recall that this property is preserved when adding free function symbols, see [13,26]).

A theory $T = (\Sigma, \mathcal{C})$ admits *quantifier elimination* iff for any arbitrary Σ-formula $\alpha(\mathbf{x})$ it is always possible to compute a quantifier-free formula $\varphi(\mathbf{x})$

such that $T \models \forall \mathbf{x}.(\alpha(\mathbf{x}) \leftrightarrow \varphi(\mathbf{x}))$. Thus, in view of the above assumption on decidability of $SMT(T)$-problem, a theory having quantifier elimination is decidable (i.e. T-satisfiability of *every* formula is decidable). Our favorite example of a theory with quantifier elimination is *Presburger Arithmetic*, hereafter denoted with $\mathbb{P}$; this is the theory in the signature $\{0, 1, +, -, =, <\}$ augmented with infinitely many unary predicates D_k (for each integer k greater than 1). Semantically, the intended class of models for $\mathbb{P}$ contains just the structure whose support is the set of the natural numbers, where $\{0, 1, +, -, =, <\}$ have the natural interpretation and D_k is interpreted as the sets of natural numbers divisible by k (these extra predicates are needed to get quantifier elimination [21]).

3   Monic-Flat Array Property Fragments

Although $\mathbb{P}$ represents the fragment of arithmetic mostly used in formal approaches for the static analysis of systems, we underline that there are many other fragments that have quantifier elimination and can be quite useful; these fragments can be both weaker (like Integer Difference Logic [20]) and stronger (like the exponentiation extension of Semënov theorem [24]) than $\mathbb{P}$. Thus, the *modular* approach proposed in this Section to model arrays is not motivated just by generalization purposes, but can have practical impact.

There exist two ways of introducing arrays in a declarative setting, the mono-sorted and the multi-sorted ways. The former is more expressive because (roughly speaking) it allows to consider indexes also as elements[1], but might be computationally more difficult to handle. We discuss decidability results for both cases, starting from the mono-sorted case.

3.1   The Mono-sorted Case

Let $T = (\Sigma, \mathcal{C})$ be a theory; the theory $\mathtt{ARR}^1(T)$ *of arrays over* T is obtained from T by adding to it infinitely many (fresh) free unary function symbols. This means that the signature of $\mathtt{ARR}^1(T)$ is obtained from Σ by adding to it unary function symbols (we use the letters $a, a_1, a_2, \ldots$ for them) and that a structure $\mathcal{M}$ is a model of $\mathtt{ARR}^1(T)$ iff (once the interpretations of the extra function symbols are disregarded) it is a structure belonging to the original class $\mathcal{C}$.

For array theories it is useful to introduce the following notation. We use $\mathbf{a}$ for a tuple $\mathbf{a} = a_1, \ldots, a_{|\mathbf{a}|}$ of distinct 'array constants' (i.e. free function symbols); if $\mathbf{t} = t_1, \ldots, t_{|\mathbf{t}|}$ is a tuple of terms, the notation $\mathbf{a}(\mathbf{t})$ represents the tuple (of length $|\mathbf{a}| \cdot |\mathbf{t}|$) of terms $a_1(t_1), \ldots, a_1(t_{|\mathbf{t}|}), \ldots, a_{|\mathbf{a}|}(t_1), \ldots, a_{|\mathbf{a}|}(t_{|\mathbf{t}|})$.

$\mathtt{ARR}^1(T)$ may be highly undecidable, even when T itself is decidable (see [17]), thus it is mandatory to limit the shape of the formulæ we want to try to decide. A prenex formula or a term in the signature of $\mathtt{ARR}^1(T)$ are said to be *flat* iff for every term of the kind $a(t)$ occurring in them (here a is any array constant), the

---

[1] This is useful in the analysis of programs, when pointers to the memory (modeled as an array) are stored into array variables.

sub-term t is always a variable. Notice that every formula is logically equivalent to a flat one; however the flattening transformations are based on rewriting as

$$\phi(a(t), ...) \rightsquigarrow \exists x (x = t \wedge \phi(a(x), ...)) \quad \text{or} \quad \phi(a(t), ...) \rightsquigarrow \forall x (x = t \rightarrow \phi(a(x), ...))$$

and consequently they may alter the quantifiers prefix of a formula. Thus it must be kept in mind (when understanding the results below), that flattening trans- formation cannot be operated on any occurrence of a term without exiting from the class that is claimed to be decidable. When we indicate a flat quantifier-free formula with the notation $\psi(\mathbf{x}, \mathbf{a}(\mathbf{x}))$, we mean that such a formula is obtained from a Σ-formula of the kind $\psi(\mathbf{x}, \mathbf{z})$ (i.e. from a quantifier-free Σ-formula where at most the free variables $\mathbf{x}, \mathbf{z}$ can occur) by replacing $\mathbf{z}$ by $\mathbf{a}(\mathbf{x})$.

Theorem 1. *If the T-satisfiability of $\exists^* \forall \exists^*$ sentences is decidable, then the $\mathrm{ARR}^1(T)$-satisfiability of $\exists^* \forall$-flat sentences is decidable.*

Proof. We present an algorithm, $\mathsf{SAT}_{\mathsf{MONO}}$, for deciding the satisfiability of the $\exists^* \forall$-flat fragment of $\mathrm{ARR}^1(T)$ (we let T be $(\Sigma, \mathcal{C})$). Subsequently, we show that $\mathsf{SAT}_{\mathsf{MONO}}$ is sound and complete. From the complexity viewpoint, notice that $\mathsf{SAT}_{\mathsf{MONO}}$ produces a quadratic instance of a $\exists^* \forall \exists^*$-satisfiability problem.

The Decision Procedure $\mathsf{SAT}_{\mathsf{MONO}}$

STEP I. Let

$$F := \exists \mathbf{c} \, \forall i. \psi(i, \mathbf{a}(i), \mathbf{c}, \mathbf{a}(\mathbf{c}))$$

be a $\exists^* \forall$-flat $\mathrm{ARR}^1(T)$-sentence, where ψ is a quantifier-free Σ-formula. Sup- pose that s is the length of $\mathbf{a}$ and t is the length of $\mathbf{c}$ (that is, $\mathbf{a} = a_1, \ldots, a_s$ and $\mathbf{c} = c_1, \ldots, c_t$). Let $\mathbf{e} = \langle e_{l,m} \rangle$ $(1 \leq l \leq s, 1 \leq m \leq t)$ be a tuple of length $s \cdot t$ of fresh variables and consider the $\mathrm{ARR}^1(T)$-formula:

$$F_1 := \exists \mathbf{c} \, \exists \mathbf{e} \, \forall i. \psi(i, \mathbf{a}(i), \mathbf{c}, \mathbf{e}) \wedge \bigwedge_{1 \leq l \leq t} \bigwedge_{1 \leq m \leq s} a_m(c_l) = e_{l,m}$$

STEP II. From F_1 build the formula

$$F_2 := \exists \mathbf{c} \, \exists \mathbf{e} \, \forall i. \left[\psi(i, \mathbf{a}(i), \mathbf{c}, \mathbf{e}) \wedge \bigwedge_{1 \leq l \leq t} (i = c_l \rightarrow \bigwedge_{1 \leq m \leq s} a_m(i) = e_{l,m}) \right]$$

STEP III. Let $\mathbf{d}$ be a fresh tuple of variables of length s; check the T-satisfiabi- lity of

$$F_3 := \exists \mathbf{c} \, \exists \mathbf{e} \, \forall i \, \exists \mathbf{d}. \left[\psi(i, \mathbf{d}, \mathbf{c}, \mathbf{e}) \wedge \bigwedge_{1 \leq l \leq t} (i = c_l \rightarrow \bigwedge_{1 \leq m \leq s} d_m = e_{l,m}) \right]$$

Correctness and Completeness of SAT$_{MONO}$. SAT$_{MONO}$ transforms an ARR$^1(T)$-formula F into an equisatisfiable T-formula F_3 belonging to the $\exists^*\forall\exists^*$ fragment. More precisely, it holds that F, F_1 and F_2 are equivalent formulæ, because

$$\bigwedge_{1\leq l\leq t} \forall i.(i = c_l \rightarrow \bigwedge_{1\leq m\leq s} a_m(i) = e_{l,m}) \equiv \bigwedge_{1\leq l\leq t} \bigwedge_{1\leq m\leq s} a_m(c_l) = e_{l,m}$$

From F_2 to F_3 and back, satisfiability is preserved because F_2 is the Skolemization of F_3, where the existentially quantified variables $\mathbf{d} = d_1, \ldots, d_s$ are substituted with the free unary function symbols $\mathbf{a} = a_1, \ldots a_s$.   ⊣

Since Presburger Arithmetic is decidable (via quantifier elimination), we get in particular that

Corollary 1. *The* ARR$^1(\mathbb{P})$-*satisfiability of* $\exists^*\forall$-*flat sentences is decidable.*

As another example matching the hypothesis of Theorem 1 (i.e. as an example of a T such that T-satisfiability of $\exists^*\forall\exists^*$-sentences is decidable) consider pure first order logic with equality in a signature with predicate symbols of any arity but with only unary function symbols [6].

3.2   The Multi-sorted Case

We are now considering a theory of arrays parametric in the theories specifying constraints over indexes and elements of the arrays. Formally, we need two ingredient theories, $T_I = (\Sigma_I, \mathcal{C}_I)$ and $T_E = (\Sigma_E, \mathcal{C}_E)$. We can freely assume that Σ_I and Σ_E are disjoint (otherwise we can rename some symbols); for simplicity, we let both signatures be mono-sorted (but extending our results to many-sorted T_E is quite straightforward): let us call INDEX the unique sort of T_I and ELEM the unique sort of T_E.

The theory ARR$^2(T_I, T_E)$ *of arrays over* T_I *and* T_E is obtained from the union of $\Sigma_I \cup \Sigma_E$ by adding to it infinitely many (fresh) free unary function symbols (these new function symbols will have domain sort INDEX and codomain sort ELEM). The models of ARR$^2(T_I, T_E)$ are the structures whose reducts to the symbols of sorts INDEX and ELEM are models of T_I and T_E, respectively.

Consider now an atomic formula $P(t_1, \ldots, t_n)$ in the language of ARR$^2(T_I, T_E)$ (in the typical situation, P is the equality predicate). Since the predicate symbols of ARR$^2(T_I, T_E)$ are from $\Sigma_I \cup \Sigma_E$ and $\Sigma_I \cap \Sigma_E = \emptyset$, P belongs either to Σ_I or to Σ_E; in the latter case, all terms t_i have sort ELEM and in the former case all terms t_i are Σ_I-terms. We say that $P(t_1, \ldots, t_n)$ is an INDEX-*atom* in the former case and that it is an ELEM-*atom* in the latter case.

When dealing with ARR$^2(T_I, T_E)$, *we shall limit ourselves to quantified variables of sort* INDEX : this limitation is justified by the benchmarks arising in applications (see Section 4).[2] A sentence in the language of ARR$^2(T_I, T_E)$ is said

---

[2] Topmost existentially quantified variables of sort ELEM can be modeled by enriching T_E with free constants.

to be *monic* iff it is in prenex form and every `INDEX` atom occurring in it contains at most one variable falling within the scope of a *universal* quantifier.

Example 1. Consider the following sentences:

(I) $\forall i.\, a(i) = i$;

(II) $\forall i_1 \forall i_2.\, (i_1 \leq i_2 \rightarrow a(i_1) \leq a(i_2))$;

(III) $\exists i_1 \exists i_2.\, (i_1 \leq i_2 \wedge a(i_1) \not\leq a(i_2))$;

(IV) $\forall i_1 \forall i_2.\, a(i_1) = a(i_2)$;

(V) $\forall i.\, (D_2(i) \rightarrow a(i) = 0)$;

(VI) $\exists i\, \forall j.\, (a_1(j) < a_2(3i))$.

The flat formula (I) is not well-typed, hence it is not allowed in $\text{ARR}^2(\mathbb{P}, \mathbb{P})$; however, it is allowed in $\text{ARR}^1(\mathbb{P})$. Formula (II) expresses the fact that the array a is sorted: it is flat but not monic (because of the atom $i_1 \leq i_2$). On the contrary, its negation (III) is flat and monic (because i_1, i_2 are now existentially quantified). Formula (IV) expresses that the array a is constant; it is flat and monic (notice that the universally quantified variables i_1, i_2 both occur in $a(i_1) = a(i_2)$ but the latter is an `ELEM` atom). Formula (V) expresses that a is initialized so to have all even positions equal to 0: it is monic and flat. Formula (VI) is monic but not flat because of the term $a_2(3i)$ occurring in it; however, in $3i$ no universally quantified variable occurs, so it is possible to produce by flattening the following sentence

$$\exists i\, \exists i'\, \forall j\, (i' = 3i \wedge a_1(j) < a_2(i'))$$

which is logically equivalent to (VI), it is flat and still lies in the $\exists^*\forall$-class. Finally, as a more complicated example, notice that the following sentence

$$\exists k\, \forall i.\, (D_2(k) \wedge a(k) = \text{`}\backslash 0\text{'} \wedge (D_2(i) \wedge i < k \rightarrow a(i) = \text{`b'}) \wedge (\neg D_2(i) \wedge i < k \rightarrow a(i) = \text{`c'}))$$

is monic and flat: it says that a represents a string of the kind $(\text{bc})^*$.

Theorem 2. *If T_I-satisfiability of $\exists^*\forall$-sentences is decidable, then $\text{ARR}^2(T_I, T_E)$-satisfiability of $\exists^*\forall^*$-monic-flat sentences is decidable.*

Proof. As we did for SAT_{MONO}, we give a decision procedure, $\text{SAT}_{\text{MULTI}}$, for the $\exists^*\forall^*$-monic-flat fragment of $\text{ARR}^2(T_I, T_E)$; for space reasons, we give here just some informal justifications, the reader is referred to [2] for proofs. First (STEP I), the procedure *guesses* the sets (called 'types') of relevant `INDEX` atoms satisfied in a model to be built. Subsequently (STEP II) it introduces a representative variable for each type together with the constraint that guessed types are exhaustive. Finally (STEP III, IV and V) the procedure applies combination techniques for purification.   ⊣

The Decision Procedure $\text{SAT}_{\text{MULTI}}$. The algorithm is non-deterministic: the input formula is satisfiable iff we can guess suitable data $\mathcal{T}, \mathcal{B}$ so that the formulæ F_I, F_E below are satisfiable.

STEP I. Let F be a $\exists^*\forall^*$-monic-flat formula; let it be

$$F := \exists \mathbf{c}\, \forall \mathbf{i}.\psi(\mathbf{i}, \mathbf{a}(\mathbf{i}), \mathbf{c}, \mathbf{a}(\mathbf{c})),$$

(where as usual ψ is a $T_I \cup T_E$-quantifier-free formula). Suppose $\mathbf{a} = a_1, \ldots, a_s$, $\mathbf{i} = i_1, \ldots, i_n$ and $\mathbf{c} = c_1, \ldots, c_t$. Consider the set (notice that all atoms in K are Σ_I-atoms and have just one free variable because F is monic)

$$K = \{A(x, \mathbf{c}) \mid A(i_k, \mathbf{c}) \text{ is an INDEX atom of } F\}_{1 \le k \le n} \cup \{x = c_l\}_{1 \le l \le t}$$

Let us call *type* a set of literals M such that: (i) each literal of M is an atom in K or its negation; (ii) for all $A(x, \mathbf{c}) \in K$, either $A(x, \mathbf{c}) \in M$ or $\neg A(x, \mathbf{c}) \in M$. Guess a set $\mathcal{T} = \{M_1, \ldots, M_q\}$ of types.

STEP II. Let $\mathbf{b} = b_1, \ldots, b_q$ be a tuple of new variables of sort INDEX and let

$$F_1 := \exists \mathbf{b} \, \exists \mathbf{c} \left[\begin{array}{l} \forall x. \left(\bigvee_{j=1}^{q} \bigwedge_{L \in M_j} L(x, \mathbf{c}) \right) \wedge \\[2ex] \bigwedge_{j=1}^{q} \bigwedge_{L \in M_j} L(b_j, \mathbf{c}) \wedge \\[2ex] \bigwedge_{\sigma: \mathbf{i} \to \mathbf{b}} \psi(\mathbf{i}\sigma, \mathbf{a}(\mathbf{i}\sigma), \mathbf{c}, \mathbf{a}(\mathbf{c})) \end{array} \right]$$

where $\mathbf{i}\sigma$ is the tuple of terms $\sigma(i_1), \ldots, \sigma(i_n)$.

STEP III. Let $\mathbf{e} = \langle e_{l,m} \rangle$ $(1 \le l \le s, 1 \le m \le t+q)$ be a tuple of length $s \cdot (t+q)$ of free constants of sort ELEM. Consider the formula

$$F_2 := \exists \mathbf{b} \, \exists \mathbf{c} \left[\begin{array}{l} \forall x. \left(\bigvee_{j=1}^{q} \bigwedge_{L \in M_j} L(x, \mathbf{c}) \right) \wedge \\[2ex] \bigwedge_{j=1}^{q} \bigwedge_{L \in M_j} L(b_j, \mathbf{c}) \wedge \\[2ex] \bar{\psi}(\mathbf{b}, \mathbf{c}, \mathbf{e}) \wedge \\[2ex] \bigwedge_{d_m, d_n \in \mathbf{b} * \mathbf{c}} \bigwedge_{l=1}^{s} (d_m = d_n \to e_{l,m} = e_{l,n}) \end{array} \right]$$

where $\mathbf{b} * \mathbf{c} := d_1, \ldots, d_{q+t}$ is the concatenation of the tuples $\mathbf{b}$ and $\mathbf{c}$ and $\bar{\psi}(\mathbf{b}, \mathbf{c}, \mathbf{e})$ is obtained from

$$\bigwedge_{\sigma: \mathbf{i} \to \mathbf{b}} \psi(\mathbf{i}\sigma, \mathbf{a}(\mathbf{i}\sigma), \mathbf{c}, \mathbf{a}(\mathbf{c}))$$

by substituting each term in the tuple $\mathbf{a}(\mathbf{b}) * \mathbf{a}(\mathbf{c})$ with the constant occupying the corresponding position in the tuple $\mathbf{e}$.

STEP IV. Let $\mathcal{B}$ a full Boolean satisfying assignment for the atoms of the formula

$$F_3 := \bar{\psi}(\mathbf{b}, \mathbf{c}, \mathbf{e}) \wedge \bigwedge_{d_m, d_n \in \mathbf{b} * \mathbf{c}} \bigwedge_{l=1}^{s} (d_m = d_n \to e_{l,m} = e_{l,n})$$

and let $\bar{\psi}_I(\mathbf{b}, \mathbf{c}), \bar{\psi}_E(\mathbf{e})$ be the (conjunction of the) sets of literals of sort INDEX and ELEM, respectively, induced by $\mathcal{B}$.

STEP V. Check the T_I-satisfiability of

$$F_I := \exists \mathbf{b}\,\exists \mathbf{c}.\ \left[\forall x.\ \left(\bigvee_{j=1}^{q}\bigwedge_{L\in M_j} L(x,\mathbf{c})\right) \wedge \bigwedge_{j=1}^{q}\bigwedge_{L\in M_j} L(b_j,\mathbf{c}) \wedge \bar{\psi}_I(\mathbf{b},\mathbf{c})\right]$$

and the T_E-satisfiability of

$$F_E := \bar{\psi}_E(\mathbf{e})$$

Notice that F_I is an $\exists^*\forall$-sentence; F_E is ground and the T_E-satisfiability of F_E (considering the $\mathbf{e}$ as variables instead of as free constants) is decidable because we assumed that all the theories we consider (hence our T_E too) have quantifier-free fragments decidable for satisfiability.

Theorem 2 applies to $\mathtt{ARR}^2(\mathbb{P},\mathbb{P})$ because $\mathbb{P}$ admits quantifier elimination. For this theory, we can determine complexity upper and lower bounds:

Theorem 3. $\mathtt{ARR}^2(\mathbb{P},\mathbb{P})$-*satisfiability of* $\exists^*\forall^*$-*monic-flat sentences is* NEXPTIME-*complete.*

Proof. We use exponentially bounded domino systems for reduction [6,19], see [2] for details.   ⊣

4 A Decidability Result for the Reachability Analysis of Flat Array Programs

Based on the decidability results described in the previous section, we can now achieve important decidability results in the context of reachability analysis for programs handling arrays of unbounded length. As a reference theory, we shall use $\mathtt{ARR}^1(\mathbb{P}^+)$ or $\mathtt{ARR}^2(\mathbb{P}^+,\mathbb{P}^+)$, where $\mathbb{P}^+$ is $\mathbb{P}$ enriched with free constant symbols and with *definable* predicate and function symbols. We do not enter into more details concerning what a definable symbol is (see, e.g., [25]), we just underline that definable symbols are nothing but useful macros that can be used to formalize case-defined functions and SMT-LIB commands like if-then-else. The addition of definable symbols does not compromise quantifier elimination, hence decidability of $\mathbb{P}^+$. Below, we let $\mathcal{T}$ be $\mathtt{ARR}^1(\mathbb{P}^+)$ or $\mathtt{ARR}^2(\mathbb{P}^+,\mathbb{P}^+)$.

Henceforth $\mathbf{v}$ will denote, in the following, the variables of the programs we will analyze. Formally, $\mathbf{v} = \mathbf{a},\mathbf{c}$ where, according to our conventions, $\mathbf{a}$ is a tuple of array variables (modeled as free unary function symbols of $\mathcal{T}$ in our framework) and $\mathbf{c}$ a tuple of scalar variables; the latter can be modeled as variables in the logical sense - in $\mathtt{ARR}^2(\mathbb{P}^+,\mathbb{P}^+)$ we can model them either as variables of sort INDEX or as free constants of sort ELEM.

A *state-formula* is a formula $\alpha(\mathbf{v})$ of $\mathcal{T}$ representing a (possibly infinite) set of configurations of the program under analysis. A *transition formula* is a formula of $\mathcal{T}$ of the kind $\tau(\mathbf{v},\mathbf{v}')$ where $\mathbf{v}'$ is obtained from copying the variables in $\mathbf{v}$ and adding a prime to each of them. For the purpose of this work, programs will be represented by their control-flow automaton.

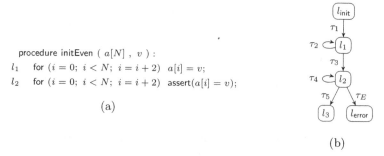

```
procedure initEven ( a[N] , v ) :
l1    for (i = 0; i < N; i = i + 2)  a[i] = v;
l2    for (i = 0; i < N; i = i + 2)  assert(a[i] = v);
```

(a)

(b)

Fig. 1. The initEven procedure (a) and its control-flow graph (b)

Definition 1 (Programs). *Given a set of variables* $\mathbf{v}$, *a program is a triple* $\mathcal{P} = (L, \Lambda, E)$, *where (i)* $L = \{l_1, \ldots, l_n\}$ *is a set of* program locations *among which we distinguish an initial location* l_{init} *and an error location* l_{error}; *(ii)* Λ *is a finite set of transition formulæ* $\{\tau_1(\mathbf{v}, \mathbf{v}'), \ldots, \tau_r(\mathbf{v}, \mathbf{v}')\}$ *and (iii)* $E \subseteq L \times \Lambda \times L$ *is a set of* actions.

We indicate by $src, \mathcal{L}, trg$ the three projection functions on E; that is, for $e = (l_i, \tau_j, l_k) \in E$, we have $src(e) = l_i$ (this is called the 'source' location of e), $\mathcal{L}(e) = \tau_j$ (this is called the 'label' of e) and $trg(e) = l_k$ (this is called the 'target' location of e).

Example 2. Consider the procedure initEven in Fig. 1. For this procedure, $\mathbf{a} = a$, $\mathbf{c} = i, v$. N is a constant of the background theory. Λ is the set of formulæ (we omit identical updates):

$$\tau_1 := i' = 0$$
$$\tau_2 := i < N \wedge a' = \lambda j. \text{if } (j = i) \text{ then } v \text{ else } a(j) \wedge i' = i + 2$$
$$\tau_3 := i \geq N \wedge i' = 0$$
$$\tau_4 := i < N \wedge a(i) = v \wedge i' = i + 2$$
$$\tau_5 := i \geq N$$
$$\tau_E := i < N \wedge a(i) \neq v$$

The procedure initEven can be formalized as the control-flow graph depicted in Fig. 1(b), where $L = \{l_{\mathsf{init}}, l_1, l_2, l_3, l_{\mathsf{error}}\}$.

Definition 2 (Program paths). *A program path (in short, path) of* $\mathcal{P} = (L, \Lambda, E)$ *is a sequence* $\rho \in E^n$, *i.e.,* $\rho = e_1, e_2, \ldots, e_n$, *such that for every* e_i, e_{i+1}, $trg(e_i) = src(e_{i+1})$. *We denote with* $|\rho|$ *the length of the path. An error path is a path* ρ *with* $src(e_1) = l_{\mathsf{init}}$ *and* $trg(e_{|\rho|}) = l_{\mathsf{error}}$. *A path* ρ *is a feasible path if* $\bigwedge_{j=1}^{|\rho|} \mathcal{L}(e_j)^{(j)}$ *is* $\mathcal{T}$-satisfiable, *where* $\mathcal{L}(e_j)^{(j)}$ *represents* $\tau_{i_j}(\mathbf{v}^{(j-1)}, \mathbf{v}^{(j)})$, *with* $\mathcal{L}(e_j) = \tau_{i_j}$.

The *(unbounded) reachability problem* for a program $\mathcal{P}$ is to detect if $\mathcal{P}$ admits a feasible error path. Proving the safety of $\mathcal{P}$, therefore, means solving the reachability problem for $\mathcal{P}$. This problem, given well known limiting results, is not decidable for an arbitrary program $\mathcal{P}$. The consequence is that, in general, reachability analysis is sound, but not complete, and its incompleteness manifests itself in (possible) divergence of the verification algorithm (see, e.g., [1]).

To gain decidability, we must first impose restrictions on the shape of the transition formulæ, for instance we can constrain the analysis to formulæ falling within decidable classes like those we analyzed in the previous section. This is not sufficient however, due to the presence of loops in the control flow. Hence we assume flatness conditions on such control flow and "accelerability" of the transitions labeling self-loops. This is similar to what is done in [7, 9, 12] for integer variable programs, but since we handle array variables we need specific restrictions for acceleration. Our result for the decidability of the safety of annotated array programs builds upon the results presented in Section 3 and the acceleration procedure presented in [3].

We first give the definition of flat^0-program, i.e., programs with only self-loops for which each location belongs to at most one loop. Subsequently we will identify sufficient conditions for achieving the full decidability of the reachability problem for flat^0-programs.

Definition 3 (flat^0-program). *A program $\mathcal{P}$ is a* flat^0*-program if for every path $\rho = e_1, \ldots, e_n$ of $\mathcal{P}$ it holds that for every $j < k$ $(j, k \in \{1, \ldots, n\})$, if $src(e_j) = trg(e_k)$ then $e_j = e_{j+1} = \cdots = e_k$.*

We now turn our attention to transition formulæ. Acceleration is a well-known formalism in the area of model-checking. It has been integrated in several frameworks and constitutes a fundamental technology for the scalability and efficiency of modern model checkers (e.g., [5]). Given a loop, represented as a transition relation τ, the accelerated transition τ^+ allows to compute *in one shot* the *precise* set of states reachable after n unwindings of that loop, for any n. This prevents divergence of the reachability analysis along τ, caused by its unwinding. What prevents the applicability of acceleration in the domain we are targeting is that accelerations are not always definable. By definition, the acceleration of a transition $\tau(\mathbf{v}, \mathbf{v}')$ is the union of the n-th compositions of τ with itself, i.e. it is $\tau^+ := \bigvee_{n>0} \tau^n$, where

$$\tau^1(\mathbf{v}, \mathbf{v}') := \tau(\mathbf{v}, \mathbf{v}'), \qquad \tau^{n+1}(\mathbf{v}, \mathbf{v}') := \exists \mathbf{v}''.(\tau(\mathbf{v}, \mathbf{v}'') \wedge \tau^n(\mathbf{v}'', \mathbf{v}')) .$$

τ^+ can be practically exploited only if there exists a formula $\varphi(\mathbf{v}, \mathbf{v}')$ equivalent, modulo the considered background theory, to $\bigvee_{n>0} \tau^n$. Based on this observation on definability of accelerations, we are now ready to state a general result about the decidability of the reachability problem for programs with arrays. The theorem we give is, as we did for results in Section 3, modular and general. We will show an instance of this result in the following section. Notationally, let us extend the projection function $\mathcal{L}$ by denoting $\mathcal{L}^+(e) := \mathcal{L}(e)^+$ if $src(e) = trg(e)$ and $\mathcal{L}^+(e) := \mathcal{L}(e)$ otherwise, where $\mathcal{L}(e)^+$ denotes the acceleration of the transition labeling the edge e.

Theorem 4. *Let $\mathcal{F}$ be a class of formulæ decidable for $\mathcal{T}$-satisfiability. The unbounded reachability problem for a flat^0-program $\mathcal{P}$ is decidable if (i) $\mathcal{F}$ is closed under conjunctions and (ii) for each $e \in E$ one can compute $\alpha(\mathbf{v}, \mathbf{v}') \in \mathcal{F}$ such that $\mathcal{T} \models \mathcal{L}^+(e) \leftrightarrow \alpha(\mathbf{v}, \mathbf{v}')$,*

Proof. Let $\rho = e_1, \ldots, e_n$ be an error path of $\mathcal{P}$; when testing its feasibility, according to Definition 3, we can limit ourselves to the case in which $e_1, \ldots, e_n$ are all distinct, provided we replace the labels $\mathcal{L}(e_k)^{(k)}$ with $\mathcal{L}^+(e_k)^{(k)}$ in the formula $\bigwedge_{j=1}^{n} \mathcal{L}(e_j)^{(j)}$ from Definition 2.[3] Thus $\mathcal{P}$ is unsafe iff, for some path $e_1, \ldots, e_n$ whose edges are all distinct, the formula

$$\mathcal{L}^+(e_1)^{(1)} \wedge \cdots \wedge \mathcal{L}^+(e_n)^{(n)} \tag{1}$$

is $\mathcal{T}$-satisfiable. Since the involved paths are finitely many and $\mathcal{T}$-satisfiability of formulæ like (1) is decidable, the safety of $\mathcal{P}$ can be decided.   ⊣

4.1 A Class of Array Programs with Decidable Reachability Problem

We now produce a class of programs with arrays – we call it simple$_{\mathcal{A}}^0$-programs– for which requirements of Theorem 4 are met. The class of simple$_{\mathcal{A}}^0$-programs contains non recursive programs implementing searching, copying, comparing, initializing, replacing and testing procedures. As an example, the initEven program reported in Fig. 1 is a simple$_{\mathcal{A}}^0$-program. Formally, a simple$_{\mathcal{A}}^0$-*program* $\mathcal{P} = (L, \Lambda, E)$ is a flat^0-program such that (i) every $\tau \in \Lambda$ is a formula belonging to one of the decidable classes covered by Corollary 1 or Theorem 3; (ii) if $e \in E$ is a self-loop, then $\mathcal{L}(e)$ is a simple$_k$-assignment.

Simple$_k$-assignments are transitions (defined below) for which the acceleration is first-order definable and is a Flat Array Property. For a natural number k, we denote by $\bar{k}$ the term $1 + \cdots + 1$ (k-times) and by $\bar{k} \cdot t$ the term $t + \cdots + t$ (k-times).

Definition 4 (simple$_k$-assignment). *Let $k \geq 0$; a simple$_k$-assignment is a transition $\tau(\mathbf{v}, \mathbf{v}')$ of the kind*

$$\phi_L(\mathbf{c}, \mathbf{a}[d]) \wedge d' = d + \bar{k} \wedge \mathbf{d}' = \mathbf{d} \wedge \mathbf{a}' = \lambda j.\text{if } (j = d) \text{ then } \mathbf{t}(\mathbf{c}, \mathbf{a}(d)) \text{ else } \mathbf{a}(j)$$

where (i) $\mathbf{c} = d, \mathbf{d}$ and (ii) the formula $\phi_L(\mathbf{c}, \mathbf{a}[d])$ and the terms $\mathbf{t}(\mathbf{c}, \mathbf{a}[d])$ are flat.

The following Lemma (which is an instance of a more general result from [3]) gives the template for the accelerated counterpart of a simple$_k$-assignment.

Lemma 1. *Let $\tau(\mathbf{v}, \mathbf{v}')$ be a simple$_k$-assignment. Then $\tau^+(\mathbf{v}, \mathbf{v}')$ is $\mathcal{T}$-equivalent to the formula*

$$\exists y > 0 \begin{pmatrix} \forall z. \big((d \leq z < d + \bar{k} \cdot y \wedge D_{\bar{k}}(z - d)) \rightarrow \phi_L(z, \mathbf{d}, \mathbf{a}(d))\big) \wedge \\ \mathbf{a}' = \lambda j.\mathbf{U}(j, y, \mathbf{v}) \wedge d' = d + \bar{k} \cdot y \wedge \mathbf{d}' = \mathbf{d} \end{pmatrix}$$

---

[3] Notice that by these replacements we can represent in one shot infinitely many paths, namely those executing self-loops any given number of times.

where the definable functions $U_h(j, y, \mathbf{v})$, $1 \leq h \leq s$ *of the tuple* $\mathbf{U}$ *are*

$$\text{if } (d \leq j < d + \bar{k} \cdot y \ \wedge D_{\bar{k}}(j - d)) \text{ then } t_h(j, \mathbf{d}, \mathbf{a}(j)) \text{ else } a_h(j) .$$

Example 3. Consider transition τ_2 from the formalization of our running example of Fig. 1. The acceleration τ_2^+ of such formula is (we omit identical updates)

$$\exists y > 0. \begin{pmatrix} \forall z.(i \leq z < i + 2y \wedge D_2(z - i) \to z < N) \wedge i' = i + 2y \ \wedge \\ a' = \lambda j. (\text{if } (i \leq j < 2y + i \wedge D_2(j - i)) \text{ then } v \text{ else } a[j]) \end{pmatrix}$$

We can now formally show that the reachability problem for simple_A^0-programs is decidable, by instantiating Theorem 4 with the results obtained so far.

Theorem 5. *The unbounded reachability problem for* simple_A^0*-programs is decidable.*

Proof. By prenex transformations, distributions of universal quantifiers over conjunctions, etc., it is easy to see that the decidable classes covered by Corollary 1 or Theorem 3 are closed under conjunctions. Since the acceleration of a simple_k-assignment fits inside these classes (just eliminate definitions via λ-abstractions by using universal quantifiers), Theorem 4 applies. ⊣

4.2 Experimental Observations

We evaluated the capabilities of available SMT-Solvers on checking the satisfiability of Flat Array Properties and for that we selected some simple_A^0-programs, both safe and unsafe. Following the procedure identified in the proof of Theorem 4 we generated 200 SMT-LIB2-compliant files with Flat Array Properties[4]. The simple_A^0-programs we selected perform some simple manipulations on arrays of unknown length, like searching for a given element, initializing the array, swapping the arrays, copying one array into another, etc. We tested CVC4 [4] (version 1.2) and Z3 [10] (version 4.3.1) on the generated SMT-LIB2 files. Experimentation has been performed on a machine equipped with a 2.66 GHz CPU and 4GB of RAM running Mac OSX 10.8.5. From our evaluation, both tools timeout on some proof-obligations[5]. These results suggest that the fragment of Flat Array Properties definitely identifies fragments of theories which are decidable, but their satisfiability is still not entirely covered by modern and highly engineered tools.

5   Conclusions and Related Work

In this paper we identified a class of Flat Array Properties, a quantified fragment of theories of arrays, admitting decision procedures. Our results are parameterized in the theories used to model indexes and elements of the array; in this sense,

---

[4] Such files have been generated automatically with our prototype tool which we make available at www.inf.usi.ch/phd/alberti/prj/booster.

[5] See the discussion in [2] for more information on the experiments.

there is some similarity with [18], although (contrary to [18]) we consider purely syntactically specified classes of formulæ. We provided a complexity analysis of our decision procedures. We also showed that the decidability of Flat Array Properties, combined with acceleration results, allows to depict a sound and complete procedure for checking the safety of a class of programs with arrays.

The modular nature of our solution makes our contributions orthogonal with respect to the state of the art: we can enrich $\mathbb{P}$ with various definable or even not definable symbols [24] and get from our Theorems 1,2 decidable classes which are far from the scope of existing results. Still, it is interesting to notice that also the special cases of the decidable classes covered by Corollary 1 and Theorem 3 are orthogonal to the results from the literature. To this aim, we make a closer comparison with [8,15]. The two fragments considered in [8,15] are characterized by rather restrictive syntactic constraints. In [15] it is considered a subclass of the $\exists^*\forall$-fragment of $\mathtt{ARR}^1(T)$ called SIL, *Single Index Logic*. In this class, formulæ are built according to a grammar allowing (i) as atoms only difference logic constraints and some equations modulo a fixed integer and (ii) as universally quantified subformulæ only formulæ of the kind $\forall \mathbf{i}.\phi(\mathbf{i}) \to \psi(\mathbf{i}, \mathbf{a}(\mathbf{i} + \bar{\mathbf{k}}))$ (here $\mathbf{k}$ is a tuple of integers) where ϕ, ψ are conjunctions of atoms (in particular, no disjunction is allowed in ψ). On the other side, SIL includes some non-flat formulæ, due to the presence of constant increment terms $\mathbf{i} + \bar{\mathbf{k}}$ in the consequents of the above universally quantified implications. Similar restrictions are in [16]. The Array Property Fragment described in [8] is basically a subclass of the $\exists^*\forall^*$-fragment of $\mathtt{ARR}^2(\mathbb{P}, \mathbb{P})$; however universally quantified subformulæ are constrained to be of the kind $\forall \mathbf{i}.\phi(\mathbf{i}) \to \psi(\mathbf{a}(\mathbf{i}))$, where in addition the INDEX part $\phi(\mathbf{i})$ must be a conjunction of atoms of the kind $i \leq j, i \leq t, t \leq i$ (with $i, j \in \mathbf{i}$ and where t does not contain occurrences of the universally quantified variables $\mathbf{i}$). These formulæ are flat but not monic because of the atoms $i \leq j$.

From a computational point of view, a complexity bound for $\mathsf{SAT}_{\mathsf{MONO}}$ has been shown in the proof of Theorem 1, while the complexity of the decision procedure proposed in [15] is unknown. On the other side, both $\mathsf{SAT}_{\mathsf{MULTI}}$ and the decision procedure described in [8] run in NEXPTIME (the decision procedure in [8] is in NP only if the number of universally quantified index variables is bounded by a constant N). Our decision procedures for quantified formulæ are also partially different, in spirit, from those presented so far in the SMT community. While the vast majority of SMT-Solvers address the problem of checking the satisfiability of quantified formulæ via instantiation (see, e.g., [8,11,14,23]), our procedures – in particular $\mathsf{SAT}_{\mathsf{MULTI}}$ – are still based on instantiation, but the instantiation refers to a set of terms enlarged with the free constants witnessing the guessed set of realized types.

From the point of view of the applications, providing a full decidability result for the unbounded reachability analysis of a class of array programs is what differentiates our work with other contributions like [1,3].

References

1. Alberti, F., Bruttomesso, R., Ghilardi, S., Ranise, S., Sharygina, N.: Lazy abstraction with interpolants for arrays. In: Bjørner, N., Voronkov, A. (eds.) LPAR-18. LNCS, vol. 7180, pp. 46–61. Springer, Heidelberg (2012)
2. Alberti, F., Ghilardi, S., Sharygina, N.: Decision procedures for flat array properties. Technical Report 2013/04, University of Lugano (October 2013), http://www.inf.usi.ch/research_publication.htm?id=77
3. Alberti, F., Ghilardi, S., Sharygina, N.: Definability of accelerated relations in a theory of arrays and its applications. In: Fontaine, P., Ringeissen, C., Schmidt, R.A. (eds.) FroCoS 2013. LNCS, vol. 8152, pp. 23–39. Springer, Heidelberg (2013)
4. Barrett, C., Conway, C.L., Deters, M., Hadarean, L., Jovanović, D., King, T., Reynolds, A., Tinelli, C.: CVC4. In: Gopalakrishnan, G., Qadeer, S. (eds.) CAV 2011. LNCS, vol. 6806, pp. 171–177. Springer, Heidelberg (2011)
5. Behrmann, G., Bengtsson, J., David, A., Larsen, K.G., Pettersson, P., Yi, W.: UPPAAL implementation secrets. In: Damm, W., Olderog, E.-R. (eds.) FTRTFT 2002. LNCS, vol. 2469, pp. 3–22. Springer, Heidelberg (2002)
6. Börger, E., Grädel, E., Gurevich, Y.: The classical decision problem. Perspectives in Mathematical Logic. Springer, Berlin (1997)
7. Bozga, M., Iosif, R., Lakhnech, Y.: Flat parametric counter automata. Fundamenta Informaticae (91), 275–303 (2009)
8. Bradley, A.R., Manna, Z., Sipma, H.B.: What's decidable about arrays? In: Emerson, E.A., Namjoshi, K.S. (eds.) VMCAI 2006. LNCS, vol. 3855, pp. 427–442. Springer, Heidelberg (2006)
9. Comon, H., Jurski, Y.: Multiple counters automata, safety analysis and presburger arithmetic. In: Vardi, M.Y. (ed.) CAV 1998. LNCS, vol. 1427, pp. 268–279. Springer, Heidelberg (1998)
10. de Moura, L., Bjørner, N.: Z3: An efficient SMT solver. In: Ramakrishnan, C.R., Rehof, J. (eds.) TACAS 2008. LNCS, vol. 4963, pp. 337–340. Springer, Heidelberg (2008)
11. Detlefs, D.L., Nelson, G., Saxe, J.B.: Simplify: a theorem prover for program checking. Technical Report HPL-2003-148, HP Labs (2003)
12. Finkel, A., Leroux, J.: How to compose Presburger-accelerations: Applications to broadcast protocols. In: Agrawal, M., Seth, A.K. (eds.) FSTTCS 2002. LNCS, vol. 2556, pp. 145–156. Springer, Heidelberg (2002)
13. Ganzinger, H.: Shostak light. In: Voronkov, A. (ed.) CADE 2002. LNCS (LNAI), vol. 2392, pp. 332–346. Springer, Heidelberg (2002)
14. Ge, Y., de Moura, L.: Complete instantiation for quantified formulas in satisfiabiliby modulo theories. In: Bouajjani, A., Maler, O. (eds.) CAV 2009. LNCS, vol. 5643, pp. 306–320. Springer, Heidelberg (2009)
15. Habermehl, P., Iosif, R., Vojnar, T.: A logic of singly indexed arrays. In: Cervesato, I., Veith, H., Voronkov, A. (eds.) LPAR 2008. LNCS (LNAI), vol. 5330, pp. 558–573. Springer, Heidelberg (2008)
16. Habermehl, P., Iosif, R., Vojnar, T.: What else is decidable about integer arrays? In: Amadio, R.M. (ed.) FOSSACS 2008. LNCS, vol. 4962, pp. 474–489. Springer, Heidelberg (2008)
17. Halpern, J.Y.: Presburger arithmetic with unary predicates is Π_1^1 complete. J. Symbolic Logic 56(2), 637–642 (1991), doi:10.2307/2274706
18. Ihlemann, C., Jacobs, S., Sofronie-Stokkermans, V.: On local reasoning in verification. In: Ramakrishnan, C.R., Rehof, J. (eds.) TACAS 2008. LNCS, vol. 4963, pp. 265–281. Springer, Heidelberg (2008)

19. Lewis, H.B.: Complexity of solvable cases of the decision problem for the predicate calculus. In: 19th Ann. Symp. on Found. of Comp. Sci. pp. 35–47. IEEE (1978)
20. Nieuwenhuis, R., Oliveras, A.: DPLL(T) with Exhaustive Theory Propagation and Its Application to Difference Logic. In: Etessami, K., Rajamani, S.K. (eds.) CAV 2005. LNCS, vol. 3576, pp. 321–334. Springer, Heidelberg (2005)
21. Oppen, D.C.: A superexponential upper bound on the complexity of Presburger arithmetic. J. Comput. System Sci. 16(3), 323–332 (1978)
22. Ranise, S., Tinelli, C.: The Satisfiability Modulo Theories Library, SMT-LIB (2006), http://www.smt-lib.org
23. Reynolds, A., Tinelli, C., Goel, A., Krstić, S., Deters, M., Barrett, C.: Quantifier instantiation techniques for finite model finding in SMT. In: Bonacina, M.P. (ed.) CADE 2013. LNCS, vol. 7898, pp. 377–391. Springer, Heidelberg (2013)
24. Semënov, A.L.: Logical theories of one-place functions on the set of natural numbers. Izvestiya: Mathematics 22, 587–618 (1984)
25. Shoenfield, J.R.: Mathematical logic. Association for Symbolic Logic, Urbana (2001) (reprint of the 1973 second printing)
26. Tinelli, C., Zarba, C.G.: Combining nonstably infinite theories. J. Automat. Reason. 34(3), 209–238 (2005)

SATMC: A SAT-Based Model Checker
for Security-Critical Systems

Alessandro Armando[1,2], Roberto Carbone[2], and Luca Compagna[3]

[1] DIBRIS, University of Genova, Genova, Italy
[2] Security & Trust, FBK, Trento, Italy
[3] Product Security Research, SAP AG, Sophia Antipolis, France
{armando,carbone}@fbk.eu, luca.compagna@sap.com

Abstract. We present SATMC 3.0, a SAT-based bounded model checker for security-critical systems that stems from a successful combination of encoding techniques originally developed for planning with techniques developed for the analysis of reactive systems. SATMC has been successfully applied in a variety of application domains (security protocols, security-sensitive business processes, and cryptographic APIs) and for different purposes (design-time security analysis and security testing). SATMC strikes a balance between general purpose model checkers and security protocol analyzers as witnessed by a number of important success stories including the discovery of a serious man-in-the-middle attack on the SAML-based Single Sign-On (SSO) for Google Apps, an authentication flaw in the SAML 2.0 Web Browser SSO Profile, and a number of attacks on PKCS#11 Security Tokens. SATMC is integrated and used as back-end in a number of research prototypes (e.g., the AVISPA Tool, Tookan, the SPaCIoS Tool) and industrial-strength tools (e.g., the Security Validator plugin for SAP NetWeaver BPM).

1 Introduction

With the convergence of the social, cloud, and mobile paradigms, information and communication technologies are affecting our everyday personal and working live to unprecedented depth and scale. We routinely use online services that stem from the fruitful combination of mobile applications, web applications, cloud services, and/or social networks. Sensitive data handled by these services often flows across organizational boundaries and both the privacy of the users and the assets of organizations are often at risk.

Solutions (e.g., security protocols and services) that aim to securely combine the ever-growing ecosystem of online services are already available. But they are notoriously difficult to get right. Many security-critical protocols and services have been designed and developed only to be found flawed years after their deployment. These flaws are usually due to the complex and unexpected interactions of the protocols and services as well as to the possible interference of malicious agents. Since these weaknesses are very difficult to spot by traditional verification techniques (e.g., manual inspection and testing), security-critical systems are a natural target for formal method techniques.

E. Ábrahám and K. Havelund (Eds.): TACAS 2014, LNCS 8413, pp. 31–45, 2014.
© Springer-Verlag Berlin Heidelberg 2014

SATMC is a SAT-based bounded model checker for security-critical systems that combines encoding techniques developed for planning [26] with techniques developed for the analysis of reactive systems [15]. The approach reduces the problem of determining whether the system violates a security goal in $k > 0$ steps to the problem of checking the satisfiability of a propositional formula (the SAT problem). Modern SAT solvers can tackle SAT problems of practical relevance in milliseconds. Since its first release in 2004 [8], SATMC has been enhanced to support Horn clauses and first-order LTL formulae. This makes SATMC 3.0 able to support the security analysis of distributed systems that exchange messages over a wide range of secure channels, are subject to sophisticated security policies, and/or aim at achieving a variety of security goals.

Since (both honest and malicious) agents can build and exchange messages of finite, but arbitrary complexity (through concatenation and a variety of cryptographic primitives), most security-critical, distributed systems are inherently infinite state. For this reason general purpose model checkers (e.g., SPIN [24], NuSMV [19])—which assume the input system to be finite state—are not suited for the analysis of a large and important set of security-critical systems (e.g., cryptographic protocols and APIs). Special purpose tools (most notably, security protocol analyzers, e.g., CL-AtSe [27], OFMC [13], Proverif [16]) are capable of very good performance and support reasoning about the algebraic properties of cryptographic operators. SATMC complements security protocol analyzers by supporting a powerful specification language for communication channels, intruder capabilities, and security goals based on first-order LTL.

SATMC strikes a balance between general purpose model checkers and security protocol analyzers. SATMC has been successfully applied in variety of application domains (namely, security protocols, security-sensitive business processes, and cryptographic APIs) and for different purposes (e.g., design-time security analysis and security testing). SATMC is integrated and used as a backend in a number of research prototypes (the AVISPA Tool [2], Tookan [18], the AVANTSSAR Platform [1], and the SPaCIoS Tool [28]) and industrial-strength tools (the Security Validator plugin for SAP NetWeaver BPM[1]). The effectiveness of SATMC is witnessed by the key role it played in the discovery of:

- a flaw in a "patched" version of the protocol for online contract signing proposed by Asokan, Shoup, and Waidner (ASW) [3],
- a serious man-in-the-middle attack on the SAML-based SSO for Google Apps [6] and, more recently, an authentication flaw in the SAML 2.0 Web Browser SSO Profile and related vulnerabilities on actual products [5],
- a number of attacks on the PKCS#11 Security Tokens [18], and
- a flaw in a two-factor and two-channel authentication protocol [7].

As shown in Figure 1, the applicability of SATMC in different domains is enabled by domain-specific connectors that translate the system and the property specifications into ASLan [12], a specification language based on set-rewriting, Horn clauses, and first-order LTL which is amenable to formal analysis. As shown

---

[1] http://scn.sap.com/docs/DOC-32838

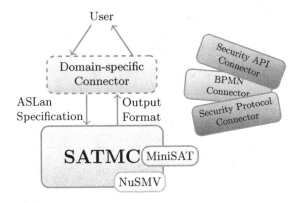

Fig. 1. High-level Overview

in the same figure, SATMC leverages NuSMV to generate the SAT encoding for the LTL formulae and MiniSAT [22] to solve the SAT problems.

Structure of the Paper. In the next section we present some success stories related to the application domains wherein SATMC has been so far employed. In Section 3 we provide the formal framework and in Section 4 we illustrate how the ASLan specification language can be used to specify security-critical systems, the abilities of the attackers, and the security goals. In Section 5 we present the bounded model checking procedure implemented in SATMC and the architecture of the tool, and we conclude in Section 6 with some final remarks.

2   Success Stories

SATMC has been successfully used to support the security analysis and testing in a variety of industry relevant application domains: security protocols, business processes, and security APIs.

Security Protocols.   Security protocols are communication protocols aiming to achieve security assurances of various kinds through the usage of cryptographic primitives. They are key to securing distributed information infrastructures, including—and most notably—the Web. The SAML 2.0 Single Sign-On protocol [21] (SAML SSO, for short) is the established standard for cross-domain browser-based SSO for enterprises. Figure 2 shows the prototypical use case for the SAML SSO that enables a Service Provider (SP) to authenticate a Client (C) via an Identity Provider (IdP): C asks SP to provide the resource at URI (step 1). SP then redirects C to IdP with the authentication request $AReq(\text{ID}, \text{SP})$, where ID uniquely identifies the request (steps 2 and 3). IdP then challenges C to provide valid credentials (gray dashed arrow). If the authentication succeeds, IdP builds and sends C a digitally signed authentication assertion $(\{AA\}_{K_{\text{IdP}}^{-1}})$ embedded into an HTTP form (step 4). This form also includes some script that automatically posts the message to SP (step 5). SP checks the assertion

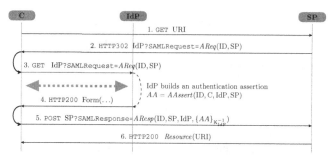

Fig. 2. SAML SSO Protocol

and then deliver the requested resource to C (step 6). Upon successful execution of the protocol, C and SP are mutually authenticated and the resource has been confidentially delivered to C. To achieve this, SAML SSO—as most of the application-level protocols—assumes that the communication between C and SP as well as that between C and IdP is carried over unilateral SSL/TLS communication channels. It must be noted that even with secure communication channels in place, designing and developing application-level security protocols such as the SAML SSO remains a challenge. These protocols are highly configurable, are described in bulky natural language specifications, and deviations from the standard may be dictated by application-specific requirements of the organization.

The SAML-based SSO for Google Apps in operation until June 2008 deviated from the standard in a few, seemingly minor ways. By using SATMC, we discovered an authentication flaw in the service that allowed a malicious SP to mount a severe man-in-the-middle attack [6]. We readily informed Google and the US-CERT of the problem. In response to our findings Google developed a patch and asked their customers to update their applications accordingly. A vulnerability report was then released by the US-CERT.[2] The severity of the vulnerability has been rated High by NIST.[3] By using the SATMC we also discovered an authentication flaw in the prototypical SAML SSO use case [5]. This flaw paves the way to launching Cross-Site Scripting (XSS) and Cross-Site Request Forgery (XSRF) attacks, as witnessed by a new XSS attack that we identified in the SAML-based SSO for Google Apps. We reported the problem to OASIS which subsequently released an *errata* addressing the issue.[4]

We also used SATMC at SAP as a back-end for security protocol analysis and testing (AVANTSSAR [1] and SPaCIoS [28]) to assist development teams in the design and development of the SAP NetWeaver SAML Single Sign-On (SAP NGSSO) and SAP OAuth 2.0 solutions. Overall, more than one hundred different protocol configurations and corresponding formal models have been analyzed, showing that both SAP NGSSO and SAP OAuth2 services are indeed well designed.

---

[2] http://www.kb.cert.org/vuls/id/612636
[3] http://web.nvd.nist.gov/view/vuln/detail?vulnId=CVE-2008-3891
[4] http://tools.oasis-open.org/issues/browse/SECURITY-12

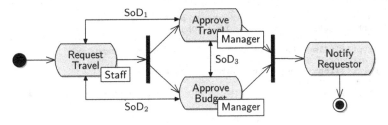

Fig. 3. A simple travel approval process with annotated security requirements

All in all, SATMC has been key to the analysis of various security protocols of industrial complexity, leading to the discovery of a number of serious flaws, including a vulnerability in a "patched" version of the optimistic fair-exchange contract signing protocol developed by Asokan, Shoup, and Weidner [3] and a protocol for strong authentication based on the GSM infrastructure [7].

Business Processes. A Business Process (BP) is a workflow of activities whose execution aims to accomplish a specific business goal. BPs must be carefully designed and executed so to comply with security and regulatory compliance requirements. Figure 3 illustrates a simple example of a BP for travel request approval: a staff member may issue a travel request. Both the reason and the budget of the travel must be approved by managers. Afterwards, the requesting user is notified whether the request is granted or not. The BP shall ensure a number of authorization requirements: only managers shall be able to approve the reason and budget of travel requests. Moreover, a manager should not be allowed to approve her own travel request (Separation of Duty). Finally, the manager that approves the travel reason should not get access to the details of the travel budget (and vice versa) to perform her job (Need-to-Know Principle). Checking whether a given BP of real-world complexity complies with these kind of requirements is difficult.

SATMC has been used to model check BPs against high-level authorization requirements [10]. Moreover, SATMC lies at the core of a Security Validation prototype for BPs developed by the Product Security Research unit at SAP. This prototype can integrate off-the-shelf Business Process Management (BPM) systems (e.g., SAP Netweaver BPM and Activity) to support BP analysts in the evaluation of BP compliance. It enables a BP analyst to easily specify the security goals and triggers SATMC via a translation of the BP workflow, data, security policy and goal into ASLan. As soon as a flaw is discovered, it is graphically rendered to the analyst [20,11].

Security APIs. A Security API is an Application Program Interface that allows untrusted code to access sensitive resources in a secure way. Figure 4 shows a few methods of the Java interface[5] for the security API defined by the PKCS#11 standard [25]. The Java interface and its implementation allow to access the PKCS#11 modules of smart cards or other hardware security modules (HSM) where

---

[5] http://javadoc.iaik.tugraz.at/pkcs11_wrapper/1.2.15/iaik/pkcs/
pkcs11/wrapper/PKCS11.html

```
// modifies the value of one or more object attributes
void C_SetAttributeValue(long hSes, long hObj, CK_ATTRIBUTE[] pAtt)
// initializes a decryption operation
void C_DecryptInit(long hSes, CK_MECHANISM pMechanism, long hKey)
// decrypt encrypted data
byte[] C_Decrypt(long hSes, byte[] pEncryptedData)
// wraps (i.e., encrypts) a key
byte[] C_WrapKey(long hSes, CK_MECHANISM pMechanism, long hWrappingKey, long hKey)
```

Fig. 4. PKCS#11: Java interface

sensitive resources (e.g., cryptographic keys, pin numbers) can be stored. These resources can be associated with attributes (cf. C_SetAttributeValue) stating, e.g., whether they can be extracted from the device or not, whether a certain key can be used to wrap (encrypt) another key, etc. For instance, if an object is set to be non-extractable, then it cannot be reset and become extractable again. More in general, changes to the attribute values and access to sensitive resources must comply the policy that the security API is designed to enforce and this must hold for any possible sequence of invocation of the methods offered by the API (C_Decrypt, C_WrapKey, etc.).

SATMC lies at the core of Tookan [18], a tool capable to automatically detect and reproduce policy violations in commercially available cryptographic security tokens, exploiting vulnerabilities in their RSA PKCS#11 based APIs. Tookan can automatically reverse-engineer real PKCS#11 tokens, deduce their functionalities, construct formal models of the API for the SATMC model checker, and then execute the attack traces found by SATMC directly against the actual token. Tookan has been able to detect a variety of severe attacks on a number of commercial tokens (e.g., SecurID800 by RSA, CardOS V4.3 B by Siemens) [23]. Cryptosense[6] is a spin-off recently established on top of the success of Tookan.

3   Formal Framework

A *fact* is an atomic formula of a first-order language. We consider a language $\mathcal{L}$ defined as the smallest set of formulae containing facts and equalities between (first-order) terms as atomic propositions as well as the formulae built with the usual propositional connectives ($\neg$, $\vee$, ...), first-order quantifiers ($\forall$ and $\exists$), and temporal operators (**F** for "some time in the future", **G** for "globally", **O** for "some time in the past", ...). A formula is *closed* if and only if all variables in it are bound by some quantifier.

Let $\mathcal{V}$ be the set of variables in $\mathcal{L}$; let $\mathcal{F}$ and $\mathcal{T}$ be the (possibly infinite) sets of ground (i.e., variable-free) facts and terms of $\mathcal{L}$ respectively. A *model* is 4-uple $M = \langle \mathcal{I}, \mathcal{R}, \mathcal{H}, \mathcal{C} \rangle$, where

- $\mathcal{I} \subseteq \mathcal{F}$ is the *initial state*,
- $\mathcal{R}$ is a set of *rewrite rules*, i.e., expressions of the form ($L \xrightarrow{r(v_1,...,v_n)} R$), where L and R are finite sets of facts, r is a *rule name* (i.e., an n-ary function

---

[6] http://cryptosense.com/

symbol uniquely associated with the rule) for $n \geq 0$, and $v_1, \ldots, v_n$ are the variables in L; it is required that the variables occurring in R also occur in L.

- $\mathcal{H}$ is a set of *Horn clauses*, i.e., expressions of the form $(h \xleftarrow{c(v_1, \ldots, v_n)} B)$, where h is a fact, B is a finite set of facts, c is a *Horn clause name* (i.e., an n-ary function symbol uniquely associated with the clause) for $n \geq 0$, and $v_1, \ldots, v_n$ are the variables occurring in the clause.

- $\mathcal{C} \subseteq \mathcal{L}$ is a set of closed formulae called *constraints*.

An *assignment* is a total function from $\mathcal{V}$ into $\mathcal{T}$, i.e., $\sigma : \mathcal{V} \to \mathcal{T}$. Assignments are extended to the facts and terms of $\mathcal{L}$ in the obvious way. Let $S \subseteq \mathcal{F}$, *the closure of* $S \subseteq \mathcal{F}$ *under* $\mathcal{H}$, in symbols $\lceil S \rceil^{\mathcal{H}}$, is the smallest set of facts containing S and such that for all $(h \xleftarrow{c(\ldots)} B) \in \mathcal{H}$ and $\sigma : \mathcal{V} \to \mathcal{T}$ if $B\sigma \subseteq \lceil S \rceil^{\mathcal{H}}$ then $h\sigma \in \lceil S \rceil^{\mathcal{H}}$. A set of facts S *is closed under* $\mathcal{H}$ iff $\lceil S \rceil^{\mathcal{H}} = S$. We interpret the facts in $\lceil S \rceil^{\mathcal{H}}$ as the propositions holding in the state represented by S, all other facts being false (closed-world assumption). Let $(L \xrightarrow{\rho} R) \in \mathcal{R}$ and $\sigma : \mathcal{V} \to \mathcal{T}$. We say that *rule (instance)* $\rho\sigma$ *is applicable in state* S if and only if $L\sigma \subseteq \lceil S \rceil^{\mathcal{H}}$ and when this is the case $S' = \mathrm{app}_{\rho\sigma}(S) = (S \setminus L\sigma) \cup R\sigma$ is the state resulting from the execution of $\rho\sigma$ in S. A *path* π is an alternating sequence of states and rules instances $S_0 \rho_1 S_1 \rho_2 \ldots$ such that $S_i = \mathrm{app}_{\rho_i}(S_{i-1})$, for $i = 1, 2, \ldots$. If, additionally, $S_0 \subseteq \mathcal{I}$, then we say that the path is *initialized*. Let $\pi = S_0 \rho_1 S_1 \ldots$ be a path; we define $\pi(i) = S_i$ and $\pi_i = S_i \rho_{i+1} S_{i+1} \ldots$; $\pi(i)$ and π_i are the i-th state of the path and the suffix of the path starting with the i-th state, respectively. We assume that paths have infinite length. (This can be always obtained by adding stuttering transitions to the system.) Let π be an initialized path of M. An LTL formula ϕ *is valid on* π *under* σ, in symbols $\pi \models_\sigma \phi$, if and only if $\pi_0 \models_\sigma \phi$, where $\pi_i \models_\sigma \phi$ is inductively defined as follows.

$$
\begin{array}{lll}
\pi_i \models_\sigma f & \text{iff} & f\sigma \in \lceil \pi(i) \rceil^{\mathcal{H}} \ (f \text{ is a fact}) \\
\pi_i \models_\sigma t_1 = t_2 & \text{iff} & t_1\sigma \text{ and } t_2\sigma \text{ are the same term} \\
\pi_i \models_\sigma \neg\phi & \text{iff} & \pi_i \not\models_\sigma \phi \\
\pi_i \models_\sigma \phi \vee \psi & \text{iff} & \pi_i \models_\sigma \phi \text{ or } \pi_i \models_\sigma \psi \\
\pi_i \models_\sigma \mathbf{F}(\phi) & \text{iff} & \text{there exists } j \geq i \text{ such that } \pi_j \models_\sigma \phi \\
\pi_i \models_\sigma \mathbf{G}\phi & \text{iff} & \text{for all } j \geq i \ \pi_j \models_\sigma \phi \\
\pi_i \models_\sigma \mathbf{O}\phi & \text{iff} & \text{there exists } 0 \leq j \leq i \text{ such that } \pi_j \models_\sigma \phi \\
\pi_i \models_\sigma \exists x.\phi & \text{iff} & \text{there exists } t \in \mathcal{T} \text{ such that } \pi_i \models_{\sigma[t/x]} \phi
\end{array}
$$

where $\sigma[t/x]$ is the assignment that associates x with t and all other variables y with $\sigma(y)$. The semantics of the remaining connectives and temporal operators, as well as of the universal quantifier, is defined analogously. Let $M_1 = \langle \mathcal{I}_1, \mathcal{R}_1, \mathcal{H}_1, \mathcal{C}_1 \rangle$ and $M_2 = \langle \mathcal{I}_2, \mathcal{R}_2, \mathcal{H}_2, \mathcal{C}_2 \rangle$. The *parallel composition of* M_1 *and* M_2 is the model $M_1 \| M_2 = \langle \mathcal{I}_1 \cup \mathcal{I}_2, \mathcal{R}_1 \cup \mathcal{R}_2, \mathcal{H}_1 \cup \mathcal{H}_2, \mathcal{C}_1 \cup \mathcal{C}_2 \rangle$. Let $M = \langle \mathcal{I}, \mathcal{R}, \mathcal{H}, \mathcal{C} \rangle$ be a model and $\phi \in \mathcal{L}$. We say that ϕ *is valid in* M, in symbols $M \models \phi$, if and only if $\pi \models_\sigma \phi$ for all initialized paths π of M and all assignments σ such that $\pi \models_\sigma \psi$ for all $\psi \in \mathcal{C}$.

Table 1. Facts and their informal meaning

	Fact	Meaning
Domain	$\mathtt{sent}(s, b, a, m, c)$	s sent m on c to a pretending to be b
Independent	$\mathtt{rcvd}(a, b, m, c)$	m (supposedly sent by b) has been received on c by a
	$\mathtt{contains}(d, ds)$	d is member of ds
	$\mathtt{ik}(m)$	the intruder knows m
Protocols	$\mathtt{state}_r(j, a, ts)$	a plays r, has internal state ts, and can execute step j
Business	$\mathtt{pa}(r, t)$	r has the permission to perform t
Processes	$\mathtt{ua}(a, r)$	a is assigned to r
	$\mathtt{executed}(a, t)$	a executed t
	$\mathtt{granted}(a, t)$	a is granted to execute t
APIs	$\mathtt{attrs}(as)$	security token has attributes as

Legenda: s, a, b: agents; m: message; c: channel; r: role; j: protocol step; ts: list of terms; t: task d: data; ds: set of data; o: resource object; as: set of attributes

4   Modeling Security-Critical Systems

We are interested in model checking problems of the form:

$$M_S \| M_I \models G \tag{1}$$

where $M_S = \langle \mathcal{I}_S, \mathcal{R}_S, \mathcal{H}_S, \mathcal{C}_S \rangle$ and $M_I = \langle \mathcal{I}_I, \mathcal{R}_I, \mathcal{H}_I, \mathcal{C}_I \rangle$ are the model of the security-sensitive system and of the intruder respectively and G is an LTL formula expressing the security properties that the combined model must enjoy.

Table 1 presents an excerpt of the facts (2nd column) used in the different application domains (1st column). Their informal meaning is explained in the rightmost column. Some facts have a fixed meaning: $\mathtt{ik}$ models the intruder knowledge, $\mathtt{sent}$ and $\mathtt{rcvd}$ are used to model communication, and $\mathtt{contains}$ expresses set membership. Other facts are domain specific: $\mathtt{state}_r(j, a, ts)$ models the state of honest agents in security protocols; $\mathtt{pa}(r, t)$, $\mathtt{ua}(a, r)$, $\mathtt{executed}(a, t)$ and $\mathtt{granted}(a, t)$ are used to represent the security policy and task execution in business processes; finally $\mathtt{attrs}(as)$ is used to model attribute-value assignments to resource objects in security APIs. Here and in the sequel we use typewriter font to write facts and rules with the additional convention that variables are capitalized (e.g., $\mathtt{C}$, $\mathtt{AReq}$), whereas constants and function symbols begin with a lower-case letter (e.g., $\mathtt{hReq}$).

Formal Modeling of Security-Critical Systems. In the case of security protocols, the initial state $\mathcal{I}_S$ contains a state-fact $\mathtt{state}_r(1, a, ts)$ for each agent a. In case of business processes, the initial state specifies which tasks are ready for execution as well as the access control policy (e.g., the user-role and the role-permission assignment relations). In case of security APIs, the initial state specifies some attribute-value assignments.

Let us now consider an example of rewriting rules in $\mathcal{R}_S$. The reception of message 2 by the client and the forwarding of message 3 in Figure 2 are modeled by the following rewriting rule:

$\text{rcvd}(C, SP, \text{hRsp}(c30x, IdP, AReq), C_{SP2C}) .$

$\text{state}_c(2, C, [SP, \dots, C_{C2IdP}]) \xrightarrow{\text{send}_2(C,\dots,C_{C2IdP})} \text{state}_c(3, C, [Areq, SP, \dots, C_{C2IdP}]) .$

$\text{sent}(C, C, IdP, \text{hReq}(\text{get}, IdP, AReq), C_{C2IdP})$

The clauses in $\mathcal{H}_S$ support the specification, e.g., of access control policies. For instance, in case of business processes, the Role-based Access Control (RBAC) model can be naturally and succinctly specified as follows:

$$\text{granted}(A, T) \xleftarrow{\text{grant}(A,R,T)} \text{ua}(A, R), \text{pa}(R, T)$$

Moreover, security-critical systems often rely on assumptions on the behavior of the principals involved (e.g., progress, availability). These assumptions can be specified by adding suitably defined LTL formulae to $\mathcal{C}_S$. Some examples are provided in the last two rows of Table 2.

Formal Modeling of the Intruder. A model that corresponds to the Dolev-Yao intruder is given by $M_{DY} = \langle \emptyset, \mathcal{R}_{DY}, \mathcal{H}_{DY}, \emptyset \rangle$, where the rewrite rules in $\mathcal{R}_{DY}$ model the ability to overhear, divert, and intercept messages and the clauses in $\mathcal{H}_{DY}$ model the inferential capabilities, e.g., the ability to decrypt messages when the key used for encryption is known to the intruder as well as that to forge new messages. The model of the Dolev-Yao intruder M_{DY} can be complemented by a model $M_{I'} = \langle \mathcal{I}_{I'}, \mathcal{R}_{I'}, \mathcal{H}_{I'}, \mathcal{C}_{I'} \rangle$, where $\mathcal{I}_{I'}$ contains the facts representing the initial knowledge in the scenario considered, $\mathcal{R}_{I'}$ and $\mathcal{H}_{I'}$ model additional, domain specific behaviors of the intruder, and $\mathcal{C}_{I'}$ may instead constrain the otherwise allowed behaviors. Thus the model of the intruder stems from the parallel combination of M_{DY} and $M_{I'}$, i.e., $M_I = (M_{DY} \| M_{I'})$.

For instance, the behavior of the intruder for security APIs can be extended using the following rule that models the Java method C_Decrypt of Figure 4:

$\text{ik}(\text{crypt}(K, R)) . \text{ik}(\text{hand}(N, \text{inv}(K))) .$

$\text{attrs}(KeyAttrs) . \text{contains}(\text{attr}(\text{decrypt}, \text{true}, N), KeyAttrs)$

$\xrightarrow{\text{decrypt\_key\_asym}(KeyAttrs,K,R,N)} \text{ik}(R) . LHS$

where LHS abbreviates the left hand side of the rule. This rule states that if *(i)* the intruder knows a cipher-text encrypted with key K and the handler N of the key $\text{inv}(K)$, and *(ii)* N has the attribute decryption set to true (i.e., the key associated with that handler can be used for decryption), then the decrypt method can be applied and the intruder can retrieve the plain-text R. (Notice that knowing the handler does not mean to know the key associated to the handler.)

As a further instance, a transport layer protocol such as SSL/TLS can be abstractly characterized by including suitable formulae in $\mathcal{C}_{I'}$. To illustrate consider the first four rows of Table 2, where, here and in the sequel, $\forall(\psi)$ stands for the universal closure of the formula ψ. The formula in the 3rd row formalizes the property of a weakly confidential channel, i.e., a channel whose output is exclusively accessible to a single, yet unknown, receiver. In our model this amounts

Table 2. LTL constraints

Property	LTL Formula
$confidential\_to(c, p)$	$\mathbf{G}\,\forall(\mathtt{rcvd}(A, B, M, c) \Rightarrow A = p)$
$authentic\_on(c, p)$	$\mathbf{G}\,\forall(\mathtt{sent}(RS, A, B, M, c) \Rightarrow (A = p \land RS = p))$
$weakly\_confidential(c)$	$\mathbf{G}\,\forall((\mathtt{rcvd}(A, B, M, c) \land \mathbf{F}\,\mathtt{rcvd}(A', B', M', c)) \Rightarrow A = A')$
$resilient(c)$	$\mathbf{G}\,\forall(\mathtt{sent}(RS, A, B, M, c) \Rightarrow \mathbf{F}\,\mathtt{rcvd}(B, A, M, c))$
$progress(a, r, j)$	$\mathbf{G}\,\forall(\mathtt{state}_r(j, a, ES) \Rightarrow \mathbf{F}\,\neg\mathtt{state}_r(j, a, ES))$
$availability(a, c)$	$\mathbf{G}\,\forall(\mathtt{rcvd}(a, P, M, c) \Rightarrow \mathbf{F}\,\neg\mathtt{rcvd}(a, P, M, c))$

to requiring that, for every state S, if a fact $\mathtt{rcvd}(a, b, m, c) \in S$, then in all the successor states the $\mathtt{rcvd}$ facts with channel c must have a as recipient (see corresponding LTL formula in the 3rd row). More details can be found in [6,4].

Security Goals. For security protocols, besides the usual secrecy and authentication goals, our property specification language $\mathcal{L}$ allows for the specification of sophisticated properties involving temporal operators and first-order quantifiers. For instance, a fair exchange goal for the ASW protocol discussed in [4] is:

$$\mathbf{G}\,\forall n_O.\forall n_R.(\mathtt{hasvc}(r, txt, n_O, n_R) \Rightarrow \mathbf{F}\,\exists n_R.\mathtt{hasvc}(o, txt, n_O, n_R))$$

stating that if an agent r has a valid contract, then we ask o to possess a valid contract relative to the same contractual text txt and secret commitment n_O.

Finally, the separation of duty property SoD$_3$ exemplified in Figure 3 can be expressed as the following LTL formula:

$$\mathbf{G}\,\forall(\mathtt{executed}(\mathtt{A}, \mathtt{approve\_travel}) \Rightarrow \mathbf{G}\,\neg\mathtt{executed}(\mathtt{A}, \mathtt{approve\_budget}))$$

This goal states that if an agent $\mathtt{A}$ has executed the task $\mathtt{approve\_travel}$ then he should not execute the task $\mathtt{approve\_budget}$.

5   SAT-Based Model Checking of Security-Critical Systems

A high-level overview of the architecture of SATMC 3.0 is depicted in Figure 5. SATMC takes as input the specification of the system M_S, (optionally) a specification of the custom intruder behavior $M_{I'}$, a security goal $G \in \mathcal{L}$, and checks whether $M_S \| M_I \models G$ via a reduction to a SAT problem. Since $M_I = (M_{DY} \| M_{I'})$, this boils down to checking whether $M_S \| M_{DY} \| M_{I'} \models G$. The **DY Attacker** module computes and carries out a number of optimizing transformations on $M_S \| M_{DY}$. These transformations specialize the (otherwise very prolific) rules and clauses of M_{DY} and produce a model $M_{S\text{-}DY}$ which is easier to analyze than (yet equivalent to) $M_S \| M_{DY}$ [9]. The module finally computes and yields the model $M_{S\text{-}DY} \| M_{I'}$ which is equivalent to $M_S \| M_I$ with

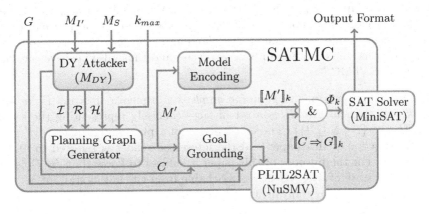

Fig. 5. SATMC Internals

$M_I = (M_{DY} \| M_{I'})$. Thus the problem of checking whether $M_S \| M_{DY} \| M_{I'} \models G$ is reduced to checking whether $M_{S\text{-}DY} \| M_{I'} \models G$.

Let $M = (M_{S\text{-}DY} \| M_{I'}) = \langle \mathcal{I}, \mathcal{R}, \mathcal{H}, \mathcal{C} \rangle$. SATMC now builds a propositional formula Φ_k such that every truth-value assignment satisfying Φ_k corresponds to a counterexample of $M \models G$ of length k and vice versa, with $k \le k_{max}$ (where the upper bound k_{max} is an additional input to SATMC). The formula Φ_k is given by the conjunction of the propositional formulae (i) $[\![M']\!]_k$ encoding the unfolding (up to k-times) of the transition relation associated with $M' = \langle \mathcal{I}, \mathcal{R}, \mathcal{H}, \emptyset \rangle$, and (ii) $[\![C \Rightarrow G]\!]_k$, where C is a conjunction of the formulae in $\mathcal{C}$, encoding the set of attack traces of length k satisfying the constraints C. The module **Model Encoding** takes as input M' and generates $[\![M']\!]_k$, while $[\![C \Rightarrow G]\!]_k$ is generated by the cascade of the **Goal Grounding** and **PLTL2SAT** modules.

The **PLTL2SAT** module leverages existing Bounded Model Checking (BMC) techniques [14]. However, the techniques available in the literature assume that (i) a propositional encoding of the transition relation of M is available and that (ii) the goal formula belongs of propositional LTL. Both assumptions are violated by the model checking problem we consider, since (i) the models we consider are defined over a set of states which is not bounded *a priori* and (ii) first-order LTL formulae are allowed. In [9] we showed that the first problem can be tackled by computing a planning graph of the problem of depth k. A planning graph [17] (module **Planning Graph Generator**) is a succinct representation of an over-approximation of the states reachable in k steps. The planning graph is also key to reducing the first-order LTL formula $(C \Rightarrow G)$ to an equivalent (in a sense that will be defined later) propositional LTL formula (via the **Goal Grounding** module) which is then reduced to SAT using techniques developed for bounded model checking of reactive systems [14] (via the **PLTL2SAT** module).

A SAT solver is finally used to check the satisfiability of the formula Φ_k (module **SAT Solving**). Although not shown in Figure 5, SATMC carries out an iterative deepening strategy on k. Initially k is set to 0, and then it is incremented till an attack is found (if any) or k_{max} is reached. If this is the case no attack traces of length up to k_{max} exist. Notice that it is possible to set k_{max} to ∞, but then the procedure may not terminate (i.e., it is a semi-decision procedure). It is worth noticing that even though the planning graph may represent spurious execution paths, the encoding in SAT is precise and thus false positives are not returned by SATMC.

The Planning Graph. A *planning graph* is a sequence of layers Γ_i for $i = 0, \ldots, k$, where each layer Γ_i is a set of facts concisely representing the set of states $\|\Gamma_i\| = \{S : S \subseteq \Gamma_i\}$. The construction of a planning graph for M' goes beyond the scope of this paper and the interested reader is referred to [9] for more details. For the purpose of this paper it suffices to know that *(i)* Γ_0 is set to the initial state of M', *(ii)* if S is reachable from the initial state of M' in i steps, then $S \in \|\Gamma_i\|$ (or equivalently $S \subseteq \Gamma_i$) for $i = 0, \ldots, k$, and *(iii)* $\Gamma_i \subseteq \Gamma_{i+1}$ for $i = 0, \ldots, k-1$, i.e., the layers in the planning graph grow monotonically.

Encoding the Model. The first step is to add a time-index to the rules and facts to indicate the state at which the rules apply or the facts hold. Facts and rules are thus indexed by 0 through k. If p is a fact, a rule, or a Horn clause and i is an index, then p^i is the corresponding time-indexed propositional variable. If $p = p_1, \ldots, p_n$ is a tuple of facts, rules, or Horn clauses and i is an index, then $p^i = p_1^i, \ldots, p_n^i$ is the corresponding time-indexed tuple of propositional variables. The propositional formula $[\![M']\!]_0$ is $I(f^0, hc^0)$, while $[\![M']\!]_k$, for $k > 0$, is of the form:

$$I(f^0, hc^0) \wedge \bigwedge_{i=0}^{k-1} T_i(f^i, \rho^i, hc^i, f^{i+1}, hc^{i+1}) \tag{2}$$

where f, ρ, and hc are tuples of facts, rules, and Horn clauses, respectively. The formula $I(f^0, hc^0)$ encodes the initial state whereas the formula $T_i(f^i, \rho^i, hc^i, f^{i+1}, hc^{i+1})$ encodes all the possible evolutions of the system from step i to step $i + 1$. The encoding of the system follows the approach proposed in [9], adapted from an encoding technique originally introduced for AI planning, extended to support Horn clauses.

Grounding First-order LTL Formulae. Planning graphs are also key to turn any first-order LTL formula ψ into a propositional LTL formula ψ_0 such that if π is an execution path of M' with k or less states that violates ψ_0, then π violates also ψ, and vice versa. This allows us to reduce the BMC problem for any first-order LTL formula ψ to the BMC for a propositional LTL formula ψ_0 (module **Goal Grounding**) which can in turn be reduced to SAT by using the techniques available in the literature. The functionalities of the module **PLTL2SAT** are currently given by the NuSMV model checker, used as a plugin by SATMC. From the key properties of the planning graph described in Section 5 it is easy to see that if a fact does not occur in Γ_k, then it is false in all states reachable from the initial state in k steps and this leads to the following fact.

Fact 1 *Let $\psi \in \mathcal{L}$, Γ_i for $i = 0, \ldots, k$ be a planning graph for M', and p a fact such that $p \notin \Gamma_k$. Then, if π is an execution path of M' with k or less states that violates ψ then π violates also $\psi[\perp/p]$ (and vice versa), where $\psi[\perp/p]$ is the formula obtained from ψ by replacing all occurrences of p with $\perp$.*

To illustrate consider the problem of generating a propositional version of:

$$\exists \mathsf{A}.\, \mathbf{F}(\neg\, \mathbf{O}\, s(\mathsf{A}, \mathsf{b}) \wedge r(\mathsf{b}, \mathsf{A})) \tag{3}$$

when $\Gamma_k = \{s(\mathsf{a1}, \mathsf{b}), r(\mathsf{b}, \mathsf{a1}), r(\mathsf{b}, \mathsf{a2})\}$. If the variable A ranges over the (finite) set of constants $D_{\mathsf{A}} = \{\mathsf{a1}, \ldots, \mathsf{an}\}$, then we can replace the existential quantifier with a disjunction of instances of the formula in the scope of the quantifier, where each instance is obtained by replacing the quantified variable, namely A, with the constants in D_{A}: $\mathbf{F}(\neg\, \mathbf{O}\, s(\mathsf{a1}, \mathsf{b}) \wedge r(\mathsf{b}, \mathsf{a1})) \vee \ldots \vee \mathbf{F}(\neg\, \mathbf{O}\, s(\mathsf{an}, \mathsf{b}) \wedge r(\mathsf{b}, \mathsf{an}))$ By repeatedly using Fact 1, this formula can be rewritten into: $\mathbf{F}(\neg\, \mathbf{O}\, s(\mathsf{a1}, \mathsf{b}) \wedge r(\mathsf{b}, \mathsf{a1})) \vee \ldots \vee \mathbf{F}(\neg\, \mathbf{O}\, \perp \wedge \perp)$ and finally be simplified to

$$\mathbf{F}(\neg\, \mathbf{O}\, s(\mathsf{a1}, \mathsf{b}) \wedge r(\mathsf{b}, \mathsf{a1})) \vee \mathbf{F}(r(\mathsf{b}, \mathsf{a2})) \tag{4}$$

Even if the resulting formula is compact thanks to the simplification induced by the planning graph, the instantiation step, namely the replacement of the existential quantifier with a disjunction of instances, can be very expensive or even unfeasible (if the domain of the existentially quantified variable is not bounded).

A better approach is to let the instantiation activity be driven by the information available in the planning graph. This can be done by generating instances of the formula by recursively traversing the formula itself in a top down fashion. As soon as an atomic formula is met, it is matched against the facts in Γ_k and if a matching fact is found then the formula is replaced with the ground counterpart found in Γ_k and the corresponding matching substitution is carried over as a constraint. The approach is iterated on backtracking in order to generate all possible instances and when no (other) matching fact in Γ_k for the atomic formula at hand is found, then we replace it with $\perp$.

To illustrate this, let us apply the approach to (3). By traversing the formula we find the atomic formula $s(\mathsf{A}, \mathsf{b})$ which matches with $s(\mathsf{a1}, \mathsf{b})$ in Γ_k with matching substitution $\{\mathsf{A} = \mathsf{a1}\}$. The atomic formula $s(\mathsf{A}, \mathsf{b})$ is instantiated to $s(\mathsf{a1}, \mathsf{b})$ and the constraint $\mathsf{A} = \mathsf{a1}$ is carried over. We are then left with the problem of finding a matching fact in Γ_k for the formula $r(\mathsf{b}, \mathsf{A})$ with $\mathsf{A} = \mathsf{a1}$, i.e., for $r(\mathsf{b}, \mathsf{a1})$. The matching fact is easily found in Γ_k and we are therefore left with the formula $(i1)$ $\mathbf{F}(\neg\, \mathbf{O}\, s(\mathsf{a1}, \mathsf{b}) \wedge r(\mathsf{b}, \mathsf{a1}))$ as our first instance. On backtracking we find that there is no other matching fact for $r(\mathsf{b}, \mathsf{a1})$ which is then replaced by $\perp$, thereby leading to the instance $(i2)$ $\mathbf{F}(\neg\, \mathbf{O}\, s(\mathsf{a1}, \mathsf{b}) \wedge \perp)$. By further backtracking we find that there is no other matching fact for $s(\mathsf{A}, \mathsf{b})$ in Γ_k and therefore we generate another instance by replacing $s(\mathsf{A}, \mathsf{b})$ with $\perp$ and carry over the constraint $\mathsf{A} \neq \mathsf{a1}$. The only fact in Γ_k matching $r(\mathsf{b}, \mathsf{A})$ while satisfying the constraint $\mathsf{A} \neq \mathsf{a1}$ is $r(\mathsf{b}, \mathsf{a2})$. We are then left with the formula $(i3)$ $\mathbf{F}(\neg\, \mathbf{O}\, \perp \wedge r(\mathsf{b}, \mathsf{a2}))$ as our third instance. No further matching fact for $r(\mathsf{b}, \mathsf{a2})$ exists. The procedure therefore turns the first-order LTL formula (3) into the disjunction of $(i1)$, $(i2)$, and $(i3)$, which can be readily simplified to (4).

6 Conclusions

We presented SATMC 3.0, a SAT-based Model Checker for security-critical systems. SATMC successfully combines techniques from AI planning and for the analysis of reactive systems to reduce the problem of determining the existence of an attack of bounded length violating a given security goal to SAT. SATMC supports the specification of security policies as Horn clauses and of security assumptions and goals as first-order LTL formulae. Its flexibility and effectiveness is demonstrated by its successful usage within three industrial relevant application domains (security protocols, business processes, and security APIs) and its integration within a number of research prototypes and industrial-strength tools. SATMC 3.0 can be downloaded at http://www.ai-lab.it/satmc.

Acknowledgments. We are grateful to Luca Zanetti for his contribution in the design and implementation of the Goal Grounding and PLTL2SAT modules. This work has partially been supported by the FP7-ICT Project SPaCIoS (no. 257876), by the PRIN project "Security Horizons" (no. 2010XSEMLC) funded by MIUR, and by the Activity "STIATE" (no. 14231) funded by the EIT ICT-Labs.

References

1. Armando, A., et al.: The AVANTSSAR Platform for the Automated Validation of Trust and Security of Service-Oriented Architectures. In: Flanagan, C., König, B. (eds.) TACAS 2012. LNCS, vol. 7214, pp. 267–282. Springer, Heidelberg (2012)
2. Armando, A., et al.: The AVISPA Tool for the Automated Validation of Internet Security Protocols and Applications. In: Etessami, K., Rajamani, S.K. (eds.) CAV 2005. LNCS, vol. 3576, pp. 281–285. Springer, Heidelberg (2005)
3. Armando, A., Carbone, R., Compagna, L.: LTL Model Checking for Security Protocols. In: 20th IEEE Computer Security Foundations Symposium (CSF), pp. 385–396. IEEE Computer Society (2007)
4. Armando, A., Carbone, R., Compagna, L.: LTL Model Checking for Security Protocols. In: JANCL, pp. 403–429. Hermes Lavoisier (2009)
5. Armando, A., Carbone, R., Compagna, L., Cuéllar, J., Pellegrino, G., Sorniotti, A.: An Authentication Flaw in Browser-based Single Sign-On Protocols: Impact and Remediations. Computers & Security 33, 41–58 (2013)
6. Armando, A., Carbone, R., Compagna, L., Cuéllar, J., Tobarra, L.: Formal Analysis of SAML 2.0 Web Browser Single Sign-On: Breaking the SAML-based Single Sign-On for Google Apps. In: Shmatikov, V. (ed.) Proc. ACM Workshop on Formal Methods in Security Engineering, pp. 1–10. ACM Press (2008)
7. Armando, A., Carbone, R., Zanetti, L.: Formal Modeling and Automatic Security Analysis of Two-Factor and Two-Channel Authentication Protocols. In: Lopez, J., Huang, X., Sandhu, R. (eds.) NSS 2013. LNCS, vol. 7873, pp. 728–734. Springer, Heidelberg (2013)
8. Armando, A., Compagna, L.: SATMC: A SAT-Based Model Checker for Security Protocols. In: Alferes, J.J., Leite, J. (eds.) JELIA 2004. LNCS (LNAI), vol. 3229, pp. 730–733. Springer, Heidelberg (2004)

9. Armando, A., Compagna, L.: SAT-based Model-Checking for Security Protocols Analysis. International Journal of Information Security 7(1), 3–32 (2008)
10. Armando, A., Ponta, S.E.: Model Checking of Security-Sensitive Business Processes. In: Degano, P., Guttman, J.D. (eds.) FAST 2009. LNCS, vol. 5983, pp. 66–80. Springer, Heidelberg (2010)
11. Arsac, W., Compagna, L., Pellegrino, G., Ponta, S.E.: Security Validation of Business Processes via Model-Checking. In: Erlingsson, Ú., Wieringa, R., Zannone, N. (eds.) ESSoS 2011. LNCS, vol. 6542, pp. 29–42. Springer, Heidelberg (2011)
12. AVANTSSAR. Deliverable 2.1: Requirements for modelling and ASLan v.1 (2008), http://www.avantssar.eu
13. Basin, D., Mödersheim, S., Viganò, L.: OFMC: A Symbolic Model-Checker for Security Protocols. International Journal of Information Security (2004)
14. Biere, A.: Bounded Model Checking. In: Biere, A., Heule, M., van Maaren, H., Walsh, T. (eds.) Handbook of Satisfiability. Frontiers in Artificial Intelligence and Applications, vol. 185, pp. 457–481. IOS Press (2009)
15. Biere, A., Cimatti, A., Clarke, E., Zhu, Y.: Symbolic Model Checking without BDDs. In: Cleaveland, W.R. (ed.) TACAS 1999. LNCS, vol. 1579, pp. 193–207. Springer, Heidelberg (1999)
16. Blanchet, B.: An Efficient Cryptographic Protocol Verifier Based on Prolog Rules. In: Computer Security Foundations Workshop (CSFW), pp. 82–96 (2001)
17. Blum, A., Furst, M.: Fast Planning Through Planning Graph Analysis. In: Proc. International Joint Conference on Artificial Intelligence, IJCAI 1995 (1995)
18. Bortolozzo, M., Centenaro, M., Focardi, R., Steel, G.: Attacking and Fixing PKCS#11 Security Tokens. In: Proc. ACM Conference on Computer and Communications Security (CCS 2010), Chicago, USA, pp. 260–269. ACM Press (2010)
19. Cimatti, A., Clarke, E., Giunchiglia, E., Giunchiglia, F., Pistore, M., Roveri, M., Sebastiani, R., Tacchella, A.: NuSMV 2: An OpenSource Tool for Symbolic Model Checking. In: Brinksma, E., Larsen, K.G. (eds.) CAV 2002. LNCS, vol. 2404, pp. 359–364. Springer, Heidelberg (2002)
20. Compagna, L., Guilleminot, P., Brucker, A.D.: Business Process Compliance via Security Validation as a Service. In: ICST 2013, pp. 455–462 (2013)
21. OASIS Consortium. SAML V2.0 Technical Overview (March 2008), http://wiki.oasis-open.org/security/Saml2TechOverview
22. Eén, N., Sörensson, N.: An Extensible SAT-solver. In: Giunchiglia, E., Tacchella, A. (eds.) SAT 2003. LNCS, vol. 2919, pp. 502–518. Springer, Heidelberg (2004)
23. Focardi, R., Luccio, F.L., Steel, G.: An Introduction to Security API Analysis. In: Aldini, A., Gorrieri, R. (eds.) FOSAD 2011. LNCS, vol. 6858, pp. 35–65. Springer, Heidelberg (2011)
24. Holzmann, G.: The Spin model checker: primer and reference manual, 1st edn. Addison-Wesley Professional (2003)
25. RSA Se: Inc. PKCS#11: Cryptographic Token Interface Standard v2.20 (2004)
26. Kautz, H., McAllester, H., Selman, B.: Encoding Plans in Propositional Logic. In: Aiello, L.C., Doyle, J., Shapiro, S. (eds.) KR 1996: Principles of Knowledge Representation and Reasoning, pp. 374–384. Morgan Kaufmann (1996)
27. Turuani, M.: The CL-Atse Protocol Analyser. In: Pfenning, F. (ed.) RTA 2006. LNCS, vol. 4098, pp. 277–286. Springer, Heidelberg (2006)
28. Viganò, L.: The SPaCIoS Project: Secure Provision and Consumption in the Internet of Services. In: ICST 2013, pp. 497–498 (2013)

IC3 Modulo Theories
via Implicit Predicate Abstraction

Alessandro Cimatti, Alberto Griggio, Sergio Mover, and Stefano Tonetta

Fondazione Bruno Kessler, Trento, Italy
{cimatti,griggio,mover,tonettas}@fbk.eu

Abstract. We present a novel approach for generalizing the IC3 algorithm for invariant checking from finite-state to infinite-state transition systems, expressed over some background theories. The procedure is based on a tight integration of IC3 with Implicit (predicate) Abstraction, a technique that expresses abstract transitions without computing explicitly the abstract system and is incremental with respect to the addition of predicates. In this scenario, IC3 operates only at the Boolean level of the abstract state space, discovering inductive clauses over the abstraction predicates. Theory reasoning is confined within the underlying SMT solver, and applied transparently when performing satisfiability checks. When the current abstraction allows for a spurious counterexample, it is refined by discovering and adding a sufficient set of new predicates. Importantly, this can be done in a completely incremental manner, without discarding the clauses found in the previous search.

The proposed approach has two key advantages. First, unlike current SMT generalizations of IC3, it allows to handle a wide range of background theories without relying on ad-hoc extensions, such as quantifier elimination or theory-specific clause generalization procedures, which might not always be available, and can moreover be inefficient. Second, compared to a direct exploration of the concrete transition system, the use of abstraction gives a significant performance improvement, as our experiments demonstrate.

1 Introduction

IC3 [5] is an algorithm for the verification of invariant properties of transition systems. It builds an over-approximation of the reachable state space, using clauses obtained by generalization while disproving candidate counterexamples. In the case of finite-state systems, the algorithm is implemented on top of Boolean SAT solvers, fully leveraging their features. IC3 has demonstrated to be extremely effective, and it is a fundamental core in all the engines in hardware verification.

There have been several attempts to lift IC3 to the case of infinite-state systems, for its potential applications to software, RTL models, timed and hybrid systems [9], although the problem is in general undecidable. These approaches are set in the framework of Satisfiability Modulo Theory (SMT) [1] and hereafter are referred to as IC3 Modulo Theories [7,18,16,25]: the infinite-state transition system is symbolically described by means of SMT formulas, and an SMT solver plays the same role of the SAT solver in the discrete case. The key difference is the need in IC3 Modulo Theories

E. Ábrahám and K. Havelund (Eds.): TACAS 2014, LNCS 8413, pp. 46–61, 2014.

for specific theory reasoning to deal with candidate counterexamples. This led to the development of various techniques, based on quantifier elimination or theory-specific clause generalization procedures. Unfortunately, such extensions are typically ad-hoc, and might not always be applicable in all theories of interest. Furthermore, being based on the fully detailed SMT representation of the transition systems, some of these solutions (e.g. based on quantifier elimination) can be highly inefficient.

We present a novel approach to IC3 Modulo Theories, which is able to deal with infinite-state systems by means of a tight integration with *predicate abstraction* (PA) [12], a standard abstraction technique that partitions the state space according to the equivalence relation induced by a set of predicates. In this work, we leverage *Implicit Abstraction* (IA) [23], which allows to express abstract transitions without computing explicitly the abstract system, and is fully incremental with respect to the addition of new predicates. In the resulting algorithm, called IC3+IA, the search proceeds as if carried out in an abstract system induced by the set of current predicates $\mathbb{P}$ – in fact, IC3+IA only generates clauses over $\mathbb{P}$. The key insight is to exploit IA to obtain an abstract version of the relative induction check. When an abstract counterexample is found, as in Counter-Example Guided Abstraction-Refinement (CEGAR), it is simulated in the concrete space and, if spurious, the current abstraction is refined by adding a set of predicates sufficient to rule it out.

The proposed approach has several advantages. First, unlike current SMT generalizations of IC3, IC3+IA allows to handle a wide range of background theories without relying on ad-hoc extensions, such as quantifier elimination or theory-specific clause generalization procedures. The only requirement is the availability of an effective technique for abstraction refinement, for which various solutions exist for many important theories (e.g. interpolation [15], unsat core extraction, or weakest precondition). Second, the analysis of the infinite-state transition system is now carried out in the abstract space, which is often as effective as an exact analysis, but also much faster. Finally, the approach is completely incremental, without having to discard or reconstruct clauses found in the previous iterations.

We experimentally evaluated IC3+IA on a set of benchmarks from heterogeneous sources [2,14,18], with very positive results. First, our implementation of IC3+IA is significantly more expressive than the SMT-based IC3 of [7], being able to handle not only the theory of Linear Rational Arithmetic (LRA) like [7], but also those of Linear Integer Arithmetic (LIA) and fixed-size bit-vectors (BV). Second, in terms of performance IC3+IA proved to be uniformly superior to a wide range of alternative techniques and tools, including state-of-the-art implementations of the bit-level IC3 algorithm ([11,22,3]), other approaches for IC3 Modulo Theories ([7,16,18]), and techniques based on k-induction and invariant discovery ([14,17]). A remarkable property of IC3+IA is that it can deal with a large number of predicates: in several benchmarks, *hundreds of predicates* were introduced during the search. Considering that an explicit computation of the abstract transition relation (e.g. based on All-SMT [19]) often becomes impractical with a few dozen predicates, we conclude that IA is fundamental to scalability, allowing for efficient reasoning in a fine-grained abstract space.

The rest of the paper is structured as follows. In Section 2 we present some background on IC3 and Implicit Abstraction. In Section 3 we describe IC3+IA and prove its formal properties. In Section 4 we discuss the related work. In Section 5 we experimentally evaluate our method. In Section 6 we draw some conclusions and present directions for future work.

2 Background

2.1 Transition Systems

Our setting is standard first order logic. We use the standard notions of theory, satisfiability, validity, logical consequence. We denote formulas with φ, ψ, I, T, P, variables with x, y, and sets of variables with $X, Y, \overline{X}, \widehat{X}$. Unless otherwise specified, we work on quantifier-free formulas, and we refer to 0-arity predicates as Boolean variables, and to 0-arity uninterpreted functions as (theory) variables. A literal is an atom or its negation. A *clause* is a disjunction of literals, whereas a *cube* is a conjunction of literals. If s is a cube $l_1 \wedge \ldots \wedge l_n$, with $\neg s$ we denote the clause $\neg l_1 \vee \ldots \vee \neg l_n$, and vice versa. A formula is in conjunctive normal form (CNF) if it is a conjunction of clauses, and in disjunctive normal form (DNF) if it is a disjunction of cubes. With a little abuse of notation, we might sometimes denote formulas in CNF $C_1 \wedge \ldots \wedge C_n$ as sets of clauses $\{C_1, \ldots, C_n\}$, and vice versa. If $X_1, \ldots, X_n$ are a sets of variables and φ is a formula, we might write $\varphi(X_1, \ldots, X_n)$ to indicate that all the variables occurring in φ are elements of $\bigcup_i X_i$. For each variable x, we assume that there exists a corresponding variable x' (the *primed version* of x). If X is a set of variables, X' is the set obtained by replacing each element x with its primed version ($X' = \{x' \mid x \in X\}$), $\overline{X}$ is the set obtained by replacing each x with $\overline{x}$ ($\overline{X} = \{\overline{x} \mid x \in X\}$) and X^n is the set obtained by adding n primes to each variable ($X^n = \{x^n \mid x \in X\}$).

Given a formula φ, φ' is the formula obtained by adding a prime to each variable occurring in φ. Given a theory T, we write $\varphi \models_T \psi$ (or simply $\varphi \models \psi$) to denote that the formula ψ is a logical consequence of φ in the theory T.

A *transition system (TS)* S is a tuple $S = \langle X, I, T \rangle$ where X is a set of (state) variables, $I(X)$ is a formula representing the initial states, and $T(X, X')$ is a formula representing the transitions. A *state* of S is an assignment to the variables X. A *path* of S is a finite sequence $s_0, s_1, \ldots, s_k$ of states such that $s_0 \models I$ and for all $i, 0 \leq i < k$, $(s_i, s'_{i+1}) \models T$.

Given a formula $P(X)$, the *verification problem* denoted with $S \models P$ is the problem to check if for all paths $s_0, s_1, \ldots, s_k$ of S, for all $i, 0 \leq i \leq k, s_i \models P$. Its dual is the *reachability problem*, which is the problem to find a path $s_0, s_1, \ldots, s_k$ of S such that $s_k \models \neg P$. $P(X)$ represents the "good" states, while $\neg P$ represents the "bad" states.

Inductive invariants are central to solve the verification problem. P is an inductive invariant iff (i) $I(X) \models P(X)$; and (ii) $P(X) \wedge T(X, X') \models P(X')$. A weaker notion is given by relative inductive invariants: given a formula $\phi(X)$, P is inductive relative to ϕ iff (i) $I(X) \models P(X)$; and (ii) $\phi(X) \wedge P(X) \wedge T(X, X') \models P(X')$.

2.2 IC3 with SMT

IC3 [5] is an efficient algorithm for the verification of finite-state systems, with Boolean state variables and propositional logic formulas. IC3 was subsequently extended to the

SMT case in [7,16]. In the following, we present its main ideas, following the description of [7]. For brevity, we have to omit several important details, for which we refer to [5,7,16].

Let S and P be a transition system and a set of good states as in §2.1. The IC3 algorithm tries to prove that $S \models P$ by finding a formula $F(X)$ such that: (i) $I(X) \models F(X)$; (ii) $F(X) \wedge T(X, X') \models F(X')$; and (iii) $F(X) \models P(X)$.

In order to construct an inductive invariant F, IC3 maintains a sequence of formulas (called *trace*) $F_0(X), \ldots, F_k(X)$ such that: (i) $F_0 = I$; (ii) $F_i \models F_{i+1}$; (iii) $F_i(X) \wedge T(X, X') \models F_{i+1}(X')$; (iv) for all $i < k$, $F_i \models P$. Therefore, each element of the trace F_{i+1}, called *frame*, is inductive relative to the previous one, F_i. IC3 strengthens the frames by finding new relative inductive clauses by checking the unsatisfiability of the formula:

$$RelInd(F, T, c) := F \wedge c \wedge T \wedge \neg c'. \tag{1}$$

More specifically, the algorithm proceeds incrementally, by alternating two phases: a blocking phase, and a propagation phase. In the *blocking* phase, the trace is analyzed to prove that no intersection between F_k and $\neg P(X)$ is possible. If such intersection cannot be disproved on the current trace, the property is violated and a counterexample can be reconstructed. During the blocking phase, the trace is enriched with additional formulas, which can be seen as strengthening the approximation of the reachable state space. At the end of the blocking phase, if no violation is found, $F_k \models P$.

The *propagation* phase tries to extend the trace with a new formula F_{k+1}, moving forward the clauses from preceding F_i's. If, during this process, two consecutive frames become identical (i.e. $F_i = F_{i+1}$), then a fixpoint is reached, and IC3 terminates with F_i being an inductive invariant proving the property.

In the *blocking* phase IC3 maintains a set of pairs (s, i), where s is a set of states that can lead to a bad state, and $i > 0$ is a position in the current trace. New formulas (in the form of clauses) to be added to the current trace are derived by (recursively) proving that a set s of a pair (s, i) is unreachable starting from the formula F_{i-1}. This is done by checking the satisfiability of the formula $RelInd(F_{i-1}, T, \neg s)$. If the formula is unsatisfiable, then $\neg s$ is *inductive relative to* F_{i-1}, and IC3 strengthens F_i by adding $\neg s$ to it[1], thus *blocking* the bad state s at i. If, instead, (1) is satisfiable, then the overapproximation F_{i-1} is not strong enough to show that s is unreachable. In this case, let p be a subset of the states in $F_{i-1} \wedge \neg s$ such that all the states in p lead to a state in s' in one transition step. Then, IC3 continues by trying to show that p is not reachable in one step from F_{i-2} (that is, it tries to block the pair $(p, i - 1)$). This procedure continues recursively, possibly generating other pairs to block at earlier points in the trace, until either IC3 generates a pair $(q, 0)$, meaning that the system does not satisfy the property, or the trace is eventually strengthened so that the original pair (s, i) can be blocked.

A key difference between the original Boolean IC3 and its SMT extensions in [7,16] is in the way sets of states to be blocked or generalized are constructed. In the blocking phase, when trying to block a pair (s, i), if the formula (1) is satisfiable, then a new pair $(p, i - 1)$ has to be generated such that p is a cube in the *preimage of s wrt. T*. In the propositional case, p can be obtained from the model μ of (1) generated by

---

[1] $\neg s$ is actually *generalized* before being added to F_i. Although this is fundamental for the IC3 effectiveness, we do not discuss it for simplicity.

the SAT solver, by simply dropping the primed variables occurring in μ. This cannot be done in general in the first-order case, where the relationship between the current state variables X and their primed version X' is encoded in the theory atoms, which in general cannot be partitioned into a primed and an unprimed set. The solution proposed in [7] is to compute p by existentially quantifying (1) and then applying an *under-approximated* existential elimination algorithm for linear rational arithmetic formulas. Similarly, in [16] a theory-aware generalization algorithm for linear rational arithmetic (based on interpolation) was proposed, in order to strengthen $\neg s$ before adding it to F_i after having successfully blocked it.

2.3   Implicit Abstraction

Predicate Abstraction. Abstraction [10] is used to reduce the search space while preserving the satisfaction of some properties such as invariants. If $\widehat{S}$ is an abstraction of S, if a condition is reachable in S, then also its abstract version is reachable in $\widehat{S}$. Thus, if we prove that a set of states is not reachable in $\widehat{S}$, the same can be concluded for the concrete transition system S.

In Predicate Abstraction [12], the abstract state-space is described with a set of predicates. Given a TS S, we select a set $\mathbb{P}$ of predicates, such that each predicate $p \in \mathbb{P}$ is a formula over the variables X that characterizes relevant facts of the system. For every $p \in \mathbb{P}$, we introduce a new abstract variable x_p and define $X_{\mathbb{P}}$ as $\{x_p\}_{p \in \mathbb{P}}$. The abstraction relation $H_{\mathbb{P}}$ is defined as $H_{\mathbb{P}}(X, X_{\mathbb{P}}) := \bigwedge_{p \in \mathbb{P}} x_p \leftrightarrow p(X)$. Given a formula $\phi(X)$, the abstract version $\widehat{\phi}_{\mathbb{P}}$ is obtained by existentially quantifying the variables X, i.e., $\widehat{\phi}_{\mathbb{P}} = \exists X.(\phi(X) \wedge H_{\mathbb{P}}(X, X_{\mathbb{P}}))$. Similarly for a formula over X and X', $\widehat{\phi}_{\mathbb{P}} = \exists X, X'.(\phi(X, X') \wedge H_{\mathbb{P}}(X, X_{\mathbb{P}}) \wedge H_{\mathbb{P}}(X', X'_{\mathbb{P}}))$. The abstract system with $\widehat{S}_{\mathbb{P}} = \langle X_{\mathbb{P}}, \widehat{I}_{\mathbb{P}}, \widehat{T}_{\mathbb{P}} \rangle$ is obtained by abstracting the initial and the transition conditions. In the following, when clear from the context, we write just $\widehat{\phi}$ instead of $\widehat{\phi}_{\mathbb{P}}$.

Since most model checkers deal only with quantifier-free formulas, the computation of $\widehat{S}_{\mathbb{P}}$ requires the elimination of the existential quantifiers. This may result in a bottleneck and some techniques compute weaker/more abstract systems (cfr., e.g., [21]).

Implicit Predicate Abstraction. Implicit predicate abstraction [23] embeds the definition of the predicate abstraction in the encoding of the path. This is based on the following formula:

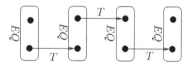

Fig. 1. Abstract path

$$EQ_{\mathbb{P}}(X, \overline{X}) := \bigwedge_{p \in \mathbb{P}} p(X) \leftrightarrow p(\overline{X}) \quad (2)$$

which relate two concrete states corresponding to the same abstract state. The formula $\widehat{Path}_{k,\mathbb{P}} := \bigwedge_{1 \leq h < k}(T(\overline{X}^{h-1}, X^h) \wedge EQ_{\mathbb{P}}(X^h, \overline{X}^h)) \wedge T(\overline{X}^{k-1}, X^k)$ is satisfiable iff there exists a path of k steps in the abstract state space. Intuitively, instead of having a contiguous sequence of transitions, the encoding represents a sequence of disconnected transitions where every gap between two transitions is forced to lay in the same abstract state (see Fig. 1). $BMC_{\mathbb{P}}^k$ encodes the abstract bounded model checking problem and

is obtained from $\widehat{Path}_{k,\mathbb{P}}$ by adding the abstract initial and target conditions: $\mathrm{BMC}_{\mathbb{P}}^k =$
$I(X^0) \wedge EQ_{\mathbb{P}}(X^0, \overline{X}^0) \wedge \widehat{Path}_{k,\mathbb{P}} \wedge EQ_{\mathbb{P}}(X^k, \overline{X}^k) \wedge \neg P(\overline{X}^k).$

3   IC3 with Implicit Abstraction

3.1   Main Idea

The main idea of IC3+IA is to mimic how IC3 would work on the abstract state space defined by a set of predicates $\mathbb{P}$, but using IA to avoid quantifier elimination to compute the abstract transition relation. Therefore, clauses, frames and cubes are restricted to have predicates in $\mathbb{P}$ as atoms. We call these clauses, frames and cubes respectively $\mathbb{P}$-clauses, $\mathbb{P}$-formulas, and $\mathbb{P}$-cubes. Note that for any $\mathbb{P}$-formula ϕ (and thus also for $\mathbb{P}$-cubes and $\mathbb{P}$-clauses), $\widehat{\phi} = \phi[X_{\mathbb{P}}/\mathbb{P}] \wedge \exists X.(\bigwedge_{p \in \mathbb{P}} x_p \leftrightarrow p(X))$.

The key point of IC3+IA is to use an abstract version of the check (1) to prove that an abstract clause $\widehat{c}$ is inductive relative to the abstract frame $\widehat{F}$:

$$AbsRelInd(F, T, c, \mathbb{P}) := F(X) \wedge c(X) \wedge$$
$$EQ_{\mathbb{P}}(X, \overline{X}) \wedge T(\overline{X}, \overline{X}') \wedge EQ_{\mathbb{P}}(\overline{X}', X') \wedge \neg c(X') \quad (3)$$

Theorem 1. *Consider a set $\mathbb{P}$ of predicates, $\mathbb{P}$-formulas F and a $\mathbb{P}$-clause c. $RelInd(\widehat{F}, \widehat{T}, \widehat{c})$ is satisfiable iff $AbsRelInd(F, T, c, \mathbb{P})$ is satisfiable. In particular, if $s \models AbsRelInd(F, T, c, \mathbb{P})$, then $\widehat{s} \models RelInd(\widehat{F}, \widehat{T}, \widehat{c})$.*

Proof. Suppose $s \models AbsRelInd(F, T, c, \mathbb{P})$. Let us denote with $\overline{t}$ and t the projections of s respectively over $\overline{X} \cup \overline{X}'$ and over $X \cup X'$. Then $\overline{t} \models T$ and therefore $\widehat{\overline{t}} \models \widehat{T}$. Since $s \models EQ_{\mathbb{P}}(X, \overline{X}) \wedge EQ_{\mathbb{P}}(\overline{X}', X')$, $\widehat{t}$ and $\widehat{\overline{t}}$ are the same abstract transition and therefore $\widehat{t} \models \widehat{T}$. Since $t \models F \wedge c$, then $\widehat{t} \models \widehat{F} \wedge \widehat{c}$. Since $t \models \neg c'$, then $\widehat{t} \models \widehat{(\neg c')}$ and since c is a Boolean combination of $\mathbb{P}$, then $\widehat{t} \models \neg \widehat{c}'$. Thus, $\widehat{s} \models \widehat{t} \models RelInd(\widehat{F}, \widehat{T}, \widehat{c})$.

For the other direction, suppose $\overline{t} \models RelInd(\widehat{F}, \widehat{T}, \widehat{c})$. Then there exists an assignment t to $X \cup X'$ such that $t \models T$ and $\widehat{t} = \overline{t}$. Therefore, $t \models F(X) \wedge c(X) \wedge EQ_{\mathbb{P}}(X, X) \wedge T(X, X') \wedge EQ_{\mathbb{P}}(X', X') \wedge \neg c(X')$, which concludes the proof.

3.2   The Algorithm

The IC3+IA algorithm is shown in Figure 2. The IC3+IA has the same structure of IC3 as described in [11]. Additionally, it keeps a set of predicates $\mathbb{P}$, which are used to compute new clauses. The only points where IC3+IA differs from IC3 (shown in red in Fig. 2) are in picking $\mathbb{P}$-cubes instead of concrete states, the use of *AbsRelInd* instead of *RelInd*, and in the fact that a spurious counterexample may be found and, in that case, new predicates must be added.

More specifically, the algorithm consists of a loop, in which each iteration is divided into the blocking and the propagation phase. The blocking phase starts by picking a cube c of predicates representing an abstract state in the last frame violating the property. This is recursively blocked along the trace by checking if $AbsRelInd(F_{i-1}, T, \neg c, \mathbb{P})$

```
bool IC3+IA (I, T, P, ℙ):
1.    ℙ = ℙ ∪ {p | p is a predicate in I or in P}
2.    trace = [I]   # first elem of trace is init formula
3.    trace.push()   # add a new frame to the trace
4.    while True:
          # blocking phase
5.        while there exists a ℙ-cube c s.t. c ⊨ trace.last() ∧ ¬P:
6.            if not recBlock(c, trace.size() − 1):
                 # a pair (s₀, 0) is generated
7.               if the simulation of π = (s₀, 0); . . . ; (sₖ, k) fails:
8.                   ℙ := ℙ ∪ refine(I, T, P, ℙ, π)
9.               else return False   # counterexample found

          # propagation phase
10.       trace.push()
11.       for i = 1 to trace.size() − 1:
12.           for each clause c ∈ trace[i]:
13.               if AbsRelInd(trace[i], T, c, ℙ) ⊨ ⊥:
14.                   add c to trace[i+1]
15.           if trace[i] == trace[i+1]: return True   # property proved

# simplified recursive description, in practice based on priority queue [5,11]
bool recBlock(s, i):
1.    if i == 0: return False   # reached initial states
2.    while AbsRelInd(trace[i-1], T, ¬s, ℙ) ⊭ ⊥:
3.        extract a ℙ-cube c from the Boolean model of AbsRelInd(trace[i-1], T, ¬s, ℙ)
             # c is an (abstract) predecessor of s
4.        if not recBlock(c, i − 1): return False
5.    g = generalize(¬s, i)   # standard IC3 generalization [5,11] (using AbsRelInd)
6.    add g to trace[i]
7.    return True
```

Fig. 2. High-level description of IC3+IA (with changes wrt. the Boolean IC3 in red)

is satisfiable. If the relative induction check succeeds, F_i is strengthened with a generalization of $\neg c$. If the check fails, the recursive blocking continues with an *abstract predecessor* of c, that is, a ℙ-cube in $F_i \wedge \neg c$ that leads to c in one step. This recursive blocking results in either strengthening of the trace or in the generation of an *abstract counterexample*. If the counterexample can be simulated on the concrete transition system, then the algorithm terminates with a violation of the property. Otherwise, it refines the abstraction, adding new predicates to ℙ so that the abstract counterexample is no more a path of the abstract system. In the propagation phase, ℙ-clauses of a frame F_i that are inductive relative to F_i using $\widehat{T}$ are propagated to the following frame F_{i+1}. As for IC3, if two consecutive frames are equal, we can conclude that the property is satisfied by the abstract transition system, and therefore also by the concrete one.

3.3   Simulation and Refinement

During the search the procedure may find a counterexample in the abstract space. As usual in the CEGAR framework, we simulate the counterexample in the concrete system to either find a real counterexample or to refine the abstraction, adding new predicates to $\mathbb{P}$. Technically, IC3+IA finds a set of counterexamples $\pi = (s_0, 0); \ldots ; (s_k, k)$ instead of a single counterexample, as described in [7] (i.e. this behaviour depends on the generalization of a cube performed by ternary simulation or don't care detection). We simulate π as usual via bounded model checking. Formally, we encode all the paths of S up to k steps restricted to π with: $I(X^0) \wedge \bigwedge_{i<k} T(X^i, X^{i+1}) \wedge P(X^k) \wedge \bigwedge_{i \leq k} s_k(X^k)$. If the formula is satisfiable, then there exists a concrete counterexample that witnesses $S \not\models P$, otherwise π is spurious and we refine the abstraction adding new predicates. The *refine*$(I, T, \mathbb{P}, \pi)$ procedure is orthogonal to IC3+IA, and can be carried out with several techniques, like interpolation, unsat core extraction or weakest precondition, for which there is a wide literature. The only requirement of the refinement is to remove the spurious counterexamples π. In our implementation we used interpolation to discover predicates, similarly to [15].

Also, note that in our approach the set of predicates increases monotonically after a refinement (i.e. we always add new predicates to the existing set of predicates). Thus, the transition relation is monotonically strengthened (i.e. since $\mathbb{P} \subseteq \mathbb{P}'$, $\widehat{T}_{\mathbb{P}'} \to \widehat{T}_{\mathbb{P}}$). This allows us to *keep all the clauses* in the IC3+IA frames after a refinement, enabling a fully incremental approach.

3.4 Correctness

Lemma 1 (Invariants). *The following conditions are invariants of* IC3+IA:

1. $F_0 = I$;
2. *for all* $i < k$, $F_i \models F_{i+1}$;
3. *for all* $i < k$, $F_i(X) \wedge EQ_{\mathbb{P}}(X, \overline{X}) \wedge T(\overline{X}, \overline{X}') \wedge EQ_{\mathbb{P}}(\overline{X}', X') \models F_{i+1}(X')$;
4. *for all* $i < k$, $F_i \models P$.

Proof. Condition 1 holds, since initially $F_0 = I$, and F_0 is never changed. We prove that the conditions (2-4) are loop invariants for the main IC3+IA loop (line 4). The invariant conditions trivially hold when entering the loop.

Then, the invariants are preserved by the inner loop at line 5. The loop may change the content of a frame F_{i+1} adding a new clause c while recursively blocking a cube $(p, i + 1)$. c is added to F_{i+1} if the abstract relative inductive check $AbsRelInd(F_i, T, c, \mathbb{P})$ holds. Clearly, this preserves the conditions 2-3. In the loop the set of predicates $\mathbb{P}$ may change at line 8. Note that the invariant conditions still hold in this case. In particular, 3 holds because if $\mathbb{P} \subseteq \mathbb{P}'$, then $EQ_{\mathbb{P}'} \models EQ_{\mathbb{P}}$. When the inner loop ends, we are guaranteed that $F_k \models P_{\mathbb{P}}$ holds. Thus, condition 4 is preserved when a new frame is added to the abstraction in line 10. Finally, the propagation phase clearly maintains all the invariants (2-4), by the definition of abstract relative induction $AbsRelInd(F_i, T, c, \mathbb{P}')$.

Lemma 2. *If* IC3+IA *$(I, T, P, \mathbb{P})$ returns true, then* $\widehat{S}_{\mathbb{P}} \models \widehat{P}_{\mathbb{P}}$.

Proof. The invariant conditions of the IC3 algorithm hold for the abstract frames: 1) $\widehat{F_0} = \widehat{I}$; for all $i < k$, 2) $\widehat{F_i} \models \widehat{F_{i+1}}$; 3) $\widehat{F_i} \wedge \widehat{T} \models \widehat{F'_{i+1}}$; and 4) $\widehat{F_i} \models \widehat{P}$.

Conditions 1), 2), and 4) follow from Lemma 1, since I, P, and F_i are $\mathbb{P}$-cubes. Condition 3) follows from Lemma 1, since $\widehat{T} = \exists \overline{X}, \overline{X}'.EQ_{\mathbb{P}}(X, \overline{X}) \wedge T(\overline{X}, \overline{X}') \wedge EQ_{\mathbb{P}}(\overline{X}', X')$ by definition.

By assumption IC3+IA returns *true* and thus $\widehat{F_{k-1}} = \widehat{F_k}$. Since the conditions (1-4) hold, we have that $\widehat{F_{k-1}}$ is an inductive invariant that proves $\widehat{S} \models \widehat{P}$.

Theorem 2 (Soundness). *Let* $S = \langle X, I, T \rangle$ *be a transition system and* P *a safety property and* $\mathbb{P}$ *be a set of predicates over* X. *The result of* IC3+IA $(I, T, P, \mathbb{P})$ *is correct.*

Proof. If IC3+IA $(I, T, P, \mathbb{P})$ returns *true*, then $\widehat{S_{\mathbb{P}}} \models \widehat{P_{\mathbb{P}}}$ by Lemma 2, and thus $S \models P$. If IC3+IA $(I, T, P, \mathbb{P})$ returns *false*, then the simulation of the abstract counterexample in the concrete system succeeded, and thus $S \not\models P$.

Lemma 3 (Abstract counterexample). *If* IC3+IA *finds a counterexample* π, *then* $\widehat{\pi}$ *is a path of* $\widehat{S}$ *violating* $\widehat{P}$.

Proof. For all i, $0 \leq i \leq$ trace.size, if $\pi[i] = (s_i, i)$ then s_i is a $\mathbb{P}$-cube satisfying F_i. Moreover, $s_k \models \neg P$. By Lemma 1, $F_0 = I$ and therefore $s_0 \models I$. Since s_0, s_k, I, and P are $\mathbb{P}$-formulas, $\widehat{s_0} \models \widehat{I}$ and $\widehat{s_k} \models \neg \widehat{P}$. Again by Lemma 1, for all i, $F_i(X) \wedge EQ_{\mathbb{P}}(X, \overline{X}) \wedge T(\overline{X}, \overline{X}') \wedge EQ_{\mathbb{P}}(\overline{X}', X') \models F_{i+1}(X')$, and thus $s_i \wedge s'_{i+1} \models \exists \overline{X}, \overline{X}'.EQ_{\mathbb{P}}(X, \overline{X}) \wedge T(\overline{X}, \overline{X}') \wedge EQ_{\mathbb{P}}(\overline{X}', X')$. Therefore, $\widehat{s_i} \wedge \widehat{s_{i+1}}' \models \widehat{T}$.

Theorem 3 (Relative completeness). *Suppose that for some set* $\mathbb{P}$ *of predicates,* $\widehat{S} \models \widehat{P}$. *If, at a certain iteration of the main loop,* IC3+IA *has* $\mathbb{P}$ *as set of predicates, then* IC3+IA *returns true.*

Proof. Let us consider the case in which, at a certain iteration of the main loop, $\mathbb{P}$ is as defined in the premises of theorem. At every following iteration of the loop, IC3+IA either finds an abstract counterexample π or strengthens a frame F_i with a new $\mathbb{P}$-clause. The first case is not possible, since, by Lemma 3, $\widehat{\pi}$ would be a path of $\widehat{S}$ violating the property. Therefore, at every iteration, IC3+IA strengthens some frame with a new $\mathbb{P}$-clause. Since the number of $\mathbb{P}$-clauses is finite and, by Lemma 1, for all i, $F_i \models F_{i+1}$, IC3+IA will eventually find that $F_i = F_{i+1}$ for some i and return true.

4   Related Work

This work combines two lines of research in verification, abstraction and IC3.

Among the existing abstraction techniques, predicate abstraction [12] has been successfully applied to the verification of infinite-state transition systems, such as software [20]. Implicit abstraction [23] was first used with k-induction to avoid the explicit computation of the abstract system. In our work, we exploit implicit abstraction in IC3 to avoid theory-specific generalization techniques, widening the applicability of IC3 to transition systems expressed over some background theories. Moreover, we provided the first integration of implicit abstraction in a CEGAR loop.

The IC3 [5] algorithm has been widely applied to the hardware domain [11,6] to prove safety and also as a backend to prove liveness [4]. In [24], IC3 is combined with a lazy abstraction technique in the context of hardware verification. The approach has some similarities with our work, but it is limited to Boolean systems, it uses a "visible variables" abstraction rather than PA, and applies a modified concrete version of IC3 for refinement.

Several approaches adapted the original IC3 algorithm to deal with infinite-state systems [7,16,18,25]. The techniques presented in [7,16] extend IC3 to verify systems described in the linear real arithmetic theory. In contrast to both approaches, we do not rely on theory specific generalization procedures, which may be expensive, such as quantifier elimination [7] or may hinder some of the IC3 features, like generalization (e.g. the interpolant-based generalization of [16] does not exploit relative induction). Moreover, IC3+IA searches for a proof in the abstract space. The approach presented in [18] is restricted to timed automata since it exploits the finite partitioning of the region graph. While we could restrict the set of predicates that we use to regions, our technique is applicable to a much broader class of systems, and it also allows us to apply conservative abstractions. IC3 was also extended to the bit-vector theory in [25] with an ad-hoc extension, that may not handle efficiently some bit-vector operators. Instead, our approach is not specific for bit-vectors.

5   Experimental Evaluation

We have implemented the algorithm described in the previous section in the SMT extension of IC3 presented in [7]. The tool uses MATHSAT [8] as backend SMT solver, and takes as input either a symbolic transition system or a system with an explicit control-flow graph (CFG), in the latter case invoking a specialized "CFG-aware" variant of IC3 (TreeIC3, also described in [7]). The discovery of new predicates for abstraction refinement is performed using the interpolation procedures implemented in MATH-SAT, following [15]. In this section, we experimentally evaluate the effectiveness of our new technique. We will call our implementation of the various algorithms as follows: IC3(LRA) is the "concrete" IC3 extension for Linear Rational Arithmetic (LRA) as presented in [7]; TREEIC3+ITP(LRA) is the CFG-based variant of [7], also working only over LRA, and exploiting interpolants whenever possible[2]; IC3+IA(T) is IC3 with Implicit Abstraction for an arbitrary theory T; TREEIC3+IA(T) is the CFG-based IC3 with Implicit Abstraction for an arbitrary theory T.

All the experiments have been performed on a cluster of 64-bit Linux machines with a 2.7 Ghz Intel Xeon X5650 CPU, with a memory limit set to 3Gb and a time limit of 1200 seconds (unless otherwise specified). The tools and benchmarks used in the experiments are available at https://es.fbk.eu/people/griggio/papers/tacas14-ic3ia.tar.bz2.

5.1   Performance Benefits of Implicit Abstraction

In the first part of our experiments, we evaluate the impact of Implicit Abstraction for the performance of IC3 modulo theories. In order to do so, we compare IC3+IA(LRA) and TREEIC3+IA(LRA) against IC3(LRA) and TREEIC3+ITP(LRA) on the same set of benchmarks used in [7], expressed in the LRA theory. We also compare both

---

[2] See [7] for more details.

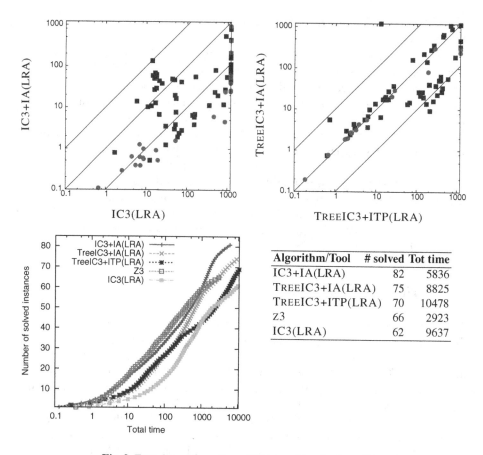

Fig. 3. Experimental results on LRA benchmarks from [7]

variants against the SMT extension of IC3 for LRA presented in [16] and implemented in the z3 SMT solver.[3]

The results are reported in Figure 3. In the scatter plots at the top, safe instances are shown as blue squares, and unsafe ones as red circles. The plot at the bottom reports the number of solved instances and the total accumulated execution time for each tool. From the results, we can clearly see that using abstraction has a very significant positive impact on performance. This is true for both the fully symbolic and the CFG-based IC3, but it is particularly important in the fully symbolic case: not only IC3+IA(LRA) solves 20 more instances than IC3(LRA), but it is also more than one order of magnitude faster in many cases, and there is no instance that IC3(LRA) can solve but IC3+IA(LRA) can't. In fact, Implicit Abstraction is so effective for these benchmarks that IC3+IA(LRA) outperforms also TREEIC3+IA(LRA), even though IC3(LRA) is significantly less efficient than TREEIC3+ITP(LRA). One of the reasons for the smaller performance gain obtained in the CFG-based algorithm might be

---

[3] We used the Git revision 3d910028bf of z3.

that TREEIC3+ITP(LRA) already tries to avoid expensive quantifier elimination operations whenever possible, by populating the frames with clauses extracted from interpolants, and falling back to quantifier elimination only when this fails (see [7] for details). Therefore, in many cases TREEIC3+ITP(LRA) and TREEIC3+IA(LRA) end up computing very similar sets of clauses. However, implicit abstraction still helps significantly in many instances, and there is only one problem that is solved by TREEIC3+ITP(LRA) but not by TREEIC3+IA(LRA). Moreover, both abstraction-based algorithms outperform all the other ones, including Z3.

We also tried a traditional CEGAR approach based on explicit predicate abstraction, using a bit-level IC3 as model checking algorithm and the same interpolation procedure of IC3+IA(LRA) for refinement. As we expected, this configuration ran out of time or memory on most of the instances, and was able to solve only 10 of them.

Finally, we did a preliminary comparison with a variant of IC3 specific for timed automata, ATMOC [18]. We randomly selected a subset of the properties provided with ATMOC, ignoring the trivial ones (i.e. properties that are 1-step inductive or with a counterexample of length < 3). IC3+IA(LRA) performs very well also in this case, solving 100 instances in 772 seconds, while ATMOC solved 41 instances in 3953 seconds (Z3 and IC3(LRA) solved 100 instances in 1535 seconds and 46 instances in 3347 seconds respectively). For lack of space we do not report the plots.

Impact of Number of Predicates. The refinement step may introduce more predicates than those actually needed to rule out a spurious counterexample (e.g. the interpolation-based refinement adds all the predicates found in the interpolant). In principle, such redundant predicates might significantly hurt performance. Using the implicit abstraction framework, however, we can easily implement a procedure that identifies and removes (a subset of) redundant predicates after each successful refinement step. Suppose that IC3+IA finds a spurious counterexample trace $\pi = (s_0, 0); \ldots ; (s_k, k)$ with the set of predicates $\mathbb{P}$, and that $refine(I, T, \mathbb{P}, \pi)$ finds a set $\mathbb{P}_n$ of new predicates. The reduction procedure exploits the encoding of the set of paths of the abstract system $S_{\mathbb{P} \cup \mathbb{P}_n}$ up to k steps, $\mathrm{BMC}^k_{\mathbb{P} \cup \mathbb{P}_n}$. If $\mathbb{P} \cup \mathbb{P}_n$ are sufficient to rule out the spurious counterexample, $\mathrm{BMC}^k_{\mathbb{P} \cup \mathbb{P}_n}$ is unsatisfiable. We ask the SMT solver to compute the unsatisfiable core of $\mathrm{BMC}^k_{\mathbb{P} \cup \mathbb{P}_n}$, and we keep only the predicates of $\mathbb{P}_n$ that appear in the unsatisfiable core.

In order to evaluate the effectiveness of this simple approach, we compare two versions of IC3+IA(LRA) with and without the reduction procedure. Perhaps surprisingly, although the reduction procedure is almost always effective in reducing the total number of predicates, the effects on the execution time are not very big. Although redundancy removal seems to improve performance for the more difficult instances, overall the two versions of IC3+IA(LRA) solve the same number of problems. However, this shows that the algorithm is much less sensitive to the number of predicates added than approaches based on an explicit computation of the abstract transition relation e.g. via All-SMT, which often show also in practice (and not just in theory) an exponential increase in run time with the addition of new predicates. IC3+IA(LRA) manages to solve problems for which it discovers several hundreds of predicates, reaching the peak of 800 predicates and solving most of safe instances with more than a hundred predicates. These numbers are typically way out of reach for explicit abstraction techniques, which blow up with a few dozen predicates.

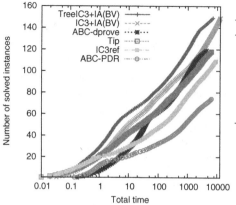

Algorithm/Tool	# solved	Tot time
TREEIC3+IA(BV)	150	7056
IC3+IA(BV)	150	12753
ABC-DPROVE	120	4298
TIP	119	6361
IC3REF	110	9041
ABC-PDR	75	6447

Fig. 4. Experimental results on BV benchmarks from software verification

5.2   Expressiveness Benefits of Implicit Abstraction

In the second part of our experimental analysis, we evaluate the effectiveness of Implicit Abstraction as a way of applying IC3 to systems that are not supported by the methods of [7], by instantiating IC3+IA(T) (and TREEIC3+IA(T)) over the theories of Linear Integer Arithmetic (LIA) and of fixed-size bit-vectors (BV).

IC3 for BV.   For evaluating the performance of IC3+IA(BV) and TREEIC3+IA(BV), we have collected over 200 benchmark instances from the domain of software verification. More specifically, the benchmark set consists of: all the benchmarks used in §5.1, but using BV instead of LRA as background theory; the instances of the `bitvector` set of the Software Verification Competition SV-COMP [2]; the instances from the test suite of InvGen [13], a subset of which was used also in [25].

We have compared the performance of our tools with various implementations of the Boolean IC3 algorithm, run on the translations of the benchmarks to the bit-level Aiger format: the PDR implementation in the ABC model checker (ABC-PDR) [11], TIP [22], and IC3REF [3], the new implementation of the original IC3 algorithm as described in [5]. Finally, we have also compared with the DPROVE algorithm of ABC (ABC-DPROVE), which combines various different techniques for bit-level verification, including IC3.[4] We also tried Z3, but it ran out of memory on most instances. It seems that Z3 uses a Datalog-based engine for BV, rather than PDR.

The results of the evaluation on BV are reported in Figure 4. As we can see, both IC3+IA(BV) and TREEIC3+IA(BV) outperform the bit-level IC3 implementations. In this case, the CFG-based algorithm performs slightly better than the fully-symbolic one, although they both solve the same number of instances.

IC3 for LIA.   For our experiments on the LIA theory, we have generated benchmarks using the Lustre programs available from the webpage of the KIND model checker for Lustre [14]. Since such programs do not have an explicit CFG, we have only evaluated

---

[4] We used ABC version `374286e9c7bc`, TIP `4ef103d81e` and IC3REF `8670762eaf`.

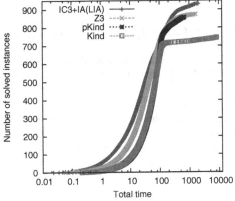

Algorithm/Tool	# solved	Tot time
IC3+IA(LIA)	933	2064
Z3	875	1654
PKIND	859	720
KIND	746	8493

Fig. 5. Experimental results on LIA benchmarks from Lustre programs [14]

IC3+IA(LIA), by comparing it with Z3 and with the latest versions of KIND as well as its parallel version PKIND [17].[5] The results are summarized in Figure 5. Also in this case, IC3+IA(LIA) outperforms the other systems.

6   Conclusion

In this paper we have presented IC3+IA, a new approach to the verification of infinite state transition systems, based on an extension of IC3 with implicit predicate abstraction. The distinguishing feature of our technique is that IC3 works in an abstract state space, since the counterexamples to induction and the relative inductive clauses are expressed with the abstraction predicates. This is enabled by the use of implicit abstraction to check (abstract) relative induction. Moreover, the refinement in our procedure is fully incremental, allowing to keep all the clauses found in the previous iterations.

The approach has two key advantages. First, it is very general: the implementations for the theories of LRA, BV, and LIA have been obtained with relatively little effort. Second, it is extremely effective, being able to efficiently deal with large numbers of predicates. Both advantages are confirmed by the experimental results, obtained on a wide set of benchmarks, also in comparison against dedicated verification engines.

In the future, we plan to apply the approach to other theories (e.g. arrays, non-linear arithmetic) investigating other forms of predicate discovery, and to extend the technique to liveness properties.

Acknowledgments. This work was carried out within the D-MILS project, which is partially funded under the European Commission's Seventh Framework Programme (FP7).

---

[5] We used version 1.8.6c of KIND and PKIND. PKIND differs from KIND because it runs in parallel k-Induction and an automatic invariant generation procedure. We run KIND with options "-compression -n 100000" and PKIND with options "-compression -with-inv-gen -n 100000".

References

1. Barrett, C.W., Sebastiani, R., Seshia, S.A., Tinelli, C.: Satisfiability modulo theories. In: Handbook of Satisfiability, vol. 185, pp. 825–885. IOS Press (2009)
2. Beyer, D.: Second Competition on Software Verification - (Summary of SV-COMP 2013). In: Piterman, N., Smolka, S.A. (eds.) TACAS 2013. LNCS, vol. 7795, pp. 594–609. Springer, Heidelberg (2013)
3. Bradley, A.: IC3ref, `https://github.com/arbrad/IC3ref`
4. Bradley, A., Somenzi, F., Hassan, Z., Zhang, Y.: An incremental approach to model checking progress properties. In: Proc. of FMCAD (2011)
5. Bradley, A.R.: SAT-Based Model Checking without Unrolling. In: Jhala, R., Schmidt, D. (eds.) VMCAI 2011. LNCS, vol. 6538, pp. 70–87. Springer, Heidelberg (2011)
6. Chokler, H., Ivrii, A., Matsliah, A., Moran, S., Nevo, Z.: Incremental formal verification of hardware. In: Proc. of FMCAD (2011)
7. Cimatti, A., Griggio, A.: Software Model Checking via IC3. In: Madhusudan, P., Seshia, S.A. (eds.) CAV 2012. LNCS, vol. 7358, pp. 277–293. Springer, Heidelberg (2012)
8. Cimatti, A., Griggio, A., Schaafsma, B.J., Sebastiani, R.: The MathSAT5 SMT Solver. In: Piterman, N., Smolka, S.A. (eds.) TACAS 2013. LNCS, vol. 7795, pp. 93–107. Springer, Heidelberg (2013)
9. Cimatti, A., Mover, S., Tonetta, S.: Smt-based scenario verification for hybrid systems. Formal Methods in System Design 42(1), 46–66 (2013)
10. Clarke, E., Grumberg, O., Long, D.: Model Checking and Abstraction. ACM Trans. Program. Lang. Syst. 16(5), 1512–1542 (1994)
11. Een, N., Mishchenko, A., Brayton, R.: Efficient implementation of property-directed reachability. In: Proc. of FMCAD (2011)
12. Graf, S., Saïdi, H.: Construction of Abstract State Graphs with PVS. In: Grumberg, O. (ed.) CAV 1997. LNCS, vol. 1254, pp. 72–83. Springer, Heidelberg (1997)
13. Gupta, A., Rybalchenko, A.: InvGen: An efficient invariant generator. In: Bouajjani, A., Maler, O. (eds.) CAV 2009. LNCS, vol. 5643, pp. 634–640. Springer, Heidelberg (2009)
14. Hagen, G., Tinelli, C.: Scaling Up the Formal Verification of Lustre Programs with SMT-Based Techniques. In: Cimatti, A., Jones, R.B. (eds.) FMCAD, pp. 1–9. IEEE (2008)
15. Henzinger, T., Jhala, R., Majumdar, R., McMillan, K.: Abstractions from proofs. In: POPL, pp. 232–244 (2004)
16. Hoder, K., Bjørner, N.: Generalized property directed reachability. In: Cimatti, A., Sebastiani, R. (eds.) SAT 2012. LNCS, vol. 7317, pp. 157–171. Springer, Heidelberg (2012)
17. Kahsai, T., Tinelli, C.: Pkind: A parallel k-induction based model checker. In: Barnat, J., Heljanko, K. (eds.) PDMC. EPTCS, vol. 72, pp. 55–62 (2011)
18. Kindermann, R., Junttila, T., Niemelä, I.: SMT-based induction methods for timed systems. In: Jurdziński, M., Ničković, D. (eds.) FORMATS 2012. LNCS, vol. 7595, pp. 171–187. Springer, Heidelberg (2012)
19. Lahiri, S.K., Nieuwenhuis, R., Oliveras, A.: SMT techniques for fast predicate abstraction. In: Ball, T., Jones, R.B. (eds.) CAV 2006. LNCS, vol. 4144, pp. 424–437. Springer, Heidelberg (2006)
20. McMillan, K.L.: Lazy Abstraction with Interpolants. In: Ball, T., Jones, R.B. (eds.) CAV 2006. LNCS, vol. 4144, pp. 123–136. Springer, Heidelberg (2006)

21. Sharygina, N., Tonetta, S., Tsitovich, A.: The synergy of precise and fast abstractions for program verification. In: SAC, pp. 566–573 (2009)
22. Sorensson, N., Claessen, K.: Tip, https://github.com/niklasso/tip
23. Tonetta, S.: Abstract Model Checking without Computing the Abstraction. In: Cavalcanti, A., Dams, D.R. (eds.) FM 2009. LNCS, vol. 5850, pp. 89–105. Springer, Heidelberg (2009)
24. Vizel, Y., Grumberg, O., Shoham, S.: Lazy abstraction and SAT-based reachability in hardware model checking. In: Cabodi, G., Singh, S. (eds.) FMCAD, pp. 173–181. IEEE (2012)
25. Welp, T., Kuehlmann, A.: QF_BV model checking with property directed reachability. In: Macii, E. (ed.) DATE, pp. 791–796 (2013)

SMT-Based Verification of Software Countermeasures against Side-Channel Attacks

Hassan Eldib, Chao Wang, and Patrick Schaumont

Department of ECE, Virginia Tech, Blacksburg, VA 24061, USA
{heldib,chaowang,schaum} @vt.edu

Abstract. A common strategy for designing countermeasures against side channel attacks is using randomization techniques to remove the statistical dependency between sensitive data and side-channel emissions. However, this process is both labor intensive and error prone, and currently, there is a lack of automated tools to formally access how secure a countermeasure really is. We propose the first SMT solver based method for formally verifying the security of a countermeasures against such attacks. In addition to checking whether the sensitive data are *masked*, we also check whether they are *perfectly masked*, i.e., whether the joint distribution of any d intermediate computation results is independent of the secret key. We encode this verification problem into a series of quantifier-free first-order logic formulas, whose satisfiability can be decided by an off-the-shelf SMT solver. We have implemented the new method in a tool based on the LLVM compiler and the Yices SMT solver. Our experiments on recently proposed countermeasures show that the method is both effective and efficient for practical use.

1 Introduction

Security analysis of the hardware and software systems implemented in embedded devices is becoming increasingly important, since an adversary may have physical access to such devices and therefore can launch a whole new class of side-channel attacks, which utilize secondary information resulting from the execution of sensitive algorithms on these devices. For example, the power consumption of a typical embedded device executing the instruction tmp=text⊕key depends on the value of the secret key [12]. This value can be reliably deduced using a statistical method known as *differential power analysis* (DPA [10,19]). In recent years, many commercial systems in the embedded space have shown weaknesses against such attacks [16,14,1].

A common mitigation strategy against such attacks is using randomization techniques to remove the statistical dependency between the sensitive data and the side-channel information. This can be done in multiple ways. Boolean masking, for example, uses an XOR operation of a random number r with a sensitive variable a to obtain a masked (randomized) variable: $a_m = a \oplus r$ [1,17]. Later, the sensitive variable can be restored by a second XOR operation with the same random number: $a_m \oplus r = a$. Other randomization based countermeasures have used additive masking ($a_m = a + r \ mod \ n$), multiplicative masking ($a_m = a * r \ mod \ n$), and application-specific code transformations such as RSA blinding ($a_m = ar^e \ mod \ N$).

E. Ábrahám and K. Havelund (Eds.): TACAS 2014, LNCS 8413, pp. 62–77, 2014.

However, designing and implementing such side-channel countermeasures are labor intensive and error prone, and currently, there is a lack of formal verification tools to evaluate how secure a countermeasure really is. Software countermeasures are particularly challenging to design, since the source of the information leakage is not the cryptographic software but the microprocessor hardware that executes the software. From the perspective of average software developers – who may not know all the architectural details of the device – it is difficult to predict the myriad possible ways in which side-channel information may be leaked. Furthermore, bugs in implementation can also break an otherwise secure countermeasure.

In this paper, we propose a new method for formally verifying the security of masking countermeasures. Our method uses an SMT solver to check if any intermediate computation result of a software statistically depends on the sensitive data. Since this is a statistical property, it cannot be directly checked by conventional formal verification methods [5,20,21,11]. Although in the literature, there exists some work on tackling the problem using type-based information flow analysis techniques [18], these methods are often overly conservative, leading to the classification of countermeasures as secure when they are not. In contrast, our method always returns the precise result. Although Bayrak *et al.* [2] also used a constraint solver in their method, the analysis is significantly less precise than ours. They check whether a variable is *masked* by some random variable, but not whether it is *perfectly masked*, i.e., whether the probability distribution is dependent on the sensitive data. To the best of our knowledge, our method is the first automated verification method that checks for *perfect masking*. This is important because with *order-d* perfect masking, an implementation is provably secure against any type of *order-d* (and lower-order) power analysis attack [9].

Fig. 1 (left) illustrates the difference between naive and perfect masking. Here, k is the sensitive data, r1 and r2 are the random variables, and o1, o2, o3, and o4 are the results of four different masking schemes. Assume that all variables are Boolean, we can construct the truth table in Fig. 1 (right). Although o1, o2, o3 all seem to depend on the values of the random variables r1 and r2, they are vulnerable to side-channel attacks. To see why, consider the case when o1 is logical 1. In this case, we know for sure that k is 1, regardless of the values of the random variables. Similarly, when o2 is logical 0, we know for sure that k is 0. Although o3 does not *directly* leak the sensitive information about k as in o1 and o2, the masking is still not perfect. When o3 is logical 1 (or 0), there is a 75% chance that k is logical 1 (or 0). Therefore, an adversary may launch a power analysis attack to deduce the value of k.

			k	r1	r2	o1	o2	o3	o4
			0	0	0	0	0	0	0
o1	=	$k \wedge (r1 \wedge r2)$	0	0	1	0	0	0	1
o2	=	$k \vee (r1 \wedge r2)$	0	1	0	0	0	0	1
o3	=	$k \oplus (r1 \wedge r2)$	0	1	1	0	1	1	0
o4	=	$k \oplus (r1 \oplus r2)$	1	0	0	0	1	1	1
			1	0	1	0	1	1	0
			1	1	0	0	1	1	0
			1	1	1	1	1	0	1

Fig. 1. Masking examples: o1, o2, o3 are not perfectly masked, but o4 is perfectly masked

In contrast, o4 is *perfectly masked* in that the output is statistically independent of the sensitive data. When k is logical 1 (or 0), there is 50% chance that o4 is logical 1 (or 0). Therefore, it is provably secure against any first-order power analysis attack, where the adversary can observe one intermediate computation result. The example in Fig. 1 also demonstrates a weakness of the method in [2]: Since it only checks whether a variable is masked, but not whether its probability distribution depends on the key, it would (falsely) classify all of o1, o2, o3, o4 as secure. In contrast, our new method can differentiate o4 from the other three, since only o4 is perfectly masked.

We have implemented our new method in a verification tool based on the LLVM compiler and the Yices SMT solver [6]. We encode the verification problem into a series of quantifier-free first-order logic formulas, whose satisfiability can be decided by Yices. Our SMT encoding scheme is significantly different from the ones used by standard verification methods, because the *perfect masking* property checked by our tool is statistical in nature. For comparison, we also implemented the method in [2] in our tool. We have conducted experiments on a large set of recently proposed countermeasures, including the ones applied to AES and the MAC-Keccak reference code submitted to Round 3 of NIST's SHA-3 competition. Our results show that the new method is effective in detecting flaws in the masking implementation. Furthermore, the method is scalable enough to handle programs of practical size and complexity.

The remainder of this paper is organized as follows. We establish notation in Section 2, before presenting our SMT based verification algorithm in Section 3. Then, we illustrate the entire verification process using an example in Section 4. We present our incremental verification method in Section 5, which further improves the scalability of our SMT-based method. We present our experimental results in Section 6, and finally give our conclusions in Section 7.

2   Preliminaries

In this section, we define the type of side-channel attacks considered in this paper and review the notion of *perfect masking*.

Side-Channel Attacks. Following the notation used by Blömer *et al.* [4], we assume that the program to be verified implements a function $c \leftarrow enc(x, k)$, where x is the plaintext, k is the secret key, and c is the ciphertext. Let $I_1(x, k, r)$, $I_2(x, k, r)$, ..., $I_t(x, k, r)$ be the sequence of intermediate computation results inside the function, where r is an s-bit random number in the domain $\{0, 1\}^s$. The purpose of using r is to make all intermediate results statistically independent of the secret key (k).

When $enc(x, k)$ is a linear function in the Boolean domain, masking and de-masking are straightforward. However, when $enc(x, k)$ is a non-linear function, masking and de-masking often require a complete redesign of the implementation. However, this manual design process is both labor intensive and error prone, and currently, there is a lack of automated tools to assess how secure a countermeasure really is.

We assume that an adversary knows the pair (x, c) of plaintext and ciphertext in $c \leftarrow enc(x, k)$. For each pair (x, c), the adversary also knows the joint distribution of at most d intermediate computation results $I_1(x, k, r), \ldots, I_d(x, k, r)$, through access to some aggregated quantity such as the power dissipation. However, the adversary does not have access to r, which is produced by a true random number generator. The goal of the adversary is to compute the secret key (k). In embedded computing, for instance, these are realistic assumptions. In their seminal work, Kocher *et al.* [10] demonstrated that for $d = 1$ and 2, the sensitive data can be reliably deduced using a statistical method known as differential power analysis (DPA).

Perfect Masking. Given a pair (x, k) of plaintext and secret key for the function $enc(x, k)$, and d intermediate results $I_1(x, k, r), \ldots, I_d(x, k, r)$, we use $D_{x,k}(R)$ to denote the joint distribution of $I_1, \ldots, I_d$ – while assuming that the s-bit random number r is uniformly distributed in the domain $\{0, 1\}^s$. Following Blömer *et al.* [4], we do not put restrictions on the technical capability of an adversary. As long as there is information leak, we consider the implementation to be vulnerable.

Definition 1. *Given an implementation of function $enc(x, k)$ and a set of intermediate results $\{I_i(x, k, r)\}$, we say that the implementation is order-d perfectly masked if, for all d-tuples $\langle I_1, \ldots, I_d \rangle$, we have*

$$D_{x,k}(R) = D_{x',k'}(R) \quad \textit{for any two pairs } (x, k) \textit{ and } (x', k') .$$

The notion of *perfect masking* used here is more accurate than the *sensitivity* [2]. There, an intermediate result is considered to be *sensitive* if (1) it depends on at least one *secret* input and (2) it is independent of any *random* input. We have demonstrated the difference between them using the example in Fig. 1, where o1, o2, o3, o4 are all *insensitive*, but only o4 is *perfectly masked*. In general, if an intermediate result is perfectly masked, it is guaranteed to be insensitive. However, an insensitive intermediate result may not be perfectly masked.

To check for violations of *perfect masking*, we need to decide whether there exists a d-tuple $\langle I_1, \ldots, I_d \rangle$ such that $D_{x,k}(R) \neq D_{x',k'}(R)$ for some (x, k) and (x', k'). Here, the main challenge is to compute $D_{x,k}(R)$. We will present our solution in Section 3.

In this work, we focus on verifying security-critical programs, e.g. those that implement cryptographic algorithms, as opposed to arbitrary software programs. (Our method would be too expensive for verifying general-purpose software.) In general, the class of programs that we consider here do not have input-dependent control flow, meaning that we can easily remove all the loops and function calls from the code using standard loop unrolling and function inlining techniques. Furthermore, the program can be transformed into a branch-free representation, where the if-else branches are merged. Finally, since all variables are bounded integers, we can convert the program to a purely Boolean program through bit-blasting. Therefore, in this paper, we shall present our new verification method on the bit-level representation of a branch-free program. Our goal is to verify that all intermediate bits of the program are perfectly masked.

3 SMT Based Verification of Perfect Masking

We first illustrate the overall flow of our verification method using the program in Fig. 2. The program is a masked version of $c \leftarrow (k1 \wedge k2)$, where $k1$ and $k2$ are two secret

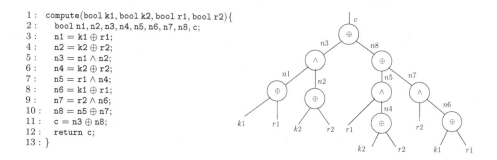

```
1 :   compute(bool k1, bool k2, bool r1, bool r2){
2 :     bool n1, n2, n3, n4, n5, n6, n7, n8, c;
3 :     n1 = k1 ⊕ r1;
4 :     n2 = k2 ⊕ r2;
5 :     n3 = n1 ∧ n2;
6 :     n4 = k2 ⊕ r2;
7 :     n5 = r1 ∧ n4;
8 :     n6 = k1 ⊕ r1;
9 :     n7 = r2 ∧ n6;
10 :    n8 = n5 ⊕ n7;
11 :    c = n3 ⊕ n8;
12 :    return c;
13 : }
```

Fig. 2. Example: a program and its graphic representation ($\oplus$ denotes XOR; $\wedge$ denotes AND)

keys, $r1$ and $r2$ are random variables with independent and uniform distribution in $\{0,1\}$, and c is the computation result. The objective of masking is to make the power consumption of the device executing this code independent from the values of the secret keys. This masking scheme originated from Blömer et al. [4]. The return value c is logically equivalent to $(k1 \wedge k2) \oplus (r1 \wedge r2)$. The corresponding demasking function, which is not shown in the figure, is $c \oplus (r1 \wedge r2)$. Therefore, demasking would produce a result that is logically equivalent to the desired value $(k1 \wedge k2)$.

Our method will determine if all the intermediate variables of the program are perfectly masked. We use the Clang/LLVM compiler to parse the input Boolean program and construct the data-flow graph, where the root represents the output and the leaf nodes represent the input bits. Each internal node represents the result of a Boolean operation of one of the following types: AND, OR, NOT, and XOR. For the example in Fig. 2, our method starts by parsing the program and creating a graph representation. This is followed by traversing the graph in a topological order, from the program inputs (leaf nodes) to the return value (root node). For each internal node, which represents an intermediate result, we check whether it is perfectly masked. The order in which we check the internal nodes is as follows: $n1, n2, n3, n4, n5, n6, n7, n8$, and finally, c.

The Theory. As the starting point, we mark all the plaintext bits in x as public, the key bits in k as secret, and the mask bits in r as random. Then, for each intermediate computation result $I(x, k, r)$ of the program, we check whether it is perfectly masked. Following Definition 1, we formulate this check as a satisfiability problem as follows:

$$\exists x.\exists k, k' \ . \ \left(\Sigma_{r\in\{0,1\}^s}I(x,k,r) \neq \Sigma_{r\in\{0,1\}^s}I(x,k',r)\right)$$

Here, x represents the plaintext bits, k and k' represent two different valuations of the key bits, and r is the random number uniformly distributed in the domain $\{0,1\}^s$, where s is the number of random bits. For any fixed (x, k, k'),

- $\Sigma_{r\in\{0,1\}^s}I(x,k,r)$ is the number of satisfying assignments for $I(x,k,r)$, and
- $\Sigma_{r\in\{0,1\}^s}I(x,k',r)$ is the number of satisfying assignment for $I(x,k',r)$.

Assume that r is uniformly distributed in the domain $\{0,1\}^s$, the above summations can be used to indicate the probabilities of I being logical 1 under two different key values k and k'.

If the above formula is satisfiable, there exists a plaintext x and two different keys (k, k') such that the distribution of $I(x, k, r)$ differs from the distribution of $I(x, k', r)$. In other words, some information of the secret key is leaked through I, and therefore we say that I is not perfectly masked. If the above formula is unsatisfiable, then such information leakage is not possible, and therefore we say that I is perfectly masked.

Another way to understand the above satisfiability problem is to look at the negation. Instead of checking the *satisfiability* of the formula above, we check the *validity* of the formula below:

$$\forall x. \forall k, k'. \ \left(\Sigma_{r \in \{0,1\}^s} I(x, k, r) = \Sigma_{r \in \{0,1\}^s} I(x, k', r) \right)$$

If this formula is valid – meaning that it holds for all valuations of x, k and k' – then we say that I is perfectly masked.

The Encoding. Let Φ denote the SMT formula to be created for checking intermediate result $I(x, k, r)$. Let s be the number of random bits in r. Our encoding method ensures that Φ is satisfiable if and only if I is not perfectly masked. We define Φ as follows:

$$\Phi := \left(\bigwedge_{r=0}^{2^s-1} \Psi_k^r \right) \wedge \left(\bigwedge_{r=0}^{2^s-1} \Psi_{k'}^r \right) \wedge \Psi_{b2i} \wedge \Psi_{sum} \wedge \Psi_{diff} \ ,$$

where the subformulas are defined as follows:

- ***Program logic*** (Ψ_k^r): Each subformula Ψ_k^r encodes a copy of the functionality of $I(x, k, r)$, with the random variable r set to a concrete value in $\{0, \ldots, 2^s - 1\}$ and the key set to value k or k'. All copies share the same plaintext variable x.
- ***Boolean-to-int*** (Ψ_{b2i}): It encodes the conversion of the Boolean valued output of $I(x, k, r)$ to an integer (true becomes 1 and false becomes 0), so that the integer values can be summed up later to compute $\Sigma_{r=1}^{2^s} I(x, k, r)$.
- ***Sum-up-the-1s*** (Ψ_{sum}): It encodes the two summations of the logical 1s in the outputs of the 2^s program logic copies, one for $I(x, k, r)$ and the other for $I(x, k', r)$.
- ***Different sums*** (Ψ_{diff}): It asserts that the two summations should have different results.

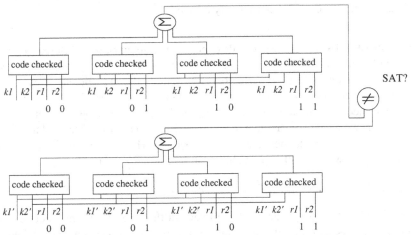

Fig. 3. SMT encoding for checking the statistical dependence of an output on secret data $(k1, k2)$

Fig. 3 is a pictorial illustration of our SMT encoding for an intermediate result $I(k1, k2, r1, r2)$, where $k1, k2$ are the secret key bits and $r1, r2$ are two random bits. Here, the first four boxes, encoding $\Psi_k^0, \ldots, \Psi_k^3$, are the four copies of the program logic for key bits $(k1k2)$, with the random bits set to 00, 01, 10, and 11, respectively. The other four boxes, encoding $\Psi_{k'}^0, \ldots, \Psi_{k'}^3$, are the four copies of the program logic for key bits $(k1'k2')$, with the random bits set to 00, 01, 10, and 11, respectively. The formula checks for security against first-order DPA attacks – whether there exist two sets of keys ($k1$ $k2$ and $k1'$ $k2'$) under which the distributions of I are different.

The Running Example. Consider node $n8$ in Fig. 2 as the node under verification. The function is defined as `n8 = (r1 & (k2 xor r2)) xor (r2 & (k1 xor r1))`. The SMT formula that our method generates – by instantiating `r1r2` to 00, 01, 10, and 11 – is the conjunction of all of the formulas listed below:

```
n8_1 = (0 & (k2 xor 0)) xor (0 & (k1 xor 0))          // four copies of I(k, r)
n8_2 = (0 & (k2 xor 1)) xor (1 & (k1 xor 0))
n8_3 = (1 & (k2 xor 0)) xor (0 & (k1 xor 1))
n8_4 = (1 & (k2 xor 1)) xor (1 & (k1 xor 1))
n8_1' = (0 & (k2' xor 0)) xor (0 & (k1' xor 0))       // four copies of I(k',r)
n8_2' = (0 & (k2' xor 1)) xor (1 & (k1' xor 0))
n8_3' = (1 & (k2' xor 0)) xor (0 & (k1' xor 1))
n8_4' = (1 & (k2' xor 1)) xor (1 & (k1' xor 1))
(( num1 = 1 ) & n8_1 ) | ((num1=0) & not n8_1 )       // convert bool to integer
(( num2 = 1 ) & n8_2 ) | ((num2=0) & not n8_2 )
(( num3 = 1 ) & n8_3 ) | ((num3=0) & not n8_3 )
(( num4 = 1 ) & n8_4 ) | ((num4=0) & not n8_4 )
(( num1' = 1 ) & n8_1') | ((num1'=0) & not n8_1')     // convert bool to integer
(( num2' = 1 ) & n8_2') | ((num2'=0) & not n8_2')
(( num3' = 1 ) & n8_3') | ((num3'=0) & not n8_3')
(( num4' = 1 ) & n8_4') | ((num4'=0) & not n8_4')
(num1 + num2 + num3 + num4) != (num1' + num2' + num3' + num4')    // the check
```

We solve the conjunction of the above formulas using an off-the-shelf SMT solver called Yices [6]. In this particular example, the formula is satisfiable. For example, one of the satisfying assignments is `k1k2=00` and `k1'k2'=01`. We shall show in the next section that, when the key bits are 00, the probability for $n8$ to be logical 1 is 0%; but when the key bits are 01, the probability is 50%. This makes it vulnerable to first-order DPA attacks. Therefore, $n8$ is not perfectly masked.

High-Order Attacks. For a masked code to be resistant to *first-order* differential power analysis (DPA) attacks, all the intermediate results must be perfectly masked. However, even if each intermediate result is perfectly masked, it is still not sufficient to resist *high-order* DPA attacks, where an adversary can simultaneously observe leakage from more than one intermediate computation result. For a masking scheme to be resistant to *order-d* DPA attacks, we need to ensure that the joint distribution of any d intermediate results (where $d = 2, 3, \ldots$) is independent of the secret key. That is, for any d intermediate results $I_1, \ldots, I_d$, we check the satisfiability of the following formula:

$$\exists x. \exists k, k' \, . \, \left(\Sigma_{r \in \{0,1\}^s} \Sigma_{i=1}^d I_i(x, k, r) \neq \Sigma_{r \in \{0,1\}^s} \Sigma_{i=1}^d I_i(x, k', r) \right)$$

Our encoding can be easily extended to implement this new check. In practice, most countermeasures assume that the adversary has access to the side-channel leakage of either one or two intermediate results, which corresponds to first-order and second-order attacks. In our actual implementation, we handle both first-order and second-order attacks. In our experiments, we also evaluate our new method on verifying countermeasures against both first-order and second-order attacks (where $d = 1$ or 2).

4 The Working Example

Consider the automated verification of our running example in Fig. 2. For each internal node I, we first identify all the transitive fan-in nodes of I in the program to form a *code region* for the subsequent SMT solver based analysis. In the worst case, the extracted code region should start from the instruction (node) to be verified, and cover all the transitive fan-in nodes on which it depends. Then, the extracted code region is given to our SMT based verification procedure, whose goal is to prove (or disprove) that the node is statistically independent of the secret key.

Following a topological order, our method starts with node $n1$, which is defined in Line 3 of the program in Fig. 2. The extracted code region consists of $n1 = k1 \oplus r1$ itself. Since it involves only one key and one random variable in the XOR operation, a simple static analysis can prove that it is perfectly masked. Therefore, although we could have verified it using SMT, we skip it for efficiency reasons. Such simple static analysis is able to prove that $n2$, $n4$ and $n6$ are also perfectly masked.

Next, we check if $n3$ is perfectly masked. The truth table of $n3$ is shown in Fig. 4 (left). In all four valuations of $k1$ and $k2$, the probability of $n3$ being logical 1 is 25%. Therefore, $n3$ is perfectly masked. When we apply our SMT based method, the solver is not able to find any satisfying assignment for $k1$ and $k2$ under which the probability distributions of $n3$ are different. Note that our method does not check the probability of the output being logical 0, since having an equal probability distribution of logical 1 is equivalent to having an equal probability distribution for logical 0.

k1	k2	r1	r2	n3
0	0	0	0	0
0	0	0	1	0
0	0	1	0	0
0	0	1	1	1
0	1	0	0	0
0	1	0	1	0
0	1	1	0	1
0	1	1	1	0
1	0	0	0	0
1	0	0	1	1
1	0	1	0	0
1	0	1	1	0
1	1	0	0	1
1	1	0	1	0
1	1	1	0	0
1	1	1	1	0

k1	k2	r1	r2	n8
0	0	0	0	0
0	0	0	1	0
0	0	1	0	0
0	0	1	1	0
0	1	0	0	0
0	1	0	1	0
0	1	1	0	1
0	1	1	1	1
1	0	0	0	0
1	0	0	1	1
1	0	1	0	0
1	0	1	1	1
1	1	0	0	0
1	1	0	1	1
1	1	1	0	1
1	1	1	1	0

k1	k2	r1	r2	c
0	0	0	0	0
0	0	0	1	0
0	0	1	0	0
0	0	1	1	1
0	1	0	0	0
0	1	0	1	0
0	1	1	0	0
0	1	1	1	1
1	0	0	0	0
1	0	0	1	0
1	0	1	0	0
1	0	1	1	1
1	1	0	0	1
1	1	0	1	1
1	1	1	0	1
1	1	1	1	0

Fig. 4. The truth-tables for internal nodes $n3$, $n8$, and c of the example program in Fig. 2

The verification steps for nodes $n5$ and $n7$ are similar to that of $n3$ – all of them are perfectly masked.

Next, we check if $n8$ is perfectly masked. The proof would fail because, as shown in the truth table in Fig. 4 (middle), the probability for $n8$ to be logical 1 is not the same under different valuations of the keys. For example, if the keys are 00, then $n8$ would be 0 regardless of the values of the random variables. Recall that we have shown the detailed SMT encoding for $n8$ in Section 3. Using our method, the solver can quickly find two configurations of the key bits (for example, 00 and 11) under which the probabilities of $n8$ being logical 1 are different. Therefore, $n8$ is not perfectly masked.

The remaining node is c, whose truth table is shown in Fig. 4 (right). Similar to $n8$, our SMT based method will be able to show that it is not perfectly masked.

It is worth pointing out that the result of applying the *Sleuth* method [2] would have been different. Although $n8$ and c are clearly vulnerable to first-order DPA attacks, the *Sleuth* method, based on the notion of *sensitivity*, would have classified them as "securely masked." This demonstrates a major advantage of our new method over *Sleuth*.

5   The Incremental Verification Algorithm

Note that the size of the formula created by our SMT encoding is linear in the size of the program and exponential in the number of random variables – for s random bits, we need to make 2^{s+1} copies of the program logic. This is the main bottleneck for applying our method to large programs. In this section, we propose an incremental verification algorithm, which applies SMT solver based analysis only to small code regions – one at a time – as opposed to the entire fan-in cone of the node under verification. This is crucial for scaling the method up to programs of practical size.

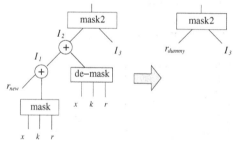

$$I_2 := I_1 \oplus de\text{-}mask(x, k, r)$$
$$\quad := r_{new} \oplus mask(x, k, r) \oplus de\text{-}mask(x, k, r)$$
$$\quad := r_{new} \oplus (\ldots)$$
$$\quad := r_{dummy}$$

Before verifying *mask2*, if we have already proved that I_2 is *perfectly masked*, and r_{new} is a new random variable not used elsewhere, then for the purpose of checking *mask2* only, we can substitute I_2 with r_{new} while verifying *mask2*.

Fig. 5. Incremental verification: applying the SMT based analysis to a small fan-in region only

Extracting the Verification Region. In practice, a common strategy in implementing randomization based countermeasures is to have a chain of modules, where the inputs of each module are masked before executing its logic, and are demasked afterward. To avoid having an unmasked intermediate value, the inputs to the successor module are masked with fresh random variables, before they are demasked from the random variables of the previous module. This can be illustrated by the example in Fig. 5, where the output of *mask(x,k,r)* is masked with the new random variable r_{new} before it is demasked from the old random variable r.

Due to *associativity* of the $\oplus$ operator, reordering the masking and demasking operations would not change the logical result. For example, in Fig. 5, the instruction being verified is in *mask2()*. Since the newly added random variable r_{new} is not used inside *mask()* or *de-mask()*, or in the support of I_3, we can replace the entire fan-in cone of I_2 by a new random variable r_{dummy} (or even r_{new} itself) while verifying *mask2()*. We shall see in the experimental results section that such opportunities are abundant in real-world applications. Therefore, in this subsection, we present a sound algorithm for extracting a small code region from the fan-in cone of the node under verification.

Our algorithm relies on some auxiliary data structures associated with the current node i under verification: *supportV[i]*, *uniqueM[i]* and *perfectM[i]*.

- *supportV[i]* is the set of inputs in the support of the function of node i.
- *uniqueM[i]* is the set of random inputs that each reaches i along only one path.
- *perfectM[i]* is a subset of *uniqueM[i]* where each random variable, by itself, guarantees that node i is perfectly masked.

These tables can be computed by a traversal of the program nodes as described in Algorithm 1. For example, for node I_1 in Fig. 5, *supportV[I_1]*= $\{x, k, r, r_{new}\}$, *uniqueM[I_1]* = $\{r, r_{new}\}$, and *perfectM[I_1]*= $\{r_{new}\}$, assuming r is not repeated in the mask block. For node I_2, we have *supportV[I_2]*= $\{x, k, r, r_{new}\}$, *uniqueM[I_2]*= $\{r_{new}\}$, since r reaches I_2 twice and so may have been de-masked, and *perfectM[I_2]*= $\{r_{new}\}$.

Algorithm 1. Computing the auxiliary tables for all internal nodes of the program.

```
 1. supportV[i] ← { v } for each input node i with variable v
 2. uniqueM[i] ← { v } for each input node i with random mask variable v
 3. perfectM[i] ← { v } for each input node i with random mask variable v
 4. for each (internal node i in a leaf-to-root topological order) {
 5.     L ← LEFTCHILD(i)
 6.     R ← RIGHTCHILD(i)
 7.     supportV[i] ← supportV[L] ∪ supportV[R]
 8.     uniqueM ← (uniqueM[L] ∪ uniqueM[R]) \ (supportV[L] ∩ supportV[R])
 9.     if (i is an XOR node)
10.         perfectM[i] ← uniqueM[i] ∩ (perfectM[L]∪perfectM[R])
11.     else
12.         perfectM[i] ← { }
13. }
```

Our idea of extracting a small code region for SMT based analysis is formalized in Algorithm 2. Given the node i under verification, and *uniqueM[i]* as the set of random variables that each reaches i along only one path, we call GETREGION(i,*uniqueM[i]*) to compute the region. Inside GETREGION, *uniqueM[i]* is renamed to *freshMasksATi*. More specifically, we start by checking each transitive fan-in node n of the current node i. If n is a leaf node (Line 2), then we add n and the input variable v to the region. If n is not a leaf node, we check if there is a random variable $r \in$*uniqueMATi* that, by itself, can perfectly mask node n (Line 4). In Fig. 5, for example, r_{new}, by itself, can uniformly mask node I_2. If such random variable r exists, then we add pair (n, r) to the region and return – skipping the entire fan-in cone of n. Otherwise, we recursively invoke GETREGION to traverse the two child nodes of n.

Algorithm 2. Extracting a code region for node i for the subsequent SMT based analysis.

```
1.  GETREGION (n, uniqueMATi) {
2.    if (n is an input node with variable v)
3.      region.add ← (n, v)
4.    else if (∃ random variable r ∈ perfectM[n] ∩ uniqueMATi)
5.      region.add ← (n, r)
6.    else
7.      region.add ← (n, {})
8.      region.add ← GETREGION(n.Left,  uniqueMATi)
9.      region.add ← GETREGION(n.Right, uniqueMATi)
10.   return region
11. }
```

The Overall Algorithm. Algorithm 3 shows the overall flow of our incremental verification method. Given the program and the lists of secret, random and plaintext variables, our method systematically scans through all the internal nodes from the inputs to the return value. For each node i, our method first extracts a small code region (Line 4). Then, we invoke the SMT based analysis. If the node is not perfectly masked, we add it to the list of *bad* nodes.

Algorithm 3. Incremental verification of perfect masking.

```
1.  VERIFYPERFECTMASKING (Prog, keys, rands, plains) {
2.    badNodes ← { }
3.    for each (internal node i ∈ Prog in a topological order ) {
4.        region ← GETREGION(i, uniqueM[i])
5.        notPerfect ← CHECKMASKINGBYSMT (i, region, keys, rands, plains )
6.        if (notPerfect)
7.          badNodes.add( i )
8.    }
9.    return badNodes
10. }
```

To optimize the performance of Algorithm 3, we conduct a simple static analysis between Line 4 and Line 5 to quickly check whether it is fruitful to invoke the SMT solver. The first one checks if the region contains any secret keys, if not then the solver is not invoked and the instruction is perfectly masked. The second analysis checks some syntactic conditions – if all of these conditions are satisfied, the current node i is guaranteed to be perfectly masked. In such case, we also avoid invoking the SMT solver. The implemented syntactic conditions are listed as follows:

- The instruction has no secret input as its child. This guarantees that when a secret variable is introduced, its masking operation will be verified.
- None of the random variables appears in both operand's *supportV* tables. This guarantees that no perfectly masking of a secret variable in any of the operands may be affected.

– Both operands are perfectly masked. This guarantees to find all the resultant imperfect masked instructions due to an initial imperfectly masked instruction.

To further optimize the performance of Algorithm 3, we implement a method for identifying random variables that are *don't cares* for the node i under verification, and use the information to reduce the cost of the SMT based analysis. Prior to the SMT encoding, for each random variable $r \in supportV[i]$, we check if the value of r can ever affect the output of i. If the answer is no, then r is a *don't care*. During our SMT encoding, we will set r to logical 0 rather than treat r as a random variable, to to reduce the size of the SMT formula. This can lead to a significant performance improvement since the formula size is exponential in the number of relevant random variables.

We check whether $r \in support[i]$ is a *don't care* for node i by constructing a SAT formula and solving it using the SMT solver. The SAT formula is defined as follows:

$$\Psi_{region}^{r=0} \wedge \Psi_{region}^{r=1} \wedge \Psi_{diffO} \, ,$$

where $\Psi_{region}^{r=0}$ encodes the program logic of the region, with the random bit r set to 0, $\Psi_{region}^{r=1}$ encodes the program logic of the region, with the random bit r set to 1, and Φ_{diffO} asserts that the outputs of these two copies differ. If the above formula is unsatisfiable, then r is a *don't care* for node i.

6 Experiments

We have implemented our method in a verification tool called *SC Sniffer*, based on the LLVM compiler and the Yices SMT solver [6]. It runs in two modes: monolithic and incremental. The monolithic mode applies our SMT based encoding to the entire fan-in cone of each node in the program, whereas the incremental method tries to restrict the SMT encoding to a localized region. In addition, we implemented the *Sleuth* method [2] for experimental comparison. The main difference is that our method not only checks whether a node is masked (as in *Sleuth*), but also checks whether it is perfectly masked, i.e. it is statistically independent of the secret key.

We have evaluated our tool on some recently proposed countermeasures. Our experiments were designed to answer the following research questions:

– How effective is our new method? We know that in theory, the new method is more accurate than the *Sleuth* method. But does it have a significant advantage over the *Sleuth* method in practice?
– How scalable is our new method, especially in verifying applications of realistic code size and complexity? We have extended our SMT based method with incremental verification. Is it effective in practice?

Table 1 shows the statistics of the benchmarks. Column 1 shows the name of each benchmark example. Column 2 shows a short description of the implemented algorithm. Column 3 shows the number of lines of code – here, each instruction is a bit level operation. Column 4 shows the number of nodes that represent the intermediate computation results. Columns 5-7 show the number of input bits that are the secret key, the plaintext, and the random variable, respectively.

Table 1. The benchmark statistics: in addition to the program name and a short description, we show the total lines of code, the numbers of intermediate nodes and the various inputs

Name	Description	Code Size	Nodes	Keys	Plains	Rands
P1	CHES13 Masked Key Whitening	79	47	16	16	16
P2	CHES13 De-mask and then Mask	67	31	8	0	16
P3	CHES13 AES Shift Rows [2nd-order]	21	21	2	0	2
P4	CHES13 Messerges Boolean to Arithmetic (bit0) [2-order]	23	24	1	0	2
P5	CHES13 Goubin Boolean to Arithmetic (bit0) [2-order]	27	60	1	0	2
P6	Logic Design for AES S-Box (1st implementation)	32	9	2	0	2
P7	Logic Design for AES S-Box (2nd implementation)	40	6	2	0	3
P8	Masked Chi function MAC-Keccak (1st implementation)	59	19	3	0	4
P9	Masked Chi function MAC-Keccak (2nd implementation)	60	19	3	0	4
P10	Syn. Masked Chi func MAC-Keccak (1st implementation)	66	22	3	0	4
P11	Syn. Masked Chi func MAC-Keccak (2nd implementation)	66	22	3	0	4
P12	MAC-Keccak 512b Perfect masked	285k	128k	288	288	805
P13	MAC-Keccak 512b De-mask and then mask – compiler error	285k	128k	288	288	805
P14	MAC-Keccak 512b Not-perfect Masking of Chi function (v1)	285k	128k	288	288	805
P15	MAC-Keccak 512b Not-perfect Masking of Chi function (v2)	285k	152k	288	288	805
P16	MAC-Keccak 512b Not-perfect Masking of Chi function (v3)	285k	128k	288	288	805
P17	MAC-Keccak 512b Unmasking of Pi function	285k	131k	288	288	805

Table 2. Experimental results: comparing our *SC Sniffer* method with the *Sleuth* method [2]

Name	Sleuth [2]				SC Sniffer (monolithic)				SC Sniffer (incremental)				
	masked	nodes failed	nodes checked	time	masked perfect	nodes failed	nodes checked	time	masked perfect	nodes failed	nodes checked	SMT mask	time
P1	No	16	47	0.16s	No	16	47	0.22s	No	16	47	16	0.09s
P2	No	8	31	0.21s	No	8	31	0.20s	No	8	31	8	0.09s
P3	No	9	21	1.17s	No	9	21	1.27s	No	9	21	18	0.46s
P4	No	2	24	0.58s	No	2	24	0.65s	No	2	24	8	0.57s
P5	No	2	60	1.19s	No	2	60	1.40s	No	2	60	20	1.12s
P6	Yes	0	9	0.06s	No	2	9	0.10s	No	2	9	2	0.08s
P7	Yes	0	6	0.04s	No	1	6	0.07s	No	1	6	1	0.03s
P8	No	1	19	0.15s	No	3	19	0.26s	No	3	19	3	0.11s
P9	Yes	0	19	0.13s	No	2	19	0.27s	No	2	19	2	0.10s
P10	Yes	0	22	0.18s	No	1	22	0.32s	No	1	22	2	0.14s
P11	Yes	0	22	0.20s	No	1	22	0.37s	No	1	22	3	0.18s
P12	Yes	0	128k	91m53s	-	0	34	mem-out	Yes	0	128K	0	10m48s
P13	No	2560	128k	92m59s	No	1	46	mem-out	No	2560	128K	2560	14m10s
P14	Yes	0	128k	97m38s	-	0	31	mem-out	No	1024	128K	1024	18m20s
P15	Yes	0	152k	132m10s	-	0	32	mem-out	No	512	152K	1024	37m37s
P16	No	512	128k	113m12s	-	0	40	mem-out	No	1536	128K	1536	17m24s
P17	No	4096	131k	103m56s	-	0	34	mem-out	No	4096	131K	4096	17m35s

The benchmarks are classified into three groups. The first group of test cases (P1 to P5) are taken from the *Sleuth* benchmark [2], all of which contain intermediate variables that are not masked at all. More specifically, P1 is the masking key whitening code on Page 12 of the *Sleuth* paper. P2 is the AES8 example, a smart card implementation of AES resistant to power analysis, originated from Herbst *et al.* [8]. P3 is the code on Page 13 of the *Sleuth* paper, also originated from Herbst *et al.* [8]. P4 is the code on Page 18 of the *Sleuth* paper, originated from Messerges [13]. P5 is the code on Page 18 of the *Sleuth* paper, originated from Goubin [7].

The second group of test cases (P6 to P11) are examples where most of the intermediate variables are masked, but none of the masking schemes is perfect. P6 and P7 are the two examples used by Blömer *et al.* [4] (on Page 7). P8 and P9 are the SHA3 MAC-Keccak computation reordered examples, originated from Bertoni *et al.* [3] (Eq. 5.2 on Page 46). P10 and P11 are two experimental masking schemes for the Chi function in SHA3, none of which is perfectly masked.

The third group of test cases (P12 to P17) comes from the regeneration of MAC-Keccak reference code submission to NIST in the SHA-3 competition [15]. There are a total of 285k lines of Boolean operation code. The difference among these test cases is that they are protected by various countermeasures, some of which are perfectly masked (e.g. P12) whereas others are not.

Table 2 shows the experimental results run on a machine with a 3.4 GHz Intel i7-2600 CPU, 4 GB RAM, and a 32-bit Linux OS. We have compared the performance of three methods: *Sleuth*, New (monolithic), and New (incremental). Here, *Sleuth* is the method proposed by Bayrak *et al.* [2], while the other two are our own method. In this table, Column 1 shows the name of each test program. Columns 2-5 show the results of running *Sleuth*, including whether the program passed the check, the number of nodes failed the check, and the total number of nodes checked. Columns 6-9 show the results of running our new monolithic method. Here, mem-out means that the method requires more than 4 GB of RAM. Columns 10-14 show the results of running our new incremental method. Here, we also show the number of SMT based masking checks made, which is often much smaller than the number of nodes checked, because many of them are resolved by our static analysis.

First, the results show that our new algorithm is more accurate than *Sleuth* in deciding whether a node is securely masked. Every node that failed the security check of *Sleuth* would also fail the security check of our new method. However, there are many nodes that passed the check of *Sleuth*, but failed the check of our new method. These are the nodes that are masked, but their probability distributions are still dependent on the sensitive inputs – in other words, they are not perfectly masked.

Second, the results show that our incremental method is significantly more scalable than the monolithic method. On the first two groups of test cases, where the programs are small, both methods can complete, and the difference in run time is small. However, on large programs such as the Keccak reference code, the monolithic method could not finish since it quickly ran out of the 4 GB RAM, whereas the incremental method can finish in a reasonable amount of time. Moreover, although the *Sleuth* method implements a significantly simpler (and hence weaker) check, it is also based on a monolithic verification approach. Our results in Table 2 show that, on large examples, our incremental method is significantly faster than *Sleuth*.

As a measurement of the scalability of the algorithms, we have conducted experiments on a 1-bit version of test program P1 for 1 to 10 encryption rounds. In each parameterized version, the input for each round is the output from the previous round. We ran the experiment twice, once with an unmasked instruction in each round, and once with all instructions perfectly masked. The results of

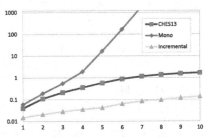

the two experiments are almost identical, and therefore, we only plot the result for the perfectly masked version. In the right figure, the x-axis shows the program size, and the y-axis shows the verification time in seconds. Among the three methods, our incremental method is the most scalable.

7   Conclusions

We have presented the first fully automated method for formally verifying whether a software implementation is *perfectly masked* by uniformly random inputs, and therefore is secure against power analysis based side-channel attacks. Our new method relies on translating the verification problem into a set of constraint solving problems, which can be decided by off-the-shelf solvers such as Yices. We have also presented an incremental checking procedure to drastically improve the scalability of the SMT based algorithm. We have conducted experiments on a large set of recently proposed countermeasures. Our results show that the new method is not only more precise than existing methods, but also scalable for practical use.

Acknowledgments. This work is supported in part by the NSF grant CNS-1128903 and the ONR grant N00014-13-1-0527.

References

1. Balasch, J., Gierlichs, B., Verdult, R., Batina, L., Verbauwhede, I.: Power analysis of Atmel CryptoMemory – recovering keys from secure EEPROMs. In: Dunkelman, O. (ed.) CT-RSA 2012. LNCS, vol. 7178, pp. 19–34. Springer, Heidelberg (2012)
2. Bayrak, A.G., Regazzoni, F., Novo, D., Ienne, P.: Sleuth: Automated verification of software power analysis countermeasures. In: Bertoni, G., Coron, J.-S. (eds.) CHES 2013. LNCS, vol. 8086, pp. 293–310. Springer, Heidelberg (2013)
3. Bertoni, G., Daemen, J., Peeters, M., Assche, G.V., Keer, R.V.: Keccak implementation overview, http://keccak.neokeon.org/Keccak-implementation-3.2.pdf
4. Blömer, J., Guajardo, J., Krummel, V.: Provably secure masking of AES. In: Handschuh, H., Hasan, M.A. (eds.) SAC 2004. LNCS, vol. 3357, pp. 69–83. Springer, Heidelberg (2004)
5. Clarke, E.M., Grumberg, O., Peled, D.A.: Model Checking. MIT Press, Cambridge (1999)
6. Dutertre, B., de Moura, L.: A fast linear-arithmetic solver for DPLL(T). In: Ball, T., Jones, R.B. (eds.) CAV 2006. LNCS, vol. 4144, pp. 81–94. Springer, Heidelberg (2006)
7. Goubin, L.: A sound method for switching between boolean and arithmetic masking. In: Koç, Ç.K., Naccache, D., Paar, C. (eds.) CHES 2001. LNCS, vol. 2162, pp. 3–15. Springer, Heidelberg (2001)
8. Herbst, C., Oswald, E., Mangard, S.: An AES smart card implementation resistant to power analysis attacks. In: Zhou, J., Yung, M., Bao, F. (eds.) ACNS 2006. LNCS, vol. 3989, pp. 239–252. Springer, Heidelberg (2006)
9. Joye, M., Paillier, P., Schoenmakers, B.: On second-order differential power analysis. In: Rao, J.R., Sunar, B. (eds.) CHES 2005. LNCS, vol. 3659, pp. 293–308. Springer, Heidelberg (2005)
10. Kocher, P.C., Jaffe, J., Jun, B.: Differential power analysis. In: Wiener, M. (ed.) CRYPTO 1999. LNCS, vol. 1666, pp. 388–397. Springer, Heidelberg (1999)

11. Li, B., Wang, C., Somenzi, F.: A satisfiability-based approach to abstraction refinement in model checking. Electronic Notes in Theoretical Computer Science 89(4) (2003)
12. Mangard, S., Oswald, E., Popp, T.: Power Analysis Attacks - Revealing the Secrets of Smart Cards. Springer (2007)
13. Messerges, T.S.: Securing the AES finalists against power analysis attacks. In: Schneier, B. (ed.) FSE 2000. LNCS, vol. 1978, pp. 150–164. Springer, Heidelberg (2001)
14. Moradi, A., Barenghi, A., Kasper, T., Paar, C.: On the vulnerability of FPGA bitstream encryption against power analysis attacks: Extracting keys from Xilinx Virtex-II FPGAs. In: ACM Conference on Computer and Communications Security, pp. 111–124 (2011)
15. NIST. Keccak reference code submission to NIST's SHA-3 competition (Round 3), http://csrc.nist.gov/groups/ST/hash/sha-3/Round3/documents/Keccak_FinalRnd.zip
16. Paar, C., Eisenbarth, T., Kasper, M., Kasper, T., Moradi, A.: Keeloq and side-channel analysis-evolution of an attack. In: FDTC, pp. 65–69 (2009)
17. Prouff, E., Rivain, M.: Masking against side-channel attacks: A formal security proof. In: Johansson, T., Nguyen, P.Q. (eds.) EUROCRYPT 2013. LNCS, vol. 7881, pp. 142–159. Springer, Heidelberg (2013)
18. Sabelfeld, A., Myers, A.C.: Language-based information-flow security. IEEE Journal on Selected Areas in Communications 21(1), 5–19 (2003)
19. Taha, M., Schaumont, P.: Differential power analysis of MAC-Keccak at any key-length. In: Sakiyama, K., Terada, M. (eds.) IWSEC 2013. LNCS, vol. 8231, pp. 68–82. Springer, Heidelberg (2013)
20. Wang, C., Hachhtel, G.D., Somenzi, F.: Abstraction Refinement for Large Scale Model Checking. Springer (2006)
21. Yang, Z., Wang, C., Ivančić, F., Gupta, A.: Mixed symbolic representations for model checking software programs. In: Formal Methods and Models for Codesign, pp. 17–24 (July 2006)

Detecting Unrealizable Specifications of Distributed Systems*

Bernd Finkbeiner and Leander Tentrup

Saarland University, Germany

Abstract. Writing formal specifications for distributed systems is difficult. Even simple consistency requirements often turn out to be unrealizable because of the complicated information flow in the distributed system: not every information is available in every component, and information transmitted from other components may arrive with a delay or not at all, especially in the presence of faults. The problem of checking the distributed realizability of a temporal specification is, in general, undecidable. Semi-algorithms for synthesis, such as bounded synthesis, are only useful in the positive case, where they construct an implementation for a realizable specification, but not in the negative case: if the specification is unrealizable, the search for the implementation never terminates. In this paper, we introduce *counterexamples to distributed realizability* and present a method for the detection of such counterexamples for specifications given in linear-time temporal logic (LTL). A counterexample consists of a set of paths, each representing a different sequence of inputs from the environment, such that, no matter how the components are implemented, the specification is violated on *at least one* of these paths. We present a method for finding such counterexamples both for the classic distributed realizability problem and for the distributed realizability problem with faulty nodes. Our method considers, incrementally, larger and larger sets of paths until a counterexample is found. While counterexamples for full LTL may consist of infinitely many paths, we give a semantic characterization such that the required number of paths can be bounded. For this fragment, we thus obtain a decision procedure. Experimental results, obtained with a QBF-based prototype implementation, show that our method finds simple errors very quickly, and even problems with high combinatorial complexity, like the Byzantine Generals' Problem, are tractable.

1 Introduction

The goal of program synthesis, and systems engineering in general, is to build systems that satisfy a given specification. Sometimes, however, this goal is unattainable, because the conditions of the specification are *impossible* to satisfy in an

---

* This work was partially supported by the German Research Foundation (DFG) as part of SFB/TR 14 AVACS and by the Saarbrücken Graduate School of Computer Science, which receives funding from the DFG as part of the Excellence Initiative of the German Federal and State Governments.

E. Ábrahám and K. Havelund (Eds.): TACAS 2014, LNCS 8413, pp. 78–92, 2014.

implementation. A textbook example for such a case is the *Byzantine Generals'
Problem*, introduced in the early 1980s by Lamport et al. [1]. Three generals
of the Byzantine army, consisting of one commander and two lieutenants, need
to agree on whether they should "attack" or "retreat." For this purpose, the
commander sends an order to the lieutenants, and all generals then exchange
messages with each other, reporting, for example, to one general which messages
they have received from the other general. The problem is that one of the generals is a traitor and can therefore not be assumed to tell the truth: the tale of the
Byzantine generals is, after all, just an illustration for the problem of achieving
fault tolerance in distributed operating systems, where we would like to achieve
consensus even if a certain subset of the nodes is faulty. Of course, we cannot
expect the traitor to agree with the loyal generals, but we might still expect a
loyal lieutenant to agree with the order issued by a loyal commander, and two
loyal lieutenants to reach a consensus in case the commander is the traitor. This
specification is, however, unrealizable in the setting of the three generals (and,
more generally, in all settings where at least a third of the nodes are faulty).

Detecting unrealizable specifications is of great value because it avoids spend-
ing implementation effort on specifications that are impossible to satisfy. If the
system consists of a single process, then unrealizable specifications can be detected with *synthesis* algorithms, which detect unrealizability as a byproduct of
attempting to construct an implementation. For distributed systems, the problem is more complicated: in order to show that there is no way for the three
generals to achieve consensus, we need to argue about the knowledge of each
general. The key observation in the Byzantine Generals' Problem is that the
loyal generals have no way of knowing who, among the other two generals, is
the traitor and who is the second loyal general. For example, the situation where
the commander is the traitor and orders one lieutenant to "attack" and the other
to "retreat" is *indistinguishable*, from the point of view of the loyal lieutenant
who is ordered to attack, from the situation where the commander is loyal and
orders both lieutenants to attack, while the traitor claims to have received a
"retreat" order. Since the specification requires the lieutenant to act differently
(agree with the other lieutenant vs. agree with the commander) in the two indistinguishable situations, we reach a contradiction.

Since realizability for distributed systems is in general an undecidable problem [2], the only available decision procedures are limited to special cases, such as
pipeline and ring architectures [3, 4]. There are semi-algorithms for distributed
synthesis, such as *bounded synthesis* [5], but the focus is on the search for implementations rather than on the search for inconsistencies: if an implementation
exists, the semi-algorithm terminates with such an implementation, otherwise it
runs forever. In this paper, we take the opposite approach and study *counterexamples to realizability*. Intuitively, a counterexample collects a sufficient number
of scenarios such that, no matter what the implementation does, an error will
occur in *at least one* of the chosen scenarios. As specifications, we consider formulas of linear-time temporal logic (LTL). It is straightforward to encode the
Byzantine Generals' Problem in LTL. Another interesting example is the famous

CAP Theorem, a fundamental result in the theory of distributed computation conjectured by Brewer [6]. The CAP Theorem states that it is impossible to design a distributed system that provides Consistency, Availability, and Partition tolerance (CAP) simultaneously. We assume there is a fixed number n of nodes, that every node implements the same service, and that there are direct communication links between all nodes. We use the variables req_i and out_i to denote input and output of node i, respectively. The consistency and availability requirements can then be encoded as the LTL formulas $\bigwedge_{1 \leq i < n}(\text{out}_i \leftrightarrow \text{out}_{i+1})$ and $(\bigvee_{1 \leq i \leq n} \text{req}_i) \leftrightarrow (\bigcirc \bigvee_{1 \leq i \leq n} \text{out}_i)$. The partition tolerance is modeled in a way that there is always at most one node partitioned from the rest of the system.

In both examples, a finite set of input sequences suffices to force the system into violating the specification on at least one of the input sequences. In this paper, we present an efficient method for finding such counterexamples. It turns out that searching for counterexamples is much easier than the classic synthesis approach of establishing unrealizability by the non-existence of strategy trees [2, 3, 4]. The difficulty in synthesis is to enforce the consistency condition that the strategy of a process must act the same way in all situations the process cannot distinguish. On the strategy trees, this consistency condition is not an ω-regular (or even decidable) property. When analyzing a counterexample, on the other hand, we only check consistency on a specific set of sequences, not on a full tree. This restricted consistency condition is an ω-regular property and can, in fact, simply be expressed in LTL as part of the temporal specification. Our QBF-based prototype implementation finds counterexamples for the Byzantine Generals' Problem and the CAP Theorem within just a few seconds.

Related Work. To the best of the authors' knowledge, there has been no attempt in the literature to characterize unrealizable specifications for distributed systems beyond the restricted class of architectures with decidable synthesis problems, such as pipelines and rings [3, 4]. By contrast, there is a rich literature concerning unrealizability for open systems, that is, single-process systems interacting with the environment [7, 8, 9]. In robotics, there have been recent attempts to analyze unrealizable specifications [10]. The results are also focused on the reason for unsatisfiability, while our approach tries to determine if a specification is unrealizable. Moreover, they only consider the simpler non-distributed synthesis of GR(1) specifications, which is a subset of LTL. There are other approaches concerning unrealizable specifications in the non-distributed setting that also use counterexamples [11, 12]. There, the system specifications are assumed to be correct and the information from the counterexamples are used to modify environment assumptions in order to make the specifications realizable. The Byzantine Generals' Problem is often used as an illustration for the knowledge-based reasoning in epistemic logics, see [13] for an early formalization. Concerning the synthesis of fault-tolerant distributed systems, there is an approach to synthesize fault-tolerant systems in the special case of strongly connected system architectures [14].

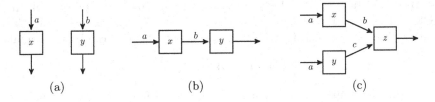

Fig. 1. Distributed architectures

2 Distributed Realizability

A specification is *realizable* if there exists an implementation that satisfies the specification. For distributed systems, the realizability problem is typically stated with respect to a specific system architecture. Figure 1 shows some typical example architectures: an architecture consisting of *independent* processes, a *pipeline* architecture, and a *join* architecture. The architecture describes the communication topology of the distributed system. For example, an edge from x to y labeled with b indicates that b is a shared variable between processes x and y, where x writes to b and y reads b. The classic *distributed realizability problem* is to decide whether there exists an implementation (or *strategy*) for each process in the architecture, such that the joint behavior satisfies the specification. In this paper, we are furthermore interested in the synthesis of fault-tolerant distributed systems, where the processes and the communication between processes may become faulty.

In order to have a uniform and precise definition for the various realizability problems of interest, we use a logical representation. Extended coordination logic (ECL) [15] is a game-based extension of linear-time temporal logic (LTL). ECL uses the *strategy quantifier* $\exists C \rhd s$ to express the existence of an implementation for a process output s based on input variables C.

ECL Syntax. ECL formulas contain two types of variables: the set $\mathcal{C}$ of *input* (or *coordination*) variables, and the set $\mathcal{S}$ of *output* (or *strategy*) variables. In addition to the usual LTL operators Next $\bigcirc$, Until $\mathcal{U}$, and Release $\mathcal{R}$, ECL has the strategy quantifier $\exists C \rhd s$, which introduces an output variable s whose values must be chosen based on the inputs in C. The syntax is given by the grammar

$$\varphi ::= x \mid \neg x \mid \varphi \vee \varphi \mid \varphi \wedge \varphi \mid \bigcirc \varphi \mid \varphi \, \mathcal{U} \, \varphi \mid \varphi \, \mathcal{R} \, \varphi \mid \exists C \rhd s. \, \varphi \mid \forall C \rhd s. \, \varphi \ ,$$

where $x \in \mathcal{C} \, \dot\cup \, \mathcal{S}$, $C \subseteq \mathcal{C}$, and $s \in \mathcal{S}$. Beside the standard abbreviations true $\equiv x \vee \neg x$, false $= x \wedge \neg x$, $\Diamond \varphi \equiv$ true $\mathcal{U} \, \varphi$, and $\Box \varphi \equiv$ false $\mathcal{R} \, \varphi$, we use $\bigcirc_n \varphi$ as an abbreviation of n consecutive Next operators.

We denote by $\mathcal{Q}$ the (possibly empty) *quantification prefix* of a formula and call the remainder the *body*. For $Q \in \{\exists, \forall\}$, we use $\mathcal{Q}_Q$ if the prefix contains only Q-quantifiers. For the purposes of this paper, it suffices to consider the fragment ECL$_\exists$ that only contains existential quantifiers. We furthermore assume that the body is quantifier-free, i.e., that the formulas are in *prenex normal form (PNF)*.

Examples. We demonstrate how to express distributed realizability problems in ECL$_\exists$ with the example architectures from Fig. 1. The realizability of an LTL formula ψ_1 in the architecture from Fig. 1(a) is expressed by the ECL$_\exists$ formula

$$\exists\{a\} \triangleright x. \exists\{b\} \triangleright y. \psi_1 . \tag{1}$$

Interprocess communication via a shared variable b, as in the pipeline architecture from Fig. 1(b), is expressed by separating the information read from b from the output written to b. In the following ECL$_\exists$ formula we use output variable x to denote the output written to b:

$$\exists\{b\} \triangleright y. \exists\{a, b\} \triangleright x. \Box (b = x) \to \psi_2 \tag{2}$$

The LTL specification ψ_2 is qualified by the input-output relation $\Box (b = x)$, which expresses that ψ_2 is required to hold under the assumption that the information written to b by process x is also the information read from b by process y. This separation between sent and received information is useful to model faults that disturb the transmission. Failing processes can be specified by omitting the input-output relations that refer to the failing processes. As an example, consider the architecture in Fig. 1(c). The ECL$_\exists$ formula

$$\exists\{a\} \triangleright x, y. \exists\{b, c\} \triangleright z. \left(\Box (c = y) \to \psi_3\right) \wedge \left(\Box (b = x) \to \psi_3\right) \tag{3}$$

specifies that there exists an implementation such that ψ_3 is guaranteed to hold even if process x or y (but not both) fails.

For a formula Φ, we differentiate two types of coordination variables, *external* and *internal*. A coordination variable $c \in \mathcal{C}$ is external iff it is a true input from the environment, i.e., not contained in any input-output relation of Φ. For example, the input a in (3) is external while b and c are internal.

ECL Semantics. We give a quick definition of the ECL$_\exists$ semantics for formulas in PNF and refer the reader to [15] for details and for the semantics of full ECL. The semantics is based on *trees* as a representation for strategies and computations. Given a finite set of directions Υ and a finite set of labels Σ, a (full) Σ-*labeled* Υ-*tree* $\mathcal{T}$ is a pair $\langle \Upsilon^*, l \rangle$, where $l : \Upsilon^* \to \Sigma$ assigns each *node* $v \in \Upsilon$ a label $l(v)$. For two trees $\mathcal{T}$ and $\mathcal{T}'$, we define the joint valuation $\mathcal{T} \oplus \mathcal{T}'$ to be the widened tree with the union of both labels. We refer to [15] for a formal definition. A path σ in a Σ-labeled Υ-tree $\mathcal{T}$ is an ω-word $\sigma_0 \sigma_1 \sigma_2 \ldots \in \Upsilon^\omega$ and the corresponding labeled path $\sigma^{\mathcal{T}}$ is $(l(\epsilon), \sigma_0)(l(\sigma_0), \sigma_1)(l(\sigma_0 \sigma_1), \sigma_2)(l(\sigma_0 \sigma_1 \sigma_2), \sigma_3) \ldots \in (\Upsilon \times \Sigma)^\omega$.

For a strategy variable s that is bound by some quantifier $Q\mathcal{C} \triangleright s. \varphi$, we refer to $\mathcal{C}$ as the *scope* of s, denoted by Scope(s). The meaning of a strategy variable s is a *strategy* or *implementation* $f_s : (2^{\text{Scope}(s)})^* \to 2^{\{s\}}$, i.e., a function that maps a history of valuations of input variables to a valuation of the output variable s. We represent the computation of a strategy f_s as the tree $\langle (2^{\text{Scope}(s)})^*, f_s \rangle$ where f_s serves as the labeling function (cf. Fig. 2(a)–(b)). ECL$_\exists$ formulas are interpreted over *computation trees*, that are the joint valuations of the computations for

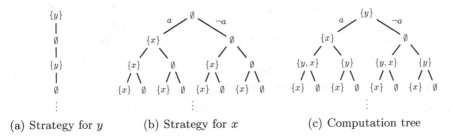

(a) Strategy for y (b) Strategy for x (c) Computation tree

Fig. 2. In (a) and (b) we sketch example strategies for y and x satisfying the ECL$_\exists$ formula $\exists \emptyset \rhd y.\, \exists \{a\} \rhd x.\, \Box (\bigcirc x \leftrightarrow a) \wedge \Box (y \leftrightarrow \bigcirc \neg y)$. In (c) we visualize the resulting computation tree on which the body (LTL) formula is evaluated.

strategies belonging to the strategy variables in $\mathcal{S}$, i.e., $\bigoplus_{s \in \mathcal{S}} \langle (2^{\mathrm{Scope}(s)})^*, f_s \rangle$ (cf. Fig. 2(c)). Given an ECL$_\exists$ formula $\mathcal{Q}_\exists.\, \varphi$ in prenex normal form over strategy variables $\mathcal{S}$ and coordination variables $\mathcal{C}$, the formula is satisfied if there exists a computation tree $\mathcal{T}$ (over $\mathcal{S}$), such that all paths in $\mathcal{T}$ satisfy the LTL formula φ, i.e., $\forall \sigma \in (2^\mathcal{C})^\omega.\, \sigma^\mathcal{T}, 0 \vDash \varphi$ where the satisfaction of an LTL formula on a labeled path $\sigma^\mathcal{T}$ on position $i \geq 0$ is defined as usual.

3 Counterexamples to Distributed Realizability

We now introduce *counterexamples to realizability*, which correspond to *counterexamples to satisfiability* for the ECL$_\exists$ formula that represents the realizability problem. The satisfiability problem for an ECL$_\exists$ formula in prenex form asks for an implementation for all strategy variables in the quantification prefix of the formula such that the temporal specification in the body is satisfied.

Let $\Phi = \mathcal{Q}_\exists.\, \varphi$ be an ECL$_\exists$ formula in prenex form over coordination variables $\mathcal{C}$ and strategy variables $\mathcal{S}$, where the body of the formula is the LTL formula φ. A *counterexample to satisfiability* for Φ is a (possibly infinite) set of paths $\mathcal{P} \subseteq (2^\mathcal{C})^\omega$, such that, no matter what strategies are chosen for the strategy variables in $\mathcal{S}$, there exists a path $\sigma \in \mathcal{P}$ that violates the body φ. Formally, $\mathcal{P} \subseteq (2^\mathcal{C})^\omega$ is a counterexample to satisfiability iff, for all strategies $f_s : (2^{\mathrm{Scope}(s)})^* \to 2^{\{s\}}$ for each $s \in \mathcal{S}$, it holds that there exists a path $\sigma \in \mathcal{P}$ such that $\sigma^\mathcal{T}, 0 \vDash \neg \varphi$ where $\mathcal{T} = \bigoplus_{s \in \mathcal{S}} \langle (2^{\mathrm{Scope}(s)})^*, f_s \rangle$.

Proposition 1. *An ECL$_\exists$ formula Φ over coordination variables $\mathcal{C}$ and strategy variables $\mathcal{S}$ is unsatisfiable if and only if there exists a counterexample to satisfiability $\mathcal{P} \subseteq (2^\mathcal{C})^\omega$.*

Proof. By the semantics of ECL$_\exists$ and $\mathcal{P} = (2^\mathcal{C})^\omega$.   □

In the remainder of the paper, we focus on counterexamples to realizability problems. The distributed realizability problem *without* faults correspond to ECL$_\exists$ formulas of the form $\Phi = \mathcal{Q}_\exists.\, \varphi_{\mathrm{path}} \to \varphi$, where the φ_{path} defines the system architecture $\mathcal{A}_\Phi$: there is an edge from one strategy variable to another if the input-output relation occurs in φ_{path}. A *finite* counterexample to satisfiability of Φ is a finite set of paths $\mathcal{P} \subseteq (2^{\mathcal{C}_{\mathrm{ext}}})^\omega$ corresponding to external coordination variables, such that for any implementation $\mathcal{T}$ there exists a path $\sigma \in \mathcal{P}$ such that an extension $\sigma' \in (2^{\mathcal{C}})^\omega$ of σ violates φ. Note that the extension of σ by the valuation of the internal coordination variables is uniquely specified by the input path σ and the system implementation $\mathcal{T}$.

Corollary 2. *If there exists a finite counterexample to satisfiability $\mathcal{P} \subseteq (2^{\mathcal{C}_{ext}})^\omega$ for an $ECL_\exists$ formula $\Phi = \mathcal{Q}_\exists. \varphi_{path} \to \varphi$ over coordination variables $\mathcal{C}$ and strategy variables $\mathcal{S}$, then Φ is unsatisfiable.*

As an example consider again the $ECL_\exists$ formula (1) $\exists\{a\} \rhd x.\exists\{b\} \rhd y.\psi_1$, corresponding to the architecture from Fig. 1(a) in the previous section. Let $\psi_1 := \Box(\bigcirc y \leftrightarrow a)$, i.e., y must output the input a with an one-step delay. A simple counterexample for this formula consists of two paths $\mathcal{P}_1 := \{\emptyset^\omega, \{a\}^\omega\}$ that differ in the values of a, but not in the values of b. Since process x cannot distinguish the two paths, but must produce different outputs, we arrive at a contradiction. Consider the same formula for the pipeline architecture specified by (2) $\exists\{b\} \rhd y.\exists\{a, b\} \rhd x.\Box(b = x) \to \psi_2$. Due to the delay when forwarding the input a over shared variable b, the formula becomes unsatisfiable. $\mathcal{P}_1$ is a finite counterexample in this case, too: Given an implementation of x and y, we extend both paths such that the input-output specification $\Box(b = x)$ is satisfied.

The distributed realizability problem *with* faults correspond to $ECL_\exists$ formulas of the form $\Phi = \mathcal{Q}_\exists. \bigwedge_{1 \le i \le n} (\varphi_{\mathrm{path}_i} \to \varphi_i)$. If $\varphi_i = \varphi$ for all i, the formula states that there exists an implementation such that the specification φ should hold in all architectures induced by the path specifications $\varphi_{\mathrm{path}_i}$. Omitted channel specifications in one of these formulas represent an arbitrary error at this channel. In this case, a counterexample identifies for each implementation one of these architectures where a contradiction occurs. A *finite* counterexample to satisfiability of Φ are n finite sets of paths $\mathcal{P}_i \subseteq (2^{\mathcal{C}_{\mathrm{ext}}^i})^\omega$ each corresponding to external coordination variables $\mathcal{C}_{\mathrm{ext}}^i$ in the respective architecture i, such that for any implementation $\mathcal{T}$ there exists an architecture j and a path $\sigma \in \mathcal{P}_j$ such that an extension $\sigma' \in (2^{\mathcal{C}})^\omega$ of σ violates φ_j.

Corollary 3. *An $ECL_\exists$ formula $\Phi = \mathcal{Q}_\exists. \bigwedge_{1 \le i \le n} (\varphi_{path_i} \to \varphi_i)$ over coordination variables $\mathcal{C}$ and strategy variables $\mathcal{S}$ is unsatisfiable if there exists a finite counterexample to satisfiability of Φ.*

A counterexample for the ECL specification (3) introduces paths for inputs as well as for every faulty node by introducing paths that model the exact channel specification and additional paths that model the arbitrary node failures. The target node that reads from a shared variable can, in contrast to incomplete information, react differently on the given paths, but the reaction must be consistent regarding its observations on all paths. Consider for example the specification $\psi_3 := (\bigcirc_2 z \leftrightarrow a)$ for the ECL formula in (3), that is, process z should output the input a of nodes x and y. In both architectures we introduce additional paths for the coordination variable that is omitted in the channel specification, i.e., b and c for the first and second conjunct, respectively. Process z cannot tell which of its inputs come from a faulty node. Since z must produce the same output on two paths it cannot distinguish, the implementation of z contradicts the specification in either architecture.

4   From ECL$_\exists$ to QPTL

We encode the existence of finite counterexample to realizability as a formula of *quantified propositional temporal logic (QPTL)*. QPTL extends LTL with a *path quantifier* $\exists p$, where a path $\sigma \in 2^{\mathrm{AP}}$ satisfies $\exists p.\, \varphi$ at position $i \geq 0$, denoted by $\sigma, i \vDash \exists p.\, \varphi$, if there exists a path $\sigma' \in 2^{\mathrm{AP} \cup \{p\}}$ which coincides with σ except for the newly introduced atomic proposition p, such that $\sigma', i \vDash \varphi$. In the encoding, we use the path quantifier to explicitly name the paths in the counterexample.

Realizability without Faults. We consider first the distributed realizability problems *without* faults, represented by ECL$_\exists$ formula $\Phi = \mathcal{Q}_\exists.\, \varphi_{\text{path}} \rightarrow \varphi$. We assume, without loss of generality, that the architecture $\mathcal{A}_\Phi$ is acyclic. Finkbeiner and Schewe [4] gave a realizability-preserving transformation to acyclic architectures that removes *feedback edges*.

Lemma 4 ([4]). *Any ECL$_\exists$ formula $\Phi = \mathcal{Q}_\exists.\, \varphi_{path} \rightarrow \varphi$ can be transformed into an equisatisfiable formula $\Phi' = \mathcal{Q}'_\exists.\, \varphi'_{path} \rightarrow \varphi'$ such that the system architecture $\mathcal{A}_{\Phi'}$ is acyclic.*

We search for a finite counterexample of Φ by bounding the number of paths regarding the *external* coordination variables. The bound on the number of paths is given as a function $K : \mathcal{C} \rightarrow \mathbb{N}$ that maps each coordination variable to the number of branchings that should be considered for this variable. For example, for coordination variables a and b, and $K(a) = K(b) = 1$, we encode 4 different paths, one per possible combination for the two paths for each variable. We fix an arbitrary strict order $\prec\, \subseteq \mathcal{C} \times \mathcal{C}$ between the coordination variables. For a set $C \subseteq \mathcal{C}$, we identify $K(C)$ by the vector $\mathbb{N}^{|C|}$ where the position of the value $K(c)$ for a coordination variable $c \in C$ is determined by $\prec$. For our encoding in QPTL, we use the following helper functions:

- deps(v) returns the set of coordination variables that *influence* variable v. A coordination variable c influences variable v if c belongs to a directed path that leads to v in $\mathcal{A}_\Phi$. For example in the architecture of Fig. 1(c), b and x are influenced by a while z is influenced by a, b, and c. A coordination variable is influenced by itself.
- branches(C, K) returns the set of branches belonging to coordination variables C. A branch is referenced by a tuple $\mathbb{N}^{|C|}$ and the set of branches is $\{(n_{c_1}, \ldots, n_{c_k}) \mid \{c_1 \prec \cdots \prec c_k\} = C$ and $1 \leq n_c \leq 2^{K(c)}$ for all $c \in C\}$
- paths($C; K$) and strategies(S, K) create the (path) variables in the QPTL formula that belong to the variables of the ECL$_\exists$ formula. For a variable $v \in C \cup S$ it introduces for each branch $\pi \in$ branches(deps(v), K) a separate variable p_π^v that represents the variable v belonging to this branch π.

- header(S, K) creates the alternating introductions of strategies and paths according to the acyclic architecture $\mathcal{A}_\Phi$. For every strategy variable $s \in S$ we introduce all paths belonging to coordination variables $c \in \mathrm{Scope}(s)$ prior to s and avoid duplicate path introductions:

$$\exists\, \mathrm{paths}(\mathrm{Scope}(s_1), K) \,\forall\, \mathrm{strategies}(\{s_1\}, K)$$
$$\exists\, \mathrm{paths}(\mathrm{Scope}(s_2) \setminus \mathrm{Scope}(s_1), K) \,\forall\, \mathrm{strategies}(\{s_2\}, K)$$
$$\ldots$$
$$\exists\, \mathrm{paths}\Big(\mathrm{Scope}(s_n) \setminus \Big(\bigcup_{i=1,\ldots,n-1} \mathrm{Scope}(s_i)\Big), K\Big) \,\forall\, \mathrm{strategies}(\{s_n\}, K) \ ,$$

where $s_1, \ldots, s_n$ are sorted in ascending order according to their informedness, i.e., the subset relation on their scopes.

- consistent(S, K) specifies the consistency condition for the variables belonging to the strategy variables on the different branches. The variables $p_{\pi_1}^s, \ldots, p_{\pi_k}^s$ belonging to a strategy variable $s \in S$ must be equal as long as the coordination variables in the scope of s on the branches $\pi_1, \ldots, \pi_k$ are equal. This can be specified in LTL as there are only finitely many branches.

The QPTL encoding for ECL$_\exists$ formula Φ and function $K : \mathcal{C} \to \mathbb{N}$ is

$$\mathrm{unsat}_{\mathrm{dist}}(\Phi, K) := \mathrm{header}(\mathcal{S}, K).\, \mathrm{consistent}(\mathcal{S}, K) \to$$
$$\Big(\bigwedge_{\pi \in \mathrm{branches}(\mathcal{C}, K)} \varphi_{\mathrm{path}}(\pi)\Big) \wedge \Big(\bigvee_{\pi \in \mathrm{branches}(\mathcal{C}, K)} \neg\varphi(\pi)\Big) \ , \qquad (4)$$

where $\varphi(\pi)$ is the initialization of LTL formula φ on the branch π, that is we exchange v by $p_{\pi'}^v$ for $v \in \mathcal{C} \cup \mathcal{S}$ where π' is the subvector of π that contains the values for coordination variables in $\mathrm{deps}(v)$.

Theorem 5 (Correctness). *Given an ECL$_\exists$ formula $\Phi = \mathcal{Q}_\exists.\, \varphi_{path} \to \varphi$ over coordination variables $\mathcal{C}$ and strategy variables $\mathcal{S}$ with an acyclic system architecture $\mathcal{A}_\Phi$. Φ is unsatisfiable if there exists a function $K : \mathcal{C} \to \mathbb{N}$ such that the QPTL formula $\mathrm{unsat}_{dist}(\Phi, K)$ is satisfiable.*

Realizability with Node Failures. In the case of possible failures, the ECL$_\exists$ formulas Φ has the more general form $\mathcal{Q}_\exists.\, \bigwedge_{1 \leq i \leq n} (\varphi_{\mathrm{path}_i} \to \varphi_i)$. In this specific setting we cannot assume acyclic architectures in general. The architecture belonging to Φ is acyclic if the architecture belonging to the conjunction of all paths specifications $\bigwedge_{1 \leq i \leq n} \varphi_{\mathrm{path}_i}$ is acyclic. An edge is a *common feedback edge* if and only if it is a feedback edge in all architectures. As before, we can eliminate common feedback edges but this does not give us acyclic architectures in general as depicted in Fig. 3. In the following, we assume acyclic architectures after removing common feedback edges.

The QPTL encoding of ECL$_\exists$ formula Φ and functions $K_1 \ldots K_n : \mathcal{C} \to \mathbb{N}$ is

$$\mathrm{unsat}_{\mathrm{fault}}(\Phi, K_1, \ldots, K_n) := \mathrm{header}(\mathcal{S}, K).\, \mathrm{consistent}(\mathcal{S}, K) \to$$
$$\bigvee_{1 \leq i \leq n} \Big(\bigwedge_{\pi \in \mathrm{branches}(\mathcal{C}, K_i)} \varphi_{\mathrm{path}_i}(\pi)\Big) \wedge \Big(\bigvee_{\pi \in \mathrm{branches}(\mathcal{C}, K_i)} \neg\varphi_i(\pi)\Big) \ , \qquad (5)$$

where $K : \mathcal{C} \to \mathbb{N}$ is defined as $K(c) := \max_{1 \leq i \leq n} K_i(c)$ for every $c \in \mathcal{C}$.

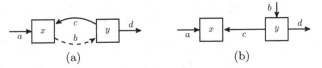

Fig. 3. Example illustrating common feedback edges: Edge c is a feedback edge in architecture (a), but not in architecture (b), thus it is also not a common feedback edge when considering both architectures

Theorem 6 (Correctness). *Given an $ECL_\exists$ formula $\Phi = Q_\exists \cdot \bigwedge_{1 \leq i \leq n} \left(\varphi_{path_i} \to \varphi_i \right)$ over coordination variables C and strategy variables S with an acyclic system architecture A_Φ after removing common feedback edges. Φ is unsatisfiable if there exist functions $K_1 \ldots K_n : C \to \mathbb{N}$ such that the QPTL formula $unsat_{fault}(\Phi, K_1, \ldots, K_n)$ is satisfiable.*

Example. We consider again the Byzantine Generals' Problem with three nodes g_1, g_2, and g_3. The first general is the commander who forwards the input v that states whether to attack the enemy or not. The encoding as $ECL_\exists$ formula is

$$\Phi_{bgp} := \exists\{v\} \triangleright g_{12}, g_{13}. \exists\{c_{12}\} \triangleright g_{23}. \exists\{c_{13}\} \triangleright g_{32}. \exists\{c_{12}, c_{32}\} \triangleright g_2. \exists\{c_{13}, c_{23}\} \triangleright g_3.$$

$$(\text{operational}_{2,3} \to \text{consensus}_{2,3}) \wedge \bigwedge_{i \in \{2,3\}} (\text{operational}_{1,i} \to \text{correctval}_i) \ ,$$

where the quantification prefix introduces the strategies for the generals g_2 and g_3, as well as the communication between the three generals as depicted in the architecture in Fig. 4(a). Note that we omit the vote of the commander g_1 as it is not used in the specification. In the temporal part, we specify which failures can occur. The first conjunct, corresponding to Fig. 4(b), states that the commander is faulty ($\text{operational}_{2,3}$) which implies that the other two generals have to reach a consensus whether to attack or not ($\text{consensus}_{2,3}$). The other two cases, depicted in Fig. 4(c)–(d), are symmetric and state that whenever one general is faulty the other one should agree on the decision made by the commander. The QPTL encoding $unsat_{fault}(\Phi_{bgp}, K_1, K_2, K_3)$ is given as

$$\exists \text{paths}(\{v\}, K). \ \forall \text{strategies}(\{g_{12}, g_{13}\}, K). \ \exists \text{paths}(\{c_{12}, c_{13}\}, K).$$

$$\forall \text{strategies}(\{g_{23}, g_{32}\}, K). \ \exists \text{paths}(\{c_{23}, c_{32}\}, K). \ \forall \text{strategies}(\{g_2, g_3\}, K).$$

$$\text{consistent}(\{g_{12}, g_{13}, g_{23}, g_{32}, g_2, g_3\}, K) \to$$

$$\left(\left(\bigwedge_{\pi \in \text{branches}(C, K_1)} \text{operational}_{2,3}(\pi) \wedge \bigvee_{\pi \in \text{branches}(C, K_1)} \neg\text{consensus}_{2,3}(\pi) \right) \vee \right.$$

$$\left(\bigwedge_{\pi \in \text{branches}(C, K_2)} \text{operational}_{1,3}(\pi) \wedge \bigvee_{\pi \in \text{branches}(C, K_2)} \neg\text{correctval}_3(\pi) \right) \vee$$

$$\left. \left(\bigwedge_{\pi \in \text{branches}(C, K_3)} \text{operational}_{1,2}(\pi) \wedge \bigvee_{\pi \in \text{branches}(C, K_3)} \neg\text{correctval}_2(\pi) \right) \right) \ .$$

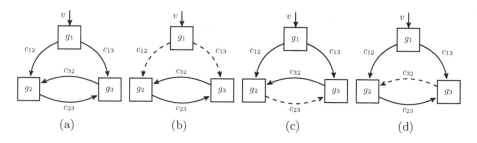

Fig. 4. The Byzantine Generals' architecture. Figure (a) shows the architecture in cases all generals are loyal. Figures (b)–(d) show the possible failures, indicated by the dashed communication links.

5   From QPTL to QBF

Presently available QPTL solver were unable to handle even small instances of our problem. We therefore simplify the problem using the following steps. Instead of checking the QPTL formula directly, we encode the formula as an equivalent *monadic second order logic of one successor (S1S)* formula using a straightforward translation. We then interpret the S1S formula with a WS1S formula, which can be checked using the WS1S solver Mona [16]. Some of our smaller instances were solved by Mona, but the Byzantine Generals' Problem failed due to memory constraints in the BDD library.

Taking the simplifications even further, we not only bound the *number* of paths but also the *length* of the paths by translating the problem to the satisfiability problem of *quantified Boolean formulas (QBF)*. The encoding translates a QPTL variable x to Boolean variables $x_0, \ldots, x_{k-1}$, each representing one step in the system where k is the length of the paths. We build the QBF formula by *unrolling* the QPTL formula for k-steps: Each variable in the quantification prefix of the QPTL formula is transformed into k Boolean variables in the QBF prefix, e.g., the 3-unrolling of $\exists x. \forall y. \varphi$ is $\exists x_0, x_1, x_2. \forall y_0, y_1, y_2. \varphi_{unroll}$. The unrolling of the remaining LTL formula is given by the expansion law for Until, $\varphi \, \mathcal{U} \, \psi \equiv \psi \vee (\varphi \wedge \bigcirc \varphi \, \mathcal{U} \, \psi)$. After the unrolling, the QBF formula is transformed into Conjunctive Normal Form (CNF) and encoded in the QDIMACS file format, that is the standard format for QBF solvers. Already with this encoding we could solve more examples than using the WS1S approach.

In this simple translation, one cause of high complexity is due to the consistency conditions between the strategy variables across different paths. However, most of these variables are not used for the counterexample itself but appear only in the consistency condition. One optimization removes these unnecessary variables from the encoding. Therefore, we collect all strategy variables and (when possible) their temporal occurrence from the LTL specification. For every used strategy variable we build the *dependency graph* that contains all variables which can influence the outcome of the strategy. In the last step, we remove all variables that are not contained in any dependency graph.

6 Completeness

Proposition 1 states that the characterization of unsatisfiable formulas with counterexamples is complete. Our method, however, searches for counterexamples involving only a bounded number of external paths and the following example shows this leads to incompleteness. Consider the $ECL_\exists$ formula $\Phi_{inf} := \exists \emptyset \triangleright y.\,\varphi_{inf}$ with temporal specification $\varphi_{inf} := \Diamond (y \neq x)$ where x is a free coordination variable. Φ_{inf} is unsatisfiable because for every strategy $f_y : \emptyset^* \to 2^{\{y\}}$ there exists a path $\sigma \in (2^{\{x\}})^\omega$ that simulates exactly the output of the strategy, as the formula is evaluated over the full binary x-tree. Assume for contradiction that a finite set of paths $P \subseteq (2^{\{x\}})^\omega$ suffices to satisfy $\neg\varphi_{inf}$ against any strategy f_y. Interpreting the outcome of the strategy as a path and considering all possible strategies gives us a full binary tree $\mathcal{T}$. Let ρ be a path from $\mathcal{T}$ that is not contained in P (after renaming y in ρ to x). Such a path must exists because there are infinite many different paths in $\mathcal{T}$. Choose the strategy f_y^ρ that belongs to ρ. For all paths in P it holds that $\Diamond (y \neq x)$ and thus no path satisfies $\neg\varphi_{inf}$.

However, in practice finite external counterexamples are sufficient to detect many errors in specifications. In this section we give a semantic characterization of the finite path satisfiability based only on the LTL specification.

Given an $ECL_\exists$ formula $\Phi = \mathcal{Q}_\exists.\,\varphi_{path} \to \varphi$. We assume w.l.o.g. that φ only contains coordination variables $\mathcal{C}_e \subseteq \mathcal{C}$ that are not used as a channel as otherwise one could replace a variable $c \in \mathcal{C} \setminus \mathcal{C}_e$ by the strategy variable corresponding to the channel. The semantics of the LTL formula $\neg\varphi$, denoted by $[\![\neg\varphi]\!]$, gives us a language $\mathcal{L} \subseteq (2^\mathcal{S} \times 2^{\mathcal{C}_e})^\omega$. From $\mathcal{L}$ we obtain the relation $\mathcal{R} \subseteq (2^\mathcal{S})^\omega \times (2^{\mathcal{C}_e})^\omega$ between paths of strategy variables and paths of coordination variables. We say that an LTL formula ψ over variables $\mathcal{S} \times \mathcal{C}_e$ admits finite external paths if there exists a function $r : (2^\mathcal{S})^\omega \to (2^{\mathcal{C}_e})^\omega$ such that (1) for all $\sigma \in (2^\mathcal{S})^\omega$ it holds that $r(\sigma) = \rho \Leftrightarrow \sigma \,\mathcal{R}\, \rho$, and (2) $\{r(\sigma) \mid \sigma \in (2^\mathcal{S})^\omega\}$ is finite.

Let $\mathcal{RA}_\psi$ be the deterministic Rabin word automata for LTL formula ψ. $\mathcal{RA}_\psi$ contains a *path split* if there exist a state q in the automaton where (1) there are two outgoing edges labeled with (s,p) and (s',p') where $s \neq s'$ and $p \neq p'$, and (2) from q we can build accepting runs visiting q infinitely often and containing exclusively the (s,p)-edge or (s',p')-edge.

Theorem 7. *An LTL formula ψ over variables $\mathcal{S} \times \mathcal{C}_e$ admits finite external paths if and only if the automaton $\mathcal{RA}_\psi$ has no path split.*

7 Experimental Results

We have carried out our experiments on a 2.6 GHz Opteron system. For solving the QBF instances, we used a combination of the QBF preprocessor Bloqqer [17] in version 031 and the QBF solver DepQBF [18] in version 1.0. For solving the WS1S instances, we used Mona [16] in version 1.4-15.

Table 1 demonstrates that the Byzantine Generals' Problem remains, despite the optimizations described above, a nontrivial combinatorial problem: we need to find a suitable set of paths for every possible combination of the strategies of the generals. The bound given in the first column reads as follows: The first component is the number of branchings for the input variable v in all three architectures. The last three components state the number of branchings for the outputs of the faulty nodes in their respective architectures. For example, bound $(1, 1, 0, 0)$ means that we have two branches for v, c_{12}, and c_{13}, while we have only one branch for c_{23} and c_{32}. More precisely, starting from always zero functions K_1, K_2, K_3, the bound $(1, 1, 0, 0)$ sets $K_1(v) = K_2(v) = K_3(v) = K_1(c_{12}) = K_1(c_{13}) = 1$ and $K_2(c_{23}) = K_3(c_{32}) = 0$. To prove the unrealizability, we need one branching for the input v and one branching for every coordination variable that serves as a shared variable for a faulty node, i.e., the bound $(1, 1, 1, 1)$. The number of branches and thereby the formula size grows exponentially with the number of branchings for the input variables.

Table 1. Result of the *Byzantine Generals' Problem* example

Bound	Result	# Clauses	# Variables	Memory (MB)	Time (s)
$(0, 0, 0, 0)$	Unsatisfiable	57	44	5.06	0.00
$(1, 0, 0, 0)$	Unsatisfiable	228	143	5.71	0.05
$(1, 1, 0, 0)$	Unsatisfiable	2286	1095	17.83	2.16
$(1, 1, 1, 0)$	Unsatisfiable	2904	1375	18.41	2.42
$(1, 1, 1, 1)$	Satisfiable	3522	1655	28.88	11.95

The table shows the time and memory consumption of Bloqqer 031 and DepQBF 1.0 when solving the encoding of the Byzantine Generals' Problem in QBF with a fixed length of 3 unrollings.

The CAP Theorem for two nodes is encoded as the $\text{ECL}_\exists$ formula

$$\exists\{\text{req}_1\} \triangleright \text{com}_1. \exists\{\text{req}_1, \text{chan}_2\} \triangleright \text{out}_1. \exists\{\text{req}_2\} \triangleright \text{com}_2. \exists\{\text{req}_2, \text{chan}_1\} \triangleright \text{out}_2.$$
$$(\square(\text{chan}_1 = \text{com}_1) \rightarrow \square((\text{out}_1 = \text{out}_2) \wedge ((\text{req}_1 \vee \text{req}_2) \leftrightarrow \bigcirc_2(\text{out}_1 \vee \text{out}_2)))) \wedge$$
$$(\square(\text{chan}_2 = \text{com}_2) \rightarrow \square((\text{out}_1 = \text{out}_2) \wedge ((\text{req}_1 \vee \text{req}_2) \leftrightarrow \bigcirc_2(\text{out}_1 \vee \text{out}_2)))) .$$

The architecture is similar to Fig. 1(a) with the difference that there is a direct communication channel between the two processes $(\text{chan}_1, \text{chan}_2)$. The formula states that the system should be available and consistent despite an failure of one process. Table 2 shows that our method is able to find conflicts in a specification with an architecture up to 50 nodes within reasonable time. When we drop either Consistency, Availability, or Partition tolerance, the corresponding instances (AP, CP, and CA) become satisfiable. Hence, our tool does not find counterexamples in these cases.

Discussion. We evaluate the different encodings that we have used in the following. There does not exist an algorithm that decides whether a given $\text{ECL}_\exists$ formula is unsatisfiable. We used a sound approach where we bound the number of paths and encoded the problem in QPTL. The reason for incompleteness was

Table 2. Result of the *CAP Theorem* example

Instance	Result	# Clauses	# Variables	Memory (MB)	Time (s)
ap_2	Unsatisfiable	1232	619	9.22	0.29
ca_2	Unsatisfiable	1408	763	12.47	0.87
cp_2	Unsatisfiable	48	42	5.05	0.00
cap_2	Satisfiable	110	84	5.05	0.00
cap_5	Satisfiable	665	426	5.06	0.05
cap_10	Satisfiable	2590	1556	6.49	0.35
cap_25	Satisfiable	15865	9146	35.47	2.83
cap_50	Satisfiable	62990	35796	87.84	44.03

The table shows the time and memory consumption of Bloqqer 031 and DepQBF 1.0 when solving the encoding of the CAP Theorem in QBF with a fixed length of 2 unrollings.

shown in Sec. 6; in some cases one may need infinite many paths to show unsatisfiability. Our encoding in WS1S (Mona) loses the ability to find counterexample paths of infinite length, e.g., the $ECL_\exists$ formula $\exists \emptyset \triangleright y. \Diamond \Box (\bigcirc y \leftrightarrow x)$ with free coordination variable x is unsatisfiable where two paths that are infinitely often different are sufficient to prove it. The QPTL encoding is capable of finding these paths while the WS1S encoding is not. However, Mona could not solve any satisfiable instance given in Tables 1 and 2. Lastly, for the translation in QBF we do not only restrict ourself to paths of finite length (WS1S), but we also bound the paths to length k where k is an additional parameter. With this encoding we approximate the reactive behavior of our system by a finite prefix. It turned out that despite of this restriction we could prove unsatisfiability for many interesting specifications. In practice, one would first use the QBF abstraction in order to find "cheap" counterexamples. After hitting the number of paths that the QBF solver can no longer handle within reasonable time, one proceeds with more costly abstractions like the WS1S encoding.

8   Conclusion

We introduced counterexamples for distributed realizability and showed how to automatically derive counterexamples from given specifications in $ECL_\exists$. We used encodings in QPTL, WS1S, and QBF. Our experiments showed that the QBF encoding was the most efficient. Even problems with high combinatorial complexity, such as the Byzantine Generals' Problem, are handled automatically. Given that QBF solvers are likely to improve in the future, even larger instances should become tractable. Possible future directions include building a set of benchmarks, evaluating more solvers, and use the information about an counterexample given by QBF certification [19] to build counterexamples for the specification. As the bound given for the encoding is not uniform, i.e., there is a bound for each coordination variable, and the observation that the performance depend on the chosen bound, it is crucial to find suitable heuristics that rank the importance of the coordination variables. Also, more types of failures could be incorporated into our model, e.g., variations of the failure duration like *transient*, or *intermittent*. Lastly, it would be also conceivable to use similar methods to derive a larger class of *infinite* counterexamples.

References

1. Lamport, L., Shostak, R.E., Pease, M.C.: The byzantine generals problem. ACM Trans. Program. Lang. Syst. 4(3), 382–401 (1982)
2. Pnueli, A., Rosner, R.: Distributed reactive systems are hard to synthesize. In: Proc. FOCS 1990, pp. 746–757 (1990)
3. Kupferman, O., Vardi, M.Y.: Synthesizing distributed systems. In: LICS, pp. 389–398. IEEE Computer Society (2001)
4. Finkbeiner, B., Schewe, S.: Uniform distributed synthesis. In: LICS, pp. 321–330. IEEE Computer Society (2005)
5. Finkbeiner, B., Schewe, S.: Bounded synthesis. International Journal on Software Tools for Technology Transfer 15(5-6), 519–539 (2013)
6. Brewer, E.A.: Towards robust distributed systems (abstract). In: PODC, p. 7. ACM (2000)
7. Church, A.: Logic, arithmetic and automata. In: Proc. 1962 Intl. Congr. Math., Upsala, pp. 23–25 (1963)
8. Abadi, M., Lamport, L., Wolper, P.: Realizable and unrealizable specifications of reactive systems. In: Ronchi Della Rocca, S., Ausiello, G., Dezani-Ciancaglini, M. (eds.) ICALP 1989. LNCS, vol. 372, pp. 1–17. Springer, Heidelberg (1989)
9. Kupferman, O., Vardi, M.Y.: Synthesis with incomplete information. In: Proc. of ICTL (1997)
10. Raman, V., Kress-Gazit, H.: Analyzing unsynthesizable specifications for high-level robot behavior using LTLMoP. In: Gopalakrishnan, G., Qadeer, S. (eds.) CAV 2011. LNCS, vol. 6806, pp. 663–668. Springer, Heidelberg (2011)
11. Li, W., Dworkin, L., Seshia, S.A.: Mining assumptions for synthesis. In: MEMOCODE, pp. 43–50. IEEE (2011)
12. Chatterjee, K., Henzinger, T.A., Jobstmann, B.: Environment assumptions for synthesis. In: van Breugel, F., Chechik, M. (eds.) CONCUR 2008. LNCS, vol. 5201, pp. 147–161. Springer, Heidelberg (2008)
13. Halpern, J.Y., Moses, Y.: Knowledge and common knowledge in a distributed environment. In: PODC, pp. 50–61. ACM (1984)
14. Dimitrova, R., Finkbeiner, B.: Synthesis of fault-tolerant distributed systems. In: Liu, Z., Ravn, A.P. (eds.) ATVA 2009. LNCS, vol. 5799, pp. 321–336. Springer, Heidelberg (2009)
15. Finkbeiner, B., Schewe, S.: Coordination logic. In: Dawar, A., Veith, H. (eds.) CSL 2010. LNCS, vol. 6247, pp. 305–319. Springer, Heidelberg (2010)
16. Henriksen, J.G., Jensen, J.L., Jørgensen, M.E., Klarlund, N., Paige, R., Rauhe, T., Sandholm, A.: Mona: Monadic second-order logic in practice. In: Brinksma, E., Steffen, B., Cleaveland, W.R., Larsen, K.G., Margaria, T. (eds.) TACAS 1995. LNCS, vol. 1019, pp. 89–110. Springer, Heidelberg (1995)
17. Biere, A., Lonsing, F., Seidl, M.: Blocked clause elimination for QBF. In: Bjørner, N., Sofronie-Stokkermans, V. (eds.) CADE 2011. LNCS, vol. 6803, pp. 101–115. Springer, Heidelberg (2011)
18. Lonsing, F., Biere, A.: DepQBF: A dependency-aware QBF solver. JSAT 7(2-3), 71–76 (2010)
19. Balabanov, V., Jiang, J.H.R.: Unified QBF certification and its applications. Formal Methods in System Design 41(1), 45–65 (2012)

Synthesizing Safe Bit-Precise Invariants[*]

Arie Gurfinkel[1], Anton Belov[2], and Joao Marques-Silva[2]

[1] Carnegie Mellon University, USA
[2] University College Dublin, Ireland

Abstract. Bit-precise software verification is an important and difficult problem. While there has been an amazing progress in SAT solving, Satisfiability Modulo Theory of Bit Vectors, and bit-precise Bounded Model Checking, proving bit-precise safety, i.e. synthesizing a safe inductive invariant, remains a challenge. Although the problem is decidable and is reducible to propositional safety by bit-blasting, the approach does not scale in practice. The alternative approach of lifting propositional algorithms to bit-vectors is difficult. In this paper, we propose a novel technique that uses unsound approximations (i.e., neither over- nor under-) for synthesizing sound bit-precise invariants. We prototyped the technique using Z3/PDR engine and applied it to bit-precise verification of benchmarks from SVCOMP'13. Even with our preliminary implementation we were able to demonstrate significant (orders of magnitude) performance improvements with respect to bit-precise verificaton using Z3/PDR directy.

1 Introduction

The problem of program safety (or reachability) verification is to decide whether a given program can violate an assertion (i.e., can reach a bad state). The problem is reducible to finding either a finite counter-example, or a safe inductive invariant that certifies unreachability of a bad state. The problem of bit-precise program safety, Safety(BV), further requires that the program operations are represented soundly relative to low-level bit representation of data. Arguably, verification techniques that are not bit-precise are unsound, and do not reflect the actual behavior of a program. Unlike many other problems in software verification, bit-precise verification (without memory allocation and concurrency) is decidable. However, in practice it appears to be more challenging that verification of programs relative to integers or rationals (both undecidable).

The recent decade has seen an amazing progress in SAT solvers, in Satisfiability Modulo Theory of Bit-Vectors, SMT(BV), and in Bounded Model Checkers

[*] This material is based upon work funded and supported by the Department of Defense under Contract No. FA8721-05-C-0003 with Carnegie Mellon University for the operation of the Software Engineering Institute, a federally funded research and development center. This material has been approved for public release and unlimited distribution. DM-0000869. The second and third authors are financially supported by SFI PI grant BEACON (09/IN.1/I2618), and by FCT grants ATTEST (CMU-PT/ELE/0009/2009) and POLARIS (PTDC/EIA-CCO/123051/2010).

E. Ábrahám and K. Havelund (Eds.): TACAS 2014, LNCS 8413, pp. 93–108, 2014.
© Springer-Verlag Berlin Heidelberg 2014

(BMC) based on these techniques. A SAT solver decides whether a given propositional formula is satisfiable. Current solvers can handle very large problems and are routinely used in many industrial applications (including Hardware and Software verification). SMT(BV) extends SAT-solver techniques to the theory of bit-vectors – that is propositional formulas whose atoms are predicates about bit-vectors. Most successful SMT(BV) solvers (e.g., Boolector [6], STP [17], Z3 [12], MathSAT [9]) are based on reducing the problem to SAT via *pre-processing* and *bit-blasting*. The bit-blasting step takes a BV formula φ and constructs an equivalent propositional formula ψ, where each propositional variable of ψ corresponds to a bit of some bit-vector variable of φ. The, more important, pre-processing step typically consists of equisatisfiable reductions that reduce the size of the input formula. While the pre-processor is not as powerful as the SAT-solver (typically pre-processor is required to run in polynomial time), it does not maintain equivalence. The pre-processing phase of SMT(BV) solvers is crucial for their performance. For example, in our experiments with Boolector, the different between straight forward bit-blasting and pre-processing is several order of magnitude.

There has also been a tremendous progress in applying those techniques to program verification. In particular, there are several mature Bounded Model Checkers, including CBMC [10], LLBMC [32], and ESBMC [11], that decide existence of a bounded bit-precise counterexamples of C programs. These tools are based on ultimate reduction of BMC to SAT, either via their own custom bit-blasting and pre-processing steps (e.g., CBMC) or by leveraging SMT(BV) solvers described above (e.g., LLBMC). While BMC tools are great at finding counterexamples (even in industrial applications), *proving* bit-precise safety, i.e., synthesizing a bit-precise invariant, remains a challenge. For example, none of the tools submitted to the Software Verification Competition in 2013 (SVCOMP'13) are both bit-precise and effective at invariant synthesis.

As we described above, Safety(BV) is decidable. In fact, it is reducible to safety problem over propositional logic, Safety(Prop), via the simple bit-blasting mentioned above. Thus, the naive solution is to reduce Safety(BV) to Safety(Prop) and decide it using tools for propositional verification. This, however, does not scale. Our experiments with Z3/PDR (the Model Checker of Z3), show that the approach is ineffective for almost all benchmarks in SVCOMP'13. The main issue is that the reduction of Safety(BV) to Safety(Prop) is incompatible with the pre-processing techniques that make bit-blasting for SMT(BV) so effective.

An alternative approach of lifting effective Model Checking technique from propositional level to BV appears to be difficult, with only a few somewhat successful attempts (e.g., [26,19]). For example, techniques based on interpolation (e.g., [31,27,1]) require world-level interpolation for BV [25,19] that satisfies additional properties (e.g., sequence and tree properties) [21]. While, techniques based on PDR [22], require novel world-level inductive generalization strategies. Both are difficult problems in themselves.

Thus, instead of lifting existing techniques, we are interested in finding a way to use existing verification engines to improve scalability of the naive bit-blasting-based solution. Our key insight is based on the observation that most program verifiers abstract program arithmetic by integer (or rational) arithmetic. This is unsound in the presence of overflows (see [19] for an example), but the results are often "almost" correct. More importantly, they are useful to the users. Thus, we are interested in how to reuse such unsound invariants in a sound way.

Our procedure is based on an iterative *guess-and-check* loop. Given a Safety(BV) problem P, we begin by trying to solve P using a Safety(BV) solver. If this takes too long, we abort it, and construct an approximation (neither over- nor under-) P_T of P in another theory T (e.g., Linear Rational Arithmetic), decide the safety of P_T using a solver for Safety(T), and obtain an inductive safe invariant Inv_T. We then *port* Inv_T in a sound way to P, strengthen P with it, and repeat bit-blasting-based verification. In the best case, the ported version of Inv_T is a safe and inductive invariant for P and the process terminates immediately. In the worst case, Inv_T contributes facts that might help the next verification effort.

We make the following contributions. First, we formally define a framework that allows to use unsound invariants soundly in a verification loop. Second, we instantiate the framework for the theories of Bit Vectors and Linear Arithmetic. In particular, we describe an algorithm for computing Maximal Inductive Subformula for SMT(BV) and show how it interacts with the pre-processing step. Third, we have implemented the proposed framework using Z3/PDR for Safety(Prop) and Boolector for SMT(BV) and have evaluated it on the benchmarks from SVCOMP'13. Even with our preliminary implementation, we are able to synthesize safe invariants for most programs.

Related Work. The use of over- and under-approximation and relaxation of a problem from one theory into another is common in both SMT-solving and Model Checking. For example, Bryant et al. [7], use over- and under-approximation to decide formulas in SMT(BV). Komuravelli et al. [24] similarly use over- and under-approximations for Software Model Checking. While we do not require our approximations to be sound, we employ similar techniques to lift proof certificates (inductive invariants in our case) are in principle similar.

Computing Maximal Inductive Subformula (MIS) is similar to mining an inductive invariant from a set of possible annotations, as for example in [16,23]. The key novelty in our approach is in the reduction from MIS problem to a Minimal Unsatisfiable Subformula (MUS) problem that allows the use of efficient MUS extractors for SAT.

The works conceptually closest to ours are in the area of Upgrade Checking [15], Multi-Property Verification [8], and Regression Verification [18,28,4]. A common theme in the above approaches is that they attempt to lift a safety invariant from one given program P_1 to another, related but not equivalent, program P_2. The key difference is that we do not assume existence of a proven program P_1, but, instead, synthesize P_1 and its safety proof automatically.

2   Preliminaries

We assume some familiarity with program verification, logic, SMT and SAT.

Safety Verification. A transition system P is a tuple $(\mathcal{V}, \mathit{Init}, \mathit{Tr}, \mathit{Bad})$, where $\mathcal{V}$ is a set of variables, Init, Bad, and Tr are formulas (with free variables in $\mathcal{V}$) denoting the initial and the bad states, and the transition relation, respectively.

A transition system P is UNSAFE iff there exists a natural number N such that the following formula is satisfiable:

$$\mathit{Init}(v_0) \wedge \left(\bigwedge_{i=0}^{N-1} \mathit{Tr}(v_i, v_{i+1}) \right) \wedge \mathit{Bad}(v_N) \tag{1}$$

When P is UNSAFE and $s \in \mathit{Bad}$ is the reachable state, the path from $s_0 \in \mathit{Init}$ to $s \in \mathit{Bad}$ is called a counterexample (CEX).

A transition system P is SAFE if and only if there exists a formula Inv, called *a safe invariant*, that satisfies the following conditions:

$$\mathit{Init}(v) \rightarrow \mathit{Inv}(v) \qquad \mathit{Inv}(v) \wedge \mathit{Tr}(v, u) \rightarrow \mathit{Inv}(u) \qquad \mathit{Inv}(v) \rightarrow \neg \mathit{Bad}(v) \tag{2}$$

A formula Inv that satisfies the first two conditions is called an *invariant* of P, while a formula Inv that satisfies the third condition is called *safe*. A *safety verification problem* is to decide whether a transition system P is SAFE or UNSAFE. Thus, a safety verification problem is equivalent to the problem of establishing an existence of a safe invariant. In SAT-based Model Checking, the verification problem is decided by iteratively synthesizing an invariant Inv or finding a CEX.

Minimal Unsatisfiability. A CNF formula F, viewed as a set of clauses, is *minimal unsatisfiable (MU)* if (i) F is unsatisfiable, and (ii) for any clause $C \in F$, $F \setminus \{C\}$ is satisfiable. A CNF formula F' is a *minimal unsatisfiable subformula (MUS)* of a formula F if $F' \subseteq F$ and F' is MU. Motivated by several applications, minimal unsatisfiability and related concepts have been extended to CNF formulas where clauses are partitioned into disjoint sets called *groups*.

Definition 1. *[33] Given an explicitly partitioned unsatisfiable CNF formula* $G = G_0 \cup G_1 \cup \cdots \cup G_k$ *(a group-MUS instance or a group-CNF formula), where* G_i*'s are pair-wise disjoint sets of clauses called* groups*, a group-MUS of G is a subset $\mathcal{G}$ of $\{G_1, \ldots, G_k\}$ such that (i) $G_0 \cup \bigcup \mathcal{G}$ is unsatisfiable, and (ii) for any group $G \in \mathcal{G}$, $G_0 \cup \bigcup (\mathcal{G} \setminus \{G\})$ is satisfiable.*

Notice that group-0, G_0, plays the special role of a "background" subformula, with respect to which the set of groups $\{G_1, \ldots, G_k\}$ is minimized. In particular, if G_0 is unsatisfiable, the group-MUS of G is $\emptyset$.

3   Synthesizing Safe Bit-Precise Invariants

3.1   High-Level Description of the Approach

Given a transition system $P = (\mathcal{V}, \mathit{Init}, \mathit{Tr}, \mathit{Bad})$, let the *target* theory $\mathcal{T}_T$ be the theory[1], or a combination of theories, that define the formulas in P. Let

---

[1] The term "theory" is used as in the context of Satisfiability Modulo Theories.

$\mathcal{T}_W$ be another theory, referred to as a *working* theory, with the intention that reasoning in $\mathcal{T}_W$ is easier in practice than reasoning in $\mathcal{T}_T$. Our approach relies on a mapping $M_{T \to W}$ that translates formulas over $\mathcal{T}_T$ to formulas over $\mathcal{T}_W$. Although the correctness of the approach is not affected by the choice of $M_{T \to W}$, its effectiveness is. We would like to map between formulas that are somewhat close to each other semantically. Thus, we assume that $M_{T \to W}$ maps the *terms* and the *atomic formulas* of $\mathcal{T}_T$ to those of $\mathcal{T}_W$ and is an identity mapping for the symbols shared between the two theories. The mapping is extended to all formulas of $\mathcal{T}_T$ by structural induction, i.e., given a formula $F(v)$ over $\mathcal{T}_T$, the corresponding formula $F_W(v)$ over $\mathcal{T}_W$ is constructed by inductively applying $M_{T \to W}$ on the structure of $F(v)$. Similarly, to translate formulas from $\mathcal{T}_W$ to $\mathcal{T}_T$, we work with a mapping $M_{W \to T}$ from the terms and the atomic formulas of the working theory $\mathcal{T}_W$ to those of $\mathcal{T}_T$, extended to all formulas of $\mathcal{T}_W$.

Example 1. Let $\mathcal{T}_T = \mathrm{BV}^*(32)$ — a sub-theory of the quantifier-free fragment of the first-order theory of 32 bit bit-vector arithmetic (cf., [7]) obtained by removing all the non-arithmetic functions and predicates, as well as the multiplication and the division on bit-vectors. Let $\mathcal{T}_W = \mathrm{LA}$ — the quantifier-free fragment of the first order-theory of linear arithmetic, together with the propositional logic. The mapping $M_{T \to W}$ is defined as follows: (i) the propositional fragment of $\mathcal{T}_T$ maps to the propositional fragment of $\mathcal{T}_W$ as is; (ii) bit-vector variables map to LA variables; (iii) the arithmetic functions and predicates of $\mathrm{BV}(32)$ map to their natural counterparts in LA, e.g., $+^{[32]}$ to $+$, $<^{[32]}$ to $<$, etc. Then, if

$$Init(x^{[32]}, y^{[32]}, z) = (x^{[32]} +^{[32]} y^{[32]} >^{[32]} 0^{[32]}) \wedge z,$$

where $x^{[32]}$ and $y^{[32]}$ are bit-vector and z propositional variables, the corresponding LA formula $Init_W(x, y, z)$ is

$$Init(x, y, z) = (x + y > 0) \wedge z.$$

The inverse mapping $M_{W \to T}$ from LA to $\mathrm{BV}(32)$ is constructed in a similar manner, with the slight complication related to LA constants, which might be non-integer, too large to fit into the required bit-width, or negative. One possibility to deal with non-integer constants is to truncate the fractional digits, i.e., map 0.5 to $0^{[32]}$. Other options include rounding up the constants when possible, e.g., by translating $(x > 0.5)$ to $(x^{[32]} \geq^{[32]} 1^{[32]})$, but $(x < 0.5)$ to $(x^{[32]} \leq^{[32]} 0^{[32]})$. For this paper, we adopt the former, simpler, approach, and leave the investigation of more sophisticated translations to future work. To convert an integer LA constant to $\mathrm{BV}(32)$ we take the lower 32 bit of its 2s-complement representation.

Remark 1. Clearly, our sub-theory $\mathrm{BV}^*(32)$ of the full theory $\mathrm{BV}(32)$ was chosen to simplify the construction of the mapping to and from LA. Generally, such restriction of the original target theory might not be necessary if the working theory $\mathcal{T}_W$ supports uninterpreted functions.

The pseudocode in Algorithm 1 provides the high-level description of our verification framework (MISper). Given a transition system $P = (\mathcal{V}, Init, Tr, Bad)$

Algorithm 1: MISper — safety verification framework

Input : $P = (\mathcal{V}, Init, Tr, Bad)$ — a transition system over theory $\mathcal{T}_T$
Output: st $\in$ {SAFE, UNSAFE, UNKNOWN}

1 **forever do**
2 | **under resource limits do**
3 | | $(st, Inv, Cex) \leftarrow$ Safety$(\mathcal{T}_T)(P)$ // solve in the target theory
4 | | if st $\neq$ UNKNOWN **then return** st
5 | $(\mathcal{T}_W, M_{T\to W}, M_{W\to T}) \leftarrow$ pick a working theory and mappings
6 | $P_W \leftarrow M_{T\to W}(P)$ // translate P to the working theory
7 | $(st, Inv_W, Cex_W) \leftarrow$ Safety$(\mathcal{T}_W)(P_W)$
8 | **if** st $\neq$ SAFE **then**
9 | | **return** UNKNOWN   // options: deal with CEX; try another $\mathcal{T}_W$
10 | $Cand \leftarrow M_{W\to T}(Inv_W)$ // get the candidate invariant for P
11 | **if** $Cand$ is safe invariant for P **then**
12 | | **return** SAFE
13 | $Cand_I \leftarrow$ ComputeMIS($Cand$)
14 | $Tr(u, v) \leftarrow Cand_I(u) \wedge Tr(u, v) \wedge Cand_I(v)$ // strengthen tr. rel.

---

over the target theory $\mathcal{T}_T$ (e.g., BV*(32) from Example 1), we first attempt to solve P with a solver for Safety$(\mathcal{T}_T)$ under heuristically chosen resource limits[2]. If the solver fails to prove or disprove the safety of P, we pick a working theory $\mathcal{T}_W$, and a pair of corresponding mappings $M_{T\to W}$ and $M_{W\to T}$ (e.g., $\mathcal{T}_W = $ LA and the mappings are as in Example 1). Then, we attempt to verify the safety of $P_W = M_{T\to W}(P) = (\mathcal{U}, M_{T\to W}(Init), M_{T\to W}(Tr), M_{T\to W}(Bad))$, where $\mathcal{U}$ are the fresh variables introduced by $M_{T\to W}$, using a solver for Safety$(\mathcal{T}_W)$. Since P_W is in general neither under- nor over- approximation of P, the (un)safety of the former does not imply the (un)safety of the latter. Since the focus of this paper is on synthesis of invariants for verification, we omit the detailed discussion of how to handle the UNSAFE status of P_W. One option is to simply return UNKNOWN, as in Algorithm 1. Alternatively, the CEX for P_W can be mapped to $\mathcal{T}_T$ via $M_{W\to T}$ and checked on P — if the mapped CEX is also a CEX for P, return UNSAFE. Otherwise, the mapping can be refined to eliminate the CEX, and the safety verification of P_W under the new mapping repeated. If, on the other hand, P_W *is* safe, we take the safe invariant Inv_W of P_W, and translate it back to the target theory $\mathcal{T}_T$ to obtain a *candidate-invariant* formula $Cand = M_{W\to T}(Inv_W)$. If $Cand$ is a safe invariant of P, then the safety of P is established, and the algorithm returns SAFE. Otherwise, we attempt to compute a subformula $Cand_I$ of $Cand$ that is an invariant of P — this is done in the function ComputeMIS on line 13 of Algorithm 1, which we describe in detail in Section 3.2. Once an invariant of P is obtained, we restrict the transition relation of P by replacing the formula $Tr(u, v)$ in P with the formula $Cand_I(u) \wedge Tr(u, v) \wedge Cand_I(v)$, and attempt to verify the safety of the new

---

[2] This step is optional on the first iteration of the main loop of Algorithm 1.

transition system (the next iteration of the main loop). Since $Cand_I$ is the actual invariant of P, the (un)safety of strengthened transition system implies the (un)safety of the input system P.

This verification framework can be instantiated in numerous ways and leaves a number of open heuristic choices. We postpone the description of an instantiation of the framework used in our experiments to Section 4.

3.2   Computing Invariants

Given a candidate invariant $Cand$ for a transition system $P = (\mathcal{V}, \mathit{Init}, \mathit{Tr}, \mathit{Bad})$, obtained as described in Section 3.1, we are interested in computing a subformula $Cand_I$ of $Cand$ that is an invariant with respect to P, that is, $Cand_I(u) \wedge Tr(u, v) \models Cand_I(v)$. Similarly to the previous work on invariant extraction (e.g., [8,24]), we proceed under the assumption that the candidate invariant $Cand(u)$ is given as a *conjunction* of formulas $Cand(u) = L_1(u) \wedge \cdots \wedge L_n(u)$. We refer to the conjuncts L_i of $Cand$ as *lemmas*. Then, the invariant $Cand_I$ can be always be constructed as a (possibly empty) conjunction of some of the lemmas in $Cand$. In our setting, this assumption is justified by the fact that many verification tools, particularly those based on PDR [5,13] and its extensions (e.g., Z3/PDR [22]) do indeed produce invariants in this form. In the worst case, $Cand$ itself can be treated as the (only) conjunct, which, while affecting the effectiveness of our approach, does not affect its correctness. We note that the ideas discussed in this section can be extended to candidate invariants of arbitrary structure, though such extension is outside of the scope of this paper.

For notational convenience we treat $Cand$ as a *set* of lemmas $\{L_1, \ldots, L_n\}$, and formalize the invariant computation problem as follows:

Definition 2. *Given a set of lemmas $\mathcal{L} = \{L_1, \ldots, L_n\}$ and a transition relation $Tr(u, v)$, a subset $\mathcal{L}' \subseteq \mathcal{L}$ is inductive if $(\bigwedge_{L \in \mathcal{L}'} L(u)) \wedge Tr(u, v) \models \bigwedge_{L \in \mathcal{L}'} L(v)$. An inductive subset $\mathcal{L}' \subseteq \mathcal{L}$ is maximal if no strict superset of $\mathcal{L}'$ is inductive. Finally, an inductive subset $\mathcal{L}' \subseteq \mathcal{L}$ is maximum if the cardinality of $\mathcal{L}'$ is maximum among all inductive subsets of $\mathcal{L}$.*

It is not difficult to see that a union of two inductive subsets is inductive, and so any set of lemmas $\mathcal{L}$ has a *unique* maximal, and hence a *unique* maximum, inductive subset $\mathcal{L}'$. We refer to $\mathcal{L}'$ as the *MIS* (maximal/maximum inductive subset) of $\mathcal{L}$. Thus, in our framework, given a candidate invariant $Cand$ of transition system P, the actual invariant $Cand_I$ of P is obtained by computing the MIS of $Cand$ — this is motivated by the fact that we aim to strengthen the transition relation as much as possible prior to the next iteration of the algorithm.

Approaches to MIS Computation. The existing approaches to computation of MISes can be categorized into *eager* and *lazy*. Given a set of lemmas $\mathcal{L} = \{L_1, \ldots, L_n\}$ and the transition relation Tr, the eager approach (taken, for example, in [8]) starts by checking whether $\mathcal{L}(u) \wedge Tr(u, v) \models \mathcal{L}(v)$. This is typically done by testing the unsatisfiability of the formula $\mathcal{L}(u) \wedge Tr(u, v) \wedge \neg \mathcal{L}(v)$ with an SMT (or a SAT) solver. If the formula satisfiable, i.e., $\mathcal{L}$ is not inductive, the model returned by the solver must falsify one or more lemmas in $\mathcal{L}(v)$. These lemmas are then removed *both* from $\mathcal{L}(u)$ and from $\mathcal{L}(v)$, and the test is repeated. The process continues until for some subset $\mathcal{L}' \subseteq \mathcal{L}$, $\mathcal{L}'(u) \wedge Tr(u,v) \models \mathcal{L}'(v)$. The final subset $\mathcal{L}'$ is obviously inductive. Furthermore, for any set of lemmas $\mathcal{L}'' \subseteq \mathcal{L} \setminus \mathcal{L}'$ there must have been a point in the execution of the algorithm where it obtained a model for a formula $\mathcal{L}'(u) \wedge \mathcal{L}''(u) \wedge Tr(u,v)$ that falsifies at least one lemma in $\mathcal{L}''(v)$, as otherwise this lemma would be included in $\mathcal{L}'$. Hence, $\mathcal{L}'$ is maximal, and therefore is a MIS of $\mathcal{L}$.

In the lazy approach to MIS computation (e.g., [16,24]), when the set $\mathcal{L}$ is not inductive, the lemmas in the consequent $\mathcal{L}(v)$ that are falsified by the model of $\mathcal{L}(u) \wedge Tr(u,v)$ are initially removed *only* from $\mathcal{L}(v)$. The process continues until for some $\mathcal{L}' \subseteq \mathcal{L}$, $\mathcal{L}(u) \wedge Tr(u,v) \models \mathcal{L}'(v)$ — notice that the premise still contains all of the lemmas of $\mathcal{L}$. We refer to such sets $\mathcal{L}'$ as *semi-inductive* with respect to $\mathcal{L}$ and Tr. Observe that the semi-inductive subset $\mathcal{L}'$ obtained in this manner is *maximal* and also *maximum*, by the argument analogous to that used to establish the uniqueness of MISes. Once the maximum semi-inductive subset $\mathcal{L}'$ of $\mathcal{L}$ is computed, the lemmas excluded from $\mathcal{L}'$ are removed from $\mathcal{L}(u)$, and the algorithm checks whether $\mathcal{L}'(u) \wedge Tr(u,v) \models \mathcal{L}'(v)$, i.e., whether $\mathcal{L}'$ is inductive. If not, the algorithm repeats the process, by first computing a maximum semi-inductive subset of $\mathcal{L}'$, then checking its inductiveness, and so on. The, eventually obtained, inductive subset of $\mathcal{L}$ is the MIS of $\mathcal{L}$ — this can be justified in essentially the same way as for the eager approach.

One potential advantage of the lazy approach is that, since, compared to the eager approach, there are often more lemmas in the premises, the SMT/SAT solver is likely to work with stronger formulas. Furthermore, if a solver retains information between invocations — for example, derived facts and history-based heuristic parameters, as in *incremental* SAT solvers — more information can be reused between iterations, thus speeding-up the MIS computation.

One additional feature of the lazy approach, pointed out and used in [24], is that the computation of semi-inductive subsets can be reduced to the computation of Minimal Unsatisfiable Subformulas (MUSes), or, more precisely, to the computation of group-MUSes (recall Definition 1). This observation is particularly useful in cases when satisfiability problem in the theory that defines the invariants can be soundly reduced to propositional satisfiability, as it allows to leverage the large body of recent work and tools for the computation of MUSes (e.g., [2,30,34]). We take advantage of this observation in the implementation of our framework since, in our case, the invariants are quantifier-free formula over (a sub-theory of) the theory of bit-vectors, and the satisfiability of such formulas can be soundly reduced to SAT via bit-blasting. The reduction to group-MUS computation and the overall MIS extraction flow are presented below.

Computing MISes with Group-MUSes. For a set of lemmas $\mathcal{L} = \{L_1, \ldots, L_n\}$ and a transition relation formula Tr, we first rewrite the formula $\mathcal{L}(u) \wedge Tr(u,v) \wedge \neg\mathcal{L}(v)$, used to check the inductiveness of $\mathcal{L}$, as a formula $A_{\mathcal{L}, Tr}$ defined in the following way:

$$A_{\mathcal{L}, Tr} = \left(\bigwedge_{L_i \in \mathcal{L}} (pre_i \rightarrow L_i(u)) \right) \wedge Tr(u, v) \wedge \left(\bigvee_{L_i \in \mathcal{L}} (post_i \wedge \neg L_i(v)) \right), \quad (3)$$

where pre_i and $post_i$ for $i \in [1, n]$ are fresh propositional variables, one for each lemma $L_i \in \mathcal{L}$. One of the purposes of these variables is similar to that of the indicator variables used in assumption-based incremental SAT solving (cf. [14]) — the variables can be used to emulate the removal of lemmas from formulas $\mathcal{L}(u)$ and $\mathcal{L}(v)$. Setting pre_i to true (resp. false) causes the lemma L_i to be included (resp. excluded) from $\mathcal{L}(u)$, while setting $post_i$ to true (resp. false) has the same effect on the lemma L_i in $\mathcal{L}(v)$. The names of the variables reflect the fact that they control either the "*pre*condition" or the "*post*condition" lemmas. With this in mind, a computation of the MIS of $\mathcal{L}$ with respect to Tr can be implemented on top of an incremental SMT solver by loading the formula $A_{\mathcal{L}, Tr}$ into the solver, and checking the satisfiability of the formula under a set of assumptions. For example, the set $\mathcal{L}$ is inductive if and only if the formula is unsatisfiable under assumptions $\bigcup_{i \in [1, n]} \{pre_i, post_i\}$. When a lemma $L_i \in \mathcal{L}$ needs to be removed from $\mathcal{L}(u)$ and/or $\mathcal{L}(v)$, we simply assert the formula $(\neg pre_i)$ and/or $(\neg post_i)$ to the solver.

However, as explained above, our intention is to take advantage of propositional MUS extractors, using the fact that quantifier-free bit-vector formulas can be soundly converted to propositional logic. The *pre* and *post* variables serve a purpose in this context as well. Assume that we have a polytime computable function $B2P$, which given a quantifier-free formula F_{BV} over the theory BV, and a set of *propositional* variables $X = \{x_1, \ldots, x_k\}$ that occur in F_{BV} returns a propositional formula $F_{Prop} = B2P(F_{BV}, X)$, in CNF, with the following property: for any assignment τ to the variables in X, the formula $F_{BV}[\tau]$ is satisfiable if and only if so is the formula $F_{Prop}[\tau]$. Following [29], we say that the formulas F_{BV} and F_{Prop} are *var-equivalent* on X in this case. Note that var-equivalence of F_{BV} and F_{Prop} on X does not imply F_{Prop} contains all variables of X — for example, $F_{Prop} = \top$ is var-equivalent to F_{BV} if $F_{BV}[\tau]$ is satisfiable for every assignment τ for X.

Now, for a set of lemmas $\mathcal{L} = \{L_1, \ldots, L_n\}$ and a transition relation Tr over BV, let $A_{\mathcal{L}, Tr}$ be the formula defined in (3), let $Pre = \{pre_i \mid i \in [1, n]\}$, $Post = \{post_i \mid i \in [1, n]\}$. Consider the group-CNF formula $G_{\mathcal{L}, Tr}$ constructed in the following way:

$G_{\mathcal{L}, Tr} = G_0 \cup G_1 \cup \cdots \cup G_n$, where:
$\quad G_0 = C_{\mathcal{L}, Tr} \cup \{(pre_i) \mid i \in [1, n]\}$, with $C_{\mathcal{L}, Tr} = B2P(A_{\mathcal{L}, Tr}, Pre \cup Post)$
$\quad G_i = \{(\neg post_i)\}$ for $i \in [1, n]$

That is, the group G_0 of $G_{\mathcal{L}, Tr}$ is the formula $C_{\mathcal{L}, Tr}$ — a CNF formula var-equivalent to $A_{\mathcal{L}, Tr}$ on the set $Pre \cup Post$ — together with the positive unit clauses for *pre* variables. Each group G_i in $G_{\mathcal{L}, Tr}$ consists of a single negative unit clause for the variable $post_i$.

Proposition 1. *Let $\mathcal{G}$ be a group-MUS of the group-CNF formula $G_{\mathcal{L},Tr}$. Then, the set of lemmas $\mathcal{L}' = \{L_k \mid k \in [1,n]$ and $G_k \notin \mathcal{G}\}$ is the maximum semi-inductive subset of $\mathcal{L}$ with respect to Tr. Furthermore, $\mathcal{G} = \emptyset$ iff $\mathcal{L}$ is inductive.*

Intuitively, Proposition 1 follows from the fact that the function $B2P$ preserves var-equivalence. The formulas $A_{\mathcal{L},Tr}$ and $C_{\mathcal{L},Tr}$ are var-equivalent on the variables $Pre \cup Post$. Thus, any group-MUS $\mathcal{G}$ of the group-CNF formula $G_{\mathcal{L},Tr}$ is exactly a group-MUS of the "group-BV" formula obtained by taking $A_{\mathcal{L},Tr}$ together with the appropriate unit clauses as group-0 and the rest of groups as in $G_{\mathcal{L},Tr}$. Furthermore, whenever a group G_i is included in $\mathcal{G}$, the corresponding variable $post_i$ is forced to 0, and so the lemma $L_i(v)$ is disabled in $A_{\mathcal{L},Tr}$. Since $G_0 \cup \bigcup \mathcal{G}$ is unsatisfiable, so is the formula $A_{\mathcal{L},Tr}$ with the rest of the post-lemmas (i.e., the set $\mathcal{L}'$) enabled, thus implying the semi-inductiveness of $\mathcal{L}'$. The maximality of the latter is implied by the minimality of $\mathcal{G}$.

Proof. First, observe that the formula $G_{\mathcal{L},Tr}$ is unsatisfiable. This is because $G_{\mathcal{L},Tr} \equiv C_{\mathcal{L},Tr}[\tau]$, where $\tau = \{pre_i \to 1, post_i \to 0 \mid i \in [1,n]\}$ is the assignment entailed by the unit clauses in $G_{\mathcal{L},Tr}$. Since $B2P$ preserves var-equivalence on $Pre \cup Post$, the formula $C_{\mathcal{L},Tr}[\tau]$ is equisatisfiable with the formula $A_{\mathcal{L},Tr}[\tau]$ (cf. (3)), which, in turn, is unsatisfiable since τ sets all $post$ variables to 0.

Let now $\mathcal{G}$ be a group-MUS of $G_{\mathcal{L},Tr}$. Since $G_0 \cup \bigcup \mathcal{G}$ is unsatisfiable (recall Definition 1), so is the formula $C_{\mathcal{L},Tr}[\tau_{\mathcal{G}}]$, where $\tau_{\mathcal{G}} = \{pre_i \to 1 \mid i \in [1,n]\} \cup \{post_j \to 1 \mid G_j \notin \mathcal{G}\} \cup \{post_k \to 0 \mid G_k \in \mathcal{G}\}$, and, therefore, the formula $A_{\mathcal{L},Tr}[\tau_{\mathcal{G}}]$. Note, however, that the latter is equivalent to $\mathcal{L}(u) \wedge Tr(u,v) \wedge \neg \mathcal{L}'(v)$, where $\mathcal{L}'$ is as defined in the statement of the proposition. Hence, $\mathcal{L}'$ is semi-inductive.

Finally, w.l.o.g. take any $\mathcal{G}' \subset \mathcal{G}$. Since $\mathcal{G}$ is a group-MUS of $G_{\mathcal{L},Tr}$, the formula $G_0 \cup \bigcup \mathcal{G}'$ is satisfiable. Following the previous argument with the assignment $\tau_{\mathcal{G}'}$ we have that the formula $A_{\mathcal{L},Tr}[\tau_{\mathcal{G}'}]$ is satisfiable, and so is the formula $\mathcal{L}(u) \wedge Tr(u,v) \wedge \neg \mathcal{L}''(v)$, where $\mathcal{L}'' = \mathcal{L} \cup \{L_k \mid G_k \in \mathcal{G} \setminus \mathcal{G}'\}$. We conclude that any $\mathcal{L}'' \supset \mathcal{L}'$ is not semi-inductive, and so $\mathcal{L}'$ is maximal.

The "only-if" part of the second claim of the proposition follows immediately from the first claim. For the "if" part, assume that $\mathcal{L}$ is inductive, and let τ be the assignment that enables all lemmas of $\mathcal{L}$, i.e., $\tau = \{pre_i \to 1, post_i \to 1 \mid i \in [1,n]\}$. Then, the formula $A_{\mathcal{L},Tr}[\tau]$ is unsatisfiable. Since the $post$ variables appear in $A_{\mathcal{L},Tr}$ only in positive polarity, changing the value of any of the $post$ variables to 0 cannot make the formula satisfiable. Thus, for $\tau' = \{pre_i \to 1 \mid i \in [1,n]\}$ the formula $A_{\mathcal{L},Tr}[\tau']$ is also unsatisfiable, and since $B2P$ preserves var-equivalence, so is the CNF formula $C_{\mathcal{L},Tr}[\tau']$. But, $C_{\mathcal{L},Tr}[\tau'] \equiv G_0$, and so the group-MUS of $G_{\mathcal{L},Tr}$ is $\emptyset$. $\square$

The MIS Computation Algorithm. Based on Proposition 1, we can compute the maximum semi-inductive subset of the set of lemmas $\mathcal{L}$ by invoking any off-the-shelf group-MUS extractor (e.g., MUSer2 [3]). The $post$ variables are essential for this reduction, as the translation function $B2P$ can, and in practice does, significantly modify the structure of the input BV formula through the application of various BV-specific preprocessing techniques. The purpose of pre

---

Algorithm 2: ComputeMIS for invariants in BV

Input : $(\mathcal{L}, \mathit{Tr})$ — a set of lemmas and a transition relation, in BV
Output: $\mathcal{L}' \subseteq \mathcal{L}$ — the MIS of $\mathcal{L}$ with respect to Tr

1 construct $A_{\mathcal{L}, \mathit{Tr}}$ `// the BV formula defined in eq. (3)`
2 $C_{\mathcal{L}, \mathit{Tr}} \leftarrow B2P(A_{\mathcal{L}, \mathit{Tr}}, \mathit{Pre} \cup \mathit{Post})$ `// compute a var-equivalent CNF`
3 $\mathcal{L}' \leftarrow \mathcal{L}$
4 **forever do**
5 $\quad$ construct $G_{\mathcal{L}, \mathcal{L}', \mathit{Tr}}$ `// the group-CNF defined in eq. (4)`
6 $\quad$ $\mathcal{G} \leftarrow \text{ComputeGMUS}(G_{\mathcal{L}, \mathcal{L}', \mathit{Tr}})$ `// compute a group-MUS`
7 $\quad$ **if** $\mathcal{G} = \emptyset$ **then**   `// $\mathcal{L}'$ is inductive, cf. Prop. 1`
8 $\quad\quad$ ⌊ **return** $\mathcal{L}'$
9 $\quad$ $\mathcal{L}' = \{L_k \mid k \in [1, n] \text{ and } G_k \notin \mathcal{G}\}$ `// remove lemmas included in $\mathcal{G}$`

---

variables is slightly more technical. Assume that in the first iteration of the lazy MIS computation algorithm a maximal semi-inductive set $\mathcal{L}'$ of $\mathcal{L}$ is computed, and that $\mathcal{L}' \subset \mathcal{L}$. At this point, some of the lemmas $\mathcal{L}(u)$ (i.e., the precondition lemmas) have to be removed from $\mathcal{L}$. One possibility is to build a new formula $A_{\mathcal{L}', \mathit{Tr}}$ analogously to that in equation (3), apply the function $B2P$ to it, and proceed with the computation of the maximum semi-inductive subset of $\mathcal{L}'$. An alternative is to re-use the CNF formula $C_{\mathcal{L}, \mathit{Tr}}$, obtained by translating the original formula $A_{\mathcal{L}, \mathit{Tr}}$ via $B2P$, and simply add negative unit clauses $(\neg \mathit{pre}_i)$ and $(\neg \mathit{post}_i)$ for each of the lemmas removed from $\mathcal{L}$. This way we avoid re-invoking $B2P$, and open up the possibility of reusing more information between the invocations of the group-MUS extractor. As the group-CNF formula $G_{\mathcal{L}, \mathit{Tr}}$ does need to be modified between iterations by taking into account removal of some of the lemmas, for a set $\mathcal{L}' \subseteq \mathcal{L}$ of *remaining* lemmas we define the group-CNF formula $G_{\mathcal{L}, \mathcal{L}', \mathit{Tr}}$ as follows:

$$G_{\mathcal{L}, \mathcal{L}', \mathit{Tr}} = G_0 \cup \{G_i \mid L_i \in \mathcal{L}'\}, \text{ where:}$$
$$G_0 = C_{\mathcal{L}, \mathit{Tr}} \cup \{(\mathit{pre}_i) \mid L_i \in \mathcal{L}'\} \cup \{(\neg \mathit{pre}_j), (\neg \mathit{post}_j) \mid L_j \in \mathcal{L} \setminus \mathcal{L}'\} \quad (4)$$
$$G_i = \{(\neg \mathit{post}_i)\} \text{ for } L_i \in \mathcal{L}'.$$

The pseudocode of the MIS computation algorithm based on the ideas presented above is presented in Algorithm 2. Given a set of BV lemmas $\mathcal{L}$ and a transition relation formula Tr, the algorithm constructs the formula $A_{\mathcal{L}, \mathit{Tr}}$, defined in (3), and converts the formula to CNF using a var-equivalence preserving function $B2P$. The set $\mathcal{L}'$ that will eventually represent the resulting MIS is initialized to $\mathcal{L}$. The main loop of the algorithm reflects the outer loop of the lazy MIS computation approach. On every iteration, the maximum semi-inductive subset of $\mathcal{L}'$ is computed via the reduction to group-MUS computation, as justified by Proposition 1. If the group-MUS is empty, then, according to Proposition 1, the set $\mathcal{L}'$ itself is inductive, and, therefore, based on the correctness of the lazy MIS computation algorithm, is the MIS of $\mathcal{L}$. Otherwise, $\mathcal{L}'$ is updated to the computed maximum semi-inductive subset represented by the extracted

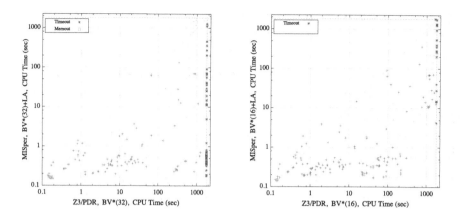

Fig. 1. Performance of Z3/PDR and MISper for the target theories $BV^*(32)$ (left) and $BV^*(16)$ (right) in terms of CPU runtime. Timeout of 1800 seconds is represented by the dashed (green) lines; orders of magnitude are represented by diagonals.

group-MUS (line 9). Note that the removal of the lemmas from the premise formula $\mathcal{L}(u)$ performed at this stage during the lazy MIS computation is implicit in the construction of the group-CNF formula $G_{\mathcal{L},\mathcal{L}',Tr}$ in the next iteration of the main loop (cf. (4)). The termination of the algorithm is guaranteed by the fact that on every iteration at least one lemma is removed from $\mathcal{L}'$, and so, in the worst case, there will be an iteration of the main loop with $\mathcal{L}' = \emptyset$. Since, in this case, $\mathcal{L}'$ is inductive, by Proposition 1 the computed group-MUS will be $\emptyset$, and the algorithm terminates.

4   Implementation and Empirical Evaluation

Our prototype implementation of MISper framework was instantiated with the restriction BV^* of the theory of bit-vectors, described in Example 1, as the target theory $\mathcal{T}_T$, and the theory of linear arithmetic LA as working theory $\mathcal{T}_W$. The mappings $M_{T\to W}$ and $M_{W\to T}$ between the theories are as described in Example 1. We used Z3/PDR engine for the implementation of the Safety(BV) and Safety(LA) procedures. The Horn SMT systems used as an input to Z3/PDR were obtained from the UFO framework. To check the safety and the inductiveness of the candidate invariants *Cand* in BV we used the bit-vector engine of Z3. To perform var-equivalent translation of BV formulas to CNF during invariant extraction (function *B2P* in Algorithm 2) we used the front-end of the SMT(BV) solver Boolector [6]. Though we were unable to formally establish the var-equivalence of the translation, we validated the inductiveness of computed invariants independently. Finally, we used the MUS extractor MUSer2 to compute group-MUSes in Algorithm 2.

Experimental Setup and Results. To evaluate the performance of the proposed framework empirically we selected 214 bit-precise verification benchmarks

Table 1. Performance of Z3/PDR and MISper for the target theories BV*(32) and BV*(16). Within each horizontal section, the first row (all) presents the data for all 214 instances, while the second row (unsol.) presents the data for those instances that were not solved by Z3/PDR. "Solved" means that the tool returned SAFE within the timeout/memout of 1800 sec/4 GB. Column Z3/PDR shows the data for Z3/PDR — each cell contains the number of solved instances (#sol), followed by the average and the median of the CPU times on the solved instances (avg/med). Column MISper displays the same data for MISper. Column MISper:*Cand* displays the data for instances solved by MISper by proving the safety of the candidate invariant *Cand* (Alg. 1, line 12). Column MISper:MIS displays the data for instances solved by MISper by computing MIS of *Cand*, and invoking Z3/PDR on strengthened system (Alg. 1, lines 13-14). For example, the first row in the table shows that out of 214 instances, Z3/PDR solved 116, while MISper solved 174, out of which 165 were solved immediately after the conversion of LA invariant to BV*(32), and 9 were solved after extracting invariants.

bit width	inst.	count	Z3/PDR #sol(avg/med)	MISper #sol(avg/med)	MISper:*Cand* #sol(avg/med)	MISper:MIS #sol(avg/med)
32	all	214	116(127.54/8.27)	**174**(28.34/0.43)	165(8.50/0.42)	9(391.95/133.94)
	unsol.	98	—	58(75.90/1.03)	52(21.89/0.70)	6(544.05/366.18)
16	all	214	165(176.69/8.20)	**182**(69.32/0.38)	165(8.37/0.36)	17(660.91/399.32)
	unsol.	49	—	18(624.79/376.24)	6(50.80/21.45)	12(911.78/1094.58)

from the set of SAFE benchmarks used in 2013 Competition on Software Verification, SVCOMP'13[3]. We translated the benchmarks to Horn SMT formulas over the theories BV*(32) and BV*(16) (recall Example 1), after replacing the unsupported bit-vector operations by fresh variables — hence, the resulting systems are an over-approximation of the original programs[4]. We compared the performance of Z3/PDR engine with that of MISper, instantiated with the theory of linear arithmetic (LA) as a working theory $\mathcal{T}_W$. All experiments were performed on Intel Xeon X3470, 32 GB, running Linux 2.6. For each experiment, we set a CPU time limit of 1800 seconds, and a memory limit of 4 GB.

The scatter plots in Figure 1, complemented by Table 1, summarize the results of our experiments. In 32-bit experiments, MISper solved all 116 instances solved by Z3/PDR, and additional 58 on which Z3/PDR exceeded the allotted resources (174 in total). Furthermore, judging from the scatter plot (left), on the vast majority of instances MISper was at least one order of magnitude faster than Z3/PDR, and, in some cases, the performance improvement exceeded three orders of magnitude. The 16-bit benchmarks were, not surprisingly, easier for Z3/PDR than 32-bit, and so it succeeded to solve quite significantly more problems (165). Nevertheless, MISper significantly outperforms Z3/PDR in this setting as well, solving 17 more benchmarks, and still demonstrating multiple orders of magnitude performance improvements. We found only one instance solved by Z3/PDR, but unsolved by MISper (exceeded time limit). To summarize, the results clearly demonstrate the effectiveness of the proposed framework.

---

[3] http://sv-comp.sosy-lab.org/2013.

[4] The benchmarks are available at http://bitbucket.org/arieg/misp.

A number of interesting additional observations can be made by analyzing the data in Table 1. Consider the 58 instances unsolved by Z3/PDR and solved by MISper in the 32-bit experiments (second row of Table 1). In 52 of these the safe invariants obtained in LA were transferred to directly to BV. Thus, in many practical cases, while the safety of the program can be easily established without taking into account its bit-precise semantics, the BV-based engine seems to get bogged down by discovering information that, in the end, is mostly irrelevant. In these situations, our approach allows to "find needles in the haystack", and quickly. In the remaining 6 cases, the bit-precise semantics do come into play. However, the MIS-based invariant synthesis allows to transfer information that is useful for bit-precise reasoning — this is evidenced by at least 3x average speed-up of bit-precise reasoning on the strengthened system, with close to 6x speed-up on 3 instances out of 6. The 16-bit experiments confirm the usefulness of the partially transferred invariants further: out of 18 instances unsolved by Z3/PDR, only on 6 the LA invariant could be transferred directly to BV, while on remaining 12 the partial information allowed to speed-up the verification by at least 2x on average.

5   Conclusion

In this paper, we introduced a bit-precise program verification framework MISper. The key idea behind the framework is to transfer, at least partially, information obtained during the verification of an unsound approximation of the original program in the form of bit-precise invariants. We describe a novel approach to computing such invariants that allows to take advantage of the state-of-the-art propositional MUS extractors. The results of the experiments with our proto-type implementation of the framework suggest that the proposed approach is promising. Furthermore, the verification tool FrankenBit [20] that integrates our prototype implementation of MISper with LLBMC [32], has won two awards at the 2014 Competition on Software Verification (SVCOMP'14).

References

1. Albarghouthi, A., Gurfinkel, A., Chechik, M.: From Under-Approximations to Over-Approximations and Back. In: Flanagan, C., König, B. (eds.) TACAS 2012. LNCS, vol. 7214, pp. 157–172. Springer, Heidelberg (2012)
2. Belov, A., Lynce, I., Marques-Silva, J.: Towards efficient MUS extraction. AI Commun. 25(2) (2012)
3. Belov, A., Marques-Silva, J.: MUSer2: An Efficient MUS Extractor. JSAT 8(1/2) (2012)
4. Beyer, D., Löwe, S., Novikov, E., Stahlbauer, A., Wendler, P.: Precision reuse for efficient regression verification. In: ESEC/SIGSOFT FSE (2013)
5. Bradley, A.R.: SAT-Based Model Checking without Unrolling. In: Jhala, R., Schmidt, D. (eds.) VMCAI 2011. LNCS, vol. 6538, pp. 70–87. Springer, Heidelberg (2011)

6. Brummayer, R., Biere, A.: Boolector: An Efficient SMT Solver for Bit-Vectors and Arrays. In: Kowalewski, S., Philippou, A. (eds.) TACAS 2009. LNCS, vol. 5505, pp. 174–177. Springer, Heidelberg (2009)

7. Bryant, R.E., Kroening, D., Ouaknine, J., Seshia, S.A., Strichman, O., Brady, B.A.: Deciding Bit-Vector Arithmetic with Abstraction. In: Grumberg, O., Huth, M. (eds.) TACAS 2007. LNCS, vol. 4424, pp. 358–372. Springer, Heidelberg (2007)

8. Chockler, H., Ivrii, A., Matsliah, A., Moran, S., Nevo, Z.: Incremental formal verification of hardware. In: FMCAD (2011)

9. Cimatti, A., Griggio, A., Schaafsma, B.J., Sebastiani, R.: The MathSAT5 SMT Solver. In: Piterman, N., Smolka, S.A. (eds.) TACAS 2013. LNCS, vol. 7795, pp. 93–107. Springer, Heidelberg (2013)

10. Clarke, E., Kroening, D., Lerda, F.: A Tool for Checking ANSI-C Programs. In: Jensen, K., Podelski, A. (eds.) TACAS 2004. LNCS, vol. 2988, pp. 168–176. Springer, Heidelberg (2004)

11. Cordeiro, L., Fischer, B., Marques-Silva, J.: SMT-Based Bounded Model Checking for Embedded ANSI-C Software. IEEE Trans. Software Eng. 38(4) (2012)

12. de Moura, L., Bjørner, N.: Z3: An Efficient SMT Solver. In: Ramakrishnan, C.R., Rehof, J. (eds.) TACAS 2008. LNCS, vol. 4963, pp. 337–340. Springer, Heidelberg (2008)

13. Eén, N., Mishchenko, A., Brayton, R.K.: Efficient implementation of property directed reachability. In: FMCAD (2011)

14. Eén, N., Sörensson, N.: Temporal induction by incremental SAT solving. Electr. Notes Theor. Comput. Sci. 89(4) (2003)

15. Fedyukovich, G., Sery, O., Sharygina, N.: Function Summaries in Software Upgrade Checking. In: Eder, K., Lourenço, J., Shehory, O. (eds.) HVC 2011. LNCS, vol. 7261, pp. 257–258. Springer, Heidelberg (2012)

16. Flanagan, C., Leino, K.R.M.: Houdini, an Annotation Assistant for ESC/Java. In: Oliveira, J.N., Zave, P. (eds.) FME 2001. LNCS, vol. 2021, pp. 500–517. Springer, Heidelberg (2001)

17. Ganesh, V., Dill, D.L.: A Decision Procedure for Bit-Vectors and Arrays. In: Damm, W., Hermanns, H. (eds.) CAV 2007. LNCS, vol. 4590, pp. 519–531. Springer, Heidelberg (2007)

18. Godlin, B., Strichman, O.: Regression verification. In: DAC (2009)

19. Griggio, A.: Effective word-level interpolation for software verification. In: FMCAD (2011)

20. Gurfinkel, A., Belov, A.: FrankenBit: Bit-Precise Verification with Many Bits (Competition Contribution). In: Ábrahám, E., Havelund, K. (eds.) TACAS 2014. LNCS, vol. 8413, pp. 408–411. Springer, Heidelberg (2014)

21. Gurfinkel, A., Rollini, S.F., Sharygina, N.: Interpolation properties and SAT-based model checking. In: Van Hung, D., Ogawa, M. (eds.) ATVA 2013. LNCS, vol. 8172, pp. 255–271. Springer, Heidelberg (2013)

22. Hoder, K., Bjørner, N.: Generalized Property Directed Reachability. In: Cimatti, A., Sebastiani, R. (eds.) SAT 2012. LNCS, vol. 7317, pp. 157–171. Springer, Heidelberg (2012)

23. Kahsai, T., Ge, Y., Tinelli, C.: Instantiation-Based Invariant Discovery. In: Bobaru, M., Havelund, K., Holzmann, G.J., Joshi, R. (eds.) NFM 2011. LNCS, vol. 6617, pp. 192–206. Springer, Heidelberg (2011)

24. Komuravelli, A., Gurfinkel, A., Chaki, S., Clarke, E.M.: Automatic Abstraction in SMT-Based Unbounded Software Model Checking. In: Sharygina, N., Veith, H. (eds.) CAV 2013. LNCS, vol. 8044, pp. 846–862. Springer, Heidelberg (2013)

25. Kroening, D., Weissenbacher, G.: Lifting Propositional Interpolants to the Word-Level. In: FMCAD (2007)
26. Kroening, D., Weissenbacher, G.: Interpolation-Based Software Verification with WOLVERINE. In: Gopalakrishnan, G., Qadeer, S. (eds.) CAV 2011. LNCS, vol. 6806, pp. 573–578. Springer, Heidelberg (2011)
27. Kuncak, V., Rybalchenko, A. (eds.): VMCAI 2012. LNCS, vol. 7148. Springer, Heidelberg (2012)
28. Lahiri, S.K., Hawblitzel, C., Kawaguchi, M., Rebêlo, H.: SYMDIFF: A Language-Agnostic Semantic Diff Tool for Imperative Programs. In: Madhusudan, P., Seshia, S.A. (eds.) CAV 2012. LNCS, vol. 7358, pp. 712–717. Springer, Heidelberg (2012)
29. Lang, J., Liberatore, P., Marquis, P.: Propositional Independence: Formula-Variable Independence and Forgetting. J. Artif. Intell. Res. (JAIR) 18 (2003)
30. Marques-Silva, J., Janota, M., Belov, A.: Minimal Sets over Monotone Predicates in Boolean Formulae. In: Sharygina, N., Veith, H. (eds.) CAV 2013. LNCS, vol. 8044, pp. 592–607. Springer, Heidelberg (2013)
31. McMillan, K.L.: Lazy Abstraction with Interpolants. In: Ball, T., Jones, R.B. (eds.) CAV 2006. LNCS, vol. 4144, pp. 123–136. Springer, Heidelberg (2006)
32. Merz, F., Falke, S., Sinz, C.: LLBMC: Bounded Model Checking of C and C++ Programs Using a Compiler IR. In: Joshi, R., Müller, P., Podelski, A. (eds.) VSTTE 2012. LNCS, vol. 7152, pp. 146–161. Springer, Heidelberg (2012)
33. Nadel, A.: Boosting minimal unsatisfiable core extraction. In: FMCAD (2010)
34. Nadel, A., Ryvchin, V., Strichman, O.: Efficient MUS Extraction with Resolution. In: FMCAD (2013)

PEALT: An Automated Reasoning Tool for Numerical Aggregation of Trust Evidence

Michael Huth and Jim Huan-Pu Kuo

Department of Computing, Imperial College London
London, SW7 2AZ, United Kingdom
{m.huth,jimhkuo}@imperial.ac.uk

Abstract. We present a tool PEALT that supports the understanding and validation of mechanisms that numerically aggregate trust evidence of potentially heterogenous sources. Such mechanisms are expressed in the policy composition language Peal and subjected to vacuity checking, sensitivity analysis of thresholds, and policy refinement. Verification code is generated by either compiling away numerical references prior to constraint solving or by delegating numerical reasoning to Z3, the common back-end constraint solver of PEALT. The former gives compact diagnostics but restricts value ranges and may be space intensive. The latter generates compact verification code, but gives verbose diagnostics, and may struggle with multiplicative reasoning. We experimentally compare code generation and verification running times of these methods on randomly generated analyses and on a non-random benchmark modeling majority voting. Our findings suggest both methods have complementary value and may scale up well for the analysis of most realistic case studies.

1 Introduction

Trust is a fundamental factor that influences decisions pertaining to human interactions, be they social or economic in nature. Mayer et al. [11] offer a definition of trust as *"... the willingness to be vulnerable, based on positive expectation about the behavior of others."* These expectations of the trustor would be informed by trust signals exchanged with the trustee of a planned interaction. Trust has an economic incentive, it avoids the use of costly measures that guarantee *assurance* in the absence of trust-enabled interaction. We note that assurance is the established means of realizing "IT security". Traditionally, trust signals (e.g. body language) could be observed both in spatial and temporal proximity to a planned interaction. Modern IT infrastructures, however, disembed agents in space and in time from such signals and interaction resources, making it hard to use existing trust mechanics such as those proposed in [17] in this setting [10].

This identifies a need for a *calculus* in which trust and distrust signals can be expressed and aggregated to support decision making in a variety of applications (e.g. financial transactions, software installations, and run-time monitoring of hardware). In our proposed methodology, signals of trust or distrust have no effect in their absence but evaluate to a score in their presence. These scores

E. Ábrahám and K. Havelund (Eds.): TACAS 2014, LNCS 8413, pp. 109–123, 2014.

may be determined by techniques suitable for the types of signals, e.g. machine learning if signals are features, metrics if signals indicate trustworthiness of IT infrastructures, etc. This then makes it challenging to devise a calculus for combining scores of different types in a manner that articulates the expectations in trust-mediated interactions. Let us give some examples of this.

Trust of an individual in an online transaction will depend, amongst other things, on the monetary value of that transaction, the reputation of the seller, and contextual information such as recommendations from friends. IT infrastructures in highly dynamic and volatile environments such as military operating theatres can no longer be secured in a binary "secure or insecure" manner. They have to react to risks in agile manners [1], suggesting the use of compositional metrics for run-time trust management. Similarly, run-time systems may want to monitor executing code by measuring signals from execution characteristics – such as the threat level of parsed input (e.g. input such as meta-data may serve as an attack surface [19]), the domain of a remote procedure call, etc. – and aggregate such evidence to control execution paths. We refer to [8] for a case study of such execution control in the Scala programming language, where methods are annotated with *expectation blocks* – a precursor of the language Peal [4] – whose aggregation computes what corresponds to the score of a policy set in Peal.

These examples suggest a trust calculus needs to express evidence that is not only rooted in trust (e.g. an asset value), needs to be extensible for domain-specific expressions of signals (e.g. those of a social network), and requires a means of calculating trust from observed signals (e.g. compositional metrics). In [4], such a language Peal was proposed in which signals are abstract predicates whose truth triggers a score, and where score aggregation captures reasoning about levels of trust. In [4], several analyses were also defined that assess if trust calculations perform as expected by specifiers. Verification of trust calculations is thus a key ingredient of such an approach, and the focus of this paper.

We here express the analysis of Peal expressions as constraints that can be analyzed with the SMT solver Z3, and so capture *logical dependencies* of (dis)trust signals. Specifically, we refine and extend the language Peal of [4] to support a richer calculus, we implement analyses proposed in [4] in the SMT solver Z3 on this richer language via two different methods of automated Z3 code generation in PEALT, and we experimentally explore the trade-offs of both methods.

Outline of paper. Section 2 contains background on Peal and the SMT solver Z3. Design and implementation of PEALT are outlined in Section 3. In Section 4, we describe two methods for converting conditions used in analyses into Z3 input. The validation of PEALT via experiments and other activities is reported in Section 5. Section 6 contains related work, and Section 7 concludes the paper.

2   Background

Peal: a **P***luggable* **E***vidence* **A***ggregation* **L***anguage.* The syntax of language Peal is shown in Figure 1. In Peal, a rule *rule* consists of a predicate or signal q_j and its declared score s_j, has no effect if predicate q_j is false (no signal), and has score s_j as effect otherwise (signal present). Policies *pol* have form as in

$$p_i = op\,((q_1\ s_1)\dots(q_n\ s_n))\ default\ s \qquad \text{or} \qquad p_i = op\,()\ default\ s \qquad (1)$$

contain zero or more rules, a default score s, and an aggregation operator *op*. Policy p_i returns default score s if all its rules have false predicates; otherwise it returns the result of applying *op* to all scores s_j of true predicates q_j. The

$$
\begin{aligned}
op &::= min \mid max \mid + \mid * \\
rule &::= if\ (q)\ score \\
pol &::= op\,(rule^*)\ default\ score \\
pSet &::= pol \mid max(pSet, pSet) \mid min(pSet, pSet) \\
cond &::= th < pSet \mid pSet \le th
\end{aligned}
$$

Fig. 1. Syntax of Peal where q ranges over some language of predicates, and *th* and *score* range over real numbers (potentially restricted by domains or analysis methods)

design of Peal is layered as in [4]. Supported aggregation operators are *min* (e.g. for *distrust* signals), *max* (e.g. for trust signals), $+$ (e.g. for accumulative signals), and $*$ (e.g. for aggregating independent probabilistic evidence). Policies are composed into policy sets (*pSet*) using *max* and *min*. Finally, policy sets are compared to thresholds *th* using inequalities in conditions *cond*. The intuition is that scores and thresholds are real numbers but that some analysis methods may constrain the ranges of said values. The latter is one reason why the PEALT input language under-specifies such design choices. The meaning of policy composition is context-dependent. For example, if a condition $th < min(pS1, pS2)$ is used in support of recommending an action, e.g., then *min* acts as a *pessimistic* composition since the score of any of its arguments may falsify this condition.

SMT solver Z3. Satisfiability modulo theories [5] is supported with robust and powerful tools, that combine the state-of-the-art of deductive theorem proving with that of SAT solving for propositional logic. The SMT solver Z3 has a declarative input language for defining constants, functions, and assertions about them [12]. Figure 2 shows Z3 input code to illustrate that language and its principal analysis directives. On the left, constants of Z3 type Bool and Real are declared. Then an assertion defines that the Boolean constant q1 means that x is less than $y + 1$, and the next assertion insists that q1 be true. The directives check-sat and get-model instruct Z3 to find a witness of the satisfiability of the conjunction of all visible assertions, and to report such a witness (called a model). On the right, we see what Z3 reports for the input on the left: sat states that there is a model; other possible replies are unsat (there cannot be a model), and unknown (Z3 does not know whether or not a model exists).

```
(declare-const q1 Bool)          sat
(declare-const x,y Real)         (model
(assert (= q1 (< x (+ y 1))))      (define-fun y () Real 0.0 )
(assert q1)                        (define-fun q1 () Bool true )
(check-sat)                        (define-fun x () Real 0.0
(get-model)                      )
```

Fig. 2. Left: Z3 input with directives to find and generate a model. Right: Z3 output for this input, a model that makes all input assertions true. (Both edited to save space.)

3   Workflow and Input Language of PEALT

The tool is rendered as a web application which accepts analysis declarations. The declared analyses can be converted to Z3 input code, followed by calling Z3 and getting feedback on running such code. The tool also allows generation of random declarations or creation of majority-voting condition instances – the latter stress test the explicit method for Z3 code generation described below. A typical workflow of using PEALT would be to generate/write/edit Peal conditions and their analyses, to run these analyses on the Z3 code the tool compiles, and to study the Z3 output to decide whether further such actions are needed. Analyses such as `different?` c1 c2 have keywords ending in ? and list conditions as arguments. Users may specify any number of analyses. Generated Z3 input code will execute each declared analysis in turn using a visibility stack discipline for assertions, as detailed in Section 4.

Example 1. Figure 3 shows an example of PEALT input that may model trust perceptions when downloading a software installation and where a non-matching hash of the download, e.g., is mitigated by the fact that the download was done in a browser X that may non-maliciously change file signatures in that process. In the example, both analyses have negative outcome.

Keywords `POLICIES` etc. divide declarations into sorts: policies, policy sets, conditions, domain-specific declarations, and analyses. Keyword *if* is omitted from rules in PEALT input for sake of succinctness. A simple naming construct `name = expr` is used to uniformly bind expressions from the syntactic categories for policies, policy sets, conditions, and analyses to names that can be referenced without any scope restrictions. The syntax for policies, policy sets, and conditions is hoped to be intuitive enough given the definition of Peal. Domain-specific declarations are written in zone `DOMAIN_SPECIFICS`, are expressed directly in Z3 code, and assume that all predicates within rules of declared policies are declared in Z3 input as Z3 type `Bool` already.

We implemented two different ways of generating Z3 input code for declarations entered into PEALT: an explicit and a symbolic one, whose details we will provide below. Intuitively, explicit code generation compiles away any references to numerical values to capture logically – without loss of arithmetic precision – the declared analyses; whereas symbolic code generation statically encodes the

```
POLICIES
b1 = min ((companyDevice 0.1) (uncertifiedOrigin 0.2) (nonMatchingHash 0.2)) default 1
b2 = + ((downloadWithBrowserX 0.1) (useIOS 0.2) (useLinux 0.1) (recentPatch 0.1)) default 0
POLICY_SETS
pSet = min(b1, b2)
CONDITIONS
cond1 = 0.2 < pSet
cond2 = 0.1 < pSet
DOMAIN_SPECIFICS
(declare-const numberOfDaysSinceLastPatch Real)
(assert (= recentPatch (< numberOfDaysSinceLastPatch 7)))
ANALYSES
ana1 = always_true? cond1
ana2 = equivalent? cond1 cond2
```

Fig. 3. Trust perceptions of software download in PEALT, with two analyses

operational semantics of **Peal** through use of numerical declarations in order for Z3 to be able to reason about all possible dynamic settings. Z3 code generation may produce an exponential blow-up in the explicit method whereas the symbolic one typically finds it harder to reason about multiplication.

Users can specify which code generation method (explicit or symbolic) to use, whether to just compile Z3 input code, and whether to also run it and display results. Users also have the option of downloading the generated Z3 code (as it may be large). For the explicit method, one may just generate results of all analyses in pretty-printed, minimal form. We don't offer this for the symbolic method as its code generation prevents the creation of minimal output models. PEALT is written in Scala 2.10.2 using the Lift web framework. After converting Peal declarations into Z3 input code, PEALT interfaces with the SMT solver Z3 (version 4.3.1) by launching it as an external process via Scala's *ProcessBuilder*.

4   Z3 Code Generation

Our tool only generates code for conditions that are *used*: i.e. that are declared in the input panel *and* occur in at least one declared analysis as argument. Let `c1` be the declared name of such a condition for declaration $c1 = cond$. We generate Z3 code that declares `c1` as Z3 type `Bool` and adds an assert statement that binds the name `c1` to $\phi[cond]$ via (`assert` (= `c1` $\phi[cond]$)) where $\phi[cond]$ is Z3 code for the logical formula generated for condition `cond`.

The code generated for $\phi[cond]$ explicitly or implicitly lists all signal scenarios that *may* occur if we ignore any logical dependencies between signals. This means that we delegate to our analysis backend, the Z3 SMT solver, the task of only generating scenarios in analyses that are also *logically feasible*. We now describe two methods for generating Z3 code for $\phi[cond]$, starting with the explicit one.

Explicit code generation. For sake of succinctness, we state $\phi[cond]$ here as a formula of propositional logic over predicates and not as Z3 input. The definition of $\phi[cond]$ is given by structural induction over the policy set argument in *cond*, as shown in Figure 4. In the first four equations, *min* and *max* compositions of policy sets create disjunctions or conjunctions of simpler code generation problems, depending on the type of inequality in *cond*. The first equation, for example, expresses that the minimum of (the score of) two policy sets is less than or equal to a threshold iff that it the case for one of these two policy sets.

The next four equations define auxiliary predicates Q_1 to Q_4 that we can use to specify the remaining cases of conditions that involve only a sole policy. All such conditions first generate the code context for the *non-default* case: in (6), the default score of the sole policy in the condition is compatible with the inequality. Therefore, we generate a disjunction whose first disjunct captures the default case when all predicates of all rules are false, and whose second disjunct captures the non-default case. In (7), the default score of the sole policy is incompatible with the inequality of its condition *cond* and so only the non-default case may apply. Therefore, we generate a conjunction that forces at least one predicate and the formula generated for the non-default case to be true.

It remains to describe the code generation for the non-default case $\phi_{op}^{ndf}[cond]$: in (8), code generation of $\phi_{op}^{ndf}[cond]$ adds a top-level negation and reverts the condition type when Q_3 holds – where $dual(pol \leq th)$ equals $th < pol$ and $dual(th < pol)$ equals $pol \leq th$. This means that we only have to deal with the same inequality type in the remaining cases, that enumerate scenarios. The enumeration process for *max* and *min* in (9) is clear. For example, $\phi_{max}^{ndf}[th < pol]$ is a disjunction of all predicates in *pol* whose scores are strictly larger than *th*.

The code generation in (10) applies to conditions $pol \leq th$ for $*$ policies *pol*, and conditions $th < pol$ for $+$ policies *pol*. In these cases, we enumerate all minimal scenarios of present signals that make the condition true. These scenarios are minimal in that any smaller subset of present signals won't make the condition true. The code therefore generates a disjunction of monomials where each monomial describes such a minimal scenario. Concretely, as $+$ is monotone and the inequality is $th < pol$, we only need to generate *minimal* index sets X such that the sum of all s_i with i in X is above *th*. These X are the elements of set $\mathcal{M}_+$ which is computed by $enum_+$ in Figure 5. The Boolean guard in the *while*-loop of $enum_+$ makes use of the partial sums t_i to ensure that recursive calls to $enum_+$ are only made when they will still enumerate at least one new element of $\mathcal{M}_+$. The correctness proof for $enum_+$ is straightforward: all such minimal index sets X are generated in some recursive execution path (completeness), and all enumerated index sets are indeed minimal (soundness, which requires the scores to be sorted in ascending order). Algorithm $enum_*$ enumerates all minimal scenarios in the case of a $*$ policy in $pol \leq th$ and is dual to $enum_+$: it reverts all inequalities for *th*, lists scores in descending order, and therefore retains the requirement to compute *minimal* index sets. The correctness proof for $enum_*$ is that for $enum_+$ modulo that duality.

Let us discuss what restrictions use of this explicit code generation imposes on the PEALT input language. It requires that all scores within $*$ policies be within $[0, 1]$ so that $*$ is anti-tone; that all scores within $+$ policies be non-negative to get a correct interpretation of *minimal* index sets in $enum_+$; whereas scores within *max* and *min* policies may be any real numbers, since the inequalities

$$\phi[min(pS_1, pS_2) \le th] \overset{\text{def}}{=} \phi[pS_1 \le th] \vee \phi[pS_2 \le th] \tag{2}$$

$$\phi[max(pS_1, pS_2) \le th] \overset{\text{def}}{=} \phi[pS_1 \le th] \wedge \phi[pS_2 \le th] \tag{3}$$

$$\phi[th < min(pS_1, pS_2)] \overset{\text{def}}{=} \phi[th < pS_1] \wedge \phi[th < pS_2] \tag{4}$$

$$\phi[th < max(pS_1, pS_2)] \overset{\text{def}}{=} \phi[th < pS_1] \vee \phi[th < pS_2] \tag{5}$$

$$Q_1(pol, cond) \overset{\text{def}}{=} (s \le th, cond = pol \le th) \vee (th < s, cond = th < pol)$$

$$Q_2(pol, cond) \overset{\text{def}}{=} (th < s, cond = pol \le th) \vee (s \le th, cond = th < pol)$$

$$Q_3(op, cond) \overset{\text{def}}{=} (op \in \{+, max\}, cond = pol \le th) \vee (op \in \{*, min\}, cond = th < pol)$$

$$Q_4(op, cond) \overset{\text{def}}{=} (op = *, cond = pol \le th) \vee (op = +, cond = th < pol)$$

$$\phi[cond] \overset{\text{def}}{=} (\neg q_1 \wedge \cdots \wedge \neg q_n) \vee \phi_{op}^{ndf}[cond] \qquad \text{(when } Q_1(pol, cond) \text{ is true)} \tag{6}$$

$$\phi[cond] \overset{\text{def}}{=} (q_1 \vee \cdots \vee q_n) \wedge \phi_{op}^{ndf}[cond] \qquad \text{(when } Q_2(pol, cond) \text{ is true)} \tag{7}$$

$$\phi_{op}^{ndf}[cond] \overset{\text{def}}{=} \neg \phi_{op}^{ndf}[dual(cond)] \qquad \text{(when } Q_3(op, cond) \text{ is true)} \tag{8}$$

$$\phi_{max}^{ndf}[th < pol] \overset{\text{def}}{=} \bigvee_{i | th < s_i} q_i \qquad \phi_{min}^{ndf}[pol \le th] \overset{\text{def}}{=} \bigvee_{i | s_i \le th} q_i \tag{9}$$

$$\phi_{op}^{ndf}[cond] \overset{\text{def}}{=} \bigvee_{X \in \mathcal{M}_{op}} \bigwedge_{i \in X} q_i \qquad \text{(when } Q_4(op, cond) \text{ is true)} \tag{10}$$

Fig. 4. Explicit code generation (recursively): pol has form as in (1); predicates Q_1 to Q_4 drive the compilation logic; the computation of sets $\mathcal{M}_{op}$ is detailed in Figure 5

```
enum_+(X, acc, index, op) {                    enum_*(X, acc, index, op) {
  if (th < acc) { output X; }                    if (acc ≤ th) { output X; }
  else {                                         else {
    j = index - 1;                                 j = index - 1;
    while ((0 ≤ j) ∧ (th < op(acc, t_j))) {        while ((0 ≤ j) ∧ (op(acc, t_j) ≤ th)) {
      enum_+(X ∪ {j}, op(acc, s_j), j, op);          enum_*(X ∪ {j}, op(acc, s_j), j, op);
      j = j - 1; }}}                                 j = j - 1; }}}
```

Fig. 5. Left: algorithm $enum_+$ computes $\mathcal{M}_+$ where scores s_i are sorted in ascending order. Right: algorithm $enum_*$ computes $\mathcal{M}_*$ where s_i are sorted in descending order. Initial call context is $(\{\}, 0, n, +)$ for $enum_+$ and $(\{\}, 1, n, *)$ for $enum_*$.

in (9) have the intended meaning for all sign combinations. Z3 code generated for the PEALT input in Figure 3 is shown in Figure 6. PEALT uses the **push** and **pop** directives of Z3 in order to add constraints specific to an analysis onto the top of the assertion visibility stack that Z3 maintains, and to discharge these assertions before turning to the next analysis. The Z3 code generated for analyses is verbatim the same for the symbolic code generation to which we turn next.

```
(declare-const recentPatch Bool)
(declare-const useLinux Bool)
(declare-const uncertifiedOrigin Bool)
(declare-const companyDevice Bool)
(declare-const downloadWithBrowserX Bool)
(declare-const useIOS Bool)
(declare-const nonMatchingHash Bool)
(declare-const cond2 Bool)
(declare-const cond1 Bool)
(assert (= cond1 (and (or (and (not companyDevice) (not uncertifiedOrigin) (not nonMatchingHash))
              (not (or companyDevice uncertifiedOrigin nonMatchingHash)))
              (and (or downloadWithBrowserX useIOS useLinux recentPatch)
              (or (and useIOS recentPatch) (and useIOS useLinux) (and useIOS downloadWithBrowserX)
              (and recentPatch useLinux downloadWithBrowserX))))))
(assert (= cond2 (and (or (and (not companyDevice) (not uncertifiedOrigin) (not nonMatchingHash))
              (not companyDevice)) (and (or downloadWithBrowserX useIOS useLinux recentPatch)
              (or useIOS (and recentPatch useLinux) (and recentPatch downloadWithBrowserX)
              (and useLinux downloadWithBrowserX))))))

(echo "Result of analysis [ana1 = always_true? cond1]:")
(push)
(declare-const always_true_ana1 Bool)
(assert (= always_true_ana1 cond1))
(assert (not always_true_ana1))
(check-sat)
(get-model)
(pop)

(echo "Result of analysis [ana2 = equivalent? cond1 cond2]:")
(push)
(declare-const equivalent_ana2 Bool)
(assert (= equivalent_ana2 (or (and cond1 (not cond2)) (and (not cond1) cond2))))
(assert equivalent_ana2)
(check-sat)
(get-model)
(pop)
```

Fig. 6. Explicitly generated code for input from Figure 3 (hand edited to save space)

Symbolic code generation. This method also binds the name c1 of declaration c1 = cond to its condition via (assert (= c1 $\phi[cond]$)). But for each policy p_i occurring in *cond*, it also declares a constant *cond_p_i* of Z3 type Bool and then generates $\phi[cond]$ as a positive Boolean formula over the constants *cond_p_i*. This process follows the same logic as for explicit code generation in (2) to (5). For each declared constant cond_p_i of Z3 type Bool, it then adds an assert statement (assert (= cond_p_i $\phi[cond\_p_i]$)) that defines the meaning of *cond_p_i*. For policies p_i of form as in (1), the code generated is similar to the one of the explicit method when *op* equals *min* or *max* – we refer to [7] for further details.

Let *op* equal $*$ or $+$ and policy p_i occur in at least one condition within some declared analysis. Then the code generation for $\phi[cond\_p_i]$ in Figure 7 trades off the space complexity of enumerating elements in $\mathcal{M}_+$ and $\mathcal{M}_*$ with the time complexity of solving real-valued inequalities in the Z3 SMT solver. For each predicate q_j within p_i, we declare a constant $p_i\_score\_q_j$ of Z3 type Real, and add two assertions that, combined, model that the value of $p_i\_score\_q_j$ is s_j iff q_j is true, and that this value equals the unit of $+$ (respectively, $*$) iff q_j is false. This means that we can precisely model the *effect* of the non-default case (when at least one q_j is true) by aggregating all values $p_i\_score\_q_j$ with *op*, and by comparing that aggregated result to the threshold in the specified manner

($<$ or $\geq$). Crucially, the values of $p_i\_score\_q_j$ for predicates that happen to be false won't contaminate this aggregated value as they are units for operator op.

The encoding for symbolic code generation is therefore *linear* in the size of *cond*. Using this encoding, we can now express $\phi[cond\_p_i]$ in Z3 by directly encoding the "operational" semantics of $cond\_p_i$: either the default score satisfies the inequality and all policy predicates are false, or at least one policy predicate is true and the aggregation of all values $p_i\_score\_q_j$ with op satisfies the inequality. These Z3 declarations and expressions are stated in Figure 7.

```
(declare-const p_i_score_q_j Real)
(assert (implies q_j (= s_i p_i_score_q_j)))
(assert (implies (not (= <unit> p_i_score_q_j)) q_j))

(or (and (cop th s) (not (or q_1 ... q_n)))
    (and (or q_1 ... q_n)
         (cop th (op p_i_score_q_1 ... p_i_score_q_n))))
```

Fig. 7. Top: declarations for $p_i\_score\_q_j$ where s_j is s_j, and <unit> is 0.0 for + policies p_i and 1.0 for * policies p_i. Bottom: Z3 code for $\phi[cond\_p_i]$ for the first case in (1); comparison operator cop is $<$ for $th < p_i$ or $\geq$ for $th \geq p_i$, and th denotes th.

The symbolic code generation described above imposes no restrictions on the ranges of scores s_i. PEALT allows us to replace s_i with an arithmetic expression such as any real numbers c, real variables x, or products thereof $(c \cdot x)$.

Analyses. Analysis `implies?` checks whether the first condition logically implies the second one, which is a form of policy refinement. Analyses `always_false?` and `satisfiable?` are "equivalent" but capture different intent of the user, ditto for analysis `equivalent?` versus analysis `different?`. A typical use of analysis `different?` is to check whether conditions differ for $0.5 < pSet$ and $0.6 < pSet$, i.e. whether $pSet$ is sensitive to the increase of threshold value from 0.5 to 0.6.

Specification of domain specifics. Users may add domain-specific constraints or knowledge as Z3 code within zone `DOMAIN_SPECIFICS`: e.g. to declare variables with which one can then define the exact meaning of predicates used in rules (e.g. as a means of adding parameters to signals), to encode required properties of the modeling domain, and to perhaps add assertions that guide the search of a model of some analysis. The use of raw Z3 code means that any code generation method will simply copy and paste this code into the generated Z3 input code. We realize that our decision to automatically generate Z3 declarations of all variables occurring in rules might confuse novice users, though, when they try to declare these as Z3 types within zone `DOMAIN_SPECIFICS` explicitly.

Witness generation. For each declared analysis, Z3 will try to decide it when running PEALT. If the Z3 output is `unsat`, then we know that there is no witness to the query – e.g. for `always_true?` this would mean that Z3 decides that the condition cannot be false, and so the answer is "yes, always true". If the Z3 output is sat, then we report the correct answer (e.g. for always_true? we say "no, not always true") and generate supporting evidence for this answer. For explicit code generation, the generated models tend to be very short (few crucial truth values of predicates q_i and supporting values of variables used to define these q_i if applicable). PEALT can post-processes this raw Z3 output to extract this information in pretty-printed form, an example thereof is seen in Figure 8. For symbolic code generation, model list truth values for *almost all* declared predicates q_i that occur in at least one $*$ or $+$ policy. The reason for this seems to stem from the assertions we declare for variables p_i_score_q_j in Figure 7. We mean to investigate how to shorten such evidence in future work.

```
Result of analysis [ana1 = always_true? cond1]
cond1 is NOT always true
For example, when useLinux is true, recentPatch is true,
nonMatchingHash is true, companyDevice is false
```

Fig. 8. Sample of pretty printed evidence for satisfiability witness computed from explicitly generated code for always_true? from Figure 3 (hand edited to save space)

Execution constraints. To summarize, explicit code generation of policies within analyzed conditions requires that no $*$ policy has scores outside $[0, 1]$ and that no other policy has negative or non-constant scores. For symbolic code generation, we only have to ensure that *min* and *max* policies have constant scores (negative ones are allowed), and we mean to lift the latter restriction in future work.

5   Validation

We report experimental results for code generation methods and execution of generated code on random and non-random analyses. We also discuss other tool validation activities we conducted. All experiments were run on a test server with two, 6-core, Intel E5 CPUs running at 2.5GHz and 48G of RAM.

Non-random benchmark. We use condition $0.5 < p_{mv(n)}$ with $+$ policy $p_{mv(n)}$, default score 0, and n many rules each with score $1/n$. The condition is true when more than half of the predicates are true ("majority voting"). There are no logical dependencies of predicates in $p_{mv(n)}$ and the size of $\mathcal{M}_+$ is exponential in n. We can generate explicitly Z3 input code for values of n up to 27 (when code takes up half a gigabyte), and code generation takes more than five minutes for n being 23. By comparison, we could generate symbolically such code and verify that this condition is true, within five minutes each, for n up to 49408.

Randomly generated analyses. We also implemented a feature

$$randPeal\ n, m_{min}, m_{max}, m_+, m_*, p, th, \delta$$

that randomly generates a policy set *pSet*, two conditions $th < pSet$ and $th + \delta < pSet$ and analyses the first one with always_true?, the second one with always_false?, and then applies different? to both conditions. Predicates are randomly selected from a pool of p many predicates (with $n \leq p$). Scores are chosen from $[0, 1]$ uniformly at random. In $pSet$, there are n policies for each operator op of Peal (i.e. $4n$ policies in total) and each op policy has m_{op} many rules. For the maximal k with $2^k \leq 4n$, we combine 2^k policies using alternating max and min compositions on their full binary parse tree; the result is further composed with the remaining $4n - 2^k$ policies (if applicable) by grouping these in min pairs, and by adding these pairs in alternating min and max compositions to the binary policy tree. This stress tests policy composition above and beyond what one would expect in practical specifications.

We then conducted three experiments that share an execution and termination logic: experimental input to $randPeal$ has only one degree of freedom and we use unbounded binary search to see (within granularity of 10 and for five randomly generated condition pairs) whether both code generation methods can generate Z3 code within five minutes, and whether Z3 can perform each analysis within that same time frame. If this fails for one of these condition pairs, we stop binary expansion and go to a bisection mode to find the boundary.

Experiment 1 picks for operator min input headers $1, x, 1, 1, 1, 3x, 0.5, 0.1$ so it explores how many (x) rules a sole min policy can handle within five minutes. The same evaluation is done for the other three operators. We also investigated a variant of this experiment – Exp 1 (DS) – for which we also add as many assertions as there are declared predicates in the conditions, as described in [7]. This uses a function calledBy that models method call graphs with at most one incoming edge (using a forall axiom in Z3 code) and declares a third of these predicates to mean that a specific method called. The other two thirds define predicates as linear inequalities between real, respectively integer, variables (which may stem from method input headers) – please see [7] for details.

Experiment 2 picks for operator min the input headers $n, c, 1, 1, 1, 3c, 0.5, 0.1$ where c equals $x/10$ for the boundary value of x found in Experiment 1. We here explore how many min policies we can handle for a sizeable number of rules. The same evaluation is done for the other three operators. Experiment 3 picks for operator min input headers $n, n, 1, 1, 1, 3n, 0.5, 0.1$ so that we explore how many (the n) min policies with the same number of rules we can handle within five minutes. The same evaluation is done for the other three operators.

Results of these experiments are displayed in Figure 9. In their discussion we need to recognize that random analyses can have very different analysis times for the same configuration type. So a termination "boundary" does not mean that we cannot verify larger instances within five minutes, it just means that we encountered an instance at the reported boundary that took longer than that.

In the first experiment, Z3 code generation seems faster than execution of that Z3 code. We also see that up to two million rules can be handled for min and max for both code generation methods within two minutes. For $*$, explicit code generation seems to be one order of magnitude better than symbolic code generation, although the Z3 execution in the latter case appears to be faster. For $+$, on the other hand, symbolic code generation now seems to be an order

Exp 1	ex min	sy min	ex max	sy max	ex *	sy *	ex +	sy +
rules	1867904	1802240	2101248	2162688	120	16	144	5784
code	26s	20s	32s	22s	5s	0.1s	14s	0.6s
Z3	110s	181s	74s	132s	48s	3s	72s	133s

Exp 1 (DS)	ex min	sy min	ex max	sy max	ex *	sy *	ex +	sy +
rules	8064	6280	6544	7240	136	16	128	1848
code	0.9	0.8	0.8s	0.8	8s	0.1s	1s	1s
Z3	133s	88s	136s	150s	60s	14s	40s	91s

Exp 2	ex min	sy min	ex max	sy max	ex *	sy *	ex +	sy +
pol,rul	48,186790	56,180224	40,210124	56,216268	65888,12	4192,2	17488,14	24,578
code	264s	76s	169s	87s	279s	84s	277s	0.8s
Z3 time	438s	205s	44s	249s	4s	108s	2s	160s

Exp 3	ex min	sy min	ex max	sy max	ex *	sy *	ex +	sy +
pol=rul	2128	2552	2136	2936	88	16	96	160
code	271s	71s	293s	99s	85s	0.2s	160s	1s
Z3	8s	63s	8s	120s	17s	144s	26s	23s

Fig. 9. Experimental results: columns show code generation method ("ex"plicit or "sy"mbolic) and operator; rows show number of rules for policies of chosen operator in analyses, time (rounded to seconds) to generate Z3 code, and time to execute Z3 code

of magnitude better than the explicit one – handling thousands of rules in just over two minutes. When we add the domain-specific constraints in Exp 1 (DS), we notice that *min* and *max* can only handle about seven-thousand rules in a similar amount of time (compared to two million beforehand). The results for * for both methods and for + for explicit code generation seem about the same as without domain-specific constraints. But + now only can handle less than two-thousand rules for symbolic code generation. In the second experiment, the number of rules used for *max* and *min* is about two-hundred thousand. We can deal with about fifty policies with that many rules within five minutes, noting that code generation now takes more time. It is noteworthy that explicit code generation can handle over sixty-thousand * policies with 12 rules each, but that this drops to less than twenty-thousand + policies; the symbolic approach does not scale that well in comparison. In the third experiment, both methods can handle between two to three thousand policies with that many rules for *max* and *min*. For operators * and +, the explicit method spends most of its time in code generation whereas the symbolic one spends the bulk of its time in Z3 execution. For operator *, explicit code generation is still about an order of magnitude better whereas for + it is not significantly better.

Ideally, we would like to extend these experiments to larger data points. But such an attempt quickly reaches the memory boundary of our powerful server in explicit code generation. We also believe that practical case studies would not use more than a few dozen or hundreds of rules for each + and * policy declared, and so both approaches may actually work well then.

Software validation and future work. We have not yet encountered a Z3 output **unknown** for PEALT analyses, although this is easy to achieve by adding complex constraints as domain specifics. We validated both code generation methods by running them side by side on randomly generated analyses and checking whether they would produce conflicting answers (**unsat** and **sat**). During the development of PEALT, we encountered a few of these conflicts which helped to identify implementation bugs. Of course, this does not mean what we proved the correctness of our Z3 code generator (written in Scala), and doing so would be unwise as this generator will evolve with the tool language. Therefore, we want to independently verify the evidence computed by Z3, in future work. This will also verify that no **double** rounding errors in Z3 corrupted analysis outcomes. In future work, we also want to understand whether we can construct proofs for outputs **unsat** such that these proofs are meaningful for the analyses in question.

6   Related Work

The language in Figure 1 extends that in [4]: it supports policies without rules, * policies, negative and non-constant scores for symbolic code generation, and logical dependencies of predicates q_i within PEALT. The symbolic code generation in PEALT uses the same enumeration process for + and * on *minimal* index sets (and not maximal ones as in [4]). PEALT implements most analyses of [4] *with* logical dependencies, leaving more complex ones of [4] for future work.

The determination of scores is a fundamental concern in our approach, and where PEALT is meant to provide confidence in such scorings and their implications. The process of arriving at scores depends on the application domain, we offer two examples thereof from the literature. TrustBAC [3] extends role-based access control with levels of trust, scores in $[-1, 1]$, that are bound to roles in RBAC sessions. These levels are derived from a trust vector that reflects user behavior, user recommendations, and other sources. No analysis of these levels and their implications is offered. In [16], we see an example of how a sole score may reflect the integrity of an information infrastructure, as a formula that accounts for known vulnerabilities, threats that can exploit such vulnerabilities, and the likelihood for each vulnerability to exist in the given infrastructure. We should keep in mind that any such metrics are heuristics, and so it is important to analyze their impact on decision making, especially if other factors also influence such decisions. PEALT allows us, in principle, to conduct such analyses. Extant work enriches security elements with quantities, e.g. credential chains [18], security levels [15], trust-management languages [2], reputation [9], and combinations of reputation and trust [13,14]. But we are not aware of substantial tool support for analyzing the effect of such enrichments when combined with other aspects of evidence. Shinren [6] offers the ability to reason about both trust and distrust explicitly and in a declarative manner, with the support of priority composition operators for layers of trust and distrust. Although Peal is in principle expressive enough to encode most of this functionality, doing so would not constitute good engineering practice: this is a good example for when conditions of Peal would be expressions to be composed in upstream languages such as Shinren.

7   Conclusions

We have created a tool PEALT in which one can study different mechanisms of aggregating numerical trust evidence. We extended the policy-composition language Peal of [4] and modified the generation of verification conditions reported in [4] for Peal conditions to make them dischargeable with an SMT solver. We proposed two different means of generating such verification conditions and discussed both conceptual and experimental advantages and disadvantages of such methods. The explicit method compiles away any references to numerical values and so arrives at a purely logical formulation. The price for this may be an explosion in the length of the resulting formula and in the restriction of score ranges for certain policy composition operators (e.g. multiplication). The symbolic method creates formulas with only linear size in the conditions but shifts the computational burden to Z3 and its reasoning about linear arithmetic. Both methods delegate to Z3 logical feasibility checks of trust scenarios discovered in analyses. Our current PEALT prototype supports verification of policy refinement, vacuity checking, sensitivity analysis of thresholds in conditions, and non-constant scores (for symbolic code generation) to express metrics. We think PEALT is a good example of the benefits that can be gained by connecting to a powerful back-end such as the SMT solver Z3 for analyses. The version of the source code used in this paper is available on `https://bitbucket.org/jimhkuo/pealt`.

Acknowledgments. We thank Jason Crampton and Charles Morisset for very fruitful discussions on PEALT, anonymous reviewers for helpful comments, and Intel® Corporation for funding this work in its *Trust Evidence* research project.

References

1. Announcement of Cybersecurity Collaborative Research Alliance. Press Release, US Army Research Laboratory (October 15, 2013)
2. Bistarelli, S., Martinelli, F., Santini, F.: A semantic foundation for trust management languages with weights: An application to the *RT* family. In: Rong, C., Jaatun, M.G., Sandnes, F.E., Yang, L.T., Ma, J. (eds.) ATC 2008. LNCS, vol. 5060, pp. 481–495. Springer, Heidelberg (2008)
3. Chakraborty, S., Ray, I.: TrustBAC: integrating trust relationships into the RBAC model for access control in open systems. In: Proceedings of the Eleventh ACM Symposium on Access Control Models and Technologies, SACMAT 2006, pp. 49–58. ACM, New York (2006)
4. Crampton, J., Huth, M., Morisset, C.: Policy-based access control from numerical evidence. Tech. Rep. 2013/6, Imperial College London, Department of Computing (October 2013) ISSN 1469-4166 (Print), ISSN 1469-4174 (Online)

5. De Moura, L., Bjørner, N.: Satisfiability modulo theories: introduction and applications. Commun. ACM 54(9), 69–77 (2011)
6. Dong, C., Dulay, N.: Shinren: Non-monotonic trust management for distributed systems. In: Nishigaki, M., Jøsang, A., Murayama, Y., Marsh, S. (eds.) IFIPTM 2010. IFIP AICT, vol. 321, pp. 125–140. Springer, Heidelberg (2010)
7. Huth, M., Kuo, J.H.P.: PEALT: A reasoning tool for numerical aggregation of trust evidence. Tech. Rep. 2013/7, Imperial College London, Department of Computing (2013) ISSN 1469-4166 (Print)
8. Huth, M., Kuo, J.H.-P.: Towards verifiable trust management for software execution(extended abstract). In: Huth, M., Asokan, N., Čapkun, S., Flechais, I., Coles-Kemp, L. (eds.) TRUST 2013. LNCS, vol. 7904, pp. 275–276. Springer, Heidelberg (2013)
9. Jøsang, A., Ismail, R.: The beta reputation system. In: Proceedings of the 15th Bled Conference on Electronic Commerce, Bled, Slovenia, June 17-19 (2002)
10. Kirlappos, I., Sasse, M.A., Harvey, N.: Why trust seals don't work: A study of user perceptions and behavior. In: Katzenbeisser, S., Weippl, E., Camp, L.J., Volkamer, M., Reiter, M., Zhang, X. (eds.) TRUST 2012. LNCS, vol. 7344, pp. 308–324. Springer, Heidelberg (2012)
11. Mayer, R., Davis, J., Schoorman, F.D.: An integrative model of organizational trust. Academy of Management Review 20(3), 709–734 (1995)
12. de Moura, L., Bjørner, N.: Z3: An efficient SMT solver. In: Ramakrishnan, C.R., Rehof, J. (eds.) TACAS 2008. LNCS, vol. 4963, pp. 337–340. Springer, Heidelberg (2008)
13. Mui, L.: Computational Models of Trust and Reputation: Agents, Evolutionary Games, and Social Networks. Ph.D. thesis, Massachusetts Institute of Technology (2002)
14. Muller, T., Schweitzer, P.: On beta models with trust chains. In: Fernández-Gago, C., Martinelli, F., Pearson, S., Agudo, I. (eds.) IFIPTM. IFIP AICT, vol. 401, pp. 49–65. Springer, Heidelberg (2013)
15. Ni, Q., Bertino, E., Lobo, J.: Risk-based access control systems built on fuzzy inferences. In: Proceedings of the 5th ACM Symposium on Information, Computer and Communications Security, ASIACCS 2010, pp. 250–260. ACM, New York (2010), http://doi.acm.org/10.1145/1755688.1755719
16. Nurse, J.R.C., Creese, S., Goldsmith, M., Rahman, S.S.: Supporting human decision-making online using information-trustworthiness metrics. In: Marinos, L., Askoxylakis, I. (eds.) HAS/HCII 2013. LNCS, vol. 8030, pp. 316–325. Springer, Heidelberg (2013)
17. Riegelsberger, J., Sasse, M.A., McCarthy, J.D.: The mechanics of trust: A framework for research and design. Int. J. Hum.-Comput. Stud. 62(3), 381–422 (2005)
18. Schwoon, S., Jha, S., Reps, T.W., Stubblebine, S.G.: On generalized authorization problems. In: CSFW, pp. 202–218. IEEE Computer Society (2003)
19. Shapiro, R., Bratus, S., Smith, S.W.: "Weird Machines" in ELF: A Spotlight on the Underappreciated Metadata. In: Proceedings of the 7th USENIX Workshop on Offensive Technologies (WOOT 2013), 12 pages. USENIX (2013)

GRASShopper

Complete Heap Verification with Mixed Specifications

Ruzica Piskac[1], Thomas Wies[2,*], and Damien Zufferey[3]

[1] Yale University, USA
[2] New York University, USA
[3] MIT CSAIL, USA

Abstract. We present GRASShopper, a tool for compositional verification of heap-manipulating programs against user-provided specifications. What makes our tool unique is its decidable specification language, which supports mixing of assertions expressed in separation logic and first-order logic. The user of the tool can thus take advantage of the succinctness of separation logic specifications and the discipline of local reasoning. Yet, at the same time, she can revert to classical logic in the cases where decidable separation logic fragments are less suited, such as reasoning about constraints on data and heap structures with complex sharing. We achieve this combination of specification languages through a translation to programs whose specifications are expressed in a decidable fragment of first-order logic called GRASS. This logic is well-suited for automation using satisfiability modulo theory solvers. Unlike other tools that provide similar features, our decidability guarantees enable GRASShopper to produce detailed counterexamples for incorrect or underspecified programs. We have found this feature to be invaluable when debugging specifications. We present the underlying philosophy of the tool, describe the major technical challenges, and discuss implementation details. We conclude with an evaluation that considers challenging benchmarks such as sorting algorithms and a union/find data structure.

1 Introduction

We present GRASShopper, a new tool for compositional verification of heap manipulating programs against user-provided specifications. GRASShopper takes programs in a C-like procedural language as input. The tool checks that procedures mutually satisfy their contracts, that all memory accesses are safe, and that there are no memory leaks. The unique feature of the input language is that it admits specifications that freely mix assertions expressed in separation logic and first-order logic.

Separation logic (SL) [19] is an extension of Hoare logic for proving the correctness of heap-manipulating programs. SL assertions specify regions in the heap rather than the global state of the heap. This distinction to classical logic gives rise to a discipline of local reasoning where the specification of a program fragment C only concerns C's *footprint*, i.e., the portion of memory on which C operates. This approach typically yields succinct and natural specifications that closely resemble a programmer's intuition about program correctness. Separation logic has therefore spawned extensive research

---

* Supported in part by NSF grant CCS-1320583.

E. Ábrahám and K. Havelund (Eds.): TACAS 2014, LNCS 8413, pp. 124–139, 2014.

into developing tool support for automated verification of programs against SL specifications [3,4,9,27]. The cores of such tools are specialized theorem provers for checking entailments between SL assertions [2,6,7,21]. Much of the work on such provers aims at decidable fragments of separation logic to guarantee a robust user experience.

Despite the elegance of separation logic, there are certain situations where it is more appropriate to express specifications in classical logic. This includes, for example, situations in which data structures exhibit complex sharing or involve constraints about data, e.g., arithmetic constraints. Reasoning about such constraints is not directly supported by SL theorem provers. The question is then how to extend these provers without giving up on decidability and completeness guarantees.

Typically, theory reasoning is realized by using a satisfiability modulo theories (SMT) solver that is integrated with the SL entailment procedure [5]. However, the interplay between SL reasoning and theory reasoning is intricate, e.g. equalities inferred by the theory solvers must be propagated back to the SL solver. Guaranteeing completeness of such a combined procedure is brittle and often involves the reimplementation of infrastructure that is already provided by the SMT solver.

In our previous work, we developed a new approach for checking SL entailments that reduces to checking satisfiability of formulas expressed in a decidable fragment of first-order logic [22]. We refer to this fragment as the logic of graph reachability and stratified sets (GRASS). Formulas in this logic express properties of the structure of graphs, such as whether nodes in the graph are inter-reachable, as well as properties of sets of nodes. The combination of these two features enables a natural encoding of the semantics of SL assertions. The advantage of this approach is that we can now delegate all reasoning to the SMT solver, exploiting existing infrastructure for combinations [18] and extensions [25] of first-order theories to handle reasoning about data robustly.

In this paper, we present GRASShopper, a tool which extends our previous work with support for local reasoning. Inspired by implicit dynamic frames [20,24], we present a translation of programs with mixed separation logic and first-order logic specifications to programs with GRASS specifications. The translation and verification of the resulting program is fully automated. The key challenge in this approach is to ensure that the encoding of SL assertions and the support for local reasoning remains within a decidable logic. To this end, we present a decidable extension of the GRASS logic that suffices to express that reachability information concerning heap paths outside the footprint of a code fragment is preserved by the execution of that code fragment.

We implemented the decision procedure for our extension of GRASS on top of the SMT solver Z3 [8] and integrated this decision procedure into GRASShopper. We used the tool to automatically verify list-manipulating programs such as sorting algorithms whose specifications involve constraints on data. We further considered programs whose specifications are difficult to express in decidable SL fragments alone. One example is the find operation of a union/find data structure. The postcondition of this operation must describe a heap region that consists of an unbounded number of list segments. With our approach we can easily express this postcondition using a quantified constraint in classical logic, while using SL assertions to describe the precondition. The seamless yet robust combination of separation logic and classical logic in a specification language that supports local reasoning is the key contribution of this work.

```
1   struct Node { var data : int; var next: Node; }
2   predicate blseg(x: Node, y: Node, lb: int, ub: int) {
3       x = y ∨ x ≠ y * acc(x) * lb ⩽ x.data ⩽ ub * blseg(x.next, y, lb, ub)
4   }
5   predicate bslseg(x: Node, y: Node, lb: int, ub: int) {
6       x = y ∨ x ≠ y * acc(x) * lb ⩽ x.data ⩽ ub * bslseg(x.next, y, x.data, ub)
7   }
8   procedure quicksort(x: Node, y: Node, ghost lb: int, ghost ub: int) returns (rx: Node)
9       requires blseg(x, y, lb, ub);
10      ensures bslseg(rx, y, lb, ub);
11  { if (x≠y ∧ x.next≠y) {
12      var pivot: Node, z: Node;
13      rx, pivot := split(x, y, lb);
14      rx := quicksort(rx, pivot, lb, pivot.data);
15      z := quicksort(pivot.next, y, pivot.data, ub);
16      pivot.next := z;
17    } else { rx := x; }
18  }
```

Fig. 1. A partial implementation of a quicksort algorithm on singly-linked lists

2   Overview and Running Example

We illustrate our approach through an example that implements a quicksort algorithm for linked lists storing integer values. The implementation and specification is shown in Figure 1. We use the syntax of GRASShopper's input language (modulo mark-up).

The procedure quicksort takes two pointers x and y as input, marking the start and end points of the list segment that is to be sorted. This property is expressed by the SL assertion in the precondition of quicksort: the inductive predicate blseg(x, y, lb, ub). The predicate states that x and y are indeed the start and end points of an acyclic list segment. Furthermore, it states that the data values of this list segment are bounded from below and above by the values lb and ub, respectively. These values are passed to quicksort as additional ghost parameters. The atomic predicate acc(x) in the definition of blseg represents a heap region that consists of the single heap cell x. That is, acc(x) means that x is in the footprint of the predicate. Such SL assertions are combined to assertions describing larger heap regions using *spatial conjunction*, denoted by '*'. Spatial conjunction asserts that the composed heap regions are disjoint in memory. Hence, blseg describes an *acyclic* list segment. Note that atomic assertions such as x = y only express constraints on values but describe empty heap regions. In particular, x = y ∨ x ≠ y is not a tautology. Such constraints are called *pure* in SL jargon. Further note that spatial conjunction binds stronger than classical conjunction and disjunction.

The footprint of blseg(x, y, lb, ub) is also the initial footprint of procedure quicksort which, by induction, consists of all heap cells between x and y, excluding y. The quicksort procedure returns a pointer rx to the head of the sorted list segment, which we specify in the postcondition using the predicate bslseg(rx, y, lb, ub). For exposition purposes, we do not specify that the output list is a permutation of the input list.

In the recursive case, quicksort picks a pivot and splits the list into two segments, one containing all values smaller than pivot.data, and one containing all other values. To simplify the presentation, we have factored out the code for the actual splitting in

```
1   procedure split(x: Node, y: Node, ghost lb: int, ghost ub: int) returns (rx: Node, pivot: Node)
2     requires blseg(x, y, lb, ub) * x ≠ y;
3     ensures blseg(rx, pivot, lb, pivot.data) * blseg(pivot, y, pivot.data, ub);
4     ensures Btwn(next, rx, pivot, y) * pivot ≠ y * lb ≤ pivot.data ≤ ub;
```

Fig. 2. Specification of the procedure split used by quicksort

a separate procedure split. After splitting, quicksort recursively calls itself on the two sublists and concatenates the two sorted list segments.

We provide the specification of split but not its implementation. It is shown in Fig. 2. The specification is agnostic to implementation details such as whether only the data values are reordered in the list or the entire nodes. Multiple ensures, respectively, requires clauses in a procedure contract are implicitly connected by spatial conjunction.

The procedure split also demonstrates the convenience of a specification language that allows mixing of separation logic and reachability logic. The conjunct Btwn(next, rx, pivot, y) in the second ensures clause is a predicate in our logic GRASS. The predicate states that the node pivot lies between rx and y on the direct next path connecting the two nodes. That is, the two list segments described by the first ensures clause do not form a panhandle list. A panhandle list can occur if y is a dangling pointer to an unallocated node and split allocates that node and inserts it into the list segment from rx to pivot, thereby creating a cycle. Without the additional reachability constraint, the specification of split would be too weak to prove the correctness of quicksort because the final sorted list segment returned by quicksort must be acyclic. If we used either only separation logic or only reachability logic, the specification of procedure split would be considerably more complicated (assuming we stayed inside decidable fragments).

3   Verifying Programs with GRASShopper

The verification of the input program provided to GRASShopper proceeds in three steps: first we translate the program to an equivalent program whose specification is expressed solely in our first-order logic fragment GRASS; in the second step we encode the translated program into verification conditions (also expressed in GRASS) using standard verification condition generation; finally we decide the generated verification conditions using our GRASS solver. All three steps are fully automated in GRASShopper. We now explain these steps using the quicksort procedure as a running example.

3.1   Translation to GRASS Programs

We first describe the translation of the input program to a GRASS program. The translation must capture the semantics of Hoare triples in separation logic and preserve the ability to reason about correctness locally. For a Hoare triple $\{P\}C\{Q\}$ to be valid in separation logic, the precondition P must subsume the footprint of the program fragment C. That is, P specifies the portion of memory that C is allowed to access. This semantics enables local reasoning, which is distilled into the so-called *frame rule*. The frame rule states that if $\{P\}C\{Q\}$ is valid, then so is $\{P * F\}C\{Q * F\}$ for any SL assertion F. That is, C does not affect the state of memory regions disjoint from its footprint. The assertion F is referred to as the *frame* of the rule application.

The frame rule enables compositional symbolic execution of program fragments. For example in quicksort, the symbolic state after the call to split in line 13 is described by the postcondition of split. The first subsequent recursive call to quicksort then only operates on the first sublist blseg(rx,pivot,lb,ub) of that symbolic state, leaving blseg(pivot,y,lb,ub) in the frame. The frame rule then implies that this second sublist is not modified by the first recursive call. All such applications of the frame rule for procedure calls are made explicit in the GRASS program.

The translation to a GRASS program proceeds one procedure at a time. Each resulting procedure is equivalent to its counterpart in the input program, modulo auxiliary ghost state. This auxiliary ghost state makes the semantics of separation logic specifications explicit and encodes the applications of the frame rule. Figure 3 shows the result of the translation for the quicksort procedure. The translation works as follows.

Alloc. First, we introduce a global ghost variable Alloc (line 2), which is used to model allocation and deallocation instructions. That is, at any point of execution, Alloc denotes the set of all Node objects that are currently allocated on the heap.

Footprints and Implicit Frame Inference. Each procedure maintains its own footprint throughout its execution using the dedicated local ghost variable FP. That is, at any point of a procedure's execution, FP contains the set of all heap nodes that the procedure has permission to access or modify at that point. Each heap access or modification is therefore guarded by an assert statement that checks whether the modification is permitted by the current footprint (see, e.g., lines 25 and 29). The translation maintains the invariant that footprints contain only allocated nodes. That is, both allocation and deallocation instructions affect FP.

For each procedure call, the footprint of the caller is passed to the callee and the callee returns the new footprint of the caller. That is, it is the callee's responsibility to inform the caller about allocation and deallocation operations that affect the caller's footprint. For this purpose, each procedure is instrumented with an additional ghost input parameter FP_Caller and an additional ghost return parameter FP_Caller'.

The contract of the translated procedure governs the transfer of permissions between caller and callee via the exchanged footprints and ties the footprints to the translations of the separation logic specifications in the original procedure contract. The initial value of FP in the translated procedure is determined by the footprint of the separation logic assertions in the precondition of the input procedure, which itself must be a subset of the callers footprint (line 16).

Note that the ghost variable FP is declared as an implicit ghost input parameter of the procedure (line 13). The semantics of an implicit ghost parameter is that it is existentially quantified across the entire procedure contract[1]. That is, during verification condition generation, the precondition of the contract is asserted at the call site with all implicit ghost parameters existentially quantified. When the solver checks the generated verification condition for this assertion, it needs to find a witness for FP, thereby implicitly inferring the frame of the procedure call that is used in the application of

---

[1] We adhere to the usual semantics of procedure contracts where input parameters occuring in ensures clauses refer to the initial values of these parameters.

```
1   struct Node { var data : Int; var next: Node; }
2   ghost var Alloc: set<Node>;
3   function blseg_fp(x: Node, y: Node) returns (Footprint: set<Node>) {
4       Footprint = {z: Node :: Btwn(next, x, z, y) ∧ z ≠ y}
5   }
6   predicate blseg_struct(x: Node, y: Node, lb: int, ub: int) {
7       Btwn(next, x, y, y) ∧ ∀z ∈ blseg_fp(x, y) :: lb ≤ z.data ≤ ub
8   }
9   predicate bslseg_struct(x: Node, y: Node, lb: int, ub: int) {
10      blseg_struct(x,y,lb,ub) ∧ ∀z,w ∈ blseg_fp(x, y) :: Btwn(next,z,w,y) ⇒ z.data ≤ w.data
11  }
12  procedure quicksort(x: Node, y: Node, ghost lb: int, ghost ub: int,
13          ghost FP_Caller: set<Node>, implicit ghost FP: set<Node>)
14      returns (rx: Node, ghost FP_Caller': set<Node>)
15      requires blseg_struct(x, y, lb, ub);
16      requires FP = blseg_fp(x, y) ∧ FP ⊆ FP_Caller;
17      free requires FP_Caller ⊆ Alloc ∧ null ∉ Alloc;
18      modifies next, data, Alloc;
19      ensures bslseg_struct(rx, y, lb, ub);
20      ensures blseg_fp(rx, y) = (Alloc ∩ FP) ∪ (Alloc \ old(Alloc));
21      free ensures FP_Caller' = (FP_Caller \ FP) ∪ (Alloc ∩ FP) ∪ (Alloc \ old(Alloc));
22      free ensures FP_Caller' ⊆ Alloc ∧ null ∉ Alloc;
23      free ensures Frame(old(Alloc), FP, old(next), next) ∧ Frame(old(Alloc), FP, old(data), data);
24  { FP_Caller := FP_Caller \ FP;
25      assert x = y ∨ x ∈ FP;
26      if (x≠y ∧ x.next≠y) {
27          var pivot: Node, z: Node;
28          rx, pivot, FP := split(x, y, lb, FP);
29          assert pivot ∈ FP;
30          rx, FP := quicksort(rx, pivot, lb, pivot.data, FP);
31          z, FP := quicksort(pivot.next, y, pivot.data, ub, FP);
32          pivot.next := z;
33      } else { rx := x; }
34      FP_Caller' := FP_Caller ∪ FP; }
```

Fig. 3. Translation of quicksort program from Figure 1 to an equivalent GRASS program

the frame rule. After the precondition has been asserted, it is assumed with the implicit ghost parameters replaced by fresh Skolem constants. These Skolem constants then also occur in the assumed postcondition at the call site.

Encoding the Frame Rule. The free requires and ensures clauses in the contract constitute the actual encoding of the frame rule. The free annotation means that the corresponding clause does not need to be checked but can be freely assumed by the callee, respectively, caller. These clauses follow from the soundness of the frame rule and the invariants concerning Alloc and the footprints that are guaranteed by the translation. We discuss the most important parts of the encoding in more detail:

– First, consider the ensures clause in line 20: $blseg\_fp(rx, y) = (Alloc \cap FP) \cup (Alloc \backslash old(Alloc))$. This clause states that the footprint of the postcondition, denoted by $blseg\_fp(rx, y)$, accounts for all memory in the initial footprint that has not been deallocated, and all memory that has been freshly allocated (but not deallocated again) during execution of quicksort. This clause thus implies that the procedure does not leak memory.

- Next, consider the ensures clause in line 21: FP_Caller′ = (FP_Caller\FP) ∪ (Alloc ∩ FP) ∪ (Alloc**old**(Alloc)). This clause states that the new footprint of the caller, FP_Caller′, is the caller's old footprint with the initial footprint of quicksort replaced by quicksort's final footprint (as defined in line 20).
- Finally, the clause in line 23 states that the fields next and data are not modified in the frame of the call. We express this using the predicate Frame. The frame of the call is given by the set old(Alloc) \ FP. We discuss the predicate Frame in more detail in the next section, as the choice of its encoding is crucial for the completeness of our translation.

Translation of SL Assertions. Finally, we describe the translation of the SL assertions in the contract of the input procedure. This translation generalizes our previous work on deciding entailment in separation logic of linked lists via reduction to GRASS [22].

First, each inductive SL predicate $p(x)$ in the input program is translated to a GRASS predicate p_struct(x) and a function p_fp(x). The predicate p_struct(x) collects all constraints concerning the structure of the heap region that is described by the SL predicate $p(x)$, while the function p_fp(x) denotes the footprint of $p(x)$. For example, consider the predicate blseg(x,y,lb,ub) in the input program. As expected, its footprint function blseg_fp(x,y) denotes the set of all nodes z on the next path between x and y, excluding y. This is expressed in terms of a set comprehension. Such set comprehensions are expanded to universally quantified constraints in the back-end solver. Note that if y is not reachable from x in the heap, then blseg_fp(x,y) denotes the empty set. For convenience, we reuse the same footprint function for the translation of the predicate bslseg. The predicate blseg_struct(x,y,lb,ub) states that x is indeed reachable from y (which is expressed by the predicate Btwn(x,y,y)) and that the nodes in the footprint store data values in the interval [lb,ub]. Our tool uses a sound heuristic to generate the translations of the user-defined inductive predicates. The heuristic cannot be complete for arbitrary inductively defined predicates, as the problem of checking entailment for such predicates becomes undecidable. However, our back-end solver is complete for the translations of a large class of predicates describing linked list structures, including the ones in the quicksort example.

With the translation of inductive predicates in place, the translation of an SL assertion H to a GRASS formula is then given by a function $tr(H, X)$, where X is a set variable that denotes the footprint of the assertion. The definition of $tr(H, X)$ is defined recursively on the structure of H as follows:

- if $H = p(x)$, then $tr(H, X) \equiv$ p_struct$(x) \wedge X =$ p_fp(x);
- if $H = \text{acc}(x)$ where x is a node variable, then $tr(H, X) \equiv X = \{x\}$;
- if $H = \text{acc}(Y)$ where Y is a node set variable, then $tr(H, X) \equiv X = Y$;
- if $H = F$ where F is a pure constraint, then $tr(H, X) \equiv F \wedge X = \varnothing$;
- if $H = H_1 * H_2$, then $tr(H, X) \equiv \exists X_1, X_2 :: tr(H_1, X_1) \wedge tr(H_2, X_2) \wedge X = X_1 \uplus X_2$, where X_1, X_2 are fresh node set variables;
- if $H = H_1 + H_2$, then $tr(H, X) \equiv \exists X_1, X_2 :: tr(H_1, X_1) \wedge tr(H_2, X_2) \wedge X = X_1 \cup X_2$, where X_1, X_2 are fresh node set variables.

For convenience, we also include nondisjoint spatial composition in our SL assertion language, which we denote by $H_1 + H_2$. This operator is useful to specify overlayed data structures concisely, respectively, specify alternative views of the same data structure. Note that the *points-to* predicate x.next $\mapsto$ y that is commonly used in separation logic fragments is simply a short-hand for the assertion acc(x) $*$ x.next $=$ y.

Example 1. In Figure 3, the translation tr(blseg(x,y,lb,ub), FP) of the original precondition of the quicksort procedure is the conjunction of the clause in line 15 and the first set equality in the clause in line 16.

Apart from the treatment of inductive predicates, the translation of SL assertions is surprisingly close to the way in which their semantics is traditionally defined. To the expert reader, this might seem problematic, at first. Namely, when checking the generated verification conditions, the back-end solver for GRASS negates some of the resulting constraints to reduce the problem to satisfiability queries. Thus, some of the auxiliary existentially quantified set variables that are introduced in the translation of spatial operators[2] become universally quantified. This might raise concerns about decidability. However, the translation function is defined in such a way that all existentially quantified set variables are uniquely defined by set equalities. That is, the negated constraints of the form $\forall X :: X = T \Rightarrow F$ can be transformed back into equivalent constraints of the form $\exists X :: X = T \wedge F$.

3.2 Frame Axioms and Completeness

We next discuss how we ensure both completeness of the translation to GRASS programs and decidability of checking the generated verification conditions (relative to certain assumptions about the specifications in the input program).

To enable efficient verification condition generation where all case splitting is differed to the back-end SMT solver, we model fields such as next and data as arrays. This allows us to encode field updates conveniently as store operations, which are supported by the array theory in the SMT solver. However, we also need to model the effect of procedure calls on fields, and how modifications of fields affect reachability information captured by the Btwn predicate.

Ultimately, both completeness and decidability hinge on the interpretation of the frame axioms Frame(A, FP, f, f'), which we use to encode the application of the frame rule. Here, A and FP are the values of Alloc and FP before a procedure call, and f and f' are arrays that encode the state of a field such as next before and after the call. In principle, it is sufficient to consider the following interpretation of Frame, which states that the field f is not modified in the frame of the call:

$$\text{Frame}(\text{Alloc}, \text{FP}, f, f') \equiv \forall x \in (\text{Alloc} \backslash \text{FP}) :: x.f = x.f' \qquad (1)$$

The translation to GRASS programs that we outlined in the previous section would then be complete if we considered an axiomatic semantics where GRASS formulas are interpreted in a first-order logic with transitive closure. Transitive closure enables

---

[2] As well as the quantified implicit ghost parameter FP in call-site checks of preconditions.

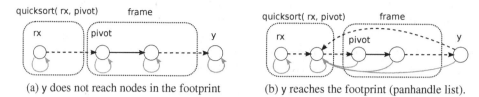

(a) y does not reach nodes in the footprint   (b) y reaches the footprint (panhandle list).

Fig. 4. Two of the possible heaps at the call site on line 14. The footprint of the recursive call to quicksort and the portion of the frame that belongs to the caller's footprint are enclosed in dotted boxes. Solid black edges denote next pointers, dashed black edges indicate next paths, and solid red edges represent the *ep* function.

us to tie the interpretation of a predicate Btwn(next,x,y,z) on a semantic level to the interpretation of next in a given program state. However, the problem of checking the generated verification conditions would be undecidable [11].

An alternative approach is to tie the interpretation of Btwn(next,x,y,z) to the interpretation of next on an axiomatic level. In general, transitive closure cannot be axiomatized in first-order logic. However, we are considering the special case of finite structures, for which first-order axiomatizations of transitive closure exist. In fact, several *reachability logics* for reasoning about heap structures have been proposed that can be decided efficiently (see, e.g., [16, 26]). The problem now is to preserve precise reachability information in the presence of field modifications, i.e., how do Btwn(next,x,y,z) and Btwn(next',x,y,z) relate if next' is obtained from next by some (possibly unbounded) sequence of updates. For single heap updates p.next := q, the effect on the reachability predicate can be encoded using appropriate axioms [16]. However, to preserve reachability information for heap paths in the frame of a procedure call (which may execute an unbounded number of heap updates) we need a more general mechanism.

To preserve reachability information in the frame, we need an interface between the frame and the footprint of the callee that distinguishes the portions of a path belonging to the frame from those portions belonging to the footprint. We define this interface using the *entry point function*. The entry point for a heap node x with respect to a set X and field f, denoted $ep(X, f, x)$, is defined as the first node in X that is reachable from x via f. If such a node does not exist, then $ep(X, f, x) = x$.

Example 2. Figure 4 illustrates two different heap states that may occur at the call site of the recursive call to quicksort on line 14 in Figure 1. The evaluation of the entry point function is depicted by red arrows.

We axiomatize *ep* in terms of the predicate Btwn as follows:

$$\forall x :: \text{Btwn}(f, x, ep(X, f, x), ep(X, f, x))$$
$$\forall x :: ep(X, f, x) \in X \lor ep(X, f, x) = x$$
$$\forall x, y :: \text{Btwn}(f, x, y, y) \land y \in X \Rightarrow ep(X, f, x) \in X \land \text{Btwn}(f, x, ep(X, f, x), y)$$

Using the entry point function we can now correctly update the reachability information for paths that cross the boundary into the footprint of the callee. The corresponding frame axiom for pointer fields such as next is then as follows:

$$\text{Frame}(A, FP, f, f') \equiv \forall x \in (A \backslash FP) :: x.f = x.f' \land$$
$$\forall x, y, z \in (A \backslash FP) :: \text{ReachWO}(f, x, y, ep(FP, f, x)) \Rightarrow$$
$$(\text{Btwn}(f, x, z, y) \Leftrightarrow \text{Btwn}(f', x, z, y)) \land$$
$$\forall x, y, z \in A :: x \notin FP \land x = ep(FP, f, x) \Rightarrow$$
$$(\text{Btwn}(f, x, y, z) \Leftrightarrow \text{Btwn}(f', x, y, z))$$

The two additional axioms specify that the order of nodes is preserved for the path segments between any node x and its entry point into FP, respectively, the full path starting in x if no node in FP is reachable from x. The predicate $\text{ReachWO}(f, x, y, z)$ means that x can reach y via f without going through z. We express this as follows:

$$\text{ReachWO}(f, x, y, z) \equiv \text{Btwn}(f, x, y, z) \lor \text{Btwn}(f, x, y, y) \land \neg\text{Btwn}(f, x, z, z)$$

For nonpointer fields such as data, equation 1 is already sufficient.

3.3   Deciding the Verification Conditions

The verification conditions that are generated from the GRASS programs are augmented with theory axioms to encode the semantics of predicates such as Btwn as well as operations on sets. The resulting formulas are in first-order logic, checked for (un)satisfiability modulo first-order theories that are natively supported by SMT solvers, e.g., linear arithmetic and free function symbols. The generated formulas contain both existential and universal quantifiers, however, no $\forall\exists$ quantifier alternations. To ensure that we can use the SMT solver as an actual decision procedure for checking satisfiability of the generated formulas, we preprocess these quantifiers before we pass the formula to the SMT solver. Preprocessing depends on the kind of the quantifier:

- Existentially quantified subformulas are simply skolemized. We implemented optimization such as maximizing the scope of existential quantifiers and reusing existentially quantified variables as much as possible to minimize the number of generated Skolem constants.
- Universally quantified subformulas are first hoisted to the top level of the formula (by introducing propositional variables as place holders) and then further processed depending on their type. We distinguish three types that we further describe below.

Effective Propositional Fragment (EPR). The EPR fragment (aka the Bernays-Schönfinkel-Ramsey class) consists of formulas in which universally quantified variables do not occur below function symbols. This fragment can be decided quite efficiently using Z3's model-based quantifier instantiation mechanism. Hence, all EPR formulas are passed directly to Z3. For formulas that are not in EPR, we make a finer distinction.

Stratified Sort Fragment. If universal quantified variables appear below function symbols, then instantiating these variables may create new ground terms, which in turn can be used for instantiation, causing the SMT solver to diverge. One special case, though, are axioms satisfying stratified sort restrictions [1]. Examples of such formulas are the quantified constraints in the predicates blseg_struct and bslseg_struct of Figure 3. The sort of the quantified variables z and w is Node, while the sort of the instantiated terms z.data and w.data is int. Since we do not quantify over int variables, the generated ground terms do not enable new quantifier instantiations. Formulas in the stratified sort fragment are directly passed to Z3.

Local Theory Extensions. The remaining quantified constraints are more difficult. In general, we provide no completeness guarantee for our handling of quantifiers because we allow users to specify unrestricted quantified pure constraints in their specifications. However, we can guarantee completeness for specifications written in separation logic for linked lists mixed with quantifier-free pure GRASS constraints (as well as some types of user-specified quantified constraints). We designed our translation carefully so that the remaining quantified formulas are in decidable fragments (in particular, the frame and theory axioms). To decide these fragments, we build on local theory extensions [25]. Local theory extensions are described by axioms for which instantiation can be restricted to ground terms appearing in the verification condition (or some finite set of ground terms that can be computed from this formula). We preprocess such axioms by partially instantiating all variables below function symbols with the relevant sets of ground terms. The partially instantiated axioms are then in the EPR fragment and passed to Z3. We discuss one example of a local theory extension in more detail below. To reduce the number of generated partial instances, we compute the congruence closure for the ground part of the verification condition to group ground terms into equivalence classes. We then only need to consider one representative term per equivalence class during instantiation.

Example 3. One example of a local theory extension is the theory extension defining the entry point functions in Section 3.2 together with the generated frame axioms concerning ep. Note that in all models of this extension, the entry point function is idempotent for fixed X and f. Hence, we only need to instantiate these axioms once for each Node ground term x. One potential problem may arise from the interactions between the ep functions for different footprint sets and fields. That is, instantiating one ep term for one X, f and ground term t may expose a new entry point $e = ep(X', f', ep(X, f, t))$ for another pair X', f' such that, in some model, e is different from all previously generated ground terms. However, such a situation cannot occur if all footprints are defined by a union of a bounded number of list segments. This holds true for separation logic of linked lists. Even in the general case, the counterexamples that witness incompleteness are rather degenerate and we doubt they can occur in actual program executions.

4   Mixing Separation Logic and First-Order Logic Specifications

The key advantage of our approach is that it allows the user to seamlessly mix SL and GRASS specifications. Some data structures are difficult to specify in separation logic because they involve complex sharing, or their footprints are not easily definable using simple inductive predicates. In Figure 5, we show the specifications of the find and union procedures of a union-find data structure implemented as a forest of inverted trees. This data structure exhibits both of the above problems.

Complex Sharing. A path that goes from a node to its representative in a union-find structure can be expressed as a list segment. However, describing the entire structure is

```
1  predicate lseg_set(x: Node, y: Node, X: set<Node>) {
2      (x = y * X = ∅) ∨ (x ≠ y * acc(x) * x ∈ X * lseg_set(x.next, y, X \ {x}))
3  }
4  procedure find(x: Node, ghost root_x: Node, implicit ghost X: set<Node>)
5      returns (res: Node)
6      requires lseg_set(x, root_x, X) * root_x.next ↦ null;
7      ensures res = root_x * acc(X) * (∀ z ∈ X :: z.next = res) * res.next ↦ null;
8
9  procedure union(x: Node, y: Node, ghost root_x: Node, ghost root_y: Node,
10                 implicit ghost X: set<Node>, implicit ghost Y: set<Node>)
11     requires lseg_set(x, root_x, X) + lseg_set(y, root_y, Y);
12     requires root_x.next ↦ null + root_y.next ↦ null;
13     ensures (acc(X) + acc(Y)) * (root_y.next ↦ null + acc(root_x));
14     ensures (∀ z ∈ X :: z.next = root_x) * (∀ z ∈ Y :: z.next = root_y);
15     ensures root_x = root_y ∨ root_x.next = root_y;
```

Fig. 5. Operations on a union-find data structure with mixed specifications

more difficult. For instance, in the union procedure if x and y are in different equivalence classes, then the two paths in the data structure are disjoint. However, if they are in the same class, then their paths may be partially shared. It is difficult to express this in traditional SL fragments without explicitly distinguishing the two cases. We can cover both cases conveniently using the spatial connective + for nondisjoint union.

Structural Constraints Expressed in First-Order Logic. When path compaction is used in the find procedure, then the postcondition of find is not expressible in terms of a bounded number of inductive predicates. The reason is that path compaction turns a list segment of unbounded length into an unbounded number of points-to predicates. Therefore, expressing the postcondition requires some form of universal quantification. We can express this quite easily using the constraint $F \equiv \forall z \in X :: z.\text{next} = \text{root\_x}$, where X is the initial footprint of the procedure described by an SL assertion. Note that the additional predicate acc(X) in the postcondition specifies that X is also the final footprint of the procedure. Hence, F only constrains the structure of the heap region that is captured by the footprint. Note that this example also uses implicit ghost parameters of procedures to existentially quantify over the explicit footprint X.

When mixing separation logic and classical logic, then additional well-formedness checks are needed to guarantee that reachability predicates and other heap-dependent pure formulas do not constrain heap regions outside of the footprint that is specified by the nonpure SL assertions. Otherwise, the application of the frame rule would become unsound. However, these additional checks can be automated in the same manner as the checks of the actual verification conditions.

5   Implementation and Evaluation

We have implemented all the features described in this paper in GRASShopper. The tool is implemented in OCaml and available under a BSD license. The source code distribution including all benchmarks can be downloaded from the project web page [10].

Benchmarks	# LOC	# VCs	time in s
SLL (loop)	156	56	1.9
SLL (rec.)	142	70	3.1
sorted SLL	171	55	6.6
DLL	195	59	11
sorting algorithms	230	98	15
union-find	35	8	4.8
SLL.filter (deref. null pointer)		7	0.4
DLL.insert (missing update)		8	3.1
quicksort (underspec. split)		12	0.9
union-find (bug in postcond.)		4	12.8

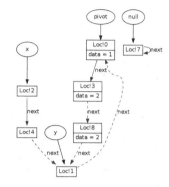

Fig. 6. The left-hand side shows the summary of the experiments for the collections of correct benchmarks as well as some benchmarks that contain bugs in the code or specification. The right-hand side shows the generated counterexample for the underspecified quicksort program.

GRASShopper takes as input an annotated C-like program and generates verification conditions, which are checked using a back-end SMT solver. The solver is integrated via the standard interface defined by SMT-LIB 2. Currently, we use Z3 [8] as back-end solver but we are working on incorporating CVC4 as well as other solvers.

Evaluation. We have collected 37 examples of correct heap-manipulating programs working over singly and doubly-linked lists. This includes basic manipulations of the data structures (traverse, dispose, copy, reverse, concat, filter, remove, insert) for the singly-linked lists (SLL) and doubly-linked lists (DLL). The singly-linked list examples come in three flavors: an imperative style loop-based implementation, a recursive implementation, and one based on sorted lists. Beyond these benchmarks, we implement four different sorting algorithms (insertion sort, merge sort, quicksort, strand sort) and a union-find data structure. In addition, we applied the tool to programs that contain bugs or have incorrect specifications. The table in Fig. 6 summarizes our results. The table shows the number of lines of code for each set of examples, the total number of verification conditions, and the total running time of GRASShopper on those examples. All examples have been correctly verified, respectively, falsified. The number of lines of code includes the specifications but excludes the definitions of the data structures.

Counterexample Generation. When a verification condition cannot be proved, i.e., the formula sent to the SMT solver is satisfiable, GRASShopper uses the model returned by the solver to construct a counterexample. Due to the preprocessing of quantifiers, the model returned by the SMT solver is actually a partial model of the GRASS formula. This means that instead of having all pointer fields defined, some of them are summarized by reachability constraints. These reachability constraints encode paths of unbounded length in the heap. From this information we construct a graph in Graphviz format that represents an entire family of counterexamples.

For example, when we were writing the quicksort example in Fig. 1, we had to iterate a few times before we obtained a correct version. At some point, we had a postcondition for split that was missing the Btwn predicate, as described in Section 2. The corresponding counterexample produced by GRASShopper is shown in Fig. 6. The graph clearly shows the panhandle list. The full counterexample also includes valuations for the footprint sets of the caller and callee. The final footprint FP_Caller' returned by split is {Loc!0, Loc!1, Loc!2, Loc!3, Loc!4, Loc!8} and the footprint that was expected by the postcondition of quicksort is {Loc!2, Loc!4}. The two sets should be equal.

6   Related Work and Conclusion

Since the pioneering work on the Smallfoot tool [2, 3], several efficient decision procedures for entailment checking in separation logic of linked lists have been developed [7, 21]. Other procedures target more expressive fragments, e.g., nested lists [6] or structures with tree backbones [12]. Currently, GRASShopper only supports structures with a flat list backbone but we are working on extending the tool to handle more complex data structures.

In our previous work [22], we proposed an approach to deciding entailment in separation logic via a reduction to first-order logic and presented a technique for frame inference. However, this technique relied on model enumeration, which is very expensive. We now propose an alternative where the frame rule is encoded in the SMT query.

Qiu et al. [23] introduced DRYAD a logic to specify heap shapes. To reason about DRYAD formulas, they use natural proofs, a heuristic to bound the proof search space. For instance, the unfolding of recursive definitions is limited to the ground terms in the formulas. This is similar to our approach of quantifier instantiation based on local theory extensions, but without completeness guarantees.

Closely related to our approach is the work on using effectively propositional logic (EPR) for reasoning about programs that manipulate linked lists [13, 14]. As in this paper, the authors of [14] use idempotent entry point functions to express that heap paths in the frame of a procedure call do not change. Their approach yields a sound and complete procedure for modular checking of EPR specifications. We have developed the same idea independently, motivated by the goal of verifying programs with specifications that mix separation logic with first-order theories. The union/find data structure has also been considered in [14]. Beside the different motivation, the main technical difference between our work and [14] is that we are not restricted to programs with acyclic lists. Incidentally, the more general reachability predicate that we use for reasoning about cycles yields a simpler encoding of the frame rule.

Our SL translation and the handling of the frame rule is in part inspired by work on implicit dynamic frames [20, 24]. Per se, the implicit dynamic frames approach provides no decidability guarantees for the first-order logic fragment used by the SL encoding. In particular, tools such as VeriFast [15] and Chalice [17], which are based on this approach, use pattern-based quantifier instantiation heuristics to check the resulting verification conditions. These heuristics are in general incomplete and often fail to produce models for satisfiable formulas. Instead, we designed the target fragment of our SL encoding carefully so that decidability is preserved by the translation while still admitting efficient implementations on top of SMT solvers. We find the ability of our implementation to produce counterexamples invaluable when debugging specifications.

References

1. Abadi, A., Rabinovich, A., Sagiv, M.: Decidable fragments of many-sorted logic. In: Dershowitz, N., Voronkov, A. (eds.) LPAR 2007. LNCS (LNAI), vol. 4790, pp. 17–31. Springer, Heidelberg (2007)
2. Berdine, J., Calcagno, C., O'Hearn, P.W.: A decidable fragment of separation logic. In: Lodaya, K., Mahajan, M. (eds.) FSTTCS 2004. LNCS, vol. 3328, pp. 97–109. Springer, Heidelberg (2004)
3. Berdine, J., Calcagno, C., O'Hearn, P.W.: Smallfoot: Modular automatic assertion checking with separation logic. In: de Boer, F.S., Bonsangue, M.M., Graf, S., de Roever, W.-P. (eds.) FMCO 2005. LNCS, vol. 4111, pp. 115–137. Springer, Heidelberg (2006)
4. Berdine, J., Cook, B., Ishtiaq, S.: SLAYER: Memory Safety for Systems-Level Code. In: Gopalakrishnan, G., Qadeer, S. (eds.) CAV 2011. LNCS, vol. 6806, pp. 178–183. Springer, Heidelberg (2011)
5. Botincan, M., Parkinson, M.J., Schulte, W.: Separation logic verification of C programs with an SMT solver. Electr. Notes Theor. Comput. Sci. 254, 5–23 (2009)
6. Bouajjani, A., Drăgoi, C., Enea, C., Sighireanu, M.: Accurate invariant checking for programs manipulating lists and arrays with infinite data. In: Chakraborty, S., Mukund, M. (eds.) ATVA 2012. LNCS, vol. 7561, pp. 167–182. Springer, Heidelberg (2012)
7. Cook, B., Haase, C., Ouaknine, J., Parkinson, M., Worrell, J.: Tractable reasoning in a fragment of separation logic. In: Katoen, J.-P., König, B. (eds.) CONCUR 2011. LNCS, vol. 6901, pp. 235–249. Springer, Heidelberg (2011)
8. de Moura, L., Bjørner, N.: Z3: An efficient SMT solver. In: Ramakrishnan, C.R., Rehof, J. (eds.) TACAS 2008. LNCS, vol. 4963, pp. 337–340. Springer, Heidelberg (2008)
9. Dudka, K., Peringer, P., Vojnar, T.: Predator: A practical tool for checking manipulation of dynamic data structures using separation logic. In: Gopalakrishnan, G., Qadeer, S. (eds.) CAV 2011. LNCS, vol. 6806, pp. 372–378. Springer, Heidelberg (2011)
10. GRASShopper tool wep page, http://cs.nyu.edu/wies/software/grasshopper (last accessed: October 2013)
11. Immerman, N., Rabinovich, A., Reps, T., Sagiv, M., Yorsh, G.: The boundary between decidability and undecidability for transitive-closure logics. In: Marcinkowski, J., Tarlecki, A. (eds.) CSL 2004. LNCS, vol. 3210, pp. 160–174. Springer, Heidelberg (2004)
12. Iosif, R., Rogalewicz, A., Simacek, J.: The tree width of separation logic with recursive definitions. In: Bonacina, M.P. (ed.) CADE 2013. LNCS, vol. 7898, pp. 21–38. Springer, Heidelberg (2013)
13. Itzhaky, S., Banerjee, A., Immerman, N., Nanevski, A., Sagiv, M.: Effectively-propositional reasoning about reachability in linked data structures. In: Sharygina, N., Veith, H. (eds.) CAV 2013. LNCS, vol. 8044, pp. 756–772. Springer, Heidelberg (2013)
14. Itzhaky, S., Lahav, O., Banerjee, A., Immerman, N., Nanevski, A., Sagiv, M.: Modular reasoning on unique heap paths via effectively propositional formulas. In: POPL (2014)
15. Jacobs, B., Smans, J., Philippaerts, P., Vogels, F., Penninckx, W., Piessens, F.: VeriFast: A powerful, sound, predictable, fast verifier for C and java. In: Bobaru, M., Havelund, K., Holzmann, G.J., Joshi, R. (eds.) NFM 2011. LNCS, vol. 6617, pp. 41–55. Springer, Heidelberg (2011)
16. Lahiri, S., Qadeer, S.: Back to the future: revisiting precise program verification using SMT solvers. In: POPL (2008)
17. Leino, K.R.M., Müller, P., Smans, J.: Verification of concurrent programs with chalice. In: Aldini, A., Barthe, G., Gorrieri, R. (eds.) FOSAD 2007/2008/2009. LNCS, vol. 5705, pp. 195–222. Springer, Heidelberg (2009)

18. Nelson, G., Oppen, D.C.: Simplification by cooperating decision procedures. ACM TOPLAS 1(2), 245–257 (1979)
19. O'Hearn, P., Reynolds, J., Yang, H.: Local reasoning about programs that alter data structures. In: Fribourg, L. (ed.) CSL 2001 and EACSL 2001. LNCS, vol. 2142, pp. 1–19. Springer, Heidelberg (2001)
20. Parkinson, M.J., Summers, A.J.: The relationship between separation logic and implicit dynamic frames. Logical Methods in Computer Science 8(3) (2012)
21. Pérez, J.A.N., Rybalchenko, A.: Separation logic + superposition calculus = heap theorem prover. In: PLDI, pp. 556–566. ACM (2011)
22. Piskac, R., Wies, T., Zufferey, D.: Automating Separation Logic Using SMT. In: Sharygina, N., Veith, H. (eds.) CAV 2013. LNCS, vol. 8044, pp. 773–789. Springer, Heidelberg (2013)
23. Qiu, X., Garg, P., Stefanescu, A., Madhusudan, P.: Natural proofs for structure, data, and separation. In: PLDI, pp. 231–242 (2013)
24. Smans, J., Jacobs, B., Piessens, F.: Implicit dynamic frames: Combining dynamic frames and separation logic. In: Drossopoulou, S. (ed.) ECOOP 2009. LNCS, vol. 5653, pp. 148–172. Springer, Heidelberg (2009)
25. Sofronie-Stokkermans, V.: Hierarchic reasoning in local theory extensions. In: Nieuwenhuis, R. (ed.) CADE 2005. LNCS (LNAI), vol. 3632, pp. 219–234. Springer, Heidelberg (2005)
26. Totla, N., Wies, T.: Complete instantiation-based interpolation. In: POPL. ACM (2013)
27. Yang, H., Lee, O., Berdine, J., Calcagno, C., Cook, B., Distefano, D., O'Hearn, P.W.: Scalable shape analysis for systems code. In: Gupta, A., Malik, S. (eds.) CAV 2008. LNCS, vol. 5123, pp. 385–398. Springer, Heidelberg (2008)

Alternating Runtime and Size Complexity Analysis of Integer Programs[*]

Marc Brockschmidt[1], Fabian Emmes[2], Stephan Falke[3], Carsten Fuhs[4], and Jürgen Giesl[2]

[1] Microsoft Research, Cambridge, UK
[2] RWTH Aachen University, Germany
[3] Karlsruhe Institute of Technology, Germany
[4] University College London, UK

Abstract. We present a modular approach to automatic complexity analysis. Based on a novel alternation between finding symbolic time bounds for program parts and using these to infer size bounds on program variables, we can restrict each analysis step to a small part of the program while maintaining a high level of precision. Extensive experiments with the implementation of our method demonstrate its performance and power in comparison with other tools.

1 Introduction

There exist numerous methods to prove termination of imperative programs, e.g., [2,6,8,9,12,13,15–17,19,25,33–35]. In many cases, however, termination is not sufficient, but the program should terminate in reasonable (e.g., (pseudo-) polynomial) time. To prove this, it is often crucial to derive (possibly non-linear) bounds on the values of variables that are modified repeatedly in loops.

We build upon the well-known observation that rank functions for termination proofs also provide a runtime complexity bound [3,4,6,7,32]. However, this only holds for proofs using a *single* rank function. Larger programs are usually handled by a disjunctive [16,28,35] or lexicographic [6,12,13,17,19,21,23,25] combination of rank functions. Here, deriving a complexity bound is much harder.

To illustrate this, consider the program on the right and a variant where the instruction "x = x + i" is removed. For both variants, the lexicographic rank function $\langle f_1, f_2 \rangle$ proves termination, where f_1 measures states by the value of i and f_2 is just the value of x. However, the program without the instruction "x = x + i" has linear runtime, while the program on the right has quadratic runtime. The crucial difference between the two programs is in the *size* of x after the first loop.

```
while i > 0 do
    i = i - 1
    x = x + i
done
while x > 0 do
    x = x - 1
done
```

To handle such effects, we introduce a novel modular approach which *alternates* between finding *runtime bounds* and finding *size bounds*. In contrast to standard invariants, our size bounds express a relation to the size of the variables at the program start, where we measure the *size* of integers by their absolute values. Our method derives runtime bounds for isolated parts of the program

[*] Supported by the DFG grant GI 274/6-1.

E. Ábrahám and K. Havelund (Eds.): TACAS 2014, LNCS 8413, pp. 140–155, 2014.

and uses these to deduce (often non-linear) size bounds for program variables at certain locations. Further runtime bounds can then be inferred using size bounds for variables that were modified in preceding parts of the program. By splitting the analysis in this way, we only need to consider small program parts in each step, and the process continues until all loops and variables have been handled.

For the example, our method proves that the first loop is executed linearly often using the rank function i. Then, it deduces that i is bounded by the size of its initial value $|i_0|$ in all loop iterations. Combining these bounds, it infers that x is incremented by a value bounded by $|i_0|$ at most $|i_0|$ times, i.e., x is bounded by the sum of its initial size $|x_0|$ and $|i_0|^2$. Finally, our method detects that the second loop is executed x times, and combines this with our bound $|x_0| + |i_0|^2$ on x's value when entering the second loop. In this way, we can conclude[1] that the program's runtime is bounded by $|i_0| + |i_0|^2 + |x_0|$. This novel combination of runtime and size bounds allows us to handle loops whose runtime depends on variables like x that were modified in earlier loops. Thus, our approach succeeds on many programs that are beyond the reach of previous techniques.

Sect. 2 introduces the basic notions for our approach. Then Sect. 3 and Sect. 4 present our techniques to compute runtime and size bounds, respectively. Sect. 5 discusses related work and provides an extensive experimental evaluation. Proofs for all theorems as well as several extensions of our approach can be found in [14].

2   Preliminaries

```
Input: List x
ℓ₀: List y = null
ℓ₁: while x ≠ null do
        y = new List(x.val, y)
        x = x.next
    done
    List z = y
ℓ₂: while z ≠ null do
        List u = z.next
ℓ₃:    while u ≠ null do
            z.val += u.val
            u = u.next
        done
        z = z.next
    done
```

Consider the program on the right. For an input list x, the loop at location ℓ_1 creates a list y by reversing the elements of x. The loop at location ℓ_2 iterates over the list y and increases each element by the sum of its successors. So if y was $[5, 1, 3]$, it will be $[5+1+3, 1+3, 3]$ after the second loop. This example is a representative for methods using several algorithms in sequence.

We regard sequential imperative integer programs with (potentially non-linear) arithmetic and unbounded non-determinism. Our approach is compatible with methods that abstract features like heap usage to integers [2, 4, 15, 19, 29, 34]. So the above program could be abstracted automatically to the integer program below. Here, list variables are replaced by integer variables that correspond to the lengths of the lists.

We fix a (finite) set of program variables $\mathcal{V} = \{v_1, \ldots, v_n\}$ and represent integer programs as directed graphs. Nodes are program *locations* $\mathcal{L}$ and edges are program *transitions* $\mathcal{T}$. The set $\mathcal{L}$ contains a *canonical start location* ℓ_0. W.l.o.g., we assume that no transition leads back to ℓ_0 and that all transitions $\mathcal{T}$ are reachable from ℓ_0. All transitions originating in ℓ_0 are called *initial transitions*. The

---

[1] Since each step of our method over-approximates the runtime or size of a variable, we actually obtain the bound $2 + |i_0| + \max\{|i_0|, |x_0|\} + |i_0|^2$, cf. Sect. 4.2.

transitions are labeled by formulas over the variables $\mathcal{V}$ and primed post-variables $\mathcal{V}' = \{v_1', \ldots, v_n'\}$ which represent the values of the variables after the transition. In the following graph, we represented these formulas by imperative commands. For instance, t_3 is labeled by the formula $z > 0 \wedge u' = z - 1 \wedge x' = x \wedge y' = y \wedge z' = z$.

We used standard invariant-generation techniques (based on the Octagon domain [30]) to propagate simple integer invariants, adding the condition $z > 0$ to the transitions t_4 and t_5.

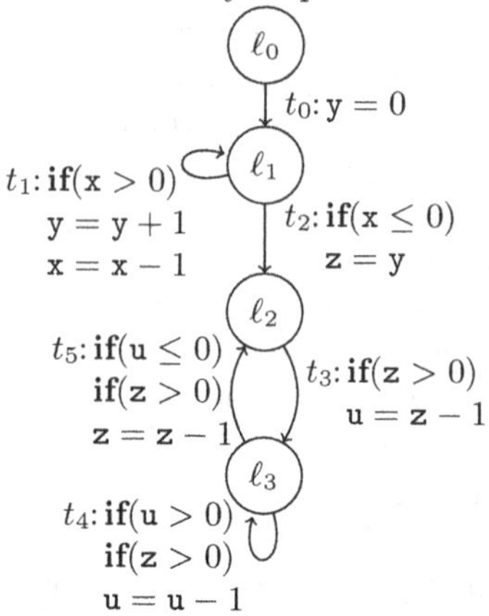

Definition 1 (Programs). *A transition is a tuple (ℓ, τ, ℓ') where $\ell, \ell' \in \mathcal{L}$ are locations and τ is a formula relating the (pre-)variables $\mathcal{V}$ and the post-variables $\mathcal{V}'$. A program is a set of transitions $\mathcal{T}$. A configuration $(\ell, \boldsymbol{v})$ consists of a location $\ell \in \mathcal{L}$ and a valuation $\boldsymbol{v} : \mathcal{V} \to \mathbb{Z}$. We write $(\ell, \boldsymbol{v}) \to_t (\ell', \boldsymbol{v}')$ for an evaluation* step *with a transition $t = (\ell, \tau, \ell')$ iff the valuations $\boldsymbol{v}, \boldsymbol{v}'$ satisfy the formula τ of t. We drop the index t if we do not care about the used transition and write $(\ell, \boldsymbol{v}) \to^k (\ell', \boldsymbol{v}')$ if k evaluation steps lead from configuration $(\ell, \boldsymbol{v})$ to $(\ell', \boldsymbol{v}')$.*

The graph (right column):

ℓ_0

$t_0: y = 0$

$t_1: \mathbf{if}(x > 0)$
$\quad y = y + 1$
$\quad x = x - 1$

ℓ_1

$t_2: \mathbf{if}(x \leq 0)$
$\quad z = y$

ℓ_2

$t_5: \mathbf{if}(u \leq 0)$
$\quad \mathbf{if}(z > 0)$
$\quad z = z - 1$

$t_3: \mathbf{if}(z > 0)$
$\quad u = z - 1$

ℓ_3

$t_4: \mathbf{if}(u > 0)$
$\quad \mathbf{if}(z > 0)$
$\quad u = u - 1$

So for the program above, we have $(\ell_1, \boldsymbol{v}_1) \to_{t_2} (\ell_2, \boldsymbol{v}_2)$ for any valuations where $\boldsymbol{v}_1(x) = \boldsymbol{v}_2(x) \leq 0$, $\boldsymbol{v}_1(y) = \boldsymbol{v}_2(y) = \boldsymbol{v}_2(z)$, and $\boldsymbol{v}_1(u) = \boldsymbol{v}_2(u)$.

Let $\mathcal{T}$ always denote the analyzed program. Our goal is to find bounds on the runtime and the sizes of program variables, where these bounds are expressed as functions in the sizes of the input variables $v_1, \ldots, v_n$. For our example, our method will detect that its runtime is bounded by $3 + 4 \cdot |x| + |x|^2$ (i.e., it is quadratic in $|x|$). We measure the *size* of variable values $\boldsymbol{v}(v_i)$ by their absolute values $|\boldsymbol{v}(v_i)|$. For a valuation $\boldsymbol{v}$ and a vector $\boldsymbol{m} = (m_1, \ldots, m_n) \in \mathbb{N}^n$, let $\boldsymbol{v} \leq \boldsymbol{m}$ abbreviate $|\boldsymbol{v}(v_1)| \leq m_1 \wedge \ldots \wedge |\boldsymbol{v}(v_n)| \leq m_n$. We define *runtime complexity* by a function rc that maps the sizes $\boldsymbol{m}$ of the program variables to the maximal number of evaluation steps that are possible from a start configuration $(\ell_0, \boldsymbol{v})$ with $\boldsymbol{v} \leq \boldsymbol{m}$. To analyze complexity in a modular way, we construct a *runtime approximation* $\mathcal{R}$ such that for any $t \in \mathcal{T}$, $\mathcal{R}(t)$ over-approximates the number of times that t can be used in an evaluation. In Def. 2, $\to^* \circ \to_t$ is the relation that allows to perform arbitrary many evaluation steps followed by a step with transition t.

As we generate new bounds by composing previously found bounds, we only use weakly monotonic functions $\mathcal{R}(t)$ (i.e., $m_i \geq m_i'$ implies $(\mathcal{R}(t))(m_1, \ldots, m_i, \ldots, m_n) \geq (\mathcal{R}(t))(m_1, \ldots, m_i', \ldots, m_n)$). We define the set of *upper bounds* $\mathfrak{C}$ as the weakly monotonic functions from $\mathbb{N}^n \to \mathbb{N}$ and ?, where $?(\boldsymbol{m}) = \omega$ for all $\boldsymbol{m} \in \mathbb{N}^n$. We have $\omega > n$ for all $n \in \mathbb{N}$. In our implementation, we restrict $\mathcal{R}(t)$ to functions constructed from max, min, ?, and polynomials from $\mathbb{N}[v_1, \ldots, v_n]$.

Definition 2 (Runtime Complexity and Approximation). *The* runtime complexity $\mathrm{rc} : \mathbb{N}^n \to \mathbb{N} \cup \{\omega\}$ *is defined as[2]* $\mathrm{rc}(\boldsymbol{m}) = \sup\{k \in \mathbb{N} \mid \exists \boldsymbol{v}_0, \ell, \boldsymbol{v} . \boldsymbol{v}_0 \leq$

---

[2] Here, $\mathrm{rc}(\boldsymbol{m}) = \omega$ means non-termination or arbitrarily long runtime. Such programs result from non-determinism, e.g., $i = \mathbf{nondet}()$; $\mathbf{while}\ i > 0\ \mathbf{do}\ i = i - 1\ \mathbf{done}$.

$m \wedge (\ell_0, v_0) \to^k (\ell, v)\}$. A function $\mathcal{R} : \mathcal{T} \to \mathfrak{C}$ is a runtime approximation iff $(\mathcal{R}(t))(m) \geq \sup\{k \in \mathbb{N} \mid \exists v_0, \ell, v \cdot v_0 \leq m \wedge (\ell_0, v_0)(\to^* \circ \to_t)^k (\ell, v)\}$ holds for all transitions $t \in \mathcal{T}$ and all $m \in \mathbb{N}^n$. The initial runtime approximation $\mathcal{R}_0$ is defined as[3] $\mathcal{R}_0(t) = 1$ for all initial transitions t and $\mathcal{R}_0(t) = ?$ otherwise.

For *size complexity*, we analyze how large the value of a program variable can become. Analogous to $\mathcal{R}$, we use a *size approximation* $\mathcal{S}$, where $\mathcal{S}(t, v')$ is a bound on the size of the variable v *after* a certain transition t was used in an evaluation. For any transition $t \in \mathcal{T}$ and $v \in \mathcal{V}$, we call $|t, v'|$ a *result variable*.

Definition 3 (Result Variables and Size Approximation). *Let* RV $= \{|t, v'| \mid t \in \mathcal{T}, v \in \mathcal{V}\}$ *be the set of* result variables. *A function* $\mathcal{S} : $ RV $\to \mathfrak{C}$ *is a* size approximation *iff* $(\mathcal{S}(t, v'))(m) \geq \sup\{|v(v)| \mid \exists v_0, \ell, v \cdot v_0 \leq m \wedge (\ell_0, v_0)(\to^* \circ \to_t)(\ell, v)\}$ *holds for all* $|t, v'| \in$ RV *and all* $m \in \mathbb{N}^n$. *The initial size approximation* $\mathcal{S}_0$ *is defined as* $\mathcal{S}_0(t, v') = ?$ *for all* $|t, v'| \in$ RV. *A pair* $(\mathcal{R}, \mathcal{S})$ *is a* complexity approximation *if* $\mathcal{R}$ *is a runtime and* $\mathcal{S}$ *is a size approximation.*

Our approach starts with the initial approximation $(\mathcal{R}_0, \mathcal{S}_0)$ and improves it by iterative refinement. An approximation for the runtime complexity rc of the whole program $\mathcal{T}$ can be obtained by adding the runtime bounds $\mathcal{R}(t)$ for its transitions, i.e., $(\sum_{t \in \mathcal{T}} \mathcal{R}(t)) \geq$ rc. The overall bound $\sum_{t \in \mathcal{T}} \mathcal{R}(t) = 3 + 4 \cdot |\mathbf{x}| + |\mathbf{x}|^2$ for our example was obtained in this way. Here for $f, g \in \mathfrak{C}$, the comparison, addition, multiplication, maximum, and the minimum are defined point-wise. So $f \geq g$ holds iff $f(m) \geq g(m)$ for all $m \in \mathbb{N}^n$ and $f + g$ is the function with $(f + g)(m) = f(m) + g(m)$, where $\omega + n = \omega$ for all $n \in \mathbb{N} \cup \{\omega\}$.

3   Computing Runtime Bounds

To find runtime bounds automatically, we use (lexicographic combinations of) *polynomial rank functions* (PRFs). Such rank functions are widely used in termination analysis and many techniques are available to generate PRFs automatically [6, 8, 9, 12, 19–21, 33]. In Sect. 3.1 we recapitulate the basic approach to use PRFs for the generation of time bounds. In Sect. 3.2, we improve it to a novel modular approach which infers time bounds by combining PRFs with information about variable sizes and runtime bounds found earlier.

3.1   Runtime Bounds from Polynomial Rank Functions

A PRF $\mathcal{P}ol : \mathcal{L} \to \mathbb{Z}[v_1, \ldots, v_n]$ assigns an integer polynomial $\mathcal{P}ol(\ell)$ over the program variables to each location ℓ. Then configurations (ℓ, v) are measured as the value of the polynomial $\mathcal{P}ol(\ell)$ for the numbers $v(v_1), \ldots, v(v_n)$. To obtain time bounds, we search for PRFs where no transition increases the measure of configurations, and at least one transition decreases it. To rule out that this decrease continues forever, we also require that the measure has a lower bound.

Definition 4 (PRF). *We call* $\mathcal{P}ol : \mathcal{L} \to \mathbb{Z}[v_1, \ldots, v_n]$ *a polynomial rank function (PRF) for* $\mathcal{T}$ *iff there is a non-empty* $\mathcal{T}_\succ \subseteq \mathcal{T}$ *such that the following holds:*

---

[3] Here, "1" denotes the constant function which maps all arguments $m \in \mathbb{N}^n$ to 1.

- *for all $(\ell, \tau, \ell') \in \mathcal{T}$, we have $\tau \Rightarrow (\mathcal{P}ol(\ell))(v_1, \ldots, v_n) \geq (\mathcal{P}ol(\ell'))(v'_1, \ldots, v'_n)$*
- *for all $(\ell, \tau, \ell') \in \mathcal{T}_{\succ}$, we have $\tau \Rightarrow (\mathcal{P}ol(\ell))(v_1, \ldots, v_n) > (\mathcal{P}ol(\ell'))(v'_1, \ldots, v'_n)$*
  and $\tau \Rightarrow (\mathcal{P}ol(\ell))(v_1, \ldots, v_n) \geq 1$

The constraints on a PRF $\mathcal{P}ol$ are the same constraints needed for termination proofs, allowing to re-use existing PRF synthesis techniques and tools. They imply that the transitions in $\mathcal{T}_{\succ}$ can only be used a limited number of times, as each application of a transition from $\mathcal{T}_{\succ}$ decreases the measure, and no transition increases it. Hence, if the program is called with input $m_1, \ldots, m_n$, no transition $t \in \mathcal{T}_{\succ}$ can be used more often than $(\mathcal{P}ol(\ell_0))(m_1, \ldots, m_n)$ times. Consequently, $\mathcal{P}ol(\ell_0)$ is a runtime bound for the transitions in $\mathcal{T}_{\succ}$. Note that no such bound is obtained for the remaining transitions in $\mathcal{T}$.

In the program from Sect. 2, we could use $\mathcal{P}ol_1$ with $\mathcal{P}ol_1(\ell) = \mathsf{x}$ for all $\ell \in \mathcal{L}$, i.e., we measure configurations by the value of x. No transition increases this measure and t_1 decreases it. The condition $\mathsf{x} > 0$ ensures that the measure is positive whenever t_1 is used, i.e., $\mathcal{T}_{\succ} = \{t_1\}$. Hence $\mathcal{P}ol_1(\ell_0)$ (i.e., the value x at the beginning of the program) is a bound on the number of times t_1 can be used.

Such PRFs lead to a basic technique for inferring time bounds. As mentioned in Sect. 2, to obtain a modular approach afterwards, we only allow weakly monotonic functions as complexity bounds. For any polynomial $p \in \mathbb{Z}[v_1, \ldots, v_n]$, let $[p]$ result from p by replacing all coefficients and variables with their absolute value (e.g., for $\mathcal{P}ol_1(\ell_0) = \mathsf{x}$ we have $[\mathcal{P}ol_1(\ell_0)] = |\mathsf{x}|$ and if $p = 2 \cdot v_1 - 3 \cdot v_2$ then $[p] = 2 \cdot |v_1| + 3 \cdot |v_2|$). As $[p](m_1, \ldots, m_n) \geq p(m_1, \ldots, m_n)$ holds for all $m_1, \ldots, m_n \in \mathbb{Z}$, this is a sound approximation, and $[p]$ is weakly monotonic. In our example, the initial runtime approximation $\mathcal{R}_0$ can now be refined to $\mathcal{R}_1$, with $\mathcal{R}_1(t_1) = [\mathcal{P}ol_1(\ell_0)] = |\mathsf{x}|$ and $\mathcal{R}_1(t) = \mathcal{R}_0(t)$ for all other transitions t.

Theorem 5 (Complexities from PRFs). *Let $\mathcal{R}$ be a runtime approximation and $\mathcal{P}ol$ be a PRF for $\mathcal{T}$. Let[4] $\mathcal{R}'(t) = [\mathcal{P}ol(\ell_0)]$ for all $t \in \mathcal{T}_{\succ}$ and $\mathcal{R}'(t) = \mathcal{R}(t)$ for all other $t \in \mathcal{T}$. Then, $\mathcal{R}'$ is also a runtime approximation.*

3.2 Modular Runtime Bounds from PRFs and Size Bounds

The basic method from Thm. 5 only succeeds in finding complexity bounds for simple examples. In particular, it often fails for programs with non-linear runtime. Although corresponding SAT- and SMT-encodings exist [20], generating a suitable PRF $\mathcal{P}ol$ of a non-linear degree is a complex synthesis problem (and undecidable in general). This is aggravated by the need to consider all of $\mathcal{T}$ at once, which is required to check that no transition of $\mathcal{T}$ increases $\mathcal{P}ol$'s measure.

Therefore, we now present a new *modular* technique that only considers isolated program *parts* $\mathcal{T}' \subseteq \mathcal{T}$ in each PRF synthesis step. The bounds obtained from these "local" PRFs are then lifted to a bound expressed in the input values. To this end, we combine them with bounds on the size of the variables when entering the program part $\mathcal{T}'$ and with a bound on the number of times that

---

[4] To ensure that $\mathcal{R}'(t)$ is at most as large as the previous bound $\mathcal{R}(t)$, one could also define $\mathcal{R}'(t) = \min\{[\mathcal{P}ol(\ell_0)], \mathcal{R}(t)\}$. A similar improvement is possible for all other techniques in the paper that refine the approximations $\mathcal{R}$ or $\mathcal{S}$.

$\mathcal{T}'$ can be reached in evaluations of the full program $\mathcal{T}$. This allows us to use existing efficient procedures for the automated generation of (often linear) PRFs for the analysis of programs with (possibly non-linear) runtime.

For instance, consider the *subset* $\mathcal{T}_1' = \{t_1, \ldots, t_5\}$ of the transitions in our program. Using the constant PRF $\mathcal{P}ol_2$ with $\mathcal{P}ol_2(\ell_1) = 1$ and $\mathcal{P}ol_2(\ell_2) = \mathcal{P}ol_2(\ell_3) = 0$, we see that t_1, t_3, t_4, t_5 do not increase the measure of configurations and that t_2 decreases it. Hence, in executions that are *restricted to* $\mathcal{T}_1'$ and that start in ℓ_1, t_2 is used at most $\lceil \mathcal{P}ol_2(\ell_1) \rceil = 1$ times. To obtain a global result, we consider how often $\mathcal{T}_1'$ is reached in a full program run. As $\mathcal{T}_1'$ can only be reached by the transition t_0, we *multiply* its runtime approximation $\mathcal{R}_1(t_0) = 1$ with the local bound $\lceil \mathcal{P}ol_2(\ell_1) \rceil = 1$ obtained for the sub-program $\mathcal{T}_1'$. Thus, we can refine the runtime approximation $\mathcal{R}_1$ to $\mathcal{R}_2(t_2) = \mathcal{R}_1(t_0) \cdot \lceil \mathcal{P}ol_2(\ell_1) \rceil = 1 \cdot 1 = 1$ and we set $\mathcal{R}_2(t) = \mathcal{R}_1(t)$ for all other t.

In general, to estimate how often a sub-program $\mathcal{T}'$ is reached in an evaluation, we consider the transitions $\tilde{t} \in \mathcal{T}$ that lead to an "entry location" ℓ in $\mathcal{T}'$. We *multiply* the runtime bound of such transitions $\tilde{t}$ with the bound $\lceil \mathcal{P}ol(\ell) \rceil$ for runs starting in ℓ. In our example, t_0 is the only transition leading to $\mathcal{T}_1' = \{t_1, \ldots, t_5\}$ and thus, the runtime bound $\mathcal{R}_1(t_0) = 1$ is multiplied with $\lceil \mathcal{P}ol_2(\ell_1) \rceil$.

Next, we consider the remaining transitions $\mathcal{T}_2' = \{t_3, t_4, t_5\}$ for which we have no bound yet. We use $\mathcal{P}ol_3(\ell_2) = \mathcal{P}ol_3(\ell_3) = \mathbf{z}$ where $(\mathcal{T}_2')_\succ = \{t_5\}$. So *restricted to the sub-program* $\mathcal{T}_2'$, t_5 is used at most $\lceil \mathcal{P}ol_3(\ell_2) \rceil = |\mathbf{z}|$ times. Here, $\mathbf{z}$ refers to the value when entering $\mathcal{T}_2'$ (i.e., after transition t_2). To translate this bound into an expression in the input values, we substitute the variable $\mathbf{z}$ by its maximal size after using the transition t_2, i.e., by the *size bound* $\mathcal{S}(t_2, \mathbf{z}')$. As the runtime of the loop at ℓ_2 depends on the size of $\mathbf{z}$, our approach *alternates* between computing runtime and size bounds. Our method to compute size bounds will determine that the size of $\mathbf{z}$ after the transition t_2 is at most $|\mathbf{x}|$, cf. Sect. 4. Hence, we replace the variable $\mathbf{z}$ in $\lceil \mathcal{P}ol_3(\ell_2) \rceil = |\mathbf{z}|$ by $\mathcal{S}(t_2, \mathbf{z}') = |\mathbf{x}|$.

So in general, the polynomials $\lceil \mathcal{P}ol(\ell) \rceil$ for the entry locations ℓ of $\mathcal{T}'$ only provide a bound in terms of the variable values at location ℓ. To find bounds expressed in the variable values at the start location ℓ_0, we use our *size approximation* $\mathcal{S}$ and replace all variables in $\lceil \mathcal{P}ol(\ell) \rceil$ by our approximation for their sizes at location ℓ. For this, we define the *application* of polynomials to functions. Let $p \in \mathbb{N}[v_1, \ldots, v_n]$ and $f_1, \ldots, f_n \in \mathfrak{C}$. Then $p(f_1, \ldots, f_n)$ is the function with $(p(f_1, \ldots, f_n))(\boldsymbol{m}) = p(f_1(\boldsymbol{m}), \ldots, f_n(\boldsymbol{m}))$ for all $\boldsymbol{m} \in \mathbb{N}^n$. Weak monotonicity of $p, f_1, \ldots, f_n$ also implies weak monotonicity of $p(f_1, \ldots, f_n)$, i.e., $p(f_1, \ldots, f_n) \in \mathfrak{C}$.

For example, when analyzing how often t_5 is used in the sub-program $\mathcal{T}_2' = \{t_3, t_4, t_5\}$ above, we applied the polynomial $\lceil \mathcal{P}ol_3(\ell_2) \rceil$ for the start location ℓ_2 of $\mathcal{T}_2'$ to the size bounds $\mathcal{S}(t_2, v')$ for the variables $\mathbf{x}$, $\mathbf{y}$, $\mathbf{z}$, $\mathbf{u}$ (i.e., to their sizes before entering $\mathcal{T}_2'$). As $\lceil \mathcal{P}ol_3(\ell_2) \rceil = |\mathbf{z}|$ and $\mathcal{S}(t_2, \mathbf{z}') = |\mathbf{x}|$, we obtained $\lceil \mathcal{P}ol_3(\ell_2) \rceil (\mathcal{S}(t_2, \mathbf{x}'), \mathcal{S}(t_2, \mathbf{y}'), \mathcal{S}(t_2, \mathbf{z}'), \mathcal{S}(t_2, \mathbf{u}')) = |\mathbf{x}|$.

To compute a global bound, we also have to examine how often $\mathcal{T}_2'$ can be executed in a full program run. As $\mathcal{T}_2'$ is only reached by t_2, we obtain $\mathcal{R}_3(t_5) = \mathcal{R}_2(t_2) \cdot |\mathbf{x}| = 1 \cdot |\mathbf{x}| = |\mathbf{x}|$. For all other transitions t, we again have $\mathcal{R}_3(t) = \mathcal{R}_2(t)$.

In Thm. 6, our technique is represented by the procedure TimeBounds. It takes the current complexity approximation $(\mathcal{R}, \mathcal{S})$ and a sub-program $\mathcal{T}'$, and computes a PRF for $\mathcal{T}'$. Based on this, $\mathcal{R}$ is refined to the approximation $\mathcal{R}'$.

Theorem 6 (TimeBounds). *Let* $(\mathcal{R}, \mathcal{S})$ *be a complexity approximation and* $\mathcal{T}' \subseteq \mathcal{T}$ *such that* $\mathcal{T}'$ *contains no initial transitions. Let* $\mathcal{L}' = \{\ell \mid (\ell, \tau, \ell') \in \mathcal{T}'\}$ *contain all entry locations of* $\mathcal{T}'$ *and let* $\mathcal{P}ol$ *be a PRF for* $\mathcal{T}'$. *For any* $\ell \in \mathcal{L}'$, *let* $\mathcal{T}_\ell$ *contain all transitions* $(\tilde{\ell}, \tilde{\tau}, \ell) \in \mathcal{T} \setminus \mathcal{T}'$ *leading to* ℓ. *Let* $\mathcal{R}'(t) = \sum_{\ell \in \mathcal{L}', \tilde{t} \in \mathcal{T}_\ell} \mathcal{R}(\tilde{t}) \cdot [\mathcal{P}ol(\ell)](\mathcal{S}(\tilde{t}, v_1'), \ldots, \mathcal{S}(\tilde{t}, v_n'))$ *for* $t \in \mathcal{T}'_\succ$ *and* $\mathcal{R}'(t) = \mathcal{R}(t)$ *for all* $t \in \mathcal{T} \setminus \mathcal{T}'_\succ$. *Then,* TimeBounds$(\mathcal{R}, \mathcal{S}, \mathcal{T}') = \mathcal{R}'$ *is also a runtime approximation.*

Here one can see why we require complexity bounds to be weakly monotonic. The reason is that $\mathcal{S}(\tilde{t}, v')$ over-approximates the size of v at some location ℓ. Hence, to ensure that $[\mathcal{P}ol(\ell)](\mathcal{S}(\tilde{t}, v_1'), \ldots, \mathcal{S}(\tilde{t}, v_n'))$ correctly over-approximates how often transitions of $\mathcal{T}'_\succ$ can be applied in parts of evaluations that only use transitions from $\mathcal{T}'$, $[\mathcal{P}ol(\ell)]$ must be weakly monotonic.

By Thm. 6, we now obtain bounds for the remaining transitions in our example. For $\mathcal{T}'_3 = \{t_3, t_4\}$, we use $\mathcal{P}ol_4(\ell_2) = 1$, $\mathcal{P}ol_4(\ell_3) = 0$, and hence $(\mathcal{T}'_3)_\succ = \{t_3\}$. The transitions t_2 and t_5 lead to $\mathcal{T}'_3$, and thus, we obtain $\mathcal{R}_4(t_3) = \mathcal{R}_3(t_2) \cdot 1 + \mathcal{R}_3(t_5) \cdot 1 = 1 + |x|$ and $\mathcal{R}_4(t) = \mathcal{R}_3(t)$ for all other transitions t.

For $\mathcal{T}'_4 = \{t_4\}$, we use $\mathcal{P}ol_5(\ell_3) = u$ with $(\mathcal{T}'_4)_\succ = \mathcal{T}'_4$. The part $\mathcal{T}'_4$ is only entered by the transition t_3. So to get a global bound, we substitute u in $[\mathcal{P}ol_5(\ell_3)] = |u|$ by $\mathcal{S}(t_3, u')$ (in Sect. 4, we will determine $\mathcal{S}(t_3, u') = |x|$). Thus, $\mathcal{R}_5(t_4) = \mathcal{R}_4(t_3) \cdot \mathcal{S}(t_3, u') = (1 + |x|) \cdot |x| = |x| + |x|^2$ and $\mathcal{R}_5(t) = \mathcal{R}_4(t)$ for all other $t \in \mathcal{T}$. So while the runtime of $\mathcal{T}'_4$ on its own is linear, the loop at location ℓ_3 is reached a linear number of times, i.e., its transition t_4 is used *quadratically* often. Thus, the overall program runtime is bounded by $\sum_{t \in \mathcal{T}} \mathcal{R}_5(t) = 3 + 4 \cdot |x| + |x|^2$.

4   Computing Size Bounds

The procedure TimeBounds improves the runtime approximation $\mathcal{R}$, but up to now the size approximation $\mathcal{S}$ was only used as an input. To infer bounds on the sizes of variables, we proceed in three steps. First, we find *local size bounds* that approximate the effect of a single transition on the sizes of variables. Then, we construct a *result variable graph* that makes the flow of data between variables explicit. Finally, we analyze each strongly connected component (SCC) of this graph independently. Here, we combine the local size bounds with our runtime approximation $\mathcal{R}$ to estimate how often transitions modify a variable value.

By a series of SMT queries, we find local size bounds $\mathcal{S}_l(t, v')$ that describe how the size of the post-variable v' is related to the pre-variables of a transition t. So while $\mathcal{S}(t, v')$ is a bound on the size of v after using t in a full program run, $\mathcal{S}_l(t, v')$ is a bound on v after a single use of t.

Definition 7 (Local Size Approximation). *We call* $\mathcal{S}_l : \mathsf{RV} \to \mathfrak{C}$ *a local size approximation iff* $(\mathcal{S}_l(t, v'))(m) \geq \sup\{|v'(v)| \mid \exists \ell, v, \ell', v'. v \leq m \wedge (\ell, v) \to_t (\ell', v')\}$ *for all* $|t, v'| \in \mathsf{RV}$ *and all* $m \in \mathbb{N}^n$.

In our example, we obtain $\mathcal{S}_l(t_1, y') = |y| + 1$, as t_1 increases y by 1. Similarly, $|t_1, x'|$ is bounded by $|x|$. As t_1 is only executed if x is positive, decreasing x by

1 does not increase its *absolute* value. The bound $\max\{0, |x| - 1\}$ would also be allowed, but our approach does not compute better global size bounds from it.

To track how variables influence each other, we construct a result variable graph (RVG) whose nodes are the result variables. An RVG for our example is shown below. Here, we display local size bounds in the RVG to the left of the result variables, separated by "$\geq$" (e.g., "$|x| \geq |t_1, x'|$" means $\mathcal{S}_l(t_1, x') = |x|$).

The RVG has an edge from a result variable $|\tilde{t}, \tilde{v}'|$ to $|t, v'|$ if the transition $\tilde{t}$ can be used directly before t and if $\tilde{v}$ occurs in the local size bound $\mathcal{S}_l(t, v')$. Such an edge means that the size of $\tilde{v}'$ in the post-location of the transition $\tilde{t}$ may influence the size of v' in t's post-location.

$$
\begin{array}{llll}
|x| \geq |t_0, x'| & 0 \geq |t_0, y'| & |z| \geq |t_0, z'| & |u| \geq |t_0, u'| \\
|x| \geq |t_1, x'| & |y|+1 \geq |t_1, y'| & |z| \geq |t_1, z'| & |u| \geq |t_1, u'| \\
|x| \geq |t_2, x'| & |y| \geq |t_2, y'| & |y| \geq |t_2, z'| & |u| \geq |t_2, u'| \\
|x| \geq |t_3, x'| & |y| \geq |t_3, y'| & |z| \geq |t_3, z'| & |z| \geq |t_3, u'| \\
|x| \geq |t_4, x'| & |y| \geq |t_4, y'| & |z| \geq |t_4, z'| & |u| \geq |t_4, u'| \\
|x| \geq |t_5, x'| & |y| \geq |t_5, y'| & |z| \geq |t_5, z'| & |u| \geq |t_5, u'|
\end{array}
$$

To state which variables may influence a function $f \in \mathfrak{C}$, we define its *active variables* as $\mathsf{actV}(f) = \{v_i \in \mathcal{V} \mid \exists m_1, \ldots, m_n, m_i' \in \mathbb{N}.$ $f(m_1, \ldots, m_i, \ldots, m_n) \neq f(m_1, \ldots, m_i', \ldots, m_n)\}$. Let $\mathsf{pre}(t)$ denote the transitions that may precede t in evaluations, i.e., $\mathsf{pre}(t) = \{\tilde{t} \in \mathcal{T} \mid \exists v_0, \ell, v.$ $(\ell_0, v_0) \rightarrow^* \circ \rightarrow_{\tilde{t}} \circ \rightarrow_t (\ell, v)\}$. While $\mathsf{pre}(t)$ is undecidable in general, there exist several techniques to compute over-approximations of $\mathsf{pre}(t)$, cf. [19,21]. For example, one can disregard the formulas of the transitions and approximate $\mathsf{pre}(t)$ by all transitions that end in t's source location.

Definition 8 (RVG). *Let $\mathcal{S}_l$ be a local size approximation. An RVG has $\mathcal{T}$'s result variables as nodes and the edges $\{(|\tilde{t}, \tilde{v}'|, |t, v'|) \mid \tilde{t} \in \mathsf{pre}(t), \tilde{v} \in \mathsf{actV}(\mathcal{S}_l(t, v'))\}$.*

For the transition t_2 which sets $z = y$, we obtain $\mathcal{S}_l(t_2, z') = |y|$. Hence, we have $\mathsf{actV}(\mathcal{S}_l(t_2, z')) = y$. The program graph implies $\mathsf{pre}(t_2) = \{t_0, t_1\}$, and thus, our RVG contains edges from $|t_0, y'|$ to $|t_2, z'|$ and from $|t_1, y'|$ to $|t_2, z'|$.

Each SCC of the RVG represents a set of result variables that may influence each other. To lift the local approximation $\mathcal{S}_l$ to a global one, we consider each SCC on its own. We treat the SCCs in topological order, reflecting the data flow. As usual, an SCC is a maximal subgraph with a path from each node to every other node. An SCC is *trivial* if it consists of a single node without an edge to itself. In Sect. 4.1, we show how to deduce global bounds for trivial SCCs and in Sect. 4.2, we handle non-trivial SCCs where transitions are applied repeatedly.

4.1   Size Bounds for Trivial SCCs of the RVG

$\mathcal{S}_l(t, v')$ approximates the size of v' after the transition t w.r.t. t's pre-variables. But our goal is to obtain a *global* bound $\mathcal{S}(t, v')$ that approximates v' w.r.t. *the initial values* of the variables at the program start. For trivial SCCs that consist of a result variable $\alpha = |t, v'|$ with an initial transition t, the local bound $\mathcal{S}_l(\alpha)$ is also the global bound $\mathcal{S}(\alpha)$, as the start location ℓ_0 has no incoming transitions. For example, regard the trivial SCC with the result variable $|t_0, \mathbf{y}'|$. As $0 \geq |t_0, \mathbf{y}'|$ holds, its global size bound is also 0, and we set $\mathcal{S}(t_0, \mathbf{y}') = 0$.

Next, we consider trivial SCCs $\alpha = |t, v'|$ with incoming edges from other SCCs. Now $\mathcal{S}_l(\alpha)(\mathbf{m})$ is an upper bound on the size of v' after using the transition t in a configuration where the sizes of the variables are at most $\mathbf{m}$. To obtain a global bound, we replace $\mathbf{m}$ by upper bounds on t's input variables. The edges leading to α come from result variables $|\tilde{t}, v'_i|$ where $\tilde{t} \in \mathsf{pre}(t)$ and $v_i \in \mathsf{actV}(\mathcal{S}_l(\alpha))$. Thus, a bound for the result variable $\alpha = |t, v'|$ is obtained by applying $\mathcal{S}_l(\alpha)$ to $\mathcal{S}(\tilde{t}, v'_1), \ldots, \mathcal{S}(\tilde{t}, v'_n)$, for all $\tilde{t} \in \mathsf{pre}(t)$.

As an example consider the result variable $|t_2, \mathbf{z}'|$. Its local size bound is $\mathcal{S}_l(t_2, \mathbf{z}') = |\mathbf{y}|$. To express this bound in terms of the input variables, we consider the predecessors $|t_0, \mathbf{y}'|$ and $|t_1, \mathbf{y}'|$ of $|t_2, \mathbf{z}'|$ in the RVG. So $\mathcal{S}_l(t_2, \mathbf{z}')$ must be applied to $\mathcal{S}(t_0, \mathbf{y}')$ and $\mathcal{S}(t_1, \mathbf{y}')$. If SCCs are handled in topological order, one already knows that $\mathcal{S}(t_0, \mathbf{y}') = 0$ and $\mathcal{S}(t_1, \mathbf{y}') = |\mathbf{x}|$. Thus, $\mathcal{S}(t_2, \mathbf{z}') = \max\{0, |\mathbf{x}|\} = |\mathbf{x}|$.

Thm. 9 presents the resulting procedure SizeBounds. Based on the current approximation $(\mathcal{R}, \mathcal{S})$, it improves the global size bound for the result variable in a non-trivial SCC of the RVG. Non-trivial SCCs will be handled in Thm. 10.

Theorem 9 (SizeBounds for Trivial SCCs). *Let $(\mathcal{R}, \mathcal{S})$ be a complexity approximation, let $\mathcal{S}_l$ be a local size approximation, and let $\{\alpha\} \subseteq \mathsf{RV}$ be a trivial SCC of the RVG. We define $\mathcal{S}'(\alpha') = \mathcal{S}(\alpha')$ for $\alpha' \neq \alpha$ and*

- *$\mathcal{S}'(\alpha) = \mathcal{S}_l(\alpha)$, if $\alpha = |t, v'|$ for some initial transition t*
- *$\mathcal{S}'(\alpha) = \max\{\mathcal{S}_l(\alpha)(\mathcal{S}(\tilde{t}, v'_1), \ldots, \mathcal{S}(\tilde{t}, v'_n)) \mid \tilde{t} \in \mathsf{pre}(t)\}$, otherwise*

Then $\mathsf{SizeBounds}(\mathcal{R}, \mathcal{S}, \{\alpha\}) = \mathcal{S}'$ is also a size approximation.

4.2 Size Bounds for Non-trivial SCCs of the RVG

Finally, we show how to improve the size bounds for result variables in non-trivial SCCs of the RVG. Such an SCC corresponds to a loop and hence, each of its *local* changes can be applied several times. By combining the time bounds $\mathcal{R}(t)$ for its transitions t with the local size bounds $\mathcal{S}_l(t, v')$, we approximate the overall effect of these repeated changes. To simplify this approximation, we use the following classification of result variables α depending on their local size bound $\mathcal{S}_l(\alpha)$:

- $\alpha \in \doteq$ (α is an "equality") if the result variable is not larger than its pre-variables or a constant, i.e., iff there is a number $e_\alpha \in \mathbb{N}$ with $\max\{e_\alpha, m_1, \ldots, m_n\} \geq (\mathcal{S}_l(\alpha))(m_1, \ldots, m_n)$ for all $m_1, \ldots, m_n \in \mathbb{N}$.
- $\alpha \in \dot{+}$ (α "adds a constant") if the result variable only increases over the pre-variables by a constant, i.e., iff there is a number $e_\alpha \in \mathbb{N}$ with $e_\alpha + \max\{m_1, \ldots, m_n\} \geq (\mathcal{S}_l(\alpha))(m_1, \ldots, m_n)$ for all $m_1, \ldots, m_n \in \mathbb{N}$.
- $\alpha \in \dot{\Sigma}$ (α "adds variables") if the result variable is not larger than the sum of the pre-variables and a constant, i.e., iff there is a number $e_\alpha \in \mathbb{N}$ with $e_\alpha + \sum_{i \in \{1, \ldots, n\}} m_i \geq (\mathcal{S}_l(\alpha))(m_1, \ldots, m_n)$ for all $m_1, \ldots, m_n \in \mathbb{N}$.

So for our example, we get $\{|t_3, \mathbf{z}'|, |t_4, \mathbf{z}'|, |t_5, \mathbf{z}'|\} \subseteq \doteq$ since $\mathcal{S}_l(t_3, \mathbf{z}') = \mathcal{S}_l(t_4, \mathbf{z}') = \mathcal{S}_l(t_5, \mathbf{z}') = |\mathbf{z}|$. Similarly, we have $|t_1, \mathbf{y}'| \in \dot{+}$ as $\mathcal{S}_l(t_1, \mathbf{y}') = |\mathbf{y}| + 1$.

In the following, local size bounds like $2 \cdot |\mathbf{x}|$ are not handled because we are currently interested only in bounds that can be expressed by *polynomials* (and max and min). If a change bounded by $2 \cdot |\mathbf{x}|$ is applied $|\mathbf{y}|$ times, the resulting value is bounded only by the exponential function $2^{|\mathbf{y}|} \cdot |\mathbf{x}|$. Of course, our approach could be extended to infer such exponential size bounds as well. In Sect. 5, we discuss the limitations and possible extensions of our approach.

Similar to $\mathsf{pre}(t)$ for transitions t, let $\mathsf{pre}(\alpha)$ for a result variable α be those $\tilde{\alpha} \in RV$ with an edge from $\tilde{\alpha}$ to α in the RVG. To deduce a bound on the size of the result variables α in an SCC C, we first consider the size of values *entering* the SCC C. Hence, we require that the resulting size bound $\mathcal{S}(\alpha)$ for $\alpha \in C$ should be at least as large as the sizes $\mathcal{S}(\tilde{\alpha})$ of the *inputs* $\tilde{\alpha}$, i.e., of those result variables $\tilde{\alpha}$ outside the SCC C that have an edge to some $\alpha \in C$. Moreover, if the SCC C contains result variables $\alpha = |t, v'| \in \doteq$, then the transition t either does not increase the size at all, or increases it to the constant e_α. Hence, the bound $\mathcal{S}(\alpha)$ for the result variables α in C should also be at least $\max\{e_\alpha \mid \alpha \in \doteq\}$.[5]

For example, when computing the global size bounds for the result variables in the SCC $C = \{|t_3, \mathbf{z}'|, |t_4, \mathbf{z}'|, |t_5, \mathbf{z}'|\}$ in our example, the only predecessor of this SCC is $|t_2, \mathbf{z}'|$ with $\mathcal{S}(t_2, \mathbf{z}') = |\mathbf{x}|$. For each $\alpha \in C$, the corresponding constant e_α is 0. Thus, for all $\alpha \in C$ we obtain $\mathcal{S}(\alpha) = \max\{|\mathbf{x}|, 0\} = |\mathbf{x}|$.

To handle result variables $\alpha \in \dotplus \setminus \doteq$ that add a constant e_α, we consider how often this addition is performed. Thus, while TimeBounds from Thm. 6 uses the size approximation $\mathcal{S}$ to improve the runtime approximation $\mathcal{R}$, SizeBounds uses $\mathcal{R}$ to improve $\mathcal{S}$. We define $\mathcal{R}(|t, v'|) = \mathcal{R}(t)$ for all result variables $|t, v'|$. Then, since $\mathcal{R}(\alpha)$ is a bound on the number of times that e_α is added, the repeated traversal of α's transition increases the overall size by at most $\mathcal{R}(\alpha) \cdot e_\alpha$.

For instance, consider the result variable $\alpha = |t_1, \mathbf{y}'|$ in our example. Its local size bound is $\mathcal{S}_l(t_1, \mathbf{y}') = |\mathbf{y}| + 1$, i.e., each traversal of t_1 increases $\mathbf{y}$ by $e_\alpha = 1$. As before, we use the size bounds on the predecessors of the SCC $\{\alpha\}$ as a basis. So the input value when entering the SCC is $\mathcal{S}(t_0, \mathbf{y}') = 0$. Since t_1 is executed at most $\mathcal{R}(\alpha) = \mathcal{R}(t_1) = |\mathbf{x}|$ times, we obtain the global bound $\mathcal{S}(\alpha) = \mathcal{S}(t_0, \mathbf{y}') + \mathcal{R}(\alpha) \cdot e_\alpha = 0 + |\mathbf{x}| \cdot 1 = |\mathbf{x}|$.

Finally, we discuss how to handle result variables $\alpha \in \dot{\Sigma} \setminus \dotplus$. To this end, consider the program from Sect. 1 again. Its program graph is depicted on the right. Our method detects the runtime bounds $\mathcal{R}(t_0) = 1$, $\mathcal{R}(t_1) = |\mathbf{i}|$, and $\mathcal{R}(t_2) = 1$. To obtain size bounds, we first generate the RVG (see the next page). Now we can infer the global size bounds $\mathcal{S}(t, \mathbf{i}') = |\mathbf{i}|$ for all $t \in \mathcal{T}$ and $\mathcal{S}(t_0, \mathbf{x}') = |\mathbf{x}|$. Next we regard the result variable $\alpha = |t_1, \mathbf{x}'|$ with the local bound $\mathcal{S}_l(\alpha) = |\mathbf{x}| + |\mathbf{i}|$. Thus, we have $\alpha \in \dot{\Sigma} \setminus \dotplus$.

For result variables α that sum up several program variables, we require that only *one* comes from α's own SCC in the RVG. Otherwise, we would also consider loops like **while** $z > 0$ **do** $x = x + y$; $y = x$; $z = z - 1$; **done** that increase the size of $\mathbf{x}$ exponentially. To express our requirement formally, let $V_\alpha = \{v \mid |t, v'| \in \mathsf{pre}(\alpha) \cap C\}$ be those variables whose result variables in C have an edge to

---

$t_1: \mathbf{if}(\mathbf{i} > 0)$

$\quad \mathbf{i} = \mathbf{i} - 1$

$\quad \mathbf{x} = \mathbf{x} + \mathbf{i}$

$t_2: \mathbf{if}(\mathbf{i} \leq 0)$

$t_3: \mathbf{if}(\mathbf{x} > 0)$

$\quad \mathbf{x} = \mathbf{x} - 1$

ℓ_0

t_0

ℓ_1

ℓ_2

---

[5] Again, "e_α" denotes the constant function mapping all values from $\mathbb{N}^n$ to e_α.

α. We require $|\mathcal{V}_\alpha| = 1$, i.e., no two result variables $|t, v'|, |\tilde{t}, \tilde{v}'|$ in α's SCC C with $v \neq \tilde{v}$ may have edges to α. But we allow incoming edges from arbitrary result variables *outside* the SCC. The requirement is satisfied in our RVG, as $\alpha = |t_1, \mathbf{x}'|$ is a predecessor of itself and its SCC contains no other result variables. Thus, $\mathcal{V}_\alpha = \{\mathbf{x}\}$. Of course, α also has predecessors of the form $|t, \mathbf{i}'|$ outside the SCC.

$$
\begin{array}{cc}
|\mathbf{i}| \geq |t_0, \mathbf{i}'| & |\mathbf{x}| \geq |t_0, \mathbf{x}'| \\
\downarrow \quad \nearrow \quad \searrow \quad \downarrow \quad \nearrow \\
|\mathbf{i}| \geq |t_1, \mathbf{i}'| \longrightarrow |\mathbf{x}| + |\mathbf{i}| \geq |t_1, \mathbf{x}'| \\
\downarrow \quad\quad\quad \downarrow \\
|\mathbf{i}| \geq |t_2, \mathbf{i}'| & |\mathbf{x}| \geq |t_2, \mathbf{x}'| \\
\downarrow \quad \nearrow \quad\quad \downarrow \quad \nearrow \\
|\mathbf{i}| \geq |t_3, \mathbf{i}'| & |\mathbf{x}| \geq |t_3, \mathbf{x}'|
\end{array}
$$

For each variable v, let f_v^α be an upper bound on the size of those result variables $|t, v'| \notin C$ that have edges to α, i.e., $f_v^\alpha = \max\{\mathcal{S}(t, v') \mid |t, v'| \in \mathsf{pre}(\alpha) \setminus C\}$. The execution of α's transition then means that the value of the variable in $\mathcal{V}_\alpha$ can be increased by adding f_v^α (for all $v \in \mathsf{actV}(\mathcal{S}_l(\alpha)) \setminus \mathcal{V}_\alpha$) plus the constant e_α. Again, this can be repeated at most $\mathcal{R}(\alpha)$ times. So the overall size is bounded by adding $\mathcal{R}(\alpha) \cdot (e_\alpha + \sum_{v \in \mathsf{actV}(\mathcal{S}_l(\alpha)) \setminus \mathcal{V}_\alpha} f_v^\alpha)$.

In our example with $\alpha = |t_1, \mathbf{x}'|$, we have $\mathcal{V}_\alpha = \{\mathbf{x}\}$, $\mathsf{actV}(\mathcal{S}_l(\alpha)) = \mathsf{actV}(|\mathbf{x}| + |\mathbf{i}|) = \{\mathbf{i}, \mathbf{x}\}$, and $f_\mathbf{i}^\alpha = \max\{\mathcal{S}(t_0, \mathbf{i}'), \mathcal{S}(t_1, \mathbf{i}')\} = |\mathbf{i}|$. When entering α's SCC, the input is bounded by the preceding transitions, i.e., by $\max\{\mathcal{S}(t_0, \mathbf{i}'), \mathcal{S}(t_1, \mathbf{i}'), \mathcal{S}(t_0, \mathbf{x}')\} = \max\{|\mathbf{i}|, |\mathbf{x}|\}$. By traversing α's transition t_1 repeatedly (at most $\mathcal{R}(\alpha) = \mathcal{R}(t_1) = |\mathbf{i}|$ times), this value may be increased by adding $\mathcal{R}(\alpha) \cdot (e_\alpha + f_\mathbf{i}^\alpha) = |\mathbf{i}| \cdot (0 + |\mathbf{i}|) = |\mathbf{i}|^2$. Hence, we obtain $\mathcal{S}(\alpha) = \max\{|\mathbf{i}|, |\mathbf{x}|\} + |\mathbf{i}|^2$. Consequently, we also get $\mathcal{S}(t_2, \mathbf{x}') = \mathcal{S}(t_3, \mathbf{x}') = \max\{|\mathbf{i}|, |\mathbf{x}|\} + |\mathbf{i}|^2$. Thm. 10 extends the procedure SizeBounds from Thm. 9 to non-trivial SCCs.

Theorem 10 (SizeBounds for Non-Trivial SCCs). *Let $(\mathcal{R}, \mathcal{S})$ be a complexity approximation, $\mathcal{S}_l$ a local size approximation, and $C \subseteq \mathsf{RV}$ a non-trivial SCC of the RVG. If there is an $\alpha \in C$ with $\alpha \notin \dot{\Sigma}$ or both $\alpha \in \dot{\Sigma} \dot{+}$ and $|\mathcal{V}_\alpha| > 1$, then we set $\mathcal{S}' = \mathcal{S}$. Otherwise, for all $\alpha \notin C$ let $\mathcal{S}'(\alpha) = \mathcal{S}(\alpha)$. For all $\alpha \in C$, we set*

$$
\begin{aligned}
\mathcal{S}'(\alpha) = \max(\ &\{\mathcal{S}(\tilde{\alpha}) \mid \text{there is an } \alpha \in C \text{ with } \tilde{\alpha} \in \mathsf{pre}(\alpha) \setminus C\} \ \cup \ \{e_\alpha \mid \alpha \in \dot{=}\}\ ) \\
&+ \textstyle\sum_{\alpha \in \dot{+} \setminus \dot{=}} \mathcal{R}(\alpha) \cdot e_\alpha \\
&+ \textstyle\sum_{\alpha \in \dot{\Sigma} \setminus \dot{+}} \mathcal{R}(\alpha) \cdot (e_\alpha + \textstyle\sum_{v \in \mathsf{actV}(\mathcal{S}_l(\alpha)) \setminus \mathcal{V}_\alpha} f_v^\alpha)
\end{aligned}
$$

Then $\mathsf{SizeBounds}(\mathcal{R}, \mathcal{S}, C) = \mathcal{S}'$ is also a size approximation.

In our example, by the inferred size bounds we can derive a runtime bound for the last transition t_3. When calling TimeBounds on $\mathcal{T}' = \{t_3\}$, it finds the PRF $\mathcal{P}ol(\ell_2) = \mathbf{x}$, implying that $\mathcal{T}'$'s runtime is linear. When reaching $\mathcal{T}'$, the size of $\mathbf{x}$ is bounded by $\mathcal{S}(t_2, \mathbf{x}')$. So $\mathcal{R}(t_3) = \mathcal{R}(t_2) \cdot [\mathcal{P}ol(\ell_2)](\mathcal{S}(t_2, \mathbf{i}'), \mathcal{S}(t_2, \mathbf{x}')) = 1 \cdot \mathcal{S}(t_2, \mathbf{x}') = \max\{|\mathbf{i}|, |\mathbf{x}|\} + |\mathbf{i}|^2$. So a bound on the overall runtime is $\sum_{t \in \mathcal{T}} \mathcal{R}(t) = 2 + |\mathbf{i}| + \max\{|\mathbf{i}|, |\mathbf{x}|\} + |\mathbf{i}|^2$, i.e., it is linear in $|\mathbf{x}|$ and quadratic in $|\mathbf{i}|$.

5   Implementation and Related Work

We presented a new alternating modular approach for runtime and size complexity analysis of integer programs. Each step only considers a small part of the program, and runtime bounds help to infer size bounds and vice versa.

Our overall procedure to compute the runtime and size approximations $\mathcal{R}$ and

$\mathcal{S}$ is displayed on the right. After starting with the initial approximations $\mathcal{R}_0, \mathcal{S}_0$, the procedure TimeBounds (Thm. 6) is used to improve the runtime bounds for those transitions $\mathcal{T}'$ for which we have no bound yet.[6] After-

$$(\mathcal{R}, \mathcal{S}) := (\mathcal{R}_0, \mathcal{S}_0)$$
while there are t, v with $\mathcal{R}(t) = ?$ or $\mathcal{S}(t, v') = ?$ **do**
    $\mathcal{T}' := \{t \in \mathcal{T} \mid \mathcal{R}(t) = ?\}$
    $\mathcal{R} := \text{TimeBounds}(\mathcal{R}, \mathcal{S}, \mathcal{T}')$
    for all SCCs C of the RVG in topological order **do**
        $\mathcal{S} := \text{SizeBounds}(\mathcal{R}, \mathcal{S}, C)$
    done
done

wards, the procedure SizeBounds (Thm. 9 and 10) considers the SCCs of the result variable graph in topological order to update the size approximation.

When all bounds have been determined, $\mathcal{R}$ and $\mathcal{S}$ are returned. Of course, we do not always succeed in finding bounds for all transitions and variables. Thus, while the procedure keeps on improving the bounds, at any point during its run, $\mathcal{R}$ and $\mathcal{S}$ are over-approximations of the actual runtimes and sizes. Hence, the procedure can be interrupted at any time and it always returns correct bounds.

Several methods to determine symbolic complexity bounds for programs have been developed in recent years. The approaches of [3,4] (implemented in COSTA and its backend PUBS) and [37] (implemented in Loopus) also use an iterative procedure based on termination proving techniques to find runtime bounds for isolated loops, which are then combined to an overall result. However, [3,4] handles all loop transitions at once and [37] is restricted to termination proofs via the size-change principle [28]. The approach of [6] (implemented in Rank) first proves termination by a lexicographic combination of linear rank functions, similar to our Thm. 6. However, while Thm. 6 combines these rank functions with size bounds, [6] approximates the reachable state space using Ehrhart polynomials. The tool SPEED [24] instruments programs by counters and employs an invariant generation tool to obtain bounds on these counters. The ABC system [11] also determines symbolic bounds for nested loops, but does not treat sequences of loops. Finally, our technique in Sect. 4.2 to infer size bounds by estimating the effect of repeated local changes has some similarities to the approach of [10] which defines syntactic criteria for programs to have polynomial complexity.

The work on determining the *worst-case execution time* (WCET) for real-time systems [36] is largely orthogonal to symbolic loop bounds. It distinguishes processor instructions according to their complexity, but requires loop bounds to be provided by the user. Recently, recurrence solving has been used as an automatic pre-processing step for WCET analysis in the tool r-TuBound [27].

There is also a wealth of work on complexity for declarative paradigms. For instance, *resource aware* ML [26] analyzes amortized complexity for recursive functional programs with inductive data types, but it does not handle programs whose complexity depends on integers. There are also numerous techniques for complexity analysis of term rewriting and logic programming [7,18,22,31,32].

---

[6] After generating a PRF $\mathcal{P}ol$ for $\mathcal{T}'$, it is advantageous to extend $\mathcal{T}'$ by all remaining transitions (ℓ, τ, ℓ') from $\mathcal{T} \setminus \mathcal{T}'$ where the measure $\mathcal{P}ol$ is also (weakly) decreasing, i.e., where $\tau \Rightarrow (\mathcal{P}ol(\ell))(v_1, \ldots, v_n) \geq (\mathcal{P}ol(\ell'))(v_1', \ldots, v_n')$. Calling the procedure TimeBounds with this extended set $\mathcal{T}'$ yields better results and may also improve previously found runtime bounds. We used this strategy for the example in Sect. 3.

Our approach builds upon well-known basic concepts (like lexicographic rank functions), but uses them in a novel way to obtain a more powerful technique than previous approaches. In particular, in contrast to previous work, our approach deals with non-linear information flow between different program parts.

To evaluate our approach, we implemented a prototype KoAT and compared it with PUBS [3, 4] and Rank [6]. We also contacted the authors of SPEED [24] and Loopus [37], but were not able to obtain these tools. We did not compare KoAT to ABC [11], RAML [26], or r-TuBound [27], as their input or analysis goals differ considerably from ours. As benchmarks, we collected 682 programs from the literature on termination and complexity of integer programs. These include all 36 examples from the evaluation of Rank, all but one of the 53 examples used to evaluate PUBS,[7] all 27 examples from the evaluations of SPEED, and the examples from the current paper (which can be handled by KoAT, but not by PUBS or Rank). Where examples were available as C programs, we used the tool KITTeL [19] to transform them into integer programs automatically. The collection contains 48 recursive examples, which cannot be analyzed with Rank, and 20 examples with non-linear arithmetic, which can be handled by neither Rank nor PUBS. The remaining examples are compatible with all tested tools. All examples, the results of the three tools, and a binary of KoAT are available at [1].

The table illustrates how often each tool could infer a specific runtime bound for the example set. Here, 1, $\log n$, n, $n \log n$, n^2,

	1	$\log n$	n	$n \log n$	n^2	n^3	$n^{>3}$	EXP	Time
KoAT	121	0	145	0	59	3	3	0	1.1 s
PUBS	116	5	131	5	22	7	0	6	0.8 s
Rank	56	0	19	0	8	1	0	0	0.5 s

n^3, and $n^{>3}$ represent their corresponding asymptotic classes and EXP is the class of exponential functions. In the column "Time", we give the average runtime on those examples where the respective tool was successful. The average runtime on those 65 examples where *all* tools succeeded were 0.5 s for KoAT, 0.2 s for PUBS, and 0.6 s for Rank. The benchmarks were executed on a computer with 6GB of RAM and an Intel i7 CPU clocked at 3.07 GHz, using a timeout of 60 seconds for each example. A longer timeout did not yield additional results.

On this collection, our approach was more powerful than the two other tools and still efficient. In fact, KoAT is only a simple prototype whose efficiency could still be improved considerably by fine-tuning its implementation. As shown in [1], there are 77 examples where KoAT infers a bound of a lower asymptotic class than PUBS, 548 examples where the bounds are in the same class, and 57 examples where the bound of PUBS is (asymptotically) more precise than KoAT's. Similarly, there are 259 examples where KoAT is asymptotically more precise than Rank, 410 examples where they are equal, and 13 examples where Rank is more precise. While KoAT is the only of the three tools that can also handle non-linear arithmetic, even when disregarding the 20 examples with non-linear arithmetic, KoAT can detect runtime bounds for 325 examples, whereas PUBS succeeds only for 292 programs and Rank only finds bounds for 84 examples.

A limitation of our implementation is that it only generates (possibly non-linear) PRFs to detect *polynomial* bounds. In contrast, PUBS uses PRFs to find *logarithmic* and *exponential* complexity bounds as well [3]. Such an extension

---

[7] We removed one example with undefined semantics.

could also be directly integrated into our method. Moreover, we are restricted to weakly monotonic bounds in order to allow their modular composition. Another limitation is that our size analysis only handles certain forms of local size bounds in non-trivial SCCs of the result variable graph. For that reason, it often over-approximates the sizes of variables that are both incremented and decremented in the same loop. Due to all these imprecisions, our approach sometimes infers bounds that are asymptotically larger than the actual asymptotic costs.

Our method is easily *extended*. In [14], we provide an extension to handle (possibly recursive) procedure calls in a modular fashion. Moreover, we show how to treat other forms of bounds (e.g., on the number of sent network requests) and how to compute bounds for separate program parts in advance or in parallel.

Future work will be concerned with refining the precision of the inferred runtime and size approximations and with improving our implementation (e.g., by extending it to infer also non-polynomial complexities). Moreover, instead of abstracting heap operations to integers, we intend to investigate an extension of our approach to apply it directly to programs operating on the heap. Finally, similar to the coupling of COSTA with the tool KeY in [5], we want to automatically *certify* the complexity bounds found by our implementation KoAT.

Acknowledgments. We thank A. Ben-Amram, B. Cook, C. von Essen, C. Otto for valuable discussions and C. Alias and S. Genaim for help with the experiments.

References

1. http://aprove.informatik.rwth-aachen.de/eval/IntegerComplexity/
2. Albert, E., Arenas, P., Codish, M., Genaim, S., Puebla, G., Zanardini, D.: Termination analysis of Java Bytecode. In: Barthe, G., de Boer, F.S. (eds.) FMOODS 2008. LNCS, vol. 5051, pp. 2–18. Springer, Heidelberg (2008)
3. Albert, E., Arenas, P., Genaim, S., Puebla, G.: Closed-form upper bounds in static cost analysis. JAR 46(2), 161–203 (2011)
4. Albert, E., Arenas, P., Genaim, S., Puebla, G., Zanardini, D.: Cost analysis of object-oriented bytecode programs. TCS 413(1), 142–159 (2012)
5. Albert, E., Bubel, R., Genaim, S., Hähnle, R., Puebla, G., Román-Díez, G.: Verified resource guarantees using COSTA and KeY. In: Khoo, S.-C., Siek, J.G. (eds.) PEPM 2011, pp. 73–76. ACM Press (2011)
6. Alias, C., Darte, A., Feautrier, P., Gonnord, L.: Multi-dimensional rankings, program termination, and complexity bounds of flowchart programs. In: Cousot, R., Martel, M. (eds.) SAS 2010. LNCS, vol. 6337, pp. 117–133. Springer, Heidelberg (2010)
7. Avanzini, M., Moser, G.: A combination framework for complexity. In: van Raamsdonk, F. (ed.) RTA 2013. LIPIcs, vol. 21, pp. 55–70. Dagstuhl Publishing (2013)
8. Bagnara, R., Mesnard, F., Pescetti, A., Zaffanella, E.: A new look at the automatic synthesis of linear ranking functions. IC 215, 47–67 (2012)
9. Ben-Amram, A.M., Genaim, S.: On the linear ranking problem for integer linear-constraint loops. In: Giacobazzi, R., Cousot, R. (eds.) POPL 2013, pp. 51–62. ACM Press (2013)
10. Ben-Amram, A.M., Jones, N.D., Kristiansen, L.: Linear, polynomial or exponential? Complexity inference in polynomial time. In: Beckmann, A., Dimitracopoulos, C., Löwe, B. (eds.) CiE 2008. LNCS, vol. 5028, pp. 67–76. Springer, Heidelberg (2008)

11. Blanc, R., Henzinger, T.A., Hottelier, T., Kovács, L.: ABC: Algebraic bound computation for loops. In: Clarke, E.M., Voronkov, A. (eds.) LPAR 2010. LNCS (LNAI), vol. 6355, pp. 103–118. Springer, Heidelberg (2010)

12. Bradley, A.R., Manna, Z., Sipma, H.B.: Linear ranking with reachability. In: Etessami, K., Rajamani, S.K. (eds.) CAV 2005. LNCS, vol. 3576, pp. 491–504. Springer, Heidelberg (2005)

13. Brockschmidt, M., Cook, B., Fuhs, C.: Better termination proving through cooperation. In: Sharygina, N., Veith, H. (eds.) CAV 2013. LNCS, vol. 8044, pp. 413–429. Springer, Heidelberg (2013)

14. Brockschmidt, M., Emmes, F., Falke, S., Fuhs, C., Giesl, J.: Alternating runtime and size complexity analysis of integer programs. Tech. Rep. AIB 2013-12, RWTH Aachen (2013), available from [1] and from http://aib.informatik.rwth-aachen.de

15. Brockschmidt, M., Musiol, R., Otto, C., Giesl, J.: Automated termination proofs for Java programs with cyclic data. In: Madhusudan, P., Seshia, S.A. (eds.) CAV 2012. LNCS, vol. 7358, pp. 105–122. Springer, Heidelberg (2012)

16. Cook, B., Podelski, A., Rybalchenko, A.: Termination proofs for systems code. In: Schwartzbach, M., Ball, T. (eds.) PLDI 2006, pp. 415–426. ACM Press (2006)

17. Cook, B., See, A., Zuleger, F.: Ramsey vs. Lexicographic termination proving. In: Piterman, N., Smolka, S.A. (eds.) TACAS 2013. LNCS, vol. 7795, pp. 47–61. Springer, Heidelberg (2013)

18. Debray, S., Lin, N.: Cost analysis of logic programs. TOPLAS 15, 826–875 (1993)

19. Falke, S., Kapur, D., Sinz, C.: Termination analysis of C programs using compiler intermediate languages. In: Schmidt-Schauß, M. (ed.) RTA 2011. LIPIcs, vol. 10, pp. 41–50. Dagstuhl Publishing (2011)

20. Fuhs, C., Giesl, J., Middeldorp, A., Schneider-Kamp, P., Thiemann, R., Zankl, H.: SAT solving for termination analysis with polynomial interpretations. In: Marques-Silva, J., Sakallah, K.A. (eds.) SAT 2007. LNCS, vol. 4501, pp. 340–354. Springer, Heidelberg (2007)

21. Fuhs, C., Giesl, J., Plücker, M., Schneider-Kamp, P., Falke, S.: Proving termination of integer term rewriting. In: Treinen, R. (ed.) RTA 2009. LNCS, vol. 5595, pp. 32–47. Springer, Heidelberg (2009)

22. Giesl, J., Ströder, T., Schneider-Kamp, P., Emmes, F., Fuhs, C.: Symbolic evaluation graphs and term rewriting: A general methodology for analyzing logic programs. In: De Schreye, D., Janssens, G., King, A. (eds.) PPDP 2012, pp. 1–12. ACM Press (2012)

23. Giesl, J., Thiemann, R., Schneider-Kamp, P., Falke, S.: Mechanizing and improving dependency pairs. JAR 37(3), 155–203 (2006)

24. Gulwani, S., Mehra, K.K., Chilimbi, T.M.: SPEED: Precise and efficient static estimation of program computational complexity. In: Shao, Z., Pierce, B.C. (eds.) POPL 2009, pp. 127–139. ACM Press (2009)

25. Harris, W.R., Lal, A., Nori, A.V., Rajamani, S.K.: Alternation for termination. In: Cousot, R., Martel, M. (eds.) SAS 2010. LNCS, vol. 6337, pp. 304–319. Springer, Heidelberg (2010)

26. Hoffmann, J., Aehlig, K., Hofmann, M.: Multivariate amortized resource analysis. TOPLAS 34(3) (2012)

27. Knoop, J., Kovács, L., Zwirchmayr, J.: r-TuBound: Loop bounds for WCET analysis (Tool paper). In: Bjørner, N., Voronkov, A. (eds.) LPAR 2012. LNCS, vol. 7180, pp. 435–444. Springer, Heidelberg (2012)

28. Lee, C.S., Jones, N.D., Ben-Amram, A.M.: The size-change principle for program termination. In: Hankin, C., Schmidt, D. (eds.) POPL 2001, pp. 81–92. ACM Press (2001)

29. Magill, S., Tsai, M.H., Lee, P., Tsay, Y.K.: Automatic numeric abstractions for heap-manipulating programs. In: Hermenegildo, M.V., Palsberg, J. (eds.), POPL 2010, pp. 211–222 (2010)
30. Miné, A.: The Octagon abstract domain. HOSC 19(1), 31–100 (2006)
31. Navas, J., Mera, E., López-García, P., Hermenegildo, M.V.: User-definable resource bounds analysis for logic programs. In: Dahl, V., Niemelä, I. (eds.) ICLP 2007. LNCS, vol. 4670, pp. 348–363. Springer, Heidelberg (2007)
32. Noschinski, L., Emmes, F., Giesl, J.: Analyzing innermost runtime complexity of term rewriting by dependency pairs. JAR 51(1), 27–56 (2013)
33. Podelski, A., Rybalchenko, A.: A complete method for the synthesis of linear ranking functions. In: Steffen, B., Levi, G. (eds.) VMCAI 2004. LNCS, vol. 2937, pp. 239–251. Springer, Heidelberg (2004)
34. Spoto, F., Mesnard, F., Payet, É.: A termination analyser for Java Bytecode based on path-length. TOPLAS 32(3) (2010)
35. Tsitovich, A., Sharygina, N., Wintersteiger, C.M., Kroening, D.: Loop summarization and termination analysis. In: Abdulla, P.A., Leino, K.R.M. (eds.) TACAS 2011. LNCS, vol. 6605, pp. 81–95. Springer, Heidelberg (2011)
36. Wilhelm, R., Engblom, J., Ermedahl, A., Holsti, N., Thesing, S., Whalley, D.B., Bernat, G., Ferdinand, C., Heckmann, R., Mitra, T., Mueller, F., Puaut, I., Puschner, P.P., Staschulat, J., Stenström, P.: The worst-case execution-time problem: overview of methods and survey of tools. TECS 7(3), 36:1–36:53 (2008)
37. Zuleger, F., Gulwani, S., Sinn, M., Veith, H.: Bound analysis of imperative programs with the size-change abstraction. In: Yahav, E. (ed.) SAS 2011. LNCS, vol. 6887, pp. 280–297. Springer, Heidelberg (2011)

Proving Nontermination via Safety

Hong-Yi Chen[1], Byron Cook[2,1], Carsten Fuhs[1],
Kaustubh Nimkar[1], and Peter O'Hearn[1]

[1] University College London, UK
[2] Microsoft Research, UK

Abstract. We show how the problem of nontermination proving can be reduced to a question of underapproximation search guided by a safety prover. This reduction leads to new nontermination proving implementation strategies based on existing tools for safety proving. Our preliminary implementation beats existing tools. Furthermore, our approach leads to easy support for programs with unbounded nondeterminism.

1 Introduction

The problem of proving program *non*termination represents an interesting complement to termination as, unlike safety, termination's falsification cannot be witnessed by a finite trace. While the problem of proving termination has now been extensively studied, the search for reliable and scalable methods for proving nontermination remains open.

In this paper we develop a new method of proving nontermination based on a reduction to safety proving that leverages the power of existing tools. An iterative algorithm is developed which uses counterexamples to a fixed safety property to refine an underapproximation of a program. With our approach, existing safety provers can now be employed to prove nontermination of programs that previous techniques could not handle. Not only does the new approach perform better, it also leads to nontermination proving tools supporting programs with nondeterminism, for which previous tools had only little support.

Limitations. Our proposed nontermination procedure can only prove nontermination. On terminating programs the procedure is likely to diverge (although some heuristics are proposed which aim to avoid this). While our method could be extended to further programming language features (*e.g.* heap, recursion), in practice the supported features of an underlying safety prover determine applicability. Our implementation uses a safety prover for non-recursive programs with linear integer arithmetic commands.

```
if (k ≥ 0)
   skip;
else
   i := −1;

while (i ≥ 0) {
   i := nondet();
}

i := 2;
```

Example. Before discussing our procedure in a formal setting, we begin with a simple example given to the right. In this program the command i := nondet() represents nondeterministic value introduction into the variable i. The loop in this program

E. Ábrahám and K. Havelund (Eds.): TACAS 2014, LNCS 8413, pp. 156–171, 2014.
© Springer-Verlag Berlin Heidelberg 2014

is nonterminating when the program is invoked with appropriate inputs and when appropriate choices for nondet assignment are made. We are interested in automatically detecting this nontermination. The basis of our procedure is the search for an underapproximation of the original program that *never* terminates. As "never terminates" can be encoded as safety property (defined later as *closed recurrence* in Sect. 2), we can then iterate a safety prover together with a method of underapproximating based on counterexamples. We have to be careful, however, to find the right underapproximation in order to avoid unsoundness.

In order to find the desired underapproximation for our example, we introduce an assume statement at the beginning with the initial precondition true. We also place assume(true) statements after each use of nondet. We then put an assert(false) statement at points where the loop under consideration exits (thus encoding the "never terminates" property). See Fig. 1(a).

We can now use a safety checker to search for paths that violate this assertion. Any error path clearly cannot contribute towards the nontermination of the loop. After detecting such a path we calculate restrictions on the introduced assume statements such that the path is no longer feasible when the restriction is applied.

Initially as a first counterexample to safety, we might get the path $k < 0$, $i :=$ -1, $i < 0$, from a safety prover. We now want to determine from which states we can reach assert(false) and eliminate those states. Using a precondition computation similar to Calcagno *et al.* [6] we find the condition $k < 0$. The trick is to use the standard weakest precondition rule for assignments, but to use $pre(\mathtt{assume}(Q), P) \triangleq P \wedge Q$ instead of the standard $wp(\mathtt{assume}(Q), P) \triangleq Q \Rightarrow P$. This way, we only consider executions that actually reach the error location. To rule out the states $k < 0$ we can add the negation (*e.g.* $k \geq 0$) to the precondition assume statement. See Fig. 1(b).

In our procedure we try again to prove the assertion statement unreachable, using the program in Fig. 1(b). In this instance we might get the path $k \geq$ 0, skip, $i < 0$, which again violates the assertion. For this path we would discover the precondition $k \geq 0 \wedge i < 0$, and to rule out these states we refine the precondition assume statement with "assume($k \geq 0 \wedge i \geq 0$);". See Fig. 1(c).

On this program our safety prover will again fail, perhaps resulting in the path $k \geq 0$, skip, $i \geq 0$, $i := \mathtt{nondet}()$, $i < 0$. Then our procedure would stop computing the precondition at the command $i := \mathtt{nondet}()$ (for reasons discussed later). Here we would learn that at the nondeterministic command the result must be $i < 0$ to violate the assertion, thus we would refine the assume statement just after the nondet with the negation of $i < 0$: "assume($i \geq 0$);" See Fig. 1(d).

The program in Fig. 1(d) cannot violate the assertion, and thus we have hopefully computed the desired underapproximation to the transition relation needed in order to prove nontermination. However, for soundness, it is essential to ensure that the loop in Fig. 1(d) is still reachable, even after the successive restrictions to the state-space. We encode this condition as a safety problem. See Fig. 1(e). This time we add assert(false) before the loop and aim to prove that the assertion is violated. The existence of a path violating the assertion ensures that the loop in Fig. 1(d) is reachable. Here the assertion and thus the

<table>
<tr><td>

```
assume(true);

if (k ≥ 0)
    skip;
else
    i := −1;

while (i ≥ 0) {
    i := nondet();
    assume(true);
}

assert(false);

i := 2;
```
(a)

</td><td>

```
assume(k ≥ 0);

if (k ≥ 0)
    skip;
else
    i := −1;

while (i ≥ 0) {
    i := nondet();
    assume(true);
}

assert(false);

i := 2;
```
(b)

</td><td>

```
assume(k ≥ 0 ∧ i ≥ 0);

if (k ≥ 0)
    skip;
else
    i := −1;

while (i ≥ 0) {
    i := nondet();
    assume(true);
}

assert(false);

i := 2;
```
(c)

</td></tr>
<tr><td>

```
assume(k ≥ 0 ∧ i ≥ 0);

if (k ≥ 0)
    skip;
else
    i := −1;

while (i ≥ 0) {
    i := nondet();
    assume(i ≥ 0);
}

assert(false);

i := 2;
```
(d)

</td><td>

```
assume(k ≥ 0 ∧ i ≥ 0);

if (k ≥ 0)
    skip;
else
    i := −1;

assert(false);

while (i ≥ 0) {
    i := nondet();
    assume(i ≥ 0);
}
```
(e)

</td><td>

```
assume(k ≥ 0 ∧ i ≥ 0);
assume(k ≥ 0);

skip;
while (i ≥ 0) {
    i := nondet();
    assume(i ≥ 0);
}
```
(f)

</td></tr>
</table>

Fig. 1. Original instrumented program **(a)** and its successive underapproximations **(b)**, **(c)**, **(d)**. Reachability check for the loop **(e)**, and nondeterminism-assume that must be checked for satisfiability **(f)**.

loop are still reachable. The path violating the assertion is our desired path to the loop which we refer to as *stem*. Fig. 1(f) shows the stem and the loop.

Finally we need to ensure that the assume statement in Fig. 1(f) can always be satisfied with some i by any reachable state from the restricted pre-state. This is necessary: our underapproximations may accidentally have eliminated not only the paths to the loop's exit location, but also all of the nonterminating paths inside the loop. Once this check succeeds we have proved nontermination.

2 Closed Recurrence Sets

In this section we define a new concept which is at the heart of our procedure, called *closed recurrence*. Closed recurrence extends the known concept of (open) recurrence [16] in a way that facilitates automation, e.g. via a safety prover.

Preliminaries. Let S be the set of states. Given a transition relation $R \subseteq S \times S$, for a state s with $R(s, s')$, we say that s' is a successor of s under R.

We will be considering programs P with finitely many program locations $\mathbb{L}$ and a set of memory states M, so the program's state space S is given as $S = \mathbb{L} \times M$. For instance, for a program on n integer variables, we have $M = \mathbb{Z}^n$, and a memory state amounts to a valuation of the program variables.

A program P on locations $\mathbb{L}$ is represented via its *control-flow graph (CFG)* $(\mathbb{L}, \Delta, l_i, l_f, l_e)$. The program locations are the CFG's nodes and Δ is a set of edges between locations labeled with commands. We designate special locations in $\mathbb{L}$: l_i is the initial location, l_f the final location, and l_e the error location. Each $(l, T, l') \in \Delta$ is a directed edge from l to l' labeled with a command T. We write $R_T \subseteq M \times M$ for the relation on memory states induced by T in the usual way.

We say that a memory state s at node l has a successor s' along the edge (l, T, l') iff $R_T(s, s')$ holds. A path π in a CFG is a sequence of edges (l_0, T_0, l_1) $(l_1, T_1, l_2) \ldots (l_{n-1}, T_{n-1}, l_n)$. The composite transition relation R_π of a path π is the composition $R_{T_0} \circ R_{T_1} \circ \ldots \circ R_{T_{n-1}}$ of the individual relations. We also describe a path π by the sequence of nodes it visits, e.g. $l_0 \to l_1 \to \ldots \to l_{n-1} \to l_n$.

Commands. We represent by V the set of all program variables. A deterministic assignment statement is of the form $\mathsf{i} := \mathsf{exp}$ where $\mathsf{i} \in V$ and exp is an expression over program variables. A nondeterministic assignment statement is of the form $\mathsf{i} := \mathsf{nondet}(); \mathsf{assume}(\mathsf{Q});$ where $\mathsf{i} \in V$, $\mathsf{nondet}()$ is a nondeterministic choice and Q is a boolean expression over V representing the restriction that the $\mathsf{nondet}()$ choice must obey. Conditional statements are encoded using assume commands (from Nelson [22]): $\mathsf{assume}(\mathsf{Q})$, where Q is a boolean expression over V. W.l.o.g. l_i has 0 incoming and 1 outgoing edge, labeled with $\mathsf{assume}(\mathsf{Q})$, where initially usually $\mathsf{Q} \triangleq \mathsf{true}$. For readability, in our example CFGs we often write Q for $\mathsf{assume}(\mathsf{Q})$. Our algorithm will later strengthen Q in the assume-statements.

We define the indegree of a node l in a CFG to be the number of incoming edges to l. Similarly, the outdegree of a node l in a CFG is the number of outgoing edges from l. A node $l \in \mathbb{L} \setminus \{l_i, l_f, l_e\}$ must be of one of the following types.

1. A deterministic assignment node: l has outdegree exactly 1 and the outgoing edge is labeled with a deterministic assignment statement or skip. Any memory state s at l has a unique successor s' along the edge.
2. A deterministic conditional node: l has outdegree 2 with one edge labeled $\mathsf{assume}(\varphi)$, the other edge labeled $\mathsf{assume}(\neg\varphi)$. Any memory state s at l has a unique successor s' along one edge and no successor along the other edge.
3. A nondeterministic assignment node: l has outdegree exactly 1 and the outgoing edge is labeled with a nondeterministic assignment statement. A memory state s at l may have zero or more successors along the outgoing edge depending on the condition present in the $\mathsf{assume}(\mathsf{Q})$ statement.

In our construction of a CFG, a lone statement assume(Q) from an input program is modeled by a deterministic conditional node, with one edge labeled assume(Q) and the other edge labeled assume(¬Q) leading to the end location l_f.

Example. Consider the CFG for our initial example given in Fig. 2. Here we have the initial location $l_i = 0$, the final location $l_f = 7$, and the error location $l_e = 8$. The nodes 2, 3 and 6 are deterministic assignment nodes, nodes 1 and 4 are deterministic conditional nodes, and node 5 is a nondeterministic assignment node.

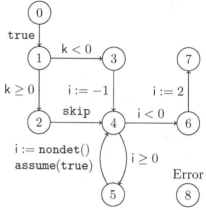

Fig. 2. CFG for initial example

CFG loops. Given a program with its CFG, a loop L in the CFG is a set of nodes s.t.

- There exists a path from any node of L to any other node of L.
- (W.l.o.g.) we assume that there is only one node h of L s.t. there exists a node $n \notin L$ with an edge from n to h. The node h is called the *header node* of L.

The subgraph of CFG containing all nodes of L is called the *loop body* of L. Header h of L is a deterministic conditional node with one edge that is part of the loop body, the *guard edge* of L. The other edge of h goes to a node $e \notin L$. We call this edge the *exit edge* of L and e the *exit location* of L.[1]

Example. In Fig. 2, the only loop is $L = \{4, 5\}$, and its header node h is 4. The exit location of L is 6.

Given a loop L in program P, we define a *loop path* π_L as any finite path through L's body of the form $(l_0 = l_h) \to l_1 \to \dots \to l_{n-1} \to (l_n = l_h)$, where l_h is the header node of L and $\forall p.(0 < p < n) \to l_p \neq l_h$. We define the *composite transition relation* R_L of L as $R_L(s, s')$ *iff* there exists a loop path π s.t. $R_\pi(s, s')$. Here R_L can be an infinite (or empty) set. The initial states I_L for R_L are the set of reachable states at the loop header before the loop is entered for the first time.

Preconditions. When computing preconditions of assume statements we borrow from Calcagno *et al.* [6]: $pre(\text{assume}(Q), P) \triangleq P \wedge Q$, called the "assume as assert trick". This lets us interpret assume statements (often from conditional branches) in a way that allows us to determine in a precondition the states from which an error location can be reached in a safety counterexample path. For assignment statements we will use the standard weakest precondition [12].

Example. Note that the weakest precondition of an assignment with nondeterminism is a little subtle. Let i := nondet(); assume(true); be the nondet statement under consideration. The weakest precondition for the postcondition $(i < j)$ is false (equivalent to $\forall i. \ i < j$). However the weakest precondition for the postcondition $(i < j \vee k > 0)$ is $(k > 0)$.

---

[1] Languages like Java or C allow loops with additional exit edges also from locations other than the loop header, which are implemented by commands like break or goto. We also support such more general loops, via a program transformation.

Recurrence sets. A relation R with initial states I is nonterminating *iff* there exists an infinite transition sequence $s_0 \xrightarrow{R} s_1 \xrightarrow{R} s_2 \xrightarrow{R} \ldots$ with $s_0 \in I$. Gupta *et al.* [16] characterize nontermination of a relation R by the existence of a *recurrence set, viz.* a nonempty set of states $\mathcal{G}$ such that for each $s \in \mathcal{G}$ there exists a transition to some $s' \in \mathcal{G}$. In particular, an infinite transition sequence $s_0 \xrightarrow{R} s_1 \xrightarrow{R} s_2 \xrightarrow{R} \ldots$ itself gives rise to the recurrence set $\{s_0, s_1, s_2, \ldots\}$. Here we extend the notion of a recurrence set to include initial states. A transition relation R with initial states I has an (open) recurrence set of states $\mathcal{G}(s)$ *iff* (1) and (2) hold. A transition relation R with

$$\exists s. \mathcal{G}(s) \wedge I(s) \qquad (1)$$
$$\forall s \exists s'. \mathcal{G}(s) \to R(s, s') \wedge \mathcal{G}(s') \quad (2)$$

initial states I is nonterminating *iff* it has a recurrence set of states.

A set $\mathcal{G}$ is a *closed recurrence set* for a transition relation R with initial states I *iff* the conditions (3)–(5) hold. In contrast to open recurrence sets, we now require a

$$\exists s. \mathcal{G}(s) \wedge I(s) \qquad (3)$$
$$\forall s \exists s'. \mathcal{G}(s) \to R(s, s') \qquad (4)$$
$$\forall s \forall s'. \mathcal{G}(s) \wedge R(s, s') \to \mathcal{G}(s') \quad (5)$$

purely universal property: for each $s \in \mathcal{G}$ and *for each* of its successors s', also s' must be in the recurrence set (Condition (5)). So instead of requiring that we *can* stay in the recurrence set, we now demand that we *must* stay in the recurrence set. This now helps us to incorporate nondeterministic transition systems too.

Now what if a state s in our recurrence set $\mathcal{G}$ has no successor s' at all? Our alleged infinite transition sequence would reach a sudden halt, yet our universal formula would trivially hold. Thus, we impose that each $s \in \mathcal{G}$ has *some* successor s' (Condition (4)). But this existential statement need not mention that s' must be in $\mathcal{G}$ again—our previous *universal* statement already takes care of this.

Theorem 1 (Closed Recurrence Sets are Recurrence Sets). *Let $\mathcal{G}$ be a closed recurrence set for R with initial states I. Then $\mathcal{G}$ is also an (open) recurrence set for R with initial states I.*

The proofs for all theorems can be found in the technical report [7].   □

Underapproximation. We call a transition relation R' with initial states I' an underapproximation of transition relation R with initial states I *iff* $R' \subseteq R$, $I' \subseteq I$. Then *every* nonterminating program contains a closed recurrence set as an underapproximation (*i.e.*, together with underapproximation, closed recurrence sets characterize nontermination).

Theorem 2 (Open Recurrence Sets Always Contain Closed Recurrence Sets). *There exists a recurrence set $\mathcal{G}$ for a transition relation R with initial states I iff there exist an underapproximation R' with initial states I' and $\mathcal{G}' \subseteq \mathcal{G}$ such that $\mathcal{G}'$ is a closed recurrence set for R' with initial states I'.*

3 Algorithm

Our nontermination proving procedure PROVER is detailed in Fig. 3. Its input is a program P given by its CFG, and a loop to be considered for nontermination. To prove nontermination of the entire program P we need to find only one nonterminating loop L. This can be done in parallel. Alternatively, the procedure

PROVER (CFG P, Loop L)
    $h :=$ header node of L
    $e :=$ exit node of L in P
    $P' :=$ UNDERAPPROXIMATE(P, e)
    $L' :=$ refined loop L in P'
    if $\neg$ REACHABLE(P', h) **then**
        return Unknown, $\bot$
    fi
    $\Pi := \{\pi \mid \pi$ feasible path to h in $P'\}$
    for all $\pi \in \Pi$ **do**
        $P' := \pi :: L'$ // concatenation
        if VALIDATE(P') **then**
            return NonTerminating, P'
        fi
    done
    return Unknown, $\bot$

UNDERAPPROXIMATE (CFG P, Node e)
    $\kappa := [\,]$
    while REACHABLE(P, e) **do**
        $\pi :=$ feasible path to e in P
        $\kappa := \pi :: \kappa$
        $P :=$ REFINE(P, π)
        if the n most recent paths in κ
            are repeating **then**
            $P :=$ STRENGTHEN$(P, \text{FIRST}(\kappa))$
        fi
    done
    return P

REFINE (CFG P, Path π)
    $(l_0\ T_0\ l_1)(l_1\ T_1\ l_2)\ldots(l_{n-1}\ T_{n-1}\ l_n) := \pi$
    Calculate WPs $\psi_1, \psi_2 \ldots \psi_{n-1}$ along π
        so $\{\psi_1\}T_1\{\psi_2\}T_2\ldots\{\psi_{n-1}\}T_{n-1}\{\text{true}\}$
        are valid Hoare-triples.
    Find p s.t. $\psi_p \neq \text{false} \wedge \forall q < p.\ \psi_q = \text{false}$
    $P := P|_{(T_{p-1}, \neg\psi_p)}$
    return P

STRENGTHEN (CFG P, Path π)
    $(l_0\ T_0\ l_1)(l_1\ T_1\ l_2)\ldots(l_{n-1}\ T_{n-1}\ l_n) := \pi$
    Calculate WPs $\psi_1, \psi_2 \ldots \psi_{n-1}$ along π
        so $\{\psi_1\}T_1\{\psi_2\}T_2\ldots\{\psi_{n-1}\}T_{n-1}\{\text{true}\}$
        are valid Hoare-triples.
    Find p s.t. $\psi_p \neq \text{false} \wedge \forall q < p.\ \psi_q = \text{false}$
    $W := \{v \mid v$ gets updated in subpath
        $(l_p\ T_p\ l_{p+1})\ldots(l_{n-1}T_{n-1}l_n)\}$
    $\rho_p := \text{QE}(\exists W.\ \psi_p)$
    $P := P|_{(T_{p-1}, \neg\rho_p)}$
    return P

VALIDATE (CFG P')
    $L' :=$ the outermost loop in P'
    $\mathbb{M} := \{l \mid l$ is nondet assignment node in $L'\}$
    for all $l \in \mathbb{M}$ **do**
        Calculate invariant inv_l at node l in P'
        let nondet statement at l be
            v := nondet(); assume(φ);
        if $inv_l \rightarrow \exists v.\ \varphi$ is not valid **then**
            return false
        fi
    done
    return true

Fig. 3. Algorithm PROVER for underapproximation to synthesize a reachable nonterminating loop. To prove nontermination of P, PROVER should be run on all loops L.

can be implemented sequentially, but then timeouts are advisable in PROVER, as the procedure might diverge and cause another loop to not be considered.

The subprocedure UNDERAPPROXIMATE performs the search for an underapproximation such that we can prove the loop is never exited. While the loop exit is still REACHABLE (*a.k.a.* "unsafe"), we use the subprocedure REFINE to examine paths returned from an off-the-shelf safety prover. Here the notation $P|_{(T_i, \varphi)}$ denotes P with an additional assume(φ) added to the transition T_i. From the postcondition **true** (used to indicate success in reaching the loop exit), we use a backwards precondition analysis to find out which program states will inevitably end up in the loop exit. We continue this precondition calculation until either we have reached the beginning of the path or until just before we have reached a nondeterministic assignment that leads to the precondition **false**. We then negate this condition as our underapproximating refinement.

In some cases our refinement is too weak, leading to divergence. The difficulty is that in cases the same loop path will be considered repeatedly, but at each instance the loop will be unrolled for an additional iteration. To avoid this problem we impose a limit n for the number of paths that go along the same locations (possibly with more and more repetitions). We call such paths *repeating*. If we reach this limit, we use the subprocedure STRENGTHEN to strengthen the precondition, inspired by a heuristic by Cook and Koskinen [8]. Here we again calculate a precondition, but when we have found ψ_p, we quantify out all the variables that are written to after ψ_p and apply quantifier elimination (QE) to get ρ_p. We then refine with $\neg\rho_p$. This leads to a more aggressive pruning of the transition relation. This heuristic can lead to additional incompleteness.

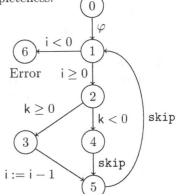

Example. Consider the instrumented program to the right. Suppose we have initially $\varphi \triangleq i \geq 0$. We might get $cex_1 : 0 \to 1 \to 2 \to 3 \to 5 \to 1 \to 6$ as a first counterexample. The REFINE procedure finds the weakest precondition $k \geq 0 \wedge i = 0$ at location 1. Adding its negation to φ and simplifying the formula gives us $\varphi \triangleq (i \geq 0) \wedge (k < 0 \vee i \geq 1)$. Now we may get $cex_2 : 0 \to 1 \to 2 \to 3 \to 5 \to 1 \to 2 \to 3 \to 5 \to 1 \to 6$ as next counterexample, and REFINE updates $\varphi \triangleq (i \geq 0) \wedge (k < 0 \vee i \geq 2)$. Now we may get $cex_3 : 0 \to 1 \to 2 \to 3 \to 5 \to 1 \to 2 \to 3 \to 5 \to 1 \to 2 \to 3 \to 5 \to 1 \to 6$ as next counterexample. Note that cex_1, cex_2, cex_3 are repeating counterexamples and if we just use the REFINE procedure, UNDERAPPROXIMATE gets stuck in a sequence of infinite counterexamples. Now STRENGTHEN identifies the repeating counterexamples, considers cex_1 and calculates the weakest precondition $\psi_1 \triangleq k \geq 0 \wedge i = 0$. It then existentially quantifies out variable i as it gets modified later along cex_1. We get $\exists i. \ k \geq 0 \wedge i = 0$, and quantifier elimination yields $\rho_1 \triangleq k \geq 0$. Clearly ψ_1 entails ρ_1. Adding $\neg\rho_1$ to φ and simplifying the formula we get $\varphi \triangleq i \geq 0 \wedge k < 0$. Now all repeating counterexamples are eliminated, the program is safe, and we have obtained a closed recurrence set witnessing nontermination of the original program.

In the UNDERAPPROXIMATE procedure, once there are no further counterexamples to safety of P, we know that in P the loop exit is not reachable. The procedure returns the final underapproximation (denoted by P') that is safe.

When UNDERAPPROXIMATE returns to PROVER, we check if in P' the original loop L after refinements has a closed recurrence set. We refer to the refined loop as L'. In order to check the existence of a closed recurrence set, we first need to ensure that L' is reachable in P' even after the refinements. We again pose this problem as a safety/reachability problem. This time we mark the header node of L' as an error location in P' and hope that P' is unsafe. If P' is safe then clearly we have failed to prove nontermination and we report the result as unknown. If P' is unsafe, then the counterexample to its safety is a path to the header of L'. We enumerate all such paths to the header of L' in a set Π (generated lazily in our implementation). For each such path $\pi \in \Pi$ we then create a simplified CFG P' by concatenating π to L', thus eliminating other paths to L'.

At this point, we are sure that the header of L' is reachable and there is no path that can reach the exit location of L'. However refinements in UNDERAP-PROXIMATE may have restricted the **nondet** statements inside L' by strengthening the **assume** statements associated with them. Thus a reachable state at the nondeterministic assignment node may not have a successor along its outgoing edge. This would bring our alleged infinite execution to a halt. The safety checker cannot detect this since then the path just gets blocked at this node, and the error location at the exit of L' cannot be reached.

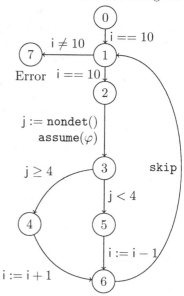

Example. Consider the instrumented program in Fig. 4. Suppose initially $\varphi \triangleq$ **true**. The original program (without instrumentation) is clearly terminating. Our algorithm might give $cex_1 : 0 \to 1 \to 2 \to 3 \to 4 \to 6 \to 1 \to 7$ as the first counterexample. The **nondet** statement at node 2 gets restricted by updating $\varphi \triangleq (j \leq 3 \vee i == 9)$. Now we might get $cex_2 : 0 \to 1 \to 2 \to 3 \to 5 \to 6 \to 1 \to 7$ as the next counterexample. Our algorithm restricts the **nondet** statement at node 2 by updating $\varphi \triangleq (j \leq 3 \vee i == 9) \wedge (j \geq 4 \vee i == 11)$.

However now there are no further counterexamples, and the safety checker returns safe. The state $s \vDash i = 10$ at node 2 has no successor along the outgoing edge as there is

Fig. 4. Program showing why we need VALIDATE procedure

no way to satisfy the condition φ and the execution is halted, so it would be unsound to report the result as Nonterminating.

Note that at first it may appear that adding another outgoing edge to node 2 with $j :=$ **nondet**(); **assume**($\neg\varphi$); and marking the next node as an error node would help us catch the halted execution. However the problem is that this would discover again all of the previously eliminated counterexamples as well. Thus we need a special check by the VALIDATE procedure, which we describe next.

VALIDATE takes as input the final underapproximation P'. It first calculates a location invariant at every nondet. assignment node inside the outermost loop L' in P'. Let l be a nondet. assignment node with: $v :=$ **nondet**(); **assume**(φ); Let *inv* be a location invariant at l. VALIDATE then checks if (6) is valid. This formula checks if for all reachable states at l, a choice can be made for the **nondet** assignment obeying φ (and thus Condition

$$inv \to \exists v. \varphi \quad (6)$$

(4) holds). VALIDATE returns **true** *iff* (6) holds for all **nondet** statements in L'.

Example. Consider the program in Fig. 1(f). Using a standard invariant generator we calculate the invariant $i \geq 0$ before line 4. Substituting in (6) we get, $i \geq 0 \to \exists i'. i' \geq 0$. Clearly the formula is valid. Note that in most of the cases even the weakest invariant **true** can be sufficient to prove validity of (6). In this example as well we can easily prove that **true** $\rightarrow \exists i'. i' \geq 0$ is valid.

Moreover, consider the program in Fig. 4. Suppose $\varphi \triangleq (j \leq 3 \vee i == 9) \wedge (j \geq 4 \vee i == 11)$. Using an invariant generator, we obtain the location invariant $i = 10$ at location 2. Then (6) becomes $i = 10 \rightarrow \exists j. (j \leq 3 \vee i = 9) \wedge (j \geq 4 \vee i = 11)$. Clearly the formula is not valid. In this case VALIDATE returns **false**.

If VALIDATE returns **true**, we are sure that every reachable state at the non-deterministic assignment node in L' has a successor along the edge. At this point, we report nontermination and return the final underapproximation P' of P as a proof of nontermination for P: P' is a closed recurrence set.

Note that as invariants are overapproximations, we may report unknown in some cases even when the discovered underapproximation actually does have a closed recurrence set. However, the check is essential to retain soundness.

Theorem 3 (Correctness of Prover for Nontermination). *Let P be a program and L a loop in P. Suppose* PROVER $(P, L) = Nonterminating, P'$. *Then P is nonterminating.*

4   Nested Loops

Our algorithm can handle nested loops easily. That is a part of the beauty of the reduction to safety, as existing safety provers (*e.g.* SLAM, IMPACT, *etc.*) handle nested loops with ease. Note that technically we only need to consider an outermost loop. Consider the instrumented program with nested loops to the right.

```
if (i == 10) {
    while (i > 0) {
        i := i − 1;
        while (i == 0)
            skip;
    }
    assert(false);
}
```

Here the outer loop decreases the value of i 10 times and then it is the inner loop that is nonterminating. However, it suffices only to consider the outermost loop for safety as the **assert(false)** at the end of the outer loop is not reachable, but the head of the outer loop is reachable, so that we have proved nontermination.

Tricky example. We close with an example that partially explains the advantage seen for our tool over TNT (discussed in Sect. 5). Consider the program to the right (already shown with our algorithm's instrumentation, initially with $\varphi \triangleq$ **true**). This program clearly does not terminate, yet TNT will fail to prove it. In fact, our implementation of TNT which follows the strategy discussed for enumerating lassos [16] diverges looking at larger and larger cyclic paths (*i.e.* straight-line code from a location

```
assume(φ);
while (k ≥ 0) {
    k := k + 1;
    j := k;
    while (j ≥ 1)
        j := j − 1;
}
assert(false);
```

back to that location). The difficulty here is that each cyclic path is well-founded. Consider *e.g.* this cyclic path from the head h of the outer loop back to h:

$$k \geq 0, \quad k := k + 1, \quad j := k, \quad j \geq 1, \quad j := j - 1, \quad j < 1, \quad k \geq 0$$

This path is well-founded. In fact the path cannot be repeated. The root of the problem is the command sequence $j \geq 1$, $j := j - 1$, $j < 1$, which tells us that j goes from exactly 1 to 0. Because $j = 1$ before entering the inner loop, we know that $k = 1$, thus by the $k := k + 1$ command we know that $k = 0$ at the start of the loop's execution. Thus the command sequence respects the following condition: $k' > k \wedge k' \leq 1$, and thus it is well-founded. Hence, the lasso-based tool TNT will never be able to prove nontermination of this program. The tool APROVE cannot prove such *aperiodic* nontermination for nested loops either [5].

Our approach, however, does not fall victim to this problem. It will find the path: $k < 0$, resulting in $\varphi \triangleq k \geq 0$. As assert(false) is unreachable with this restriction (and the loop is still reachable), we have proved nontermination.

5   Related Work

Automatic tools for proving nontermination of term rewriting systems include [14,23]. However, while nontermination analysis for term rewriting considers the *entire* state space as legitimate initial states for a (possibly infinite) evaluation sequence, our setting also factors in reachability from the initial states.

Static nontermination analysis has also been investigated for logic programs (*e.g.* [24,31]). Most related to our setting are techniques for constraint-logic programs (CLPs) [25]. Termination tools for CLPs (*e.g.* [25]) can in cases be used to prove nontermination of imperative programs (*e.g.* JULIA [26] can show nontermination for Java Bytecode programs if the abstraction to CLPs is exact, but gives no witness like a recurrence set to the user). The main difficulty for imperative programs is that typically overapproximating abstractions (in general unsound for nontermination) are used for converting languages like Java and C to CLPs.

TNT [16] uses a characterization of nontermination by recurrence sets. We build upon this notion and introduce *closed* recurrence sets in our formalization, as an intermediate concept during our nontermination proof search. In contrast to us, TNT is restricted to programs with *periodic* "lasso-shaped" counterexamples to termination. We support unbounded nondeterminism in the program's transition relation, whereas TNT is restricted to deterministic commands.

The tool INVEL [30] analyzes nontermination of Java programs using a combination of theorem proving and invariant generation. However, INVEL does not provide a witness for nontermination. Like Brockschmidt *et al.* [5], we were unable to obtain a working version of INVEL. Note that in the empirical evaluation by Brockschmidt *et al.* [5], the APROVE tool (which we have compared against) subsumed INVEL on INVEL's data set. Finally, INVEL is only applicable to deterministic (integer) programs, yet our approach allows nondeterminism as well.

Atig *et al.* [1] describe a technique for proving nontermination of multithreaded programs, via a reduction to nontermination reasoning for sequential programs. Our work complements Atig *et al.*, as we provide improvements to the underlying sequential tools that future multithreaded tools can make use of.

The tool TREX [19] combines existing nontermination proving techniques with a TERMINATOR-like [9] iterative procedure. Our new method should complement TREX nicely, as ours is more powerful than the underlying nontermination proving approach previously used [16].

APROVE [13] uses SMT to prove nontermination of Java programs [5]. First nontermination of a loop regardless of its context is shown, then reachability of this loop with suitable values. Drawbacks are that they require recurrence sets to be singletons (after program slicing) or the loop conditions to be invariants.

Gurfinkel *et al.* [18] present the CEGAR-based model checker YASM which supports arbitrary CTL properties, such as EG *pc* $\neq$ END, denoting nontermination. YASM implements a method of both under and over-approximating the input program. Unfortunately, together with the author of YASM we were not able to get the tool working on our examples [17]. We suspect that our approach will be faster, as it uses current safety proving techniques, *i.e.* IMPACT [20] rather than SLAM-style technology [2]. This is a feature of our approach: *any* off-the-shelf software model checker can be turned into a nontermination prover.

Nontermination proving for finite-state systems is essentially a question of safety [3]. Nontermination and/or related temporal logics are also supported for more expressive systems, *e.g.* pushdown automata [28].

Recent work on CTL proving for programs uses an off-the-shelf nontermination prover [8]. We use a few steps when treating nondeterminism which look similar to the approach from [8]. The key difference is that our work *provides* a nontermination prover, whereas the previous work *requires* one off-the-shelf.

Gulwani *et al.* [15] (Claim 3), make a false claim that is similar to our own. Their claim is false, as a nondeterministic program can be constructed which represents a counterexample. Much of the subtlety in our approach comes from our method of dealing with nondeterminism.

6   Experiments

We have built a preliminary implementation of our approach within the tool T2 [10,4][2] and conducted an empirical evaluation with it against these tools:

- TNT [16], the original TNT tool was not available, and thus we have reimplemented its constraint-based algorithm with Z3 [11] as SMT backend.
- APROVE [13], via the Java Bytecode frontend, using the SMT-based nontermination analysis by Brockschmidt *et al.* [5].
- JULIA [29], which implements an approach via a reduction to constraint logic programming described by Payet and Spoto [26].

As a benchmark set, we used a set of 492 benchmarks for termination analysis from a variety of applications also used in prior tool evaluations (*e.g.* Windows device drivers, the APACHE web server, the POSTGRESQL server, integer approximations of numerical programs from a book on numerical recipes [27], integer approximations of benchmarks from LLBMC [21] and other tool evaluations).[3]

Of these, 81 are known to be nonterminating and 254 terminating. For 157 examples, the termination status is unknown. These examples include a program whose termination would imply the Collatz conjecture, and the remaining examples are too large to render a manual analysis feasible. On average a CFG in

---

[2] We will make our implementation available in the next source code release of T2.

[3] Download: http://www0.cs.ucl.ac.uk/staff/C.Fuhs/safety-nontermination

	(a)			(b)			(c)		
	Nonterm	TO	No Res	Nonterm	TO	No Res	Nonterm	TO	No Res
Fig. 3	51	0	30	0	45	209	82	3	72
APROVE	0	61	20	0	142	112	0	139	18
JULIA	3	8	70	0	40	214	0	91	66
TNT	19	3	59	0	48	206	32	12	113

Fig. 5. Evaluation success overview, showing the number of problems solved for each tool. Here **(a)** represents the results for known nonterminating examples, **(b)** is known terminating examples, **(c)** is (previously) unknown examples.

our test suite has 18.4 nodes (max. 427 nodes) and 2.4 loops (max. 120 loops).

Unfortunately each tool requires a different machine configuration, and thus a direct comparison is difficult. Experiments with our procedure were performed on a dualcore Intel Core 2 Duo U9400 (1.4 GHz, 2 GB RAM, Windows 7). TNT was run on Intel Core i5-2520M (2.5 GHz, 8 GB RAM, Ubuntu Linux 12.04). We ran APROVE on Intel Core i7-950 (3.07 GHz, 6 GB RAM, Debian Linux 7.2). Note that the TNT-/APROVE-machines are significantly faster than the machine our new procedure was run on, thus we can make some adjusted comparison between the tools. For JULIA, an unknown cloud-based configuration was used. All tools were run with a timeout of 60s. When a tool returned early with no definite result, we display this in the plots using the special "NR" (no result) value.

We ran three sets of experiments: (a) all the examples previously known to be nonterminating, (b) all the examples previously known to be terminating, and (c) all the examples where no previous results are known. With (a) we assess the efficiency of the algorithm, (b) is used to demonstrate its soundness, and (c) checks if our algorithm scales well on relatively large and complicated examples. The results of the three sets of experiments are given in Fig. 5, which shows for each tool and for each set (a)–(c) the numbers of benchmarks with nontermination proofs ("Nonterm"), timeouts ("TO"), and no results ("No Res"). (Proofs of *termination*, found by APROVE and JULIA, are also listed as "No Res".)

On the 89 deterministic instances of our benchmark set, our implementation proves nontermination of 33 examples, and TNT of 21 examples. We have also experimented with different values for the number of repeated paths before invoking STRENGTHEN. The results are reported in Fig. 6 (runtimes are for successful nontermination proofs).

# Paths	Nonterm	Time [s]
2	133	272
4	133	301
6	129	264
∞	123	272

Fig. 6. Repeated paths before calling STRENGTHEN

Fig. 7 charts the difference in power and performance between our implementation and TNT in a scatter plot, in log scale. Here we have included all programs from (a)–(c). Each 'x'-mark in the plot represents an example from the benchmark. The value of the x-axis plots the runtime of TNT and the y-axis value plots the runtime of our procedure on the same example. Points under the diagonal are in favor of our procedure. Thus, the more 'x'-marks there are in the lower-righthand corner, the better our tool has performed.

Discussion. Figs. 5(a&c) demonstrate that our technique is overwhelmingly the most successful tool (Fig. 5(b) confirms simply that no tool has demonstrable

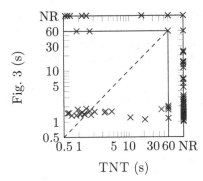

Fig. 7. Evaluation results of our procedure vs. TNT. Scatter plot in log scale. Timeout=60s. NR="No Result", indicating failure of the tool.

soundness bugs). The poor precision of APROVE & JULIA is mainly due to the non-deterministic updates originally present in many of the benchmarks and also introduced by the (automated) conversion of the benchmarks to Java (the two tools' input syntax). This shows the lack of reliable support of non-determinism in today's nontermination tools.

The TNT algorithm requires outright that nondeterminism must not occur in the input. Our implementation of TNT softens this requirement slightly: parts of the program with `nondet`-assignments are allowed as long as they are not used during the synthesis of recurrence sets.

Finally, we observe in Fig. 6 that the STRENGTHEN procedure provides additional precision for our approach without harming performance.

7   Conclusion

We have introduced a new method of proving nontermination. The idea is to split the reasoning in two parts: a safety prover is used to prove that a loop in an underapproximation of the original program *never* terminates; meanwhile failed safety proofs are used to calculate the underapproximation. We have shown that nondeterminism can be easily handled in our framework while previous tools often fail. Furthermore, we have shown that our approach leads to performance improvements against previous tools where they are applicable.

Our technique is not restricted to linear integer arithmetic: Given suitable tools for safety proving and for precondition inference, in principle our approach is applicable to *any* program setting (note that the STRENGTHEN procedure is just an optimization). For future work, *e.g.* heap programs are a highly promising candidate for nontermination analysis via abduction tools for separation logic [6].

Acknowledgments. We thank Marc Brockschmidt, Fabian Emmes, Florian Frohn and Fausto Spoto for help with the experiments and Tony Hoare, Jules Villard and the anonymous reviewers for insightful comments.

References

1. Atig, M.F., Bouajjani, A., Emmi, M., Lal, A.: Detecting fair non-termination in multithreaded programs. In: Madhusudan, P., Seshia, S.A. (eds.) CAV 2012. LNCS, vol. 7358, pp. 210–226. Springer, Heidelberg (2012)
2. Ball, T., Rajamani, S.K.: The SLAM toolkit. In: Berry, G., Comon, H., Finkel, A. (eds.) CAV 2001. LNCS, vol. 2102, pp. 260–264. Springer, Heidelberg (2001)

3. Biere, A., Artho, C., Schuppan, V.: Liveness checking as safety checking. In: Proc. FMICS 2002 (2002)
4. Brockschmidt, M., Cook, B., Fuhs, C.: Better termination proving through cooperation. In: Sharygina, N., Veith, H. (eds.) CAV 2013. LNCS, vol. 8044, pp. 413–429. Springer, Heidelberg (2013)
5. Brockschmidt, M., Ströder, T., Otto, C., Giesl, J.: Automated detection of nontermination and NullPointerExceptions for Java Bytecode. In: Beckert, B., Damiani, F., Gurov, D. (eds.) FoVeOOS 2011. LNCS, vol. 7421, pp. 123–141. Springer, Heidelberg (2012)
6. Calcagno, C., Distefano, D., O'Hearn, P.W., Yang, H.: Compositional shape analysis by means of bi-abduction. J. ACM 58(6), 26 (2011)
7. Chen, H.-Y., Cook, B., Fuhs, C., Nimkar, K., O'Hearn, P.: Proving nontermination via safety. Technical Report RN/13/23, UCL (2014)
8. Cook, B., Koskinen, E.: Reasoning about nondeterminism in programs. In: Proc. PLDI 2013 (2013)
9. Cook, B., Podelski, A., Rybalchenko, A.: TERMINATOR: Beyond safety. In: Ball, T., Jones, R.B. (eds.) CAV 2006. LNCS, vol. 4144, pp. 415–418. Springer, Heidelberg (2006)
10. Cook, B., See, A., Zuleger, F.: Ramsey vs. Lexicographic termination proving. In: Piterman, N., Smolka, S.A. (eds.) TACAS 2013. LNCS, vol. 7795, pp. 47–61. Springer, Heidelberg (2013)
11. de Moura, L., Bjørner, N.: Z3: An efficient SMT solver. In: Ramakrishnan, C.R., Rehof, J. (eds.) TACAS 2008. LNCS, vol. 4963, pp. 337–340. Springer, Heidelberg (2008)
12. Dijkstra, E.W.: A Discipline of Programming. Prentice-Hall (1976)
13. Giesl, J., Schneider-Kamp, P., Thiemann, R.: AProVE 1.2: Automatic termination proofs in the dependency pair framework. In: Furbach, U., Shankar, N. (eds.) IJCAR 2006. LNCS (LNAI), vol. 4130, pp. 281–286. Springer, Heidelberg (2006)
14. Giesl, J., Thiemann, R., Schneider-Kamp, P.: Proving and disproving termination of higher-order functions. In: Gramlich, B. (ed.) FroCos 2005. LNCS (LNAI), vol. 3717, pp. 216–231. Springer, Heidelberg (2005)
15. Gulwani, S., Srivastava, S., Venkatesan, R.: Program analysis as constraint solving. In: Proc. PLDI 2008 (2008)
16. Gupta, A., Henzinger, T.A., Majumdar, R., Rybalchenko, A., Xu, R.-G.: Proving non-termination. In: Proc. POPL 2008 (2008)
17. Gurfinkel, A.: Private communication (2012)
18. Gurfinkel, A., Wei, O., Chechik, M.: YASM: A software model-checker for verification and refutation. In: Ball, T., Jones, R.B. (eds.) CAV 2006. LNCS, vol. 4144, pp. 170–174. Springer, Heidelberg (2006)
19. Harris, W.R., Lal, A., Nori, A.V., Rajamani, S.K.: Alternation for termination. In: Cousot, R., Martel, M. (eds.) SAS 2010. LNCS, vol. 6337, pp. 304–319. Springer, Heidelberg (2010)
20. McMillan, K.L.: Lazy abstraction with interpolants. In: Ball, T., Jones, R.B. (eds.) CAV 2006. LNCS, vol. 4144, pp. 123–136. Springer, Heidelberg (2006)
21. Merz, F., Falke, S., Sinz, C.: LLBMC: Bounded model checking of C and C++ programs using a compiler IR. In: Joshi, R., Müller, P., Podelski, A. (eds.) VSTTE 2012. LNCS, vol. 7152, pp. 146–161. Springer, Heidelberg (2012)
22. Nelson, G.: A generalization of Dijkstra's calculus. ACM TOPLAS 11(4) (1989)
23. Payet, É.: Loop detection in term rewriting using the eliminating unfoldings. Theor. Comput. Sci. 403(2-3) (2008)

24. Payet, É., Mesnard, F.: Nontermination inference of logic programs. ACM TOPLAS 28(2) (2006)
25. Payet, É., Mesnard, F.: A non-termination criterion for binary constraint logic programs. TPLP 9(2) (2009)
26. Payet, É., Spoto, F.: Experiments with non-termination analysis for Java Bytecode. In: Proc. BYTECODE 2009 (2009)
27. Press, W.H., Teukolsky, S.A., Vetterling, W.T., Flannery, B.P.: Numerical Recipes: The Art of Scientific Computing. Cambridge Univ. Press (1989)
28. Song, F., Touili, T.: Pushdown model checking for malware detection. In: Flanagan, C., König, B. (eds.) TACAS 2012. LNCS, vol. 7214, pp. 110–125. Springer, Heidelberg (2012)
29. Spoto, F., Mesnard, F., Payet, É.: A termination analyzer for Java bytecode based on path-length. ACM TOPLAS 32(3) (2010)
30. Velroyen, H., Rümmer, P.: Non-termination checking for imperative programs. In: Beckert, B., Hähnle, R. (eds.) TAP 2008. LNCS, vol. 4966, pp. 154–170. Springer, Heidelberg (2008)
31. Voets, D., De Schreye, D.: A new approach to non-termination analysis of logic programs. In: Hill, P.M., Warren, D.S. (eds.) ICLP 2009. LNCS, vol. 5649, pp. 220–234. Springer, Heidelberg (2009)

Ranking Templates for Linear Loops

Jan Leike[1,2] and Matthias Heizmann[1,*]

[1] University of Freiburg, Germany
[2] Max Planck Institute for Software Systems, Germany

Abstract. We present a new method for the constraint-based synthesis
of termination arguments for linear loop programs based on *linear ranking templates*. Linear ranking templates are parametrized, well-founded
relations such that an assignment to the parameters gives rise to a ranking function. This approach generalizes existing methods and enables us
to use templates for many different ranking functions with affine-linear
components. We discuss templates for multiphase, piecewise, and lexicographic ranking functions. Because these ranking templates require both
strict and non-strict inequalities, we use Motzkin's Transposition Theorem instead of Farkas Lemma to transform the generated $\exists\forall$-constraint
into an $\exists$-constraint.

1   Introduction

The scope of this work is the constraint-based synthesis of termination arguments. In our setting, we consider *linear loop programs*, which are specified by
a boolean combination of affine-linear inequalities over the program variables.
This allows for both, deterministic and non-deterministic updates of the program
variables. An example of a linear loop program is given in Figure 1.

Usually, linear loop programs do not occur as stand-alone programs. Instead,
they are generated as a finite representation of an infinite path in a control flow
graph. For example, in (potentially spurious) counterexamples in termination
analysis [9,13,17,18,21,22], non-termination analysis [12], stability analysis [8,23],
or cost analysis [1,11].

We introduce the notion of *linear ranking templates* (Section 3). These are
parameterized relations specified by linear inequalities such that any assignment
to the parameters yields a well-founded relation. This notion is general enough
to encompass all existing methods for linear loop programs that use constraint-
based synthesis of ranking functions of various kinds (see Section 6 for an assessment). Moreover, ours is the first method for synthesis of lexicographic ranking
functions that does not require a mapping between loop disjuncts and lexicographic components.

In this paper we present the following linear ranking templates.

---

* This work is supported by the German Research Council (DFG) as part of the
Transregional Collaborative Research Center "Automatic Verification and Analysis
of Complex Systems" (SFB/TR14 AVACS).

E. Ábrahám and K. Havelund (Eds.): TACAS 2014, LNCS 8413, pp. 172–186, 2014.

$$\textbf{while} \ (q > 0): \qquad\qquad q > 0$$
$$q := q - y; \qquad\qquad \land q' = q - y$$
$$y := y + 1; \qquad\qquad \land y' = y + 1$$

Fig. 1. A linear loop program given as program code (left) and as a formula defining a binary relation (right)

- The *multiphase ranking template* specifies a ranking function that proceeds through a fixed number of phases in the program execution. Each phase is ranked by an affine-linear function; when this function becomes non-positive, we move on to the next phase (Subsection 4.1).
- The *piecewise ranking template* specifies a ranking function that is a piecewise affine-linear function with affine-linear predicates to discriminate between the pieces (Subsection 4.2).
- The *lexicographic ranking template* specifies a lexicographic ranking function that corresponds to a tuple of affine-linear functions together with a lexicographic ordering on the tuple (Subsection 4.3).

These linear ranking templates can be used as a 'construction kit' for composing linear ranking templates that enable more complex ranking functions (Subsection 4.4). Moreover, variations on the linear ranking templates presented here can be used and completely different templates could be conceived.

Our method is described in Section 5 and can be summarized as follows. The input is a linear loop program as well as a linear ranking template. From these we construct a constraint to the parameters of the template. With Motzkin's Theorem we can transform the constraint into a purely existentially quantified constraint (Subsection 5.1). This ∃-constraint is then passed to an SMT solver which checks it for satisfiability. A positive result implies that the program terminates. Furthermore, a satisfying assignment will yield a ranking function, which constitutes a termination argument for the given linear loop program.

Related approaches invoke Farkas' Lemma for the transformation into ∃-constraints [2,5,6,7,14,20,24,25]. The piecewise and the lexicographic ranking template contain both strict and non-strict inequalities, yet only non-strict inequalities can be transformed using Farkas' Lemma. We solve this problem by introducing the use of Motzkin's Transposition Theorem, a generalization of Farkas' Lemma. As a side effect, this also enables both, strict and non-strict inequalities in the program syntax. To our knowledge, all of the aforementioned methods can be improved by the application of Motzkin's Theorem instead of Farkas' Lemma.

Our method is complete in the following sense. If there is a ranking function of the form specified by the given linear ranking template, then our method will discover this ranking function. In other words, the existence of a solution is never lost in the process of transforming the constraint.

In contrast to some related methods [14,20] the constraint we generate is not linear, but rather a nonlinear algebraic constraint. Theoretically, this constraint can be decided in exponential time [10]. Much progress on nonlinear SMT solvers has been made and present-day implementations routinely solve nonlinear constraints of various sizes [16].

A related setting to linear loop programs are *linear lasso programs*. These consist of a linear loop program and a program stem, both of which are specified by boolean combinations of affine-linear inequalities over the program variables. Our method can be extended to linear lasso programs through the addition of affine-linear inductive invariants, analogously to related approaches [5,7,14,25].

2   Preliminaries

In this paper we use $\mathbb{K}$ to denote a field that is either the rational numbers $\mathbb{Q}$ or the real numbers $\mathbb{R}$. We use ordinal numbers according to the definition in [15]. The first infinite ordinal is denoted by ω; the finite ordinals coincide with the natural numbers, therefore we will use them interchangeably.

2.1   Motzkin's Transposition Theorem

Intuitively, Motzkin's Transposition Theorem [26, Corollary 7.1k] states that a given system of linear inequalities has no solution if and only if a contradiction can be derived via a positive linear combination of the inequalities.

Theorem 1 (Motzkin's Transposition Theorem). *For $A \in \mathbb{K}^{m \times n}$, $C \in \mathbb{K}^{\ell \times n}$, $b \in \mathbb{K}^m$, and $d \in \mathbb{K}^\ell$, the formulae (M1) and (M2) are equivalent.*

$$\forall x \in \mathbb{K}^n. \ \neg(Ax \leq b \ \wedge \ Cx < d) \tag{M1}$$

$$\exists \lambda \in \mathbb{K}^m \ \exists \mu \in \mathbb{K}^\ell. \ \lambda \geq 0 \ \wedge \ \mu \geq 0$$
$$\wedge \ \lambda^T A + \mu^T C = 0 \ \wedge \ \lambda^T b + \mu^T d \leq 0 \tag{M2}$$
$$\wedge \ (\lambda^T b < 0 \ \vee \ \mu \neq 0)$$

If ℓ is set to 1 in Theorem 1, we obtain the affine version of Farkas' Lemma [26, Corollary 7.1h]. Therefore Motzkin's Theorem is strictly superior to Farkas' Lemma, as it allows for a combination of both strict and non-strict inequalities. Moreover, it is logically optimal in the sense that it enables transformation of *any* universally quantified formula from the theory of linear arithmetic.

2.2   Linear Loop Programs

In this work, we consider programs that consist of a single loop. We use binary relations over the program's states to define its transition relation.

We denote by x the vector of n variables $(x_1, \ldots, x_n)^T \in \mathbb{K}^n$ corresponding to program states and by $x' = (x_1', \ldots, x_n')^T \in \mathbb{K}^n$ the variables of the next state.

Definition 1 (Linear loop program). *A* linear loop program $\mathrm{LOOP}(x, x')$ *is a binary relation defined by a formula with the free variables x and x' of the form*

$$\bigvee_{i \in I} \left(A_i \binom{x}{x'} \leq b_i \ \wedge \ C_i \binom{x}{x'} < d_i \right)$$

for some finite index set I, some matrices $A_i \in \mathbb{K}^{n \times m_i}$, $C_i \in \mathbb{K}^{n \times k_i}$, and some vectors $b_i \in \mathbb{K}^{m_i}$ and $d_i \in \mathbb{K}^{k_i}$. The linear loop program $\text{LOOP}(x, x')$ is called conjunctive, iff there is only one disjunct, i.e., $\#I = 1$.

Geometrically the relation LOOP corresponds to a union of convex polyhedra.

Definition 2 (Termination). We say that a linear loop program $\text{LOOP}(x, x')$ terminates iff the relation $\text{LOOP}(x, x')$ is well-founded.

Example 1. Consider the following program code.

$$\textbf{while } (q > 0):$$
$$\textbf{if } (y > 0):$$
$$q := q - y - 1;$$
$$\textbf{else}:$$
$$q := q + y - 1;$$

We represent this as the following linear loop program:

$$(q > 0 \ \wedge \ y > 0 \ \wedge \ y' = y \ \wedge \ q' = q - y - 1)$$
$$\vee (q > 0 \ \wedge \ y \leq 0 \ \wedge \ y' = y \ \wedge \ q' = q + y - 1)$$

This linear loop program is not conjunctive. Furthermore, there is no infinite sequence of states $x_0, x_1, \ldots$ such that for all $i \geq 0$, the two successive states (x_i, x_{i+1}) are contained in the relation LOOP. Hence the relation $\text{LOOP}(x, x')$ is well-founded and the linear loop program terminates.

3 Ranking Templates

A *ranking template* is a template for a well-founded relation. More specifically, it is a parametrized formula defining a relation that is well-founded for all assignments to the parameters. If we show that a given program's transition relation LOOP is a subset of an instance of this well-founded relation, it must be well-founded itself and thus we have a proof for the program's termination. Moreover, an assignment to the parameters of the template gives rise to a ranking function. In this work, we consider ranking templates that can be encoded in linear arithmetic.

We call a formula whose free variables contain x and x' a *relation template*. Each free variable other than x and x' in a relation template is called *parameter*. Given an assignment ν to all parameter variables of a relation template $\text{T}(x, x')$, the evaluation $\nu(\text{T})$ is called an *instantiation of the relation template* T. We note that each instantiation of a relation template $\text{T}(x, x')$ defines a binary relation.

When specifying templates, we use parameter variables to define affine-linear functions. For notational convenience, we will write $f(x)$ instead of the term $s_f^T x + t_f$, where $s_f \in \mathbb{K}^n$ and $t_f \in \mathbb{K}$ are parameter variables. We call f an *affine-linear function symbol*.

Definition 3 (Linear ranking template). *Let* $\mathrm{T}(x, x')$ *be a template with parameters* D *and affine-linear function symbols* F *that can be written as a boolean combination of atoms of the form*

$$\sum_{f \in F} \left(\alpha_f \cdot f(x) + \beta_f \cdot f(x') \right) + \sum_{d \in D} \gamma_d \cdot d \, \rhd \, 0,$$

where $\alpha_f, \beta_f, \gamma_d \in \mathbb{K}$ *are constants and* $\rhd \in \{\geq, >\}$. *We call* T *a linear ranking template* over D *and* F *iff every instantiation of* T *defines a well-founded relation.*

Example 2. We call the following template with parameters $D = \{\delta\}$ and affine-linear function symbols $F = \{f\}$ the *Podelski-Rybalchenko ranking template* [20].

$$\delta > 0 \, \wedge \, f(x) > 0 \, \wedge \, f(x') < f(x) - \delta \tag{1}$$

In the remainder of this section, we introduce a formalism that allows us to show that every instantiation of the Podelski-Rybalchenko ranking template defines a well-founded relation. Let us now check the additional syntactic requirements for 1 to be a linear ranking template:

$$\delta > 0 \equiv \left(0 \cdot f(x) + 0 \cdot f(x') \right) + 1 \cdot \delta > 0$$
$$f(x) > 0 \equiv \left(1 \cdot f(x) + 0 \cdot f(x') \right) + 0 \cdot \delta > 0$$
$$f(x') < f(x) - \delta \equiv \left(1 \cdot f(x) + (-1) \cdot f(x') \right) + (-1) \cdot \delta > 0$$

The next lemma states that we can prove termination of a given linear loop program by checking that this program's transition relation is included in an instantiation of a linear ranking template.

Lemma 1. *Let* LOOP *be a linear loop program and let* T *be a linear ranking template with parameters* D *and affine-linear function symbols* F. *If there is an assignment* ν *to* D *and* F *such that the formula*

$$\forall x, x'. \left(\mathrm{LOOP}(x, x') \to \nu(\mathrm{T})(x, x') \right) \tag{2}$$

is valid, then the program LOOP *terminates.*

Proof. By definition, $\nu(\mathrm{T})$ is a well-founded relation and (2) is valid iff the relation LOOP is a subset of $\nu(\mathrm{T})$. Thus LOOP must be well-founded. □

In order to establish that a formula conforming to the syntactic requirements is indeed a ranking template, we must show the well-foundedness of its instantiations. According to the following lemma, we can do this by showing that an assignment to D and F gives rise to a ranking function. A similar argument was given in [3]; we provide significantly shortened proof by use of the Recursion Theorem, along the lines of [15, Example 6.12].

Definition 4 (Ranking Function). *Given a binary relation R over a set Σ, we call a function ρ from Σ to some ordinal α a ranking function for R iff for all $x, x' \in \Sigma$ the following implication holds.*

$$(x, x') \in R \implies \rho(x) > \rho(x')$$

Lemma 2. *A binary relation R is well-founded if and only if there exists a ranking function for R.*

Proof. Let ρ be a ranking function for R. The image of a sequence decreasing with respect to R under ρ is a strictly decreasing ordinal sequence. Because the ordinals are well-ordered, this sequence cannot be infinite.

Conversely, the graph $G = (\Sigma, R)$ with vertices Σ and edges R is acyclic by assumption. Hence the function ρ that assigns to every element of Σ an ordinal number such that $\rho(x) = \sup \{\rho(x') + 1 \mid (x, x') \in R\}$ is well-defined and exists due to the Recursion Theorem [15, Theorem 6.11]. $\square$

Example 3. Consider the terminating linear loop program LOOP from Example 1. A ranking function for LOOP is $\rho : \mathbb{R}^2 \to \omega$, defined as follows.

$$\rho(q, y) = \begin{cases} \lceil q \rceil, & \text{if } q > 0, \text{ and} \\ 0 & \text{otherwise.} \end{cases}$$

Here $\lceil \cdot \rceil$ denotes the ceiling function that assigns to every real number r the smallest natural number that is larger or equal to r. Since we consider the natural numbers to be a subset of the ordinals, the ranking function ρ is well-defined.

We use assignments to a template's parameters and affine-linear function symbols to construct a ranking function. These functions are real-valued and we will transform them into functions with codomain ω in the following way.

Definition 5. *Given an affine-linear function f and a real number $\delta > 0$ called the step size, we define the ordinal ranking equivalent of f as*

$$\widehat{f}(x) = \begin{cases} \left\lceil \frac{f(x)}{\delta} \right\rceil, & \text{if } f(x) > 0, \text{ and} \\ 0 & \text{otherwise.} \end{cases}$$

For better readability we used this notation which does not explicitly refer to δ. In our presentation the step size δ is always clear from the context in which an ordinal ranking equivalent $\widehat{f}$ is used.

Example 4. Consider the linear loop program LOOP(x, x') from Example 1. For $\delta = \frac{1}{2}$ and $f(q) = q + 1$, the ordinal ranking equivalent of f with step size δ is

$$\widehat{f}(q, y) = \begin{cases} \lceil 2(q + 1) \rceil, & \text{if } q + 1 > 0, \text{ and} \\ 0 & \text{otherwise.} \end{cases}$$

The assignment from Example 4 to δ and f makes the implication (2) valid. In order to invoke Lemma 1 to show that the linear loop program given in Example 1 terminates, we need to prove that the Podelski-Rybalchenko ranking template is a linear ranking template. We use the following technical lemma.

Lemma 3. *Let f be an affine-linear function of step size $\delta > 0$ and let x and x' be two states. If $f(x) > 0$ and $f(x) - f(x') > \delta$, then $\widehat{f}(x) > 0$ and $\widehat{f}(x) > \widehat{f}(x')$.*

Proof. From $f(x) > 0$ follows that $\widehat{f}(x) > 0$. Therefore $\widehat{f}(x) > \widehat{f}(x')$ in the case $\widehat{f}(x') = 0$. For $\widehat{f}(x') > 0$, we use the fact that $f(x) - f(x') > \delta$ to conclude that $\frac{f(x)}{\delta} - \frac{f(x')}{\delta} > 1$ and hence $\widehat{f}(x') > \widehat{f}(x)$. □

An immediate consequence of this lemma is that the Podelski-Rybalchenko ranking template is a linear ranking template: any assignment ν to δ and f satisfies the requirements of Lemma 3. Consequently, $\widehat{f}$ is a ranking function for $\nu(\mathrm{T})$, and by Lemma 2 this implies that $\nu(\mathrm{T})$ is well-founded.

4 Examples of Ranking Templates

4.1 Multiphase Ranking Template

The multiphase ranking template is targeted at programs that go through a finite number of phases in their execution. Each phase is ranked with an affine-linear function and the phase is considered to be completed once this function becomes non-positive.

Example 5. Consider the linear loop program from Figure 1. Every execution can be partitioned into two phases: first y increases until it is positive and then q decreases until the loop condition $q > 0$ is violated. Depending on the initial values of y and q, either phase might be skipped altogether.

Definition 6 (Multiphase Ranking Template). *We define the k-phase ranking template with parameters $D = \{\delta_1, \dots, \delta_k\}$ and affine-linear function symbols $F = \{f_1, \dots, f_k\}$ as follows.*

$$\bigwedge_{i=1}^{k} \delta_i > 0 \tag{3}$$

$$\wedge \bigvee_{i=1}^{k} f_i(x) > 0 \tag{4}$$

$$\wedge\, f_1(x') < f_1(x) - \delta_1 \tag{5}$$

$$\wedge \bigwedge_{i=2}^{k} \left(f_i(x') < f_i(x) - \delta_i \,\vee\, f_{i-1}(x) > 0 \right) \tag{6}$$

We say that the multiphase ranking function given by an assignment to $f_1, \ldots, f_k$ and $\delta_1, \ldots, \delta_k$ is *in phase i*, iff $f_i(x) > 0$ and $f_j(x) \leq 0$ for all $j < i$. The condition (4) states that there is always some i such that the multiphase ranking function is in phase i. (5) and (6) state that if we are in a phase $\geq i$, then f_i has to be decreasing by at least $\delta_i > 0$. Note that the 1-phase ranking template coincides with the Podelski-Rybalchenko ranking template.

Multiphase ranking functions are related to *eventually negative expressions* introduced by Bradley, Manna, and Sipma [6]. However, in contrast to our approach, they require a template tree that specifies in detail how each loop transition interacts with each phase.

Lemma 4. *The k-phase ranking template is a linear ranking template.*

Proof. The k-phase ranking template conforms to the syntactic requirements to be a linear ranking template. Let an assignment to the parameters D and the affine-linear function symbols F of the k-phase template be given. Consider the following ranking function with codomain $\omega \cdot k$.

$$\rho(x) = \begin{cases} \omega \cdot (k - i) + \widehat{f_i}(x) & \text{if } f_j(x) \leq 0 \text{ for all } j < i \text{ and } f_i(x) > 0, \\ 0 & \text{otherwise.} \end{cases} \quad (7)$$

Let $(x, x') \in \text{T}$. By Lemma 2, we need to show that $\rho(x') < \rho(x)$. From (4) follows that $\rho(x) > 0$. Moreover, there is an i such that $f_i(x) > 0$ and $f_j(x) \leq 0$ for all $j < i$. By (5) and (6), $f_j(x') \leq 0$ for all $j < i$ because $f_j(x') < f_j(x) - \delta_j \leq 0 - \delta_j \leq 0$, since $f_\ell(x) \leq 0$ for all $\ell < j$.

If $f_i(x') \leq 0$, then $\rho(x') \leq \omega \cdot (k - i) < \omega \cdot (k - i) + \widehat{f_i}(x) = \rho(x)$. Otherwise, $f_i(x') > 0$ and from (6) follows $f_i(x') < f_i(x) - \delta_i$. By Lemma 3, $\widehat{f_i}(x) > \widehat{f_i}(x')$ for the ordinal ranking equivalent of f_i with step size δ_i. Hence

$$\rho(x') = \omega \cdot (k - i) + \widehat{f_i}(x') < \omega \cdot (k - i) + \widehat{f_i}(x) = \rho(x). \qquad \square$$

Example 6. Consider the program from Figure 1. The assignment

$$f_1(q, y) = 1 - y, \qquad f_2(q, y) = q + 1, \qquad \delta_1 = \delta_2 = \tfrac{1}{2}$$

yields a 2-phase ranking function for this program.

Example 7. There are terminating conjunctive linear loop programs that do not have a multiphase ranking function:

$$q > 0 \ \wedge \ q' = q + z - 1 \ \wedge \ z' = -z$$

Here, the sign of z is alternated in each iteration. The function $\rho(q, y, z) = \lceil q \rceil$ is decreasing in every second iteration, but not decreasing in each iteration.

Example 8. Consider the following linear loop program.

$$(q > 0 \ \wedge \ y > 0 \ \wedge \ y' = 0)$$
$$\vee \ (q > 0 \ \wedge \ y \leq 0 \ \wedge \ y' = y - 1 \ \wedge \ q' = q - 1)$$

For a given input, we cannot give an upper bound on the execution time: starting with $y > 0$, after the first loop execution, y is set to 0 and q is set to *some arbitrary value*, as no restriction to q' applies in the first disjunct. In particular, this value does not depend on the input. The remainder of the loop execution then takes $\lceil q \rceil$ iterations to terminate.

However we can prove the program's termination with the 2-phase ranking function constructed from $f_1(q, y) = y$ and $f_2(q, y) = q$.

4.2   Piecewise Ranking Template

The piecewise ranking template formalizes a ranking function that is defined piecewise using affine-linear predicates to discriminate the pieces.

Definition 7 (Piecewise Ranking Template). *We define the k-piece ranking template with parameters $D = \{\delta\}$ and affine-linear function symbols $F = \{f_1, \ldots, f_k, g_1, \ldots, g_k\}$ as follows.*

$$\delta > 0 \tag{8}$$

$$\wedge \bigwedge_{i=1}^{k} \bigwedge_{j=1}^{k} \left(g_i(x) < 0 \ \vee \ g_j(x') < 0 \ \vee \ f_j(x') < f_i(x) - \delta \right) \tag{9}$$

$$\wedge \bigwedge_{i=1}^{k} f_i(x) > 0 \tag{10}$$

$$\wedge \bigvee_{i=1}^{k} g_i(x) \geq 0 \tag{11}$$

We call the affine-linear function symbols $\{g_i \mid 1 \leq i \leq k\}$ *discriminators* and the affine-linear function symbols $\{f_i \mid 1 \leq i \leq k\}$ *ranking pieces*.

The disjunction (11) states that the discriminators cover all states; in other words, the piecewise defined ranking function is a total function. Given the k different pieces $f_1, \ldots, f_k$ and a state x, we use f_i as a ranking function only if $g_i(x) \geq 0$ holds. This choice need not be unambiguous; the discriminators may overlap. If they do, we can use any one of their ranking pieces. According to (10), all ranking pieces are positive-valued and by (9) piece transitions are well-defined: the rank of the new state is always less than the rank any of the ranking pieces assigned to the old state.

Lemma 5. *The k-piece ranking template is a linear ranking template.*

Proof. The k-piece ranking template conforms to the syntactic requirements to be a linear ranking template. Let an assignment to the parameter δ and the affine-linear function symbols F of the k-piece template be given. Consider the following ranking function with codomain ω.

$$\rho(x) = \max \left\{ \widehat{f_i}(x) \mid g_i(x) \geq 0 \right\} \tag{12}$$

The function ρ is well-defined, because according to (11), the set $\{\widehat{f}_i(x) \mid g_i(x) \geq 0\}$ is not empty. Let $(x, x') \in \mathrm{T}$ and let i and j be indices such that $\rho(x) = \widehat{f}_i(x)$ and $\rho(x') = \widehat{f}_j(x')$. By definition of ρ, we have that $g_i(x) \geq 0$ and $g_j(x) \geq 0$, and (9) thus implies $f_j(x') < f_i(x) - \delta$. According to Lemma 3 and (10), this entails $\widehat{f}_j(x') < \widehat{f}_i(x)$ and therefore $\rho(x') < \rho(x)$. Lemma 2 now implies that T is well-founded. □

Example 9. Consider the following linear loop program.

$$(q > 0 \ \wedge \ p > 0 \ \wedge \ q < p \ \wedge \ q' = q - 1)$$
$$\vee \ (q > 0 \ \wedge \ p > 0 \ \wedge \ p < q \ \wedge \ p' = p - 1)$$

In every loop iteration, the minimum of p and q is decreased by 1 until it becomes negative. Thus, this program is ranked by the 2-piece ranking function constructed from $f_1(p, q) = p$ and $f_2(p, q) = q$ with step size $\delta = \frac{1}{2}$ and discriminators $g_1(p, q) = q - p$ and $g_2(p, q) = p - q$. Moreover, this program does not have a multiphase or lexicographic ranking function: both p and q may increase without bound during program execution due to non-determinism and the number of switches between p and q being the minimum value is also unbounded.

4.3 Lexicographic Ranking Template

Lexicographic ranking functions consist of lexicographically ordered components of affine-linear functions. A state is mapped to a tuple of values such that the loop transition leads to a decrease with respect to the lexicographic ordering for this tuple. Therefore no function may increase unless a function of a lower index decreases. Additionally, at every step, there must be at least one function that decreases.

Several different definitions for lexicographic ranking functions have been utilized [2,4,5]; a comparison can be found in [4]. Each of these definitions for lexicographic linear ranking functions can be formalized using linear ranking templates; in this publication we are following the definition of [2].

Definition 8 (Lexicographic Ranking Template). *We define the k-lexicographic ranking template with parameters $D = \{\delta_1, \ldots, \delta_k\}$ and affine-linear function symbols $F = \{f_1, \ldots, f_k\}$ as follows.*

$$\bigwedge_{i=1}^{k} \delta_i > 0 \tag{13}$$

$$\wedge \ \bigwedge_{i=1}^{k} f_i(x) > 0 \tag{14}$$

$$\wedge \ \bigwedge_{i=1}^{k-1} \left(f_i(x') \leq f_i(x) \ \vee \ \bigvee_{j=1}^{i-1} f_j(x') < f_j(x) - \delta_j \right) \tag{15}$$

$$\wedge \ \bigvee_{i=1}^{k} f_i(x') < f_i(x) - \delta_i \tag{16}$$

The conjunction (14) establishes that all lexicographic components $f_1, \ldots, f_k$ have positive values. In every step, at least one component must decrease according to (16). From (15) follows that all functions corresponding to components of smaller index than the decreasing function may increase.

Lemma 6. *The k-lexicographic ranking template is a linear ranking template.*

Proof. The k-lexicographic ranking template conforms to the syntactic requirements to be a linear ranking template. Let an assignment to the parameters D and the affine-linear function symbols F of the k-lexicographic template be given. Consider the following ranking function with codomain ω^k.

$$\rho(x) = \sum_{i=1}^{k} \omega^{k-i} \cdot \widehat{f}_i(x) \tag{17}$$

Let $(x, x') \in \mathrm{T}$. From (14) follows $f_j(x) > 0$ for all j, so $\rho(x) > 0$. By (16) and Lemma 3, there is a minimal i such that $\widehat{f}_i(x') < \widehat{f}_i(x)$. According to (15), $\widehat{f}_1(x') \leq \widehat{f}_1(x)$ and hence inductively $\widehat{f}_j(x') \leq \widehat{f}_j(x)$ for all $j < i$, since i was minimal.

$$\rho(x') = \sum_{j=1}^{k} \omega^{k-j} \cdot \widehat{f}_j(x') \leq \sum_{j=1}^{i-1} \omega^{k-j} \cdot \widehat{f}_j(x) + \sum_{j=i}^{k} \omega^{k-j} \cdot \widehat{f}_j(x')$$

$$< \sum_{j=1}^{i-1} \omega^{k-j} \cdot \widehat{f}_j(x) + \omega^{k-i} \cdot \widehat{f}_i(x) \leq \rho(x)$$

Therefore Lemma 2 implies that T is well-founded.   □

4.4   Composition of Templates

The multiphase ranking template, the piecewise ranking template, and the lexicographic ranking template defined in the previous sections can be used as a 'construction kit' for more general linear ranking templates. Each of our templates contains lower bounds ((4), (10), (11), and (14)) and decreasing behavior ((5), (6), (9), (15), and (16)). We can compose templates by replacing the lower bound conditions and decreasing behavior conditions to affine-linear function symbols in our linear ranking templates with the corresponding conditions of another template. This is possible because linear ranking templates allow arbitrary boolean combination of inequalities and are closed under this kind of substitution. For example, we can construct a template for a lexicographic ranking function whose lexicographic components are multiphase functions instead of affine-linear functions (see Figure 2). This encompasses the approach applied by Bradley et al. [6].

$$\bigwedge_{i=1}^{k} \bigwedge_{j=1}^{\ell} \delta_{i,j} > 0$$

$$\wedge \bigwedge_{i=1}^{k} \bigvee_{j=1}^{\ell} f_{i,j}(x) > 0$$

$$\wedge \bigwedge_{i=1}^{k-1} \left(\left(f_{i,1}(x') \leq f_{i,1}(x) \wedge \bigwedge_{j=2}^{\ell} \left(f_{i,j}(x') \leq f_{i,j}(x) \vee f_{i,j-1}(x) > 0 \right) \right) \right.$$

$$\left. \vee \bigvee_{t=1}^{i-1} \left(f_{t,1}(x') < f_{t,1}(x) - \delta_{t,1} \wedge \bigwedge_{j=2}^{\ell} \left(f_{t,j}(x') < f_{t,j}(x) - \delta_{t,j} \vee f_{t,j-1}(x) > 0 \right) \right) \right)$$

$$\wedge \bigvee_{i=1}^{k} \left(f_{i,1}(x') < f_{i,1}(x) - \delta_{i,1} \wedge \bigwedge_{j=2}^{\ell} \left(f_{i,j}(x') < f_{i,j}(x) - \delta_{i,j} \vee f_{i,j-1}(x) > 0 \right) \right)$$

Fig. 2. A k-lexicographic ranking template with ℓ phases in each lexicographic component with the parameters $D = \{\delta_{i,j}\}$ and affine-linear function symbols $F = \{f_{i,j}\}$

5 Synthesizing Ranking Functions

Our method for ranking function synthesis can be stated as follows. We have a finite pool of linear ranking templates. This pool will include the multiphase, piecewise, and lexicographic ranking templates in various sizes and possibly combinations thereof. Given a linear loop program whose termination we want to prove, we select a linear ranking template from the pool. With this template we build the constraint (2) to the linear ranking template's parameters. If this constraint is satisfiable, this gives rise to a ranking function according to Lemma 2. Otherwise, we try again using the next linear ranking template from the pool until the pool has been exhausted. In this case, the given linear loop program does not have a ranking function of the form specified by any of the pool's linear ranking templates and the proof of the program's termination failed. See Figure 3 for a specification of our method in pseudocode.

Following related approaches [2,5,6,7,14,20,24,25], we transform the $\exists\forall$-constraint (2) into an $\exists$-constraint. This transformation makes the constraint more easily solvable because it reduces the number of non-linear operations in the constraint: every application of an affine-linear function symbol f corresponds to a non-linear term $s_f^T x + t_f$.

5.1 Constraint Transformation Using Motzkin's Theorem

Fix a linear loop program LOOP and a linear ranking template T with parameters D and affine-linear function symbols F. We write LOOP in disjunctive normal form and T in conjunctive normal form:

Input: linear loop program LOOP and a list of linear ranking templates $\mathcal{T}$
Output: a ranking function for LOOP or **null** if none is found

```
foreach т ∈ 𝒯 do:
    let φ = ∀x, x'. (LOOP(x, x') → т(x, x'))
    let ψ = transformWithMotzkin(φ)
    if SMTsolver.checkSAT(ψ):
        let (D, F) = т.getParameters()
        let ν = getAssignment(ψ, D, F)
        return т.extractRankingFunction(ν)
return null
```

Fig. 3. Our ranking function synthesis algorithm described in pseudocode. The function **transformWithMotzkin** transforms the $\exists\forall$-constraint φ into an $\exists$-constraint ψ as described in Subsection 5.1.

$$\text{LOOP}(x, x') \equiv \bigvee_{i \in I} A_i\left(\begin{smallmatrix}x\\x'\end{smallmatrix}\right) \leq b_i$$

$$\text{T}(x, x') \equiv \bigwedge_{j \in J} \bigvee_{\ell \in L_j} \text{T}_{j,\ell}(x, x')$$

We prove the termination of LOOP by solving the constraint (2). This constraint is implicitly existentially quantified over the parameters D and the parameters corresponding to the affine-linear function symbols F.

$$\forall x, x'. \left(\left(\bigvee_{i \in I} A_i\left(\begin{smallmatrix}x\\x'\end{smallmatrix}\right) \leq b_i \right) \rightarrow \left(\bigwedge_{j \in J} \bigvee_{\ell \in L_j} \text{T}_{j,\ell}(x, x') \right) \right) \tag{18}$$

First, we transform the constraint (18) into an equivalent constraint of the form required by Motzkin's Theorem.

$$\bigwedge_{i \in I} \bigwedge_{j \in J} \forall x, x'. \neg \left(A_i\left(\begin{smallmatrix}x\\x'\end{smallmatrix}\right) \leq b_i \wedge \left(\bigwedge_{\ell \in L_j} \neg \text{T}_{j,\ell}(x, x') \right) \right) \tag{19}$$

Now, Motzkin's Transposition Theorem will transform the constraint (19) into an equivalent existentially quantified constraint.

This $\exists$-constraint is then checked for satisfiability. If an assignment is found, it gives rise to a ranking function. Conversely, if no assignment exists, then there cannot be an instantiation of the linear ranking template and thus no ranking function of the kind formalized by the linear ranking template. In this sense our method is sound and complete.

Theorem 2 (Soundness). *If the transformed $\exists$-constraint is satisfiable, then the linear loop program terminates.*

Theorem 3 (Completeness). *If the $\exists\forall$-constraint (2) is satisfiable, then so is the transformed $\exists$-constraint.*

6 Related Work

The first complete method of ranking function synthesis for linear loop programs through constraint solving was due Podelski and Rybalchenko [20]. Their approach considers termination arguments in form of affine-linear ranking functions and requires only linear constraint solving. We explained the relation to their method in Example 2.

Bradley, Manna, and Sipma propose a related approach for linear lasso programs [5]. They introduce affine-linear inductive supporting invariants to handle the stem. Their termination argument is a lexicographic ranking function with each component corresponding to one loop disjunct. This not only requires nonlinear constraint solving, but also an ordering on the loop disjuncts. The authors extend this approach in [6] by the use of *template trees*. These trees allow each lexicographic component to have a ranking function that decreases not necessarily in every step, but *eventually*.

In [14] the method of Podelski and Rybalchenko is extended. Utilizing supporting invariants analogously to Bradley et al., affine-linear ranking functions are synthesized. Due to the restriction to non-decreasing invariants, the generated constraints are linear.

A collection of example-based explanations of constraint-based verification techniques can be found in [24]. This includes the generation of ranking functions, interpolants, invariants, resource bounds and recurrence sets.

In [4] Ben-Amram and Genaim discuss the synthesis of affine-linear and lexicographic ranking functions for linear loop programs over the integers. They prove that this problem is generally co-NP-complete and show that several special cases admit a polynomial time complexity.

References

1. Albert, E., Arenas, P., Genaim, S., Puebla, G.: Closed-form upper bounds in static cost analysis. J. Autom. Reasoning 46(2), 161–203 (2011)
2. Alias, C., Darte, A., Feautrier, P., Gonnord, L.: Multi-dimensional rankings, program termination, and complexity bounds of flowchart programs. In: Cousot, R., Martel, M. (eds.) SAS 2010. LNCS, vol. 6337, pp. 117–133. Springer, Heidelberg (2010)
3. Ben-Amram, A.M.: Size-change termination, monotonicity constraints and ranking functions. In: Bouajjani, A., Maler, O. (eds.) CAV 2009. LNCS, vol. 5643, pp. 109–123. Springer, Heidelberg (2009)
4. Ben-Amram, A.M., Genaim, S.: Ranking functions for linear-constraint loops. In: POPL (2013)
5. Bradley, A.R., Manna, Z., Sipma, H.B.: Linear ranking with reachability. In: Etessami, K., Rajamani, S.K. (eds.) CAV 2005. LNCS, vol. 3576, pp. 491–504. Springer, Heidelberg (2005)
6. Bradley, A.R., Manna, Z., Sipma, H.B.: The polyranking principle. In: Caires, L., Italiano, G.F., Monteiro, L., Palamidessi, C., Yung, M. (eds.) ICALP 2005. LNCS, vol. 3580, pp. 1349–1361. Springer, Heidelberg (2005)

7. Colón, M.A., Sankaranarayanan, S., Sipma, H.B.: Linear invariant generation using non-linear constraint solving. In: Hunt Jr., W.A., Somenzi, F. (eds.) CAV 2003. LNCS, vol. 2725, pp. 420–432. Springer, Heidelberg (2003)
8. Cook, B., Fisher, J., Krepska, E., Piterman, N.: Proving stabilization of biological systems. In: Jhala, R., Schmidt, D. (eds.) VMCAI 2011. LNCS, vol. 6538, pp. 134–149. Springer, Heidelberg (2011)
9. Cook, B., Podelski, A., Rybalchenko, A.: Terminator: Beyond safety. In: Ball, T., Jones, R.B. (eds.) CAV 2006. LNCS, vol. 4144, pp. 415–418. Springer, Heidelberg (2006)
10. Grigor'ev, D.Y., Vorobjov Jr., N.N.: Solving systems of polynomial inequalities in subexponential time. Journal of Symbolic Computation 5(1-2), 37–64 (1988)
11. Gulwani, S., Zuleger, F.: The reachability-bound problem. In: PLDI, pp. 292–304 (2010)
12. Gupta, A., Henzinger, T.A., Majumdar, R., Rybalchenko, A., Xu, R.G.: Proving non-termination. In: POPL, pp. 147–158 (2008)
13. Harris, W.R., Lal, A., Nori, A.V., Rajamani, S.K.: Alternation for termination. In: Cousot, R., Martel, M. (eds.) SAS 2010. LNCS, vol. 6337, pp. 304–319. Springer, Heidelberg (2010)
14. Heizmann, M., Hoenicke, J., Leike, J., Podelski, A.: Linear ranking for linear lasso programs. In: Van Hung, D., Ogawa, M. (eds.) ATVA 2013. LNCS, vol. 8172, pp. 365–380. Springer, Heidelberg (2013)
15. Jech, T.: Set Theory, 3rd edn. Springer (2006)
16. Jovanović, D., de Moura, L.: Solving non-linear arithmetic. In: Gramlich, B., Miller, D., Sattler, U. (eds.) IJCAR 2012. LNCS, vol. 7364, pp. 339–354. Springer, Heidelberg (2012)
17. Kroening, D., Sharygina, N., Tonetta, S., Tsitovich, A., Wintersteiger, C.M.: Loop summarization using abstract transformers. In: Cha, S(S.), Choi, J.-Y., Kim, M., Lee, I., Viswanathan, M. (eds.) ATVA 2008. LNCS, vol. 5311, pp. 111–125. Springer, Heidelberg (2008)
18. Kroening, D., Sharygina, N., Tsitovich, A., Wintersteiger, C.M.: Termination analysis with compositional transition invariants. In: Touili, T., Cook, B., Jackson, P. (eds.) CAV 2010. LNCS, vol. 6174, pp. 89–103. Springer, Heidelberg (2010)
19. Leike, J.: Ranking function synthesis for linear lasso programs. Master's thesis, University of Freiburg, Germany (2013)
20. Podelski, A., Rybalchenko, A.: A complete method for the synthesis of linear ranking functions. In: Steffen, B., Levi, G. (eds.) VMCAI 2004. LNCS, vol. 2937, pp. 239–251. Springer, Heidelberg (2004)
21. Podelski, A., Rybalchenko, A.: Transition invariants. In: LICS, pp. 32–41 (2004)
22. Podelski, A., Rybalchenko, A.: Transition predicate abstraction and fair termination. In: POPL, pp. 132–144 (2005)
23. Podelski, A., Wagner, S.: A sound and complete proof rule for region stability of hybrid systems. In: Bemporad, A., Bicchi, A., Buttazzo, G. (eds.) HSCC 2007. LNCS, vol. 4416, pp. 750–753. Springer, Heidelberg (2007)
24. Rybalchenko, A.: Constraint solving for program verification: Theory and practice by example. In: Touili, T., Cook, B., Jackson, P. (eds.) CAV 2010. LNCS, vol. 6174, pp. 57–71. Springer, Heidelberg (2010)
25. Sankaranarayanan, S., Sipma, H.B., Manna, Z.: Constraint-based linear-relations analysis. In: Giacobazzi, R. (ed.) SAS 2004. LNCS, vol. 3148, pp. 53–68. Springer, Heidelberg (2004)
26. Schrijver, A.: Theory of linear and integer programming. Wiley-Interscience series in discrete mathematics and optimization. Wiley (1999)

FDR3 — A Modern Refinement Checker for CSP

Thomas Gibson-Robinson, Philip Armstrong, Alexandre Boulgakov,
and Andrew W. Roscoe

Department of Computer Science, University of Oxford
Wolfson Building, Parks Road, Oxford, OX1 3QD, UK
{thomas.gibson-robinson,philip.armstrong,
alexandre.boulgakov,bill.roscoe}@cs.ox.ac.uk

Abstract. FDR3 is a complete rewrite of the CSP refinement checker
FDR2, incorporating a significant number of enhancements. In this paper
we describe the operation of FDR3 at a high level and then give a detailed
description of several of its more important innovations. This includes
the new multi-core refinement-checking algorithm that is able to achieve
a near linear speed up as the number of cores increase. Further, we
describe the new algorithm that FDR3 uses to construct its internal
representation of CSP processes—this algorithm is more efficient than
FDR2's, and is able to compile a large class of CSP processes to more
efficient internal representations. We also present experimental results
that compare FDR3 to related tools, which show it is unique (as far as
we know) in being able to scale beyond the bounds of main memory.

1 Introduction

FDR (Failures Divergence Refinement) is the most widespread refinement
checker for the process algebra CSP [1,2,3]. FDR takes a list of CSP processes,
written in machine-readable CSP (henceforth CSP_M) which is a lazy functional
language, and is able to check if the processes refine each other according to
the CSP denotational models (e.g. the traces, failures and failures-divergences
models). It is also able to check for more properties, including deadlock-freedom,
livelock-freedom and determinism, by constructing equivalent refinement checks.

FDR2 was released in 1996, and has been widely used both within industry
and in academia for verifying systems [4,5,6]. It is also used as a verification
backend for several other tools including: Casper [7] which verifies security protocols; SVA [8] which can verify simple shared-variable programs; in addition to
several industrial tools (e.g. ModelWorks and ASD).

FDR3 has been under development for the last few years as a complete rewrite
of FDR2. It represents a major advance over FDR2, not only in the size of system
that can be checked (we have verified systems with over ten billion states in a
few hours), but also in terms of its ease of use. FDR3 has also been designed
and engineered to be a stable platform for future development of CSP model-
checking tools, in addition to tools for *CSP-like* languages [2]. In this paper we
give an outline of FDR3, highlighting a selection of the advances made.

E. Ábrahám and K. Havelund (Eds.): TACAS 2014, LNCS 8413, pp. 187–201, 2014.

In Section 4 we describe the new multi-core refinement-checking algorithm that achieves a near linear increase in performance as the number of cores increases. Section 6 gives some experimental results that compare the performance of the new algorithm to FDR2, Spin [9], DiVinE [10], and LTSmin [11].

In Section 5 we detail the new *compilation* algorithm, which constructs FDR's internal representation of CSP processes (i.e. labelled-transition systems) from CSP_M processes. This algorithm is an entirely new development and is able to compile many CSP processes into more *efficient* labelled-transition systems. It is also related to the operational semantics of CSP, unlike the FDR2 algorithm which was based on heuristics.

In addition to the advances that we present in this paper, FDR3 incorporates a number of other new features. Most notably, the graphical user interface has been entirely rethought, and includes: a new CSP_M type checker; a built-in version of ProBE, the CSP process animator; and a new debugger that emphasises interactions between processes. See the FDR3 manual [12] for further details.

Before describing the new advances, in Section 2 we briefly review CSP. In Section 3 we then outline the high-level design and structure of FDR3.

2   CSP

CSP [1,2,3] is a *process algebra* in which programs or *processes* that communicate events from a set Σ with an environment may be described. We sometimes structure events by sending them along a *channel*. For example, *c.3* denotes the value 3 being sent along the channel *c*. Further, given a channel *c* the set $\{\!|c|\!\} \subseteq \Sigma$ contains those events of the form *c.x*.

The simplest CSP process is the process $STOP$ that can perform no events. The process $a \to P$ offers the environment the event $a \in \Sigma$ and then behaves like P. The process $P \;\square\; Q$ offers the environment the choice of the events offered by P and by Q and is not resolved by the internal action τ. $P \sqcap Q$ non-deterministically chooses which of P or Q to behave like. $P \rhd Q$ initially behaves like P, but can timeout (via τ) and then behaves as Q.

$P \;_A\|_B\; Q$ allows P and Q to perform only events from A and B respectively and forces P and Q to synchronise on events in $A \cap B$. $P \underset{A}{\parallel} Q$ allows P and Q to run in parallel, forcing synchronisation on events in A and arbitrary interleaving of events not in A. The *interleaving* of two processes, denoted $P \;|||\; Q$, runs P and Q in parallel but enforces no synchronisation. $P \setminus A$ behaves as P but hides any events from A by transforming them into the internal event τ. This event does not synchronise with the environment and thus can always occur. $P[\![R]\!]$, behaves as P but renames the events according to the relation R. Hence, if P can perform a, then $P[\![R]\!]$ can perform each b such that $(a, b) \in R$, where the choice (if more than one such b) is left to the environment (like $\square$). $P \;\triangle\; Q$ initially behaves like P but allows Q to *interrupt* at any point and perform a visible event, at which point P is discarded and the process behaves like Q. $P \;\Theta_A\; Q$ initially behaves like P, but if P ever performs an event from A, P is discarded and $P \;\Theta_A\; Q$ behaves like Q. *Skip* is the process that immediately *terminates*.

The sequential composition of P and Q, denoted $P \,;\, Q$, runs P until it terminates at which point Q is run. Termination is indicated using a $\checkmark$: *Skip* is defined as $\checkmark \to STOP$ and, if the left argument of $P \,;\, Q$ performs a $\checkmark$, $P \,;\, Q$ performs a τ to the state Q (i.e. P is discarded and Q is started).

Recursive processes can be defined either equationally or using the notation $\mu X \cdot P$. In the latter, every occurrence of X within P represents a recursive call.

An argument P of a CSP operator Op is **on** iff it can perform an event. P is **off** iff no such rule exists. For example, the left argument of the exception operator is **on**, whilst the right argument is **off**.

The simplest approach to giving meaning to a CSP expression is by defining an operational semantics. The operational semantics of a CSP process naturally creates a *labelled transition system* (LTS) where the edges are labelled by events from $\Sigma \cup \{\tau\}$ and the nodes are process states. Formally, an LTS is a 3-tuple consisting of a set of nodes, an initial node, and a relation $\xrightarrow{a}$ on the nodes: i.e. it is a directed graph where each edge is labelled by an event. The usual way of defining the operational semantics of CSP processes is by presenting *Structured Operational Semantics* (SOS) style rules in order to define $\xrightarrow{a}$. For instance, the operational semantics of the exception operator are defined by:

$$\frac{P \xrightarrow{a} P'}{P \, \Theta_A \, Q \xrightarrow{a} Q} \; a \in A \qquad \frac{P \xrightarrow{b} P'}{P \, \Theta_A \, Q \xrightarrow{b} P' \, \Theta_A \, Q} \; b \notin A \qquad \frac{P \xrightarrow{\tau} P'}{P \, \Theta_A \, Q \xrightarrow{\tau} P' \, \Theta_A \, Q}$$

The interesting rule is the first, which specifies that if P performs an event $a \in A$, then $P \, \Theta_A \, Q$ can perform the event a and behave like Q.

The SOS style of operational semantics is far more expressive than is required to give an operational semantics to CSP, and indeed can define operators which, for a variety of reasons, make no sense in CSP models. As pointed out in [3], it is possible to re-formulate CSP's semantics in the highly restricted *combinator* style of operational semantics, which largely concentrates on the relationships between events of argument processes and those of the constructed system. This style says, *inter alia*, that only **on** arguments can influence events, that any τ action of an **on** argument must be allowed to proceed freely, and that an argument process has changed state in the result state if and only if it has participated in the action. Cloning of **on** arguments is not permitted. Any language with a combinator operational semantics can be translated to CSP with a high degree of faithfulness [3] and is compositional over every CSP model. FDR3 is designed so that it can readily be extended to such *CSP-like* languages.

CSP also has a number of *denotational models*, such as the traces, failures and failures-divergences models. In these models, each process is represented by a set of behaviours: the traces model represents a process by the set of sequences of events it can perform; the failures model represents a process by the set of events it can *refuse* after each trace; the failures-divergences model augments the failures model with information about when a process can perform an unbounded number of τ events. Two processes are equal in a denotational model iff they have the same set of behaviours. If every behaviour of *Impl* is a behaviour of *Spec* in the denotational model X, then *Spec is refined by Impl*, denoted $Spec \sqsubseteq_X Impl$.

3   The Overall Structure of FDR3

As FDR3 is a refinement checker (deadlock freedom, determinism, etc. are converted into refinement checks), we consider how FDR3 decides if $P \sqsubseteq Q$.

Since P and Q will actually be CSP_M expressions, FDR3 needs to *evaluate* them to produce a tree of CSP operator applications. For example, if P was the CSP_M expression if true then c?x -> STOP else STOP, this would evaluate to c.0 -> STOP [] c.1 -> STOP. Notice that the functional language has been removed: all that remains is a tree of trivial operator applications, as follows.

Definition 1. A *syntactic process* P is generated according to the grammar: $P ::= Operator(P_1, \ldots, P_M) \mid N$ where the P_i are also syntactic processes, *Operator* is any CSP operator (e.g. external choice, prefix etc) and N is a *process name*. A *syntactic process environment* Γ is a function from process name to syntactic process such that $\Gamma(N)$ is never a process name.

The *evaluator* converts CSP_M expressions to syntactic processes. Since CSP_M is a lazy functional language, the complexity of evaluating CSP_M depends on how the CSP_M code has been written. This is written in Haskell and is available as part of the open-source Haskell library libcspm [13], which implements a parser, type-checker and evaluator for CSP_M.

Given a syntactic process, FDR3 then converts this to an LTS which is used to represent CSP processes during refinement checks. In order to support various features (most importantly, the *compressions* such as *normalisation*), FDR internally represents processes as *generalised labelled transition systems* (GLTSs), rather than LTSs. These differ from LTSs in that the individual states can be labelled with properties according to the semantic model in use. For example, if the failures model is being used, a GLTS would allow states to be labelled with refusals. The *compiler* is responsible for converting syntactic processes into GLTSs. The primary challenge for the compiler is to decide which of FDR3's internal representations of GLTSs (which have various trade-offs) should be used to represent each syntactic process. This algorithm is detailed in Section 5.

After FDR3 has constructed GLTSs for the specification and implementation processes, FDR3 checks for refinement. Firstly, as with FDR2, the specification GLTS is *normalised* [3] to yield a deterministic GLTS with no τ's. Normalising large specifications is expensive, however, generally specifications are relatively small. FDR3 then checks if the implementation GLTS refines the normalised specification GLTS according to the algorithm presented in Section 4.

Like FDR2, FDR3 supports a variety of compressions which can be used to cut the state space of a system. FDR3 essentially supports the compressions of [3], in some cases with significantly improved algorithms, which we will report on separately. It also supports the *chase* operator of FDR2 which forces τ actions and is a useful pruner of state spaces where it is semantically valid.

Like recent versions of FDR2, FDR3 supports the Timed CSP language [14,15]. It uses the strategy outlined in [16,3] of translating the continuous Timed CSP language to a variant of untimed CSP with prioritisation and relying on

function REFINES(S, I, $\mathcal{M}$)
    $done \leftarrow \{\}$ ▷ The set of states that have been visited
    $current \leftarrow \{(root(S), root(I))\}$ ▷ States to visit on the current ply
    $next \leftarrow \{\}$ ▷ States to visit on the next ply
    while $current \neq \{\}$ **do**
        for $(s, i) \leftarrow current \setminus done$ **do**
            Check if i refines s according to $\mathcal{M}$
            $done \leftarrow done \cup \{(s, i)\}$
            for $(e, i') \in transitions(I, i)$ **do**
                if $e = \tau$ **then** $next \leftarrow next \cup \{(s, i')\}$
                else $t \leftarrow transitions(S, s, e)$
                    if $t = \{\}$ **then** Report trace error   ▷ S cannot perform the event
                    else $\{s'\} \leftarrow t$
                        $next \leftarrow next \cup \{(s', i')\}$
        $current \leftarrow next$
        $next \leftarrow \{\}$

Fig. 1. The single-threaded refinement-checking algorithm where: S is the normalised specification GLTS; I is the implementation GLTS; $\mathcal{M}$ is the denotational model to perform the check in; $root(X)$ returns the root of the GLTS X; $transitions(X, s)$ returns the set of all (e, s') such that there is a transition from s to s' in the GLTS X labelled by the event e; $transitions(X, s, e)$ returns only successors under event e

theorems of *digitisation* [17]. In order to support this, FDR3 also supports the *prioritise* operator [3,18], which has other interesting applications as shown there.

4 Parallel Refinement Checking

We now describe the new multi-core refinement-checking algorithm that FDR3 uses to decide if a *normalised* GLTS P (recall that normalisation produces a GLTS with no τ's and such that for each state and each event, there is a unique successor state) is refined by another GLTS Q. We begin by outlining the refinement checking algorithm of [2] and describing the FDR2 implementation [19]. We then define the parallel refinement-checking algorithm, before contrasting our approach with the approaches taken by others to parallelise similar problems.

In this paper we concentrate on parallelising refinement checking on shared-memory systems. We also concentrate on refinement checking in models that do not consider divergence: we will report separately on parallelising this.

The Single-Threaded Algorithm Refinement checking proceeds by performing a search over the implementation, checking that every reachable state is compatible with every state of the specification after the same trace. A breadth-first search is performed since this produces a minimal counterexample when the check fails. The single threaded algorithm [2,19] is given in Figure 1.

The interesting aspect of an implementation of the above algorithm is how it stores the sets of states (i.e. *current*, *next* and *done*). FDR2 uses B-Trees for

function WORKER(S, I, $\mathcal{M}$, w)

    $done_w, current_w, next_w \leftarrow \{\}, \{\}, \{\}$

    $finished_w \leftarrow true$

    if $hash(root(S), root(I)) = w$ **then**

        $current_w \leftarrow \{(root(S), root(I))\}$

        $finished_w \leftarrow false$

    while $\vee_{w \in Workers} \neg finished_w$ **do**

        Wait for other workers to ensure the plys start together

        $finished_w \leftarrow true$

        for $(s, i) \leftarrow current_w \setminus done_w$ **do**

            $finished_w \leftarrow false$

            Check if i refines s according to $\mathcal{M}$

            $done_w \leftarrow done_w \cup \{(s, i)\}$

            for $(i', e) \in transitions(I, i)$ **do**

                if $e = \tau$ **then** $w' \leftarrow hash(s, i') \mod \#Workers$

                    $next_{w'} \leftarrow next_{w'} \cup \{(s, i')\}$

                else $t \leftarrow transitions(S, s, e)$

                    if $t = \{\}$ **then** Report Trace Error

                    else $\{s'\} \leftarrow t$

                        $w' \leftarrow hash(s', i') \mod \#Workers$

                        $next_{w'} \leftarrow next_{w'} \cup \{(s', i')\}$

        Wait for other workers to finish their ply

        $current_w \leftarrow next_w$

        $next_w \leftarrow \{\}$

Fig. 2. Each worker in a parallel refinement check executes the above function. The set of all workers is given by *Workers*. *Hash*(s, i) is an efficient hash function on the state pair (s, i). All other functions are as per Figure 1.

all of the above sets [19], primarily because this allowed checks to efficiently use disk-based storage when RAM was exhausted (in contrast to, e.g. hash tables, where performance often decays to the point of being unusable once RAM has been exhausted). This brings the additional benefit that inserts into *done* (from *current*) can be performed in sorted order. Since B-Trees perform almost optimally under such workloads, this makes insertions into the *done* tree highly efficient. To improve efficiency, inserts into the *next* tree are buffered, with the buffer being sorted before insertion. The storage that the B-Tree uses is also compressed, typically resulting in memory requirements being halved.

Parallelisation Parallelising FDR3's refinement checking essentially reduces to parallelising the breadth-first search of Figure 1. Our algorithm partitions the state space based on a hash function on the node pairs. Each worker is assigned a partition and has local *current*, *next* and *done* sets. When a worker visits a transition, it computes the worker who is responsible for the destination by hashing the new state pair. This algorithm is presented in Figure 2.

Whilst the abstract algorithm is straightforward, the implementation has to be carefully designed in order to obtain good performance. As before, our primary consideration is minimising memory usage. In fact, this becomes even more critical in the parallel setting since memory will be consumed at a far greater rate: with 16 cores, FDR3 can visit up to 7 billion states per hour consuming 70GB of storage. Thus, we need to allow checks to exceed the size of the available RAM. Given the above, B-Trees are a natural choice for storing the sets.

All access to the *done* and *current* B-Trees is restricted to the worker who owns those B-Trees, meaning that there are no threading issues to consider. The *next* B-Trees are more problematic: workers can generate node pairs for other workers. Thus, we need to provide some way of accessing the *next* B-Trees of other workers in a thread-safe manner. Given the volume of data that needs to be put into *next* (which can be an order of magnitude greater than the volume put into *done*), locking the tree is undesirable. One option would be to use fine-grained locking on the B-Tree, however this is difficult to implement efficiently.

Instead of using complex locks, we have generalised the buffering that is used to insert into *next* under the single-threaded algorithm. Each worker w has a set of buffers, one for each other worker, and a list of buffers it has received from other workers that require insertion into this worker's *next*. When a buffer of worker w for worker $w' \neq w$ fills up, it immediately passes it to the target worker. Workers periodically check the stack of pending buffers to be flushed, and when a certain size is exceeded, they perform a bulk insert into *next* by performing a n-way merge of all of the pending buffers to produce a single sorted buffer.

One potential issue this algorithm could suffer from is uneven distribution amongst the workers. We have not observed this problem: the workers have terminated at roughly the same time. If necessary this could be addressed by increasing the number of partitions, with workers picking a partition to work on.

We give experimental results that show the algorithm is able to achieve a near linear speed up in Section 6.

Related Work There have been many algorithms proposed for parallelising BFS, e.g. [20,21,22,23]. In general, these solutions do not attempt to optimise memory usage of performance once RAM has been exhausted to the same degree.

The authors of [20] parallelised the FDR2 refinement checker for cluster systems that used MPI. The algorithm they used was similar to our algorithm in that nodes were partitioned amongst the workers and that B-Trees were used for storage. The main difference comes from the communication of *next*: in their approach this was deferred until the end of each round where a bulk exchange was done, whereas in our model we use a complex buffer system.

The authors of [21] propose a solution that is optimised for performing a BFS on sparse graphs. This uses a novel tree structure to efficiently (in terms of time) store the bag of nodes that are to be visited on the next ply. This was not suitable for FDR since it does not provide a general solution for eliminating duplicates in *next*, which would cause FDR3 to use vastly more memory.

The author of [23] enhances the Spin Model Checker [9] to support parallel BFS. In this solution, which is based on [24], *done* is a lock-free hash-table and is shared between all of the workers, whilst new states are randomly assigned to a number of subsets which are lock-free linked lists. This approach is not suitable for FDR since hash-tables are known not to perform well once RAM has been exhausted (due to their essentially random access pattern). Storing *next* in a series of linked-lists is suitable for Spin since it can efficiently check if a node is in *done* using the lock-free hash-table. This is not the case for FDR, since there is no way of efficiently checking if a node is in the *done* B-Tree of a worker.

5   Compiler

As outlined in Section 3, the compiler is responsible for converting syntactic processes into GLTSs. This is a difficult problem due to the generality of CSP since operators can be combined in almost arbitrary ways. In order to allow the processes to be represented efficiently, FDR3 has a number of different GLTS types as described in Section 5.1, and a number of different way of constructing each GLTS, as described in Section 5.2. In Section 5.3 we detail the new algorithm that the compiler uses to decide which of FDR3's representations of GLTSs to use. This is of critical importance: if FDR3 were to choose the wrong representation this could cause the time to check a property and the memory requirements to greatly increase.

5.1   GLTSs

FDR3 has two main representations of GLTSs: Explicit and Super-Combinator machines. Explicit machines require memory proportional to the number of states and transitions during a refinement check. In contrast, Super-Combinator machines only require storage proportional to the number of states, since the transitions can be computed on-the-fly. Equally, it takes longer to calculate the transitions of a Super-Combinator machine than the corresponding Explicit machine.

An Explicit GLTS is simply a standard graph data structure. Nodes in an Explicit GLTS are process states whilst the transitions are stored in a sorted list. A *Super-Combinator* machine represents the LTS by a series of component LTSs along with a list of rules to combine the transitions of the components. Nodes for a Super-Combinator machine are tuples, with one entry for each component machine. For example, a Super-Combinator for $P \,|||\, Q$ consists of the components $\langle P, Q \rangle$ and the rules:

$$\{((\langle 1 \mapsto a \rangle, a) \mid a \in \alpha P \cup \{\tau\}\} \cup \{((\langle 2 \mapsto a \rangle, a) \mid a \in \alpha Q \cup \{\tau\}\}$$

where αX is the alphabet of the process X (i.e. the set of events it can perform). These rules describe how to combine the actions of P and Q into actions of the whole machine. A single rule is of the form (f, e) where f is a partial function from the index of a component machine (e.g. in the above example, 1 represents P) to the event that component must perform. e is the event the overall machine performs if all components perform their required events.

Rules can also be split into *formats*, which are sets of rules. For example, a Super-Combinator for $P \,;\, Q$ would start in format *1*, which has the rules:

$$\{((\langle 1 \mapsto a \rangle, a, 1) \mid a \in \alpha P \cup \{\tau\}, a \neq \checkmark\} \cup \{((\langle 1 \mapsto \checkmark \rangle, \tau, 2) \mid a \in \alpha Q \cup \{\tau\}\}.$$

The second format has the rules: $\{(\langle 2 \mapsto a \rangle, a, 2) \mid a \in \alpha Q \cup \{\tau\}\}$. Thus, the first format allows P to perform visible events and stay in format 1 (as indicated by the third element of the tuple), but if P performs a $\checkmark$ and terminates, the second format is started which allows Q to perform visible events.

Rules can also specify that component machines should be *restarted*. For example, to represent $P = X \,;\, P$ as a Super-Combinator, there needs to be a way of *restarting* the process X after a $\checkmark$. Thus, we add to the rules a list of components whose states should be discarded and replaced by their root states:

$$\{(\{1 \mapsto a\}, a, 1, \langle\rangle) \mid a \in \alpha X \cup \{\tau\}, a \neq \checkmark)\} \cup \{(\{1 \mapsto \checkmark\}, \tau, 1, \langle 1 \rangle)\}.$$

The first rule set allows X to perform non-$\checkmark$ events as usual. However, if X ever performs a $\checkmark$ this is converted into a τ and component 1 (i.e. X) is restarted.

FDR also recursively combines the rules for Super-Combinator machines. For example, $(P \,|||\, Q) \,|||\, R$ is not represented as two different Super-Combinator machines, but instead the rules for $P \,|||\, Q$ and $\cdot \,|||\, R$ are combined. This process is known as *supercompilation*. As you might expect from the name, supercombinators are closely related to combinator operational semantics: the "super" essentially co-incides with the joining together using supercompilation.

5.2 Strategies

There are several different *strategies* that FDR3 can use to construct Explicit or Super-Combinator machines from syntactic processes. These strategies differ in the type of processes that they can support (e.g. some cannot support recursive processes), the time they take to execute and the type of the resulting GLTS.

The *low-level* is the simplest strategy and supports any process. An Explicit LTS is constructed simply by directly applying CSP's operational semantics.

The *high-level* compiles a process to a Super-Combinator. This is not able to compile *recursive* processes, such as $P \mathrel{\widehat{=}} a \rightarrow P$. The supercombinator rules are directly constructed using the operational semantics of CSP.

The *mixed-level* is a hybrid of the low and high-level strategies where, intuitively, non-recursive parts of processes are compiled as per the high-level strategy whilst recursive parts are compiled as per the low-level strategy. For example, consider $P \mathrel{\widehat{=}} a \rightarrow P \mathrel{\square} b \rightarrow (X \,|||\, Y)$: compiling $X \,|||\, Y$ at the high-level is preferable since it does not require the cartesian product of X and Y to be formed. If P is compiled at the mixed-level, $X \,|||\, Y$ is compiled at the high-level, and $a \rightarrow P \mathrel{\square} b \rightarrow \cdot$ is compiled into an Explicit machine. These are wrapped in a Super-Combinator machine that *starts* $X \,|||\, Y$ when the Explicit machine performs the b. The supercombinator has two formats, the first with the rules: $\{(\{1 \mapsto a\}, a, 1), (\{1 \mapsto b\}, b, 2)\}$ and the second with: $\{(\{2 \mapsto a\}, a, 2) \mid a \in \alpha(X \,|||\, Y) \cup \{\tau\}\}$. Thus, when the first process performs b, the Super-Combinator moves to the second format in which $X \,|||\, Y$ is run. The next section formalises the set of process that can be compiled in this way.

The *recursive high-level* strategy is new in FDR3. This compiles to a Super-Combinator machine and allows some recursive processes (which we formalise in the next section) to be compiled. This is used to compile processes such as $P \mathbin{\widehat{=}} (X \mathbin{|||} Y) \mathbin{;} P$ which are recursive, but are desirable to compile to Super-Combinator machines for efficiency reasons (as above, constructing $X \mathbin{|||} Y$ is expensive). In this particular case, $X \mathbin{|||} Y$ is compiled to a Super-Combinator machine, and then a recursive supercombinator is constructed with the rules:

$$\{((\{1 \mapsto a\}, a, 1, \langle\rangle) \mid a \in \alpha(X \mathbin{|||} Y) \cup \{\tau\}, a \neq \checkmark)\} \cup \{((\{1 \mapsto \checkmark\}, \tau, 1, \langle1\rangle))\}.$$

Recall that the last component in the above rules indicates that component 1 should be reset. Thus, the above rules indicate that $X \mathbin{|||} Y$ can perform non-$\checkmark$ events normally, but a $\checkmark$ will cause $X \mathbin{|||} Y$ to be reset to its initial state.

The majority of processes can be compiled at the recursive high-level, with the exception of those that recurse through an **on** argument of an operator (e.g. $P = a \rightarrow P \mathbin{\square} b \rightarrow P$). For example, consider the process $P = X \mathbin{;} (P \mathbin{\square} \ldots)$: since $\square$ is not discarded by a τ, it follows that this recursion is safe only when X always performs a visible event before a $\checkmark$ (otherwise there would be an infinite series of $\square$'s applied). This cannot be determined statically (i.e. without accessing the transitions of X), and thus it is not possible to determine if the process can be compiled at the recursive high-level. Thankfully, such processes are sufficiently rare in the context where recursive high-level is of use.

5.3   Picking a Strategy

We now describe the new algorithm that FDR3 uses to decide how to compile a syntactic process. The input to the compilation algorithm is a syntactic process environment (Definition 1) and the output is a list of strategies that specify how each syntactic processes should be compiled. The algorithm guarantees to produce a strategy such that executing the strategy yields a valid GLTS that corresponds to the input process. The algorithm also uses heuristics to attempt to reduce the time and memory usage during the subsequent refinement check.

All operators have a preferred *level* of compilation, either *low* (indicating Explicit is preferred) or high (indicating Super-Combinator is preferred). For example, prefix prefers the low whilst interleave prefers high. In general, FDR3 aims to compile an operator at its preferred level. If this is high, this may require using the mixed and recursive high-level strategies on surrounding processes (a preference for high is more important). When this is not possible (because, e.g., the processes do not permit the mixed level), the low-level strategy is used.

The first step is to calculate the strongly connected components (SCCs) of recursive processes. This is done by performing a DFS on the recursion graph that is naturally formed from the syntactic process environment. Then, we compute which SCCs can be compiled at the recursive high-level, and which SCCs would prefer to be compiled at the recursive high-level (by incorporating preferences, e.g. prefix prefers to recurse at low, but ; prefers high). The graph is also used to check for invalid processes, such as $P = P \mathbin{\square} P$: formally, for each process name P we check that on each path back to P, at least one **off** argument is traversed.

Using the recursion graph, FDR3 computes which strategy to use to compile a syntactic process P. This cannot be done in ignorance of the *context* of P,

function STRATEGY(P, r) ▷ P is a syntactic process, r is an event type
   $as \leftarrow \langle\rangle$ ▷ The strategy for each argument of P
  for each argument Q of P **do**
     $forceLow \leftarrow false$ ▷ Set to *true* if this must be compiled at low
     if Q is an **on** argument of P **then**
        $r' \leftarrow r \sqcap discards(P, Q)$
        $forceLow \leftarrow r = None$
     else   ▷ Q is **off**
        if $r \sqcap turnedOnBy(P, Q) = None$ **then**   ▷ This might get turned **on** by
           $forceLow \leftarrow true$ ▷ an event that does not discard the context
        else $r' \leftarrow Any$ ▷ The context is discarded when Q is turned **on**
     if $forceLow$ **then** $as \leftarrow as ^\frown \langle Low \rangle$
     else $as \leftarrow as ^\frown \langle Strategy(Q, r') \rangle$
  $allLow \leftarrow \bigwedge_{a \in as} a = Low$
  if (P is recursive $\vee\ r \neq Any$) $\wedge\ recursionType(P) \neq High$ **then**
    if $allLow$ **then return** *Low*
    else return *Mixed*
  else if P is recursive **then return** *RecursiveHigh*
  else if P prefers *Low* **then**
    if $allLow$ **then return** *Low*
    else return *Mixed*
  else return *High*

Fig. 3. The algorithm FDR3 uses to decide how to compile syntactic processes

since this may dictate how a process is compiled. For example, $P = a \rightarrow P \sqcap Q$ requires Q to be compiled at the low-level, since P is a low-level recursion and Q appears as an **on** argument of an operator that is on the recursion path. Thus, when compiling a syntactic process, we need to be aware of the surrounding context $C[\cdot]$, (e.g. $C_1[X] \mathrel{\widehat{=}} X \mathbin{|||} STOP$). When deciding on the strategy for P, the relevant fact about the context is what events P can perform to cause the context to be *discarded*. For example, nothing can discard the context C_1, whilst any visible event discards the context $C_2[X] \mathrel{\widehat{=}} X \mathbin{\square} STOP$. As we are interested in statically analysing processes, we approximate these sets as follows.

Definition 2. An *event type* is either *None*, *Invisible*, *Visible* or *Any*. The relation $<$ is defined as *None* $<$ *Invisible*, *None* $<$ *Visible*, *Invisible* $<$ *Any*, *Visible* $<$ *Any*. Note $<$ is a partial order on event types. The meet of e_1 and e_2 is denoted by $e_1 \sqcap e_2$.

Definition 3. Let Q be an argument of a syntactic process P. If Q is **on**, then $discards(P, Q)$ returns the event type that Q performs to cause P to be discarded and Q to be left running (e.g. $discards(X \mathbin{\square} Y, X) = Visible$, whilst $discards(X \mathbin{|||} Y, X) = None$). If Q is **off**, then $turnedOnBy(P, Q)$ returns the event type that P performs in order to turn **on** Q. For example, $turnedOnBy(X ; Y, Y) = Invisible$ whilst $turnedOnBy(X \mathbin{\Theta.} Y, Y) = Visible$.

Thus it is possible to use *discards* along with the meet on event types to compute when a context will be discarded.

Figure 3 defines a function $Strategy(P, r)$ that returns the strategy that should be used to compile the syntactic process P in a context that is discarded by events of event type r. Informally, given a process P and an event type r this firstly recursively visits each of its arguments, passing down an appropriate event restriction (which is computed using *discards* for **on** arguments and *turnedOnBy* for **off** arguments). It may also force some arguments to be low-level if the restriction becomes *None*. Then, a compilation strategy for P is computed by considering the preferences of the operator, whether the operator is recursive and the deduced strategies for the arguments. The overriding observation behind this choice is that compilation at high is only allowed when the process is non-recursive, and when there is no surrounding context (i.e. $r = Anything$).

5.4   Related Work

FDR2 has support for Explicit and Super-Combinator GLTSs, along with a GLTS definition for each CSP operator (e.g. external choice etc). We believe that the FDR3 representation is superior, since it requires fewer GLTS types to be maintained and because it makes the GLTSs independent of CSP, making other process algebras easier to support. As mentioned in Section 5.2, FDR2 did not make use of the recursive high-level, and was unable to automatically compile processes such as $P = (X \,|||\, Y)\,;\, P$ at the high-level. We have found that the recursive high-level has dramatically decreased compilation time on many examples.

The biggest difference is in the algorithm that each uses to compile syntactic processes. FDR2 essentially used a series of heuristics to accomplish this and would always start trying to compile the process at its preferred level, backtracking where necessary. This produced undesirable behaviour on certain processes. We believe that since the new algorithm is based on the operational semantics of CSP, it is simpler and can be easily applied to other CSP-like process algebras.

6   Experiments

We compare the performance of a pre-release version of FDR 3.1.0 to FDR 2.94, Spin 6.25, DiVinE 3.1 beta 1, and LTSmin 2.0, on a complete traversal of a graph. The experiments were performed on a Linux server with two 8 core 2GHz Xeons with hyperthreading (i.e. 32 virtual cores), 128GB RAM, and five 100GB SSDs. All input files are available from the first author's webpage. — denotes a check that took over 6 hours, * denotes a check that was not attempted, and † denotes a check that could not be completed due to insufficient memory. Times refer to the total time required to run each program whilst memory figures refer to the maximum *Resident Set Size* plus any on-disk storage used.

Figure 4a compares the performance of FDR2 and FDR3. FDR3 with 1 worker substantially outperforms FDR2. This is because FDR3's B-Tree has been heavily optimised and because FDR3 makes fewer allocations during refinement checks. FDR3 with 1 worker also uses less memory than FDR2: this is due to a new compaction algorithm used to compress B-Tree blocks that only

Input	States (10^6)	Transitions (10^6)	Time (s) & Storage (GB)			FDR3-32 Speedup
			FDR2	FDR3-1	FDR3-32	
bully.7	129	1354	2205 (4.8)	1023 (2.2)	85 (5.5)	12.0
cuberoll.0	7524	20065	—	—	3546 (74.5)	—
ddb.0	65	377	722 (1.4)	405 (0.5)	31 (2.36)	13.1
knightex.5.5	67	259	550 (1.4)	282 (0.6)	23 (2.4)	12.3
knightex.3.11	19835	67321	*	*	26235 (298.5)	—
phils.10	60	533	789 (1.3)	431 (0.5)	32 (2.0)	13.5
solitare.0	187	1487	2059 (4.4)	1249 (1.6)	84 (3.8)	14.9
solitare.1	1564	13971	19318 (35.1)	11357 (11.7)	944 (17.5)	12.0
solitaire.2	11622	113767	*	*	9422 (113.3)	—
tnonblock.7	322	635	2773 (6.7)	937 (2.6)	109 (6.8)	8.6

(a) Times comparing FDR2, FDR3 with 1 worker, and FDR3 with 32 workers.

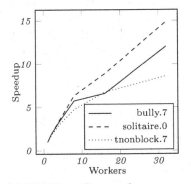

(b) FDR3's scaling performance.

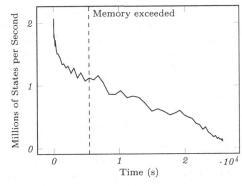

(c) Disk storage performance on knightex.3.11.

Fig. 4. Experimental results demonstrating FDR3's performance

stores the difference between keys. The extra memory used for the parallel version is for extra buffers and the fact that the B-Tree blocks do not compress as well.

The speed-ups that Figures 4a and 4b exhibit between 1 and 32 workers vary according to the problem. solitaire is sped up by a factor of 15 which is almost optimal given the 16 cores. Conversely, tnonblock.7 is only sped up by a factor of 9 because it has many small plys, meaning that the time spent waiting for other workers at the end of a ply is larger.

Figure 4c shows how the speed that FDR3 visits states at changes during the course of verifying knightex.3.11, which required 300GB of storage (FDR3 used 110GB of memory as a cache and 190GB of on-disk storage). During a refinement check, the rate at which states are explored will decrease because the B-Trees increase in size. Observe that there is no change in the decrease of the state visiting rate after memory is exceeded. This demonstrates that B-Trees are effectively able to scale to use large amounts of on-disk storage.

Figure 5 compares the performance of FDR3, Spin, DiVinE and LTSmin. For in-memory checks Spin, DiVinE and LTSmin complete the checks up to three

Input	Time (s) & Storage (GB)			
	Spin-32	FDR3-32	DiVinE-32	LTSmin-32
`knightex.5.5`	12 (5.8)	23 (2.4)	13 (4.6)	28 (33.1)
`knightex.3.10`	396 (115.0)	943 (22.7)	†	395 (35.5)
`knightex.3.11`	†	26235 (298.5)	†	†
`solitaire.0`	89 (15.5)	85 (3.9)	85 (14.3)	73 (36.4)

Fig. 5. A comparison between FDR3, Spin, DiVinE and LTSmin. `knightex.3.10` has 2035×10^6 states and 6786×10^6 transitions.

times faster than FDR3 but use up to four times more memory. We believe that FDR3 is slower because supercombinators are expensive to execute in comparison to the LTS representations that other tools use, and because B-Trees are slower to insert into than hashtables. FDR3 was the only tool that was able to complete `knightex.3.11` which requires use of on-disk storage; Spin, DiVinE and LTSmin were initially fast, but dramatically slowed once main memory was exhausted.

7 Conclusions

In this paper we have presented FDR3, a new refinement checker for CSP. We have described the new compiler that is more efficient, more clearly defined and produces better representations than the FDR2 compiler. Further, we have detailed the new parallel refinement-checking algorithm that is able to achieve a near-linear speed-up as the number of cores increases whilst ensuring efficient memory usage. Further, we have demonstrated that FDR3 is able to scale to enormous checks that far exceed the bounds of memory, unlike related tools.

This paper concentrates on parallelising refinement checks on shared-memory systems. It would be interesting to extend this to support clusters instead: this would allow even larger checks to be run. It would also be useful to consider how to best parallelise checks in the failures-divergence model. This is a difficult problem, in general, since this uses a depth-first search to find cycles.

FDR3 is available for 64-bit Linux and Mac OS X from https://www.cs.ox.ac.uk/projects/fdr/. FDR3 is free for personal use or academic research, whilst commercial use requires a licence.

Acknowledgements. This work has benefitted from many useful conversations with Michael Goldsmith, Colin O'Halloran, Gavin Lowe, and Nick Moffat. We would also like to thank the anonymous reviewers for their useful comments.

References

1. Hoare, C.A.R.: Communicating Sequential Processes. Prentice-Hall, Inc., Upper Saddle River (1985)
2. Roscoe, A.W.: The Theory and Practice of Concurrency. Prentice Hall (1997)

3. Roscoe, A.W.: Understanding Concurrent Systems. Springer (2010)
4. Lawrence, J.: Practical Application of CSP and FDR to Software Design. In: Abdallah, A.E., Jones, C.B., Sanders, J.W. (eds.) CSP25. LNCS, vol. 3525, pp. 151–174. Springer, Heidelberg (2005)
5. Mota, A., Sampaio, A.: Model-checking CSP-Z: strategy, tool support and industrial application. Science of Computer Programming 40(1) (2001)
6. Fischer, C., Wehrheim, H.: Model-Checking CSP-OZ Specifications with FDR. In: IFM 1999. Springer (1999)
7. Lowe, G.: Casper: A Compiler for the Analysis of Security Protocols. Journal of Computer Security 6(1-2) (1998)
8. Roscoe, A.W., Hopkins, D.: SVA, a Tool for Analysing Shared-Variable Programs. In: Proceedings of AVoCS 2007 (2007)
9. Holzmann, G.: Spin Model Checker: The Primer and Reference Manual. Addison-Wesley Professional (2003)
10. Barnat, J., Brim, L., Havel, V., Havlíček, J., Kriho, J., Lenčo, M., Ročkai, P., Štill, V., Weiser, J.: DiVinE 3.0 – An Explicit-State Model Checker for Multithreaded C & C++ Programs. In: Sharygina, N., Veith, H. (eds.) CAV 2013. LNCS, vol. 8044, pp. 863–868. Springer, Heidelberg (2013)
11. Laarman, A., van de Pol, J., Weber, M.: Multi-Core LTSMIN: Marrying Modularity and Scalability. In: Bobaru, M., Havelund, K., Holzmann, G.J., Joshi, R. (eds.) NFM 2011. LNCS, vol. 6617, pp. 506–511. Springer, Heidelberg (2011)
12. University of Oxford, Failures-Divergence Refinement—FDR 3 User Manual (2013), https://www.cs.ox.ac.uk/projects/fdr/manual/
13. University of Oxford, libcspm (2013), https://github.com/tomgr/libcspm
14. Reed, G.M., Roscoe, A.W.: A Timed Model for Communicating Sequential Processes. Theoretical Computer Science 58 (1988)
15. Armstrong, P., Lowe, G., Ouaknine, J., Roscoe, A.W.: Model checking Timed CSP. In: Proceedings of HOWARD (Festschrift for Howard Barringer) (2012)
16. Ouaknine, J.: Discrete Analysis of Continuous Behaviour in Real-Time Concurrent Systems. DPhil Thesis (2001)
17. Barringer, H., Kuiper, R., Pnueli, A.: A really abstract concurrent model and its temporal logic. In: Proceedings of the 13th ACM SIGACT-SIGPLAN Symposium on Principles of Programming Languages. ACM (1986)
18. Roscoe, A.W., Hopcroft, P.J.: Slow abstraction via priority. In: Liu, Z., Woodcock, J., Zhu, H. (eds.) Theories of Programming and Formal Methods. LNCS, vol. 8051, pp. 326–345. Springer, Heidelberg (2013)
19. Roscoe, A.W.: Model-Checking CSP. In: A Classical Mind: Essays in Honour of CAR Hoare (1994)
20. Goldsmith, M., Martin, J.: The parallelisation of FDR. In: Proceedings of the Workshop on Parallel and Distributed Model Checking (2002)
21. Leiserson, C.E., Schardl, T.B.: A work-efficient parallel breadth-first search algorithm (or how to cope with the nondeterminism of reducers). In: Proc. 22nd ACM Symposium on Parallelism in Algorithms and Architectures, SPAA 2010 (2010)
22. Korf, R.E., Schultze, P.: Large-scale parallel breadth-first search. In: Proc. 20th National Conference on Artificial Intelligence, vol. 3. AAAI (2005)
23. Holzmann, G.J.: Parallelizing the Spin Model Checker. In: Donaldson, A., Parker, D. (eds.) SPIN 2012. LNCS, vol. 7385, pp. 155–171. Springer, Heidelberg (2012)
24. Laarman, A., van de Pol, J., Weber, M.: Boosting multi-core reachability performance with shared hash tables. In: Formal Methods in Computer-Aided Design (2010)

Concurrent Depth-First Search Algorithms

Gavin Lowe

Department of Computer Science, University of Oxford
Wolfson Building, Parks Road, Oxford, OX1 3QD, United Kingdom
gavin.lowe@cs.ox.ac.uk

Abstract. We present concurrent algorithms, based on depth-first search, for three problems relevant to model checking: given a state graph, to find its strongly connected components, which states are in loops, and which states are in "lassos". Our algorithms typically exhibit about a four-fold speed-up over the corresponding sequential algorithms on an eight-core machine.

1 Introduction

In this paper we present concurrent versions of algorithms based on depth-first search, all variants of Tarjan's Algorithm [17]. We consider algorithms for three closely related problems:

1. To find the strongly connected components (SCCs) of a graph (i.e., the maximal subsets S of the graph's nodes such that for any pair of nodes $n, n' \in S$, there is a path from n to n');
2. To find which nodes are part of a cycle in the graph (i.e., such that there is a non-empty path from the node to itself);
3. To find which nodes are part of a "lasso" (i.e., such that there is a path from the node to a node on a cycle).

Our main interest in these algorithms is as part of the development of the FDR3 model checker [6,18] for CSP [16]. In order to carry out checks in the failures-divergences model, it is necessary to detect which nodes are divergent, i.e. can perform an unbounded number of internal τ events; this is equivalent to detecting whether the node is part of a lasso in the transition graph restricted to τ-transitions (Problem 3).

FDR's main failures-divergences refinement checking algorithm performs a concurrent breadth-first search of the product of the state graphs of the system and specification processes, testing whether each system state is compatible with the corresponding specification state. In particular, this involves testing whether the system state is divergent; hence several divergences tests need to be performed concurrently starting at different nodes.

Further, FDR can perform various compressions upon the transition graphs of processes. One of these, `tau_loop_factor`, works by identifying all nodes within an SCC in the transition graph restricted to τ-transitions (Problem 1).

E. Ábrahám and K. Havelund (Eds.): TACAS 2014, LNCS 8413, pp. 202–216, 2014.

Problem 2 has applications in other areas of model checking: the automata-theoretic approach for LTL model checking [19] involves searching for a cycle containing an accepting state in the graph formed as the product of the Büchi property automaton and the system.

We present concurrent algorithms for each of the above three problems. Our implementations typically exhibit about a four-fold speed-up over the corresponding sequential algorithms on an eight-core machine; the speed-ups are slightly better on graphs with a higher ratio of transitions to states.

These are challenging problems for the following reasons. In many graphs, threads will encounter nodes that are currently being considered by other threads; we need to ensure that the threads do not duplicate work, do not interfere with one another, but do obtain information from one another: depth-first search seems to be an area where it is difficult to achieve a high degree of independence between threads. Further, many graphs contain a *super-component* that contains a large proportion of the graph's nodes; for Problems 1 and 2, it seems impossible to avoid having the nodes of this super-component being considered sequentially.

In [14], Reif showed that computation of depth-first search post-ordering of vertices is P-complete. This is often used to claim that parallelising algorithms based on depth-first search is difficult (assuming $NC \neq P$): no algorithm can run in poly-logarithmic time with a polynomial number of processors. Nevertheless, it is possible to achieve significant speed-ups, at least for a fairly small number of processors (as is common in current computers), for the types of graphs that are typical of those encountered in model checking.

In Section 2 we review the sequential version of Tarjan's Algorithm. In Section 3 we present our concurrent algorithm. In Section 4 we describe some aspects of our prototype implementation, and highlight a few tricky aspects. In Section 5 we report on some experiments, comparing our algorithm to the sequential version. We sum up and discuss related work in Section 6.

2   Tarjan's Algorithm

In this section we review the sequential Tarjan's Algorithm [17]. We start by describing the original version, for finding SCCs; we then discuss how to adapt the algorithm to find loops or lassos.

Tarjan's Algorithm performs a depth-first search of the graph. The algorithm uses a stack, denoted tarjanStack, to store those nodes that have been encountered in the search but not yet placed into an SCC. Each node n is given two variables: index, which is a sequence counter, corresponding to the order in which nodes were encountered; and lowlink which records the smallest index of a node n' in the stack that is reachable via the descendents of n fully considered so far. The following function (presented in pseudo-Scala) to update a node's low-link will be useful.

```
def updateLowlink(update: Int) = { lowlink = min(lowlink, update) }
```

```
1   var index = 0
2   // Set node's index and lowlink, and add it to the stacks
3   def addNode(node) = {
4     node.index = index; node.lowlink = index; index += 1
5     controlStack.push(node); tarjanStack.push(node)
6   }
7   addNode(startNode)
8   while(controlStack.nonEmpty){
9     val node = controlStack.top
10    if (node has an unexplored edge to child ){
11      if ( child   previously  unseen) addNode(child)
12      else if ( child  is  in  tarjanStack ) node.updateLowlink(child.index)
13      // otherwise, child is complete, nothing to do
14    }
15    else{ // backtrack from node
16      controlStack.pop
17      if (controlStack.nonEmpty) controlStack.top.updateLowlink(node.lowlink)
18      if (node.lowlink == node.index){
19        start  new SCC
20        do{
21          w = tarjanStack.pop; add w to SCC; mark w as complete
22        } until (w == node)
23      }
24    }
25  }
```

Fig. 1. Sequential Tarjan's Algorithm

Also, each node has a status: either *complete* (when it has been placed in an SCC), *in-progress* (when it has been encountered but not yet been placed in an SCC), or *unseen* (when it has not yet been encountered).

Tarjan's Algorithm is normally described recursively; however, we consider here an iterative version. We prefer an iterative version for two reasons: (1) as is well known, iteration is normally more efficient than recursion; (2) when we move to a concurrent version, we will want to suspend searches; this will be easier with an iterative version. We use a second stack, denoted controlStack, that corresponds to the control stack of the recursive version, and keeps track of the nodes to backtrack to.

We present the sequential Tarjan's Algorithm for finding SCCs (Problem 1) in Figure 1. The search starts from the node startNode. When an edge is explored to a node that is already in the stack, the low-link of the edge's source is updated (line 12). Similarly, when the search backtracks, the next node's low-link is updated (line 17). On backtracking from a node, if its low-link equals its index, all the nodes above it on the Tarjan stack form an SCC, and so are removed from that stack and collected (lines 18–23).

The following observation will be useful later.

Observation 1.   1. For each node in the tarjanStack, there's a path in the graph
to each subsequent node in the tarjanStack.

2. For any node n in the tarjanStack, if n is nearer the top of that stack than
controlStack.top, then there is a path from n to controlStack.top (and hence the
two nodes are in the same SCC).

3. If nodes n and l are such that n.lowlink $= l$.index, then all the nodes between n
and l in the tarjanStack are in the same SCC.

If, instead, we are interested in finding cycles (Problem 2) then: (1) at line 12,
if node $==$ child then we mark the node as in a cycle; and (2) after line 22, if the
SCC has more than one node, we mark all its nodes as in a cycle.

If we are interested in finding lassos (Problem 3) then: (1) at line 12, we
immediately mark node and all the other nodes in the Tarjan stack as being in
a lasso; and (2) if we encounter a complete node (line 13), if it is in a lasso, we
mark all the nodes in the Tarjan stack as being in a lasso.

3   Concurrent Tarjan's Algorithm

We now describe our concurrent version of Tarjan's Algorithm. We again start
with an algorithm for finding SCCs, presented in Figure 2; we later consider how
to adapt this for the other problems.

Each search is independent, and has its own control stack and Tarjan stack.
A search is started at an arbitrary node startNode that has not yet been considered by any other search (we describe this aspect of our implementation in
Section 4.2). Each search proceeds much as in the standard Tarjan's Algorithm,
as long as it does not encounter a node that is part of another current search.
However, if the search encounters a node child that is not complete but is not
in its own stack (line 13) —so it is necessarily in the stack of another search—
then the search suspends (detailed below). When child is completed, the search
can be resumed (line 24). This design means that each node is in the stacks of
at most one search; each node has a field search identifying that search (set at
line 5).

A difficulty occurs if suspending a search would create a cycle of searches, each
blocked on the next. Clearly we need to take some action to ensure progress. We
transfer the relevant nodes of those searches into a single search, and continue,
thereby removing the blocking-cycle. We explain our procedure in more detail
with an example, depicted in Figure 3; it should be clear how to generalise
this example. The bottom-left of the figure depicts the graph G being searched;
the top-left depicts the tarjanStacks of the searches (oriented downwards, so the
"tops" of the stacks are towards the bottom of the page).

Suppose search s_1 is blocked at n_1 waiting for node c_2 of search s_2 to complete,
because s_1 encountered an edge from n_1 to c_2 (corresponding to node and child,
respectively, in Figure 2). Similarly, suppose search s_2 is blocked at n_2 waiting
for node c_3 of search s_3 to complete; and search s_3 is blocked at n_3 waiting
for node c_1 of search s_1 to complete. This creates a blocking cycle of suspended
searches (see Figure 3, top-left). Note that the nodes between c_1 and n_1, between

```
1   var index = 0
2   // Set node's index, lowlink and search, and add it to the stacks
3   def addNode(node) = {
4      node.index = index; node.lowlink = index; index += 1
5      node.search = thisSearch; controlStack.push(node); tarjanStack.push(node)
6   }
7   addNode(StartNode)
8   while(controlStack.nonEmpty){
9      val node = controlStack.top
10     if(node has an unexplored edge to child){
11        if(child previously unseen) addNode(child)
12        else if(child is in tarjanStack) node.updateLowlink(child.index)
13        else if(child is not complete) // child is in−progress in a different search
14           suspend waiting for child to complete
15        // otherwise, child is complete, nothing to do
16     }
17     else{ // backtrack from node
18        controlStack.pop
19        if(controlStack.nonEmpty) controlStack.top.updateLowlink(node.lowlink)
20        if(node.lowlink == node.index){
21           start new SCC
22           do{
23              w = tarjanStack.pop; add w to SCC
24              mark w as complete and unblock any searches suspended on it
25           } until(w == node)
26        }
27     }
28  }
```

Fig. 2. Concurrent Tarjan's Algorithm (changes from Fig. 1 underlined)

c_2 and n_2, and between c_3 and n_3 are all in the same SCC, by Observation 1(1); we denote this SCC by "C".

Let t_1 be the top of the Tarjan stack of s_1: t_1 might equal n_1; or s_1 might have backtracked from t_1 to n_1. Note that all the nodes between n_1 and t_1 are in the same SCC as n_1, by Observation 1(2), and hence in the SCC C. Similarly, let t_2 and t_3 be the tops of the other Tarjan stacks; all the nodes between n_2 and t_2, and between n_3 and t_3 are likewise in C.

Let l_1 be the earliest node of s_1 known (according to the low-links of s_1) to be in the same SCC as c_1: l_1 is the earliest node reachable by following low-links from the nodes between c_1 to t_1 (inclusive), and then (perhaps) following subsequent low-links; equivalently, l_1 is the last node in s_1 that is no later than c_1 and such that all low-links of nodes between l_1 and t_1 are at least l_1 (a simple traversal of the Tarjan stack can identify l_1). Hence all the nodes from l_1 to t_1 are in the SCC C (by Observation 1(3)). Let l_2 and l_3 be similar.

Consider the graph G' formed by transforming the original graph by adding edges from n_1 to l_2, and from n_3 to l_1, as illustrated in Figure 3 (middle top

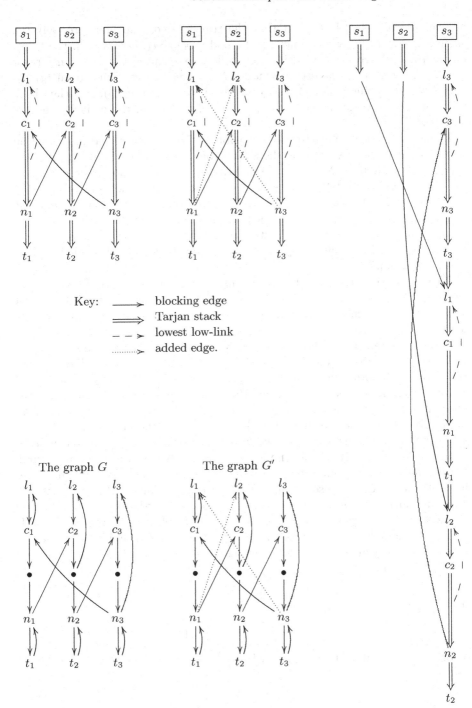

Key:
- → blocking edge
- ⟹ Tarjan stack
- – – → lowest low-link
- ·······› added edge.

Fig. 3. Illustration of the blocking cycle reduction

and middle bottom). It is clear that the transformed graph has precisely the same SCCs as the original, since all the nodes below l_1, l_2 and l_3 in the figure are in the same SCC C. Consider the following scenario for the transformed graph: the search s_3 explores via nodes l_3, c_3, n_3 (backtracking from t_3), l_1, c_1, n_1 (backtracking from t_1), l_2, c_2, n_2 (backtracking from t_2), and then back to c_3; meanwhile, the searches s_1 and s_2 reach l_1 and l_2, respectively, and are suspended.

We transform the stacks to be compatible with this scenario, as illustrated in Figure 3 (right), by transferring the nodes from l_1 to n_1, and from l_2 to n_2 onto the stack of search s_3. Note, in particular, that the indexes and lowlinks have to be updated appropriately (letting $\delta_1 = s_3.\mathsf{index} - l_1.\mathsf{index}$, we add δ_1 onto the index and lowlink of each node transferred from s_1 and update $s_3.\mathsf{index}$ to be one larger than the greatest of the new indexes; we then repeat with s_2).

We then resume search s_3. We start by considering the edge from n_2 to c_3, and so update the lowlink of n_2. Searches s_1 and s_2 remain suspended until l_1 and l_2 are completed.

We now consider the other two problems. If we are interested in finding cycles (Problem 2) then we adapt the algorithm as for the sequential algorithm: (1) at line 12, if node == child then we mark the node as in a cycle; and (2) after line 25, if the SCC has more than one node, we mark all its nodes as in a cycle.

If we are interested in finding lassos (Problem 3) then we again adapt the algorithm as for the sequential algorithm: (1) at line 12, we immediately mark node and all the other nodes in the Tarjan stack as being in a lasso; and (2) if we encounter a complete node (line 15), if it is in a lasso, we mark all the nodes in the Tarjan stack as being in a lasso. Further, if a search encounters an in-progress node (line 13), if that node is in a lasso, then there is no need to suspend the search: instead all the nodes in the Tarjan stack can also be marked as in a lasso. Similarly, when a node is marked as being in a lasso, any search blocked on it can be unblocked; when such a search is unblocked, all the nodes in its Tarjan stack can also be marked as in a lasso. Finally, the procedure for reducing blocking cycles can be greatly simplified, using the observation that all the nodes in the Tarjan stacks are in a lasso: the search that discovered the cycle (s_3 in the example) marks all its nodes as in a lasso, and so unblocks the search blocked on it (s_2 in the example); that search similarly marks its nodes as in a lasso, and so on.

4   Implementation

In this section we give some details of our prototype implementation of the algorithm, and highlight a few areas where care is required. Our implementation[1] uses Scala [12].

---

[1] Available from http://www.cs.ox.ac.uk/people/gavin.lowe/parallelDFS.html.

4.1   Suspending and Resuming Searches

Each node n includes a field blocked : List[Search], storing the searches that have encountered this node and are blocked on it. When the node is completed, those searches can be resumed (line 24 of Figure 2). Note that testing whether n is complete (line 13 of Figure 2) and updating blocked has to be done atomically. In addition, each suspended search has a field waitingFor, storing the node it is waiting on.

We record which searches are blocked on which others in a map suspended from Search to Search, encapsulated in a Suspended object. The Suspended object has an operation suspend(s: Search, n: Node) to record that s is blocked on n.

When s suspends blocked by a node of s', we detect if this would create a blocking cycle by transitively following the suspended map to see if it includes a blocking path from s' to s. If so, nodes are transferred to s, and s is resumed as outlined in the previous section. This is delicate. Below, let s_b be one of the searches from which nodes are transferred and that remains blocked.

1. Each node's search, index and lowlink are updated, as described in the previous section.
2. Each s_b with remaining nodes has its waitingFor field updated to the appropriate node of s (the l_i nodes of Figure 3); and those nodes have their blocked fields updated.
3. The suspended map is updated: each s_b that has had *all* its nodes transferred is removed; each other s_b is now blocked by s; and any other search s' that was blocked on one of the nodes transferred to s is now also blocked on s.

The Suspended object acts as a potential bottleneck. Perhaps surprisingly, it is possible to allow several calls to suspend to proceed semi-concurrently. Considered as a graph, the suspended map forms a forest of reverse arborescences, i.e. a forest of trees, with all edges in a tree oriented towards a single sink search; further, only the sink searches are active. Hence, concurrent reductions of blocking cycles act on distinct reverse arborescences and so distinct searches.

We may not allow two concurrent attempts to detect a blocking cycle (consider the case where each of two searches is blocked on the other: the cycle will not be detected). Further, if no blocking cycle is found, the suspended map needs to be updated before another attempt to find a blocking cycle; and the suspended map must not be updated between reading the search field of the blocking node n and completing the search for a blocking cycle (to prevent n being transferred to a different search in the meantime)[2]. Finally, the suspended map itself must be thread-safe (we simply embed updates in **synchronized** blocks).

Other than as described in the previous paragraph, calls to suspend may act concurrently. In particular, suppose a call suspend(s,n) detects a blocking cycle. It updates search fields (item 1, above) *before* the suspended map (item 3). Suppose, further, a second call, suspend(s',n'), acts on the same reverse arborescence,

---

[2] We believe that the amount of locking here can be reduced; however, this locking does not seem to be a major bottleneck in practice.

and consider the case that n' is one of the nodes transferred to s. We argue that the resulting race is benign. The second call will not create a blocking cycle (since only the sink search of the reverse arborescence, s, can create a blocking cycle); this will be correctly detected, even in the half-updated state. Further, suspended(s') gets set correctly: if suspend(s',n') sets suspended(s') to n'.search before suspend(s,n) updates n'.search, then the latter will subsequently update suspended(s') to s (in item 3); if suspend(s,n) sets n'.search to s before suspend(s',n') reads it, then both will set suspended(s') to s.

4.2   Scheduling

Our implementation uses a number of worker threads (typically one per processor core), which execute searches. We use a Scheduler object to provide searches for workers, thereby implementing a form of task-based parallelism.

The Scheduler keeps track of searches that have been unblocked as a result of the blocking node becoming complete (line 24 of Figure 2). A dormant worker can resume one of these. (Note that when a search is unblocked, the update to the Scheduler is done *after* the updates to the search itself, so that it is not resumed in an inconsistent state.)

The algorithm can proceed in one of two different modes: *rooted*, where the search starts at a particular node, but the state space is not known in advance; and *unrooted*, where the state space is known in advance, and new searches can start at arbitrary nodes. In an unrooted search, the Scheduler keeps track of all nodes from which no search has been started. A dormant worker can start a new search at one of these (assuming it has not been reached by another search in the meantime). Similarly, in a rooted search the Scheduler keeps track of nodes encountered in the search but not yet expanded: when a search encounters a new node n, it passes n's previously unseen successors, except the one it will consider next, to the Scheduler. Again, a dormant worker can start a new search from such a node.

4.3   Enhancements

We now describe a few details of our implementation that have an effect upon efficiency.

We use a map from node identifiers (Ints) to Node objects that store information about nodes. We have experimented with many representations of this map. Our normal implementation is based on the hash table described by Laarman et al. in [7]. However, this implementation uses a fixed-size table, rather than resizing the table, thus going against the design of FDR (we have extended the hash table to allow resizing, but this makes the implementation somewhat slower). On some problems (including our experiments on random graphs in the next section), the implementation works better with a sharded hash table[3] with

---

[3] A sharded hash table can be thought of as a collection of M individual hash tables, each with its own lock; an entry with hash value h is stored in the table with index $h \bmod M$.

open addressing. Even with these implementation, the algorithms spend about 40% of their time within this map. (Other implementations are worse; using a Java ConcurrentHashMap increases the running time by a factor of two!)

It is clearly advantageous to avoid suspending searches, if possible. Therefore, the implementation tries to choose (at line 10 of Figure 2) a child node that is not in-progress in a different search, if one exists.

Some nodes have no successors. It is advantageous, when starting a search from such a node, to avoid creating a Search object with its associated stacks, but instead to just mark the node as complete and to create a singleton SCC containing it.

5   Experiments

In this section we report the results of timing experiments. The experiments were carried out on an eight-core machine (an Intel® Xeon® E5620) with 12GB of RAM. Each of the results is averaged over ten runs, after a warm-up round.

We have performed timing experiments on a suite of CSP files. We have extracted the graphs of τ-transitions for all implementation processes in the FDR3 test suite (including most of the CSP models from [15,16,1]) and the CSP models from [10]. The top of Figure 4 gives statistics about a selection of the graphs with between 200,000 and 5,000,000 states (we omit eleven such, in the interests of space), plus a slightly smaller file tring2.1 which we discuss below[4]. For each graph we give the number of states (i.e. nodes), the number of transitions (i.e. edges), the number of SCCs, the size of the largest SCC, the number of trivial SCCs (with a single state), the number of states on a loop, and the number of states on a lasso.

The bottom of Figure 4 gives corresponding timing results. For each of the three problems, we give times (in ms) for each of the concurrent and sequential algorithms, and the ratio between them (which represents the speed-up factor). The penultimate row gives totals for these running times, and their ratios. The final row gives data for tring2.1. Even on a single-threaded program, the JVM uses a fair amount of concurrency. The sequential algorithm typically uses about 160% of a single core (as measured by top). Hence the maximum speed-up one should expect is a factor of about five.

We have performed these experiments in unrooted mode, because it more-closely simulates our main intended use within FDR, namely for detecting divergences (i.e. τ-lassos) during failures-divergences checks. Such a check performs a breadth-first search of the product of the system and specification processes; for each pair of states encountered, if the specification state does not allow a divergence, then FDR checks that the system state does not have a divergence. The overall effect is normally that a lasso search is started at every reachable system state.

The concurrent algorithms normally give significant speed-ups. Further, the speed-up tends to be larger for larger graphs, particularly for graphs with more

---

[4] The file matmult.6 contains no τ-transitions, only visible transitions.

Graph	States	Transitions	SCCs	Largest SCC	Trivial SCCs	Loop states	Lasso states
cloudp.0	691692	1020880	691692	1	691692	0	0
cloudp.2	480984	643790	480984	1	480984	0	0
soldiers.0	714480	688110	714480	1	714480	0	0
comppuz.0	1235030	1558042	1235030	1	1235030	0	0
solitaire.0	494372	2271250	494372	1	494372	0	0
solitaire.1	4001297	5387623	4001297	1	4001297	0	0
matmul.6	2252800	0	2252800	1	2252800	0	0
virtroute.2	390625	1937500	390625	1	390625	0	0
tabp2.0	430254	310312	430254	1	430254	0	0
tabp2.1	427192	308978	427192	1	427192	0	0
tabp2.2	437908	316254	437908	1	437908	0	0
tringm.1	921403	925998	921403	1	921403	0	0
alt12.2.0	344221	1034608	344221	1	344221	0	0
alt12.2.1	344221	1114628	251927	2400	241821	102400	277229
alt12.3.0	575627	1283160	575627	1	575627	0	0
alt12.3.1	575627	1507604	447053	6560	439291	136336	440255
alt11.2.0	589149	1757856	589149	1	589149	0	0
alt11.2.1	589149	1883340	389713	1442	368629	220520	512131
alt11.3.0	990167	2227720	990167	1	990167	0	0
alt11.3.1	990167	2576732	652431	3168	628759	361408	886425
tring2.1	175363	355287	45822	129542	45821	131594	175363

	SCCs			Loops			Lassos		
Graph	Conc	Seq	Ratio	Conc	Seq	Ratio	Conc	Seq	Ratio
cloudp.0	174	697	3.99	158	562	3.54	159	348	2.18
cloudp.2	127	414	3.24	120	317	2.63	118	167	1.42
soldiers.0	193	708	3.66	185	579	3.12	186	331	1.78
comppuz.0	334	1626	4.86	304	1399	4.59	305	990	3.24
solitaire.0	191	668	3.50	178	573	3.22	175	423	2.41
solitaire.1	1531	5058	3.30	1034	4396	4.25	1035	3220	3.11
matmul.6	543	2533	4.67	543	2161	3.97	543	1365	2.51
virtroute.2	138	457	3.31	129	381	2.95	129	261	2.03
tabp2.0	152	370	2.43	142	279	1.96	143	137	0.96
tabp2.1	153	370	2.41	141	278	1.97	144	137	0.95
tabp2.2	157	379	2.40	144	286	1.98	145	140	0.97
tringm.1	281	869	3.09	258	699	2.71	258	390	1.51
alt12.2.0	118	404	3.42	111	338	3.03	108	232	2.14
alt12.2.1	118	383	3.23	111	316	2.84	125	263	2.10
alt12.3.0	172	766	4.43	161	652	4.03	159	469	2.94
alt12.3.1	186	744	4.00	174	630	3.61	189	520	2.75
alt11.2.0	178	805	4.51	164	692	4.20	163	503	3.07
alt11.2.1	188	760	4.04	174	642	3.67	198	558	2.81
alt11.3.0	276	1226	4.44	256	1042	4.07	254	741	2.92
alt11.3.1	287	1178	4.10	274	983	3.58	315	845	2.68
Total	8505	34092	4.01	7554	28964	3.83	7816	21258	2.72
tring2.1	461	207	0.45	420	125	0.30	76	118	1.55

Fig. 4. Results for tests on CSP files: statistics about the graphs, and timing results

transitions. However, beyond a few million states, the speed-ups drop off again, I believe because of issues of memory contention.

The results for tring2.1 deserve comment. This graph has a large SCC, accounting for over 70% of the states. The first two concurrent algorithms consider the nodes of this SCC sequentially and so (because the concurrent algorithms are inevitably more complex) are slightly slower than the sequential algorithms. However, the algorithm for lassos gives more scope for considering the nodes of this SCC concurrently, and therefore gives a speed-up.

The above point is also illustrated in Figure 5. This figure considers a number of random graphs, each with $N = 200,000$ states. For each pair of nodes n and n', an edge is included from n to n' with probability p; this gives an expected number

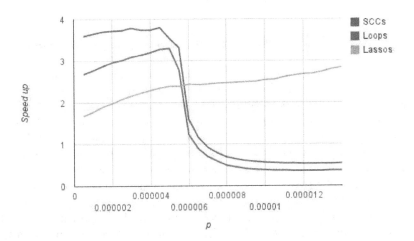

p	SCCs	Largest SCCs	Loop states	Lasso states	p	SCCs	Largest SCCs	Loop states	Lasso states
0.0000005	200000	1	0	0	0.0000075	131836	68165	68167	116882
0.0000010	200000	1	0	1	0.0000080	117613	82387	82390	128340
0.0000015	200000	1	0	0	0.0000085	104296	95704	95706	138443
0.0000020	200000	1	1	1	0.0000090	92685	107316	107318	146591
0.0000025	200000	1	1	2	0.0000095	82651	117350	117351	153129
0.0000030	200000	1	1	3	0.0000100	73020	126981	126982	159418
0.0000035	199999	2	2	7	0.0000105	64830	135171	135171	164467
0.0000040	199998	3	4	20	0.0000110	57715	142286	142287	168734
0.0000045	199994	6	8	120	0.0000115	51080	148921	148922	172610
0.0000050	199908	72	96	2573	0.0000120	45565	154436	154437	175740
0.0000055	194020	5973	5984	34743	0.0000125	40710	159291	159292	178494
0.0000060	179848	20149	20155	63368	0.0000130	36322	163679	163679	180849
0.0000065	164038	35959	35966	84903	0.0000135	32422	167579	167580	183109
0.0000070	147928	52071	52075	101907	0.0000140	28929	171072	171072	184999

Fig. 5. Experiments on random graphs

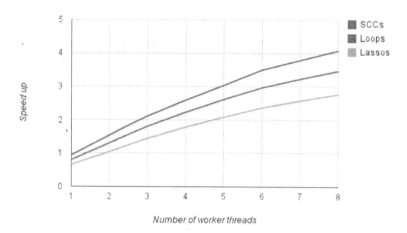

Fig. 6. Speed ups on CSP files as a function of the number of worker threads

of edges equal to N^2p. (Note that such graphs do not share many characteristics with the graphs one typically model checks!) The graph plots the speed-up for the three algorithms for various values of p; the tables give statistical information about the graphs considered (giving averages, rounded to the nearest integer in each case). For p greater than about 0.000005, the graph has a large SCC, and the algorithms for SCCs and loops become less efficient. However, the algorithm for finding lassos becomes progressively comparatively more efficient as p, and hence the number of edges, increases; indeed, for higher values of p, the speed-up plateaus at about 5.

It is worth noting that graphs corresponding to the τ-transitions of CSP processes rarely have very large SCCs. The graph tring2.1 corresponds to a CSP process designed for checking in the traces model, as opposed to the failures-divergences model, so the problems considered in this paper are not directly relevant to it.

Figure 6 considers how the speed up varies as a function of the number of worker threads. It suggests that the algorithm scales well.

6   Conclusions

In this paper we have presented three concurrent algorithms for related problems: finding SCCs, loops and lassos in a graph. The algorithms give appreciable speed-ups, typically by a factor of about four on an eight-core machine.

It is not surprising that we fall short of a speed-up equal to the number of cores. As noted above, the JVM uses a fair amount of concurrency even on single-threaded programs. Also, the concurrent algorithms are inevitably more complex than the sequential ones. Further, I believe that they are slowed down by contention for the memory bus, because the algorithms frequently need to read data from RAM.

I believe there is some scope for reducing the memory contention, in particular by reducing the size of Node objects: many of the attributes of Nodes are necessary only for *in-progress* nodes, so could be stored in the relevant Search object. Further, I intend to investigate whether it's possible to reduce the amount of locking of objects done by the prototype implementation.

We intend to incorporate the lasso and SCC algorithms into the FDR3 model checker. In particular, it will be interesting to see whether the low-level nature of C++ (in which FDR3 is implemented) permits optimisations that give better memory behaviour.

As noted earlier, a large proportion of the algorithms' time is spent within the map storing information about nodes. I would like to experiment with different implementations.

Related Work. We briefly discuss here some other concurrent algorithms addressing one or more of our three problems. We leave an experimental comparison with these algorithms for future work.

Gazit and Miller [5] describe an algorithm based upon the following idea. The basic step is to choose an arbitrary *pivot* node, and calculate its SCC as the intersection of its descendents and ancestors; these descendents and ancestors can be calculated using standard concurrent algorithms. This basic step is repeated with a new pivot whose SCC has not been identified, until all SCCs are identified. A number of improvements to this algorithm have been proposed [13,11,2].

Several papers have proposed algorithms for finding loops, in the particular context of LTL model checking [8,4,9,3]. These algorithms are based on the SWARM technique: multiple worker threads perform semi-independent searches of the graph, performing a nested depth-first search to detect a loop containing an accepting state; the workers share only information on whether a node has been fully explored, and whether it has been considered within an inner depth-first search.

Acknowledgements. I would like to thank Tom Gibson-Robinson for many interesting and useful discussions that contributed to this paper. I would also like to thank the anonymous referees for their useful comments.

References

1. Armstrong, P., Lowe, G., Ouaknine, J., Roscoe, A.W.: Model checking timed CSP. In: Proceedings of HOWARD-60 (2012)
2. Barnat, J., Chaloupka, J., van de Pol, J.: Distributed algorithms for SCC decomposition. Journal of Logic and Computation 21(1), 23–44 (2011)
3. Evangelista, S., Laarman, A., Petrucci, L., van de Pol, J.: Improved multi-core nested depth-first search. In: Chakraborty, S., Mukund, M. (eds.) ATVA 2012. LNCS, vol. 7561, pp. 269–283. Springer, Heidelberg (2012)
4. Evangelista, S., Petrucci, L., Youcef, S.: Parallel nested depth-first searches for LTL model checking. In: Bultan, T., Hsiung, P.-A. (eds.) ATVA 2011. LNCS, vol. 6996, pp. 381–396. Springer, Heidelberg (2011)

5. Fleischer, L.K., Hendrickson, B.A., Pinar, A.: On identifying strongly connected components in parallel. In: Rolim, J.D.P. (ed.) IPDPS-WS 2000. LNCS, vol. 1800, pp. 505–511. Springer, Heidelberg (2000)

6. Gibson-Robinson, T., Armstrong, P., Boulgakov, A., Roscoe, A.W.: FDR3 — A modern refinement checker for CSP. In: Ábrahám, E., Havelund, K. (eds.) TACAS 2014. LNCS, vol. 8413, pp. 180–194. Springer, Heidelberg (2014)

7. Laarman, A., van de Pol, J., Weber, M.: Boosting multi-core reachability performance with shared hash tables. In: Proceedings of 10th International Conference on Formal Methods in Computer-Aided Design, FMCAD 2010 (2010)

8. Laarman, A., Langerak, R., van de Pol, J., Weber, M., Wijs, A.: Multi-core nested depth-first search. In: Bultan, T., Hsiung, P.-A. (eds.) ATVA 2011. LNCS, vol. 6996, pp. 321–335. Springer, Heidelberg (2011)

9. Laarman, A.W., van de Pol, J.C.: Variations on multi-core nested depth-first search. In: Proceedings of the 10th International Workshop on Parallel and Distributed Methods in Verification. Electronic Proceedings in Theoretical Computer Science, vol. 72, pp. 13–28 (2011)

10. Lowe, G.: Implementing generalised alt: A case study in validated design using CSP. In: Communicating Process Architectures (2011)

11. McLendon III, W., Hendrickson, B., Plimpton, S.J., Rauchwerger, L.: Finding strongly connected components in distributed graphs. Journal of Parallel and Distributed Computing 65(8), 901–910 (2005)

12. Odersky, M., Spoon, L., Venners, B.: Programming in Scala. Artima (2008)

13. Orzan, S.: On Distributed Verification and Verified Distribution. PhD thesis, Free University of Amsterdam (2004)

14. Reif, J.H.: Depth-first search is inherently sequential. Information Processing Letters 20(5), 229–234 (1985)

15. Roscoe, A.W.: Theory and Practice of Concurrency. Prentice Hall (1998)

16. Roscoe, A.W.: Understanding Concurrent Systems. Springer (2010)

17. Tarjan, R.: Depth-first search and linear graph algorithms. SIAM Journal of Computing 1(2), 146–160 (1972)

18. University of Oxford. Failures-Divergence Refinement—FDR 3 User Manual (2013), http://www.cs.ox.ac.uk/projects/fdr/manual/index.html

19. Vardi, M.Y., Wolper, P.: An automata-theoretic approach to automatic program verification. In: Proceedings of Logic in Computer Science (1986)

Basic Problems in Multi-View Modeling*

Jan Reineke[1] and Stavros Tripakis[2]

[1] Saarland University, Germany
[2] UC Berkeley, USA and Aalto University, Finland

Abstract. Modeling all aspects of a complex system within a single model is a difficult, if not impossible, task. Multi-view modeling is a methodology where different aspects of the system are captured by different models, or *views*. A key question then is *consistency*: if different views of a system have some degree of overlap, how can we guarantee that they are consistent, i.e., that they do not contradict each other? In this paper we formulate this and other basic problems in multi-view modeling within an abstract formal framework. We then instantiate this framework in a discrete, finite-state system setting, and study how some key verification and synthesis problems can be solved in that setting.

1 Introduction

Real systems are usually complex objects, and grasping all the details of a system at the same time is often difficult. In addition, each of the various stakeholders in the system are concerned with different system aspects. For these reasons, modeling and design teams usually deal only with partial and incomplete *views* of a system, which are easier to manage separately. For example, when designing a digital circuit, architects may be concerned with general (boolean) functionality issues, while ignoring performance. Other stakeholders, however, may be concerned about timing aspects such as the delay of the critical path, which ultimately affects the clock rate at which the circuit can be run. Yet other stakeholders may be interested in a different aspect, namely, energy consumption of the circuit which affects battery life.

Modeling and simulation are often used to support system design. In this paper, when we talk about views, we refer concretely to the different *models* of a system that designers build. Such models may be useful as models of an *existing* system: the system exists, and a model is built in order to study the system. Then, the model is only a partial or incomplete view of the system, since it focuses on certain aspects and omits others. For example, an energy consumption model for an airplane ignores control, air dynamics, and other aspects. Models may also be used for a *system-to-be-built*: an energy consumption model as in the example above could be developed as part of the design process, even before the airplane is built.

---

* This research is partially supported by the National Science Foundation and the Academy of Finland, via projects *ExCAPE: Expeditions in Computer Augmented Program Engineering* and *COSMOI: Compositional System Modeling with Interfaces*, by the Deutsche Forschungsgemeinschaft as part of the Transregional Collaborative Research Centre SFB/TR 14 *AVACS*, and by the centers *TerraSwarm* and *iCyPhy (Industrial Cyber-Physical Systems)* at UC Berkeley.

E. Ábrahám and K. Havelund (Eds.): TACAS 2014, LNCS 8413, pp. 217–232, 2014.

For large systems, each aspect of the system is typically designed by a dedicated design team. These teams often use different modeling languages and tools to capture different views, which is generally referred to as *multi-view modeling* (MVM). MVM presents a number of challenges, such as the crucial issue of *consistency*: if different views of the system are captured by different models, and these models have some degree of overlap, how can we guarantee that the models are consistent, i.e., that they do not contradict each other? Understanding the precise meaning of such questions, and developing techniques to answer them, ideally fully automatically, is the main goal of this paper.

Toward this goal, we begin in Section 2 by introducing an example of simple 3-dimensional structure modeling. Even though our focus is on dynamic behaviors, we will use this static system as an illustrative running example to demonstrate the salient concepts of our formal MVM framework. The latter is itself presented in Section 3. The main concepts are as follows: (1) views can be derived from systems using abstraction functions, which map system behaviors to view behaviors; (2) conformance formalizes how "faithful" a view is to a system; (3) consistency of a set of views is defined as existence of a witness system to which all views conform; (4) view reduction allows to "optimize" views by using the information contained in other views; (5) orthogonality captures independence between views.

The framework proposed in Section 3 is abstract, in the sense that it does not refer to specific notions of behaviors, neither to concrete representations of systems and views. In the rest of the paper we instantiate this abstract framework for the case of discrete systems. The latter, defined in Section 4, are finite-state symbolic transition systems consisting of a set of state variables, a predicate over the state variables characterizing the set of initial states, and a predicate characterizing the transition relation.

In Section 5 we study projections as abstraction functions for discrete systems. Fully-observable systems, where all variables are observable, are not closed under projection, therefore we also consider systems with internal (unobservable) variables. We show how to effectively solve a number of verification and synthesis problems on discrete systems and views, including view conformance and consistency checking.

2 Running Example: 3D Objects

To illustrate the concept of views we introduce a running example. Consider the 3D structure shown at the left of Figure 1. It can be modeled as a set of points in a $4 \times 4 \times 4$ space, each point (x, y, z) representing a "box" appearing at coordinate (x, y, z), for $x, y, z \in \{1, 2, 3, 4\}$. The object shown to the left of the figure contains 16 such boxes, and the corresponding set contains 16 points.

Three views of the object are shown to the right of the figure: a top view, a front view, and a side view. These views can be formalized as 2D projections. Let S be the set of points representing the 3D object. Then the three views can be formalized as sets $V_{top}, V_{front}, V_{side}$, where: $V_{top} = \{(x, y) \mid \exists z : (x, y, z) \in S\}, V_{front} = \{(x, z) \mid \exists y : (x, y, z) \in S\}, V_{side} = \{(y, z) \mid \exists x : (x, y, z) \in S\}$.

The above projections can be seen as *abstractions* of S. In fact, they are generally *strict* abstractions in the sense that some information about S is lost during the abstraction. In the case of Figure 1, e.g., the same views would be obtained if one were to add

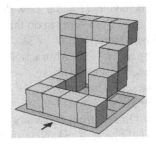

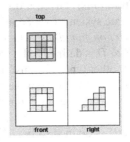

Fig. 1. A 3D structure (left) and 3 views of it (right) – image produced using this tool: http://www.fi.uu.nl/toepassingen/02015/toepassing_wisweb.en.html

to the object the missing boxes so that no box under the "staircase structure" hangs in the air.

3   Views: A Formalization

Systems: We define a *system* semantically, as a set of behaviors. As in [15], there is no restriction on the type of behaviors: they could be discrete traces, continuous trajectories, hybrid traces, or something else. We only assume given a domain of possible behaviors, $\mathcal{U}$. Then, a *system S over domain of behaviors $\mathcal{U}$* is a subset of $\mathcal{U}$: $S \subseteq \mathcal{U}$.

View Domains: A view is intuitively an "incomplete picture" of a system. It can be incomplete in different ways:

- Some behaviors may be missing from the view, i.e., the view may contain only a *subset* of system behaviors. (As we shall see when we discuss conformance, the view may also be a *superset*.)
- Some parts of a behavior itself may be missing in the view. E.g., if the behavior refers to a state vector with, say, 10 state variables, the view could refer only to 2 state variables. In this case the view can be seen as a *projection*.
- More generally, the view may be obtained by some other kind of *transformation* (not necessarily a projection) to behaviors. E.g., the original system behaviors may contain temperature as a state variable, but the view only contains temperature averages over some period of time.

From the above discussion, it appears that: semantically, views can be formalized as sets of behaviors, just like systems are. However, because of projections or other transformations, the domain of behaviors of a view is not necessarily the same as the domain of system behaviors, $\mathcal{U}$. Therefore, we let $\mathcal{D}_i$ be the domain of behaviors of view i (there can be more than one view, hence the subscript i). When we refer to a general view domain, we drop the subscript and simply write $\mathcal{D}$.

In the case of our running example, $\mathcal{U} = \{1, 2, 3, 4\}^3$, and $\mathcal{D}_{top} = \mathcal{D}_{front} = \mathcal{D}_{side} = \{1, 2, 3, 4\}^2$.

Views: A view is a set of behaviors over a given view domain. That is, a *view V over view domain $\mathcal{D}$* is defined to be a subset of $\mathcal{D}$: $V \subseteq \mathcal{D}$.

Abstraction Functions: Given a domain of behaviors $\mathcal{U}$ and a view domain $\mathcal{D}$, we would like to relate systems over $\mathcal{U}$ and views over $\mathcal{D}$. In order to do this, we will first introduce *abstraction functions*, which map behaviors from $\mathcal{U}$ to $\mathcal{D}$. An *abstraction function from $\mathcal{U}$ to $\mathcal{D}$* is defined to be a mapping $a : \mathcal{U} \to \mathcal{D}$. Abstraction functions can be projections or other types of transformations, as discussed above.

In the case of our running example, the abstraction functions $a_{top}, a_{front}, a_{side}$ are 3D-to-2D projections on the corresponding planes.

An abstraction function a can be naturally "lifted" from behaviors to systems. If $S \subseteq \mathcal{U}$, then $a(S)$ is defined to be: $a(S) := \{a(\sigma) \mid \sigma \in S\}$. Note that $a(S) \subseteq \mathcal{D}$, therefore, $a(S)$ is a view over $\mathcal{D}$.

Conformance: Given system $S \subseteq \mathcal{U}$, view $V \subseteq \mathcal{D}$, and abstraction function $a : \mathcal{U} \to \mathcal{D}$, we say that V *is a complete view of S w.r.t. a* if $V = a(S)$. The notion of complete view is a reasonable way of capturing how "faithful" a given view is to a certain system. For example, if S is an object containing two boxes, $S = \{(1,1,1),(2,2,2)\}$ and a_{top} is the top view, then $V_1 = \{(1,1),(2,2)\}$ is complete w.r.t. a_{top}, whereas $V_2 = \{(2,2)\}$ and $V_3 = \{(1,1),(2,2),(3,3)\}$ are not complete.

But faithfulness need not always require a strict equality as in the condition $V = a(S)$. Depending on the usage one makes of a view, weaker conditions may be appropriate. Because of this, we introduce the notion of *conformance*. Conformance is defined with respect to a partial order $\sqsupseteq$ on the set of all views over view domain $\mathcal{D}$. That is, $\sqsupseteq$ is a partial order on $2^{\mathcal{D}}$, the powerset of $\mathcal{D}$. Then, we say that V *conforms to S w.r.t. a and $\sqsupseteq$*, denoted $V \sqsupseteq_a S$, if $V \sqsupseteq a(S)$.

For example, if one uses the top view to decide whether it is safe to drop a box to the floor without touching another box during landing, then a view that safely approximates the set of free (x, y) positions could be acceptable. In this case, the partial order $\sqsupseteq$ is $\supseteq$, i.e., conformance is defined as $V \supseteq a_{top}(S)$. Indeed, dropping a box to $(x, y) \notin V$ would be safe, since $(x, y) \notin V$ and $V \supseteq a_{top}(S)$ imply $(x, y) \notin a_{top}(S)$. In another scenario, it may be more appropriate to require that the view *under*-approximates $a(S)$, thus *over*-approximates the set of free (x, y) positions. For example, if one uses the top view to decide whether it is safe to drop an object so that it does *not* hit the floor, then it is more appropriate to define conformance as $V \subseteq a_{top}(S)$. In this case, $\sqsupseteq$ is $\subseteq$.

An Alternative Formalization – Starting with Conformance: In the way we formalized things so far, we started with an abstraction function a and a partial order $\sqsupseteq$, and defined the conformance relation $\sqsupseteq_a$ with respect to those. As an alternative, we can start with a conformance relation $\models \subseteq 2^{\mathcal{D}} \times 2^{\mathcal{U}}$, which relates a view V and a system S, i.e., $V \models S$, and derive an abstraction function a. We can do this provided that $\models$ satisfies the conditions described below, and that the domain of views equipped with $\sqsupseteq$, denoted $(2^{\mathcal{D}}, \sqsupseteq)$, forms a complete lattice. Let $\bigsqcap$ denote the greatest lower bound in this lattice. Note that the interpretation of the lattice is that the smaller an element the more accurate it is, and $x \sqsupseteq y$ says that y is smaller than x. Therefore, when $\sqsupseteq$ is $\supseteq$, top is $\mathcal{D}$, bottom is $\emptyset$, and $\bigsqcap$ is $\bigcap$. When $\sqsupseteq$ is $\subseteq$, $\bigsqcap$ is $\bigcup$. Then, $\models$ induces an abstraction function a defined as follows:

$$a_{\models}(S) := \bigsqcap \{V \subseteq \mathcal{D} \mid V \models S\}.$$

For this to work, however, we need $\models$ to have the two following properties:

1. (monotonicity) $V_1 \models S \wedge V_2 \sqsupseteq V_1 \Rightarrow V_2 \models S$.
2. (conformance preserved by $\sqcap$) $\forall W \subseteq 2^{\mathcal{D}} : (\forall V \in W : V \models S) \Rightarrow (\sqcap W) \models S$.

Condition 1 says that if V_1 conforms to S then any view greater than V_1 also conforms to S. Condition 2 says that if a set of views all conform to a system S, then their greatest lower bound also conforms to S. Any relation $\sqsupseteq_a$ defined by an abstraction function a and an order $\sqsupseteq$ forming a complete lattice has these two properties by construction.

Consistency: Consider a set of views, $V_1, V_2, ..., V_n$, over view domains $\mathcal{D}_1, \mathcal{D}_2, ..., \mathcal{D}_n$. For each view domain $\mathcal{D}_i$, consider given a conformance relation $\models_i$ (which could be derived from given abstraction function a_i and partial order $\sqsupseteq_i$, or defined as a primitive notion as explained above). We say that $V_1, V_2, ..., V_n$ *are consistent w.r.t.* $\models_1, \models_2, ..., \models_n$ if there exists a system S over $\mathcal{U}$ such that $\forall i = 1, ..., n : V_i \models_i S$. We call such a system S a *witness* to the consistency of $V_1, V_2, ..., V_n$. Clearly, if no such S exists, then one must conclude that the views are inconsistent, as there is no system from which these views could be derived. When $\sqsupseteq_i$ is $=$ for all i, i.e., when $V_i = a_i(S)$ for all i, we say that $V_1, ..., V_n$ are *strictly consistent*. Note that if $\sqsupseteq_i$ is $\supseteq$ for all i, then consistency trivially holds as the empty system is a witness, since $V_i \supseteq \emptyset = a_i(\emptyset)$ for all i. Also, if $\sqsupseteq_i$ is $\subseteq$ for all i and every a_i satisfies $a_i(\mathcal{U}) = \mathcal{D}_i$, then consistency trivially holds as the system $\mathcal{U}$ is a witness, since $V_i \subseteq \mathcal{D}_i = a_i(\mathcal{U})$ for all i.

In our 3D objects example, if V_{top} is non-empty but V_{side} is empty, then the two views are inconsistent w.r.t. strict conformance $V = a(S)$. A less trivial case is when $V_{top} = \{(1,1)\}$ and $V_{side} = \{(2,2)\}$. Again the two views are inconsistent (w.r.t. $=$): V_{top} asserts that some box must be in the column with (x, y) coordinates $(1, 1)$, but V_{side} implies that there is no box whose y coordinate is 1.

The last example may mislead to believe that consistency (w.r.t. $=$) is equivalent to "intersection of inverse projection of views being non-empty." This is not true. Even in the case where abstraction functions are projections, non-empty intersection of inverse projections is a necessary, but not a sufficient condition for consistency. To see this, consider views $V_{top} = \{(1,1), (3,3)\}$ and $V_{side} = \{(2,2), (1,2)\}$ in the context of our running example. These two views are inconsistent w.r.t. $=$. Yet the intersection of their inverse projections is non-empty, and equal to $\{(1,1,2)\}$.

View Reduction: Given a set of views $V_1, ..., V_n$ of a system S, it may be possible to "reduce" each view V_i based on the information contained in the other views, and as a result obtain views $V_1', ..., V_n'$ that are "more accurate" views of S. We use the term *reduction* inspired from similar work in abstract interpretation [5,10].

For example, if we assume that conformance is defined as $V \supseteq a(S)$, then the views $V_{top} = \{(1,1), (3,3)\}$ and $V_{side} = \{(2,2), (1,2)\}$ can be reduced to $V_{top}' = \{(1,1)\}$ and $V_{side}' = \{(1,2)\}$. V_{top}' is still a valid top view, in the sense that for every system S, if both $V_{top} \supseteq a_{top}(S)$ and $V_{side} \supseteq a_{side}(S)$, then $V_{top}' \supseteq a_{top}(S)$. In addition, V_{top}' is more accurate than V_{top} in the sense that V_{top}' is a strict subset of V_{top}. Indeed, V_{top} does not contain the "bogus" square $(3,3)$ which cannot occur in S, as we learn from V_{side}.

Let us now define the notion of view reduction formally. First, given a conformance relation between views and systems, $\models \subseteq 2^{\mathcal{D}} \times 2^{\mathcal{U}}$, we define the concretization function $c_{\models}$ which, given a view V, returns the set of all systems which V conforms to:

$$c_{\models}(V) := \{S \subseteq \mathcal{U} \mid V \models S\} = \{S \subseteq \mathcal{U} \mid V \sqsupseteq a_{\models}(S)\}.$$

Note that $V_1, ..., V_n$ are consistent w.r.t. $\models_1, ..., \models_n$ iff $\bigcap_{i=1}^n c_{\models_i}(V_i) \neq \emptyset$. Also observe that, by definition, $a_{\models}(S) \models S$. As a consequence, $S \in c_{\models}(a_{\models}(S))$ for all $S \subseteq \mathcal{U}$.

We next lift $a_{\models}$ to sets of systems. For this, we will again assume that $(2^{\mathcal{D}}, \sqsupseteq)$ forms a lattice, with $\bigsqcap$ denoting its greatest lower bound.[1] Then, if $\mathcal{S}$ is a set of systems over $\mathcal{U}$, we define $a_{\models}(\mathcal{S})$ to be the "most accurate" view that conforms to all systems in $\mathcal{S}$:

$$a_{\models}(\mathcal{S}) := \bigsqcap\{V \subseteq \mathcal{D} \mid c_{\models}(V) \supseteq \mathcal{S}\} = \bigsqcap\{V \subseteq \mathcal{D} \mid \forall S \in \mathcal{S} : V \models S\}.$$

Lemma 1. *The most accurate view that conforms to a set of systems $\mathcal{S}$ can also be determined from the individual systems' abstractions:*

$$a_{\models}(\mathcal{S}) = \bigsqcup\{a_{\models}(S) \mid S \in \mathcal{S}\}.$$

Missing proofs to lemmas and theorems can be found in the technical report [17].

Given the above, and assuming n view domains with corresponding conformance relations, $(\mathcal{D}_1, \models_1), ..., (\mathcal{D}_n, \models_n)$, view reduction can be defined as follows:

$$reduce_i(V_1, V_2, ..., V_n) := a_{\models_i}\left(\bigcap_{i=1}^n c_{\models_i}(V_i)\right).$$

Lemma 2. *Reduction is a reductive operation, i.e., $V_i \sqsupseteq reduce_i(V_1, V_2, ..., V_n)$ for all i. The set of witnesses to the consistency of views $V_1, ..., V_n$ is invariant under reduction, i.e., $\bigcap_{i=1}^n c_{\models_i}(reduce_i(V_1, V_2, ..., V_n)) = \bigcap_{i=1}^n c_{\models_i}(V_i)$ for all i.*

The second part of the lemma implies that reduction is idempotent, i.e., for all i: $reduce_i(V_1, ..., V_n) = reduce_i(V_1', ..., V_n')$, where $V_i' = reduce_i(V_1, V_2, ..., V_n)$.

Orthogonality: In some fortunate cases different aspects of a system are independent of each other. Intuitively, what this means is that each aspect can be defined separately without the need for communication between development teams to avoid inconsistencies.

Formally, we say that view domains $\mathcal{D}_1, ..., \mathcal{D}_n$ are *orthogonal* if all sets of non-empty views $V_1, ..., V_n$ from these view domains are mutually irreducible, i.e., if $reduce_i(V_1, ..., V_n) = V_i$ for all $i = 1, ..., n$. The view domains from our example of 3D objects, capturing projections onto two dimensions, are *not* orthogonal, as the reduction example involving the domains shows. On the other hand, view domains corresponding to the projection onto *individual* dimensions would indeed be orthogonal to each other.

Alternatively, orthogonal view domains can be defined by requiring that all sets of non-empty views $V_1, ..., V_n$ from these domains are consistent w.r.t. $=$.

The following lemma shows that the two definitions of orthogonal domains are equivalent, if we assume that conformance is defined based on abstraction functions and the superset and equality relations as the partial orders on views.

---

[1] Note that when $\sqsupseteq$ is a set-theoretic relation such as $\subseteq$ or $\supseteq$, this obviously holds and $\bigsqcap$ is $\bigcup$ or $\bigcap$. When $\sqsupseteq$ is $=$ then $(2^{\mathcal{D}}, =)$ is not a lattice, and the definition of view reduction given below does not apply. This is not a problem, as in that case we require views to be complete.

Lemma 3. *Given non-empty views $V_1, ..., V_n$, the following statements are equivalent:*

1. $V_1, ..., V_n$ *are consistent w.r.t.* $=_{a_1}, ..., =_{a_n}$.
2. $V_1, ..., V_n$ *are mutually irreducible w.r.t.* $\supseteq_{a_1}, ..., \supseteq_{a_n}$.
3. $V_1, ..., V_n$ *are mutually irreducible w.r.t.* $\subseteq_{a_1}, ..., \subseteq_{a_n}$.

A system $S \subseteq \mathcal{U}$ is called *view definable* w.r.t. $\models_1, ..., \models_n$ if there exist views $V_1 \subseteq \mathcal{D}_1, ..., V_n \subseteq \mathcal{D}_n$, such that $c_{\models_1}(V_1) \cap \cdots \cap c_{\models_n}(V_n) = \{S\}$. In the example of 3D objects, with 2D projections, the empty object $S = \{\}$ is view definable, as it is defined by the empty views. Similarly, all objects $S_{i,j,k} = \{(i, j, k)\}$ are view definable. Note that a general cube is not view definable, as there are other objects (e.g., a hollow cube) which have the same 2D projections.

Verification and Synthesis Problems Related to Views

View conformance checking: given (concrete representation of) system S, view V, and a certain conformance relation, does V conform to S?

View synthesis: given system S and abstraction function a, synthesize (concrete representation of) $a(S)$. Alternatively, given S and conformance relation $\models$, construct smallest view V such that $V \models S$, that is, construct $a_\models(S)$.

View consistency checking: given views $V_1, ..., V_n$ and conformance relations $\models_1, ..., \models_n$, check whether $V_1, ..., V_n$ are consistent w.r.t. $\models_1, ..., \models_n$.

System synthesis from views: given consistent views $V_1, ..., V_n$ and conformance relations $\models_1, ..., \models_n$, construct a system S such that for all i, $V_i \models_i S$.

View reduction: given views $V_1, ..., V_n$ compute $reduce_i(V_1, V_2, ..., V_n)$ for given i.

4 Discrete Systems

Our goal in the rest of this paper is to instantiate the view framework developed in Section 3. We instantiate it for a class of discrete systems, and we also provide answers to some of the corresponding algorithmic problems.

We will consider finite-state discrete systems. The state space of such a system can be represented by a set of boolean variables, X, resulting in 2^n potential states, where $n = |X|$ is the size of X. A *state* s over X is a *valuation over X*, i.e., a function $s : X \rightarrow \mathbb{B}$, where $\mathbb{B} := \{0, 1\}$ is the set of booleans. For convenience, we sometimes consider other finite domains with the understanding that they can be encoded as booleans. A *behavior over X* is a finite or infinite sequence of states over X, $\sigma = s_0 s_1 s_2 \cdots$. $\mathcal{U}(X)$ denotes the set of all possible behaviors over X.

Semantically, a discrete system S over X is a set of behaviors over X, i.e., $S \subseteq \mathcal{U}(X)$. For computation, we need a concrete representation of discrete systems. We will start with a simple representation where all system variables are observable. We will then discuss limitations of this representation and consider an extension where the system can also have internal (unobservable) variables in addition to the observable ones.

Fully-Observable Discrete Systems: A *fully-observable* discrete system (FOS) is represented concretely by a triple (X, θ, ϕ). X is the (finite) set of (boolean) variables. All variables in X are considered observable. θ is a boolean expression over X, characterizing the set of initial states of the system. Given state s, we write $\theta(s)$ to denote the fact that s satisfies θ, i.e., s is an initial state. ϕ is a boolean expression over $X \cup X'$, where X' is the set of primed copies of variables in X, $X' := \{x' \mid x \in X\}$, representing the next state variables, as usual. ϕ characterizes pairs of states (s, s'), each representing a transition of S, i.e., a move from state s to state s'. We write $\phi(s, s')$ to denote that the pair (s, s') satisfies ϕ, i.e., that there is a transition from s to s'.

A behavior of a system (X, θ, ϕ) is a finite or infinite sequence of states over X, $\sigma = s_0 s_1 s_2 \cdots$, such that $\theta(s_0)$ and $\forall i : \phi(s_i, s_{i+1})$, i.e., s_0 is an initial state and there is a transition from each s_i to s_{i+1} (if the latter exists). A state s is *reachable* if there is a finite behavior $s_0 s_1 \cdots s_n$, such that $s = s_n$.

We sometimes use $S = (X, \theta, \phi)$ to denote the concrete (syntactic) representation of discrete system S, and $[\![S]\!]$ to denote its semantics, i.e., its set of behaviors.

Projection (variable hiding): Projection, or variable hiding, is a natural operation on systems, which can also serve as a basic abstraction function for views, as we shall see below. Here, we define projection and motivate the introduction of internal variables in the concrete representation of discrete systems.

Let s be a state over a set of variables X. Given subset $Y \subseteq X$, the projection function h_Y projects s onto the set of variables Y, that is, h_Y hides from s all variables in $X \backslash Y$. $h_Y(s)$ is defined to be the new state s' over Y, that is, the function $s' : Y \to \mathbb{B}$, such that $s'(x) = s(x)$ for all $x \in Y$.

Projection can be lifted to behaviors in the standard way. If $\sigma = s_0 s_1 \cdots$ is a behavior over X, then $h_Y(\sigma)$ is a behavior over Y defined by $h_Y(\sigma) := h_Y(s_0)h_Y(s_1) \cdots$. Projection can also be lifted to systems. If S is a discrete system over X then $h_Y([\![S]\!]) := \{h_Y(\sigma) \mid \sigma \in [\![S]\!]\}$.

Non-closure Properties

Non-closure Under Projection: The projection $h_Y([\![S]\!])$ is defined semantically, as a set of behaviors. It is natural to ask whether the syntactic representation of discrete systems is closed under projection. That is, is it true that for any $S = (X, \theta, \phi)$, and $Y \subseteq X$, there exists $S' = (Y, \theta', \phi')$, such that $[\![S']\!] = h_Y([\![S]\!])$? This is not generally true:

Lemma 4. *There exists a FOS $S = (X, \theta, \phi)$, and $Y \subseteq X$, such that there is no FOS $S' = (Y, \theta', \phi')$, such that $[\![S']\!] = h_Y([\![S]\!])$.*

Proof. Consider the finite-state system $S = (\{x, y\}, x = 0 \wedge y = true, (x' = (x + 1) \bmod 5) \wedge (y' \leftrightarrow (x' = 0)))$, where $x \in \{0, 1, 2, 3, 4\}$ and $y \in \mathbb{B}$. Let $Y = \{y\}$. Then $h_Y([\![S]\!]) = \{y_0 y_1 \cdots \mid \forall i : y_i \leftrightarrow i \bmod 5 = 0\}$. We claim that there is no $S' = (Y, \theta', \phi')$ such that $[\![S']\!] = h_Y([\![S]\!])$. The reason is that S' needs to count modulo five in order to produce the correct output. But S' has only one boolean variable y. □

As it turns out, we can check whether closure under projection holds for a given system: see Theorem 2 in Section 5.

Non-closure Under Union

Lemma 5. *Fully-observable systems over a set of variables X are not closed under union, i.e., there exist $S_1 = (X, \theta_1, \phi_1)$, $S_2 = (X, \theta_2, \phi_2)$ such that there is no $S = (X, \theta, \phi)$ such that $[\![S]\!] = [\![S_1]\!] \cup [\![S_2]\!]$.*

Proof. Consider as an example $S_1 = (\{x\}, \theta_1 = x, \phi_1 = x \wedge \neg x')$ and $S_2 = (\{x\}, \theta_2 = \neg x, \phi_1 = \neg x \wedge x')$. Both systems allow exactly one transition, from $x \mapsto true$ to $x \mapsto false$ and vice versa. A system that represents the union of S_1 and S_2 needs to include both transitions. Then, however, it also includes arbitrarily long behaviors alternating between $x \mapsto true$ and $x \mapsto false$. □

Discrete Systems with Internal Variables: The above non-closure properties motivate us to study, in addition to fully-observable discrete systems, a generalization which extends them with a set of *internal, unobservable* state variables. Most practical modeling languages also allow the construction of models with both internal and observable state variables.

Accordingly, we extend the definition of a discrete system to be in general a tuple (X, Z, θ, ϕ), where X, Z are disjoint (finite) sets of variables. X models the observable and Z the internal variables. θ is a boolean expression over $X \cup Z$ and ϕ is a boolean expression over $X \cup Z \cup X' \cup Z'$. In such a system, we need to distinguish between behaviors, and observable behaviors. A behavior of a system $S = (X, Z, \theta, \phi)$ is a finite or infinite sequence σ over $X \cup Z$, defined as above. The observable behavior corresponding to σ is $h_X(\sigma)$, which is a behavior over X. From now on, $[\![S]\!]$ denotes the set of all behaviors (over $X \cup Z$) of S, and $[\![S]\!]_o$ denotes the set of observable behaviors (over X) of S.

Note that we allow Z to be empty. In that case, the system has no internal variables, i.e., it is a FOS. We will continue to represent a FOS by a triple $S = (X, \theta, \phi)$. A FOS S satisfies $[\![S]\!] = [\![S]\!]_o$.

Closure Properties: We have already shown (Lemma 5) that FOS are not closed under union. They are however closed under intersection:

Lemma 6. *Given two FOS $S_1 = (X, \theta_1, \phi_1)$ and $S_2 = (X, \theta_2, \phi_2)$, a FOS S such that $[\![S]\!] = [\![S_1]\!] \cap [\![S_2]\!]$ is $S_1 \wedge S_2 = (X, \theta_1 \wedge \theta_2, \phi_1 \wedge \phi_2)$.*

General discrete systems (with internal variables) are closed under intersection, union, as well as projection.

Lemma 7. *Let $S_1 = (X, Z_1, \theta_1, \phi_1)$ and $S_2 = (X, Z_2, \theta_2, \phi_2)$ be two systems, such that $Z_1 \cap Z_2 = \emptyset$. Let $Y \subseteq X$ and let z be a fresh variable not in $X \cup Z_1 \cup Z_2$. Let:*

$$S_\cap = (X, Z_1 \cup Z_2, \theta_1 \wedge \theta_2, \phi_1 \wedge \phi_2),$$
$$S_\cup = \big(X, Z_1 \cup Z_2 \cup \{z\}, (\theta_1 \wedge z) \vee (\theta_2 \wedge \neg z).(z \to \phi_1 \wedge z') \wedge (\neg z \to \phi_2 \wedge \neg z')\big),$$
$$S_h = (Y, Z_1 \cup (X \setminus Y), \theta_1, \phi_1).$$

Then, $[\![S_\cap]\!]_o = [\![S_1]\!]_o \cap [\![S_2]\!]_o$, $[\![S_\cup]\!]_o = [\![S_1]\!]_o \cup [\![S_2]\!]_o$, and $[\![S_h]\!]_o = h_Y([\![S_1]\!]_o)$.

5   Views of Finite-State Discrete Systems

Having defined discrete systems, we now turn to instantiating the view framework for such systems.

Discrete Views, View Domains, and Abstraction Functions: Discrete views are finite-state discrete systems. They are represented in general by tuples of the form (X, Z, θ, ϕ), and when $Z = \emptyset$, by triples of the form (X, θ, ϕ).

In this paper, we will study projection as the abstraction function for the discrete view framework. That is, a system will be a discrete system S over a set of observable variables X, and therefore the domain of system behaviors will be $\mathcal{U} = \mathcal{U}(X)$. A view will be a discrete system V over a subset of observable variables $Y \subseteq X$. Therefore, the view domain of V is $\mathcal{D} = \mathcal{U}(Y)$. Note that both S and V may have (each their own) internal variables.

Let $S = (X, Z, \theta, \phi)$ be a discrete system, $V = (Y, W, \theta', \phi')$ be a discrete view, with $Y \subseteq X$, and $\sqsupseteq$ be one of the orders $=$, $\subseteq$, or $\supseteq$. To make notation lighter, we will write $V \sqsupseteq h_Y(S)$ instead of $[\![V]\!]_o \sqsupseteq h_Y([\![S]\!])$. Note, that $h_Y([\![S]\!]) = h_Y([\![S]\!]_o)$. More generally, when comparing systems or views, we compare them w.r.t. their observable behaviors. For instance, when writing $V_1 \sqsupseteq V_2$, we mean $[\![V_1]\!]_o \sqsupseteq [\![V_2]\!]_o$.

Least and Greatest Fully-Observable Views: Let S be a discrete system over set of observable variables X. Given a set $Y \subseteq X$, one might ask whether there is a "canonical" view V of S w.r.t. Y. Clearly, if we allow V to have internal variables, the answer is yes: it suffices to turn all variables in $X \setminus Y$ into internal variables in V. Then, by Lemma 7, V represents precisely the projection of S to Y, i.e., it is a complete view, it satisfies $V = h_Y(S)$, and therefore trivially also $V \supseteq h_Y(S)$ and $V \subseteq h_Y(S)$. Note that this is true independently of whether S has internal variables or not.

In this section we study the question for the case where we forbid V from having internal variables, i.e., we restrict views to be fully-observable. As FOS are not closed under projection, there are systems that have no complete fully-observable view. On the other hand, there can be multiple views V over Y such that $V \supseteq h_Y(S)$ or $V \subseteq h_Y(S)$. In particular, $(Y, true, true) \supseteq h_Y(S)$ and $(Y, false, false) \subseteq h_Y(S)$, for any S and Y. Thus, the question arises, whether there is a *least* fully-observable view $lv(S, Y)$ of S with $lv(S, Y) \supseteq h_Y(S)$, such that for any fully-observable view V' with $V' \supseteq h_Y(S)$, we have $V' \supseteq lv(S, Y)$. Similarly, one may ask whether there is a *greatest* fully-observable view $gv(S, Y)$ w.r.t. $\subseteq_{h_Y}$. These questions are closely related to whether views are closed under intersection and union. In particular, we can use closure under intersection to show that a least view always exists. A greatest view, on the other hand, does not necessarily exist.

Theorem 1. *Let* $S = (X, Z, \theta, \phi)$ *be any discrete system and let* $Y \subseteq X$. *Let* ψ_S *characterize the set of reachable states of* S. *Then the FOS*

$$(Y, \theta_Y = \exists (X \cup Z) \setminus Y : \theta, \phi_Y = \exists (X \cup Z) \setminus Y : \psi_S \wedge \exists (X' \cup Z') \setminus Y' : \phi)$$

is the unique fully-observable least view $lv(S, Y)$, *that is,* $lv(S, Y) \supseteq h_Y(S)$, *and for any fully-observable view* V' *over* Y *with* $V' \supseteq h_Y(S)$, *we have* $V' \supseteq lv(S, Y)$.

As Lemma 4 shows, the projection of a system cannot generally be represented as a fully-observable view. As it turns out, we can effectively check whether this is the case for a given system S, by checking whether the least view of S conforms to S w.r.t. $=$.

Theorem 2. *Given discrete system S over X and $Y \subseteq X$, there exists a fully-observable view V over Y with $V = h_Y(S)$ iff $[\![lv(S, Y)]\!] = h_Y([\![S]\!])$.*

Theorem 2 implies that it is decidable to check whether a system admits a fully-observable complete view V.

Theorem 3. *There is a discrete system S over X and a subset $Y \subseteq X$ for which there is no unique greatest fully-observable view $gv(S, Y)$ with $gv(S, Y) \subseteq h_Y(S)$, such that for any fully-observable view V' with $V' \subseteq h_Y(S)$, we have $V' \subseteq gv(S, Y)$.*

Proof. Consider the FOS $S = (\{x, y\}, \theta = (x \wedge y) \vee (\neg x \wedge \neg y), \phi = (x \wedge \neg x' \wedge y \wedge y') \vee (\neg x \wedge x' \wedge \neg y \wedge \neg y'))$. The FOS S_1 and S_2 from the proof of Lemma 5 are both views of S for $Y = \{x\}$, yet they are incomparable and there is no FOS view conforming to S w.r.t. $\subseteq$ that is greater than both of them as their union is not a view of S.   □

View Conformance Checking for Discrete Systems and Views

Problem 1. Given discrete system $S = (X, Z, \theta, \phi)$, discrete view $V = (Y, W, \theta_V, \phi_V)$, where $Y \subseteq X$ and $Z \cap W = \emptyset$, and partial order $\sqsupseteq \in \{=, \subseteq, \supseteq\}$, check whether $V \sqsupseteq h_Y(S)$.

Problem 2. Given discrete systems $S_1 = (X, Z_1, \theta_1, \phi_1)$ and $S_2 = (X, Z_2, \theta_2, \phi_2)$, where $Z_1 \cap Z_2 = \emptyset$, and partial order $\sqsupseteq \in \{=, \subseteq, \supseteq\}$, check whether $[\![S_1]\!]_o \sqsupseteq [\![S_2]\!]_o$.

Theorem 4. *Problem 1 can be reduced to Problem 2 in polynomial time. Problem 2 is in PSPACE.*

Proof. For the first part of the theorem, observe that discrete systems are closed under projection. An instance of Problem 1 can be transformed into an instance of Problem 2, simply by shifting the variables $X \setminus Y$ of S from the observable to the internal variables.

For the second part of the theorem, we limit our attention to the case $\sqsupseteq = \subseteq$, as the other two cases then follow trivially. Problem 2 can be reduced to the finite state automaton inequivalence problem, which is known to be in PSPACE [9]. As discrete systems are closed under union, we construct a system $S_\cup$, with $[\![S_\cup]\!]_o = [\![S_1]\!]_o \cup [\![S_2]\!]_o$. Then $[\![S_\cup]\!]_o = [\![S_2]\!]_o$ iff $[\![S_1]\!]_o \subseteq [\![S_2]\!]_o$. From $S_\cup$ and S_2 we can construct NFAs $M_\cup$ and M_2 that accept a sequence σ iff σ is an observable behavior of $S_\cup$ and S_2, respectively.   □

Theorem 5. *Problem 1 is in P for partial order $\sqsupseteq = \supseteq$ if the discrete view V is a FOS.*

Proof. First, notice that if $Y \subseteq X$, then $V = (Y, \theta_V, \phi_V)$ is a view of $S = (X, Z, \theta, \phi)$ if and only if it is a view of the fully-observable system $S' = (X \cup Z, \theta, \phi)$. This is because $h_Y(S) = h_Y(S')$. Thus, in the following, we will assume S to be a FOS with $S = (X, \theta, \phi)$.

Let ψ_S denote the reachable states of S. ψ_S can, e.g., be computed incrementally using BDDs. Let $Z := X \setminus Y$ and $Z' := X' \setminus Y'$. Then, $V \sqsupseteq_{h_Y} S$, if and only if the following two conditions hold, which can be effectively checked:

1. $\forall Y, Z : \theta(Y, Z) \to \theta_V(Y) \equiv \forall s : \theta(s) \to \theta_V(h_Y(s))$, and
2. $\forall Y, Z, Y', Z' : \psi_S(Y, Z) \to (\phi((Y, Z), (Y', Z')) \to \phi_V(Y, Y')) \equiv \forall s, s' : \psi_S(s) \to (\phi(s, s') \to \phi_V(h_Y(s), h_Y(s')))$.

We need to show that Conditions 1 and 2 from above hold, if and only if $V \sqsupseteq_{h_Y} S$.
Let us first show that Conditions 1 and 2 imply $V \sqsupseteq_{h_Y} S$:
We show this by induction over the length n of behaviors σ of S.
Base case: let $\sigma = s_0 \in [\![S]\!]$ be any behavior of length 1 of S. Then $\theta(s_0)$ must hold, which, by Condition 1 implies $\theta_V(h(s_0))$, which implies that $h(s_0) \in [\![V]\!]$.
Induction step: let $\sigma = s_0 s_1 \cdots s_{n-1} s_n \in [\![S]\!]$ be a sequence of length $n + 1$. As S is by definition prefix-closed, $s_0 s_1 \cdots s_{n-1}$ is also in S. By the induction hypothesis, we know that $h(s_0)h(s_1) \cdots h(s_{n-1})$ is in $[\![V]\!]$. As $\sigma \in S$, s_{n-1} is reachable, thus $\psi_S(s_{n-1})$ holds. Thus, we can apply Condition 2, and deduce from the fact that $\phi(s_{n-1}, s_n)$, that $\phi_V(h(s_{n-1}), h(s_n))$. This in turn implies that $h(s_0)h(s_1) \cdots h(s_{n-1})$ $h(s_n)$ is a behavior of V.
Now, let us show the opposite direction, i.e., that $V \sqsupseteq_{h_Y} S$ implies Conditions 1 and 2. We show this by contraposition. Assume Condition 1 does not hold. Then, there is a valuation vY of Y and a valuation vZ of Z, such that $\theta(vYvZ)$ holds (where $vYvZ$ is the valuation that agrees with vY on Y and with vZ on Z), but $\theta_V(vY)$ does not. Clearly, $h(vYvZ) = vY$. So, $vYvZ \in [\![S]\!]$, but $h(vYvZ) \notin [\![V]\!]$, which implies that $V \sqsupseteq_{h_Y} S$ does not hold. Now assume that Condition 2 does not hold. This implies that there are valuations vY, vZ and vY', vZ', such that $\psi_S(vYvZ)$ and $\phi(vYvZ, vY'vZ')$ hold, but $\phi_V(vY, vY')$ does not. As $vYvZ$ is thus reachable, there must be a behavior $s_0 \cdots (vYvZ) \in [\![S]\!]$. By $\phi(vYvZ, vY'vZ')$, we also have that $s_0 \cdots (vYvZ)(vY'vZ') \in [\![S]\!]$. Yet, because $\phi_V(vY, vY')$ does not hold, $h(s_0) \cdots h(vYvZ)h(vY'vZ') \notin [\![V]\!]$, which concludes the proof. $\qquad\square$

Theorem 6. *Problem 1 is PSPACE-hard even if the discrete view V is fully-observable for $|Y| \geq 1$ and partial orders $=, \subseteq$. Problem 1 is also PSPACE-hard for $|Y| \geq 1$ and partial order $\supseteq$ if V is not restricted to be fully-observable.*

In [13], it is shown that checking the universality of non-deterministic finite automata (NFA), having the property that all states are final, is PSPACE-hard for alphabets of size at least 2. In the technical report [17], we show how to reduce this problem to Problem 1.

View Consistency Checking for Discrete Systems and Views

Problem 3. Given partial order $\sqsupseteq \in \{=, \subseteq, \supseteq\}$ and discrete views $V_1, ..., V_n$, with $V_i = (Y_i, W_i, \theta_i, \phi_i)$ for $i = 1, ..., n$, check whether there exists discrete system $S = (X, Z, \theta, \phi)$, with $X \supseteq Y_i$ for all i, such that $V_i \sqsupseteq_{h_{Y_i}} S$ for all i.

Problem 3 asks to check whether a given number of views are consistent w.r.t. projection as abstraction function and a given partial order among $=, \subseteq, \supseteq$. Note that we can assume without loss of generality that the witness system has set of observable variables $X = \bigcup_{i=1}^{n} Y_i$, as any extra variables could be made internal.
Problem 3 is trivially solved by the "all" system $\theta = \phi = true$ for $\subseteq$ and by the "empty" system $\theta = \phi = false$ for $\supseteq$. For $=$, if we restrict the witness system to be a

FOS, then Problem 3 is trivially decidable as there are only finitely many systems with $X = \bigcup_{i=1}^{n} Y_i$. Clearly, this is not very efficient. Theorems 7-9 (which also apply to general discrete systems, non necessarily FOS) provide a non-brute-force method.

Theorem 7. *For a set of views $V_1, \ldots, V_n$, with $V_i = (Y_i, W_i, \theta_i, \phi_i)$ for all i, there always exists a computable unique greatest witness system $gw(V_1, \ldots, V_n) = (X, Z, \theta, \phi)$, with $X = \bigcup_{i=1}^{n} Y_i$, w.r.t. partial order $\supseteq$.*

Proof. First, observe that $S_i = (X, W_i, \theta_i, \phi_i)$ is the unique greatest witness system for V_i for systems with the set of variables X, i.e., $V_i \supseteq_{h_{Y_i}} S_i$ and for all $S = (X, W, \theta, \phi)$ such that $V_i \supseteq_{h_{Y_i}} S$, we have $[\![S_i]\!] \supseteq [\![S]\!]$. In fact, $V_i =_{h_{Y_i}} S_i$. Given two views V_i, V_j, the unique greatest witness system for both views is $S_{i,j} = (X, W_i \cup W_j, \theta_i \wedge \theta_j, \phi_i \wedge \phi_j)$, whose behaviors are exactly the intersection of the behaviors of S_i and S_j (see Lemma 7). Adding any behavior to $S_{i,j}$ would violate either $V_i \supseteq_{h_{Y_i}} S_{i,j}$ or $V_j \supseteq_{h_{Y_j}} S_{i,j}$ Generalizing the above, $S_\wedge = (X_\wedge = \bigcup_{i=1}^{n} Y_i, Z_\wedge = \bigcup_{i=1}^{n} W_i, \theta_\wedge = \bigwedge_{i=1}^{n} \theta_i, \phi_\wedge = \bigwedge_{i=1}^{n} \phi_i)$ is the unique greatest witness system for the set of views $V_1, \ldots, V_n$. $\square$

Theorem 8. *Consistency with respect to $=$ holds if and only if the greatest witness system $gw(V_1, \ldots, V_n)$ derived in Theorem 7 is a witness with respect to $=$.*

Theorem 9. *Problem 3 is PSPACE-complete for partial order $=$.*

Theorem 10. *There are discrete views $V_1, \ldots, V_n$, with $V_i = (Y_i, W_i, \theta_i, \phi_i)$ for all i, for which there is no unique least witness system $lw(V_1, \ldots, V_n) = (X, Z, \theta, \phi)$, with $X = \bigcup_{i=1}^{n} Y_i$, w.r.t. partial order $\subseteq$.*

Proof. Consider the following two views $V_x = (\{x\}, \theta_x = x, \phi_x = true)$ and $V_y = (\{y\}, \theta_y = y, \phi_y = true)$. We provide two witness systems S_1, S_2, both consistent with V_x, V_y, such that their intersection is not consistent with V_x and V_y, which proves that there is no unique least witness system for V_x, V_y w.r.t. $\subseteq$:

$$S_1 = (\{x, y\}, \theta_1 = x \wedge y, \phi_1 = (x \Leftrightarrow y) \wedge (x' \Leftrightarrow y'))$$
$$S_2 = (\{x, y\}, \theta_2 = x \wedge y, \phi_2 = x' \vee y')$$

In every behavior of S_1, x and y take the same value, whereas in S_2, x and y are never both *false*. In their intersection $S_\cap = (\{x, y\}, \theta_1 \wedge \theta_2, \phi_1 \wedge \phi_2)$, neither x nor y can thus ever be *false*. So $S_\cap$ is neither consistent with V_x nor with V_y. $\square$

View Reduction for Discrete Systems and Views

Problem 4. Given partial order $\sqsupseteq \in \{=, \subseteq, \supseteq\}$ and discrete views $V_1, \ldots, V_n$, with $V_i = (Y_i, W_i, \theta_i, \phi_i)$ for $i = 1, \ldots, n$, compute $reduce_i(V_1, \ldots, V_n)$ for all $i = 1, \ldots, n$.

Theorem 11. *For partial order $\supseteq$, Problem 4 is solved by the projection of the greatest witness system to the observable variables of the respective view: let $gw(V_1, \ldots, V_n) = (X, Z, \theta, \phi)$, with $X = \bigcup_{i=1}^{n} Y_i$, be the greatest witness system to the consistency of $V_1, \ldots, V_n$ w.r.t. partial order $\supseteq$. Then:*

$$reduce_i(V_1, \ldots, V_n) = (Y_i, Z \cup (X \setminus Y_i), \theta, \phi).$$

For partial order $\subseteq$, Problem 4 is often trivial. Specifically, if the sets of observable variables of all views are incomparable, then no information can be transferred from one view to another:

Theorem 12. *Let $V_1, ..., V_n$ be discrete views with $V_i = (Y_i, W_i, \theta_i, \phi_i)$. Assume $Y_i \setminus Y_j \neq \emptyset$ for all i, j. Then, assuming $\sqsupseteq$ is $\subseteq$, the following holds for all i:*

$$reduce_i(V_1, ..., V_n) = V_i.$$

6 Discussion

MVM is not a new topic, and terms such as "view" and "viewpoint" often appear in system engineering literature, including standards such as ISO 42010 [12]. Despite this fact, and the fact that MVM is a crucial concern in system design, an accepted mathematical framework for reasoning about views has so far been lacking. This is especially true for *behavioral* views, that is, views describing the dynamic behavior of the system, as opposed to its static structure. Behavioral views are the main focus of our work.

Discrete behavioral views could also be captured in a temporal logic formalism such as LTL. View consistency could then be defined as satisfiability of the conjunction $\phi_1 \wedge \cdots \wedge \phi_n$, where each ϕ_i is a view (possibly over a different set of variables). This definition is however weaker than our definition of strict consistency (w.r.t. $=$). Satisfiability of $\phi_1 \wedge \cdots \wedge \phi_n$ is equivalent to checking that the intersection of the inverse projections of views is non-empty, which, as we explained earlier, is a necessary but not sufficient condition for strict consistency.

The same fundamental difference exists between our framework and view consistency as formulated in the context of interface theories, where a special type of interface conjunction is used [11] (called "fusion" in [2] and "shared refinement" in [7,18]).

Behavioral abstractions/views are also the topic of [15,16]. Their framework is close to ours, in the sense that it also uses abstraction functions to map behaviors between different levels of abstraction (or between systems and views). The focus of both [15,16] is to ease the verification task in a heterogeneous (e.g., both discrete and continuous) setting. Our main focus is checking view consistency. The notion of "heterogeneous consistency" [15] is different from our notion of view consistency. The notion of "conjunctive implication" [15] is also different, as views which have an empty intersection of their inverse projections trivially satisfy conjunctive implication, yet these views can be inconsistent in our framework. Problems such as view consistency checking are not considered in [15,16].

Consistency between architectural views, which capture structural but not behavioral aspects of a system, is studied in [3]. Consistency problems are also studied in [8] using a static, logic-based framework. Procedures such as join and normalization in relational databases also relate to notions of static consistency.

An extensive survey of different approaches for multi-view modeling can be found in [14]. [14] also gives a partial and preliminary formalization, but does not discuss algorithmic problems. [4] discusses an informal methodology for selecting formalisms, languages, and tools based on viewpoint considerations. A survey of trends in multi-paradigm modeling can be found in [1]. Trends and visions in multi-view modeling are also the topic of [19]. The latter paper also discusses pragmatics of MVM in the context of the Ptolemy tool. However formal aspects of MVM and algorithmic problems such as checking consistency are not discussed.

Implicitly, MVM is supported by multi-modeling languages such as UML, SysML, and AADL. For instance, AADL defines separate "behavior and error annexes" and having separate models in these annexes can result in inconsistencies. But capabilities such as conformance or consistency checking are typically not provided by the tools implementing these standards. Architectural consistency notions in a UML-like framework are studied in [6].

This work is a first step toward a formal and algorithm-supported framework for multi-view modeling. A natural direction for future work is to study algorithmic problems such as consistency checking in a heterogeneous setting. Although the framework of Section 3 is general enough to capture heterogeneity, in this paper we restricted our attention to algorithmic MVM problems for discrete systems, as we feel that we first need a solid understanding of MVM in this simpler case.

Other directions for future work including investigating other types of abstraction functions, generalizing the methods developed in Section 5, e.g., so that $\subseteq, =, \supseteq$ can be arbitrarily combined, and studying algorithmic problems related to orthogonality.

References

1. Amaral, V., Hardebolle, C., Karsai, G., Lengyel, L., Levendovszky, T.: Recent advances in multi-paradigm modeling. In: Ghosh, S. (ed.) MODELS 2009. LNCS, vol. 6002, pp. 220–224. Springer, Heidelberg (2010)
2. Benveniste, A., Caillaud, B., Ferrari, A., Mangeruca, L., Passerone, R., Sofronis, C.: Multiple viewpoint contract-based specification and design. In: de Boer, F.S., Bonsangue, M.M., Graf, S., de Roever, W.-P. (eds.) FMCO 2007. LNCS, vol. 5382, pp. 200–225. Springer, Heidelberg (2008)
3. Bhave, A., Krogh, B.H., Garlan, D., Schmerl, B.: View consistency in architectures for cyber-physical systems. In: ICCPS 2011, pp. 151–160 (2011)
4. Broman, D., Lee, E.A., Tripakis, S., Törngren, M.: Viewpoints, Formalisms, Languages, and Tools for Cyber-Physical Systems. In: MPM (2012)
5. Cousot, P., Cousot, R.: Systematic design of program analysis frameworks. In: POPL, pp. 269–282. ACM (1979)
6. Dijkman, R.M.: Consistency in Multi-Viewpoint Architectural Design. PhD thesis, University of Twente (2006)
7. Doyen, L., Henzinger, T., Jobstmann, B., Petrov, T.: Interface theories with component reuse. In: EMSOFT, pp. 79–88 (2008)
8. Finkelstein, A., Gabbay, D., Hunter, A., Kramer, J., Nuseibeh, B.: Inconsistency handling in multiperspective specifications. IEEE TSE 20(8), 569–578 (1994)
9. Garey, M.R., Johnson, D.S.: Computers and Intractability: A Guide to the Theory of NP-Completeness. W. H. Freeman (1979)
10. Granger, P.: Improving the results of static analyses programs by local decreasing iteration. In: Shyamasundar, R.K. (ed.) FSTTCS 1992. LNCS, vol. 652, pp. 68–79. Springer, Heidelberg (1992)
11. Henzinger, T.A., Ničković, D.: Independent implementability of viewpoints. In: Calinescu, R., Garlan, D. (eds.) Monterey Workshop 2012. LNCS, vol. 7539, pp. 380–395. Springer, Heidelberg (2012)

12. ISO/IEC/IEEE 42010:2011. Systems and software engineering - Architecture description, the latest edition of the original IEEE Std 1471:2000, Recommended Practice for Architectural Description of Software-intensive Systems. IEEE and ISO (2011)

13. Kao, J.-Y., Rampersad, N., Shallit, J.: On NFAs where all states are final, initial, or both. Theoretical Computer Science 410(47-49), 5010–5021 (2009)

14. Persson, M., Törngren, M., et al.: A Characterization of Integrated Multi-View Modeling for Embedded Systems. In: EMSOFT (2013)

15. Rajhans, A., Krogh, B.H.: Heterogeneous verification of cyber-physical systems using behavior relations. In: HSCC 2012, pp. 35–44. ACM (2012)

16. Rajhans, A., Krogh, B.H.: Compositional heterogeneous abstraction. In: HSCC 2013, pp. 253–262. ACM (2013)

17. Reineke, J., Tripakis, S.: Basic problems in multi-view modeling. Technical Report UCB/EECS-2014-3, EECS Department, University of California, Berkeley (January 2014)

18. Tripakis, S., Lickly, B., Henzinger, T.A., Lee, E.A.: A theory of synchronous relational interfaces. ACM Trans. on Progr. Lang. and Sys. (TOPLAS) 33(4) (July 2011)

19. von Hanxleden, R., Lee, E.A., Motika, C., Fuhrmann, H.: Multi-view modeling and pragmatics in 2020. In: Calinescu, R., Garlan, D. (eds.) Monterey Workshop 2012. LNCS, vol. 7539, pp. 209–223. Springer, Heidelberg (2012)

GPUexplore: Many-Core On-the-Fly State Space Exploration Using GPUs

Anton Wijs* and Dragan Bošnački

Eindhoven University of Technology, The Netherlands

Abstract In recent years, General Purpose Graphics Processors (GPUs) have been successfully applied in multiple application domains to drastically speed up computations. Model checking is an automatic method to formally verify the correctness of a system specification. Such specifications can be viewed as implicit descriptions of a large directed graph or state space, and for most model checking operations, this graph must be analysed. Constructing it, or on-the-fly exploring it, however, is computationally intensive, so it makes sense to try to implement this for GPUs. In this paper, we explain the limitations involved, and how to overcome these. We discuss the possible approaches involving related work, and propose an alternative, using a new hash table approach for GPUs. Experimental results with our prototype implementations show significant speed-ups compared to the established sequential counterparts.

1 Introduction

General Purpose Graphics Processing Units (GPUs) are being applied successfully in many areas of research to speed up computations. Model checking [1] is an automatic technique to verify that a given specification of a complex, safety-critical (usually embedded) system meets a particular functional property. It involves very time and memory demanding computations. Many computations rely on *on-the-fly state space exploration*. This incorporates interpreting the specification, resulting in building a graph, or state space, describing all its potential behaviour. Hence, the state space is not explicitly given, but implicitly, through the specification. The state space size is not known a priori.

GPUs have been successfully applied to perform computations for probabilistic model checking, when the state space is given a priori [2–4]. However, no attempts as of yet have been made to perform the exploration itself entirely using GPUs, due to it not naturally fitting the data parallel approach of GPUs, but in this paper, we propose a way to do so. Even though current GPUs have a limited amount of memory, we believe it is relevant to investigate the possibilities of GPU state space exploration, if only to be prepared for future hardware

---

* This work was sponsored by the NWO Exacte Wetenschappen, EW (NWO Physical Sciences Division) for the use of supercomputer facilities, with financial support from the Nederlandse Organisatie voor Wetenschappelijk Onderzoek (Netherlands Organisation for Scientific Research, NWO).

E. Ábrahám and K. Havelund (Eds.): TACAS 2014, LNCS 8413, pp. 233–247, 2014.
© Springer-Verlag Berlin Heidelberg 2014

developments (for example, GPUs are already being integrated in CPUs). We also believe that the results reported in this paper can be relevant for solving other on-the-fly graph problems. In this paper, we describe several options to implement basic state space exploration, i.e. reachability analysis, for explicit-state model checking on GPUs. We focus on CUDA-enabled GPUs of NVIDIA, but the options can also be implemented using other interfaces. We experimentally compare these options, and draw conclusions. Where relevant, we use techniques from related work, but practically all related implementations are focussed on explicit graph searching, in which the explicit graph is given, as opposed to on-the-fly constructing the graph. The structure of the paper is as follows: in Section 2, the required background information is given. Then, Section 3 contains the description of several implementations using different extensions. In Section 4, experimental results are shown, and finally, Section 5 contains conclusions and discusses possible future work.

2   Background and Related Work

2.1   State Space Exploration

The first question is how a specification should be represented. Most descriptions, unfortunately, are not very suitable for our purpose, since they require the dynamic construction of a database of data terms during the exploration. GPUs are particularly unsuitable for dynamic memory allocation. We choose to use a slightly modified version of the *networks of LTSs* model [5]. In such a network, the possible behaviour of each process or component of the concurrent system design is represented by a *process* LTS, or *Labelled Transition System*. An LTS is a directed graph in which the vertices represent states of a process, and the edges represent transitions between states. Moreover, each edge has a label indicating the event that is fired by the process. Finally, an LTS has an initial state s_I. A network of LTSs is able to capture the semantics of specifications with *finite-state* processes at a level where all data has been abstracted away and only states remain. It is used in particular in the CADP verification toolbox [6]. Infinite-state processes are out of the scope here, and are considered future work.

In the remainder of this paper, we use the following notations: a network contains a vector Π of n process LTSs, with $n \in \mathbb{N}$. Given an integer $n > 0$, $1..n$ is the set of integers ranging from 1 to n. A vector $\overline{v}$ of size n contains n elements indexed by $1..n$. For $i \in 1..n$, $\overline{v}[i]$ denotes element i in $\overline{v}$, hence $\Pi[i]$ refers to the ith LTS.

Besides a finite number of LTSs, a network also contains a finite set $\mathcal{V}$ of *synchronisation rules*, describing how behaviour of different processes should synchronise. Through this mechanism, it is possible to model synchronous communication between processes. Each rule $\langle \overline{t}, \alpha \rangle$ consists of a vector $\overline{t}$ of size n, describing the process events it is applicable on, and a result α, i.e. the system event resulting from a successful synchronisation. As an example, consider the first two LTSs from the left in Figure 1, together defining a network with $n = 2$

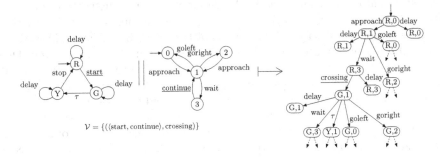

Fig. 1. Exploring the state space of a traffic light specification

of a simple traffic light system specification, where process 0 represents the behaviour of a traffic light (the states representing the colours of the light) and process 1 represents a pedestrian. We also have $\mathcal{V} = \{(\langle start, continue \rangle, crossing)\}$, meaning that there is only a single synchronisation rule, expressing that the *start* event of process 0 can only be fired if event *continue* of process 1 is fired at the same time, resulting in the event *crossing* being fired by the system as a whole.

In general, synchronisation rules are not required to involve all processes; in order to express that a rule is not applicable on a process $i \in 1..n$, we use a dummy value $\bullet$ indicating this, and define $\bar{t}[i] = \bullet$.

State space exploration now commences as follows: first, the two initial states of the processes (indicated by an incoming transition without a source state) are combined into a system state vector $\bar{s} = \langle R, 0 \rangle$. In general, given a vector $\bar{s}$, the corresponding state of $\Pi[i]$, with $i \in 1..n$, is $\bar{s}[i]$. The set of outgoing transitions (and their corresponding target states or successors of $\bar{s}$) can now be determined using two checks for each transition $\bar{s}[i] \xrightarrow{a} p_i$, with p_i a state of process i:

1. $\neg \exists \langle \bar{t}, \alpha \rangle \in \mathcal{V}.\bar{t}[i] = a \implies \bar{s} \xrightarrow{a} \bar{s}'$ with $\bar{s}'[i] = p_i \wedge \forall j \in 1..n \setminus \{i\}.\bar{s}'[j] = \bar{s}[j]$

2. $\forall \langle \bar{t}, \alpha \rangle \in \mathcal{V}.\bar{t}[i] = a \wedge (\forall j \in 1..n \setminus \{i\}.\bar{t}[j] \neq \bullet \implies \bar{s}[j] \xrightarrow{\bar{t}[j]} p_j) \implies \bar{s} \xrightarrow{\alpha} \bar{s}'$
   with $\forall j \in 1..n.(\bar{t}[j] = \bullet \wedge \bar{s}'[j] = \bar{s}[j]) \vee (\bar{t}[j] \neq \bullet \wedge \bar{s}'[j] = p_j)$

The first check is applicable for all *independent* transitions, i.e. transitions on which no rule is applicable, hence they can be fired individually, and therefore directly 'lifted' to the system level. The second check involves applying synchronisation rules. In Figure 1, part of the system state space obtained by applying the defined checks on the traffic network is displayed on the right.

2.2 GPU Programming

NVIDIA GPUs can be programmed using the CUDA interface, which extends the C and FORTRAN programming languages. These GPUs contain tens of streaming multiprocessors (SM) (see Figure 2, with N the number of SMs), each containing a fixed number of streaming processors (SP), e.g. 192 for the Kepler K20 GPU, and fast on-chip *shared memory*. Each SM employs single instruction, multiple data (SIMD) techniques, allowing for data parallelisation. A single instruction stream is performed by a fixed size group of threads called a *warp*. Threads in a warp share a program counter, hence perform instructions in lock-step. Due to this, *branch divergence* can occur within a warp, which should be avoided: for instance, consider the if-then-else construct **if (C) then A else B**. If a warp needs to execute this, and for at least one thread **C** holds, then *all* threads must step through **A**. It is therefore possible that the threads must step together through both **A** and **B**, thereby decreasing performance. The size of a warp is fixed and depends on the GPU type, usually it is 32, we refer to it as *WarpSize*. A *block* of threads is a larger group assigned to a single SM. The threads in a block can use the shared memory to communicate with each other. An SM, however, can handle many blocks in parallel. Instructions to be performed by GPU threads can be defined in a function called a *kernel*. When launching a kernel, one can specify how many thread blocks should execute it, and how many threads each block contains (usually a power of two). Each SM then schedules all the threads of its assigned blocks up to the warp level. Data parallelisation can be achieved by using the predefined keywords *BlockId* and *ThreadId*, referring to ID of the block a thread resides in, and the ID of a thread within its block, respectively. Besides that, we refer with *WarpNr* to the global ID of a warp, and with *WarpTId* to the ID of a thread within its warp. These can be computed as follows: $WarpNr = ThreadId/WarpSize$ and $WarpTId = ThreadId \% WarpSize$.

Most of the data used by a GPU application resides in *global memory* or device memory. It embodies the interface between the host (CPU) and the kernel (GPU). Depending on the GPU type, its size is typically between 1 and 6 GB. It has a high bandwidth, but also a high latency, therefore memory caches are used. The cache line of most current NVIDIA GPU L1 and L2 caches is 128 Bytes, which directly corresponds with each thread in a warp fetching a 32-bit integer. If memory accesses in a kernel can be coalesced within each warp, efficient fetching can be

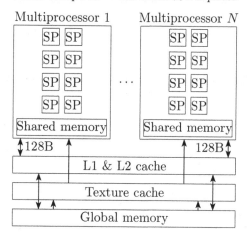

Fig. 2. Hardware model of CUDA GPUs

achieved, since then, the threads in a warp perform a single fetch together, nicely filling one cache line, instead of different fetches, which would be serialised by the GPU, thereby losing many clock-cycles. This plays an important role in the hash table implementation we propose.

Finally, read-only data structures in global memory can be declared as *textures*, by which they are connected to a *texture cache*. This may be beneficial if access to the data structure is expected to be random, since the cache may help in avoiding some global memory accesses.

2.3 Sparse Graph Search on GPUs

In general, the most suitable search strategy for parallelisation is *Breadth-First Search* (BFS), since each search level is a set of vertices that can be distributed over multiple workers. Two operations dominate in BFS: *neighbour gathering*, i.e. obtaining the list of vertices reachable from a given vertex via one edge, and *status lookup*, i.e. determining whether a vertex has already been visited before. There exist many parallelisations of BFS; here, we will focus on GPU versions. Concerning model checking, [7] describes the only other GPU on-line exploration we found, but it uses both the CPU and GPU, restricting the GPU to neighbour gathering, and it uses bitstate hashing, hence it is not guaranteed to be exhaustive. In [8], explicit state spaces are analysed.

The vast majority of GPU BFS implementations are quadratic parallelisations, e.g. [9, 10]. To mitigate the dependency of memory accesses on the graph structure, each vertex is considered in each iteration, yielding a complexity of $\mathcal{O}(|V|^2 + |E|)$, with V the set of vertices and E the set of edges. In [11], entire warps are used to obtain the neighbours of a vertex.

There are only a few linear parallelisations in the literature: in [12], a hierarchical scheme is described using serial neighbour gathering and multiple queues to avoid high contention on a single queue. In [13], an approach using prefix sum is suggested, and a thorough analysis is made to determine how gatherings and lookups need to be placed in kernels for maximum performance.

All these approaches are, however, not directly suitable for on-the-fly exploration. First of all, they implement status lookups by maintaining an array, but in on-the-fly exploration, the required size of such an array is not known a priori. Second of all, they focus on using an adjacency matrix, but for on-the-fly exploration, this is not available, and the memory access patterns are likely to be very different.

Related to the first objection, the use of a hash table seems unavoidable. Not many GPU hash table implementations have been reported, but the ones in [14, 15] are notable. They are both based on *Cuckoo-hashing* [16]. In Cuckoo hashing, collisions are resolved by shuffling the elements along to new locations using multiple hash functions. Whenever an element must be inserted, and hash function h_1 refers it to a location l already populated by another element, then the latter element is replaced using the next hash function for that element, i.e. if it was placed in l using hash function h_i, then function $h_{i+1} \bmod k_c$, with k_c the number of hash functions, is used. In [15], it is suggested to set $k_c = 4$.

Finally, in [14, 15], a comparison is made to radix sorting, in particular of [17]. On a GPU, sorting can achieve high throughput, due to the regular access patterns, making list insertion and sorting faster than hash table insertion. Lookups, however, are slower than hash table lookups if one uses binary searches, as is done in [14, 15]. An alternative is to use B-trees for storing elements, improving

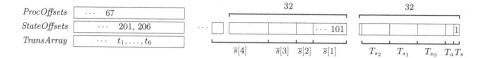

Fig. 3. Encodings of a network, a state vector and a transition entry

memory access patterns by grouping the elements in warp-segments.[1] Although we have chosen to use a hash table approach (for on-the-fly exploration, we experience that the sorting approach is overly complicated, requiring many additional steps), we will use this idea of warp-segments for our hash table.

3   GPU Parallelisation

Alg. 1 provides a high-level view of state space exploration. As in BFS, one can clearly identify the two main operations, namely *successor generation* (line 4), analogous to neighbour gathering, and *duplicate detection* (line 5), analogous to status lookup. Finally, in lines 6-7, states are added to the work sets, *Visited* being the set of visited states and *Open* being the set of states yet to be explored (usually implemented as a queue). In the next subsections, we will discuss our approach to implementing these operations.

3.1   Data Encoding

As mentioned before, memory access patterns are usually the main cause for performance loss in GPU graph traversal. The first step to minimise this effect is to choose appropriate encodings of the data. Figure 3 presents on the left how we encode a network into three 32-bit

---

Algorithm 1. State space exploration

Require: network $\langle \Pi, \mathcal{V} \rangle$, initial state $\overline{s_I}$
    $Open, Visited \leftarrow \{\overline{s_I}\}$
2: **while** $Open \neq \emptyset$ **do**
    $\overline{s} \leftarrow Open; Open \leftarrow Open \setminus \overline{s}$
4:    **for all** $\overline{s}' \in \mathbf{constructSystemSuccs}(\overline{s})$ **do**
      if $\overline{s}' \notin Visited$ **then**
6:      $Visited \leftarrow Visited \cup \{\overline{s}'\}$
      $Open \leftarrow Open \cup \{\overline{s}'\}$

---

integer arrays. The first, called *ProcOffsets*, contains the start offset for each of the $\Pi[i]$ in the second array. The second array, *StateOffsets*, contains the offsets for the source states in the third array. Finally, the third array, *TransArray*, actually contains encodings of the outgoing transitions of each state. As an example, let us say we are interested in the outgoing transitions of state 5 of process LTS 8, in some given network. First, we look at position 8 in *ProcOffsets*, and find that the states of that process are listed starting from position 67. Then, we look at position 67+5 in *StateOffsets*, and we find that the outgoing transitions of state 5 are listed starting at position 201 in *TransArray*. Moreover, at position 67+6, we find the end of that list. Using these positions, we can iterate over the outgoing transitions in *TransArray*.

---

[1] See http://www.moderngpu.com (visited 18/4/2013).

One can imagine that these structures are practically going to be accessed randomly when exploring. However, since this data is never updated, we can store the arrays as textures, thereby using the texture caches to improve access.

Besides this, we must also encode the transition entries themselves. This is shown on the right of Figure 3. Each entry fills a 32-bit integer as much as possible. It contains the following information: the lowest bit (T_s) indicates whether or not the transition depends on a synchronisation rule. The next $\log_2(c_a)$ number of bits, with c_a the number of different labels in the entire network, encodes the transition label (T_a). We encode the labels, which are basically strings, by integer values, sorting the labels occurring in a network alphabetically. After that, each $\log_2(c_s)$ bits, with c_s the number of states in the process LTS owning this transition, encodes one of the target states. If there is non-determinism w.r.t. label T_a from the source state, multiple target states will be listed, possibly continuing in subsequent transition entries.

In the middle of Figure 3, the encoding of state vectors is shown. These are simply concatenations of encodings of process LTS states. Depending on the number of bits needed per LTS state, which in turn depends on the number of states in the LTSs, a fixed number of 32-bit integers is required per vector.

Finally, the synchronisation rules need to be encoded. To simplify this, we rewrite networks such that we only have rules involving a single label, e.g. $(\langle a, a \rangle, a)$. In practice, this can usually be done without changing the meaning. For the traffic light system, we could rewrite *start* and *continue* to *crossing*. It allows encoding the rules as bit sequences of size n, where for each process LTS, 1 indicates that the process should participate, and 0 that it should not participate in synchronisation. Two integer arrays then suffice, one containing these encodings, the other containing the offsets for all the labels.

3.2 Successor Generation

At the start of a search iteration, each block fetches a tile of new state vectors from the global memory. How this is done is explained at the end of Section 3.3. The tile size depends on the block size *BlockSize*.

On GPUs, one should realise fine-grained parallelism to obtain good speedups. Given the fact that each state vector consists of n states, and the outgoing transitions information needs to be fetched from physically separate parts of the memory, it is reasonable to assign n threads to each state vector to be explored. In other words, in each iteration, the tile size is at most *BlockSize*/n vectors. Assigning multiple threads per LTS for fetching, as in [11], does not lead to further speedups, since the number of transition entries to fetch is usually quite small due to the sparsity of the LTSs, as observed before by us in [4].

We group the threads into vector groups of size n to assign them to state vectors. Vector groups never cross warp boundaries, unless $n > 32$. The positive effect of this is that branch divergence can be kept to a minimum, since the threads in a vector group work on the same task. For a vector $\bar{s}$, each thread with ID i w.r.t. its vector group (the VGID) fetches the outgoing transitions of $\bar{s}[i + 1]$. Each transition entry T with $T_s = 0$ can directly be processed, and the corresponding target state vectors are stored for duplicate detection (see Section 3.3). For all transitions with $T_s = 1$, to achieve cooperation between the threads while limiting the amount of used shared memory, the threads iterate over their transitions in order of label ID (LID). To facilitate this, the entries in each segment of outgoing transitions belonging to a particular state in *TransArray* are sorted on LID before exploration starts.

Successors reached through synchronisation are constructed in iterations. In each iteration, the threads assigned to $\bar{s}$ fetch the entries with lowest LID and $T_s = 1$ from their list of outgoing transitions, and store these in a designated buffer in the shared memory. The size of this buffer can be determined before exploration as n times the maximum

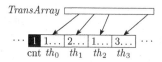

Fig. 4. Fetching transitions

number of entries with the same LID and $T_s = 1$ from any process state in the network. Then, the thread with VGID 0, i.e. the vector group leader, determines the lowest LID fetched within the vector group. Figure 4 illustrates this for a vector with $n = 4$. Threads th_0 to th_3 have fetched transitions with the lowest LIDs for their respective process states that have not yet been processed in the successor generation, and thread th_0 has determined that the next lowest LID to be processed by the vector group is 1. This value is written in the *cnt* location. Since transitions in *TransArray* are sorted per state by LID, we know that all possible transitions with LID = 1 have been placed in the vector group buffer. Next, all threads that fetched entries with the lowest LID, in the example threads th_0 and th_2, start scanning the encodings of rules in $\mathcal{V}$ applicable on that LID. We say that thread i owns rule r iff there is no $j \in 1..n$ with $j < i$ and $r[j] \neq \bullet$. If a thread encounters a rule that it owns, then it checks the buffer contents to determine whether the rule is applicable. If it is, it constructs the target state vectors and stores them for duplicate detection. In the next iteration, all entries with lowest LID are removed, the corresponding threads fetch new entries, and the vector group leader determines the next lowest LID to be processed.

3.3   Closed Set Maintenance

Local State Caching. As explained in Section 2, we choose to use a global memory hash table to store states. Research has shown that in state space exploration, due to the characteristics of most networks, there is a strong sense of locality, i.e. in each search iteration, the set of new state vectors is relatively small, and most of the already visited vectors have been visited about two iterations earlier [18, 19]. This allows effective use of block local *state caches* in shared memory. Such a cache, implemented as a linear probing hash table, can be consulted quickly, and many duplicates can already be detected, reducing the number of global memory accesses. We implemented the caches in a lockless way, apart from using a *compare-and-swap* (CAS) operation to store the first integer of a state vector.

When processing a tile, threads add successors to the cache. When finished, the block scans the cache, to check the presence of the successors in the global hash table. Thus, caches also allow threads to cooperatively perform global duplicate detection and insertion of new vectors.

Global Hash Table. For the global hash table, we initially used the Cuckoo hash table of [15]. Cuckoo hashing has the nice property that lookups are done in constant time, namely, it requires k_c memory accesses, with k_c the number of hash functions used.

However, an important aspect of Cuckoo hashing is that elements are relocated in case collisions occur. In [15], key-value pairs are stored in 64-bit integers, hence insertions can be done atomically using CAS operations. Our state vectors, though, can encompass more than 64 bits, ruling out completely atomic insertions. After having created our own extension of the hash table of [15] that allows for larger elements, we experienced in experiments that the number of explored states far exceeded the actual number of reachable states, showing that in many cases, threads falsely conclude that a vector was not present (a *false negative*). We concluded that this is mainly due to vector relocation, involving non-atomic removal and insertion, which cannot be avoided for large vectors; once a thread starts removing a vector, it is not present anymore in the hash table until the subsequent insertion has finished, and any other thread looking for the vector will not be able to locate it during that time. It should however be noted, that although the false negatives may negatively influence the performance, they do not affect the correctness of our method.

To decrease the number of false negatives, as an alternative, we choose to implement a hash table using buckets, linear probing and bounded double hashing. It is implemented using an array, each consecutive *WarpSize* 32-bit integers forming a bucket. This plays to the strength of warps: when a block of threads is performing duplicate detection, all the threads in a warp cooperate on checking the presence of a particular $\bar{s}$. The first hash function h_1, built as specified in [15], is used to find the primary bucket. A warp can fetch a bucket with one memory access, since the bucket size directly corresponds with one cache line. Subsequently, the bucket contents can be checked in parallel by the warp. This is similar to the *walk-the-line* principle of [20], instead that here, the walk is done in parallel, so we call it *warp-the-line*. Note that each bucket can contain up to *WarpSize*/c vectors, with c the number of 32-bit integers required for a vector. If the vector is not present and there is a free location, the vector is inserted. If the bucket is full, h_2 is used to jump to another bucket, and so on. This is similar to [21], instead that we do not move elements between buckets.

The pseudo-code for scanning the local cache and looking up and inserting new vectors (i.e. find-or-put) in the case that state vectors fit in a single 32-bit integer is displayed in Alg. 2. The implementation contains the more general case. The cache is declared **extern**, meaning that the size is given when launching the kernel. Once a work tile has been explored and the successors are in the cache, each thread participates in its warp to iterate over the cache contents (lines 6, 27). If a vector is new (line 8, note that empty slots are marked 'old'), insertion in the hash table will be tried up to $H \in \mathbb{N}$ times. In lines 11-13, warp-the-line is performed, each thread in a warp investigating the appropriate bucket slot. If any

Algorithm 2. Hash table find-or-put for single integer state vectors

```
    extern volatile _shared_ unsigned int cache []
 2: < process work tile and fill cache with successors >
    WarpNr ← ThreadId / WarpSize
 4: WarpTId ← ThreadId % WarpSize
    i ← WarpNr
 6: while i < |cache| do
        s̄ ← cache[i]
 8:     if isNewVector(s̄) then
            for j = 0 to H do
10:             BucketId ← h₁(s̄)
                entry ← Visited[BucketId + WarpTId]
12:             if entry = s̄ then
                    setOldVector(cache[i])
14:             s̄ ← cache[i]
                if isNewVector(s̄) then
16:                 for l = 0 to WarpSize do
                        if Visited[BucketId + l] = empty then
18:                         if WarpTId = 0 then
                                old = atomicCAS(&Visited[BucketId + l], empty, s̄)
20:                             if old = empty then
                                    setOldVector(s̄)
22:                         if ¬isNewVector(s̄) then
                                break
24:                 if ¬isNewVector(s̄) then
                        break
26:             BucketId ← BucketId + h₂(s̄)
        i ← i + BlockSize/WarpSize
```

thread sets $\bar{s}$ as old in line 13, then all threads will detect this in line 15, since $\bar{s}$ is read from shared memory. If the vector is not old, then it is attempted to insert it in the bucket (lines 15-23). This is done by the warp leader ($WarpTId = 0$, line 18), by performing a CAS. CAS takes three arguments, namely the address where the new value must be written, the expected value at the address, and the new value. It only writes the new value if the expected value is encountered, and returns the encountered value, therefore a successful write has happened if **empty** has been returned (line 20). Finally, in case of a full bucket, h_2 is used to jump to the next one (line 26).

As discussed in Section 4, we experienced good speedups and no unresolved collisions using a double hashing bound of 8, and, although still present, far fewer false negatives compared to Cuckoo hashing. Finally, it should be noted that chaining is not a suitable option on a GPU, since it requires memory allocation at runtime, and the required sizes of the chains are not known a priori.

Recall that the two important data structures are *Open* and *Visited*. Given the limited amount of global memory, and that the state space size is unknown a priori, we prefer to initially allocate as much memory as possible for *Visited*. But also the required size of *Open* is not known in advance, so how much memory should be allocated for it without potentially wasting some? We choose to combine the two in a single hash table by using the highest bit in each vector encoding to indicate whether it should still be explored or not. The drawback is that unexplored vectors are not physically close to each other in memory, but the typically large number of threads can together scan the memory relatively fast, and using one data structure drastically simplifies implementation. It has the added benefit that load-balancing is handled by the hash functions, due to the fact that the distribution over the hash table achieves distribution over the workers. A consequence is that the search will not be strictly BFS, but this is not a requirement. At the start of an iteration, each block gathers a tile of new vectors by scanning predefined parts of the hash table, determined by the block ID. In the next section, several possible improvements on scanning are discussed.

3.4   Further Extensions

On top of the basic approach, we implemented the following extensions. First of all, instead of just one, we allow a variable number of search iterations to be performed within one kernel launch. This improves duplicate detection using the caches due to them maintaining more of the search history (shared memory data is lost once a kernel terminates). Second of all, building on the first extension, we implemented a technique we call *forwarding*. When multiple iterations are performed per launch, and a block is not in its final iteration, its threads will add the unexplored successors they generated in the current iteration to their own work tile for the next one. This reduces the need for scanning for new work.

4   Implementation and Experiments

We implemented the exploration techniques in CUDA for C.[2] The implementation was tested using 25 models from different sources; some originate from the distributions of the state-of-the-art model checking toolsets CADP [6] and mCRL2 [22], and some from the BEEM database [23]. In addition, we added two we created ourselves. Here, we discuss the results for a representative subset.

Sequential experiments have been performed using EXP.OPEN [5] with GENERATOR, both part of CADP. These are highly optimised for sequential use. Those experiments were performed on a machine with an INTEL XEON E5520 2.27 GHz CPU, 1TB RAM, running Fedora 12. The GPU experiments were done on machines running CentOS Linux, with a Kepler K20 GPU, an INTEL E5-2620 2.0 GHz CPU, and 64 GB RAM. The GPU has 13 SMs, 6GB global memory (realising a hash table with about 1.3 billion slots), and 48kB (12,288 integers) shared memory per block. We chose not to compare with the GPU tool of [7], since it is a CPU-GPU hybrid, and therefore does not clearly allow to study to what extent a GPU can be used by itself for exploration. Furthermore, it uses bitstate hashing, thereby not guaranteeing exhaustiveness.

We also conducted experiments with the model checker LTSMIN [24] using the six CPU cores of the machines equipped with K20s. LTSMIN uses the most scalable multi-core exploration techniques currently available.

Table 1 displays the characteristics of the models we consider here. The first five are models taken from and inspired by those distributed with the mCRL2 toolset (in general '.1' suffixed models indicate that we extended the existing

---

[2] The implementation and experimental data is available at
http://www.win.tue.nl/~awijs/GPUexplore.

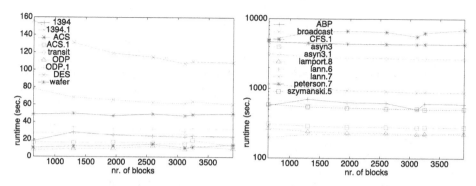

Fig. 5. Performance with varying nr. of blocks (iters=10)

models to obtain larger state spaces), the next two have been created by us, the seven after that originate from CADP, and the final five come from the BEEM database. The latter ones have first been translated manually to mCRL2, since our input, network of LTSs, uses an action-based representation of system behaviour, but BEEM models are state-based, hence this gap needs to be bridged.

Table 1. Benchmark characteristics

Model	#States	#Transitions
1394	198,692	355,338
1394.1	36,855,184	96,553,318
acs	4,764	14,760
acs.1	200,317	895,004
wafer stepper.1	4,232,299	19,028,708
ABP	235,754,220	945,684,122
broadcast	60,466,176	705,438,720
transit	3,763,192	39,925,524
CFS.1	252,101,742	1,367,483,201
asyn3	15,688,570	86,458,183
asyn3.1	190,208,728	876,008,628
ODP	91,394	641,226
ODP.1	7,699,456	31,091,554
DES	64,498,297	518,438,860
lamport.8	62,669,317	304,202,665
lann.6	144,151,629	648,779,852
lann.7	160,025,986	944,322,648
peterson.7	142,471,098	626,952,200
szymanski.5	79,518,740	922,428,824

An important question is how the exploration should be configured, i.e. how many blocks should be launched, and how many iterations should be done per kernel launch. We tested different configurations for 512 threads per block (other numbers of threads resulted in reduced performance) using double hashing with forwarding; Figure 5 shows our results launching a varying number of blocks (note the logscale of the right graph), each performing 10 iterations per kernel launch. The ideal number of blocks for the K20 seems to be 240 per SM, i.e. 3120 blocks. For GPU standards, this is small, but launching more often negatively affects performance, probably due to the heavy use of shared memory.

Figure 6 shows some of our results on varying the number of iterations per kernel launch. Here, it is less clear which value leads to the best results, either 5 or 10 seems to be the best choice. With a lower number, the more frequent hash table scanning becomes noticable, while with higher numbers, the less frequent passing along of work from SMs to each other leads to too much redundancy, i.e. re-exploration of states, causing the exploration to take more time.

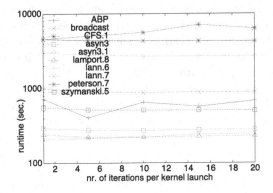

Fig. 6. Performance with varying nr. of iterations per kernel (blocks=3120)

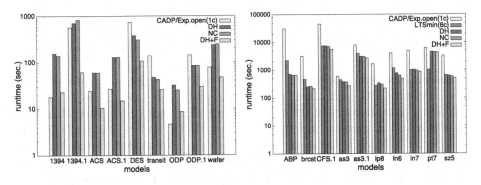

Fig. 7. Runtime results for various tools

For further experimentation, we opted for 10 iterations per launch. Figure 7 shows our runtime results (note the log scale). The GPU extension combinations used are Double Hashing (DH), DH+Forwarding (DH+F), and DH without local caches (NC). The smaller state spaces are represented in the left graph. Here, DH and NC often do not yet help to speed up exploration; the overhead involved can lead to longer runtimes compared to sequential runs. However, DH+F is more often than not faster than sequential exploration. The small differences between DH and NC, and the big ones between NC and DH+F (which is also the case in the right graph) indicate that the major contribution of the caches is forwarding, as opposed to localised duplicate detection, which was the original motivation for using them. DH+F speeds up DH on average by 42%.

It should be noted that for vectors requiring multiple integers, GPU exploration tends to perform on average 2% redundant work, i.e. some states are re-explored. In those cases, data races occur between threads writing and reading vectors, since only the first integer of a vector is written with a CAS. However, we consider these races benign, since it is important that all states are explored, not how many times, and adding additional locks hurts the performance.

The right graph in Figure 7 includes results for LTSMIN using six CPU cores. This shows that, apart from some exceptions, our GPU implementation on average has a performance similar to using about 10 cores with LTSMIN, based on the fact that LTSMIN demonstrates near-linear speedups when the number of cores is increased. In case of the exceptions, such as the ABP case, about two orders of magnitude speedup is achieved. This may seem disappointing, considering that GPUs have an enormous computation potential. However, on-the-fly exploration is not a straightforward task for a GPU, and a one order of magnitude speedup seems reasonable. Still, we believe these results are very promising, and merit further study. Existing multi-core exploration techniques, such as in [24], scale well with the number of cores. Unfortunately, we cannot test whether this holds for our GPU exploration, apart from varying the number of blocks; the number of SMs cannot be varied, and any number beyond 15 on a GPU is not yet available.

Concluding, our choices regarding data encoding and successor generation seem to be effective, and our findings regarding a new GPU hash table, local caches and forwarding can be useful for anyone interested in GPU graph exploration.

5   Conclusions

We presented an implementation of on-the-fly GPU state space exploration, proposed a novel GPU hash table, and experimentally compared different configurations and combinations of extensions. Compared to state-of-the-art sequential implementations, we measured speedups of one to two orders of magnitude. We think that GPUs are a viable option for state space exploration. Of course, more work needs to be done in order to really use GPUs to do model checking. For future work, we will experiment with changing the number of iterations per kernel launch during a search, support LTS networks with data, pursue checking safety properties, and experiment with partial searches [25, 26].

References

1. Baier, C., Katoen, J.P.: Principles of Model Checking. The MIT Press (2008)
2. Bošnački, D., Edelkamp, S., Sulewski, D., Wijs, A.: Parallel Probabilistic Model Checking on General Purpose Graphics Processors. STTT 13(1), 21–35 (2011)
3. Bošnački, D., Edelkamp, S., Sulewski, D., Wijs, A.: GPU-PRISM: An Extension of PRISM for General Purpose Graphics Processing Units. In: Joint HiBi/PDMC Workshop (HiBi/PDMC 2010), pp. 17–19. IEEE (2010)
4. Wijs, A.J., Bošnački, D.: Improving GPU Sparse Matrix-Vector Multiplication for Probabilistic Model Checking. In: Donaldson, A., Parker, D. (eds.) SPIN 2012. LNCS, vol. 7385, pp. 98–116. Springer, Heidelberg (2012)
5. Lang, F.: Exp.Open 2.0: A Flexible Tool Integrating Partial Order, Compositional, and On-The-Fly Verification Methods. In: Romijn, J.M.T., Smith, G.P., van de Pol, J. (eds.) IFM 2005. LNCS, vol. 3771, pp. 70–88. Springer, Heidelberg (2005)
6. Garavel, H., Lang, F., Mateescu, R., Serwe, W.: CADP 2010: A Toolbox for the Construction and Analysis of Distributed Processes. In: Abdulla, P.A., Leino, K.R.M. (eds.) TACAS 2011. LNCS, vol. 6605, pp. 372–387. Springer, Heidelberg (2011)

7. Edelkamp, S., Sulewski, D.: Efficient Explicit-State Model Checking on General Purpose Graphics Processors. In: van de Pol, J., Weber, M. (eds.) SPIN 2000. LNCS, vol. 6349, pp. 106–123. Springer, Heidelberg (2010)
8. Barnat, J., Bauch, P., Brim, L., Češka, M.: Designing Fast LTL Model Checking Algorithms for Many-Core GPUs. J. Par. Distr. Comput. 72, 1083–1097 (2012)
9. Deng, Y., Wang, B., Shuai, M.: Taming Irregular EDA Applications on GPUs. In: ICCAD 2009, pp. 539–546 (2009)
10. Harish, P., Narayanan, P.J.: Accelerating Large Graph Algorithms on the GPU Using CUDA. In: Aluru, S., Parashar, M., Badrinath, R., Prasanna, V.K. (eds.) HiPC 2007. LNCS, vol. 4873, pp. 197–208. Springer, Heidelberg (2007)
11. Hong, S., Kim, S., Oguntebi, T., Olukotun, K.: Accelerating CUDA Graph Algorithms At Maximum Warp. In: PPoPP 2011, pp. 267–276. ACM (2011)
12. Luo, L., Wong, M., Hwu, W.M.: An Effective GPU Implementation of Breadth-First Search. In: DAC 2010, pp. 52–55. IEEE Computer Society Press (2010)
13. Merrill, D., Garland, M., Grimshaw, A.: Scalable GPU Graph Traversal. In: PPoPP 2012, pp. 117–128. ACM (2012)
14. Alcantara, D., Sharf, A., Abbasinejad, F., Sengupta, S., Mitzenmacher, M., Owens, J., Amenta, N.: Real-time Parallel Hashing on the GPU. ACM Trans. Graph. 28(5), 154 (2009)
15. Alcantara, D., Volkov, V., Sengupta, S., Mitzenmacher, M., Owens, J., Amenta, N.: Building an Efficient Hash Table on the GPU. In: GPU Computing Gems Jade Edition. Morgan Kaufmann (2011)
16. Pagh, R.: Cuckoo Hashing. In: Meyer auf der Heide, F. (ed.) ESA 2001. LNCS, vol. 2161, pp. 121–133. Springer, Heidelberg (2001)
17. Merrill, D., Grimshaw, A.: High Performance and Scalable Radix Sorting: a Case Study of Implementing Dynamic Parallelism for GPU Computing. Parallel Processing Letters 21(2), 245–272 (2011)
18. Pelánek, R.: Properties of State Spaces and Their Applications. STTT 10(5), 443–454 (2008)
19. Mateescu, R., Wijs, A.: Hierarchical Adaptive State Space Caching Based on Level Sampling. In: Kowalewski, S., Philippou, A. (eds.) TACAS 2009. LNCS, vol. 5505, pp. 215–229. Springer, Heidelberg (2009)
20. Laarman, A., van de Pol, J., Weber, M.: Boosting Multi-core Reachability Performance with Shared Hash Tables. In: FMCAD 2010, pp. 247–255 (2010)
21. Dietzfelbinger, M., Mitzenmacher, M., Rink, M.: Cuckoo Hashing with Pages. In: Demetrescu, C., Halldórsson, M.M. (eds.) ESA 2011. LNCS, vol. 6942, pp. 615–627. Springer, Heidelberg (2011)
22. Cranen, S., Groote, J.F., Keiren, J.J.A., Stappers, F.P.M., de Vink, E.P., Wesselink, W., Willemse, T.A.C.: An overview of the mCRL2 Toolset and Its Recent Advances. In: Piterman, N., Smolka, S.A. (eds.) TACAS 2013. LNCS, vol. 7795, pp. 199–213. Springer, Heidelberg (2013)
23. Pelánek, R.: BEEM: Benchmarks for Explicit Model Checkers. In: Bošnački, D., Edelkamp, S. (eds.) SPIN 2007. LNCS, vol. 4595, pp. 263–267. Springer, Heidelberg (2007)
24. Laarman, A., van de Pol, J., Weber, M.: Multi-Core LTSMIN: Marrying Modularity and Scalability. In: Bobaru, M., Havelund, K., Holzmann, G.J., Joshi, R. (eds.) NFM 2011. LNCS, vol. 6617, pp. 506–511. Springer, Heidelberg (2011)
25. Torabi Dashti, M., Wijs, A.J.: Pruning State Spaces with Extended Beam Search. In: Namjoshi, K.S., Yoneda, T., Higashino, T., Okamura, Y. (eds.) ATVA 2007. LNCS, vol. 4762, pp. 543–552. Springer, Heidelberg (2007)
26. Wijs, A.: What To Do Next?: Analysing and Optimising System Behaviour in Time. PhD thesis, VU University Amsterdam (2007)

Forward Reachability Computation for Autonomous Max-Plus-Linear Systems[*]

Dieky Adzkiya[1], Bart De Schutter[1], and Alessandro Abate[2,1]

[1] Delft Center for Systems and Control
TU Delft – Delft University of Technology, The Netherlands
{d.adzkiya,b.deschutter,a.abate}@tudelft.nl
[2] Department of Computer Science
University of Oxford, United Kingdom
alessandro.abate@cs.ox.ac.uk

Abstract. This work discusses the computation of forward reachability for autonomous (that is, deterministic) Max-Plus-Linear (MPL) systems, a class of continuous-space discrete-event models that are relevant for applications dealing with synchronization and scheduling. Given an MPL model and a set of initial states, we characterize and compute its "reach tube," namely the sequential collection of the sets of reachable states (these sets are regarded step-wise as "reach sets"). We show that the exact computation of the reach sets can be quickly and compactly performed by manipulations of difference-bound matrices, and derive explicit worst-case bounds for the complexity of these operations. The concepts and techniques are implemented within the toolbox VeriSiMPL, and are practically elucidated by a running example. We further display the computational performance of the approach by two concluding numerical benchmarks: the technique comfortably handles reachability computations over twenty-dimensional MPL models (i.e., models with twenty continuous variables), and it clearly outperforms an alternative state-of-the-art approach in the literature.

1 Introduction

Reachability analysis is a fundamental problem in the areas of formal methods and of systems theory. It is concerned with assessing whether a certain set of states of a system is attainable from a given set of initial conditions. The problem is particularly interesting and compelling over models with continuous components – either in time or in the (state) space. For the first class of models, reachability has been widely investigated over discrete-space systems, such as timed automata [1,2], or (timed continuous) Petri nets [3], or hybrid automata [4]. On the other hand, much research has been done to enhance and scale the

---

[*] This work has been supported by the European Commission STREP project MoVeS 257005, by the European Commission Marie Curie grant MANTRAS 249295, by the European Commission IAPP project AMBI 324432, by the European Commission NoE Hycon2 257462, and by the NWO VENI grant 016.103.020.

E. Ábrahám and K. Havelund (Eds.): TACAS 2014, LNCS 8413, pp. 248–262, 2014.
© Springer-Verlag Berlin Heidelberg 2014

reachability analysis of continuous-space models. Among the many approaches for deterministic dynamical systems, we report here the use of face lifting [5], the computation of flow-pipes via polyhedral approximations [6,7], the formulation as solution of Hamilton-Jacobi equations [8] (related to the study of forward and backward reachability [9]), the use of ellipsoidal techniques [10,11], differential inclusions [12], support functions [13], and Taylor models [14].

Max-Plus-Linear (MPL) models are discrete-event systems [15] with continuous variables that express the timing of the underlying sequential events. Autonomous MPL models are characterized by deterministic dynamics. MPL models are employed to describe the timing synchronization between interleaved processes, and as such are widely employed in the analysis and scheduling of infrastructure networks, such as communication and railway systems [16] and production and manufacturing lines [17]. They are related to a subclass of timed Petri nets, namely timed-event graphs [15], however not directly to time Petri nets [18] nor to timed automata [1]. MPL models are classically analyzed over properties such as transient and periodic regimes [15]. They can be simulated (though not verified) via the max-plus toolbox Scilab [19].

Reachability analysis of MPL systems from a *single* initial condition has been investigated in [20,21] by the computation of the reachability matrix (as for discrete-time linear dynamical systems). It has been shown in [22, Sect. 4.13] that the reachability problem for autonomous MPL systems with a single initial condition is decidable – this result however does not hold for a general, uncountable set of initial conditions. Under the limiting assumption that the set of initial conditions is expressed as a max-plus polyhedron [23,24], forward reachability analysis can be performed over the max-plus algebra. In conclusion, to the best of our knowledge, there exists no computational toolbox for general reachability analysis of MPL models, nor it is possible to leverage software for related timed-event graphs or timed Petri nets. As an alternative, reachability computation for MPL models can be studied using the Multi-Parametric Toolbox (MPT) [25] (cf. Section 4).

In this work, we extend the state-of-the-art results for forward reachability analysis of MPL models by considering an arbitrary (possibly uncountable) set of initial conditions, and present a new computational approach to forward reachability analysis of MPL models. We first alternatively characterize MPL dynamics by Piece-wise Affine (PWA) models, and show that the dynamics can be fully represented by Difference-Bound Matrices (DBM) [26, Sect. 4.1], which are structures that are quite simple to manipulate. We further claim that DBM are closed over PWA dynamics, which leads to being able to map DBM-sets through MPL models. We then characterize and compute, given a set of initial states, its "reach tube," namely the sequential collection of the sets of reachable states (aggregated step-wise as "reach sets"). With an emphasis on computational and implementation aspects, we provide a quantification of the worst-case complexity of the algorithms discussed throughout the work. Notice that although DBM are a structure that has been used in reachability analysis of timed automata, this does not imply that we can employ related techniques for reachability analysis of MPL systems, since the two modeling frameworks are not equivalent.

While this new approach reduces reachability analysis of MPL models to a computationally feasible task, the foundations of this contribution go beyond mere manipulations of DBM: the technique is inspired by the recent work in [27], which has developed an approach to the analysis of MPL models based on finite-state abstractions. In particular, the procedure for forward reachability computation on MPL models discussed in this work is implemented in the VeriSiMPL ("very simple") software toolbox [28], which is freely available. While the general goals of VeriSiMPL go beyond the topics of this work and are thus left to the interested reader, in this article we describe the details of the implementation of the suite for reachability analysis within this toolbox over a running example. With an additional numerical case study, we display the scalability of the tool as a function of model dimension (the number of its continuous variables): let us emphasize that related approaches for reachability analysis of discrete-time dynamical systems based on finite abstractions do not reasonably scale beyond models with a few variables [29], whereas our procedure comfortably handles models with about twenty continuous variables. In this numerical benchmark we have purposely generated the underlying dynamics randomly: this allows deriving empirical outcomes that are general and not biased towards possible structural features of a particular model. Finally, we successfully benchmark the computation of forward reachability sets against an alternative approach based on the well-developed MPT software tool [25].

2   Models and Preliminaries

2.1   Max-Plus-Linear Systems

Define $\mathbb{R}_\varepsilon$, ε and e respectively as $\mathbb{R} \cup \{\varepsilon\}$, $-\infty$ and 0. For $\alpha, \beta \in \mathbb{R}_\varepsilon$, introduce the two operations $\alpha \oplus \beta = \max\{\alpha, \beta\}$ and $\alpha \otimes \beta = \alpha + \beta$, where the element ε is considered to be absorbing w.r.t. $\otimes$ [15, Definition 3.4]. Given $\beta \in \mathbb{R}$, the max-algebraic power of $\alpha \in \mathbb{R}$ is denoted by $\alpha^{\otimes \beta}$ and corresponds to $\alpha\beta$ in the conventional algebra. The rules for the order of evaluation of the max-algebraic operators correspond to those of conventional algebra: max-algebraic power has the highest priority, and max-algebraic multiplication has a higher priority than max-algebraic addition [15, Sect. 3.1].

The basic max-algebraic operations are extended to matrices as follows. If $A, B \in \mathbb{R}_\varepsilon^{m \times n}$; $C \in \mathbb{R}_\varepsilon^{m \times p}$; $D \in \mathbb{R}_\varepsilon^{p \times n}$; and $\alpha \in \mathbb{R}_\varepsilon$, then $[\alpha \otimes A](i,j) = \alpha \otimes A(i,j)$; $[A \oplus B](i,j) = A(i,j) \oplus B(i,j)$; $[C \otimes D](i,j) = \bigoplus_{k=1}^{p} C(i,k) \otimes D(k,j)$; for $i = 1, \ldots, m$ and $j = 1, \ldots, n$. Notice the analogy between $\oplus$, $\otimes$ and $+$, $\times$ for matrix and vector operations in conventional algebra. Given $m \in \mathbb{N}$, the m-th max-algebraic power of $A \in \mathbb{R}_\varepsilon^{n \times n}$ is denoted by $A^{\otimes m}$ and corresponds to $A \otimes \cdots \otimes A$ (m times). Notice that $A^{\otimes 0}$ is an n-dimensional max-plus identity matrix, i.e. the diagonal and nondiagonal elements are e and ε, respectively. In this paper, the following notation is adopted for reasons of convenience. A vector with each component that is equal to 0 (or $-\infty$) is also denoted by e (resp., ε).

Furthermore, for practical reasons, the state space is taken to be $\mathbb{R}^n$, which also implies that the state matrix has to be row-finite (cf. Definition 1).

An autonomous (that is, deterministic) MPL model [15, Remark 2.75] is defined as:

$$x(k) = A \otimes x(k-1) , \tag{1}$$

where $A \in \mathbb{R}_\varepsilon^{n \times n}$, $x(k-1) = [x_1(k-1) \ldots x_n(k-1)]^T \in \mathbb{R}^n$ for $k \in \mathbb{N}$. The independent variable k denotes an increasing discrete-event counter, whereas the state variable x defines the (continuous) timing of the discrete events. Autonomous MPL models are characterized by deterministic dynamics. Related to the state matrix A is the notion of regular (or row-finite) matrix and that of irreducibility.

Definition 1 (Regular (Row-Finite) Matrix, [16, Sect. 1.2]) *A max-plus matrix $A \in \mathbb{R}_\varepsilon^{n \times n}$ is called regular (or row-finite) if A contains at least one element different from ε in each row.*

A matrix $A \in \mathbb{R}_\varepsilon^{n \times n}$ is irreducible if the nondiagonal elements of $\bigoplus_{k=1}^{n-1} A^{\otimes k}$ are finite (not equal to ε). If A is irreducible, there exists a unique max-plus eigenvalue $\lambda \in \mathbb{R}$ [15, Th. 3.23] and the corresponding eigenspace $E(A) = \{x \in \mathbb{R}^n : A \otimes x = \lambda \otimes x\}$ [15, Sect. 3.7.2].

Example: Consider the following autonomous MPL model from [16, Sect. 0.1], representing the scheduling of train departures from two connected stations $i = 1, 2$ ($x_i(k)$ denotes the time of the k-th departure for station i):

$$x(k) = \begin{bmatrix} 2 & 5 \\ 3 & 3 \end{bmatrix} \otimes x(k-1) , \text{ or equivalently },$$

$$\begin{bmatrix} x_1(k) \\ x_2(k) \end{bmatrix} = \begin{bmatrix} \max\{2 + x_1(k-1), 5 + x_2(k-1)\} \\ \max\{3 + x_1(k-1), 3 + x_2(k-1)\} \end{bmatrix} . \tag{2}$$

Matrix A is a row-finite matrix and irreducible since $A(1,2) \neq \varepsilon \neq A(2,1)$.   □

Proposition 1 ([16, Th. 3.9]) *Let $A \in \mathbb{R}_\varepsilon^{n \times n}$ be an irreducible matrix with max-plus eigenvalue $\lambda \in \mathbb{R}$. There exist $k_0, c \in \mathbb{N}$ such that $A^{\otimes(k+c)} = \lambda^{\otimes c} \otimes A^{\otimes k}$, for all $k \geq k_0$. The smallest k_0 and c verifying the property are defined as the length of the transient part and the cyclicity, respectively.*

Proposition 1 allows to establish the existence of a periodic behavior. Given an initial condition $x(0) \in \mathbb{R}^n$, there exists a finite $k_0(x(0))$, such that $x(k+c) = \lambda^{\otimes c} \otimes x(k)$, for all $k \geq k_0(x(0))$. Notice that we can seek the length of the transient part $k_0(x(0))$ specifically for the initial condition $x(0)$, which is in general less conservative than the global $k_0 = k_0(A)$, as in Proposition 1. Upper bounds for the length of the transient part k_0 and for its computation have been discussed in [30].

Example: In the example (2), from Proposition 1 we obtain a max-plus eigenvalue $\lambda = 4$, cyclicity $c = 2$, and a (global) length of the transient part $k_0 = 2$.

The length of the transient part specifically for $x(0) = [3,0]^T$ can be computed observing the trajectory

$$\begin{bmatrix} 3 \\ 0 \end{bmatrix}, \begin{bmatrix} 5 \\ 6 \end{bmatrix}, \begin{bmatrix} 11 \\ 9 \end{bmatrix}, \begin{bmatrix} 14 \\ 14 \end{bmatrix}, \begin{bmatrix} 19 \\ 17 \end{bmatrix}, \begin{bmatrix} 22 \\ 22 \end{bmatrix}, \begin{bmatrix} 27 \\ 25 \end{bmatrix}, \begin{bmatrix} 30 \\ 30 \end{bmatrix}, \begin{bmatrix} 35 \\ 33 \end{bmatrix}, \begin{bmatrix} 38 \\ 38 \end{bmatrix}, \dots$$

The periodic behavior occurs (as expected) after 2 event steps, i.e. $k_0([3,0]^T) = 2$, and shows a period equal to 2, namely $x(4) = 4^{\otimes 2} \otimes x(2) = 8 + x(2)$, and similarly $x(5) = 4^{\otimes 2} \otimes x(3)$. Furthermore $x(k+2) = 4^{\otimes 2} \otimes x(k)$ for $k \geq 2$.   □

2.2   Piece-Wise Affine Systems

This section discusses Piece-wise Affine (PWA) systems [31] generated by an autonomous MPL model. In the following section, PWA systems will play an important role in forward reachability analysis. PWA systems are characterized by a cover of the state space, and by affine (linear plus constant) dynamics that are active within each set of the cover.

Every autonomous MPL model characterized by a row-finite matrix $A \in \mathbb{R}_{\varepsilon}^{n \times n}$ can be expressed as a PWA system in the event domain. The affine dynamics are characterized, along with its corresponding region, by the coefficients $g = (g_1, \dots, g_n) \in \{1, \dots, n\}^n$ or, more precisely, as:

$$R_g = \bigcap_{i=1}^{n} \bigcap_{j=1}^{n} \{x \in \mathbb{R}^n : A(i, g_i) + x_{g_i} \geq A(i, j) + x_j\} \; ; \tag{3}$$

$$x_i(k) = x_{g_i}(k-1) + A(i, g_i) , \qquad 1 \leq i \leq n . \tag{4}$$

Implementation: VeriSiMPL employs a backtracking algorithm to generate the PWA system. Recall that we are looking for all coefficients $g = (g_1, \dots, g_n)$ such that R_g is not empty. In the backtracking approach, the partial coefficients are $(g_1, \dots, g_k)$ for $k = 1, \dots, n$ and the corresponding region is

$$R_{(g_1, \dots, g_k)} = \bigcap_{i=1}^{k} \bigcap_{j=1}^{n} \{x \in \mathbb{R}^n : A(i, g_i) + x_{g_i} \geq A(i, j) + x_j\} .$$

Notice that if the region associated with a partial coefficient $(g_1, \dots, g_k)$ is empty, then the regions associated with the coefficients $(g_1, \dots, g_n)$ are also empty, for all $g_{k+1}, \dots, g_n$. The set of all coefficients can be represented as a potential search tree. For a 2-dimensional MPL model, the potential search tree is given in Fig. 1. The backtracking algorithm traverses the tree recursively, starting from the root, in a depth-first order. At each node, the algorithm checks whether the corresponding region is empty: if the region is empty, the whole sub-tree rooted at the node is skipped (pruned).

The function `maxpl2pwa` is used to construct a PWA system from an autonomous MPL model. The autonomous MPL model is characterized by a row-finite state matrix (`Ampl`), whereas the PWA system is characterized by a collection of regions (`D`) and a set of affine dynamics (`A,B`). The affine dynamics that are active in the

j-th region are characterized by the j-th column of both A and B. Each column of A and the corresponding column of B contain the coefficients $[g_1, \ldots, g_n]^T$ and the constants $[A(1, g_1), \ldots, A(n, g_n)]^T$, respectively. The data structure of D will be discussed in Section 2.3.

Considering the autonomous MPL example in (2), the following script generates the PWA system:

```
>> Ampl = [2 5;3 3], [A,B,D] = maxpl2pwa(Ampl)
```

It will become clear in Section 2.3 that the nonempty regions of the PWA system produced by the script are: $R_{(1,1)} = \{x \in \mathbb{R}^2 : x_1 - x_2 \geq 3\}$, $R_{(2,1)} = \{x \in \mathbb{R}^2 : e \leq x_1 - x_2 \leq 3\}$, and $R_{(2,2)} = \{x \in \mathbb{R}^2 : x_1 - x_2 \leq e\}$. The affine dynamics corresponding to a region R_g are characterized by g, e.g. those for region $R_{(2,1)}$ are given by $x_1(k) = x_2(k-1) + 5$, $x_2(k) = x_1(k-1) + 3$. □

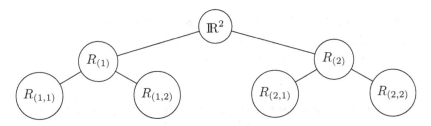

Fig. 1. Potential search tree for a 2-dimensional MPL model

2.3 Difference-Bound Matrices

This section introduces the definition of a DBM [26, Sect. 4.1] and of its canonical-form representation. DBM provide a simple and computationally advantageous representation of the MPL dynamics, and will be further used in the next section to represent the initial conditions and reach sets.

Definition 2 (Difference-Bound Matrix) *A DBM is the intersection of finitely many sets defined by $x_j - x_i \bowtie_{i,j} \alpha_{i,j}$, where $\bowtie_{i,j} \in \{<, \leq\}$, $\alpha_{i,j} \in \mathbb{R} \cup \{+\infty\}$, for $0 \leq i \neq j \leq n$ and the value of x_0 is always equal to 0.*

The special variable x_0 is used to represent bounds on a single variable: $x_i \leq \alpha$ can be written as $x_i - x_0 \leq \alpha$. A "stripe" is defined as a DBM that does not contain x_0. Definition 2 can be likewise given over the input and the corresponding augmented space.

Implementation: VeriSiMPL represents a DBM in $\mathbb{R}^n$ as a 1×2 cell: the first element is an $(n+1)$-dimensional real-valued matrix representing the upper bound α, and the second element is an $(n+1)$-dimensional Boolean matrix representing the value of $\bowtie$. More precisely, the $(i+1, j+1)$-th element represents the upper bound and the strictness of the sign of $x_j - x_i$, for $i = 0, \ldots, n$ and $j = 0, \ldots, n$ (cf. Definition 2). Furthermore, a collection of DBM is also represented as a 1×2 cell, where the corresponding matrices are stacked along the third dimension.   □

Each DBM admits an equivalent and unique canonical-form representation, which is a DBM with the tightest possible bounds [26, Sect. 4.1]. The Floyd-Warshall algorithm can be used to obtain the canonical-form representation of a DBM, with a complexity that is cubic w.r.t. its dimension. One advantage of the canonical-form representation is that it is easy to compute orthogonal projections w.r.t. a subset of its variables, which is simply performed by deleting rows and columns corresponding to the complementary variables [26, Sect. 4.1].

Implementation: The Floyd-Warshall algorithm has been implemented in the function `floyd_warshall`. Given a collection of DBM, this function generates its canonical-form representation. The following MATLAB script computes the canonical-form representation of $D = \{x \in \mathbb{R}^4 : x_1 - x_4 \leq -3, x_2 - x_1 \leq -3, x_2 - x_4 \leq -3, x_3 - x_1 \leq 2\}$:

```
>> D = cell(1,2), ind = sub2ind([5,5],[4,1,4,1]+1,[1,2,2,3]+1)
>> D{1} = Inf(5), D{1}(1:6:25) = 0, D{1}(ind) = [-3,-3,-3,2]
>> D{2} = false(5), D{2}(1:6:25) = true, D{2}(ind) = true
>> Dcf = floyd_warshall(D)
```

Let us discuss the steps in the construction of the DBM D. We first initialize D with $\mathbb{R}^4$ as `D = cell(1,2)`, `D{1} = Inf(5)`, `D{1}(1:6:25) = 0`, `D{2} = false(5)`, `D{2}(1:6:25) = true`. The variable `ind` contains the location, in linear index format, of each inequality in the matrix. We define the upper bounds and the strictness in `D{1}(ind) = [-3,-3,-3,2]` and `D{2}(ind) = true`, respectively. The output is `Dcf` $= \{x \in \mathbb{R}^4 : x_1 - x_4 \leq -3, x_2 - x_1 \leq -3, x_2 - x_4 \leq -6, x_3 - x_1 \leq 2, x_3 - x_4 \leq -1\}$. Notice that the bounds of $x_2 - x_4$ and $x_3 - x_4$ are tighter. Moreover, the orthogonal projection of D (or Dcf) w.r.t. $\{x_1, x_2\}$ is $\{x \in \mathbb{R}^2 : x_2 - x_1 \leq -3\}$.   □

The following result plays an important role in the computation of reachability for MPL models.

Proposition 2 ([27, Th. 1]) *The image of a DBM with respect to affine dynamics (in particular the PWA expression (4) generated by an MPL model) is a DBM.*

Implementation: The procedure to compute the image of a DBM in $\mathbb{R}^n$ w.r.t. the affine dynamics (4) involves: 1) computing the cross product of the DBM and $\mathbb{R}^n$; then 2) determining the DBM generated by the expression of the affine dynamics (each equation can be expressed as the difference between variables at event k and $k - 1$); 3) intersecting the DBM obtained in steps 1 and 2; 4) generating the canonical-form representation; finally 5) projecting the DBM over the variables at event k, i.e. $\{x_1(k), \ldots, x_n(k)\}$. The worst-case complexity critically depends on computing the canonical-form representation (in the fourth step) and is $\mathcal{O}(n^3)$.

The procedure has been implemented in **dbm_image**. It computes the image of a collection of DBM w.r.t. the corresponding affine dynamics. The following example computes the image of $D = \{x \in \mathbb{R}^2 : e \leq x_1 - x_2 \leq 3\}$ w.r.t. $x_1(k) = x_2(k-1) + 5$, $x_2(k) = x_1(k-1) + 3$:

```
>> D = cell(1,2), ind = sub2ind([3,3],[2,1]+1,[1,2]+1)
>> D{1} = Inf(3), D{1}(1:4:9) = 0, D{1}(ind) = [3,0]
>> D{2} = false(3), D{2}(1:4:9) = true, D{2}(ind) = true
>> A = [2;1], B =[5;3], Dim = dbm_image(A,B,D)
```

The image is $\text{Dim} = \{x \in \mathbb{R}^2 : -1 \leq x_1 - x_2 \leq 2\}$, which is a DBM.   □

The result in Proposition 2 allows computing the image of a DBM in $\mathbb{R}^n$ w.r.t. the MPL model characterized by a row-finite matrix $A \in \mathbb{R}_\varepsilon^{n \times n}$. In order to do so, we leverage the corresponding PWA system dynamics and separate the procedure in the following steps: 1) intersecting the DBM with each region of the PWA system; then 2) computing the image of nonempty intersections according to the corresponding affine dynamics (cf. Theorem 2). The worst-case complexity depends on the last step and is $\mathcal{O}(|\text{R}(A)| \cdot n^3)$, where $|\text{R}(A)|$ is the number of regions in the PWA system generated by matrix A.

Proposition 2 can be extended as follows.

Corollary 1 *The image of a union of finitely many DBM w.r.t. the PWA system generated by an MPL model is a union of finitely many DBM.*

3   Forward Reachability Analysis

The goal of forward reachability analysis is to quantify the set of possible states that can be attained under the model dynamics, from a set of initial conditions. Two main notions can be defined.

Definition 3 (Reach Set) *Given an MPL model and a nonempty set of initial positions $X_0 \subseteq \mathbb{R}^n$, the reach set X_N at the event step $N > 0$ is the set of all states $\{x(N) : x(0) \in X_0\}$ obtained via the MPL dynamics.*

Definition 4 (Reach Tube) *Given an MPL model and a nonempty set of initial positions $X_0 \subseteq \mathbb{R}^n$, the reach tube is defined by the set-valued function $k \mapsto X_k$ for any given $k > 0$ where X_k is defined.*

Unless otherwise stated, in this work we focus on *finite-horizon* reachability: in other words, we compute the reach set for a finite index N (cf. Definition 3) and the reach tube for $k = 1, \ldots, N$, where $N < \infty$ (cf. Definition 4). While the reach set can be obtained as a by-product of the (sequential) computations used to obtain the reach tube, we will argue that it can be as well calculated by a tailored procedure (one-shot).

In the computation of the quantities defined above, the set of initial conditions $X_0 \subseteq \mathbb{R}^n$ will be assumed to be a union of finitely many DBM. In the more general case of arbitrary sets, these will be over- or under-approximated by DBM. As it will become clear later, this will in general shape the reach set X_k at event step $k > 0$ as a union of finitely many DBM. For later use, we assume that X_k is a union of $|X_k|$ DBM and in particular that the set of initial conditions X_0 is a union of $|X_0|$ DBM.

3.1 Sequential Computation of the Reach Tube

This approach uses the one-step dynamics for autonomous MPL systems iteratively. In each step, we leverage the DBM representation and the PWA dynamics to compute the reach set.

Given a set of initial conditions X_0, the reach set X_k is recursively defined as the image of X_{k-1} w.r.t. the MPL dynamics as

$$X_k = \mathcal{I}(X_{k-1}) = \{A \otimes x : x \in X_{k-1}\} \ .$$

In the dynamical systems and automata literature the mapping $\mathcal{I}$ is also known as *Post* [32, Definition 2.3]. Under the assumption that X_0 is a union of finitely many DBM, by Corollary 1 it can be shown by induction that the reach set X_k is also a union of finitely many DBM, for each $k \in \mathbb{N}$.

Implementation: Given a state matrix A and a set of initial conditions X_0, the general procedure for obtaining the reach tube works as follows: first, we construct the PWA system generated by A; then, for each $k = 1, \ldots, N$, the reach set X_k is obtained by computing $\mathcal{I}(X_{k-1})$.

The worst-case complexity of the procedure (excluding that related to the generation of PWA system) can be assessed as follows. The complexity of computing $\mathcal{I}(X_{k-1})$ is $\mathcal{O}(|X_{k-1}| \cdot |\mathsf{R}(A)| \cdot n^3)$, for $k = 1, \ldots, N$. This results in an overall complexity of $\mathcal{O}(|\mathsf{R}(A)| \cdot n^3 \sum_{k=0}^{N-1} |X_k|)$. Notice that quantifying explicitly the cardinality $|X_k|$ of the DBM union at each step k is not possible in general (cf. Benchmark in Section 4).

The procedure has been implemented in `maxpl_reachtube_for`. The inputs are the PWA system (`A`, `B`, `D`), the initial states (`D0`), and the event horizon (`N`). The set of initial states `D0` is a collection of finitely many DBM and the event horizon `N` is a natural number. The output is a $1 \times (N+1)$ cell. For each $1 \leq i \leq N+1$, the i-th element contains the reach set X_{i-1}, which is a collection of finitely many DBM (cf. Section 2.3).

Let us consider the unit square as the set of initial conditions $X_0 = \{x \in \mathbb{R}^2 : 0 \leq x_1 \leq 1, 0 \leq x_2 \leq 1\}$. The following MATLAB script computes the reach tube for two steps:

```
>> Ampl = [2 5;3 3], [A,B,D] = maxpl2pwa(Ampl), N = 2
>> D0 = cell(1,2), ind = sub2ind([3,3],[1,2,0,0]+1,[0,0,1,2]+1)
>> D0{1} = Inf(3), D0{1}(1:4:9) = 0, D0{1}(ind) = [0,0,1,1]
>> D0{2} = false(3), D0{2}(1:4:9) = true, D0{2}(ind) = true
>> DON = maxpl_reachtube_for(A,B,D,D0,N)
```

The reach sets are DBM given by $X_1 = \{x \in \mathbb{R}^2 : 1 \leq x_1 - x_2 \leq 2, 5 \leq x_1 \leq 6, 3 \leq x_2 \leq 4\}$, $X_2 = \{x \in \mathbb{R}^2 : 0 \leq x_1 - x_2 \leq 1, 8 \leq x_1 \leq 9, 8 \leq x_2 \leq 9\}$, and are shown in Fig. 2 (left). $\qquad\square$

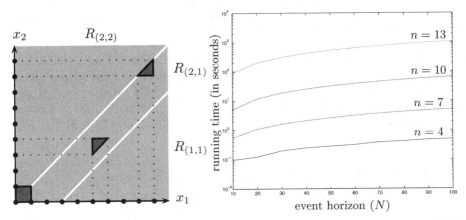

Fig. 2. (Left plot) Reach tube for autonomous MPL model over 2 event steps. (Right plot) Time needed to generate reach tube of autonomous models for different models size and event horizons, cf. Section 4.

Recall that, given a set of initial conditions X_0 and a finite event horizon $N \in \mathbb{N}$, in order to compute X_N, we have to calculate $X_1, \ldots, X_{N-1}$. If the autonomous MPL system is irreducible, we can exploit the periodic behavior (cf. Proposition 1) to simplify the computation.

Proposition 3 *Let $A \in \mathbb{R}_\varepsilon^{n \times n}$ be an irreducible matrix with max-plus eigenvalue $\lambda \in \mathbb{R}$ and cyclicity $c \in \mathbb{N}$. There exists a $k_0(X_0) = \max_{x \in X_0} k_0(x)$, such that $X_{k+c} = \lambda^{\otimes c} \otimes X_k$, for all $k \geq k_0(X_0)$.*

Proof. Recall that for each $x(0) \in \mathbb{R}^n$, there exists a $k_0(x(0))$ such that $x(k + c) = \lambda^{\otimes c} \otimes x(k)$, for all $k \geq k_0(x(0))$. Since $k_0(X_0) = \max_{x \in X_0} k_0(x)$, for each $x(0) \in X_0$, we have $x(k+c) = \lambda^{\otimes c} \otimes x(k)$, for $k \geq k_0(X_0)$. Recall from Definition 3 that $X_k = \{x(k) : x(0) \in X_0\}$, for all $k \in \mathbb{N}$. $\qquad\square$

Thus if the autonomous MPL system is irreducible, we only need to compute $X_1, \ldots, X_{k_0(X_0) \wedge N}$ in order to calculate X_N, for any $N \in \mathbb{N}$, where $k_0(X_0) \wedge N = \min\{k_0(X_0), N\}$.

If the initial condition X_0 is a stripe, the infinite-horizon reach tube can be computed in a finite time, as stated in the following theorem.

Theorem 1 *Let $A \in \mathbb{R}_\varepsilon^{n \times n}$ be an irreducible matrix with cyclicity $c \in \mathbb{N}$. If X_0 is a union of finitely many stripes, then $\bigcup_{i=0}^{k_0(X_0)+c-1} X_i = \bigcup_{i=0}^{k} X_i$, for all $k \geq k_0(X_0) + c - 1$.*

Proof. First we will show that X_k is a union of finitely many stripes for all $k \in \mathbb{N}$. By using the procedure to compute the image of a DBM w.r.t. an affine dynamics, it can be shown that the image of a stripe w.r.t. affine dynamics (generated by an MPL model) is a stripe. Following the arguments after Theorem 2, it can be shown that the image of a union of finitely many stripes w.r.t. the PWA system generated by an MPL model is a union of finitely many stripes.

Since a stripe is a collection of equivalence classes [16, Sect. 1.4], then $X_0 \otimes \alpha = X_0$, for each $\alpha \in \mathbb{R}$. From Proposition 3 and the previous observations, $X_{k+c} = X_k$ for all $k \geq k_0(X_0)$. ☐

Example: The set of initial conditions can also be described as a stripe, for example $X_0 = \{x \in \mathbb{R}^2 : -1 \leq x_1 - x_2 \leq 1\}$. The reach sets are stripes given by $X_1 = \{x \in \mathbb{R}^2 : 1 \leq x_1 - x_2 \leq 2\}$ and $X_2 = \{x \in \mathbb{R}^2 : 0 \leq x_1 - x_2 \leq 1\}$. Additionally, we obtain $X_1 = X_{2k-1}$ and $X_2 = X_{2k}$, for all $k \in \mathbb{N}$. It follows that the infinite-horizon reach tube is $\bigcup_{k=0}^{+\infty} X_k = \bigcup_{k=0}^{2} X_k = \{x \in \mathbb{R}^2 : -1 \leq x_1 - x_2 \leq 2\}$. ☐

3.2 One-Shot Computation of the Reach Set

In this section we discuss a procedure for computing the reach set for a specific event step N using a tailored (one-shot) procedure. Given a set of initial conditions X_0, we compute the reach set at event step N by using

$$X_N = (\mathcal{I} \circ \cdots \circ \mathcal{I})(A) = \mathcal{I}^N(A) = \{A^{\otimes N} \otimes x : x \in X_0\} .$$

Using Corollary 1, it can be seen that the reach set X_N is a union of finitely many DBM.

Implementation: Given a state matrix A, a set of initial conditions X_0 and a finite index N, the general procedure for obtaining X_N is: 1) computing $A^{\otimes N}$; then 2) constructing the PWA system generated by it; finally 3) computing the image of X_0 w.r.t. the obtained PWA system.

Let us quantify the total complexity of the first and third steps in the procedure. The complexity of computing N-th max-algebraic power of an $n \times n$ matrix (cf. Section 2.1) is $\mathcal{O}(\lceil \log_2(N) \rceil \cdot n^3)$. Excluding the generation of the PWA system – step 2), see above – the overall complexity of the procedure is $\mathcal{O}(\lceil \log_2(N) \rceil \cdot n^3 + |X_0| \cdot |R(A^{\otimes N})| \cdot n^3)$.

The procedure has been implemented in `maxpl_reachset_for`. The inputs are the state matrix (`Ampl`), the initial states (`D0`), and the event horizon (`N`). The set of initial states `D0` is a collection of finitely many DBM (cf. Section 2.3) and the event horizon `N` is a natural number. The output is a 1×2 cell: the first element is the set of initial states and the second one is the reach set at event step `N`. Recall that both the initial states and the reach set are a collection of finitely many DBM.

Let us consider the unit square as the set of initial conditions $X_0 = \{x \in \mathbb{R}^2 : 0 \leq x_1 \leq 1, 0 \leq x_2 \leq 1\}$. The following MATLAB script computes the reach set for two steps:

```
>> Ampl = [2 5;3 3], N = 2
>> D0 = cell(1,2), ind = sub2ind([3,3],[1,2,0,0]+1,[0,0,1,2]+1)
>> D0{1} = Inf(3), D0{1}(1:4:9) = 0, D0{1}(ind) = [0,0,1,1]
>> D0{2} = false(3), D0{2}(1:4:9) = true, D0{2}(ind) = true
>> DON = maxpl_reachset_for(Ampl,D0,N)
```

As expected, the reach set is a DBM given by $X_2 = \{x \in \mathbb{R}^2 : 0 \le x_1 - x_2 \le 1, 8 \le x_1 \le 9, 8 \le x_2 \le 9\}$.   □

Intuitively, the sequential approach involves step-wise computations, and yields correspondingly more information than the one-shot procedure as an output. The complexities of both the sequential and one-shot computations depend on the number of PWA regions corresponding to, respectively, the models related to matrix A and $A^{\otimes N}$. Thus, in order to compare the performance of both methods, we need to assess the cardinality of the PWA regions generated by $A^{\otimes k}$, for different values of k: from our experiments, it seems that the cardinality of PWA regions grows if k increases, hence the one-shot approach may not always result in drastic computational advantages. More work is needed to conclusively assess this feature.

4   Numerical Benchmark

4.1   Implementation and Setup

The technique for forward reachability computation on MPL models discussed in this work is implemented in the VeriSiMPL ("very simple") version 1.3, which is freely available at [28]. VeriSiMPL is a software tool originally developed to obtain finite abstractions of Max-Plus-Linear (MPL) models, which enables their verification against temporal specifications via a model checker. The algorithms have been implemented in MATLAB 7.13 (R2011b) and the experiments have been run on a 12-core Intel Xeon 3.47 GHz PC with 24 GB of memory.

In order to test the practical efficiency of the proposed algorithms, we compute the runtime needed to determine the reach tube of an autonomous MPL system, for event horizon $N = 10$ and an increasing dimension n of the MPL model. We also keep track of the number of regions of the PWA system generated from the MPL model. For any given n, we generate matrices A with 2 finite elements (in a max-plus sense) that are randomly placed in each row. The finite elements are randomly generated integers between 1 and 100. The set of initial conditions is selected as the unit hypercube, i.e. $\{x \in \mathbb{R}^n : 0 \le x_1 \le 1, \ldots, 0 \le x_n \le 1\}$.

Over 10 independent experiments, Table 1 reports the average time needed to generate the PWA system and to compute the reach tube, as well as the corresponding number of regions. As confirmed by Table 1, the time needed to compute the reach tube is monotonically increasing w.r.t. the dimension of the MPL model (as we commented previously this is not the case for the cardinality of reach sets, which hinges on the structure of the MPL models). For a fixed model size and dynamics, the growth of the computational time for forward reachability is linear (in the plot, logarithmic over logarithmic time scale) with the event horizon as shown in Fig. 2 (right). We have also performed reachability computations for the case of the set of initial conditions described as a stripe, which has yielded results that are analogue to those in Table 1.

Table 1. Numerical benchmark, autonomous MPL model: computation of the reach tube (average over 10 experiments)

size of MPL model	time for generation of PWA system	number of regions of PWA system	time for generation of reach tube	number of regions of X_{10}
3	0.09 [sec]	5.80	0.09 [sec]	4.20
5	0.14 [sec]	22.90	0.20 [sec]	6.10
7	0.52 [sec]	89.60	0.72 [sec]	13.40
9	2.24 [sec]	340.80	2.25 [sec]	4.10
11	10.42 [sec]	1.44×10^3	15.49 [sec]	3.20
13	46.70 [sec]	5.06×10^3	5.27 [min]	16.90
15	3.48 [min]	2.01×10^4	25.76 [min]	10.10
17	15.45 [min]	9.07×10^4	3.17 [hr]	68.70
19	67.07 [min]	3.48×10^5	7.13 [hr]	5.00

4.2 Comparison with Alternative Reachability Computations

To the best of the authors knowledge, there exist no approaches for general forward reachability computation over MPL models. Forward reachability can be alternatively assessed only leveraging the PWA characterization of the model dynamics (cf. Section 2). Forward reachability analysis of PWA models can be best computed by the Multi-Parametric Toolbox (MPT, version 2.0) [25]. However, the toolbox has some implementation requirements: the state space matrix A has to be invertible – this is in general not the case for MPL models; the reach sets X_k have to be bounded – in our case the reach sets can be unbounded, particularly when expressed as stripes; further, MPT deals only with full-dimensional polytopes – whereas the reach sets of interest may not necessarily be so; finally, MPT handles convex regions and over-approximates the reach sets X_k when necessary – our approach computes instead the reach sets exactly.

For the sake of comparison, we have constructed randomized examples (with invertible dynamics) and run both procedures in parallel, with focus on computation time rather than the actual obtained reach tubes. Randomly generating the underlying dynamics allows deriving general results that are not biased towards possible structural features of the model. MPT can handle in a reasonable time frame models with dimension up to 10: in this instance (as well as lower-dimensional ones) we have obtained that our approach performs better (cf. Table 2). Notice that this is despite MPT being implemented in the C language, whereas VeriSiMPL runs in MATLAB: this leaves quite some margin of computational improvement to our techniques.

Table 2. Time for generation of the reach tube of 10-dimensional autonomous MPL model for different event horizons (average over 10 experiments)

event horizon	20	40	60	80	100
VeriSiMPL	11.02 [sec]	17.94 [sec]	37.40 [sec]	51.21 [sec]	64.59 [sec]
MPT	47.61 [min]	1.19 [hr]	2.32 [hr]	3.03 [hr]	3.73 [hr]

5   Conclusions and Future Work

This work has discussed the computation of forward reachability analysis of Max-Plus-Linear models by fast manipulations of DBM through PWA dynamics.

Computationally, we are interested in further optimizing the software for reachability computations, by leveraging symbolic techniques based on the use of decision diagrams and by developing an implementation in the C language. We are presently exploring a comparison of the proposed approach with Flow* [14].

We plan to investigate *backward* reachability, as well as reachability of *non-autonomous* models, which embed non-determinism in the form of a control input, by tailoring or extending the techniques discussed in this work.

References

1. Alur, R., Dill, D.: A theory of timed automata. Theoretical Computer Science 126(2), 183–235 (1994)
2. Behrmann, G., David, A., Larsen, K.G.: A tutorial on uppaal. In: Bernardo, M., Corradini, F. (eds.) SFM-RT 2004. LNCS, vol. 3185, pp. 200–236. Springer, Heidelberg (2004)
3. Kloetzer, M., Mahulea, C., Belta, C., Silva, M.: An automated framework for formal verification of timed continuous Petri nets. IEEE Trans. Ind. Informat. 6(3), 460–471 (2010)
4. Henzinger, T.A., Rusu, V.: Reachability verification for hybrid automata. In: Henzinger, T.A., Sastry, S.S. (eds.) HSCC 1998. LNCS, vol. 1386, pp. 190–204. Springer, Heidelberg (1998)
5. Dang, T., Maler, O.: Reachability analysis via face lifting. In: Henzinger, T.A., Sastry, S.S. (eds.) HSCC 1998. LNCS, vol. 1386, pp. 96–109. Springer, Heidelberg (1998)
6. Chutinan, A., Krogh, B.: Computational techniques for hybrid system verification. IEEE Trans. Autom. Control 48(1), 64–75 (2003)
7. CheckMate, http://users.ece.cmu.edu/~krogh/checkmate/
8. Mitchell, I., Bayen, A., Tomlin, C.: A time-dependent Hamilton-Jacobi formulation of reachable sets for continuous dynamic games. IEEE Trans. Autom. Control 50(7), 947–957 (2005)
9. Mitchell, I.M.: Comparing forward and backward reachability as tools for safety analysis. In: Bemporad, A., Bicchi, A., Buttazzo, G. (eds.) HSCC 2007. LNCS, vol. 4416, pp. 428–443. Springer, Heidelberg (2007)
10. Kurzhanskiy, A., Varaiya, P.: Ellipsoidal techniques for reachability analysis of discrete-time linear systems. IEEE Trans. Autom. Control 52(1), 26–38 (2007)

11. Kurzhanskiy, A., Varaiya, P.: Ellipsoidal toolbox. Technical report, EECS Department, University of California, Berkeley (May 2006)
12. Asarin, E., Schneider, G., Yovine, S.: Algorithmic analysis of polygonal hybrid systems, part i: Reachability. Theoretical Computer Science 379(12), 231–265 (2007)
13. Le Guernic, C., Girard, A.: Reachability analysis of hybrid systems using support functions. In: Bouajjani, A., Maler, O. (eds.) CAV 2009. LNCS, vol. 5643, pp. 540–554. Springer, Heidelberg (2009)
14. Chen, X., Ábrahám, E., Sankaranarayanan, S.: Flow*: An Analyzer for Non-linear Hybrid Systems. In: Sharygina, N., Veith, H. (eds.) CAV 2013. LNCS, vol. 8044, pp. 258–263. Springer, Heidelberg (2013)
15. Baccelli, F., Cohen, G., Olsder, G., Quadrat, J.P.: Synchronization and Linearity, An Algebra for Discrete Event Systems. John Wiley and Sons (1992)
16. Heidergott, B., Olsder, G., van der Woude, J.: Max Plus at Work–Modeling and Analysis of Synchronized Systems: A Course on Max-Plus Algebra and Its Applications. Princeton University Press (2006)
17. Roset, B., Nijmeijer, H., van Eekelen, J., Lefeber, E., Rooda, J.: Event driven manufacturing systems as time domain control systems. In: Proc. 44th IEEE Conf. Decision and Control and European Control Conf. (CDC-ECC 2005), pp. 446–451 (December 2005)
18. Merlin, P., Farber, D.J.: Recoverability of communication protocols–implications of a theoretical study. IEEE Trans. Commun. 24(19), 1036–1043 (1976)
19. Plus, M.: Max-plus toolbox of Scilab (1998),
    http://www.cmap.polytechnique.fr/~gaubert/MaxplusToolbox.html
20. Gazarik, M., Kamen, E.: Reachability and observability of linear systems over max-plus. Kybernetika 35(1), 2–12 (1999)
21. Gaubert, S., Katz, R.: Reachability and invariance problems in max-plus algebra. In: Benvenuti, L., De Santis, A., Farina, L. (eds.) Positive Systems. LNCIS, vol. 294, pp. 15–22. Springer, Heidelberg (2003)
22. Gaubert, S., Katz, R.: Reachability problems for products of matrices in semirings. International Journal of Algebra and Computation 16(3), 603–627 (2006)
23. Gaubert, S., Katz, R.: The Minkowski theorem for max-plus convex sets. Linear Algebra and its Applications 421(2-3), 356–369 (2007)
24. Zimmermann, K.: A general separation theorem in extremal algebras. Ekonom.-Mat. Obzor 13(2), 179–201 (1977)
25. Kvasnica, M., Grieder, P., Baotić, M.: Multi-parametric toolbox, MPT (2004)
26. Dill, D.: Timing assumptions and verification of finite-state concurrent systems. In: Sifakis, J. (ed.) CAV 1989. LNCS, vol. 407, pp. 197–212. Springer, Heidelberg (1990)
27. Adzkiya, D., De Schutter, B., Abate, A.: Finite abstractions of max-plus-linear systems. IEEE Trans. Autom. Control 58(12), 3039–3053 (2013)
28. Adzkiya, D., Abate, A.: VeriSiMPL: Verification via biSimulations of MPL models. In: Joshi, K., Siegle, M., Stoelinga, M., D'Argenio, P.R. (eds.) QEST 2013. LNCS, vol. 8054, pp. 274–277. Springer, Heidelberg (2013),
    http://sourceforge.net/projects/verisimpl/
29. Yordanov, B., Belta, C.: Formal analysis of discrete-time piecewise affine systems. IEEE Trans. Autom. Control 55(12), 2834–2840 (2010)
30. Charron-Bost, B., Függer, M., Nowak, T.: Transience bounds for distributed algorithms. In: Braberman, V., Fribourg, L. (eds.) FORMATS 2013. LNCS, vol. 8053, pp. 77–90. Springer, Heidelberg (2013)
31. Sontag, E.D.: Nonlinear regulation: The piecewise-linear approach. IEEE Trans. Autom. Control 26(2), 346–358 (1981)
32. Baier, C., Katoen, J.P.: Principles of Model Checking. The MIT Press (2008)

Compositional Invariant Generation
for Timed Systems

Lacramioara Aştefănoaei, Souha Ben Rayana,
Saddek Bensalem, Marius Bozga, and Jacques Combaz

UJF-Grenoble, CNRS VERIMAG UMR 5104, Grenoble F-38041, France*

Abstract. In this paper we address the state space explosion problem inherent to model-checking timed systems with a large number of components. The main challenge is to obtain pertinent global timing constraints from the timings in the components alone. To this end, we make use of auxiliary clocks to automatically generate new invariants which capture the constraints induced by the synchronisations between components. The method has been implemented as an extension of the D-Finder tool and successfully experimented on several benchmarks.

1 Introduction

Compositional methods in verification have been developed to cope with state space explosion. Generally based on divide et impera principles, these methods attempt to break monolithic verification problems into smaller sub-problems by exploiting either the structure of the system or the property or both. Compositional reasoning can be used in different manners e.g., for deductive verification, assume-guarantee, contract-based verification, compositional generation, etc.

The development of compositional verification for timed systems remains however challenging. State-of-the-art tools [7,13,25,18] for the verification of such systems are mostly based on symbolic state space exploration, using efficient data structures and particularly involved exploration techniques. In the timed context, the use of compositional reasoning is inherently difficult due to the synchronous model of time. Time progress is an action that synchronises continuously all the components of the system. Getting rid of the time synchronisation is necessary for analysing independently different parts of the system (or of the property) but becomes problematic when attempting to re-compose the partial verification results. Nonetheless, compositional verification is actively investigated and several approaches have been recently developed and employed in timed interfaces [2] and contract-based assume-guarantee reasoning [15,22].

In this paper, we propose a different approach for exploiting compositionality for analysis of timed systems using invariants. In contrast to exact reachability analysis, invariants are symbolic approximations of the set of reachable states of the system. We show that rather precise invariants can be computed compositionally, from the separate analysis of the components in the system and from

---

* Work partially supported by the European Integrated Projects 257414 ASCENS, 288175 CERTAINTY, and STREP 318772 D-MILS.

E. Ábrahám and K. Havelund (Eds.): TACAS 2014, LNCS 8413, pp. 263–278, 2014.
© Springer-Verlag Berlin Heidelberg 2014

their composition glue. This method is proved to be sound for the verification of safety properties. However, it is not complete.

The starting point is the verification method of [9], summarised in Figure 1. The method exploits compositionality as explained next. Consider a system consisting of components B_i interacting by means of a set γ of multi-party interactions, and let Ψ be a system property of interest. Assume that all B_i as well as the composition through γ can be independently characterised by means of component invariants $CI(B_i)$, respectively interaction invariants $II(\gamma)$. The connection between the invariants and the system property Ψ can be intuitively understood as follows: if Ψ can be proved to be a logical consequence of the conjunction of components and interaction invariants, then Ψ holds for the system.

In the rule (VR) the symbol " $\vdash$ " is used to underline that the logical implication can be effectively proved (for instance with an SMT solver) and the notation "$B \models \Box \Psi$" is to be read as "Ψ holds in every reachable state of B".

$$\frac{\vdash \bigwedge_i CI(B_i) \wedge II(\gamma) \to \Psi}{\|_\gamma B_i \models \Box \Psi} \quad (VR)$$

Fig. 1. Compositional Verification

The verification rule (VR) in [9] has been developed for untimed systems. Its direct application to timed systems may be weak as interaction invariants do not capture global timings of interactions between components. The key contribution of this paper is to improve the invariant generation method so to better track such global timings by means of auxiliary *history clocks* for actions and interactions. At component level, history clocks expose the local timing constraints relevant to the interactions of the participating components. At composition level, extra constraints on history clocks are enforced due to the simultaneity of interactions and to the synchrony of time progress.

As an illustration, let us consider as running example the timed system in Figure 2 which depicts a "controller" component serving n "worker" components, one at a time. The interactions between the controller and the workers are defined by the set of synchronisations $\{(a \mid b_i), (c \mid d_i) \mid i \leq n\}$. Periodically, after every 4 units of time, the controller synchronises its action a with the action b_i of any worker i whose clock shows at least $4n$ units of time. Initially, such a worker exists because the controller waits for $4n$ units of time before interacting with workers. The cycle repeats forever because there is always a worker "willing" to do b, that is, the system is deadlock-free. Proving deadlock-freedom of the system requires to establish that when the controller is at location lc_1 there is at least one worker such that $y_i - x \geq 4n - 4$.

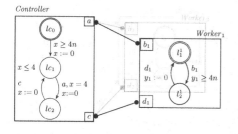

Fig. 2. A Timed System

Unfortunately, this property cannot be shown if we use (VR) as it is in [9]. Intuitively, this is because the proposed invariants are too weak to infer such cross constraints relating the clocks of the controller and the clocks of the workers:

interaction invariants $II(\gamma)$ relates only locations of components and thus at most eliminates unreachable configurations like $(lc_1, \ldots, l_2^i, \ldots)$, while the component invariants can only state local conditions on clocks such as that $x \leq 4$ at lc_1. Using history clocks allows to recover additional constraints. For example, after the first execution of the loop, each time when the controller is at location lc_1, there exists a worker i whose clock has an equal value as that of the controller. Similarly, history clocks allow to infer that different $(a \mid b_i)$ interactions are separated by at least 4 time units. These constraints altogether are then sufficient to prove the deadlock freedom property.

Related Work. Automatic generation of invariants for concurrent systems is a long-time studied topic. Yet, to our knowledge, specific extensions or applications for timed systems are rather limited. As an exception, the papers [5,17] propose a monolithic, non-compositional method for finding invariants in the case of systems represented as a single timed automaton.

Compositional verification for timed systems has been mainly considered in the context of timed interface theories [2] and contract-based assume guarantee reasoning [15,22]. These methods usually rely upon choosing a "good" decomposition structure and require individual abstractions for components to be deterministic timed I/O automata. Finding the abstractions is in general difficult, however, their construction can be automated by using learning techniques [22] in some cases. In contrast to the above, we are proposing a fully automated method generating, in a compositional manner, an invariant approximating the reachable states of a timed system. Abstractions serve also for compositional minimisation, for instance [10] minimises by constructing timed automata quotients with respect to simulation; these quotients are in turn composed for model-checking. Our approach is orthogonal in that we do not compose at all. Compositional deductive verification as in [16] is also orthogonal on our work in that, by choosing a particular class of local invariants to work with, we need not focus on elaborate proof systems but reason at a level closer to intuition.

The use of additional clocks has been considered, for instance, in [8]. There, extra reference clocks are added to components to faithfully implement a partial order reduction strategy for symbolic state space exploration. Time is allowed to progress desynchronised for individual components and re-synchronised only when needed, i.e., for direct interaction within components. Clearly, the history clocks in our work behave in a similar way, however, our use of clocks is as a helper construction in the generation of invariants and we are totally avoiding state space exploration. Finally, another successful application of extra clocks has been provided in [23] for timing analysis of asynchronous circuits. There, specific history clocks are reset on input signals and used to provide a new time basis for the construction of an abstract model of output signals of the circuit.

Organisation of the paper. Section 2 recalls the needed definitions for modelling timed systems and their properties. Section 3 presents our method for compositional generation of invariants. Section 4 describes the prototype implementing the method and some case studies we experimented with. Section 5 concludes.

2   Timed Systems and Properties

In the framework of the present paper, components are timed automata and systems are compositions of timed automata with respect to multi-party interactions. The timed automata we use are essentially the ones from [3], however, sligthly adapted to embrace a uniform notation throughout the paper.

Definition 1 (Syntax of a Component). *A component is a timed automaton* $(L, l_0, A, T, \mathcal{X}, \mathsf{tpc})$ *where L is a finite set of locations, l_0 is an initial location, A a finite set of actions, $T \subseteq L \times (A \times \mathcal{C} \times 2^{\mathcal{X}}) \times L$ is a set of edges labeled with an action, a guard, and a set of clocks to be reset, $\mathcal{X}$ is a finite set of clocks[1], and $\mathsf{tpc} : L \to \mathcal{C}$ assigns a time progress condition[2] to each location. $\mathcal{C}$ is the set of clock constraints. A clock constraint is defined by the grammar:*

$$C ::= true \mid false \mid x\#ct \mid x - y\#ct \mid C \wedge C$$

with $x, y \in \mathcal{X}$, $\# \in \{<, \leq, =, \geq, >\}$ and $ct \in \mathbb{Z}$. Time progress conditions are restricted to conjunctions of constraints as $x \leq ct$.

Before recalling the semantics of a component, we first fix some notation. Let $\mathbf{V}$ be the set of all clock valuation functions $\mathbf{v} : \mathcal{X} \to \mathbb{R}_{\geq 0}$. For a clock constraint C, $C(\mathbf{v})$ denotes the evaluation of C in $\mathbf{v}$. The notation $\mathbf{v} + \delta$ represents a new $\mathbf{v}'$ defined as $\mathbf{v}'(x) = \mathbf{v}(x) + \delta$ while $\mathbf{v}[r]$ represents a new $\mathbf{v}'$ which assigns any x in r to 0 and otherwise preserves the values from $\mathbf{v}$.

Definition 2 (Semantics of a Component). *The semantics of a component $B = (L, l_0, A, T, X, \mathsf{tpc})$ is given by the labelled transition system $(Q, A, \to)$ where $Q \subseteq L \times \mathbf{V}$ denotes the states of B and $\to \subseteq Q \times (A \cup \mathbb{R}_{\geq 0}) \times Q$ denotes the transitions according to the rules:*

- $(l, \mathbf{v}) \xrightarrow{\delta} (l, \mathbf{v} + \delta)$ *if* $(\forall \delta' \in [0, \delta]).(\mathsf{tpc}(l)(\mathbf{v} + \delta'))$ *(time progress);*
- $(l, \mathbf{v}) \xrightarrow{a} (l', \mathbf{v}[r])$ *if* $(l, (a, g, r), l') \in T$, $g(\mathbf{v}) \wedge \mathsf{tpc}(l')(\mathbf{v}[r])$ *(action step).*

Because the semantics defined above is in general infinite, we work with the so called zone graph [19] as a finite symbolic representation. The symbolic states in a zone graph are pairs (l, ζ) where l is a location of B and ζ is a *zone*, a set of clock valuations defined by clock constraints. Given a symbolic state (l, ζ), its successor with respect to a transition t of B is denoted as $\mathsf{succ}(t, (l, \zeta))$ and defined by means of its timed and its discrete successor:

- $\mathsf{time\text{-}succ}((l, \zeta)) = (l, \nearrow \zeta \cap \mathsf{tpc}(l))$
- $\mathsf{disc\text{-}succ}(t, (l, \zeta)) = (l', (\zeta \cap g)[r] \cap \mathsf{tpc}(l'))$ if $t = (l, (\_, g, r), l')$
- $\mathsf{succ}(t, (l, \zeta)) = \mathsf{norm}(\mathsf{time\text{-}succ}(\mathsf{disc\text{-}succ}(t, (l, \zeta))))$

---

[1] Clocks are local. This is essential for avoiding side effects which would break compositionality and local analysis.

[2] To avoid confusion with invariant properties, we prefer to adopt the terminology of "time progress condition" from [11] instead of "location invariants".

where $\nearrow, [r],$ norm are usual operations on zones: $\nearrow \zeta$ is the forward diagonal projection of ζ, i.e., it contains any valuation $\mathbf{v}'$ for which there exists a real δ such that $\mathbf{v}' - \delta$ is in ζ; $\zeta[r]$ is the set of all valuations in ζ after applying the resets in r; norm(ζ) corresponds to normalising ζ such that computation of the set of all successors terminates. Since we are seeking component invariants which are over-approximations of the reachable states, a more thorough discussion on normalisation is not relevant for the present paper. The interested reader may refer to [12] for more precise definitions.

A symbolic execution of a component starting from a symbolic state s_0 is a sequence of symbolic states $s_0, s_1, \ldots, s_n, \ldots$ such that for any $i > 0$ there exists a transition t for which s_i is succ(t, s_{i-1}).

Given a component B with initial symbolic state s_0 and transitions T, the set of reachable symbolic states $Reach(B)$ is $Reach(s_0)$ where $Reach$ is defined recursively for an arbitrary s as:

$$Reach(s) = \{s\} \cup \bigcup_{t \in T} Reach(\text{succ}(t, s)).$$

In our framework, components communicate by means of *interactions*, which are synchronisations between their actions. Given n components B_i, $1 \le i \le n$, with disjoint sets of actions A_i, an interaction is a subset of actions $\alpha \subseteq \cup_i A_i$ containing at most one action per component, that is, of the form $\alpha = \{a_i\}_{i \in I}$, with $a_i \in A_i$ for all $i \in I \subseteq \{1, \ldots, n\}$. Given a set of interactions $\gamma \subseteq 2^{\cup_i A_i}$, we denote by $Act(\gamma)$ the set of actions involved in γ, that is, $Act(\gamma) = \cup_{\alpha \in \gamma} \alpha$. A *timed system* is the composition of components B_i for a set of interactions γ such that $Act(\gamma) = \cup_i A_i$.

Definition 3 (Timed System). *For n components $B_i = (L_i, l_0^i, A_i, T_i, \mathcal{X}_i, \text{tpc}_i)$ with $A_i \cap A_j = \emptyset$, $\mathcal{X}_i \cap \mathcal{X}_j = \emptyset$, for any $i \ne j$, the composition $\|_\gamma B_i$ w.r.t. a set of interactions γ is defined by a timed automaton $(L, \bar{l}_0, \gamma, T_\gamma, \mathcal{X}, \text{tpc})$ where $\bar{l}_0 = (l_0^1, \ldots, l_0^n)$, $\mathcal{X} = \cup_i \mathcal{X}_i$, $L = \times_i L_i$, $\text{tpc}(\bar{l}) = \wedge_i \text{tpc}(l_i)$, and T_γ is such that for any interaction $\alpha = \{a_i\}_{i \in I}$ we have that $\bar{l} \xrightarrow{\alpha, g, r} \bar{l}'$ where $\bar{l} = (l_1, \ldots, l_n)$, $g = \wedge_{i \in I} g_i$, $r = \cup_{i \in I} r_i$, and $\bar{l}'(i) = $ if $(i \notin I)$ l_i else l_i' for $l_i \xrightarrow{a_i, g_i, r_i} l_i'$.*

In the timed system $\|_\gamma B_i$ a component B_i can execute an action a_i only as part of an interaction α, $a_i \in \alpha$, that is, along with the execution of all other actions $a_j \in \alpha$, which corresponds to the usual notion of multi-party interaction. Notice that interactions can only restrict the behavior of components, i.e. the states reached by B_i in $\|_\gamma B_i$ belong to $Reach(B_i)$. This property is exploited by the verification rule (VR) presented throughout this paper.

To give a logical characterisation of components and interactions we use invariants. An invariant Φ is a state property which holds in every reachable state of a component (or of a system) B, in symbols, $B \models \Box\Phi$. We use $CI(B_i)$ and $II(\gamma)$, to denote component, respectively interaction invariants. For component invariants, our choice is to work with their reachable set. More precisely, for a component B with initial state s_0, $CI(B)$ is the disjunction of $(l \wedge \zeta)$ and where, to ease the reading, we abuse notation and use l as a place holder for a state predicate "$at(l)$" which holds in any symbolic state with location l, that is, the semantics of $at(l)$ is given by $(l, \zeta) \models at(l)$. As an example, the component invariants for the scenario in Figure 2 with one worker are:

$$CI(Controller) = (lc_0 \wedge x \geq 0) \vee (lc_1 \wedge x \leq 4) \vee (lc_2 \wedge x \geq 0)$$
$$CI(Worker_i) = (l_1^i \wedge y_i \geq 0) \vee (l_2^i \wedge y_i \geq 4).$$

Interaction invariants are over-approximations of global state spaces allowing us to disregard certain tuples of local states as unreachable. Interaction invariants relate locations of different atomic components. They are either boolean e.g., $l_1 \vee l_2 \vee l_3$ or linear e.g., $l_1 + l_2 + l_3 = 1$. These particular examples ensure that at least (resp. exactly) one of the locations l_1, l_2, l_3 are active at any time. Interaction invariants are computed on the synchronization skeleton of the composition, that is, a 1-safe Petri net obtained by composing component behaviours according to the interaction glue. The methods rely on boolean ([9]) / algebraic ([21]) constraint solving and avoid any form of state-space exploration. In the case of the running example, when the controller is interacting with one worker, the interaction invariant $II(\{(a \mid b_1), (c \mid d_1)\})$ is $(lc_2 \vee l_1^1) \wedge (l_2^1 \vee lc_0 \vee lc_1)$.

The proposed invariants[3] have the feature that they are inductive. We recall that an invariant Φ is inductive if it holds initially and if for a state s s.t. $s \models \Phi$ we have that $s' \models \Phi$ for any successor s' of s. Moreover, inductive invariants have the property that their conjunction is also an inductive invariant.

3   Timed Invariant Generation

As explained in the introduction, a direct application of (VR) may not be useful in itself in the sense that the component and the interaction invariants alone are usually not enough to prove global properties, especially when the properties involve relations between clocks in different components. More precisely, though component invariants encode timings of local clocks, there is no direct way – the interaction invariant is orthogonal on timing aspects – to constrain the bounds on the differences between clocks in different components. To give a concrete illustration, consider the safety property $\Psi_{Safe} = (lc_1 \wedge l_1^1 \rightarrow x \leq y_1)$ that holds in the running example with one worker. It is not difficult to see that Ψ_{Safe} cannot be deduced from $CI(Controller) \wedge CI(Worker_1) \wedge II(\{(a \mid b_1), (c \mid d_1)\})$.

3.1   History Clocks for Actions

In this section we show how we can, by means of some auxiliary constructions, apply (VR) more successfully. To this end, we "equip" components (and later, interactions) with *history clocks*, a clock per action; then, at interaction time, the clocks corresponding to the actions participating in the interaction are reset.

---

[3] The rule (VR) is generic enough to work with other types of invariants. For example, one could use over-approximations of the reachable set in the case of component invariants, however, this comes at the price of losing precision.

This basic transformation allows us to automatically compute a new invariant of the system with history clocks. This new invariant, together with the component and interaction invariants, is shown to be, after projection of history clocks, an invariant of the initial system.

Definition 4 (Components with History Clocks). *Given a component model* $B = (L, l_0, A, T, \mathcal{X}, \mathsf{tpc})$, *its extension wrt history clocks is a timed automaton* $B^h = (L, l_0, A, T^h, \mathcal{X} \cup \mathcal{H}_A, \mathsf{tpc})$ *where:*

- $\mathcal{H}_A = \{h_a \mid a \in A\} \cup \{h_0\}$ *is the set of history clocks associated to actions and* h_o, *a history clock dedicated to initialisation. Together with the clocks in* $\mathcal{X}$, h_0 *is initialised to zero. All other clocks in* $\mathcal{H}_A$ *may be initialised to any arbitrary positive value.*
- $T^h = \{(l, (a, g, r \cup [h_a := 0]), l') \mid (l, (a, g, r), l') \in T\}.$

Since there is no timing constraint involving history clocks, these have no influence on the behaviour. The extended model is, in fact, bisimilar to the original model. Moreover, any invariant of the composition of B_i^h corresponds to an invariant of $\|_\gamma B_i$. For the ease of reading, we abuse notation and use $\exists \mathcal{H}_A$ to stand for $\exists h_0 \exists h_{a_1} \exists h_{a_2} \dots \exists h_{a_n}$ for $A = \{a_1, a_2, \dots, a_n\}$.

Proposition 1 *Any symbolic execution in* B^h *corresponds to a symbolic execution (where all constraints on history clocks are ignored) in* B. *Moreover, if* $\|_\gamma B_i^h \models \Box \Phi$ *then* $\|_\gamma B_i \models \Box(\exists \mathcal{H}_A).\Phi$.

The only operation acting on history clocks is reset. Its effect is that immediately after an interaction takes place, all history clocks involved in the interaction are equal to zero. All other history clocks preserve their previous values, thus they are at least greater in value than all those being reset. This basic but useful observation is exploited in the following definition, which builds, recursively, all the inequalities that could hold given an interaction set γ.

Definition 5 (Interaction Inequalities for History Clocks). *Given an interaction set* γ, *we define the following interaction inequalities* $\mathcal{E}(\gamma)$:

$$\mathcal{E}(\gamma) = \bigvee_{\alpha \in \gamma} \left(\left(\bigwedge_{\substack{a_i, a_j \in \alpha \\ a_k \notin \alpha}} h_{a_i} = h_{a_j} \leq h_{a_k} \right) \wedge \mathcal{E}(\gamma \ominus \alpha) \right).$$

where $\gamma \ominus \alpha = \{\beta \setminus \alpha \mid \beta \in \gamma \wedge \beta \nsubseteq \alpha\}$.

Remark 1. We can use the interpreted function "min" as syntactic sugar to have a more compact expression for $\mathcal{E}(\gamma)$:

$$\mathcal{E}(\gamma) = \bigvee_{\alpha \in \gamma} \left(\bigwedge_{a_i, a_j \in \alpha} h_{a_i} = h_{a_j} \leq \min_{a_k \notin \alpha} h_{a_k} \wedge \mathcal{E}(\gamma \ominus \alpha) \right).$$

Example 1. For $\gamma = \{(a \mid b_1), (c \mid d_1)\}$, corresponding to the interactions between the controller and one worker in Figure 2, the compact form of $\mathcal{E}(\gamma)$ is:

$$\left(h_a = h_{b_1} \leq \min(h_c, h_{d_1}) \wedge h_c = h_{d_1} \right) \vee \left(h_c = h_{d_1} \leq \min(h_a, h_{b_1}) \wedge h_a = h_{b_1} \right).$$

$\mathcal{E}(\gamma)$ characterises the relations between history clocks during any possible execution of a system. It can be shown, by induction, that this characterisation is, in fact, an inductive invariant of the extended system.

Proposition 2 $\mathcal{E}(\gamma)$ *is an inductive invariant of* $\|_\gamma B_i^h$.

By Proposition 2, and using the fact that component and interaction invariants are inductive, we have that also their conjunction is an inductive invariant of the system with history clocks. As a consequence of Proposition 1, we can eliminate the history clocks from $\wedge_i CI(B_i^h) \wedge II(\gamma) \wedge \mathcal{E}(\gamma)$ and obtain an invariant of the original system. This invariant is usually stronger than $CI(B_i) \wedge II(\gamma)$ and yields more successful applications of the rule (VR).

Example 2. We reconsider the sub-system of a controller and a worker from Figure 2. We illustrate how the safety property ψ_{Safe} introduced in the beginning of the section can be shown to hold by using the newly generated invariant. The invariants for the components with history clocks are:

$$CI(Controller^h) = (lc_0 \wedge h_0 = x) \vee$$
$$(lc_1 \wedge x \le 4 \wedge h_a \le h_0 \wedge (h_a = h_c \ge 4 + x \ \vee x = h_c \le h_a)) \vee$$
$$(lc_2 \wedge x = h_a \wedge h_c \le h_0 \wedge (h_c \ge h_a + 8 \vee h_c = h_a + 4))$$
$$CI(Worker_1^h) = (l_1^1 \wedge (y_1 = h_0 \vee y_1 = h_{d_1} \le h_{b_1} \le h_0)) \vee$$
$$(l_2^1 \wedge h_0 \ge y_1 = h_{d_1} \ge 4 + h_{b_1})$$

By using the interaction invariant described in Section 2 and the equality constraints $\mathcal{E}(\gamma)$ from Example 1, after the elimination of the existential quantifiers in $(\exists h_0.\exists h_a.\exists h_{b_1}.\exists h_c.\exists h_{d_1})(CI(Controller^h) \wedge CI(Worker_1^h) \wedge II(\gamma) \wedge \mathcal{E}(\gamma))$ we obtain the following invariant Φ:

$$\Phi = (l_1^1 \wedge lc_0 \wedge (\boldsymbol{y_1 \le x})) \vee (l_1^1 \wedge lc_1 \wedge (\boldsymbol{y_1 = x \vee y_1 \ge x + 4})) \vee$$
$$(l_2^1 \wedge lc_2 \wedge (\boldsymbol{y_1 = x + 4 \vee y_1 \ge x + 8})).$$

It can be easily checked that $\Phi \wedge \neg \Psi_{Safe}$ has no satisfying model and this proves that Ψ_{Safe} holds for the system. We used bold fonts in Φ to highlight relations between x and y_1 which are not in $CI(Controller) \wedge CI(Worker_1) \wedge II(\gamma)$.

To sum up, the basic steps described so far are: (1) extend the input components B_i to components with history clocks B_i^h; (2) compute component invariants $CI(B_i^h)$ and (3) equality constraints $\mathcal{E}(\gamma)$ from the interactions γ; (4) finally, eliminate the history clocks in $\wedge_i CI(B_i^h) \wedge \mathcal{E}(\gamma) \wedge II(\gamma)$, and obtain a stronger invariant by means of which the application of (VR) is more successful.

We conclude the section with a remark on the size of $\mathcal{E}(\gamma)$. Due to the combination of recursion and disjunction, $\mathcal{E}(\gamma)$ can be large. Much more compact formulae can be obtained by exploiting non-conflicting interactions, i.e., interactions that do not share actions.

Proposition 3 *For* $\gamma = \gamma_1 \cup \gamma_2$ *with* $Act(\gamma_1) \cap Act(\gamma_2) = \emptyset$, $\mathcal{E}(\gamma) \equiv \mathcal{E}(\gamma_1) \wedge \mathcal{E}(\gamma_2)$.

Corollary 4 *If the interaction model γ has only disjoint interactions, i.e., for any $\alpha_1, \alpha_2 \in \gamma$, $\alpha_1 \cap \alpha_2 = \emptyset$, then $\mathcal{E}(\gamma) \equiv \bigwedge_{\alpha \in \gamma} \left(\bigwedge_{a_i, a_j \in \alpha} h_{a_i} = h_{a_j} \right)$.*

Example 3. The interaction set γ in Example 1 is not conflicting. Thus, by applying Corollary 4, we can simplify the expression of $\mathcal{E}(\gamma)$ to $(h_a = h_{b_1}) \wedge (h_c = h_{d_1})$.

3.2 History Clocks for Interactions

The equality constraints on history clocks allow to relate the local constraints obtained individually on components. In the case of non-conflicting interactions, the relation is rather "tight", that is, expressed as conjunction of equalities on history clocks. In contrast, the presence of conflicts lead to a significantly weaker form. Intuitively, every action in conflict can be potentially used in different interactions. The uncertainty on its exact use leads to a disjunctive expression as well as to more restricted equalities and inequalities amongst history clocks.

Nonetheless, the presence of conflicts themselves can be additionally exploited for the generation of new invariants. That is, in contrast to equality constraints obtained from interaction, the presence of conflicting actions enforce disequalities (or separation) constraints between all interactions using them. In what follows, we show a generic way to automatically compute such invariants enforcing differences between the timings of the interactions themselves. To effectively implement this, we proceed in a similar manner as in the previous section: we again make use of history clocks and corresponding resets but this time we associate them to interactions, at the system level.

Definition 6 (Systems with Interaction History Clocks). *Given a system $\|_\gamma B_i$, its extension wrt history clocks for interactions is $\|_{\gamma^h} B_i^h, \Gamma^*$ where:*

- *Γ^* is an auxiliary TA having one location l with no invariant, and for each interaction α in γ a clock h_α, i.e., $\Gamma^* = (\{l^*\}, A_\gamma, T, \mathcal{H}_\gamma, \emptyset)$ where:*
  - *the set of actions $A_\gamma = \{a_\alpha \mid \alpha \in \gamma\}$*
  - *the set of clocks $\mathcal{H}_\gamma = \{h_\alpha \mid \alpha \in \gamma\}$*
  - *$T = \{(l^*, a_\alpha, true, h_\alpha := 0, l^*) \mid \alpha \in \gamma\}$*
- *$\gamma^h = \{(a_\alpha \mid \alpha) \mid \alpha \in \gamma\}$ with $(a_\alpha \mid \alpha)$ denoting $\{a_\alpha\} \cup \{a \mid a \in \alpha\}$.*

Using a similar argument as for Proposition 1, it can be shown that any invariant of $\|_{\gamma^h} B_i^h, \Gamma^*$ corresponds to an invariant of $\|_\gamma B_i$ by first showing that any execution of $\|_{\gamma^h} B_i^h, \Gamma^*$ corresponds to an execution of $\|_\gamma B_i$.

Proposition 5 *Any execution in $\|_{\gamma^h} B_i^h, \Gamma^*$ corresponds to an execution in $\|_\gamma B_i$. Moreover, if $\|_{\gamma^h} B_i^h, \Gamma^* \models \Box\, \Phi$ then $\|_\gamma B_i \models \Box\, \exists \mathcal{H}_\gamma \exists \mathcal{H}_A.\Phi$ where the new notation $\exists \mathcal{H}_\gamma$ stands for $\exists h_{\alpha_1} \exists h_{\alpha_2} \ldots \exists h_{\alpha_n}$ when $\gamma = \{\alpha_1, \alpha_2, \ldots, \alpha_n\}$.*

We use history clocks for interactions to express additional constraints on their timing. The starting point is the observation that when two conflicting interactions compete for the same action a, no matter which one is first, the other one must wait until the component which owns a is again able to execute a. This is referred to as a "separation constraint" for conflicting interactions.

Definition 7 (Separation Constraints for Interaction Clocks). *Given an interaction set γ, the induced separation constraints, $\mathcal{S}(\gamma)$, are defined as follows:*

$$\mathcal{S}(\gamma) = \bigwedge_{a \in Act(\gamma)} \bigwedge_{\substack{\alpha \neq \beta \in \gamma \\ a \in \alpha \cap \beta}} \mid h_\alpha - h_\beta \mid \geq k_a$$

where $\mid \mid$ stands for absolute values and k_a denotes the minimum between the first occurrence time of a and the minimal time elapse between two consecutive occurrences of a. It is computed[4] locally on the component executing a.

Example 4. In our running example the only shared actions are a and c within the controller, and both k_a and k_c are equal to 4, thus the expression of the separation constraints reduces to:

$$\mathcal{S}(\gamma) \equiv \bigwedge_{i \neq j} |h_{c|d_i} - h_{c|d_j}| \geq 4 \wedge \bigwedge_{i \neq j} |h_{a|b_i} - h_{a|b_j}| \geq 4.$$

Proposition 6 $\mathcal{S}(\gamma)$ *is an inductive invariant of* $\|_{\gamma^h} B_i^h, \Gamma^*$.

Proof. By induction on the length of computations. For the base case, we assume that the initial values of the history clocks for interactions in Γ^* are such that they satisfy $\mathcal{S}(\gamma)$. Obviously, such a satisfying initial model always exists: it suffices to take all h_α with a minimal distance between them greater than the maximum k_a, in an arbitrary order.

For the inductive step, let s be the state reached after i steps, s' a successor, α an interaction such that $s \xrightarrow{\alpha} s'$, a an arbitrary action and $\beta \in \gamma$ such that $a \in \beta$. For any $\beta' \neq \alpha$, $\mid h_\beta - h_{\beta'} \mid \geq k_a$ is unchanged from s to s' (α is the only interaction for which h_α is reset from s to s') and thus holds by induction. We now turn to $\mid h_\beta - h_\alpha \mid$ which at s' evaluates to h_β. Let s_a be the most recent state reached by an interaction containing a. If no such interaction exists, that is, if a has no appearance in the i steps to s, let s_a be the initial state. On the path from s_a to s', h_β could not have been reset (otherwise, s_a would not be the most recent one). Thus $h_\beta \geq k_a$ by the definition of k_a.   □

The invariant $\mathcal{S}(\gamma)$ is defined over the history clocks for interactions. Previously, the invariant $\mathcal{E}(\gamma)$ has been expressed using history clocks for actions. In order to "glue" them together in a meaningful way, we need some connection between history and interaction clocks. This connection is formally addressed by the constraints $\mathcal{E}^*$ defined below.

Definition 8 ($\mathcal{E}^*$). *Given an interaction set γ, we define $\mathcal{E}^*(\gamma)$ as follows:*

$$\mathcal{E}^*(\gamma) = \bigwedge_{a \in Act(\gamma)} h_a = \min_{\alpha \in \gamma, a \in \alpha} h_\alpha.$$

---

[4] For instance, by reduction to a shortest path problem in weighted graphs [14].

By a similar argument as the one in Proposition 2, it can be shown that $\mathcal{E}^*(\gamma)$ is an inductive invariant of the extended system. The connection between $\mathcal{E}$ and $\mathcal{E}^*$ is given in Proposition 7.

Proposition 7 $\mathcal{E}^*(\gamma)$ *is an inductive invariant of* $\|_{\gamma^h} B_i^h, \Gamma^*$. *Moreover, the equivalence* $\exists \mathcal{H}_\gamma . \mathcal{E}^*(\gamma) \equiv \mathcal{E}(\gamma)$ *is a valid formula.*

Proof. To see that $\mathcal{E}^*(\gamma)$ is an invariant it suffices to note that, for any action a, there is always an interaction α containing a such that h_a and h_α are both reset in the same time.

The connection between $\mathcal{E}$ and $\mathcal{E}^*$ is shown by induction on the number of interactions in γ. We only present the base case, $\gamma = \{\alpha\}$, (the inductive one as well as all proofs can be found in [4]):

$$\mathcal{E}(\gamma) = \bigwedge_{a_i, a_j \in \alpha} h_{a_i} = h_{a_j} \equiv \exists h_\alpha . \Big(\bigwedge_{a_i \in \alpha} h_{a_i} = h_\alpha \Big) \equiv$$

$$\exists \mathcal{H}_\gamma . \Big(\bigwedge_{a_i \in Act(\gamma)} h_{a_i} = \min_{\alpha \in \gamma, a_i \in \alpha} h_\alpha \Big) \equiv \exists \mathcal{H}_\gamma . \mathcal{E}^*(\gamma).$$

$\square$

From Proposition 7, together with Propositions 5 and 6, it follows that $\exists \mathcal{H}_A \exists \mathcal{H}_\gamma . (\wedge_i CI(B_i^h) \wedge II(\gamma) \wedge \mathcal{E}^*(\gamma) \wedge \mathcal{S}(\gamma))$ is an invariant of $\|_\gamma B_i$. This new invariant is in general stronger than $\wedge_i CI(B_i^h) \wedge II(\gamma) \wedge \mathcal{E}(\gamma)$ and it provides better state space approximations for timed systems with conflicting interactions.

Example 5. To get some intuition about the invariant generated using separation constraints, let us reconsider the running example with two workers. The subformula which we emphasise here is the conjunction of $\mathcal{E}^*$ and $\mathcal{S}$. The interaction inequalities for history clocks are:

$$\mathcal{E}^*(\gamma) \equiv h_{b_1} = h_{a|b_1} \wedge h_{b_2} = h_{a|b_2} \wedge h_a = \min_{i=1,2}(h_{a|b_i}) \wedge$$

$$h_{d_1} = h_{c|d_1} \wedge h_{d_2} = h_{c|d_2} \wedge h_c = \min_{i=1,2}(h_{c|d_i})$$

by recalling the expression of $\mathcal{S}(\gamma)$ from Example 4 we obtain that:

$$\exists \mathcal{H}_\gamma . \mathcal{E}^*(\gamma) \wedge \mathcal{S}(\gamma) \equiv |h_{b_2} - h_{b_1}| \geq 4 \wedge |h_{d_2} - h_{d_1}| \geq 4$$

and thus, after quantifier elimination in $\exists \mathcal{H}_A \exists \mathcal{H}_\gamma . (CI(Controller^h) \wedge_i CI(Worker_i^h) \wedge II(\gamma) \wedge \mathcal{E}^*(\gamma) \wedge \mathcal{S}(\gamma))$, we obtain the following invariant Φ:

$$\Phi = (l_1^1 \wedge l_1^2 \wedge lc_0 \wedge x = y_1 = y_2) \vee$$
$$(l_1^1 \wedge l_1^2 \wedge lc_1 \wedge x \leq 4 \wedge ((y_1 = x \wedge \boldsymbol{y_2 - y_1 \geq 4} \vee y_1 \geq x + 8 \vee$$
$$y_2 = x \wedge \boldsymbol{y_1 - y_2 \geq 4} \vee y_2 \geq x + 8))) \vee$$
$$(l_2^1 \wedge l_1^2 \wedge lc_2 \wedge (y_1 \geq x + 8 \vee (y_2 = x + 4 \wedge \boldsymbol{y_1 - y_2 \geq 4}))) \vee$$
$$(l_1^2 \wedge l_2^1 \wedge lc_2 \wedge (y_2 \geq x + 8 \vee (y_1 = x + 4 \wedge \boldsymbol{y_2 - y_1 \geq 4})))$$

We emphasised in the expression of Φ the newly discovered constraints. All in all, Φ is strong enough to prove that the system is deadlock free.

4   Implementation and Experiments

The method has been implemented in a Scala (`scala-lang.org/`) prototype (`www-verimag.imag.fr/~lastefan/tas`) which is currently being integrated with the D-Finder tool [9] for verification of Real-Time BIP systems [1]. The prototype takes as input components B_i, an interaction set γ and a global safety property Ψ and checks whether the system satisfies Ψ. Internally, it uses PPL (`bugseng.com/products/ppl`) to manipulate zones (essentially polyhedra) and to compute component invariants. It generates Z3 (`z3.codeplex.com`) Python code to check the satisfiability of the formula $\wedge_i CI(B_i) \wedge II(\gamma) \wedge \Phi^* \wedge \neg\Psi$ where Φ^*, depending on whether γ is conflicting, stands for $\mathcal{E}(\gamma)$ or $\mathcal{E}^*(\gamma) \wedge \mathcal{S}(\gamma)$. If the formula is not satisfiable, the prototype returns `no solution`, that is, the system is guaranteed to satisfy Ψ. Otherwise, it returns a substitution for which the formula is satisfiable, that is, the conjunction of invariants is true while Ψ is not. This substitution may correspond to a false positive in the sense that the state represented by the substitution could be unreachable.

For experiments, we chose three classical benchmarks which we discuss below.

Train Gate Controller: This is a classical example from [3]. The system is composed of a controller, a gate and a number of trains. For simplicity, Figure 3 depicts only one train interacting with the controller and the gate. The controller lowers and raises the gate when a train enters, respectively exits. The safety property of interest is that when a train is at location `in`, the gate has been lowered: $\wedge_i(in_i \to g_2)$. When there is only one train in the system, $\mathcal{E}(\gamma)$ is enough to show safety. When there are more trains, we use the separation constraints.

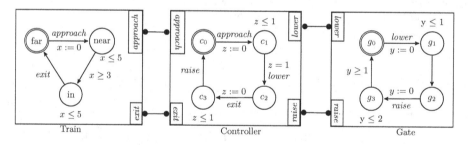

Fig. 3. A Controller Interacting with a Train and a Gate

Fischer Protocol: This is a well-studied protocol for mutual exclusion [20]. The protocol specifies how processes can share a resource one at a time by means of a shared variable to which each process assigns its own identifier number. After θ time units, the process with the id stored in the variable enters the critical state and uses the resource. We use an auxiliary component `Id Variable` to mimic the role of the shared variable. To keep the size of the generated invariants manageable, we restrict to the acyclic version. The system with two concurrent processes is represented in Figure 4. The property of interest is mutual exclusion: $(cs_i \wedge cs_j) \to i = j$. The component `Id Variable` has combinatorial behavior and a large number of actions $(2n + 1)$, thus the generated invariant is huge except for very small values of n. To overcome this issue, we extracted from the structure of the generated invariant a weaker inductive one which we verified for validity locally with Uppaal. Basically, it encodes information like $h_{eq_i} < h_{set_i} \rightarrow h_{eq_i} < h_{eq_0} \wedge h_{set_i} < h_{eq_0}$ for any index i. This invariant, together with the component invariants for the processes and together with $\mathcal{E}(\gamma)$ is sufficient to show that mutual exclusion holds.

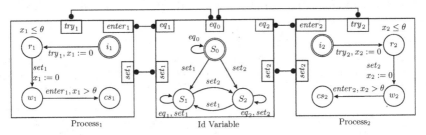

Fig. 4. The Fischer Protocol

Temperature Controller: This example is an adaptation from [9]. It represents a simplified model of a nuclear plant. The system consists of a controller interacting with an arbitrary number n of rods (two, in Figure 5) in order to maintain the temperature between the bounds 450 and 900: when the temperature in the reactor reaches 900 (resp. 450), a rod must be used to cool (resp. heat) the reactor. The rods are enabled to cool only after $900n$ units of time. The global property of interest is the absence of deadlock, that is, the system can run continuously and keep the temperature between the bounds. To express this property in our prototype, we adapt from [24] the definition of *enabled* states, while in Uppaal, we use the query A[] not deadlock. For one rod, $\mathcal{E}(\gamma)$ is enough to show the property. For more rods, because interactions are conflicting, we need the separation constraints which basically bring as new information conjunctions as $\wedge_i(h_{rest_{\pi(i)}} - h_{rest_{\pi(i-1)}} \geq 1350)$ for π an ordering on rods.

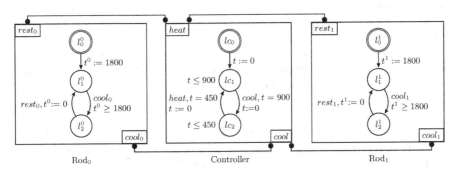

Fig. 5. A Controller Interacting with 2 Rods

The experiments were run on a Dell machine with Ubuntu 12.04, an Intel(R) Core(TM)i5-2430M processor of frequency 2.4GHz×4, and 5.7GiB memory. The results, synthesised in Table 1, show the potential of our method in terms of accuracy (no false positives) and scalability. For larger numbers of components, the size of the resulting invariants was not problematic for Z3. However, it may be the case that history clocks considerably increase the size of the generated formulae. It can also be observed that Uppaal being highly optimised, it has better scores on the first example in particular and on smaller systems in general. The timings for our prototype are obtained with the Unix command time while the results for Uppaal come from the command verifyta which comes with the Uppaal 4.1.14 distribution.

Table 1. Results from Experiments. The marking "*" highlights the cases when $\mathcal{E}$ alone was enough to prove the property. The expressions of form "$x + y$" are to be read as "the formula $\bigwedge_i CI(B_i) \wedge II(\gamma) \wedge \mathcal{E}(\gamma)$, resp. $\mathcal{E}^*(\gamma) \wedge \mathcal{S}(\gamma)$, has length x, resp. y".

Model & Property	Size	Time/Space	
		$\mathcal{E}^* \wedge \mathcal{S}$	Uppaal
Train Gate Controller & mutual exclusion	1*	0m0.156s/2.6kB+140B	0ms/8 states
	2	0m0.176s/3.2kB+350B	0ms/13 states
	64	0m4.82s/530kB+170kB	0m0.210s/323 states
	124	0m17.718s/700kB+640kB	0m1.52s/623 states
Fischer & mutual exclusion	2*	0m0.144/3kB	0m0.008s/14 states
	4*	0m0.22s/6.5kB	0m0.012s/156 states
	6*	0m0.36s/12.5kB	0m0.03s/1714 states
	14*	0m2.840s/112kB	no result in 4 hours
Temperature Controller & absence of deadlock	1*	0m0.172s/840B+60B	0m0.01s/4 states
	8	0m0.5s/23kB+2.4kB	11m0.348s/57922 states
	16	0m2.132s/127kB+9kB	no result in 6 hours
	124	0m19.22s/460kB+510kB	idem

5   Conclusion and Future Work

We presented a fully automated compositional method to generate global invariants for timed systems described as parallel compositions of timed automata components using multi-party interactions. The soundness of the method proposed has been proven. In addition, it has been implemented and successfully tested on several benchmarks. The results show that our method may outperform existing exhaustive exploration-based techniques for large systems, thanks to the use of compositionality and over-approximations.

This work is currently being extended in several directions. First, in order to achieve a better integration within D-Finder tool [9] and the Real-Time BIP framework [1] we are working on handling *urgencies* [6] on transitions. Actually, urgencies provide an alternative way to constrain time progress, which is more intuitive to use by programmers but much difficult to handle in a compositional way. A second extension concerns the development of heuristics to reduce the size of the generated invariants. As an example, symmetry-based reduction is potentially interesting for systems containing identical, replicated components. Finally, we are considering specific extensions to particular classes of timed systems and properties, in particular, for schedulability analysis of systems with mixed-critical tasks.

References

1. Abdellatif, T., Combaz, J., Sifakis, J.: Model-based implementation of real-time applications. In: EMSOFT (2010)
2. de Alfaro, L., Henzinger, T.A., Stoelinga, M.: Timed interfaces. In: Sangiovanni-Vincentelli, A.L., Sifakis, J. (eds.) EMSOFT 2002. LNCS, vol. 2491, pp. 108–122. Springer, Heidelberg (2002)
3. Alur, R., Dill, D.L.: A theory of timed automata. Theor. Comput. Sci. (1994)
4. Astefanoaei, L., Rayana, S.B., Bensalem, S., Bozga, M., Combaz, J.: Compositional invariant generation for timed systems. Technical Report TR-2013-5, Verimag Research Report (2013)
5. Badban, B., Leue, S., Smaus, J.-G.: Automated invariant generation for the verification of real-time systems. In: WING@ETAPS/IJCAR (2010)
6. Basu, A., Bozga, M., Sifakis, J.: Modeling heterogeneous real-time components in BIP. In: SEFM (2006)
7. Behrmann, G., David, A., Larsen, K.G., Håkansson, J., Pettersson, P., Yi, W., Hendriks, M.: UPPAAL 4.0. In: QEST (2006)
8. Bengtsson, J., Jonsson, B., Lilius, J., Yi, W.: Partial order reductions for timed systems. In: Sangiorgi, D., de Simone, R. (eds.) CONCUR 1998. LNCS, vol. 1466, pp. 485–500. Springer, Heidelberg (1998)
9. Bensalem, S., Bozga, M., Sifakis, J., Nguyen, T.-H.: Compositional verification for component-based systems and application. In: Cha, S(S.), Choi, J.-Y., Kim, M., Lee, I., Viswanathan, M. (eds.) ATVA 2008. LNCS, vol. 5311, pp. 64–79. Springer, Heidelberg (2008)
10. Berendsen, J., Vaandrager, F.W.: Compositional abstraction in real-time model checking. In: Cassez, F., Jard, C. (eds.) FORMATS 2008. LNCS, vol. 5215, pp. 233–249. Springer, Heidelberg (2008)
11. Bornot, S., Sifakis, J.: An algebraic framework for urgency. Information and Computation (1998)
12. Bouyer, P.: Forward analysis of updatable timed automata. Form. Methods Syst. Des. (2004)
13. Bozga, M., Daws, C., Maler, O., Olivero, A., Tripakis, S., Yovine, S.: Kronos: A model-checking tool for real-time systems. In: Vardi, M.Y. (ed.) CAV 1998. LNCS, vol. 1427, pp. 546–550. Springer, Heidelberg (1998)
14. Courcoubetis, C., Yannakakis, M.: Minimum and maximum delay problems in real-time systems. Formal Methods in System Design (1992)
15. David, A., Larsen, K.G., Legay, A., Møller, M.H., Nyman, U., Ravn, A.P., Skou, A., Wasowski, A.: Compositional verification of real-time systems using Ecdar. STTT (2012)
16. de Boer, F.S., Hannemann, U., de Roever, W.-P.: Hoare-style compositional proof systems for reactive shared variable concurrency. In: Ramesh, S., Sivakumar, G. (eds.) FSTTCS 1997. LNCS, vol. 1346, pp. 267–283. Springer, Heidelberg (1997)
17. Fietzke, A., Weidenbach, C.: Superposition as a decision procedure for timed automata. Mathematics in Computer Science (2012)
18. Gardey, G., Lime, D., Magnin, M., Roux, O(H.): Romeo: A tool for analyzing time petri nets. In: Etessami, K., Rajamani, S.K. (eds.) CAV 2005. LNCS, vol. 3576, pp. 418–423. Springer, Heidelberg (2005)
19. Henzinger, T.A., Nicollin, X., Sifakis, J., Yovine, S.: Symbolic model checking for real-time systems. Inf. Comput. (1994)
20. Lamport, L.: A fast mutual exclusion algorithm. ACM Trans. Comput. Syst. (1987)

21. Legay, A., Bensalem, S., Boyer, B., Bozga, M.: Incremental generation of linear invariants for component-based systems. In: ACSD (2013)
22. Lin, S.-W., Liu, Y., Hsiung, P.-A., Sun, J., Dong, J.S.: Automatic generation of provably correct embedded systems. In: Aoki, T., Taguchi, K. (eds.) ICFEM 2012. LNCS, vol. 7635, pp. 214–229. Springer, Heidelberg (2012)
23. Salah, R.B., Bozga, M., Maler, O.: Compositional timing analysis. In: EMSOFT (2009)
24. Tripakis, S.: Verifying progress in timed systems. In: Katoen, J.-P. (ed.) ARTS 1999. LNCS, vol. 1601, pp. 299–314. Springer, Heidelberg (1999)
25. Wang, F.: Redlib for the formal verification of embedded systems. In: ISoLA (2006)

Characterizing Algebraic Invariants by Differential Radical Invariants*

Khalil Ghorbal and André Platzer

Carnegie Mellon University, Pittsburgh, PA, 15213, USA
{kghorbal,aplatzer}@cs.cmu.edu

Abstract We prove that any invariant algebraic set of a given polynomial vector field can be algebraically represented by one polynomial and a finite set of its successive Lie derivatives. This so-called *differential radical characterization* relies on a sound abstraction of the reachable set of solutions by the smallest variety that contains it. The characterization leads to a differential radical invariant proof rule that is sound and complete, which implies that invariance of algebraic equations over real-closed fields is decidable. Furthermore, the problem of generating invariant varieties is shown to be as hard as minimizing the rank of a symbolic matrix, and is therefore NP-hard. We investigate symbolic linear algebra tools based on Gaussian elimination to efficiently automate the generation. The approach can, e.g., generate nontrivial algebraic invariant equations capturing the airplane behavior during take-off or landing in longitudinal motion.

Keywords: invariant algebraic sets, polynomial vector fields, real algebraic geometry, Zariski topology, higher-order Lie derivation, automated generation and checking, symbolic linear algebra, rank minimization, formal verification

1 Introduction

Reasoning about the solutions of differential equations by means of their conserved functions and expressions is ubiquitous all over science studying dynamical processes. It is even crucial in many scientific fields (e.g. control theory or experimental physics), where a guarantee that the behavior of the system will remain within a certain predictable region is required. In computer science, the interest of the automated generation of these conserved expressions, so-called *invariants*, was essentially driven and motivated by the formal verification of different aspects of hybrid systems, i.e. systems combining discrete dynamics with differential equations for the continuous dynamics.

The verification of hybrid systems requires ways of handling both the discrete and continuous dynamics, e.g., by proofs [15], abstraction [21,27], or approximation [10]. Fundamentally, however, the study of the safety of hybrid systems can be shown to reduce constructively to the problem of generating invariants for their differential equations [18]. We focus on this core problem in this paper. We study the case of *algebraic*

---

* This material is based upon work supported by the National Science Foundation by NSF CAREER Award CNS-1054246, NSF EXPEDITION CNS-0926181 and grant no. CNS-0931985. This research is also partially supported by the Defense Advanced Research Agency under contract no. DARPA FA8750-12-2-0291.

E. Ábrahám and K. Havelund (Eds.): TACAS 2014, LNCS 8413, pp. 279–294, 2014.
© Springer-Verlag Berlin Heidelberg 2014

invariant equation, i.e. invariants described by a polynomial equation of the form $h = 0$ for a polynomial h. We also only consider algebraic differential equations (or algebraic vector fields), i.e. systems of ordinary differential equations in (vectorial) explicit form $\frac{d\boldsymbol{x}}{dt} = \boldsymbol{p}(\boldsymbol{x})$, with a polynomial right-hand side, $\boldsymbol{p}$. The class of algebraic vector fields is far from restrictive and many analytic nonalgebraic functions, such as the square root, the inverse, the exponential or trigonometric functions, can be exactly modeled as solutions of ordinary differential equations with a polynomial vector field (a concrete example will be given in Section 6.2).

While algebraic invariant equations are not the only invariants of interest for hybrid systems [19,17], they are still intimately related to all other algebraic invariants, such as semialgebraic invariants. We, thus, believe that the characterization we achieve in this paper to be an important step forward in understanding the invariance problem of polynomial vector fields, and hence the hybrid systems with polynomial vector fields.

Our results indicate that algebraic geometry is well suited to reason about and effectively compute algebraic invariant equations. Relevant concepts and results from algebraic geometry will be introduced and discussed as needed. The proofs of all presented results are available in [5].

Content. In Section 2, we introduce a precise algebraic abstraction of the reachable set of the solution of a generic algebraic initial value problem. This abstraction is used to give a necessary and sufficient condition for a polynomial h to have the reachable set of the solution as a subset of the set of its roots. Section 3 builds on top of this characterization to, firstly, check the invariance of a variety candidate (Section 3.1) and, secondly, give an algebraic characterization for a variety to be an invariant for a polynomial vector field (Section 3.2). The characterization of invariant varieties is exploited in Section 4 where the generation of invariant varieties is reduced to symbolic linear algebra computation. The contributions of this work are summarized in Section 5. Finally, Section 6 presents three case studies to highlight the importance of our approach through concrete and rather challenging examples.

2   Sound and Precise Algebraic Abstraction by Zariski Closure

We consider autonomous[1] algebraic initial value problems (see Def. 1 below). A nonautonomous system with polynomial time dependency can be reformulated as an autonomous system by adding a clock variable that reflects the progress of time. In this section, we investigate algebraic invariant equations for the considered initial value problems. This study is novel and will turn out to be fruitful from both the theoretical and practical points of view. The usual approach which assumes the initial value to be in a region of the space, often an algebraic set, will be discussed in Section 3.

Let $\boldsymbol{x} = (x_1, \ldots, x_n) \in \mathbb{R}^n$, and $\boldsymbol{x}(t) = (x_1(t), \ldots, x_n(t))$, where $x_i : \mathbb{R} \to \mathbb{R}$, $t \mapsto x_i(t)$. The initial value $\boldsymbol{x}(t_\iota) = (x_1(t_\iota), \ldots, x_n(t_\iota)) \in \mathbb{R}^n$, for some $t_\iota \in \mathbb{R}$, will be denoted by $\boldsymbol{x}_\iota$. We do not consider any additional constraint on the dynamics, that is the evolution domain corresponds to the domain of definition.

---

[1] Autonomous means that the rate of change of the system over time depends only on the system's state, not on time.

Definition 1 (Algebraic Initial Value Problem). *Let p_i, $1 \leq i \leq n$, be multivariate polynomials of the polynomial ring $\mathbb{R}[\boldsymbol{x}]$. An algebraic initial value problem is a pair of an explicit algebraic ordinary differential equations system (or polynomial vector field), $\boldsymbol{p}$, and an initial value, $\boldsymbol{x}_\iota \in \mathbb{R}^n$:*

$$\frac{dx_i}{dt} = \dot{x}_i = p_i(\boldsymbol{x}), 1 \leq i \leq n, \ \boldsymbol{x}(t_\iota) = \boldsymbol{x}_\iota \ . \tag{1}$$

Since polynomial functions are smooth (C^∞, i.e. they have derivatives of any order), they are locally Lipschitz-continuous. By Cauchy-Lipschitz theorem (a.k.a. Picard-Lindelöf theorem), there exists a unique maximal solution to the initial value problem (1) defined on some nonempty open set $U_t \subseteq \mathbb{R}$. A global solution defined for all $t \in \mathbb{R}$ may not exist in general. For instance, the maximal solution $x(t)$ of the 1-dimensional system $\{\dot{x} = x^2, x(t_\iota) = x_\iota \neq 0\}$ is defined on $\mathbb{R} \setminus \{t_\iota + x_\iota^{-1}\}$.

Algebraic invariant equations for initial value problems are defined as follows.

Definition 2 (Algebraic Invariant Equation (Initial Value Problem))

An algebraic invariant equation for the initial value problem (1) is an expression of the form $h(\boldsymbol{x}(t)) = 0$ that holds true for all $t \in U_t$, where $h \in \mathbb{R}[\boldsymbol{x}]$ and $\boldsymbol{x} : U_t \rightarrow \mathbb{R}^n$, is the (unique) maximal solution of (1).

Notice that any (finite) disjunction of conjunctions of algebraic invariant equations over the reals is also an algebraic invariant equation (w.r.t. Def. 2) using the following equivalence ($\mathbb{R}[\boldsymbol{x}]$ is an integral domain):

$$\bigvee_i \bigwedge_j f_{i,j} = 0 \longleftrightarrow \prod_i \sum_j f_{i,j}^2 = 0 \ . \tag{2}$$

In Def. 2, the function $h(\boldsymbol{x}(t))$, and hence the polynomial $h(\boldsymbol{x})$, depend on the fixed but unknown initial value $\boldsymbol{x}_\iota$. We implicitly assume this dependency for a clearer notation and will emphasize it whenever needed. Also, observe that $h(\boldsymbol{x}(t))$, seen as a real valued function of time t, is only defined over the open set $U_t \subseteq \mathbb{R}$ since the solution $\boldsymbol{x}(t)$ is itself only defined over U_t. The polynomial function $h : \mathbb{R}^n \rightarrow \mathbb{R}; \boldsymbol{x} \mapsto h(\boldsymbol{x})$ is, however, defined for all $\mathbb{R}^n$.

Definition 3 (Orbit). *The reachable set, or orbit, of the solution of Eq. (1), $\boldsymbol{x}(t)$ is defined as $\mathcal{O}(\boldsymbol{x}_\iota) \overset{def}{=} \{\boldsymbol{x}(t) \mid t \in U_t\} \subseteq \mathbb{R}^n$.*

The complete geometrical characterization of the orbit requires the exact solution of Eq. (1). Very few initial value problems admit an analytic solution, although a local approximation can be always given using Taylor series approximations (such approximation is for instance used in [10] for the verification of hybrid systems). In this work, we introduce a sound abstraction of the orbit, $\mathcal{O}(\boldsymbol{x}_\iota)$, using (affine) varieties[2]. The idea is to embed the orbit (which is not a variety in general) in a variety to be defined. The embedding we will be using is a well-known topological closure operation in algebraic

---

[2] In the literature, some authors use the terminology algebraic sets so that varieties is reserved for irreducible algebraic sets. Here we will use both terms equally.

geometry called the *Zariski closure* ([6, Chapter 1]). Varieties, which are sets of points, can be represented and computed efficiently using their algebraic counterpart: ideals of polynomials. Therefore, we first recall three useful definitions: an ideal of the ring $\mathbb{R}[x]$, the variety of a subset of $\mathbb{R}[x]$, and finally the vanishing ideal of a subset of $\mathbb{R}^n$.

Definition 4 (Ideal). *An ideal I is a subset of $\mathbb{R}[x]$ that contains the polynomial zero (0), is stable under addition, and external multiplication. That is, for all $h_1, h_2 \in I$, the sum $h_1 + h_2 \in I$; and if $h \in I$, then, $qh \in I$ for all $q \in \mathbb{R}[x]$.*

For a finite natural number r, we denote by $\langle h_1, \ldots, h_r \rangle$ the subset of $\mathbb{R}[x]$ generated by the polynomials $\{h_1, \ldots, h_r\}$, i.e. the set of linear combinations of the polynomials h_i (where the coefficients are themselves polynomials):

$$\langle h_1, \ldots, h_r \rangle \stackrel{\text{def}}{=} \left\{ \sum_{i=1}^{r} g_i h_i \mid g_1, \ldots, g_r \in \mathbb{R}[x] \right\} .$$

By Def. 4, the set $\langle h_1, \ldots, h_r \rangle$ is an ideal. More interestingly, by Hilbert's Basis Theorem [7], any ideal I of the Noetherian ring $\mathbb{R}[x]$ can be *finitely generated* by, say $\{h_1, \ldots, h_r\}$, so that $I = \langle h_1, \ldots, h_r \rangle$.

Given $Y \subseteq \mathbb{R}[x]$, the variety (over the reals), $V(Y)$, is a subset of $\mathbb{R}^n$ defined by the common roots of all polynomials in Y. That is,

$$V(Y) \stackrel{\text{def}}{=} \{x \in \mathbb{R}^n \mid \forall h \in Y, h(x) = 0\} .$$

The vanishing ideal (over the reals), $I(S)$, of $S \subseteq \mathbb{R}^n$ is the set of all polynomials that evaluates to zero for all $x \in S$:

$$I(S) \stackrel{\text{def}}{=} \{h \in \mathbb{R}[x] \mid \forall x \in S, h(x) = 0\} .$$

The Zariski closure $\bar{\mathcal{O}}(x_\iota)$ of the orbit $\mathcal{O}(x_\iota)$ is defined as the variety of the vanishing ideal of $\mathcal{O}(x_\iota)$:

$$\bar{\mathcal{O}}(x_\iota) \stackrel{\text{def}}{=} V(I(\mathcal{O}(x_\iota))) . \tag{3}$$

That is, $\bar{\mathcal{O}}(x_\iota)$ is defined as the set of all points that are common roots of all polynomials that are zero everywhere on the orbit $\mathcal{O}(x_\iota)$. The variety $\bar{\mathcal{O}}(x_\iota)$ soundly overapproximates all reachable states $x(t)$ in the orbit of $\mathcal{O}(x_\iota)$, including the initial value x_ι:

Proposition 1 (Soundness of Zariski Closure). $\mathcal{O}(x_\iota) \subseteq \bar{\mathcal{O}}(x_\iota)$.

Therefore, all safety properties that hold true for $\bar{\mathcal{O}}(x_\iota)$, are also true for $\mathcal{O}(x_\iota)$. The soundness in Proposition 1 corresponds to the reflexivity property of the Zariski closure: for any subset S of $\mathbb{R}^n$, $S \subseteq V(I(S))$. Besides, the algebraic geometrical fact that the Zariski closure $\bar{\mathcal{O}}(x_\iota)$ is the *smallest*[3] variety containing $\mathcal{O}(x_\iota)$ corresponds to the fact that $\bar{\mathcal{O}}(x_\iota)$ is the most precise algebraic abstraction of $\mathcal{O}(x_\iota)$.

---

[3] Smallest here is to be understood w.r.t. to the usual geometrical sense, that is, any other variety containing $\mathcal{O}(x_\iota)$, contains also its closure $\bar{\mathcal{O}}(x_\iota)$.

Observe that if the set of generators of $I(\mathcal{O}(\boldsymbol{x}_\iota))$ is only the zero polynomial, $I(\mathcal{O}(\boldsymbol{x}_\iota)) = \langle 0 \rangle$, then $\bar{\mathcal{O}}(\boldsymbol{x}_\iota) = \mathbb{R}^n$ (the whole space) and the Zariski closure fails to be informative. For instance, for (non-degenerated) one dimensional vector fields ($n = 1$) that evolve over time, the only univariate polynomial that has infinitely many roots is the zero polynomial. This points out the limitation of the closure operation used in this work and raises interesting question about how to deal with such cases (this will be left as future work).

The closure operation abstracts time. This means that $\bar{\mathcal{O}}(\boldsymbol{x}_\iota)$ defines a subset of $\mathbb{R}^n$ within which the solution always evolves without saying anything about where the system will be at what time (which is what a solution would describe and which is exactly what the abstraction we are defining here gets rid off). In particular, $\bar{\mathcal{O}}(\boldsymbol{x}_\iota)$ is independent of whether the system evolves forward or backward in time.

Although, we know that $I(\mathcal{O}(\boldsymbol{x}_\iota))$ is finitely generated, computing all its generators may be intractable. By the real Nullstellensatz, vanishing ideals over $\mathbb{R}$ are in fact exactly the real radical ideals [1, Section 4.1]. In real algebraic geometry, real radical ideals are notoriously hard[4] to compute. However, we shall see in the sequel that *Lie derivation* will give us a powerful computational handle that permits to tightly approximate (and even compute in some cases) $I(\mathcal{O}(\boldsymbol{x}_\iota))$. The Lie derivative of a polynomial along a vector field is defined as follows.

Definition 5 (Lie Derivative). *The Lie derivative of $h \in \mathbb{R}[\boldsymbol{x}]$ along the vector field $\boldsymbol{p} = (p_1, \ldots, p_n)$ is defined by:*

$$\mathfrak{L}_{\boldsymbol{p}}(h) \overset{\text{def}}{=} \sum_{i=1}^{n} \frac{\partial h}{\partial x_i} p_i \;. \tag{4}$$

Higher-order Lie derivatives are defined recursively: $\mathfrak{L}_{\boldsymbol{p}}^{(k+1)}(h) \overset{\text{def}}{=} \mathfrak{L}_{\boldsymbol{p}}(\mathfrak{L}_{\boldsymbol{p}}^{(k)}(h))$, *with* $\mathfrak{L}_{\boldsymbol{p}}^{(0)}(h) \overset{\text{def}}{=} h$.

We state an important property of the ideal $I(\mathcal{O}(\boldsymbol{x}_\iota))$. Similar result is known under different formulations ([23, Theorem 3.1] and [16, Lemma 3.7]).

Proposition 2. *$I(\mathcal{O}(\boldsymbol{x}_\iota))$ is a differential ideal for $\mathfrak{L}_{\boldsymbol{p}}$, i.e. it is stable under the action of the $\mathfrak{L}_{\boldsymbol{p}}$ operator. That is, for all $h \in I(\mathcal{O}(\boldsymbol{x}_\iota))$, $\mathfrak{L}_{\boldsymbol{p}}(h) \in I(\mathcal{O}(\boldsymbol{x}_\iota))$.*

In the next section, we give a necessary and sufficient condition for a polynomial h to be in $I(\mathcal{O}(\boldsymbol{x}_\iota))$, that is for the expression $h = 0$ to be an algebraic invariant equation for the initial value problem (1), i.e. h evaluates to 0 all along the orbit of $\boldsymbol{x}_\iota$.

3 Differential Radical Characterization

In this section, we study the algebraic properties of the Zariski closure $\bar{\mathcal{O}}(\boldsymbol{x}_\iota)$ defined in the previous section. We then define and characterize invariant algebraic sets of polynomial vector fields.

---

[4] Given an ideal $I \subseteq \mathbb{R}[\boldsymbol{x}]$, the degree of the polynomials that generate its real radical is bounded by the degree of polynomials that generate I to the power of $2^{O(n^2)}$ [14, Theorem 5.9].

For $h \in \mathbb{R}[x]$, we recursively construct an ascending chain of ideals of $\mathbb{R}[x]$ by appending successive Lie derivatives of h to the list of generators:

$$\langle h \rangle \subset \langle h, \mathfrak{L}_p^{(1)}(h) \rangle \subset \cdots \subset \langle h, \ldots, \mathfrak{L}_p^{(N-1)}(h) \rangle = \langle h, \ldots, \mathfrak{L}_p^{(N)}(h) \rangle .$$

Since the ring $\mathbb{R}[x]$ is Noetherian, the chain above has necessarily a finite length: the maximal ideal (in the sense of inclusion), so-called the *differential radical ideal*[5] of h, will be denoted by $\sqrt[\mathfrak{L}p]{\langle h \rangle}$. Its *order* is the smallest N such that:

$$\mathfrak{L}_p^{(N)}(h) \in \langle \mathfrak{L}_p^{(0)}(h), \ldots, \mathfrak{L}_p^{(N-1)}(h) \rangle . \tag{5}$$

The following theorem, an important contribution of this work, states a necessary and sufficient condition for a polynomial h to be in $I(\mathcal{O}(x_\iota))$.

Theorem 1 (Differential Radical Characterization). *Let $h \in \mathbb{R}[x]$, and let N denote the order of $\sqrt[\mathfrak{L}p]{\langle h \rangle}$. Then, $h \in I(\mathcal{O}(x_\iota))$ if and only if*

$$\bigwedge_{0 \leq i \leq N-1} \mathfrak{L}_p^{(i)}(h)(x_\iota) = 0 . \tag{6}$$

The statement of Theorem 1 is general and assumes nothing about $x_\iota \in \mathbb{R}^n$. A natural question to ask is how differential radical characterization can be used to reason about *invariant regions* of a given polynomial vector field. By invariant (or stable) regions, we mean, regions $S \subset \mathbb{R}^n$ from which the trajectory of the solution of the initial value problem (1), with $x_\iota \in S$, can never escape. In particular, we focus on invariant algebraic sets where S is variety.

Definition 6 (Invariant Variety). *The variety S is an invariant variety for the vector field p if and only if $\forall x_\iota \in S, \mathcal{O}(x_\iota) \subseteq S$.*

Dual to the geometrical point of view in Def. 6, the algebraic point of view is given by extending the definition of algebraic invariant equation for initial value problems (Def. 2), to algebraic invariant equation for polynomial vector fields.

Definition 7 (Algebraic Invariant Equation (Vector Field)). *The expression $h = 0$ is an algebraic invariant equation for the vector field p if and only if $V(\langle h \rangle)$ is an invariant variety for p.*

Unlike Def. 2, Def. 7, or its geometrical counterpart, Def. 6, corresponds to the typical object of studies in hybrid system verification as they permit the abstraction of the continuous part by means of algebraic equations. In the two following sections, we show how differential radical characterization (Theorem 1) can be used to address two particular questions: *checking* the invariance of a variety candidate (Section 3.1) and *characterizing* invariant varieties (Section 3.2).

We will say that the polynomial h is a *differential radical invariant* (for p) if and only if $V\left(\sqrt[\mathfrak{L}p]{\langle h \rangle}\right)$ is an invariant variety for p.

---

[5] The construction of $\sqrt[\mathfrak{L}p]{\langle h \rangle}$ is very similar to the construction of the radical of an ideal except with higher-order Lie derivatives in place of higher powers of polynomials.

3.1 Checking Invariant Varieties by Differential Radical Invariants

The problem we solve in this section is as follows: given a polynomial vector field p, can we decide whether the equation $h = 0$ is an algebraic invariant equation for the vector field p ? Dually, we want to check whether the variety $V(\langle h \rangle)$ is invariant for p. Theorem 2 solves the problem.

Theorem 2. *Let $h \in \mathbb{R}[x]$, and let N denote the order of $\sqrt[\mathcal{L}_p]{\langle h \rangle}$. Then, $V(\langle h \rangle)$ is an invariant variety for the vector field p (or equivalently $h = 0$ is an algebraic invariant equation for p) if and only if*

$$h = 0 \rightarrow \bigwedge_{1 \leq i \leq N-1} \mathcal{L}_p^{(i)}(h) = 0 \ . \tag{7}$$

Corollary 1 (Decidability). *It is decidable whether the expression $h = 0$ is an algebraic invariant equation for the vector field p assuming real algebraic coefficients for h and p.*

The *sound* and *complete* related proof rule from Theorem 2 can be written as follows (N denotes the order of $\sqrt[\mathcal{L}_p]{\langle h \rangle}$):

$$\text{(DRI)} \ \frac{h = 0 \rightarrow \bigwedge_{1 \leq i \leq N-1} \mathcal{L}_p^{(i)}(h) = 0}{(h = 0) \rightarrow [\dot{x} = p](h = 0)} \ . \tag{8}$$

Using the naive trick in Eq. (2), theoretically, the proof rule can be easily extended to check for the invariance of any finite disjunction of conjunctions of algebraic invariant equations for p. This means that we can check for the invariance of any variety for p, given its algebraic representation. However, in practice, other techniques, outside the scope of this paper, should be considered to try to keep the degree of the involved polynomials as low as possible.

3.2 Differential Radical Characterization of Invariant Varieties

In the previous section, we were given a variety candidate of the form $V(\langle h \rangle)$ and asked whether we can decide for its invariance. In this section, we characterize all invariant varieties of a vector field p using a differential radical criterion. The following theorem fully characterizes invariant varieties of polynomial vector fields.

Theorem 3 (Characterization of Invariant Varieties). *A variety S is an invariant variety for the vector field p if and only if there exists a polynomial h such that $S = V\left(\sqrt[\mathcal{L}_p]{\langle h \rangle}\right)$. As a consequence, every invariant variety corresponds to an algebraic invariant equation involving a polynomial and its higher-order Lie derivatives (N denotes the order of $\sqrt[\mathcal{L}_p]{\langle h \rangle}$):*

$$\bigwedge_{0 \leq i \leq N-1} \mathcal{L}_p^{(i)}(h) = 0 \ . \tag{9}$$

Observe how Theorem 3 proves, from the differential radical characterization point of view, the well-known fact about invariant polynomial functions [17, Theorem 3]: if $\mathfrak{L}_{\boldsymbol{p}}(h(\boldsymbol{x})) = 0$, then, for any $c \in \mathbb{R}$, $\sqrt[\mathfrak{L}_{\boldsymbol{p}}]{\langle h(\boldsymbol{x}) - c \rangle} = \langle h(\boldsymbol{x}) - c \rangle$, and so $s = v(\langle h(\boldsymbol{x}) - c \rangle)$ is an invariant variety for $\boldsymbol{p}$.

An algebraic invariant equation for $\boldsymbol{p}$ is defined semantically (Def. 7) as a polynomial that evaluates to zero if it is zero initially (admits $\boldsymbol{x}_\iota$ as a root). Differential radical invariants are, on the other hand, defined as a structured, syntactically computable, conjunction of polynomial equations involving one polynomial and its successive Lie derivatives. By Theorem 3, both coincide.

The explicit formulation of Eq. (5), namely

$$\mathfrak{L}_{\boldsymbol{p}}^{(N)}(h) = \sum_{i=0}^{N-1} g_i \mathfrak{L}_{\boldsymbol{p}}^{(i)}(h), \tag{10}$$

for some $g_i \in \mathbb{R}[\boldsymbol{x}]$, is computationally attractive as it only involves polynomial arithmetic on higher-order Lie derivatives of one polynomial, h, which in turn can be computed automatically by symbolic differentiation. Section 4 exploits this fact to automatically generate differential radical invariants and consequently invariant varieties.

4   Effective Generation of Invariant Varieties

In the previous section, we have seen (Theorem 3) that differential radical ideals characterize invariant varieties. Based on Eq. (10), we explain in this section how we automatically construct differential radical ideals given a polynomial vector field $\boldsymbol{p}$ by deriving a set of constraints that the coefficients of a parametrized polynomial have to satisfy.

The degree of a polynomial in $\mathbb{R}[\boldsymbol{x}]$ is defined as the maximum degree among the (finite) set of degrees of its monomials[6]. When the degrees of all nonzero monomials of a polynomial h are equal, we say that h is *homogeneous*, or a *form*, of degree d.

By introducing an extra variable x_0 and multiplying all monomials by a suitable power of x_0, any polynomial of $\mathbb{R}[\boldsymbol{x}]$ can be homogenized to a form in $\mathbb{R}[x_0][\boldsymbol{x}]$. The additional variable x_0 is considered as a time-independent function: its time derivative is zero ($\dot{x}_0 = p_0 = 0$). "De-homogenizing" the vector field corresponds to instantiating x_0 with 1, which gives back the original vector field. Geometrically, the homogenization of polynomials corresponds to the notion of projective varieties in projective geometry, where the homogenized polynomial is the algebraic representative of the original variety in the projective plane [3, Chapter 8].

From a computational prospective, working in the projective plane offers a more symmetric representation: all monomials of a form have the same degree. The arithmetic of degrees over forms is also simplified: the degree of a product is the sum of the degrees of the operands. In the reminder of this section, we only consider forms of $\mathbb{R}[x_0, \dots, x_n]$. The symbol $\boldsymbol{x}$ will denote the vector of all involved variables.

---

[6] The degree of the zero polynomial (0) is undefined. We assume in this work that all finite degrees are acceptable for the zero polynomial.

If h denotes a form of degree d, and d' the maximum degree among the degrees of p_i, then the degree of the polynomial $\mathfrak{L}_{\boldsymbol{p}}^{(k)}(h)$ is given by:

$$\deg(\mathfrak{L}_{\boldsymbol{p}}^{(k)}(h)) = d + k(-1 + d') \ . \tag{11}$$

Recall that a form of degree d in $\mathbb{R}[x_0, \dots, x_n]$ has

$$m_d \stackrel{\text{def}}{=} \binom{n+d}{d} \tag{12}$$

monomials (the binomial coefficient of $n+d$ and d). A parametrized form $h_{\boldsymbol{\alpha}}$ of degree d can therefore be represented by its symbolic coefficients' vector $\boldsymbol{\alpha} : \mathbb{R}^{m_d}$. For this representation to be canonical, one needs to fix an order over monomials of the same degree. We will use the usual lexicographical order, except for x_0: $x_1 > x_2 > \cdots > x_n > x_0$. We first compare the degrees of x_1, if equal, we compare the degrees of x_2 and so on till reaching x_n and then x_0. For instance, for $n = 2$, a parametrized form $h_{\boldsymbol{\alpha}}$ of degree $d = 1$ is equal to $\alpha_1 x_1 + \alpha_2 x_2 + \alpha_3 x_0$. Its related coefficients' vector is $\boldsymbol{\alpha} = (\alpha_1, \alpha_2, \alpha_3)$.

Let $h_{\boldsymbol{\alpha}}$ be a parametrized form of degree d and let $\boldsymbol{\alpha} = (\alpha_1, \dots, \alpha_{m_d})$ denote the coefficients' vector with respect to the monomial order defined above. Since all polynomials in Eq. (10) are forms in projective coordinates, the degree of each term $g_i \mathfrak{L}_{\boldsymbol{p}}^{(i)}(h_{\boldsymbol{\alpha}})$ matches exactly the degree of $\mathfrak{L}_{\boldsymbol{p}}^{(N)}(h_{\boldsymbol{\alpha}})$. Hence, by Eq. (11): $\deg(g_i) = (N - i)(-1 + d')$. The coefficients' vector of each form g_i is then a vector, $\boldsymbol{\beta}_i$, of size $m_{(N-i)(-1+d')}$ (see Eq. (12)). So that we obtain $m_{d+N(-1+d')}$ biaffine equations: linear in α_i, $1 \le i \le m_d$, and affine $\boldsymbol{\beta}_{i,j}$, $0 \le i \le N - 1$, $1 \le j \le m_{(N-i)(-1+d')}$. A concrete example is as follows.

Example 1. Suppose we have $n = 2$, $d' = 1$, $p_1 = a_1 x_1 + a_2 x_2$ and $p_2 = b_1 x_1 + b_2 x_2$. For $d = 1$, the parametrized form $h_{\boldsymbol{\alpha}}$ is equal to $\alpha_1 x_1 + \alpha_2 x_2 + \alpha_3 x_0$. Let $N = 1$. The first-order Lie derivative, $\mathfrak{L}_{\boldsymbol{p}}(h_{\boldsymbol{\alpha}})$, has the same degree, 1, and is equal to $\alpha_1(a_1 x_1 + a_2 x_2) + \alpha_2(b_1 x_1 + b_2 x_2)$. In this case, g is a form of degree 0, that is a real number. So it has one coefficient $\beta \in \mathbb{R}$. We, therefore, obtain $m_1 = \binom{3}{1} = 3$ constraints:

$$
\begin{array}{ll}
(-a_1 + \beta)\alpha_1 + (-b_1)\alpha_2 = 0 \\
(-a_2)\alpha_1 + (-b_2 + \beta)\alpha_2 = 0 \\
(\beta)\alpha_3 \qquad\qquad\qquad\quad = 0
\end{array}
\leftrightarrow
\begin{pmatrix} -a_1 + \beta & -b_1 & 0 \\ -a_2 & -b_2 + \beta & 0 \\ 0 & 0 & \beta \end{pmatrix} \cdot \begin{pmatrix} \alpha_1 \\ \alpha_2 \\ \alpha_3 \end{pmatrix} = 0 \ .
$$

As suggested in Example 1, for a given d and N, and if we concatenate all vectors $\boldsymbol{\beta}_i$ into one vector $\boldsymbol{\beta}$, the equational constraints can be rewritten as a symbolic linear algebra problem of the following form:

$$M_{d,N}(\boldsymbol{\beta})\boldsymbol{\alpha} = 0, \tag{13}$$

where $\boldsymbol{\alpha}$ and $\boldsymbol{\beta}$ are decoupled. The matrix $M_{d,N}(\boldsymbol{\beta})$ is called the *matrix representation* of the ideal membership problem $\mathfrak{L}_{\boldsymbol{p}}^{(N)}(h_{\boldsymbol{\alpha}}) \in ? \langle h_{\boldsymbol{\alpha}}, \dots, \mathfrak{L}_{\boldsymbol{p}}^{(N-1)}(h_{\boldsymbol{\alpha}}) \rangle$.

Recall that the *kernel* (or null-space) of a matrix $M \in \mathbb{R}^{r \times c}$, with r rows and c columns is the subspace of $\mathbb{R}^c$ defined as the preimage of the vector $0 \in \mathbb{R}^c$:

$$\ker(M) \stackrel{\text{def}}{=} \{x \in \mathbb{R}^c \mid Mx = 0\} \ .$$

Let $s = \dim(\ker(M_{d,N}(\beta))) \leq m_d$. If, for all β, $s = 0$, then the kernel is $\{0\}$. Hence, $\alpha = 0$ and, for the chosen N, we have $h_\alpha = 0$: the only differential radical ideal generated by a form of degree d is the trivial ideal $\langle 0 \rangle$. If, however, $s \geq 1$, then, by Theorem 3, we generate an invariant (projective) variety for p. In this case, de-homogenizing is not always possible. In fact, the constraint on the initial value could involve x_0, which prevents the de-homogenization (see Example 2). Otherwise, we recover an invariant (affine) variety for the original vector field. This is formally stated in the following theorem.

Theorem 4 (Effective Generation of Projective Invariant Varieties)

Let h_α denote a parametrized form of degree d. There exists a real vector β such that $\dim(\ker(M_{d,N}(\beta))) \geq 1$ if and only if for $\alpha \in \ker(M_{d,N}(\beta))$, $V\left(\sqrt[\mathcal{L}_p]{\langle h_\alpha \rangle}\right) \subset \mathbb{R}^{n+1}$ is a projective invariant variety for the homogenized vector field.

When $s = \dim(\ker(M_{d,N}(\beta))) \geq 1$, the subspace $\ker(M_{d,N}(\beta))$ is spanned by s vectors, $e_1, \ldots, e_s \in \mathbb{R}^{m_d}$, and for $\alpha = \gamma_1 e_1 + \cdots + \gamma_s e_s$, for arbitrarily $(\gamma_1, \ldots, \gamma_s) \in \mathbb{R}^s$, the variety $V\left(\sqrt[\mathcal{L}_p]{\langle h_\alpha \rangle}\right)$ is a *family* of invariant varieties of p (parametrized with γ).

In the sequel, we give a sufficient condition, so that, for any given initial value, one gets a variety (different from the trivial whole space) that embeds the reachable set of the trajectory, $\mathcal{O}(x_\iota)$. For instance, for conservative Hamiltonian system, if the total energy function, h, is polynomial (such as the energy function of the perfect pendulum), then, for any initial value x_ι, $\mathcal{O}(x_\iota) \subseteq V\left(\sqrt[\mathcal{L}_p]{\langle h(x) - h(x_\iota)\rangle}\right) = V(\langle h(x) - h(x_\iota)\rangle)$.

For a generic $x_\iota \in \mathbb{R}^n$, if x_ι satisfies Eq. (6), then, by Theorem 1, $h_\alpha \in I(\mathcal{O}(x_\iota))$, and $\bar{\mathcal{O}}(x_\iota) \subseteq V\left(\sqrt[\mathcal{L}_p]{\langle h_\alpha \rangle}\right)$ ([5, Corollary 1]). However, for x_ι to satisfy Eq. (6), α must be in the intersection of N hyperplanes, $H_0, \ldots, H_{N-1}$, each defined explicitly by the condition $\mathfrak{L}_p^{(i)}(h_\alpha)(x_\iota) = 0$:

$$H_i \stackrel{\text{def}}{=} \left\{ \alpha \in \mathbb{R}^{m_d} \mid \mathfrak{L}_p^{(i)}(h_\alpha)(x_\iota) = 0 \right\}. \tag{14}$$

Proposition 3 (Effective Sound Approximation of $\mathcal{O}(x_\iota)$). *Let h_α be a parametrized form of degree d, and $M_{d,N}(\beta)$ the matrix representation of Eq. (10). Let $H_i \subseteq \mathbb{R}^{m_d}$, $0 \leq i \leq N-1$, be the hyperplanes defined in Eq. (14). Then, $\mathcal{O}(x_\iota) \subseteq V\left(\sqrt[\mathcal{L}_p]{\langle h_\alpha \rangle}\right)$, if there exists β such that:*

$$\dim(\ker(M_{d,N}(\beta))) > m_d - \dim\left(\bigcap_{i=0}^{N-1} H_i\right). \tag{15}$$

The remainder of this section discusses our approach to maximize the dimension of the kernel of $M_{d,N}(h)$, as well as the complexity of the underlying computation.

Gaussian Elimination. Let $\beta = (\beta_1, \ldots, \beta_s) : \mathbb{R}^s$. By Theorem 4, we want to find an instance, β^*, of β that maximizes $\dim \ker(M_{d,N}(\beta))$, where all the elements of $M_{d,N}(\beta)$ are affine in β. At each iteration, our algorithm [5, Algorithm 1] assigns new values to the remaining coefficients in β for the matrix $M_{d,N}(\beta)$ to maximize the dimension of its kernel. A set, $\mathcal{M}$, gathers all the instantiations of $M_{d,N}(\beta)$. The procedure ends when no further assignment can be done. The algorithm is in fact a typical `MapReduce` procedure which can be parallelized. A naive approach would be to first extract a basis for the matrix $M_{d,N}(\boldsymbol{\beta})$ (which requires symbolic computation capabilities for linear algebra), then, solves for βs that zero the determinant. In practice, however, row-reducing speeds up the computation: we row-reduce $M_{d,n}(\boldsymbol{\beta})$, and record any divisions by the pivot element: we then branch with any β that zero the denominator.

Example 2. We apply the algorithm sketched above to Example 1. The determinant of the matrix $M_{1,1}(\beta)$ is $\beta(\beta^2 - (a_1 + b_2)\beta - a_2 b_1 + a_1 b_2)$. Since we do not have any constraints on the parameters a_1, a_2, b_1, b_2, the only generic solution for the determinant is $\beta = 0$. The kernel of $M_{1,1}(0)$, of dimension 1, is generated by $(0, 0, 1)$. The only candidates in this case are $h_\alpha(\boldsymbol{x}) = \gamma x_0$, $\gamma \in \mathbb{R}$. If we de-homogenize (set x_0 to 1), then, $\gamma = 0$ and we find the trivial invariant variety, $\mathbb{R}^n$.

The result of Example 2 is expected as it studies a generic linear vector field without any a priori constraints on the parameters. This triggers, naturally, an interesting feature of the differential radical characterization: its ability to synthesize vector fields to enforce an invariant variety. For instance, in Example 2, let $\delta \overset{\text{def}}{=} (a_1 - b_2)^2 + 4a_2 b_1$. If $\delta \geq 0$, and $a_2 \neq 0$, then the kernel of $M_{1,1}(\beta)$ is generated by the vector $(a_1 - b_2 \pm \sqrt{\delta}, 2a_2, 0)$ (which is an eigenvector of the matrix $M_{1,1}(\beta)$). By Theorem 4, we have an invariant variety given by: $(a_1 - b_2 \pm \sqrt{\delta})x_1 + 2a_2 x_2 = 0$. This is also expected for linear systems as eigenvectors span stable subspaces.

Complexity. By Theorem 4, the generation of invariant varieties is equivalent to maximizing the dimension of the kernel of the matrix $M_{d,N}(\boldsymbol{\beta})$ over unconstrained β, which is in turn equivalent to the following unconstrained minimal rank problem:

$$\min_{\boldsymbol{\beta}} \text{rank}(M_{d,N}(\boldsymbol{\beta})), \tag{16}$$

where the elements of the vector β are in $\mathbb{R}$. If the vector field p has no parameters, then the entries of the matrix $M_{d,N}(\boldsymbol{\beta})$ are either elements of β or real numbers. Under these assumptions, the problem (16) is in PSPACE [2, Corollary 20] over the field of real numbers[7], and is at least NP-hard (see [2, Corollary 12] and [8, Theorem 8.2]) independently from the underlying field. In fact, deciding whether the rank of $M_{d,N}(\boldsymbol{\beta})$ is less than or equal to a given fixed bound is no harder than deciding the corresponding existential first-order theory.

On the other hand, there is an NP-hard lower bound for the feasibility of the original set of (biaffine) equations in β and α given in Eq. (13). In the simpler bilinear case and, assuming, as above, that the vector field has no parameters, finding a nontrivial solution ($\alpha = 0$ is trivial) is also NP-hard [8, Theorems 3.7 and 3.8].

5   Related Work and Contributions

The contribution of this work is fourfold.

---

[7] The complexity class depends on the underlying field and is worse for fields with nonzero characteristic.

Sound and Precise Algebraic Abstraction of Reachable Sets (Section 2). Unlike previous work [28,23,12,11], we start by studying algebraic initial value problems. We propose a sound abstraction (Proposition 1) to embed (overapproximate) the reachable set. Our abstraction relies on the Zariski closure operator over affine varieties (closed sets of the Zariski topology), which allows a clean and sound geometrical abstraction. From there, we define the vanishing ideal of the closure, and give a necessary and sufficient condition (Theorem 1) for a polynomial equation to be an invariant for algebraic initial value problems.

Checking Invariant Varieties by Differential Radical Invariants (Section 3.1). The differential radical characterization allows to check for and falsify the invariance of a variety candidate. Unlike already existing proof rules [28,12,17], which are sound but can only prove a restrictive class of invariants. From Theorem 2, we derive a sound and complete proof rule (Eq. (8)) and prove that the problem is decidable (Corollary 1) over the real-closed algebraic fields.

Differential Radical Characterization of Invariant Varieties (Section 3.2). The differential radical criterion completely characterizes all invariant varieties of polynomial vector fields. This new characterization (Theorem 3) permits to relate invariant varieties to a purely algebraic, well-behaved, conjunction of polynomial equations involving one polynomial and its successive Lie derivatives (Eq. (9)). It naturally generalizes [9,26] where linear vector fields are handled and [24,12] where only a restrictive class of invariant varieties is considered.

Effective Generation of Invariant Varieties (Section 4). Unlike [28,23,11,22], we do not use quantifier elimination procedures nor Gröbner Bases algorithms for the generation of invariant varieties. We have developed and generalized the use of symbolic linear algebra tools to effectively generate families of invariant varieties (Theorem 4) and to soundly overapproximate reachable sets (Proposition 3). In both cases, the problem requires maximizing the dimension of the kernel of a symbolic matrix. The complexity is shown to be NP-hard, but in PSPACE, for polynomial vector fields without parameters. We also generalize the previous related work on polynomial-consecution. In particular, Theorems 2 and 4 in [12] are special cases of, respectively, Theorem 4 and Proposition 3, when the order of differential radical ideals is exactly 1.

6 Case Studies

The following challenging example comes up as a subsystem we encountered when studying aircraft dynamics: $p_1 = -x_2$, $p_2 = x_1$, $p_3 = x_4^2$, $p_4 = x_3 x_4$.

It appears frequently whenever Euler angles and the three dimensional rotational matrix is used to describe the dynamics of rigid body motions. For some chosen initial value, such as $x_\iota = (1, 0, 0, 1)$, it is an exact algebraic encoding of the trigonometric functions : $x_1(t) = \cos(t)$, $x_2(t) = \sin(t)$, $x_3(t) = \tan(t)$, $x_4(t) = \sec(t)$. When $d = 2$ and $N = 1$, the matrix $M_{2,1}(\beta)$ is 35×15, with 90 (out of 525) nonzero elements, and $|\beta| = 5$. The maximum dimension of $\ker(M_{2,1}(\beta))$ is 3 attained for $\beta = \mathbf{0}$. The condition of Proposition 3 is satisfied and, for any x_ι, we find the following algebraic invariant equations for the corresponding initial value problem:

$$h_1 = x_1^2 + x_2^2 - x_{\iota 1}^2 - x_{\iota 2}^2 = 0, \quad h_2 = -x_3^2 + x_4^2 + x_{\iota 3}^2 - x_{\iota 4}^2 = 0 \ .$$

In particular, for the initial value $x_\iota = (1, 0, 0, 1)$, one recovers two trigonometric identities, namely $\cos(t)^2 + \sin(t)^2 - 1 = 0$ for h_1 and $-\tan(t)^2 + \sec(t)^2 - 1 = 0$ for h_2.

For $N = 3$, the matrix $M_{2,3}(\beta)$ is 126×15, with 693 (out of 1890) nonzero elements, and $|\beta| = 55$. We found a β for which the dimension of $\ker(M_{2,3}(\beta))$ is 5. By Theorem 4, we have a family of invariant varieties for p encoded by the following differential radical invariant: $h = \gamma_1 - x_3^2 \gamma_2 + x_4^2 \gamma_2 + x_2 x_4 \gamma_3 + x_1^2 \gamma_4 + x_2^2 \gamma_4 + x_1 x_4 \gamma_5$, where γ_i, $1 \le i \le 5$, are real numbers. In particular, when $(\gamma_1, \gamma_2, \gamma_3, \gamma_4, \gamma_5) = (1, 0, 0, 0, 1)$, we have the following algebraic invariant equation for p:

$$-1 + x_1 x_4 = 0 \wedge -x_2 x_4 + x_3 = 0 \wedge -1 - x_3^2 + x_4^2 = 0 \ . \tag{17}$$

Interestingly, since $x_\iota = (1, 0, 0, 1)$ satisfies the above equations, we recover, respectively, the following trigonometric identities:

$$-1 + \cos(t)\sec(t) = 0 \wedge -\sin(t)\sec(t) + \tan(t) = 0 \wedge -1 - \tan(t)^2 + \sec(t)^2 = 0 \ .$$

We stress the fact that Eq. (17) is *one* algebraic invariant equation for p. In fact, any conjunct alone, a part from $-1 - x_3^2 + x_4^2 = 0$, of Eq. (17) is not an algebraic invariant equation for p. Indeed, we can falsify the candidate $-1 + x_1 x_4 = 0$ using Theorem 2: the implication $-1 + x_1 x_4 = 0 \longrightarrow -x_2 x_4 + x_3 = 0$ is obviously false in general.

Notice that h_1 and h_2 can be found separately by splitting the original vector field into two separate vector fields since the pairs (p_1, p_2) and (p_3, p_4) can be decoupled. However, by decoupling, algebraic invariant equation such as Eq. (17) cannot be found. This clearly shows that in practice, splitting the vector field into independent ones should be done carefully when it comes to generating invariant varieties. This is somehow counter-intuitive as decoupling for the purpose of solving is always desirable. In fact, any decoupling breaks an essential link between all involved variables: time.

We proceed to discuss collision avoidance of two airplanes (Section 6.1) and then the use of invariant varieties to tightly capture the vertical motion of an airplane (Section 6.2).

6.1 Collision Avoidance

We revisit the linear vector field encoding Dubin's vehicle model for aircrafts [4]. Although the system was discussed in many recent papers [20,23,11], we want to highlight an additional algebraic invariant equation that *links* both airplanes when turning with the same angular velocity. The differential equation system is given by:

$$p_1 = \dot{x}_1 = d_1, \quad p_2 = \dot{x}_2 = d_2, \quad p_3 = \dot{d}_1 = -\omega_1 d_2, \quad p_4 = \dot{d}_2 = \omega_1 d_1,$$
$$p_5 = \dot{y}_1 = e_1, \quad p_6 = \dot{y}_2 = e_2, \quad p_7 = \dot{e}_1 = -\omega_2 e_2, \quad p_8 = \dot{e}_2 = \omega_2 e_1 \ .$$

The angular velocities ω_1 and ω_2 can be either zero (straight line flight) or equal to a constant ω which denotes the standard rate turn (typically $180°/2mn$ for usual commercial airplanes). When the two airplanes are manoeuvring with the same standard rate turn ω, apart from the already known invariants, we discovered the following differential radical invariant (which corresponds to a family of invariant varieties):

$$h_1 = \gamma_1 d_1 + \gamma_2 d_2 + \gamma_3 e_1 + \gamma_4 e_2 = 0 \wedge h_2 = \gamma_2 d_1 - \gamma_1 d_2 + \gamma_4 e_1 - \gamma_3 e_2 = 0,$$

for an arbitrarily $(\gamma_1, \ldots, \gamma_4) \in \mathbb{R}^4$. We have $\sqrt[\varepsilon_p]{\langle h_1 \rangle} = \sqrt[\varepsilon_p]{\langle h_2 \rangle} = \langle h_1, h_2 \rangle$. Observe also that $V(\langle h_1 \rangle)$ and $V(\langle h_2 \rangle)$ are not invariant varieties for p.

6.2   Longitudinal Motion of an Airplane

The full dynamics of an aircraft are often separated (decoupled) into different modes where the differential equations take a simpler form by either fixing or neglecting the rate of change of some configuration variables [25]. The first standard separation used in stability analysis gives two main modes: longitudinal and lateral-directional. We study the 6th order longitudinal equations of motion as it captures the vertical motion (climbing, descending) of an airplane. We believe that a better understanding of the envelope that soundly contains the trajectories of the aircraft will help tightening the surrounding safety envelope and hence help trajectory management systems to safely allow more dense traffic around airports. The current safety envelope is essentially a rough cylinder that doesn't account for the real capabilities allowed by the dynamics of the airplane. We use our automated invariant generation techniques to characterize such an envelope. The theoretical improvement and the effective underlying computation techniques described earlier in this work allow us to push further the limits of automated invariant generation. We first describe the differential equations (vector field) then show the non-trivial energy functions (invariant functions for the considered vector field) we were able to generate. Let g denote the gravity acceleration, m the total mass of an airplane, M the aerodynamic and thrust moment w.r.t. the y axis, (X, Z) the aerodynamics and thrust forces w.r.t. axis x and z, and I_{yy} the second diagonal element of its inertia matrix. The restriction of the nominal flight path of an aircraft to the vertical plane reduces the full dynamics to the following 6 differential equations [25, Chapter 5] (u: axial velocity, w: vertical velocity, x: range, z: altitude, q: pitch rate, θ: pitch angle):

$$\dot{u} = \frac{X}{m} - g\sin(\theta) - qw \qquad \dot{x} = \cos(\theta)u + \sin(\theta)w \qquad \dot{\theta} = q$$

$$\dot{w} = \frac{Z}{m} + g\cos(\theta) + qu \qquad \dot{z} = -\sin(\theta)u + \cos(\theta)w \qquad \dot{q} = \frac{M}{I_{yy}} \,.$$

We encode the trigonometric functions using two additional variables for $\cos(\theta)$ and $\sin(\theta)$, making the total number of variables equal to 8. The parameters are considered unconstrained. Unlike [23], we do not consider them as new time independent variables. So that the total number of state variables (n) and hence the degree of the vector field are unchanged. Instead, they are carried along the symbolic row-reduction computation as symbols in $M_{d,N}(\beta)$. For the algebraic encoding of the above vector field ($n = 8$), the matrix $M_{3,1}(\beta)$ is 495×165, with 2115 (out of 81675) nonzero elements, and $|\beta| = 9$. We were able to automatically generate the following three invariant functions:

$$\frac{Mz}{I_{yy}} + g\theta + \left(\frac{X}{m} - qw\right)\cos(\theta) + \left(\frac{Z}{m} + qu\right)\sin(\theta),$$
$$\frac{Mx}{I_{yy}} - \left(\frac{Z}{m} + qu\right)\cos(\theta) + \left(\frac{X}{m} - qw\right)\sin(\theta), \quad -q^2 + \frac{2M\theta}{I_{yy}} .$$

We substituted the intermediate variables that encode sin and cos back to emphasize the fact that algebraic invariants and algebraic differential systems are suitable to encode many real complex dynamical systems. Using our Mathematica implementation, the computation took 1 hour on a recent laptop with 4GB and 1.7GHz Intel Core i5.

Acknowledgments. We thank the anonymous reviewers for their careful reading and detailed comments. We also would like to very much thank JEAN-BAPTISTE JEANNIN and ANDREW SOGOKON for the multiple questions, various comments and fruitful objections they both had on an early version of this work. We are finally grateful to ERIC GOUBAULT and SYLVIE PUTOT for the relevant references they pointed out to us on the integrability theory of nonlinear systems.

7 Conclusion

For polynomial vector fields, we give an algebraic characterization of invariant varieties. This so-called differential radical characterization makes it possible to decide for the invariance of a given variety candidate. It is, in addition, computationally attractive: generating invariant varieties requires minimizing the rank of a symbolic matrix and is hence at least NP-hard. The case studies show how the technique applies successfully to rather complex systems. We also revisited some known problems in the literature to exemplify the benefits of having a necessary and sufficient condition: all other known sound approaches generate a special class of invariant varieties (i.e. miss others).

In the future, we plan to investigate upper bounds for the order of the differential radical ideal of a given polynomial. Also, invariant varieties are not the only invariant of interest for polynomial vector fields, we want to consider semialgebraic sets as they play a prominent role in both hybrid systems and control theory. Finally, the effective use of algebraic invariants in general in the context of hybrid systems is still a challenging problem that we want to explore in more depth.

References

1. Bochnak, J., Coste, M., Roy, M.F.: Real Algebraic Geometry. A series of modern surveys in mathematics. Springer (2010)
2. Buss, J.F., Frandsen, G.S., Shallit, J.: The computational complexity of some problems of linear algebra. J. Comput. Syst. Sci. 58(3), 572–596 (1999)
3. Cox, D.A., Little, J., O'Shea, D.: Ideals, Varieties, and Algorithms: An Introduction to Computational Algebraic Geometry and Commutative Algebra. Springer (2007)
4. Dubins, L.E.: On curves of minimal length with a constraint on average curvature, and with prescribed initial and terminal positions and tangents. American Journal of Mathematics 79(3), 497–516 (1957)

5. Ghorbal, K., Platzer, A.: Characterizing algebraic invariants by differential radical invariants. Tech. Rep. CMU-CS-13-129, School of Computer Science, Carnegie Mellon University, Pittsburgh, PA, 15213 (November 2013), http://reports-archive.adm.cs.cmu.edu/anon/2013/abstracts/13-129.html

6. Hartshorne, R.: Algebraic Geometry. Graduate Texts in Mathematics. Springer (1977)

7. Hilbert, D.: Über die Theorie der algebraischen Formen. Mathematische Annalen 36(4), 473–534 (1890)

8. Hillar, C.J., Lim, L.H.: Most tensor problems are NP-hard. J. ACM 60(6), 45 (2013)

9. Lafferriere, G., Pappas, G.J., Yovine, S.: Symbolic reachability computation for families of linear vector fields. J. Symb. Comput. 32(3), 231–253 (2001)

10. Lanotte, R., Tini, S.: Taylor approximation for hybrid systems. In: Morari, Thiele (eds.) [13], pp. 402–416

11. Liu, J., Zhan, N., Zhao, H.: Computing semi-algebraic invariants for polynomial dynamical systems. In: Chakraborty, S., Jerraya, A., Baruah, S.K., Fischmeister, S. (eds.) EMSOFT, pp. 97–106. ACM (2011)

12. Matringe, N., Moura, A.V., Rebiha, R.: Generating invariants for non-linear hybrid systems by linear algebraic methods. In: Cousot, R., Martel, M. (eds.) SAS 2010. LNCS, vol. 6337, pp. 373–389. Springer, Heidelberg (2010)

13. Morari, M., Thiele, L. (eds.): HSCC 2005. LNCS, vol. 3414. Springer, Heidelberg (2005)

14. Neuhaus, R.: Computation of real radicals of polynomial ideals II. Journal of Pure and Applied Algebra 124(13), 261–280 (1998)

15. Platzer, A.: Differential dynamic logic for hybrid systems. J. Autom. Reasoning 41(2), 143–189 (2008)

16. Platzer, A.: Logical Analysis of Hybrid Systems: Proving Theorems for Complex Dynamics. Springer, Heidelberg (2010)

17. Platzer, A.: A differential operator approach to equational differential invariants - (invited paper). In: Beringer, L., Felty, A.P. (eds.) ITP. LNCS, vol. 7406, pp. 28–48. Springer (2012)

18. Platzer, A.: Logics of dynamical systems. In: LICS, pp. 13–24. IEEE (2012)

19. Platzer, A.: The structure of differential invariants and differential cut elimination. Logical Methods in Computer Science 8(4), 1–38 (2012)

20. Platzer, A., Clarke, E.M.: Computing differential invariants of hybrid systems as fixedpoints. In: Gupta, A., Malik, S. (eds.) CAV 2008. LNCS, vol. 5123, pp. 176–189. Springer, Heidelberg (2008)

21. Rodríguez-Carbonell, E., Kapur, D.: An abstract interpretation approach for automatic generation of polynomial invariants. In: Giacobazzi, R. (ed.) SAS 2004. LNCS, vol. 3148, pp. 280–295. Springer, Heidelberg (2004)

22. Rodríguez-Carbonell, E., Tiwari, A.: Generating polynomial invariants for hybrid systems. In: Morari, Thiele (eds.) [13], pp. 590–605

23. Sankaranarayanan, S.: Automatic invariant generation for hybrid systems using ideal fixed points. In: Johansson, K.H., Yi, W. (eds.) HSCC, pp. 221–230. ACM (2010)

24. Sankaranarayanan, S., Sipma, H.B., Manna, Z.: Constructing invariants for hybrid systems. Formal Methods in System Design 32(1), 25–55 (2008)

25. Stengel, R.F.: Flight Dynamics. Princeton University Press (2004)

26. Tiwari, A.: Approximate reachability for linear systems. In: Maler, O., Pnueli, A. (eds.) HSCC 2003. LNCS, vol. 2623, pp. 514–525. Springer, Heidelberg (2003)

27. Tiwari, A.: Abstractions for hybrid systems. Formal Methods in System Design 32(1), 57–83 (2008)

28. Tiwari, A., Khanna, G.: Nonlinear systems: Approximating reach sets. In: Alur, R., Pappas, G.J. (eds.) HSCC 2004. LNCS, vol. 2993, pp. 600–614. Springer, Heidelberg (2004)

Quasi-Equal Clock Reduction: More Networks, More Queries

Christian Herrera, Bernd Westphal, and Andreas Podelski

Albert-Ludwigs-Universität Freiburg, 79110 Freiburg, Germany

Abstract. Quasi-equal clock reduction for networks of timed automata replaces equivalence classes of clocks which are equal except for *unstable phases*, i.e., points in time where these clocks differ on their valuation, by a single representative clock. An existing approach yields significant reductions of the overall verification time but is limited to so-called well-formed networks and *local queries*, i.e., queries which refer to a single timed automaton only. In this work we present two new transformations. The first, for networks of timed automata, summarises unstable phases without losing information under weaker well-formedness assumptions than needed by the existing approach. The second, for queries, now supports the full query language of Uppaal. We demonstrate that the cost of verifying non-local properties is much lower in transformed networks than in their original counterparts with quasi-equal clocks.

1 Introduction

Real-time systems often use distributed architectures and communication protocols to exchange data in real-time. Examples of such protocols are the classes of TDMA-based protocols [1] and EPL-based protocols [2].

Real-time systems can be modelled and verified by using *networks of timed automata* [3]. In [4] a technique that reduces the number of clocks that model the local timing behaviour and synchronisation activity of distributed components is presented in order to reduce the verification runtime of properties in networks of timed automata that fulfill a set of syntactical criteria called *well-formedness*. In systems implementing, e.g., TDMA or EPL protocols this technique eliminates the unnecessary verification overhead caused by the interleaving semantics of timed automata, where the automata reset their clocks one by one at the end of each communication phase. This interleaving induces sets of reachable intermediate configurations which grow exponentially in the number of components in the system. Model checking tools like *Uppaal* [5] explore these configurations even when they are irrelevant for the property being verified. This exploration unnecessarily increases the overall memory consumption and runtime verification of the property.

The notion of *quasi-equal* clocks was presented in [4] to characterise clocks that evolve at the same rate and whose valuation only differs in *unstable phases*,

---

[1] CONACYT (Mexico) and DAAD (Germany) sponsor the work of the first author.

E. Ábrahám and K. Havelund (Eds.): TACAS 2014, LNCS 8413, pp. 295–309, 2014.
© Springer-Verlag Berlin Heidelberg 2014

i.e., points in time where these clocks are reset one by one. Sets of quasi-equal clocks induce *equivalence classes* in networks of timed automata.

Although the technique introduced in [4] shows promising results for transformed networks, the technique has two severe drawbacks. Namely, it loses all the information from intermediate configurations and it supports only *local queries*, i.e., properties defined over single timed automaton of well-formed networks. A concrete consequence of these drawbacks can be observed in the system with quasi-equal clocks presented in [6] which implements an EPL protocol. In the transformed model of this system it is not possible to perform the sanity check that a given automaton receives configuration data from other system components right before this automaton resets its quasi-equal clock. The check involves querying information of several automata from intermediate configurations. System properties are quite often expressed in terms of several automata.

To overcome these limitations, in this work we revisit the reduction of quasi-equal clocks in networks of timed automata, and we present an approach based on the following new idea. For each set of quasi-equal clocks we summarise unstable configurations using dedicated locations of automata introduced during network transformation. Queries which explicitly refer to unstable configurations are rewritten to refer to the newly introduced summary location instead. The dedicated summary locations also allow us to support *complex* resetting edges in the original model, i.e. edges with synchronisation of assignments other than clock resets. This allows us to extend the queries that we support as per our new approach which is also a source-to-source transformation, i.e. our approach can be used with a wide range of model-checking tools.

Our approach aims to provide the modelling engineer with a system optimisation technique which allows him to naturally model systems without caring to optimise them for verification. Our contributions are: (1) We now support properties referring to multiple timed automata, in particular properties which query (possibly overlapping) unstable configurations. (2) We enlarge the applicability of our new approach by relaxing the well-formedness criteria presented in [4]. Our approach allows us to prove in a much simpler and more elegant way (without a need for the reordering lemma from [4]) that transformed networks are weakly bisimilar to their original counterparts. We show that properties wrt. an original network are fully preserved in the transformed network, i.e., the transformed network satisfies a transformed property if and only if the original network satisfies the original property. We evaluate our approach on six real world examples, three of them new, where we observe significant improvements in the verification cost of non-local queries compared to the cost of verifying them in the original networks.

The paper is organized as follows. In Section 2, we provide basic definitions. Section 3 introduces the formal definition of *well-formed* networks and presents the algorithm that implements our approach. In Section 4, we formalise the relation of a well-formed network and its transformed network and prove the correctness of our approach. In Section 5, we compare the verification time of six real world examples before and after applying our approach. Section 6 concludes.

Related Work. The methods in [7–9] eliminate clocks by using static analysis over single timed automaton, networks of timed automata and parametric timed automata, respectively. The approaches in [7, 8] reduce the number of clocks in timed automata by detecting *equal* and *active* clocks. Two clocks are equal in a location if both are reset by the same incoming edge, so just one clock for each set of equal clocks is necessary to determine the future behavior of the system. A clock is active at a certain location if this clock appears in the invariant of that location, or in the guard of an outgoing edge of such a location, or another active clock takes its value when taking an outgoing edge. Non-active clocks play no role in the future evolution of the system and therefore can be eliminated. In [9] the same principle of active clocks is used in parametric timed automata. Our benchmarks use at most one clock per component which is always active, hence the equal and active approach is not applicable on them.

The work in [10, 11] uses *observers*, i.e., single components encoding properties of a system, to reduce clocks in systems. For each location of the observer, the technique can deactivate clocks if they do not play a role in the future evolution of this observer. Processing our benchmarks in order to encode properties as per the observers approach may be more expensive than our method (one observer per property), and may not guarantee the preservation of information from intermediate configurations which in the case of our EPL benchmark is needed. In general using observers to characterise non-local queries is not straightforward.

In sequential timed automata [12], one set of quasi-equal clocks is syntactically declared. Those quasi-equal clocks are implicitly reduced by applying the sequential composition operator. The work in [13] avoids the use of shared clocks in single timed automaton by replacing shared clocks with fresh ones if the evolution of these automata does not depend on these clocks. This approach increments the number of clocks (in contrast to ours). Our benchmarks do not use shared clocks. The approach in [14] detects quasi-equal clocks in networks of timed automata. Interestingly, the authors demonstrate the feasibility of their approach in benchmarks that we also use in this paper.

2 Preliminaries

Following the presentation in [15], we here recall the following definitions.

Let $\mathcal{X}$ be a set of *clocks*. The set $\Phi(\mathcal{X})$ of *simple clock constraints* over $\mathcal{X}$ is defined by the grammar $\varphi ::= x \sim c \mid x - y \sim c \mid \varphi_1 \wedge \varphi_2$ where $x, y \in \mathcal{X}$, $c \in \mathbb{Q}_{\geq 0}$, and $\sim \in \{<, \leq, \geq, >\}$. Let $\Phi(\mathcal{V})$ be a set of *integer constraints* over *variables* $\mathcal{V}$. The set $\Phi(\mathcal{X}, \mathcal{V})$ of *constraints* comprises $\Phi(\mathcal{X})$, $\Phi(\mathcal{V})$, and conjunctions of clock and integer constraints. We use $clocks(\varphi)$ and $vars(\varphi)$ to respectively denote the set of clocks and variables occurring in a constraint φ. We assume the canonical satisfaction relation "$\models$" between *valuations* ν : $\mathcal{X} \cup \mathcal{V} \to Time \cup \mathbb{Z}$ and constraints, with $Time = \mathbb{R}_{\geq 0}$. A timed automaton $\mathcal{A}$ is a tuple $(L, B, \mathcal{X}, \mathcal{V}, I, E, \ell_{ini})$, which consists of a finite set of *locations* L, where $\ell_{ini} \in L$ is the initial location, a finite set B of *actions* comprising the *internal action* τ, finite sets $\mathcal{X}$ and $\mathcal{V}$ of clocks and variables, a mapping

$I : L \rightarrow \Phi(\mathcal{X})$, that assigns to each location a *clock constraint*, and a set of *edges* $E \subseteq L \times B \times \Phi(\mathcal{X}, \mathcal{V}) \times \mathcal{R}(\mathcal{X}, \mathcal{V}) \times L$. An edge $e = (\ell, \alpha, \varphi, \vec{r}, \ell') \in E$ from location ℓ to ℓ' involves an action $\alpha \in B$, a *guard* $\varphi \in \Phi(\mathcal{X}, \mathcal{V})$, and a *reset vector* $\vec{r} \in \mathcal{R}(\mathcal{X}, \mathcal{V})$. A reset vector is a finite, possibly empty sequence of *clock resets* $x := 0$, $x \in \mathcal{X}$, and *assignments* $v := \psi_{int}$, where $v \in \mathcal{V}$ and ψ_{int} is an integer expression over $\mathcal{V}$. We write $\mathcal{X}(\mathcal{A})$, $\ell_{ini}(\mathcal{A})$, etc., to denote the set of clocks, the initial location, etc., of $\mathcal{A}$; $clocks(\vec{r})$ and $vars(\vec{r})$ to denote the sets of clocks and variables occurring in $\vec{r}$, respectively. We use $\beta(e)$ to denote the set of basic elements (locations, reset vector, etc.) of an edge $e \in E(\mathcal{A})$. We use the following operation of complementation on actions $\overline{\cdot}$, which is defined by $\overline{\alpha!} = \alpha?$, $\overline{\alpha?} = \alpha!$ and $\overline{\tau} = \tau$. A *network* $\mathcal{N}$ *(of timed automata)* consists of a finite set $\mathcal{A}_1, \ldots, \mathcal{A}_N$ of timed automata with pairwise disjoint sets of clocks and pairwise disjoint sets of locations and a set $\mathcal{B}(\mathcal{N}) \subseteq \bigcup_{i=1}^{N} B(\mathcal{A}_i)$ of *broadcast channels*. We write $\mathcal{A} \in \mathcal{N}$ if and only if $\mathcal{A} \in \{\mathcal{A}_1, \ldots, \mathcal{A}_N\}$.

The operational semantics of the network $\mathcal{N}$ is the labelled transition system $\mathcal{T}(\mathcal{N}) = (Conf(\mathcal{N}), Time \cup \{\tau\}, \{\xrightarrow{\lambda} | \lambda \in Time \cup \{\tau\}\}, \mathcal{C}_{ini})$. The set of configurations $Conf(\mathcal{N})$ consists of pairs of *location vectors* $\langle \ell_1, \ldots, \ell_N \rangle$ from $\times_{i=1}^{N} L(\mathcal{A}_i)$ and valuations of $\bigcup_{1 \le i \le N} \mathcal{X}(\mathcal{A}_i) \cup \mathcal{V}(\mathcal{A}_i)$ which satisfy the constraint $\bigwedge_{i=1}^{N} I(\ell_i)$. We write $\ell_{s,i}$, $1 \le i \le N$, to denote the location which automaton $\mathcal{A}_i$ assumes in configuration $s = \langle \vec{\ell}_s, \nu_s \rangle$ and $\nu_{s,i}$ to denote $\nu_s|_{\mathcal{V}(\mathcal{A}_i) \cup \mathcal{X}(\mathcal{A}_i)}$. Between two configurations $s, s' \in Conf(\mathcal{N})$ there can be four kinds of transitions. There is a *delay transition* $\langle \vec{\ell}_s, \nu_s \rangle \xrightarrow{t} \langle \vec{\ell}_{s'}, \nu_{s'} \rangle$ if $\nu_s + t' \models \bigwedge_{i=1}^{N} I_i(\ell_{s,i})$ for all $t' \in [0, t]$, where $\nu_s + t'$ denotes the valuation obtained from ν_s by time shift t'. There is a *local transition* $\langle \vec{\ell}_s, \nu_s \rangle \xrightarrow{\tau} \langle \vec{\ell}_{s'}, \nu_{s'} \rangle$ if there is an edge $(\ell_{s,i}, \tau, \varphi, \vec{r}, \ell_{s',i}) \in E(\mathcal{A}_i)$, $1 \le i \le N$, such that $\vec{\ell}_{s'} = \vec{\ell}_s[\ell_{s,i} := \ell_{s',i}]$, $\nu_s \models \varphi$, $\nu_{s'} = \nu_s[\vec{r}]$, and $\nu_{s'} \models I_i(\ell_{s',i})$. There is a *synchronization transition* $\langle \vec{\ell}_s, \nu_s \rangle \xrightarrow{\tau} \langle \vec{\ell}_{s'}, \nu_{s'} \rangle$ if there are $1 \le i, j \le N$, $i \ne j$, a channel $b \in B(\mathcal{A}_i) \cap B(\mathcal{A}_j)$, and edges $(\ell_{s,i}, b!, \varphi_i, \vec{r}_i, \ell_{s',i}) \in E(\mathcal{A}_i)$ and $(\ell_{s,j}, b?, \varphi_j, \vec{r}_j, \ell_{s',j}) \in E(\mathcal{A}_j)$ such that $\vec{\ell}_{s'} = \vec{\ell}_s[\ell_{s,i} := \ell_{s',i}][\ell_{s,j} := \ell_{s',j}]$, $\nu_s \models \varphi_i \wedge \varphi_j$, $\nu_{s'} = \nu_s[\vec{r}_i][\vec{r}_j]$, and $\nu_{s'} \models I_i(\ell_{s',i}) \wedge I_j(\ell_{s',j})$. Let $b \in \mathcal{B}$ be a broadcast channel and $1 \le i_0 \le N$ such that $(\ell_{s,i_0}, b!, \varphi_{i_0}, \vec{r}_{i_0}, \ell_{s',i_0}) \in E(\mathcal{A}_{i_0})$. Let $1 \le i_1, \ldots, i_k \le N$, $k \ge 0$, be those indices different from i_0 such that there is an edge $(\ell_{s,i_j}, b?, \varphi_{i_j}, \vec{r}_{i_j}, \ell_{s',i_j}) \in E(\mathcal{A}_{i_j})$. There is *broadcast transition* $\langle \vec{\ell}_s, \nu_s \rangle \xrightarrow{\tau} \langle \vec{\ell}_{s'}, \nu_{s'} \rangle$ in $\mathcal{T}(\mathcal{N})$ if $\vec{\ell}_{s'} = \vec{\ell}_s[\ell_{s,i_0} := \ell_{s',i_0}] \cdots [\ell_{s,i_k} := \ell_{s',i_k}]$, $\nu_s \models \bigwedge_{j=0}^{k} \varphi_{i_j}$, $\nu_{s'} = \nu_s[\vec{r}_{i_0}] \cdots [\vec{r}_{i_k}]$, and $\nu_{s'} \models \bigwedge_{j=0}^{k} I_{i_j}(\ell_{s',i_j})$. $\mathcal{C}_{ini} = \{\langle \vec{\ell}_{ini}, \nu_{ini} \rangle\} \cap Conf(\mathcal{N})$, where $\vec{\ell}_{ini} = \langle \ell_{ini,1}, \ldots, \ell_{ini,N} \rangle$ and $\nu_{ini}(x) = 0$ for each $x \in \mathcal{X}(\mathcal{A}_i), 1 \le i \le N$. A finite or infinite sequence $\sigma = s_0 \xrightarrow{\lambda_1} s_1 \xrightarrow{\lambda_2} s_2 \ldots$ is called *transition sequence* (starting in $s_0 \in \mathcal{C}_{ini}$) of $\mathcal{N}$. Sequence σ is called *computation* of $\mathcal{N}$ if and only if it is infinite and $s_0 \in \mathcal{C}_{ini}$. We denote the set of all computations of $\mathcal{N}$ by $\Pi(\mathcal{N})$. A configuration s is called *reachable* (in $\mathcal{T}(\mathcal{N})$) if and only if there exists a computation $\sigma \in \Pi(\mathcal{N})$ such that s occurs in σ.

The set of *basic formulae* over $\mathcal{N}$ is given by the grammar $\beta ::= \ell \mid \neg \ell \mid \varphi$ where $\ell \in L(\mathcal{A}_i)$, $1 \le i \le n$, and $\varphi \in \Phi(\mathcal{X}(\mathcal{N}), \mathcal{V}(\mathcal{N}))$. Basic formula β is satisfied by configuration $s \in Conf(\mathcal{N})$ if and only if $\ell_{s,i} = \ell$, $\ell_{s,i} \ne \ell$, or $\nu_s \models \varphi$, resp. A *reachability query EPF* over $\mathcal{N}$ is $\exists \Diamond CF$ where CF is a *configuration formula* over $\mathcal{N}$, i.e., any logical connection of basic formulae. We use $\beta(CF)$ to denote the set of basic formulae in CF. $\mathcal{N}$ satisfies $\exists \lozenge \, CF$, denoted by $\mathcal{N} \models \exists \lozenge \, CF$, if and only if there is a configuration s reachable in $\mathcal{T}(\mathcal{N})$ s.t. $s \models CF$.

We recall from [4] the following definitions. Given a network $\mathcal{N}$ with clocks $\mathcal{X}$, two clocks $x, y \in \mathcal{X}$ are called *quasi-equal*, denoted by $x \simeq y$, if and only if for all computation paths of $\mathcal{N}$, the valuations of x and y are equal, or the valuation of one of them is equal to 0, i.e., if $\forall s_0 \xrightarrow{\lambda_1} s_1 \xrightarrow{\lambda_2} s_2 \cdots \in \Pi(\mathcal{N}) \; \forall i \in \mathbb{N}_0 \bullet \nu_{s_i} \models (x = 0 \lor y = 0 \lor x = y)$. In the following, we use $\mathcal{EC}_{\mathcal{N}}$ to denote the set $\{Y \in \mathcal{X}/\simeq \; | \; 1 < |Y|\}$ of equivalence classes of *quasi-equal* clocks of $\mathcal{N}$ with at least two elements. For each $Y \in \mathcal{X}/\simeq$, we assume a designated representative denoted by $rep(Y)$. For $x \in Y$, we use $rep(x)$ to denote $rep(Y)$. Given a constraint $\varphi \in \Phi(\mathcal{X}, \mathcal{V})$, we write $\Gamma(\varphi)$ to denote the constraint that is obtained by syntactically replacing each occurrence of a clock $x \in \mathcal{X}$ in φ, by the representative $rep(x)$. Given an automaton $\mathcal{A} \in \mathcal{N}$, a set of clocks $X \subseteq \mathcal{X}(\mathcal{A})$, and a set of variables $V \subseteq \mathcal{V}(\mathcal{A})$, we use $\mathcal{SE}_X(\mathcal{A})$ to denote the set of *simple resetting edges* of $\mathcal{A}$ which reset clocks from X, have action τ, no variables occur in their guards, and do not update any variables, i.e., $\mathcal{SE}_X(\mathcal{A}) = \{(\ell, \alpha, \varphi, \vec{r}, \ell') \in E(\mathcal{A}) \; | \; clocks(\vec{r}) \cap X \neq \emptyset \land \alpha = \tau \land vars(\varphi) = \emptyset \land vars(\vec{r}) = \emptyset\}$. We use $\mathcal{CE}_X(\mathcal{A})$ to denote the set of *complex resetting edges* of $\mathcal{A}$ which reset clocks from X and have an action different from τ or update some variables, i.e., $\mathcal{CE}_X(\mathcal{A}) = \{(\ell, \alpha, \varphi, \vec{r}, \ell') \in E(\mathcal{A}) \; | \; clocks(\vec{r}) \cap X \neq \emptyset \land (vars(\vec{r}) \cap V \neq \emptyset \; \lor \; \alpha \neq \tau)\}$. We use $\mathcal{LS}_X(\mathcal{A})$ and $\mathcal{LC}_X(\mathcal{A})$ to respectively denote the set of locations (source and destination) of simple and complex resetting edges wrt. X of $\mathcal{A}$. We use $\mathcal{E}_X(\mathcal{A}) = \mathcal{SE}_X(\mathcal{A}) \cup \mathcal{CE}_X(\mathcal{A})$ to denote the set of resetting edges of $\mathcal{A}$ which reset clocks from X, and $\mathcal{RES}_X(\mathcal{N})$ to denote the set of automata in $\mathcal{N}$ which have a resetting edge, i.e., $\mathcal{RES}_X(\mathcal{N}) = \{\mathcal{A} \in \mathcal{N} \; | \; \mathcal{E}_X(\mathcal{A}) \neq \emptyset\}$. A location ℓ (ℓ') is called is called *reset (successor) location* wrt. $Y \in \mathcal{EC}_{\mathcal{N}}$ in $\mathcal{N}$ if and only if there is a resetting edge in $\mathcal{SE}_Y(\mathcal{A}) \cup \mathcal{CE}_Y(\mathcal{A})$ from (to) ℓ (ℓ'). We use $\mathcal{RL}_Y(\mathcal{N})$ $(\mathcal{RL}_Y^+(\mathcal{N}))$ to denote the set of reset (successor) locations wrt. Y in $\mathcal{N}$ and we set $\mathcal{RL}_{\mathcal{EC}_{\mathcal{N}}}(\mathcal{N}) := \bigcup_{Y \in \mathcal{EC}_{\mathcal{N}}} \mathcal{RL}_Y(\mathcal{N})$ and similarly $\mathcal{RL}_{\mathcal{EC}_{\mathcal{N}}}^+(\mathcal{N})$.

A configuration $s \in Conf(\mathcal{N})$ is called *stable* wrt. $Y \in \mathcal{EC}_{\mathcal{N}}$ if and only if all clocks in Y have the same value in s, i.e., if $\forall x \in Y \bullet \nu_s(x) = \nu_s(rep(x))$. We use $\mathcal{SC}_{\mathcal{N}}^Y$ to denote the set of all configurations that are stable wrt. Y and $\mathcal{SC}_{\mathcal{N}}$ to denote the set $\bigcap_{Y \in \mathcal{EC}_{\mathcal{N}}} \mathcal{SC}_{\mathcal{N}}^Y$ of *globally stable* configurations of $\mathcal{N}$. Configurations not in $\mathcal{SC}_{\mathcal{N}}$ are called *unstable*. An edge e of a timed automaton $\mathcal{A}$ in network $\mathcal{N}$ is called *delayed* if and only if time must pass before e can be taken, i.e., if $\forall s_0 \xrightarrow{\lambda_1}_{E_1} s_1 \ldots s_{n-1} \xrightarrow{\lambda_n}_{E_n} s_n \in \Pi(\mathcal{N}) \bullet e \in E_n \implies \exists 0 \leq j < n \bullet \lambda_j \in Time \setminus \{0\} \land \forall j \leq i < n \bullet E(\mathcal{A}) \cap E_i = \emptyset$. Where we write $s_i \xrightarrow{\lambda_i}_{E_i} s_{i+1}$, $i \in \mathbb{N}^{>0}$, to denote that the transition $s_i \xrightarrow{\lambda_i} s_{i+1}$ is justified by the set of edges E_i; E_i is empty for delay transitions, i.e., if $\lambda_i \in Time$. We say $\mathcal{EC}_{\mathcal{N}}$-reset edges are *pre/post delayed in network* $\mathcal{N}$ if and only if all edges originating in reset or reset successor locations are delayed, i.e., if $\forall e = (\ell, \alpha, \varphi, \vec{r}, \ell') \in E(\mathcal{N}) \bullet \ell \in \mathcal{RL}_{\mathcal{EC}_{\mathcal{N}}}(\mathcal{N}) \cup \mathcal{RL}_{\mathcal{EC}_{\mathcal{N}}}^+(\mathcal{N}) \implies e$ is delayed.

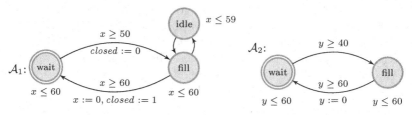

Fig. 1. Model of a chemical plant controller with quasi-equal clocks

3   Reducing Clocks in Networks of Timed Automata

Consider the following motivating example of a distributed chemical plant controller. At the end of every minute, the controller fills two containers with gas, one for at most 10 seconds and the other for at most 20 seconds. Figure 1 shows a model of this system in form of the network $\mathcal{N}_1$ which is composed of automata $\mathcal{A}_1$ and $\mathcal{A}_2$ with respective clocks x and y. Additionally, automaton $\mathcal{A}_1$ has the boolean variable *closed* that is set to true, i.e., *closed* := 1, when $\mathcal{A}_1$ has filled its container. Both automata start in a waiting phase at the point in time 0 and after filling the containers they wait for the next round. Both clocks x and y, together with the variable *closed* are respectively reset and updated at the point in time 60. Yet, in the strict interleaving semantics of networks of timed automata, these resets occur one after the other.

According to the definition of quasi-equal clocks, clocks x and y are quasi-equal because their valuations are only different from each other when they are reset at the point in time 60. Now consider verifying in $\mathcal{N}_1$, whether the container of automaton $\mathcal{A}_1$ is closed before automaton $\mathcal{A}_2$ resets its clock. A query that states this property is $\exists \Diamond \phi$ with configuration formula $\phi : closed = 1 \wedge y \geq 60$. Clearly in $\mathcal{N}_1$, this query is satisfied only when clocks x and y have different valuations, i.e., in unstable configurations. Property $\exists \Diamond \phi$ cannot be treated by the approach in [4] since that approach supports only local queries, i.e., queries which refer to properties of at most one automaton. The approach in [4] completely eliminates all unstable configurations, those where quasi-equal clocks have different valuations, since no alternative representation of them was proposed for transformed models. Furthermore, $\mathcal{N}_1$ does not satisfy the well-formedness criteria of [4] because the resetting edge also assigns a variable.

3.1   Transformational Reduction of Quasi-Equal Clocks

In the following we present an algorithm which reduces a given set of quasi-equal clocks in networks of timed automata and preserves all possible queries. For simplicity, we impose a set of syntactical criteria called well-formedness rules over networks of timed automata.

Definition 1 (Well-formed Network). *A network $\mathcal{N}$ is called well-formed if and only if it satisfies the following restrictions for each set of quasi-equal clocks $Y \in \mathcal{EC}_\mathcal{N}$:*

(R1) *An edge resets at most one clock $x \in Y$, in the constraint (guard) of this edge there is a clause of the form $x \geq C_Y$, and the source location of that edge has an invariant $x \leq C_Y$ for some constant $C_Y > 0$, i.e.,*

$$\exists C_Y \in \mathbb{N}^{>0} \ \forall \mathcal{A} \in \mathcal{N} \ \forall (\ell, \alpha, \varphi, \vec{r}, \ell') \in \mathcal{E}_Y(\mathcal{A}) \ \exists x \in Y, \varphi_0 \in \beta(\varphi) \bullet$$
$$clocks(\vec{r}) = \{x\} \wedge I(\ell) = x \leq C_Y \wedge \varphi_0 = x \geq C_Y$$
$$\wedge \forall \varphi_1 \in \beta(\varphi) \bullet clocks(\varphi_1) \neq \emptyset \implies \varphi_1 = \varphi_0.$$

(R2) *Resetting edges do not coincide on source locations.*

$$\forall \mathcal{A} \in \mathcal{N} \ \forall (\ell_i, \alpha_i, \varphi_i, \vec{r}_i, \ell_i') \neq (\ell_j, \alpha_j, \varphi_j, \vec{r}_j, \ell_j') \in \mathcal{E}_Y(\mathcal{A}) \ \bullet \ \ell_i \neq \ell_j.$$

(R3) *For pairs of edges that synchronise on some channel $a \in B(\mathcal{N})$, either all edges reset a clock from Y, or none of these edges resets a clock from Y, or the output $a!$ is in one edge resetting a clock from Y, and the inputs $a?$ are in the edges of automata which do not reset clocks from Y, i.e.,*

$$\forall \mathcal{A}_1 \neq \mathcal{A}_2 \in \mathcal{N} \ \forall e_i = (\ell_i, \alpha_i, \varphi_i, \vec{r}_i, \ell_i') \in E(\mathcal{A}_i), i = 1, 2, \alpha_1 = \overline{\alpha_2} \bullet$$
$$(e_1 \notin \mathcal{E}_Y(\mathcal{A}_1) \wedge e_2 \notin \mathcal{E}_Y(\mathcal{A}_2)) \vee (e_1 \in \mathcal{E}_Y(\mathcal{A}_1) \wedge e_2 \in \mathcal{E}_Y(\mathcal{A}_2))$$
$$\vee (\exists i \in \{1, 2\}, a \in B(\mathcal{N}) \bullet \alpha_i = a! \wedge e_i \in \mathcal{E}_Y(\mathcal{A}_i) \wedge \mathcal{A}_{3-i} \notin \mathcal{RES}_Y(\mathcal{N})).$$

(R4) *At most one clock from Y occurs in the guard of any edge, i.e.,*

$$\forall (\ell, \alpha, \varphi, \vec{r}, \ell') \in E(\mathcal{N}) \bullet |clocks(\varphi) \cap Y| \leq 1.$$

The transformation algorithm presented here which was developed in order to support all queries and in particular those interested in unstable configurations, allows us to easily relax the syntactical restrictions presented in [4]. The relaxations done in this work are the following. By restriction *R1*, now looped edges or those edges from initial locations can reset clocks from $Y \in \mathcal{EC}_\mathcal{N}$ as well as update variables, and we now allow the guard of such edges to conjoin integer constraints over variables. By *R2* we now allow more edges from a reset location (but still only one resetting edge from it). By *R3*, we now allow a resetting edge to have a limited but still useful synchronisation. The new well-formedness criteria are less restrictive then they look on first sight. They allow us to extend the applicability of our new approach by treating three new case studies. Note that the network in Figure 1 satisfies the new well-formedness criteria.

In the following we describe the transformation algorithm $\mathcal{K}$. It works with two given inputs, a well-formed network $\mathcal{N}$ and a set of equivalence classes $\mathcal{EC}_\mathcal{N} = \{Y_1, \ldots, Y_n\}$ of quasi-equal clocks. The output of $\mathcal{K}$ is the transformed network $\mathcal{N}' = \{\mathcal{A}_1', \ldots, \mathcal{A}_n'\} \cup \{\mathcal{R}_Y \mid Y \in \mathcal{EC}_\mathcal{N}\}$ with broadcast channels $B(\mathcal{N}') = B(\mathcal{N}) \cup \{reset_Y \mid Y \in \mathcal{EC}_\mathcal{N}\}$. The automata $\mathcal{A}_i'$ are obtained by applying repeatedly (in any order) the algorithm $\mathcal{K}_0$ to $\mathcal{A}_i$ for each equivalence class in $\mathcal{EC}_\mathcal{N}$, i.e., $\mathcal{A}_i' = \mathcal{K}_0(\ldots \mathcal{K}_0(\mathcal{A}_i, Y_1), \ldots Y_n)$. Algorithm $\mathcal{K}_0$ is defined as follows.

$$\mathcal{K}_0(\mathcal{A}, Y) = \begin{cases} \mathcal{A} & , \text{if } \mathcal{A} \notin \mathcal{RES}_Y(\mathcal{N}), \\ (L', B', \mathcal{X}', \mathcal{V}', I', E', \ell_{ini}') & , \text{otherwise} \end{cases}$$

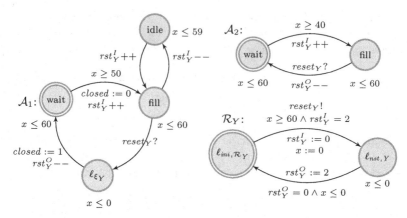

Fig. 2. The model the chemical plant controller after applying $\mathcal{K}$

where per equivalence class

- intermediate locations for each complex resetting edge are added, $L' = L(\mathcal{A}) \cup \Xi_Y(\mathcal{A})$ with $\Xi_Y(\mathcal{A}) = \{\ell_{\xi_{Y,e}} \mid e \in \mathcal{CE}_Y(\mathcal{A})\}$, $\ell'_{ini} = \ell_{ini}(\mathcal{A})$,
- the broadcast channel $reset_Y$ is added, $B' = B(\mathcal{A}) \cup \{reset_Y\}$; clocks except for each representative clock are deleted, $\mathcal{X}' = (\mathcal{X}(\mathcal{A}) \setminus Y) \cup \{rep(Y)\}$; and rst variables are added, $\mathcal{V}' = \mathcal{V} \cup \{rst_Y^I, rst_Y^O\}$,
- quasi-equal clocks occurring in invariants are replaced by the respective representative clock, $I'(\ell) = I(\ell)[y/rep(y) \mid y \in Y]$ for $\ell \in L(\mathcal{A})$; and a zero delay invariant is added to each intermediate location $I'(\ell) = rep(y) \leq 0$ for $\ell \in \Xi_Y(\mathcal{A})$; On non-resetting edges each quasi-equal clock is replaced by the respective representative clock; the input $reset_Y$? is placed and the reset of quasi-equal clocks is removed from simple edges; and intermediate locations and reset successor locations are linked, respectively,

$$
\begin{aligned}
E' = \{ & (\ell, \alpha, \varphi[y/rep(y) \mid y \in Y], \vec{r}; \rho_e, \ell') \mid e = (\ell, \alpha, \varphi, \vec{r}, \ell') \in E(\mathcal{A}) \setminus \mathcal{E}_Y(\mathcal{A})\} \\
\cup \{ & (\ell, reset_Y?, \varphi[y \sim c/true \mid y \in Y], \vec{r}[y := 0/\epsilon \mid y \in Y]; \rho_e, \ell') \mid \\
& e = (\ell, \tau, \varphi, \vec{r}, \ell') \in \mathcal{SE}_Y(\mathcal{A})\} \\
\cup \{ & (\ell_{\xi_{Y,e}}, \alpha, \varphi[y \sim c/true \mid y \in Y], \vec{r}[y := 0/\epsilon \mid y \in Y]; \rho_e, \ell'), \\
& (\ell, reset_Y?, true, \epsilon, \ell_{\xi_{Y,e}}) \mid e = (\ell, \alpha, \varphi, \vec{r}, \ell') \in \mathcal{CE}_Y(\mathcal{A})\}
\end{aligned}
$$

where the reset sequence $\rho_e = r_1; r_2; r_3$ depends on the edge e as follows:

- $r_1 = rst_Y^I := rst_Y^I + 1$ if e is to a reset location in $\mathcal{RL}_Y(\mathcal{N})$, and $r_1 = \epsilon$ otherwise,
- $r_2 = rst_Y^I := rst_Y^I - 1$ if e is from a reset location in $\mathcal{RL}_Y(\mathcal{N})$ and $e \notin \mathcal{E}_Y(\mathcal{A})$, and $r_2 = \epsilon$ otherwise, and
- $r_3 = rst_Y^O := rst_Y^O - 1$ if $e \in \mathcal{E}_Y(\mathcal{A})$, and $r_3 = \epsilon$ otherwise.

The *resetter* $\mathcal{R}_Y$ for equivalence class Y is the timed automaton

$$
(\{\ell_{ini,\mathcal{R}_Y}, \ell_{nst,Y}\}, \{reset_Y\}, \{rep(Y)\}, \{rst_Y^I := iL_Y, rst_Y^O := n_Y\}, I, E, \ell_{ini,\mathcal{R}_Y}).
$$

It initializes the variable rst_Y^I to $iL_Y := |\{\mathcal{A} \in \mathcal{N} \mid \ell_{ini,\mathcal{A}} \in \mathcal{RL}_Y(\mathcal{N})\}|$, i.e. the number of automata whose initial location is a reset location of Y, and rst_Y^O to $n_Y := |\mathcal{RES}_Y(\mathcal{N})|$, i.e. the number of automata that reset the clocks of Y. There are two locations with the invariants $I(\ell_{ini,\mathcal{R}_Y}) = true$ and $I(\ell_{nst,Y}) = rep(Y) \leq 0$. The set of edges E consists of

$$(\ell_{ini,\mathcal{R}_Y}, reset_Y!, (rst_Y^I = n_Y \wedge rep(Y) \geq C_Y), rst_Y^I := 0; rep(Y) := 0, \ell_{nst,Y})$$
$$\text{and } (\ell_{nst,Y}, \tau, (rst_Y^O = 0 \wedge rep(Y) \leq 0), rst_Y^O := n_Y, \ell_{ini,\mathcal{R}_Y})$$

where C_Y is the time at which the clocks in Y are reset (cf. *R1*).

Example 1. Applying $\mathcal{K}$ to $\mathcal{N}_1$ from Figure 1 yields network $\mathcal{N}_1'$ (cf. Figure 2). Similar to the algorithm in [4], only the representative clock of each equivalence class remains. All guards and invariants with quasi-equal clocks are re-written to refer to the representative clock, and the reset operation is delegated to the resetter. The variable rst_Y^I together with well-formedness enforces a *blocking* multicast synchronisation between resetter and the automata in $\mathcal{RES}_Y(\mathcal{N})$.

In order to support non-local queries, and in particular queries for possibly overlapping unstable configurations, the approach presented here introduces one resetter *per* equivalence class with *two* locations each. The location $\ell_{nst,Y}$ represents all unstable configuration wrt. Y. To support complex edges, and thus non-trivial behaviour during unstable phases, complex edges are basically split into two. The first one synchronises with the resetter and the second one carries out the actions of the original complex edge. As long as the second edge has not been taken, the system is unstable. The variable rst_Y^O is introduced to indicate to automaton $\mathcal{R}_Y$ when this unstability finishes. Its value gives the number of automata which still need to take their reset edge in the current unstable phase.

In $\mathcal{N}_1'$, we have thereby eliminated the interleaving induced by resetting the clocks x and y in $\mathcal{N}_1$, but the interleaving wrt. variable updates during reset of quasi-equal clocks is preserved by splitting the complex edge into two. Note that in transformed networks, configurations with the locations $\ell_{nst,Y_1}, \ldots, \ell_{nst,Y_n}$, where $1 < n$, reflect overlapping unstable phases, i.e. instability wrt. multiple equivalence classes at one point in time.

The following function Ω syntactically transforms properties over a well-formed network $\mathcal{N}$ into properties over $\mathcal{N}' = \mathcal{K}(\mathcal{N}, \mathcal{EC_N})$. Function Ω treats queries for source or destination locations of resetting edges special and outputs an equivalent property which can be verified in $\mathcal{N}'$.

For instance, consider a simple resetting edge $e \in \mathcal{SE}_Y(\mathcal{A})$ of some $\mathcal{A} \in \mathcal{N}$. The source location ℓ of e can be assumed in $\mathcal{N}$ in different configurations: either the reset time is not yet reached, or the reset time is reached but $\mathcal{A}$ did not reset yet, while other automata in $\mathcal{RES}_Y(\mathcal{N})$ may have reset their clocks already. In $\mathcal{N}'$, all edges resulting from simple edges fire at once on the broadcast synchronisation, so all source locations are left together. Because the resetter moves to $\ell_{nst,Y}$, a configuration of $\mathcal{N}'$ which assumes location $\ell_{nst,Y}$ represents all similar configurations of $\mathcal{N}$ where all simple edges are in their source or destination location. Thus the location ℓ is reachable in $\mathcal{N}$ if and only if (i) $\mathcal{N}'$ reaches $\ell_{nst,Y}$, or (ii) if ℓ is reached while being stable, i.e., not being in $\ell_{nst,Y}$.

A similar reasoning is applied to properties querying elements of a complex resetting edge wrt. Y, but instead of using $\ell_{nst,Y}$ we use the intermediate location $\ell_{\xi_{Y,e}}$ from $\mathcal{N}'$, since this location represents unstability before updating any variable that occurs in a complex edge.

In this sense, configurations involving location $\ell_{nst,Y}$ summarise unstable phases of $\mathcal{N}$. Assuming $\ell_{nst,Y}$ in $\mathcal{N}'$ represents both cases for a simple edge, that it has already been taken or not, and that the clock x reset by this edge is still C_Y or already 0. Although involving two choices, there are essentially two cases (not four): having taken the reset edge and being unstable implies that, x is 0 and some other clocks are still C_Y, or x is still C_Y and some other clocks are already 0. To this end, we introduce fresh existentially quantified variables $\tilde{\ell}$ and $\tilde{x}$ in Ω_0 and conjoin it with a consistency conjunction. By $R1$, we only need to consider 0 and C_Y as values of $\tilde{x}$, thus the existential quantification can be rewritten into a big disjunction, and hence is a proper query.

Definition 2 (Function Ω). *Let $Y \in \mathcal{EC}_\mathcal{N}$ be sets of clocks of a well-formed network $\mathcal{N}$ and let $\mathcal{N}' = \mathcal{K}(\mathcal{N}, \mathcal{EC}_\mathcal{N})$. Let C_Y be the constant described in restriction R1. Let $\ell_{nst,Y}$ be the unique non initial location of $\mathcal{R}_Y$, the resetter automaton wrt. Y in $\mathcal{N}'$. Let β be a basic formula over $\mathcal{N}$. Then the function Ω is defined as follows where $\mathcal{L}_Y = \mathcal{LS}_Y(\mathcal{N}) \cup (\mathcal{LC}_Y(\mathcal{N}) \cap \mathcal{RL}_Y(\mathcal{N}))$:*

$$\Omega_0(\beta) = \begin{cases} (\ell \wedge \neg\ell_{nst,Y}) \vee (\ell_{nst,Y} \wedge \tilde{\ell}) & , \text{ if } \beta = \ell, \ell \in \mathcal{L}_Y. \\ (\neg\ell \wedge \neg\ell_{nst,Y}) \vee (\ell_{nst,Y} \wedge \neg\tilde{\ell}) & , \text{ if } \beta = \neg\ell, \ell \in \mathcal{L}_Y. \\ (\Gamma(\varphi) \wedge \neg\ell_{nst,Y}) \vee (\ell_{nst,Y} \wedge \tilde{\varphi}) & , \text{ if } \beta = \varphi, \tilde{\varphi} = \varphi[x/\tilde{x} \mid x \in \mathcal{X}(\mathcal{N})]. \\ \beta & , \text{ otherwise} \end{cases}$$

$$\Omega(CF) = \exists \tilde{x}_1, .., \tilde{x}_k \ \exists \tilde{\ell}_1, .., \tilde{\ell}_m \bullet \Omega_0(CF) \wedge \bigwedge_{\substack{(\ell,\alpha,\varphi,\vec{r},\ell') \\ \in \mathcal{CE}_Y(\mathcal{A}), \\ \ell_i = \ell}} (\tilde{\ell}_i \implies \ell_{\xi_{Y,e}}) \wedge \bigwedge_{\substack{1 \leq i \neq j \leq m, \\ 1 \leq p \leq n \\ \ell_i, \tilde{\ell}_j \in L_p,}} \neg(\tilde{\ell}_i \wedge \tilde{\ell}_j)$$

$$\wedge \bigwedge_{\substack{1 \leq i \leq k, 1 \leq j \leq m, \\ x_j \in \mathcal{X}_p \cap Y, 1 \leq p \leq n, \\ \ell_i \in L_p \cap (\mathcal{RL}_Y(\mathcal{N}) \setminus \mathcal{RL}_Y^+(\mathcal{N}))}} (\tilde{\ell}_i \implies \tilde{x}_j = C_Y) \wedge \bigwedge_{\substack{1 \leq i \leq k, 1 \leq j \leq m, \\ x_j \in \mathcal{X}_p \cap Y, 1 \leq p \leq n, \\ \ell_i \in L_p \cap (\mathcal{RL}_Y^+(\mathcal{N}) \setminus \mathcal{RL}_Y(\mathcal{N}))}} (\tilde{\ell}_i \implies \tilde{x}_j = 0) \wedge \bigwedge_{\substack{(\ell,\alpha,\varphi,\vec{r},\ell') \\ \in \mathcal{SE}_Y(\mathcal{A}), \\ \ell_i \in \{\ell,\ell'\}}} (\tilde{\ell}_i \implies \ell')$$

For example, for $\Omega(\phi)$ we obtain, after some simplifications given that $\mathcal{A}_2$ has only simple resetting edges, the following transformed formula:

$$\exists \tilde{x} \in \{0, C_Y\} \bullet closed = 1 \wedge ((x \leq 60 \wedge \neg\ell_{nst,Y}) \vee (\ell_{nst,Y} \wedge \tilde{x} \geq 60)).$$

4   Formal Relation of a Well-formed Network and Its Transformed Network

In order to prove our approach correct we establish a weak bisimulation relation between a well-formed network and its respective transformed network. To this end, we firstly extend the notion of (un)stability to $\mathcal{N}'$ as follows.

Definition 3 (Stable Configuration of $\mathcal{N}'$). *Let $\mathcal{N}$ be a network and let $Y \in \mathcal{EC}_{\mathcal{N}}$ be a set of quasi-equal clocks. Let $\mathcal{N}' = \mathcal{K}(\mathcal{N}, \mathcal{EC}_{\mathcal{N}})$.*

A configuration $r \in Conf(\mathcal{N}')$ is called stable wrt. Y *if and only if the initial location $\ell_{ini, \mathcal{R}_Y}$ of resetter $\mathcal{R}_Y \in \mathcal{N}'$ occurs in r, i.e., if $r \models \ell_{ini, \mathcal{R}_Y}$. We use $SC_{\mathcal{N}'}^Y$ to denote the set of all configurations that are stable wrt. Y and $SC_{\mathcal{N}'}$ to denote the set $\bigcap_{Y \in \mathcal{EC}_{\mathcal{N}}} SC_{\mathcal{N}'}^Y$ of* globally stable *configurations of $\mathcal{N}'$. We call a configuration $r \notin SC_{\mathcal{N}'}$* unstable.

We recall that configurations induced when each clock from $Y \in \mathcal{EC}_{\mathcal{N}}$ is reset in well-formed networks $\mathcal{N}$, are summarised in transformed networks $\mathcal{N}'$ in configurations where the $\ell_{nst, \mathcal{R}_Y}$-location occurs together with the valuations of rst_Y^I and rst_Y^O reflecting these resets. Hence with the valuations from rst_Y^I and rst_Y^O we unfold information summarised in these configurations from $\mathcal{N}'$.

Lemma 1 (Weak Bisimulation)

Any well-formed network $\mathcal{N}$ where $\mathcal{EC}_{\mathcal{N}}$-reset edges are pre/post delayed, is weakly bisimilar to $\mathcal{N}' = \mathcal{K}(\mathcal{N}, \mathcal{EC}_{\mathcal{N}})$, i.e., there is a weak bisimulation relation $\mathcal{S} \subseteq Conf(\mathcal{N}) \times Conf(\mathcal{N}')$ such that

1. *$\forall s \in \mathcal{C}_{ini}(\mathcal{N}) \, \exists r \bullet (s, r) \in \mathcal{S}$ and $\forall r \in \mathcal{C}_{ini}(\mathcal{N}') \, \exists s \bullet (s, r) \in \mathcal{S}$.*
2. *For all config. formulae CF over $\mathcal{N}$, $\forall (s, r) \in \mathcal{S} \bullet s \models CF \implies r \models \Omega(CF)$ and $\forall r \in CONS_{\mathcal{EC}_{\mathcal{N}}} \bullet r \models \Omega(CF) \implies \exists s \in Conf(\mathcal{N}) \bullet (s, r) \in \mathcal{S} \wedge s \models CF$.*
3. *For all $(s, r) \in \mathcal{S}$,*
   (a) *if $s \xrightarrow{\lambda} s'$ with*
      i. *$s \in SC_{\mathcal{N}}^Y$, $s' \notin SC_{\mathcal{N}}^Y$, where $Y \in \mathcal{EC}_{\mathcal{N}}$, and justified by a simple resetting edge, there is r' such that $r \xrightarrow{\lambda} r'$ and $(s', r') \in \mathcal{S}$.*
      ii. *$s, s' \notin SC_{\mathcal{N}}^Y$, or $s \notin SC_{\mathcal{N}}^Y$ and $s' \in SC_{\mathcal{N}_0}^Y$ where $Y \in \mathcal{EC}_{\mathcal{N}}$, and justified by a simple resetting edge, then $r \xrightarrow{\tau} r$ and $(s', r) \in \mathcal{S}$.*
      iii. *$s, s' \in SC_{\mathcal{N}}^Y$, or $s \in SC_{\mathcal{N}}^Y$ and $s' \notin SC_{\mathcal{N}}^Y$, where $Y \in \mathcal{EC}_{\mathcal{N}}$, and justified by the set $CE_Y \subseteq \mathcal{CE}_Y(\mathcal{N})$ of complex resetting edges wrt. Y, then there exist r', r'' such that $r \xrightarrow{\tau} r' \xrightarrow{\lambda} r''$ and $(s, r'), (s', r'') \in \mathcal{S}$.*
      iv. *$s \notin SC_{\mathcal{N}}^Y$, $s' \in SC_{\mathcal{N}}^Y$, where $Y \in \mathcal{EC}_{\mathcal{N}}$, and justified by $CE_Y \subseteq \mathcal{CE}_Y(\mathcal{N})$, there is r' s.t. $r \xrightarrow{\lambda} r'$ and $(s', r') \in \mathcal{S}$.*
      v. *$s, s' \in SC_{\mathcal{N}}^Y$, $\ell_r = \ell_{nst, \mathcal{R}_Y}$ for some $Y \in \mathcal{EC}_{\mathcal{N}}$, and $\lambda = d > 0$, there exist r', r'' such that $r \xrightarrow{\tau} r' \xrightarrow{\lambda} r''$ and $(s, r'), (s', r'') \in \mathcal{S}$.*
      vi. *Otherwise there exists r' such that $r \xrightarrow{\lambda} r'$ and $(s', r') \in \mathcal{S}$.*
   (b) *if $r \xrightarrow{\lambda} r'$ with*
      i. *$r \in SC_{\mathcal{N}'}^Y, r' \notin SC_{\mathcal{N}'}^Y$, where $Y \in \mathcal{EC}_{\mathcal{N}}$, $\nu_{r'}(rst_Y^O) < N$, where $N = \nu_r(rst_Y^O)$, there exist $s_1, \ldots, s_n$ where $n = N - \nu_{r'}(rst_Y^O)$, such that $s \xrightarrow{\tau} s_1 \xrightarrow{\tau} \ldots \xrightarrow{\tau} s_n$ and $(s_i, r') \in \mathcal{S}$, $1 \le i \le n$.*
      ii. *$r \in SC_{\mathcal{N}'}^Y, r' \notin SC_{\mathcal{N}'}^Y$, $\nu_{r'}(rst_Y^O) = \nu_r(rst_Y^O)$, where $Y \in \mathcal{EC}_{\mathcal{N}}$, then $s \xrightarrow{0} s$ and $(s, r') \in \mathcal{S}$.*
      iii. *$\ell_r = \ell_{nst, \mathcal{R}_Y}, \ell_{r'} \neq \ell_{nst, \mathcal{R}_Y}$, $Y \in \mathcal{EC}_{\mathcal{N}}$, then $s \xrightarrow{0} s$ and $(s, r') \in \mathcal{S}$.*
      iv. *Otherwise there exists s' such that $s \xrightarrow{\lambda} s'$ and $(s', r') \in \mathcal{S}$.*

Proof (sketch). Let $\mathcal{N}$ be a well-formed network and let $\mathcal{N}' = \mathcal{K}(\mathcal{N}, \mathcal{EC}_{\mathcal{N}})$. For each $Y \in \mathcal{EC}_{\mathcal{N}}$ use the following six conditions to obtain a weak bisimulation

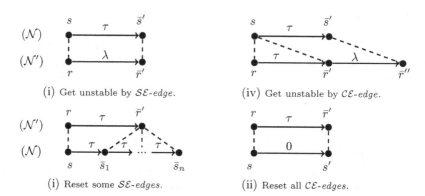

(i) Get unstable by $\mathcal{SE}$-edge.   (iv) Get unstable by $\mathcal{CE}$-edge.

(i) Reset some $\mathcal{SE}$-edges.   (ii) Reset all $\mathcal{CE}$-edges.

Fig. 3. Some involved weak bisimulations cases between the transition system (TS) of a well-formed network $\mathcal{N}$ and the TS of the network $\mathcal{N}' = \mathcal{K}(\mathcal{N}, \mathcal{EC}_{\mathcal{N}})$. Dots with the legend $(\bar{s})s$ and $(\bar{r})r$ represent (unstable) stable configurations of $\mathcal{N}$ and $\mathcal{N}'$, respectively. Arrows represent transitions between configurations of the same TS. Configurations s and r are in transition simulation if they are linked by a dotted line.

relation $\mathcal{S}$ between configurations $s \in Conf(\mathcal{N})$ and *consistent* configurations $r \in CONS_{\mathcal{EC}_{\mathcal{N}}}$ of $\mathcal{N}'$, i.e., configurations whose valuations of variables rst_Y^I match the number of reset locations wrt. Y assumed in r, and if r is unstable, variables rst_Y^O match the number of intermediate locations assumed in r, otherwise match $|Y|$. (1) any pair (s,r) matches the valuations of variables and non-quasi-equal clocks. (2) automata from $\mathcal{N}$ and $\mathcal{N}'$ which do not reset clocks from Y must coincide on locations. (3) relate stable configurations from $\mathcal{N}$ where all quasi-equal clocks from Y have the valuation C_Y and the variable $rst_Y^I = |Y|$, to either stable configurations in $\mathcal{N}'$ where the clock $rep(Y) = C_Y$, or to unstable configurations which reflect the synchronisation on the channel $reset_Y$. (4) take unstable configurations from $\mathcal{N}$ and $\mathcal{N}'$ and relate them if they show the effect of taking the same complex resetting edge. (5) relate unstable configurations wrt. Y in $\mathcal{N}$ to the unstable configuration in $\mathcal{N}'$ whose variable $rst_Y^O = 0$ and the location $\ell_{r,\mathcal{R}_Y} = \ell_{nst,\mathcal{R}_Y}$. (6) relate stable configurations from $\mathcal{N}$ which show the effect of resetting each clock from Y, to the unstable configuration of $\mathcal{N}'$ which shows the same effect, i.e., the valuation of the variable $rst_Y^O = 0$. This last restriction allows $\mathcal{N}'$ to make the return transition to stability.

During stability phases there is a strong bisimulation (one-to-one) between the networks $\mathcal{N}$ and $\mathcal{N}'$. Only during unstability phases there is a weak bisimulation (one-to-many) in both directions. There are cases (reset of simple edges) where $\mathcal{N}$ simulates one step of $\mathcal{N}'$ with multiple steps, and cases (reset of complex edges) where $\mathcal{N}'$ simulates one step of $\mathcal{N}$ with multiple steps. Figure 3 shows some involved simulation steps between unstable phases in $\mathcal{N}$ and $\mathcal{N}'$.   □

Theorem 1. *Let $\mathcal{N}$ be a well-formed network where $\mathcal{EC}_{\mathcal{N}}$-resets are pre/post delayed. Let CF be a configuration formula over $\mathcal{N}$. Then*

$$\mathcal{K}(\mathcal{N}, \mathcal{EC}_{\mathcal{N}}) \models \exists \Diamond \, \Omega(CF) \iff \mathcal{N} \models \exists \Diamond \, CF.$$

Table 1. Column XX-$N(K)$ gives the figures for case study XX with N sensors (and K applied). 'C' gives the number of clocks in the model, 'kStates' the number of visited states times 10^3, 'M' memory usage in MB, and '$t(s)$' verification time in seconds. FraTTA transformed each of our benchmarks in at most 5 seconds. (Env.: Intel i3, 2.3GHz, 3GB, Ubuntu 11.04, verifyta 4.1.3.4577 with default options.)

Network	C	kStates	M	$t(s)$	Network	C	kStates	M	$t(s)$
EP-21	21	3,145.7	507.4	498.4	FS-8	14	5,217.7	181.4	758.7
EP-21K	1	5,242.9	624.9	167.5	FS-8K	5	1,081.9	41.6	32.8
EP-22	22	6,291.5	1,025.9	1,291.7	FS-10	16	17,951.3	568.2	4,271.2
EP-22K	1	10,485.8	1,269.6	358.3	FS-10K	5	1,215.0	44.1	39.0
EP-23	23	-	-	-	FS-11	17	-	-	-
EP-23K	1	18,431.8	2,490.2	646.8	FS-126K	5	9,512.3	300.5	1,529.8
TT-6	7	2,986.0	114.9	38.1	CD-14	16	7,078.1	591.8	1,384.3
TT-6K	1	2,759.6	106.7	30.6	CD-14K	2	442	52.5	42.3
TT-7	8	16,839.9	611.5	276.4	CD-16	18	13,441.1	1,996.4	3,806.3
TT-7K	1	15,746.7	577.3	262.7	CD-16K	2	2,031.9	240.9	389.0
TT-8	9	-	-	-	CD-17	19	-	-	-
TT-8K	1	66,265.9	2,367.7	1,227.6	CD-18K	2	9,1975.3	1,142.8	2,206.1
LS-7	18	553.3	74.5	22.7	CR-6	6	264.5	18.7	2.9
LS-7K	6	605.3	83.2	11.5	CR-6K	1	129.4	18.2	1.5
LS-9	22	8,897.6	1,283.5	686.6	CR-7	7	7,223.7	496.5	136.3
LS-9K	6	9,106.3	1,417.9	238.8	CR-7K	1	2,530.1	342.4	42.5
LS-11	26	-	-	-	CR-8	8	-	-	-
LS-11K	6	7,694.0	2,188.2	460.6	CR-8K	1	5,057.6	785.0	109.4

Proof. Use Lemma 1 and induction over the lenght of paths to show that CF holds in $\mathcal{N}$ if and only if $\Omega(CF)$ holds in $\mathcal{K}(\mathcal{N}, \mathcal{EC}_\mathcal{N})$. $\square$

5   Experimental Results

We applied our approach to six industrial case studies using *FraTTA* [16], our implementation of $\mathcal{K}$. The three case studies *FS* [17], *CR* [18], *CD* [19] are from the class of TDMA protocols and appear in [4]. The relaxed well-formedness criteria (compared to [4]) allowed us to include the three new case studies *EP* [6], *TT* [20], *LS* [21]. We verified non-local queries as proposed by the respective authors of these case studies. None of these queries could be verified with the approach presented in [4]. Our motivating case study is inspired by the network from [6] which use the Ethernet PowerLink protocol in Alstom Power Control Systems. The network consists of N sensors and one master. The sensors exchange information with the master in two phases, the first is isochronous and the second asynchronous. An error occurs if a sensor fails to update the configuration data as sent by the master in the beginning of the isochronous phase. Specifically, each sensor should update its internal data before the master has reset its clock. The query $configData := \forall\square\ \mathcal{A}.configData = 1 \wedge \mathcal{A}.x = 0 \wedge \mathcal{M}.y > 0$, where $\mathcal{A}$ is a sensor and $\mathcal{M}$ is the master, x and y are quasi-equal clocks from the same equivalence class, and *configData* is a boolean variable set to true by the edge that resets x when $\mathcal{A}$ has successfully updated its configuration data, checks whether this network is free from errors as explained before. Note that query *configData* is non-local and in addition refers to an unstable configuration. We refer the reader to [17–21] for more information on the other case studies.

Table 1 gives figures for the verification of the non-local queries in instances of the original and the transformed model. The rows without results indicate the smallest instances for which we did not obtain results within 24 hours. For all examples except for TT, we achieved significant reductions in verification time. The quasi-equal clocks in the TT model are reset by a broadcast transition so there is no interleaving of resets in the original model. Still, verification of the transformed TT instances *including* transformation time is faster than verification of the original ones. Regarding memory consumption, note that verification of the K-models of EP and LS takes slightly more memory than verification of the original counterparts. We argue that this is due to all resetting edges being *complex* in these two networks. Thus, our transformation preserves the full interleaving of clock resets and the whole set of unstable locations whose size is exponential in the number of participating automata, and it adds the transitions to and from location ℓ_{nst}. The shown reduction of the verification time is due to a smaller size of the DBMs that Uppaal uses to represent zones [22] and whose size grows quadratically in the number of clocks. If the resetting edges are *simple* (as in FS, CD, and CR), our transformation removes all those unstable configurations.

6   Conclusion

Our new technique reduces the verification time of networks of timed automata with quasi-equal clocks. It represents all clocks from an equivalence class by one representative, and it eliminates those configurations induced by automata that reset quasi-equal clocks one by one. All interleaving transitions which are induced by simple resetting edges are replaced by just two transitions in the transformed networks. We use *nst*-locations to summarise unstable configurations. This allows us to also reduce the runtime of non-local properties or properties explicitly querying unstable phases. With variables *rstI*, *rstO* we unfold information summarised in *nst*-locations, and together with a careful syntactical transformation of properties, we reflect all properties of original networks in transformed ones. Our new approach fixes the two severe drawbacks of [4], which only supports local queries and whose strong well-formedness conditions rules out many industrial case-studies. Our experiments show the feasibility and potential of the new approach, even if some interleavings are preserved and only the number of clocks is reduced.

References

1. Rappaport, T.S.: Wireless communications, vol. 2. Prentice Hall (2002)
2. Cena, G., Seno, L., et al.: Performance analysis of ethernet powerlink networks for distributed control and automation systems. CSI 31(3), 566–572 (2009)

3. Alur, R., Dill, D.: A theory of timed automata. TCS 126(2), 183–235 (1994)
4. Herrera, C., Westphal, B., Feo-Arenis, S., Muñiz, M., Podelski, A.: Reducing quasi-equal clocks in networks of timed automata. In: Jurdziński, M., Ničković, D. (eds.) FORMATS 2012. LNCS, vol. 7595, pp. 155–170. Springer, Heidelberg (2012)
5. Behrmann, G., David, A., Larsen, K.G.: A tutorial on UPPAAL. In: Bernardo, M., Corradini, F. (eds.) SFM-RT 2004. LNCS, vol. 3185, pp. 200–236. Springer, Heidelberg (2004)
6. Limal, S., Potier, S., Denis, B., Lesage, J.: Formal verification of redundant media extension of ethernet powerlink. In: ETFA, pp. 1045–1052. IEEE (2007)
7. Daws, C., Yovine, S.: Reducing the number of clock variables of timed automata. In: RTSS, pp. 73–81. IEEE (1996)
8. Daws, C., Tripakis, S.: Model checking of real-time reachability properties using abstractions. In: Steffen, B. (ed.) TACAS 1998. LNCS, vol. 1384, pp. 313–329. Springer, Heidelberg (1998)
9. André, É.: Dynamic clock elimination in parametric timed automata. In: FSFMA, OASICS, pp. 18–31, Schloss Dagstuhl - Leibniz-Zentrum fuer Informatik (2013)
10. Braberman, V., Garbervestky, D., Kicillof, N., Monteverde, D., Olivero, A.: Speeding up model checking of timed-models by combining scenario specialization and live component analysis. In: Ouaknine, J., Vaandrager, F.W. (eds.) FORMATS 2009. LNCS, vol. 5813, pp. 58–72. Springer, Heidelberg (2009)
11. Braberman, V.A., Garbervetsky, D., Olivero, A.: Improving the verification of timed systems using influence information. In: Katoen, J.-P., Stevens, P. (eds.) TACAS 2002. LNCS, vol. 2280, pp. 21–36. Springer, Heidelberg (2002)
12. Muñiz, M., Westphal, B., Podelski, A.: Timed automata with disjoint activity. In: Jurdziński, M., Ničković, D. (eds.) FORMATS 2012. LNCS, vol. 7595, pp. 188–203. Springer, Heidelberg (2012)
13. Balaguer, S., Chatain, T.: Avoiding shared clocks in networks of timed automata. In: Koutny, M., Ulidowski, I. (eds.) CONCUR 2012. LNCS, vol. 7454, pp. 100–114. Springer, Heidelberg (2012)
14. Muñiz, M., Westphal, B., Podelski, A.: Detecting quasi-equal clocks in timed automata. In: Braberman, V., Fribourg, L. (eds.) FORMATS 2013. LNCS, vol. 8053, pp. 198–212. Springer, Heidelberg (2013)
15. Olderog, E.-R., Dierks, H.: Real-time systems - formal specification and automatic verification. Cambridge University Press (2008)
16. Fitriani, K.: FraTTA: Framework for transformation of timed automata, Master Team Project, Albert-Ludwigs-Universität Freiburg (2013)
17. Dietsch, D., Feo-Arenis, S., et al.: Disambiguation of industrial standards through formalization and graphical languages. In: RE, pp. 265–270. IEEE (2011)
18. Gobriel, S., Khattab, S., Mossé, D., et al.: RideSharing: Fault tolerant aggregation in sensor networks using corrective actions. In: SECON, pp. 595–604. IEEE (2006)
19. Jensen, H., Larsen, K., Skou, A.: Modelling and analysis of a collision avoidance protocol using SPIN and Uppaal. In: 2nd SPIN Workshop (1996)
20. Steiner, W., Elmenreich, W.: Automatic recovery of the TTP/A sensor/actuator network. In: WISES, pp. 25–37, Vienna University of Technology (2003)
21. Kordy, P., Langerak, R., et al.: Re-verification of a lip synchronization protocol using robust reachability. In: FMA. EPTCS, vol. 20, pp. 49–62 (2009)
22. Bengtsson, J., Yi, W.: Timed automata: Semantics, algorithms and tools. In: Desel, J., Reisig, W., Rozenberg, G. (eds.) ACPN 2003. LNCS, vol. 3098, pp. 87–124. Springer, Heidelberg (2004)

Are Timed Automata Bad for a Specification Language? Language Inclusion Checking for Timed Automata*

Ting Wang[1], Jun Sun[2], Yang Liu[3], Xinyu Wang[1], and Shanping Li[1]

[1] College of Computer Science and Technology, Zhejiang University, China
[2] ISTD, Singapore University of Technology and Design, Singapore
[3] School of Computer Engineering, Nanyang Technological University, Singapore

Abstract. Given a timed automaton $\mathcal{P}$ modeling an implementation and a timed automaton $\mathcal{S}$ as a specification, language inclusion checking is to decide whether the language of $\mathcal{P}$ is a subset of that of $\mathcal{S}$. It is known that this problem is undecidable and "this result is an obstacle in using timed automata as a specification language" [2]. This undecidability result, however, does not imply that all timed automata are bad for specification. In this work, we propose a zone-based semi-algorithm for language inclusion checking, which implements simulation reduction based on Anti-Chain and LU-simulation. Though it is not guaranteed to terminate, we show that it does in many cases through both theoretical and empirical analysis. The semi-algorithm has been incorporated into the PAT model checker, and applied to multiple systems to show its usefulness and scalability.

1 Introduction

Timed automata, introduced by Alur and Dill in [2], have emerged as one of the most popular models to specify and analyze real-time systems. It has been shown that the reachability problem for timed automata is decidable using the construction of region graphs [2]. Efficient zone-based methods for checking both safety and liveness properties have later been developed [14,21]. In [2], it has also been shown that timed automata in general cannot be determinized, and the language inclusion problem is undecidable, which "is an obstacle in using timed automata as a specification language".

In order to avoid undecidability, a number of subclasses of timed automata which are determinizable (and perhaps serve as a good specification language) have been identified, e.g., event-clock timed automata [3,17], timed automata restricted to at most one clock [16] and integer resets timed automata [18]. Recently, Baier *et al.* [4] described a method for determinizing arbitrary timed automaton, which under a boundedness condition, yields an equivalent deterministic timed automaton in finite time. Furthermore, they show that the boundedness condition is satisfied by several subclasses of timed automata which are known to be determinizable. However, the method is based on region graphs and it is well-known that region graphs are inefficient and lead to state space explosion. Compared to region graphs, zone graphs are often used in existing tools for real-time system verification, such as UPPAAL [14] and KRONOS [23]. Zone-based approaches have also been used to solve problems which are related to the language

---

* This research is sponsored in part by NSFC Program (No.61103032) of China.

E. Ábrahám and K. Havelund (Eds.): TACAS 2014, LNCS 8413, pp. 310–325, 2014.
© Springer-Verlag Berlin Heidelberg 2014

inclusion problem, like the universality problem (which asks whether a timed automaton accepts all timed words) for timed automata with one-clock only [1]. However, to the best of our knowledge, there has not been any zone-based method proposed for language inclusion checking for arbitrary timed automata.

In this work we develop a zone-based method to solve the language inclusion problem. Formally, given an implementation timed automaton $\mathcal{P}$ and a specification timed automaton $\mathcal{S}$, the language inclusion problem is to decide whether the language of $\mathcal{P}$ is a subset of that of $\mathcal{S}$. It is known that the problem can be converted to a reachability problem on the synchronous product of $\mathcal{P}$ and determinization of $\mathcal{S}$ [16]. Inspired by [1,4], the main contribution of this work is that we present a semi-algorithm with a transformation that determinizes $\mathcal{S}$ and constructs the product on-the-fly, where zones are used as a symbolic representation. Furthermore, simulation relations between the product states are used, which can be obtained through LU-simulation [5] and Anti-Chain [22]. With the simulation relations, many product states may be skipped, which often contributes to the termination of our semi-algorithm.

Our semi-algorithm can be applied to arbitrary timed automata, though it may not terminate sometimes. To argue that timed automata can nonetheless serve as a specification language, we investigate when our approach is terminating, both theoretically and empirically. Firstly, we prove that, with the clock boundedness condition [4], we are able to construct a suitable well-quasi-order on the product state space to ensure termination. It thus implies that our semi-algorithm is always terminating for subclasses of timed automata which are known to be determinizable. Furthermore, we prove that for some classes of timed automata which may violate the boundedness condition, our semi-algorithm is always terminating as long as there is a well-quasi-order on the abstract state space explored. Secondly, using randomly generated timed automata, we show that our approach terminates for many timed automata which are not determinizable (and violating the boundedness condition) because of the simulation reduction. Thirdly, we collect a set of commonly used patterns for specifying timed properties [8,12] and show that our approach is always terminating for all of those properties. Lastly, our semi-algorithm has been implemented in the PAT [19] framework, and applied to a number of benchmark systems to demonstrate its effectiveness and scalability.

The remainders of the paper is organized as follows. Section 2 reviews the notions of timed automata. Section 3 shows how to reduce language inclusion checking to a reachability problem, which is then solved using a zone-based approach. Section 4 reports the experimental results. Section 5 reviews related work. Section 6 concludes.

2 Background

In this section, we review the relevant background and define the language inclusion problem. We start with defining labeled transition systems (LTS). An LTS is a tuple $\mathcal{L} = (S, Init, \Sigma, T)$, where S is a set of states; $Init \subseteq S$ is a set of initial states; Σ is an alphabet; and $T \subseteq S \times \Sigma \times S$ is a labeled transition relation. A run of $\mathcal{L}$ is a finite sequence of alternating states and events $\langle s_0, e_1, s_1, e_2, \cdots, e_n, s_n \rangle$ such that $(s_i, e_i, s_{i+1}) \in T$ for all $0 \leq i \leq n-1$. We say the run starts with s_0 and ends with s_n. A state s' is reachable from s iff there is a run starting with s and ending with s'. A state is always reachable from itself. A run is rooted if it starts with a state in $Init$. A state is reachable if there is a rooted run which ends at the state. Given a state $s \in S$ and an event $e \in \Sigma$, we write $post(s, e, \mathcal{L})$ to denote $\{s' | (s, e, s') \in T\}$. We write $post(s, \mathcal{L})$ to denote $\{s' | \exists e \in \Sigma \cdot (s, e, s') \in T\}$, i.e., the set of successors of s.

Let $F \subseteq S$ be a set of target states. Given two states s_0 and s_1 in S, we say that s_0 is simulated by s_1 with respect to F if $s_0 \in F$ implies that $s_1 \in F$; and for any $e \in \Sigma$, $(s_0, e, s'_0) \in T$ implies there exists $(s_1, e, s'_1) \in T$ such that s'_0 is simulated by s'_1. In order to check whether a state in F is reachable, if we know that s is simulated by s', then s can be skipped during system exploration if s' has been explored already. This is known as simulation reduction [7].

The original definition of timed automata is finite-state timed Büchi automata [2] equipped with real-valued clock variables and Büchi accepting condition (to enforce progress). Later, timed safety automata were introduced in [11] which adopt an intuitive notion of progress. That is, instead of having accepting states, each state in timed safety automata is associated with a local timing constraint called a *state invariant*. An automaton can stay at a state as long as the valuation of the clocks satisfies the state invariant. The reader can refer to [9] for the expressiveness of timed safety automata. In the following, we focus on timed safety automata as they are supported in the state-of-art model checker UPPAAL [14] and are often used in practice. Hereafter, they are simply referred to as timed automata.

Let $\mathbb{R}^+$ be the set of non-negative real numbers. Given a set of clocks C, we define $\Phi(C)$ as the set of clock constraints. Each clock constraint is inductively defined by: $\delta := true | x \sim n | \delta_1 \wedge \delta_2 | \neg \delta_1$ where $\sim \in \{=, \leq, \geq, <, >\}$; x is a clock in C and $n \in \mathbb{R}^+$ is a constant. Without loss of generality, we assume that n is an integer constant. The set of downward constraints obtained with $\sim \in \{\leq, <\}$ is denoted as $\Phi_{\leq,<}(C)$. A clock valuation v for a set of clocks C is a function which assigns a real value to each clock. A clock constraint can be viewed as the set of clock valuations which satisfy the constraint. A clock valuation v satisfies a clock constraint δ, written as $v \in \delta$, iff δ evaluates to be true using the clock values given by v. For $d \in \mathbb{R}^+$, let $v + d$ denote the clock valuation v' s.t. $v'(c) = v(c) + d$ for all $c \in C$. For $X \subseteq C$, let clock resetting notion $[X \mapsto 0]v$ denote the valuation v' such that $v'(c) = v(c)$ for all $c \in C \wedge c \notin X$, and $v'(x) = 0$ for all $x \in X$. We write $C = 0$ to be the clock valuation where each clock $c \in C$ reads 0.

Formally, a timed automaton is a tuple $\mathcal{A} = (S, Init, \Sigma, C, L, T)$ where S is a finite set of states; $Init \subseteq S$ is a set of initial states; Σ is an alphabet; C is a finite set of clocks; $L : S \rightarrow \Phi_{\leq,<}(C)$ labels each state with an invariant; $T \subseteq S \times \Sigma \times \Phi(C) \times 2^C \times S$ is a labeled transition relation. Intuitively, a transition $(s, e, \delta, X, s') \in T$ can be fired if δ is satisfied. After event e occurs, clocks in X are set to zero. The (concrete) semantics of $\mathcal{A}$ is an infinite-state LTS, denoted as $\mathcal{C}(\mathcal{A}) = (S_c, Init_c, \mathbb{R}^+ \times \Sigma, T_c)$ such that S_c is a set of configurations of $\mathcal{A}$, each of which is a pair (s, v) where $s \in S$ is a state and v is a clock valuation; $Init_c = \{(s, C = 0) | s \in Init\}$ is a set of initial configurations; and T_c is a set of concrete transitions of the form $((s, v), (d, e), (s', v'))$ such that there exists a transition $(s, e, \delta, X, s') \in T$; $v + d \in \delta$; $v + d \in L(s)$; $[X \mapsto 0](v + d) = v'$; and $v' \in L(s')$. Intuitively, the system idles for d time units at state s and then take the transition (generating event e) to reach state s'. An example timed automaton is shown in Fig. 1(a). The initial state is p_0. The automaton has a state

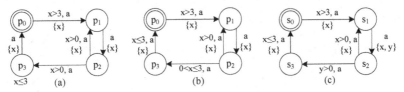

Fig. 1. Timed automata examples

invariant $x \leq 3$ on state p_3 which implies that if the control is at p_3, it must transit to the next state before the value of clock x is larger than 3.

A timed automaton $\mathcal{A}$ is deterministic iff $Init$ contains only one state and for any two transitions $(s_0, e_0, \delta_0, X_0, s'_0) \in T$ and $(s_1, e_1, \delta_1, X_1, s'_1) \in T$, if $s_0 = s_1$ and $e_0 = e_1$, then δ_0 and δ_1 are mutually exclusive. Otherwise, $\mathcal{A}$ is non-deterministic. For instance, The timed automaton in Fig. 1(c) is non-deterministic as the two transitions from state s_2 are both labeled with a and the guards are not mutually exclusive.

Given $\langle(s_0, v_0), (d_1, e_1), (s_1, v_1), (d_2, e_2), \cdots (s_n, v_n)\rangle$ as a run of $\mathcal{C}(\mathcal{A})$, we can obtain a timed word: $\langle(D_1, e_1), (D_2, e_2), \cdots, (D_n, e_n)\rangle$ so that $D_i = \sum_{j=1}^{i} d_j$ for all $1 \leq i \leq n$. We define the $\mathcal{L}(\mathcal{A}, (s, v))$ to be the set of timed words obtained from the set of all runs starting with (s, v). The language of $\mathcal{A}$, written as $\mathcal{L}(\mathcal{A})$, is defined as the language obtained from any rooted run of $\mathcal{A}$. Two timed automata are equivalent if they define the same language. In practice, a system model is often composed of several automata executing in parallel. We skip the details on parallel composition of timed automata and remark our approach in this work applies to networks of timed automata. The language inclusion checking problem is then defined as follows. Given a timed automaton $\mathcal{P}$ and a timed automaton $\mathcal{S}$, how do we check whether $\mathcal{L}(\mathcal{P}) \subseteq \mathcal{L}(\mathcal{S})$?

In order to simplify the presentation in later sections, we first transform a given timed automaton to an equivalent one without state invariants, which will not affect our approach. The idea is to move the state invariants to transition guards. Given a timed automaton $\mathcal{A}$ and a state s with state invariant $L(s)$, we construct a timed automaton $\mathcal{A}'$ with the following two steps. Firstly, if (s, e, δ, X, s') is a transition from s, change it to $(s, e, \delta \wedge L(s), X, s')$. Secondly, if (s', e, δ, X, s) is a transition leading to s, for any clock constraint of the form $x \sim n$ where $\sim \in \{\leq, <\}$ in $L(s)$, if $x \notin X$, conjunct δ with $x \sim n$. For instance, given the timed automaton in Fig. 1(a), we construct the timed automaton in Fig. 1(b). The state invariant $x \leq 3$ of state p_3 is added to the transition from p_2 to p_3 and the transition from p_3 to p_0. By a simple argument, it can be shown that $\mathcal{L}(\mathcal{A}) = \mathcal{L}(\mathcal{A}')$. Notice that this transformation is not sound if the language of a timed automaton is defined differently, e.g., with a non-Zenoness assumption. In the following, we assume that all timed automata are without state invariants.

3 Language Inclusion Checking

In this section, we present our method on solving the language inclusion checking problem. We fix $\mathcal{P} = (S_p, Init_p, \Sigma_p, C_p, L_p, T_p)$ and $\mathcal{S} = (S_s, Init_s, \Sigma_s, C_s, L_s, T_s)$ to be the two timed automata such that S_p and S_s are disjoint as well as C_p and C_s.[1]

---

[1] The proofs in this section can be found at
   http://www.comp.nus.edu.sg/~pat/refine_ta/paper.pdf

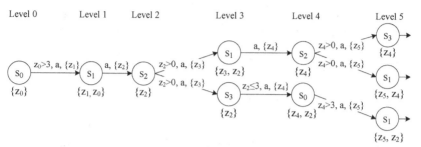

Fig. 2. Unfolding a timed automaton into an infinite timed tree

3.1 Unfolding Specification

In our method, we construct on-the-fly an unfolding of S in the form of an infinite timed tree which is equivalent to S. The idea is adopted from the approach in [4]. Before we present the formal definition, we illustrate the unfolding using an example. Fig. 2 shows the infinite timed tree after unfolding the automaton shown in Fig. 1(c). The idea is to introduce a fresh clock at every level and use the newly introduced clocks to replace ordinary clocks, i.e., x and y in this example. The benefit of doing this becomes clear later. At level 0, we are at state s_0 and introduce a clock z_0. Now since clock x and clock y are started at the same time as z_0 and the clocks will not be reset before the transition from s_0 takes place, we can use z_0 to replace x and y in the transition guard from s_0 at level 0 to s_1 at level 1. Because at level 0, the reading of clock z_0 is relevant to the future system behavior, we say that z_0 is active. In the tree, we label every node with a pair (s, A) where s is a state and A is a set of active clocks. Notice that not all clocks are active. For instance, clock z_0 and clock z_1 are no longer active at level 2.

One transition from the level 0 node leads to the node of level 1, corresponding to the transition from state s_0 to state s_1 in Fig. 1(c). The clock constraint $x > 3$ is rewritten to $z_0 > 3$ using only active clocks from the source node. A fresh clock z_1 is introduced along the transition. Notice that the node at level 1 is labelled with a set of two active clocks. z_1 is active at state s_1 at level 1 since it can be used to replace clock x which is reset along the transition, whereas z_0 is active because it is used to replace clock y which is not reset along the transition. The set of active clocks of the node at level 2 is a singleton z_2 since both of the clocks x and y are reset along the transition. z_0 and z_1 are not active as their reading is irrelevant to future transitions from s_2. Following the same construction, we build the tree level by level.

In the following, we define the unfolding of S. Let $Z = \langle z_0, z_1, z_2, \cdots \rangle$ be an infinite sequence of clocks. The unfolding S is an infinite timed tree, which can be viewed as a timed automaton $S_\infty = (St_\infty, Init_\infty, \Sigma_\infty, Z, T_\infty)$ with infinitely many states. Furthermore, we assume that S_∞ is associated with function $level$ such that $level(n)$ is the level of node n in the tree for all $n \in St_\infty$. A state n in St_∞ is in the form of (s, A) where $s \in S_s$ and A is a set of clocks. Given any state n, we define a function $f_n : C_s \mapsto Z$ which maps ordinary clocks in C_s to active clocks in Z. In an abuse of notations, given a clock constraint δ on C_s, we write $f_n(\delta)$ to denote the clock constraint obtained by replacing clocks in C_s with those in Z according to f_n. Given any state

$n = (s, A)$, we define A to be $\{f_n(c) | c \in C_s\}$. The initial states $Init_\infty$ and transition relation T_∞ are unfolded as follows.

- For any $s \in Init_s$, there is a level-0 node $n = (s, \{z_0\})$ in St_∞ with $level(n) = 0$, $f_n(c) = z_0$ for all $c \in C_s$.
- For each node $n = (s, A)$ at level i and for each transition $(s, e, \delta, X, s') \in T_s$, we add a node $n' = (s', A')$ at level $i + 1$ such that $f_{n'}(c) = f_n(c)$ if $c \in C_s \setminus X$, $f_{n'}(c) = z_{i+1}$ if $c \in X$; $level(n') = i + 1$. We add a transition $(n, e, f_n(\delta), \{z_{i+1}\}, n')$ to T_∞.

Note that transitions at the same level have the same set of resetting clocks, which contains one clock. Given a node $n = (s, A)$ in the tree, observe that not every clock x in A is active as the clock may never be used to guard any transition from s. Hereafter, we assume that inactive clocks are always removed.

3.2 Zone Abstraction for Language Inclusion Checking

It can be shown that S and S_∞ are equivalent [4]. Intuitively, S and S_∞ have the same language, thus the language inclusion problem can be converted to the language inclusion problem between $\mathcal{P}$ and S_∞. To solve the problem, we have to deal with two sources of infinity. One is that there are infinitely many clocks and the other is there are infinitely many clock valuations for each clock. In the following, we tackle the latter with zone abstraction [14].

In this work, we define a zone (which may or may not be convex) as the maximum set of clock valuations satisfying a clock constraint. Given a clock constraint δ, let $\delta^\uparrow$ denote the zone reached by delaying an arbitrary amount of time. For $X \subseteq C$, let $[X \mapsto 0]\delta$ denote the zone obtained by setting clocks in X to 0; and let $\delta[X]$ denote the projection of δ on X.

We define an LTS $\mathcal{Z}_\infty = (S, Init, \Sigma, T)$, which is a zone graph generated from the synchronous product of $\mathcal{P}$ and the determinization of S_∞. A state in S is an abstract configuration of the form (s_p, X_s, δ) such that $s_p \in S_p$; X_s is a set of nodes in S_∞ as defined in Section 3.1; and δ is a clock constraint. Recall that a state of S_∞ is of the form (s_s, A) where $s_s \in S_s$ and A is a set of active clocks. Given a set of states X_s of S_∞, we write $Act(X_s)$ to denote the set of all active clocks, i.e., $\{c | \exists (s_s, A) \in X_s \cdot c \in A\}$. δ constraints all clocks in $Act(X_s)$.

The $Init$ of the zone graph is defined as: $\{(s_p, Init_\infty, (Act(Init_\infty) = 0)^\uparrow) | s_p \in Init_p\}$. Σ equals to Σ_p. Next, we define T by showing how to generate successors of a given abstract configuration (s_p, X_s, δ). For every state $(s_s, A) \in X_s$, let $T_\infty(e, X_s)$ be the set of transitions in T_∞ which start with a state in X_s and are labeled with event e. Notice that the guard conditions of transitions in $T_\infty(e, X_s)$ may not be mutually exclusive. We define a set of constraints $Cons(e, X_s)$ such that each element in $Cons(e, X_s)$ is a constraint which conjuncts, for each transition in $T_\infty(e, X_s)$, either the transition guard or its negation. Notice that elements in $Cons(e, X_s)$ are by definition mutually exclusive. Given (s_p, X_s, δ) and an outgoing transition (s_p, e, g_p, X_p, s_p') from s_p in $\mathcal{P}$, for each $g \in Cons(e, X_s)$ we generate a successor (s_p', X_s', δ') as follows.

- For any state $(s_s, A) \in X_s$ and any transition $((s_s, A), e, g_s, Y, (s_s', A')) \in T_\infty$, if $\delta \wedge g_p \wedge g \wedge g_s$ is not false, then $(s_s', A') \in X_s'$.

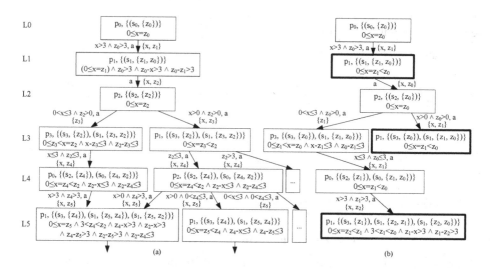

Fig. 3. Zone graphs: (a) $\mathcal{Z}_\infty$ and (b) $\mathcal{Z}_r^{LU}$

- All states in X_s are at the same level and thus all transitions in $T_\infty(e, X_s)$ have the same resetting clock. Let Y be that clock and $\delta' = ([Y \cup X_p \mapsto 0](\delta \wedge g \wedge g_p))^\uparrow$.
- The transition from (s_p, X_s, δ) to (s'_p, X'_s, δ') is labeled with the tuple $(e, g_p \wedge g, X_p \cup Y)$.

We illustrate the above using the example in Fig. 3(a). Given the abstract configuration in level 4, which is $(p_2, \{(s_2, \{z_4\}), (s_0, \{z_4, z_2\})\}, 0 \le x = z_4 < z_2 \wedge z_2 - x \le 3 \wedge z_2 - z_4 \le 3)$. As shown in Fig. 2, there are two transitions from state $(s_2, \{z_4\})$ which are labeled with event a and one from state $(s_0, \{z_4, z_2\})$, which makes up $T_s(a, \{(s_2, \{z_4\}), (s_0, \{z_4, z_2\})\})$. The two transitions from $(s_2, \{z_4\})$ have the same guard $z_4 > 0$ and the one from $(s_0, \{z_4, z_2\})$ has the guard $z_4 > 3$. The set $Cons(e, X_s)$ contains the following constraints: $z_4 > 0 \wedge z_4 > 3$, $z_4 \le 0 \wedge z_4 > 3$, $z_4 > 0 \wedge z_4 \le 3$, and $z_4 \le 0 \wedge z_4 \le 3$. Taking the transition form p_2 to p_1 as an example, we generate four potential successors for each of constraints in $Cons(e, X_s)$, as shown above. Two of them are infeasible as the resultant constraints are false. The rest two are shown in Fig. 3(a) (the first two from left at level 5). Since z_2 is no longer active for the second successor, the clock constraint of the second successor is modified to $0 \le x = z_5 < z_4 \wedge z_4 - x \le 3 \wedge z_4 - z_5 \le 3$ so as to remove constraints on z_2. Similarly, we can generate other configurations in Fig. 3(a).

In the following, we reduce the language inclusion checking problem to a reachability problem in $\mathcal{Z}_\infty$. Notice that one of constraints in $Cons(e, X_s)$ conjuncts the negations of all guards of transitions in $T_\infty(e, X_s)$. Let us denote the constraint as neg. For instance, given the same abstract state in the middle of level 4 in Fig. 3(a), the constraint neg in $Cons(e, X_s)$ is: $z_4 \le 0 \wedge z_4 \le 3$, which is equivalent to $z_4 \le 0$. Conjuncted with the guard condition $x > 0$ and the initial constraint $0 \le x = z_4 < z_2 \wedge z_2 - x \le 3 \wedge z_2 - z_4 \le 3$, it becomes false and hence no successor is generated for neg. Given neg, assume the corresponding successor is (s'_p, X'_s, δ'). It is easy to see that X'_s is empty. If δ' is not false, intuitively there exists a time point such that $\mathcal{P}$ can perform e whereas $\mathcal{S}$ cannot, which implies language inclusion is not true. Thus, we have the following theorem.

Theorem 1. $\mathcal{L}(\mathcal{P}) \subseteq \mathcal{L}(\mathcal{S})$ *iff there is no reachable state* $(s_p, \emptyset, \delta)$ *in* $\mathcal{Z}_\infty$. □

Theorem 1 therefore reduces our language inclusion problem to a reachability problem on $\mathcal{Z}_\infty$. If a state in the form of $(s_p, \emptyset, \delta)$ is reachable, then we can conclude that the language inclusion is false. The remaining problem is that there may be infinitely many clocks. In the following, we show how to reduce the number of clocks, which is inspired by [4]. Intuitively, given any abstract state (s_p, X_s, δ) in the zone graph $\mathcal{Z}_\infty$, instead of always using a new clock in Z, we can reuse a clock which is not currently active, or equivalently not in $Act(X_s)$. For instance, given the state on level 1 in Fig. 3(a), there are two active clocks z_0 and z_1. For the successor of this state on level 2, instead of using z_2, we can reuse z_0 and systematically rename z_2 to z_0 afterwards. The result of renaming is shown partially in Fig. 3(b) (notice that some zones in Fig. 3(b) are different from the ones in Fig. 3(a) and some states have been removed, because of simulation reduction shown next). We denote the zone graph after renaming as $\mathcal{Z}_r$. We also denote the successors of an abstract state ps in $\mathcal{Z}_r$ as $post(ps, \mathcal{Z}_r)$. By a simple argument, it can be shown that there is a reachable state $(s_p, \emptyset, \delta)$ in $\mathcal{Z}_\infty$ iff there is a reachable state $(s'_p, \emptyset, \delta')$ in $\mathcal{Z}_r$.

3.3 Simulation Reduction

We have so far reduced the language inclusion checking problem to a reachability problem in the potentially infinite-state LTS $\mathcal{Z}_r$. Next, we reduce the size of $\mathcal{Z}_r$ by exploring simulation relation between states in $\mathcal{Z}_r$. We first extend the lower-upper bounds (hereafter LU-bounds) simulation relation defined in [5] to language inclusion checking.

We define two functions L and U. Given a state s in $\mathcal{Z}_r$ and a clock $x \in C_p \cup Z$, we perform a depth-first-search to collect all transitions reachable from s without going through a transition which resets x. Next, we set $L(s, x)$ (resp. $U(s, x)$) to be the maximal constant k such that there exists a constraint $x > k$ or $x \geq k$ (resp. $x < k$ or $x \leq k$) in a guard of those transitions. If such a constant does not exist, we set $L(s, x)$ (resp. $U(s, x)$) to $-\infty$. We remark that $L(s, x)$ is always the same as $U(s, x)$ for a clock in Z because both guard conditions and their negations are used in constructing $\mathcal{Z}_r$. For instance, if we denote the state at level 0 in Fig. 3(b) as s_0, which can be seen as the initial state in $\mathcal{Z}_r$, the function L is then defined such that $L(s_0, x) = 3$, $L(s_0, z_0) = 3$.

Next, we define a relation between two zones using the LU-bounds and show that the relation constitutes a simulation relation. Given two clock valuations v and v' at a state s and the two functions L and U, we write $v \preccurlyeq_{LU} v'$ if for each clock c, either $v'(c) = v(c)$ or $L(s, c) < v'(c) < v(c)$ or $U(s, c) < v(c) < v'(c)$. Next, given two zones δ_1 and δ_2, we write $\delta_1 \preccurlyeq_{LU} \delta_2$ to denote that for all $v_1 \in \delta_1$, there is a $v_2 \in \delta_2$ such that $v_1 \preccurlyeq_{LU} v_2$. The following shows that $\preccurlyeq_{LU}$ constitutes a simulation relation.

Lemma 1. *Let* (s, X, δ_i) *where* $i \in \{0, 1\}$ *be two states of* $\mathcal{Z}_r$ *and* F *be the set of states* $\{(s', \emptyset, \delta')\}$ *in* $\mathcal{Z}_r$. (s, X, δ_1) *simulates* (s, X, δ_0) *w.r.t.* F *if* $\delta_0 \preccurlyeq_{LU} \delta_1$. □

With the above lemma, given an abstract state (s, X, δ) of $\mathcal{Z}_r$, we can enlarge the time constraint δ so as to include all clock valuations which are simulated by some valuations in δ without changing the result of reachability analysis. In the following, we write $LU(\delta)$ to denote the set $\{v | \exists v' \in \delta \cdot v \preccurlyeq_{LU} v'\}$[2]. We construct an LTS, denoted as $\mathcal{Z}_r^{LU}$ which replaces each state (s, X, δ) in $\mathcal{Z}_r$ with $(s, X, LU(\delta))$. We denote the successors of a state ps in $\mathcal{Z}_r^{LU}$ as $post(ps, \mathcal{Z}_r^{LU})$. By a simple argument, we can show that there is a reachable state $(s, \emptyset, \delta)$ in $\mathcal{Z}_r$ iff there is a reachable state $(s', \emptyset, \delta')$ in $\mathcal{Z}_r^{LU}$. For instance, given the $\mathcal{Z}_r$ after renaming $\mathcal{Z}_\infty$ shown in Fig. 3(a), Fig. 3(b) shows the corresponding $\mathcal{Z}_r^{LU}$.

Next, we incorporate another simulation relation in our work which is inspired by the Anti-Chain algorithm [22]. The idea is that given two abstract states (s, X, δ) and (s', X', δ') of $\mathcal{Z}_r^{LU}$, we can infer a simulation relation by comparing X and X'. One problem is that states in X and X' may have different sets of active clocks. The exact names of the clocks however do not matter semantically. In order to compare X and X' (and compare δ and δ'), we define clock mappings. A mapping from $Act(X')$ to $Act(X)$ is a injection function $f : Act(X') \rightarrow Act(X)$ which maps every clock in $Act(X')$ to one in $Act(X)$. We write $X' \subseteq_f X$ if there exists a mapping f such that for all $(s'_s, A') \in X'$, there exists $(s_s, A) \in X$ such that $s_s = s'_s$ and for all $x \in A'$, $f(x) \in A$. Notice that there might be clocks in $Act(X)$ which are not mapped to. We write $range(f)$ to denote the set of clocks which are mapped to in $Act(X)$. With an abuse of notations, given a constraint δ' constituted by clocks in $Act(X')$, we write $f(\delta')$ to denote the constraint obtained by renaming the clocks accordingly to f. We write $\delta \subseteq_f \delta'$ if $\delta[range(f)] \subseteq f(\delta')$, i.e., the clock valuations which satisfy the constraint $\delta[range(f)]$ (obtained by projecting δ onto clocks in $Act(X')$) satisfy δ' after clock renaming. Next, we define a relation between two abstract configurations. We write $(s, X, \delta) \sqsubseteq (s', X', \delta')$ iff the following are satisfied: $s = s'$ and there exists a mapping f such that $X' \subseteq_f X$ and $\delta \subseteq_f \delta'$. The next lemma establishes that $\sqsubseteq$ is a simulation relation.

Lemma 2. *Let (s, X, δ) and (s', X', δ') be states in $\mathcal{Z}_r^{LU}$. Let $F = \{(s, \emptyset, \delta_0)\}$ be the set of target states. (s', X', δ') simulates (s, X, δ) w.r.t. F if $(s, X, \delta) \sqsubseteq (s', X', \delta')$.* □

For example, let ps_0 denote the state at level 1 in Fig. 3(a). Let ps_1 denote the bold-lined state at level 1 and ps_2 denote the one at level 5 in Fig. 3(b). With the LU simulation relation, ps_0 can be replaced by ps_1. A renaming function f can be defined from clocks in ps_1 to clocks in ps_2, i.e., $f(z_0) = z_1$ and $f(z_1) = z_2$. After renaming, ps_1 becomes $(p_1, \{(s_1, \{z_2, z_1\})\}, 0 \leq x = z_2 < z_1)$. Therefore, $ps_2 \sqsubseteq ps_1$ and hence we do not need to explore from ps_2. Similarly, we do not need to explore from the bold-lined state at level 3 in Fig. 3(b), namely ps_3. Notice that without the LU simulation reduction $ps_3 \sqsubseteq ps_1$ cannot hold, and the successors of ps_3 must be explored.

3.4   Algorithm

In the following, we present our semi-algorithm. Let $\mathcal{Z}_r^{LU}$ be the tuple $(S, Init, \Sigma, T)$ where $Init$ is a set $(init_p, Init_s, LU((C_p = 0 \wedge z_0 = 0)^\uparrow))$. Algorithm 1 constructs

---

[2] Notice that we may not be able to represent this set as a convex time constraint [5].

Algorithm 1. Language inclusion checking

```
1: let working := Init;
2: let done := ∅;
3: while working ≠ ∅ do
4:     remove ps = (s_p, X_s, δ) from working;
5:     add ps into done and remove all ps' ∈ done s.t. ps' ⊑ ps;
6:     for all (s'_p, X'_s, δ') ∈ post(ps, Z_r^{LU}) do
7:         if X'_s = ∅ then
8:             return false;
9:         end if
10:        if ∄ ps' ∈ done such that (s'_p, X'_s, δ') ⊑ ps' then
11:            put (s'_p, X'_s, δ') into working;
12:        end if
13:    end for
14: end while
15: return true;
```

Z_r^{LU} on-the-fly while performing reachability analysis with simulation reduction. It maintains two data structures. One is a set *working* which stores states in S which are yet to be explored. The other is a set *done* which contains states which have already been explored. Initially, *working* is set to be $Init$ and *done* is empty. During the loop from line 3 to line 14, each time a state is removed from *working* and added to *done*. Notice that in order to keep *done* small, whenever a state ps is added into *done*, all states which are simulated by ps are removed. We generate successors of ps at line 6. For each successor, if it is a target state, we return false at line 8. If it is simulated by a state in *done*, it is ignored. Otherwise, it is added into *working* so that it will be explored later. Lastly, we return true at line 15 after exploring all states. We remark that *done* is an *Anti-Chain* [22] as any pair of states in *done* is incomparable. The following theorem states that the semi-algorithm always produces correct results.

Theorem 2. *Algorithm 1 returns true iff* $\mathcal{L}(\mathcal{P}) \subseteq \mathcal{L}(\mathcal{S})$. □

Next, we establish sufficient conditions for the termination of semi-algorithm with the theorems of *well quasi-order* (WQO [15]). A *quasi-order* (QO) on a set $\mathcal{A}$ is a pair $(\mathcal{A}, \preccurlyeq)$ where $\preccurlyeq$ is a reflective and transitive binary relation in $\mathcal{A} \times \mathcal{A}$. A QO is a WQO if for each infinite sequence $\langle a_0, a_1, a_2, \ldots \rangle$ composed of the elements in $\mathcal{A}$, there exists $i < j$ such that $a_j \preccurlyeq a_i$. Therefore if a WQO can be found among states in Z_r^{LU} with the simulation relation $\sqsubseteq$, our semi-algorithm terminates, as stated in the following theorem.

Theorem 3. *Let S be the set of states of Z_r^{LU}. If $(S, \sqsubseteq)$ is a WQO, Algorithm 1 is terminating.* □

The above theorem implies that our semi-algorithm always terminates given the subclass of timed automata satisfying the clock boundedness condition [4], including strongly non-Zeno timed automata, event-clock timed automata and timed automata with integer resets. That is, if the boundedness condition is satisfied, Z_r^{LU} has a bounded number of clocks and if the number of clocks are bounded, obviously the set S is finite (with maximum ceiling zone normalization). Since $(S, =)$ is a WQO if S is finite by a property of WQO, and '=' implies '$\sqsubseteq$', $(S, \sqsubseteq)$ is also a WQO for this special case. Furthermore, the theorem also shows that the semi-algorithm is terminating for all single-clock timed automata, as a WQO has been shown in [1], which may not satisfy the boundedness condition.

4   Evaluation

Our method has been implemented with 46K lines of C# code and integrated into the PAT model checker [19][3]. We remark that in our setting, a zone may not be convex (for instance, due to negation used in constructing $\mathcal{Z}_r$) and thus cannot be represented as a single difference bound matrix (DBM). Rather it can be represented either as a difference bound logic formula, as shown in [3], or as a set of DBMs. In this work, the latter approach is adopted for the efficiency reason. In the following, we evaluate our approach in order to answer three research questions. All experiment data are obtained using a PC with Intel(R) Core(TM) i7-2600 CPU at 3.40 GHz and 8.0 GB RAM.

The first question is: are timed automata good to specify commonly used timed properties? That is, if timed automata are used to model the properties, will our semi-algorithm terminate? In [8,12], the authors summarized a set of commonly used patterns for real-time properties. Some of the patterns are shown below where a, b, c are events; x is a clock and h denotes all the other events. Most of the patterns are self-explanatory and therefore we refer to the readers to [8,12] for details. We remark that although the patterns below are all single-clock timed automata, a specification may be the parallel composition of multiple patterns and hence have multiple clocks. Observe that all timed automata below are deterministic except (g). A simple investigation shows that (g) satisfies the clock boundedness condition and hence our semi-algorithm terminates for all the properties below.

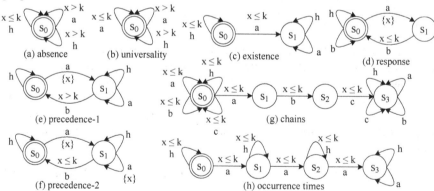

(a) absence   (b) universality   (c) existence   (d) response
(e) precedence-1   (g) chains   (f) precedence-2   (h) occurrence times

The second question is: is the semi-algorithm useful in practice? That is, given a real-world system, is it scalable? In the following, we model and verify benchmark

---

[3] PAT and the experiment details can be found at
http://www.comp.nus.edu.sg/~pat/refine_ta

Table 1. Experiments on Language Inclusion Checking for Timed Systems

System	$|C_s|$	Det	$\sqsubseteq +LU$			LU			$\sqsubseteq$		
			stored	total	time	stored	total	time	stored	total	time
Fischer*8	1	Yes	91563	224208	28.3	138657	300384	516.7	-	-	-
Fischer*6	6	No	38603	78332	537.0	-	-	-	-	-	-
Fischer*6	2	No	27393	58531	6.8	36218	70348	30.3	-	-	-
Fischer*7	2	No	121782	271895	42.9	159631	326772	661.7	-	-	-
Railway*8	1	Yes	796154	1124950	142.1	-	-	-	-	-	-
Railway*6	6	No	23265	33427	7.2	27903	39638	20.4	-	-	-
Railway*7	7	No	180034	260199	66.7	222806	318698	1352.8	-	-	-
Lynch*5	1	Yes	3852	11725	0.6	16193	48165	6.0	45488	421582	377.2
Lynch*7	1	Yes	79531	400105	34.9	-	-	-	-	-	-
Lynch*5	2	No	8091	29686	2.4	63623	208607	151.3	56135	324899	290.1
Lynch*6	2	No	35407	162923	16.7	477930	1828668	5751.1	-	-	-
FDDI*7	7	Yes	1198	1590	7.4	8064	9592	36.4	8452	11836	125.5
CSMA*7	1	Yes	9840	36255	4.5	-	-	-	-	-	-

timed systems using our semi-algorithm and evaluate its performance. The benchmark systems include Fischer's mutual exclusion protocol (Fischer for short, similarly hereinafter), Lynch-Shavit's mutual exclusion protocol (Lynch), railway control system (Railway), fiber distributed data interface (FDDI), and CSMA/CD protocol (CSMA). The results are shown in Table 1. The systems are all built as networks of timed automata, and the number of processes is shown in column 'System'. The verified properties are requirements on the systems specified using the timed patterns. Some of the properties contain one timed automaton with one clock, while the rest are networks of timed automata with more than one clock (one clock for each timed automaton). In the table, column '$|C_s|$' is the number of clocks (processes) in the specification. The systems in the same group, e.g., Fischer*6 and Fischer*7 both with $|C_s| = 2$, have the same specification. Notice that the number of processes in a system and the one in the specification can be different because we can 'hide' events in the systems and use h in the specifications as shown in the patterns. Column 'Det' shows whether the specification is deterministic or not. The results of our semi-algorithm are shown in column '$\sqsubseteq +LU$'. In order to show the effectiveness of simulation reduction, we show the results without $\sqsubseteq$ reduction in column LU and the results without LU-reduction in column $\sqsubseteq$. For each algorithm, column 'stored' denotes the number of stored states; column 'total' denotes the total number of generated states; column 'time' denotes the verification time in seconds. Symbol '-' means either the verification time is more than 2 hours or out-of-memory exception happens. Notice that our semi-algorithm terminates in all cases and all verification results are true. Comparing *stored* and *total*, we can see that many states are skipped due to simulation reduction. From the verification time we can see that both simulation relations are helpful in reducing the state space. To the best of our knowledge, there is no existing tool supporting language inclusion checking of these models.

Table 2. Experiments on Random Timed Automata

$|S|$	$|C|$	$Dt = 0.6$	$Dt = 0.8$	$Dt = 1.0$	$Dt = 1.1$	$Dt = 1.3$
4	1	1.00\0.99\0.98	0.99\0.93\0.74	0.99\0.82\0.59	0.99\0.63\0.39	0.89\0.18\0.09
4	2	0.99\0.98\0.94	0.98\0.87\0.68	0.94\0.72\0.51	0.85\0.49\0.33	0.45\0.12\0.06
4	3	0.99\0.98\0.93	0.95\0.82\0.65	0.89\0.67\0.52	0.75\0.42\0.28	0.31\0.10\0.06
6	1	1.00\0.99\0.98	0.99\0.97\0.90	0.99\0.61\0.41	0.97\0.43\0.29	0.83\0.13\0.08
6	2	0.99\0.99\0.98	0.99\0.96\0.88	0.88\0.49\0.32	0.79\0.34\0.22	0.44\0.09\0.05
6	3	0.99\0.99\0.98	0.99\0.94\0.85	0.78\0.44\0.29	0.69\0.31\0.21	0.34\0.11\0.07
8	1	1.00\0.99\0.99	0.99\0.92\0.83	0.96\0.53\0.40	0.94\0.37\0.31	0.55\0.08\0.07
8	2	0.99\0.99\0.99	0.99\0.91\0.84	0.84\0.48\0.37	0.73\0.32\0.25	0.25\0.10\0.09
8	3	0.99\0.99\0.99	0.98\0.91\0.83	0.78\0.47\0.38	0.70\0.40\0.32	0.20\0.08\0.07

The last question is: how good are timed automata as a specification language? We consider a timed automaton specification is 'good' if given an implementation model, our semi-algorithm answers conclusively on the language inclusion problem. To answer this question, we extend the approach on generating non-deterministic finite automata in [20] to automatically generate random timed automata, and then apply our semi-algorithm for language inclusion checking. Without loss of generality, a generated timed automaton has always one initial state and the alphabet is $\{0, 1\}$. In addition, the following parameters are used to control the random generation process: the number of state $|S|$, the number of clocks $|C|$, a parameter Dt for transition density and a clock ceiling. For each event in the alphabet, we generate k transitions (and hence the transition density for the event is $Dt = k/|S|$) and distribute the transitions randomly among all $|S|$ states. For each transition, the clock constraint and the resetting clocks are generated randomly according to the clock ceiling. We remark that if both implementation and specification models are generated randomly, language inclusion almost always fails. Thus, in order to have cases where language inclusion does hold, we generate a group of implementation specification pairs by generating an implementation first, and then adding transitions to the implementation to get the specification.

The experimental results are shown in Table 2[4]. For each different combinations of $|S|$, $|C|$ and Dt, we compute three numbers shown in the form of $a \setminus b \setminus c$. a is the percentage of cases in which our semi-algorithm terminates; c is the percentage of the cases satisfying the boundedness condition (and therefore being determinizable [4]). The gap between a and c thus shows the effectiveness of our approach on timed automata which may be non-determinizable. In order to show the effectiveness of simulation reduction, b is the percentage of cases in which our semi-algorithm terminates without simulation reduction (and with maximum ceiling zone normalization). We generate 1000 random pairs to calculate each number. In all cases $a > b$ and $b > c$, e.g., a is much larger than

---

[4] Notice that there are cases where there is only one clock in the specification and yet our semi-algorithm is not terminating. This is because of using a set of DBMs to represent zones. That is, because there is no efficient procedure to check whether a zone z is a subset of another (which is represented as the union of multiple DBMs), the LU-simulation that we discover is partial and we may unnecessarily explore more states, infinitely more in some cases.

b and c when $Dt \geq 1.0$. This result implies that our semi-algorithm terminates even if the specification may not be 'determinizable', which we credit to simulation reduction and the fact that the semi-algorithm is on-the-fly (so that language inclusion checking can be done without complete determinization). When transition density increases, the gap between a and b increases (e.g., when $Dt \geq 1.0$, b is always much smaller that a), which evidences the effectiveness of our simulation reduction. In general, the lower the density is, the more likely it is that the semi-algorithm terminates. We calculate the transition density of the timed property patterns and the benchmark systems. We find that all the events have transition densities less than or equal to 1.0 except the absence pattern. Based on the results presented in Table 2, we conclude that in practice, our semi-algorithm has a high probability of terminating. This perhaps supports the view that timed automata could serve as a good specification language.

5 Related Work

The work in [2] is the first study on the language inclusion checking problem for timed automata. The work shows that timed automata are not closed under complement, which is an obstacle in automatically comparing the languages of two timed automata. Naturally, this conclusion leads to work on identifying determinizable subclasses of timed automata, with reduced expressiveness. Several subclasses of timed automata have been identified, i.e., event-clock timed automata [3,17], timed automata with integer resets [18] or with one clock [16] and strongly non-Zeno timed automata [4].

Our work is inspired by the work in [4] which presents an approach for deciding when a timed automaton is determinizable. The idea is to check whether the timed automaton satisfies a clock boundedness condition. The authors show that the condition is satisfied by event-clock timed automata, timed automata with integer resets and strongly non-Zeno timed automata. Using region construction, it is shown in [4] that an equivalent deterministic timed automaton can be constructed if the given timed automaton satisfies the boundedness condition. The work is closely related to [1], in which the authors proposed a zone-based approach for determinizing timed automata with one clock. Our work combines [1,4] and extends them with simulation reduction so as to provide an approach which could be useful for arbitrary timed automata in practice.

In addition, a game-based approach for determinizing timed automata has been proposed in [6,13]. This approach produces an equivalent deterministic timed automaton or a deterministic over-approximation, which allows one to enlarge the set of timed automata that can be automatically determinized compared to the one in [4]. In comparison, our approach could determinize timed automata which fail the boundedness condition in [4], and can cover the examples shown in [6]. The work is remotely related to work in [10]. In particular, it has been shown that under digitization with the definition of weakly monotonic timed words, whether the language of a closed timed automaton is included in the language of an open timed automaton is decidable [10].

6 Conclusion

In summary, the contributions of this work are threefold. First, we develop a zone-based approach for language inclusion checking of timed automata, which is further combined with simulation reduction for better performance. Second, we investigate, both theoretical and empirically, when the semi-algorithm is terminating. Lastly, we implement the semi-algorithm in the PAT framework and apply it to benchmark systems. As far as the authors know, our implementation is the first tool which supports using arbitrary timed automata as a specification language. More importantly, with the proposed semi-algorithm and the empirical results, we would like to argue that timed automata do serve a specification language in practice. As for the future work, we would like to investigate the language inclusion checking problem with the assumption of non-Zenoness.

References

1. Abdulla, P.A., Ouaknine, J., Quaas, K., Worrell, J.B.: Zone-Based Universality Analysis for Single-Clock Timed Automata. In: Arbab, F., Sirjani, M. (eds.) FSEN 2007. LNCS, vol. 4767, pp. 98–112. Springer, Heidelberg (2007)
2. Alur, R., Dill, D.L.: A Theory of Timed Automata. Theory of Computer Science 126(2), 183–235 (1994)
3. Alur, R., Fix, L., Henzinger, T.A.: Event-clock Automata: A Determinizable Class of Timed Automata. Theoretical Computer Science 211, 253–273 (1999)
4. Baier, C., Bertrand, N., Bouyer, P., Brihaye, T.: When Are Timed Automata Determinizable? In: Albers, S., Marchetti-Spaccamela, A., Matias, Y., Nikoletseas, S., Thomas, W. (eds.) ICALP 2009, Part II. LNCS, vol. 5556, pp. 43–54. Springer, Heidelberg (2009)
5. Behrmann, G., Bouyer, P., Larsen, K.G., Pelánek, R.: Lower and Upper Bounds in Zone-based Abstractions of Timed Automata. International Journal on Software Tools for Technology Transfer 8(3), 204–215 (2004)
6. Bertrand, N., Stainer, A., Jéron, T., Krichen, M.: A Game Approach to Determinize Timed Automata. In: Hofmann, M. (ed.) FOSSACS 2011. LNCS, vol. 6604, pp. 245–259. Springer, Heidelberg (2011)
7. Dill, D.L., Hu, A.J., Wong-Toi, H.: Checking for Language Inclusion Using Simulation Preorders. In: Larsen, K.G., Skou, A. (eds.) CAV 1991. LNCS, vol. 575, pp. 255–265. Springer, Heidelberg (1992)
8. Gruhn, V., Laue, R.: Patterns for Timed Property Specifications. Electronic Notes in Theoretical Computer Science 153(2), 117–133 (2006)
9. Henzinger, T.A., Kopke, P.W., Wong-Toi, H.: The Expressive Power of Clocks. In: Fülöp, Z. (ed.) ICALP 1995. LNCS, vol. 944, pp. 417–428. Springer, Heidelberg (1995)
10. Henzinger, T.A., Manna, Z., Pnueli, A.: What Good are Digital Clocks? In: Kuich, W. (ed.) ICALP 1992. LNCS, vol. 623, pp. 545–558. Springer, Heidelberg (1992)
11. Henzinger, T.A., Nicollin, X., Sifakis, J., Yovine, S.: Symbolic Model Checking for Realtime Systems. Journal of Information and Computation 111(2), 193–244 (1994)
12. Konrad, S., Cheng, B.H.C.: Real-time Specification Patterns. In: ICSE, pp. 372–381 (2005)
13. Krichen, M., Tripakis, S.: Conformance Testing for Real-Time Systems. Formal Methods in System Design 34(3), 238–304 (2009)
14. Larsen, K.G., Petterson, P., Wang, Y.: UPPAAL in a Nutshell. Journal on Software Tools for Technology Transfer 1(1-2), 134–152 (1997)
15. Marcone, A.: Foundations of BQO Theory. Transactions of the American Mathematical Society 345(2), 641–660 (1994)
16. Ouaknine, J., Worrell, J.: On The Language Inclusion Problem for Timed Automata: Closing a Decidability Gap. In: LICS, pp. 54–63 (2004)
17. Raskin, J., Schobbens, P.: The Logic of Event Clocks - Decidability, Complexity and Expressiveness. Journal of Automata, Languages, and Combinatories 4(3), 247–286 (1999)

18. Suman, P.V., Pandya, P.K., Krishna, S.N., Manasa, L.: Timed Automata with Integer Resets: Language Inclusion and Expressiveness. In: Cassez, F., Jard, C. (eds.) FORMATS 2008. LNCS, vol. 5215, pp. 78–92. Springer, Heidelberg (2008)
19. Sun, J., Liu, Y., Dong, J.S., Pang, J.: PAT: Towards flexible verification under fairness. In: Bouajjani, A., Maler, O. (eds.) CAV 2009. LNCS, vol. 5643, pp. 709–714. Springer, Heidelberg (2009)
20. Tabakov, D., Vardi, M.Y.: Experimental Evaluation of Classical Automata Constructions. In: Sutcliffe, G., Voronkov, A. (eds.) LPAR 2005. LNCS (LNAI), vol. 3835, pp. 396–411. Springer, Heidelberg (2005)
21. Tripakis, S.: Verifying progress in timed systems. In: Katoen, J.-P. (ed.) ARTS 1999. LNCS, vol. 1601, pp. 299–314. Springer, Heidelberg (1999)
22. De Wulf, M., Doyen, L., Henzinger, T.A., Raskin, J.-F.: Antichains: A New Algorithm for Checking Universality of Finite Automata. In: Ball, T., Jones, R.B. (eds.) CAV 2006. LNCS, vol. 4144, pp. 17–30. Springer, Heidelberg (2006)
23. Yovine, S.: Kronos: a Verification Tool for Real-time Systems. Journal on Software Tools for Technology Transfer 1(1-2), 123–133 (1997)

Formal Design of Fault Detection and Identification Components Using Temporal Epistemic Logic

Marco Bozzano, Alessandro Cimatti, Marco Gario, and Stefano Tonetta

Fondazione Bruno Kessler, Trento, Italy
{bozzano,cimatti,gario,tonettas}@fbk.eu

Abstract. Automated detection of faults and timely recovery are fundamental features for autonomous critical systems. Fault Detection and Identification (FDI) components are designed to detect faults on-board, by reading data from sensors and triggering predefined alarms.

The design of effective FDI components is an extremely hard problem, also due to the lack of a complete theoretical foundation, and of precise specification and validation techniques.

In this paper, we present the first formal framework for the design of FDI for discrete event systems. We propose a logical language for the specification of FDI requirements that accounts for a wide class of practical requirements, including novel aspects such as maximality and non-diagnosability. The language is equipped with a clear semantics based on temporal epistemic logic. We discuss how to validate the requirements and how to verify that a given FDI component satisfies them. Finally, we develop an algorithm for the synthesis of correct-by-construction FDI components, and report on the applicability of the framework on an industrial case-study coming from aerospace.

1 Introduction

The correct operation of complex critical systems (e.g., trains, satellites, cars) increasingly relies on the ability to detect when and which faults occur during operation. This function, called Fault Detection and Identification (FDI), provides information that is vital to drive the containment of faults and their recovery. This is especially true for fail-operational systems, where the occurrence of faults should not compromise the ability to carry on critical functions, as opposed to fail-safe systems, where faults are typically handled by going to a safe state. FDI is typically carried out by dedicated modules, called FDI components, running in parallel with the system. An FDI component processes sequences of observations, made available by predefined sensors, and is required to trigger a set of predefined alarms in a timely and accurate manner. The alarms are then used by recovery modules to autonomously guarantee the survival of the system.

Faults are often not directly observable, and their occurrence can only be inferred by observing the effects that they have on the observable parts of the system. Moreover, faults may have complex dynamics, and may interact with each other in complex ways. For these reasons, the design of FDI components

E. Ábrahám and K. Havelund (Eds.): TACAS 2014, LNCS 8413, pp. 326–340, 2014.
© Springer-Verlag Berlin Heidelberg 2014

is a very challenging task, as witnessed by a recent Invitation To Tender issued by the European Space Agency [1]. The key reasons are the lack of a clear and complete theoretical foundation, supported by clear and effective specification and validation techniques. As a consequence, the design often results in very conservative assumptions, so that the overall system features suboptimal behaviors, and is not trusted during critical phases.

In this paper, we propose a formal foundation to support the design of FDI by introducing a *pattern based* language for the specification of FDI requirements. Intuitively, an FDI component is specified by stating which are the observable signals (the inputs of the FDI component), the desired alarms (in terms of the unobservable state), and defining the relation between the two. The language supports various forms of delay (exact, finite, bounded) between the occurrence of faults, and the raising of the corresponding alarm. The patterns are provided with an underlying formal semantics expressed in epistemic temporal logic [2], where the *knowledge* operator is used to express the certainty of a condition, based on the available observations. The formalization encodes properties such as *alarm correctness* (whenever an alarm is raised by the FDI component, then the associated condition did occur), and *alarm completeness* (if an alarm is not raised, then either the associated condition did not occur, or it would have been impossible to detect it, given the available observations). Moreover, we precisely characterize two aspects that are important for the specification of FDI requirements. The first one is the *diagnosability* of the plant, i.e., whether the sensors convey enough information to detect the required conditions. We explain how to deal with non-diagnosable plants by introducing the more fine grained concept of *trace diagnosability*, where diagnosability is localized to individual traces. The second is the *maximality* of the diagnoser, that is, the ability of the diagnoser to raise an alarm as soon as and whenever possible.

Within our framework, we cover the problems of (i) validation of a given specification, (ii) verification of a given diagnoser with respect to a given specification, and (iii) automated synthesis of a diagnoser from a given specification, using a synchronous and perfect-recall semantics for the epistemic operator. Moreover, we provide formal proofs for the correctness of the synthesis algorithm, we show that the specification language correctly captures the formal semantics and we clearly define the relation between diagnosability, maximality and correctness. The framework has been validated on an industrial setting, in a project funded by the European Space Agency [1]. The framework provides the conceptual foundation underlying a design toolset, which has been applied to the specification, verification and synthesis of an FDI component for a satellite.

It is important to remark the deep difference between the design of FDI components and diagnosis. A diagnosis system can benefit from powerful computing platform, it can provide partial diagnoses, and can possibly require further (postmortem) inspections. This is typical of approaches that rely on logical reasoning engines (e.g., SAT solvers [3]). An FDI component, on the contrary, runs onboard (as part of the on-line control strategy) and is subject to restrictions such as timing and computation power. FDI design thus requires a deeper theory, which accounts for the issues of delay in raising the alarms, trace diagnosability, and maximality. Furthermore, a consistency-based approach [3] is not applicable to the design of FDI: in order to formally verify the effectiveness of an FDI component as part of an overall fault-management strategy, a formal model of the FDI component (e.g., as an automaton) is required.

This paper is structured as follows. Section 2 provides some introductory background. Section 3 formalizes the notion of FDI. Section 4 presents the specification language. In Section 5 we discuss how to validate the requirements, and how to verify an FDI component with respect to the requirements. In Section 6 we present an algorithm for the synthesis of correct-by-construction FDI components. The results of evaluating our approach in an industrial setting are presented in Section 7. Section 8 compares our work with previous related works. Section 9 concludes the paper with a hint on future work.

2   Background

Plants and FDIs are represented as *transition systems*. A transition system is a tuple $S = \langle V, V_o, W, W_o, I, T \rangle$, where V is the set of state variables, $V_o \subseteq V$ is the set of observable state variables; W is the set of input variables, $W_o \subseteq W$ is the set of observable input variables; I is a formula over V defining the initial states, T is a formula over V, W, V' (with V' being the next version of the state variables) defining the transition relation.

A *state* s is an assignment to the state variables V. We denote with s' the corresponding assignment to V'. An *input* i is an assignment to the input variables W. The *observable part* $obs(s)$ of a state s is the projection of s on the subset V_o of observable state variables. The observable part $obs(i)$ of an input i is the projection of i on the subset W_o of observable input variables. Given an assignment a to a set of variables X and $X_1 \subseteq X$, we denote the projection of a over X_1 with $a_{|X_1}$. Thus, $obs(s) = s_{|V_o}$ and $obs(i) = i_{|W_o}$.

A *trace* of S is a sequence $\pi = s_0, i_1, s_1, i_2, s_2, \ldots$ of states and inputs such that s_0 satisfies I and, for each $k \geq 0$, $\langle s_k, i_{k+1}, s_{k+1} \rangle$ satisfies T. W.l.o.g. we consider infinite traces only. The observable part of π is $obs(\pi) = obs(s_0), obs(i_1), obs(s_1), obs(i_2), obs(s_2), \ldots$. Given a sequence $\pi = s_0, i_1, s_1, i_2, s_2, \ldots$ and an integer $k \geq 0$, we denote with σ^k the finite prefix $s_0, i_1, \ldots, s_k$ of π containing the first $k+1$ states. We denote with $\pi[k]$ the $k+1$-th state s_k. We say that s is *reachable* in S iff there exists a trace π of S such that $s = \pi[k]$ for some $k \geq 0$. We say that S is deterministic if i) there are no two initial states s_0 and s_0' s.t. $obs(s_0) = obs(s_0')$ ii) there are no two transitions $\langle s, i_1, s_1' \rangle$ and $\langle s, i_2, s_2' \rangle$ from a reachable state s s.t. $obs(i_1) = obs(i_2)$ and $obs(s_1') = obs(s_2')$.

Let $S^1 = \langle V^1, V_o^1, W^1, W_o^1, I^1, T^1 \rangle$ and $S^2 = \langle V^2, V_o^2, W^2, W_o^2, I^2, T^2 \rangle$ be two transition systems with $\emptyset = (V^1 \setminus V_o^1) \cap V^2 = V^1 \cap (V^2 \setminus V_o^2) = (W^1 \setminus W_o^1) \cap W^2 = W^1 \cap (W^2 \setminus W_o^2)$. We define the *synchronous product* $S^1 \times S^2$ as the transition system $\langle V^1 \cup V^2, V_o^1 \cup V_o^2, W^1 \cup W^2, W_o^1 \cup W_o^2, I^1 \wedge I^2, T^1 \wedge T^2 \rangle$. Every state s of $S^1 \times S^2$ can be considered as the product $s^1 \times s^2$ such that $s^1 = s_{|V^1}$ is a state of S^1 and $s^2 = s_{|V^2}$ is a state of S^2.

We say that S^1 is *compatible* with S^2 iff i) for every initial state s^2 of S^2, there exists an initial state s^1 of S^1 such that $s^1_{|V_o^1 \cap V_o^2} = s^2_{|V_o^1 \cap V_o^2}$ and ii) for every reachable state $s^1 \times s^2$ of $S^1 \times S^2$, for every transition $\langle s^2, i^2, s'^2 \rangle$ of S^2, there exists a transition $\langle s^1, i^1, s'^1 \rangle$ such that $i^1_{|W_o^1 \cap W_o^2} = i^2_{|W_o^1 \cap W_o^2}$ and $s'^1_{|V_o^1 \cap V_o^2} = s'^2_{|V_o^1 \cap V_o^2}$.

3 Formal Framework

3.1 Diagnoser

A diagnoser is a machine D that synchronizes with observable traces of the plant P. D has a set $\mathcal{A}$ of Boolean alarm variables that are activated in response to the monitoring of P. We use *diagnoser* and *FDI component* interchangeably, and call *system* the composition of the plant and the FDI component.

Formally, given a set $\mathcal{A}$ of alarms and a plant transition system $P = \langle V^P, V_o^P, W^P, W_o^P, I^P, T^P \rangle$, a diagnoser is a deterministic transition system $D(\mathcal{A}, P) = \langle V^D, V_o^D, W^D, W_o^D, I^D, T^D \rangle$ such that: $V_o^P \subseteq V_o^D$, $W_o^P \subseteq W_o^D$, $\mathcal{A} \subseteq V_o^D$ and $D(\mathcal{A}, P)$ is compatible with P; when clear from the context, we use D to indicate $D(\mathcal{A}, P)$. Given a trace π_P of P we denote with $D(\pi_P)$ the trace of D matching π_P. Only observable variables can be shared among the two systems and used to perform synchronization. This gives raise to the problem of partial observability: the diagnoser cannot perfectly track the evolution of the original system. This makes the diagnoser synthesis problem hard.

3.2 Detection, Identification, and Diagnosis Conditions

The first element for the specification of the FDI requirements is given by the conditions that must be monitored. Here, we distinguish between detection and identification, which are the two extreme cases of the diagnosis problem; the first deals with knowing whether a fault occurred in the system, while the second tries to identify the characteristics of the fault. Between these two cases there can be intermediate ones: we might want to restrict the detection to a particular subsystem, or identification among two similar faults might not be of interest.

For example, a data acquisition system composed of a sensor and a filter might have several possible faults: the sensor might fail in a single way ($sdie$) while the filter might fail in two ways ($fdie_{high}$ or $fdie_{low}$). The *detection* task is the problem of understanding when (at least) one of the two components has failed. The *identification* task tries to understand exactly which fault occurred. Similarly, e.g., if we can replace the filter whenever it fails, it might suffice to know that one of $fdie_{high}$ or $fdie_{low}$ occurred (this is sometimes called *isolation*).

FDI components are generally used to recognize faults. However, there is no reason to restrict our interest to faults. Recovery procedures might differ depending on the current state of the plant, therefore, it might be important to consider other unobservable information of the system.

We call the condition of the plant to be monitored *diagnosis condition*, denoted with β. We assume that for any point in time along a trace execution of

β	
EXACTDEL$(A, \beta, 2)$	
BOUNDDEL$(A, \beta, 4)$	
FINITEDEL(A, β)	

Fig. 1. Examples of alarm responses to the diagnosis condition β

the plant (and therefore also of the system), β is either true or false based on what happened before that time point. Therefore, β can be an atomic condition (including faults), a sequence of atomic conditions, or Boolean combination thereof. If β is a fault, the fault must be identified; if β is a disjunction of faults, instead, it suffices to perform the detection, without identifying the exact fault.

3.3   Alarm Conditions

The second element of the specification of FDI requirements is the relation between a diagnosis condition and the raising of an alarm. This also leads to the definition of when the FDI is correct and complete with regard to a set of alarms.

An *alarm condition* is composed of two parts: the diagnosis condition and the delay. The delay relates the time between the occurrence of the diagnosis condition and the corresponding alarm; it might be the case that the occurrence of a fault can go undetected for a certain amount of time. It is important to specify clearly how long this interval can be at most. Interaction with industrial experts led us to identify three patterns of *alarm conditions*, which we denote with EXACTDEL(A, β, n), BOUNDDEL(A, β, n), and FINITEDEL(A, β):

1. EXACTDEL(A, β, n) specifies that whenever β is true, A must be triggered exactly n steps later and A can be triggered only if n steps earlier β was true; formally, for any trace π of the system, if β is true along π at the time point i, then A is true in $\pi[i + n]$ (Completeness); if A is true in $\pi[i]$, then β must be true in $\pi[i - n]$ (Correctness).

2. BOUNDDEL(A, β, n) specifies that whenever β is true, A must be triggered within the next n steps and A can be triggered only if β was true within the previous n steps; formally, for any trace π of the system, if β is true along π at the time point i then A is true in $\pi[j]$, for some $i \le j \le i+n$ (Completeness); if A is true in $\pi[i]$, then β must be true in $\pi[j']$ for some $i - n \le j' \le i$ (Correctness).

3. FINITEDEL(A, β) specifies that whenever β is true, A must be triggered in a later step and A can be triggered only if β was true in some previous step; formally, for any trace π of the system, if β is true along π at the time point i then A is true in $\pi[j]$ for some $j \ge i$ (Completeness); if A is true in $\pi[i]$, then β must be true along π in some time point between 0 and i (Correctness).

Figure 1 provides an example of admissible responses for the various alarms to the occurrences of the same diagnosis condition β; note how in the case of BOUNDDEL$(A, \beta, 4)$ the alarm can be triggered at any point as long as it is within the next 4 time-steps. FINITEDEL(A, β) is of particular theoretical interest since it captures the idea of diagnosis as defined in previous works [4].

An alarm condition is actually a property of the whole system since it relates a condition of the plant with an alarm of the diagnoser. Thus, when we say that a diagnoser D of P satisfies an alarm condition, we mean that the traces of the system $D \times P$ satisfy it.

Considering our previous example of the data acquisition system, we can define the following toy specification. $\beta_1 = (sdie \lor fdie_{high} \lor fdie_{low})$ indicates the fault detection condition, therefore we define the FINITEDEL(A_1, β_1) as the finite-delay fault detection. Another example could be identification of the sensor death $(\beta_2 = sdie)$ within a bound: BOUNDDEL$(A_2, \beta_2, 5)$. Finally, we could be interested in knowing that some fault occurred in the filter with some precise delay information: EXACTDEL$(A_3, (fdie_{high} \lor fdie_{low}), 2)$.

3.4 Diagnosability

Given an alarm condition, we need to know whether it is possible to build a diagnoser for it. In fact, there is no reason in having a specification that cannot be realized. This property is called *diagnosability* and was introduced in [5].

In this section, we define the concept of diagnosability for the different types of alarm conditions. We proceed by first giving the definition of diagnosability in the traditional way (à la Sampath) in terms of observationally equivalent traces w.r.t. the diagnosis condition. Then, we prove that a plant P is diagnosable iff there exists a diagnoser that satisfies the specification. In the following, we will not provide definitions for finite-delay since they can be obtained by generalizing the ones for bounded-delay.

Definition 1 *Given a plant P and a diagnosis condition β, we say that* EXACTDEL(A, β, d) *is diagnosable in P iff for any pair of traces σ_1, σ_2 and for all $i \geq 0$, if $obs(\sigma_1^{i+d}) = obs(\sigma_2^{i+d})$ then $\sigma_1, i \models \beta$ iff $\sigma_2, i \models \beta$.*

Definition 2 *Given a plant P and a diagnosis condition β, we say that* BOUNDDEL(A, β, d) *is diagnosable in P iff for any pair of traces σ_1, σ_2 and for all $i \geq 0$ there exists a j, $i \leq j \leq i + d$, s.t. if $obs(\sigma_1^j) = obs(\sigma_2^j)$ and $\sigma_1, i \models \beta$ then $\sigma_2, k \models \beta$ for some k, $j - d \leq k \leq j$.*

An exact-delay alarm condition is not diagnosable in P iff there exists a pair of traces that violates the conditions of Definition 1: this would be a pair of traces σ_1 and σ_2 such that for some $i \geq 0$, $\sigma_1, i \models \beta$, $obs(\sigma_1^{i+d}) = obs(\sigma_2^{i+d})$, and $\sigma_2, i \not\models \beta$. We call such a pair a *critical pair*. Definition 2 is a generalization of Sampath's definition of diagnosability:

Theorem 1. *Let α be a propositional formula and β_α a condition that holds in a point of a trace if α holds in some point of its prefix, then α is d-delay diagnosable (as in [5]) in P iff* BOUNDDEL(A, β_α, d) *is diagnosable in P.*

The following theorem shows that if a component satisfies the diagnoser specification then the monitored plant must be diagnosable for that specification. In Section 6 on synthesis we will show also the converse, i.e., if the specification is diagnosable then a diagnoser exists.

Theorem 2. *Let D be a diagnoser for P. If D satisfies an alarm condition then the alarm condition is diagnosable in P.*

The above definition of diagnosability might be stronger than necessary, since diagnosability is defined as a global property of the plant. Imagine the situation in which there is a critical pair and after removing this critical pair from the possible executions of the system, our system becomes diagnosable. This suggests that the system was "almost" diagnosable, and an ideal diagnoser would be able to perform a correct diagnosis in all the cases except one (i.e., the one represented by the critical pair). To capture this idea, we redefine the problem of diagnosability from a global property expressed on the plant, to a local property (expressed on points of single traces).

Definition 3 *Given a plant P, a diagnosis condition β and a trace σ_1 such that for some $i \geq 0$ $\sigma_1, i \models \beta$, we say that $\mathrm{EXACTDEL}(A, \beta, d)$ is trace diagnosable in $\langle \sigma_1, i \rangle$ iff for any trace σ_2 such that $obs(\sigma_1^{i+d}) = obs(\sigma_2^{i+d})$ then $\sigma_2, i \models \beta$.*

Definition 4 *Given a plant P, a diagnosis condition β, and a trace σ_1 such that for some $i \geq 0$ $\sigma_1, i \models \beta$, we say that $\mathrm{BOUNDDEL}(A, \beta, d)$ is trace diagnosable in $\langle \sigma_1, i \rangle$ iff there exists j, $i \leq j \leq i + d$ such that, for any trace σ_2 such that $obs(\sigma_1^j) = obs(\sigma_2^j)$ then $\sigma_2, k \models \beta$ for some $j - d \leq k \leq j$.*

A specification that is trace diagnosable in a plant along all points of all traces is diagnosable in the classical sense, and we say it is *system* diagnosable.

3.5   Maximality

As shown in Figure 1, bounded- and finite-delay alarms are correct if they are raised within the valid bound. However, there are several possible variations of the same alarm in which the alarm is active in different instants or for different periods. We address this problem by introducing the concept of *maximality*. Intuitively, a maximal diagnoser is required to raise the alarms as soon as possible and as long as possible (without violating the correctness condition).

Definition 5 *D is a maximal diagnoser for an alarm condition with alarm A in P iff for every trace π_P of P, $D(\pi_P)$ contains the maximum number of points i such that $D(\pi_P), i \models A$ in the sense that if $D(\pi_P), i \not\models A$ then there does not exist another correct diagnoser D' of P such that $D'(\pi_P), i \models A$.*

4   Formal Specification

In this section, we present the Alarm Specification Language with Epistemic operators (ASL_K). This language allows designers to define requirements on the FDI alarms including aspects such as delays, diagnosability and maximality.

Diagnosis conditions and alarm conditions are formalized using LTL with past operators [6] (from here on, simply LTL). The definitions of trace diagnosability and maximality, however, cannot be captured by using a formalization based on LTL. Therefore, in order to capture these two concepts, we rely on temporal epistemic logic. The intuition is that this logic enables us to reason on set of observationally equivalent traces instead that on single traces (like in LTL). We assume the familiarity of the reader to LTL, but we provide a brief introduction to temporal epistemic logic, and then show how it can be used to verify diagnosability, define requirements for non-diagnosable cases and express the concept of maximality.

4.1 Temporal Epistemic Logic

Epistemic logic has been used to describe and reason about knowledge of agents and processes. There are several ways of extending epistemic logic with temporal operators. We use the logic KL_1 [2] and extended it with past operators.

A formula in KL_1 is defined as $\beta ::= p \mid \beta \wedge \beta \mid \neg\beta \mid O\beta \mid Y\beta \mid F\beta \mid X\beta \mid K\beta$. Note how this is an extension of LTL on the past, with the addition of the epistemic operator K. The intuitive semantics of $O\beta$ is that β was true in the past, while $Y\beta$ means that in the previous state β was true; the intuitive semantics of $K\beta$ is that the diagnoser *knows* that β holds in the current execution. The formal semantics of the epistemic operator K is given on indistinguishable traces:

$$\sigma_1, n \models K\beta \text{ iff } \forall \sigma_2, obs(\sigma_1^n) = obs(\sigma_2^n) \Rightarrow \sigma_2, n \models \beta.$$

Therefore, $K\beta$ holds at time n in a trace σ_1, if β holds in all traces that are observational equivalent to σ_1 at time n. This definition implicitly forces *perfect-recall* in the semantics of the epistemic operator, since we define the epistemic equivalence between traces and not between states. Moreover, the traces are compared with a synchronous semantics. Therefore, the semantics of our transition system is synchronous and with perfect-recall (compare [2]).

4.2 Diagnosis and Alarm Conditions as LTL Properties

Let $\mathcal{P}$ be a set of propositions representing either faults or elementary conditions for the diagnosis. The set $\mathcal{D_P}$ of *diagnosis conditions* over $\mathcal{P}$ is any formula β built with the following rule: $\beta ::= p \mid \beta \wedge \beta \mid \neg\beta \mid O\beta \mid Y\beta$ with $p \in \mathcal{P}$. We use the abbreviations $Y^n\phi = YY^{n-1}\phi$ (with $Y^0\phi = \phi$), $O^{\leq n}\phi = \phi \vee Y\phi \vee \cdots \vee Y^n\phi$ and $F^{\leq n}\phi = \phi \vee X\phi \vee \cdots \vee X^n\phi$.

We define the *Alarm Specification Language* (ASL) in Figure 2, where we associate to each type of alarm condition an LTL formalization encoding the concepts of correctness and completeness. *Correctness*, the first conjunct, intuitively says that whenever the diagnoser raises an alarm, then the fault must have occurred. *Completeness*, the second conjunct, intuitively encodes that whenever the fault occurs, the alarm will be raised. In the following, for simplicity, we abuse notation and indicate with φ both the alarm condition and the associated LTL; for an alarm condition φ, we denote with A_φ the associated alarm variable A, and with $\tau(\varphi)$ the following formulae: $\tau(\varphi) = Y^n\beta$ for $\varphi = \text{ExactDel}(A, \beta, n)$; $\tau(\varphi) = O^{\leq n}\beta$ for $\varphi = \text{BoundDel}(A, \beta, n)$; $\tau(\varphi) = O\beta$ for $\varphi = \text{FiniteDel}(A, \beta)$.

Alarm Condition	LTL Formulation
$\textrm{ExactDel}(A, \beta, n)$	$G(A \rightarrow Y^n \beta) \wedge G(\beta \rightarrow X^n A)$
$\textrm{BoundDel}(A, \beta, n)$	$G(A \rightarrow O^{\leq n} \beta) \wedge G(\beta \rightarrow F^{\leq n} A)$
$\textrm{FiniteDel}(A, \beta)$	$G(A \rightarrow O\beta) \wedge G(\beta \rightarrow FA)$

Fig. 2. Alarm conditions as LTL (ASL)

Alarm Condition	Diagnosability condition
$\textrm{ExactDel}(A, \beta, n)$	$G(\beta \rightarrow X^n KY^n \beta)$
$\textrm{BoundDel}(A, \beta, n)$	$G(\beta \rightarrow F^{\leq n} KO^{\leq n} \beta)$
$\textrm{FiniteDel}(A, \beta)$	$G(\beta \rightarrow FKO\beta)$

β

$KO^{\leq 4}\beta$

A (Maximal)

A (Non-Maximal)

(a) Diagnosability Property.   **(b)** Example of Maximality.

Fig. 3. Diagnosability and Maximality

4.3 Diagnosability as Epistemic Property

We can write the diagnosability tests for the different alarm conditions directly as epistemic properties that can be verified on single points of the traces (trace diagnosability) or on the entire plant (system diagnosability) (Figure 3.a). For example, the diagnosability test for $\textrm{ExactDel}(A, \beta, n)$ says that it is always the case that whenever β occurs, exactly n steps afterwards, the diagnoser *knows* that n steps before β occurred. Since K is defined on observationally equivalent traces, the only way to falsify the formula would be to have a trace in which β occurs, and another one (observationally equivalent at least for the next n steps) in which β did not occur; but this is in contradiction with the definition of diagnosability (Definition 1).

4.4 Maximality as Epistemic Property

The property of maximality says that the diagnoser will raise the alarm as soon as it is possible to know the diagnosis condition, and the alarm will stay up as long as possible. The property $K\tau(\varphi) \rightarrow A$ encodes this behavior:

Theorem 3. *D is maximal for φ in P iff $D \times P \models G(K\tau(\varphi) \rightarrow A_\varphi)$.*

Whenever the diagnoser knows that $\tau(\varphi)$ is satisfied, it will raise the alarm. For bounded- and finite-delay alarms, this guarantees also that the alarm will stay up if possible, since $K\tau(\varphi) \rightarrow XKY\tau(\varphi)$. An example of maximal and non-maximal alarm is given in Figure 3.b. Note that according to our definition, the set of maximal alarms is a subset of the non-maximal ones.

4.5 $\textrm{ASL}_K$ Specifications

The formalization of $\textrm{ASL}_K$ (Figure 4) is obtained by extending ASL (Figure 2) with the concepts of maximality and diagnosability, defined as epistemic properties. When *maximality* is required we add a third conjunct following Theorem 3.

Template	$maximality = False$	$maximality = True$
$diag = System$		
EXACTDEL	$G(A \to Y^n\beta) \wedge G(\beta \to X^n A)$	$G(A \to Y^n\beta) \wedge G(\beta \to X^n A) \wedge$ $G(KY^n\beta \to A)$
BOUNDDEL	$G(A \to O^{\leq n}\beta) \wedge G(\beta \to F^{\leq n}A)$	$G(A \to O^{\leq n}\beta) \wedge G(\beta \to F^{\leq n}A) \wedge$ $G(KO^{\leq n}\beta \to A)$
FINITEDEL	$G(A \to O\beta) \wedge G(\beta \to FA)$	$G(A \to O\beta) \wedge G(\beta \to FA) \wedge$ $G(KO\beta \to A)$
$diag = Trace$		
EXACTDEL	$G(A \to Y^n\beta) \wedge$ $G((\beta \to X^n KY^n\beta) \to (\beta \to X^n A))$	$G(A \to Y^n\beta) \wedge$ $G((\beta \to X^n KY^n\beta) \to (\beta \to X^n A)) \wedge$ $G(KY^n\beta \to A)$
BOUNDDEL	$G(A \to O^{\leq n}\beta) \wedge$ $G((\beta \to F^{\leq n}KO^{\leq n}\beta) \to (\beta \to F^{\leq n}A))$	$G(A \to O^{\leq n}\beta) \wedge$ $G((\beta \to F^{\leq n}KO^{\leq n}\beta) \to (\beta \to F^{\leq n}A)) \wedge$ $G(KO^{\leq n}\beta \to A)$
FINITEDEL	$G(A \to O\beta) \wedge$ $G((\beta \to FKO\beta) \to (\beta \to FA))$	$G(A \to O\beta) \wedge$ $G((\beta \to FKO\beta) \to (\beta \to FA)) \wedge$ $G(KO\beta \to A)$

Fig. 4. ASL_K specification patterns

When $diag = trace$ instead, we precondition the completeness to the trace diagnosability (as defined in Figure 3.a); this means that the diagnoser will raise an alarm whenever the diagnosis condition is satisfied and the diagnoser is able to know it. The formalizations presented in the table can be simplified, but are left as-is to simplify their comprehension. For example, in the case $diag = trace$, we do not need to verify the completeness due to the following result:

Theorem 4. *Given a diagnoser D for a plant P and a trace diagnosable alarm condition φ, if D is maximal for φ, then D is complete.*

A similar result holds for EXACTDEL in the non-maximal case, that becomes: $G(A \to Y^n\beta) \wedge G(KY^n\beta \to A)$. Finally, the implications for the completeness in the trace diagnosability case can be rewritten as, e.g., $G((\beta \wedge FKO\beta) \to (FA))$. Another interesting result is the following:

Theorem 5. *Given a diagnoser D for a plant P and a system diagnosable condition φ, if D is maximal for φ and φ is diagnosable in P then D is complete.*

An ASL_K specification is built by instantiating the patterns defined in Figure 4. For example, we would write $EXACTDEL_K(A, \beta, n, trace, True)$ for an exact-delay alarm A for β with delay n, that satisfies the trace diagnosability property and is maximal. An introductory example on the usage of ASL_K for the specification of a diagnoser is provided in [7].

5   Validation and Verification of ASL_K Specifications

Thanks to the formal characterization of ASL_K, it is possible to apply formal methods for the validation and verification of a set of FDI requirements. In *validation* we verify that the requirements capture the interesting behaviors and exclude the spurious ones, before proceeding with the design of the diagnoser. In *verification*, we check that a candidate diagnoser fulfills a set of requirements.

Validation In the following we focus on the validation of an alarm specification, but the same ideas can be applied to a set of diagnosis conditions. We consider a set of environmental assumptions E and a specification $\mathcal{A}_P$. The environment assumption E may include both assumption on the plant's input and an abstraction of the plant. It can vary in a spectrum starting from trivially no assumption ($E = \top$), to some LTL properties, to a detailed model of the plant, going through several intermediate levels. The idea is that throughout the different phases of the development process, we have access to better versions of the plant model, and therefore the analysis can be refined. For example, it might be possible to provide some assumption on the maximum number of faults in the system, or on their dynamics, before a complete description of the subsystems is available.

Known techniques for requirements validation (e.g.,[8]) include checking their consistency, their compatibility with some possible scenarios, whether they entail some expected properties and if they are realizable, i.e., if there exists an implementation satisfying the requirements. In the following we instantiate these checks for the alarm specification.

In Section 6, we prove that we can always synthesize a diagnoser satisfying $\mathcal{A}_P$, with the only assumption that if $\mathcal{A}_P$ contains some system diagnosable alarm condition, then that condition is diagnosable in the plant. This means that any specification $\mathcal{A}_P$ is consistent by construction (just consider a diagnosable plant). Moreover, the check for realizability reduces to checking that the plant is diagnosable for the system diagnosable conditions in $\mathcal{A}_P$. The diagnosability check can be performed via epistemic model-checking (Section 4.3) or it can be reduced to an LTL model-checking problem using the twin-plant construction [9].

As check of possible scenarios, we would like that alarms should eventually be activated, but also that alarms are not always active. This means that for a given alarm condition $\varphi \in \mathcal{A}_P$, we are interested in verifying that there is a trace $\pi \in E$ and a trace $\pi' \in E$ s.t. $\pi \models FA_\varphi$ and $\pi' \models F\neg A_\varphi$. This can be done by checking the unsatisfiability of $(E \wedge \varphi) \to G\neg A_\varphi$ and $(E \wedge \varphi) \to GA_\varphi$.

As check of entailed properties, it is interesting to understand whether there is some correlation between alarms in order to simplify the model, or to guarantee some redundancy requirement. To check whether $A_{\varphi'}$ is a more general alarm than A_φ (subsumption) we verify that $(E \wedge \varphi \wedge \varphi') \to G(A_\varphi \to A_{\varphi'})$ is a tautology. A trivial example of subsumption of alarms is given by the definition of maximality: any non-maximal alarm is subsumed by its corresponding maximal version. Finally, we can verify that two alarms are mutually exclusive by checking the validity of $(E \wedge \varphi \wedge \varphi') \to G\neg(A_\varphi \wedge A_{\varphi'})$. In general, the validation of alarm conditions requires reasoning in temporal epistemic logic, however, the validation of diagnosis condition only requires reasoning on LTL with past.

Verification. The verification of a system w.r.t. a specification can be performed via model-checking techniques using the semantics of the alarm conditions:

Definition 6 *Let D be a diagnoser for alarms $\mathcal{A}$ and plant P. We say that D satisfies a set $\mathcal{A}_P$ of ASL_K specifications iff for each φ in $\mathcal{A}_P$ there exists an alarm $A_\varphi \in \mathcal{A}$ and $D \times P \models \varphi$.*

To perform this verification steps, we need in general a model checker for KL_1 with synchronous perfect recall such as MCK [10]. However, if the specification falls in the pure LTL fragment (ASL) we can verify it with an LTL model-checker such as NuSMV [11] thus benefiting from the efficiency of the tools in this area. Moreover, a diagnoser is required to be compatible with the plant. Therefore, we need to take care that the synchronous composition of the plant with the diagnoser does not reduce the behaviors of the plant. This would imply that there is a state and an observation that are possible for the plant, but not taken into account by the diagnoser. Compatibility can be checked with dedicated tools such as Ticc [12] based on game theory. However, here we require compatibility in all environments and therefore, compatibility can be checked by model checking by adding a sink state to the diagnoser, so that if we are in a state and we receive an observation that was not covered by the original diagnoser, we go to the sink state. Once we modified the diagnoser, we verify that $D \times P \models G \neg SinkState$.

6 Synthesis of a Diagnoser from an ASL_K Specification

In this section, we sketch an algorithm to synthesize a diagnoser that satisfies a given specification $\mathcal{A}_P$. The algorithm considers the most expressive case of ASL_K (maximal/trace diagnosable), satisfying, therefore all other cases.

The idea of the algorithm is to generate an automaton that encodes the set of possible states in which the plant could be after each observations. The result is achieved by generating the power-set of the states of the plant, and defining a suitable transition relation among the elements of this set that only considers the observable information. We call the sets in the power-set *belief states*. Each belief state of the automaton can be annotated with the alarms that are satisfied in all the states of the belief state, obtaining the diagnoser.

Our algorithm resembles the construction by Sampath [5] and Schumann [13]. The main differences are that we consider LTL Past expression as diagnosis condition, and not only fault events as done in previous works. Moreover, instead of providing a set of possible diagnosis, we provide alarms: we need to be certain that the alarm condition is satisfied in all possible diagnosis in order to raise the alarm. This gives raise to a 3-valued alarm system, in which we *know* that the fault occurred, *know* that the fault did *not* occurred or are uncertain.

Given a plant $P = \langle V^P, V_o^P, W^P, W_o^P, I^P, T^P \rangle$, let S be the set of states of P. The *belief automaton* is defined as $\mathcal{B}(P) = \langle B, E, B_0, R \rangle$ where $B = 2^S$, $E = 2^{W_o^P \cup V_o^P}$ and $B_0 \subseteq B$ and $R : (B \times E) \to B$ are defined as follows.

We define $B_0 = \{b \mid \text{there exists } u \in 2^{V_o^P} \text{ s.t. for all } s \in b, s \models I^P \text{ and } obs(s) = u\}$: we assume that the diagnoser can be initialized by observing the plant, and each initial belief state must, therefore, be compatible with one of the possible initial observations on the plant. The transition function R is defined as follows $R(b, e) = \{s' \mid \exists s \in b \text{ s.t. } \langle s, i, s' \rangle \models T^P, obs(s') = e_{|V_o^P}, obs(i) = e_{|W_o^P}\}$: the belief state $b' = R(b, e)$ is a successor of b iff all the states in b' are compatible with the observations from a state in b.

The diagnoser is obtained by annotating each state of the belief automaton with the corresponding alarms. To do this we explore the belief automaton, and annotate with A_φ all the states b that satisfy the temporal property $\tau(\varphi)$: $b \models A_\varphi$ iff $\forall s \in b.s \models \tau(\varphi)$. It might occur that neither $K\tau(\varphi)$ nor $K\neg\tau(\varphi)$ hold in a state. In this case there is at least a state in the belief state in which $K\tau(\varphi)$ holds and one in which it does not hold. This pair of states represents uncertainty, and are caused by non-diagnosabile traces.

We define D_φ as the diagnoser for φ. For the propositional case $\tau(\varphi) = p$, $D_\varphi = \langle V^{D_\varphi}, V_o^{D_\varphi}, W^{D_\varphi}, W_o^{D_\varphi}, I^{D_\varphi}, T^{D_\varphi} \rangle$ is a symbolic representation of $\mathcal{B}(P)$ with $V_o^{D_\varphi} = V_o^P \cup \{A_\varphi\}$, $W_o^{D_\varphi} = W_o^P$ and such that every state b of D_φ represents a state in B (with abuse of notation we do not distinguish between the two) and, for all $v \in V_o^{D_\varphi}$, $v \in obs(b)$ iff for all $s \in b$, $v \in s$, and such that every observation e of D_φ represents an observation in E and $obs(e) = e_{|W_o^{D_\varphi}}$. The following holds:

Theorem 6 (Compatibility). D_φ is compatible with P.

Theorem 7 (Correctness, Completeness and Maximality). D_φ is correct (i.e. $D_\varphi \times P \models G(A_\varphi \to \tau(\varphi))$), maximal (i.e. $D_\varphi \times P \models G(K(\tau(\varphi)) \to A_\varphi)$) and complete (under the assumption that if φ is system diagnosable, then φ is diagnosable in P).

All other alarm conditions can be reduced to the propositional case. We build a new plant P' by adding a monitor variable $\overline{\tau}$ to P s.t., $P' = P \times (G(\tau(\varphi) \leftrightarrow \overline{\tau}))$, where we abuse notation to indicate the automaton that encodes the monitor variable. By rewriting the alarm condition as $\varphi' = \text{ExactDel}(A_\varphi, \overline{\tau}, 0)$, we obtain that $D \times P \models \varphi$ iff $D \times P' \models \varphi'$.

7   Industrial Experience

The framework described in this paper has been motivated by, and used in, the AUTOGEF project [1], funded by the European Space Agency. The main goal of the project was the definition of a set of requirements for an on-board Fault Detection, Identification and Recovery (FDIR) component and its synthesis. The problem was tackled by synthesizing the Fault Detection (FDI) and Fault Recovery (FR) components separately, with the idea that the FDI provides sufficient diagnosis information for the FR to act on.

The AUTOGEF framework was evaluated using scalable benchmark examples. Moreover, Thales Alenia Space evaluated AUTOGEF on a case study based on the EXOMARS Trace Gas Orbiter. This case-study is a significant exemplification of the framework described in this paper, since it covers all the phases of the FDIR development process. The system behavior (including faulty behavior) was modeled using a formal language and table- and pattern-based description of the mission phases/modes and observability characteristics of the system. The specification of FDIR requirements by means of patterns greatly simplified the accessibility of the tool to engineers that were not experts in formal methods. Specification of alarms was carried out in the case of finite delay, under the assumption of trace diagnosability and maximality of the diagnoser. Moreover, different faults and alarms were associated with specific mission phase/mode and configurations of the system, which enabled generation of specific alarms (and recoveries) for each configuration. The specification was validated, by performing diagnosability analysis on the system model. The synthesis routines were run on a system composed of 11 components, with 10 faults in total, and generated an FDI component with 754 states. Finally, the correctness of the diagnoser was verified by using model-checking routines. Synthesis and verification capabilities have been implemented on top of the NuSMV model checker. We remark that the ability to define trace diagnosable alarms was crucial for the synthesis of the diagnoser, since most of the modeled faults were not system diagnosable.

Successful completion of the project, and positive evaluations from the industrial partner and ESA, suggest that a first step towards a formal model-based design process for FDIR was achieved.

8   Related Work

Previous works on formal FDI development have considered the specification and synthesis in isolation. Our approach differs with the state of the art because we provide a comprehensive view on the problem. Due to the lack of specification formalism for diagnosers, the problem of verifying their correctness, completeness and maximality was, to the best of our knowledge, unexplored.

Concerning specification and synthesis [14] is close to our work. The authors present a way to specify the diagnoser using LTL properties, and present a synthesis algorithm for this specification. However, problems such as maximality and trace diagnosability are not taken into account. Interesting in [14] is the handling of diagnosis condition with future operators.

Some approaches exist that define diagnosability as epistemic properties. Two notable examples are [15] and [16], where the latter extends the definition of diagnosability to a probabilistic setting. However, these works focus on finite-delay diagnosability only, and do not consider other types of delays and the problem of trace diagnosability.

Finally, we extend the results on diagnosability checking from [9] in order to provide an alternative way of checking diagnosability and redefine the concept of diagnosability at the trace level.

9   Conclusions and Future Work

This paper presents a formal framework for the design of FDI components, that covers many practically-relevant issues such as delays, non-diagnosability and maximality. The framework is based on a formal semantics provided by temporal epistemic logic. We covered the specification, validation, verification and synthesis steps of the FDI design, and evaluated the applicability of each step on a case-study from aerospace. To the best of our knowledge, this is the first work that provides a formal and unified view to all the phases of FDI design.

In the future, we plan to explore the following research directions. First, we will extend FDI to deal with asynchronous and infinite-state systems. In this work we addressed the development of FDI for finite state synchronous systems only. However, it would be of practical interest to consider infinite state systems and timed/hybrid behaviors. Another interesting line of research is the development of optimized ad-hoc techniques for reasoning on the fragment of temporal epistemic logic that we are using, both for verification and validation, and evaluating and improving the scalability of the synthesis algorithms. Finally, we will work on integrating the FDI component with the recovery procedures.

References

1. European Space Agency: ITT AO/1-6570/10/NL/LvH "Dependability Design Approach for Critical Flight Software". Technical report (2010)
2. Halpern, J.Y., Vardi, M.Y.: The complexity of reasoning about knowledge and time. Lower bounds. Journal of Computer and System Sciences 38(1), 195–237 (1989)
3. Grastien, A., Anbulagan, A., Rintanen, J., Kelareva, E.: Diagnosis of discrete-event systems using satisfiability algorithms. In: AAAI, vol. 1, pp. 305–310 (2007)
4. Rintanen, J., Grastien, A.: Diagnosability testing with satisfiability algorithms. In: Veloso, M.M. (ed.) IJCAI, pp. 532–537 (2007)
5. Sampath, M., Sengupta, R., Lafortune, S., Sinnamohideen, K., Teneketzis, D.C.: IEEE Transactions on Control Systems Technology 4, 105–124 (1996)
6. Lichtenstein, O., Pnueli, A., Zuck, L.: The glory of the past. In: Parikh, R. (ed.) Logics of Programs, vol. 193, pp. 196–218. Springer, Heidelberg (1985)
7. Bozzano, M., Cimatti, A., Gario, M., Tonetta, S.: Formal Specification and Synthesis of FDI through an Example. In: Workshop on Principles of Diagnosis, DX 2013 (2013), https://es.fbk.eu/people/gario/dx2013.pdf
8. Cimatti, A., Roveri, M., Susi, A., Tonetta, S.: Validation of requirements for hybrid systems: A formal approach. ACM Transactions on Software Engineering and Methodology 21(4), 22 (2012)
9. Cimatti, A., Pecheur, C., Cavada, R.: Formal Verification of Diagnosability via Symbolic Model Checking. In: IJCAI, pp. 363–369 (2003)
10. Gammie, P., van der Meyden, R.: MCK: Model checking the logic of knowledge. In: Alur, R., Peled, D.A. (eds.) CAV 2004. LNCS, vol. 3114, pp. 479–483. Springer, Heidelberg (2004)
11. Cimatti, A., Clarke, E., Giunchiglia, E., Giunchiglia, F., Pistore, M., Roveri, M., Sebastiani, R., Tacchella, A.: NuSMV 2: An OpenSource Tool for Symbolic Model Checking. In: Brinksma, E., Larsen, K.G. (eds.) CAV 2002. LNCS, vol. 2404, pp. 359–364. Springer, Heidelberg (2002)
12. Adler, B.T., de Alfaro, L., da Silva, L.D., Faella, M., Legay, A., Raman, V., Roy, P.: TICC: A Tool for Interface Compatibility and Composition. In: Ball, T., Jones, R.B. (eds.) CAV 2006. LNCS, vol. 4144, pp. 59–62. Springer, Heidelberg (2006)
13. Schumann, A.: Diagnosis of discrete-event systems using binary decision diagrams. In: Workshop on Principles of Diagnosis (DX 2004), pp. 197–202 (2004)
14. Jiang, S., Kumar, R.: Failure diagnosis of discrete event systems with linear-time temporal logic fault specifications. IEEE Transactions on Automatic Control, pp. 128–133 (2001)
15. Ezekiel, J., Lomuscio, A., Molnar, L., Veres, S.: Verifying Fault Tolerance and Self-Diagnosability of an Autonomous Underwater Vehicle. In: IJCAI, pp. 1659–1664 (2011)
16. Huang, X.: Diagnosability in concurrent probabilistic systems. In: Proceedings of the 2013 International Conference on Autonomous Agents and Multi-agent Systems (2013)

Monitoring Modulo Theories

Normann Decker, Martin Leucker, and Daniel Thoma

Institute for Software Engineering and Programming Languages
Universität zu Lübeck, Germany
{decker,leucker,thoma}@isp.uni-luebeck.de

Abstract. This paper considers a generic approach to enhance traditional runtime verification techniques towards first-order theories in order to reason about data. This allows especially for the verification of multi-threaded, object-oriented systems. It presents a general framework lifting the monitor synthesis for propositional temporal logics to a temporal logic over structures within some first-order theory. To evaluate such temporal properties, SMT solving and classical monitoring of propositional temporal properties is combined. The monitoring procedure was implemented for linear-time temporal logic (LTL) based on the Z3 SMT solver and evaluated regarding runtime performance.

1 Introduction

In this paper we consider runtime verification of multi-threaded, object-oriented systems, representing a major class of today's practical software. As opposed to other verification techniques such as model checking or theorem proving, runtime verification (RV) does not aim at the analysis of the whole system but on evaluating a correctness property on a particular run, based on log-files or on-the-fly. To this end, typically a monitor is synthesized from some high-level specification that is monitoring the run at hand.

In recent years, a variety of synthesis algorithms has been developed, differing in the underlying expressiveness of the specification formalism and the resulting monitoring approach. Typically, a variant of linear-time temporal logic (LTL) is employed as specification language and monitoring is automata-based or rewriting-based.

Within the setting of multiple, in general arbitrarily many instances of program parts, for example in terms of threads or objects, a software engineer is naturally interested in verifying that the interaction of individual instances follows general rules. The ability of taking the dynamics of data structures and values into account is a desirable feature for specification and verification approaches. As such, the expressiveness of plain propositional temporal logics such as LTL does not suffice, as they do not allow for specifying complex properties on data.

In this paper, we enhance traditional runtime verification techniques for propositional temporal logics by first-order theories for reasoning about data, based on SMT solvers. In result, we obtain a powerful tool for verifying complex properties at runtime which exceeds the expressiveness of previous approaches. The implementation in our tool jUnit[RV] [1] also shows that the framework is suitable for practical applications.

E. Ábrahám and K. Havelund (Eds.): TACAS 2014, LNCS 8413, pp. 341–356, 2014.
© Springer-Verlag Berlin Heidelberg 2014

Today's SMT solvers are highly optimized tools that can check the satisfiability of formulae over a variety of first-order theories such as arithmetics, arrays, lists and uninterpreted functions. They allow for reasoning on a large class of data structures used in modern software systems. We hence aim at integrating their capabilities with the efficient monitoring approaches for temporal properties. We formulate example properties showing the specific strength of our framework in terms of expressiveness. Our benchmarks for monitoring Java programs show that such specifications can be monitored efficiently.

Combining Monitoring and SMT. In the following we outline the idea of our approach my means of a running example. Consider a mutual exclusion property where a resource must not be accessed while it is locked, stated in LTL as $G(\text{lock} \rightarrow \neg\text{access}\, U\, \text{unlock})$. If there are several resource objects available at runtime, this is too restrictive and one might specifically limit foreign access to locked resources. Using variables r and p, p', intended to represent resources and processes, respectively, and suitable predicates, the property can be stated as

$$G(\text{lock}(p, r) \rightarrow (\forall p' \neq p : \neg\text{access}(p', r))\, U\, \text{unlock}(p, r)). \tag{1}$$

The free variables r and p are then implicitly universally quantified. Formally, all variables range over some universe that is fixed by the application. In our example, this could be the set of object identifiers in a certain Java program.

Data theories. To define a formal semantics for expressions as those above we note that we essentially use an LTL formula and exchanged propositions by first-order formulae. In LTL, propositions are evaluated at a position in some word, i.e. a letter. To evaluate first-order formulae, such a letter must now be a first-order structure describing a system state. In the example we fixed the universe to object IDs and used a binary predicate "=" indicating equality. This is covered by the first-order theory of natural numbers with equality and can be handled by essentially all SMT solvers. It is possible to use more powerful theories, e.g., with linear order or arithmetics. Section 3.4 provides more examples.

What remains are the predicates that are not part of the theory. These specifically characterize the current system state or, more accurately, are interpreted by the current system state in terms of the current observation. We call them *observation predicates*, in the example we use binary predicates lock, unlock and access. Inspecting the program states, we obtain, at any time, an observation g that interprets all observation predicates in terms of relations on the universe.

The first-order formulae reason about the data structures under a specific observation. We therefore refer to this logic as *data logic*. Data logic formulae may have free variables, such as p and r in the example. Summing up, we can define the semantics of a data logic formula in terms of (1) an observation interpreting the observation predicates (and possibly observation functions), (2) a theory that fixes the interpretation of all other predicates and functions and (3) a valuation that assigns a value from the universe to each free variable.

Temporal data logic. In the example, the data logic replaces the propositional part that LTL is based on. To the logic expressing the temporal aspect, we generically refer to as the *temporal logic*. Our assumptions on the temporal logic must be that it is linear (defined on words) and that it only uses atomic propositions to "access" the word. For example, the semantics of some temporal operator must not depend on the current letter directly but only on the semantics of some proposition. We formally define that requirement in Section 3 but for now only remark that typical temporal logics like LTL, the linear μ-calculus or the temporal logic of calls and returns (CaRet) [2] fit into that schema.

Given a suitable temporal logic and data logic we can define the formalism we aim at. Taking the temporal logic and replacing the atomic propositions by data formulae, we obtain what we call a *temporal data logic*. The theory and universe is fixed by the data logic and the semantics of temporal data logic formulae can thus be defined over a *sequence of observations*. The free variables are bound universally so the formula is evaluated over the observation sequence for all possible valuations. The semantics of the formula is the conjunction (more generally the infimum) of these results.

Monitor construction. Assuming a monitor construction for the (propositional) temporal logic, we can evaluate a sequence of observations on-the-fly. The idea is to construct a *symbolic* monitor that deals atomically with data formulae. In the example formula (Equation 1) we treat $\mathsf{lock}(p, r)$, $\forall p' \neq p : \neg\mathsf{access}(p', r)$ and $\mathsf{unlock}(p, r)$ as three atomic propositions, say χ_1, χ_2 and χ_3. We obtain a temporal logic formula $\mathbf{G}(\chi_1 \to \chi_2 \mathbf{U} \chi_3)$ over a set of atomic propositions $AP = \{\chi_1, \chi_2, \chi_3\}$. A monitor can then be constructed that reads words over the finite symbolic alphabet $\Sigma := 2^{AP}$.

The free variables in the formula are p and r and range over the universe of natural numbers $\mathbb{N}$. Given a valuation $\theta : \{p, r\} \to \mathbb{N}$ for those, mapping, e.g., p to $\theta(p) = 1$ and r to $\theta(r) = 2$, we can map an observation g to the letter $a \in \Sigma$ that contains all formulae that are satisfied by g. For example, say g interprets the observation predicates as $\mathsf{lock}_g = \{(1, 2), (10, 7)\}$ and $\mathsf{access}_g = \mathsf{unlock}_g = \emptyset$ (because objects 1 and 10 happen to lock the resources 2 and 7, respectively, and otherwise nothing happened in the current execution step of the program). Then, under θ, g is mapped to $a = \{\chi_1, \chi_2\} \in \Sigma$ since χ_1 and χ_2 hold but χ_3 does not. The observation g might be mapped to some other symbolic letter for another valuation θ'. If, for example, $\theta'(p) = 2$ then χ_1 does not hold and g is projected to $a' = \{\chi_2\} \in \Sigma$.

In Section 4 we present a monitoring algorithm that maintains a copy of the symbolic monitor for each valuation. For a new observation, the algorithm simulates the individual transition for each copy by projecting the observation under the specific valuation. As the universe is in general infinite, the number of monitor instances is infinite as well but the algorithm uses a data structure to finitely represent the state of all monitor instances.

Related Work. In runtime verification, handling data values to reason about the computation of a system more precisely has always been a concern. One of the first works extending LTL by parameters is by Stolz and Bodden [3]. Binding of parameters of propositions takes place in a PROLOG-style fashion and the resulting approach is reasonable for the intended applications. However, no precise denotational semantics is given.

The works on Eagle and RuleR [4,5] allow the formulation of first-order safety properties. The corresponding systems come with a rewriting-based semantics and are well-suited for specifying safety properties of especially finite, yet perhaps expanding traces. In [6] a runtime verification approach for the temporal evaluation of integer-modulo-constraints was presented. The underlying logic has a decidable satisfiability problem and the overall approach is anticipatory. However, only limited computations can be followed. To reason about the temporal evolution of data values along some computation, some form of bounded unrolling like in bounded model checking [7] can be used. For runtime verification, however, such an approach is not suitable, as the observed trace cannot be bounded.

Closely related to our work is that of Chen and Rosu [8]. It considers the setting of sequences of actions which are parameterized by identifiers (ID). The main idea is to divide the sequence of a program into sub-sequences, called slices, containing only a single ID, and monitor each slice independently. Hence, in contrast to our approach, no interdependencies between the different slices can be checked. Moreover, our monitoring approach is not limited to plain IDs but allows the user to reason more generally over data in terms of arbitrary (decidable) first-order theories. The work considers a dedicated temporal logic (LTL) together with the dedicated notion of parameters, whereas in our framework an arbitrary linear temporal logic is extended by a first-order theory.

Recently, Bauer et al. presented an approach combining LTL with a variant of first-order logic for runtime verification [9]. However, their approach restricts quantification to finite sets always determined in advance by the system observation. This allows for finitely instantiating quantifiers during monitor execution, but also profoundly limits the expressiveness of first-order logic. Basically, it is only possible to evaluate first-order formulae over finite system observations, and not to express properties in a declarative manner.

2   Preliminaries

First-Order Logic. A *signature* $S = (P, F, ar)$ consists of finite sets P, F of predicate and function symbols, respectively, each of some arity defined by $ar : P \cup F \to \mathbb{N}$. An *extension* of S is a signature $T = (P', F', ar')$ such that $P \subseteq P'$, $F \subseteq F'$ and $ar' \subseteq ar$.

The *syntax* of first-order formulae over the signature S is defined in the usual way using operators $\vee$ (or), $\wedge$ (and), $\neg$ (negation), variables $x_0, x_1, \ldots$, predicate and function symbols $p \in P$, $f \in F$, quantifiers $\forall$ (universal), $\exists$ (existential). *Free* variables are not in the scope of some quantifier and are assumed to come from some set $\mathcal{V}$. The set of all first-order formulae over a signature S is denoted FO[S]. We consider constants as function symbols f with $ar(f) = 0$. A *sentence* is a formula without free variables.

An *S-structure* is a tuple $s = (\mathcal{U}, \mathfrak{s})$ comprising a non-empty *universe* $\mathcal{U}$ and a function $\mathfrak{s}$ mapping each predicate symbol $p \in P$ to a relation $p_s \subseteq \mathcal{U}^n$ of arity $n = ar(p)$ and each function symbol $f \in F$ to a function $f_s : \mathcal{U}^m \to \mathcal{U}$ of arity $m = ar(f)$. A *T-structure* $t = (\mathcal{T}, \mathfrak{t})$ is an *extension* of s if T is an extension of S, $\mathcal{T} = \mathcal{U}$ and $\mathfrak{s}(r) = \mathfrak{t}(r)$ for all symbols $r \in P \cup F$.

A *valuation* is a mapping $\theta : \mathcal{V} \to \mathcal{U}$ of free variables to values. The set of all such mappings may be denoted $\mathcal{U}^{\mathcal{V}}$. The semantics of first-order formulae is defined as usual. We write $(s, \theta) \models \chi$ if a formula χ is satisfied for some structure s and valuation θ. For sentences, we refer to a sole satisfying structure as a *model*, omitting a valuation. The *theory* $\mathfrak{T}$ of an S-structure s is the set of all sentences χ such that s is a model for χ.

Temporal Specifications. We use AP to denote a finite set of *atomic propositions* and $\Sigma := 2^{AP}$ for the finite alphabet over AP. For arbitrary, possibly infinite alphabets we mostly use Γ. A *word* over some alphabet Γ is a sequence of letters from Γ and Γ^*, Γ^ω denote the sets of finite and infinite words over Γ, respectively. The syntax of *linear-time temporal logic (LTL)* is defined in the usual way over atomic propositions AP using negation, boolean connectives and temporal operators X (next), U (until), G (globally) and F (eventually). We refer to the standard LTL semantics over infinite words $w \in \Sigma^\omega$ as LTL_ω given for an LTL formula φ by a mapping $[\![\varphi]\!]_\omega : \Sigma^\omega \to \mathbb{B}$ where $\mathbb{B} = \{\top, \bot\}$ denotes the two-valued boolean lattice. The finitary three-valued LTL semantics LTL_3 [10], is given for φ by a mapping $[\![\varphi]\!]_3 : \Sigma^* \to \mathbb{B}_3$ where $\mathbb{B}_3 = \{\top, ?, \bot\}$ denotes the three-valued boolean lattice ordered $\top > ? > \bot$. It is defined for $w \in \Sigma^*$ as $[\![\varphi]\!]_3(w) := \top$ if $\forall u \in \Sigma^\omega : [\![\varphi]\!]_\omega(wu) = \top$, $[\![\varphi]\!]_3(w) := \bot$ if $\forall u \in \Sigma^\omega : [\![\varphi]\!]_\omega(wu) = \bot$ and $[\![\varphi]\!]_3(w) := ?$ otherwise.

Monitor. A *monitor* $\mathcal{M} = (Q, \Gamma, \delta, q_0, \lambda, \Lambda)$ for a temporal property is a Moore machine where Q is a possibly infinite set of states, Γ is a possibly infinite input alphabet, $\delta : Q \times \Gamma \to Q$ is a deterministic transition function and $\lambda : Q \to \Lambda$ is a labeling function mapping states to labels from the set Λ.

3   Temporal Data Logic

The aim of the framework is to enable the user to specify and check complex properties of execution traces. As described above we consider two aspects, time and data. Note that we refer to *discrete* time, as opposed to continuous notions like in timed automata. In this section we therefore formalize how and under which assumptions two logics considering time (temporal logic) and data (data logic) can be combined to a specification formalism (temporal data logic) that can express the timely behaviour of a system with respect to the data it processes. The clear separation of the aspects will give rise to a monitoring procedure.

3.1   Temporal Logic

The notion of a temporal logic (*TL*) that we consider for our monitoring framework is inspired by the intuition for LTL which is widely used for behavioural specifications, in particular in runtime verification. However, our monitoring approach does only rely on some specific properties that also come with other, also more expressive logics. In the following we identify the required features of a suitable temporal logic for our framework.

We require the desired temporal behaviour to be specified in a finitary, linear logic, that is, the semantics is defined on *finite words* over some alphabet Γ. The truth values of the semantics need to come from a complete semi-lattice $(\mathbb{S}, \sqcap)$ since we will handle multiple monitor instances and combine individual verdicts.

Second, there must be a *monitor construction* for the logic in question since our framework is intended to generically lift such a construction for handling data. We assume that such a construction turns a *TL* formula φ into a Moore machine $\mathcal{M}_\varphi$ with output $\mathcal{M}_\varphi(w) = [\![\varphi]\!](w)$ for $w \in \Gamma^*$. The restriction to Moore machines is not essential, our constructions are applicable to similar models, including Mealy machines and we do not rely on a finite state space.

As we aim at replacing atomic propositions, we require that the semantics of the temporal logic can only distinguish letters by means of the semantics of such propositions. This allows for lifting the semantics from a propositional to a complex alphabet where letters have more internal structure.

Proposition semantics. We formalize the distinction of positional and temporal aspects of a temporal logic formula using a *proposition semantics* $ps : AP \to 2^\Gamma$ mapping propositions $p \in AP$ to the set of letters $ps(p) \subseteq \Gamma$ that satisfy the proposition. Given, that the semantics of some propositional temporal logic can be defined by only referring to letters using a proposition semantics, it can be substituted without influencing the temporal aspect.

We refer to the canonical semantics for $\Gamma = \Sigma = 2^{AP}$ as $\mathsf{ps}_{AP} : AP \to 2^\Sigma$, with $\mathsf{ps}_{AP}(p) := \{a \subseteq AP \mid p \in a\}$. It is the "sharpest" in the sense that it distinguishes maximally many letters by means of combinations of propositions.

Symbolic abstraction. For an alphabet Γ, atomic propositions AP and a proposition semantics $ps : AP \to 2^\Gamma$, let $\pi_{ps} : \Gamma \to \Sigma$ be a projection with $\pi_{ps}(g) := \{p \in AP \mid g \in ps(p)\}$, mapping a letter $g \in \Gamma$ to the set of propositions that hold for it. For convenience, we lift the projection to words $g_1 \ldots g_n$ ($g_i \in \Gamma$) by $\pi_{ps}(g_1 \ldots g_n) := \pi_{ps}(g_1) \ldots \pi_{ps}(g_n)$. Using π_{ps}, we consider the letters form Σ as symbolic abstractions of Γ wrt. AP and ps in the sense that π_{ps} maintains all the structure of Γ that is relevant for evaluating (boolean combinations of) propositions form AP.

As argued above, for the purpose of lifting a temporal logic over atomic propositions to propositions carrying data, i.e., structure, it is essential that the semantics of propositions can be encapsulated and exchanged without influencing the temporal aspect. We can formalize this requirement on a temporal logic TL using the symbolic abstraction. We assume the semantics of a TL formula φ to be a mapping that takes linear sequences from Γ^* and assigns a truth value from the complete semi-lattice $\mathbb{S}$. If the semantics satisfies our criterion we can make the proposition semantics $ps : AP \to 2^\Gamma$ an explicit parameter and assume the semantics of a formula φ is given by a mapping $[\![\varphi]\!](ps) : \Gamma^* \to \mathbb{S}$, or, generally, $[\![\varphi]\!] : (AP \to 2^\Gamma) \to (\Gamma^* \to \mathbb{S})$. Moreover, projecting the input word to a symbolic word and evaluating $[\![\varphi]\!](\mathsf{ps}_{AP})$ on it must not change the result.

Definition 1 (Propositional semantics). *Let AP be a set of atomic propositions and Γ an alphabet. A semantics $[\![\varphi]\!] : (AP \to 2^\Gamma) \to (\Gamma^* \to \mathbb{S})$ is propositional iff for all proposition semantics $ps : AP \to 2^\Gamma$ and all words $\gamma \in \Gamma^*$*

$$[\![\varphi]\!](ps)(\gamma) = [\![\varphi]\!](\mathsf{ps}_{AP})(\pi_{ps}(\gamma)).$$

Based on that notion of propositional semantics we can summarize the formal criteria for a temporal logic to be suitable for our monitoring framework.

Definition 2 (Temporal logic). *A temporal logic is a specification formalism TL over a set of atomic propositions AP that enjoys the following properties.*

1. *The semantics of formulae φ is given for finite words over an input alphabet Γ by a mapping $[\![\varphi]\!]_{TL} : (AP \to 2^\Gamma) \to (\Gamma^* \to \mathbb{S})$ where $(\mathbb{S}, \sqcap)$ is a complete semi-lattice.*
2. *The semantics is propositional.*
3. *A monitor construction is available that turns a formula φ into a Moore machine $\mathcal{M}_\varphi$ with output $\mathcal{M}_\varphi(w) = [\![\varphi]\!]_{TL}(\mathsf{ps}_{AP})(w)$ for $w \in \Sigma^*$.*

3.2 Data Logic

To reason about data values our framework can use a so called *data logic DL* based on any first-order theory for which satisfiability is decidable. We assume the theory is represented by some structure which can be extended by additional predicate and function symbols that will represent observations from the system that shall be monitored.

Definition 3 (Data logic). *Let $T = (P, F, \text{ar})$ be a signature, $t = (\mathcal{D}, \mathfrak{a})$ some T-structure and P', F' be additional predicate and function symbols with arity defined by $\text{ar}' : P' \cup F' \to \mathbb{N}$, called observation symbols.*

A data logic DL is a tuple $(t, G, \mathcal{V}, \mathcal{D})$ such that $G = (P \cup P', F \cup F', \text{ar} \cup \text{ar}')$ is an extension of T and $\mathcal{V}$ is a finite set of first-order variables.

A DL formula is a first-order formula over the signature G and possibly free variables from $\mathcal{V}$. A DL formula is called observation-independent, if it does not contain observation symbols. An observation is a G-structure $g = (\mathcal{D}, \mathfrak{g})$ that is an extension of t. The set of all observations is denoted Γ.

The semantics of a DL formula is defined over tuples $(g, \theta) \in \Gamma \times \mathcal{D}^\mathcal{V}$ consisting of an observation and a valuation $\theta : \mathcal{V} \to \mathcal{D}$ of free variables in the usual way.

For an instance of the monitoring framework the structure t representing the theory is fixed. An observation-independent *DL* formula φ with free variables $x_1, \ldots, x_n \in \mathcal{V}$ can be evaluated just wrt. t, without considering an observation. A decision procedure for the theory of t can thus be applied directly. Further, φ can be interpreted as a constraint on the domain of variable valuations $\mathcal{D}^\mathcal{V}$ by considering the set $\Theta_\varphi := \{\theta \in \mathcal{D}^\mathcal{V} \mid (t, \theta) \models \varphi\}$.

3.3 Temporal Data Logic

Given a temporal and a data logic as described above, we can now define their combination, the temporal data logic *TDL*. In *TDL* formulae we use brackets $\langle$ and $\rangle$ to clarify which parts come from the data logic.

Definition 4 (Temporal data logic). *Let TL be a temporal logic and $DL = (t, G, \mathcal{V}, \mathcal{D})$ a data logic. Let AP be a finite set $\{\langle \chi_1 \rangle, \ldots, \langle \chi_n \rangle\}$ where $\chi_1, \ldots, \chi_n$ are DL formulae with free variables from $\mathcal{V}$.*

A TDL formula is a TL formula over AP. A structured word is a finite sequence $\gamma \in \Gamma^*$ of DL observations. For a valuation $\theta \in \mathcal{D}^\mathcal{V}$, let the proposition semantics $\text{ps}_\theta : AP \to 2^\Gamma$ be defined by $\text{ps}_\theta(\langle \chi \rangle) := \{g \in \Gamma \mid (g, \theta) \models \chi\}$ for $\langle \chi \rangle \in AP$. The semantics of a TDL formula φ is a mapping $[\![\varphi]\!]_{TDL} : \Gamma^* \to \mathbb{S}$ defined for $\gamma \in \Gamma^*$ by

$$[\![\varphi]\!]_{TDL}(\gamma) := \bigsqcap_{\theta \in \mathcal{D}^\mathcal{V}} [\![\varphi]\!]_{TL}(\text{ps}_\theta)(\gamma).$$

Recall, for ps_θ we obtain a projection $\pi_{\text{ps}_\theta} : \Gamma^* \to \Sigma^*$ from structured to symbolic words. In the following we abbreviate π_{ps_θ} by π_θ. From Definition 2 of the temporal logic it follows that we can evaluate the semantics of some *TDL* formula *symbolically*, which is an essential step in lifting a monitor construction for *TL* to the data setting.

Table 1. Example properties using LTL and CaRet with data

mutex $\mathrm{G}(\langle\mathsf{lock}(f,t)\rangle \to \langle\forall t' \neq t : \neg\mathsf{access}(f,t')\rangle\,\mathrm{U}\langle\mathsf{unlock}(f,t)\rangle)$
access $(\langle\mathsf{open}(x)\rangle\,\mathrm{R}\,\neg\langle\mathsf{access}(x)\rangle) \wedge \mathrm{G}(\langle\mathsf{close}(x)\rangle \to \mathrm{G}\,\neg\langle\mathsf{access}(x)\rangle)$
iterator $\mathrm{G}((\langle\mathsf{iterator}(i)\rangle \vee \langle\mathsf{next}(i)\rangle) \to \mathrm{X}(\langle\mathsf{hasNext}(i,\mathsf{true})\rangle\,\mathrm{R}\,\neg\langle\mathsf{next}(i)\rangle))$
modified $\mathrm{G}(\langle\mathsf{iterator}(c,i)\rangle \to \mathrm{G}(\langle\mathsf{add}(c)\rangle \to (\neg\langle\mathsf{next}(i)\rangle\,\mathrm{U}\langle\mathsf{finalize}(i)\rangle)))$
server $\mathrm{G}(\langle\mathsf{request}(t,x)\rangle \to \mathrm{F}\langle\exists t' : \mathsf{response}(t',x,t)\rangle)$
response $\mathrm{G}(\langle\mathsf{request}(t)\rangle \wedge \langle x = \mathsf{time}\rangle \to (\langle\mathsf{time} < x+100\rangle\,\mathrm{U}\langle\mathsf{response}(t)\rangle))$
counter $\mathrm{G}(\langle\mathsf{p}(x)\rangle \to \mathrm{X}\langle\mathsf{p}(x+1)\rangle)$
velocity $\mathrm{G}(\langle\mathsf{s} = x \wedge \mathsf{t} = y\rangle \to \mathrm{X}\langle\mathsf{s} - x < \mathsf{vmax} \cdot (\mathsf{t} - y)\rangle)$
matching $\mathrm{G}((\langle\mathsf{call}\rangle \wedge \langle\mathsf{printOpen}(x)\rangle) \to \mathrm{X}^{\mathrm{a}}\langle\mathsf{printClose}(x)\rangle)$
bound $\mathrm{G}(\langle\mathsf{open}(x)\rangle \to \mathrm{X}(\neg\langle\mathsf{ret}\rangle \to \mathrm{G}^{\mathrm{a}}(\langle\mathsf{open}(y)\rangle \to \langle x > y\rangle)))$
depth $\mathrm{G}(\langle\mathsf{open}(x)\rangle \to \mathrm{X}((\neg\langle\mathsf{ret}\rangle \wedge \mathrm{F}^{\mathrm{a}}\langle\mathsf{open}(x-1)\rangle) \vee (\langle\mathsf{ret}\rangle \wedge \langle x = 0\rangle)))$

Proposition 1. *Let φ be a TDL formula, $\mathcal{D}^{\mathcal{V}}$ the valuation space for free variables in φ, $\chi_1,\ldots,\chi_n$ the data logic formulae used in φ and $AP = \{\langle\chi_1\rangle,\ldots,\langle\chi_n\rangle\}$. For $\gamma \in \Gamma^*$ we have $[\![\varphi]\!]_{TDL}(\gamma) = \bigsqcap_{\theta\in\mathcal{D}^{\mathcal{V}}}[\![\varphi]\!]_{TL}(\mathsf{ps}_{AP})(\pi_\theta(\gamma))$.*

3.4 LTL and CaRet with Data

We now exemplify the instantiation of our framework by means of LTL. More precisely, we show that the the finitary, three-valued LTL$_3$ semantics $[\![\varphi]\!]_3 : \Sigma^* \to \mathbb{B}_3$ can be formulated to comply Definition 2. It is defined over $\Sigma = 2^{AP}$ based on the infinitary LTL$_\omega$ semantics. The inductive definition of LTL$_\omega$ only refers to letters for atomic propositions. This can be easily reformulated in terms of an arbitrary proposition semantics $ps : AP \to 2^\Gamma$ over an arbitrary alphabet Γ. Instead of defining $[\![p]\!]_\omega(w) = \top$ iff $p \in w_0$, we let $[\![p]\!]_\omega(ps)(\gamma) := \top$ if $\gamma_0 \in ps(p)$ and $[\![p]\!]_\omega(ps)(\gamma) := \bot$ otherwise, for $\gamma \in \Gamma^\omega$. The rest of the definition remains untouched. The definition of the three-valued semantics $[\![\varphi]\!]_3$ does not at all refer to letters directly but only to LTL$_\omega$. With these simple modifications LTL$_3$ fits to the notion of temporal logic in the sense of Definition 2. The corresponding monitor construction proposed in [10,11] can be applied.

Proposition 2. *The MMT framework can be instantiated for LTL$_3$.*

The mutual exclusion property presented earlier is one example for a specification based on LTL and the theory of IDs. Other common examples of temporal properties are the correct use of iterators or global request/response properties. In the propositional versions of such properties the objects in question, iterators, resources or requests, are assumed to be unique. Adding data in terms of IDs, for example, allows for a much more realistic formulation. Table 1 lists formulations of these properties and also others that cannot be expressed without distinguishing at least identities. The property *modified* requires that an iterator must not be used after the collection it corresponds to has been changed. Further, counting (*counter*) or arithmetic constraints (*response*, *velocity*), also on real numbers, are valuable features for a realistic specification.

RLTL and CaRet: Regular and nesting properties. Regular LTL [12] is an extension of LTL based on regular expressions. CaRet [2] is a temporal logic with calls and returns expressing non-regular properties. In addition to the LTL operators, CaRet allows for abstract temporal operators such as X^a and G^a, moving forward by jumping on a word from a calling position to matching return position, reflecting the intuition of procedure calls. For RLTL and CaRet monitor constructions have been proposed [6,13]. Despite both are more complex the same arguments as for LTL apply. Example properties are listed in Table 1 and express matching call- and return values and nesting-depth bounds.

4   Monitoring

In this section we present our monitoring procedure for *TDL* formulae. It relies on the observation made in Proposition 1, namely that the *TDL* semantics for an input word $\gamma \in \Gamma^*$ is characterized by the *TL* semantics for projections of γ.

Any *TDL* formula can be interpreted as *TL* formula when considering all occurring data logic formulae as individual symbols. With this interpretation we can employ the monitor construction for *TL* to obtain a monitor over a finite alphabet constructed from these symbols.

Definition 5 (Symbolic monitor). *Let φ be a TDL formula and $\chi_1, \ldots, \chi_n$ the data logic formulae used in φ and $AP = \{\langle \chi_1 \rangle, \ldots, \langle \chi_n \rangle\}$. The symbolic alphabet for φ is the finite set $\Sigma := 2^{AP}$. The symbolic monitor for φ is the monitor $\mathcal{M}_\Sigma$ constructed for φ interpreted as TL formula over AP.*

The symbolic monitor $\mathcal{M}_\Sigma$ for a *TDL* formula φ computes the semantics $[\![\varphi]\!](\mathsf{ps}_{AP}) : \Sigma^* \to \mathbb{S}$. Following Proposition 1, what remains is to maintain a monitor for each valuation $\theta \in \mathcal{D}^\mathcal{V}$ and to individually compute the corresponding projection π_θ on the input.

Within this section we present an algorithm for efficiently maintaining these, in general infinitely many, monitor instances. It uses a data structure, called constraint tree, that represents finitely many equivalence classes of symbolic monitors. The constraint tree also allows for easy computation of the infimum of the outputs of all monitor instances, which is the semantics of the property on the input trace read so far.

4.1   Representing and Evaluating Observations

While observations are formally defined as first-order structures, we want to use them algorithmically and must therefore choose a representation. An actual implementation of an SMT solver already fixes how to represent all objects essential for handling a certain theory, such as first-order formulae, predicates and function symbols. We have defined observations to be extensions of a structure representing the theory and want to handle them practically using an SMT solver. Consequently, we assume them to be extensions of the structure that the tool uses to represent and handle a theory. For the purpose of the implementation, it is a reasonable assumption that the semantics of observation symbols be expressible or, more precisely, expressed within the considered data theory.

Formally, for $DL = (t, G, \mathcal{V}, \mathcal{D})$ where t is a T-structure, we assume that any observation $g \in \Gamma$ induces a mapping $\hat{g} : FO[G] \to FO[T]$ s.t. for all *DL* formulae χ and all valuations $\theta \in \mathcal{D}^\mathcal{V}$ we have $(g, \theta) \models \chi$ iff $(t, \theta) \models \hat{g}(\chi)$. Note that this can be realized by substituting observation predicates by some observation-independent formula that characterizes its semantics wrt. g. Function symbols f can be replaced using existential substitution replacing expressions of the form $e(f(e'))$ by $\exists z : e(z) \land \xi_f(e', z)$ where an observation-free DL formula ξ_f characterizes the semantics of f wrt. g.

As noted earlier, we can also employ observation-free formulae ρ to describe sets of valuations $\Theta_\rho \subseteq \mathcal{D}^\mathcal{V}$. While this does not allow for representing any arbitrary set of valuations, the expressiveness of the data theory suffices to express any relevant set. If ρ represents an equivalence class wrt. some formula $\hat{g}(\chi)$, meaning $(t, \theta) \models \hat{g}(\chi)$ holds for all $\theta \in \Theta_\rho$ or none, we have that $(t, \theta) \models \hat{g}(\chi)$ iff there is any $\theta' \in \mathcal{D}^\mathcal{V}$ such that $(t, \theta') \models \hat{g}(\chi) \land \rho$.

Let χ be a DL formula and $g \in \Gamma$ an observation. Let ρ be an observation-free DL formula such that for all $\theta_1, \theta_2 \in \Theta_\rho$ we have $(t, \theta_1) \models \hat{g}(\chi)$ iff $(t, \theta_2) \models \hat{g}(\chi)$. Then, for all $\theta \in \Theta_\rho$, $(g, \theta) \models \chi$ iff $\hat{g}(\chi) \land \rho$ is satisfiable. Note that $\hat{g}(\chi) \land \rho$ is an observation-free DL formula and that checking it for satisfiability is exactly what we assume an SMT solver be able to do.

4.2 Constraint Trees

We next introduce constraint trees, a data structure storing the configurations of a set of instances of some symbolic monitor. It maintains sets of valuations $\Theta \subseteq \mathcal{D}^\mathcal{V}$ represented by constraints and stores for each such set a monitor state. The desired property regarding the use in our monitoring algorithm is that the sets of constraints induce a partition of the valuation space.

Definition 6 (Constraint tree). *Let $\mathcal{M}_\Sigma$ be a symbolic monitor with states Q and DL a data logic. A constraint tree is a tuple $T = (I, L, S_1, S_2, C, \lambda_I, \lambda_L)$ such that $(I \cup L, S_1, S_2)$ is a finite, non-empty binary tree with internal nodes I, leaf nodes L and successor relations $S_1, S_2 \subseteq I \times (I \cup L)$, C is a set of observation-independent DL formulae called constraints, $\lambda_I : I \to C$ labels internal nodes with constraints and $\lambda_L : L \to Q$ labels leaf nodes with monitor states.*

Let the DL formula $\rho(v_0 \ldots v_i)$ be the conjunction over all constraints along the path $v_0 \ldots v_{i-1}$, where all S_2-successors are negated and $\rho(v_0) = \text{true}$. A path constraint in T is a DL formula $\rho(v_0 \ldots v_n)$ such that $v_0 \ldots v_n$ is a maximal path in T. A constraint tree T is consistent if the set of all path constraints in T induces a partition of $\mathcal{D}^\mathcal{V}$. The set of all constraint trees is denoted $\mathcal{T}$.

In a constraint tree T, each inner node represents a constraint that is used to separate the valuation space $\mathcal{D}^\mathcal{V}$. S_1-branches represent the parts where the particular constraint holds while in the S_2-branches it does not.

Constraint trees $T = (I, L, E, C, \lambda_I, \lambda_L)$ will be used to represent 'mappings $t : \mathcal{D}^\mathcal{V} \to Q$ assigning a monitor state $q \in Q$ to each valuation $\theta \in \mathcal{D}^\mathcal{V}$. If T is consistent, every valuation θ satisfies exactly one path constraint ρ in T which in turn corresponds to a unique path ending in some leaf node $v \in L$. The mapping is thereby defined as $t(\theta) = \lambda_L(v)$. Note that t would not be necessarily well-defined for constraint trees that are not consistent. Where convenient, we may identify a path constraint ρ with the set Θ_ρ of valuations satisfying it and write, e.g., $\theta \in \rho$ if some valuation $\theta \in \Theta_\rho$ satisfies ρ.

4.3   Symbolic Monitor Execution

In the following we present an algorithm incrementally processing a sequence of observations in order to compute the semantics of some *TDL* formula φ. It maintainings a consistent constraint tree as a finite representation of a mapping of valuations to states of the symbolic monitor $\mathcal{M}_\Sigma = (Q, \Sigma, \delta, q_0, \lambda, \mathbb{S})$ for φ.

The algorithm starts on the trivial constraint tree consisting only of one leaf node labeled by the initial state q_0. This means that the monitor instances for all valuations are in state q_0. Intuitively, for an input word $\gamma \in \Gamma$ the algorithm executes one monitor instance for each valuation $\theta \in \mathcal{D}^\mathcal{V}$ on the respective projection $\pi_\theta(\gamma)$. For the empty word $\gamma = \epsilon$, all projections are equal and all instances are in the same state. When reading a new observation $g \in \Gamma$ which is, for all valuations, projected to the same symbolic letter $a \in \Sigma$, all monitor instances read the same projection and their state changes equally to $\delta(q_0, a)$. Otherwise, if g is mapped to different symbolic letters for different valuations, the so far uniformly handled valuation space is *split*.

Consider two valuations $\theta, \theta' \in \mathcal{D}^\mathcal{V}$ and an input symbol $g \in \Gamma$ such that their projections $a = \pi_\theta(g) \neq b = \pi_{\theta'}(g)$ are different. Then there is some proposition $\langle\chi\rangle \in AP$ that distinguishes a and b, e.g., let $\langle\chi\rangle \in a$ and $\langle\chi\rangle \notin b$. In general, the behaviour of all monitor instances reading a letter including $\langle\chi\rangle$ may diverge from those reading a letter not including $\langle\chi\rangle$. Therefore, the algorithm records this fact by splitting the valuation space in two parts, one for which χ holds under observation g and another for which it does not. A new node is added to the tree, labeled by the constraint $\hat{g}(\chi)$ precisely distinguishing the two parts. A part may be split up further in the same way in case other propositions again distinguish valuations from it. Additional nodes are created in the constraint tree accordingly and so the path constraint ρ on the path to a leaf node $v \in L$ characterizes exactly the set of valuations Θ_ρ for which the projection of the observation g is equal and thus the state of all corresponding monitor instances. This process is continued when reading further observations. For each part Θ_ρ represented in the constraint tree, a new observation $h \in \Gamma$ is processed by checking for each proposition $\langle\chi\rangle \in AP$ if there are valuations in Θ_ρ that observe a projection including $\langle\chi\rangle$ by checking satisfiability of $\rho \wedge \hat{h}(\chi)$ and if there are others observing a projection not including $\langle\chi\rangle$ by checking the satisfiability of $\rho \wedge \neg\hat{h}(\chi)$. If one of the formulae is empty, meaning that one of the hypothetical new parts $\Theta_{\rho \wedge \hat{h}(\chi)} = \Theta_\rho \cap \Theta_{\hat{h}(\chi)}$ and $\Theta_{\rho \wedge \neg\hat{h}(\chi)} = \Theta_\rho \cap \overline{\Theta_{\hat{h}(\chi)}}$ is empty, the new observation h is projected equally wrt. $\langle\chi\rangle$ for all valuations in the part which is thus not split by $\hat{h}(\chi)$. Only if both new parts are non-empty, the part is split by adding a new node to the constraint tree labeled by $\hat{h}(\chi)$. Once all necessary splits are performed for an observation, all propositions are evaluated yielding the projections for each (possibly new) part. According to those, the leaf nodes are updated using the transition function of the symbolic monitor.

The procedure described above is listed explicitly as Algorithm 1. There, for the set of all constraint trees $\mathcal{T}$, we use constructors $\texttt{InnerCTree} : \text{FO}[S] \times \mathcal{T} \times \mathcal{T} \to \mathcal{T}$ and $\texttt{LeafCTree} : Q \to \mathcal{T}$ for sub-trees and leafs, respectively, where $\text{FO}[S]$ is the set of observation-independent *DL* formulae. For $T = \texttt{LeafCTree}(q)$ we assume that T consists of a single node $v \in L$ that is labeled by $\lambda_L(v) = q$ and for $T = \texttt{InnerCTree}(\varphi, T_1, T_2)$ we assume that T has at least three nodes

---

Algorithm 1. Split constraints and simulate monitor steps

```
1   function split =
2       //recursively process subtrees, accumulate constraints
3       case (P, ρ, a, InnerCTree(φ, t₀, t₁), g) then
4           InnerCTree(φ,split(P, ρ ∧ ¬φ, a, t₀, g),split(P, ρ ∧ φ, a, t₁, g))

6       //evaluate propositions, split partition if necessary
7       case ({⟨χ⟩} ∪ P, ρ, a, LeafCTree(s), g) then
8           T₀ = if SAT(ρ ∧ ¬ĝ(χ)) then
9                   split(P, ρ ∧ ¬ĝ(χ), a, LeafCTree(s), g)
10              else Empty
11          T₁ = if SAT(ρ ∧ ĝ(χ)) then
12                   split(P, ρ ∧ ĝ(χ), a ∪ {⟨χ⟩}, LeafCTree(s), g)
13              else Empty
14          if (t₀ = Empty) then t₁
15          else if (t₁ = Empty) then t₀
16          else InnerCTree(ĝ(χ), t₀, t₁)

18      //store new state
19      case (∅, ρ, a, LeafCTree(s), g) then
20          LeafCTree(δ(s,a))

22  function step(t: CTree, g ∈ Γ): CTree =
23      split(AP, true, ∅, t, g)
```

---

v, v_1, v_2 such that v is the root of T labeled by $\lambda_I(v) = \varphi$, v_1, v_2 are the roots of T_1 and T_2, respectively, and $(v, v_1) \in S_1$ and $(v, v_2) \in S_2$.

Based on constraint trees as data structure and the algorithm for modifying constraint trees regarding a new observation we can now define the data monitor for a *TDL* formula, where, as before, the data logic *DL* is defined over observations Γ and the temporal logic *TL* uses truth values $\mathbb{S}$.

Definition 7 (Data monitor). *Let φ be a TDL formula, $\Sigma = 2^{AP}$ the symbolic alphabet and $\mathcal{M}_\Sigma = (Q, \Sigma, \delta, q_0, \lambda_Q, \mathbb{S})$ the symbolic monitor for φ.*

The data monitor *for φ is a Moore machine $\mathcal{M}_\Gamma = (\mathcal{T}, \Gamma, \text{step}, T_0, \lambda_\mathcal{T}, \mathbb{S})$ using constraint trees $\mathcal{T}$ as states.*

The transition function $\text{step} : \mathcal{T} \times \Gamma \to \mathcal{T}$ is given by Algorithm 1 and the initial tree T_0 consists of a single leaf node labeled with the initial state q_0 of $\mathcal{M}_\Sigma$. For a constraint tree $T \in \mathcal{T}$ where the leaf nodes L are labeled by λ_L, the monitor output is defined by $\lambda_\mathcal{T} : \mathcal{T} \to \mathbb{S}$ with $\lambda(T) = \bigsqcap_{v \in L} \lambda_\Sigma(\lambda_L(v))$.

4.4   Correctness

Proposition 3 (Termination). *On a constraint tree T, the function step in Algorithm 1 terminates and has a running time in $\mathcal{O}(|T| \cdot |\Sigma|)$ where $|T|$ is the number of nodes in T and $|\Sigma| = 2^{|AP|}$ is the number of abstract symbols.*

The monitoring procedure presented above is correct in that the data monitor $\mathcal{M}_\Gamma$ for a *TDL* formula φ computes the correct semantics for all input words.

Theorem 1 (Correctness). *Let φ be a TDL formula and $\mathcal{M}_\Gamma$ the data monitor for φ. Then, for all $\gamma \in \Gamma^*$, $M_\Gamma(\gamma) = [\![\varphi]\!]_{TDL}(\gamma)$.*

In order to prove correctness, we first settle some observations. Recall that the semantics $[\![\varphi]\!]_{TDL}$ can be represented as the conjunction $\bigsqcap_{\theta \in \mathcal{D}^V} [\![\varphi]\!]_{TL}(\text{ps}_{AP})$ $(\pi_{\text{ps}_\theta}(\gamma))$ over projections $\pi_{\text{ps}_\theta}(\gamma)$ (Proposition 1). We fix the data logic *DL* for this section and write π_θ for π_{ps_θ} in the following.

Despite the conjunction above is infinite, given a finite word $\gamma \in \Gamma^*$, the valuation space $\mathcal{D}^{\mathcal{V}}$ can be partitioned into finitely many equivalence classes $\Theta_1, \ldots, \Theta_n$ such that the projection of γ is unique for each class Θ_i, i.e., $\forall_{\theta, \theta' \in \Theta_i}$: $\pi_\theta(\gamma) = \pi_{\theta'}(\gamma)$. It therefore suffices to maintain this set of equivalence classes which can in turn be finitely represented by constraints ρ_i. Let $w_i = \pi_\theta(\gamma) \in \Sigma^*$ for $\theta \in \Theta_i$ be the projection of γ for the class Θ_i ($i \in \{1, \ldots, n\}$). The semantics can then be computed as the finite conjunction $[\![\varphi]\!]_{TDL}(\gamma) = \bigsqcap_{i=1}^n [\![\varphi]\!]_{TL}(\mathsf{ps}_{AP})(w_i)$.

It remains to reason that this partition exists which we do by showing that it is in fact computed by the monitoring algorithm. More precisely, we show that the constraint tree T that is the configuration of the monitor $\mathcal{M}_\Gamma$ after reading a word γ is consistent. That is, the path constraints ρ represented by T cover the whole valuation space and are disjoint. Moreover, for all valuations $\theta \in \rho$ of such an equivalence class ρ, the symbolic monitor $\mathcal{M}_\Sigma$ behaves the same on all corresponding projections $\pi_\theta(\gamma)$.

Lemma 1. *Let $\mathcal{M}_\Gamma = (\mathcal{T}, \Gamma, \delta_\Gamma, t_0, \lambda_\Gamma)$ and $\mathcal{M}_\Sigma = (Q, \Sigma, \delta_\Sigma, q_0, \lambda_\Sigma)$ be the data monitor and the symbolic monitor, respectively, for some TDL formula φ. Let for $\gamma \in \Gamma^*$ be $T = \delta_\Gamma(T_0, \gamma)$ and R_T the set of path constraints in T. If T is consistent, $T(\rho)$ denote for $\rho \in R_T$ the unique label of the leaf in T corresponding to ρ. Then, (i) $\{\Theta_\rho \mid \rho \in R_T\}$ is a partition of $\mathcal{D}^{\mathcal{V}}$ and (ii) $\forall_{\rho \in R_T} \forall_{\theta \in \Theta_\rho} : T(\rho) = \delta_\Sigma(q_0, \pi_\theta(\gamma))$.*

We can now proof that the data monitor computes the correct semantics.

Proof (Theorem 1).
Let $T = \delta_\Gamma(T_0, \gamma)$. We have, using Lemma 1 (i) and (ii),

$$\mathcal{M}_\Gamma(\gamma) = \lambda_\Gamma(T) = \prod_{v \in L} \lambda_\Sigma(\lambda_L(v)) \overset{(i)}{=} \prod_{\rho \in R_T} \lambda_\Sigma(T(\rho)) \overset{(ii)}{=} \prod_{\rho \in R_T} \prod_{\theta \in \rho} \delta_\Sigma(q_0, \pi_\theta(\gamma))$$

$$\overset{(i)}{=} \prod_{\theta \in \mathcal{D}^{\mathcal{V}}} \delta_\Sigma(q_0, \pi_\theta(\gamma)) = \prod_{\theta \in \mathcal{D}^{\mathcal{V}}} [\![\varphi]\!]_{TL}(\mathsf{ps}_{AP})(\pi_\theta(\gamma)) = [\![\varphi]\!]_{TDL}(\gamma)$$

$\square$

4.5   Remarks and Optimizations

Impartiality and anticipation. An impartial semantics distinguishes between preliminary and final verdicts. A final verdict for some word indicates that it will not change for any continuation. Impartiality is desirable as monitoring can be stopped as a soon as a final verdict is encountered (c.f. [14,6]). In the context of our framework this gains even more importance. When the underlying monitor is impartial, a branch already yielding a final verdict can be pruned. This immensely improves runtime performance. If the symbolic monitor is impartial, the data monitor (partially) inherits this property in the typical cases. Another desired property is anticipation, i.e., evaluating to a final verdict as early as possible. While in general not transfered from the symbolic to the data monitor, this may still lead to better performance.

Dedicated theories as first-class citizens. The monitoring framework is also flexible in the sense that one can trade efficiency for generality. When the properties intended to monitor are simple enough it is reasonable to extend the algorithm to directly evaluate constraints. As we show in the experiments this works well, in particular for properties concerning only object IDs.

5 Experimental Results

We implemented our framework based on jUnit^{RV} [1], a tool for monitoring temporal properties for applications running on the Java Virtual Machine. The previous version of jUnit^{RV} supported classical LTL specifications referring to, e.g., the invocation of a method of some class. With the approach proposed here it is now possible, for example, to specify properties that relate to individual objects and their evolution in time. The implementation is based on a generic interface to an SMT solver. We present benchmarks using the SMT solver Z3 [15]. For comparison, we additionally implemented a dedicated solver for the theory of IDs (i.e., conjunctions of equality constraints on natural numbers). For the benchmarks, we have chosen representative properties from Table 1. The property *mutex* is a typical example for interaction patterns in object-oriented systems. It was evaluated on a program with resource objects and user objects randomly accessing them. The *iterator* example was evaluated on a simple program using randomly one of two iterator objects for traversing a list. Third, we evaluated a typical client-server response pattern (*server*) on a program simulating a number of server threads that receive requests and responses. For handling existential quantification, we rely on Z3. For comparison, we also evaluate the property $G(\langle \text{request}(t, x) \rangle \rightarrow F\langle \text{response}(x, t) \rangle)$ (*server2*) as a variation that can be handled by our simple solver. The *counter* property covers the counting of natural numbers which is a very elementary aspect in computer programs and uses an unbounded number of different data values. A property involving a rather complex theory is *velocity*. The free variables refer to real numbers as data values and the constraints that have to be checked are multi-dimensional.

In our experiments we measured the execution time of a program with an integrated monitor over the number of monitoring steps. The measurements were taken up to 10^4 steps. Very simple programs were used, since the measured runtime is thereby essentially the runtime of the monitoring algorithm. The linear graphs obtained for every example show that the execution time for a monitoring step is constant. The most complex properties, *velocity* and *server* induce the most overhead due to a higher computational cost by the SMT solver. However, even the performance for *velocity* of 4.2 ms/step is acceptable for many applications. Thus, employing an SMT solver is viable whenever performance is not a main concern, for instance in case a monitoring step is not expected to happen frequently wrt. to the overall computation steps. Our dedicated implementation is much faster (by factor 100) and hence can only be distinguished in the right-hand diagram. These results demonstrate, that performance can be improved for specific settings and the approach can still be employed when performance is more critical. As mentioned before, the number of calls to the SMT solver is linear in the size of the constraint tree. Hence, the overhead may increase up to linearly in the number of runtime objects that need to be tracked. In our

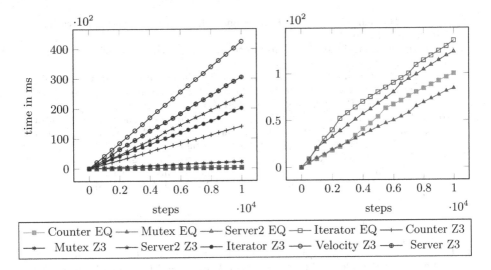

Fig. 1. Experimental results

example the maximal size of the constraint tree was six. All experiments were carried out on an Intel i5 (750) CPU.

6 Conclusion

With the combination of propositional temporal logics and first-order theories, the framework we propose in this paper allows for a precise, yet high-level and universal formulation of behavioural properties. This helps the user to avoid modeling errors by formulating specifications describing a system on a higher level of abstraction than required for an actual implementation.

The clear separation of the aspects of time and data allows for efficient runtime verification as the different aspects are handled separately in terms of a symbolic monitor construction and solving satisfiability for first-order theories. The independent application of techniques from monitoring and SMT solving benefits from improvements in both fields.

Our implementation and the experimental evaluation show that the approach is applicable in the setting of object-oriented systems and that the runtime overhead is reasonably small. Note that this is despite the properties expressible in our framework are hard to analyze. The satisfiability problem, for example, is already undecidable for the combination of LTL and the very basic theory of identities.

References

1. Decker, N., Leucker, M., Thoma, D.: jUnit[RV]–Adding Runtime Verification to jUnit. In: Brat, G., Rungta, N., Venet, A. (eds.) NFM 2013. LNCS, vol. 7871, pp. 459–464. Springer, Heidelberg (2013)
2. Alur, R., Etessami, K., Madhusudan, P.: A temporal logic of nested calls and returns. In: Jensen, K., Podelski, A. (eds.) TACAS 2004. LNCS, vol. 2988, pp. 467–481. Springer, Heidelberg (2004)

3. Stolz, V., Bodden, E.: Temporal assertions using AspectJ. Electr. Notes Theor. Comput. Sci. (2006)

4. Goldberg, A., Havelund, K.: Automated runtime verification with EAGLE. In: MSVVEIS. INSTICC Press (2005)

5. Barringer, H., Rydeheard, D.E., Havelund, K.: Rule systems for run-time monitoring: From EAGLE to RULER. In: Sokolsky, O., Taşıran, S. (eds.) RV 2007. LNCS, vol. 4839, pp. 111–125. Springer, Heidelberg (2007)

6. Dong, W., Leucker, M., Schallhart, C.: Impartial anticipation in runtime-verification. In: Cha, S(S.), Choi, J.-Y., Kim, M., Lee, I., Viswanathan, M. (eds.) ATVA 2008. LNCS, vol. 5311, pp. 386–396. Springer, Heidelberg (2008)

7. Biere, A., Clarke, E., Raimi, R., Zhu, Y.: Verifying safety properties of a powerPC^{TM} microprocessor using symbolic model checking without BDDs. In: Halbwachs, N., Peled, D.A. (eds.) CAV 1999. LNCS, vol. 1633, pp. 60–71. Springer, Heidelberg (1999)

8. Chen, F., Roşu, G.: Parametric trace slicing and monitoring. In: Kowalewski, S., Philippou, A. (eds.) TACAS 2009. LNCS, vol. 5505, pp. 246–261. Springer, Heidelberg (2009)

9. Bauer, A., Küster, J.-C., Vegliach, G.: From propositional to first-order monitoring. In: Legay, A., Bensalem, S. (eds.) RV 2013. LNCS, vol. 8174, pp. 59–75. Springer, Heidelberg (2013)

10. Bauer, A., Leucker, M., Schallhart, C.: Monitoring of real-time properties. In: Arun-Kumar, S., Garg, N. (eds.) FSTTCS 2006. LNCS, vol. 4337, pp. 260–272. Springer, Heidelberg (2006)

11. Bauer, A., Leucker, M., Schallhart, C.: Runtime verification for LTL and TLTL. ACM Trans. Softw. Eng. Methodol. (2011)

12. Leucker, M., Sánchez, C.: Regular linear temporal logic. In: Jones, C.B., Liu, Z., Woodcock, J. (eds.) ICTAC 2007. LNCS, vol. 4711, pp. 291–305. Springer, Heidelberg (2007)

13. Decker, N., Leucker, M., Thoma, D.: Impartiality and anticipation for monitoring of visibly context-free properties. In: Legay, A., Bensalem, S. (eds.) RV 2013. LNCS, vol. 8174, pp. 183–200. Springer, Heidelberg (2013)

14. Bauer, A., Leucker, M., Schallhart, C.: The good, the bad, and the ugly, but how ugly is ugly? In: Sokolsky, O., Taşıran, S. (eds.) RV 2007. LNCS, vol. 4839, pp. 126–138. Springer, Heidelberg (2007)

15. de Moura, L., Bjørner, N.: Z3: An efficient SMT solver. In: Ramakrishnan, C.R., Rehof, J. (eds.) TACAS 2008. LNCS, vol. 4963, pp. 337–340. Springer, Heidelberg (2008)

Temporal-Logic Based Runtime Observer Pairs
for System Health Management
of Real-Time Systems[*],[**]

Thomas Reinbacher[1], Kristin Yvonne Rozier[2], and Johann Schumann[3]

[1] Vienna University of Technology, Austria
treinbacher@ecs.tuwien.ac.at
[2] NASA Ames Research Center, Moffett Field, CA, USA
Kristin.Y.Rozier@nasa.gov
[3] SGT, Inc., NASA Ames, Moffett Field, CA, USA
Johann.M.Schumann@nasa.gov

Abstract. We propose a real-time, Realizable, Responsive, Unobtrusive Unit (rt-R2U2) to meet the emerging needs for System Health Management (SHM) of new safety-critical embedded systems like automated vehicles, Unmanned Aerial Systems (UAS), or small satellites. SHM for these systems must be able to handle unexpected situations and adapt specifications quickly during flight testing between closely-timed consecutive missions, not mid-mission, necessitating fast reconfiguration. They must enable more advanced probabilistic reasoning for diagnostics and prognostics while running aboard limited hardware without affecting the certified on-board software. We define and prove correct translations of two real-time projections of Linear Temporal Logic to two types of efficient observer algorithms to continuously assess the status of the system. A *synchronous* observer yields an instant abstraction of the satisfaction check, whereas an *asynchronous* observer concretizes this abstraction at a later, a priori known, time. By feeding the system's real-time status into a statistical reasoning unit, e.g., based on Bayesian networks, we enable advanced health estimation and diagnosis. We experimentally demonstrate our novel framework on real flight data from NASA's Swift UAS. By on-boarding rt-R2U2 aboard an existing FPGA already built into the standard UAS design and seamlessly intercepting sensor values through read-only observations of the system bus, we avoid system integration problems of software instrumentation or added hardware. The flexibility of our approach with regard to changes in the monitored specification is not due to the reconfigurability offered by FPGAs; it is a benefit of the modularity of our observers and would also be available on non-reconfigurable hardware platforms such as ASICs.

1 Introduction

Autonomous and automated systems, including Unmanned Aerial Systems (UAS), rovers, and satellites, have a large number of components, e.g., sensors, actuators, and

---

[*] A full version with appendices containing full proofs of correctness for all observer algorithms is available at http://research.kristinrozier.com/TACAS14.html. This work was supported in part by the Austrian Research Agency FFG, grant 825891, and NASA grant NNX08AY50A.

[**] The rights of this work are transferred to the extent transferable according to title 17 U.S.C. 105.

E. Ábrahám and K. Havelund (Eds.): TACAS 2014, LNCS 8413, pp. 357–372, 2014.
© Springer-Verlag Berlin Heidelberg 2014

software, that must function together reliably at mission time. System Health Management (SHM) [17] can detect, isolate, and diagnose faults and possibly initiate recovery activities on such real-time systems. Effective SHM requires assessing the status of the system with respect to its specifications and estimating system health during mission time. Johnson et al. [17, Ch.1] recently highlighted the need for new, formal-methods based capabilities for modeling complex relationships among different sensor data and reasoning about timing-related requirements; computational expense prevents the current best methods for SHM from meeting operational needs.

We need a new SHM framework for real-time systems like the Swift [16] electric UAS (see Fig. 1), developed at NASA Ames. SHM for such systems requires:

RESPONSIVENESS: the SHM framework must continuously monitor the system. Deviations from the monitored specifications must be detected within a tight and a priori known time bound, enabling mitigation or rescue measures, e.g., a controlled emergency landing to avoid damage on the ground. Reporting intermediate status and satisfaction of timed requirements as early as possible is required for enabling responsive decision-making.

UNOBTRUSIVENESS: the SHM framework must not alter crucial properties of the system including *functionality* (not change behavior), *certifiability* (avoid re-certification of flight software/hardware), *timing* (not interfere with timing guarantees), and *tolerances* (not violate size, weight, power, or telemetry bandwidth constraints). Utilizing commercial-off-the-shelf (COTS) and previously proven system components is absolutely required to meet today's tight time and budget constraints; adding the SHM framework to the system must not alter these components as changes that require them to be re-certified cancel out the benefits of their use. Our goal is to create the most effective SHM capability with the limitation of read-only access to the data from COTS components.

REALIZABILITY: the SHM framework must be usable in a plug-and-play manner by providing a generic interface to connect to a wide variety of systems. The specification language must be easily understood and expressive enough to encode e.g. temporal relationships and flight rules. The framework must adapt to new specifications without a lengthy re-compilation. We must be able to efficiently monitor different requirements during different mission stages, like takeoff, approach, measurement, and return.

1.1 Related Work

Existing methods for Runtime Verification (RV) [4] assess system status by automatically generating, mainly software-based, observers to check the state of the system against a formal specification. Observations in RV are usually made accessible via software instrumentation [15]; they report only when a specification has passed or failed. Such instrumentation violates our requirements as it may make re-certification of the system onerous, alter the original timing behavior, or increase resource consumption [23]. Also, reporting only the outcomes of specifications violates our responsiveness requirement.

Systems in our applications domain often need to adhere to timing-related rules like: *after receiving the command 'takeoff' reach an altitude of* 600 ft *within five minutes.* These flight rules can be easily expressed in temporal logics; often in some flavor of linear temporal logic (LTL), as studied in [7]. Mainly due to promising complexity results [6,11], restrictions of LTL to its past-time fragment have most often been used for RV. Though specifications including past time operators may be natural for some other domains [19], flight rules require future-time reasoning. To enable more intuitive specifications, others have studied monitoring of future-time claims; see [22] for a survey and [5, 11, 14, 21, 27, 28] for algorithms and frameworks. Most of these observer algorithms, however, were designed with a software implementation in mind and require a powerful computer. There are many hardware alternatives, e.g. [12], however all either resynthesize monitors from scratch or exclude checking real-time properties [2]. Our unique approach runs the logic synthesis tool once to synthesize as many real-time observer blocks as we can fit on our platform, e.g., FPGA or ASIC; our Sec. 4.1 only interconnects these blocks. Others have proposed using Bayesian inference techniques [10] to estimate the health of a system. However, modeling timing-related behavior with dynamic Bayesian networks is very complex and quickly renders practical implementations infeasible.

1.2   Approach and Contributions

We propose a new paired-observer SHM framework allowing systems like the Swift UAS to assess their status against a temporal logic specification while enabling advanced health estimation, e.g., via discrete Bayesian networks (BN) [10] based reasoning. This novel combination of two approaches, often seen as orthogonal to each other, enables us to check timing-related aspects with our paired observers while keeping BN health models free of timing information, and thus computationally attractive. Essentially, we can enable better real-time SHM by utilizing paired temporal observers to optimize BN-based decision making. Following our requirements, we call our new SHM framework for real-time systems a rt-R2U2 (real-time, Realizable, Responsive, Unobtrusive Unit).

Our rt-R2U2 synthesizes a pair of observers for a real-time specification φ given in Metric Temporal Logic (MTL) [1] or a specialization of LTL for mission-time bounded characteristics, which we define in Sec. 2. To ensure RESPONSIVENESS of our rt-R2U2, we design two kinds of observer algorithms in Sec. 3 that verify whether φ holds at a discrete time and run them in parallel. *Synchronous* observers have small hardware footprints (max. eleven two-input gates per operator; see Theorem 3 in Sec. 4) and return an instant, three-valued abstraction {**true, false, maybe**}) of the satisfaction check of φ with every new tick of the Real Time Clock (RTC) while their *asynchronous* counterparts concretize this abstraction at a later, a priori known time. This unique approach allows us to signal early failure *and acceptance* of every specification whenever possible via the asynchronous observer. Note that previous approaches to runtime monitoring signal only specification failures; signaling *acceptance*, and particularly *early acceptance* is unique to our approach and required for supporting other system components such as prognostics engines or decision making units. Meanwhile, our synchronous observer's three-valued output gives intermediate information that a specification has not yet passed/failed, enabling probabilistic decision making via a Bayesian Network as described in [26].

We implement the rt-R2U2 in hardware as a self-contained unit, which runs externally to the system, to support UNOBTRUSIVENESS; see Sec. 4. Safety-critical embedded systems often use industrial, vehicle bus systems, such as CAN and PCI, interconnecting hardware and software components, see Fig 1. Our rt-R2U2 provides

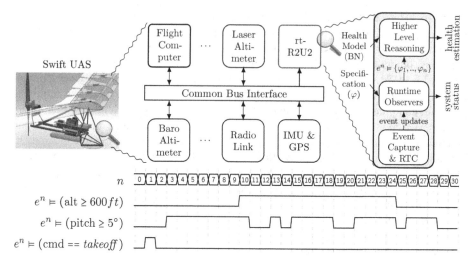

Fig. 1. rt-R2U2: An instance of our SHM framework rt-R2U2 for the NASA Swift UAS. Swift subsystems (top): The laser altimeter maps terrain and determines elevation above ground by measuring the time for a laser pulse to echo back to the UAS. The barometric altimeter determines altitude above sea level via atmospheric pressure. The inertial measurement unit (IMU) reports velocity, orientation (yaw, pitch, and roll), and gravitational forces using accelerometers, gyroscopes, and magnetometers. Running example (bottom): predicates over Swift UAS sensor data on execution e; ranging over the readings of the barometric altimeter, the pitch sensor, and the takeoff command received from the ground station; n is the time stamp as issued by the Real-Time-Clock.

generic read-only interfaces to these bus systems supporting our UNOBTRUSIVENESS requirement and sidestepping instrumentation. Events collected on these interfaces are time stamped by a RTC; progress of time is derived from the observed clock signal, resulting in a discrete time base $\mathbb{N}_0$. Events are then processed by our runtime observer pairs that check whether a specification holds on a sequence of collected events. Other RV approaches for on-the-fly observers exhibit high overhead [13,20,24] or use powerful database systems [3], thus, violate our requirements.

To meet our REALIZABILITY requirement, we design an efficient, highly parallel hardware architecture, yet keep it programmable to adapt to changes in the specification. Unlike existing approaches, our observers are designed with an efficient hardware implementation in mind, therefore, avoid recursion and expensive search through memory and aim at maximizing the benefits of the parallel nature of hardware. We synthesize rt-R2U2 *once* and generate a configuration, similar to machine code, to interconnect and configure the static hardware observer blocks of rt-R2U2, adapting to new specifications without running CAD or compilation tools like previous approaches. UAS have very limited bandwidth constraints; transferring a lightweight configuration is preferable to transferring a new image for the whole hardware design. The checks computed by these runtime observers represent the system's status and can be utilized by a higher level reasoner, such as a human operator, Bayesian network, or otherwise, to compute a health estimation, i.e., a conditional probability expressing the belief that a certain subsystem is healthy, given the status of the system. In this paper, we compute these health estimations by adapting the BN-based inference algorithms of [10] in hardware. Our contributions include synthesis and integration of the synchronous/asynchronous observer pairs, a modular hardware implementation, and execution of a proof-of-concept rt-R2U2 running on a self-contained Field Programmable Gate Array (FPGA) (Sec. 5).

2   Real-Time Projections of LTL

MTL replaces the temporal operators of LTL with operators that respect time bounds [1].

Definition 1 (Discrete-Time MTL). *For atomic proposition* $\sigma \in \Sigma$, σ *is a formula. Let time bound* $J = [t, t']$ *with* $t, t' \in \mathbb{N}_0$. *If* φ *and* ψ *are formulas, then so are:*

$$\neg\varphi \mid \varphi \wedge \psi \mid \varphi \vee \psi \mid \varphi \rightarrow \psi \mid \mathcal{X}\varphi \mid \varphi \mathcal{U}_J \psi \mid \Box_J \varphi \mid \Diamond_J \varphi.$$

Time bounds are specified as intervals: for $t, t' \in \mathbb{N}_0$, we write $[t, t']$ for the set $\{i \in \mathbb{N}_0 \mid t \leq i \leq t'\}$. We use the functions $\min, \max, \mathrm{dur}$, to extract the lower time bound (t), the upper time bound (t'), and the duration ($t' - t$) of J. We define the satisfaction relation of an MTL formula as follows: an execution $e = (s_n)$ for $n \geq 0$ is an infinite sequence of states. For an MTL formula φ, time $n \in \mathbb{N}_0$ and execution e, we define φ *holds at time n of execution e*, denoted $e^n \vDash \varphi$, inductively as follows:

$e^n \vDash true$ is **true**, $e^n \vDash \sigma$ iff σ holds in s_n, $e^n \vDash \neg\varphi$ iff $e^n \nvDash \varphi$,

$e^n \vDash \varphi \wedge \psi$ iff $e^n \vDash \varphi$ and $e^n \vDash \psi$, $e^n \vDash \mathcal{X}\varphi$ iff $e^{n+1} \vDash \varphi$,

$e^n \vDash \varphi \mathcal{U}_J \psi$ iff $\exists i (i \geq n) : (i - n \in J \wedge e^i \vDash \psi \wedge \forall j (n \leq j < i) : e^j \vDash \varphi)$.

With the dualities $\Diamond_J \varphi \equiv \mathbf{true}\, \mathcal{U}_J\, \varphi$ and $\neg \Diamond_J \neg\varphi \equiv \Box_J\, \varphi$ we arrive at two additional operators: $\Box_J\, \varphi$ (*φ is an invariant within the future interval J*) and $\Diamond_J \varphi$ (*φ holds eventually within the future interval J*). In order to efficiently encode specifications in practice, we introduce two special cases of $\Box_J\, \varphi$ and $\Diamond_J \varphi$: $\blacksquare_\tau \varphi \equiv \Box_{[0,\tau]}\, \varphi$ (*φ is an invariant within the next τ time units*) and $\blacklozenge_\tau \varphi \equiv \Diamond_{[0,\tau]} \varphi$ (*φ holds eventually within the next τ time units*). For example, the flight rule from Sec. 1, "After receiving the takeoff command reach an altitude of $600\,ft$ within five minutes," is efficiently captured in MTL by $(cmd == takeoff) \rightarrow \blacklozenge_5(alt \geq 600\,ft)$, assuming a time-base of one minute and the atomic propositions $(alt \geq 600\,ft)$ and $(cmd == takeoff)$ as in Fig. 1.

Systems in our application domain are usually bounded to a certain mission time. For example, the Swift UAS has a limited air-time, depending on the available battery capacity and predefined waypoints. We capitalize on this property to intuitively monitor standard LTL requirements using a mission-time bounded projection of LTL.

Definition 2 (Mission-Time LTL). *For a given LTL formula* ξ *and a mission time* $t_m \in \mathbb{N}_0$, *we denote by* ξ_m *the mission-time bounded equivalent of* ξ, *where* ξ_m *is obtained by replacing every* $\Box\varphi$, $\Diamond\varphi$, *and* $\varphi\, \mathcal{U}\, \psi$ *operator in* ξ *by the* $\blacksquare_\tau \varphi$, $\blacklozenge_\tau \varphi$, *and* $\varphi\, \mathcal{U}_J\, \psi$ *operators of MTL, where* $J = [0, t_m]$ *and* $\tau = t_m$.

Inputs to rt-R2U2 are time-stamped events, collected incrementally from the system.

Definition 3 (Execution Sequence). *An execution sequence for an MTL formula* φ, *denoted by* $\langle T_\varphi \rangle$, *is a sequence of tuples* $T_\varphi = (v, \tau_e)$ *where* $\tau_e \in \mathbb{N}_0$ *is a time stamp and* $v \in \{\mathbf{true}, \mathbf{false}, \mathbf{maybe}\}$ *is a verdict.*

We use a superscript integer to access a particular element in $\langle T_\varphi \rangle$, e.g., $\langle T_\varphi^0 \rangle$ is the first element in execution sequence $\langle T_\varphi \rangle$. We write $T_\varphi . \tau_e$ to access τ_e and $T_\varphi . v$ to access v of such an element. We say T_φ holds if $T_\varphi.v$ is **true** and T_φ does not hold if $T_\varphi.v$ is **false**. For a given execution sequence $\langle T_\varphi \rangle = \langle T_\varphi^0 \rangle, \langle T_\varphi^1 \rangle, \langle T_\varphi^2 \rangle, \langle T_\varphi^3 \rangle, \ldots$, the tuple accessed by $\langle T_\varphi^i \rangle$ corresponds to a section of an execution e as follows: for all times $n \in [\langle T_\varphi^{i-1} \rangle.\tau_e + 1, \langle T_\varphi^i \rangle.\tau_e]$, $e^n \models \varphi$ in case $\langle T_\varphi^i \rangle.v$ is **true** and $e^n \nvDash \varphi$ in case $\langle T_\varphi^i \rangle.v$ is **false**. In case $\langle T_\varphi^i \rangle$ is **maybe**, neither $e^n \models \varphi$ nor $e^n \nvDash \varphi$ is defined.

In the remainder of this paper, we will frequently refer to execution sequences collected from the Swift UAS as shown in Fig. 1. The predicates shown are atomic propositions over sensor data in our specifications and are sampled with every new time stamp n issued by the RTC. For example, $\langle T_{\text{pitch} \geq 5°} \rangle = ((\textbf{false}, 0), (\textbf{false}, 1), (\textbf{false}, 2), (\textbf{true}, 3), \ldots, (\textbf{true}, 17), (\textbf{true}, 18))$ describes $e^n \models (\text{pitch} \geq 5°)$ sampled over $n \in [0, 18]$ and $\langle T_{\text{pitch} \geq 5°} \rangle$ holds 19 elements.

3 Asynchronous and Synchronous Observers

The problem of monitoring a real-time specification has been studied extensively in the past; see [8, 22] for an overview. Solutions include: (a) translating the temporal formula into a finite-state automaton that accepts all the models of the specification [11, 12, 14, 28], (b) restricting MTL to its *safety* fragment and waiting until the operators' time bounds have elapsed to decide the truth value afterwards [5, 21], and (c) restricting LTL to its past-time fragment [6, 11, 24]. Compiling new observers to automata as in (a) requires re-running the logic synthesis tool to yield a new hardware observer, in automaton or autogenerated VHDL code format as described in [12], which may take dozens of minutes to complete, violating the REALIZABILITY requirement. Observers generated by (b) are in conflict with the RESPONSIVENESS requirement and (c) do not natively support flight rules. Our observers provide UNOBTRUSIVENESS via a self-contained hardware implementation. To enable such an implementation, our design needs to refrain from dynamic memory, linked lists, and recursion – commonly used in existing software-based observers, however, not natively available in hardware.

Our two types of runtime observers differ in the times when new outputs are generated and in the resource footprints required to implement them. A *synchronous* (time-triggered) observer is trimmed towards a minimalistic hardware footprint and computes a three-valued abstraction of the satisfaction check for the specification with each tick of the RTC, without considering events happening after the current time. An *asynchronous* (event-triggered) observer concretizes this abstraction at a later, a priori known, time and makes use of synchronization queues to take events into account that occur after the current time.[1] Our novel parallel composition of these two observers updates the status of the system at every tick of the RTC, yielding great responsiveness. An inconclusive answer when we can't yet know **true/false** is still beneficial as the higher-level reasoning part of our rt-R2U2 supports reasoning with inconclusive inputs. This allows us to derive an intermediate estimation of system health with the option to initiate fault mitigation actions even without explicitly knowing all inputs. If exact reasoning is required, we can re-evaluate system health when the *asynchronous* observer provides exact answers.

---

[1] Similar terms have been used by others [9] to refer to monitoring with pairs of observers that do not update with the RTC, incur delays dangerous to a UAS, and require system interaction that violates our requirements (Sec. 1).

In the remainder of this section, we discuss[2] both *asynchronous* and *synchronous* observers for the operators $\neg\, \varphi$, $\varphi \wedge \psi$, $\blacksquare_\tau\, \varphi$, $\square_J\, \varphi$, and $\varphi\, \mathcal{U}_J\, \psi$. Informally, an MTL observer is an algorithm that takes execution sequences as input and produces another execution sequence as output. For a given unary operator $\bullet$, we say that an observer algorithm implements $e^n \vDash \bullet\, \varphi$, iff for all execution sequences $\langle T_\varphi \rangle$ as input, it produces an execution sequence as output that evaluates $e^n \vDash \bullet\, \varphi$ (analogous for binary operators).

3.1 Asynchronous Observers

The main characteristic of our asynchronous observers is that they are *evaluated with every new input tuple* and that for every generated output tuple T we have that $T.v \in \{\mathbf{true}, \mathbf{false}\}$ and $T.\tau_e \in [0, n]$. Since verdicts are exact evaluations of a future-time specification φ for each clock tick they may resolve φ for clock ticks prior to the current time n if the information required for this resolution was not available until n.

Our observers distinguish two types of transitions of the signals described by execution sequences. We say transition $\underline{\quad\Gamma}$ of execution sequence $\langle T_\varphi \rangle$ occurs at time $n = \langle T_\varphi^i \rangle.\tau_e + 1$ iff $(\langle T_\varphi^i \rangle.v \oplus \langle T_\varphi^{i+1} \rangle.v) \wedge \langle T_\varphi^{i+1} \rangle.v$ holds. Similarly, we say transition $\overline{\Gamma\quad}$ of execution sequence $\langle T_\varphi \rangle$ occurs at time $n = \langle T_\varphi^i \rangle.\tau_e + 1$ iff $(\langle T_\varphi^i \rangle.v \oplus \langle T_\varphi^{i+1} \rangle.v) \wedge \langle T_\varphi^i \rangle.v$ holds ($\oplus$ denotes the Boolean exclusive-or). For example, transitions $\underline{\quad\Gamma}$ and $\overline{\Gamma\quad}$ of $\langle T_{\text{pitch} \geq 5°} \rangle$ in Fig. 1 occur at times 3 and 11, respectively.

Negation ($\neg\, \varphi$). The observer for $\neg\, \varphi$, as stated in Alg. 1, is straightforward: for every input T_φ we negate the truth value of $T_\varphi.v$. The observer generates $(\ldots, (\mathbf{true}, 2), (\mathbf{false}, 3), \ldots)$.

Invariant within the Next τ Time Stamps ($\blacksquare_\tau\, \varphi$). An observer for $\blacksquare_\tau\, \varphi$ requires registers $m_{\uparrow\varphi}$ and m_{τ_s} with domain $\mathbb{N}_0$: $m_{\uparrow\varphi}$ holds the time stamp of the latest $\underline{\quad\Gamma}$ transition of $\langle T_\varphi \rangle$ whereas m_{τ_s} holds the start time of the next tuple in $\langle T_\varphi \rangle$. For the observer in Alg. 2, the check $m \leq (T_\varphi.\tau_e - \tau)$ in line 8 tests whether φ held for at least the previous τ time stamps. To illustrate the algorithm, consider an observer for $\blacksquare_5$ (pitch $\geq 5°$) and the execution in Fig. 1. At time $n = 0$, we have $m_{\uparrow\varphi} = 0$ and since $\langle T_{\text{pitch} \geq 5°}^0 \rangle$ does not hold the output is $(\mathbf{false}, 0)$. Similarly, the outputs for $n \in [1, 2]$ are $(\mathbf{false}, 1)$ and $(\mathbf{false}, 2)$. At time $n = 3$, a $\underline{\quad\Gamma}$ transition of $\langle T_{\text{pitch} \geq 5°} \rangle$ occurs, thus $m_{\uparrow\varphi} = 3$. Since the check in line 8 does not hold, the algorithm does not generate a new output, i.e., returns $(\lrcorner, \lrcorner)$ designating output is delayed until a later time, which repeats at times $n \in [4, 7]$. At $n = 8$, the check in line 8 holds and the algorithm returns $(\mathbf{true}, 3)$. Likewise, the outputs for $n \in [9, 10]$ are $(\mathbf{true}, 4)$ and $(\mathbf{true}, 5)$. At $n = 11$, $\langle T_{\text{pitch} \geq 5°}^{11} \rangle$ does not hold and the algorithm outputs $(\mathbf{false}, 11)$. We note the ability of the observer to *re-synchronize* its output with respect to its inputs and the RTC. For $n \in [8, 10]$, outputs are given for a time prior to n, however, at $n = 11$ the observer re-synchronizes: the output $(\mathbf{false}, 11)$ signifies that $e^n \nvDash \blacksquare_5$ (pitch $\geq 5°$) for $n \in [6, 11]$. By the equivalence $\blacklozenge_\tau\, \varphi \equiv \neg\blacksquare_\tau\neg\varphi$, we immediately arrive at an observer for $\blacklozenge_\tau\, \varphi$ from Alg. 2 by negating both the input and the output tuple.

---

[2] Proofs of correctness for every observer algorithm appear in the Appendix.

Algorithm 1. Observer for $\neg \varphi$.

1: At each new input T_φ:
2: $T_\xi \leftarrow (\neg T_\varphi.v, T_\varphi.\tau_e)$
3: **return** T_ξ

Algorithm 2. Observer for $\blacksquare_\tau \varphi$. Initially, $m_{\uparrow \varphi} = m_{\tau_s} = 0$.

1: At each new input T_φ:
2: $T_\xi \leftarrow T_\varphi$
3: **if** $\underline{\Gamma}$ transition of T_ξ occurs **then**
4: $\quad m_{\uparrow \varphi} \leftarrow m_{\tau_s}$
5: **end if**
6: $m_{\tau_s} \leftarrow T_\varphi.\tau_e + 1$
7: **if** T_ξ holds **then**
8: $\quad$ **if** $m_{\uparrow \varphi} \leq (T_\xi.\tau_e - \tau)$ holds **then**
9: $\quad\quad T_\xi.\tau_e \leftarrow T_\xi.\tau_e - \tau$
10: $\quad$ **else**
11: $\quad\quad T_\xi \leftarrow (\lrcorner, \lrcorner)$
12: $\quad$ **end if**
13: **end if**
14: **return** T_ξ

Algorithm 3. Observer for $\varphi \wedge \psi$.

1: At each new input (T_φ, T_ψ):
2: **if** T_φ holds and T_ψ holds and $q_\varphi \neq ()$ holds and $q_\psi \neq ()$ holds **then**
3: $\quad T_\xi \leftarrow (\textbf{true}, \min(T_\varphi.\tau_e, T_\psi.\tau_e))$
4: **else if** $\neg T_\varphi$ holds and $\neg T_\psi$ holds and $q_\varphi \neq ()$ and $q_\psi \neq ()$ holds **then**
5: $\quad T_\xi \leftarrow (\textbf{false}, \max(T_\varphi.\tau_e, T_\psi.\tau_e))$
6: **else if** $\neg T_\varphi$ holds and $q_\varphi \neq ()$ holds **then**
7: $\quad T_\xi \leftarrow (\textbf{false}, T_\varphi.\tau_e)$
8: **else if** $\neg T_\psi$ holds and $q_\psi \neq ()$ holds **then**
9: $\quad T_\xi \leftarrow (\textbf{false}, T_\psi.\tau_e)$
10: **else**
11: $\quad T_\xi \leftarrow (\lrcorner, \lrcorner)$
12: **end if**
13: $\text{dequeue}(q_\varphi, q_\psi, T_\xi.\tau_e)$
14: **return** T_ξ

Algorithm 4. Observer for $\square_J \varphi$.

1: At each new input T_φ:
2: $T_\xi \leftarrow \blacksquare_{\mathrm{dur}(J)} T_\varphi$
3: **if** $(T_\xi.\tau_e - \min(J) \geq 0)$ **then**
4: $\quad T_\xi.\tau_e \leftarrow T_\xi.\tau_e - \min(J)$
5: **else**
6: $\quad T_\xi \leftarrow (\lrcorner, \lrcorner)$
7: **end if**
8: **return** T_ξ

Algorithm 5. Observer for $\varphi \mathcal{U}_J \psi$. Initially, $m_{pre} = m_{\uparrow \varphi} = 0$, $m_{\downarrow \varphi} = -\infty$, and $p = \textbf{false}$.

1: At each new input (T_φ, T_ψ) in lockstep mode:
2: **if** $\underline{\Gamma}$ transition of T_φ occurs **then**
3: $\quad m_{\uparrow \varphi} \leftarrow \tau_e - 1$
4: $\quad m_{pre} \leftarrow -\infty$
5: **end if**
6: **if** $\overline{}\!\!\mathsf{L}$ transition of T_φ occurs and T_ψ holds **then**
7: $\quad T_\varphi.v, p \leftarrow \textbf{true}, \textbf{true}$
8: $\quad m_{\downarrow \varphi} \leftarrow \tau_e$
9: **end if**
10: **if** T_φ holds **then**
11: $\quad$ **if** T_ψ holds **then**
12: $\quad\quad$ **if** $(m_{\uparrow \varphi} + \min(J) < \tau_e)$ holds **then**
13: $\quad\quad\quad m_{pre} \leftarrow \tau_e$
14: $\quad\quad\quad$ **return** $(\textbf{true}, \tau_e - \min(J))$
15: $\quad\quad$ **else if** p holds **then**
16: $\quad\quad\quad$ **return** $(\textbf{false}, m_{\downarrow \varphi})$
17: $\quad\quad$ **end if**
18: $\quad$ **else if** $(m_{pre} + \mathrm{dur}(J) \leq \tau_e)$ holds **then**
19: $\quad\quad$ **return** $(\textbf{false}, \max(m_{\uparrow \varphi}, \tau_e - \max(J)))$
20: $\quad$ **end if**
21: **else**
22: $\quad p \leftarrow \textbf{false}$
23: $\quad$ **if** $(\min(J) = 0)$ holds **then**
24: $\quad\quad$ **return** $(T_\psi.v, \tau_e)$
25: $\quad$ **end if**
26: $\quad$ **return** $(\textbf{false}, \tau_e)$
27: **end if**
28: **return** $(\lrcorner, \lrcorner)$

Invariant within Future Interval ($\square_J \varphi$). The observer for $\square_J \varphi$, as stated in Alg. 4, builds on an observer for $\blacksquare_\tau \varphi$ and makes use of the equivalence $\blacksquare_\tau \varphi \equiv \square_{[0,\tau]} \varphi$. Intuitively, the observer for $\blacksquare_\tau \varphi$ returns true iff φ holds for at least the next τ time units. We can thus construct an observer for $\square_J \varphi$ by reusing the algorithm for $\blacksquare_\tau \varphi$, assigning $\tau = \mathrm{dur}(J)$ and shifting the obtained output by $\min(J)$ time stamps into the past. From the equivalence $\diamondsuit_J \varphi \equiv \neg \square_J \neg \varphi$, we can immediately derive an observer for $\diamondsuit_J \varphi$ from the observer for $\square_J \varphi$. To illustrate the algorithm, consider an observer for $\square_{5,10}$ (alt $\geq 600 ft$) over the execution in Fig. 1. For $n \in [0, 4]$ the algorithm returns $(\lrcorner, \lrcorner)$, since $((T^{0...4}_{\mathrm{alt} \geq 600 ft}).\tau_e - 5) \geq 0$ (line 3 of Alg. 4) does not hold. At $n = 5$ the underlying observer for $\blacksquare_5$ (alt $\geq 600 ft$) returns $(\textbf{false}, 5)$, which is transformed (by line 4) into the output $(\textbf{false}, 0)$. For similar arguments, the outputs for $n \in [6, 9]$ are $(\textbf{false}, 1)$, $(\textbf{false}, 2)$, $(\textbf{false}, 3)$, and $(\textbf{false}, 4)$. At $n \in [10, 14]$, the observer for $\blacksquare_5$ (alt $\geq 600 ft$) returns $(\lrcorner, \lrcorner)$. At $n = 15$, $\blacksquare_5$ (alt $\geq 600 ft$) yields $(\textbf{true}, 10)$, which is transformed (by line 4) into the output is $(\textbf{true}, 5)$. Note also that $\mathcal{X} \varphi \equiv \square_{[1,1]} \varphi$.

The remaining observers for the binary operators $\varphi \wedge \psi$ and $\varphi \, \mathcal{U}_J \, \psi$ take tuples (T_φ, T_ψ) as inputs, where T_φ is from $\langle T_\varphi \rangle$ and T_ψ is from $\langle T_\psi \rangle$. Since $\langle T_\varphi \rangle$ and $\langle T_\psi \rangle$ are execution sequences produced by two different observers, the two elements of the input tuple (T_φ, T_ψ) are not necessarily generated at the same time. Our observers for binary MTL operators thus use two FIFO-organized *synchronization queues* to buffer parts of $\langle T_\varphi \rangle$ and $\langle T_\psi \rangle$, respectively. For a synchronization queue q we denote by $q = (\,)$ its emptiness and by $|q|$ its size.

Conjunction ($\varphi \wedge \psi$). The observer for $\varphi \wedge \psi$, as stated in Alg. 3, reads inputs (T_φ, T_ψ) from two synchronization queues, q_φ and q_ψ. Intuitively, the algorithm follows the rules for conjunction in Boolean logic with additional emptiness checks on q_φ and q_ψ. The procedure **dequeue**$(q_\varphi, q_\psi, T_\xi.\tau_e)$ drops all entries T_φ in q_φ for which the following holds: $T_\varphi.\tau_e \leq T_\xi.\tau_e$ (analogous for q_ψ). To illustrate the algorithm, consider an observer for $\blacksquare_5$ (alt $\geq 600\,ft$) $\wedge$ (pitch $\geq 5°$) and the execution in Fig. 1. For $n \in [0, 9]$ the two observers for the involved subformulas immediately output (**false**, n). For $n \in [10, 14]$, the observer for $\blacksquare_5$ (alt $\geq 600\,ft$) returns $(\_, \_)$, while in the meantime, the atomic proposition (pitch $\geq 5°$) toggles its truth value several times, i.e., (**true**, 10), (**false**, 11), (**false**, 12), (**true**, 13), (**false**, 14). These tuples need to be buffered in queue $q_{\text{pitch} \geq 5°}$ until the observer for $\blacksquare_5$ (alt $\geq 600\,ft$) generates its next output, i.e., (**true**, 10) at $n = 15$. We apply the function **aggregate**$(\langle T_\varphi \rangle)$, which repeatedly replaces two consecutive elements $\langle T_\varphi^i \rangle, \langle T_\varphi^{i+1} \rangle$ in $\langle T_\varphi \rangle$ by $\langle T_\varphi^{i+1} \rangle$ iff $\langle T_\varphi^i \rangle.v = \langle T_\varphi^{i+1} \rangle.v$, to the content of $q_{\text{pitch} \geq 5°}$ once every time an element is added to $q_{\text{pitch} \geq 5°}$. Therefore, at $n = 15$: $q_{\text{pitch} \geq 5°} = ((\textbf{true}, 10), (\textbf{false}, 12), (\textbf{true}, 13), (\textbf{false}, 14), (\textbf{true}, 15))$ and $q_{\blacksquare_5 \, (\text{alt} \geq 600ft)} = ((\textbf{true}, 10))$. The observer returns (**true**, 10) (line 3) and **dequeue**$(q_\varphi, q_\psi, 10)$ yields: $q_{\text{pitch} \geq 5°} = ((\textbf{false}, 12), (\textbf{true}, 13), (\textbf{false}, 14), (\textbf{true}, 15))$ and $q_{\blacksquare_5 \, (\text{alt} \geq 600ft)} = (\,)$.

Until within Future Interval ($\varphi \, \mathcal{U}_J \, \psi$). The observer for $\varphi \, \mathcal{U}_J \, \psi$, as stated in Alg. 5, reads inputs (T_φ, T_ψ) from two synchronization queues and makes use of a Boolean flag p and three registers $m_{\uparrow\varphi}$, $m_{\downarrow\varphi}$, and m_{pre} with domain $\mathbb{N}_0 \cup \{-\infty\}$: $m_{\uparrow\varphi}$ ($m_{\downarrow\varphi}$) holds the time stamp of the latest $\_\!\_\!\Gamma$ transition ($\neg\!\_\!\_$ transition) of $\langle T_\varphi \rangle$ and m_{pre} holds the latest time stamp where the observer detected $\varphi \, \mathcal{U}_J \, \psi$ to hold. Input tuples (T_φ, T_ψ) for the observer are read from synchronization queues in a *lockstep* mode: (T_φ, T_ψ) is split into (T'_φ, T'_ψ), where $T'_\varphi.\tau_e = T'_\psi.\tau_e$ and the time stamp $T''_\varphi.\tau_e$ of the next tuple (T''_φ, T''_ψ) is $T'_\varphi.\tau_e + 1$. This ensures that the observer outputs only a single tuple at each run and avoids output buffers, which would account for additional hardware resources (see correctness proof in the Appendix for a discussion). Intuitively, if T_φ does not hold (lines 22-26) the observer is synchronous to its input and immediately outputs (**false**, $T_\varphi.\tau_e$). If T_φ holds (lines 11-20) the time stamp n' of the output tuple is not necessarily *synchronous* to the time stamp $T_\varphi.\tau_e$ of the input anymore, however, bounded by $(T_\varphi.\tau_e - \max(J)) \leq n' \leq T_\varphi.\tau_e$ (see Lemma "*unrolling*" in the Appendix). To illustrate the algorithm, consider an observer for (pitch $\geq 5°$) $\mathcal{U}_{[5,10]}$ (alt $\geq 600\,ft$) over the execution in Fig. 1. At time $n = 0$, we have $m_{pre} = 0$, $m_{\uparrow\varphi} = 0$, and $m_{\downarrow\varphi} = -\infty$ and since $\langle T_{\text{pitch} \geq 5°}^0 \rangle$ does not hold, the observer outputs (**false**, 0) in line 26. The outputs for $n \in [1, 2]$ are (**false**, 1) and (**false**, 2). At time $n = 3$, a $\_\!\_\!\Gamma$ transition of $\langle T_{\text{pitch} \geq 5°} \rangle$ occurs, thus we assign $m_{\uparrow\varphi} = 2$ and $m_{pre} = -\infty$ (lines 3 and 4). Since

$\langle T^3_{\text{pitch} \geq 5°} \rangle$ holds and $\langle T^3_{\text{alt} \geq 600ft} \rangle$ does not hold, the predicate in line 18 is evaluated, which holds and the algorithm returns $\langle \textbf{false}, \max(2, 3 - 10) \rangle = \langle \textbf{false}, 2 \rangle$. Thus, the observer does not yield a new output in this case, which repeats for times $n \in [4, 9]$. At time $n = 10$, a $\_\!\!\Gamma$ transition of $\langle T_{\text{alt} \geq 600ft} \rangle$ occurs and the predicate in line 12 is evaluated. Since $(2 + 5) < 10$ holds, the algorithm returns $(\textbf{true}, 5)$, revealing that $e^n \models (\text{pitch} \geq 5°) \, \mathcal{U}_{[5,10]} \, (\text{alt} \geq 600ft)$ for $n \in [3, 5]$. At time $n = 11$, a $\neg\!\!\llcorner$ transition of $\langle T_{\text{pitch} \geq 5°} \rangle$ occurs and since $\langle T^{11}_{\text{alt} \geq 600ft} \rangle$ holds, p and the truth value of the current input $\langle T^{11}_{\text{pitch} \geq 5°} \rangle.v$ are set **true** and $m_{\downarrow \varphi} = 11$. Again, line 12 is evaluated and the algorithm returns $(\textbf{true}, 6)$. At time $n = 12$, since $\langle T^{12}_{\text{pitch} \geq 5°} \rangle$ does not hold, we clear p in line 22 and the algorithm returns $(\textbf{false}, 12)$ in line 26, i.e., $e^n \not\models (\text{pitch} \geq 5°) \, \mathcal{U}_{[5,10]} \, (\text{alt} \geq 600ft)$ for $n \in [7, 12]$. At time $n = 13$, a $\_\!\!\Gamma$ transition of $\langle T_{\text{pitch} \geq 5°} \rangle$ occurs, thus $m_{\uparrow \varphi} = 12$ and $m_{pre} = -\infty$. The predicates in line 12 and 15 do not hold, the algorithm returns no new output in line 28. At time $n = 14$, a $\neg\!\!\llcorner$ transition of $\langle T_{\text{pitch} \geq 5°} \rangle$ occurs, thus p and $\langle T^{14}_{\text{pitch} \geq 5°} \rangle.v$ are set **true** and $m_{\downarrow \varphi} = 14$. The predicate in line 15 holds, and the algorithm outputs $(\textbf{false}, 14)$, revealing that $e^n \not\models (\text{pitch} \geq 5°) \, \mathcal{U}_{[5,10]} \, (\text{alt} \geq 600ft)$ for $n \in [13, 14]$.

3.2 Synchronous Observers

The main characteristic of our synchronous observers is that they are evaluated at every tick of the RTC and that their output tuples T are guaranteed to be synchronous to the current time stamp n. Thus, for each time n, a synchronous observer outputs a tuple T with $T.\tau_e = n$. This eliminates the need for synchronization queues. Inputs and outputs of these observers are execution sequences with three-valued verdicts. The underlying abstraction is given by $\widehat{\textbf{eval}} : \boxtimes \rightarrow \{\textbf{true}, \textbf{false}, \textbf{maybe}\}$, where $\boxtimes \in \{\neg\varphi, \varphi \wedge \psi, \blacksquare_\tau \varphi, \square_J \varphi, \varphi \, \mathcal{U}_J \, \psi\}$. The implementation of $\widehat{\textbf{eval}} (\neg\varphi)$ and $\widehat{\textbf{eval}} (\varphi \wedge \psi)$ follows the rules for Kleene logic [18]. For the remaining operators we define the verdict $T_\xi.v$ of the output tuple $(T_\xi.v, n)$, generated for inputs $(T_\varphi.v, n)$ (respectively $(T_\psi.v, n)$ for $\varphi \, \mathcal{U}_J \, \psi$), as:

$$\widehat{\textbf{eval}} (\blacksquare_\tau \varphi) = \begin{cases} \textbf{true} & \text{if } T_\varphi.v \text{ holds and } \tau = 0, \\ \textbf{false} & \text{if } T_\varphi.v \text{ does not hold}, \\ \textbf{maybe} & \text{otherwise.} \end{cases}$$

$$\widehat{\textbf{eval}} (\square_J \varphi) = \textbf{maybe}.$$

$$\widehat{\textbf{eval}} (\varphi \, \mathcal{U}_J \, \psi) = \begin{cases} \textbf{true} & \text{if } T_\varphi.v \text{ and } T_\psi.v \text{ holds} \\ & \text{and } \min(J) = 0, \\ \textbf{false} & \text{if } T_\varphi.v \text{ does not hold}, \\ \textbf{maybe} & \text{otherwise.} \end{cases}$$

To illustrate our synchronous observer algorithms, consider the previously discussed formula $\blacksquare_5 (\text{alt} \geq 600ft) \wedge (\text{pitch} \geq 5°)$, which we want to evaluate using the synchronous observer:

$$\xi = \widehat{\textbf{eval}} (\widehat{\textbf{eval}} (\blacksquare_5 (\text{alt} \geq 600ft)) \wedge (\text{pitch} \geq 5°))$$

For $n \in [0, 9]$, as in the case of the *asynchronous* observer, we can immediately output $(\textbf{false}, n)$. At $n = 10$, $\widehat{\textbf{eval}} (\blacksquare_5 (\text{alt} \geq 600ft))$ yields $(\textbf{maybe}, n)$, thus, the observer is inconclusive about the truth value of $e^{10} \models \xi$. At $n \in [11, 12]$ since $(\text{pitch} \geq 5°)$ does not hold, the outputs are $(\textbf{false}, n)$. For analogous arguments, the output at $n = 13$ is $(\textbf{maybe}, 13)$, at $n = 14$ $(\textbf{false}, 14)$, and at $n = 15$ $(\textbf{maybe}, 15)$. In this way, at times

$n \in \{11, 12, 14\}$ the synchronous observer completes early evaluation of ξ, producing output that would, without the abstraction, be guaranteed by the exact asynchronous observer with a delay of 5 time units, i.e., at times $n \in \{16, 17, 19\}$.

4 Mapping Observers into Efficient Hardware

We introduce a mapping of the observer pairs into efficient hardware blocks and a synthesis procedure to generate a configuration for these blocks from an arbitrary MTL specification. This configuration is loaded into the control unit of our rt-R2U2, where it changes the interconnections between a pool of (static) hardware observer blocks and assigns memory regions for synchronization queues. This approach enables us to quickly change the monitored specification (within resource limitations) without re-compiling the rt-R2U2's hardware, supporting our REALIZABILITY requirement.

Asynchronous observers require arithmetic operations on time stamps. Registers and flags as required by the observer algorithm are mapped to circuits that can store information, such as flip-flops. For the synchronization queues we turn to block RAMs (abundant on FPGAs), organized as ring buffers. Time stamps are internally stored in registers of width $w = \lceil log_2(n) \rceil + 2$, to indicate $-\infty$ and to allow overflows when performing arithmetical operations on time stamps. Subtraction and relational operators as required by the observer for $\blacksquare_\tau \, \varphi$ (Fig. 2) can be built around adders. For example, the check in line 8 of Alg. 2 is implemented using two w-bit wide adders: one for $q = T_\varphi.\tau_e - \tau$ and one to decide whether $m_{\uparrow\varphi} \geq q$. A third adder runs in parallel and assigns a new value to m_{τ_s} (line 6 of Alg. 2). Detecting a $\_\!\!\!\Gamma$ transition on $\langle T_\varphi \rangle$ maps to an XOR gate and an AND gate, implementing the circuit $(T_\varphi^{i-1}.v \oplus T_\varphi^i.v) \wedge T_\varphi^i.v$, where $T_\varphi^{i-1}.v$ is the truth value of the previous input, stored in a flip-flop. The multiplexer either writes a new output or sets a flag to indicate $(\_, \_)$.

Synchronous observers do not require calculations on time stamps and directly map to basic digital logic gates. Fig. 2 shows a circuit representing an $\widehat{\mathbf{eval}}\,(\blacksquare_\tau \, \varphi)$ observer that accounts for one two-input AND gate, one two-input OR gate, and two Inverter gates. Inputs (i_1, i_2) and outputs (y_1, y_2) are encoded (to project the three-valued logic into Boolean logic) such as: **true** $(0, 0)$, **false** $(0, 1)$, and **maybe** $(1, 0)$. Input j is set if $\tau_e = 0$ and cleared otherwise.

4.1 Synthesizing a Configuration for the rt-R2U2

The synthesis procedure to translate an MTL specification ξ into a configuration such that the rt-R2U2 instantiates observers for both ξ and $\widehat{\mathbf{eval}}\,(\xi)$, works as follows:

- Preprocessing. By the equivalences given in Sect. 2 rewrite ξ to ξ', such that operators in ξ' are from $\{\neg\,\varphi, \varphi \wedge \psi, \blacksquare_\tau \, \varphi, \square_J \, \varphi, \varphi \, \mathcal{U}_J \, \psi\}$ (**SA1**).
- Parsing. Parse ξ' to obtain an Abstract Syntax Tree (AST), denoted by AST(ξ'). The leaves of this tree are the atomic propositions Σ of ξ' (**SA2**).
- Allocating observers. For all nodes q in AST(ξ') allocate both the corresponding synchronous and the asynchronous hardware observer block (**SA3**).
- Adding synchronization queues. $\forall q \in$ AST(ξ'): If q is of type $\varphi \wedge \psi$ or $\varphi \, \mathcal{U}_J \, \psi$ add queues q_φ and q_ψ to the inputs of the respective asynchronous observer (**MA1**).

Algorithm 6. Assigning synchronization queue sizes for $AST(\xi')$. Let S be a set of nodes; Initially: $w = 0$, add all Σ nodes of $AST(\xi')$ to S; The function wcd : $\boxplus \rightarrow \mathbb{N}_0$ calculates the *worst-case-delay* an asynchronous observer may introduce by: $wcd(\neg \varphi) = wcd(\varphi \wedge \psi) = 0$, $wcd(\blacksquare_\tau \varphi) = \tau$, $wcd(\square_J \varphi) = wcd(\varphi \, \mathcal{U}_J \, \psi) = \max(J)$.

```
 1: while S is not empty do
 2:     s, w ← get next node from S, 0
 3:     if s is type φ U_J ψ or φ ∧ ψ then
 4:         w ← max(|q_φ|, |q_ψ|) + wcd(s)
 5:     end if
 6:     while s is not a synchronization queue do
 7:         s, w ← get predecessor of s in AST(ξ'), w + wcd(s)
 8:     end while
 9:     Set |q| = w; (q is opposite synchronization queue of s)
10:     Add all φ U_J ψ and φ ∧ ψ nodes that have unassigned synchronization queue sizes to S
11: end while
```

- Interconnect and dimensioning. Connect observers and queues according to $AST(\xi')$. Execute Alg. 6 (**MA2**).

Let $\{\sigma_1, \sigma_2, \sigma_3\} \in \Sigma$ and $\xi = \sigma_1 \rightarrow (\lozenge_{10} (\sigma_2) \vee \lozenge_{100}(\sigma_3))$ be an MTL formula we want to synthesize a configuration for. SA1 yields $\xi' = \neg(\sigma_1 \wedge \neg(\neg\blacksquare_{10} (\neg\sigma_2)) \wedge \neg(\neg\blacksquare_{100} (\neg\sigma_3)))$ which simplifies to $\xi = \neg(\sigma_1 \wedge \blacksquare_{10} (\neg\sigma_2) \wedge \blacksquare_{100} (\neg\sigma_3))$. SA2 yields $AST(\xi')$. SA3 instantiates two $\varphi \wedge \psi$, three $\neg \varphi$, one $\blacksquare_{10} T_\varphi$ and one $\blacksquare_{100} T_\varphi$ observers, both synchronous and asynchronous. MA1, introduces queues $q_{\sigma_1}, q_{\xi_2}, q_{\xi_3}, q_{\xi_4}$ and MA2 interconnects observers and queues and assigns $|q_{\sigma_1}| = 100$, $|q_{\xi_2}| = 100$, $|q_{\xi_3}| = 10$, and $|q_{\xi_4}| = 0$, see Fig. 2.

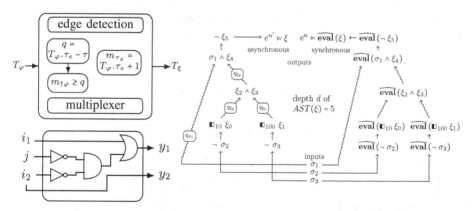

Fig. 2. Left: hardware implementations for $\blacksquare_\tau \varphi$ (top) and $\overline{\mathbf{eval}} (\blacksquare_\tau \varphi)$ (bottom). Right: subformulas of $AST(\xi)$, observers, and queues synthesized for ξ. Mapping the observers to hardware yields two levels of parallelism: (i) asynchronous (left) and the synchronous observers (right) run in parallel and (ii) observers for subformulas run in parallel, e.g., $\blacksquare_{10} \xi_0$ and $\blacksquare_{100} \xi_1$.

4.2 Circuit Size and Depth Complexity Results

Having discussed how to determine the size of the synchronization queues for our asynchronous MTL observers, we are now in the position to prove space and time complexity bounds.

Theorem 1 (Space Complexity of Asynchronous Observers). *The respective asynchronous observer for a given MTL specification φ has a space complexity, in terms of memory bits, bounded by $(2 + \lceil \log_2(n) \rceil) \cdot (2 \cdot m \cdot p)$, where m is the number of binary observers (i.e., $\varphi \wedge \psi$ or $\varphi \mathcal{U}_J \psi$) in φ, p is the worst-case delay of a single predecessor chain in $\mathrm{AST}(\varphi)$, and $n \in \mathbb{N}_0$ is the time stamp it is executed.*

Theorem 2 (Time Complexity of Asynchronous Observers). *The respective asynchronous observer for a given MTL specification φ has an asymptotic time complexity of $\mathcal{O}\big(\log_2 \log_2 \max(p, n) \cdot d \big)$, where p is the maximum worst-case-delay of any observer in $\mathrm{AST}(\varphi)$, d the depth of $\mathrm{AST}(\varphi)$, and $n \in \mathbb{N}_0$ the time stamp it is executed.*

For our synchronous observers, we prove upper bounds in terms of two-input gates on the size of resulting circuits. Actual implementations may yield significant better results on circuit size, depending on the performance of the logic synthesis tool.

Theorem 3 (Circuit-Size Complexity of Synchronous Observers). *For a given MTL formula φ, the circuit to monitor $\widehat{\mathbf{eval}}\,(\varphi)$ has a circuit-size complexity bounded by $11 \cdot m$, where m is the number of observers in $\mathrm{AST}(\varphi)$.*

Theorem 4 (Circuit-Depth Complexity of Synchronous Observers). *For a given MTL formula φ, the circuit to monitor $\widehat{\mathbf{eval}}\,(\varphi)$ has a circuit-depth complexity of $4 \cdot d$.*

5 Applying the rt-R2U2 to NASA's Swift UAS

We implemented our rt-R2U2 as a register-transfer-level VHDL hardware design, which we simulated in MENTOR GRAPHICS MODELSIM and synthesized for different FPGAs using the industrial logic synthesis tool ALTERA QUARTUS II.[3] With our rt-R2U2, we analyzed raw flight data from NASA's Swift UAS collected during test flights. The higher-level reasoning is performed by a *health model*, modeled as a Bayesian network (BN) where the nodes correspond to discrete random variables. Fig. 3 shows the relevant excerpt for reasoning about altitude. Directed edges encode conditional dependencies between variables, e.g., the sensor reading S_L depends on the health of the laser altimeter sensor H_L. Conditional probability tables at each node define the local dependencies. During health estimation, verdicts computed by our observer algorithms are provided as virtual sensor values to the observable nodes S_L, S_B, S_S; e.g., the laser altimeter measuring an altitude increase would result in setting S_L to state *inc*. Then, the posteriors of the multivariate probability distribution encoded in the BN are calculated [10]; for details of modeling and reasoning see [25].

Our temporal specifications are evaluated by our runtime observers and describe flight rules (φ_1, φ_2) and virtual sensors:

---

[3] Simulation traces are available in the Appendix; tools can be downloaded at
http://www.mentor.com and http://www.altera.com.

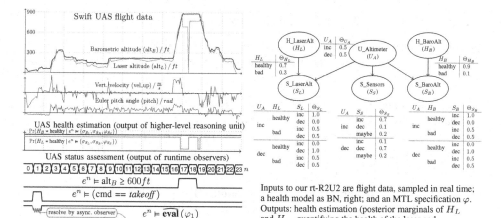

Fig. 3. Adding SHM to the Swift UAS

$$\varphi_1 = (\text{cmd} == \text{takeoff}) \rightarrow \blacklozenge_{10} (\text{alt}_B \geq 600\,ft)$$
$$\varphi_2 = (\text{cmd} == \text{takeoff}) \rightarrow \blacklozenge_* (\text{cmd} == \text{land})$$

φ_1 encodes our running example flight rule; φ_2 is a mission-bounded LTL property requiring that the command *land* is received after *takeoff*, within the projected mission time, indicated by $*$. Fig. 3 shows the execution sequences produced by both the asynchronous ($e^n \vDash \varphi_1$) and the synchronous ($e^n \vDash \overline{\textbf{eval}}\,(\varphi_1)$) observers for flight rule φ_1. To keep the presentation accessible we scaled the timeline to just 24 time stamps; the actual implementation uses a resolution of 2^{32} time stamps. The synchronous observer is able to prove the validity of φ_1 immediately at all time stamps but one ($n = 1$), where the output is $(\textbf{maybe}, 1)$, indicated by ⌇⌇. The asynchronous observer will resolve this inconclusive output at time $n = 11$, by generating the tuple $(\textbf{false}, 1)$, revealing a violation of φ at time $n = 1$. The verdicts of $\sigma_{S_{L\uparrow}}, \sigma_{S_{L\downarrow}}, \sigma_{S_{B\uparrow}}, \sigma_{S_{B\downarrow}}, \varphi_{S_{S\uparrow}}$, and $\varphi_{S_{S\downarrow}}$ are mapped to inputs S_L, S_B, S_S of the health model:

$$\sigma_{S_{L\uparrow}} = (\text{alt}_L - \text{alt}'_L) > 0 \qquad \sigma_{S_{L\downarrow}} = (\text{alt}_L - \text{alt}'_L) < 0$$
$$\sigma_{S_{B\uparrow}} = (\text{alt}_B - \text{alt}'_B) > 0 \qquad \sigma_{S_{B\downarrow}} = (\text{alt}_B - \text{alt}'_B) < 0$$

$\sigma_{S_{B\uparrow}}$ observes if the first derivation of the barometric altimeter reading is positive, thus, holds if the sensors values indicate that the UAS is ascending. We set S_B to *inc* if $\sigma_{S_{B\uparrow}}$ holds and to *dec* if $\sigma_{S_{B\downarrow}}$ holds. The specifications $\varphi_{S_{S\uparrow}}$ and $\varphi_{S_{S\downarrow}}$ subsume the pitch and the velocity readings to an additional, indirect altitude sensor. Due to sensor noise, simple threshold properties on the IMU signals would yield a large number of false positives. Instead $\varphi_{S_{S\uparrow}}$ and $\varphi_{S_{S\downarrow}}$ use $\blacksquare_\tau \varphi$ observers as filters, by requiring that the pitch and the velocity signals exceed a threshold for multiple time steps.

$$\varphi_{S_{S\uparrow}} = \blacksquare_{10} (\text{pitch} \geq 5°) \land \blacksquare_5 (\text{vel\_up} \geq 2\tfrac{m}{s})$$
$$\varphi_{S_{S\downarrow}} = \blacksquare_{10} (\text{pitch} < 2°) \land \blacksquare_5 (\text{vel\_up} \leq -2\tfrac{m}{s})$$

Our real-time SHM analysis matched post-flight analysis by test engineers, including successfully pinpointing a laser altimeter failure, see Fig 3: the barometric altimeter, pitch, and the velocity readings indicated an *increase* in altitude ($\sigma_{S_{B\uparrow}}$ and $\varphi_{S_{S\uparrow}}$

held) while the laser altimeter indicated a *decrease* ($\sigma_{S_{L\downarrow}}$ held). The posterior marginal $\Pr(H_L = \text{healthy} \mid e^n \vDash \{\sigma_{S_L}, \sigma_{S_B}, \varphi_{S_S}\})$ of the node H_L, inferred from the BN, dropped from 70% to 8%, indicating a low degree of trust in the laser altimeter reading during the outage; engineers attribute the failure to the UAS exceeding its operational altitude.

6 Conclusion

We presented a novel SHM technique that enables both real-time assessment of the system status of an embedded system with respect to temporal-logic-based specifications and also supports statistical reasoning to estimate its health at runtime. To ensure REALIZABILITY, we observe specifications given in two real-time projections of LTL that naturally encode future-time requirements such as flight rules. Real-time health modeling, e.g., using Bayesian networks allows mitigative reactions inferred from complex relationships between observations. To ensure RESPONSIVENESS, we run both an over-approximative, but *synchronous* to the real-time clock (RTC), and an exact, but *asynchronous* to the RTC, observer in parallel for every specification. To ensure UNOBTRUSIVENESS to flight-certified systems, we designed our observer algorithms with a light-weight, FPGA-based implementation in mind and showed how to map them into efficient, but reconfigurable circuits. Following on our success using rt-R2U2 to analyze real flight data recorded by NASA's Swift UAS, we plan to analyze future missions of the Swift or small satellites with the goal of deploying rt-R2U2 onboard.

References

1. Alur, R., Henzinger, T.A.: Real-time Logics: Complexity and Expressiveness. In: LICS, pp. 390–401. IEEE (1990)
2. Backasch, R., Hochberger, C., Weiss, A., Leucker, M., Lasslop, R.: Runtime verification for multicore SoC with high-quality trace data. ACM Trans. Des. Autom. Electron. Syst. 18(2), 18:1–18:26 (2013)
3. Barre, B., Klein, M., Soucy-Boivin, M., Ollivier, P.-A., Hallé, S.: MapReduce for parallel trace validation of LTL properties. In: Qadeer, S., Tasiran, S. (eds.) RV 2012. LNCS, vol. 7687, pp. 184–198. Springer, Heidelberg (2013)
4. Barringer, H., et al.: RV 2010. LNCS, vol. 6418. Springer, Heidelberg (2010)
5. Basin, D., Klaedtke, F., Müller, S., Pfitzmann, B.: Runtime monitoring of metric first-order temporal properties. In: FSTTCS, pp. 49–60 (2008)
6. Basin, D., Klaedtke, F., Zălinescu, E.: Algorithms for monitoring real-time properties. In: Khurshid, S., Sen, K. (eds.) RV 2011. LNCS, vol. 7186, pp. 260–275. Springer, Heidelberg (2012)
7. Bauer, A., Leucker, M., Schallhart, C.: Comparing LTL semantics for runtime verification. J. Log. and Comp. 20, 651–674 (2010)
8. Bauer, A., Leucker, M., Schallhart, C.: Runtime verification for LTL and TLTL. ACM Trans. Softw. Eng. M. 20, 14:1–14:64 (2011)
9. Colombo, C., Pace, G., Abela, P.: Safer asynchronous runtime monitoring using compensations. FMSD 41, 269–294 (2012)
10. Darwiche, A.: Modeling and Reasoning with Bayesian Networks, 1st edn. Cambridge University Press, New York (2009)
11. Divakaran, S., D'Souza, D., Mohan, M.R.: Conflict-tolerant real-time specifications in metric temporal logic. In: TIME, pp. 35–42 (2010)

12. Finkbeiner, B., Kuhtz, L.: Monitor circuits for LTL with bounded and unbounded future. In: Bensalem, S., Peled, D.A. (eds.) RV 2009. LNCS, vol. 5779, pp. 60–75. Springer, Heidelberg (2009)

13. Fischmeister, S., Lam, P.: Time-aware instrumentation of embedded software. IEEE Trans. Ind. Informatics 6(4), 652–663 (2010)

14. Geilen, M.: An improved on-the-fly tableau construction for a real-time temporal logic. In: Hunt Jr., W.A., Somenzi, F. (eds.) CAV 2003. LNCS, vol. 2725, pp. 394–406. Springer, Heidelberg (2003)

15. Havelund, K.: Runtime verification of C programs. In: Suzuki, K., Higashino, T., Ulrich, A., Hasegawa, T. (eds.) TestCom/FATES 2008. LNCS, vol. 5047, pp. 7–22. Springer, Heidelberg (2008)

16. Ippolito, C., Espinosa, P., Weston, A.: Swift UAS: An electric UAS research platform for green aviation at NASA Ames Research Center. In: CAFE EAS IV (April 2010)

17. Johnson, S., Gormley, T., Kessler, S., Mott, C., Patterson-Hine, A., Reichard, K., Philip Scandura, J.: System Health Management: with Aerospace Applications. Wiley & Sons (2011)

18. Kleene, S.C.: Introduction to Metamathematics. North Holland (1996)

19. Lichtenstein, O., Pnueli, A., Zuck, L.: The glory of the past. In: Parikh, R. (ed.) Logic of Programs 1985. LNCS, vol. 193, pp. 196–218. Springer, Heidelberg (1985)

20. Lu, H., Forin, A.: The design and implementation of P2V, an architecture for zero-overhead online verification of software programs. Tech. Rep. MSR-TR-2007-99 (2007)

21. Maler, O., Nickovic, D., Pnueli, A.: On synthesizing controllers from bounded-response properties. In: Damm, W., Hermanns, H. (eds.) CAV 2007. LNCS, vol. 4590, pp. 95–107. Springer, Heidelberg (2007)

22. Maler, O., Nickovic, D., Pnueli, A.: Checking temporal properties of discrete, timed and continuous behaviors. In: Avron, A., Dershowitz, N., Rabinovich, A. (eds.) Pillars of Computer Science. LNCS, vol. 4800, pp. 475–505. Springer, Heidelberg (2008)

23. Pike, L., Niller, S., Wegmann, N.: Runtime verification for ultra-critical systems. In: Khurshid, S., Sen, K. (eds.) RV 2011. LNCS, vol. 7186, pp. 310–324. Springer, Heidelberg (2012)

24. Reinbacher, T., Függer, M., Brauer, J.: Real-time runtime verification on chip. In: Qadeer, S., Tasiran, S. (eds.) RV 2012. LNCS, vol. 7687, pp. 110–125. Springer, Heidelberg (2013)

25. Schumann, J., Mbaya, T., Mengshoel, O., Pipatsrisawat, K., Srivastava, A., Choi, A., Darwiche, A.: Software health management with Bayesian Networks. Innovations in Systems and SW Engineering 9(4), 271–292 (2013)

26. Schumann, J., Rozier, K.Y., Reinbacher, T., Mengshoel, O.J., Mbaya, T., Ippolito, C.: Towards real-time, on-board, hardware-supported sensor and software health management for unmanned aerial systems. In: PHM (2013)

27. Tabakov, D., Rozier, K.Y., Vardi, M.Y.: Optimized temporal monitors for SystemC. Formal Methods in System Design 41(3), 236–268 (2012)

28. Thati, P., Roşu, G.: Monitoring Algorithms for Metric Temporal Logic specifications. ENTCS 113, 145–162 (2005)

Status Report on Software Verification
(Competition Summary SV-COMP 2014)

Dirk Beyer

University of Passau, Germany

Abstract. This report describes the 3rd International Competition on Software Verification (SV-COMP 2014), which is the third edition of a thorough comparative evaluation of fully automatic software verifiers. The reported results represent the state of the art in automatic software verification, in terms of effectiveness and efficiency. The verification tasks of the competition consist of nine categories containing a total of 2 868 C programs, covering bit-vector operations, concurrent execution, control-flow and integer data-flow, device-drivers, heap data structures, memory manipulation via pointers, recursive functions, and sequentialized concurrency. The specifications include reachability of program labels and memory safety. The competition is organized as a satellite event at TACAS 2014 in Grenoble, France.

1 Introduction

Software verification is an important part of software engineering, which is responsible for guaranteeing safe and reliable performance of the software systems that our economy and society relies on. The latest research results need to be implemented in verification tools, in order to transfer the theoretical knowledge to engineering practice. The Competition on Software Verification (SV-COMP) [1] is a systematic comparative evaluation of the effectiveness and efficiency of the state of the art in software verification. The benchmark repository of SV-COMP [2] is a collection of verification tasks that represent the current interest and abilities of tools for software verification. For the purpose of this competition, the verification tasks are arranged in nine categories, according to the characteristics of the programs and the properties to verify. Besides the verification tasks that are used in this competition and written in the programming language C, the SV-COMP repository also contains tasks written in Java [3] and as Horn clauses [4].

The main objectives of the Competition on Software Verification are to:

1. provide an overview of the state of the art in software-verification technology,
2. establish a repository of software-verification tasks that is widely used,
3. increase visibility of the most recent software verifiers, and
4. accelerate the transfer of new verification technology to industrial practice.

---

[1] http://sv-comp.sosy-lab.org

[2] https://svn.sosy-lab.org/software/sv-benchmarks/trunk

[3] https://svn.sosy-lab.org/software/sv-benchmarks/trunk/java

[4] https://svn.sosy-lab.org/software/sv-benchmarks/trunk/clauses

E. Ábrahám and K. Havelund (Eds.): TACAS 2014, LNCS 8413, pp. 373–388, 2014.
© Springer-Verlag Berlin Heidelberg 2014

The large attendance at the past competition sessions at TACAS witnesses that the community is interested in the topic and that the competition really helps achieving the above-mentioned objectives (1) and (3). Also, objective (2) is achieved: an inspection of recent publications on algorithms for software verification reveals that it becomes a standard for evaluating new algorithms to use the established verification benchmarks from the SV-COMP repository.

The difference of SV-COMP to other competitions [5][6][7][8][9][10][11][12][13] is that we focus on evaluating tools for *fully automatic* verification of program *source code* in a standard programming language [1,2]. The experimental evaluation is performed on dedicated machines that provide the same *limited* amount of resources to each verification tool.

2   Procedure

The procedure for the competition was not changed in comparison to the previous editions [1,2], and consisted of the phases (1) *benchmark submission* (collect and classify new verification tasks), (2) *training* (teams inspect verification tasks and train their verifiers), and (3) *evaluation* (verification runs with all competition candidates and review of the system descriptions by the competition jury). All systems and their descriptions were again archived and stamped for identification with SHA hash values. Also, before public announcement of the results, all teams received the preliminary results of their verifier for approval. After the competition experiments for the 'official' categories were finished, some teams participated in demonstration categories, in order to experiment with new categories and new rules for future editions of the competition.

3   Definitions and Rules

As a new feature of the competition and to streamline the specification of the various properties, we introduced a syntax for properties (described below). The definition of verification tasks was not changed (taken from [2]).

Verification Tasks. A verification task consists of a C program and a property. A verification run is a non-interactive execution of a competition candidate on a single verification task, in order to check whether the following statement is correct: "The program satisfies the property." The result of a verification run is a triple (ANSWER, WITNESS, TIME). ANSWER is one of the following outcomes:

---

[5] http://www.satcompetition.org
[6] http://www.smtcomp.org
[7] http://ipc.icaps-conference.org
[8] http://www.qbflib.org/competition.html
[9] http://fmv.jku.at/hwmcc12
[10] http://www.cs.miami.edu/~tptp/CASC
[11] http://termination-portal.org
[12] http://fm2012.verifythis.org
[13] http://rers-challenge.org

TRUE: The property is satisfied (i.e., no path that violates the property exists).

FALSE: The property is violated (i.e., there exists a path that violates the property) and a counterexample path is produced and reported as WITNESS.

UNKNOWN: The tool cannot decide the problem, or terminates by a tool crash, or exhausts the computing resources time or memory (i.e., the competition candidate does not succeed in computing an answer TRUE or FALSE).

For the counterexample path that must be produced as WITNESS for the result FALSE, we did not require a particular fixed format. (Future editions of SV-COMP will support machine-readable error witnesses, such that error witnesses can be automatically validated by a verifier.) The TIME is measured as consumed CPU time until the verifier terminates, including the consumed CPU time of all processes that the verifier started. If TIME is equal to or larger than the time limit, then the verifier is terminated and the ANSWER is set to 'timeout' (and interpreted as UNKNOWN). The verification tasks are partitioned into nine separate categories and one category *Overall* that contains all verification tasks. The categories, their defining category-set files, and the contained programs are explained under Verification Tasks on the competition web site.

Properties. The specification to be verified is stored in a file that is given as parameter to the verifier. In the repository, the specifications are available in .prp files in the main directory.

The definition init(main()) gives the initial states of the program by a call of function main (with no parameters). The definition LTL(f) specifies that formula f holds at every initial state of the program. The LTL (linear-time temporal logic) operator G f means that f globally holds (i.e., everywhere during the program execution), and the operator F f means that f eventually holds (i.e., at some point during the program execution). The proposition label(ERROR) is true if the C label ERROR is reached, and the proposition end is true if the program execution terminates (e.g., return of function main, program exit, abort).

Label Unreachability. The reachability property p_{error} is encoded in the program source code using a C label and expressed using the following specification (the interpretation of the LTL formula is given in Table 1):

```
CHECK( init(main()), LTL(G ! label(ERROR)) )
```

The new syntax (in comparison to previous SV-COMP editions) allows a more general specification of the reachability property, by decoupling the specification from the program source code, and thus, not requiring the label to be named ERROR.

Memory Safety. The memory-safety property $p_{memsafety}$ (only used in one category) consists of three partial properties and is expressed using the following specification (interpretation of formulas given in Table 1):

```
CHECK( init(main()), LTL(G valid-free) )
CHECK( init(main()), LTL(G valid-deref) )
CHECK( init(main()), LTL(G valid-memtrack) )
```

Table 1. Formulas used in the competition, together with their interpretation

Formula	Interpretation
G ! label(ERROR)	The C label ERROR is not reachable on any finite execution of the program.
G valid-free	All memory deallocations are valid (counterexample: invalid free). More precisely: There exists no finite execution of the program on which an invalid memory deallocation occurs.
G valid-deref	All pointer dereferences are valid (counterexample: invalid dereference). More precisely: There exists no finite execution of the program on which an invalid pointer dereference occurs.
G valid-memtrack	All allocated memory is tracked, i.e., pointed to or deallocated (counterexample: memory leak). More precisely: There exists no finite execution of the program on which the program lost track of some previously allocated memory.
F end	All program executions are finite and end on proposition end (counterexample: infinite loop). More precisely: There exists no execution of the program on which the program never terminates.

Table 2. Scoring schema for SV-COMP 2013 and 2014 (taken from [2])

Reported result	Points	Description
UNKNOWN	0	Failure to compute verification result
FALSE correct	+1	Violation of property in program was correctly found
FALSE incorrect	−4	Violation reported but property holds (false alarm)
TRUE correct	+2	Correct program reported to satisfy property
TRUE incorrect	−8	Incorrect program reported as correct (missed bug)

The verification result FALSE for the property $p_{\text{memsafety}}$ is required to include the violated partial property: $\text{FALSE}(p)$, with $p \in \{p_{\text{valid-free}}, p_{\text{valid-deref}}, p_{\text{valid-memtrack}}\}$, means that the (partial) property p is violated. According to the requirements for verification tasks, all programs in category *MemorySafety* violate at most one (partial) property $p \in \{p_{\text{valid-free}}, p_{\text{valid-deref}}, p_{\text{valid-memtrack}}\}$. Per convention, function malloc is assumed to always return a valid pointer, i.e., the memory allocation never fails, and function free always deallocates the memory and makes the pointer invalid for further dereferences.

Program Termination. The termination property $p_{\text{termination}}$ (only used in a demonstration category) is based on the proposition end and expressed using the following specification (interpretation in Table 1):

CHECK(init(main()), LTL(F end))

Evaluation by Scores and Run Time. The scoring schema was not changed from SV-COMP 2013 to 2014 and is given in Table 2. The ranking is decided based on the sum of points and for equal sum of points according to success run time, which is the total CPU time over all verification tasks for which the verifier reported a correct verification result. Sanity tests on obfuscated versions of verification tasks (renaming of variable and function names; renaming of file)

Table 3. Competition candidates with their system-description references and representing jury members

Competition candidate	Ref.	Jury member	Affiliation
BLAST 2.7.2	[31]	Vadim Mutilin	ISP RAS, Moscow, Russia
CBMC	[24]	Michael Tautschnig	Queen Mary U, London, UK
CPACHECKER	[25]	Stefan Löwe	U Passau, Germany
CPALIEN	[27]	Petr Muller	TU Brno, Czech Republic
CSEQ-LAZY	[20]	Bernd Fischer	Stellenbosch U, South Africa
CSEQ-MU	[33]	Gennaro Parlato	U Southampton, UK
ESBMC 1.22	[26]	Lucas Cordeiro	FUA, Manaus, Brazil
FRANKENBIT	[15]	Arie Gurfinkel	SEI, Pittsburgh, USA
LLBMC	[11]	Stephan Falke	KIT, Karlsruhe, Germany
PREDATOR	[9]	Tomas Vojnar	TU Brno, Czech Republic
SYMBIOTIC 2	[32]	Jiri Slaby	Masaryk U, Brno, Czech Rep.
THREADER	[29]	Corneliu Popeea	TU Munich, Germany
UFO	[14]	Aws Albarghouthi	U Toronto, Canada
ULTIMATE AUTOMIZER	[16]	Matthias Heizmann	U Freiburg, Germany
ULTIMATE KOJAK	[10]	Alexander Nutz	U Freiburg, Germany

did not reveal any discrepancy of the results. *Opting-out from Categories* and and *Computation of Score for Meta Categories* were defined as in SV-COMP 2013 [2]. The *Competition Jury* consists again of the chair and one member of each participating team. Team representatives are indicated in Table 3.

4   Participating Teams

Table 3 provides an overview of the participating competition candidates. The detailed summary of the achievements for each verifier is presented in Sect. 5. A total of 15 competition candidates participated in SV-COMP 2014: BLAST 2.7.2 [14], CBMC [15], CPACHECKER [16], CPALIEN [17], CSEQ-LAZY [18], CSEQ-MU, ESBMC 1.22 [19], FRANKENBIT [20], LLBMC [21], PREDATOR [22], SYMBIOTIC 2 [23], THREADER [24], UFO [25], ULTIMATE AUTOMIZER [26], and ULTIMATE KOJAK [27].

---

[14] http://forge.ispras.ru/projects/blast
[15] http://www.cprover.org/cbmc
[16] http://cpachecker.sosy-lab.org
[17] http://www.fit.vutbr.cz/~imuller/cpalien
[18] http://users.ecs.soton.ac.uk/gp4/cseq/cseq.html
[19] http://www.esbmc.org
[20] http://bitbucket.org/arieg/fbit
[21] http://llbmc.org
[22] http://www.fit.vutbr.cz/research/groups/verifit/tools/predator
[23] https://sf.net/projects/symbiotic
[24] http://www7.in.tum.de/tools/threader
[25] http://bitbucket.org/arieg/ufo
[26] http://ultimate.informatik.uni-freiburg.de/automizer
[27] http://ultimate.informatik.uni-freiburg.de/kojak

Table 4. Technologies and features that the verification tools offer (*incl. demo track*)

Verification tool (incl. demo track)	CEGAR	Predicate Abstraction	Symbolic Execution	Bounded Model Check.	Explicit-Value Analysis	Interval Analysis	Shape Analysis	Bit-precise Analysis	ARG-based Analysis	Lazy Abstraction	Interpolation	Concurrency Support	Ranking Functions
APROVE			✓										✓
BLAST 2.7.2	✓	✓							✓	✓	✓		
CBMC				✓				✓				✓	
CPALIEN					✓		✓						
CPACHECKER	✓	✓		✓	✓	✓	✓	✓	✓	✓	✓		
CSEQ-LAZY				✓								✓	
CSEQ-MU				✓								✓	
ESBMC 1.22				✓				✓				✓	
FUNCTION						✓							✓
FRANKENBIT				✓				✓			✓		
LLBMC				✓									
PREDATOR							✓						
SYMBIOTIC 2			✓										
T2	✓	✓				✓			✓	✓	✓		✓
TAN	✓	✓	✓	✓		✓		✓		✓			✓
THREADER	✓	✓							✓		✓	✓	
UFO	✓	✓		✓		✓			✓	✓	✓		
ULTIMATE AUTOMIZER	✓	✓								✓	✓		
ULTIMATE KOJAK	✓	✓								✓	✓		
ULTIMATE BÜCHI	✓	✓								✓	✓		✓

Table 4 lists the features and technologies that are used in the verification tools. Counterexample-guided abstraction refinement (CEGAR) [8], predicate abstraction [13], bounded model checking [6], lazy abstraction [19], and interpolation for predicate refinement [18] are implemented in many verifiers. Other features that were implemented include symbolic execution [22], the construction of an abstract reachability graph (ARG) as proof of correctness [3], and shape analysis [21]. Only a few tools support the verification of concurrent programs. Computing ranking functions [28] for proving termination is a feature that is implemented in tools that participated in the demo category on termination.

Table 5. Quantitative overview over all results — Part 1 (score / CPU time)

Competition candidate Representing jury member	BitVectors 86 points max. 49 verif. tasks	Concurrency 136 points max. 78 verif. tasks	ControlFlow 1261 points max. 843 verif. tasks	DeviceDrivers 2766 points max. 1428 verif. tasks	HeapManip. 135 points max. 80 verif. tasks
BLAST 2.7.2 V. Mutilin, Moscow, Russia	—	—	508 32 000 s	**2 682** 13 000 s	—
CBMC M. Tautschnig, London, UK	**86** 2 300 s	**128** 29 000 s	397 42 000 s	2 463 390 000 s	**132** 12 000 s
CPACHECKER S. Löwe, Passau, Germany	**78** 690 s	0 0.0 s	**1009** 9 000 s	2 613 28 000 s	107 210 s
CPALIEN P. Muller, Brno, Czech Republic	—	—	455 6 500 s	—	71 70 s
CSEQ-LAZY B. Fischer, Stellenbosch, ZA	—	**136** 1 000 s	—	—	—
CSEQ-MU G. Parlato, Southampton, UK	—	**136** 1 200 s	—	—	—
ESBMC 1.22 L. Cordeiro, Manaus, Brazil	77 1 500 s	32 30 000 s	949 35 000 s	2 358 140 000 s	97 970 s
FRANKENBIT A. Gurfinkel, Pittsburgh, USA	—	—	**986** 6 300 s	**2 639** 3 000 s	—
LLBMC S. Falke, Karlsruhe, Germany	**86** 39 s	0 0.0 s	**961** 13 000 s	0 0.0 s	107 130 s
PREDATOR T. Vojnar, Brno, Czech Republic	-92 28 s	0 0.0 s	511 3 400 s	50 9.9 s	**111** 9.5 s
SYMBIOTIC 2 J. Slaby, Brno, Czech Republic	39 220 s	-82 5.7 s	41 39 000 s	980 2 200 s	105 15 s
THREADER C. Popeea, Munich, Germany	—	100 3 000 s	—	—	—
UFO A. Albarghouthi, Toronto, Canada	—	—	912 14 000 s	**2 642** 5 700 s	—
ULTIMATE AUTOMIZER M. Heizmann, Freiburg, Germany	—	—	164 6 000 s	—	—
ULTIMATE KOJAK A. Nutz, Freiburg, Germany	-23 1 100 s	0 0.0 s	214 5 100 s	0 0.0 s	18 35 s

Table 6. Quantitative overview over all results — Part 2 (score / CPU time)

Competition candidate Representing jury member	MemorySafety 98 points max. 61 verif. tasks	Recursive 39 points max. 23 verif. tasks	Sequentialized 364 points max. 261 verif. tasks	Simple 67 points max. 45 verif. tasks	Overall 4718 points max. 2868 verif. tasks
BLAST 2.7.2 V. Mutilin, Moscow, Russia	—	—	—	30 5 400 s	—
CBMC M. Tautschnig, London, UK	4 11 000 s	30 11 000 s	237 47 000 s	66 15 000 s	3 501 560 000 s
CPACHECKER S. Löwe, Passau, Germany	95 460 s	0 0.0 s	97 9 200 s	67 430 s	2 987 48 000 s
CPALIEN P. Muller, Brno, Czech Republic	9 690 s	—	—	—	—
CSEQ-LAZY B. Fischer, Stellenbosch, ZA	—	—	—	—	—
CSEQ-MU G. Parlato, Southampton, UK	—	—	—	—	—
ESBMC 1.22 L. Cordeiro, Manaus, Brazil	-136 1 500 s	-53 4 900 s	244 38 000 s	31 27 000 s	975 280 000 s
FRANKENBIT A. Gurfinkel, Pittsburgh, USA	—	—	—	37 830 s	—
LLBMC S. Falke, Karlsruhe, Germany	38 170 s	3 0.38 s	208 11 000 s	0 0.0 s	1 843 24 000 s
PREDATOR T. Vojnar, Brno, Czech Republic	14 39 s	-18 0.12 s	-46 7 700 s	0 0.0 s	-184 11 000 s
SYMBIOTIC 2 J. Slaby, Brno, Czech Republic	-130 7.5 s	6 0.93 s	-32 770 s	-22 13 s	-220 42 000 s
THREADER C. Popeea, Munich, Germany	—	—	—	—	—
UFO A. Albarghouthi, Toronto, Canada	—	—	83 4 800 s	67 480 s	—
ULTIMATE AUTOMIZER M. Heizmann, Freiburg, Germany	—	12 850 s	49 3 000 s	—	399 10 000 s
ULTIMATE KOJAK A. Nutz, Freiburg, Germany	0 0.0 s	9 54 s	9 1 200 s	0 0.0 s	139 7 600 s

Table 7. Overview of the top-three verifiers for each category (CPU time in s)

Rank	Candidate	Score	CPU Time	Solved Tasks	False Alarms	Missed Bugs
BitVectors						
1	LLBMC	86	39	49		
2	CBMC	86	2 300	49		
3	CPACHECKER	78	690	45		
Concurrency						
1	CSEQ-LAZY	136	1 000	78		
2	CSEQ-MU	136	1 200	78		
3	CBMC	128	29 000	76	1	
ControlFlow						
1	CPACHECKER	1009	9 000	764	2	
2	FRANKENBIT	986	6 300	752		2
3	LLBMC	961	13 000	783		14
DeviceDrivers						
1	BLAST 2.7.2	2 682	13 000	1 386		2
2	UFO	2 642	5 700	1 354	2	3
3	FRANKENBIT	2 639	3 000	1 383	5	5
HeapManipulation						
1	CBMC	132	12 000	78		
2	PREDATOR	111	9.5	68		
3	LLBMC	107	130	66		
MemorySafety						
1	CPACHECKER	95	460	59		
2	LLBMC	38	170	31		
3	PREDATOR	14	39	43	12	
Recursive						
1	CBMC	30	11 000	22		1
2	ULTIMATE AUTOMIZER	12	850	9		
3	ULTIMATE KOJAK	9	54	7		
SequentializedConcurrency						
1	ESBMC 1.22	244	38 000	187	2	
2	CBMC	237	47 000	225		10
3	LLBMC	208	11 000	191	3	3
Simple						
1	CPACHECKER	67	430	45		
2	UFO	67	480	45		
3	CBMC	66	15 000	44		
Overall						
1	CBMC	3 501	560 000	2 597	3	90
2	CPACHECKER	2 987	48 000	2 421	12	
3	LLBMC	1 843	24 000	1 123	3	17

5   Results and Discussion

The results that we obtained in the competition experiments and reported in this article represent the state of the art in fully automatic and publicly available software-verification tools. The results show achievements in effectiveness (number of verification tasks that can be solved, correctness of the results) and efficiency (resource consumption in terms of CPU time). All reported results were approved by the participating teams.

The verification runs were natively executed on dedicated unloaded compute servers with a 3.4 GHz 64-bit Quad Core CPU (Intel i7-2600) and a GNU/Linux operating system (x86_64-linux). The machines had (at least) 16 GB of RAM, of which exactly 15 GB were made available to the verification tools. The run-time limit for each verification run was 15 min of CPU time. The tables report the run time in seconds of CPU time; all measured values are rounded to two significant digits. One complete competition run with all candidates on all verification tasks required a total of 51 days of CPU time.

Tables 5 and 6 present a quantitative overview over all tools and all categories. The tools are listed in alphabetical order; every table cell for competition results lists the score in the first row and the CPU time for successful runs in the second row. We indicated the top-three candidates by formatting their score in bold face and in larger font size. The entry '—' means that the verifier opted-out from the respective category. For the calculation of the score and for the ranking, the scoring schema in Table 2 was applied, the scores for meta categories (*Overall* and *ControlFlow*, consisting of several sub-categories) were computed using normalized scores as defined in last year's report [2].

Table 7 reports the top-three verifiers for each category. The run time refers to successfully solved verification tasks. The columns 'False Alarms' and 'Missed Bugs' report the number of verification tasks for which the tool reported wrong results: reporting a counterexample path but the property holds (false positive) and claiming that the program fulfills the property although it actually contains a bug (false negative), respectively.

Score-Based Quantile Functions for Quality Assessment. As described in the previous competition report [2], score-based quantile functions are a helpful visualization of the results. The competition web page [28] presents such a plot for each category, while we illustrate in Fig. 1 only the category *Overall* (all verification tasks). A total of eight verifiers participated in category *Overall*, for which the quantile plot shows the overall performance over all categories. (Note that the scores are normalized as described last year [2].)

Overall Quality Measured in Scores (Right End of Graph). CBMC is the winner of this category, because the x-coordinate of the right-most data point represents the highest total score (and thus, the total value) of the completed verification work (cf. Table 7; right-most x-coordinates match the score values in the table).

Amount of Incorrect Verification Work (Left End of Graph). The left-most data points of the quantile functions represent the total negative score of a verifier

---

[28] http://sv-comp.sosy-lab.org/2014/results

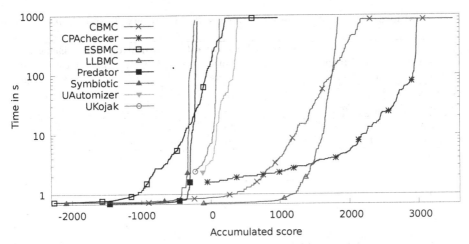

Fig. 1. Quantile functions: For each competition candidate, we plot all data points (x, y) such that the maximum run time of the n fastest correct verification runs is y and x is the accumulated score of all incorrect results and those n correct results. A logarithmic scale is used for the time range from 1 s to 1000 s, and a linear scale is used for the time range between 0 s and 1 s. The graphs are decorated with symbols at every 15-th data point.

(x-coordinate), i.e., amount of incorrect verification work. Verifiers should start with a score close to zero; CPACHECKER is best in this aspect (also the right-most columns of category *Overall* in Table 7 report this: only 12 false alarms and no missed bug for all 2 868 verification tasks).

Characteristics of the Verification Tools. The plot visualizations also help understanding how the verifiers work internally: (1) The y-coordinate of the left-most data point refers to the 'easiest' verification task for the verifier. We can see that verifiers that are based on a Java virtual machine need some start-up time (CPACHECKER, ULTIMATE). (2) The y-coordinate of the right-most data point refers to the successfully solved verification task that the verifier spent most time on (this is mostly just below the time limit). We can read the ranking of verifiers in this category from right to left. (3) The area below a graph is proportional to the accumulated CPU time for successfully solved tasks. We can identify the most resource-efficient verifiers by looking at the graphs close to the x-axis. (4) Also the shape of the graph can give interesting insights: From the two horizontal lines just below the time limit (at 850 s and 895 s, resp.), we can see that two of the bounded model checkers (CBMC, ESBMC 1.22) return a result just before the time limit is reached. The quantile plot for category *DeviceDrivers64* (not available here, but on the competition web page) shows an interesting bend at about 20 s of run time for verifier CPACHECKER: the verifier gives up with one strategy (without abstraction) and performs an internal restart for using another strategy (with abstraction and CEGAR-based refinement).

Table 8. Quantitative overview over results in category *Termination*

Competition candidate Representing team member	Termination-crafted 89 points max. 47 verif. tasks	Termination-ext 265 points max. 199 verif. tasks	Errors false alarms missed bugs
APROVE [12]	**58**	**0**	
J. Giesl, Aachen, Germany	360 s	0 s	
FUNCTION [34]	**20**	**0**	
C. Urban, Paris, France	220 s	0 s	
T2 [7]	**46**	**50**	
M. Brockschmidt, Cambridge, UK	80 s	64 s	
TAN [23]	**12**	**23**	2
C. Wintersteiger, Oxford, UK	33 s	590 s	1
ULTIMATE BÜCHI [17]	**57**	**117**	
M. Heizmann, Freiburg, Germany	250 s	4 800 s	

Robustness, Soundness, and Completeness. The best tools of each category show that state-of-the-art verification technology significantly progressed in terms of wrong verification results. Table 7 reports, in its last two columns, the number of false alarms and missed bugs, respectively, for the best verifiers in each category: There is a low number of false alarms (wrong bug reports), which witnesses that verification technology can avoid wasted developer time being spent on investigation of spurious bug reports. Also in terms of soundness, the results look promising, considering that the most missed bugs (wrong safety claims) were reported by bounded model checkers. In three categories, the top-three verifiers did not report any wrong result.

Demonstration Categories. For the first time in SV-COMP, we performed experiments in demonstration categories, i.e., categories for which we wanted to try out new applications of verification, new properties, or new rules. For the demonstration categories, we neither rank the results nor assign awards.

Termination. Checking program termination is also an important objective of software verification. We started with two sets of verification tasks: category *Termination-crafted* is a community-contributed set of verification tasks that were designed by verification researchers for the purpose of evaluating termination checkers (programs were collected from well-known papers in the area), and category *Termination-ext* is a selection of verification tasks from existing categories for which the result was determined during the demonstration runs.

Table 9. Re-verification of verification results using error witnesses; verification time in s of CPU time; path length in number of edges; expected result is 'false' in all cases

Verification task	CBMC verification	Path length	CPACHECKER re-verification
parport_false	37	179	11
eureka_01_false	0.36	42	64
Tripl.2.ufo.BOUNDED-10.pals.c	0.81	356	53
Tripl.2.ufo.UNBOUNDED.pals.c	0.80	355	44
gigaset.ko_false	44	140	120
tcm_vhost-ko–32_7a	26	197	62
vhost_net-ko–32_7a	21	89	72
si4713-i2c-ko–111_1a	430	75	12

Table 8 shows the results, which are promising: five teams participated, namely APROVE [29], FUNCTION [30], T2 [31], TAN [32], and ULTIMATE BÜCHI [33]. Also, the quality of the termination checkers was extremely good: almost all tools had no false positive ('false alarms', the verifier reported the program would not terminate although it does) and no false negative ('missed bug', the verifier reported termination but infinite looping is possible).

Device-Driver Challenge. Competitions are always looking for hard problems. We received some unsolved problems from the LDV project [34]. Three teams participated and could compute answers to 6 of the 15 problems: CBMC found 3, CPACHECKER found 4, and ESBMC found 2 solutions to the problems.

Error-Witnesses. One of the objectives of program verification is to provide a witness for the verification result. This is an open problem of verification technology: there is no commonly supported witness format yet, and the verifiers are not producing accurate witnesses that can be automatically assessed for validity [35]. The goal of this demonstration category is to change this (restricted to error witnesses for now): in cooperation with interested groups we defined a format for error witnesses and the verifiers were asked to produce error paths in that format, in order to validate their error paths with *another* verification tool.

Three tools participated in this category: CBMC, CPACHECKER, and ESBMC. The demo revealed many interesting insights on practical issues of using a common witness format, serving as a test before introducing it as a requirement to

---

[29] http://aprove.informatik.rwth-aachen.de

[30] http://www.di.ens.fr/~urban/FuncTion.html

[31] http://research.microsoft.com/en-us/projects/t2

[32] http://www.cprover.org/termination/cta/index.shtml

[33] http://ultimate.informatik.uni-freiburg.de/BuchiAutomizer

[34] http://linuxtesting.org/project/ldv

[35] There was research already on reusing previously computed error paths, but by the same tool and in particular, using tool-specific formats: for example, ESBMC was extended to reproduce errors via instantiated code [30], and CPACHECKER was used to re-check previously computed error paths by interpreting them as automata that control the state-space search [5].

the next edition of the competition. We will report here only a few cases to show how this technique can help. We selected a group of verification tasks (with expected verification result 'false') that CBMC could solve, but CPACHECKER was not able to compute a verification result. We started CPACHECKER again on the verification task, now together with CBMC's error witness. Table 9 reports the details of eight such runs: CPACHECKER can prove the error witnesses of CBMC valid, although it could not find the bug in the program without the hints from the witness. In some cases this is efficient (first and last row) and sometimes it is quite inefficient: the matching algorithm needs improvement. The matching is based purely on syntactical hints (sequence of tokens of the source program). This technique of re-verifying a program with a different verification tool significantly increases the confidence in the verification result (and makes false-alarms unnecessary).

6   Conclusion

The third edition of the Competition on Software Verification had more participants than before: the participation in the 'official' categories increased from eleven to fifteen teams, and five teams took part in the demonstration on termination checking. The number of benchmark problems increased to a total of 2 868 verification tasks (excluding demonstration categories). The organizer and the jury made sure that the competition follows the high quality standards of the TACAS conference, in particular to respect the important principles of fairness, community support, transparency, and technical accuracy.

The results showcase the progress in developing new algorithms and data structures for software verification, and in implementing efficient tools for fully-automatic program verification. The best verifiers have shown good quality in the categories that they focus on, in terms of robustness, soundness, and completeness. The participants represent a variety of general approaches — SMT-based model checking, bounded model checking, symbolic execution, and program analysis showed their different, complementing strengths. Also, the SV-COMP repository of verification tasks has grown considerably: it now contains termination problems and problems for regression verification [4], but also Horn clauses and some Java programs in addition to C programs.

Acknowledgement. We thank K. Friedberger for his support during the evaluation phase and for his work on the benchmarking infrastructure, the competition jury for making sure that the competition is well-grounded in the community, and the teams for making SV-COMP possible through their participation.

References

1. Beyer, D.: Competition on software verification (SV-COMP). In: Flanagan, C., König, B. (eds.) TACAS 2012. LNCS, vol. 7214, pp. 504–524. Springer, Heidelberg (2012)
2. Beyer, D.: Second competition on software verification. In: Piterman, N., Smolka, S.A. (eds.) TACAS 2013. LNCS, vol. 7795, pp. 594–609. Springer, Heidelberg (2013)

3. Beyer, D., Henzinger, T.A., Jhala, R., Majumdar, R.: The software model checker BLAST. Int. J. Softw. Tools Technol. Transfer 9(5-6), 505–525 (2007)
4. Beyer, D., Löwe, S., Novikov, E., Stahlbauer, A., Wendler, P.: Precision reuse for efficient regression verification. In: Proc. ESEC/FSE, pp. 389–399. ACM (2013)
5. Beyer, D., Wendler, P.: Reuse of verification results - conditional model checking, precision reuse, and verification witnesses. In: Bartocci, E., Ramakrishnan, C.R. (eds.) SPIN 2013. LNCS, vol. 7976, pp. 1–17. Springer, Heidelberg (2013)
6. Biere, A., Cimatti, A., Clarke, E., Zhu, Y.: Symbolic model checking without BDDs. In: Cleaveland, W.R. (ed.) TACAS 1999. LNCS, vol. 1579, pp. 193–207. Springer, Heidelberg (1999)
7. Brockschmidt, M., Cook, B., Fuhs, C.: Better termination proving through cooperation. In: Sharygina, N., Veith, H. (eds.) CAV 2013. LNCS, vol. 8044, pp. 413–429. Springer, Heidelberg (2013)
8. Clarke, E.M., Grumberg, O., Jha, S., Lu, Y., Veith, H.: Counterexample-guided abstraction refinement for symbolic model checking. J. ACM 50(5), 752–794 (2003)
9. Dudka, K., Peringer, P., Vojnar, T.: Predator: A shape analyzer based on symbolic memory graphs (Competition contribution). In: Ábrahám, E., Havelund, K. (eds.) TACAS 2014. LNCS, vol. 8413, pp. 412–414. Springer, Heidelberg (2014)
10. Ermis, E., Nutz, A., Dietsch, D., Hoenicke, J., Podelski, A.: Ultimate Kojak (Competition contribution). In: Ábrahám, E., Havelund, K. (eds.) TACAS 2014. LNCS, vol. 8413, pp. 421–423. Springer, Heidelberg (2014)
11. Falke, S., Merz, F., Sinz, C.: LLBMC: Improved bounded model checking of C programs using LLVM (Competition contribution). In: Piterman, N., Smolka, S.A. (eds.) TACAS 2013. LNCS, vol. 7795, pp. 623–626. Springer, Heidelberg (2013)
12. Giesl, J., Schneider-Kamp, P., Thiemann, R.: AProVE 1.2: Automatic termination proofs in the dependency pair framework. In: Furbach, U., Shankar, N. (eds.) IJCAR 2006. LNCS (LNAI), vol. 4130, pp. 281–286. Springer, Heidelberg (2006)
13. Graf, S., Saïdi, H.: Construction of abstract state graphs with Pvs. In: Grumberg, O. (ed.) CAV 1997. LNCS, vol. 1254, pp. 72–83. Springer, Heidelberg (1997)
14. Albarghouthi, A., Gurfinkel, A., Li, Y., Chaki, S., Chechik, M.: UFO: Verification with interpolants and abstract interpretation. In: Piterman, N., Smolka, S.A. (eds.) TACAS 2013. LNCS, vol. 7795, pp. 637–640. Springer, Heidelberg (2013)
15. Gurfinkel, A., Belov, A.: FrankenBit: Bit-precise verification with many bits (Competition contribution). In: Ábrahám, E., Havelund, K. (eds.) TACAS 2014. LNCS, vol. 8413, pp. 408–411. Springer, Heidelberg (2014)
16. Heizmann, M., Christ, J., Dietsch, D., Hoenicke, J., Lindenmann, M., Musa, B., Schilling, C., Wissert, S., Podelski, A.: Ultimate automizer with unsatisfiable cores (Competition contribution). In: Ábrahám, E., Havelund, K. (eds.) TACAS 2014. LNCS, vol. 8413, pp. 418–420. Springer, Heidelberg (2014)
17. Heizmann, M., Hoenicke, J., Leike, J., Podelski, A.: Linear ranking for linear lasso programs. In: Van Hung, D., Ogawa, M. (eds.) ATVA 2013. LNCS, vol. 8172, pp. 365–380. Springer, Heidelberg (2013)
18. Henzinger, T.A., Jhala, R., Majumdar, R., McMillan, K.L.: Abstractions from proofs. In: Proc. POPL, pp. 232–244. ACM (2004)
19. Henzinger, T.A., Jhala, R., Majumdar, R., Sutre, G.: Lazy abstraction. In: Proc. POPL, pp. 58–70. ACM (2002)
20. Inverso, O., Tomasco, E., Fischer, B., La Torre, S., Parlato, G.: Lazy-CSeq: A lazy sequentialization tool for C (Competition contribution). In: Ábrahám, E., Havelund, K. (eds.) TACAS 2014. LNCS, vol. 8413, pp. 398–401. Springer, Heidelberg (2014)

21. Jones, N.D., Muchnick, S.S.: A flexible approach to interprocedural data-flow analysis and programs with recursive data structures. In: POPL, pp. 66–74 (1982)
22. King, J.C.: Symbolic execution and program testing. Commun. ACM 19(7), 385–394 (1976)
23. Kröning, D., Sharygina, N., Tsitovich, A., Wintersteiger, C.M.: Termination analysis with compositional transition invariants. In: Touili, T., Cook, B., Jackson, P. (eds.) CAV 2010. LNCS, vol. 6174, pp. 89–103. Springer, Heidelberg (2010)
24. Kröning, D., Tautschnig, M.: CBMC – C bounded model checker (Competition contribution). In: Ábrahám, E., Havelund, K. (eds.) TACAS 2014. LNCS, vol. 8413, pp. 389–391. Springer, Heidelberg (2014)
25. Löwe, S., Mandrykin, M., Wendler, P.: CPACHECKER with sequential combination of explicit-value analyses and predicate analyses (Competition contribution). In: Ábrahám, E., Havelund, K. (eds.) TACAS 2014. LNCS, vol. 8413, pp. 392–394. Springer, Heidelberg (2014)
26. Morse, J., Ramalho, M., Cordeiro, L., Nicole, D., Fischer, B.: ESBMC 1.22 (Competition contribution). In: Ábrahám, E., Havelund, K. (eds.) TACAS 2014. LNCS, vol. 8413, pp. 405–407. Springer, Heidelberg (2014)
27. Muller, P., Vojnar, T.: CPALIEN: Shape analyzer for CPAChecker (Competition contribution). In: Ábrahám, E., Havelund, K. (eds.) TACAS 2014. LNCS, vol. 8413, pp. 395–397. Springer, Heidelberg (2014)
28. Podelski, A., Rybalchenko, A.: A complete method for the synthesis of linear ranking functions. In: Steffen, B., Levi, G. (eds.) VMCAI 2004. LNCS, vol. 2937, pp. 239–251. Springer, Heidelberg (2004)
29. Popeea, C., Rybalchenko, A.: Threader: A verifier for multi-threaded programs (Competition contribution). In: Piterman, N., Smolka, S.A. (eds.) TACAS 2013. LNCS, vol. 7795, pp. 633–636. Springer, Heidelberg (2013)
30. Rocha, H., Barreto, R., Cordeiro, L., Neto, A.D.: Understanding programming bugs in ANSI-C software using bounded model checking counter-examples. In: Derrick, J., Gnesi, S., Latella, D., Treharne, H. (eds.) IFM 2012. LNCS, vol. 7321, pp. 128–142. Springer, Heidelberg (2012)
31. Shved, P., Mandrykin, M., Mutilin, V.: Predicate analysis with BLAST 2.7. In: Flanagan, C., König, B. (eds.) TACAS 2012. LNCS, vol. 7214, pp. 525–527. Springer, Heidelberg (2012)
32. Slaby, J., Strejček, J.: Symbiotic 2: More precise slicing (Competition contribution). In: Ábrahám, E., Havelund, K. (eds.) TACAS 2014. LNCS, vol. 8413, pp. 415–417. Springer, Heidelberg (2014)
33. Tomasco, E., Inverso, O., Fischer, B., La Torre, S., Parlato, G.: MU-CSeq: Sequentialization of C programs by shared memory unwindings (Competition contribution). In: Ábrahám, E., Havelund, K. (eds.) TACAS 2014. LNCS, vol. 8413, pp. 402–404. Springer, Heidelberg (2014)
34. Urban, C., Miné, A.: An abstract domain to infer ordinal-valued ranking functions. In: Shao, Z. (ed.) ESOP 2014. LNCS, vol. 8410, pp. 412–431. Springer, Heidelberg (2014)

CBMC – C Bounded Model Checker
(Competition Contribution)

Daniel Kroening[1] and Michael Tautschnig[2]

[1] University of Oxford, UK
[2] Queen Mary University of London, UK

Abstract CBMC implements bit-precise bounded model checking for C programs and has been developed and maintained for more than ten years. CBMC verifies the absence of violated assertions under a given loop unwinding bound. Other properties, such as SV-COMP's ERROR labels or memory safety properties are reduced to assertions via automated instrumentation. Only recently support for efficiently checking concurrent programs, including support for weak memory models, has been added. Thus, CBMC is now capable of finding counterexamples in all of SV-COMP's categories. As back end, the competition submission of CBMC uses MiniSat 2.2.0.

1 Overview

The C Bounded Model Checker (CBMC) [2] demonstrates the violation of assertions in C programs, or proves safety of the assertions under a given bound. CBMC implements a bit-precise translation of an input C program, annotated with assertions and with loops unrolled to a given depth, into a formula. If the formula is satisfiable, then an execution leading to a violated assertion exists. For SV-COMP, satisfiability of the formula is decided using MiniSat 2.2.0 [4].

2 Architecture

Bounded model checkers such as CBMC reduce questions about program paths to constraints that can be solved by off-the-shelf SAT or SMT solvers. With the SAT back end, and given a program annotated with assertions, CBMC outputs a CNF formula the solutions of which describe program paths leading to assertion violations. In order to do so, CBMC performs the following main steps, which are outlined in Figure 1, and are explained below.

Front end. The *command-line front end* first configures CBMC according to user-supplied parameters, such as the bit-width. The *C parser* utilises an off-the-shelf C preprocessor (such as `gcc -E`) and builds a parse tree from the preprocessed source. Source file- and line information is maintained in annotations. *Type checking* populates a symbol table with type names and symbol identifiers by traversing the parse tree. Each symbol is assigned bit-level type information. CBMC aborts if any inconsistencies are detected at this stage.

E. Ábrahám and K. Havelund (Eds.): TACAS 2014, LNCS 8413, pp. 389–391, 2014.
© Springer-Verlag Berlin Heidelberg 2014

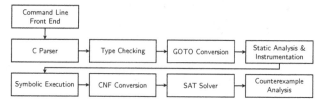

Fig. 1. CBMC architecture

Intermediate Representation. CBMC uses *GOTO programs* as intermediate representation. In this language, all non-linear control flow, such as if or switch-statements, loops and jumps, is translated to equivalent *guarded goto* statements. These statements are branch instructions that include (optional) conditions. CBMC generates one GOTO program per C function found in the parse tree. Furthermore, it adds a new main function that first calls an initialisation function for global variables and then calls the original program entry function.

At this stage, CBMC performs a light-weight static analysis to resolve function pointers to a case split over all candidate functions, resulting in a static call graph. Furthermore, assertions to guard against invalid pointer operations or memory leaks are inserted.

Middle end. CBMC performs symbolic execution by eagerly unwinding loops up to a fixed bound, which can be specified by the user on a per-loop basis or globally, for all loops. In the course of this unwinding step, CBMC also translates GOTO statements to static single assignment (SSA) form. Constant propagation and expression simplification are key to efficiency, and prevent exploration of certain infeasible branches. At the end of this process the program is represented as a system of equations over renamed program variables in guarded statements. The guards determine whether an assignment is actually performed in a given concrete program execution. In [1] we presented an extension to perform efficient bounded model checking of concurrent programs, which symbolically encodes partial orders over read and write accesses to shared variables.

Back end. While CBMC also supports SMT solvers as back ends, we use MiniSat 2.2.0 in this competition. Consequently, the resulting equation is translated into a CNF formula by bit-precise modelling of all expressions plus the Boolean guards [3]. A model computed by the SAT solver corresponds to a path violating at least one of the assertions in the program under scrutiny, and the model is translated back to a sequence of assignments to provide a human-readable counterexample. Conversely, if the formula is unsatisfiable, no assertion can be violated *within the given unwinding bounds*.

3   Strengths and Weaknesses

As a bounded model checker, and in absence of additional loop transformations or k-induction, CBMC cannot provide proofs of correctness for programs with unbounded loops in general. Yet we decided to enforce termination with a TRUE/FALSE answer within the time bounds specified in SV-COMP to provide best-effort answers. Consequently there may be unsound results on certain benchmarks. To reduce the number of such results, the wrapper script (see below) runs CBMC with increasing loop bounds of 2, 6, 12, 17, 21, and 40 until the timeout is reached. These values were obtained as educated guesses informed by the training phase.

Apart from this fundamental limitation, we observed several errors (both false positives and false negatives) caused by current limitations in treatment of pointers. This affects at least one benchmark in the Concurrency category and possibly several in MemorySafety.

The strengths of bounded model checking, on the other hand, are its predictable performance and amenability to the full spectrum of categories.

4   Tool Setup

The competition submission is based on CBMC version 4.5. The full source code of the competing version is available at

http://svn.cprover.org/svn/cbmc/releases/cbmc-4.5-sv-comp-2014/.

To process a benchmark FOO.c (with properties in FOO.prp), the script cbmc-wrapper.sh should be invoked as follows:

cbmc-wrapper.sh --propertyfile FOO.prp --32 FOO.c

for all categories with a 32-bit memory model; for those with a 64-bit memory model, --32 should be replaced by --64.

5   Software Project

CBMC is maintained by Daniel Kroening with patches supplied by the community. It is made publicly available under a BSD-style license. The source code and binaries for popular platforms are available at http://www.cprover.org/cbmc.

References

1. Alglave, J., Kroening, D., Tautschnig, M.: Partial orders for efficient bounded model checking of concurrent software. In: Sharygina, N., Veith, H. (eds.) CAV 2013. LNCS, vol. 8044, pp. 141–157. Springer, Heidelberg (2013)
2. Clarke, E., Kroening, D., Lerda, F.: A tool for checking ANSI-C programs. In: Jensen, K., Podelski, A. (eds.) TACAS 2004. LNCS, vol. 2988, pp. 168–176. Springer, Heidelberg (2004)
3. Clarke, E.M., Kroening, D., Yorav, K.: Behavioral consistency of C and Verilog programs using Bounded Model Checking. In: DAC, pp. 368–371 (2003)
4. Eén, N., Sörensson, N.: An extensible SAT-solver. In: Giunchiglia, E., Tacchella, A. (eds.) SAT 2003. LNCS, vol. 2919, pp. 502–518. Springer, Heidelberg (2004)

CPACHECKER with Sequential Combination of Explicit-Value Analyses and Predicate Analyses
(Competition Contribution)

Stefan Löwe[1], Mikhail Mandrykin[2], and Philipp Wendler[1]

[1] University of Passau, Germany
[2] Institute for System Programming of Russian Academy of Science, Russia

Abstract. CPACHECKER is a framework for software verification, built on the foundations of CONFIGURABLE PROGRAM ANALYSIS (CPA). For the SV-COMP'14, we file a CPACHECKER configuration that runs up to five analyses in sequence. The first two analyses of our approach utilize the explicit-value domain for modeling the state space, while the remaining analyses are based on predicate abstraction. In addition to that, a bit-precise counterexample checker comes into action whenever an analysis finds a counterexample. The combination of conceptually different analyses is key to the success of our verification approach, as the diversity of verification tasks is taken into account.

1 Software Architecture

CPACHECKER, which is built on the foundations of CONFIGURABLE PROGRAM ANALYSIS (CPA), strives for high extensibility and reuse. As such, auxiliary analyses, such as tracking the program counter, modeling the call stack, and keeping track of function pointers, all of which is required for virtually any verification tool, are implemented as independent CPAs. The same is true for the main analyses, such as, e.g., the explicit-value analysis and the analysis based on predicate abstraction, which are also available as decoupled CPAs within CPACHECKER.

All these CPAs can be enabled and flexibly recombined on a per-demand basis without the need of changing adjacent CPAs. Other algorithms, like CEGAR, counterexample checks, parallel or sequential combinations of analyses, as the one being filed to this year's SV-COMP'14, can be plugged together by simply passing the according configuration options to the CPACHECKER framework.

CPACHECKER, which is written in JAVA, uses the C parser of the Eclipse CDT project[1], and MathSAT5[2] for solving SMT formulae and interpolation queries.

---

[1] http://www.eclipse.org/cdt/
[2] http://mathsat.fbk.eu/

E. Ábrahám and K. Havelund (Eds.): TACAS 2014, LNCS 8413, pp. 392–394, 2014.

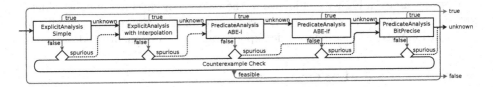

Fig. 1. Overview of the sequential combination used for reachability problems

2   Verification Approach

CPACHECKER gets as input a specification and the source of a C program, which is then transformed into a control flow automaton (CFA) of the input program. During the analysis, this CFA is traversed, gradually building the abstract reachability graph (ARG). The nodes of the ARG represent the reachable states of the program, containing all relevant information, such as the program counter, the call stack and the information collected by the main CPAs, like explicit variable assignments or boolean combinations of predicates about program variables.

For reachability problems, we use a sequential combination [1] of up to five analyses using explicit-value analysis and predicate abstraction. The general approach of our sequential combination is as follows. Once any analysis in the sequence reports the verdict *true*, this result is returned. In case a counterexample is found and validated by a subsequent counterexample check, the verdict *false* is returned. If the counterexample is found to be spurious, or when the current analysis reaches a predefined time limit, the next analysis takes over.

The sequence starts with an explicit-value analysis without abstraction or refinement for 20 seconds. The motivation here is, that many control-flow intense programs can be solved with this approach in very little time. However, this simple analysis easily falls prey to state-space explosion. This is why a more sophisticated analysis of the same domain, including an abstract-refine loop [3], is started in case the first one does not come up with a result. Next in line are three analyses using predicate abstraction with adjustable block encoding [2]. The reason for switching to analyses that are conceptually different is motivated by the fact, that different programs have different characteristics. The third and fourth analyses model program variables as real variables and use only linear arithmetic. The first of these two configurations computes predicate abstractions only at loop heads (ABE-l) and runs for at most ten minutes. The second one additionally abstracts at function call and return sites (ABE-lf), and shows different performance characteristics. The final analysis, a bit-precise predicate analysis, is used if all previous analyses failed to provide a result (reasoning about bit vectors is too expensive to use it on all programs). In addition, an analysis similar to the last one, but lacking the abstract-refine loop, checks finite counterexamples found by any of the previously mentioned analyses. The bounded model checker CBMC[3] is used to check counterexamples of the last

---

[3] http://www.cprover.org/cbmc

analysis for an even higher confidence in the result. For checking memory safety properties, we use a bounded analysis consisting of concrete memory graphs in combination with an instance of the explicit-value analysis mentioned above.

3   Strengths and Weaknesses

Similarly to our last years submissions, though far more sophisticated, the key idea of the submitted configuration is the combination of conceptually different analyses. In addition, the predicate analysis now has support for bit vectors, and also allows for more precise and efficient support for pointer aliasing by encoding possibly aliased memory locations with uninterpreted functions. However, CPACHECKER lacks support for multi-threaded or recursive programs. Efficient tracking of heap memory remains an issue, yet solvable, e.g., by summarization.

4   Setup and Configuration

CPACHECKER is available at `http://cpachecker.sosy-lab.org`. The submitted version is `1.2.11-svcomp14b`. The command line for running CPACHECKER is

```
scripts/cpa.sh -sv-comp14 -disable-java-assertions -heap 10000m -spec property.prp program.i
```

Please add the parameter `-64` for C programs assuming a 64-bit environment. For machines with less RAM, the amount of memory given to the Java VM needs to be adjusted with the parameter `-heap`. CPACHECKER will print the verification result and the name of the output directory to the console. Additional information (such as the error path) will be written to files in this directory.

5   Project and Contributors

CPACHECKER is an open-source project led by Dirk Beyer from the Software Systems Lab at the University of Passau. Several other research groups use and contribute to CPACHECKER, such as the Institute for System Programming of the Russian Academy of Sciences, the University of Paderborn and the University of Technology in Brno. We would like to thank all contributors for their work on CPACHECKER. The full list can be found at `http://cpachecker.sosy-lab.org`.

References

1. Beyer, D., Henzinger, T.A., Keremoglu, M.E., Wendler, P.: Conditional model checking: A technique to pass information between verifiers. In: Proc. FSE. ACM (2012)
2. Beyer, D., Keremoglu, M.E., Wendler, P.: Predicate abstraction with adjustable-block encoding. In: Proc. FMCAD, pp. 189–197, FMCAD (2010)
3. Beyer, D., Löwe, S.: Explicit-state software model checking based on CEGAR and interpolation. In: Cortellessa, V., Varró, D. (eds.) FASE 2013. LNCS, vol. 7793, pp. 146–162. Springer, Heidelberg (2013)

CPALIEN: Shape Analyzer for CPAChecker*
(Competition Contribution)

Petr Muller and Tomáš Vojnar

FIT, Brno University of Technology, IT4Innovations Centre of Excellence, Czech Republic

Abstract. CPALIEN is a configurable program analysis framework instance. It uses an extension of the symbolic memory graphs (SMGs) abstract domain for shape analysis of programs manipulating the heap. In particular, CPALIEN extends SMGs with a simple integer value analysis in order to handle programs with both pointers and integer data. The current version of CPALIEN is an early prototype intended as a basis for a future research in the given area. The version submitted for SV-COMP'14 does not contain any shape abstraction, but it is still powerful enough to participate in several categories.

1 Verification Approach

CPALIEN is an analyzer of pointer manipulating programs written in the C language. It intends to handle industrial, often highly optimized code. CPALIEN is able to detect common memory manipulation errors like invalid dereferences, invalid deallocations, and memory leaks.

CPALIEN is an offspring of the successful Predator shape analyzer [1]. Predator implements a sound shape analysis of programs manipulating list-like data structures of various kinds. While Predator's ability to handle programs with complex lists is great (as witnessed by the tool winning gold medals in the appropriate categories in the first two SV-COMP competitions), we were unsuccessful with extending Predator to handle other data structures than lists and to also handle data other than pointers.

Therefore, we decided to redesign Predator's abstract domain of Symbolic Memory Graphs (SMGs) within the extensible framework of CPAChecker, another successful verification framework [4], which, however, so far lacked a support for shape analysis. Consequently, CPALIEN is implemented as an extension of CPAChecker and hence as an instance of the underlying Configurable Program Analysis (CPA) [3] framework.

Compared with the use of SMGs in Predator [2], the abstract domain of CPALIEN does not yet use any shape abstractions, which means the analysis will not terminate on programs building unbounded dynamic data structures (unless an error is found). On the other hand, CPALIEN combines usage of SMGs with a simple integer value analysis. Where possible, integer values are tracked explicitly for variables. When explicit values are not available, we infer information about value equality or nonequality from assumptions. The combination of this light-weight explicit integer value analysis and

* This work was supported by the Czech Science Foundation project 14-11384S and the EU/Czech IT4Innovations Centre of Excellence project CZ.1.05/1.1.00/02.0070.

E. Ábrahám and K. Havelund (Eds.): TACAS 2014, LNCS 8413, pp. 395–397, 2014.

pointer analysis based on SMGs works well for enough test cases from the SV-COMP benchmark to get a positive score in categories where we participate.

The CPA framework allows one to merge the encountered states to reduce the generated state space. This feature is, however, not used in CPALIEN. To compute the covering relation, which is used by the high-level CPA reachability algorithm to determine the end of the state space search, CPALIEN uses the SMG join operation. CPALIEN also uses several specialized helper analyses provided by the CPAChecker framework to deal with certain specific tasks. These helper analyses are the *Location*, *CallStack*, and *FunctionPointer* CPAs.

2 ` Software Architecture

CPALIEN builds upon the CPAChecker framework for implementation, execution, and combination of instances of the CPA formalism. CPAChecker implements a reachability analysis algorithm over a generic CPA and also provides several other algorithms. CPALIEN is an implementation of a CPA instance, consisting of the abstract domain definition and the transfer relation between the states. Symbolic execution is driven by CPAChecker. CPAChecker also provides a C language parsing capability, wrapping a C parser present in the Eclipse CDT. Both CPAChecker and CPALIEN are written in Java.

3   Strengths and Weaknesses

A general strength of CPALIEN comes with implementation in the generic CPAChecker framework, offering a potential for the future in terms of combining the SMG-based shape analysis with other analyses.

Currently, CPALIEN is, however, mainly focused on heap manipulating programs as its integer value analysis plays just a supporting role without an ambition to handle harder problems. Moreover, CPALIEN is an early prototype, and it so far lacks any shape abstraction. Therefore, CPALIEN does not terminate on many of the benchmark test cases from the *Memory Safety* category for which CPALIEN is suited otherwise. For the *Heap Manipulation* category, the results are better: there are significantly more correct answers, with just a few timeouts and only a single false positive reported. Even the simple integer value analysis combined with the SMG domain managed to provide a correct answer for many test cases from the *Control Flow and Integer Value* category, especially those in the *Product Lines* sub-category.

Generally, the results correspond with the prototype status of the tool. Apart from the already mentioned missing abstraction, the tool still has many implementation issues. It also has deficiencies to handle some C language elements, like implicit type conversions. Another roadblock is CPALIEN's handling of external functions (functions with the body unavailable to the verifier). CPALIEN takes a stance that any unknown function can contain incorrect code, therefore the memory safety of programs calling unknown functions cannot be proved. An UNKNOWN answer is given for these cases. Therefore, CPALIEN's results could be improved by modeling the common C library functions, because many programs use them.

With these limitations being reflected by the results, we still argue that after their resolution, CPALIEN will form a promising base for further research on shape analysis and its integration with other specialized analyses, providing heap analysis capabilities still missing in the CPAChecker ecosystem.

4 Tool Setup and Configuration

CPALIEN is available online at the project page:

```
http://www.fit.vutbr.cz/research/groups/verifit/tools/cpalien/
```

It is a modified version of the upstream CPAChecker, containing code not yet present in the upstream repository. For the participation in the competition, we have prepared a tarball. The only dependency needed to run CPALIEN is Java version 7.

For running the verifier, we have prepared a wrapper script to provide the output required by the competition rules. The script is run in the following way:

```
$ ./cpalien.sh target_program.c
```

Upon completion, a single line with the answer is provided. More information about the verification result, such as the error path, is provided in the `output` directory. The tool does not adhere to competition requirements with respect to property files: it does not allow a property file to be passed as a parameter. This was caused by our incorrect reading of the requirements. The property file is expected to be present in the same directory as the verification task.

CPALIEN participates in the *Heap Manipulation*, *Memory Safety* and *Control Flow and Integer Variable* categories. We opt out from the remaining ones.

5 Software Project and Contributors

CPALIEN is an extension of the CPAChecker project, building on the CPAChecker heavily. CPALIEN is developed by the VeriFIT [1] group at the Brno University of Technology. A significant part of the SMG code was contributed by Alexander Driemeyer from University of Passau, whom we would like to thank. CPAChecker is a project developed mainly by the Software Systems Lab[2] at the University of Passau. Both CPALIEN and CPAChecker are distributed under the Apache 2.0 license.

References

1. Dudka, K., Peringer, P., Vojnar, T.: Predator: A Practical Tool for Checking Manipulation of Dynamic Data Structures Using Separation Logic. In: Gopalakrishnan, G., Qadeer, S. (eds.) CAV 2011. LNCS, vol. 6806, pp. 372–378. Springer, Heidelberg (2011)
2. Dudka, K., Peringer, P., Vojnar, T.: Byte-Precise Verification of Low-Level List Manipulation. In: Logozzo, F., Fähndrich, M. (eds.) SAS 2013. LNCS, vol. 7935, pp. 215–237. Springer, Heidelberg (2013)
3. Beyer, D., Henzinger, T.A., Théoduloz, G.: Configurable Software Verification: Concretizing the Convergence of Model Checking and Program Analysis. In: Damm, W., Hermanns, H. (eds.) CAV 2007. LNCS, vol. 4590, pp. 504–518. Springer, Heidelberg (2007)
4. Beyer, D., Keremoglu, M.E.: CPACHECKER: A Tool for Configurable Software Verification. In: Gopalakrishnan, G., Qadeer, S. (eds.) CAV 2011. LNCS, vol. 6806, pp. 184–190. Springer, Heidelberg (2011)

---

[1] http://www.fit.vutbr.cz/research/groups/verifit/
[2] http://www.sosy-lab.org/

Lazy-CSeq: A Lazy Sequentialization Tool for C [*]
(Competition Contribution)

Omar Inverso[1], Ermenegildo Tomasco[1], Bernd Fischer[2],
Salvatore La Torre[3], and Gennaro Parlato[1]

[1] Electronics and Computer Science, University of Southampton, UK
[2] Division of Computer Science, Stellenbosch University, South Africa
[3] Dipartimento di Informatica, Università degli Studi di Salerno, Italy
{oi2c11,et1m11,gennaro}@ecs.soton.ac.uk, bfischer@cs.sun.ac.za,
slatorre@unisa.it

Abstract. We describe a version of the lazy sequentialization schema by La Torre, Madhusudan, and Parlato that is optimized for bounded programs, and avoids the re-computation of the local state of each process at each context switch. Lazy-CSeq implements this sequentialization schema for sequentially consistent C programs using POSIX threads. Experiments show that it is very competitive.

1 Introduction

Sequentialization translates concurrent programs into (under certain assumptions) equivalent non-deterministic sequential programs and so reduces concurrent verification to its sequential counterpart. The widely used (e.g., in CSeq [2,3] or Rek [1]) sequentialization schema by Lal and Reps (LR) [6] considers only round-robin schedules with K rounds, which bounds the number of context switches between the different threads. LR first replaces the shared global memory by K indexed copies. It then executes the individual threads to completion, simulating context switches by non-deterministically incrementing the index. The first thread works with the initial memory guesses, while the remaining threads work with the values left by their predecessors. The initial guesses are also stored in a second set of copies; after all threads have terminated these are used to ensure consistency (i.e., the last thread has ended its execution in each round with initial guesses for the next round).

LR explores a large number of configurations unreachable by the concurrent program, due to the completely non-deterministic choice of the global memory copies and the late consistency check. The lazy sequentialization schema by La Torre, Madhusudan, and Parlato (LMP) [4,5] avoids this non-determinism, but at each context switch it re-computes from scratch the local state of each process. This can lead to verification conditions of exponential size when constructing the formula in a bounded model checking approach (due to function inlining). However, for bounded programs this re-computation can be avoided and the sequentialized program can instead jump to the context switch points. Lazy-CSeq implements this improved *bounded LMP schema* (bLMP) for sequentially consistent C programs that use POSIX threads.

[*] This work was partially funded by the MIUR grant FARB 2011-2012, Università degli Studi di Salerno (Italy).

E. Ábrahám and K. Havelund (Eds.): TACAS 2014, LNCS 8413, pp. 398–401, 2014.
© Springer-Verlag Berlin Heidelberg 2014

2 Verification Approach

Overview. bLMP considers only round-robin schedules with K rounds. It further assumes that the concurrent program (and thus in particular the number of possible threads) is bounded and that all jumps are forward jumps, which are both enforced in Lazy-CSeq by unrolling. Unlike LR, however, bLMP does not run the individual threads to completion in one fell swoop; instead, it repeatedly calls the sequentialized thread functions in a round-robin fashion. For each thread it maintains the program locations at which the previous round's context switch has happened and thus the computation must resume in the next round. The sequentialized thread functions then jump (in multiple hops) back to these stored locations. bLMP also keeps the thread-local variables persistent (as `static`) and thus, unlike the original LMP, does not need to re-compute their values from saved copies of previous global memory states before it resumes the computation.

Data Structures. bLMP only stores and maintains, for each thread, a flag denoting whether the thread is active, the thread's original arguments, and an integer denoting the program location at which the previous context switch has happened. Since it does not need any copy of the shared global memory, heap allcotion needs no special treatment during the sequentialization and can be delegated entirely to the backend model checker.

Main Driver. The sequentialized program's main function orchestrates the analysis. It consists of a sequence of small code snippets, one for each thread and each round, that check the thread's active flag (maintained by Lazy-CSeq's implementation of the `pthread_create` and `pthread_join` functions), and, if this is set, non-deterministically increment the next context switch point `pc_cs` (which must be smaller than the thread's size), call the sequentialized thread function with the original arguments, and store the context switch point for the next round. Lazy-CSeq obtains from the un-

```
if (active_tr[thr_idx] == 1) {
    pc_cs = pc[thr_idx] + nondet_uint();
    assume(pc_cs <= SIZE_<thr_idx>);
    thread_<thr_tdx>(thr_args[thr_idx]);
    pc[thr_idx] = pc_cs;
}
```

rolling phase the set of thread instances that the original concurrent program can possibly create within the given bounds. This allows the static construction of the main driver. Note that the choice of the context switch points in the driver is the only additional non-determinism introduced by the sequentialization.

Thread Translation. The sequentialized program also contains a function for each thread instance (including the original `main`) identified during the unrolling phase. Within the function each statement is guarded by a check whether its location is before the stored location or after the next context switch non-deterministically chosen by the driver. In the former case, the statement has already been executed in a previous round, and the simulation jumps ahead one hop; in the latter case, the statement will be executed in a future round, and the simulation jumps to the thread's exit. Each jump target (corresponding either directly to a `goto` label or indirectly to a branch of an `if` statement) is also guarded by an additional check to ensure that the jump does not jump over the context switch. Since bLMP only explores states reachable in the original concurrent program, `assert` statements need no special treatment during the sequentialization and can be delegated entirely to the backend model checker.

3   Architecture, Implementation, and Availability

Architecture. Lazy-CSeq is implemented as a source-to-source transformation tool in Python (v2.7.1). Like CSeq [2,3] and MU-CSeq [7] it uses the `pycparser` (v2.10, `github.com/eliben/pycparser`) to parse a C program into an abstract syntax tree (AST). However, in order to produce the right jump targets Lazy-CSeq unrolls all loops and replicates the thread functions. The sequentialized program can then be processed independently by any sequential verification tool for C. Lazy-CSeq has been tested with CBMC (v4.5, `www.cprover.org/cbmc/`) and ESBMC (v1.22, `www.esbmc.org`).

A small wrapper script bundles up translation and verification. It also invokes Lazy-CSeq repeatedly, with the parameters `-f2 -w2 -r2 -d135`, `-f4 -w4 -r1 -d145`, `-f16 -w1 -r1 -d220`, and `-f11 -w1 -r11 -d150`. Here f and w are the unwind bound for `for` (i.e. bounded) and `while` (i.e. potentially unbounded) loops, respectively, r is the number of rounds, and d is the depth option for the backend. We leave the analysis running to completion every time, without timeouts or memory limits. When the result is TRUE, the scripts restarts the analysis with the next set of parameters. As soon the script gets FALSE, it returns FALSE. Only if the analysis using the last set of parameters is finished and the results is TRUE, then the scripts returns TRUE.

Availability and Installation. Lazy-CSeq can be downloaded from `http://users.ecs.soton.ac.uk/gp4/cseq/lazy-cseq-0.1.zip`; it also requires installation of the `pycparser`. It can be installed as global Python script. In the competition we only used CBMC as a sequential verification backend; this must be installed in the same directory as Lazy-CSeq.

Call. Lazy-CSeq should be called in the installation directory as follows:
`lazy-cseq.py -i<file> --spec<specfile> --witness<logfile>`
Strengths and Weaknesses. Since Lazy-CSeq is not a full verification tool but only a concurrency pre-processor, we only competed in the Concurrency category. Here it achieved a perfect score.

References

1. Chaki, S., Gurfinkel, A., Strichman, O.: Time-bounded analysis of real-time systems. In: FM-CAD, pp. 72–80 (2011)
2. Fischer, B., Inverso, O., Parlato, G.: CSeq: A Sequentialization Tool for C (Competition Contribution). In: Piterman, N., Smolka, S.A. (eds.) TACAS 2013. LNCS, vol. 7795, pp. 616–618. Springer, Heidelberg (2013)
3. Fischer, B., Inverso, O., Parlato, G.: CSeq: A Concurrency Pre-Processor for Sequential C Verification Tools. In: ASE, pp. 710–713 (2013)

4. La Torre, S., Madhusudan, P., Parlato, G.: Reducing context-bounded concurrent reachability to sequential reachability. In: Bouajjani, A., Maler, O. (eds.) CAV 2009. LNCS, vol. 5643, pp. 477–492. Springer, Heidelberg (2009)
5. La Torre, S., Madhusudan, P., Parlato, G.: Sequentializing parameterized programs. In: FIT, EPTCS 87, pp. 34–47 (2012)
6. Lal, A., Reps, T.W.: Reducing concurrent analysis under a context bound to sequential analysis. Formal Methods in System Design 35(1), 73–97 (2009)
7. Tomasco, E., Inverso, O., Fischer, B., La Torre, S., Parlato, G.: MU-CSeq: Sequentialization of C Programs by Shared Memory Unwindings (Competition Contribution). In: Ábrahám, E., Havelund, K. (eds.) TACAS 2014. LNCS, vol. 8413, pp. 402–404. Springer, Heidelberg (2014)

MU-CSeq: Sequentialization of C Programs by Shared Memory Unwindings*
(Competition Contribution)

Ermenegildo Tomasco[1], Omar Inverso[1], Bernd Fischer[2],
Salvatore La Torre[3], and Gennaro Parlato[1]

[1] Electronics and Computer Science, University of Southampton, UK
[2] Division of Computer Science, Stellenbosch University, South Africa
[3] Dipartimento di Informatica, Università di Salerno, Italy
{et1m11,oi2c11,gennaro}@ecs.soton.ac.uk, bfischer@cs.sun.ac.za,
slatorre@unisa.it

Abstract. We implement a new sequentialization algorithm for multi-threaded C programs with dynamic thread creation as a new CSeq module. The novel basic idea of this algorithm is to fix (by a nondeterministic guess) the sequence of write operations in the shared memory and then simulate the behavior of the program according to any scheduling that respects this choice. Simulation is done thread-by-thread and the thread creation mechanism is replaced by function calls.

1 Introduction

Sequentialization translates a concurrent program into a corresponding sequential one while preserving a given verification property (e.g., reachability). The idea is to reuse in the domain of concurrent programs the technology developed for the analysis of sequential programs. This simplifies and speeds up the development of robust tools for concurrent programs. It also allows the designers to focus only on the concurrency aspects and provides them with a framework in which they can quickly check the effectiveness of their solutions. A sequentialization tool can be designed as a front-end for a number of analysis tools that share the same input language, and thus many alternatives are immediately available.

We design a new sequentialization algorithm for multi-threaded C programs with dynamic thread creation. Its main novelty is the idea of *memory unwinding* (MU). We fix (by a nondeterministic guess) the sequence of write operations in the shared memory and then simulate the behavior of the program according to any scheduling that respects this choice. We can then use of the number of writes in the shared memory as a parameter of the bounded analysis, which is orthogonal to considering the number of context switches underlying previous research on sequentializations based on the notion of bounded context-switching (e.g., [10,6,7,2,1,8,9]). Moreover, MU-CSeq naturally accommodates the simulation of dynamic thread creation by function calls.

We implement MU-CSeq as a new module of the tool CSeq [3,4]. Other modules of CSeq implement the Lal/Reps algorithm [6] and a lazy-sequentialization scheme aimed to exploit bounded model checking [5].

---

* This work was partially funded by the MIUR grant FARB 2011-2012, Università degli Studi di Salerno (Italy).

E. Ábrahám and K. Havelund (Eds.): TACAS 2014, LNCS 8413, pp. 402–404, 2014.

2 Verification Approach

Overview. MU-CSeq translates a multi-threaded C program P, into a standard C program P'. The source-to-source translation is parameterized over the number of writes N_w in the shared memory and the maximum number of threads N_t. The overall scheme consists of guessing a sequence σ of N_w writes and then simulating any execution of P that matches σ. The simulation is done thread-by-thread, starting from the original main function; when a new thread is created the simulation of the current thread is suspended until the simulation of the new thread has ended. When the number of threads passes the bound N_t, each new thread creation operation is just ignored.

Modules of P'. The main function of P' is in charge of guessing a consistent sequence of writes σ and starting the simulation of P. P' has a function for each function (including the main) and each thread of P. The translation of P modules into the corresponding modules of P' consists of: 1) adding a few lines of control code to handle creation and execution of threads, and 2) replacing the reads and writes in the shared memory with calls to _read and _write functions, respectively.

Guessing the Sequence of Writes. We use a global two-dimensional array _mem that corresponds to the temporal unwinding of the shared memory according to the memory updates. Here, each column corresponds to an updating event (i.e., a *write*) in σ and each row corresponds to a variable. The entry _mem[i,j] contains the value of the i-th shared variable after the j-th write in σ. We use a second global array _sigma to store for each write the involved variable and the thread that has executed the write. To guess the writes, we assign non-deterministic values to these arrays. The main function of P' then uses assume statements to check the consistency of the values stored in the guessed arrays before starting the simulation of P.

Accessing Global Memory. On executing each thread t, we store in a variable *thr_pos* the index of the last executed write in σ. This variable is updated by _read and _write. On calling _write for the assignment $x=e$, *thr_pos* is updated to the corresponding index and then _mem[x,thr_pos]=e is checked. By calling _read for reading variable x, first *thr_pos* is nondeterministically updated to any index between its current value and the next write in σ by t, and then _mem[x,thr_pos] is returned.

Thread Creation and Execution. Thread creation and execution are implemented as function calls in P'. Thus, if a thread t_2 is created from a thread t_1, the simulation of t_1 stops until the call to t_2 has terminated. Before the simulation of t_2 starts, the current value of *thr_pos* is stored in a local variable such that when t_2 has terminated, the simulation of t_1 restarts from this index. Accordingly, the simulation of t_2 starts from the current value of *thr_pos*. When either the last statement of thread t_2 is reached, or a write after the last guessed write for t_2 is executed, or an index greater than N_w is guessed for a read, then all the calls of thread t_2 are returned, including the call that has started the thread simulation. After the return we check that all write operations that t_2 has to execute actually happened.

3 Architecture, Tool Setup, and Configuration

Architecture. Our sequentialization is implemented as a source-to-source transformation in Python (v2.7.1), within the CSeq tool. It uses pycparser (v2.10, `github.com/eliben/pycparser` to parse a C program into an abstract syntax tree (AST), and then traverses the AST to construct the sequentialized version, as outlined above. The resulting program can be processed independently by any verification tool for C. MU-CSeq has been tested with CBMC (v4.2, `www.cprover.org/cbmc/`) and ESBMC (v1.22, `www.esbmc.org`). For the competition we use a wrapper script that bundles up the translation and calls CBMC for verification. We use the parameters `-w24 -t17 -f17 -unwind1 -depth4000 -MaxThreadCreate3`, where w (resp., t) is the bound on the number of write operations (resp., of spawned threads), f is the unwind bound for `for` and `unwind` is the unwind bound for the remaining loops, `depth` is the depth option for the backend, and `MaxThreadCreate` is the bound on the number of threads that are spawned in any `while` loop. No timeouts or memory limits are used in the analysis. The wrapper returns the output from CBMC.

Availability and Installation. MU-CSeq can be downloaded from `http://users.ecs.soton.ac.uk/gp4/cseq/mu-cseq-0.1.zip`; it also requires installation of the `pycparser`. It can be installed as global Python script. In the competition we only used CBMC as a sequential verification backend; this must be installed in the same directory as MU-CSeq.

Call. The tool should be called in the installation directory as follows:
`mu-cseq.py -i<file> --spec<specfile> --witness<logfile>`

Strengths and Weaknesses. Since MU-CSeq is not a full verification tool but only a concurrency pre-processor, we only competed in the `Concurrency` category. Here it achieved a perfect score.

References

1. Bouajjani, A., Emmi, M., Parlato, G.: On sequentializing concurrent programs. In: Yahav, E. (ed.) SAS 2011. LNCS, vol. 6887, pp. 129–145. Springer, Heidelberg (2011)
2. Emmi, M., Qadeer, S., Rakamaric, Z.: Delay-bounded scheduling. In: POPL, pp. 411–422 (2011)
3. Fischer, B., Inverso, O., Parlato, G.: CSeq: A Sequentialization Tool for C (Competition Contribution). In: Piterman, N., Smolka, S.A. (eds.) TACAS 2013. LNCS, vol. 7795, pp. 616–618. Springer, Heidelberg (2013)
4. Fischer, B., Inverso, O., Parlato, G.: CSeq: A Concurrency Pre-Processor for Sequential C Verification Tools. In: ASE, pp. 710–713 (2013)
5. Inverso, O., Tomasco, E., Fischer, B., La Torre, S., Parlato, G.: Lazy-CSeq: A Lazy Sequentialization tool for C (Competition Contribution). In: Ábrahám, E., Havelund, K. (eds.) TACAS 2014. LNCS, vol. 8413, pp. 398–401. Springer, Heidelberg (2014)
6. Lal, A., Reps, T.W.: Reducing concurrent analysis under a context bound to sequential analysis. Formal Methods in System Design 35(1), 73–97 (2009)
7. La Torre, S., Madhusudan, P., Parlato, G.: Reducing context-bounded concurrent reachability to sequential reachability. In: Bouajjani, A., Maler, O. (eds.) CAV 2009. LNCS, vol. 5643, pp. 477–492. Springer, Heidelberg (2009)
8. La Torre, S., Madhusudan, P., Parlato, G.: Sequentializing parameterized programs. In: FIT, EPTCS 87, pp. 34–47 (2012)
9. La Torre, S., Parlato, G.: Scope-bounded Multistack Pushdown Systems: Fixed-Point, Sequentialization, and Tree-Width. In: FSTTCS. LIPIcs, vol. 18, pp. 173–184 (2012)
10. Qadeer, S., Wu, D.: KISS: keep it simple and sequential. In: PLDI, pp. 14–24 (2004)

ESBMC 1.22
(Competition Contribution)

Jeremy Morse[1], Mikhail Ramalho[2], Lucas Cordeiro[2],
Denis Nicole[1], and Bernd Fischer[3]

[1] Electronics and Computer Science, University of Southampton, UK
[2] Electronic and Information Research Center, Federal University of Amazonas, Brazil
[3] Division of Computer Science, Stellenbosch University, South Africa
esbmc@ecs.soton.ac.uk

Abstract. We have implemented an improved memory model for ESBMC which better takes into account C's memory alignment rules and optimizes the generated SMT formulae. This simultaneously improves ESBMC's precision and performance.

1 Overview

ESBMC is a context-bounded symbolic model checker that allows the verification of single- and multi-threaded C code with shared variables and locks. ESBMC was originally branched off CBMC (v2.9) [4] and has inherited its object-based memory model. With the increasingly large SV-COMP benchmarks this is now reaching its limits. We have thus implemented an improved memory model for ESBMC; however, we opted for an incremental change and have kept the underlying object-based model in place, rather than adapting a fully byte-precise memory model as for example used by LLBMC [7]. We believe this strikes the right balance between precision and scalability.

In this paper we focus on the differences from the ESBMC version used in last year's competition (1.20) and, in particular, on the memory model; an overview of ESBMC's architecture and more details are given in our previous work [1–3, 5].

2 Differences to ESBMC 1.20

In the last year we have mostly made changes to improve ESBMC's stability, precision, and performance. In addition to the improved memory model (see below) we made a wide range of bug fixes and replaced the string-based accessor functions of the intermediate representation (which also go back to CBMC v2.9) by proper accessor functions. This change alone improves ESBMC's speed by roughly a factor of two.

3 Memory Model

The correct implementation of operations involving pointers is a significant challenge in model checking C programs. As a bounded model checker, ESBMC reduces the

E. Ábrahám and K. Havelund (Eds.): TACAS 2014, LNCS 8413, pp. 405–407, 2014.

bounded program traces to first order logic, which requires us to eliminate pointers in the model checker. We follow CBMC's approach and use a static analysis to approximate for each pointer variable the set of data objects (i.e., memory chunks) at which it *might* point at some stage in the program execution. The data objects are numbered, and a pointer target is represented by a pair of integers identifying the data object and the offset within the object. The value of a pointer variable is then the set of (*object*, *offset*)-pairs to which the pointer may point at the current execution step. The result of a dereference is the union of the sets of values associated with each of the (*object*, *offset*)-pairs.

The performance of this approach suffers if pointer offsets cannot be statically determined, e.g., if a program reads a byte from an arbitrary offset into a structure. The resulting SMT formula is large and unwieldy, and its construction is error-prone. To avoid this, we extended the static pointer analysis to determine the weakest alignment guarantee that a particular pointer variable provides, and inserted padding in structures to make all fields align to word boundaries, as prescribed by C's semantics.

These guarantees, in combination with enforcing memory access alignment rules, allow us to significantly reduce the number of valid dereference behaviours and thus the size of the resulting formula, and to detect alignment errors which we have previously ignored. In circumstances where the underlying type of a memory allocation is unclear (e.g., dynamically allocated memory with nondeterministic size), we fall back to allocating a byte array and piecing together higher level types from the bytes.

Other models checkers (in particular LLBMC [7]) treat all memory as a single byte array, upon which all pointer accesses are decomposed into byte operations. This can lead to performance problems due to the repeated updates to the memory array that need to be reflected in the SMT formula.

4   Competition Approach

In bounded model checking, the choice of the unwinding bounds can make a huge difference. In contrast to previous years, where we only used a single experimentally determined unwinding bound, we now operate an explicit iterative deepening schema ($n = 8, 12, 16$). This replaces the iterative deepening that is implicit in the k-induction that we used last year [5]. In addition, we no longer use the partial loops option [3]. For categories other than MemorySafety we only check for the reachability of the error label and ignore all other built-in properties. We use a small script that implements iterative deepening and calls ESBMC with the main parameters set as follows:

```
esbmc --timeout 15m --memlimit 15g --64 --unwind <n>
  --no-unwinding-assertions --no-assertions --error-label ERROR
  --no-bounds-check --no-div-by-zero-check --no-pointer-check <f>
```

Here, --no-unwinding-assertions removes the unwinding assertion and thus a correctness *claim* is not a full correctness *proof*; however, this increases ESBMC's performance in the competition. The script also sets the specific parameters for the MemorySafety category. The run script and a self-contained binary for 64-bit Linux environments are available at www.esbmc.org/download.html; other versions are available on request. For the competition we used the Z3 solver (V4.0).

5   Results

With the approach described above, ESBMC correctly claims 1837 benchmarks correct and finds existing errors in 557. However, it also finds unexpected errors for 38 benchmarks and fails to find the expected errors in another 52. The failures are concentrated in the MemorySafety and Recursive categories, where we produce 36 and 15 unexpected results, respectively. In MemorySafety, these are caused by differences in the memory models respectively assumed by the competition, and implemented in ESBMC; in particular, in 22 cases ESBMC detects an unchecked dereference of a pointer to a freshly allocated memory chunk, which can lead to a null pointer violation and so mask the result expected by the benchmark. In Recursive, all unexpected results are false alarms, which are caused by bounding the programs. Additionally, ESBMC produces 259 time-outs, which mostly stem from the larger benchmarks in ldv-consumption, ldv-linux-3.4-simple, seq-mthreaded, and eca. The remaining programs fail due to parsing errors (16), conversion error (1), or different internal (mostly out-of-memory) errors during the symbolic execution (108). ESBMC produces good results for all categories but MemorySafety and Recursive; however, since we did not opt out of these, our overall result suffered substantially.

ESBMC's performance has improved greatly over last year's version (v1.20). The number of errors detected has gone up from 448 to 557, while the number of unexpected and missed errors has gone down, from 53 to 38 and from 209 to 52, respectively. The biggest improvements are in the categories Sequentialized and ControlFlowInteger.

Demonstration Section. We took part in the stateful verification, error-witness checking, and device-driver challenges tracks. In particular, we use EZProofC [6] to collect and manipulate the counterexample produced by ESBMC in order to reproduce the identified error for the first round (B1) of the error-witness checking.

Acknowledgements. The third author thanks Samsung for financial support.

References

1. Cordeiro, L., Fischer, B.: Verifying Multi-Threaded Software using SMT-based Context-Bounded Model Checking. In: ICSE, pp. 331–340 (2011)
2. Cordeiro, L., Fischer, B., Marques-Silva, J.: SMT-based bounded model checking for embedded ANSI-C software. IEEE Trans. Software Eng. 38(4), 957–974 (2012)
3. Cordeiro, L., Morse, J., Nicole, D., Fischer, B.: Context-Bounded Model Checking with ESBMC 1.17 (Competition Contribution). In: Flanagan, C., König, B. (eds.) TACAS 2012. LNCS, vol. 7214, pp. 534–537. Springer, Heidelberg (2012)
4. Kroening, D., Clarke, E., Yorav, K.: Behavioral Consistency of C and Verilog Programs Using Bounded Model Checking. In: DAC, pp. 368–371. IEEE (2003)
5. Morse, J., Cordeiro, L., Nicole, D., Fischer, B.: Handling Unbounded Loops with ESBMC 1.20 (Competition Contribution). In: Piterman, N., Smolka, S.A. (eds.) TACAS 2013. LNCS, vol. 7795, pp. 619–622. Springer, Heidelberg (2013)
6. Rocha, H., Barreto, R., Cordeiro, L., Neto, A.D.: Understanding Programming Bugs in ANSI-C Software Using Bounded Model Checking Counter-Examples. In: Derrick, J., Gnesi, S., Latella, D., Treharne, H. (eds.) IFM 2012. LNCS, vol. 7321, pp. 128–142. Springer, Heidelberg (2012)
7. Sinz, C., Falke, S., Merz, F.: A Precise Memory Model for Low-Level Bounded Model Checking. In: SSV, USENIX (2010)

FrankenBit: Bit-Precise Verification with Many Bits*
(Competition Contribution)

Arie Gurfinkel[1] and Anton Belov[2]

[1] Carnegie Mellon Software Engineering Institute, USA
[2] University College Dublin, Ireland

Abstract. Bit-precise software verification is an important and difficult problem. While there has been an amazing progress in SAT solving, Satisfiability Modulo Theory of Bit Vectors, and bit-precise Bounded Model Checking, proving bit-precise safety, i.e. synthesizing a safe inductive invariant, remains a challenge. In this paper, we present FRANKENBIT — a tool that combines bit-precise invariant synthesis with BMC counterexample search. As the name suggests, FRANKENBIT combines a large variety of existing verification tools and techniques, including LLBMC, UFO, Z3, Boolector, MiniSAT and STP.

1 Verification Approach

FRANKENBIT combines two orthogonal techniques: one searches for bit-precise counterexamples, and the other synthesizes bit-precise inductive invariants. The counterexample search is done using Bounded Model Checking, and is delegated completely to LLBMC [11]. Invariant synthesis is implemented by first unsoundly approximating programs using Linear Arithmetic (LA), then computing inductive invariants for the approximation, and using those to guide the search for bit-precise invariants. The details of this approach are described in [7].

2 Software Architecture

The architecture of FRANKENBIT is shown in Fig. 1. First, the input C source is processed and compiled into LLVM [10] bitcode using the UFO front-end (UFO-FE) [1]. This involves normalizing with a custom CIL [12] pass, compiling with `llvm-gcc`, and simplifying using customized optimizations from LLVM version 2.6. The front-end is often sufficient to decide simple verification tasks. Second, two threads are started, one used to synthesize an inductive invariant (left part of Fig. 1), and the other to search for a counterexample (right part of Fig. 1).

* This material is based upon work funded and supported by the Department of Defense under Contract No. FA8721-05-C-0003 with Carnegie Mellon University for the operation of the Software Engineering Institute, a federally funded research and development center. This material has been approved for public release and unlimited distribution. DM-0000870. The second author is financially supported by SFI PI grant BEACON (09/IN.1/I2618).

E. Ábrahám and K. Havelund (Eds.): TACAS 2014, LNCS 8413, pp. 408–411, 2014.
© Springer-Verlag Berlin Heidelberg 2014

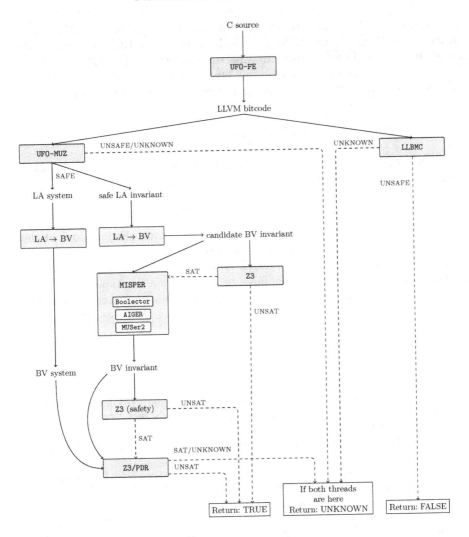

Fig. 1. FRANKENBIT: Software architecture

Invariants. Invariants are synthesized using our new algorithm MISPER [7]. First, Z3/PDR engine [8] of UFO (UFO-MUZ) abstracts the input over Linear Arithmetic (LA) and synthesizes LA invariant. If this fails, synthesis is aborted. Second, the LA invariant and abstraction are converted to bit-vectors (LA → BV). Third, the candidate bit-vector (BV) invariant is checked using Z3 [4]. If the candidate is not inductive, it is weakened until it becomes inductive using MISPER that, in turn, uses Boolector [3] for bit-blasting, aiger for CNF conversion, and MUSER2 [2] for extraction of Minimal Unsatisfiable Subformulas (MUSes). Finally, the safety of the weakened invariant is checked again with Z3 (Z3 safety), and, if necessary, strengthened using the bit-precise version of Z3/PDR.

Counterexamples. The search for counterexamples is delegated to LLBMC [11], that itself uses STP [6], and MiniSAT [5]. In order to run LLBMC on bitcode files produced by UFO-FE, they are first dis-assembled using `llvm-dis` from LLVM v2.9 and then re-assembled using `llmv-as` from LLVM v3.2.

FRANKENBIT is written in Python and borrows code from SPACER [9].

3   Tool Setup and Configuration

FRANKENBIT is available for download from `bitbucket.org/arieg/fbit/wiki /svcomp14.wiki`. The options for running the tool are:

```
./bin/fbit.py [-m64] --cex=TRACE --spec=SPEC input
```

where `-m64` turns on 64-bit model, `--cex` and `--spec` are the locations of the counter-example and the specification files, respectively, and `input` is a C file. The result is printed on the output terminal: `TRUE`, `FALSE`, `UNKNOWN`, if the property evaluates, respectively, to true, false, or unknown on the `input`.

FRANKENBIT is participating in the following categories: `Simple`, `Control Flow and Integer Variables`, and `Device Drivers Linux 64-bit`.

References

1. Albarghouthi, A., Gurfinkel, A., Li, Y., Chaki, S., Chechik, M.: UFO: Verification with Interpolants and Abstract Interpretation (Competition Contribution). In: Piterman, N., Smolka, S.A. (eds.) TACAS 2013. LNCS, vol. 7795, pp. 637–640. Springer, Heidelberg (2013)
2. Belov, A., Marques-Silva, J.: MUSer2: An Efficient MUS Extractor. JSAT 8(1/2) (2012)
3. Brummayer, R., Biere, A.: Boolector: An Efficient SMT Solver for Bit-Vectors and Arrays. In: Kowalewski, S., Philippou, A. (eds.) TACAS 2009. LNCS, vol. 5505, pp. 174–177. Springer, Heidelberg (2009)
4. de Moura, L., Bjørner, N.: Z3: An Efficient SMT Solver. In: Ramakrishnan, C.R., Rehof, J. (eds.) TACAS 2008. LNCS, vol. 4963, pp. 337–340. Springer, Heidelberg (2008)
5. Eén, N., Sörensson, N.: An Extensible SAT-solver. In: Giunchiglia, E., Tacchella, A. (eds.) SAT 2003. LNCS, vol. 2919, pp. 502–518. Springer, Heidelberg (2004)
6. Ganesh, V., Dill, D.L.: A Decision Procedure for Bit-Vectors and Arrays. In: Damm, W., Hermanns, H. (eds.) CAV 2007. LNCS, vol. 4590, pp. 519–531. Springer, Heidelberg (2007)
7. Gurfinkel, A., Belov, A., Marques-Silva, J.: Synthesizing Safe Bit-Precise Invariants. In: Ábrahám, E., Havelund, K. (eds.) TACAS 2014. LNCS, vol. 8413, pp. 93–108. Springer, Heidelberg (2014)
8. Hoder, K., Bjørner, N.: Generalized Property Directed Reachability. In: Cimatti, A., Sebastiani, R. (eds.) SAT 2012. LNCS, vol. 7317, pp. 157–171. Springer, Heidelberg (2012)

9. Komuravelli, A., Gurfinkel, A., Chaki, S., Clarke, E.M.: Automatic Abstraction in SMT-Based Unbounded Software Model Checking. In: Sharygina, N., Veith, H. (eds.) CAV 2013. LNCS, vol. 8044, pp. 846–862. Springer, Heidelberg (2013)
10. Lattner, C., Adve, V.S.: LLVM: A Compilation Framework for Lifelong Program Analysis & Transformation. In: CGO, pp. 75–88. IEEE Computer Society (2004)
11. Merz, F., Falke, S., Sinz, C.: LLBMC: Bounded Model Checking of C and C++ Programs Using a Compiler IR. In: Joshi, R., Müller, P., Podelski, A. (eds.) VSTTE 2012. LNCS, vol. 7152, pp. 146–161. Springer, Heidelberg (2012)
12. Necula, G.C., McPeak, S., Rahul, S.P., Weimer, W.: CIL: Intermediate Language and Tools for Analysis and Transformation of C Programs. In: Horspool, R.N. (ed.) CC 2002. LNCS, vol. 2304, pp. 213–228. Springer, Heidelberg (2002)

Predator: A Shape Analyzer
Based on Symbolic Memory Graphs*
(Competition Contribution)

Kamil Dudka, Petr Peringer, and Tomáš Vojnar

FIT, Brno University of Technology, IT4Innovations Centre of Excellence, Czech Republic

Abstract. Predator is a shape analyzer that uses the abstract domain of symbolic memory graphs in order to support various forms of low-level memory manipulation commonly used in optimized C code. This paper briefly describes the verification approach taken by Predator and its strengths and weaknesses revealed during its participation in the Software Verification Competition (SV-COMP'14).

1 Verification Approach

Predator is a shape analyzer that uses the abstract domain of *symbolic memory graphs (SMGs)* in order to support various forms of low-level memory manipulation commonly used in optimized C code. Compared to separation logic-based works [1], which our work is inspired by, SMGs allow one to easily apply various graph-based algorithms to efficiently manipulate with the low-level memory representation.

The formal definition of SMGs can be found in [2] together with algorithms of all the operations needed for use of SMGs in a fully automatic shape analysis. This is in particular the case of a specialised unary abstraction operator and a binary join operator that aid termination of the SMG-based shape analysis. The join operator is based on an algorithm that simultaneously traverses a pair of input SMGs and merges their corresponding nodes. The core of the join algorithm is also used by the algorithm implementing the abstraction operator to merge pairs of neighbouring nodes, together with their sub-SMGs (describing the data structures nested below them), into a single list segment. For checking entailment of SMGs, Predator again reuses the join algorithm (extended to compare generality of the SMGs being joined).

Predator requires all external functions to be properly modelled wrt. memory safety in order to exclude any side effects that could possibly break soundness of the analysis. Our distribution of Predator includes models of memory allocation functions (like `malloc` or `free`) and selected memory manipulating functions (`memset`, `memcpy`, `memmove`, etc.).

Since SV-COMP'13, the core algorithms of shape analysis were reimplemented in order to match their description presented in [2]. Consequently, the current implementation is much easier to follow, but at the same time also faster and more precise (as witnessed by the results of SV-COMP'14).

---

* This work was supported by the Czech Science Foundation project 14-11384S and the EU/Czech IT4Innovations Centre of Excellence project CZ.1.05/1.1.00/02.0070.

E. Ábrahám and K. Havelund (Eds.): TACAS 2014, LNCS 8413, pp. 412–414, 2014.

2   Software Architecture

Predator is implemented as a GCC (GNU Compiler Collection) plug-in, which makes the tool easy to use without a need to manually preprocess the source code. GCC as an industrial-strength compiler takes care of parsing the C code into an intermediate representation (known as GIMPLE). The input code is symbolically executed by Predator using the algorithms proposed in [2] with the aim to precisely interpret various low-level memory operations (such as pointer arithmetic, valid use of pointers with invalid targets, operations with memory blocks, or reinterpretation of the memory contents). Predator is written in C++ and requires Boost libraries, mainly to enable using legacy compilers for building it. The Predator GCC plug-in can be loaded into any GCC with a plug-in support up to GCC 4.8.2 (which was the latest release in 2013).

Compared to SV-COMP'13, Predator uses an improved algorithm for live variable analysis (based on a points-to analysis). The improved live variable analysis makes the shape analysis run five times faster in certain cases (e.g. the Merge-Sort algorithm case study from [2]).

3   Strengths and Weaknesses

The main strength of Predator is its byte-precise representation of reachable memory configurations, which makes it possible to successfully verify certain low-level pointer-intensive programs in the *MemorySafety* and *HeapManipulation* categories. The key design principle of Predator is soundness, which was again confirmed by reaching zero false negatives on the whole benchmark of SV-COMP'14. On the other hand, Predator does not check spuriousness of possible counterexamples for now, which caused numerous false positives (and consequently a significant loss of score). Since SV-COMP'13, the *MemorySafety* category has been extended by case studies that cause problems to Predator either by operating on data structures not covered by the current abstraction algorithm (trees and skip lists), or by the requirement to track non-pointer data along with the shapes of data structures (for example, tracking the length of lists). Compared to the SV-COMP'13 version, Predator now finally achieved the full score in the *ProductLines* subcategory. Moreover, the correct results were now delivered five times faster than the partially correct results in this (sub)category last year.

Results in the *ControlFlowInteger BitVectors* categories still suffer from a high ratio of false positives caused mainly by a too coarse analysis of integers. Due to undefined external functions, Predator was not able to analyze many test cases in the *DeviceDrivers64* and *Concurrency* categories.

4   Tool Setup and Configuration

The source code of the Predator release[1] used in the competition can be downloaded from the project web page. The file README-SVCOMP-2014 included in the archive

---

[1] http://www.fit.vutbr.cz/research/groups/verifit/tools/predator
/download/predator-2013-10-30-d1bd405.tar.gz

describes how to build Predator from source code and how to apply the tool on the competition benchmarks. After successfully building the tool from sources, the `sl_build` directory contains a script named `check-property.sh`, which needs to be invoked once for each input program. Besides the name of the input program, the script requires a mandatory option `--propertyfile` specifying the property to be verified. Compiler flags needed to compile the input program with GCC must be specified after the file name of the input program. For programs relying on a particular target architecture (such as preprocessed C sources), it is important to use the `-m32` or `-m64` compiler flags to specify the architecture. The script also provides a voluntary option `--trace` that allows one to write the error trace to a file. The verification result is printed to the standard output on success. Otherwise, the verification outcome should be treated as UNKNOWN. The script does not check for exceeding any resource limits on its own.

Although we use a global configuration of Predator for all categories, the tool provides many useful compile-time options via the `sl/config.h` configuration file. The default configuration is tweaked to obtain good overall results in both the competition benchmark and Predator's regression test-suite. The configuration can be further tweaked to improve the results in a particular category, however, at the cost of loosing some points in other categories.

5   Software Project and Contributors

Predator is an open source software project developed at Brno University of Technology (BUT) and distributed under the GNU General Public License version 3, which allows Predator to be used for both commercial and non-commercial purposes. There is no binary distribution of Predator, but it can be easily built from sources on any up to date distribution of Linux. The interaction with the compiler is facilitated by the Code Listener infrastructure [3], which is shared with Forester (a shape analyser based on forest automata [4]), including a suite of regression tests. Both Code Listener and Forester are projects also developed at BUT. Besides our development teams, we have numerous external contributors listed in the `docs/THANKS` file inside the distribution of Predator. Collaboration on further development of Predator is welcome.

References

1. Berdine, J., Calcagno, C., Cook, B., Distefano, D., O'Hearn, P.W., Wies, T., Yang, H.: Shape Analysis for Composite Data Structures. In: Damm, W., Hermanns, H. (eds.) CAV 2007. LNCS, vol. 4590, pp. 178–192. Springer, Heidelberg (2007)
2. Dudka, K., Peringer, P., Vojnar, T.: Byte-Precise Verification of Low-Level List Manipulation. In: Logozzo, F., Fähndrich, M. (eds.) SAS 2013. LNCS, vol. 7935, pp. 215–237. Springer, Heidelberg (2013)
3. Dudka, K., Peringer, P., Vojnar, T.: An Easy to Use Infrastructure for Building Static Analysis Tools. In: Moreno-Díaz, R., Pichler, F., Quesada-Arencibia, A. (eds.) EUROCAST 2011, Part I. LNCS, vol. 6927, pp. 527–534. Springer, Heidelberg (2012)
4. Habermehl, P., Holík, L., Rogalewicz, A., Šimáček, J., Vojnar, T.: Forest Automata for Verification of Heap Manipulation. In: Gopalakrishnan, G., Qadeer, S. (eds.) CAV 2011. LNCS, vol. 6806, pp. 424–440. Springer, Heidelberg (2011)

Symbiotic 2: More Precise Slicing*
(Competition Contribution)

Jiri Slaby and Jan Strejček

Faculty of Informatics, Masaryk University
Botanická 68a, 60200 Brno, Czech Republic
{slaby,strejcek}@fi.muni.cz

Abstract. SYMBIOTIC 2 keeps the concept and the structure of the original bug-finding tool SYMBIOTIC, but it uses a more precise slicing based on a field-sensitive pointer analysis instead of field-insensitive analysis of the original tool. The paper discusses this improvement and its consequences. We also briefly recall basic principles of the tool, its strong and weak points, installation, and running instructions. Finally, we comment the results achieved by SYMBIOTIC 2 in the competition.

1 Verification Approach and Software Architecture

Both SYMBIOTIC [6] and SYMBIOTIC 2 implement our verification approach proposed earlier [4]. The approach combines three standard techniques, namely *code instrumentation*, *program slicing* [7], and *symbolic execution* [3]. While the approach was originally designed for the detection of bugs described by state-machines, SYMBIOTIC 2 still supports only one kind of bugs: reachability of an ERROR label. Hence, we briefly recall the approach restricted just to this simple kind of errors. We explain the structure of the tool simultaneously.

1. Code instrumentation inserts assert(0) to each ERROR label. It is performed by a bash script calling sed. The instrumented code is translated into the LLVM bitcode by the CLANG compiler.
2. Program slicing removes instructions of the instrumented code that do not affect reachability of the inserted assert(0) statements. This code size reduction is crucial for the overall efficiency of SYMBIOTIC 2. The slicer is implemented in C++ as a plug-in for the LLVM optimizer opt.
3. Symbolic execution either reaches assert(0), or correctly finishes the execution without reaching assert(0), or it runs out of time or memory etc. These possibilities correspond to answers FALSE, TRUE, UNKNOWN, respectively. We use the symbolic executor KLEE [2] whose outputs are translated to TRUE/FALSE/UNKNOWN by a simple bash script.

The whole pipeline is executed stepwise by another bash script.

All improvements of SYMBIOTIC 2 over the tool SYMBIOTIC competing in SV-COMP 2013 are in the slicer. We have fixed some bugs in the original slicer

---

* The authors are supported by the Czech Science Foundation grant P202-10-1469.

(invalid treatment of several instructions and functions with variable number of arguments). While the original fixpoint algorithm for slicing [7] is relatively simple, it gets more complicated for programs with pointers as one instruction can influence the following one without any syntactic overlap. We need to use a pointer analysis (also called points-to analysis) to know which pointers can point to the same target. Both SYMBIOTIC and SYMBIOTIC 2 use Andersen's pointer analysis [1], SYMBIOTIC 2 replaces the original field-insensitive analysis by a field-sensitive one. This means that every field of a `struct` is now handled as a different pointer target. Similarly, we handle the first 64 elements of each array as distinct targets. The field-sensitive analysis is computationally more demanding. Thus we have also added some type filters that speed up the pointer analysis and make its results more accurate. All these improvements of the slicer significantly reduce the number of incorrect answers produced by SYMBIOTIC 2. For example, SYMBIOTIC 2 produces only correct answers for the category *ProductLines* while SYMBIOTIC produces 131 incorrect answers for the same category.

2   Strengths and Weaknesses

Our tool is applicable to all competition benchmarks satisfying two restrictions: the studied property is `ERROR` label reachability and the benchmark code is a sequential C program. Hence, the results of SYMBIOTIC 2 in the competition categories *MemorySafety* and *Concurrency* should be ignored (we missed the opt-out deadline). The first restriction can be removed by the implementation of a more sophisticated code instrumentation. The second restriction comes directly from the approach as symbolic execution and program slicing are primarily designed for sequential programs.

We first discuss strong and weak aspects of the approach and then we talk about additional strong and weak aspects of the tool. Our approach is based on symbolic execution which should produce only correct answers. On the other hand, symbolic execution suffers from the path explosion problem and relies on expensive (and often even undecidable) SMT solving. Hence, application of symbolic execution leads to many `UNKNOWN` answers, which is also the main weakness of the approach. To reduce this weakness, we combine symbolic execution with slicing which is the only theoretical source of incorrect answers (namely false positives) of our approach. Indeed, slicing can in some cases remove an infinite loop and a potential unreachable `ERROR` label located below the cycle thus become reachable. However, this situation is very rare in practice (e.g. it does not appear in the competition benchmarks) and we do not see it as a problem. An orthogonal method to reduce the high cost of symbolic execution is to use some of its variants suppressing the path explosion problem. For example, we plan to apply *compact symbolic execution* [5] instead of the classic one.

The strong aspect of the tool is its simple architecture: it is a sequence of scripts and standalone tools that are easy to replace (for example, if there is a better symbolic executor for LLVM bitcode, we can deploy it in few minutes). The main weakness of SYMBIOTIC 2 lies in the incorrect results which are sometimes reported. Even if the number of incorrect results is substantially lower than in the case of SYMBIOTIC, it is still relatively high. All the incorrect results are due to imperfection of our implementation.

3 Tool Setup and Configuration

Before using SYMBIOTIC 2, ensure that the target system contains 32-bit libraries (for 32-bit benchmarks) and LLVM with CLANG. LLVM and CLANG have to be in version 3.2 exactly. Then, SYMBIOTIC 2 can be downloaded from http://sf.net/projects/symbiotic/. Due to a bug in KLEE causing absolute paths to be built in, KLEE requires to be run from a pre-defined path. Hence we are obliged to change the current directory to /opt/ and *untar* the downloaded SYMBIOTIC 2 archive there. Running the tool is then straightforward. When the current directory is /opt/symbiotic/, the tool can be invoked for each <benchmark.c> from the set by ./runme <benchmark.c>. For benchmarks intended for 64-bit, set MFLAG=-m64 environment variable. The answers provided by SYMBIOTIC 2 are as required by the competition rules: TRUE/FALSE/UNKWNOWN. If the result for <benchmark.c> is FALSE, discovered error paths can be found in <benchmark.c>-klee-out/.

4 Software Project and Contributors

SYMBIOTIC 2 was contributed mostly by the authors of this paper and Marek Trtík. Jiri Slaby is a contact person. The tool is licensed under the GNU GPLv2 License unless specified otherwise for its parts.

References

1. Andersen, L.O.: Program Analysis and Specialization for the C Programming Language. PhD thesis, DIKU, University of Copenhagen (1994)
2. Cadar, C., Dunbar, D., Engler, D.: KLEE: Unassisted and automatic generation of high-coverage tests for complex systems programs. In: Proceedings of OSDI, pp. 209–224. USENIX Association (2008)
3. King, J.C.: Symbolic execution and program testing. Communications of ACM 19(7), 385–394 (1976)
4. Slabý, J., Strejček, J., Trtík, M.: Checking properties described by state machines: On synergy of instrumentation, slicing, and symbolic execution. In: Stoelinga, M., Pinger, R. (eds.) FMICS 2012. LNCS, vol. 7437, pp. 207–221. Springer, Heidelberg (2012)
5. Slaby, J., Strejček, J., Trtík, M.: Compact symbolic execution. In: Van Hung, D., Ogawa, M. (eds.) ATVA 2013. LNCS, vol. 8172, pp. 193–207. Springer, Heidelberg (2013)
6. Slaby, J., Strejček, J., Trtík, M.: Symbiotic: Synergy of instrumentation, slicing, and symbolic execution (competition contribution). In: Piterman, N., Smolka, S.A. (eds.) TACAS 2013. LNCS, vol. 7795, pp. 630–632. Springer, Heidelberg (2013)
7. Weiser, M.: Program slicing. In: Proceedings of ICSE, pp. 439–449. IEEE (1981)

Ultimate Automizer with Unsatisfiable Cores[*]
(Competition Contribution)

Matthias Heizmann, Jürgen Christ, Daniel Dietsch, Jochen Hoenicke,
Markus Lindenmann, Betim Musa, Christian Schilling,
Stefan Wissert, and Andreas Podelski

University of Freiburg, Germany

Abstract. ULTIMATE AUTOMIZER is an automatic software verification
tool for C programs. This tool is a prototype implementation of an
automata-theoretic approach that allows a modular verification of programs. Furthermore, this is the first implementation of a novel interpolation technique where interpolants are not obtained from an interpolating
theorem prover but from a combination of a live variable analysis, interprocedural predicate transformers and unsatisfiable cores.

1 Verification Approach

ULTIMATE AUTOMIZER verifies a C program by first executing several program
transformations and then performing an interpolation-based variant of trace
abstraction [4]. As a first step, we translate the C program into a Boogie [6]
program. The heap of the system is modeled via arrays in this Boogie program [7]. Next, the Boogie program is translated into an interprocedural control
flow graph [9]. As an optimization, we do not label the edges with single program
statements but with loop free code blocks of the program [11]. Our verification
algorithm then performs the following steps iteratively:

1. We take a sequence of statements π that leads from the start of the main
   procedure to an error location and analyze its correctness (resp. feasibility).
   In this analysis an SMT solver is used.
2. We consider this sequence of statements as a standalone program $\mathcal{P}_\pi$ and
   compute a correctness proof for $\mathcal{P}_\pi$ in form of a Hoare annotation.
3. We find a larger program $\widehat{\mathcal{P}}_\pi$ that has the same correctness proof [4].
4. We consider the preceding step as a semantical decomposition of the original
   program $\mathcal{P}$ into one part $\widehat{\mathcal{P}}_\pi$ whose correctness is already proven and one re-
   maining part $\mathcal{P}_{\text{rest}} := \mathcal{P} \backslash \widehat{\mathcal{P}}_\pi$, on which we continue. The programs $\mathcal{P}, \widehat{\mathcal{P}}_\pi, \mathcal{P}_{\text{rest}}$
   are represented by automata. This allows us to compute and represent the
   remaining part of the program $\mathcal{P}_{\text{rest}}$ (the part for which correctness was not
   yet proven). Furthermore, this automata-theoretic representation allows us
   to apply minimization [10] to represent the programs $\mathcal{P}, \widehat{\mathcal{P}}_\pi, \mathcal{P}_{\text{rest}}$ efficiently.

[*] This work is supported by the German Research Council (DFG) as part of the
Transregional Collaborative Research Center "Automatic Verification and Analysis
of Complex Systems" (SFB/TR14 AVACS)

E. Ábrahám and K. Havelund (Eds.): TACAS 2014, LNCS 8413, pp. 418–420, 2014.
© Springer-Verlag Berlin Heidelberg 2014

Our previous competition candidate [2] followed a similar approach in which the above mentioned Hoare annotation was computed by an interpolating SMT solver via Craig interpolation. Computation of Craig interpolants is known to be difficult, especially for the theory of arrays. This competition candidate follows a novel approach [8] to obtain a Hoare annotation for a sequence of statements. The predicates that represent the Hoare annotation are obtained using interprocedural predicate transformers. The arguments of these predicate transformers are not the statements of the sequence but generalized statements that are obtained from a live variable analysis and from unsatisfiable cores of the feasiblity analysis.

2   Software Architecture

ULTIMATE AUTOMIZER is one toolchain of the software analysis framework ULTIMATE which is implemented in Java. ULTIMATE offers data structures for different representations of a program, plugins which analyze or transform a program, and an interface for the communication with SMT-LIBv2 compatible theorem provers. For parsing C programs, we use the C parser of the Eclipse CDT project[1]. The operations on nested word automata are implemented in the ULTIMATE AUTOMATA LIBRARY. Our SMT queries can be answered by any SMT-LIBv2 compatible solver that supports quantifiers and the theory of arrays.

3   Discussion of Approach

Currently we model primitive data types (`int`, `float`,...) as integers $\mathbb{Z}$ or real numbers $\mathbb{R}$. We report *unknown* whenever we find a potential counterexample whose infeasibility cannot be shown because of this imprecision.

The main flaw of our implementation is the translation from C to Boogie. We failed to finish this translation in time and our submitted competition candidate is unable to verify programs that contain pointers or arrays.

4   Tool Setup and Configuration

Our competition candidate assumes that version 4.3.2.ff265c6c6ccf of the SMT solver Z3[2] is installed and that the directory of the Z3 binary is part of the PATH variable. Our competition candidate is included in a command-line version of ULTIMATE AUTOMIZER that can be downloaded from the following website:

https://ultimate.informatik.uni-freiburg.de/automizer/

The zip archive in which ULTIMATE AUTOMIZER is shipped contains the Python script `automizerSV-COMP.py` which wraps input and output for the SV-COMP.

---

[1] https://www.eclipse.org/cdt/
[2] https://z3.codeplex.com/

Using the following command, the C program `fnord.c` is verified with respect to the property file `prop.prp` and an error path is written to the file `errPath.txt`.

```
python AutomizerSvcomp.py   prop.prp   fnord.c   errPath.txt
```

5   Software Project and Contributors

Our software analysis framework ULTIMATE was started as a bachelor thesis [1]. In the last years, many students contributed plugins or improved the framework itself. A list of all developers is available on our website. An instance of ULTIMATE is running on our web server and is available via a web interface.

6   Demonstration Category Termination

We also participated in the demonstration category on termination with ULTIMATE BÜCHI AUTOMIZER which is our tool for termination analysis. The underlying approach is based on Büchi automata and has not been published yet. As a subroutine the tool ULTIMATE LASSO RANKER [3,5] is used. We thank Jan Leike and Alexander Nutz for their contributions to our termination analysis.

References

1. Dietsch, D.: STALIN: A plugin-based modular framework for program analysis. Bachelor Thesis, Albert-Ludwigs-Universität, Freiburg, Germany (2008)
2. Heizmann, M., et al.: Ultimate automizer with SMTInterpol. In: Piterman, N., Smolka, S.A. (eds.) TACAS 2013. LNCS, vol. 7795, pp. 641–643. Springer, Heidelberg (2013)
3. Heizmann, M., Hoenicke, J., Leike, J., Podelski, A.: Linear ranking for linear lasso programs. In: Van Hung, D., Ogawa, M. (eds.) ATVA 2013. LNCS, vol. 8172, pp. 365–380. Springer, Heidelberg (2013)
4. Heizmann, M., Hoenicke, J., Podelski, A.: Software model checking for people who love automata. In: Sharygina, N., Veith, H. (eds.) CAV 2013. LNCS, vol. 8044, pp. 36–52. Springer, Heidelberg (2013)
5. Leike, J.: Ranking function synthesis for linear lasso programs. Master's thesis, University of Freiburg, Germany (2013)
6. Leino, K.R.M.: This is Boogie 2. Manuscript working draft, Microsoft Research, Redmond, WA, USA (June 2008), http://research.microsoft.com/en-us/um/people/leino/papers/krml178.pdf
7. Lindenmann, M.: A simple but sufficient memory model for ultimate. Master's thesis, University of Freiburg, Germany (2012)
8. Musa, B.: Trace abstraction with unsatisfiable cores. Bachelor's thesis, University of Freiburg, Germany (2013)
9. Reps, T.W., Horwitz, S., Sagiv, S.: Precise interprocedural dataflow analysis via graph reachability. In: POPL 1995, pp. 49–61. ACM (1995)
10. Schilling, C.: Minimization of nested word automata. Master's thesis, University of Freiburg, Germany (2013)
11. Wissert, S.: Adaptive block encoding for recursive control flow graphs. Master's thesis, University of Freiburg, Germany (2013)

Ultimate Kojak
(Competition Contribution)

Evren Ermis, Alexander Nutz*, Daniel Dietsch,
Jochen Hoenicke, Andreas Podelski

University of Freiburg, Germany
{ermis,nutz,dietsch,hoenicke,podelski}@informatik.uni-freiburg.de

Abstract. ULTIMATE KOJAK is a symbolic software model checker for
C programs. It is based on CEGAR and Craig interpolation. The basic
algorithm, described in an earlier work [1], was extended to be able to
deal with recursive programs using nested word automata and nested
(tree) interpolants.

1 Verification Approach

ULTIMATE KOJAK computes inductive invariants from interpolants to prove the
correctness of a program. A program is represented by a program graph. In a
program graph, a vertex is a pair consisting of a program location and an invariant describing the abstract program state. An edge is labelled with a transition
formula that corresponds to a block of program statements. A program assertion
is represented by a transition to an error state where the transition is labelled
with the negated assertion. The goal is to show the unreachability of all error
states. The program graph is refined by the algorithm presented in a paper by
Ermis et al. [1]. This algorithm computes a sequence of interpolants for an infeasible error path and adds them to the invariant annotated at the corresponding
vertices. Since the interpolants are only invariants for the particular error path,
we also have to add new vertices for the case where the interpolants do not hold.
This is achieved by splitting every vertex on the error path into two new vertices
where each receives a new invariant: the old invariant conjoined with the interpolant for the first, and the old invariant conjoined with the negated interpolant
for the second. Afterwards, the algorithm removes all infeasible edges, thereby
refining the abstraction.

The newest version of ULTIMATE KOJAK implements this algorithm and extends it by handling inter-procedural control flow. We use nested word automata
to represent programs containing procedures [2]. These automata have `call` and
`return` transitions and support procedure summaries to prove the correctness
of recursive programs. A `return` transition conceptually has two predecessors:
the node representing the call site and the node representing the exit point of
the called procedure. Therefore our error paths are in in fact trees. To obtain

---

* Corresponding author.

E. Ábrahám and K. Havelund (Eds.): TACAS 2014, LNCS 8413, pp. 421–423, 2014.

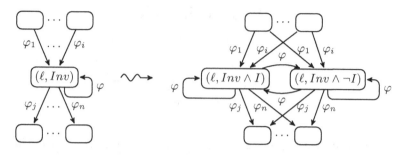

Fig. 1. We split a node that represents program location ℓ, and that has earlier been annotated with the invariant formula Inv, with the interpolant I. The node and its incoming and outgoing edges are duplicated and one copy of the node is labeled with I and the other with $\neg I$.

interpolants for these error paths, we use tree (nested) interpolation [2,3]. UL-TIMATE KOJAK utilizes block encoding [4] to summarize loop-free segments of the program, such that the focus is put on loops.

2   Software Architecture

ULTIMATE KOJAK is a toolchain in the ULTIMATE[1] Verification Framework, which is implemented in Java. ULTIMATE manages different representations of a program and passes them between its plug-ins which may analyse, transform, or visualize the representation. ULTIMATE also provides an interface for communication with SMT-LIBv2 compatible SMT solvers. For parsing C programs, we use the C parser provided by the CDT[2] project. We use Z3[3] for feasibility checks of error paths and transition formulas. Interpolation is done by our own algorithm, which is not yet published [5].

3   Discussion – Strengths and Weaknesses

In our approach, every refinement of the abstraction tends to introduce a rather high number of new edges into the graph, especially when dealing with hyper-edges (i.e. **return** edges), which may lead to a quickly growing model. Currently, interpolants are computed by our own interpolation method which may introduce quantifiers. This makes ULTIMATE KOJAK capable of handling arrays, however quantifiers that can not be easily eliminated lead to a heavy load on the SMT solver.

Due to some remaining issues in our C translation, we have problems with certain constructs, which makes us unable to verify many benchmarks, especially those where some standard library header files were inlined.

---

[1] http://ultimate.informatik.uni-freiburg.de
[2] http://eclipse.org/cdt/
[3] http://z3.codeplex.com/

In principle, ULTIMATE KOJAK can handle any program that can be formalized in a logic the attached SMT solver is capable of. Currently, we do not support bit-precise treatment of integers or concurrent programs.

4 Tool Setup and Configuration

A commandline version of ULTIMATE KOJAK can be downloaded from

http://ultimate.informatik.uni-freiburg.de/kojak

The downloaded archive contains a python script `KojakSVComp.py` that provides support for the SV-Comp-compatible input and output of the tool. The directory where the content of the archive lies is used as the working directory of the tool. The verification is started by a command like

python KojakSvComp.py prop.prp example.c errorPathOutput.txt

An installation of the SMT solver Z3 is required.[4] The Z3 executable must be in your PATH environment variable.

5 Software Project and Contributors

ULTIMATE KOJAK has been developed at the Chair of Software Engineering at the University of Freiburg as part of the ULTIMATE verification framework. Over the years numerous contributors have helped to transform a project, which initially started as a students' project, into a chair maintained verification framework on which model checkers such as ULTIMATE KOJAK and ULTIMATE AUTOMIZER[5] rely on. We would like to thank all the developers and contributors, particularly Matthias Heizmann, Jürgen Christ, Mohamed Abdelazim Sherif, Mostafa Mahmoud Mohamed, Markus Lindenmann, Betim Musa, Christian Schilling, and Stefan Wissert.

References

1. Ermis, E., Hoenicke, J., Podelski, A.: Splitting via interpolants. In: Kuncak, V., Rybalchenko, A. (eds.) VMCAI 2012. LNCS, vol. 7148, pp. 186–201. Springer, Heidelberg (2012)
2. Heizmann, M., Hoenicke, J., Podelski, A.: Nested interpolants. In: Hermenegildo, M.V., Palsberg, J. (eds.) POPL, pp. 471–482. ACM (2010)
3. Christ, J., Hoenicke, J.: Extending proof tree preserving interpolation to sequences and trees (work in progress). In: SMT Workshop, pp. 72–86 (2013)
4. Beyer, D., Cimatti, A., Griggio, A., Erkan Keremoglu, M., Sebastiani, R.: Software model checking via large-block encoding. In: FMCAD, pp. 25–32. IEEE (2009)
5. Musa, B.: Trace abstraction with unsatisfiable cores. Bachelor's thesis, University of Freiburg, Germany (2013)

---

[4] We use version 4.3.2 for Windows, any recent version should work.

[5] http://ultimate.informatik.uni-freiburg.de/automizer/

Discounting in LTL

Shaull Almagor[1], Udi Boker[2], and Orna Kupferman[1]

[1] The Hebrew University, Jerusalem, Israel
[2] The Interdisciplinary Center, Herzliya, Israel

Abstract. In recent years, there is growing need and interest in formalizing and reasoning about the quality of software and hardware systems. As opposed to traditional verification, where one handles the question of whether a system satisfies, or not, a given specification, reasoning about quality addresses the question of *how well* the system satisfies the specification. One direction in this effort is to refine the "eventually" operators of temporal logic to *discounting operators*: the satisfaction value of a specification is a value in $[0, 1]$, where the longer it takes to fulfill eventuality requirements, the smaller the satisfaction value is.

In this paper we introduce an augmentation by discounting of Linear Temporal Logic (LTL), and study it, as well as its combination with propositional quality operators. We show that one can augment LTL with an arbitrary set of discounting functions, while preserving the decidability of the model-checking problem. Further augmenting the logic with unary propositional quality operators preserves decidability, whereas adding an average-operator makes the model-checking problem undecidable. We also discuss the complexity of the problem, as well as various extensions.

1 Introduction

One of the main obstacles to the development of complex hardware and software systems lies in ensuring their correctness. A successful paradigm addressing this obstacle is *temporal-logic model checking* – given a mathematical model of the system and a temporal-logic formula that specifies a desired behavior of it, decide whether the model satisfies the formula [5]. Correctness is Boolean: a system can either satisfy its specification or not satisfy it. The richness of today's systems, however, justifies specification formalisms that are *multi-valued*. The multi-valued setting arises directly in systems with quantitative aspects (multi-valued / probabilistic / fuzzy) [9–11, 16, 23], but is applied also with respect to Boolean systems, where it origins from the semantics of the specification formalism itself [1, 7].

When considering the *quality* of a system, satisfying a specification should no longer be a yes/no matter. Different ways of satisfying a specification should induce different levels of quality, which should be reflected in the output of the verification procedure. Consider for example the specification $\mathsf{G}(request \rightarrow \mathsf{F}(response\_grant \lor response\_deny))$ ("every request is eventually responded, with either a grant or a denial"). There should be a difference between a computation that satisfies it with responses generated soon after requests and one that satisfies it with long waits. Moreover, there may be a difference between grant and deny responses, or cases in which no request is issued. The issue of generating high-quality hardware and software

E. Ábrahám and K. Havelund (Eds.): TACAS 2014, LNCS 8413, pp. 424–439, 2014.

systems attracts a lot of attention [13, 26]. Quality, however, is traditionally viewed as an art, or as an amorphic ideal. In [1], we introduced an approach for formalizing quality. Using it, a user can specify quality formally, according to the importance he gives to components such as security, maintainability, runtime, and more, and then can formally reason about the quality of software.

As the example above demonstrates, we can distinguish between two aspects of the quality of satisfaction. The first, to which we refer as "temporal quality" concerns the waiting time to satisfaction of eventualities. The second, to which we refer as "propositional quality" concerns prioritizing related components of the specification. Propositional quality was studied in [1]. In this paper we study temporal quality as well as the combinations of both aspects. One may try to reduce temporal quality to propositional quality by a repeated use of the X ("next") operator or by a use of bounded (prompt) eventualities [2, 3]. Both approaches, however, partitions the future into finitely many zones and are limited: correctness of LTL is Boolean, and thus has inherent dichotomy between satisfaction and dissatisfaction. On the other hand, the distinction between "near" and "far" is not dichotomous.

This suggests that in order to formalize temporal quality, one must extend LTL to an unbounded setting. Realizing this, researchers have suggested to augment temporal logics with *future discounting* [8]. In the discounted setting, the satisfaction value of specifications is a numerical value, and it depends, according to some discounting function, on the time waited for eventualities to get satisfied.

In this paper we add discounting to Linear Temporal Logic (LTL), and study it, as well as its combination with propositional quality operators. We introduce $LTL^{disc}[\mathcal{D}]$ – an augmentation by discounting of LTL. The logic $LTL^{disc}[\mathcal{D}]$ is actually a family of logics, each parameterized by a set $\mathcal{D}$ of discounting functions – strictly decreasing functions from $\mathbb{N}$ to $[0, 1]$ that tend to 0 (e.g., linear decaying, exponential decaying, etc.). $LTL^{disc}[\mathcal{D}]$ includes a discounting-"until" (U_η) operator, parameterized by a function $\eta \in \mathcal{D}$. We solve the model-checking threshold problem for $LTL^{disc}[\mathcal{D}]$: given a Kripke structure $\mathcal{K}$, an $LTL^{disc}[\mathcal{D}]$ formula φ and a threshold $t \in [0, 1]$, the algorithm decides whether the satisfaction value of φ in $\mathcal{K}$ is at least t.

In the Boolean setting, the automata-theoretic approach has proven to be very useful in reasoning about LTL specifications. The approach is based on translating LTL formulas to nondeterministic Büchi automata on infinite words [28]. Applying this approach to the discounted setting, which gives rise to infinitely many satisfaction values, poses a big algorithmic challenge: model-checking algorithms, and in particular those that follow the automata-theoretic approach, are based on an exhaustive search, which cannot be simply applied when the domain becomes infinite. A natural relevant extension to the automata-theoretic approach is to translate formulas to *weighted automata* [22]. Unfortunately, these extensively-studied models are complicated and many problems become undecidable for them [15]. We show that for threshold problems, we can translate $LTL^{disc}[\mathcal{D}]$ formulas into (Boolean) nondeterministic Büchi automata, with the property that the automaton accepts a lasso computation iff the formula attains a value above the threshold on that computation. Our algorithm relies on the fact that the language of an automaton is non-empty iff there is a lasso witness for the non-emptiness.

We cope with the infinitely many possible satisfaction values by using the discounting behavior of the eventualities and the given threshold in order to partition the state space into a finite number of classes. The complexity of our algorithm depends on the discounting functions used in the formula. We show that for standard discounting functions, such as exponential decaying, the problem is PSPACE-complete – not more complex than standard LTL. The fact our algorithm uses Boolean automata also enables us to suggest a solution for threshold satisfiability, and to give a partial solution to threshold synthesis. In addition, it allows to adapt the heuristics and tools that exist for Boolean automata.

Before we continue to describe our contribution, let us review existing work on discounting. The notion of discounting has been studied in several fields, such as economy, game-theory, and Markov decision processes [25]. In the area of formal verification, it was suggested in [8] to augment the μ-calculus with discounting operators. The discounting suggested there is exponential; that is, with each iteration, the satisfaction value of the formula decreases by a multiplicative factor in $(0, 1]$. Algorithmically, [8] shows how to evaluate discounted μ-calculus formulas with arbitrary precision. Formulas of LTL can be translated to the μ-calculus, thus [8] can be used in order to approximately model-check discounted-LTL formulas. However, the translation from LTL to the μ-calculus involves an exponential blowup [6] (and is complicated), making this approach inefficient. Moreover, our approach allows for arbitrary discounting functions, and the algorithm returns an exact solution to the threshold model-checking problem, which is more difficult than the approximation problem.

Closer to our work is [7], where CTL is augmented with discounting and weighted-average operators. The motivation in [7] is to introduce a logic whose semantics is not too sensitive to small perturbations in the model. Accordingly, formulas are evaluated on weighted-systems or on Markov-chains. Adding discounting and weighted-average operators to CTL preserves its appealing complexity, and the model-checking problem for the augmented logic can be solved in polynomial time. As is the case in the Boolean semantics, the expressive power of discounted CTL is limited. The fact the same combination, of discounting and weighted-average operators, leads to undecidability in the context of LTL witnesses the technical challenges of the LTL$^{\text{disc}}[\mathcal{D}]$ setting.

Perhaps closest to our approach is [19], where a version of discounted-LTL was introduced. Semantically, there are two main differences between the logics. The first is that [19] uses discounted sum, while we interpret discounting without accumulation, and the second is that the discounting there replaces the standard temporal operators, so all eventualities are discounted. As discounting functions tend to 0, this strictly restricts the expressive power of the logic, and one cannot specify traditional eventualities in it. On the positive side, it enables a clean algebraic characterization of the semantics, and indeed the contribution in [19] is a comprehensive study of the mathematical properties of the logic. Yet, [19] does not study algorithmic questions about to the logic. We, on the other hand, focus on the algorithmic properties of the logic, and specifically on the model-checking problem.

Let us now return to our contribution. After introducing $\text{LTL}^{\text{disc}}[\mathcal{D}]$ and studying its model-checking problem, we augment $\text{LTL}^{\text{disc}}[\mathcal{D}]$ with propositional quality operators. Beyond the operators min, max, and $\neg$, which are already present, two basic propositional quality operators are the multiplication of an $\text{LTL}^{\text{disc}}[\mathcal{D}]$ formula by a constant in $[0, 1]$, and the averaging between the satisfaction values of two $\text{LTL}^{\text{disc}}[\mathcal{D}]$ formulas [1]. We show that while the first extension does not increase the expressive power of $\text{LTL}^{\text{disc}}[\mathcal{D}]$ or its complexity, the latter causes the model-checking problem to become undecidable. In fact, model checking becomes undecidable even if we allow averaging in combination with a single discounting function. Recall that this is in contrast with the extension of discounted CTL with an average operator, where the complexity of the model-checking problem stays polynomial [7].

We consider additional extensions of $\text{LTL}^{\text{disc}}[\mathcal{D}]$. First, we study a variant of the discounting-eventually operators in which we allow the discounting to tend to arbitrary values in $[0, 1]$ (rather than to 0). This captures the intuition that we are not always pessimistic about the future, but can be, for example, ambivalent about it, by tending to $\frac{1}{2}$. We show that all our results hold under this extension. Second, we add to $\text{LTL}^{\text{disc}}[\mathcal{D}]$ *past* operators and their discounting versions (specifically, we allow a discounting-"since" operator, and its dual). In the traditional semantics, past operators enable clean specifications of many interesting properties, make the logic exponentially more succinct, and can still be handled within the same complexity bounds [17, 18]. We show that the same holds for the discounted setting. Finally, we show how $\text{LTL}^{\text{disc}}[\mathcal{D}]$ and algorithms for it can be used also for reasoning about weighted systems.

Due to lack of space, most proofs are omitted, and can be found in the full version, in the authors' home pages.

2   The Logic $\text{LTL}^{\text{disc}}[\mathcal{D}]$

The linear temporal logic $\text{LTL}^{\text{disc}}[\mathcal{D}]$ generalizes LTL by adding discounting temporal operators. The logic is actually a family of logics, each parameterized by a set $\mathcal{D}$ of discounting functions.

Let $\mathbb{N} = \{0, 1, ...\}$. A function $\eta : \mathbb{N} \to [0, 1]$ is a *discounting function* if $\lim_{i \to \infty} \eta(i) = 0$, and η is strictly monotonic-decreasing. Examples for natural discounting functions are $\eta(i) = \lambda^i$, for some $\lambda \in (0, 1)$, and $\eta(i) = \frac{1}{i+1}$.

Given a set of discounting functions $\mathcal{D}$, we define the logic $\text{LTL}^{\text{disc}}[\mathcal{D}]$ as follows. The syntax of $\text{LTL}^{\text{disc}}[\mathcal{D}]$ adds to LTL the operator $\varphi \mathsf{U}_\eta \psi$ (discounting-Until), for every function $\eta \in \mathcal{D}$. Thus, the syntax is given by the following grammar, where p ranges over the set AP of atomic propositions and $\eta \in \mathcal{D}$.

$$\varphi := \texttt{True} \mid p \mid \neg\varphi \mid \varphi \vee \varphi \mid \mathsf{X}\varphi \mid \varphi \mathsf{U}\varphi \mid \varphi \mathsf{U}_\eta \varphi.$$

The semantics of $\text{LTL}^{\text{disc}}[\mathcal{D}]$ is defined with respect to a *computation* $\pi = \pi^0, \pi^1, \ldots \in (2^{AP})^\omega$. Given a computation π and an $\text{LTL}^{\text{disc}}[\mathcal{D}]$ formula φ, the truth value of φ in π is a value in $[0, 1]$, denoted $[\![\pi, \varphi]\!]$. The value is defined by induction on the structure of φ as follows, where $\pi^i = \pi_i, \pi_{i+1}, \ldots$.

- $[\![\pi, \mathtt{True}]\!] = 1$.
- $[\![\pi, p]\!] = \begin{cases} 1 & \text{if } p \in \pi_0, \\ 0 & \text{if } p \notin \pi_0. \end{cases}$
- $[\![\pi, \mathsf{X}\varphi]\!] = [\![\pi^1, \varphi]\!]$.
- $[\![\pi, \varphi\mathsf{U}\psi]\!] = \sup_{i \geq 0}\{\min\{[\![\pi^i, \psi]\!], \min_{0 \leq j < i}\{[\![\pi^j, \varphi]\!]\}\}\}$.
- $[\![\pi, \varphi\mathsf{U}_\eta\psi]\!] = \sup_{i \geq 0}\{\min\{\eta(i)[\![\pi^i, \psi]\!], \min_{0 \leq j < i}\{\eta(j)[\![\pi^j, \varphi]\!]\}\}\}$.

- $[\![\pi, \varphi \vee \psi]\!] = \max\{[\![\pi, \varphi]\!], [\![\pi, \psi]\!]\}$.
- $[\![\pi, \neg\varphi]\!] = 1 - [\![\pi, \varphi]\!]$.

The intuition is that events that happen in the future have a lower influence, and the rate by which this influence decreases depends on the function η. [1] For example, the satisfaction value of a formula $\varphi\mathsf{U}_\eta\psi$ in a computation π depends on the best (supremum) value that ψ can get along the entire computation, while considering the discounted satisfaction of ψ at a position i, as a result of multiplying it by $\eta(i)$, and the same for the value of φ in the prefix leading to the i-th position.

We add the standard abbreviations $\mathsf{F}\varphi \equiv \mathtt{True}\mathsf{U}\varphi$, and $\mathsf{G}\varphi = \neg\mathsf{F}\neg\varphi$, as well as their quantitative counterparts: $\mathsf{F}_\eta\varphi \equiv \mathtt{True}\mathsf{U}_\eta\varphi$, and $\mathsf{G}_\eta\varphi = \neg\mathsf{F}_\eta\neg\varphi$. We denote by $|\varphi|$ the number of subformulas of φ.

A computation of the form $\pi = u \cdot v^\omega$, for $u, v \in (2^{AP})^*$, with $v \neq \epsilon$, is called a *lasso computation*. We observe that since a specific lasso computation has only finitely many distinct suffixes, the inf and sup in the semantics of $\mathrm{LTL}^{\mathrm{disc}}[\mathcal{D}]$ can be replaced with min and max, respectively, when applied to lasso computations.

The semantics is extended to *Kripke structures* by taking the path that admits the lowest satisfaction value. Formally, for a Kripke structure $\mathcal{K}$ and an $\mathrm{LTL}^{\mathrm{disc}}[\mathcal{D}]$ formula φ we have that $[\![\mathcal{K}, \varphi]\!] = \inf\{[\![\pi, \varphi]\!] : \pi \text{ is a computation of } \mathcal{K}\}$.

Example 1. Consider a lossy-disk: every moment in time there is a chance that some bit would flip its value. Fixing flips is done by a global error-correcting procedure. This procedure manipulates the entire content of the disk, such that initially it causes more errors in the disk, but the longer it runs, the more bits it fixes.

Let *init* and *terminate* be atomic propositions indicating when the error-correcting procedure is initiated and terminated, respectively. The quality of the disk (that is, a measure of the amount of correct bits) can be specified by the formula $\varphi = \mathsf{GF}_\eta(init \wedge \neg\mathsf{F}_\mu terminate)$ for some appropriate discounting functions η and μ. Intuitively, φ gets a higher satisfaction value the shorter the waiting time is between initiations of the error-correcting procedure, and the longer the procedure runs (that is, not terminated) in between these initiations. Note that the "worst case" nature of $\mathrm{LTL}^{\mathrm{disc}}[\mathcal{D}]$ fits here. For instance, running the procedure for a very short time, even once, will cause many errors.

3 $\mathrm{LTL}^{\mathrm{disc}}[\mathcal{D}]$ Model Checking

In the Boolean setting, the model-checking problem asks, given an LTL formula φ and a Kripke structure $\mathcal{K}$, whether $[\![\mathcal{K}, \varphi]\!] = \mathtt{True}$. In the quantitative setting, the

---

[1] Observe that in our semantics the satisfaction value of future events tends to 0. One may think of scenarios where future events are discounted towards another value in $[0, 1]$ (e.g. discounting towards $\frac{1}{2}$ as ambivalence regarding the future). We address this in Section 5.

model-checking problem is to compute $[\![\mathcal{K}, \varphi]\!]$, where φ is now an $\text{LTL}^{\text{disc}}[\mathcal{D}]$ formula. A simpler version of this problem is the threshold model-checking problem: given φ, $\mathcal{K}$, and a threshold $v \in [0, 1]$, decide whether $[\![\mathcal{K}, \varphi]\!] \geq v$. In this section we show how we can solve the latter.

Our solution uses the automata-theoretic approach, and consists of the following steps. We start by translating φ and v to an alternating weak automaton $\mathcal{A}_{\varphi,v}$ such that $L(\mathcal{A}_{\varphi,v}) \neq \emptyset$ iff there exists a computation π such that $[\![\pi, \varphi]\!] > v$. The challenge here is that φ has infinitely many satisfaction values, naively implying an infinite-state automaton. We show that using the threshold and the discounting behavior of the eventualities, we can restrict attention to a finite resolution of satisfaction values, enabling the construction of a finite automaton. Complexity-wise, the size of $\mathcal{A}_{\varphi,v}$ depends on the functions in $\mathcal{D}$. In Section 3.3, we analyze the complexity for the case of exponential-discounting functions.

The second step is to construct a nondeterministic Büchi automaton $\mathcal{B}$ that is equivalent to $\mathcal{A}_{\varphi,v}$. In general, alternation removal might involve an exponential blowup in the state space [21]. We show, by a careful analysis of $\mathcal{A}_{\varphi,v}$, that we can remove its alternation while only having a polynomial state blowup.

We complete the model-checking procedure by composing the nondeterministic Büchi automaton $\mathcal{B}$ with the Kripke structure $\mathcal{K}$, as done in the traditional, automata-based, model-checking procedure.

The complexity of model-checking an $\text{LTL}^{\text{disc}}[\mathcal{D}]$ formula depends on the discounting functions in $\mathcal{D}$. Intuitively, the faster the discounting tends to 0, the less states there will be. For exponential-discounting, we show that the complexity is NLOGSPACE in the system (the Kripke structure) and PSPACE in the specification (the $\text{LTL}^{\text{disc}}[\mathcal{D}]$ formula and the threshold), staying in the same complexity classes of standard LTL model-checking.

We conclude the section by showing how to use the generated nondeterministic Büchi automaton for addressing threshold satisfiability and synthesis.

3.1   Alternating Weak Automata

For a given set X, let $\mathcal{B}^+(X)$ be the set of positive Boolean formulas over X (i.e., Boolean formulas built from elements in X using $\wedge$ and $\vee$), where we also allow the formulas True and False. For $Y \subseteq X$, we say that Y *satisfies* a formula $\theta \in \mathcal{B}^+(X)$ iff the truth assignment that assigns *true* to the members of Y and assigns *false* to the members of $X \setminus Y$ satisfies θ. An *alternating Büchi automaton on infinite words* is a tuple $\mathcal{A} = \langle \Sigma, Q, q_{in}, \delta, \alpha \rangle$, where Σ is the input alphabet, Q is a finite set of states, $q_{in} \in Q$ is an initial state, $\delta : Q \times \Sigma \to \mathcal{B}^+(Q)$ is a transition function, and $\alpha \subseteq Q$ is a set of accepting states. We define runs of $\mathcal{A}$ by means of (possibly) infinite DAGs (directed acyclic graphs). A run of $\mathcal{A}$ on a word $w = \sigma_0 \cdot \sigma_1 \cdots \in \Sigma^\omega$ is a (possibly) infinite DAG $\mathcal{G} = \langle V, E \rangle$ satisfying the following (note that there may be several runs of $\mathcal{A}$ on w).

- $V \subseteq Q \times \mathbb{N}$ is as follows. Let $Q_l \subseteq Q$ denote all states in level l. Thus, $Q_l = \{q : \langle q, l \rangle \in V\}$. Then, $Q_0 = \{q_{in}\}$, and Q_{l+1} satisfies $\bigwedge_{q \in Q_l} \delta(q, \sigma_l)$.
- For every $l \in \mathbb{N}$, Q_l is minimal with respect to containment.
- $E \subseteq \bigcup_{l \geq 0}(Q_l \times \{l\}) \times (Q_{l+1} \times \{l+1\})$ is such that for every state $q \in Q_l$, the set $\{q' \in Q_{l+1} : E(<q, l>, <q', l+1>)\}$ satisfies $\delta(q, \sigma_l)$.

Thus, the root of the DAG contains the initial state of the automaton, and the states associated with nodes in level $l + 1$ satisfy the transitions from states corresponding to nodes in level l. The run $\mathcal{G}$ accepts the word w if all its infinite paths satisfy the acceptance condition α. Thus, in the case of Büchi automata, all the infinite paths have infinitely many nodes $\langle q, l \rangle$ such that $q \in \alpha$ (it is not hard to prove that every infinite path in $\mathcal{G}$ is part of an infinite path starting in level 0). A word w is accepted by $\mathcal{A}$ if there is a run that accepts it. The language of $\mathcal{A}$, denoted $L(\mathcal{A})$, is the set of infinite words that $\mathcal{A}$ accepts.

When the formulas in the transition function of $\mathcal{A}$ contain only disjunctions, then $\mathcal{A}$ is nondeterministic, and its runs are DAGs of width 1, where at each level there is a single node.

The alternating automaton $\mathcal{A}$ is *weak*, denoted AWA, if its state space Q can be partitioned into sets $Q_1, \ldots, Q_k$, such that the following hold: First, for every $1 \leq i \leq k$ either $Q_i \subseteq \alpha$, in which case we say that Q_i is an accepting set, or $Q_i \cap \alpha = \emptyset$, in which case we say that Q_i is rejecting. Second, there is a partial-order $\leq$ over the sets, and for every $1 \leq i, j \leq k$, if $q \in Q_i$, $s \in Q_j$, and $s \in \delta(q, \sigma)$ for some $\sigma \in \Sigma$, then $Q_j \leq Q_i$. Thus, transitions can lead only to states that are smaller in the partial order. Consequently, each run of an AWA eventually gets trapped in a set Q_i and is accepting iff this set is accepting.

3.2 From LTL$^{\text{disc}}[\mathcal{D}]$ to AWA

Our model-checking algorithm is based on translating an LTL$^{\text{disc}}[\mathcal{D}]$ formula φ to an AWA. Intuitively, the states of the AWA correspond to assertions of the form $\psi > t$ or $\psi < t$ for every subformula ψ of φ, and for certain thresholds $t \in [0, 1]$. A lasso computation is then accepted from state $\psi > t$ iff $[\![\pi, \psi]\!] > t$. The assumption about the computation being a lasso is needed only for the "only if" direction, and it does not influence the proof's generality since the language of an automaton is non-empty iff there is a lasso witness for its non-emptiness. By setting the initial state to $\varphi > v$, we are done.

Defining the appropriate transition function for the AWA follows the semantics of LTL$^{\text{disc}}[\mathcal{D}]$ in the expected manner. A naive construction, however, yields an infinite-state automaton (even if we only expand the state space on-the-fly, as discounting formulas can take infinitely many satisfaction values). As can be seen in the proof of Theorem 1, the "problematic" transitions are those that involve the discounting operators. The key observation is that, given a threshold v and a computation π, when evaluating a discounted operator on π, one can restrict attention to two cases: either the satisfaction value of the formula goes below v, in which case this happens after a bounded prefix, or the satisfaction value always remains above v, in which case we can replace the discounted operator with a Boolean one. This observation allows us to expand only a finite number of states on-the-fly.

Before describing the construction of the AWA, we need the following lemma, which reduces an extreme satisfaction of an LTL$^{\text{disc}}[\mathcal{D}]$ formula, meaning satisfaction with a value of either 0 or 1, to a Boolean satisfaction of an LTL formula. The proof proceeds by induction on the structure of the formulas.

Lemma 1. *Given an* $\text{LTL}^{disc}[\mathcal{D}]$ *formula* φ, *there exist LTL formulas* φ^+ *and* $\varphi^{<1}$ *such that* $|\varphi^+|$ *and* $|\varphi^{<1}|$ *are both* $O(|\varphi|)$ *and the following hold for every computation* π.

1. *If* $[\![\pi, \varphi]\!] > 0$ *then* $\pi \models \varphi^+$, *and if* $[\![\pi, \varphi]\!] < 1$ *then* $\pi \models \varphi^{<1}$.
2. *If* π *is a lasso, then if* $\pi \models \varphi^+$ *then* $[\![\pi, \varphi]\!] > 0$ *and if* $\pi \models \varphi^{<1}$ *then* $[\![\pi, \varphi]\!] < 1$.

Henceforth, given an $\text{LTL}^{disc}[\mathcal{D}]$ formula φ, we refer to φ^+ as in Lemma 1.

Consider an $\text{LTL}^{disc}[\mathcal{D}]$ formula φ. By Lemma 1, if there exists a computation π such that $[\![\pi, \varphi]\!] > 0$, then φ^+ is satisfiable. Conversely, since φ^+ is a Boolean LTL formula, then by [27] we know that φ^+ is satisfiable iff there exists a lasso computation π that satisfies it, in which case $[\![\pi, \varphi]\!] > 0$. We conclude with the following.

Corollary 1. *Consider an* $\text{LTL}^{disc}[\mathcal{D}]$ *formula* φ. *There exists a computation* π *such that* $[\![\pi, \varphi]\!] > 0$ *iff there exists a lasso computation* π' *such that* $[\![\pi', \varphi]\!] > 0$, *in which case* $\pi' \models \varphi^+$ *as well.*

Remark 1. The curious reader may wonder why we do not prove that $[\![\pi, \varphi]\!] > 0$ iff $\pi \models \varphi^+$ for every computation π. As it turns out, a translation that is valid also for computations with no period is not always possible. For example, as is the case with the prompt-eventuality operator of [14], the formula $\varphi = \mathsf{G}(\mathsf{F}_\eta p)$ is such that the set of computations π with $[\![\pi, \varphi]\!] > 0$ is not ω-regular, thus one cannot hope to define an LTL formula φ^+.

We start with some definitions. For a function $f : \mathbb{N} \to [0, 1]$ and for $k \in \mathbb{N}$, we define $f^{+k} : \mathbb{N} \to [0, 1]$ as follows. For every $i \in \mathbb{N}$ we have that $f^{+k}(i) = f(i + k)$.

Let φ be an $\text{LTL}^{disc}[\mathcal{D}]$ formula over AP. We define the *extended closure* of φ, denoted $xcl(\varphi)$, to be the set of all the formulas ψ of the following *classes*:

1. ψ is a subformula of φ.
2. ψ is a subformula of θ^+ or $\neg\theta^+$, where θ is a subformula of φ.
3. ψ is of the form $\theta_1 \mathsf{U}_{\eta^{+k}} \theta_2$ for $k \in \mathbb{N}$, where $\theta_1 \mathsf{U}_\eta \theta_2$ is a subformula of φ.

Observe that $xcl(\varphi)$ may be infinite, and that it has both $\text{LTL}^{disc}[\mathcal{D}]$ formulas (from Classes 1 and 3) and LTL formulas (from Class 2).

Theorem 1. *Given an* $\text{LTL}^{disc}[\mathcal{D}]$ *formula* φ *and a threshold* $v \in [0, 1]$, *there exists an AWA* $\mathcal{A}_{\varphi,v}$ *such that for every computation* π *the following hold.*

1. *If* $[\![\pi, \varphi]\!] > v$, *then* $\mathcal{A}_{\varphi,v}$ *accepts* π.
2. *If* $\mathcal{A}_{\varphi,v}$ *accepts* π *and* π *is a lasso computation, then* $[\![\pi, \varphi]\!] > v$.

Proof. We construct $\mathcal{A}_{\varphi,v} = \langle Q, 2^{AP}, Q_0, \delta, \alpha \rangle$ as follows.

The state space Q consists of two types of states. Type-1 states are assertions of the form $(\psi > t)$ or $(\psi < t)$, where $\psi \in xcl(\varphi)$ is of Class 1 or 3 and $t \in [0, 1]$. Type-2 states correspond to LTL formulas of Class 2. Let S be the set of Type-1 and Type-2 states for all $\psi \in xcl(\varphi)$ and thresholds $t \in [0, 1]$. Then, Q is the subset of S constructed on-the-fly according to the transition function defined below. We later show that Q is indeed finite.

The transition function $\delta : Q \times 2^{AP} \to \mathcal{B}^+(Q)$ is defined as follows. For Type-2 states, the transitions are as in the standard translation from LTL to AWA [27] (see the full version for details). For the other states, we define the transitions as follows. Let $\sigma \in 2^{AP}$.

$$\delta((\mathtt{True} > t), \sigma) = \begin{bmatrix} \mathtt{True} & \text{if } t < 1, \\ \mathtt{False} & \text{if } t = 1. \end{bmatrix} \qquad \delta((\mathtt{False} > t), \sigma) = \mathtt{False}.$$

$$\delta((\mathtt{True} < t), \sigma) = \mathtt{False}. \qquad \delta((\mathtt{False} < t), \sigma) = \begin{bmatrix} \mathtt{True} & \text{if } t > 0, \\ \mathtt{False} & \text{if } t = 0. \end{bmatrix}$$

$$\delta((p > t), \sigma) = \begin{bmatrix} \mathtt{True} & \text{if } p \in \sigma \text{ and } t < 1, \\ \mathtt{False} & \text{otherwise.} \end{bmatrix} \quad \delta((p < t), \sigma) = \begin{bmatrix} \mathtt{False} & \text{if } p \in \sigma \text{ or } t = 0, \\ \mathtt{True} & \text{otherwise.} \end{bmatrix}$$

$\delta((\psi_1 \vee \psi_2 > t), \sigma) = \delta((\psi_1 > t), \sigma) \vee \delta((\psi_2 > t), \sigma).$

$\delta((\psi_1 \vee \psi_2 < t), \sigma) = \delta((\psi_1 < t), \sigma) \wedge \delta((\psi_2 < t), \sigma).$

$\delta((\neg \psi_1 > t), \sigma) = \delta((\psi_1 < 1 - t), \sigma) \qquad \delta((\neg \psi_1 < t), \sigma) = \delta((\psi_1 > 1 - t), \sigma).$

$\delta((\mathsf{X}\psi_1 > t), \sigma) = (\psi_1 > t). \qquad\qquad \delta((\mathsf{X}\psi_1 < t), \sigma) = (\psi_1 < t).$

$$\delta((\psi_1 \mathsf{U} \psi_2 > t), \sigma) = \begin{bmatrix} \delta((\psi_2 > t), \sigma) \vee [\delta((\psi_1 > t), \sigma) \wedge (\psi_1 \mathsf{U} \psi_2 > t)] & \text{if } 0 < t < 1, \\ \mathtt{False} & \text{if } t \geq 1, \\ \delta(((\psi_1 \mathsf{U} \psi_2)^+), \sigma) & \text{if } t = 0. \end{bmatrix}$$

$$\delta((\psi_1 \mathsf{U} \psi_2 < t), \sigma) = \begin{bmatrix} \delta((\psi_2 < t), \sigma) \wedge [\delta((\psi_1 < t), \sigma) \vee (\psi_1 \mathsf{U} \psi_2 < t)] & \text{if } 0 < t \leq 1, \\ \mathtt{True} & \text{if } t > 1, \\ \mathtt{False} & \text{if } t = 0. \end{bmatrix}$$

$\delta((\psi_1 \mathsf{U}_\eta \psi_2 > t), \sigma) =$
$$\begin{bmatrix} \delta((\psi_2 > \frac{t}{\eta(0)}), \sigma) \vee [\delta((\psi_1 > \frac{t}{\eta(0)}), \sigma) \wedge (\psi_1 \mathsf{U}_{\eta+1} \psi_2 > t)] & \text{if } 0 < \frac{t}{\eta(0)} < 1, \\ \mathtt{False} & \text{if } \frac{t}{\eta(0)} \geq 1, \\ \delta(((\psi_1 \mathsf{U}_\eta \psi_2)^+), \sigma) & \text{if } \frac{t}{\eta(0)} = 0 \text{ (i.e., } t = 0). \end{bmatrix}$$

$\delta((\psi_1 \mathsf{U}_\eta \psi_2 < t), \sigma) =$
$$\begin{bmatrix} \delta((\psi_2 < \frac{t}{\eta(0)}), \sigma) \wedge [\delta((\psi_1 < \frac{t}{\eta(0)}), \sigma) \vee (\psi_1 \mathsf{U}_{\eta+1} \psi_2 < t)] & \text{if } 0 < \frac{t}{\eta(0)} \leq 1, \\ \mathtt{True} & \text{if } \frac{t}{\eta(0)} > 1, \\ \mathtt{False} & \text{if } \frac{t}{\eta(0)} = 0 \text{ (i.e., } t = 0). \end{bmatrix}$$

We provide some intuition for the more complex parts of the transition function: consider, for example, the transition $\delta((\psi_1 \mathsf{U}_\eta \psi_2 > t), \sigma)$. Since η is decreasing, the highest possible satisfaction value for $\psi_1 \mathsf{U}_\eta \psi_2$ is $\eta(0)$. Thus, if $\eta(0) \leq t$ (equivalently, $\frac{t}{\eta(0)} \geq 1$), then it cannot hold that $\psi_1 \mathsf{U}_\eta \psi_2 > t$, so the transition is to $\mathtt{False}$. If $t = 0$, then we only need to ensure that the satisfaction value of $\psi_1 \mathsf{U}_\eta \psi_2$ is not 0. To do so, we require that $(\psi_1 \mathsf{U}_\eta \psi_2)^+$ is satisfied. By Corollary 1, this is equivalent to the satisfiability of the former. So the transition is identical to that of the state $(\psi_1 \mathsf{U}_\eta \psi_2)^+$. Finally, if $0 < t < \eta(0)$, then (slightly abusing notation) the assertion $\psi_1 \mathsf{U}_\eta \psi_2 > t$ is true if either $\eta(0)\psi_2 > t$ is true, or both $\eta(0)\psi_1 > t$ and $\psi_1 \mathsf{U}_{\eta+1} \psi_2 > t$ are true.

The initial state of $\mathcal{A}_{\varphi,v}$ is $(\varphi > v)$. The accepting states are these of the form $(\psi_1 \mathsf{U} \psi_2 < t)$, as well as accepting states that arise in the standard translation of Boolean LTL to AWA (in Type-2 states). Note that each path in the run of $\mathcal{A}_{\varphi,v}$ eventually gets trapped in a single state. Thus, $\mathcal{A}_{\varphi,v}$ is indeed an AWA. The intuition behind the acceptance condition is as follows. Getting trapped in a state of the form $(\psi_1 \mathsf{U} \psi_2 < t)$ is allowed, as the eventuality is satisfied with value 0. On the other hand, getting stuck in other states (of Type-1) is not allowed, as they involve eventualities that are not satisfied in the threshold promised for them.

This concludes the definition of $\mathcal{A}_{\varphi,v}$. Finally, observe that while the construction as described above is infinite (indeed, uncountable), only finitely many states are reachable from the initial state ($\varphi > v$), and we can compute these states in advance. Intuitively, it follows from the fact that once the proportion between t and $\eta(i)$ goes above 1, for Type-1 states associated with threshold t and sub formulas with a discounting function η, we do not need to generate new states.

A detailed proof of $\mathcal{A}$'s finiteness and correctness is given in the full version.

Since $\mathcal{A}_{\varphi,v}$ is a Boolean automaton, then $L(\mathcal{A}) \neq \emptyset$ iff it accepts a lasso computation. Combining this observation with Theorem 1, we conclude with the following.

Corollary 2. *For an* LTL^{disc}[$\mathcal{D}$] *formula* φ *and a threshold* $v \in [0,1]$, *it holds that* $L(\mathcal{A}_{\varphi,v}) \neq \emptyset$ *iff there exists a computation* π *such that* $[\![\pi, \varphi]\!] > v$.

3.3 Exponential Discounting

The size of the AWA generated as per Theorem 1 depends on the discounting functions. In this section, we analyze its size for the class of *exponential discounting* functions, showing that it is singly exponential in the specification formula and in the threshold. This class is perhaps the most common class of discounting functions, as it describes what happens in many natural processes (e.g., temperature change, capacitor charge, effective interest rate, etc.) [8, 25].

For $\lambda \in (0,1)$ we define the *exponential-discounting* function $\exp_\lambda : \mathbb{N} \to [0,1]$ by $\exp_\lambda(i) = \lambda^i$. For the purpose of this section, we restrict to $\lambda \in (0,1) \cap \mathbb{Q}$. Let $E = \{\exp_\lambda : \lambda \in (0,1) \cap \mathbb{Q}\}$, and consider the logic LTL^{disc}[E].

For an LTL^{disc}[E] formula φ we define the set $F(\varphi)$ to be $\{\lambda_1, ..., \lambda_k :$ the operator $\mathsf{U}_{\exp_\lambda}$ appears in $\varphi\}$. Let $|\langle\varphi\rangle|$ be the length of the description of φ. That is, in addition to $|\varphi|$, we include in $|\langle\varphi\rangle|$ the length, in bits, of describing $F(\varphi)$.

Theorem 2. *Given an* LTL^{disc}[E] *formula* φ *and a threshold* $v \in [0,1] \cap \mathbb{Q}$, *there exists an AWA* $\mathcal{A}_{\varphi,v}$ *such that for every computation* π *the following hold.*

1. *If* $[\![\pi, \varphi]\!] > v$, *then* $\mathcal{A}_{\varphi,v}$ *accepts* π.
2. *If* $\mathcal{A}_{\varphi,v}$ *accepts* π *and* π *is a lasso computation, then* $[\![\pi, \varphi]\!] > v$.

Furthermore, the number of states of $\mathcal{A}_{\varphi,v}$ *is singly exponential in* $|\langle\varphi\rangle|$ *and in the description of* v.

The proof follows from the following observation. Let $\lambda \in (0,1)$ and $v \in (0,1)$. When discounting by $\exp_\lambda$, the number of states in the AWA constructed as per Theorem 1 is proportional to the maximal number i such that $\lambda^i > v$, which is at most $\log_\lambda v = \frac{\log v}{\log \lambda}$, which is polynomial in the description length of v and λ. A similar (yet more complicated) consideration is applied for the setting of multiple discounting functions and negations.

3.4 From $\mathcal{A}_{\varphi,v}$ to an NBA

Every AWA can be translated to an equivalent nondeterministic Büchi automaton (NBA, for short), yet the state blowup might be exponential BKR10,MH84. By carefully analyzing the AWA $\mathcal{A}_{\varphi,v}$ generated in Theorem 1, we show that it can be translated to an NBA with only a polynomial blowup.

The idea behind our complexity analysis is as follows. Translating an AWA to an NBA involves alternation removal, which proceeds by keeping track of entire levels in a run-DAG. Thus, a run of the NBA corresponds to a sequence of subsets of Q. The key to the reduced state space is that the number of such subsets is only $|Q|^{O(|\varphi|)}$ and not $2^{|Q|}$. To see why, consider a subset S of the states of $\mathcal{A}$. We say that S is *minimal* if it does not include two states of the form $\varphi < t_1$ and $\varphi < t_2$, for $t_1 < t_2$, nor two states of the form $\varphi U_{\eta+i} \psi < t$ and $\varphi U_{\eta+j} \psi < t$, for $i < j$, and similarly for ">". Intuitively, sets that are not minimal hold redundant assertions, and can be ignored. Accordingly, we restrict the state space of the NBA to have only minimal sets.

Lemma 2. *For an* $LTL^{disc}[\mathcal{D}]$ *formula* φ *and* $v \in [0, 1]$, *the AWA* $\mathcal{A}_{\varphi,v}$ *constructed in Theorem 1 with state space* Q *can be translated to an NBA with* $|Q|^{O(|\varphi|)}$ *states.*

3.5   Decision Procedures for $LTL^{disc}[\mathcal{D}]$

Model Checking and Satisfiability.   Consider a Kripke structure $\mathcal{K}$, an $LTL^{disc}[\mathcal{D}]$ formula φ, and a threshold v. By checking the emptiness of the intersection of $\mathcal{K}$ with $\mathcal{A}_{\neg\varphi,1-v}$, we can solve the threshold model-checking problem. Indeed, $L(\mathcal{A}_{\neg\varphi,1-v}) \cap L(\mathcal{K}) \neq \emptyset$ iff there exists a lasso computation π that is induced by $\mathcal{K}$ such that $[\![\pi, \varphi]\!] < v$, which happens iff it is not true that $[\![\mathcal{K}, \varphi]\!] \geq v$.

The complexity of the model-checking procedure depends on the discounting functions in $\mathcal{D}$. For the set of exponential-discounting functions E, we provide the following concrete complexities, showing that it stays in the same complexity classes of standard LTL model-checking.

Theorem 3. *For a Kripke structure* $\mathcal{K}$, *an* $LTL^{disc}[E]$ *formula* φ, *and a threshold* $v \in [0, 1] \cap \mathbb{Q}$, *the problem of deciding whether* $[\![\mathcal{K}, \varphi]\!] > v$ *is in NLOGSPACE in the number of states of* $\mathcal{K}$, *and in PSPACE in* $|\langle\varphi\rangle|$ *and in the description of* v.

Proof.   By Theorem 2 and Lemma 2, the size of an NBA $\mathcal{B}$ corresponding to φ and v is singly exponential in $|\langle\varphi\rangle|$ and in the description of v. Hence, we can check the emptiness of the intersection of $\mathcal{K}$ and $\mathcal{B}$ via standard "on the fly" procedures, getting the stated complexities.

Note that the complexity in Theorem 3 is only NLOGSPACE in the system, since our solution does not analyze the Kripke structure, but only takes its product with the specification's automaton. This is in contrast to the approach of model checking temporal logic with (non-discounting) accumulative values, where, when decidable, involves a doubly-exponential dependency on the size of the system [4].

Finally, observe that the NBA obtained in Lemma 2 can be used to solve the threshold-satisfiability problem: given an $LTL^{disc}[\mathcal{D}]$ formula φ and a threshold $v \in [0, 1]$, we can decide whether there is a computation π such that $[\![\pi, \varphi]\!] \sim v$, for $\sim \in \{<, >\}$, and return such a computation when the answer is positive. This is done by simply deciding whether there exists a word that is accepted by the NBA.

Threshold Synthesis.   Consider an $LTL^{disc}[\mathcal{D}]$ formula φ, and assume a partition of the atomic propositions in φ to input and output signals, we can use the NBA $\mathcal{A}_{\varphi,v}$ in order to address the *synthesis* problem, as stated in the following theorem (see the full version for the proof).

Theorem 4. *Consider an LTL$^{disc}[\mathcal{D}]$ formula φ. If there exists a transducer $\mathcal{T}$ all of whose computations π satisfy $[\![\pi, \varphi]\!] > v$, then we can generate a transducer $\mathcal{T}$ all of whose computations τ satisfy $[\![\tau, \varphi]\!] \geq v$.*

4   Adding Propositional Quality Operators

As model checking is decidable for LTL$^{disc}[\mathcal{D}]$, one may wish to push the limit and extend the expressive power of the logic. In particular, of great interest is the combining of discounting with propositional quality operators [1].

4.1   Adding the Average Operator

A well-motivated extension is the introduction of the average operator $\oplus$, with the semantics $[\![\pi, \varphi \oplus \psi]\!] = \frac{[\![\pi,\varphi]\!]+[\![\pi,\psi]\!]}{2}$. The work in [1] proves that extending LTL by this operator, as well as with other propositional quantitative operators, enables clean specification of quality and results in a logic for which the model-checking problem can be solved in PSPACE.

We show that adding the $\oplus$ operator to LTL$^{disc}[\mathcal{D}]$ gives a logic, denoted LTL$^{disc \oplus}[\mathcal{D}]$, for which the validity and model-checking problems are undecidable. The validity problem asks, given an LTL$^{disc \oplus}[\mathcal{D}]$ formula φ over the atomic propositions AP and a threshold $v \in [0,1]$, whether $[\![\pi, \varphi]\!] > v$ for every $\pi \in (2^{AP})^{\omega}$.

In the undecidability proof, we show a reduction from the 0-halting problem for two-counter machines. A *two-counter machine* $\mathcal{M}$ is a sequence $(l_1, \ldots, l_n)$ of commands involving two counters x and y. We refer to $\{1, \ldots, n\}$ as the *locations* of the machine. There are five possible forms of commands:

$$\text{INC}(c), \ \text{DEC}(c), \ \text{GOTO } l_i, \ \text{IF } c{=}0 \text{ GOTO } l_i \text{ ELSE GOTO } l_j, \ \text{HALT},$$

where $c \in \{x, y\}$ is a counter and $1 \leq i, j \leq n$ are locations. Since we can always check whether $c = 0$ before a DEC(c) command, we assume that the machine never reaches DEC(c) with $c = 0$. That is, the counters never have negative values. Given a counter machine $\mathcal{M}$, deciding whether $\mathcal{M}$ halts is known to be undecidable [20]. Given $\mathcal{M}$, deciding whether $\mathcal{M}$ halts with both counters having value 0, termed the 0-*halting problem*, is also undecidable: given a counter machine $\mathcal{M}$, we can replace every HALT command with a code that clears the counters before halting.

Theorem 5. *The validity problem for LTL$^{disc \oplus}[\mathcal{D}]$ is undecidable (for every nonempty set of discounting functions $\mathcal{D}$).*

The proof goes along the following lines: We construct from $\mathcal{M}$ an LTL$^{disc \oplus}[\mathcal{D}]$ formula φ such that $\mathcal{M}$ 0-halts iff there exists a computation π such that $[\![\pi, \varphi]\!] = \frac{1}{2}$. The idea behind the construction is as follows. The computation that φ is verified with corresponds to a description of a run of $\mathcal{M}$, where every triplet $\langle l_i, \alpha, \beta \rangle$ is encoded as the string $i x^{\alpha} y^{\beta} \#$.

The formula φ will require the following properties of the computation π (recall that the setting is quantitative, not Boolean):

1. The first configuration in π is the initial configuration of $\mathcal{M}$, namely $\langle l_1, 0, 0 \rangle$, or $1\#$ in our encoding.
2. The last configuration in π is $\langle \text{HALT}, 0, 0 \rangle$, or k in our encoding, where k is a line whose command is HALT.
3. π represents a legal run of $\mathcal{M}$, up to the consistency of the counters between transitions.
4. The counters are updated correctly between configurations.

Properties 1-3 can easily be captured by an LTL formula. Property 4 utilizes the expressive power of $\text{LTL}^{\text{disc}\oplus}[\mathcal{D}]$, as we now explain. The intuition behind Property 4 is the following. We compare the value of a counter before and after a command, such that the formula takes a value smaller than $\frac{1}{2}$ if a violation is encountered, and $\frac{1}{2}$ otherwise. Since the value of counters can change by at most 1, the essence of this formula is the ability to test equality of counters.

We start with a simpler case, to demonstrate the point. Let $\eta \in \mathcal{D}$ be a discounting function. Consider the formula $CountA := a\mathsf{U}_\eta \neg a$ and the computation $a^i b^j \#^\omega$. It holds that $[\![a^i b^j, CountA]\!] = \eta(i)$. Similarly, it holds that $[\![a^i b^j \#^\omega, a\mathsf{U}(b\mathsf{U}_\eta \neg b)]\!] = \eta(j)$. Denote the latter by $CountB$. Let $CompareAB := (CountA \oplus \neg CountB) \wedge (\neg CountA \oplus CountB)$. We now have that

$$[\![a^i b^j \#^\omega, CompareAB]\!] = \min\left\{ \frac{\eta(i)+1-\eta(j)}{2}, \frac{\eta(j)+1-\eta(i)}{2} \right\} = \frac{1}{2} - \frac{|\eta(i)-\eta(j)|}{2}, \text{ and}$$

observe that the latter is $\frac{1}{2}$ iff $i = j$ (and is less than $\frac{1}{2}$ otherwise). This is because η is strictly decreasing, and in particular an injection.

Thus, we can compare counters. To apply this technique to the encoding of a computation, we use formulas that "parse" the input and find successive occurrences of a counter.

Since, by considering a Kripke structure that generates all computations, it is easy to reduce the validity problem to the model-checking problem, we can conclude with the following.

Theorem 6. *The model-checking problem for $\text{LTL}^{\text{disc}\oplus}[\mathcal{D}]$ is undecidable.*

4.2   Adding Unary Multiplication Operators

As we have seen in Section 4.1, adding the operator $\oplus$ to $\text{LTL}^{\text{disc}}[\mathcal{D}]$ makes model checking undecidable. One may still want to find propositional quality operators that we can add to the logic preserving its decidability. In this section we describe one such operator. We extend $\text{LTL}^{\text{disc}}[\mathcal{D}]$ with the operator ∇_λ, for $\lambda \in (0, 1)$, with the semantics $[\![\pi, \nabla_\lambda \varphi]\!] = \lambda \cdot [\![\pi, \varphi]\!]$. This operator allows the specifier to manually change the satisfaction value of certain subformulas. This can be used to express importance, reliability, etc. of subformulas. For example, in $\mathsf{G}(request \rightarrow (response \vee \nabla_{\frac{2}{3}} \mathsf{X} response))$, we limit the satisfaction value of computations in which a response is given with a delay to $\frac{2}{3}$.

Note that the operator ∇_λ is similar to a one-time application of $\mathsf{U}_{\exp_\lambda^{+1}}$, thus $\nabla_\lambda \varphi$ is equivalent to $\mathtt{False}\mathsf{U}_{\exp_\lambda^{+1}} \psi$. In practice, it is better to handle ∇_λ formulas directly, by adding the following transitions to the construction in the proof of Theorem 1.

$$\delta(\nabla_\lambda \varphi > t, \sigma) = \begin{cases} \delta(\varphi > \frac{t}{\lambda}, \sigma) & \text{if } \frac{t}{\lambda} < 1, \\ \mathtt{False} & \text{if } \frac{t}{\lambda} \geq 1, \end{cases} \delta(\nabla_\lambda \varphi < t, \sigma) = \begin{cases} \delta(\varphi < \frac{t}{\lambda}, \sigma) & \text{if } \frac{t}{\lambda} \leq 1, \\ \mathtt{True} & \text{if } \frac{t}{\lambda} > 1. \end{cases}$$

5   Extensions

$\text{LTL}^{\text{disc}}[\mathcal{D}]$ **with Past Operators**   A useful augmentation of LTL is the addition of *past operators* [18]. These operators enable the specification of clearer and more succinct formulas while preserving the PSPACE complexity of model checking. In the full version, we add *discounting-past* operators to $\text{LTL}^{\text{disc}}[\mathcal{D}]$ and show how to perform model checking on the obtained logic. The solution goes via 2-way weak alternating automata and preserves the complexity of $\text{LTL}^{\text{disc}}[\mathcal{D}]$.

Weighted Systems.   In $\text{LTL}^{\text{disc}}[\mathcal{D}]$, the verified system need not be weighted in order to get a quantitative satisfaction – it stems from taking into account the delays in satisfying the requirements. Nevertheless, $\text{LTL}^{\text{disc}}[\mathcal{D}]$ also naturally fits weighted systems, where the atomic propositions have values in $[0, 1]$. In the full version we extend the semantics of $\text{LTL}^{\text{disc}}[\mathcal{D}]$ to *weighted Kripke structures*, whose computations assign weights in $[0, 1]$ to every atomic proposition. We solve the corresponding model-checking problem by properly extending the construction of the automaton $\mathcal{A}_{\varphi, v}$.

Changing the Tendency of Discounting.   One may observe that in our discounting scheme, the value of future formulas is discounted toward 0. This, in a way, reflects an intuition that we are pessimistic about the future. While in some cases this fits the needs of the specifier, it may well be the case that we are ambivalent to the future. To capture this notion, one may want the discounting to tend to $\frac{1}{2}$. Other values are also possible. For example, it may be that we are optimistic about the future, say when a system improves its performance while running and we know that components are likely to function better in the future. We may then want the discounting to tend, say, to $\frac{3}{4}$.

To capture this notion, we define the operator $O_{\eta, z}$, parameterized by $\eta \in \mathcal{D}$ and $z \in [0, 1]$, with the semantics. $[\![\pi, \varphi O_{\eta, z} \psi]\!] = \sup_{i \geq 0} \{\min\{\eta(i)[\![\pi^i, \psi]\!] + (1 - \eta(i))z, \min_{0 \leq j < i} \eta(j)[\![\pi^j, \varphi]\!] + (1 - \eta(j))z\}\}$. The discounting function η determines the rate of convergence, and z determines the limit of the discounting. In the full version, we show how to augment the construction of $\mathcal{A}_{\varphi, v}$ with the operator O in order to solve the model-checking problem.

6   Discussion

An ability to specify and to reason about quality would take formal methods a significant step forward. Quality has many aspects, some of which are propositional, such as prioritizing one satisfaction scheme on top of another, and some are temporal, for example having higher quality for implementations with shorter delays. In this work we provided a solution for specifying and reasoning about temporal quality, augmenting the commonly used linear temporal logic (LTL). A satisfaction scheme, such as ours, that is based on elapsed times introduces a big challenge, as it implies infinitely many satisfaction values. Nonetheless, we showed the decidability of the model-checking problem, and for the natural exponential-decaying satisfactions, the complexity remains as the one for standard LTL, suggesting the interesting potential of the new scheme. As for combining propositional and temporal quality operators, we showed that the problem is, in general, undecidable, while certain combinations, such as adding priorities, preserve the decidability and the complexity.

438   S. Almagor, U. Boker, and O. Kupferman

Acknowledgement. We thank Eleni Mandrali for pointing to an error in an earlier version of the paper.

References

1. Almagor, S., Boker, U., Kupferman, O.: Formalizing and reasoning about quality. In: Fomin, F.V., Freivalds, R., Kwiatkowska, M., Peleg, D. (eds.) ICALP 2013, Part II. LNCS, vol. 7966, pp. 15–27. Springer, Heidelberg (2013)
2. Almagor, S., Hirshfeld, Y., Kupferman, O.: Promptness in ω-regular automata. In: Bouajjani, A., Chin, W.-N. (eds.) ATVA 2010. LNCS, vol. 6252, pp. 22–36. Springer, Heidelberg (2010)
3. Bojańczyk, M., Colcombet, T.: Bounds in ω-regularity. In: 21st LICS, pp. 285–296 (2006)
4. Boker, U., Chatterjee, K., Henzinger, T.A., Kupferman, O.: Temporal Specifications with Accumulative Values. In: 26th LICS, pp. 43–52 (2011)
5. Clarke, E., Grumberg, O., Peled, D.: Model Checking. MIT Press (1999)
6. Dam, M.: CTL* and ECTL* as fragments of the modal μ-calculus. TCS 126, 77–96 (1994)
7. de Alfaro, L., Faella, M., Henzinger, T., Majumdar, R., Stoelinga, M.: Model checking discounted temporal properties. TCS 345(1), 139–170 (2005)
8. de Alfaro, L., Henzinger, T., Majumdar, R.: Discounting the future in systems theory. In: Baeten, J.C.M., Lenstra, J.K., Parrow, J., Woeginger, G.J. (eds.) ICALP 2003. LNCS, vol. 2719, pp. 1022–1037. Springer, Heidelberg (2003)
9. Droste, M., Rahonis, G.: Weighted automata and weighted logics with discounting. TCS 410(37), 3481–3494 (2009)
10. Droste, M., Vogler, H.: Weighted automata and multi-valued logics over arbitrary bounded lattices. TCS 418, 14–36 (2012)
11. Faella, M., Legay, A., Stoelinga, M.: Model checking quantitative linear time logic. Electr. Notes Theor. Comput. Sci. 220(3), 61–77 (2008)
12. Gastin, P., Oddoux, D.: Fast LTL to büchi automata translation. In: Berry, G., Comon, H., Finkel, A. (eds.) CAV 2001. LNCS, vol. 2102, pp. 53–65. Springer, Heidelberg (2001)
13. Kan, S.H.: Metrics and Models in Software Quality Engineering. Addison-Wesley Longman Publishing Co. (2002)
14. Kupferman, O., Piterman, N., Vardi, M.Y.: From Liveness to Promptness. In: Damm, W., Hermanns, H. (eds.) CAV 2007. LNCS, vol. 4590, pp. 406–419. Springer, Heidelberg (2007)
15. Krob, D.: The equality problem for rational series with multiplicities in the tropical semiring is undecidable. International Journal of Algebra and Computation 4(3), 405–425 (1994)
16. Kwiatkowska, M.: Quantitative verification: models techniques and tools. In: ESEC/SIGSOFT FSE, pp. 449–458 (2007)
17. Laroussinie, F., Schnoebelen, P.: A hierarchy of temporal logics with past. In: Enjalbert, P., Mayr, E.W., Wagner, K.W. (eds.) STACS 1994. LNCS, vol. 775, pp. 47–58. Springer, Heidelberg (1994)
18. Lichtenstein, O., Pnueli, A., Zuck, L.: The glory of the past. In: Parikh, R. (ed.) Logic of Programs 1985. LNCS, vol. 193, pp. 196–218. Springer, Heidelberg (1985)
19. Mandrali, E.: Weighted LTL with discounting. In: Moreira, N., Reis, R. (eds.) CIAA 2012. LNCS, vol. 7381, pp. 353–360. Springer, Heidelberg (2012)
20. Minsky, M.: Computation: Finite and Infinite Machines, 1st edn. Prentice Hall (1967)
21. Miyano, S., Hayashi, T.: Alternating finite automata on ω-words. TCS 32, 321–330 (1984)
22. Mohri, M.: Finite-state transducers in language and speech processing. Computational Linguistics 23(2), 269–311 (1997)
23. Moon, S., Lee, K., Lee, D.: Fuzzy branching temporal logic. IEEE Transactions on Systems, Man, and Cybernetics, Part B 34(2), 1045–1055 (2004)

24. Pnueli, A., Rosner, R.: On the synthesis of a reactive module. In: Proc. 16th POPL, pp. 179–190 (1989)
25. Shapley, L.: Stochastic games. Proc. of the National Academy of Science 39 (1953)
26. Spinellis, D.: Code Quality: The Open Source Perspective. Addison-Wesley Professional (2006)
27. Vardi, M.Y.: An automata-theoretic approach to linear temporal logic. In: Moller, F., Birtwistle, G. (eds.) Logics for Concurrency. LNCS, vol. 1043, pp. 238–266. Springer, Heidelberg (1996)
28. Vardi, M., Wolper, P.: An automata-theoretic approach to automatic program verification. In: 1st LICS, pp. 332–344 (1986)

Symbolic Model Checking of Stutter-Invariant Properties Using Generalized Testing Automata[*]

Ala Eddine Ben Salem[1,2], Alexandre Duret-Lutz[1],
Fabrice Kordon[2], and Yann Thierry-Mieg[2]

[1] LRDE, EPITA, Le Kremlin-Bicêtre, France
{ala,adl}@lrde.epita.fr
[2] Sorbonne Universités, UPMC Univ. Paris 06,
CNRS UMR 7606, LIP6, F-75005, Paris, France
{Fabrice.Kordon,Yann.Thierry-Mieg}@lip6.fr

Abstract. In a previous work, we showed that a kind of ω-automata known as *Transition-based Generalized Testing Automata* (TGTA) can outperform the Büchi automata traditionally used for *explicit* model checking when verifying stutter-invariant properties.

In this work, we investigate the use of these generalized testing automata to improve *symbolic* model checking of stutter-invariant LTL properties. We propose an efficient symbolic encoding of stuttering transitions in the product between a model and a TGTA. Saturation techniques available for decision diagrams then benefit from the presence of stuttering self-loops on all states of TGTA. Experimentation of this approach confirms that it outperforms the symbolic approach based on (transition-based) Generalized Büchi Automata.

1 Introduction

Model checking for Linear-time Temporal Logic (LTL) is usually based on converting the negation of the property to check into an ω-automaton $\mathcal{B}$, composing that automaton with a model $\mathcal{M}$ given as a Kripke structure, and finally checking the language emptiness of the resulting product $\mathcal{B} \otimes \mathcal{M}$ [21].

One way to implement this procedure is the *explicit approach* where $\mathcal{B}$ and $\mathcal{M}$ are represented as explicit graphs. $\mathcal{B}$ is usually a Büchi automaton or a generalization using multiple acceptance sets. We use Transition-based Generalized Büchi Automata (TGBA) for their conciseness. When the property to verify is stutter-invariant [8], testing automata [13] should be preferred to Büchi automata. Instead of observing the values of state propositions in the system, testing automata observe the *changes* of these values, making them suitable to represent stutter-invariant properties. In previous work [1], we showed how to generalize testing automata using several acceptance sets, and allowing a more efficient emptiness check. Our comparison showed these Transition-based Generalized Testing Automata (TGTA) to be superior to TGBA for model-checking of stutter-invariant properties.

Another implementation of this procedure is the *symbolic approach* where the automata and their products are represented by means of decision diagrams (a concise way to represent large sets or relations) [3]. Symbolic encodings for *generalized* Büchi

---

[*] This work has been partially supported by the project ImpRo/ANR-2010-BLAN-0317.

E. Ábrahám and K. Havelund (Eds.): TACAS 2014, LNCS 8413, pp. 440–454, 2014.

automata are pretty common [17]. With such encodings, we can compute, in one step, the sets of all direct successors (*PostImage*) or predecessors (*PreImage*) of any set of states. Using this technique, there have been a lot of propositions for symbolic emptiness-check algorithms [9, 19, 14]. These symbolic algorithms manipulate fixpoints on the transition relation which can be optimized using saturation techniques [4, 20].

However these approaches do not offer any reduction when verifying stutter-invariant properties. So far, and to the best of our knowledge, testing automata have never been used in symbolic model checking. Our goal is therefore to propose a symbolic approach for model checking using TGTA, and compare it to the symbolic approach using TGBA. In particular, we show that the computation of fixpoints on the transition relation of the product can be sped up with a dedicated evaluation of stuttering transitions. We exploit a separation of the transition relation into two terms, one of which greatly benefits from saturation techniques.

This paper is organized as follows. Section 2 presents the symbolic model-checking approach for TGBA. For generality we define our symbolic structures using predicates over state variables in order to remain independent of the decision diagrams used to actually implement the approach. Section 3 focuses on the encoding of TGTA in the same framework. We first show how a TGTA can be encoded, then we show how to improve the encoding of the Kripke structure and the product to benefit from saturation in the encoding of stuttering transitions in the TGTA. Finally, Section 4 compares the two approaches experimentally with an implementation that uses hierarchical Set Decision Diagrams (SDD) [20] (a particular type of Decision Diagrams on integer variables, on which we can apply user-defined operations). On our large, BEEM-based benchmark, our symbolic encoding of TGTA appears to to be superior to TGBA.

2 Symbolic LTL Model Checking Using TGBA

We first recall how to perform the automata-theoretic approach to LTL model checking using symbolic encodings of TGBA and Kripke structures. This setup will serve as a baseline to measure our improvements from later sections.

Through the paper, let AP designate the finite set of *atomic propositions* of the model. Any state of the model is labeled by a valuation of these atomic propositions. Let $\Sigma = 2^{AP}$ denote the set of these valuations, which we interpret either as sets or as Boolean conjunctions. For instance if $AP = \{a,b\}$, then $\Sigma = 2^{AP} = \{\{a,b\},\{a\},\{b\},\emptyset\}$ or equivalently $\Sigma = \{ab, a\bar{b}, \bar{a}b, \bar{a}\bar{b}\}$. An *execution* of the model is an infinite sequence of such valuations, i.e., an element of Σ^{ω}.

2.1 Kripke Structures and Their Symbolic Encoding

The executions of the model can be represented by a Kripke structure $\mathcal{M}$.

Definition 1 (Kripke Structure). *A* Kripke structure *over* Σ *is a tuple* $\mathcal{M} = \langle S, S_0, R, L \rangle$, *where:*

- *S is a finite set of states,*
- *$S_0 \subseteq S$ is the set of initial states,*
- *$R \subseteq S \times S$ is the transition relation,*
- *$L : S \to \Sigma$ is a state-labeling function.*

An execution $w = \ell_0\ell_1\ell_2\ldots \in \Sigma^\omega$ *is accepted by* $\mathcal{M}$ *if there exists an infinite sequence* $s_0, s_1, \ldots \in S^\omega$ *such that* $s_0 \in S_0$ *and* $\forall i \in \mathbb{N}$, $(L(s_i) = \ell_i) \wedge ((s_i, s_{i+1}) \in R)$. *The* language *accepted by* $\mathcal{M}$ *is the set* $\mathscr{L}(\mathcal{M}) \subseteq \Sigma^\omega$ *of executions it accepts.*

In symbolic model checking we encode such a structure with predicates that represent sets of states or transitions [18]. These predicates are then implemented using decision diagrams [3].

Definition 2 (Symbolic Kripke Structure). *A Kripke structure* $\mathcal{M} = \langle S, S_0, R, L \rangle$ *can be encoded by the following predicates where* $s, s' \in S$ *and* $\ell \in \Sigma$:

- $P_{S_0}(s)$ *is true iff* $s \in S_0$,
- $P_R(s, s')$ *is true iff* $(s, s') \in R$,
- $P_L(s, \ell)$ *is true iff* $L(s) = \ell$.

In the sequel, we use the notations $S_0(s)$, $R(s, s')$ *and* $L(s, \ell)$ *instead of* $P_{S_0}(s)$, $P_R(s, s')$ *and* $P_L(s, \ell)$. *A Symbolic Kripke structure is therefore a triplet of predicates* $K = \langle S_0, R, L \rangle$ *on state variables.*

Variables s and s' used above are typically implemented using decision diagrams to represent either a state or a set of states. In a typical encoding [3], states are represented by conjunctions of Boolean variables. For instance if $S = \{0, 1\}^3$, a state $s = (1, 0, 1)$ would be encoded as $s_1\bar{s}_2 s_3$. Similarly, $s_1 s_3$ would encode the set of states $\{(1, 0, 1), (1, 1, 1)\}$. With this encoding, S_0, R and L are propositional formulae which can be implemented with BDDs or other kind of decision diagrams. In our implementation, we used SDDs on integer variables [20].

2.2 TGBA and Their Symbolic Encoding

Transition-based Generalized Büchi Automata (TGBA) [11] are a generalization of the Büchi Automata (BA) commonly used for model checking. In our context, the TGBA represents the negation of the LTL property to verify. We chose to use TGBA rather than BA since they allow a more compact representation of properties [7].

Definition 3 (TGBA). *A TGBA over the alphabet* $\Sigma = 2^{AP}$ *is a tuple* $\mathcal{B} = \langle Q, Q_0, \delta, F \rangle$ *where:*

- Q *is a finite set of states,*
- $Q_0 \subseteq Q$ *is a set of initial states,*
- $\delta \subseteq Q \times \Sigma \times Q$ *is a transition relation, where each element* (q, ℓ, q') *represents a transition from state* q *to state* q' *labeled by the valuation* ℓ,
- $F \subseteq 2^\delta$ *is a set of acceptance sets of transitions.*

$\mathcal{B}$ *accepts an execution* $\ell_0\ell_1\ldots \in \Sigma^\omega$ *if there exists an infinite path* $(q_0, \ell_0, q_1)(q_1, \ell_1, q_2)$ $\ldots \in \delta^\omega$ *that visits each acceptance set infinitely often:* $q_0 \in Q_0$ *and* $\forall f \in F, \forall i \in \mathbb{N}, \exists j \geq i, (q_j, \ell_j, q_{j+1}) \in f$.

The language *accepted by* $\mathcal{B}$ *is the set* $\mathscr{L}(\mathcal{B}) \subseteq \Sigma^\omega$ *of the executions it accepts.*

We target TGBA in this paper because their use of generalized and transition-based acceptance make them more concise than traditional Büchi automata [11]. Generalized acceptance is classically used in symbolic model checking [9] and using transition-based acceptance is not a problem [17]. People working with (classical) Büchi automata can adjust to our definitions by "pushing" the acceptance of states to their outgoing transitions [7].

Any LTL formula φ can be converted into a TGBA whose language is the set of executions that satisfy φ [7]. Figure 1(a) shows a TGBA derived from the LTL formula $\mathsf{F}\,\mathsf{G}a$. The Boolean expression over $AP = \{a\}$ that labels each transition represents the valuation of atomic propositions that hold in this transition (in this example, $\Sigma = \{a, \bar{a}\}$). Any infinite path in this example is accepted if it visits infinitely often the only acceptance set containing transition $(1, a, 1)$.

Like Kripke structures, TGBAs can be encoded by predicates [18] on state variables.

Definition 4 (Symbolic TGBA)
A TGBA $\langle Q, Q_0, \delta, F \rangle$ is symbolically encoded by a triplet of predicates $\langle Q_0, \Delta, \{\Delta_f\}_{f \in F} \rangle$ where:

- *$Q_0(q)$ is true iff $q \in Q_0$,*
- *$\Delta(q, \ell, q')$ is true iff $(q, \ell, q') \in \delta$,*
- *$\forall f \in F, \Delta_f(q, \ell, q')$ is true iff $(q, \ell, q') \in f$.*

2.3   Symbolic Product of a TGBA with a Kripke Structure

We now show how to build a synchronous product by composing the symbolic representations of a TGBA with that of a Kripke structure, inspired from Sebastian *et al.* [18].

Definition 5 (Symbolic Product for TGBA). *Given a Symbolic Kripke structure $K = \langle S_0, R, L \rangle$ and a Symbolic TGBA $A = \langle Q_0, \Delta, \{\Delta_f\}_{f \in F} \rangle$ sharing a set AP of atomic propositions, the Symbolic Product $K \otimes A = \langle P_0, T, \{T_f\}_{f \in F} \rangle$ is defined by the predicates P_0, T and T_f encoding respectively the set of initial states, the transition relation and the acceptance transitions of the product:*

- *(s, q) denotes the state variables of the product (s for the Kripke structure and q for TGBA),*
- *$P_0(s, q) = S_0(s) \wedge Q_0(q)$,*
- *$T((s, q), (s', q')) = \exists \ell \left[R(s, s') \wedge L(s, \ell) \wedge \Delta(q, \ell, q') \right]$, where (s', q') encodes the next state variables,*
- *$\forall f \in F, T_f((s, q), (s', q')) = \exists \ell \left[R(s, s') \wedge L(s, \ell) \wedge \Delta_f(q, \ell, q') \right]$.*

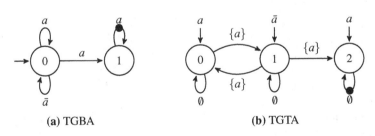

| (a) TGBA | (b) TGTA |

Fig. 1. TGBA and TGTA for the LTL property $\varphi = \mathsf{F}\,\mathsf{G}a$. Acceptance transitions are indicated by ●.

The labels ℓ are used to ensure that a transition (q, ℓ, q') of A is synchronized with a state s of K such that $L(s, \ell)$. This way, we ensure that the product recognizes only the executions of K that are also recognized by A. However we do not need to remember how product transitions are labeled to check $K \otimes A$ for emptiness. A product can be seen as a TGBA without labels on transitions.

In symbolic model checkers, the exploration of the product is based on the following *PostImage* operation [18]. For any set of states encoded by a predicate P, *PostImage*(P) $(s', q') = \exists(s, q) \left[P(s, q) \wedge T((s, q), (s', q')) \right]$ returns a predicate representing the set of states reachable in one step a state in P.

Because in TGBA the acceptance conditions are based on transitions, we also define *PostImage*(P, f) to computes the successors of P reached using only transitions from an acceptance set $f \in F$: *PostImage*$(P, f)(s', q') = \exists(s, q) \left[P(s, q) \wedge T_f((s, q), (s', q')) \right]$.

These two operations are at the heart of the symbolic emptiness check presented in the next section.

2.4 Symbolic Emptiness Check

One way to check if a product is not empty is to find a reachable Strongly Connected Component that contains transitions from all acceptance sets (we call it an *accepting SCC*). Figure 2 shows such an algorithm implemented using symbolic operations. It mimics the algorithm FEASIBLE of Kesten et al. [14] and can be seen as a forward variant of OWCTY (One Way Catch Them Young [9]) that uses *PostImage* computations instead of *PreImage*. Line 3 computes the set P of all reachable states of the product. The main loop on lines 4–8 refines P at each iteration. Lines 5–6 keep only the states of P that can be reached from a cycle in P. Lines 7–8 then remove all cycles that never visit some acceptance set $f \in F$. Eventually the main loop will reach a fixpoint where P contains all states that are reachable from an accepting SCC. The product is empty iff that set is empty.

There are many variants of such symbolic emptiness checks. We selected this variant mainly for its simplicity, as our contributions are mostly independent of the chosen algorithm: essentially, we will improve the cost of computing *Reach*(P) (used lines 3 and 8).

```
1 Input: PostImage, P₀ and F
2 begin
3 |   P ← Reach(P₀)
4 |   while P changes do
5 |   |   while P changes do
6 |   |   |   P ← PostImage(P)
7 |   |   for f in F do
8 |   |   |   P ← Reach(PostImage(P, f))
9 |   return P = ∅
```

```
1 Reach(P)
2 |   while P changes do
3 |   |   P ← P ∪ PostImage(P)
4 |   return P
```

Fig. 2. Forward-variant of OWCTY, a symbolic emptiness check

3   Symbolic Approach Using TGTA

Testing automata [10] are a kind of automata that recognize only stutter-invariant properties. In previous work [1] we generalized them as Transition-based Generalized Testing Automata (TGTA). In this section, we show how to encode a TGTA for symbolic model checking.

Definition 6. *A property, i.e., a set of infinite sequences* $\mathcal{P} \subseteq \Sigma^\omega$, *is* stutter-invariant *iff any sequence* $\ell_0 \ell_1 \ell_2 \ldots \in \mathcal{P}$ *remains in* $\mathcal{P}$ *after repeating any valuation* ℓ_i *or omitting duplicate valuations. Formally,* $\mathcal{P}$ *is stutter-invariant iff* $\ell_0 \ell_1 \ell_2 \ldots \in \mathcal{P} \iff \ell_0^{i_0} \ell_1^{i_1} \ell_2^{i_2} \ldots \in \mathcal{P}$ *for any* $i_0 > 0, i_1 > 0 \ldots$

Theorem 1. *An LTL property is stutter-invariant iff it can be expressed as an LTL formula that does not use the* X *operator [16].*

3.1   Transition-Based Generalized Testing Automata

While a TGBA observes the value of the atomic propositions AP, a TGTA observes the *changes* in these values. If a valuation of AP does not change between two consecutive valuations of an execution, we say that a TGTA executes a *stuttering transition*.

   If A and B are two valuations, $A \oplus B$ denotes the symmetric set difference, i.e., the set of atomic propositions that differ (e.g., $a\bar{b} \oplus ab = \{a\} \oplus \{a,b\} = \{b\}$). Technically, this can be implemented with an XOR operation on bitsets (hence the symbol $\oplus$).

Definition 7. *A TGTA over the alphabet* Σ *is a tuple* $\mathcal{T} = \langle Q, Q_0, U, \delta, F \rangle$ *where:*

- *Q is a finite set of states,*
- *$Q_0 \subseteq Q$ is a set of initial states,*
- *$U : Q_0 \to 2^\Sigma$ is a function mapping each initial state to a set of symbols of* Σ,
- *$\delta \subseteq Q \times \Sigma \times Q$ is the transition relation, where each element* (q, c, q') *represents a transition from state q to state q' labeled by a* changeset *c interpreted as a (possibly empty) set of atomic propositions whose value must change between q and q',*
- *$F \subseteq 2^\delta$ is a set of acceptance sets of transitions,*

and such that all stuttering transitions (i.e., transitions labeled by $\emptyset$) are self-loops and every state has a stuttering self-loop. More formally, we can define a partition of $\delta = \delta_\emptyset \cup \delta_*$ *where:*

- *$\delta_\emptyset = \{(q, \emptyset, q) \mid q \in Q\}$ is the stuttering transition relation,*
- *$\delta_* = \{(q, \ell, q') \in \delta \mid \ell \neq \emptyset\}$ is the non-stuttering transition relation.*

An execution $\ell_0 \ell_1 \ell_2 \ldots \in \Sigma^\omega$ *is accepted by* $\mathcal{T}$ *if there exists an infinite path* $(q_0, \ell_0 \oplus \ell_1, q_1)(q_1, \ell_1 \oplus \ell_2, q_2)(q_2, \ell_2 \oplus \ell_3, q_3) \ldots \in \delta^\omega$ *where:*

- *$q_0 \in Q_0$ with $\ell_0 \in U(q_0)$ (the execution is recognized by the path),*
- *$\forall f \in F, \forall i \in \mathbb{N}, \exists j \geq i, (q_j, \ell_j \oplus \ell_{j+1}, q_{j+1}) \in f$ (each acceptance set is visited infinitely often).*

The language accepted by $\mathcal{T}$ *is the set* $\mathscr{L}(\mathcal{T}) \subseteq \Sigma^\omega$ *of executions it accepts.*

   Figure 1(b) shows a TGTA recognizing the LTL formula F G a. Acceptance sets are represented using dots as in TGBAs. Transitions are labeled by changesets: e.g., the transition $(0, \{a\}, 1)$ means that the value of a changes between states 0 and 1. Initial valuations are shown above initial arrows: $U(0) = \{a\}, U(1) = \{\bar{a}\}$ and $U(2) = \{a\}$. As an illustration, the execution $\bar{a};a;a;a;\ldots$ is accepted by the run $\textcircled{1}\xrightarrow{\{a\}}\textcircled{2}\xrightarrow{\emptyset}\textcircled{2}\xrightarrow{\emptyset}\textcircled{2}\cdots$ because the value a only changes between the first two steps.

Theorem 2. *Any stutter-invariant property can be translated into an equivalent TGTA [1].*

Note that Def. 7 differs from our previous work [1] because we now enforce a partition of δ such that stuttering transitions can only be self-loops. However, the TGTA resulting from the LTL translation we presented previously [1] already have this property. We will use it to optimize symbolic computation in section 3.3.

Finally, a TGTA's symbolic encoding is similar to that of a TGBA.

Definition 8 (Symbolic TGTA)

A TGTA $\mathcal{T} = \langle Q,Q_0,U,\delta,F\rangle$ is symbolically encoded by a triplet of predicates $\langle U_0, \Delta^{\oplus}, \{\Delta_f^{\oplus}\}_{f\in F}\rangle$ where:

- $U_0(q,\ell)$ *is true iff* $(q \in Q_0) \wedge (U(q) = \ell)$
- $\Delta^{\oplus}(q,c,q')$ *is true iff* $(q,c,q') \in \delta$
- $\forall f \in F, \Delta_f^{\oplus}(q,c,q')$ *is true iff* $((q,c,q') \in f)$

3.2 Symbolic Product of a TGTA with a Kripke Structure

The product between a TGTA and a Kripke structure is similar to the TGBA case, except that we have to deal with changesets. The transitions (s,s') of a Kripke structure that must be synchronized with a transition (q,c,q') of a TGTA, are all the transitions such that the label of s and s' differs by the changeset c.

In order to reduce the number of symbolic operations when computing the Symbolic product of a TGTA with a Kripke structure, we introduce a changeset-based encoding of Kripke structure (only the transition relation changes).

Definition 9 (Changeset-based symbolic Kripke structure). *A Kripke structure $\mathcal{M} = \langle S,S_0,R,L\rangle$, can be encoded by the changeset-based symbolic Kripke structure $K^{\oplus} = \langle S_0,R^{\oplus},L\rangle$, where:*

- *the predicate $R^{\oplus}(s,c,s')$ is true iff $((s,s') \in R \wedge (L(s) \oplus L(s')) = c)$,*
- *the predicates S_0 and L have the same definition as for a Symbolic Kripke structure K (Def. 2).*

In practice, the (changeset-based or not) symbolic transition relation of the Kripke structure should be constructed directly from the model and atomic propositions of the formula to check. In Section 4.2, we discuss how we build such changeset-based Kripke structures in our setup.

The procedure requires reconstruction of the symbolic transition relation for each formula (or at least for each set of atomic propositions used in the formulas). However the cost of this construction is not significant with respect to the complexity of the overall model checking procedure (overall on our benchmark, less than 0.16% of total time was spent building these transition relations).

Adjusting the symbolic encoding of the Kripke structure to TGTA, allows us to obtain the following natural definition of the symbolic product using TGTA:

Definition 10 (Symbolic Product for TGTA). *Given a changeset-based Symbolic Kripke structure* $K^{\oplus} = \langle S_0, R, L \rangle$ *and a Symbolic TGTA* $A^{\oplus} = \langle U_0, \Delta^{\oplus}, \{\Delta_f^{\oplus}\}_{f \in F} \rangle$ *sharing the same set of atomic propositions AP, the Symbolic Product* $K^{\oplus} \otimes A^{\oplus} = \langle P_0, T, \{T_f\}_{f \in F} \rangle$ *is defined by the following predicates:*

- *The set of initial states is encoded by:* $P_0(s, q) = \exists \ell \left[S_0(s) \wedge L(s, \ell) \wedge U_0(q, \ell) \right]$
- *The transition relation of the product is:*
$$T((s, q), (s', q')) = \exists c \left[R^{\oplus}(s, c, s') \wedge \Delta^{\oplus}(q, c, q') \right]$$
- *The definition of* T_f *is similar to T by replacing* $\Delta^{\oplus}$ *with* $\Delta_f^{\oplus}$.

The definitions of *PostImage(P)* and *PostImage(P, f)* are the same as in the TGBA approach, with the new expressions of T and T_f above.

As for the product in TGBA approach, the product in TGTA approach is a TGBA (or a TGTA) without labels on transitions, and the same emptiness check algorithm (Fig. 2) can be used for the two products.

3.3 Exploiting Stuttering Transitions to Improve Saturation in the TGTA Approach

Among symbolic approaches for evaluating a fixpoint on a transition relation, the *saturation* algorithm offers gains of one to three orders of magnitude [4] in both time and memory, especially when applied to asynchronous systems [5].

The saturation algorithm does not use a breadth-first exploration of the product (i.e., each iteration in the function Reach (Fig. 2) is not a "global" *PostImage()* computation). Saturation instead recursively repeats "local" fixed-points by recognizing and exploiting transitions locality and identity transformations on state variables [5].

This algorithm considers that the system state consists of k discrete variables encoded by a Decision Diagram, and that the transition relation is expressed as a disjunction of terms called transition clusters. Each cluster typically only reads or writes a limited subset consisting of $k' \leq k$ variables, called the *support* of the cluster. During the least fixpoint computing the reachable states, saturation technique consists in reordering [12] the evaluation of ("local" fixed-points on) clusters in order to avoid the construction of (useless) intermediate Decision Diagram nodes.

The algorithm to determine an ordering for saturation is based on the support of each cluster.

We now show how to decompose the transition relation of the product $K^{\oplus} \otimes A^{\oplus}$ to exhibit clusters having a smaller support, favoring the saturation technique.

We base our decomposition on the fact that in a TGTA, all stuttering transitions are self-loops and every state has a stuttering self-loop (δ_0 in Def. 7). Therefore, stuttering transitions in the Kripke structure can be mapped to stuttering transitions in the product regardless of the TGTA state.

Let us separate stuttering and non-stuttering transitions in the transition relation T of the product between a Kripke structure and a TGTA ($K^{\oplus} \otimes A^{\oplus}$):

$$T((s, q), (s', q')) = \left(R^{\oplus}(s, \emptyset, s') \wedge \Delta^{\oplus}(q, \emptyset, q') \right) \vee \left(\exists c \left[R_*^{\oplus}(s, c, s') \wedge \Delta_*^{\oplus}(q, c, q') \right] \right)$$

where $R_*^{\oplus}$ and $\Delta_*^{\oplus}$ encode respectively the non-stuttering transitions of the model and of the TGTA:

- $\Delta_*^\oplus(q,c,q')$ is true iff $(q,c,q') \in \delta_*$ (see Def. 7)
- $R_*^\oplus(s,c,s')$ is true iff $R^\oplus(s,c,s') \wedge (c \neq \emptyset)$

According to the definition of $\delta_\emptyset$ in Def. 7, the predicate $\Delta^\oplus(q,\emptyset,q')$ encodes the set of TGTA's self-loops and can be replaced by the predicate $equal(q,q')$, simplifying T:

$$T((s,q),(s',q')) = \underbrace{\left(R^\oplus(s,\emptyset,s') \wedge equal(q,q')\right)}_{T_\emptyset((s,q),(s',q'))} \vee \underbrace{\left(\exists c \left[R_*^\oplus(s,c,s') \wedge \Delta_*^\oplus(q,c,q')\right]\right)}_{T_*((s,q),(s',q'))} \quad (1)$$

The transition relation (1) is a disjunction of T_*, synchronizing updates of both TGTA and Kripke structure, and $T_\emptyset$, corresponding to the stuttering transitions of the Kripke structure. Since all states in the TGTA have a stuttering self-loop, $T_\emptyset$ does not depend on the TGTA state. In practice, the predicate $equal(q,q')$ is an identity relation for variable q [5] and is simplified away (i.e., the term $T_\emptyset$ can be applied to a decision diagram without consulting or updating the variable q [12]). Hence q is not part of the clusters supports in $T_\emptyset$ (while q is part of the clusters supports in T_*). This gives more freedom to the saturation technique for reordering the application of clusters in $T_\emptyset$.

Note that in the product of TGBA with Kripke structure (Def. 5) there is no $T_\emptyset$ that could be extracted since there is no stuttering hypothesis in general. This severely limits the possibilities of the saturation algorithm in the TGBA approach.

In the symbolic emptiness check presented in Fig. 2, the function Reach corresponds to a least fixpoint performed using saturation. As we shall see experimentally in the next section, the better encoding of $T_\emptyset$ (without q in its support) in the product of TGTA with Kripke structure, greatly favors the saturation technique, leading to gains of roughly one order of magnitude.

4   Experimentation

We now compare the approaches presented in this paper. The symbolic model-checking approach using TGBA, presented in Section 2 serves as our baseline. We first describe our implementation and selected benchmarks, prior to discussing the results.

4.1   Implementation

All approaches are implemented on top of three libraries[1]: Spot, SDD/ITS, and LTSmin.

Spot is a model-checking library providing several bricks that can be combined to build model checkers [7]. In our implementation, we reused the modules providing a translation form an LTL formula into a TGBA and into a TGTA [1].

SDD/ITS is a library for symbolic representation of state spaces in the form of Instantiable Transition Systems (ITS): an abstract interface for symbolic Labeled Transition Systems (LTS). The symbolic encoding of ITS is based on Hierarchical Set Decision Diagrams (SDD) [20]. SDDs allow a compact symbolic representation of states and transition relation.

---

[1] Respectively http://spot.lip6.fr, http://ddd.lip6.fr, and
http://fmt.cs.utwente.nl/tools/ltsmin.

The algorithms presented in this paper can be implemented using any kind of decision diagram (such as OBDD), but use of the SDD software library allows to easily benefit from the automatic saturation mechanism described in [12].

LTSmin [2] can generate state spaces from various input formalisms (μCRL, DVE, GNA, MAPLE, PROMELA, ...) and store the obtained LTS in a concise symbolic format, called Extended Table Format (ETF). We used LTSmin to convert DVE models into ETF for our experiments. This approach offers good generality for our tool, since it can process any formalism supported by LTSmin tool.

Our symbolic model checker inputs an ETF file and an LTL formula. The LTL formula is converted into TGBA or TGTA which is then encoded using an ITS. The ETF model is also symbolically encoded using an ITS (see Sec. 4.2). The two obtained ITSs are then composed to build a symbolic product, which is also an ITS. Finally, the OWCTY emptiness check is applied to this product.

4.2   Using ETF to Build a Changeset-Based Symbolic Kripke Structure

An ETF file[2] produced by LTSmin is a text-based serialization of the symbolic representation of the transition relation of a model whose states consist in k integer variables. Transitions are described in the following tabular form:

```
0/1   0/1   *     *
1/2   *     0/1   *
. . .
```

where each column correspond to a variable, and each line describes the effect of a symbolic transition on the corresponding variables. The notation "*in/out*" means that the variable must have the value "*in*" for the transition to fire, and the value is then updated to "*out*". A "***" means that the variable is not consulted or updated by the transition. Each line may consequently encode a set of explicit transitions that differ only by the values of the starred variables: the support of a transition is the set of unstarred variables.

A changeset-based symbolic Kripke structure, as defined in Sec. 3.2, can be easily obtained from such a description. To obtain a changeset associated to a line in the file, it is enough to compute difference between values of atomic propositions associated to the *in* variables and the values associated to the *out* variables. Because they do not change, starred variables have no influence on the changeset.

Note that an empty changeset does not necessarily correspond to a line where all variables are starred. Even when *in* and *out* values are different, they may have no influence on the atomic propositions, and the resulting changeset may be empty. For instance if the only atomic proposition considered is $p = (v_1 > 1)$ (where v_1 denotes the first-column variable), then the changeset associated to the first line is $\emptyset$, and the changeset for the second line is $\{p\}$.

4.3   Benchmark

We evaluated the TGBA and TGTA approaches on the following models and formulae:

---

[2] http://fmt.cs.utwente.nl/tools/ltsmin/doc/etf.html

Table 1. Characteristics of our selected benchmark models. The stuttering-ratio represents the percentage of stuttering transitions in the model. Since the definition of stuttering depends on the atomic propositions of the formula, we give an average over the 200 properties checked against each model.

BEEM model	states $10^3 \times$	stut. ratio	BEEM model	states $10^3 \times$	stut. ratio
at.5	31 999	95%	lann.6	144 151	52%
bakery.4	157	83%	lann.7	160 025	64%
bopdp.3	1 040	91%	lifts.7	5 126	93%
elevator.4	888	74%	peterson.5	131 064	83%
brp2.3	40	79%	pgm_protocol.8	3 069	92%
fischer.5	101 028	89%	phils.8	43 046	89%
lamport_nonatomic.5	95 118	92%	production_cell.6	14 520	85%
lamport.7	38 717	93%	reader_writer.3	604	88%

- Our models come from the BEEM benchmark [15], a suite of models for explicit model checking, which contains some models that are considered difficult for symbolic model checkers [2]. Table 1 summarizes the 16 models we selected as representatives of the overall benchmark.
- BEEM provides a few LTL formulae, but they mostly represent safety properties and can thus be checked without building a product. Therefore, for each model, we randomly generated 200 stutter-invariant LTL formulae: 100 verified formulae (empty product) and 100 violated formulae (non-empty product). We consequently have a total 3200 pairs of (model, formula).

All tests were run on a 64bit Linux system running on an Intel Xeon E5645 at 2.40GHz. Executions that exceeded 30 minutes or 4GB of RAM were aborted and are reported with time and memory above these thresholds in our graphics.

In all approaches evaluated, symbolic products are encoded using the same variable ordering: we used the symbolic encoding named "log-encode with top-order" by Sebastiani et al. [18].

4.4 Results

The results of our experimental[3] comparisons are presented by the two scatter plot matrices of Fig. 3 and Fig. 4. The scatter plot highlighted at the bottom of Fig. 3 compares the time-performance of the TGTA-approach against the reference TGBA approach.[4] Each point of the scatter plot represents a measurement for a pair (*model,formula*). For the highlighted plot, the x-axis represents the TGBA approach and the y-axis represent the TGTA approach, so 3060 points below the diagonal correspond to cases where the TGTA approach is better, and the 131 points above the diagonal corresponds to points were the TGBA approach is better (In scatter plot matrices, each point below the diagonal is in favor of the approach displayed on the right, while each point above the

---

[3] The results, models, formulae and tools used in these tests, can be downloaded from http://www.lrde.epita.fr/~ala/TACAS-2014/Benchmark.html

[4] We recommend viewing these plots online.

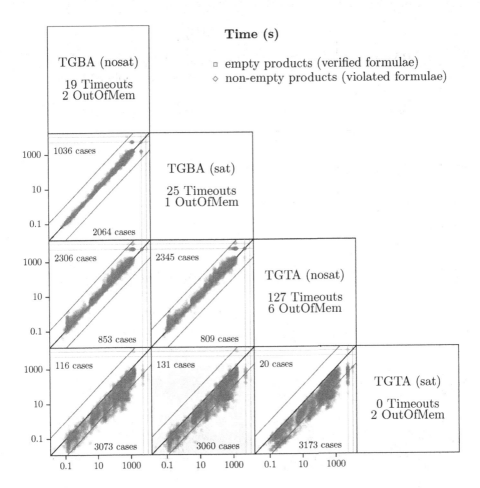

Fig. 3. Time-comparison of the TGBA and TGTA approaches, with saturation enabled "(sat)" or disabled "(nosat)", on a set of 3199 pairs (*model,formula*). Timeouts and Out-of-memory errors are plotted on separate lines on the top or right edges of the scatter plots. Each plot also displays the number of cases that are above or below the main diagonal (including timeouts and out-of-memory errors), i.e., the number of (*model,formula*) for which one approach was better than the other. Additional diagonals show the location of ×10 and /10 ratios. Points are plotted with transparency to better highlight dense areas, and lessen the importance of outliers.

diagonal is in favor of the approach displayed in the top). Axes use a logarithmic scale. The colors distinguish violated formulae (non-empty product) from verified formulae (empty products). In order to show the influence of the saturation technique, we also ran the TGBA and TGTA approaches with saturation disabled. In our comparison matrix, the labels "(sat)" and "(nosat)" indicate whether saturation was enabled or not. Fig. 4 gives the memory view of this experiment.

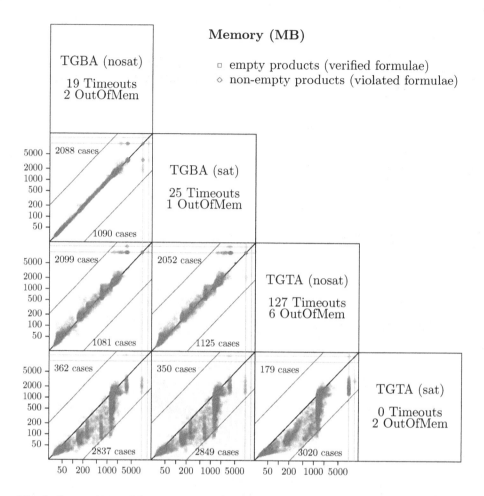

Fig. 4. Comparison of the memory-consumption of the TGBA and TGTA approaches, with or without saturation, on the same set of problems

As shown by the highlighted scatter plots in Fig. 3 and 4, the TGTA approach clearly outperforms the traditional TGBA-based scenario by one order of magnitude. This is due to the combination of two factors: saturation and exploration of stuttering.

The saturation technique does not significantly improve the model checking using TGBA (compare "TGBA (sat)" against "TGBA (nosat)" at the top of Fig. 3 and 4). In fact, the saturation technique is limited on the TGBA approach, because in the transition relation of Def. 5 each conjunction must consult the variable q representing the state of the TGBA, therefore q impacts the supports and the reordering of clusters evaluated by the saturation. This situation is different in the case of TGTA approach, where the T_0 term of the transition-relation of the product (equation (1)) does not involve the state q of the TGTA: here, saturation strongly improve performances (compare "TGTA (sat)" against "TGTA (nosat)").

Overall the improvement to this symbolic technique was only made possible because the TGTA representation makes it easy to process the stuttering behaviors separately from the rest. These stuttering transitions represent a large part of the models transitions, as shown by the stuttering-ratios of Table 1. Using these stuttering-ratios, we can estimate in our Benchmark the importance of the term $T_\emptyset$ compared to T_* in equation (1).

5 Conclusion

Testing automata [10] are a way to improve the explicit model checking approach when verifying stutter-invariant properties, but they had not been used for symbolic model checking. In this paper, we gave the first symbolic approach using testing automata, with generalized acceptance (TGTA), and compare it to a more classical symbolic approach (using TGBA).

On our benchmark, using TGTA, we were able to gain one order of magnitude over the TGBA-based approach.

We have shown that fixpoints over the transition relation of a product between a Kripke structure and a TGTA can benefit from the saturation technique, especially because part of their expression is only dependent on the model, and can be evaluated without consulting the transition relation of the property automaton. The improvement was possible only because TGTA makes it possible to process stuttering behaviors specifically, in a way that helps the saturation technique.

In future work, we plan to evaluate the use of TGTA in the context of hybrid approaches, mixing both explicit and symbolic approaches [18, 6].

References

1. Ben Salem, A.-E., Duret-Lutz, A., Kordon, F.: Model checking using generalized testing automata. In: Jensen, K., van der Aalst, W.M., Ajmone Marsan, M., Franceschinis, G., Kleijn, J., Kristensen, L.M. (eds.) ToPNoC VI. LNCS, vol. 7400, pp. 94–122. Springer, Heidelberg (2012)
2. Blom, S., van de Pol, J., Weber, M.: LTSMIN: Distributed and symbolic reachability. In: Touili, T., Cook, B., Jackson, P. (eds.) CAV 2010. LNCS, vol. 6174, pp. 354–359. Springer, Heidelberg (2010)
3. Burch, J.R., Clarke, E.M., McMillan, K.L., Dill, D.L., Hwang, L.: Symbolic model checking: 10^{20} states and beyond. In: Proc. of the Fifth Annual IEEE Symposium on Logic in Computer Science, pp. 1–33. IEEE Computer Society Press (1990)
4. Ciardo, G., Marmorstein, R., Siminiceanu, R.: Saturation unbound. In: Garavel, H., Hatcliff, J. (eds.) TACAS 2003. LNCS, vol. 2619, pp. 379–393. Springer, Heidelberg (2003)
5. Ciardo, G., Yu, A.J.: Saturation-based symbolic reachability analysis using conjunctive and disjunctive partitioning. In: Borrione, D., Paul, W. (eds.) CHARME 2005. LNCS, vol. 3725, pp. 146–161. Springer, Heidelberg (2005)
6. Duret-Lutz, A., Klai, K., Poitrenaud, D., Thierry-Mieg, Y.: Self-loop aggregation product — A new hybrid approach to on-the-fly LTL model checking. In: Bultan, T., Hsiung, P.-A. (eds.) ATVA 2011. LNCS, vol. 6996, pp. 336–350. Springer, Heidelberg (2011)
7. Duret-Lutz, A., Poitrenaud, D.: SPOT: an extensible model checking library using transition-based generalized Büchi automata. In: Proc. of MASCOTS 2004, pp. 76–83. IEEE Computer Society Press (2004)

8. Etessami, K.: Stutter-invariant languages, ω-automata, and temporal logic. In: Halbwachs, N., Peled, D.A. (eds.) CAV 1999. LNCS, vol. 1633, pp. 236–248. Springer, Heidelberg (1999)

9. Fisler, K., Fraer, R., Kanhi, G., Vardi, M.Y., Yang, Z.: Is there a best symbolic cycle-detection algorithm? In: Margaria, T., Yi, W. (eds.) TACAS 2001. LNCS, vol. 2031, pp. 420–434. Springer, Heidelberg (2001)

10. Geldenhuys, J., Hansen, H.: Larger automata and less work for LTL model checking. In: Valmari, A. (ed.) SPIN 2006. LNCS, vol. 3925, pp. 53–70. Springer, Heidelberg (2006)

11. Giannakopoulou, D., Lerda, F.: From states to transitions: Improving translation of LTL formulæ to Büchi automata. In: Peled, D.A., Vardi, M.Y. (eds.) FORTE 2002. LNCS, vol. 2529, pp. 308–326. Springer, Heidelberg (2002)

12. Hamez, A., Thierry-Mieg, Y., Kordon, F.: Hierarchical set decision diagrams and automatic saturation. In: van Hee, K.M., Valk, R. (eds.) PETRI NETS 2008. LNCS, vol. 5062, pp. 211–230. Springer, Heidelberg (2008)

13. Hansen, H., Penczek, W., Valmari, A.: Stuttering-insensitive automata for on-the-fly detection of livelock properties. In: Proc. of FMICS 2002, ENTCS, vol. 66(2) (2002)

14. Kesten, Y., Pnueli, A., Raviv, L.-O.: Algorithmic verification of linear temporal logic specifications. In: Larsen, K.G., Skyum, S., Winskel, G. (eds.) ICALP 1998. LNCS, vol. 1443, pp. 1–16. Springer, Heidelberg (1998)

15. Pelánek, R.: BEEM: Benchmarks for explicit model checkers. In: Bošnački, D., Edelkamp, S. (eds.) SPIN 2007. LNCS, vol. 4595, pp. 263–267. Springer, Heidelberg (2007)

16. Peled, D., Wilke, T.: Stutter-invariant temporal properties are expressible without the next-time operator. Information Processing Letters 63(5), 243–246 (1995)

17. Rozier, K.Y., Vardi, M.Y.: A multi-encoding approach for LTL symbolic satisfiability checking. In: Butler, M., Schulte, W. (eds.) FM 2011. LNCS, vol. 6664, pp. 417–431. Springer, Heidelberg (2011)

18. Sebastiani, R., Tonetta, S., Vardi, M.Y.: Symbolic systems, explicit properties: On hybrid approaches for LTL symbolic model checking. In: Etessami, K., Rajamani, S.K. (eds.) CAV 2005. LNCS, vol. 3576, pp. 350–363. Springer, Heidelberg (2005)

19. Somenzi, F., Ravi, K., Bloem, R.: Analysis of symbolic SCC hull algorithms. In: Aagaard, M.D., O'Leary, J.W. (eds.) FMCAD 2002. LNCS, vol. 2517, pp. 88–105. Springer, Heidelberg (2002)

20. Thierry-Mieg, Y., Poitrenaud, D., Hamez, A., Kordon, F.: Hierarchical set decision diagrams and regular models. In: Kowalewski, S., Philippou, A. (eds.) TACAS 2009. LNCS, vol. 5505, pp. 1–15. Springer, Heidelberg (2009)

21. Vardi, M.Y.: An automata-theoretic approach to linear temporal logic. In: Moller, F., Birtwistle, G. (eds.) Logics for Concurrency. LNCS, vol. 1043, pp. 238–266. Springer, Heidelberg (1996)

Symbolic Synthesis for Epistemic Specifications with Observational Semantics

Xiaowei Huang and Ron van der Meyden

School of Computer Science and Engineering
UNSW Australia
{xiaoweih,meyden}@cse.unsw.edu.au

Abstract. The paper describes a framework for the synthesis of protocols for distributed and multi-agent systems from specifications that give a program structure that may include variables in place of conditional expressions, together with specifications in a temporal epistemic logic that constrain the values of these variables. The epistemic operators are interpreted with respect to an observational semantics. The framework generalizes the notion of *knowledge-based program* proposed by Fagin et al (Dist. Comp. 1997). An algorithmic approach to the synthesis problem is developed that computes all solutions, using a reduction to epistemic model checking, that has been implemented using symbolic techniques. An application of the approach to synthesize mutual exclusion protocols is presented.

1 Introduction

In concurrent, distributed or multi-agent systems it is typical that agents must act on the basis of local data to coordinate to ensure global properties of the system. This leads naturally to the consideration of the notion of what an agent *knows* about the global state, given the state of its local data structures. *Epistemic* logic, or the logic of knowledge [9] has been developed as a formal language within which to express reasoning about this aspect of concurrent systems. In particular, *knowledge-based programs* [10], a generalization of standard programs in which agents condition their actions on formulas expressed in a temporal-epistemic logic, have been proposed as a framework for expressing designs of distributed protocols at the knowledge level. Many of the interesting analyses of problems in distributed computing based on notions of knowledge (e.g. [13]) can be cast in the form of knowledge-based programs.

Knowledge-based programs have the advantage of abstracting from the details of how information is encoded in an agent's local state, enabling a focus on *what* an agent needs to know in order to decide between its possible actions. On the other hand, this abstraction means that knowledge-based programs do not have an operational semantics. They are more like *specifications* than like programs in this regard: obtaining an implementation of a knowledge-based program requires that concrete properties of the agent's local state be found that are equivalent to the conditions on the agent's knowledge used in the program.

This gap has meant that knowledge-based analyses have been largely conducted as pencil and paper exercises to date, and only limited automated support for knowledge-based programming has been available. One approach to automation that has emerged

E. Ábrahám and K. Havelund (Eds.): TACAS 2014, LNCS 8413, pp. 455–469, 2014.

in the last ten years is the development of epistemic model checking tools [11,16]. These give a partial solution to the gap, in that they allow a putative implementation of a knowledge-based program to be verified for correctness (for examples, see [2,3]). However, this leaves open the question of how such an implementation is to be obtained, which still requires human insight.

Our contribution in this paper is to develop and implement an approach that automates the construction of implementations for knowledge-based programs for the case of the *observational semantics* for knowledge-based programs. (In earlier work [14] we dealt with stronger semantics for a more limited program syntax, see Section 7 for discussion). Our approach is to reduce the problem to model checking, enabling the investment in epistemic model checking to be leveraged to *automatically synthesize* implementations of knowledge-based programs. In particular, we build on *symbolic* techniques for epistemic model checking.

We in fact generalize the notion of knowledge-based program to a more liberal notion that we call *epistemic protocol specification*, based on a protocol template together with a set of temporal-epistemic formulas that constrain how the template is to be instantiated. This enables our techniques to be applied also to cover ideas such as the *sound local proposition* generalization of knowledge-based programs [8]. We illustrate the approach through an application of the knowledge-based programming methodology to the development of protocols for *mutual exclusion*. We give an abstract knowledge-based specification of a protocol for mutual exclusion, and show how our approach can automatically extract different protocols solving this problem.

2   A Semantic Model for Knowledge and Time

For brevity, we present the theory of our approach at the level of semantic structures, since the symbolic algorithms we use work at this level. However, the input to our synthesis system is given in a programming notation, and, for clarity of exposition, we use this notation to present examples. For motivation, the reader may prefer to read the example in Section 4 first. Details of the mapping from programming syntax to the semantic structures are fairly standard, and left to the reader's intuition.

Let V be a finite set of boolean variables and Ags be a finite set of agents. The language CTLK(V, Ags) has the syntax:

$$\phi ::= v \mid \neg\phi \mid \phi_1 \vee \phi_2 \mid EX\phi \mid E(\phi_1 U \phi_2) \mid EG\phi \mid K_i\phi$$

where $v \in V$ and $i \in Ags$. This is CTL plus the construct $K_i\phi$, which says that agent i knows that ϕ holds. We freely use standard operators that are definable in terms of the above, e.g., $AF\phi = \neg EG\neg\phi$ and $AG\phi = \neg E(true\,U\neg\phi)$.

A (finite) *model* is a tuple $M = (S, I, \longrightarrow, \{\sim_i\}_{i\in Ags}, \mathcal{F}, \pi)$ where S is a (finite) set of states, $I \subseteq S$ is a set of initial states, $\longrightarrow \subseteq S \times S$ is a transition relation, $\sim_i\colon S \times S \longrightarrow \{0, 1\}$ is an indistinguishability relation of agent i, component $\mathcal{F}$ is a fairness condition (explained below), and $\pi : S \longrightarrow \mathcal{P}(V)$ is a truth assignment (here $\mathcal{P}(V)$ denotes the powerset of V.) A *path* in M from a state $s \in S$ is a finite or infinite sequence $s = s_0 \longrightarrow s_1 \longrightarrow s_2 \longrightarrow \ldots$ We assume that $\longrightarrow$ is serial, i.e. for each $s \in S$ there exists $t \in S$ such that $s \longrightarrow t$. We model fairness using the condition $\mathcal{F}$ by taking this to be a *generalized*

Büchi fairness condition, expressed as a set of sets of states: $\mathcal{F} = \{\alpha_1, \ldots, \alpha_k\}$ where each $\alpha_i \subseteq S$. An infinite path $s = s_0 \longrightarrow s_1 \longrightarrow s_2 \longrightarrow \ldots$ is *fair* with respect to $\mathcal{F}$ if, for each $i = 1 \ldots k$, there are infinitely many indices j for which $s_j \in \alpha_i$. Let $rch(M)$ be the set of *fair reachable* states of M, i.e., the set of states s_n (for some n) such that there exists a fair path $s_0 \longrightarrow s_1 \longrightarrow \ldots \longrightarrow s_n \longrightarrow s_{n+1} \longrightarrow \ldots$ with $s_0 \in I$ an initial state. We assume that $I \subseteq rch(M)$, i.e., all initial states are the source of a fair path.

The semantics of the language is given by a satisfaction relation $M, s \models \phi$, where $s \in rch(M)$ is a fair reachable state. This relation is defined inductively as follows:

1. $M, s \models v$ if $v \in \pi(s)$,
2. $M, s \models \neg\phi$ if not $M, s \models \phi$,
3. $M, s \models \phi_1 \vee \phi_2$ if $M, s \models \phi_1$ or $M, s \models \phi_2$,
4. $M, s \models EX\phi$ if there exists $t \in rch(M)$ such that $s \longrightarrow t$ and $M, t \models \phi$,
5. $M, s \models E(\phi_1 U \phi_2)$ if there exists a fair path $s = s_0 \longrightarrow s_1 \longrightarrow \ldots \longrightarrow s_n \rightarrow \ldots$ such that $M, s_k \models \phi_1$ for $k = 0 \ldots n - 1$ and $M, s_n \models \phi_2$,
6. $M, s \models EG\phi$ if for there exists a fair path $s = s_0 \longrightarrow s_1 \longrightarrow \ldots$ with $M, s_k \models \phi$ for all $k \geq 0$,
7. $M, s \models K_i\phi$ if for all $t \in rch(M)$ with $s \sim_i t$ we have $M, t \models \phi$.

We are interested in models in which each of the agents runs a protocol in which it chooses its actions based on local information. To this end, we describe how a model may be obtained from the agents running such protocols in the context of an environment, which provides shared structure through which the agents can communicate.

An *environment* for agents Ags is a tuple $E = \langle Var_e, I_e, Acts, \longrightarrow_e, \mathcal{F}_e \rangle$, where

1. Var_e is a finite set of variables, from which we derive a set of states $S_e = \mathcal{P}(Var_e)$,
2. I_e is a subset of S_e, representing the initial states,
3. $Acts = \Pi_{i \in Ags} Acts_i$ is a set of joint actions, where each $Acts_i$ is a finite set of actions that may be performed by agent i,
4. $\longrightarrow_e \subseteq S_e \times Acts \times S_e$ is a transition relation, labelled by joint actions,
5. $\mathcal{F}_e$ is a generalized Büchi fairness condition over the states S_e.

Intuitively, a joint action a represents a choice of action a_i for each agent, performed simultaneously, and the transition relation resolves this into an effect on the state. We assume that $\longrightarrow_e$ is serial in the sense that for all $s \in S_e$ and $a \in Acts$ there exists $t \in S_e$ such that $s \xrightarrow{a} t$.

Semantically, a *concrete protocol* for agent $i \in Ags$ in such an environment E may be represented by a tuple $Prot_i = \langle PVar_i, LVar_i, OVar_i, I_i, Acts_i, \longrightarrow_i \rangle$, where

1. $PVar_i \subseteq Var_e$ is a subset of the variables of E, called the *parameter* variables of the protocol,
2. $LVar_i$ is a finite set of variables, understood as the *local variables* of the agent,
3. $OVar_i \subseteq PVar_i \cup LVar_i$ is the set of variables of the above two types that are observable to the agent, and on the basis of which the agent computes what it knows,
4. I_i is a subset of $\mathcal{P}(LVar_i)$, representing the initial states of the protocol,
5. $Acts_i$ is the set of actions that the agent is able to perform (this must match the set of actions associated to this agent in the environment),
6. $\longrightarrow_i \subseteq \mathcal{P}(PVar_i \cup LVar_i) \times Acts_i \times \mathcal{P}(LVar_i)$ is a serial labelled transition relation.

We assume that the sets Var_e and $LVar_i$, for $i \in Ags$, are mutually disjoint.[1]

Note that the transition relation $\longrightarrow_i$ indicates how an agent's local variables are updated when performing an action, which may depend on the current values of the parameter variables in the environment. This transition relation does not specify a change in the value of the parameter variables: changes to these are determined in the environment on the basis of the actions that this agent, and others, perform in the given step.

Given an environment E and a collection $\{Prot_i\}_{i \in Ags}$ of concrete protocols for the agents, we may construct a model $M(E, \{Prot_i\}_{i \in Ags}) = (S, I, \longrightarrow, \{\sim_i\}_{i \in Ags}, \mathcal{F}, \pi)$ as follows. The set of states is $S = \mathcal{P}(Var_e \cup \bigcup_{i \in Ags} LVar_i)$, i.e., the set of all assignments to the environment and local variables. We represent such states in the form $s = s_e \cup \bigcup_{i \in Ags} l_i$, where $s_e \subseteq Var_e$ and each $l_i \subseteq LVar_i$. Such a state s is taken to be an initial state in I if $s_e \in I_e$ and $l_i \in I_i$ for all agents i. That is, I is the set of states where the environment and each of the agents is in an initial state. The epistemic indistinguishability relations for agent i over the states S is defined by $s \sim_i t$ iff $s \cap OVar_i = t \cap OVar_i$, i.e., the states s and t have the same values for all of agent i's observable variables. The transition relation $\longrightarrow$ is given by $s_e \cup \bigcup_{i \in Ags} l_i \longrightarrow s'_e \cup \bigcup_{i \in Ags} l'_i$ if there exists a joint action a such that $s_e \overset{a}{\longrightarrow}_e s'_e$ and $(s_e \cap PVar_i) \cup l_i \overset{a_i}{\longrightarrow}_i l'_i$ for each agent i. We take the fairness condition $\mathcal{F}$ to contain

$$\{s_e \cup \bigcup_{i \in Ags} l_i \mid s_e \in \alpha, l_1 \in \mathcal{P}(LVar_1), \ldots, l_n \in \mathcal{P}(LVar_n)\}$$

for each $\alpha \in \mathcal{F}_e$. That is, we impose the environment's fairness constraints on the environment portion of the state. The assignment π is given by $\pi(s) = s$.

3   Epistemic Protocol Specifications

Protocol templates generalize concrete protocols by introducing some variables that may be instantiated with a boolean expression in the observable variables in order to obtain a concrete protocol. Formally, a *protocol template* for agent $i \in Ags$ is a tuple $P_i = \langle KVar_i, PVar_i, LVar_i, OVar_i, I_i, Acts_i, \longrightarrow_i \rangle$

1. $KVar_i$ is a set of variables, disjoint from all the other sets of variables, that we call the *template* variables,
2. $PVar_i, LVar_i, OVar_i, Acts_i$ are, respectively, a set of parameter variables, local variables, observable variables and actions of agent i, exactly as in a concrete protocol; as in concrete protocols, we obtain a set of local states $\mathcal{P}(LVar_i)$,
3. $I_i \subseteq \mathcal{P}(LVar_i)$ is a set of initial local states,
4. $\longrightarrow_i \subseteq \mathcal{P}(KVar_i \cup PVar_i \cup LVar_i) \times Acts_i \times \mathcal{P}(LVar_i)$ is a transition relation that describes how local states are updated, depending on the value of the template variables, parameter variables, local variables and action performed.

---

[1] We could also include a fairness condition, but exclude this here for brevity. We do not assume that $LVar_i \subseteq OVar_i$: this allows the impact on knowledge of particular local variables to be studied, and helps in managing the complexity of our technique, which scales exponentially in the number of observable variables.

An *epistemic protocol specification* is a tuple $S = \langle Ags, E, \{P_i\}_{i \in Ags}, \Phi \rangle$, consisting of a set of agents Ags, an environment E for Ags, a collection of protocol templates $\{P_i\}_{i \in Ags}$ for environment E, and a collection of epistemic logic formulas Φ over the agents Ags and variables $Var_e \cup \bigcup_{i \in Ags}(KVar_i \cup LVar_i)$.

Epistemic protocol specifications generalize the notion of knowledge-based program [9,10]. Essentially, these are epistemic protocol specifications in which, for each agent $i \in Ags$ and each template variable $v \in KVar_i$, the set Φ contains a formula of the form $AG(v \Leftrightarrow K_i\psi)$. That is, each template variable is associated with a formula of the form $K_i\psi$, expressing some property of agent i's knowledge, and we require that the meaning of the template variable be equivalent to this property.

Epistemic protocol specifications also encompass the *sound local proposition* interpretation of knowledge-based programs proposed by Engelhardt et al [8]: these associate to each template variable v a formula ϕ and require that v be interpreted by a local proposition (under the observational semantics, this is just a condition on the observable variables), such that the system satisfies $AG(v \Rightarrow \psi)$. (By the assumption of locality of v, this is equivalent to satisfying $AG(v \Rightarrow K_i\psi)$.)

To implement an epistemic protocol specification with respect to the observational semantics, we need to replace each template variable v in each agent i's protocol template by an expression over the agent's observable variables, in such a way that the specification formulas are satisfied in the model resulting from executing the resulting standard program. We now formalize this semantics.

Let θ be a substitution mapping each template variable $v \in KVar_i$, for $i \in Ags$, to a boolean expression over the observable variables $OVar_i$ of agent i's protocol P_i. If we apply this substitution to P_i, we obtain a standard protocol $P_i\theta = \langle PVar_i, LVar_i, OVar_i, I_i, Acts_i, \longrightarrow_i^\theta \rangle$, where the template variables $KVar_i$ have been removed, and all the other components are as in the protocol template, except that we derive the concrete transition relation $\longrightarrow_i^\theta \subseteq \mathcal{P}(PVar_i \cup LVar_i) \times Acts_i \times \mathcal{P}(LVar_i)$ from the transition relation $\longrightarrow_i \subseteq \mathcal{P}(KVar_i \cup PVar_i \cup LVar_i) \times Acts_i \times \mathcal{P}(LVar_i)$ in the protocol template, as follows.

Since, for each $v \in KVar_i$, the value $\theta(v)$ is an expression over the variables $OVar_i$, which is a subset of $PVar_i \cup LVar_i$, we may evaluate $\theta(v)$ on states in $\mathcal{P}(PVar_i \cup LVar_i)$. Given a state $s \in \mathcal{P}(PVar_i \cup LVar_i)$, define $s^\theta \in \mathcal{P}(KVar_i)$ by $s^\theta = \{v \in KVar_i \mid s \models \theta(v)\}$. We then define $\longrightarrow_i^\theta$ by $s \xrightarrow{a}_i^\theta l_i'$ when $s^\theta \cup s \xrightarrow{a}_i l_i'$, for $s \in \mathcal{P}(PVar_i \cup LVar_i)$ and $a \in Acts_i$ and $l_i' \in \mathcal{P}(LVar_i)$.

The substitution θ may also be applied to the specification formulas in Φ. Each $\phi \in \Phi$ is a formula over variables $Var_e \cup \bigcup_{i \in Ags}(KVar_i \cup LVar_i)$. Replacing each occurrence of a variable $v \in \bigcup_{i \in Ags} KVar_i$ by the formula $\theta(v)$ over $Var_e \cup \bigcup_{i \in Ags} LVar_i$, we obtain a formula $\phi\theta$ over $Var_e \cup \bigcup_{i \in Ags} LVar_i$. We write $\Phi\theta$ for $\{\phi\theta \mid \phi \in \Phi\}$.

We say that such a substitution θ provides an *implementation* of the epistemic protocol specification S, provided $M(E, \{P_i\theta\}_{i \in Ags}) \models \Phi\theta$. The problem we study in this paper is the following: given an environment E and an epistemic protocol specification S, synthesize an implementation θ. This is an inherently complex problem. To provide a fair comparison with the performance of our implementation, we measure it here as a function of the size of a succint representation (by means of boolean formulas for the environment and protocol components, or programs PTIME encodable by such formulas). Since the size of the output implementation θ could be of exponential size in the number of observable variables, we measure the complexity of determining the existence of an implementation: even this is already hard, as the following result shows:

Theorem 1. *The problem of determining the existence of an implementation of a given epistemic protocol specification is NEXPTIME-complete.*

4 Example: Mutual Exclusion

To illustrate our approach we use a running example concerned with mutual exclusion. Mutual exclusion protocols [7] are intended for settings where it is required that only one of a set of agents has access to a resource (e.g. a printer, or a write access to a file) at a given time. There exists a large literature on this topic, with many different approaches to its solution [17].

To model the structure of a mutual exclusion protocol, we suppose that each agent has three states: `waiting`, `trying`, and `critical`. Intuitively, while in the `waiting` state, the agent does not require the resource, and it idles for some period of time until it decides that it needs access to the resource. It then enters the `trying` state, where it waits for permission to use the resource. Once this permission has been obtained, it enters the `critical` state, within which it may use the resource. Once done, it exits the critical state and returns to the waiting state. The overall structure of the protocol is therefore a cycle `waiting` → `trying` → `critical` → `waiting`. To ensure fair sharing of the resource, we assume that no agent remains in its critical state forever.

To avoid the situation where two agents are using the resource at the same time, the specification requires that no two agents are in the `critical` state simultaneously. In order for a solution to the mutual exclusion problem to satisfy this specification, the agents need to share some information about their state and to place an appropriate guard on the transition from the `trying` state to the `critical` state. Mutual exclusion protocols differ in their approach to these requirements by providing different ways for agents to use shared variables to distribute and exploit information about their state.

Our application of our synthesis methodology assumes that the designer has some intuitions concerning what information needs to be distributed, and writes the protocol and environment in so as to reflect these ideas concerning information distribution. However, given a pattern of communication, it may still be a subtle matter to determine what information an agent can deduce from some particular values of its observable variables. We use the epistemic specification to relate the information distributed and the conditions used by the agent to make state transitions.

A general structure for a mutual exclusion protocol is given as a protocol template in Figure 1. The code uses a simple programming language, containing a Dijkstra style nondeterministic-if construct **if** $e_1 \rightarrow P_1$ [] $\ldots$ [] $e_k \rightarrow P_p$ **fi** which nondeterministically executes one of the statements P_i for which the corresponding guard e_i evaluates to true. The final e_k may be the keyword **otherwise** which represents the negation of the disjunction of the preceding e_i. If there is no otherwise clause and none of the guards in a conditional are true then the program defaults to a skip action. Evaluation of guards in **if** and **while** statements is assumed to take zero time, and a transition occurs only once an action is encountered in the execution. This applies also to an exit from a while loop.

```
/* protocol for agent i; initially state[i] = waiting */;
    while True do
        begin
        /* waiting section: wait for some amount of time before entering the trying section */
        while state[i] = waiting do
            if True → skip [] True → EnterTry fi;
        /* trying section: wait until the condition represented by template variable xᵢ holds */
        while state[i] = trying do
            if xᵢ → EnterCrit [] otherwise → skip fi;
        /* critical section: stay critical for a random amount of time,
                return to waiting when done */
        while state[i] = critical do
            if True → skip [] True → ExitCrit fi
        end
```

Fig. 1. Protocol template for a mutual exclusion solution

Variables in the programming notation are allowed to be of finite types (these are boolean encoded in the translation to the semantic level. We assume that a vector of variables state indexed by agent names records the state in {waiting, trying, critical} of each agent. Thus, mutual exclusion can be specified by the formula

$$AG \bigwedge_{i,j \in Ags,\ i \neq j} \neg(\text{state}[i] = \text{critical} \land \text{state}[j] = \text{critical}). \qquad (1)$$

The protocol template also uses three actions for the agent: **EnterTry**, **EnterCrit** and **ExitCrit**, which correspond to entering the trying, critical and waiting states respectively. We take the variables state[i] to be included in the set of environment variable Var_e. When there are n agents, with $Ags = \{0 \ldots n - 1\}$, we assume the code for the environment transition always includes the following:

```
for i = 0 ... n - 1 do
    if i.EnterTry → state[i] := trying
    [] i.EnterCrit → state[i] := critical
    [] i.ExitCrit → state[i] := waiting
    fi
```

(Here $i.a$ is a proposition that holds during the computation of any transition in which agent i performs the action a.) Additional code describing the effect of these actions may be included, which represents the way that the agents distribute information to each other concerning their state. A number of different instantiations of this additional code for these actions are discussed below.

In our epistemic specifications, we include in Φ, for each agent i, the following constraint on the template variable x_i that guards entry to the critical section:

$$AG(\mathbf{x}_i \Leftrightarrow K_i(AX(\bigwedge_{j \in Ags} (j \neq i \Rightarrow \text{state}[j] \neq \text{critical})))) \qquad (2)$$

Intuitively, this states that agent i enters its critical section when it knows that, after next transition, no other agent will be in its critical section. Note that this formula falls within the structure of the specifications for knowledge-based programs as discussed above. We also include in Φ the formula

$$\bigwedge_{i \in Ags} AG(\text{state}[i] = \text{trying} \Rightarrow AF \, \text{state}[i] = \text{critical}) \qquad (3)$$

which requires that the protocol synthesized ensures that whenever an agent starts trying, it is eventually able to enter its critical section.

One of the benefits of knowledge-based programs is that they enable the essential reasons for correctness of a protocol to be abstracted in a way that separates the information on the basis of which an agent acts from the way that this information is encoded in the state of the system. This, it is argued, allows for simpler correctness proofs that display the commonalities between different protocols solving the same problem.

This can be seen in the present specification: if the agents follow this specification, then they will not violate mutual exclusion. The proof of this is straightforward; we sketch it informally. Suppose that there is a violation of mutual exclusion, and let t be the earliest time that we have $\text{state}[i] = \text{critical} \wedge \text{state}[j] = \text{critical}$ for some pair of agents $i \neq j$. Then either i or j performs **EnterCrit** to enter its critical section at time $t - 1$. Assuming, without loss of generality, that it is agent i, we have $\mathbf{x}_i$ at time $t - 1$, so by (2), we must have $K_i(AX(\bigwedge_{k \in Ags}(k \neq i \Rightarrow \text{state}[k] \neq \text{critical})))$ at time $t - 1$. But then (since validity of $K_i \phi \Rightarrow \phi$ is immediate from the semantics of the knowledge operator), it follows that $AX(\text{state}[j] \neq \text{critical})$ at time $t - 1$, contradicting the fact that the protocol makes a transition, in the next step, to a state where $\text{state}[j] = \text{critical}$.

We note that only the implication from left to right in (2) is used in this argument, and it would also be valid if we removed the knowledge operator. This is an example of a general point that led to the "sound local proposition" generalization of knowledge-based programs proposed in [8]. However, weakening (2) to only the left to right part allows the trivial implementation $\theta(\mathbf{x}_i) = False$, where no agent ever enters its critical section. The implication from right to left in (2) amounts to saying that rather than this very weak implementation, we want the strongest possible implementation where an agent enters its critical section *whenever* it has sufficient information. Here the knowledge operator is essential since, in general, the non-local condition inside the knowledge operator will not be equivalent to a local proposition implementing $\mathbf{x}_i$.

The description above is not yet a complete solution to the mutual exclusion problem: it remains to describe how agents distribute information about their state, and how the data structures encoding this information are related to a local condition of the agent's state that can be substituted for the template variable so as to satisfy the epistemic specification. We consider here two distinct patterns of information passing, based on two overall systems architectures. In both cases $KVar_i = \{\mathbf{x}_i\}$ for all agents i.

Ring Architecture: In the *ring* architecture we consider n agents $Ags = \{0, \ldots, n-1\}$ in a ring, with agent i able to communicate with agent $i + 1 \mod n$. This communication pattern is essentially that of *token ring* protocols. In this case we assume that communication is by means of a single bit for each agent i, represented by a variable $\text{bit}[i]$. We take $Var_e = \{\text{bit}[i], \text{state}[i] \mid i = 0 \ldots n - 1\}$ and let $PVar_i = \{\text{bit}[i], \text{state}[i]\}$ and $LVar_i = \emptyset$ and $OVar_i = \{\text{bit}[i]\}$. Agent i is able to affect its own bit as well as the bit of agent $i + 1 \bmod n$ through its actions. More precisely, we add to the above code for the environment state transitions the following semantics for the **ExitCrit** actions:

for $i = 0 \ldots n - 1$ do
  if i.**ExitCrit** then begin $\text{bit}[i] := \neg\text{bit}[i]$; $\text{bit}[i + 1 \bmod n] := \neg\text{bit}[i + 1 \bmod n]$ end

That is, on exiting the critical section, the agent flips the value of its own bit, as well as the value of its successor's bit. To ensure fairness, we also add to the environment, for each agent i, the Büchi fairness constraint $\text{state}[i] \neq \texttt{waiting}$, which says that the agent does not remain forever in the waiting state, but eventually tries to go critical. This ensures that this agent takes its turn and does not forever block other agents who may be trying to enter their critical section. We also add the fairness constraints $\text{state}[i] \neq \texttt{critical}$ to ensure that no agent stays in its critical section forever. (However, we do not include $\text{state}[i] \neq \texttt{trying}$ as a fairness constraint: it is up to the protocol to ensure that an agent is eventually able to enter its critical section once it starts trying!)

Broadcast Architecture: In the *broadcast architecture*, we assume that the n agents broadcast their state to all other agents. In this case, no additional variables are needed and we take $Var_e = \{\text{state}[j] \mid j = 0 \ldots n - 1\}$. Also, for each agent i, we take $PVar_i = OVar_i = Var_e$ and $LVar_i = \emptyset$. The only code required for the actions **EnterTry**, **EnterCrit** and **ExitCrit** is that given above for updating the variables $\text{state}[i]$. We do not need to assume eventual progression from waiting to trying in this case (we allow an agent to wait forever, in this case) so the only fairness constraints are $\text{state}[i] \neq \texttt{critical}$ to ensure that no agent is forever critical.

Implementation Example: We describe an example of an implementation in the case of the ring architecture for mutual exclusion described above. We assume that initially, $\text{bit}[i] = 0$ for all agents i. Consider the substitution defined by $\theta(\mathbf{x}_i) = \neg\text{bit}[i]$ if $i = 0$ and $\theta(\mathbf{x}_i) = \text{bit}[i]$ if $i \neq 0$. (Note that these are boolean expressions in the observable variables $OVar_i = \{\text{bit}[i]\}$.) It can be shown that this yields an implementation of the epistemic protocol specification for the ring architecture (we discuss our automated synthesis of this implementation below.) Intuitively, in this implementation, agent 0 initially holds the token, represented by $\text{bit}[0] = 0$. After using the token to enter its critical section, it sets $\text{bit}[0] = 1$ to relinquish the token, and $\text{bit}[1] = 1$ in order to pass the token to agent 1. Thus, for agent 1, holding the token is represented by $\text{bit}[1]$ being true. The same holds for the remaining agents. (Obviously, there is an asymmetry in these conditions for the agents, but any solution needs to somehow break the symmetry in the initial state.) Intuitively, specification formula (2) holds because the implementation maintains the invariant that at most one of the conditions $\theta(\mathbf{x}_i)$ guarding entry to the agents' critical sections holds at any time, and when it is false, the agent is not in its critical section. Thus, the agent i for which $\theta(\mathbf{x}_i)$ is true knows that no other agent is in, or is able to enter, its critical section. Consequently, it knows that no other agent will be in its critical section at the next moment of time.

5   Reduction of Synthesis to Model Checking

We now show how the synthesis of implementations of epistemic protocol specifications S can be reduced to the problem of epistemic model checking. The approach essentially constructs a model that encodes all possible guesses of the environment, and then uses model checking to determine which guesses actually yield an implementation. The consideration of all guesses is done in bulk, using symbolic techniques.

For each agent i, let O_i be the set of boolean assignments to $OVar_i$; this represents the set of possible observations that agent i can make. We may associate to each $o \in O_i$ a conjunction ψ_o of literals over variables v in $OVar_i$, containing literal v if $o(v) = 1$ and $\neg v$ otherwise.

Since an implementation $\theta(v)$ for a template variable v is a boolean condition over observable variables, we may equivalently view this as corresponding to the set of observations on which it holds. This set can in turn be represented by its characteristic mapping from O_i to boolean values. To represent the entire implementation θ, we introduce for each agent $i \in Ags$ a set of new boolean variables X_i, containing the variables $x_{i,o,v}$, where $o \in O_i$ and $v \in KVar_i$. Let $X = \bigcup_{i \in Ags} X_i$. We call X the implementation variables of the epistemic protocol specification $\mathcal{S}$.

A candidate assignment θ for an implementation of the epistemic protocol specification, can be represented by a state χ_θ over the variables X, such that for an observation $o \in O_i$ and variable $v \in KVar_i$, we have $x_{i,o,v} \in \chi_\theta$ iff $\theta(v)$ holds with respect to assignment o. Conversely, given a state χ over the variables X, we can construct an assignment θ_χ mapping, for each agent i, the variables $KVar_i$ to boolean conditions over $OVar_i$, by

$$\theta_\chi(v) = \bigvee_{o \in O_i, \ x_{i,o,v} \in \chi} \psi_o \ .$$

To reduce synthesis to model checking, we construct a system in which the state space is based on the variables X as well as a state of a model for the implementation. Given an environment $E = \langle Var_e, I_e, Acts, \longrightarrow_e \rangle$, we define an environment $E^X = \langle Var_e^X, I_e^X, Acts, \longrightarrow_e^X \rangle$ as follows. The variables making up states are defined to be $Var_e^X = Var_e \cup X$. The initial states are given by $I_e^X = \{s \cup \chi \mid s \in I_e, \ \chi \in \mathcal{P}(X)\}$, i.e., an initial state is obtained by adding any assignment to variables X to an initial state of E. The set of actions $Acts$ is the same as in the environment E. Finally, the transition relation $\longrightarrow_e^X$ is given by $s \cup \chi \longrightarrow_e^X s' \cup \chi'$ iff $s \longrightarrow_e s'$ and $\chi = \chi'$ where $s, s' \in \mathcal{P}(Var_e)$ and $\chi, \chi' \in \mathcal{P}(X)$.

Additionally, for each agent i, we transform its protocol template $P_i = \langle KVar_i, PVar_i, LVar_i, OVar_i, I_i, Acts_i, \longrightarrow_i \rangle$ into a concrete protocol $P_i^X = \langle PVar_i^X, LVar_i, OVar_i^X, I_i, Acts_i, \longrightarrow_i^X \rangle$ for the environment E^X. The local variables $LVar_i$ and the initial states I_i are exactly as in the protocol template. The parameter variables are given by $PVar_i^X = PVar_i \cup X$, and the observable variables are given by $OVar_i^X = OVar_i \cup X$. The transition relation $\longrightarrow_i^X \subseteq \mathcal{P}(PVar_i \cup X \cup LVar_i) \times Acts_i \times \mathcal{P}(LVar_i)$ is derived from the transition relation $\longrightarrow_i \subseteq \mathcal{P}(KVar \cup PVar_i \cup LVar_i) \times Acts_i \times \mathcal{P}(LVar_i)$ as follows. For $s \in \mathcal{P}(PVar_i \cup LVar_i)$ and $\chi \in \mathcal{P}(X)$, define $\kappa(s, \chi) \in \mathcal{P}(KVar)$ by

$$\kappa(s, \chi) = \{v \in KVar_i \mid s \cup \chi \models \bigvee_{o \in O_i} \psi_o \wedge x_{i,o,v}\} \ .$$

For $l_i' \in \mathcal{P}(LVar_i)$ and $a \in Acts_i$, we then let $s \cup \chi \xrightarrow{a}{}_i^X l_i'$ iff $s \cup \kappa(s, \chi) \xrightarrow{a}{}_i l_i'$.

Intuitively, since the assignment χ to the variables X encodes an implementation θ, we make these variables an input to the transformed protocol, which uses them to make decisions that depend on the protocol template variables when executing the protocol template. In particular, when an observation $o = s \cap OVar_i \in O_i$ (equivalently, $s \models \psi_o$) satisfies $x_{i,o,v} \in \chi$, this corresponds to the template variable v taking the value true on state s according to the implementation $\theta(v)$. We therefore execute a transition of the protocol template in which v is taken to be true.

Note that the definition of the sets $OVar_i^X$ makes the variables X observable to all the agents: this effectively makes the particular implementation being run *common knowledge* to the agents, as it is in the system that we obtain from each concrete implementation. However, the combined transformed environment and transformed protocol templates represent not just one implementation, but *all possible implementations*. This is stated formally in the following result.

Theorem 2. *Let* $\mathcal{S} = \langle Ags, E, \{P_i\}_{i \in Ags}, \Phi \rangle$ *be an epistemic protocol specification, and let X be the set of implementation variables of $\mathcal{S}$. For each implementation θ of $\mathcal{S}$, we have* $M(E^X, \{P_i^X\}_{i \in Ags}), s \models \Phi\theta$ *for all initial states s of* $M(E^X, \{P_i^X\}_{i \in Ags})$ *with* $s \cap X = \chi_\theta$. *Conversely, suppose that* $\chi \in \mathcal{P}(X)$ *is such that* $M(E^X, \{P_i^X\}_{i \in Ags}), s \models \Phi\theta_\chi$ *for all initial states s of* $M(E^X, \{P_i^X\}_{i \in Ags})$ *with* $s \cap X = \chi$. *Then* θ_χ *is an implementation of* $\mathcal{S}$.

This result gives a reduction from the synthesis problem to the well understood problem of model checking. Any algorithm for model checking specifications expressible in the framework can now be applied. In particular, symbolic model checking techniques apply. We have implemented the above approach as an extension of binary-decision diagram (BDD) based epistemic model checking algorithms already implemented in the epistemic model checker MCK [11], which handles formulas in CTL^*K_n with fairness constraints using BDD based representations. The model checking techniques involved are largely standard, as in [6], with a trivial extension to handle the epistemic operators (these just require BDD's representing the set of reachable states and an equivalence on observable variables.) We make one optimization, based on the observation that the variables X encoded in the state do not actually change on any given run. We can therefore reduce the number of BDD variables required to represent the transition relation by retaining only one copy of these variables. Also, we first compute the observations $o \in O_i$ that can occur at reachable states in any putative implementation, to reduce the set X to variables $x_{i,o,v}$ where o is in fact a possible observation.

We note that the reduction does entail a blowup in the number of variables. Suppose we have n agents, with the number of observable variables of agent i being k_i. Then the size of the set X_i could be as large as $2^{k_i}|KVar_i|$, so that $|X| = \sum_{i=1...n} 2^{k_i}|KVar_i|$ is the number of new variables that need to be included in the BDD computation. With BDD-based symbolic model checking currently typically viable for numbers of the BDD variables in the order of 100's, this places an inherent limit on the size of example that we can expect to handle using our technique. Evidently, the technique favours examples in which the number of observable variables per agent is kept small. This is reflected in the results obtained for our running example, which we now discuss.

6   Solutions to the Mutual Exclusion Example

We have applied our implementation of the above reduction to the epistemic protocol specifications for mutual exclusion described in Section 4. Our technique computes the

Table 1. Running times (s) of Synthesis Experiments

No. of Agents	2	3	4	5	6	7	8
Ring (time)	0.3	1.7	5.5.	17.2	157.7	509.1	597
(No. BDD vars)	22	33	44	55	66	77	88
Broadcast (time)	0.2	194.2					
(No. BDD vars)	34	105	356				

set of all possible implementations. We now describe the implementations obtained for the two versions of this specification.

We note that, as defined above, two implementations, corresponding to substitutions θ_1 and θ_2 for the template variables, may be behaviorally equivalent, yet formally distinct. Define the equivalence relation $\sim$ on such substitutions by $\theta_1 \sim \theta_2$ if $M(E, \{P_i\theta_1\}_{i \in Ags})$ and $M(E, \{P_i\theta_2\}_{i \in Ags})$ have the same set of reachable states, and for all such reachable states s, and all template variables v, we have $M(E, \{P_i\theta_1\}_{i \in Ags}), s \models \theta_1(v)$ iff $M(E, \{P_i\theta_2\}_{i \in Ags}), s \models \theta_2(v)$. Intuitively, this means that θ_1 and θ_2 are equivalent, except on unreachable states. We treat such implementations as identical and return only one element of each equivalence class.

Ring Architecture: We have already discussed one of the possible implementations of the epistemic protocol specification for the ring architecture as the example in Section 4, viz., that in which $\theta(\mathbf{x}_0) = \neg \mathtt{bit}_0$ and $\theta(\mathbf{x}_i) = \mathtt{bit}_i$ for $i \neq 0$. Our synthesis system returns this as one of the implementations synthesized. As discussed above, this implementation essentially corresponds to a token ring protocol in which agent 0 initially holds the token. By symmetry, it is easily seen that we can take any agent k to be the one initially holding the token, and each such choice yields an implementation, with $\theta(\mathbf{x}_k) = \neg \mathtt{bit}_k$ and $\theta(\mathbf{x}_i) = \mathtt{bit}_i$ for $i \neq k$. Our synthesis system returns all these solutions, but also confirms that there are no others. Thus, up to symmetry, there is essentially just one implementation for this specification.

We note that, whatever the total number of agents n, the number of variables observable to agent i is just one, so we have $|X_i| = 2$ and we add $|X| = 2n$ variables to the underlying BDD for model checking in order to perform synthesis. This gives a slow growth rate in the number of BDD variables as we scale the number of agents, and enables us to deal with moderate size instances. Table 1 gives the performance results for our implementation as we scale the number of agents.[2] The total number of BDD variables per state (i.e., the environment variables, local protocol and program counter variables and X) is also indicated.

Broadcast Architecture: In case of the broadcast architecture, the number of variables that need to be added for synthesis increases much more rapidly. In case of n agents, we have $|X_i| = 2^{2n}$ (since we need two bits to represent each agent's state variable $\mathtt{state}[j]$), and $|X| = n2^{2n}$. Accordingly, the approach works only on modest scale examples. We describe the solutions obtained in the case of 3 agents. Our synthesis procedure computes that there exist 6 distinct solutions, which amount essentially to

---

[2] Our experiments were conducted on a Debian Linux system, 3.3GHz Intel i5-2500 CPU, with each process allocated up to 500M memory.

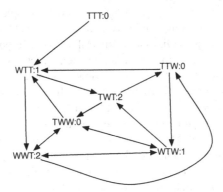

Fig. 2. Structure of a ME protocol synthesized (3 agents, broadcast architecture)

one solution under permutation of the roles of the agents. To understand this solution, note first that if any agent is in its critical section, all others know this, but cannot know whether the agent will exit its critical section in the next step. It follows that no agent is able to enter its critical section in the next step. It therefore suffices to consider the behavior of the solution on states where no agent is in its critical section, but at least one agent is in state `trying`. We describe this by means of the graph in Figure 2. Vertices in this graph indicate the protocol state inhabited by each of the agents, as well as the agent that the protocol selects for entry to the critical state, e.g., WTT:1 indicates that agent 0 is in state `waiting`, and agents 1 and 2 are in state `trying`, and that agent 1 enters its critical state in the next step. The edges point to possible successor states reached at the time the selected agent next exits its critical state. (Note that, at this time, no other agent has had the opportunity to enter its critical state, but another agent may have moved from `waiting` to `trying`, so there is some nondeterminism in the graph.) It can be verified by inspection (a focus on the upper triangle suffices, since only one agent is trying in states in the lower triangle) that the solution is fair: there is no cycle where an agent is constantly trying but never selected for entry to the critical section.

7 Related Work

Most closely related to our work in this paper are results on the complexity of verifying and deciding the existence of knowledge-based programs [20,10], with respect to what is essentially the observational semantics. The key idea of these complexity results is similar to the one we have used in our construction: guess a *knowledge assignment* that indicates at which observations (local states, in their terminology) a knowledge formula holds, and verify that this corresponds to an implementation. However, our epistemic specifications are syntactically more expressive than knowledge-based programs, and some of the details of their work are more complex, in that a labelling of runs by sub-formulas of knowledge formulas is also required. In part this is because of the focus on *linear time temporal logic* in this work, compared to our use of branching time temporal logic. This work also does not consider any concrete implementation of the theoretical results using symbolic techniques. The complexity bounds for determining the existence of an implementation of a knowledge-based program in [20,10] (NP-complete for atemporal knowledge-based programs and PSPACE-complete for programs with LTL-based knowledge conditions) are lower than our EXPTIME bound in Theorem 1 because they are based on an explicit-state rather than variable-based representation.

Our focus in this paper is on the observational semantics for knowledge. Other semantics have been studied from the point of view of synthesis. Van der Meyden and Vardi [18] consider, for the synchronous perfect recall semantics, the problem of synthesizing a protocol satisfying a formula in a linear time temporal epistemic logic in a given environment (with no limitations on the program structure of the solution). They show the problem to be decidable only in the case of a single agent. Some restrictions on environments and specifications are identified in [19] under which the problem becomes decidable. The problem can also be shown to be decidable for knowledge-based programs that run only a finitely bounded number of steps: a symbolic technique for implementing such programs with respect to synchronous semantics including perfect recall and clock based semantics is developed in [14].

A number of papers have also applied model checking of knowledge properties to synthesize distributed control strategies [4,12,15]. These works do not deal with knowledge-based programs per se, however, and it is not guaranteed that the implementing condition is equivalent to the desired knowledge property in the protocol synthesized. However, these solutions would be included in the space of solutions of specifications expressible in our more general framework.

Bonollo et al [5] have previously proposed knowledge-based specifications for distributed mutual exclusion. However, this work deals only with the specification level, and does not relate the specification developed to any concrete implementations.

Bar-David and Taubenfeld [1] considered the automated synthesis of mutual exclusion protocols. In some respects their approach is more general than ours, in that they synthesize the entire program structure, not just the implementations of conditions within a program template. However, they do not consider epistemic specifications. Also, compared to our symbolic approach, they essentially conduct a brute force search over all possible implementations up to a given size of program code, (with some optimizations to avoid redundant work) and they use explicit state model checking to verify an implementation. This limits the number of agents to which their approach can be expected to scale: they consider only two-agent systems. They mention a construction by which a two-agent solution can used to construct an n-agent solution, but this does not amount to generation of all possible solutions for the n-agent case.

8 Conclusion

Our focus in this paper has been to develop an approach that enables the space of all solutions to an epistemic protocol specification to be explored. Our implementation gives the first tool with this capability with respect to the observational semantics for knowledge, opening up the ability to more effectively explore the overall methodology of the knowledge-based approach to concurrent systems design through experimentation with examples beyond the simple mutual exclusion protocol we have considered. Applications of the tool to the synthesis of fault-tolerant protocols, where the flow of knowledge is considerably more subtle than in the reliable setting we have considered, is one area that we intend to explore in future work. Use of alternative model checking approaches to the BDD-based algorithm we have used (e.g., SAT-based algorithms) are also worth exploring.

References

1. Bar-David, Y., Taubenfeld, G.: Automatic discovery of mutual exclusion algorithms. In: Fich, F.E. (ed.) DISC 2003. LNCS, vol. 2848, pp. 136–150. Springer, Heidelberg (2003)
2. Bataineh, O.A., van der Meyden, R.: Abstraction for epistemic model checking of dining-cryptographers based protocols. In: Proc. TARK, pp. 247–256 (2011)
3. Baukus, K., van der Meyden, R.: A knowledge based analysis of cache coherence. In: Davies, J., Schulte, W., Barnett, M. (eds.) ICFEM 2004. LNCS, vol. 3308, pp. 99–114. Springer, Heidelberg (2004)
4. Bensalem, S., Peled, D., Sifakis, J.: Knowledge based scheduling of distributed systems. In: Manna, Z., Peled, D.A. (eds.) Time for Verification. LNCS, vol. 6200, pp. 26–41. Springer, Heidelberg (2010)
5. Bonollo, U., van der Meyden, R., Sonenberg, E.: Knowledge-based specification: Investigating distributed mutual exclusion. In: Bar Ilan Symposium on Foundations of AI (2001)
6. Clarke, E., Grumberg, O., Peled, D.: Model Checking. The MIT Press (1999)
7. Dijkstra, E.W.: Solution of a problem in concurrent programming control. Commun. ACM 8(9), 569 (1965)
8. Engelhardt, K., van der Meyden, R., Moses, Y.: Knowledge and the logic of local propositions. In: Proc. Conf. Theoretical Aspects of Knowledge and Rationality, pp. 29–41 (1998)
9. Fagin, R., Halpern, J., Moses, Y., Vardi, M.: Reasoning About Knowledge. MIT Press (1995)
10. Fagin, R., Halpern, J.Y., Moses, Y., Vardi, M.Y.: Knowledge-based programs. Distributed Computing 10(4), 199–225 (1997)
11. Gammie, P., van der Meyden, R.: MCK: Model checking the logic of knowledge. In: Alur, R., Peled, D.A. (eds.) CAV 2004. LNCS, vol. 3114, pp. 479–483. Springer, Heidelberg (2004)
12. Graf, S., Peled, D., Quinton, S.: Achieving distributed control through model checking. Formal Methods in System Design 40(2), 263–281 (2012)
13. Halpern, J.Y., Zuck, L.D.: A little knowledge goes a long way: Knowledge-based derivations and correctness proofs for a family of protocols. J. ACM 39(3), 449–478 (1992)
14. Huang, X., van der Meyden, R.: Symbolic synthesis of knowledge-based program implementations with synchronous semantics. In: Proc. TARK, pp. 121–130 (2013)
15. Katz, G., Peled, D., Schewe, S.: Synthesis of distributed control through knowledge accumulation. In: Gopalakrishnan, G., Qadeer, S. (eds.) CAV 2011. LNCS, vol. 6806, pp. 510–525. Springer, Heidelberg (2011)
16. Lomuscio, A., Qu, H., Raimondi, F.: MCMAS: A model checker for the verification of multi-agent systems. In: Bouajjani, A., Maler, O. (eds.) CAV 2009. LNCS, vol. 5643, pp. 682–688. Springer, Heidelberg (2009)
17. Srimani, P., Das, S.R. (eds.): Distributed Mutual Exclusion Algorithms. IEEE (1992)
18. van der Meyden, R., Vardi, M.Y.: Synthesis from knowledge-based specifications (Extended abstract). In: Sangiorgi, D., de Simone, R. (eds.) CONCUR 1998. LNCS, vol. 1466, pp. 34–49. Springer, Heidelberg (1998)
19. van der Meyden, R., Wilke, T.: Synthesis of distributed systems from knowledge-based specifications. In: Abadi, M., de Alfaro, L. (eds.) CONCUR 2005. LNCS, vol. 3653, pp. 562–576. Springer, Heidelberg (2005)
20. Vardi, M.Y.: Implementing knowledge-based programs. In: Proc. Conf. on Theoretical Aspects of Rationality and Knowledge, pp. 15–30 (1996)

Synthesis for Human-in-the-Loop Control Systems

Wenchao Li[1,*], Dorsa Sadigh[2], S. Shankar Sastry[2], and Sanjit A. Seshia[2]

[1] SRI International, Menlo Park, USA
li@csl.sri.com
[2] University of California, Berkeley, USA
{dsadigh,sastry,sseshia}@eecs.berkeley.edu

Abstract. Several control systems in safety-critical applications involve the interaction of an autonomous controller with one or more human operators. Examples include pilots interacting with an autopilot system in an aircraft, and a driver interacting with automated driver-assistance features in an automobile. The correctness of such systems depends not only on the autonomous controller, but also on the actions of the human controller. In this paper, we present a formalism for human-in-the-loop (HuIL) control systems. Particularly, we focus on the problem of synthesizing a semi-autonomous controller from high-level temporal specifications that expect occasional human intervention for correct operation. We present an algorithm for this problem, and demonstrate its operation on problems related to driver assistance in automobiles.

1 Introduction

Many safety-critical systems are *interactive*, i.e., they interact with a human being, and the human operator's role is central to the correct working of the system. Examples of such systems include fly-by-wire aircraft control systems (interacting with a pilot), automobiles with driver assistance systems (interacting with a driver), and medical devices (interacting with a doctor, nurse, or patient). We refer to such interactive control systems as *human-in-the-loop control systems*. The costs of incorrect operation in the application domains served by these systems can be very severe. Human factors are often the reason for failures or "near failures", as noted by several studies (e.g., [1,7]).

One alternative to human-in-the-loop systems is to synthesize a fully autonomous controller from a high-level mathematical specification. The specification typically captures both assumptions about the environment and correctness guarantees that the controller must provide, and can be specified in a formal language such as linear temporal logic (LTL) [15]. While this correct-by-construction approach looks very attractive, the existence of a fully autonomous controller that can satisfy the specification is not always guaranteed. For example, in the absence of adequate assumptions constraining its behavior, the environment can be modeled as being overly adversarial, causing the synthesis algorithm to conclude that no controller exists. Additionally, the high-level specification might abstract away from inherent physical limitations of the system, such as insufficient range of sensors, which must be taken into account in any real implementation. Thus, while full manual control puts too high a burden on the human operator,

---

* This work was performed when the first author was at UC Berkeley.

E. Ábrahám and K. Havelund (Eds.): TACAS 2014, LNCS 8413, pp. 470–484, 2014.
© Springer-Verlag Berlin Heidelberg 2014

some element of human control is desirable. However, at present, there is no systematic methodology to synthesize a combination of human and autonomous control from high-level specifications. In this paper, we address this limitation of the state of the art. Specifically, we consider the following question: *Can we devise a controller that is mostly automatic and requires only occasional human interaction for correct operation?* We formalize this problem of human-in-the-loop (HuIL) synthesis and establish formal criteria for solving it.

A particularly interesting domain is that of automobiles with "self-driving" features, otherwise also termed as "driver assistance systems". Such systems, already capable of automating tasks such as lane keeping, navigating in stop-and-go traffic, and parallel parking, are being integrated into high-end automobiles. However, these emerging technologies also give rise to concerns over the safety of an ultimately driverless car. Recognizing the safety issues and the potential benefits of vehicle automation, the National Highway Traffic Safety Administration (NHTSA) recently published a statement that provides descriptions and guidelines for the continual development of these technologies [13]. Particularly, the statement defines five levels of automation ranging from vehicles without any control systems automated (Level 0) to vehicles with full automation (Level 4). In this paper, we focus on Level 3 which describes a mode of automation that requires only limited driver control:

> *"Level 3 - Limited Self-Driving Automation: Vehicles at this level of automation enable the driver to cede full control of all safety-critical functions under certain traffic or environmental conditions and in those conditions to rely heavily on the vehicle to monitor for changes in those conditions requiring transition back to driver control. The driver is expected to be available for occasional control, but with sufficiently comfortable transition time. The vehicle is designed to ensure safe operation during the automated driving mode."* [13]

Essentially, this mode of automation stipulates that the human driver can act as a fail-safe mechanism and requires the driver to take over control should something go wrong. The challenge, however, lies in identifying the complete set of conditions under which the human driver has to be notified ahead of time. Based on the NHTSA statement, we identify four important criteria required for a human-in-the-loop controller to achieve this level of automation.

1. *Monitoring.* The controller should be able to determine if human intervention is needed based on monitoring past and current information about the system and its environment.
2. *Minimally Intervening.* The controller should only invoke the human operator when it is necessary, and does so in a minimally intervening manner.
3. *Prescient.* The controller can determine if a specification may be violated ahead of time, and issues an advisory to the human operator in such a way that she has sufficient time to respond.
4. *Conditionally Correct.* The controller should operate correctly until the point when human intervention is deemed necessary.

We further elaborate and formally define these concepts later in Section 3. In general, a human-in-the-loop controller, as shown in Figure 1 is a controller consists of three components: an automatic controller, a human operator, and an advisory control mechanism that orchestrates the switching between the auto-controller and the human operator.[1] In this setting, the auto-controller and the human operator can be viewed as two separate controllers, each capable of producing outputs based on inputs from the environment, while the advisory controller is responsible for determining precisely when the human operator should assume control while giving her enough time to respond.

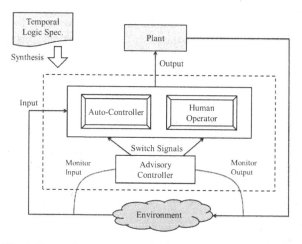

Fig. 1. Human-in-the-Loop Controller: Component Overview

In this paper, we study the construction of such controller in the context of *reactive synthesis* from LTL specifications. *Reactive synthesis* is the process of automatically synthesizing a discrete system (e.g., a finite-state Mealy transducer) that reacts to environment changes in such a way that the given specification (e.g., a LTL formula) is satisfied. There has been growing interest recently in the control and robotics communities (e.g., [20,9]) to apply this approach to automatically generate embedded control software. In summary, the main contributions of this paper are:

- A formalization of human-in-the-loop control systems and the problem of synthesizing such controllers from high-level specifications, including four key criteria these controllers must satisfy.
- An algorithm for synthesizing human-in-the-loop controllers that satisfy the aforementioned criteria.
- An application of the proposed technique to examples motivated by driver-assistance systems for automobiles.

The paper is organized as follows. Section 2 describes an motivating example discussing a *car following* example. Section 3 provides a formalism and characterization of the human-in-the-loop controller synthesis problem. Section 4 reviews material on reactive controller synthesis from temporal logic. Section 5 describes our algorithm for the problem. We then present case studies of safety critical driving scenarios in Section 6. Finally, we discuss related work in Section 7 and conclude in Section 8.

---

[1] In this paper, we do not consider explicit dynamics of the plant. Therefore it can be considered as part of the environment also.

2 Motivating Example

Consider the example in Figure 2. Car A is the autonomous vehicle, car B and C are two other cars on the road. We assume that the road has been divided into discretized regions that encode all the legal transitions for the vehicles on the map, similar to the discretization setup used in receding horizon temporal logic planning [21]. The objective of car A is to *follow* car B. Note that car B and C are part of the *environment* and cannot be controlled. The notion of following can be stated as follows. We assume that car A is equipped with sensors that allows it to see two squares ahead of itself if its view is not obstructed, as indicated by the enclosed region by blue dashed lines in Figure 2a. In this case, car B is blocking the view of car A, and thus car A can only see regions 3, 4, 5 and 6. Car A is said to be able to *follow* car B if it can always move to a position where it can see car B. Furthermore, we assume that car A and C can move at most 2 squares forward, but car B can move at most 1 square ahead, since otherwise car B can out-run or out-maneuver car A.

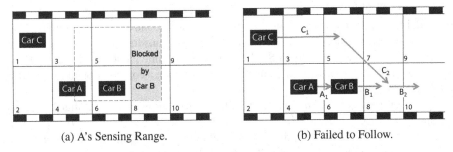

(a) A's Sensing Range.   (b) Failed to Follow.

Fig. 2. Controller Synthesis – Car A Following Car B

Given this objective, and additional safety rules such as cars not crashing into one another, our goal is to automatically synthesize a controller for car A such that:

- car A follows car B whenever possible;
- and in situations where the objective may not be achievable, *switches control* to the human driver while allowing *sufficient time* for the driver to respond and take control.

In general, it is not always possible to come up with a fully automatic controller that satisfies all requirements. Figure 2b illustrates such a scenario where car C blocks the view as well as the movement path of car A after two time steps. The brown arrows indicate the movements of the three cars in the first time step, and the purple arrows indicate the movements of car B and C in the second time step. Positions of a car X at time t is indicated by X_t. In this failure scenario, the autonomous vehicle needs to notify the human driver since it has lost track of car B.

Hence, human-in-the-loop synthesis is tasked with producing an autonomous controller along with advisories for the human driver in situations where her attention is required. Our challenge, however, is to *identify the conditions that we need to monitor and notify the driver when they may fail*. In the next section, we discuss how human constraints such as response time can be simultaneously considered in the solution, and mechanisms for switching control between the auto-controller and the human driver.

3 Formal Model of HuIL Controller

3.1 Preliminaries

Consider a Booleanized space over the input and output alphabet $\mathcal{X} = 2^X$ and $\mathcal{Y} = 2^Y$, where X and Y are two disjoint sets of variables representing inputs and outputs respectively, we model a discrete controller as a finite-state transducer. A finite-state (Mealy) transducer (FST) is a tuple $M = (Q, q_0, \mathcal{X}, \mathcal{Y}, \rho, \delta)$, where Q is the set of states, $q_0 \in Q$ is the initial state, $\rho : Q \times \mathcal{X} \to Q$ is the transition function, and $\delta : Q \times \mathcal{X} \to \mathcal{Y}$ is the output function. Given an input sequence $x = x_0 x_1 \ldots$, a run of M is the infinite sequence $q = q_0 q_1 \ldots$ of states such that $q_{k+1} = \rho(q_k, i_k)$ for all $k \geq 0$. The run q on x produces the word $M(x) = \delta(q_0, x_0)\delta(q_1, x_1)\ldots$. The language of M is then denoted by the set $\mathcal{L}(M) = \{(x, y)^\omega \mid M(x) = y\}$.

To characterize correctness of M, we assume that we can label if a state is *unsafe* or not, by using a function $\mathcal{F} : Q \to \{\texttt{true}, \texttt{false}\}$, i.e. a state q is failure-prone if $\mathcal{F}(q) = \texttt{true}$. We elaborate on $\mathcal{F}$ later in Section 5.1.

3.2 Agents as Automata

We model two of the three agents in a human-in-the-loop controller, the automatic controller $\mathcal{AC}$ and the advisory controller $\mathcal{VC}$, as finite-state transducers (FSTs). The human operator can be viewed as another FST $\mathcal{HC}$ that uses the same input and output interface as the auto-controller. The overall controller $\mathcal{HuIL}$ is then a composition of the models of $\mathcal{HC}$, $\mathcal{AC}$ and $\mathcal{VC}$.

We use a binary variable $auto$ to denote the internal advisory signal that $\mathcal{VC}$ sends to both $\mathcal{AC}$ and $\mathcal{HC}$. Hence, $\mathcal{X}^{\mathcal{HC}} = \mathcal{X}^{\mathcal{AC}} = \mathcal{X} \cup \{auto\}$, and $\mathcal{Y}^{\mathcal{VC}} = \{auto\}$. When $auto = \texttt{false}$, it means the advisory controller is requiring the human operator to take over control, and the auto-controller can have control otherwise.

We assume that the human operator (e.g., driver behind the wheel) can take control at any time by transitioning from a "non-active" state to an "active" state, e.g., by hitting a button on the dashboard or simply pressing down the gas pedal or the brake. When $\mathcal{HC}$ is in the "active" state, the human operator essentially acts as the automaton that produces outputs to the plant (e.g., a car) based on environment inputs. We use a binary variable $active$ to denote if $\mathcal{HC}$ is in the "active" state. When $active = \texttt{true}$, the output of $\mathcal{HC}$ overwrites the output of $\mathcal{AC}$, i.e. the output of $\mathcal{HC}$ is the output of $\mathcal{HuIL}$. The "overwrite" action happens when a sensor senses the human operator is in control, e.g., putting her hands on the wheel. Similarly, when $active = \texttt{false}$, the output of $\mathcal{HuIL}$ is the output of $\mathcal{AC}$. Note that even though the human operator is modeled as a FST here, since we do not have direct control of the human operator, it can in fact be any arbitrary relation mapping $\mathcal{X}$ to $\mathcal{Y}$. Considering more complex human driver models is left as a future direction [17].

3.3 Criteria for Human-in-the-Loop Controllers

One key distinguishing factor of a human-in-the-loop controller from traditional controller is the involvement of a human operator. Hence, human factors such as response time cannot be disregarded. In addition, we would like to minimize the need to engage the human operator. Based on the NHTSA statement, we derive four criteria for any effective human-in-the-loop controller, as stated below.

1. *Monitoring.* An advisory $auto$ is issued to the human operator under specific conditions. These conditions in turn need to be determined unambiguously *at runtime*, potentially based on history information but not predictions. In a reactive setting, this means we can use trace information only up to the point when the environment provides a next input from the current state.

2. *Minimally intervening.* Our mode of interaction requires only selective human intervention. An intervention occurs when $\mathcal{HC}$ transitions from the "non-active" state to the "active" state (we discuss mechanisms for suggesting a transition from "active" to "non-active" in Section 5.3, after prompted by the advisory signal $auto$ being false). However, frequent transfer of control would mean constant attention is required from the human operator, thus nullifying the benefits of having the auto-controller. In order to reduce the overhead of human participation, we want to minimize a joint objective function $\mathcal{C}$ that combines two elements: (i) the *probability* that when $auto$ is set to false, the environment will eventually force $\mathcal{AC}$ into a failure scenario, and (ii) the *cost* of having the human operator taking control. We formalize this objective function in Sec. 5.1.

3. *Prescient.* It may be too late to seek the human operator's attention when failure is imminent. We also need to allow extra time for the human to respond and study the situation. Thus, we require an advisory to be issued ahead of any failure scenario. In the discrete setting, we assume we are given a positive integer T representing human response time (which can be driver-specific), and require that $auto$ is set to false at least T number of transitions ahead of a state (in $\mathcal{AC}$) that is *unsafe*.

4. *Conditionally-Correct.* The auto-controller is responsible for correct operation as long as $auto$ is set to true. Formally, if $auto = \text{true}$ when $\mathcal{AC}$ is at a state q, then $\mathcal{F}(q) = \text{false}$. Additionally, when $auto$ is set to false, the auto-controller should still maintain correct operation in the next $T - 1$ time steps, during or after which we assume the human operator take over control. Formally, if $auto$ changes from true to false when $\mathcal{AC}$ is at a state q, let $R_T(q)$ be the set of states reachable from q within $T - 1$ transitions, then $\mathcal{F}(q') = \text{false}, \forall q' \in R_T(q)$.

Now we are ready to state the *HuIL Controller Synthesis Problem: Given a model of the system and its specification expressed in a formal language, synthesize a HuIL controller $\mathcal{HuIL}$ that is, by construction, monitoring, minimally intervening, prescient, and conditionally correct.*

In this paper, we study the synthesis of a HuIL controller in the setting of synthesis of reactive systems from linear temporal logic (LTL) specifications. We give background on this setting in Section 4, and propose an algorithm for solving the HuIL controller synthesis problem in Section 5.

4   Synthesis from Temporal Logic

4.1   Linear Temporal Logic

An LTL formula is built from atomic propositions AP, Boolean connectives (i.e. negations, conjunctions and disjunctions), and temporal operators **X** (*next*) and **U** (*until*). In this paper, we consider $AP = X \cup Y$.

LTL formulas are usually interpreted over infinite words (traces) $w \in \Sigma^\omega$, where $\Sigma = 2^{AP}$. The language of an LTL formula ψ is the set of infinite words that satisfy ψ, given by $\mathcal{L}(\psi) = \{w \in \Sigma^\omega \mid w \models \psi\}$. One classic example is the LTL formula $\mathbf{G}\,(p \to \mathbf{F}\,q)$, which means every occurrence of p in a trace must be followed by some q in the future.

An LTL formula ψ is *satisfiable* if there exists an infinite word that satisfies ψ, i.e., $\exists w \in (2^{AP})^\omega$ such that $w \models \psi$. A transducer M *satisfies* an LTL formula ψ if $\mathcal{L}(M) \subseteq \mathcal{L}(\psi)$. We write this as $M \models \psi$. *Realizability* is the problem of determining whether there exists a transducer M with input alphabet $\mathcal{X} = 2^X$ and output alphabet $\mathcal{Y} = 2^Y$ such that $M \models \psi$.

4.2   Synthesis from GR(1) Specification

Synthesis is the process of automatically finding an implementation that satisfies a given specification. However, the complexity of deciding the realizability of an LTL formula can be prohibitively high (2EXPTIME-complete [16]). Piterman et al. [14] describe a more efficient algorithm for synthesizing a subclass of LTL properties, known as Generalized Reactivity (1) [GR(1)] formulas. In this paper, we consider (unrealizable) specifications given in the GR(1) subclass. A GR(1) formula has the form $\psi = \psi^{env} \to \psi^{sys}$, where ψ^{env} represents the *environment assumptions* and ψ^{sys} represents the *system guarantees*. The syntax of GR(1) formulas is given as follows. We require ψ^l for $l \in \{env, sys\}$ to be a conjunction of sub-formulas in the following forms:

- ψ_i^l: a Boolean formula that characterizes the *initial states*.
- ψ_t^l: an LTL formula that characterizes the *transition*, in the form $\mathbf{G}\,B$, where B is a Boolean combination of variables in $X \cup Y$ and expression $\mathbf{X}\,u$ where $u \in X$ if $l = env$ and $u \in X \cup Y$ if $l = sys$.
- ψ_f^l: an LTL formula that characterizes *fairness*, in the form $\mathbf{G}\,\mathbf{F}\,B$, where B is a Boolean formula over variables in $X \cup Y$.

4.3   Games and Strategies

In general, the synthesis problem can be viewed as a two-player game between the system sys and the environment env. Following [14], a finite-state two-player game is defined by its *game graph*, represented by the tuple $\mathcal{G} = (Q^g, \theta^g, \rho^{env}, \rho^{sys}, Win)$ for input variables X controlled by the environment env and output variables Y controlled by the system sys, where $Q^g \subseteq 2^{X \cup Y}$ is the state space of the game, θ^g is a Boolean formula over $X \cup Y$ that specifies the initial states of the game structure, $\rho^{env} \subseteq Q^g \times 2^X$ is the environment transition relation relating a present state in Q^g to the possible next inputs the environment can pick in 2^X, $\rho^{sys} \subseteq Q^g \times 2^X \times 2^Y$ is the system transition relation relating a present state in Q^g and a next input in 2^X picked by the environment to the possible next outputs the system can pick in 2^Y, and Win is the winning condition. Given a set of GR(1) specifications, i.e. $\psi_i^{env}, \psi_i^{sys}, \psi_t^{env}, \psi_t^{sys}, \psi_f^{env}, \psi_f^{sys}$, we can define a game structure $\mathcal{G}$ by setting $\theta^g = \psi_i^{env} \wedge \psi_i^{sys}$, $\rho^{env} := \psi_t^{env}$ with all occurrences of $\mathbf{X}\,u$ replaced by u'^2, $\rho^{sys} = \psi_t^{sys}$ with all occurrences of $\mathbf{X}\,u$ replaced by u', and Win as $\psi_f^{env} \to \psi_f^{sys}$. A play π of $\mathcal{G}$ is a maximal sequence of states

---

[2] We use the primed copies u' of u to denote the next input/output variables.

$\pi = q_0 q_1 \dots$ of states such that $q_0 \models \theta^g$ and $(q_i, q_{i+1}) \in \rho^{env} \wedge \rho^{sys}$ for all $i \geq 0$. A play π is winning for the system iff it is infinite and $\pi \models Win$. Otherwise, π is winning for the environment. The set of states from which there exists a winning strategy for the environment is called the winning region for env.

A finite-memory strategy for env in $\mathcal{G}$ is a tuple $\mathcal{S}^{env} = (\Gamma^{env}, \gamma^{env_0}, \eta^{env})$, where Γ^{env} is a finite set representing the memory, $\gamma^{env_0} \in \Gamma^{env}$ is the initial memory content, and $\eta^{env} \subseteq Q^g \times \Gamma^{env} \times \mathcal{X} \times \Gamma^{env}$ is a relation mapping a state in $\mathcal{G}$ and some memory content $\gamma^{env} \in \Gamma^{env}$ to the possible next inputs the environment can pick and an updated memory content. A strategy $\mathcal{S}^{env}$ is winning for env from a state q if all plays starting in q and conforming to $\mathcal{S}^{env}$ are won by env. Following the terminology used in [8], if a strategy $\mathcal{S}^{env}$ is winning from an initial state q satisfying θ^g, then it is called a *counterstrategy* for env. The existence of a counterstrategy is equivalent to the specification being unrealizable. We refer the readers to [8] for details on how a counterstrategy can be extracted from intermediate results of the fix-point computation for the winning region for env. On the other hand, a winning strategy for the system can be turned into an implementation, e.g., a sequential circuit with $|X|$ inputs, $|X| + |Y|$ state-holding elements (flip-flops), and $|Y|$ outputs that satisfies the given GR(1) specification. In this paper, the synthesized implementation is effectively the auto-controller in the proposed HuIL framework, and can be viewed as a Mealy machine with state space $Q \subseteq 2^{X \cup Y}$. We refer the readers to [14] for details of this synthesis process.

4.4 Counterstrategy Graph

The counterstrategy can be conveniently viewed as a transition system. A *counterstrategy graph* G^c is a discrete transition system $G^c = (Q^c, Q_0^c \subseteq Q^c, \rho^c \subseteq Q^c \times Q^c)$, where $Q^c \subseteq Q^g \times \Gamma^{env}$ is the state space, $Q_0^c = Q_0^g \times \gamma^{env_0}$ is the set of initial states, and $\rho^c = \eta^{env} \wedge \rho^{sys}$ is the transition relation. In a nutshell, G^c describes evolutions of the game state where env adheres to η^{env} and sys adheres to ρ^{sys}. For convenience, we use a function $\theta^c : Q^c \to 2^{X \cup Y}$ to denote the game state (an assignment to X and Y) associated with a state $q^c \in Q^c$. A run π^c of G^c is a maximal sequence of states $\pi^c = q_0^c q_1^c \dots$ of states such that $q_0^c \in Q_0^c$ and $(q_i^c, q_{i+1}^c) \in \rho^c$ for all $i \geq 0$.

We can also view G^c as a directed graph, where each state in Q^c is given its own node, and there is an edge from node q_i^c to node q_j^c if given the current state at q_i^c, there exists a *next* input picked from the counterstrategy for which the system can produce a legal next output so that the game proceeds to a new state at q_j^c.

5 HuIL Controller Synthesis

Given an unrealizable specification, a counterstrategy $\mathcal{S}^{env}$ exists for env which describes moves by env such that it can force a violation of the system guarantees. The key insight of our approach for synthesizing a HuIL controller is that we can synthesize an advisory controller that monitors these moves and prompts the human operator with sufficient time ahead of any danger. These moves are essentially assumptions on the environment under which the system guarantees can be ensured. When these assumptions are not violated (the environment may behave in a benign way in reality), the auto-controller fulfills the objective of the controller. On the other hand, if any of the assumptions is violated, as flagged by the advisory controller, then the control is safely switched to the human operator in a way that she can have sufficient time to respond. The challenge, however, is to decide when an advisory should be sent to the human operator, in a way that it is also *minimally intervening* to the human operator. We use the following example to illustrate our algorithm.

Example 1. Consider $X = \{x\}, Y = \{y\}$ and the following GR(1) sub-formulas which together form $\psi = \psi^{env} \rightarrow \psi^{sys}$.

1. $\psi_f^{env} = \mathbf{G} \ (\mathbf{F} \ \neg x)$
2. $\psi_t^{sys} = \mathbf{G} \ (\neg x \rightarrow \neg y)$
3. $\psi_f^{sys} = \mathbf{G} \ (\mathbf{F} \ y)$

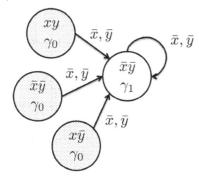

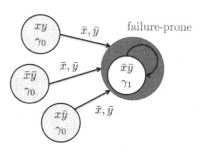

(a) Counterstrategy graph G^c for unrealizable specification ψ.

(b) Condensed graph $\hat{G}^c$ for G^c after contracting the SCC.

Specification ψ is not realizable. Figure 3a shows the computed counterstrategy graph G^c. The literal $\bar{x}$ ($\bar{y}$) denotes the negation of the propositional variable x (y). The memory content is denoted by γ_i with γ_0 being the initial memory content. The three shaded states on the left are the initial states. The literals on the edges indicate that the environment first chooses $\bar{x}$ and then the system chooses $\bar{y}$. (the system is forced to pick $\bar{y}$ due to ψ_t^{sys}). Observe that, according the counterstrategy, the system will be forced to pick $\bar{y}$ perpetually. Hence, the other system guarantee ψ_f^{sys} cannot be satisfied.

5.1   Weighted Counterstrategy Graph

Recall that a counterstrategy can be viewed as a discrete transition system or a directed graph G^c. We consider two types of *imminent* failures (violation of some system guarantee specification) described by G^c.

- **Safety violation.** For a node (state) $q_1^c \in Q^c$, if there does not exist a node q_2^c such that $(q_1^c, q_2^c) \in \rho^c$, then we say q_1^c is *failure-imminent*. In this scenario, after env picks a next input according to the counterstrategy, sys cannot find a next output such that all of the (safety) guarantees are satisfied (some ψ_i^{sys} or ψ_t^{sys} is violated).
- **Fairness violation.** If a node q^c is part of a strongly connected component (SCC) scc in Q^c, then we say q^c is *failure-doomed*. For example, the node $(\bar{x}, \bar{y}, \gamma_1)$ in Figure 3a is a failure-doomed node. Starting from q^c, env can always pick inputs in such a way that the play is forced to get stuck in scc. Clearly, all other states in scc are also *failure-doomed*.

Now we make the connection of the labeling function $\mathcal{F}$ for a controller M to the counterstrategy graph G^c which describes behaviors that M should not exhibit. Consider an auto-controller M and a state q (represented by the assignment xy) in M. $\mathcal{F}(q) = \texttt{true}$ if and only if there exist some $q^c \in Q^c$ such that $\theta^c(q^c) = xy$ and q^c is either *failure-imminent* or *failure-doomed*. In practice, it is not always the case that the environment will behave in the most adversarial way. For example, a car in front may yield if it is blocking our path. Hence, even though the specification is not realizable, it is still important to assess, at any given state, whether it will actually lead to a violation. For simplicity, we assume that the environment will adhere to the counterstrategy once it enters a *failure-doomed* state.

We can convert G^c to its directed acyclic graph (DAG) embedding $\hat{G}^c = (\hat{Q}^c, \hat{Q}^c_0, \hat{\rho}^c)$ by contracting each SCC in G^c to a single node. Figure 3b shows the condensed graph $\hat{G}^c$ of G^c shown in Figure 3a. We use a surjective function $\hat{f} : Q^c \to \hat{Q}^c$ to describe the mapping of nodes from G^c to $\hat{G}^c$. We say a node $\hat{q} \in \hat{Q}^c$ is *failure-prone* if a node $q^c \in Q^c$ is either *failure-imminent* or *failure-doomed* and $\hat{f}(q^c) = \hat{q}$.

Recall from Section 3.3 that the notion of *minimally-intervening* requires the minimization of a cost function $\mathcal{C}$, which involves the *probability* that $auto$ is set to $\texttt{false}$, Thus far, we have not associated any probabilities with transitions taken by the environment or the system. While our approach can be adapted to work with any assignment of probabilities, for ease of presentation, we make a particular choice in this paper. Specifically, we assume that at each step, the environment picks a next-input uniformly at random from the set of possible *legal* actions (next-inputs) obtained from η^{env} given the current state. In Example 1 and correspondingly Figure 3a, this means that it is equally likely for env to choose $\bar{x}$ or x from any of the states. We use $c(q)$ to denote the total number of legal actions that the environment can take from a state q.

In addition, we take into account of the cost of having the human operator perform the maneuver instead of the auto-controller. In general, this cost increases with longer human engagement. Based on these two notions, we define ϖ, which assigns a weight to an edge $e \in \hat{Q}^c \times \hat{Q}^c$ in $\hat{G}^c$, recursively as follows. For an edge between $\hat{q}_i$ and $\hat{q}_j$,

$$\varpi(\hat{q}_i, \hat{q}_j) = \begin{cases} 1 & \text{if } \hat{q}_j \text{ is } \textit{failure-prone} \\ \frac{pen(\hat{q}_i) \times len(\hat{q}_i)}{c(\hat{q}_i)} & \text{Otherwise} \end{cases}$$

where $pen : \hat{Q}^c \to \mathbb{Q}^+$ is a user-defined penalty parameter[3], and $len : \hat{Q}^c \to \mathbb{Z}^+$ is the length (number of edges) of the shortest path from a node $\hat{q}_i$ to any failure-prone node in $\hat{G}^c$. Intuitively, a state far away from any failure-prone state is less likely to cause a failure since the environment would need to make multiple consecutive moves all in an adversarial way. However, if we transfer control at this state, the human operator will have to spend more time in control, which is not desirable for a HuIL controller. Next, we describe how to use this edge-weighted DAG representation of a counterstrategy graph to derive a HuIL controller that satisfies the criteria established earlier.

5.2   Counterstrategy-Guided Synthesis

Suppose we have a counterstrategy graph G^c that summarizes all possible ways for the environment to force a violation of the system guarantees. Consider an outgoing edge

---

[3] $pen(\hat{q}_i)$ should be chosen such that $\varpi(\hat{q}_i, \hat{q}_j) < 1$.

from a non-failure-prone node $\hat{q}$ in $\hat{G}^c$ (condensed graph of G^c), this edge encodes a particular condition where the environment makes a next-move given some last move made by the environment and the system. If some of these next-moves by the environment are disallowed, such that none of the failure-prone nodes are reachable from any initial state, then we have effectively eliminated the counterstrategy. This means that if we assert the negation of the corresponding conditions as additional ψ_t^{env} (environment transition assumptions), then we can obtain a realizable specification.

Formally, we mine assumptions of the form $\phi = \bigwedge_i (\mathbf{G}\,(a_i \to \neg \mathbf{X}\, b_i))$, where a_i is a Boolean formula describing a set of assignments over variables in $X \cup Y$, and b_i is a Boolean formula describing a set of assignments over variables in X.

Under the assumption ϕ, if $(\phi \wedge \psi^{env}) \to \psi^{sys}$ is realizable, then we can automatically synthesize an auto-controller that satisfies ψ. In addition, the key observation here is that mining ϕ is *equivalent to* finding a set of edges in $\hat{G}^c$ such that, if these edges are removed from $\hat{G}^c$, then none of the failure-prone nodes is reachable from any initial state. We denote such set of edges as E^ϕ, where each edge $e \in E^\phi$ corresponds to a conjunct in ϕ. For example, if we remove the three outgoing edges from the source nodes in Figure 3b, then the failure-prone node is not reachable. Removing these three edges correspond to adding the following environment assumption, which can be monitored at runtime.

$$(\mathbf{G}\,((x \wedge y) \to \neg \mathbf{X}\, \bar{x})) \wedge (\mathbf{G}\,((\bar{x} \wedge \bar{y}) \to \neg \mathbf{X}\, \bar{x})) \wedge (\mathbf{G}\,((x \wedge \bar{y}) \to \neg \mathbf{X}\, \bar{x}))$$

Human factors play an important role in the design of a HuIL controller. The criteria established for a HuIL controller in Section 3.3 also require it to be *prescient* and *minimally intervening*. Hence, we want to mine assumptions that reflect these criteria as well. The notion of *prescient* essentially requires that none of the failure-prone nodes is reachable from a non-failure-prone node with less than T steps (edges). The weight function ϖ introduced earlier can be used to characterize the cost of a failing assumption resulting in the advisory controller prompting the human operator to take over control (by setting $auto$ to $\mathtt{false}$). Formally, we seek E^ϕ such that the total cost of switching control $\sum_{e \in E^\phi} \varpi(e)$ is minimized.

We can formulate this problem as a *s-t* min-cut problem for directed acyclic graphs. Given $\hat{G}^c$, we first compute the subset of nodes $\hat{Q}_T^c \subseteq \hat{Q}^c$ that are backward reachable within $T - 1$ steps from the set of failure-prone nodes (when $T = 1$, $\hat{Q}_T^c$ is the set of failure-prone node). We assume that $\hat{Q}_0^c \cap \hat{Q}_T^c = \emptyset$. Next, we remove the set of nodes $\hat{Q}_T^c$ from $\hat{G}^c$ and obtain a new graph $\hat{G}_T^c$. Since $\hat{G}_T^c$ is again a DAG, we have a set of source nodes and a set of terminal nodes. Thus, we can formulate a *s-t* min-cut problem by adding a new source node that has an outgoing edge (with a sufficiently large weight) to each of the source nodes and a new terminal node that has an incoming edge (with a sufficiently large weight) from each of the terminal nodes. This *s-t* min-cut problem can be easily solved by standard techniques [6]. The overall approach is summarized in Algorithm 1.

Theorem 1. *Given a GR(1) specification ψ and a response time parameter T, Algorithm 1 is guaranteed to either produce a fully autonomous controller satisfying ψ, or a HuIL controller, modeled as a composition of an auto-controller $\mathcal{AC}$, a human operator and an advisory controller $\mathcal{VC}$, that is monitoring, prescient with parameter*

Algorithm 1. Counterstrategy-Guided HuIL Controller Synthesis

---

Input: GR(1) specification $\psi = \psi^{env} \rightarrow \psi^{sys}$.
Input: T : parameter for minimum human response time.
Output: $\mathcal{AC}$ and $\mathcal{VC}$. $\mathcal{HuIL}$ is then a composition of $\mathcal{AC}$, $\mathcal{VC}$ and $\mathcal{HC}$.
   if ψ is *realizable* **then**
      Synthesize transducer $M \models \psi$ (using standard GR(1) synthesis);
      $\mathcal{HuIL} := M$ (fully autonomous).
   else
      Generate G^c from ψ (assume a single G^c; otherwise the algorithm is performed iteratively);

      Generate the DAG embedded $\hat{G}^c$ from G^c.
      Reduce $\hat{G}^c$ to $\hat{G}^c_T$;
      Assign weights to $\hat{G}^c$ using φ; by removing $\hat{Q}^c_T$ – nodes that are within $T-1$ steps of any failure-prone node;
      Formulate a *s-t* min-cut problem with $\hat{G}^c_T$;
      Solve the *s-t* min-cut problem to obtain E^ϕ;
      Add assumptions ϕ to ψ to obtain the new specification $\psi_{new} := (\phi \wedge \psi^{env}) \rightarrow \psi^{sys}$;
      Synthesize $\mathcal{AC}$ so that $M \models \psi_{new}$;
      Synthesize $\mathcal{VC}$ as a (stateless) monitor that outputs $auto = \texttt{false}$ if ϕ is violated.
   end if

T, minimally intervening[4] *with respect to the cost function* $f_C = \sum_{e \in E^\phi} w(e)$, *and* conditionally correct[5].

Proof. (Sketch) When ψ is realizable, a fully autonomous controller is synthesized and unconditionally satisfies ψ. Now consider that case when ψ is not realizable.

The HuIL controller is *monitoring* as ϕ only comprises a set of environment transitions up to the next environment input.

It is *prescient* by construction. The $auto$ flag advising the human operator to take over control is set to $\texttt{false}$ *precisely* when ϕ is violated. When ϕ is violated, it corresponds to the environment making a next-move from the current state q according to some edge $e = (\hat{q}_i, \hat{q}_j) \in E^\phi$. Consider any $q^c \in Q^c$ such that $\hat{f}(q^c) = \hat{q}_i, \theta^c(q^c) = q$. Since $\hat{q}_i \notin \hat{Q}^c_T$ by the construction of $\hat{G}^c_T$, $\hat{q}_i$ is at least T transitions away from any *failure-prone* state in $\hat{G}^c$. This means q^c must also be at least T transitions away from any *failure-imminent* state or *failure-doomed* state in Q^c. Hence, by the definition of $\mathcal{F}$ with respect to a *failure-doomed* or *failure-doomed* state in Section 5.1, q is (and $auto$ is set) at least T transitions ahead of any state that is *unsafe*.

The HuIL controller is also *conditionally correct*. By the same reasoning as above, for any state $q' \in R_T(q)$, $\mathcal{F}(q') = \texttt{false}$, i.e. q' is *safe*.

Finally, since $auto$ is set to $\texttt{false}$ precisely when ϕ is violated, and ϕ in turn is constructed based on the set of edges E^ϕ, which minimizes the cost function $f_C = \sum_{e \in E^\phi} w(e)$, the HuIL controller is *minimally-intervening* with respect to the cost function f_C.

---

[4] We assume the counterstrategy we use to mine the assumptions is an optimal one – it forces a violation of the system guarantees as quickly as possible.
[5] We assume that all failure-prone nodes are at least T steps away from any initial node.

5.3   Switching from Human Operator to Auto-Controller

Once control has been transferred to the human operator, when should the human yield control to the autonomous controller again? One idea is for the HuIL controller to continually monitor the environment after the human operator has taken control, checking if a state is reached from which the auto-controller can ensure that it satisfies the specification (under assumption ϕ), and then the advisory controller can signal a driver telling her that the auto-controller is ready to take back control. We note that alternative approaches may exist and we plan to investigate this further in future work.

6   Experimental Results

Our algorithm is implemented as an extension to the GR(1) synthesis tool RATSY [4]. Due to space constraint, we discuss only the car-following example (as shown in Section 2) here and refer the readers to `http://verifun.eecs.berkeley.edu/tacas14/` for other examples.

Recall the car-following example shown in Section 2. We describe some of the more interesting specifications below and their corresponding LTL formulas. p_A, p_B, p_C are used to denote the positions of car A, B and C respectively.

- Any position can be occupied by at most one car at a time (no crashing):

$$\mathbf{G}\left(p_A = x \to (p_B \neq x \wedge p_C \neq x)\right)$$

where x denotes a position on the discretized space. The cases for B and C are similar, but they are part of ψ_{env}.

- Car A is required to follow car B:

$$\mathbf{G}\left((v_{AB} = \texttt{true} \wedge p_A = x) \to \mathbf{X}\left(v_{AB} = \texttt{true}\right)\right)$$

where $v_{AB} = \texttt{true}$ iff car A can see car B.

- Two cars cannot cross each other if they are right next to each other. For example, when $p_C = 5$, $p_A = 6$ and $p'_C = 8$ (in the next cycle), $p'_A \neq 7$. In LTL,

$$\mathbf{G}\left(((p_C = 5) \wedge (p_A = 6) \wedge (\mathbf{X}\,p_C = 8)) \to (\mathbf{X}\,(p_A \neq 7))\right)$$

The other specifications can be found in the link described at the beginning of this section. Observe that car C can in fact force a violation of the system guarantees in one step under two situations – when $p_C = 5$, $p_B = 8$ and $p_A = 4$, or $p_C = 5$, $p_B = 8$ and $p_A = 6$. Both are situations where car C is blocking the view of car A, causing it to lose track of car B. The second failure scenario is illustrated in Figure 2b.

Applying our algorithm to this (unrealizable) specification with $T = 1$, we obtain the following assumption ϕ.

$$\phi = \mathbf{G}\left(((p_A = 4) \wedge (p_B = 6) \wedge (p_C = 1)) \to \neg\mathbf{X}\left((p_B = 8) \wedge (p_C = 5)\right)\right) \bigwedge$$

$$\mathbf{G}\left(((p_A = 4) \wedge (p_B = 6) \wedge (p_C = 1)) \to \neg\mathbf{X}\left((p_B = 6) \wedge (p_C = 3)\right)\right) \bigwedge$$

$$\mathbf{G}\left(((p_A = 4) \wedge (p_B = 6) \wedge (p_C = 1)) \to \neg\mathbf{X}\left((p_B = 6) \wedge (p_C = 5)\right)\right)$$

In fact, ϕ corresponds to three possible evolutions of the environment from the initial state. In general, ϕ can be a conjunction of conditions at different time steps as env and sys progress. The advantage of our approach is that it can produce ϕ such that we can synthesize an auto-controller that is guaranteed to satisfy the specification if ϕ is not violated, together with an advisory controller that prompts the driver (at least) T ($T = 1$ in this case) time steps ahead of a potential failure when ϕ is violated.

7   Related Work

Similar to [9], we synthesize a discrete controller from temporal logic specifications. Wongpiromsarn et al. [21] consider a receding horizon framework to reduce the synthesis problem to a set of simpler problems for a short horizon. Livingston et al. [11,12] exploit the notion of locality that allows "patching" a nominal solution. They update the local parts of the strategy as new data accumulates allowing incremental synthesis. The key innovation in this paper is that we consider synthesizing interventions to combine an autonomous controller with a human operator.

Our work is inspired by the recent works on assumption mining. Chatterjee et al. [5] construct a minimal environment assumption by removing edges from the game graph to ensure safety assumptions, then compute liveness assumptions to put additional fairness constraints on the remaining edges. Li et al. [10] and later Alur et al. [2] use a counterstrategy-guided approach to mine environment assumptions for GR(1) specifications. We adapt this approach to the synthesis of human-in-the-loop control systems.

In recent years, there has been an increasing interest in human-in-the-loop systems in the control systems community. Anderson et al. [3] study obstacle avoidance and lane keeping for semiautonomous cars. They use a model predictive control for their autonomous control. Our approach, unlike this one, seeks to provide correctness guarantees in the form of temporal logic properties. Vasudevan et al. [19] focus on learning and predicting a human model based on prior observations. Based on the measured level of threat, the controller intervenes and overwrites the driver's input. However, we believe that allowing an auto-controller to override the human inputs is unsafe especially since it is hard to fully model the environment. We propose a different paradigm where we allow the human to take control if the autonomous system predicts failure. Finally, human's reaction time while driving is an important consideration in this paper. The value of reaction time can range from 1 to 2.5 seconds for different tasks and drivers [18].

8   Conclusions

In this paper, we propose a synthesis approach for designing human-in-the-loop controllers. We consider a mode of interaction where the controller is mostly autonomous but requires occasional intervention by a human operator, and study important criteria for devising such controllers. Further, we study the problem in the context of controller synthesis from (unrealizable) temporal-logic specifications. We propose an algorithm based on mining monitorable conditions from the counterstrategy of the unrealizable specifications. Preliminary results on applying this approach to driver assistance in automobiles are encouraging. One limitation of the current approach is the use of an explicit counterstrategy graph (due to weight assignment). We plan to explore symbolic algorithms in the future.

Acknowledgment. This work was supported in part by TerraSwarm, one of six centers of STARnet, a Semiconductor Research Corporation program sponsored by MARCO and DARPA. This work was also supported by the NSF grants CCF-1116993 and CCF-1139138.

References

1. Federal Aviation Administration. The interfaces between flight crews and modern flight systems (1995)
2. Alur, R., et al.: Counter-strategy guided refinement of gr(1) temporal logic specifications. In: The Conference on Formal Methods in Computer-Aided Design, pp. 26–33 (2013)
3. Anderson, S.J., et al.: An optimal-control-based framework for trajectory planning, threat assessment, and semi-autonomous control of passenger vehicles in hazard avoidance scenarios. International Journal of Vehicle Autonomous Systems 8(2), 190–216 (2010)
4. Bloem, R., Cimatti, A., Greimel, K., Hofferek, G., Könighofer, R., Roveri, M., Schuppan, V., Seeber, R.: RATSY – A new requirements analysis tool with synthesis. In: Touili, T., Cook, B., Jackson, P. (eds.) CAV 2010. LNCS, vol. 6174, pp. 425–429. Springer, Heidelberg (2010)
5. Chatterjee, K., Henzinger, T.A., Jobstmann, B.: Environment assumptions for synthesis. In: van Breugel, F., Chechik, M. (eds.) CONCUR 2008. LNCS, vol. 5201, pp. 147–161. Springer, Heidelberg (2008)
6. Costa, M.-C., et al.: Minimal multicut and maximal integer multiflow: A survey. European Journal of Operational Research 162(1), 55–69 (2005)
7. Kohn, L.T., et al.: To err is human: Building a safer health system. Technical report, A report of the Committee on Quality of Health Care in America, Institute of Medicine (2000)
8. Könighofer, R., et al.: Debugging formal specifications using simple counterstrategies. In: Conference on Formal Methods in Computer-Aided Design, pp. 152–159 (2009)
9. Kress-Gazit, H., et al.: Temporal-logic-based reactive mission and motion planning. IEEE Transactions on Robotics 25(6), 1370–1381 (2009)
10. Li, W., et al.: Mining assumptions for synthesis. In: Conference on Formal Methods and Models for Codesign, pp. 43–50 (2011)
11. Livingston, S.C., et al.: Backtracking temporal logic synthesis for uncertain environments. In: Conference on Robotics and Automation, pp. 5163–5170 (2012)
12. Livingston, S.C., et al.: Patching task-level robot controllers based on a local μ-calculus formula. In: Conference on Robotics and Automation, pp. 4588–4595 (2013)
13. National Highway Traffic Safety Administration. Preliminary statement of policy concerning automated vehicles (May 2013)
14. Piterman, N., Pnueli, A., Sa'ar, Y.: Synthesis of reactive(1) designs. In: Emerson, E.A., Namjoshi, K.S. (eds.) VMCAI 2006. LNCS, vol. 3855, pp. 364–380. Springer, Heidelberg (2006)
15. Pnueli, A.: The temporal logic of programs. In: Annual Symposium on Foundations of Computer Science, pp. 46–57 (1977)
16. Rosner, R.: Modular synthesis of reactive systems. Ph.D. dissertation, Weizmann Institute of Science (1992)
17. Sadigh, D., et al.: Data-driven probabilistic modeling and verification of human driver behavior. In: Formal Verification and Modeling in Human-Machine Systems (2014)
18. Triggs, T.J., et al.: Reaction time of drivers to road stimuli (1982)
19. Vasudevan, R., et al.: Safe semi-autonomous control with enhanced driver modeling. In: American Control Conference, pp. 2896–2903 (2012)
20. Wongpiromsarn, T., et al.: Receding horizon temporal logic planning for dynamical systems. In: Conference on Decision and Control, pp. 5997–6004 (2009)
21. Wongpiromsarn, T., et al.: Receding horizon temporal logic planning. IEEE Transactions on Automatic Control 57(11), 2817–2830 (2012)

Learning Regular Languages over Large Alphabets

Oded Maler and Irini-Eleftheria Mens

CNRS-VERIMAG
University of Grenoble
France

Abstract. This work is concerned with regular languages defined over large alphabets, either infinite or just too large to be expressed enumeratively. We define a generic model where transitions are labeled by elements of a finite partition of the alphabet. We then extend Angluin's L^* algorithm for learning regular languages from examples for such automata. We have implemented this algorithm and we demonstrate its behavior where the alphabet is the set of natural numbers.

1 Introduction

The main contribution of this paper is a generic algorithm for learning regular languages defined over a large alphabet Σ. Such an alphabet can be infinite, like $\mathbb{N}$ or $\mathbb{R}$ or just so large, like $\mathbb{B}^n$ for very large n, that it is impossible or impractical to treat it in an enumerative way, that is, to write down $\delta(q, a)$ for every $a \in \Sigma$. The obvious solution is to use a *symbolic* representation where transitions are labeled by predicates which are applicable to the alphabet in question. Learning algorithms infer an automaton from a finite set of words (the *sample*) for which membership is known. Over small alphabets, the sample should include the set S all the shortest words that lead to each state and, in addition, the set $S \cdot \Sigma$ of all their Σ-continuations. Over large alphabets this is not a practical option and as an alternative we develop a symbolic learning algorithm over *symbolic words* which are only partially backed up by the sample. In a sense, our algorithm is a combination of automaton learning and learning of non-temporal functions. Before getting technical, let us discuss briefly some motivation.

Finite automata are among the corner stones of Computer Science. From a practical point of view they are used daily in various domains ranging from syntactic analysis, design of user interfaces or administrative procedures to implementation of digital hardware and verification of software and hardware protocols. Regular languages admit a very nice, clean and comprehensive theory where different formalisms such as automata, logic, regular expressions, semigroups and grammars are shown to be equivalent. As for learning from examples, a problem introduced by Moore [Moo56], the Nerode right-congruence relation [Ner58] which declares two *input histories* as equivalent if they lead to the same *future continuations*, provides a crisp characterization of what a *state* in a dynamical system is in terms of observable input-output behavior. All algorithms for learning automata from examples, starting with the seminal work of Gold [Gol72] and culminating in the well-known L^* algorithm of Angluin [Ang87] are based on this concept [DlH10].

E. Ábrahám and K. Havelund (Eds.): TACAS 2014, LNCS 8413, pp. 485–499, 2014.

One weakness, however, of the classical theory of regular languages is that it is rather "thin" and "flat". In other words, the alphabet is often considered as a small set devoid of any additional structure. On such alphabets, classical automata are good for expressing and exploring the temporal (sequential, monoidal) dimension embodied by the concatenation operations, but less good in expressing "horizontal" relationships. To make this statement more concrete, consider the verification of a system consisting of n automata running in parallel, making independent as well as synchronized transitions. To express the set of joint behaviors of this product of automata as a formal language, classical theory will force you to use the exponential alphabet of global states and indeed, a large part of verification is concerned with fighting this explosion using constructs such as BDDs and other logical forms that exploit the sparse interaction among components. This is done, however, without a real interaction with classical formal language theory (one exception is the theory of *traces* [DR95] which attempts to treat this issue but in a very restricted context).[1]

These and other considerations led us to use *symbolic automata* as a generic framework for recognizing languages over large alphabets where transitions outgoing from a state are labeled, semantically speaking, by *subsets* of the alphabet. These subsets are expressed syntactically according to the specific alphabet used: Boolean formulae when $\Sigma = \mathbb{B}^n$ or by some classes of inequalities when $\Sigma = \mathbb{N}$. Determinism and completeness of the transition relation, which are crucial for learning and minimization, can be enforced by requiring that the subsets of Σ that label the transitions outgoing from a given state form a *partition* of the alphabet.

Readers working on program verification or hybrid automata are, of course, aware of automata with symbolic transition guards but it should be noted that in our model *no auxiliary variables* are added to the automaton. Let us stress this point by looking at a popular extension of automata to infinite alphabets, initiated by Kaminski and Francez [KF94] using *register automata* to accept *data languages* (see [BLP10] for theoretical properties and [HSJC12] for learning algorithms). In that framework, the automaton is augmented with additional registers that can store some input letters. The registers can then be compared with newly-read letters and influence transitions. With register automata one can express, for example, the requirement that your password at login is the same as the password at sign-up. This very restricted use of memory makes register automata much simpler than more notorious automata with variables whose emptiness problem is typically undecidable. The downside is that beyond *equality* they do not really exploit the potential richness of the alphabets/theories.

Our approach is different: we do allow the *values* of the input symbols to influence transitions via predicates, possibly of a restricted complexity. These predicates involve domain *constants* and they partition the alphabet into finitely many classes. For example, over the integers a state may have transitions labeled by conditions of the form $c_1 \leq x \leq c_2$ which give real (but of limited resolution) access to the input domain. On the other hand, we insist on a finite (and small) memory so that the exact value of x *cannot* be registered and has no future influence beyond the transition it has triggered. The *symbolic transducers*, recently introduced by [VHL$^+$12], are based on the same

---

[1] This might also be the reason that Temporal Logic is more popular in verification than regular expressions because the nature of *until* is less global and less synchronous than concatenation.

principle. Many control systems, artificial (sequential machines working on quantized numerical inputs) as well as natural (central nervous system, the cell), are believed to operate in this manner.

We then develop a symbolic version of Angluin's L^* algorithm for learning regular sets from queries and counter-examples whose output is a symbolic automaton. The main difference relative to the concrete algorithm is that in the latter, every transition $\delta(q, a)$ in a conjectured automaton has at least one word in the sample that exercises it. In the symbolic case, a transition $\delta(q, a)$ where a is a *set* of concrete symbols, will be backed up in the sample only by a *subset* of a. Thus, unlike concrete algorithms where a counter-example always leads to a discovery of one or more new states, in our algorithm it may sometimes only modify the boundaries between partition blocks without creating new states.

The rest of the paper is organized as follows. In Section 2 we provide a quick summary of learning algorithms over small alphabets. In Section 3 we define symbolic automata and then extend the structure which underlies all automaton learning algorithms, namely the *observation table*, to be symbolic, where symbolic letters represent sets, and where entries in the table are supported only by partial evidence. In Section 4 we write down a symbolic learning algorithm and illustrate the behavior of a prototype implementation on learning subsets of $\mathbb{N}^*$. We conclude by a discussion of past and future work.

2   Learning Concrete Automata

We briefly survey Angluin's L^* algorithm [Ang87] for learning regular sets from membership queries and counter-examples, with slightly modified definitions to accommodate for its symbolic extension. Let Σ be a finite alphabet and let Σ^* be the set of sequences (words) over Σ. Any order relation $<$ over Σ can be naturally lifted to a lexicographic order over Σ^*. With a language $L \subseteq \Sigma^*$ we associate a *characteristic function* $f : \Sigma^* \to \{0, 1\}$.

A *deterministic finite automaton* over Σ is a tuple $\mathcal{A} = (\Sigma, Q, \delta, q_0, F)$, where Q is a non-empty finite set of *states*, $q_0 \in Q$ is the *initial* state, $\delta : Q \times \Sigma \to Q$ is the *transition function*, and $F \subseteq Q$ is the set of *final* or *accepting* states. The transition function δ can be extended to $\delta : Q \times \Sigma^* \to Q$, where $\delta(q, \epsilon) = q$ and $\delta(q, u \cdot a) = \delta(\delta(q, u), a)$ for $q \in Q$, $a \in \Sigma$ and $u \in \Sigma^*$. A word $w \in \Sigma^*$ is *accepted* by $\mathcal{A}$ if $\delta(q_0, w) \in F$, otherwise w is *rejected*. The language recognized by $\mathcal{A}$ is the set of all accepted words and is denoted by $L(\mathcal{A})$.

Learning algorithms, represented by the *learner*, are designed to infer an unknown regular language L (the *target language*). The learner aims to construct a finite automaton that recognizes the target language by gathering information from the *teacher*. The *teacher* knows the target language and can provide information about it. It can answer two types of queries: *membership queries*, i.e., whether a word belongs to the target language, and *equivalence queries*, i.e., whether a conjectured automaton suggested by the learner is the right one. If this automaton fails to accept L the teacher responds to the equivalence query by a *counter-example*, a word misclassified by the conjectured automaton.

In the L^* algorithm, the learner starts by asking membership queries. All information provided is suitably gathered in a table structure, the *observation table*. Then, when the information is sufficient, the learner constructs a *hypothesis automaton* and poses an equivalence query to the teacher. If the answer is positive then the algorithm terminates and returns the conjectured automaton. Otherwise the learner accommodates the information provided by the counter-example into the table, asks additional membership queries until it can suggest a new hypothesis and so on, until termination.

A prefix-closed set $S \uplus R \subset \Sigma^*$ is a *balanced Σ-tree* if $\forall a \in \Sigma$: 1) For every $s \in S$ $s \cdot a \in S \cup R$, and 2) For every $r \in R$, $r \cdot a \notin S \cup R$. Elements of R are called *boundary elements* or *leaves*.

Definition 1 (Observation Table). *An observation table is a tuple $T = (\Sigma, S, R, E, f)$ such that Σ is an alphabet, $S \cup R$ is a finite balanced Σ-tree, E is a subset of Σ^* and $f : (S \cup R) \cdot E \to \{0, 1\}$ is the classification function, a restriction of the characteristic function of the target language L.*

The set $(S \cup R) \cdot E$ is the *sample* associated with the table, that is, the set of words whose membership is known. The elements of S admit a tree structure isomorphic to a *spanning tree* of the transition graph rooted in the initial state. Each $s \in S$ corresponds to a state q of the automaton for which s is an *access sequence*, one of the shortest words that lead from the initial state to q. The elements of R should tell us about the back- and cross-edges in the automaton and the elements of E are "experiments" that should be sufficient to distinguish between states. This works by associating with every $s \in S \cup R$ a specialized classification function $f_s : E \to \{0, 1\}$, defined as $f_s(e) = f(s \cdot e)$, which characterizes the row of the observation table labeled by s. To build an automaton from a table it should satisfy certain conditions.

Definition 2 (Closed, Reduced and Consistent Tables). *An observation table T is:*

- *Closed if for every $r \in R$, there exists an $s \in S$, such that $f_r = f_s$;*
- *Reduced if for every $s, s' \in S$ $f_s \neq f_{s'}$;*
- *Consistent if for every $s, s' \in S$, $f_s = f_{s'}$ implies $f_{s \cdot a} = f_{s' \cdot a}, \forall a \in \Sigma$.*

Note that a reduced table is trivially consistent and that for a closed and reduced table we can define a function $g : R \to S$ mapping every $r \in R$ to the unique $s \in S$ such that $f_s = f_r$. From such an observation table $T = (\Sigma, S, R, E, f)$ one can construct an automaton $\mathcal{A}_T = (\Sigma, Q, q_0, \delta, F)$ where $Q = S$, $q_0 = \epsilon$, $F = \{s \in S : f_s(\epsilon) = 1\}$ and

$$\delta(s, a) = \begin{cases} s \cdot a & \text{when } s \cdot a \in S \\ g(s \cdot a) & \text{when } s \cdot a \in R \end{cases}$$

The learner attempts to keep the table closed at all times. The table is not closed when there is some $r \in R$ such that f_r is different from f_s for all $s \in S$. To close the table, the learner moves r from R to S and adds the Σ-successors of r to R. The extended table is then filled up by asking membership queries until it becomes closed.

Variants of the L^* algorithm differ in the way they treat counter-examples, as described in more detail in [BR04]. The original algorithm [Ang87] adds all the *prefixes* of the counter-example to S and thus possibly creating inconsistency that should be fixed. The version proposed in [MP95] for learning ω-regular languages adds all the *suffixes* of the counter-example to E. The advantage of this approach is that the table always remains consistent and reduced with S corresponding exactly to the set of states. A disadvantage is the possible introduction of redundant columns that do not contribute to further discrimination between states. The symbolic algorithm that we develop in this paper is based on an intermediate variant, referred to in [BR04] as the *reduced observation algorithm*, where some prefixes of the counter-example are added to S and some suffixes are added to E.

Example: We illustrate the behavior of the L^* algorithm while learning $L = a\Sigma^*$ over $\Sigma = \{a, b\}$. We use $+w$ to indicate a counter-example $w \in L$ rejected by the conjectured automaton, and $-w$ for the opposite case. Initially, the observation table is $T_0 = (\Sigma, S, R, E, f)$ with $S = E = \{\epsilon\}$ and $R = \Sigma$ and we ask membership queries for all words in $(S \cup R) \cdot E = \{\epsilon, a, b\}$ to obtain table T_0, shown in Fig. 1. The table is not closed so we move a to S, add its continuations, aa and ab to R and ask membership queries to obtain the closed table T_1, from which the hypothesis automaton $\mathcal{A}_1$ of Fig. 2 is derived. In response to the equivalence query for $\mathcal{A}_1$, a counter-example $-ba$ is presented, its prefixes b and ba are added to S and their successors are added to R, resulting in table T_2 of Fig. 1. This table is not consistent: two elements ϵ and b in S are equivalent but their a-successors a and ba are not. Adding a to E and asking membership queries yields a consistent table T_3 whose automaton $\mathcal{A}_3$ is the minimal automaton recognizing L.   ◢

T_0

	ϵ
ϵ	0
a	1
b	0

T_1

	ϵ
ϵ	0
a	1
b	0
aa	1
ab	1

T_2

	ϵ
ϵ	0
a	1
b	0
ba	0
aa	1
ab	1
bb	0
baa	0
bab	0

T_3

	ϵ	a
ϵ	0	1
a	1	1
b	0	0
ba	0	0
aa	1	1
ab	1	1
bb	0	0
baa	0	0
bab	0	0

Fig. 1. Observation tables of L^* while learning $a \cdot \Sigma^*$

3   Symbolic Automata

Symbolic automata are automata over large alphabets where from each state there is a small number of outgoing transitions labelled by subsets of Σ that form a *partition* of the alphabet. Let Σ be a large and possibly infinite alphabet, that we call the *concrete* alphabet. Let ψ be a *total surjective* function from Σ to a finite (symbolic) alphabet $\boldsymbol{\Sigma}$. For each *symbolic letter* $\boldsymbol{a} \in \boldsymbol{\Sigma}$ we assign a Σ-semantics $[\boldsymbol{a}]_\psi = \{a \in \Sigma : \psi(a) = \boldsymbol{a}\}$. Since ψ is total and surjective, the set $\{[\boldsymbol{a}]_\psi : \boldsymbol{a} \in \boldsymbol{\Sigma}\}$ forms a *partition* of Σ. We will

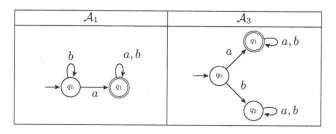

Fig. 2. Hypothesis automata for $a \cdot \Sigma^*$

often omit ψ from the notation and use $[a]$ where ψ, which is always present, is clear from the context. The Σ-semantics can be extended to symbolic words of the form $w = a_1 \cdot a_2 \cdots a_k \in \Sigma^*$ as the concatenation of the concrete one-letter languages associated with the respective symbolic letters or, recursively speaking, $[\epsilon] = \{\epsilon\}$ and $[w \cdot a] = [w] \cdot [a]$ for $w \in \Sigma^*, a \in \Sigma$.

Definition 3 (Symbolic Automaton). *A deterministic symbolic automaton is a tuple* $\mathcal{A} = (\Sigma, \boldsymbol{\Sigma}, \psi, Q, \delta, q_0, F)$, *where*

- *Σ is the input alphabet,*
- *$\boldsymbol{\Sigma}$ is a finite alphabet, decomposable into $\boldsymbol{\Sigma} = \biguplus_{q \in Q} \boldsymbol{\Sigma}_q$,*
- *$\psi = \{\psi_q : q \in Q\}$ is a family of total surjective functions $\psi_q : \Sigma \to \boldsymbol{\Sigma}_q$,*
- *Q is a finite set of states,*
- *$\delta : Q \times \boldsymbol{\Sigma} \to Q$ is a partial transition function decomposable into a family of total functions $\delta_q : \{q\} \times \boldsymbol{\Sigma}_q \to Q$,*
- *q_0 is the initial state and F is the set of accepting states.*

Automaton $\mathcal{A}$ can be viewed as representing a concrete deterministic automaton $\mathcal{A}$ whose transition function is defined as $\delta(q, a) = \delta(q, \psi_q(a))$ and its accepted concrete language is $L(\mathcal{A}) = L(\mathcal{A})$.

Remark: The association of a *symbolic language* with a symbolic automaton is more subtle because we allow different partitions of Σ and hence different input alphabets at different states, rendering the transition function *partial* with respect to $\boldsymbol{\Sigma}$. When in a state q and reading a symbol $a \notin \boldsymbol{\Sigma}_q$, the transition to be taken is well defined only when $[a] \subseteq [a']$ for some $a' \in \boldsymbol{\Sigma}_q$. The model can, nevertheless, be made deterministic and complete over a refinement of the symbolic alphabet. Let

$$\boldsymbol{\Sigma}' = \prod_{q \in Q} \boldsymbol{\Sigma}_q, \text{ with the } \Sigma\text{-semantics } [(a_1, \ldots, a_n)] = [a_1] \cap \ldots \cap [a_n]$$

and let $\tilde{\boldsymbol{\Sigma}} = \{b \in \boldsymbol{\Sigma}' : [b] \neq \emptyset\}$. We can then define an ordinary automaton $\tilde{\mathcal{A}} = (\tilde{\boldsymbol{\Sigma}}, Q, \tilde{\delta}, q_0, F)$ where, by construction, for every $b \in \tilde{\boldsymbol{\Sigma}}$ and every $q \in Q$, there is $a \in \boldsymbol{\Sigma}_q$ such that $[b] \subseteq [a]$ and hence one can define the transition function as $\tilde{\delta}(q, b) = \delta(q, a)$. This model is more comfortable for language-theoretic studies but we stick in this paper to Definition 3 as it is more efficient. A similar choice has been made in [IHS13].

Proposition 1 (Closure under Boolean Operations). *Languages accepted by deterministic symbolic automata are closed under Boolean operations.*

Proof. Closure under negation is immediate by complementing the set of accepting states. For intersection we adapt the standard product construction as follows. Let L_1, L_2 be languages recognized by the symbolic automata $\mathcal{A}_1 = (\Sigma, \Sigma_1, \psi_1, Q_1, \delta_1, q_{01}, F_1)$ and $\mathcal{A}_2 = (\Sigma, \Sigma_2, \psi_2, Q_2, \delta_2, q_{02}, F_2)$, respectively. Let $\mathcal{A} = (\Sigma, \Sigma, \psi, Q, \delta, q_0, F)$, where

- $Q = Q_1 \times Q_2$, $q_0 = (q_{01}, q_{02})$, $F = F_1 \times F_2$
- For every $(q_1, q_2) \in Q$
  - $\Sigma_{(q_1, q_2)} = \{(a_1, a_2) \in \Sigma_1 \times \Sigma_2 \mid [a_1] \cap [a_2] \neq \emptyset\}$
  - $\psi_{(q_1, q_2)}(a) = (\psi_{1, q_1}(a), \psi_{2, q_2}(a)) \; \forall a \in \Sigma$
  - $\delta((q_1, q_2), (a_1, a_2)) = (\delta_1(q_1, a_1), \delta_2(q_2, a_2)) \; \forall (a_1, a_2) \in \Sigma_{(q_1, q_2)}$

It is sufficient to observe that the corresponding implied concrete automata $\mathcal{A}_1$, $\mathcal{A}_2$ and $\mathcal{A}$ satisfy $\delta((q_1, q_2), a) = (\delta_1(q_1, a), \delta_2(q_2, a))$ and the standard proof that $L(\mathcal{A}) = L(\mathcal{A}_1) \cap L(\mathcal{A}_2)$ follows. ∎

Equivalence queries are implemented by constructing a product automaton which accepts the symmetric difference between the target language and the conjectured one, finding shortest paths to accepting states and selecting a lexicographically minimal word.

Definition 4 (Balanced Symbolic Σ-Tree). *A balanced symbolic Σ-tree is a tuple (Σ, S, R, ψ) where*

- $S \uplus R$ *is a prefix-closed subset of* Σ
- $\Sigma = \uplus_{s \in S} \Sigma_s$ *is a symbolic alphabet*
- $\psi = \{\psi_s\}_{s \in S}$ *is a family of total surjective functions of the form* $\psi_s : \Sigma \to \Sigma_s$.

It is required that for every $s \in S$ and $a \in \Sigma_s$, $s \cdot a \in S \cup R$ and for any $r \in R$ and $a \in \Sigma$, $r \cdot a \notin S \cup R$. Elements of R are called boundary elements of the tree.

We will use observation tables whose rows are symbolic words and hence an entry in the table will constitute a statement about the inclusion or exclusion of a large *set* of concrete words in the language. We will not ask membership queries concerning all those words, but only for a small representative sample that we call *evidence*.

Definition 5 (Symbolic Observation Table). *A symbolic observation table is a tuple $T = (\Sigma, \Sigma, S, R, \psi, E, f, \mu)$ such that*

- Σ *is an alphabet,*
- (Σ, S, R, ψ) *is a finite balanced symbolic Σ-tree (with R being its* boundary*),*
- E *is a subset of* Σ^*,
- $f : (S \cup R) \cdot E \to \{0, 1\}$ *is the symbolic classification function*
- $\mu : (S \cup R) \cdot E \to 2^{\Sigma^*} - \{\emptyset\}$ *is an evidence function satisfying $\mu(w) \subseteq [w]$. The image of the evidence function is prefix-closed: $w \cdot a \in \mu(w \cdot a) \Rightarrow w \in \mu(w)$.*

We use, as for the concrete case, $f_s : E \rightarrow \{0,1\}$ to denote the partial evaluation of f to some symbolic word $s \in S \cup R$, such that, $f_s(e) = f(s \cdot e)$. Note that the set E consists of *concrete* words but this poses no problem because elements of E are used only to distinguish between states and do not participate in the derivation of the symbolic automaton from the table. The notions of closed, consistent and reduced table are similar to the concrete case.

The set $M_T = (S \cup R) \cdot E$ is called the *symbolic sample* associated with T. We require that for each word $w \in M_T$ there is at least one concrete $w \in \mu(w)$ whose membership in L, denoted by $f(w)$, is known. The set of such words is called the *concrete sample* and is defined as $M_T = \{s \cdot e : s \in \mu(s), s \in S \cup R, e \in E\}$. A table where all evidences of the same symbolic word admit the same classification is called *evidence-compatible*.

Definition 6 (Table Conditions). *A table* $T = (\Sigma, \boldsymbol{\Sigma}, \boldsymbol{S}, \boldsymbol{R}, \psi, E, \boldsymbol{f}, \mu)$ *is*

- *Closed if* $\forall r \in R, \exists s = g(r) \in S, f_r = f_s$,
- *Reduced if* $\forall s, s' \in S, f_s \neq f_{s'}$,
- *Consistent if* $\forall s, s' \in S, f_s = f_{s'}$ *implies* $f_{s \cdot a} = f_{s' \cdot a}, \forall a \in \Sigma_s$.
- *Evidence compatible if* $\forall w \in M_T, \forall w_1, w_2 \in \mu(w), f(w_1) = f(w_2)$.

When a table T is evidence compatible the symbolic classification function f can be defined for every $s \in (S \cup R)$ and $e \in E$ as $f(s \cdot e) = f(s \cdot e), s \in \mu(s)$.

Theorem 1 (Automaton from Table). *From a closed, reduced and evidence compatible table* $T = (\Sigma, \boldsymbol{\Sigma}, \boldsymbol{S}, \boldsymbol{R}, \psi, E, \boldsymbol{f}, \mu)$ *one can construct a deterministic symbolic automaton compatible with the concrete sample.*

Proof. Let $\mathcal{A}_T = (\Sigma, \boldsymbol{\Sigma}, \psi, Q, \delta, q_0, F)$ where:

- $Q = S, q_0 = \epsilon$
- $F = \{s \in S \mid f_s(\epsilon) = 1\}$
- $\delta : Q \times \Sigma \rightarrow Q$ is defined as $\delta(s, a) = \begin{cases} s \cdot a & \text{when } s \cdot a \in S \\ g(s \cdot a) & \text{when } s \cdot a \in R \end{cases}$

By construction and like the L^* algorithm, $\mathcal{A}_T$ classifies correctly the symbolic sample. Due to evidence compatibility this holds also for the concrete sample. ⌐

4 The Algorithm

In this section we present a symbolic learning algorithm starting with an intuitive verbal description. From now on we assume that the alphabet is *ordered* and use a_0 to denote its minimal. We assume that the teacher always provides the smallest counter-example with respect to length *and* lexicographic order on Σ^*. Also, when we choose an evidence for a new symbolic word w in a membership query we always take the smallest possible element of $[w]$.

The algorithmic scheme is similar to the concrete L^* algorithm but differs in the treatment of counter-examples and the new concept of evidence compatibility. When the table is not closed, $S \cup R$ is extended until closure. Then a conjectured automaton $\mathcal{A}_T$

is constructed and an equivalence query is posed. If the answer is positive we are done. Otherwise the teacher provides a counter-example leading possibly to the extension of E and/or $S \cup R$. Whenever such an extension occurs, additional membership queries are posed to fill the table. The table is always kept evidence compatible and reduced except temporarily during the processing of counter-examples.

The learner starts with the symbolic table $T = (\Sigma, \mathbf{\Sigma}, \mathbf{S}, \mathbf{R}, \psi, E, \mathbf{f}, \mu)$, where $\mathbf{\Sigma} = \{a_0\}$, $\mathbf{S} = \{\epsilon\}$, $\mathbf{R} = \{a_0\}$, $E = \{\epsilon\}$, and $\mu(a_0) = \{a_0\}$. Whenever T is not closed, there is some $r \in \mathbf{R}$ such that $\mathbf{f}_r \neq \mathbf{f}_s$ for every $s \in \mathbf{S}$. To make the table closed we move r from $\mathbf{R}$ to $\mathbf{S}$ and add to $\mathbf{R}$ the word $r' = r \cdot a$, where a is a new symbolic letter with $[a] = \Sigma$, and extend the evidence function by letting $\mu(r') = \mu(r) \cdot a_0$.

When a counter-example w is presented, it is of course not part of the concrete sample. It admits a factorization $w = u \cdot a \cdot v$, where u is the largest prefix of u such that $u \in \mu(\mathbf{u})$ for some $\mathbf{u} \in \mathbf{S} \cup \mathbf{R}$. There are two cases, the second of which is particular to our symbolic algorithm.

1. $\mathbf{u} \in \mathbf{R}$: Assume that $g(\mathbf{u}) = \mathbf{s} \in \mathbf{S}$ and since the table is reduced, $\mathbf{f}_u \neq \mathbf{f}_{s'}$ for any other $\mathbf{s'} \in \mathbf{S}$. Because w is the shortest counter-example, the classification of $\mathbf{s} \cdot a \cdot v$ in the automaton is correct (otherwise $\mathbf{s} \cdot a \cdot v$, for some $\mathbf{s} \in [\mathbf{s}]$ would constitute a shorter counter-example) and different from that of $\mathbf{u} \cdot a \cdot v$. Thus we conclude that $\mathbf{u}$ deserves to be a state and should be added to $\mathbf{S}$. To distinguish between $\mathbf{u}$ and $\mathbf{s}$ we add $a \cdot v$ to E, possibly with some of its suffixes (see [BR04] for a more detailed discussion of counter-example treatment). As $\mathbf{u}$ is a new state we need to add its continuations to $\mathbf{R}$. We distinguish two cases depending on a:

   (a) If $a = a_0$ is the smallest element of Σ then a new symbolic letter a is added to $\mathbf{\Sigma}$, with $[a] = \Sigma$ and $\mu(\mathbf{u} \cdot a) = \mu(\mathbf{u}) \cdot a_0$, and the symbolic word $\mathbf{u} \cdot a$ is added to $\mathbf{R}$.

   (b) If $a \neq a_0$ then *two* new symbolic letters, a and a', are added to $\mathbf{\Sigma}$ with $[a] = \{b : b < a\}$, $[a'] = \{b : b \geq a\}$ and $\mu(\mathbf{u} \cdot a) = \mu(\mathbf{u}) \cdot a_0$, $\mu(\mathbf{u} \cdot a') = \mu(\mathbf{u}) \cdot a$. The words $\mathbf{u} \cdot a$ and $\mathbf{u} \cdot a'$ are added to $\mathbf{R}$.

2. $\mathbf{u} \in \mathbf{S}$: In this case the counter-example indicates that $\mathbf{u} \cdot a$ was wrongly assumed to be part of $[\mathbf{u} \cdot a]$ for some $a \in \Sigma_{\mathbf{u}}$, and a was wrongly assumed to be part of $[a]$. There are two cases:

   (a) There is some $a' \neq a$ such that the classification of $\mathbf{u} \cdot a' \cdot v$ by the symbolic automaton agrees with the classification of $\mathbf{u} \cdot a \cdot v$. In this case we just move a and all letters greater than a from $[a]$ to $[a']$ and no new state is added.

   (b) If there is no such a symbolic letter, we create a new a' with $[a'] = \{b \in [a] : b \geq a\}$ and update $[a]$ to be $[a] - [a']$. We let $\mu(\mathbf{u} \cdot a') = \mu(\mathbf{u}) \cdot a$ and add $\mathbf{u} \cdot a'$ to $\mathbf{R}$.

A detailed description is given in Algorithm 1 with major procedures in Algorithm 2. A statement of the form $\Sigma = \Sigma \cup \{a\}$ indicates the introduction of a new symbolic letter $a \notin \Sigma$. We use MQ and EQ as shorthands for membership and equivalence queries, respectively. Note also that for every $r \in \mathbf{R}$, $\mu(r)$ is always a singleton.

We illustrate the behavior of the algorithm on $L = \{a \cdot u : b \leq a < c, u \in \Sigma^*\}$ for two constants $b < c$ in Σ. The table is initialized to $T_0 = (\Sigma, \mathbf{\Sigma}, \mathbf{S}, \mathbf{R}, \psi, E, \mathbf{f}, \mu)$,

---

Algorithm 1. The symbolic algorithm

1: **procedure** SYMBOLIC
2:    $learned = false$
3:    Initialize the table $T = (\Sigma, \boldsymbol{\Sigma}, \boldsymbol{S}, \boldsymbol{R}, \psi, E, \boldsymbol{f}, \mu)$
4:        $\boldsymbol{\Sigma} = \{\boldsymbol{a}\}; \psi_\epsilon(a) = \boldsymbol{a}, \forall a \in \Sigma$
5:        $\boldsymbol{S} = \{\epsilon\}; \boldsymbol{R} = \{\boldsymbol{a}\}; E = \{\epsilon\}$
6:        $\mu(\boldsymbol{a}) = \{a_0\}$
7:        Ask MQ on ϵ and a_0 to fill $\boldsymbol{f}$

8:    **if** T is not closed **then**
9:        CLOSE
10:   **end if**

11:   **repeat**
12:       **if** $EQ(\mathcal{A}_T)$ **then**   ▷ $\mathcal{A}_T$ is correct
13:           $learned = true$
14:       **else**   ▷ A counter-example w is provided
15:           $M = M \cup \{w\}$
16:           COUNTER-EX(w)   ▷ Process counter-example
17:       **end if**
18:   **until** $learned$
19: **end procedure**

---

where $\boldsymbol{\Sigma} = \{a_0\}$, $\mu(a_0) = \{a_0\}$, $\boldsymbol{S} = \{\epsilon\}$, $E = \{\epsilon\}$, $\boldsymbol{R} = \{a_0\}$ and $\psi = \{\psi_\epsilon\}$ with $\psi_\epsilon(a) = a_0, \forall a \in \Sigma$. We ask membership queries to learn $f(\epsilon)$ and $f(a_0)$. Table T_0, shown in Fig. 3, is closed, reduced and evidence compatible and its related hypothesis automaton $\mathcal{A}_0$ consists of only one rejecting state, as shown in Fig. 4. The teacher responds to this conjecture by the counter-example $+b$. Since $b \notin \mu(a_0)$ and $\epsilon \in \boldsymbol{S}$, we are in Case 2-(b) of the counter-example treatment, where there is no symbolic word that classifies b correctly. We create a new symbolic letter a_1 with $\mu(a_1) = \{b\}$ and modify ψ_ϵ to $\psi_\epsilon(a) = a_0$ when $a < b$ and $\psi_\epsilon(a) = a_1$ otherwise. The derived table T_1 is not closed since for $a_1 \in \boldsymbol{R}$ there is no element $s \in \boldsymbol{S}$ such that $\boldsymbol{f}_{a_1} = \boldsymbol{f}_s$. To close the table we move a_1 from $\boldsymbol{R}$ to $\boldsymbol{S}$ and introduce a new symbolic letter a_2 to represent the continuations of a_1. We define ψ_{a_1} with $\psi_{a_1}(a) = a_2$ for all $a \in \Sigma$, $\mu(a_1 \cdot a_2) = \{b \cdot a_0\}$ and add the symbolic word $a_1 \cdot a_2$ to $\boldsymbol{R}$. We ask membership queries for the missing words and construct a new observation table T_2.

This table is closed and reduced, resulting in a new hypothesis automaton $\mathcal{A}_2$. The counter-example provided by the teacher is $-c$. This is case 2-(a) of the counter-example treatment as there exists a symbolic letter a_0 that agrees with the classification of c. We move c and all elements greater than it from $[a_1]$ to $[a_0]$, that is, $\psi_\epsilon(a) = a_0$ when $a < b$, $\psi_\epsilon(a) = a_1$ when $b \leq a < c$ and $\psi_\epsilon(a) = a_3$ otherwise. Table T_3 is closed, reduced and evidence compatible leading to the hypothesis automaton $\mathcal{A}_3$ for which $-ab$ is a counter-example where $a \in \mu(a_0)$ and $a_0 \in \boldsymbol{R}$. Thus we are now in case 1 and since the counter-example is considered to be the shortest, a_0 is a new state of the automaton, different from ϵ. We move a_0 to $\boldsymbol{S}$ and add a new symbolic letter a_4 to $\boldsymbol{\Sigma}$, which represents the transition from a_0, with $\mu(a_0 \cdot a_4) = \{a_0 \cdot a_0\}$. Now $\psi_{a_0}(a) = a_4$. However the obtained table T_4 is not reduced since $\boldsymbol{f}_\epsilon(e) = \boldsymbol{f}_{a_0}(e)$ for all $e \in E$. We

Procedures 2. Closing the table and processinging counter-examples

1: **procedure** CLOSE   ▷ Make the table closed
2:    **while** $\exists r \in R$ such that $\forall s \in S$, $f_r \neq f_s$ **do**
3:        $\Sigma' = \Sigma \cup \{a\}$; $\psi' = \psi \cup \{\psi_r\}$ with $\psi_r(a) = a$, $\forall a \in \Sigma$
4:        $S' = S \cup \{r\}$; $R' = (R - \{r\}) \cup \{r \cdot a\}$
5:        $\mu(r \cdot a) = \mu(r) \cdot a_0$
6:        Ask MQ for all words in $\{\mu(r \cdot a) \cdot e : e \in E\}$
7:        $T = (\Sigma, \Sigma', S', R', \psi', E, f', \mu')$
8:    **end while**
9: **end procedure**

1: **procedure** COUNTER-EX(w)   ▷ Process counter-example
2:    Find a factorization $w = u \cdot a \cdot v$, $a \in \Sigma$, $u, v \in \Sigma^*$ such that
3:        $\exists u \in M_T$, $u \in \mu(u)$ and $\forall u' \in M$, $u \cdot a \notin \mu(u')$
4:    **if** $u \in R$ **then**
5:        **if** $a = a_0$ **then**   ▷ Case 1(a)
6:            $\Sigma' = \Sigma \cup \{a\}$; $\psi' = \psi \cup \{\psi_u\}$, with $\psi_u(\sigma) = a$, $\forall \sigma \in \Sigma$
7:            $S' = S \cup \{u\}$; $R' = (R - \{u\}) \cup \{u \cdot a\}$; $E' = E \cup \{$suffixes of $a \cdot v\}$
8:            $\mu(u \cdot a) = \mu(u) \cdot a_0$
9:            Ask MQ for all words in $\{\mu(u \cdot a) \cdot e : e \in E'\}$
10:       **else**   ▷ Case 1(b)
11:            $\Sigma' = \Sigma \cup \{a, a'\}$
12:            $\psi' = \psi \cup \{\psi_u\}$, with $\psi_u(\sigma) = \begin{cases} a & \text{if } \sigma < a \\ a' & \text{otherwise} \end{cases}$
13:            $S' = S \cup \{u\}$; $R' = (R - \{u\}) \cup \{u \cdot a, u \cdot a'\}$; $E' = E \cup \{$suffixes of $a \cdot v\}$
14:            $\mu(u \cdot a) = \mu(u) \cdot a_0$; $\mu(u \cdot a') = \mu(u) \cdot a$
15:            Ask MQ for all words in $\{(\mu(u \cdot a) \cup \mu(u \cdot a')) \cdot e : e \in E'\}$
16:       **end if**
17:       $T' = (\Sigma, \Sigma', S', R', \psi', E', f', \mu)$
18:    **else**   ▷ Case 2(a),(b)
19:        Find $a \in \Sigma_u$ such that $a \in [a]$
20:        **if** there is no $a' \in \Sigma : f_{u \cdot a} = f_{\mu(u \cdot a')}$ on E **then**
21:            $\Sigma' = \Sigma \cup \{a'\}$; $R' = R \cup \{u \cdot a'\}$
22:            $\mu(u \cdot a') = \mu(u) \cdot a$
23:            Ask MQ for all words in $\{\mu(u \cdot a') \cdot e : e \in E\}$
24:        **end if**
25:        $\psi_u(\sigma) = \begin{cases} \psi_u(\sigma) & \text{if } \sigma \notin [a] \\ a & \text{if } \sigma \in [a] \text{ and } \sigma < a \\ a' & \text{otherwise} \end{cases}$
26:        $T = (\Sigma, \Sigma', S, R', \psi, E, f', \mu)$
27:    **end if**
28:    **if** T is not closed **then**
29:        CLOSE
30:    **end if**
31: **end procedure**

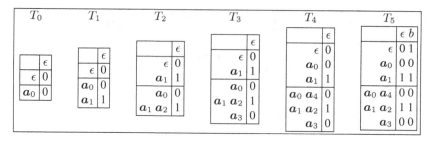

Fig. 3. Symbolic observation tables for $(b \leq a < c) \cdot \Sigma^*$

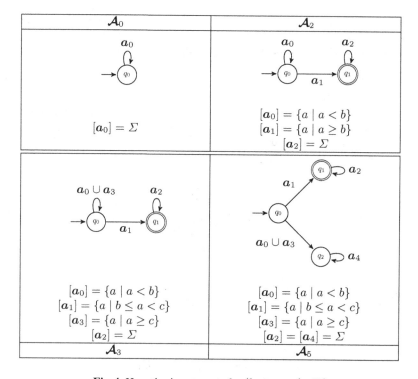

Fig. 4. Hypothesis automata for $(b \leq a < c) \cdot \Sigma^*$

add experiment b to E and fill the gaps using membership queries, resulting in table T_5 which is closed, reduced and evidence compatible. The derived automaton $\mathcal{A}_5$ is the right one and the algorithm terminates.

It is easy to see that for large alphabets our algorithm is much more efficient than L^*. For example, when $\Sigma = \{1..100\}$, $b = 20$ and $c = 50$, the L^* algorithm will need around 400 queries while ours will ask less than 10. The symbolic algorithm is influenced not by the size of the alphabet but by the resolution (partition size) with which we observe it. Fig. 5 shows a larger automaton over the same alphabet learned by our procedure.

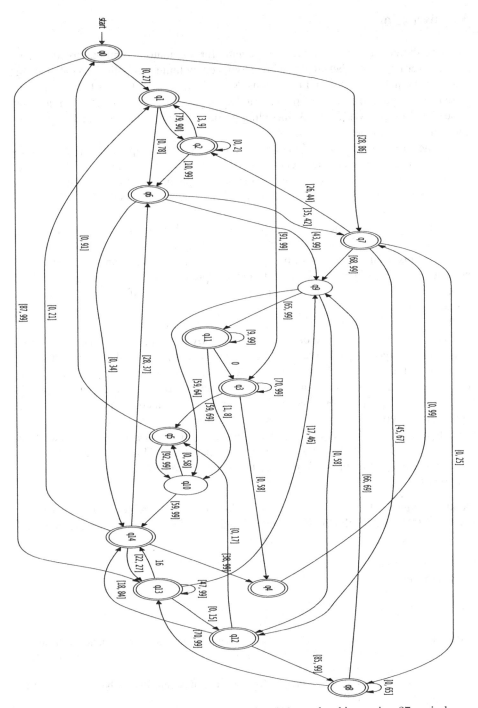

Fig. 5. An automaton learned by our procedure using 418 membership queries, 27 equivalence queries with a table of size 46 × 11

5 Discussion

We have defined a generic algorithmic scheme for automaton learning, targeting languages over large alphabets that can be recognized by finite symbolic automata having a modest number of states and transitions. Some ideas similar to ours have been proposed for the particular case of parametric languages [BJR06] and recently in a more general setting [HSM11, IHS13] including partial evidential support and alphabet refinement during the learning process.[2]

The genericity of the algorithm comes from the semantic approach (alphabet partitions) but of course, each and every domain will have its own semantic and syntactic specialization in terms of the size and shape of the alphabet partitions. In this work we have implemented an instantiation of this scheme for the alphabet $\Sigma = (\mathbb{N}, \leq)$ and the adaptation to real numbers is immediate. When dealing with numbers, the partition into a finite number of intervals (and convex sets in higher dimensions) is very natural and used in many application domains ranging from quantization of sensor readings to income tax regulations. It will be interesting to compare the expressive power and succinctness of symbolic automata with other approaches for representing numerical time series and to compare our algorithm with other inductive inference techniques for sequences of numbers.

As a first excursion into the domain, we have made quite strong assumptions on the nature of the equivalence oracle, which, already for small alphabets, is a bit too strong and pedagogical to be realistic. We assumed that it provides the shortest counterexample and also that it chooses always the minimal available concrete symbol. We can relax the latter (or both) and replace the oracle by random sampling, as already proposed in [Ang87] for concrete learning. Over large alphabets, it might be even more appropriate to employ probabilistic convergence criteria a-la *PAC learning* [Val84] and be content with a correct classification of a large fraction of the words, thus tolerating imprecise tracing of boundaries in the alphabet partitions. This topic, as well as the challenging adaptation of our framework to languages over Boolean vectors are left for future work.

Acknowledgement. This work was supported by the French project EQINOCS (ANR-11-BS02-004). We thank Peter Habermehl, Eugene Asarin and anonymous referees for useful comments and pointers to the literature.

References

[Ang87] Angluin, D.: Learning regular sets from queries and counterexamples. Information and Computation 75(2), 87–106 (1987)

[BJR06] Berg, T., Jonsson, B., Raffelt, H.: Regular inference for state machines with parameters. In: Baresi, L., Heckel, R. (eds.) FASE 2006. LNCS, vol. 3922, pp. 107–121. Springer, Heidelberg (2006)

[BLP10] Benedikt, M., Ley, C., Puppis, G.: What you must remember when processing data words. In: AMW (2010)

---

[2] Let us remark that the modification of partition boundaries is not always a refinement in the precise mathematical sense of the term.

[BR04]   Berg, T., Raffelt, H.: Model Checking. In: Broy, M., Jonsson, B., Katoen, J.-P., Leucker, M., Pretschner, A. (eds.) Model-Based Testing of Reactive Systems. LNCS, vol. 3472, pp. 557–603. Springer, Heidelberg (2005)

[DlH10] De la Higuera, C.: Grammatical inference: learning automata and grammars. Cambridge University Press (2010)

[DR95]   Diekert, V., Rozenberg, G.: The Book of Traces. World Scientific (1995)

[Gol72] Gold, E.M.: System identification via state characterization. Automatica 8(5), 621–636 (1972)

[HSJC12] Howar, F., Steffen, B., Jonsson, B., Cassel, S.: Inferring canonical register automata. In: Kuncak, V., Rybalchenko, A. (eds.) VMCAI 2012. LNCS, vol. 7148, pp. 251–266. Springer, Heidelberg (2012)

[HSM11] Howar, F., Steffen, B., Merten, M.: Automata learning with automated alphabet abstraction refinement. In: Jhala, R., Schmidt, D. (eds.) VMCAI 2011. LNCS, vol. 6538, pp. 263–277. Springer, Heidelberg (2011)

[IHS13] Isberner, M., Howar, F., Steffen, B.: Inferring automata with state-local alphabet abstractions. In: Brat, G., Rungta, N., Venet, A. (eds.) NFM 2013. LNCS, vol. 7871, pp. 124–138. Springer, Heidelberg (2013)

[KF94]   Kaminski, M., Francez, N.: Finite-memory automata. Theoretical Computer Science 134(2), 329–363 (1994)

[Moo56] Moore, E.F.: Gedanken-experiments on sequential machines. In: Automata Studies. Annals of Mathematical Studies, vol. 34, pp. 129–153. Princeton (1956)

[MP95]   Maler, O., Pnueli, A.: On the learnability of infinitary regular sets. Information and Computation 118(2), 316–326 (1995)

[Ner58] Nerode, A.: Linear automaton transformations. Proceedings of the American Mathematical Society 9(4), 541–544 (1958)

[Val84] Valiant, L.G.: A theory of the learnable. Communications of the ACM 27(11), 1134–1142 (1984)

[VHL+12] Veanes, M., Hooimeijer, P., Livshits, B., Molnar, D., Björner, N.: Symbolic finite state transducers: algorithms and applications. In: POPL, pp. 137–150 (2012)

Verification of Concurrent Quantum Protocols by Equivalence Checking

Ebrahim Ardeshir-Larijani[1,2,*], Simon J. Gay[2], and Rajagopal Nagarajan[3,**]

[1] Department of Computer Science, University of Warwick, UK
E.Ardeshir-Larijani@warwick.ac.uk
[2] School of Computing Science, University of Glasgow, UK
Simon.Gay@glasgow.ac.uk
[3] Department of Computer Science,
School of Science and Technology, Middlesex University, UK
R.Nagarajan@mdx.ac.uk

Abstract. We present a tool which uses a concurrent language for describing quantum systems, and performs verification by checking equivalence between specification and implementation. In general, simulation of quantum systems using current computing technology is infeasible. We restrict ourselves to the *stabilizer* formalism, in which there are efficient simulation algorithms. In particular, we consider concurrent quantum protocols that behave *functionally* in the sense of computing a deterministic input-output relation for all interleavings of the concurrent system. Crucially, these input-output relations can be abstracted by superoperators, enabling us to take advantage of linearity. This allows us to analyse the behaviour of protocols with arbitrary input, by simulating their operation on a finite basis set consisting of stabilizer states. Despite the limitations of the stabilizer formalism and also the range of protocols that can be analysed using this approach, we have applied our equivalence checking tool to specify and verify interesting and practical quantum protocols from teleportation to secret sharing.

1 Introduction

There have been significant advances in quantum information science over the last few decades and technologies based on these developments are at a stage well suited for deployment in a range of industrial applications. The construction of practical, general purpose quantum computers has been challenging. The only large scale quantum computer available today is manufactured by the Canadian company D-Wave. However, it does not appear to be general purpose and not everyone is convinced that it is truly quantum. On the other hand, quantum

---

* Supported by the Centre for Discrete Mathematics and its Applications (DIMAP), University of Warwick, EPSRC award EP/D063191/1.
** Partially supported by "Process Algebra Approach to Distributed Quantum Computation and Secure Quantum Communication", Australian Research Council Discovery Project DP110103473.

E. Ábrahám and K. Havelund (Eds.): TACAS 2014, LNCS 8413, pp. 500–514, 2014.

communication and cryptography have made large strides and is now well established. Physical restrictions of quantum communication, like preserving photon states over long distances, are gradually being resolved, for example, by quantum repeaters [11] and using quantum teleportation. Various Quantum Key Distribution networks have been built, including the DARPA Quantum Network in Boston, the SeCoQC network around Vienna and the Tokyo QKD Network. There is no doubt that quantum communication and quantum cryptographic protocols will become an integral part of our society's infrastructure.

On the theoretical side, quantum key distribution protocols such as BB84 have been proved to be unconditionally secure [20]. It is important to understand that this an information-theoretic proof, which does not necessarily guarantee that *implemented systems* are unconditionally secure. That is why alternative approaches, such as those based on formal methods, could be useful in analysing behaviour of implemented systems.

The area of *formal verification*, despite being a relatively young field, has found numerous applications in hardware and software technologies. Today, verification techniques span a wide spectrum from model checking and theorem proving to process calculus, all of them have helped us to grasp better understanding of interactive and complicated distributed systems. This work represents another milestone in our ongoing programme of applying formal methods to quantum systems. In this paper, we present a concurrent language for describing quantum systems, and perform verification by equivalence checking. The goal in equivalence checking is to show that the implementation of a program is identical to its specification, on all possible executions of the program. This is different from property based model checking, where an intended property is checked over all possible execution paths of a program. The key idea of this paper is to check equivalence of quantum protocols by using their superoperator semantics (Section 4). Superoperators are linear, so they are completely defined by their effect on a basis of the appropriate space. To show that two protocols are equivalent, we show that their associated superoperators are equivalent by simulating the protocols for every state in a basis of the input vector space. By choosing a basis that consists of stabilizer states, we can do this simulation efficiently.

One of the main challenges here is the *explosion of states* arising from branching and concurrency of programs. This is in addition to the need to deal with the *explosion of space* needed for specifying quantum states. For a quantum state with n *qubits*(quantum bits), we need to consider 2^n complex coefficients. To avoid this problem we restrict ourself to the *stabilizer formalism* [1]. In this formalism, quantum states can be described in polynomial space and also for certain quantum operations, the evolution of stabilizer states can be done in polynomial time. Although one cannot do universal quantum computation within the stabilizer formalism, many important protocols such as Teleportation [7], Quantum Error Correction [8] as well as *quantum entanglement* can be analysed within it. Crucially, quantum error correction is a *prerequisite* for *fault tolerant* quantum computing [24]. The latter is necessary for building a scalable quantum computer, capable of doing universal quantum computing.

Contributions. This paper extends our previous work [4] substantially in two ways. First, we now use a concurrent modelling language, which means that we can explicitly represent concurrency and communication in order to model protocols more realistically. Second, we have analysed a much wider range of examples, including several standard quantum protocols.

The paper is organised as follows. In Section 2 we give preliminaries from quantum computing and the stabilizer formalism. In Sections 3 and 4, we give the syntax and semantics of our concurrent modelling language. Section 5 describes our equivalence checking technique and Section 6 presents example protocols. In Section 7 we give details of our equivalence checking tool, and present experimental results. Section 8 reviews related work and Section 9 concludes.

2   Background

In this section, we give a very concise introduction to quantum computing. For more details, we refer to [22]. The basic element of quantum information is a *qubit* (quantum bit). Qubits are vectors in an *inner product* vector space which is called Hilbert space.[1] Quantum states are description of qubits with the general form: $|\Psi\rangle = \alpha_1 |00\ldots0\rangle + \ldots + \alpha_n |11\ldots1\rangle$, where $\alpha_i \in \mathbb{C}$ are called *amplitudes* satisfying $|\alpha_1|^2 + \ldots + |\alpha_n|^2 = 1$. The so-called Ket notation or Dirac's notation is used to distinguish unit vectors $|0\rangle$ and $|1\rangle$ from classical bits 0 and 1. Also $|00\ldots0\rangle$ corresponds to *tensor product* of unit vectors (i.e $|0\rangle \otimes 0 \ldots \otimes |0\rangle$). There are two kinds of operations on quantum states, *unitary transformations* and *measurement*. The side effect of the measurement operation is classical information, for example, the outcome of measuring the above state $|\Psi\rangle$ is a classical bit string $(00\ldots0)$ with probability $|\alpha_1|^2$, to $(11\ldots1)$ with probability $|\alpha_n|^2$. Note that measurement is a destructive operation and it changes the state of a qubit permanently. Qubits can be *entangled*. For example, a two qubit entangled state $|00\rangle + |11\rangle$, which is called a *Bell* state, cannot be decomposed into two single qubit states. Measuring one of the qubits will fix the state of the other qubit, even if they are physically separated.

Some basic quantum operations and their matrix representation are shown in the Figure 1. A model for describing a quantum system is the quantum circuit

$$X = \begin{pmatrix} 0 & 1 \\ 1 & 0 \end{pmatrix}, \ Z = \begin{pmatrix} 1 & 0 \\ 0 & -1 \end{pmatrix}, \ Y = \begin{pmatrix} 0 & -i \\ i & 0 \end{pmatrix}, \ I = \begin{pmatrix} 1 & 0 \\ 0 & 1 \end{pmatrix}$$

Fig. 1. Pauli operators

model, analogous to the classical circuit model. Each quantum circuit consists of unitary and measurement gates. Unitary gates can be applied to one and more

---

[1] Normally Hilbert space is defined with additional conditions which we are not concerned with in this paper.

qubits. In a certain kind of multiple qubit gates, which are called *controlled* gates, there is one or more control qubits and one or more target qubits. Depending on the value of the control qubit, a unitary gate is applied to the target qubit. Controlled-X (or *CNot*) and *Toffoli* [22, p. 29] gates are examples of controlled gates. Quantum circuits are normally described in the following way: single wires represent qubits, double wires represent classical bits. Single gates and measurement gates are depicted with squares, whereas controlled gates are shown with a point representing the control qubit and a circle depicting the target qubit with a vertical wire connecting them.

The *stabilizer* formalism is a useful scheme which characterises a small but important part of quantum mechanics. The core idea of the stabilizer formalism is to represent certain quantum states, which are called *stabilizer states*, with their *stabilizer group*, instead of an exponential number of complex amplitudes. For an n-qubit quantum stabilizer state $|\varphi\rangle$, the stabilizer group is defined by $Stab(|\varphi\rangle) = \{S | S |\varphi\rangle = +1 |\varphi\rangle\}$. This group can be represented elegantly by its n generators in the Pauli group (i.e P^n for P in Figure 1). Several algorithms have been developed for specifying and manipulating stabilizer states using group representation of quantum states, see [1]. Importantly, the effect of *Clifford Operators* (members of the normaliser of Pauli group, known as Clifford group) on stabilizer states can be simulated by a polynomial time algorithm. Consequently, we have the following important theorem which guarantees stabilizer states can be specified in polynomial space and certain operations and measurement can be done in polynomial time:

Theorem 1. *(Gottesman-Knill, [22, p. 464]) Any quantum computation which consists of only the following components:*

1. *State preparation, Hadamard gates, Phase gates, Controlled-Not gates and Pauli gates.*
2. *Measurement gates.*
3. *Classical control conditions on the outcomes of measurements.*

can be efficiently simulated on a classical computer.

The *density operator* is an alternative way of describing a quantum state where we need to deal with uncertainty. For instance, an ensemble of a quantum state $\{(|\phi_i\rangle, p_i)\}$, where p_is are probabilities, can be represented by the following density operator:

$$\rho := \sum_i p_i |\phi_i\rangle \langle\phi_i|$$

where $|\phi_i\rangle \langle\phi_i|$ denote outer product. Density operators are *positive* and *Hermitian*, meaning they satisfy $|\varphi\rangle$: $\langle\varphi| \rho |\varphi\rangle \geq 0$ and $\rho^\dagger = \rho$ († denotes transpose of the complex conjugate) respectively. Also a composite quantum system can be elegantly described in the language of density operators. In particular, one can obtain a *reduced* density operator by applying a *partial trace* operation on the density operator of a composite system, see [22, p. 105].

Superoperators are linear transforms on the space of density operators. Note that for an n-qubit system, the space of density operators has dimension of 2^{2n}.

Quantum information systems can be abstracted using superoperators. In the present paper, we take advantage of the linearity of superoperators: a superoperator is uniquely defined by its action on the elements of a *basis* of the space on which it acts, which in our case is a space of density operators. We can therefore check equality of superoperators by checking that for a given basis element as input, they produce the same output. In this paper, we are interested in systems which are in the stabilizer formalism. The following result [16] explicitly constructs a basis for the space of density operators which only consists of stabilizer states and hence it can be used in our equivalence checking technique.

Theorem 2. *The space of density operators for n-qubit states, considered as a $(2^n)^2$-dimensional real vector space, has a basis consisting of density matrices of n-qubit stabilizer states.*

Equality test: Another useful property of stabilizer states is that there is an efficient way of checking whether two stabilizer states are equal. One may test equality by using an algorithm for inner product of two states as in [1]. However, in [4] a novel approach is introduced which checks the linear dependence of stabilizer generators of two states. This is possible using polynomial time algorithms for obtaining stabilizer normal forms, introduced in [5]. Let $|\phi\rangle$ and $|\psi\rangle$ be stabilizer states and $Stab(|\phi\rangle)$, $Stab(|\psi\rangle)$ be their stabilizer groups, it can be easily seen that:

$$|\phi\rangle = |\psi\rangle \iff Stab(|\phi\rangle) = Stab(|\psi\rangle)$$

Therefore it suffices to show that $Stab(|\phi\rangle) \subseteq Stab(|\psi\rangle)$ and $Stab(|\phi\rangle) \supseteq Stab(|\psi\rangle)$, using independence checking approach, which results in the following proposition, proved in [4].

Proposition 1. *There is a polynomial time algorithm which decides for any stabilizer states $|\phi\rangle$ and $|\psi\rangle$, whether or not $|\phi\rangle = |\psi\rangle$.*

3   Specification of Concurrent Quantum Protocols

In this section we present a concurrent language for specifying quantum protocols, based on CCS [21]. This is different from our previous work [4] since our focus now is on concurrent communicating quantum systems. We will, however, restrict attention to protocols that receive input at the beginning and produce output at the end of their execution, rather than considering more general continuous interaction. One reason to use this language is to illustrate how designing concurrent quantum protocols can be difficult and non intuitive compared to classical protocols. For example, quantum measurement is a destructive action and if it used wrongly between parallel processes, it can destroy the effect of the whole system. Our language is similar to qCCS. [27] Communication in our system is done using *synchronous message passing or handshaking*. This structure can be extended to describe *asynchronous* communication similar to the approach of *CCS*. However, there is another reason to consider synchronicity, namely the lack of *quantum memory*. Therefore a synchronous system is closer

```
p ::= t |    t || t

t ::= nil | c!x.t | c?x.t | a:= measure x . t | U(x) . t |
      newqubit x . t | input list . t | output list . t |
      if x then U(y) . t | match list then U(x) . t

list ::= x:val | list,x:val

val  ::= 0 | 1
```

Fig. 2. Syntax of the Concurrent Language

to the current technological level of development of quantum communication. The syntax of our language is summarised in Figure 2.

Here t || t denotes parallel composition of processes and . represents process prefixes, similar to CCS. Terminated process is represented by **nil**. Prefix **input** list defines the input state of a protocol and **output** list stands for the intended output of a protocol. Often for the output we need to deallocate qubits. In [23], allocation and deallocation of qubits is presented by assuming that there is an operating system which gives/reset access to a pool of qubits (i.e qubits are not created or destroyed). However in this paper, we don't make that assumption and therefore allocation/deallocation of qubits has the physical meaning of creating or applying partial trace operation on quantum states.

For sending and receiving classical and quantum bits we use prefixes c!x and c?x. Measurement is done using prefix a:=measure x, where the outcome of measuring qubit x is assigned to a classical variable a. Conditionals, **if** and **match** impose classical conditions on the system in order to apply particular unitaries. The classical values val correspond to classical bits 0 and 1.

4 Semantics of Quantum Protocols

In this section we explain how the semantics of our specification language can be understood using superoperators. We apply π-calculus style reduction rules to our concurrent syntax in order to derive sequential interleavings, removing all communication and parallel composition. Finally, inspired by the semantics of Selinger's *quantum programming language (QPL)* [23], we argue that each sequential interleaving is equivalent to a QPL program, and thus can be characterised by a *superoperator*.

The reduction rules are in Figure 3. Here α denotes prefixes other than communication (i.e. not $c!x$ or $c?x$). Structural congruence is defined as associativity and commutativity of parallel composition, similarly to π-calculus, and is denoted by $\equiv$. Finally, τ represents the silent action and substitution of v with x is denoted by $[v/x]$. Using these rules, the transition graph for a concurrent process is a tree, because we do not have any form of loop or recursion, in which *interleavings* are represented by paths from the root to the leaves. For a protocol P, each interleaving $i \in \Im(P)$ (i.e. the set of all interleavings of P), can

$$\frac{P \equiv P' \ P' \xrightarrow{\alpha} Q' \ Q \equiv Q'}{P \xrightarrow{\alpha} Q} \quad \text{\scriptsize R-Cong} \qquad\qquad \alpha.P \xrightarrow{\alpha} P \quad \text{\scriptsize R-Act}$$

$$c!v.P \parallel c?x.Q \xrightarrow{\tau} P \parallel Q[v/x] \quad \text{\scriptsize R-Com} \qquad \frac{P \xrightarrow{\alpha} P'}{P \parallel Q \xrightarrow{\alpha} P' \parallel Q} \quad \text{\scriptsize R-Par}$$

Fig. 3. Reduction Rules

be translated to a QPL program, whose semantics is defined by a superoperator [23]. In this setting we assume that the input expression can be placed at the beginning of i, and only used once. Similarly, the output expression occurs at the end of each i, where we stop interpreting sequential interleavings. The sequential QPL program obtained in this way contains measurement operators which, when simulated, may generate branching behaviour due to quantum randomness. The semantics of QPL merges these branches by calculating a weighted sum of the density matrix representations of their final output quantum states. In the stabilizer formalism we cannot calculate these weighted sums in general, so instead we require that all of the final output quantum states are equal and hence the weighted sum becomes trivial. We further restrict our attention to protocols that are *functional* in the sense of computing a deterministic input-output relation despite their internal non-determinism due to concurrency and quantum randomness.

Definition 1 (Configuration). *Let $I^{\mathbb{Q}} : \mathbb{Q} \mapsto \mathbb{N}$ denote index of qubit variables in a quantum state. Configurations of a concurrent quantum program are defined by a tuples of the form $(\sigma, \kappa, |\phi\rangle)$, where σ represents classical variables assignment, κ represents channel variables assignment and $|\phi\rangle$ represents a quantum state corresponding to the qubit variables mapped by $I^{\mathbb{Q}}$.*

Definition 2. *A concurrent quantum protocol P is* functional *if*

1. *for a given quantum input $|\psi\rangle$ and a given interleaving $i \in \mathfrak{I}(P)$, all execution paths produce the same output quantum state; and*
2. *for a given quantum input $|\psi\rangle$, the unique output quantum state is the same across all interleavings.*

Proposition 2. *Any functional concurrent protocol P, specified with the language in Figure 2, defines a unique superoperator, which we denote by $[\![P]\!]$.*

Proof. The QPL programs corresponding to all of the interleavings of P map inputs to outputs in the same way, and therefore all define the same superoperator, which we take to be $[\![P]\!]$.

Remark 1. Quantum measurement in this paper is slightly different from QPL. Here the classical outcomes of measurement are assigned to classical variables for the modelling convenience. Nevertheless, one can easily translate our measurement expressions into QPL's if-then-else style form.

Remark 2. We *separate* classical and quantum data as in Definition 1 for a simpler implementation. Nonetheless, classical and quantum data can be mixed in a similar way as [23], using tuples of stabiliser states.

For example, the concurrent protocol

```
input x . a!x . nil | a?y . X(y) . nil |
newqubit u . b!u . nil | b?u . Z(u) . output u . nil
```

has the following interleavings, among others:

$$I_1 : input\ x; X(x); newqubit\ u; Z(u); output\ u$$
$$I_2 : input\ x; newqubit\ u; X(x); Z(u); output\ u$$
$$I_3 : newqubit\ u; input\ x; Z(u); X(x); output\ u.$$

5   Checking Equivalence of Quantum Protocols

In the following we define the equivalence between two concurrent protocols. In the classical theory of computation there are several ways of checking equivalence of concurrent systems using semantics namely: bisimulation based, automata based, game semantics and trace semantics. In this paper we focus on superoperator semantics where each interleaving of a system is described by a *superoperator*. We require that protocols be functional as in Definition 2.

In our system, we represent density matrices (mixed states) implicitly. This is done by interpreting protocols with *pure* stabilizer states on different runs of the protocol's model. However it may possible to work with mixed stabilizer states directly [1].

Having defined superoperators for concurrent quantum protocols, we explain how to verify the correctness of the protocols. We show that the specification and implementation of a protocol are equivalent by proving their corresponding supeoperators are equal. Knowing that supeoperators are linear, it suffices to execute the protocol for all elements in the stabilizer basis set of Theorem 2, to capture their effects on the input. This process is done in two phases: first functionality of specification and implementation is checked. Secondly equivalence of them will be established, in any case we require to schedule, interpret protocols in stabilizer formalism and apply equality tests on the reached states on every basis input.

The following algorithm describes how to do these two steps: for a concurrent program P, let $\Im(P, v)$ denote all possible interleavings of the program with initial state v (from basis set in the Theorem 2, denoted by $\mathfrak{B}$), produced by a scheduler and indexed by integers from 1 upwards. Let I_i denote the ith interleaving and suppose $StabSim^*(P, v, i)$ shows the final state given by that stabilizer simulation algorithm in [1] applied to I_i, on initial basis state v. Finally, let $EQ_S(v, w)$ be the equality test algorithm from Section 2. Then Figure 4 shows the equivalence checking algorithm for two concurrent programs P_1 and P_2, and establishes the following result.

```
for all v ∈ 𝔅 do
    for all i ∈ {1, 2} do
        |φ_i^v⟩ = StabSim*(P_i, v, 1)
        for all j ∈ ℑ(P_i, v) − {1} do
            if ¬EQ_S(StabSim*(P_i, v, j), |φ_i^v⟩) then
                return P_i non-functional
            end if
        end for
    end for
    if ¬EQ_S(|φ_1^v⟩, |φ_2^v⟩) then
        return P_1 ≇ P_2
    end if
end for
return P_1 ≅ P_2
```

Fig. 4. Algorithm for checking equivalence of concurrent protocols

Proposition 3. *Given two functional concurrent quantum protocols, which only use operations in the stabilizer formalism, one can systematically decide whether they are equivalent with respect to their superoperator semantics on every possible input, by iteration on the stabilizer basis.*

Proposition 4. *Checking equivalence of concurrent quantum protocols has overall (time) complexity of $O(N\,2^{2n}poly(m + n))$, where n is the number of input qubits (basis size), m is the number of qubits inside a program (i.e those created by **newqbit**) and N is the number of interleavings of processes (where $N = \frac{(\sum_i^M n_i)!}{\prod_i^M (n_i!)}$ for M processes each having n_i atomic instructions).*

Remark 3. In classical computing, the equivalence checking problem or *implementation verification* of concurrent systems (where only the containment problem is considered, not the simulation problem), is *PSPACE-complete* (see [18] for details).

6   Examples

We have analysed a range of quantum protocols covering quantum communication, quantum fault-tolerance and quantum cryptography using our equivalence checking tool. In this section, we present two of the protocols we have verified. The remaining protocols that we have analysed, in particular, fault tolerant protocols such as one bit teleportation and remote CNOT as well as error correction protocols can be found at http://go.warwick.ac.uk/eardeshir/qec.

Teleportation [7]: The goal in this protocol is to *teleport* a quantum state from Alice to Bob without physically transferring qubits, using quantum entanglement. Before starting the communication between the two parties, Alice and Bob, an entangled pair is established and shared between them. Alice then entangles the input qubit with her half of the entangled qubit by applying a

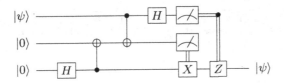

Fig. 5. Teleportation circuit

controlled-not gate followed by a Hadamard gate. She then measures her qubits and sends the classical outcome to the Bob. Depending on the four classical outcomes of Alice measurements, Bob applies certain X and Z operations and recovers the input state on his entangled qubit. The circuit which implements Quantum Teleportation is shown in the Figure 5.

However the circuit model does not provide a high level interface and does not capture the notion of *physical separation* between Alice and Bob. Through our concurrent language, we provide a programming interface and we can also describe the implementation of teleportation reflecting physical separation. The specification and implementation programs for teleportation in our concurrent language are shown in Figure 6.

```
//Implementation:
//Preparing EPR pair and sending to Alice and Bob:
newqubit y . newqubit z . H(y) . CNOT(y,z) . c!y . d!z . nil
|

//Alice's process:
(input x . c?y . CNOT(x,y) . H(x) . m := measure x . n := measure y.

b!m . b!n . nil
|

//Bob's process :
d?w . b?m . b?n . if n then X(w) . if m then Z(w) . output w . nil)
```

```
//Specification:
input x.output x.nil
```

Fig. 6. Teleportation: Specification and Implementation

Quantum Secret Sharing: This protocol was first introduced by Hillery et. al. [19]. The original problem of secret sharing involves an agent Alice sending a message to two agents Bob and Charlie, one of whom is dishonest. Alice doesn't know which one of the agents is dishonest, so she must encode the message so that Bob and Charlie must collaborate to retrieve it. For the quantum version of this protocol the three agents need to share a maximally entangled three-qubit state, called the *GHZ* state, prior to the execution of the protocol: $|000\rangle + |111\rangle$. In Figure 7, we assume that Charlie will end up with the original qubit (a variation of the protocol will allow Bob to end up with it). First, Alice entangles the input qubit with her entangled qubit from the GHZ state. Then Alice measures her qubits and sends the outcome to Charlie. Bob also measures his qubit and sends

```
// Preparing GHZ state and sending to Alice, Bob and Charlie:
newqubit a . newqubit b . newqubit c . H(a) . CNOT(a,b) . CNOT(b,c) .

d ! a . e ! b . f ! c . nil
|

//Alice, who wants to share her qubit:
(input x . d ? a . CNOT(x,a) . H(x) . m := measure x .

n:=measure a . t ! m . w ! n . nil
|

//Bob, who is chosen as a collaborator:
(e ? b . H(b) . o:=measure b . u ! o .  nil
|

//Charlie, who recovers the original quit from Alice:
f ? c . t ? m . w ? n . u ? o .

if o then Z(c) . if m then X(c) . if n then Z(c) . output c . nil))
```

Fig. 7. Secret Sharing Implementation. The specification is the same as Teleportation.

the outcome to Charlie. Finally, Charlie is able to retrieve the original qubit once he has access to the bits from Alice and Bob. The specification of secret sharing is similar to teleportation, expressed in Figure 6. The security of this protocol is a consequence of *no-cloning* theorem and is discussed in [19]. The specification for this protocol is the same as for teleportation.

We conclude with some final remarks. First, we can easily add more inputs to each of our protocols, which means that we are checking e.g. teleportation of one qubit in the presence of entanglement with other qubits. This follows from linearity, but it is never explicitly stated in standard presentations of teleportation. Second, we can model different implementations of a protocol, e.g. by changing the amount of concurrency. These differences are invisible at the level of circuit diagrams.

7   Equivalence Checker and Experimental Results

We have implemented a concurrent equivalence checker in Java [3]. The parser for the concurrent language is produced using SableCC [15]. The input of this tool is a concurrent protocol as described in Section 3. The *scheduler* generates all possible interleavings arising from execution of concurrent protocols. Each interleaving on a given input basis is passed to the interpreter which interprets programs using the Aaronson-Gottesman algorithm. The verification procedure consists of two steps. First *functionality* will be checked for a given input protocol and then, equivalence of two protocols will be determined. Both steps use the equality test algorithm in Section 2. The experimental results of verification of protocols based on the models presented in Section 6 and in [3], are summarized in the Table 8. Note that the specification of error corrections and Z/X-teleportation are the same as Figure 6, whereas remote CNOT's are specified by a single application of CNOT gate on two qubit inputs. The tool was run on a 2.5GHz Intel Core i3 machine with 4GB RAM. We would like to compare our results with those produced by the model checker QMC, but we have not been successful in running all the examples. This is partly because QMC is based on a different approach to verification i.e, temporal logic model checking, rather than equivalence checking. The tool Quantomatic is not a fully automatic tool, therefore we were not able to provide a comparison with case studies in that tool as well. The experimental results show how concurrency affects quantum systems. Not surprisingly, with more sharing of entanglement and increased classical and quantum communication, we have to deal with a larger number of interleavings. We have verified (Figure 8) sequential models of protocols in our current and previous tools [4]. Because of the complex structure of measurements in the five qubit code, we were not able to model this protocol in the sequential equivalence checker. The scheduler in our previous tool is slower than the one in our current work. This is because we were building program graphs for extracting schedules, whereas in this work schedules are directly obtained from abstract syntax tree. Comparing the results in Figure 8 shows that sequential models are analysed more quickly because they do not deal with concurrency. However, error correction protocols are inherently sequential, so their sequential and concurrent models are very similar and produce similar results.

Protocol	No. Interleaving	CM	No. Branch	SM	SEC
Teleportation	400	343	16	39	43
Dense Coding	100	120	4	22	30
Bit flip code	16	62	16	60	61
Phase flip code	16	63	16	61	62
Five qubit code	64	500	64	451	*
X-Teleportation	32	63	8	18	25
Z-Teleportation	72	78	8	19	27
Remote CNOT	78400	12074	64	112	140
Remote CNOT(A)	23040	4882	64	123	156
Quantum Secret Sharing	88480	13900	32	46	60

Fig. 8. Experimental results of equivalence checking of quantum protocols. The columns headed by CM and SM show the results of verification of concurrent and sequential models of protocols in the current tool. Column SEC shows verification times for sequential models in our previous tool [4]. The number of branches for SM and SEC models are the same. Times are in milliseconds.

8   Related Work

In recent years there have been several approaches to the formal analysis of quantum information systems. In this section we review some of the work that is most relevant to this paper.

We have already mentioned the QMC system. QMC checks properties in *Quantum Computation Tree Logic (QCTL)* [6] on models which lie within the stabilizer formalism. It can be used to check some protocols in a process-oriented style similar to that of the present paper; however, it simulates the protocols on *all* stabilizer states as inputs, not just the smaller set of stabilizer states that form a basis for the space of density matrices, and is therefore less efficient.

Our previous work [4] uses a similar approach to the present paper, but limited to sequential protocols. It therefore lacks the ability to explore, for a given protocol, different models with different degrees of concurrency.

Process calculus can also be used to analyse quantum systems. Gay and Nagarajan introduced CQP [17] based on the π-calculus; bisimulation for CQP has been developed and applied by Davidson *et al.* [10,9]. Ying *et al.* have developed qCCS [27] based on classical CCS, and studied its theory of bisimulation [14]. These are theoretical investigations which have not yet produced tools.

Wille *et al.* [26] consider two reversible circuits and then check their equivalence with respect to a target functionality (specification). To this end, techniques based on Boolean SAT and Quantum Binary Decision Diagrams [25] have been used. However, these methods are only applicable to quantum circuits with classical inputs/outputs.

Abramsky and Coecke [2] have developed diagrammatic reasoning techniques for quantum systems, based on a category-theoretic formulation of quantum mechanics. Quantomatic [12] is a tool based on this formalism, which uses graph rewriting in order to reason about quantum systems. The interface of Quantomatic is graphical, in contrast to our tool which uses a programming language syntax. Also, our tool verifies quantum protocols in a fully automatic way, whereas Quantomatic is a semi-automatic tool which needs a considerable amount of user intervention (see [13] for an example and discussion).

9 Conclusions and Future work

We have presented a technique and a tool for the verification of concurrent quantum protocols, using equivalence checking. In our work, we require that a concurrent protocol computes a function, in the sense that, (1) each interleaving yields a deterministic input-output relation; and (2) all interleavings yield the same input-output relation. The semantics of each interleaving of a quantum protocol is defined by a *superoperator*, which is a *linear* transformation from a protocol's input space to its output space. In particular, since superoperators are linear, we can analyse the behaviour of a concurrent protocol on arbitrary inputs using a suitable stabilizer basis [16]. This enables us to reduce the problem of checking equivalence over a continuum of quantum states to a tractable problem of checking equivalence over a discrete set of states. We have presented results comparing the execution times of three approaches to verification: (1) analysis of concurrent models; (2) analysis of sequentialised models with the concurrent equivalence checker; and (3) analysis of sequential models with our previous sequential equivalence checker [4].

In this work we are not able to analyse algorithms with non-stabilizer elements, like Shor's and Grover's algorithm. Also, continuously running protocols with input/output at intermediate points, need a more general notion of equivalence such as bisimulation. And of course our tool cannot be used directly when the correctness of protocols can not be specified as an equivalence, such as the security property of QKD. Nevertheless, our tool has been successfully applied to a range of examples as shown in Figure 8.

One area for future work is extending the scope of our tool to go beyond the stabilizer formalism. There are number of cases studied in [1] which involve non-stabilizer states and operations. We should be able to extend our techniques in a straightforward way, if the number of non-stabilizer operations is limited.

A more comprehensive modelling language e.g. implementing functional features, as well as improvement of the classical aspects of our tool, is highly desirable. Another area for research is extending our equivalence checking technique to other quantum modelling languages, such as CQP or qCCS. It would be interesting to investigate whether the bisimulation relations in [10] or [14] can be automated. In this paper, we have only considered an interleaving model of concurrency. Of course, one could consider other models of concurrency, for example true concurrency, and see whether it can be characterized by superoperators.

Finally, it will be interesting to develop a stabilizer based technique for analysis of security protocols such as QKD.

References

1. Aaronson, S., Gottesman, D.: Improved simulation of stabilizer circuits. Phys. Rev. A 70, 052328 (2004)
2. Abramsky, S., Coecke, B.: A categorical semantics of quantum protocols. In: Proceedings of the 19th Annual IEEE Symposium on Logic in Computer Science, pp. 415–425 (2004)
3. Ardeshir-Larijani, E.: Quantum equivalence checker (2013), http://go.warwick.ac.uk/eardeshir/qec
4. Ardeshir-Larijani, E., Gay, S.J., Nagarajan, R.: Equivalence checking of quantum protocols. In: Piterman, N., Smolka, S.A. (eds.) TACAS 2013. LNCS, vol. 7795, pp. 478–492. Springer, Heidelberg (2013)
5. Audenaert, K.M.R., Plenio, M.B.: Entanglement on mixed stabilizer states: normal forms and reduction procedures. New Journal of Physics 7(1), 170 (2005)
6. Baltazar, P., Chadha, R., Mateus, P.: Quantum computation tree logic—model checking and complete calculus. International Journal of Quantum Information 6(2), 219–236 (2008)
7. Bennett, C.H., Brassard, G., Crépeau, C., Jozsa, R., Peres, A., Wootters, W.K.: Teleporting an unknown quantum state via dual classical and Einstein-Podolsky-Rosen channels. Phys. Rev. Lett. 70, 1895–1899 (1993)
8. Calderbank, A.R., Shor, P.W.: Good quantum error-correcting codes exist. Phys. Rev. A 54, 1098–1105 (1996)
9. Davidson, T.A.S., Gay, S.J., Nagarajan, R., Puthoor, I.V.: Analysis of a quantum error correcting code using quantum process calculus. EPTCS 95, 67–80 (2012)
10. Davidson, T.A.S.: Formal Verification Techniques Using Quantum Process Calculus. PhD thesis, University of Warwick (2011)

11. de Riedmatten, H., Marcikic, I., Tittel, W., Zbinden, H., Collins, D., Gisin, N.: Long distance quantum teleportation in a quantum relay configuration. Physical Review Letters 92(4), 047904 (2004)
12. Dixon, L., Duncan, R.: Graphical reasoning in compact closed categories for quantum computation. Annals of Mathematics and Artificial Intelligence 56(1), 23–42 (2009)
13. Duncan, R., Lucas, M.: Verifying the Steane code with quantomatic. arXiv:1306.4532 (2013)
14. Feng, Y., Duan, R., Ying, M.: Bisimulation for quantum processes. In: Proceedings of the 38th Annual ACM SIGPLAN-SIGACT Symposium on Principles of Programming Languages, pp. 523–534. ACM (2011)
15. Gagnon, E.: SableCC, an object-oriented compiler framework. Master's thesis, School of Computer Science, McGill University (1998)
16. Gay, S.J.: Stabilizer states as a basis for density matrices. arXiv:1112.2156 (2011)
17. Gay, S.J., Nagarajan, R.: Communicating Quantum Processes. In: Proceedings of the 32nd ACM SIGPLAN-SIGACT Symposium on Principles of Programming Languages, pp. 145–157. ACM (2005)
18. Harel, D., Kupferman, O., Vardi, M.Y.: On the complexity of verifying concurrent transition systems. Information and Computation 173(2), 143–161 (2002)
19. Hillery, M., Bužek, V., Berthiaume, A.: Quantum secret sharing. Phys. Rev. A 59, 1829–1834 (1999)
20. Mayers, D.: Unconditional Security in Quantum Cryptography. Journal of the ACM 48(3), 351–406 (2001)
21. Milner, R.: Communication and concurrency. Prentice Hall (1989)
22. Nielsen, M.A., Chuang, I.L.: Quantum Computation and Quantum Information. Cambridge University Press (2000)
23. Selinger, P.: Towards a quantum programming language. Mathematical Structures in Computer Science 14(4), 527–586 (2004)
24. Shor, P.W.: Fault-tolerant quantum computation. In: Proceedings of the 37th Annual Symposium on Foundations of Computer Science, FOCS 1996. IEEE Computer Society, Washington, DC (1996)
25. Viamontes, G.F., Markov, I.L., Hayes, J.P.: Quantum Circuit Simulation. Springer (2009)
26. Wille, R., Grosse, D., Miller, D., Drechsler, R.: Equivalence checking of reversible circuits. In: 39th International Symposium on Multiple-Valued Logic, pp. 324–330 (2009)
27. Ying, M., Feng, Y., Duan, R., Ji, Z.: An algebra of quantum processes. ACM Trans. Comput. Logic 10(3), 19:1–19:36 (2009)

Computing Conditional Probabilities in Markovian Models Efficiently[*]

Christel Baier, Joachim Klein, Sascha Klüppelholz, and Steffen Märcker

Institute for Theoretical Computer Science
Technische Universität Dresden, Germany

Abstract. The fundamentals of probabilistic model checking for Markovian models and temporal properties have been studied extensively in the past 20 years. Research on methods for computing conditional probabilities for temporal properties under temporal conditions is, however, comparably rare. For computing conditional probabilities or expected values under ω-regular conditions in Markov chains, we introduce a new transformation of Markov chains that incorporates the effect of the condition into the model. For Markov decision processes, we show that the task to compute maximal reachability probabilities under reachability conditions is solvable in polynomial time, while it was conjectured to be computationally hard. Using adaptions of known automata-based methods, our algorithm can be generalized for computing the maximal conditional probabilities for ω-regular events under ω-regular conditions. The feasibility of our algorithms is studied in two benchmark examples.

1 Introduction

Probabilistic model checking has become a prominent technique for the quantitative analysis of systems with stochastic phenomena. Tools like PRISM [20] or MRMC [18] provide powerful probabilistic model checking engines for Markovian models and temporal logics such as probabilistic computation tree logic (PCTL) for discrete models and its continuous-time counterpart CSL (continuous stochastic logic) or linear temporal logic (LTL) as formalism to specify complex path properties. The core task for the quantitative analysis is to compute the probability of some temporal path property or the expected value of some random variable. For finite-state Markovian model with discrete probabilities, this task is solvable by a combination of graph algorithms, matrix-vector operations and methods for solving linear equation systems or linear programming techniques [25,9,15,7]. Although probabilistic model checking is a very active research topic and many researchers have suggested sophisticated methods e.g. to tackle the state explosion problem or to provide algorithms for the analysis of infinite-state

---

[*] This work was in part funded by the DFG through the CRC 912 HAEC, the cluster of excellence cfAED, the project QuaOS, the DFG/NWO-project ROCKS, and by the ESF young researcher group IMData 100098198, and the EU-FP-7 grant 295261 (MEALS).

E. Ábrahám and K. Havelund (Eds.): TACAS 2014, LNCS 8413, pp. 515–530, 2014.

stochastic models or probabilistic games, there are important classes of properties that are not directly supported by existing probabilistic model checkers. Among these are *conditional probabilities* that are well-known in probability theory and statistics, but have been neglected by the probabilistic model checking community. Exceptions are [1,2] where PCTL has been extended by a conditional probability operator and recent approaches for discrete and continuous-time Markov chains and patterns of path properties with multiple time- and cost-bounds [13,17].

The usefulness of conditional probabilities for anonymization protocols has been illustrated in [1,2]. Let us provide here some more intuitive examples that motivate the study of conditional probabilities. For systems with unreliable components one might ask for the conditional probability to complete a task successfully within a given deadline, under the condition that no failure will occur that prevents the completion of the task. If multiple tasks $\theta_1, \ldots, \theta_k$ have to be completed, assertions on the conditional probability or the conditional costs to complete task θ_i, under the condition that some other task θ_j will be completed successfully might give important insights on how to schedule the tasks without violating some service-level agreements. For another example, the conditional expected energy requirements for completing a task, under the condition that a certain utility value can be guaranteed, can provide useful insights for the design of power management algorithms. Conditional probabilities can also be useful for assume-guarantee-style reasoning. In these cases, assumptions on the stimuli of the environment can be formalized by a path property ψ and one might then reason about the quantitative system behavior using the conditional probability measure under the condition that ψ holds.

Given a purely stochastic system model $\mathcal{M}$ (e.g. a Markov chain), the analysis under conditional probability measures can be carried out using standard methods for unconditional probabilities, as we can simply rely on the mathematical definition of the conditional probability for φ (called here the *objective*) under condition ψ:

$$\mathrm{Pr}_s^{\mathcal{M}}(\varphi \,|\, \psi) \;\;=\;\; \frac{\mathrm{Pr}_s^{\mathcal{M}}(\varphi \wedge \psi)}{\mathrm{Pr}_s^{\mathcal{M}}(\psi)}$$

where s is a state in $\mathcal{M}$ with $\mathrm{Pr}_s^{\mathcal{M}}(\psi) > 0$. If both the objective φ and the condition ψ are ω-regular path properties, e.g. specified by LTL formulas or some ω-automaton, then $\varphi \wedge \psi$ is again ω-regular, and the above quotient is computable with standard techniques. This approach has been taken by Andrés and van Rossum [1,2] for the case of discrete Markov chains and PCTL path formulas, where $\varphi \wedge \psi$ is not a PCTL formula, but a ω-regular property of some simple type if nested state formulas are viewed as atoms. Recently, an automata-based approach has been developed for continuous-time Markov chains and CSL path formulas built by cascades of the until-operator with time- and cost-bounds [13]. This approach has been adapted in [17] for discrete-time Markov chains and PCTL-like path formulas with multiple bounded until-operators.

For models that support both the representation of nondeterministic and probabilistic behaviors, such as Markov decision processes (MDPs), reasoning about (conditional) probabilities requires the resolution of the nondeterministic choices by means of *schedulers*. Typically, one is interested in guarantees that can be given even for worst-case scenarios. That is, we are interested in the maximal (or minimal) conditional probability for the objective φ under condition ψ when ranging over all schedulers. Unfortunately, there is no straightforward reduction to unconditional maximal (or minimal) probabilities, simply because extrema of quotients cannot be computed by the quotient of the extremal values of the numerator and the denominator. [1,2] present a model checking algorithm for MDP and PCTL extended by a conditional probability operator. The essential features are algorithms for computing the maximal or minimal conditional probabilities for the case where both the objective and the condition are given as PCTL path formulas. These algorithms rely on transformations of the given MDP into an acyclic one and the fact that for PCTL objectives and conditions optimal schedulers that are composed by two memoryless schedulers (so-called *semi history-independent* schedulers) exist. The rough idea is to consider all semi history-independent schedulers and compute the conditional probabilities for them directly. This method suffers from the combinatorial blow-up and leads to an exponential-time algorithm. [1,2] also present reduction and bounding heuristics to omit some semi history-independent schedulers, but these cannot avoid the exponential worst-case time complexity. We are not aware of an implementation of these methods.

Contribution. The theoretical main contribution is twofold. First, for discrete Markov chains we present an alternative approach that relies on a transformation where we switch from the original Markov chain $\mathcal{M}$ to a modified Markov chain $\mathcal{M}_\psi$ such that the conditional probabilities in $\mathcal{M}$ agree with the (unconditional) probabilities in $\mathcal{M}_\psi$ for all measurable path properties φ. That is, $\mathcal{M}_\psi$ only depends on the condition ψ, but not on the objective φ. Second, for MDPs we provide a polynomial-time algorithm for computing maximal conditional probabilities when both the objective φ and the condition ψ are reachability properties. (This task was suspected to be computationally hard in [2].) Moreover, we show that adaptions of known automata-based approaches are applicable to extend this method for ω-regular objectives and conditions. In both cases, the time complexity of our methods is roughly the same as for computing (extremal) unconditional probabilities for properties of the form $\varphi \wedge \psi$.

Outline. Section 2 summarizes the relevant concepts of Markov chains and MDPs. The theoretical foundations of our approach will be presented for Markov chains in Sections 3 for MDPs in Section 4. Section 5 reports on experimental results. Section 6 contains some concluding remarks. Omitted proofs and other additional material can be found in the technical report [6].

2   Preliminaries

We briefly summarize our notations used for Markov chains and Markov decision processes. Further details can be found in textbooks on probability theory and Markovian models, see e.g. [24,19,16].

Markov Chains. A Markov chain is a pair $\mathcal{M} = (S, P)$ where S is a countable set of states and $p : s \times s \to [0, 1]$ a function, called the transition probability function, such that $\sum_{s' \in S} P(s, s') = 1$ for each state s. Paths in $\mathcal{M}$ are finite or infinite sequences $s_0 \, s_1 \, s_2 \ldots$ of states built by transitions, i.e., $P(s_{i-1}, s_i) > 0$ for all $i \geq 1$. If $\pi = s_0 \, s_1 \ldots s_n$ is a finite path then $first(\pi) = s_0$ denotes the first state of π, and $last(\pi) = s_n$ the last state of π. The notation $first(\pi)$ will be used also for infinite paths. We refer to the value

$$\Pr(\pi) \;\; = \;\; \prod_{1 \leq i \leq n} P(s_{i-1}, s_i)$$

as the probability for π. The cylinder set $Cyl(\pi)$ is the set of all infinite paths ς where π is a prefix of ς. We write $FPaths(s)$ for the set of all finite paths π with $first(\pi) = s$. Similarly, $Paths(s)$ stands for the set of infinite paths starting in s.

Given a state s, the probability space induced by $\mathcal{M}$ and s is defined using classical measure-theoretic concepts. The underlying sigma-algebra is generated by the cylinder sets of finite paths. This sigma-algebra does not depend on s. We refer to the elements of this sigma-algebra as *(measurable) path events*. The probability measure $\Pr_s^{\mathcal{M}}$ is defined on the basis of standard measure extension theorems that yield the existence of a probability measure $\Pr_s^{\mathcal{M}}$ with $\Pr_s^{\mathcal{M}}\big(Cyl(\pi) \big) = \Pr(\pi)$ for all $\pi \in FPaths(s)$, while the cylinder sets of paths π with $first(\pi) \neq s$ have measure 0 under $\Pr_s^{\mathcal{M}}$.

Markov Decision Processes (MDPs). MDPs can be seen as a generalization of Markov chains where the operational behavior in a state s consists of a nondeterministic selection of an enabled action α, followed by a probabilistic choice of the successor state, given s and α. Formally, an MDP is a tuple $\mathcal{M} = (S, Act, P)$ where S is a finite set of states, Act a finite set of actions and $P : S \times Act \times S \to [0, 1]$ a function such that for all states $s \in S$ and $\alpha \in Act$:

$$\sum_{s' \in S} P(s, \alpha, s') \in \{0, 1\}$$

We write $Act(s)$ for the set of actions that are enabled in s, i.e., $P(s, \alpha, s') > 0$ for some $s' \in S$. For technical reasons, we require that $Act(s) \neq \varnothing$ for all states s. State s is said to be *probabilistic* if $Act(s) = \{\alpha\}$ is a singleton, in which case we also write $P(s, s')$ rather than $P(s, \alpha, s')$. A *trap* state is a probabilistic state s with $P(s, s) = 1$. Paths are finite or infinite sequences $s_0 \, s_1 \, s_2 \ldots$ of states such that for all $i \geq 1$ there exists an action α_i with $P(s_{i-1}, \alpha_i, s_i) > 0$. (For our purposes, the actions are irrelevant in paths.) Several notations that have been introduced for Markov chains can now be adapted for Markov decision processes, such as $first(\pi)$, $FPaths(s)$, $Paths(s)$.

Reasoning about probabilities for path properties in MDPs requires the selection of an initial state and the resolution of the nondeterministic choices between the possible transitions. The latter is formalized via *schedulers*, often also called policies or adversaries, which take as input a finite path and select an action to be executed. For the purposes of this paper, it suffices to consider deterministic, possibly history-dependent schedulers, i.e., partial functions $\mathfrak{S} : FPaths \to Act$ such that $\mathfrak{S}(\pi) \in Act\big(last(\pi)\big)$ for all finite paths π. Given a scheduler $\mathfrak{S}$, an $\mathfrak{S}$-*path* is any path that might arise when the nondeterministic choices in $\mathcal{M}$ are resolved using $\mathfrak{S}$. Thus, $\pi = s_0 s_1 \dots s_n$ is an $\mathfrak{S}$-path iff $P\big(s_{k-1}, \mathfrak{S}(s_0 s_1 \dots s_{k-1}), s_k\big) > 0$ for all $1 \leq k \leq n$. In this case, $\mathfrak{S}[\pi]$ denotes the scheduler "$\mathfrak{S}$ after π" given by $\mathfrak{S}[\pi](t_0 t_1 \dots t_k) = \mathfrak{S}(s_0 s_1 \dots s_n t_1 \dots t_k)$ if $s_n = t_0$. The behavior of $\mathfrak{S}[\pi]$ for paths not starting in s_n is irrelevant. The probability of π under $\mathfrak{S}$ is the product of the probabilities of its transitions:

$$\mathrm{Pr}^{\mathfrak{S}}(\pi) \;=\; \prod_{i=0}^{n-1} P\big(s_{k-1}, \mathfrak{S}(s_0 s_1 \dots s_{k-1}), s_k\big)$$

Infinite $\mathfrak{S}$-paths are defined accordingly.

For a pointed MDP $(\mathcal{M}, s_{init})$, i.e. an MDP as before with some distinguished initial state $s_{init} \in S$, the behavior of $(\mathcal{M}, s_{init})$ under $\mathfrak{S}$ is purely probabilistic and can be formalized by an infinite tree-like Markov chain $\mathcal{M}_s^{\mathfrak{S}}$ where the states are the finite $\mathfrak{S}$-paths starting in s. The probability measure $\mathrm{Pr}_{\mathcal{M},s}^{\mathfrak{S}}$ for measurable sets of the infinite paths in the Markov chain $\mathcal{M}_s^{\mathfrak{S}}$, can be transferred to infinite $\mathfrak{S}$-paths in $\mathcal{M}$ starting in s. Thus, if Φ is a path event then $\mathrm{Pr}_{\mathcal{M},s}^{\mathfrak{S}}(\Phi)$ denotes its probability under scheduler $\mathfrak{S}$ for starting state s. For a worst-case analysis of a system modeled by an MDP $\mathcal{M}$, one ranges over all initial states and all schedulers (i.e., all possible resolutions of the nondeterminism) and considers the maximal or minimal probabilities for Φ. If Φ represents a desired path property, then $\mathrm{Pr}_{\mathcal{M},s}^{\min}(\Phi) = \inf_{\mathfrak{S}} \mathrm{Pr}_{\mathcal{M},s}^{\mathfrak{S}}(\Phi)$ is the probability for Φ in $\mathcal{M}$ that can be guaranteed even for the worst-case scenarios. Similarly, if Φ stands for a bad (undesired) path event, then $\mathrm{Pr}_{\mathcal{M},s}^{\max}(\Phi) = \sup_{\mathfrak{S}} \mathrm{Pr}_{\mathcal{M},s}^{\mathfrak{S}}(\Phi)$ is the least upper bound that can be guaranteed for the likelihood of Φ in $\mathcal{M}$.

Temporal-Logic Notations, Path Properties. Throughout the paper, we suppose that the reader is familiar with ω-automata and temporal logics. See e.g. [8,14,5]. We often use LTL- and CTL-like notations and identify LTL-formulas with the set of infinite words over the alphabet 2^{AP} that are models for the formulas, where AP denotes the underlying set of atomic propositions. For the Markov chain or MDP $\mathcal{M}$ under consideration we suppose then that they are extended by a labeling function $L : S \to 2^{AP}$, with the intuitive meaning that precisely the atomic propositions in $L(s)$ hold for state s. At several places, we will use temporal state and path formulas where single states or sets of states in $\mathcal{M}$ are used as atomic propositions with the obvious meaning. Similarly, if $\mathcal{M}$ arises by some product construction, (sets of) local states will be treated as atomic propositions. For the interpretation of LTL- or CTL-like formulas in $\mathcal{M}$, the probability annotations (as well as the action labels in case of an MDP) are ignored and $\mathcal{M}$ is viewed as an ordinary Kripke structure.

By a *path property* we mean any language consisting of infinite words over 2^{AP}. Having in mind temporal logical specifications, we use the logical operators $\vee, \wedge, \neg$ for union, intersection and complementation of path properties. A path property Φ is said to be measurable if the set of infinite paths π in $\mathcal{M}$ satisfying Φ is a path event, i.e., an element of the induced sigma-algebra. Indeed, all

ω-regular path properties are measurable [25]. We abuse notations and identify measurable path properties and the induced path event. Thus,

$$\mathrm{Pr}^{\mathfrak{S}}_{\mathcal{M},s}(\varphi) \quad = \quad \mathrm{Pr}^{\mathfrak{S}}_{\mathcal{M},s}\left(\left\{\, \pi \in Paths(s) \, : \, \pi \models \varphi \,\right\}\right)$$

denotes the probability for φ under scheduler $\mathfrak{S}$ and starting state s.

Assumptions. For the methods proposed in the following sections, we suppose that the state space of the given Markov chain and the MDP is finite and that all transition probabilities are rational.

3   Conditional Probabilities in Markov Chains

In what follows, let $\mathcal{M} = (S, P)$ be a finite Markov chain as in Section 2 and ψ an ω-regular condition. We present a transformation $\mathcal{M} \rightsquigarrow \mathcal{M}_\psi$ such that the conditional probabilities $\mathrm{Pr}^{\mathcal{M}}_s(\varphi \mid \psi)$ agree with the (unconditional) probabilities $\mathrm{Pr}^{\mathcal{M}_\psi}_{s_\psi}(\varphi)$ for all ω-regular objectives φ. Here, s is a state in $\mathcal{M}$ with $\mathrm{Pr}^{\mathcal{M}}_s(\psi) > 0$ and s_ψ the "corresponding" state in $\mathcal{M}_\psi$. We first treat the case where ψ is a reachability condition and then explain a generalization for ω-regular conditions.

Reachability Condition. Let $G \subseteq S$ be a set of goal states and $\psi = \lozenge G$. Intuitively, the Markov chain $\mathcal{M}_\psi$ arises from $\mathcal{M}$ by a monitoring technique that runs in parallel to $\mathcal{M}$ and operates in two modes. In the initial mode "before or at G", briefly called *before mode*, the attempt is to reach G by avoiding all states s with $s \not\models \exists \lozenge G$. The transition probabilities for the states in before mode are modified accordingly. As soon as G has been reached, $\mathcal{M}_\psi$ switches to the *normal mode* where $\mathcal{M}_\psi$ behaves as $\mathcal{M}$. In what follows, we write s^{bef} and s^{nor} for the copies of state s in the before and normal mode, respectively. For $V \subseteq S$, let $V^{bef} = \left\{s^{bef} : s \in V, s \models \exists \lozenge G\right\}$ the set of V-states where $\mathrm{Pr}^{\mathcal{M}}_s(\lozenge G)$ is positive and $V^{nor} = \left\{s^{nor} : s \in V\right\}$. The Markov chain $\mathcal{M}_\psi = (S_\psi, P_\psi)$ is defined as follows. The state space of $\mathcal{M}_\psi$ is $S_\psi = S^{bef} \cup S^{nor}$. For $s \in S \setminus G$ and $v \in S$ with $s \models \exists \lozenge G$ and $v \models \exists \lozenge G$:

$$P_\psi(s^{bef}, v^{bef}) \quad = \quad P(s, v) \cdot \frac{\mathrm{Pr}^{\mathcal{M}}_v(\lozenge G)}{\mathrm{Pr}^{\mathcal{M}}_s(\lozenge G)}$$

For $s \in G$, we define $P_\psi(s^{bef}, v^{nor}) = P(s, v)$, modeling the switch from before to normal mode. For the states in normal mode, the transition probabilities are given by $P_\psi(s^{nor}, v^{nor}) = P(s, v)$. In all other cases, $P_\psi(\cdot) = 0$. For the labeling with atomic propositions, we suppose that each state s in $\mathcal{M}$ and its copies s^{bef} and s^{nor} in $\mathcal{M}_\psi$ satisfy the same atomic propositions.

By applying standard arguments for finite Markov chains we obtain that $\mathrm{Pr}^{\mathcal{M}_\psi}_{s^{bef}}(\lozenge G^{bef}) = 1$ for all states s in $\mathcal{M}$ with $s \models \exists \lozenge G$. (This is a simple consequence of the fact that all states in S^{bef} can reach G^{bef}.) Thus, up to the switch from G to G^{bef}, the condition $\lozenge G$ (which we impose for $\mathcal{M}$) holds almost surely for $\mathcal{M}_\psi$. For each path property φ, there is a one-to-one correspondence between the infinite paths π in $\mathcal{M}$ with $\pi \models \varphi \wedge \Diamond G$ and the infinite paths π_ψ in $\mathcal{M}_\psi$ with $\pi_\psi \models \varphi$. More precisely, each path π_ψ in $\mathcal{M}_\psi$ induces a path $\pi_\psi|_\mathcal{M}$ in $\mathcal{M}$ by dropping the mode annotations. Vice versa, each path π in $\mathcal{M}$ can be augmented with mode annotations to obtain a path π_ψ in $\mathcal{M}_\psi$ with $\pi_\psi|_\mathcal{M} = \pi$, provided that π either contains some G-state or consists of states s with $s \models \exists \Diamond G$. This yields a one-to-one correspondence between the cylinder sets in $\mathcal{M}_\psi$ and the cylinder sets spanned by finite paths of $\mathcal{M}$ that never enter some state s with $s \not\models \exists \Diamond G$ without having visited G before.

Theorem 1 (Soundness of the transformation). *If Φ is a path event for $\mathcal{M}$ (i.e., a measurable set of infinite paths) then $\Phi|_\mathcal{M} = \{\pi_\psi : \pi \in \Phi, \pi \models \Diamond G \vee \Box \exists \Diamond G\}$ is measurable in $\mathcal{M}_\psi$. Moreover, for each s of $\mathcal{M}$ with $s \models \exists \Diamond G$:*

$$\mathrm{Pr}_s^\mathcal{M}(\Phi \mid \Diamond G) = \mathrm{Pr}_{s^{bef}}^{\mathcal{M}_\psi}(\Phi|_\mathcal{M})$$

Hence, $\mathrm{Pr}_s^\mathcal{M}(\varphi \mid \Diamond G) = \mathrm{Pr}_{s^{bef}}^{\mathcal{M}_\psi}(\varphi)$ for all measurable path properties φ.

Thus, once $\mathcal{M}_\psi$ has been constructed, conditional probabilities for arbitrary path properties in $\mathcal{M}$ can be computed by standard methods for computing unconditional probabilities in $\mathcal{M}_\psi$, with the same asymptotic costs. (The size of $\mathcal{M}_\psi$ is linear in the size of $\mathcal{M}$.) $\mathcal{M}_\psi$ can be constructed in time polynomial in the size of $\mathcal{M}$ as the costs are dominated by the computation of the reachability probabilities $\mathrm{Pr}_s^\mathcal{M}(\Diamond G)$. $\mathcal{M}_\psi$ can also be used to reason about the conditional expected value of a random function f on infinite paths in $\mathcal{M}$, as we have:

$$\mathsf{E}^\mathcal{M}(f \mid \Diamond G) = \mathsf{E}^{\mathcal{M}_\psi}\big(f_\psi \mid \Diamond(G^{bef} \cup G^{nor})\big)$$

where $f_\psi(\pi') = f(\pi'|_\mathcal{M})$ and $\mathsf{E}^\mathcal{N}(\cdot)$ denotes the expected-value operator in $\mathcal{N}$. An important instance is expected accumulated rewards to reach a certain set of states. See [6].

ω-regular conditions. Suppose now that the condition ψ is given by a deterministic ω-automaton $\mathcal{A}$ with, e.g., Rabin or Streett acceptance. To construct a Markov chain that incorporates the probabilities in $\mathcal{M}$ under the condition ψ, we rely on the standard techniques for the quantitative analysis of Markov chains against automata-specifications [26,5]. The details are straightforward, we just give a brief outline. First, we build the standard product $\mathcal{M} \otimes \mathcal{A}$ of $\mathcal{M}$ and $\mathcal{A}$, which is again a Markov chain. Let G be the union of the bottom strongly connected components C of $\mathcal{N} = \mathcal{M} \otimes \mathcal{A}$ that meet the acceptance condition of $\mathcal{A}$. Then, the probability $\mathrm{Pr}_s^\mathcal{M}(\psi)$ equals $\mathrm{Pr}_{\langle s, q_s \rangle}^\mathcal{N}(\Diamond G)$, where $\langle s, q_s \rangle$ is the state in $\mathcal{M} \otimes \mathcal{A}$ that "corresponds" to s. We then apply the transformation for $\mathcal{N} \rightsquigarrow \mathcal{N}_\psi$ as explained above and obtain that for all measurable path properties φ:

$$\mathrm{Pr}_s^\mathcal{M}(\varphi \mid \psi) = \mathrm{Pr}_{\langle s, q_s \rangle}^\mathcal{N}(\varphi \mid \Diamond G) = \mathrm{Pr}_{\langle s, q_s \rangle}^{\mathcal{N}_\psi}(\varphi)$$

for all states s in $\mathcal{M}$ where $\mathrm{Pr}_s^\mathcal{M}(\psi)$ is positive. This shows that the task to compute conditional probabilities for ω-regular conditions is solvable by algorithms for computing (unconditional) probabilities for ω-regular path properties.

4   Conditional Probabilities in Markov Decision Processes

We now consider the task to compute maximal conditional probabilities in MDPs. We start with the "core problem" where the objective and the condition are reachability properties. The general case of ω-regular objectives and conditions will be treated in Section 4.2.

4.1   Conditional Reachability Probabilities in MDPs

Let $(\mathcal{M}, s_{init})$ be a pointed MDP where $\mathcal{M} = (S, Act, P)$ and let $F, G \subseteq S$ such that $s_{init} \models \exists \Diamond G$, in which case $\mathrm{Pr}^{\max}_{\mathcal{M}, s_{init}}(\Diamond G) > 0$. The task is to compute

$$\max_{\mathfrak{S}} \ \mathrm{Pr}^{\mathfrak{S}}_{\mathcal{M}, s_{init}}(\Diamond F \,|\, \Diamond G) \ = \ \max_{\mathfrak{S}} \ \frac{\mathrm{Pr}^{\mathfrak{S}}_{\mathcal{M}, s_{init}}(\Diamond F \wedge \Diamond G)}{\mathrm{Pr}^{\mathfrak{S}}_{\mathcal{M}, s_{init}}(\Diamond G)}$$

where $\mathfrak{S}$ ranges over all schedulers for $\mathcal{M}$ such that $\mathrm{Pr}^{\mathfrak{S}}_{\mathcal{M}, s_{init}}(\Diamond G) > 0$. By the results of [1,2], there exists a scheduler $\mathfrak{S}$ maximizing the conditional probability for $\Diamond F$, given $\Diamond G$. (This justifies the use of max rather than sup.)

Only for simplicity, we assume that $F \cap G = \varnothing$. Thus, there are just two cases for the event $\Diamond F \wedge \Diamond G$: "either F before G, or G before F". We also suppose $s_{init} \notin F \cup G$ and that all states $s \in S$ are accessible from s_{init}.

Step 1: Normal form Transformation

We first present a transformation $\mathcal{M} \rightsquigarrow \mathcal{M}'$ such that the maximal conditional probability for "$\Diamond F$, given $\Diamond G$" agrees with the maximal conditional probability for "$\Diamond F'$, given $\Diamond G'$" in $\mathcal{M}'$ where F' and G' consist of trap states. This can be seen as some kind of normal form for maximal conditional reachability probabilities and relies on the following observation.

Lemma 1 (Scheduler improvement). *For each scheduler $\mathfrak{S}$ there is a scheduler $\mathfrak{T}$ such that for all states s with $\mathrm{Pr}^{\mathfrak{S}}_{\mathcal{M}, s}(\Diamond G) > 0$:*

(1) $\mathrm{Pr}^{\mathfrak{S}}_{\mathcal{M}, s}(\Diamond F \,|\, \Diamond G) \ \leq \ \mathrm{Pr}^{\mathfrak{T}}_{\mathcal{M}, s}(\Diamond F \,|\, \Diamond G)$

(2) $\mathrm{Pr}^{\mathfrak{T}[\pi]}_{\mathcal{M}, t}(\Diamond G) = \mathrm{Pr}^{\max}_{\mathcal{M}, t}(\Diamond G)$ *for all $t \in F$ and $\pi \in \Pi_{s \ldots t}$*

(3) $\mathrm{Pr}^{\mathfrak{T}[\pi]}_{\mathcal{M}, u}(\Diamond F) = \mathrm{Pr}^{\max}_{\mathcal{M}, u}(\Diamond F)$ *for all $u \in G$ and finite paths $\pi \in \Pi_{s \ldots u}$*

where $\Pi_{s \ldots u}$ denotes the set consisting of all finite paths $s_0 s_1 \ldots s_n$ in $\mathcal{M}$ with $s_0 = s$, $s_n = u$ and $\{s_0, s_1, \ldots, s_{n-1}\} \cap (F \cup G) = \varnothing$.

Recall that $\mathfrak{S}[\pi]$ denotes the scheduler "$\mathfrak{S}$ after π". The idea is that $\mathfrak{T}$ behaves as $\mathfrak{S}$ as long as neither F nor G has been reached. As soon as a G-state (resp. F-state) has been entered, $\mathfrak{T}$ mimics some scheduler that maximizes the probability to reach F (resp. G). This scheduler satisfies (2) and (3) by construction. Item (1) follows after some calculations (see [6]).

As a consequence of Lemma 1, for studying the maximal conditional probability for $\Diamond F$ given $\Diamond G$, it suffices to consider schedulers $\mathfrak{T}$ satisfying conditions (2) and (3). Let $\mathcal{M}'$ be the MDP that behaves as $\mathcal{M}$ as long as no state in F or G has been visited. After visiting an F-state t, $\mathcal{M}'$ moves probabilistically to a fresh goal state with probability $\mathrm{Pr}_{\mathcal{M},t}^{\max}(\Diamond G)$ or to a fail state with the remaining probability. Similarly, after visiting a G-state u, $\mathcal{M}'$ moves probabilistically to the goal state or to a new state *stop*. Formally, $\mathcal{M}' = (S', Act, P')$ where the state space of $\mathcal{M}'$ is $S' = S \cup T$ and

$$T = \{goal, stop, fail\}.$$

The transition probabilities in $\mathcal{M}'$ for the states in $S \setminus (F \cup G)$ agree with those in $\mathcal{M}$, i.e., $P'(s, \alpha, s') = P(s, \alpha, s')$ for all $s \in S \setminus (F \cup G)$, $s' \in S$ and $\alpha \in Act$. The states $t \in F$ and $u \in G$ are probabilistic in $\mathcal{M}'$ with the transition probabilities:

$$P'(t, goal) = \mathrm{Pr}_{\mathcal{M},t}^{\max}(\Diamond G) \qquad\qquad P'(u, goal) = \mathrm{Pr}_{\mathcal{M},u}^{\max}(\Diamond F)$$
$$P'(t, fail) = 1 - \mathrm{Pr}_{\mathcal{M},t}^{\max}(\Diamond G) \qquad\qquad P'(u, stop) = 1 - \mathrm{Pr}_{\mathcal{M},u}^{\max}(\Diamond F)$$

The three fresh states *goal*, *fail* and *stop* are trap states. Then, by Lemma 1:

Corollary 1 (Soundness of the normal form transformation). *For all states s in $\mathcal{M}$ with $s \models \exists \Diamond G$:*

$$\mathrm{Pr}_{\mathcal{M},s}^{\max}(\Diamond F \,|\, \Diamond G) = \mathrm{Pr}_{\mathcal{M}',s}^{\max}(\Diamond goal \,|\, \Diamond(goal \vee stop))$$

Optional simplification of $\mathcal{M}'$. Let W be the set of states w in $\mathcal{M}'$ such that for some scheduler $\mathfrak{S}$, the goal-state is reachable from w via some $\mathfrak{S}$-path, while the trap state *stop* will not be reached along $\mathfrak{S}$-paths from w. Then, all states in W can be made probabilistic with successors *goal* and *fail* and efficiently computable transition probabilities. This transformation of $\mathcal{M}'$ might yield a reduction of the reachable states, while preserving the maximal conditional probabilities for $\Diamond goal$, given $\Diamond(goal \vee stop)$. For details, see [6].

Step 2: Reduction to Ordinary Maximal Reachability Probabilities

We now apply a further transformation $\mathcal{M}' \rightsquigarrow \mathcal{M}_{\varphi|\psi}$ such that the maximal conditional probability for $\varphi = \Diamond goal$, given $\psi = \Diamond(goal \vee stop)$, in $\mathcal{M}'$ agrees with the maximal (unconditional) probability for $\Diamond goal$ in $\mathcal{M}_{\varphi|\psi}$.

Let us first sketch the ratio of this transformation. Infinite paths in $\mathcal{M}'$ that violate the condition ψ do not "contribute" to the conditional probability for $\Diamond goal$. The idea is now to "redistribute" their probabilities to all the paths satisfying the condition ψ. Speaking roughly, we aim to mimic a stochastic process that generates a sequence $\pi_0, \pi_1, \pi_2 \ldots$ of sample paths in $\mathcal{M}'$ starting in s_{init} until a path π_i is obtained where the condition ψ holds. To formalize this "redistribution procedure" by switching from $\mathcal{M}'$ to some new MDP $\mathcal{M}_{\varphi|\psi}$ we need some *restart mechanism* to discard generated prefixes of paths π_j violating ψ by returning to the initial state s_{init}, from which the next sample run π_{j+1} will be generated. Note that by discarding paths that do not satisfy ψ, the proportion of the paths satisfying $\varphi \wedge \psi$ and the paths satisfying ψ is not affected and almost surely a path satisfying ψ will be generated. Thus, the conditional probability for $\varphi \wedge \psi$ given ψ under some scheduler of the original MDP agrees with the (unconditional) probability for φ under the corresponding scheduler of the new MDP $\mathcal{M}_{\varphi|\psi}$.

The restart policy is obvious for finite paths that enter the trap state $fail$. Instead of staying in $fail$, we simply restart the computation by returning to the initial state s_{init}. The second possibility to violate ψ are paths that never enter one of the three trap states in T. To treat such paths we rely on well-known results for finite-state MDPs stating that for all schedulers $\mathfrak{S}$ almost all $\mathfrak{S}$-paths eventually enter an end component (i.e., a strongly connected sub-MDP), stay there forever and visit all its states infinitely often [11,12]. The idea is that we equip all states s that belong to some end component without any T-state with the restart-option, i.e., we add the nondeterministic alternative to return to the initial state s_{init}. To enforce that such end components will be left eventually by taking the restart-transition, one might impose strong fairness conditions for the schedulers in $\mathcal{M}_{\varphi|\psi}$. Such fairness assumptions are, however, irrelevant for maximal reachability conditions [3,4].

Let B be the set of (bad) states v such that there exists a scheduler $\mathfrak{S}$ that never visits one of the three trap states $goal$, $stop$ or $fail$ when starting in v:

$$v \in B \quad \text{iff} \quad \begin{cases} \text{there exists a scheduler } \mathfrak{S} \\ \text{such that } \mathrm{Pr}^{\mathfrak{S}}_{\mathcal{M}',v}(\Diamond T) = 0 \end{cases}$$

The MDP $\mathcal{M}_{\varphi|\psi} = (S', Act \cup \{\tau\}, P_{\varphi|\psi})$ has the same state space as the normal form MDP $\mathcal{M}'$. Its action set extends the action set of $\mathcal{M}'$ by a fresh action symbol τ for the restart-transitions. For the states $s \in S' \setminus B$ with $s \neq fail$, the new MDP $\mathcal{M}_{\varphi|\psi}$ behaves as $\mathcal{M}'$, i.e., $P_{\varphi|\psi}(s, \alpha, s') = P'(s, \alpha, s')$ for all $s \in S' \setminus (B \cup \{fail\})$, $\alpha \in Act$ and $s' \in S'$. The fresh action τ is not enabled in the states $s \in S' \setminus (B \cup \{fail\})$. For the fail-state, $\mathcal{M}_{\varphi|\psi}$ returns to the initial state, i.e., $P_{\varphi|\psi}(fail, \tau, s_{init}) = 1$ and $P_{\varphi|\psi}(fail, \tau, s') = 0$ for all states $s' \in S' \setminus \{s_{init}\}$. No other action than τ is enabled in $fail$. For the states $v \in B$, $\mathcal{M}_{\varphi|\psi}$ decides nondeterministically to behave as $\mathcal{M}$ or to return to the initial state s_{init}. That is, if $v \in B$, $\alpha \in Act$, $s' \in S'$ then $P_{\varphi|\psi}(v, \alpha, s') = P'(v, \alpha, s')$ and $P_{\varphi|\psi}(v, \tau, s_{init}) = 1$. In all remaining cases, we have $P_{\varphi|\psi}(v, \tau, \cdot) = 0$.

Paths in $\mathcal{M}'$ that satisfy $\Box B$ or that end up in $fail$, do not "contribute" to the conditional probability for $\Diamond goal$, given $\Diamond(goal \vee stop)$. Instead the probability for the infinite paths π with $\pi \in \Box B$ or $\pi \models \Diamond fail$ in $\mathcal{M}'$ are "distributed" to the probabilities for $\Diamond goal$ and $\Diamond stop$ when switching to conditional probabilities. This is mimicked by the restart-transitions to s_{init} in $\mathcal{M}_{\varphi|\psi}$.

Theorem 2 (Soundness of step 2). *For the initial state $s = s_{init}$, we have:*

$$\mathrm{Pr}^{\max}_{\mathcal{M}',s}(\Diamond goal \mid \Diamond(goal \vee stop)) = \mathrm{Pr}^{\max}_{\mathcal{M}_{\varphi|\psi},s}(\Diamond goal)$$

Algorithm and Complexity. As an immediate consequence of Theorem 2, the task to compute maximal conditional reachability probabilities in MDPs is reducible to the task to compute maximal ordinary (unconditional) reachability probabilities, which is solvable using linear programming techniques [24,7]. The size of the constructed MDP is linear in the size of $\mathcal{M}'$, which again is linear in the size of $\mathcal{M}$. The construction of $\mathcal{M}'$ and $\mathcal{M}_{\varphi|\psi}$ is straightforward. For $\mathcal{M}'$ we need to compute ordinary maximal reachability probabilities in $\mathcal{M}$. Using standard algorithms for the qualitative fragment of PCTL, the set B of bad states is computable by a graph analysis in polynomial time (see e.g. [5]). Thus, maximal conditional probabilities for reachability objectives and conditions can be computed in time polynomial in the size of $\mathcal{M}$.

4.2 Conditional Probabilities in MDPs for Other Events

Using standard automata-based techniques, our method can be generalized to deal with ω-regular properties for both the objective and the condition.

ω-regular objectives under reachability conditions. Using a standard automata-based approach, the suggested technique is also applicable to compute maximal conditional probabilities $\mathrm{Pr}^{\max}_{\mathcal{M},s}(\varphi \mid \Diamond G)$. Here, we deal with a deterministic ω-automaton $\mathcal{A}$ for φ and then compute the maximal conditional probabilities $\mathrm{Pr}^{\max}_{\mathcal{N},\langle s,q_s\rangle}(\Diamond F \mid \Diamond G)$ in the product-MDP $\mathcal{N} = \mathcal{M} \otimes \mathcal{A}$ where F is the union of all end components in $\mathcal{M} \otimes \mathcal{A}$ satisfying the acceptance condition of $\mathcal{A}$. Here, $\langle s, q_s\rangle$ denotes the state in $\mathcal{M} \otimes \mathcal{A}$ that "corresponds" to s.

(co-)safety conditions. If ψ is *regular co-safety condition* then we can use a representation of ψ by a deterministic finite automaton (DFA) $\mathcal{B}$, switch from $\mathcal{M}$ to the product-MDP $\mathcal{M} \otimes \mathcal{B}$ with the reachability condition stating that some final state of $\mathcal{B}$ should be visited. With slight modifications, an analogous technique is applicable for *regular safety conditions*, in which case we use a DFA for the bad prefixes of ψ. See [6].This approach is also applicable for MDPs with positive state rewards and if ψ is a reward-bounded reachability condition $\Diamond^{\leq r} a$.

ω-regular conditions. If the condition ψ and the objective φ are ω-regular then the task to compute $\mathrm{Pr}^{\max}_{\mathcal{M},s}(\varphi \mid \psi)$ is reducible to the task of computing maximal conditional probabilities for reachability objectives and some strong fairness condition ψ'. The idea is to simply use deterministic Streett automata $\mathcal{A}$ and $\mathcal{B}$ for φ and ψ and then to switch from $\mathcal{M}$ to the product-MDP $\mathcal{M} \otimes \mathcal{A} \otimes \mathcal{B}$. The condition ψ can then be replaced by $\mathcal{B}$'s acceptance condition. The goal set F of the objective $\Diamond F$ arises by the union of all end components in $\mathcal{M} \otimes \mathcal{A} \otimes \mathcal{B}$ where the acceptance conditions of both $\mathcal{A}$ and $\mathcal{B}$ hold.

It remains to explain how to compute $\mathrm{Pr}^{\max}_{\mathcal{M},s}(\varphi \mid \psi)$ where $\varphi = \Diamond F$ is a reachability objective and ψ is a strong fairness (i.e., Streett) condition, say:

$$\psi = \bigwedge_{1 \leq i \leq k} (\Box\Diamond R_i \to \Box\Diamond G_i)$$

We can rely on very similar ideas as for reachability conditions (see Section 4.1). The construction of a normal form MDP $\mathcal{M}'$ (step 1) is roughly the same except that we deal only with two fresh trap states: *goal* and *fail*. The restart mechanism in step 2 can be realized by switching from $\mathcal{M}'$ to a new MDP $\mathcal{M}_{\varphi|\psi}$

that is defined in the same way as in Section 4.1, except that restart-transitions are only added to those states v where $v \in R_i$ for some $i \in \{1, \ldots, k\}$, and v is contained in some end component that does not contain *goal* and does not contain any G_i-state. For further details we refer to the extended version [6]).

5   PRISM Implementation and Experiments

We have implemented most of the algorithms proposed in this paper in the popular model checker PRISM [21], extending the functionality of version 4.1. Our implementation is based on the "explicit" engine of PRISM, i.e., the analysis is carried out using an explicit representation of the reachable states and transitions. We have extended the explicit engine to handle LTL path properties for Markov chains using deterministic Rabin automata and PRISM's infrastructure.

For Markov chains, we implemented the presented transformation $\mathcal{M} \rightsquigarrow \mathcal{M}_\psi$ where ψ and φ are given as LTL formulas. The presented method for reachability conditions $\psi = \Diamond G$ has been adapted in our implementation for the more general case of constrained reachability conditions $\psi = H \, \mathsf{U} \, G$. Our implementation also supports a special treatment of conditions ψ consisting of a single step-bounded modality $\Diamond^{\leq n}$, $\mathsf{U}^{\leq n}$ or $\Box^{\leq n}$. Besides the computation of conditional probabilities, our implementation also provides the option to compute conditional expected rewards under (constrained) reachability or ω-regular conditions. We used the three types of expected rewards supported by PRISM: the expected accumulated reward until a target set F is reached or within the next $n \in \mathbb{N}$ steps, and the expected instantaneous reward obtained in the n-th step. For MDPs, our current implementation only supports the computation of maximal conditional probabilities for reachability objectives and reachability conditions based on the algorithm presented in Section 4.1.

Experiments with Markov Chains. To evaluate our transformation-based approach for Markov chains we carried out a series of experiments with the Markov chain model for the bounded retransmissions protocol presented in [10]. The model specifications are from the PRISM benchmark suite [22] (see http://www.prismmodelchecker.org/casestudies/brp.php). A sender has to transmit N fragments of a file using a simple protocol over lossy channels, where the probability of losing a message is 0.01, while the probability of losing an acknowledgment is 0.02. A parameter M specifies the maximum number of retries for each fragment. We applied our method to compute:

(B1) $\Pr_s^{\mathcal{M}}\big(\Diamond \text{ "second retry for fragment"} \mid \Box \neg \text{"finish with error"} \big)$

(B2) $\Pr_s^{\mathcal{M}}\big(\Diamond \text{ "finish with success"} \mid \Diamond \text{ "2 fragments transmitted"} \big)$

(B3) $\Pr_s^{\mathcal{M}}\big(\Box \neg \text{"retry"} \mid \Diamond \text{ "finish with success"} \wedge \Box \text{"retries} \leq 2\text{"} \big)$

All calculations for this paper were carried out on a computer with 2 Intel E5-2680 8-core CPUs at 2.70 GHz with 384Gb of RAM. Table 1 lists results for the calculation of the conditional probabilities (B1)–(B3), with $N = 128$ fragments and $M = 10$ retries. We report the number of states and the time for building the

Table 1. Statistics for the computation of (B1), (B2), (B3) for $N = 128$, $M = 10$

model $\mathcal{M}$		$\mathrm{Pr}_s^{\mathcal{M}}(\varphi \mid \psi)$ via transformation				via quotient
states	build	st. $\mathcal{M}_\psi$	$\mathcal{M} \rightsquigarrow \mathcal{M}_\psi$	calc in $\mathcal{M}_\psi$	total time	total time
(B1) 18,701	0.5 s	17,805	19.2 s	5.5 s	24.7 s	58.7 s
(B2) 18,701	0.5 s	18,679	1.7 s	17.0 s	18.7 s	39.2 s
(B3) 18,701	0.5 s	3,976	10.5 s	1.2 s	11.7 s	14.9 s

model and statistics for the calculation of $\mathrm{Pr}_s^{\mathcal{M}}(\varphi \mid \psi)$ with the method presented in Section 3 and via the quotient of $\mathrm{Pr}_s^{\mathcal{M}}(\varphi \wedge \psi)$ and $\mathrm{Pr}_s^{\mathcal{M}}(\psi)$. In addition to the total time for the calculation, for our method we list as well the size of the transformed model $\mathcal{M}_\psi$, the time spent in the transformation phase and the time spent to calculate the probabilities of φ in $\mathcal{M}_\psi$. In these experiments, our transformation method outperforms the quotient approach by separating the treatment of ψ and φ. As expected, the particular condition significantly influences the size of $\mathcal{M}_\psi$ and the time spent for the calculation in $\mathcal{M}_\psi$. We plan to allow caching of $\mathcal{M}_\psi$ if the task is to treat multiple objectives under the same condition ψ. We have carried out experiments for conditional rewards with similar scalability results as well, see [6].

Experiments with MDPs. We report on experimental studies with our implementation of the calculation of $\mathrm{Pr}_{\mathcal{M},s}^{\max}(\lozenge F \mid \lozenge G)$ for the initial state $s = s_{init}$ of the parameterized MDP presented in [23]; see also [22], http://www.prismmodelchecker.org/casestudies/wlan.php. It models a two-way handshake mechanism of the IEEE 802.11 (WLAN) medium access control scheme with two senders S_1 and S_2 that compete for the medium. As messages get corrupted when both senders send at the same time (called a collision), a probabilistic back-off mechanism is employed. The model deals with the case where a single message from S_1 and S_2 should be successfully sent. We consider here:

(W1) $\mathrm{Pr}_{\mathcal{M},s}^{\max}(\lozenge\,\text{"}c_2\text{ collisions"} \mid \lozenge\,\text{"}c_1\text{ collisions"})$

(W2) $\mathrm{Pr}_{\mathcal{M},s}^{\max}(\lozenge\text{"deadline }t\text{ expired without success of }\mathsf{S}_1\text{"} \mid \lozenge\,\text{"}c\text{ collisions"})$

The parameter N specifies the maximal number of back-offs that each sender performs. The atomic propositions "c collisions" are supported by a global counter variable in the model that counts the collisions (up to the maximal interesting value for the property). For (W2), the deadline t is encoded in the model by a global variable counting down until the deadline is expired.

Calculating (W1). Table 2 lists results for the calculation of (W1) with $c_2 = 4$ and $c_1 = 2$. We report the number of states and the time for building the model. The states in the transformed MDP $\mathcal{M}_{\varphi|\psi}$ consist of the states in the original MDP $\mathcal{M}$ plus the three trap states introduced in the transformation. We list the time for the transformation $\mathcal{M} \rightsquigarrow \mathcal{M}_{\varphi|\psi}$ and for the computation in $\mathcal{M}_{\varphi|\psi}$ separately. For comparison, we list as well the time for calculating the unconditional probabilities $\mathrm{Pr}_{\mathcal{M}}^{\max}(\varphi)$ and $\mathrm{Pr}_{\mathcal{M}}^{\max}(\psi)$ for all states in the

Table 2. Statistics for the calculation of (W1) with $c_1 = 2$ and $c_2 = 4$

	model $\mathcal{M}$		$\Pr^{\max}_{\mathcal{M},s}(\varphi \mid \psi)$				$\Pr^{\max}_{\mathcal{M}}(\varphi)$	$\Pr^{\max}_{\mathcal{M}}(\psi)$
N	states	build	$\mathcal{M} \leadsto \mathcal{M}_{\varphi\mid\psi}$	calc in $\mathcal{M}_{\varphi\mid\psi}$	total time		total	total
3	118,280	2.3 s	1.6 s	3.2 s	4.8 s		1.1 s	0.4 s
4	345,120	5.5 s	3.2 s	9.0 s	12.3 s		1.6 s	1.3 s
5	1,295,338	21.0 s	12.6 s	33.8 s	46.5 s		3.9 s	4.9 s
6	5,007,668	99.4 s	38.8 s	126.0 s	164.9 s		12.7 s	18.7 s

Table 3. Statistics for the calculation of (W2) with $N = 3$

		model $\mathcal{M}$		$\Pr^{\max}_{\mathcal{M},s}(\varphi\mid\psi)$			$\Pr^{\max}_{\mathcal{M}}(\varphi)$	$\Pr^{\max}_{\mathcal{M}}(\psi)$
t	c	states	build	$\mathcal{M} \leadsto \mathcal{M}_{\varphi\mid\psi}$	calc in $\mathcal{M}_{\varphi\mid\psi}$	total time	total	total
50	1	539,888	10.0 s	6.4 s	0.4 s	6.8 s	6.0 s	0.1 s
50	2	539,900	9.5 s	7.1 s	4.6 s	11.7 s	6.0 s	0.6 s
100	1	4,769,199	95.1 s	194.6 s	2.4 s	197.1 s	192.0 s	0.5 s
100	2	4,769,235	93.3 s	199.8 s	85.5 s	285.5 s	184.4 s	10.4 s

model, which account for a large part of the transformation. As can be seen, our approach scales reasonably well.

Calculating (W2). Table 3 lists selected results and statistics for (W2) with $N = 3$, deadline $t \in \{50, 100\}$ and number of collisions in the condition $c \in \{1, 2\}$. Again, the time for the transformation is dominated by the computations of $\Pr^{\max}_{\mathcal{M}}(\varphi)$ and $\Pr^{\max}_{\mathcal{M}}(\psi)$. However, in contrast to (W1), the time for the computation in $\mathcal{M}_{\varphi\mid\psi}$ is significantly lower. The complexity in practice thus varies significantly with the particularities of the model and the condition.

6   Conclusion

We presented new methods for the computation of (maximal) conditional probabilities via reductions to the computation of ordinary (maximal) probabilities in discrete Markov chains and MDPs. These methods rely on transformations of the model to encode the effect of conditional probabilities. For MDPs we concentrated on the computation of maximal conditional probabilities. Our techniques are, however, also applicable for reasoning about minimal conditional probabilities as: $\Pr^{\min}_{\mathcal{M},s}(\varphi \mid \psi) = 1 - \Pr^{\max}_{\mathcal{M},s}(\neg\varphi \mid \psi)$. By our results, the complexity of the problem that asks whether the (maximal) conditional probabilities meets a given probability bound is not harder than the corresponding question for unconditional probabilities. This is reflected in our experiments. In our experiments with Markov chains, our new method outperforms the naïve approach. In future work, we will extend our implementations for MDPs that currently only supports reachability objectives and conditions and study methods for the computation of maximal or minimal expected conditional accumulated rewards.

References

1. Andrés, M.E., van Rossum, P.: Conditional probabilities over probabilistic and nondeterministic systems. In: Ramakrishnan, C.R., Rehof, J. (eds.) TACAS 2008. LNCS, vol. 4963, pp. 157–172. Springer, Heidelberg (2008)
2. Andrés, M.E.: Quantitative Analysis of Information Leakage in Probabilistic and Nondeterministic Systems. PhD thesis, UB Nijmegen (2011)
3. Baier, C.: On the algorithmic verification of probabilistic systems. Universität Mannheim, Habilitation Thesis (1998)
4. Baier, C., Groesser, M., Ciesinski, F.: Quantitative analysis under fairness constraints. In: Liu, Z., Ravn, A.P. (eds.) ATVA 2009. LNCS, vol. 5799, pp. 135–150. Springer, Heidelberg (2009)
5. Baier, C., Katoen, J.-P.: Principles of Model Checking. MIT Press (2008)
6. Baier, C., Klein, J., Klüppelholz, S., Märcker, S.: Computing conditional probabilities in Markovian models efficiently. Technical report, TU Dresden (2014), http://wwwtcs.inf.tu-dresden.de/ALGI/PUB/TACAS14/
7. Bianco, A., De Alfaro, L.: Model checking of probabilistic and non-deterministic systems. In: Thiagarajan, P.S. (ed.) FSTTCS 1995. LNCS, vol. 1026, pp. 499–513. Springer, Heidelberg (1995)
8. Clarke, E., Grumberg, O., Peled, D.: Model Checking. MIT Press (2000)
9. Courcoubetis, C., Yannakakis, M.: The complexity of probabilistic verification. Journal of the ACM 42(4), 857–907 (1995)
10. D'Argenio, P.R., Jeannet, B., Jensen, H.E., Larsen, K.G.: Reachability analysis of probabilistic systems by successive refinements. In: de Alfaro, L., Gilmore, S. (eds.) PAPM-PROBMIV 2001. LNCS, vol. 2165, pp. 39–56. Springer, Heidelberg (2001)
11. de Alfaro, L.: Formal Verification of Probabilistic Systems. PhD thesis, Stanford University, Department of Computer Science (1997)
12. de Alfaro, L.: Computing minimum and maximum reachability times in probabilistic systems. In: Baeten, J.C.M., Mauw, S. (eds.) CONCUR 1999. LNCS, vol. 1664, pp. 66–81. Springer, Heidelberg (1999)
13. Gao, Y., Xu, M., Zhan, N., Zhang, L.: Model checking conditional CSL for continuous-time Markov chains. Information Processing Letters 113(1-2), 44–50 (2013)
14. Grädel, E., Thomas, W., Wilke, T. (eds.): Automata, Logics, and Infinite Games. LNCS, vol. 2500. Springer, Heidelberg (2002)
15. Hansson, H., Jonsson, B.: A logic for reasoning about time and reliability. Formal Aspects of Computing 6, 512–535 (1994)
16. Haverkort, B.: Performance of Computer Communication Systems: A Model-Based Approach. Wiley (1998)
17. Ji, M., Wu, D., Chen, Z.: Verification method of conditional probability based on automaton. Journal of Networks 8(6), 1329–1335 (2013)
18. Katoen, J.-P., Zapreev, I.S., Hahn, E.M., Hermanns, H., Jansen, D.N.: The ins and outs of the probabilistic model checker MRMC. Performance Evaluation 68(2), 90–104 (2011)
19. Kulkarni, V.: Modeling and Analysis of Stochastic Systems. Chapman & Hall (1995)
20. Kwiatkowska, M., Norman, G., Parker, D.: Probabilistic symbolic model checking with PRISM: A hybrid approach. STTT 6(2), 128–142 (2004)
21. Kwiatkowska, M., Norman, G., Parker, D.: PRISM 4.0: Verification of probabilistic real-time systems. In: Gopalakrishnan, G., Qadeer, S. (eds.) CAV 2011. LNCS, vol. 6806, pp. 585–591. Springer, Heidelberg (2011)

22. Kwiatkowska, M., Norman, G., Parker, D.: The PRISM benchmark suite. In: QEST 2012. IEEE (2012)
23. Kwiatkowska, M., Norman, G., Sproston, J.: Probabilistic model checking of the IEEE 802.11 wireless local area network protocol. In: Hermanns, H., Segala, R. (eds.) PAPM-PROBMIV 2002. LNCS, vol. 2399, pp. 169–187. Springer, Heidelberg (2002)
24. Puterman, M.: Markov Decision Processes: Discrete Stochastic Dynamic Programming. John Wiley & Sons, Inc., New York (1994)
25. Vardi, M.: Automatic verification of probabilistic concurrent finite-state programs. In: FOCS 1985, pp. 327–338. IEEE (1985)
26. Vardi, M.Y.: Probabilistic linear-time model checking: An overview of the automata-theoretic approach. In: Katoen, J.-P. (ed.) ARTS 1999. LNCS, vol. 1601, pp. 265–276. Springer, Heidelberg (1999)

Permissive Controller Synthesis for Probabilistic Systems

Klaus Dräger[3], Vojtěch Forejt[1], Marta Kwiatkowska[1],
David Parker[2], and Mateusz Ujma[1]

[1] Department of Computer Science, University of Oxford, UK
[2] School of Computer Science, University of Birmingham, UK
[3] EECS, Queen Mary, University of London, UK

Abstract. We propose novel controller synthesis techniques for probabilistic systems modelled using stochastic two-player games: one player acts as a controller, the second represents its environment, and probability is used to capture uncertainty arising due to, for example, unreliable sensors or faulty system components. Our aim is to generate robust controllers that are resilient to unexpected system changes at runtime, and flexible enough to be adapted if additional constraints need to be imposed. We develop a *permissive* controller synthesis framework, which generates *multi-strategies* for the controller, offering a choice of control actions to take at each time step. We formalise the notion of permissiveness using penalties, which are incurred each time a possible control action is blocked by a multi-strategy. Permissive controller synthesis aims to generate a multi-strategy that minimises these penalties, whilst guaranteeing the satisfaction of a specified system property. We establish several key results about the optimality of multi-strategies and the complexity of synthesising them. Then, we develop methods to perform permissive controller synthesis using mixed integer linear programming and illustrate their effectiveness on a selection of case studies.

1 Introduction

Probabilistic model checking is used to automatically verify systems with stochastic behaviour. Systems are modelled as, for example, Markov chains, Markov decision processes, or stochastic games, and analysed algorithmically to verify quantitative properties specified in temporal logic. Applications include checking the safe operation of fault-prone systems ("the brakes fail to deploy with probability at most 10^{-6}") and establishing guarantees on the performance of, for example, randomised communication protocols ("the expected time to establish connectivity between two devices never exceeds 1.5 seconds").

A closely related problem is that of *controller synthesis*. This entails constructing a model of some entity that can be controlled (e.g., a robot, a vehicle or a machine) and its environment, formally specifying the desired behaviour of the system, and then generating, through an analysis of the model, a controller that will guarantee the required behaviour. In many applications of controller synthesis, a model of the system is inherently probabilistic. For example, a robot's

E. Ábrahám and K. Havelund (Eds.): TACAS 2014, LNCS 8413, pp. 531–546, 2014.

sensors and actuators may be unreliable, resulting in uncertainty when detecting and responding to its current state; or messages sent wirelessly to a vehicle may fail to be delivered with some probability.

In such cases, the same techniques that underly probabilistic model checking can be used for controller synthesis. For, example, we can model the system as a Markov decision process (MDP), specify a property ϕ in a probabilistic temporal logic such as PCTL, and LTL, and then apply probabilistic model checking. This yields an optimal *strategy* (policy) for the MDP, which instructs the controller as to which action should be taken in each state of the model in order to guarantee that ϕ will be satisfied. This approach has been successfully applied in a variety of application domains, to synthesise, for example: control strategies for robots [21], power management strategies for hardware [16], and efficient PIN guessing attacks against hardware security modules [27].

Another important dimension of the controller synthesis problem is the presence of uncontrollable or adversarial aspects of the environment. We can take account of this by phrasing the system model as a *game* between two players, one representing the controller and the other the environment. Examples of this approach include controller synthesis for surveillance cameras [23], autonomous vehicles [11] or real-time systems [1]. In our setting, we use (turn-based) stochastic two-player games, which can be seen as a generalisation of MDPs where decisions are made by two distinct players. Probabilistic model checking of such a game yields a strategy for the controller player which guarantees satisfaction of a property ϕ, regardless of the actions of the environment player.

In this paper, we tackle the problem of synthesising *robust* and *flexible* controllers, which are resilient to unexpected changes in the system at runtime. For example, one or more of the actions that the controller can choose at runtime might unexpectedly become unavailable, or additional constraints may be imposed on the system that make some actions preferable to others. One motivation for our work is its applicability to model-driven runtime control of adaptive systems [5], which uses probabilistic model checking in an online fashion to adapt or reconfigure a system at runtime in order to guarantee the satisfaction of certain formally specified performance or reliability requirements.

We develop novel, *permissive* controller synthesis techniques for systems modelled as stochastic two-player games. Rather than generating *strategies*, which specify a single action to take at each time-step, we synthesise *multi-strategies*, which specify multiple possible actions. As in classical controller synthesis, generation of a multi-strategy is driven by a formally specified quantitative property: we focus on probabilistic reachability and expected total reward properties. The property must be guaranteed to hold, whichever of the specified actions are taken and regardless of the behaviour of the environment. Simultaneously, we aim to synthesise multi-strategies that are as *permissive* as possible, which we quantify by assigning *penalties* to actions. These are incurred when a multi-strategy blocks (does not make available) a given action. Actions can be assigned different penalty values to indicate the relative importance of allowing them. Permissive controller synthesis amounts to finding a multi-strategy whose total incurred penalty is minimal, or below some given threshold.

We formalise the permissive controller synthesis problem and then establish several key theoretical results. In particular, we show that randomised multi-strategies are strictly more powerful than deterministic ones, and we prove that the permissive controller synthesis problem is NP-hard for either class. We also establish upper bounds, showing that the problem is in NP and PSPACE for the deterministic and randomised cases, respectively.

Next, we propose practical methods for synthesising multi-strategies using mixed integer linear programming (MILP) [25]. We give an exact encoding for deterministic multi-strategies and an approximation scheme (with adaptable precision) for the randomised case. For the latter, we prove several additional results that allow us to reduce the search space of multi-strategies. The MILP solution process works incrementally, yielding increasingly permissive multi-strategies, and can thus be terminated early if required. This is well suited to scenarios where time is limited, such as online analysis for runtime control, as discussed above, or "anytime verification" [26]. Finally, we implement our techniques and evaluate their effectiveness on a range of case studies.

An extended version of this paper, with proofs, is available as [13].

Related Work. Permissive strategies in *non*-stochastic games were first studied in [2] for parity objectives, but permissivity was defined solely by comparing enabled actions. Bouyer et al. [3] showed that optimally permissive memoryless strategies exist for reachability objectives and expected penalties, contrasting with our (stochastic) setting, where they may not. The work in [3] also studies penalties given as mean-payoff and discounted reward functions, and [4] extends the results to the setting of parity games. None of [2,3,4] consider stochastic games or even randomised strategies, and they provide purely theoretical results.

As in our work, Kumar and Garg [20] consider control of stochastic systems by dynamically disabling events; however, rather than stochastic games, their models are essentially Markov chains, which the possibility of selectively disabling branches turns into MDPs. Finally, although tackling a rather different problem (counterexample generation), [28] is related in that it also uses MILP to solve probabilistic verification problems.

2   Preliminaries

We denote by $Dist(X)$ the set of discrete probability distributions over a set X. A *Dirac* distribution is one that assigns probability 1 to some $s \in X$. The *support* of a distribution $d \in Dist(X)$ is defined as $supp(d) \stackrel{\text{def}}{=} \{x \in X \mid d(x) > 0\}$.

Stochastic Games. In this paper, we use *turn-based stochastic two-player games*, which we often refer to simply as *stochastic games*. A stochastic game takes the form $\mathsf{G} = \langle S_\Diamond, S_\Box, \overline{s}, A, \delta \rangle$, where $S \stackrel{\text{def}}{=} S_\Diamond \cup S_\Box$ is a finite set of states, each associated with player $\Diamond$ or $\Box$, $\overline{s} \in S$ is an initial state, A is a finite set of actions, and $\delta : S \times A \to Dist(S)$ is a (partial) probabilistic transition function. An MDP is a stochastic game with $S_\Box = \emptyset$. Each state s of a stochastic game G has a set of *enabled* actions, given by $A(s) \stackrel{\text{def}}{=} \{a \in A \mid \delta(s,a) \text{ is defined}\}$. The unique player $\circ$ such that $s \in S_\circ$ picks the action $a \in A(s)$ to be taken in state

s. Then, the next state is determined randomly according to the distribution $\delta(s,a)$, i.e., a transition to state s' occurs with probability $\delta(s,a)(s')$. A *path* is a (finite or infinite) sequence $\omega = s_0 a_0 s_1 a_1 \ldots$ of such transitions through G. We denote by $IPath_s$ ($FPath_s$) the set of all infinite (finite) paths starting in s. We omit the subscript s when s is the initial state $\bar{s}$.

A *strategy* $\sigma : FPath \to Dist(A)$ for player $\circ \in \{\Diamond, \Box\}$ of G is a resolution of the choices of actions in each state from $S_\circ$, based on the execution so far. In standard fashion [19], a pair of strategies σ and π for $\Diamond$ and $\Box$ induces, for any state s, a probability measure $Pr^{\sigma,\pi}_{G,s}$ over $IPath_s$. A strategy σ is *deterministic* if $\sigma(\omega)$ is a Dirac distribution for all ω, and *randomised* if not. In this work, we focus purely on *memoryless* strategies, where $\sigma(\omega)$ depends only on the last state of ω, treating the strategy as a function $\sigma : S_\circ \to Dist(A)$. The case of history-dependent strategies is an interesting topic for future research. We write Σ°_G for the set of all (memoryless) player $\circ$ strategies in G.

Properties and Rewards. In order to synthesise controllers, we need a formal description of their required properties. In this paper, we use two common classes of properties: *probabilistic reachability* and *expected total reward*, which we will express in an extended version of the temporal logic PCTL [18].

For probabilistic reachability, we write properties of the form $\phi = P_{\bowtie p}[\,F\, g\,]$, where $\bowtie \in \{\leqslant, \geqslant\}$, $p \in [0,1]$ and $g \subseteq S$ is a set of target states, meaning that the probability of reaching a state in g satisfies the bound $\bowtie p$. Formally, for a specific pair of strategies $\sigma \in \Sigma^\Diamond_G$, $\pi \in \Sigma^\Box_G$ for G, the probability of reaching g under σ and π is $Pr^{\sigma,\pi}_{G,\bar{s}}(F\, g) \overset{\text{def}}{=} Pr^{\sigma,\pi}_{G,\bar{s}}(\{s_0 a_0 s_1 a_1 \cdots \in IPath_{\bar{s}} \mid s_i \in g \text{ for some } i\})$. We say that ϕ is satisfied under σ and π, denoted $G, \sigma, \pi \models \phi$, if $Pr^{\sigma,\pi}_{G,\bar{s}}(F\, g) \bowtie p$.

For rewards, we augment stochastic games with *reward structures*, which are functions of the form $r : S \times A \to \mathbb{R}_{\geqslant 0}$ mapping state-action pairs to non-negative reals. In practice, we often use these to represent "costs" (e.g. elapsed time or energy consumption), despite the terminology "rewards".

The *total reward* for reward structure r along an infinite path $\omega = s_0 a_0 s_1 a_1 \ldots$ is $r(\omega) \overset{\text{def}}{=} \sum_{j=0}^{\infty} r(s_j, a_j)$. For strategies $\sigma \in \Sigma^\Diamond_G$ and $\pi \in \Sigma^\Box_G$, the *expected total reward* is defined as $E^{\sigma,\pi}_{G,\bar{s}}(r) \overset{\text{def}}{=} \int_{\omega \in IPath_{\bar{s}}} r(\omega)\, dPr^{\sigma,\pi}_{G,\bar{s}}$. For technical reasons, we will always assume that the maximum possible reward $\sup_{\sigma,\pi} E^{\sigma,\pi}_{G,s}(r)$ is finite (which can be checked with an analysis of the game's underlying graph). An expected reward property is written $\phi = R^r_{\bowtie b}[\,C\,]$ (where C stands for *cumulative*), meaning that the expected total reward for r satisfies $\bowtie b$. We say that ϕ is satisfied under strategies σ and π, denoted $G, \sigma, \pi \models \phi$, if $E^{\sigma,\pi}_{G,\bar{s}}(r) \bowtie b$.

In fact, probabilistic reachability can be easily reduced to expected total rewards. Thus, in the techniques presented in this paper, we focus purely on expected total reward.

Controller Synthesis. To perform controller synthesis, we model the system as a stochastic game $G = \langle S_\Diamond, S_\Box, \bar{s}, A, \delta \rangle$, where player $\Diamond$ represents the controller and player $\Box$ represents the environment. A specification of the required behaviour of the system is a property ϕ, either a probabilistic reachability property $P_{\bowtie p}[\,F\, t\,]$ or an expected total reward property $R^r_{\bowtie b}[\,C\,]$.

Definition 1 (Sound strategy). *A strategy* $\sigma \in \Sigma_G^\Diamond$ *for player* $\Diamond$ *in stochastic game* G *is sound for a property* ϕ *if* G$, \sigma, \pi \models \phi$ *for any strategy* $\pi \in \Sigma_G^\Box$.

The classical *controller synthesis* problem asks whether there is a sound strategy. We can determine whether this is the case by computing the optimal strategy for player $\Diamond$ in game G [12,15]. This problem is known to be in NP $\cap$ co-NP, but, in practice, methods such as value or policy iteration can be used efficiently.

Example 1. Fig. 1 shows a stochastic game G, with controller and environment player states drawn as diamonds and squares, respectively. It models the control of a robot moving between 4 locations (s_0, s_2, s_3, s_5). When moving east ($s_0 {\rightarrow} s_2$ or $s_3 {\rightarrow} s_5$), it may be impeded by a second robot, depending on the position of the lat-

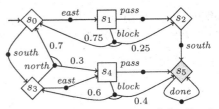

Fig. 1. A stochastic game G for Ex. 1

ter. If it is blocked, there is a chance that it does not successfully move to the next location. We use a reward structure *moves*, which assigns 1 to the controller actions *north, east, south*, and define property $\phi = \mathtt{R}_{\leqslant 5}^{moves}[\,\mathtt{C}\,]$, meaning that the expected number of moves to reach s_5 is at most 5. A sound strategy (found by minimising *moves*) chooses *south* in s_0 and *east* in s_3, yielding an expected number of moves of 3.5.

3   Permissive Controller Synthesis

We now define a framework for *permissive controller synthesis*, which generalises classical controller synthesis by producing *multi-strategies* that offer the controller flexibility about which actions to take in each state.

3.1   Multi-strategies

Multi-strategies generalise the notion of strategies, as defined in Section 2.

Definition 2 (Multi-strategy). *A (memoryless)* multi-strategy *for a game* G$=\langle S_\Diamond, S_\Box, \bar{s}, A, \delta \rangle$ *is a function* $\theta : S_\Diamond \rightarrow Dist(2^A)$ *with* $\theta(s)(\emptyset) = 0$ *for all* $s \in S_\Diamond$.

As for strategies, a multi-strategy θ is deterministic if θ always returns a Dirac distribution, and randomised otherwise. We write Θ_G^{det} and Θ_G^{rand} for the sets of all deterministic and randomised multi-strategies in G, respectively.

A deterministic multi-strategy θ chooses a set of *allowed actions* in each state $s \in S_\Diamond$, i.e., those in the unique set $B \subseteq A$ for which $\theta(s)(B) = 1$. The remaining actions $A(s) \setminus B$ are said to be *blocked* in s. In contrast to classical controller synthesis, where a strategy σ can be seen as providing instructions about precisely which action to take in each state, in permissive controller synthesis a multi-strategy provides multiple actions, any of which can be taken. A randomised multi-strategy generalises this by selecting a set of allowed actions in state s randomly, according to distribution $\theta(s)$.

We say that a controller strategy σ *complies* with multi-strategy θ if it picks actions that are allowed by θ. Formally (taking into account the possibility of randomisation), σ complies with θ if, for any state s and non-empty subset $B \subseteq A(s)$, there is a distribution $d_{s,B} \in Dist(B)$ such that, for all $a \in A(s)$, $\sigma(s)(a) = \sum_{B \ni a} \theta(s)(B) d_{s,B}(a)$.

Now, we can define the notion of a *sound* multi-strategy, i.e., one that is guaranteed to satisfy a property ϕ when complied with.

Definition 3 (Sound multi-strategy). *A multi-strategy θ for game G is sound for a property ϕ if any strategy σ that complies with θ is sound for ϕ.*

Example 2. We return to the stochastic game from Ex. 1 (see Fig. 1) and re-use the property $\phi = \mathtt{R}^{moves}_{\leqslant 5}[\,\mathtt{C}\,]$. The strategy that picks *south* in s_0 and *east* in s_3 results in an expected reward of 3.5 (i.e., 3.5 moves on average to reach s_5). The strategy that picks *east* in s_0 and *south* in s_2 yields expected reward 5. Thus a (deterministic) *multi-strategy* θ that picks $\{south, east\}$ in s_0, $\{south\}$ in s_2 and $\{east\}$ in s_3 is sound for ϕ since the expected reward is always at most 5.

3.2 Penalties and Permissivity

The motivation for multi-strategies is to offer flexibility in the actions to be taken, while still satisfying a particular property ϕ. Generally, we want a multi-strategy θ to be as *permissive* as possible, i.e. to impose as few restrictions as possible on actions to be taken. We formalise the notion of permissivity by assigning *penalties* to actions in the model, which we then use to quantify the extent to which actions are blocked by θ. Penalties provide expressivity in the way that we quantify permissivity: if it is more preferable that certain actions are allowed than others, then these can be assigned higher penalty values.

A *penalty scheme* is a pair (ψ, t), comprising a *penalty function* $\psi : S_\Diamond \times A \to \mathbb{R}_{\geqslant 0}$ and a *penalty type* $t \in \{sta, dyn\}$. The function ψ represents the impact of blocking each action in each controller state of the game. The type t dictates how penalties for individual actions are combined to quantify the permissiveness of a specific multi-strategy. For *static penalties* ($t = sta$), we simply sum penalties across all states of the model. For *dynamic penalties* ($t = dyn$), we take into account the likelihood that blocked actions would actually have been available, by using the *expected sum* of penalty values.

More precisely, for a penalty scheme (ψ, t) and a multi-strategy θ, we define the resulting penalty for θ, denoted $pen_t(\psi, \theta)$ as follows. First, we define the *local* penalty for θ at state s as $pen_{loc}(\psi, \theta, s) = \sum_{B \subseteq A(s)} \sum_{a \notin B} \theta(s, B) \psi(s, a)$. If θ is deterministic, $pen_{loc}(\psi, \theta, s)$ is simply the sum of the penalties of actions that are blocked by θ in s. If θ is randomised, $pen_{loc}(\psi, \theta, s)$ gives the expected penalty value in s, i.e. the sum of penalties weighted by the probability with which θ blocks them in s.

Now, for the static case, we sum the local penalties over all states, i.e. we put $pen_{sta}(\psi, \theta) = \sum_{s \in S_\Diamond} pen_{loc}(\psi, \theta, s)$. For the dynamic case, we use the (worst-case) expected sum of local penalties. We define an auxiliary reward structure

ψ' given by the local penalties: $\psi'(s,a) = pen_{loc}(\psi, \theta, s)$ for all $a \in A(s)$. Then:

$$pen_{dyn}(\psi, \theta) = \sup\{E_{\mathsf{G},\bar{s}}^{\sigma,\pi}(\psi') \mid \sigma \in \Sigma_{\mathsf{G}}^{\Diamond}, \pi \in \Sigma_{\mathsf{G}}^{\Box} \text{ and } \sigma \text{ complies with } \theta\}.$$

3.3 Permissive Controller Synthesis

We can now formally define the central problem studied in this paper.

Definition 4 (Permissive controller synthesis). *Consider a game* G, *a class of multi-strategies* $\star \in \{det, rand\}$, *a property* ϕ, *a penalty scheme* (ψ, t) *and a threshold* $c \in \mathbb{Q}_{\geqslant 0}$. *The* permissive controller synthesis *problem asks: does there exist a multi-strategy* $\theta \in \Theta_{\mathsf{G}}^{\star}$ *that is sound for* ϕ *and satisfies* $pen_t(\psi, \theta) \leqslant c$?

Alternatively, in a more quantitative fashion, we can aim to synthesise (if it exists) an *optimally permissive* sound multi-strategy.

Definition 5 (Optimally permissive). *Let* G, $\star$, ϕ *and* (ψ, t) *be as in Defn. 4. A sound multi-strategy* $\hat{\theta} \in \Theta_{\mathsf{G}}^{\star}$ *is* optimally permissive *if its penalty* $pen_t(\psi, \hat{\theta})$ *equals* $\inf\{pen_t(\psi, \theta) \mid \theta \in \Theta_{\mathsf{G}}^{\star} \text{ and } \theta \text{ is sound for } \phi\}$.

Example 3. We return to Ex. 2 and consider a static penalty scheme (ψ, sta) assigning 1 to the actions *north*, *east*, *south* (in any state). The deterministic multi-strategy θ from Ex. 2 is optimally permissive for $\phi = \mathbb{R}_{\leqslant 5}^{moves}[\mathsf{C}]$, with penalty 1 (just *north* in s_3 is blocked). If we instead use $\phi' = \mathbb{R}_{\leqslant 16}^{moves}[\mathsf{C}]$, the multi-strategy θ' that extends θ by also allowing *north* is now sound and optimally permissive, with penalty 0. Alternatively, the randomised multi-strategy θ'' that picks $0.7:\{north\}+0.3:\{north, east\}$ in s_3 is sound for ϕ with penalty just 0.7.

Next, we establish several fundamental results about the permissive controller synthesis problem. Proofs can be found in [13].

Optimality. Recall that two key parameters of the problem are the type of multi-strategy sought (deterministic or randomised) and the type of penalty scheme used (static or dynamic). We first note that *randomised* multi-strategies are strictly more powerful than deterministic ones, i.e. they can be more permissive (yield a lower penalty) for the same property ϕ.

Theorem 1. *The answer to a permissive controller synthesis problem (for either a* static *or* dynamic *penalty scheme) can be "no" for deterministic multi-strategies, but "yes" for randomised ones.*

This is why we explicitly distinguish between classes of multi-strategies when defining permissive controller synthesis. This situation contrasts with classical controller synthesis, where deterministic strategies are optimal for the same classes of properties ϕ. Intuitively, randomisation is more powerful in this case because of the trade-off between rewards and penalties: similar results exist in, for example, multi-objective controller synthesis on MDPs [14].

Second, we observe that, for the case of static penalties, the optimal penalty value for a given property (the infimum of achievable values) may not actually be achievable by any randomised multi-strategy.

Theorem 2. *For permissive controller synthesis using a* static *penalty scheme, an optimally permissive* randomised *multi-strategy does not always exist.*

If, on the other hand, we restrict our attention to deterministic strategies, then an optimally permissive multi-strategy *does* always exist (since the set of deterministic, memoryless multi-strategies is finite). For randomised multi-strategies with dynamic penalties, the question remains open.

Complexity. Next, we present complexity results for the different variants of the permissive controller synthesis problem. We begin with lower bounds.

Theorem 3. *The permissive controller synthesis problem is NP-hard, for either* static *or* dynamic *penalties, and* deterministic *or* randomised *multi-strategies.*

We prove NP-hardness by reduction from the Knapsack problem, where weights of items are represented by penalties, and their values are expressed in terms of rewards to be achieved. The most delicate part is the proof for randomised strategies, where we need to ensure that the multi-strategy cannot benefit from picking certain actions (corresponding to items being put to the Knapsack) with probability other than 0 or 1. For upper bounds, we have the following.

Theorem 4. *The permissive controller synthesis problem for* deterministic *(resp.* randomised*) strategies is in NP (resp. PSPACE) for* dynamic/static *penalties.*

For deterministic multi-strategies it is straightforward to show NP membership in both the dynamic and static penalty case, since we can guess a multi-strategy satisfying the required conditions and check its correctness in polynomial time. For randomised multi-strategies, with some technical effort we can encode existence of the required multi-strategy as a formula of the existential fragment of the theory of real arithmetic, solvable with polynomial space [7]. See [13].

A natural question is whether the PSPACE upper bound for randomised multi-strategies can be improved. We show that this is likely to be difficult, by giving a reduction from the square-root-sum problem. We use a variant of the problem that asks, for positive rationals $x_1, \ldots, x_n$ and y, whether $\sum_{i=1}^{n} \sqrt{x_i} \leqslant y$. This problem is known to be in PSPACE, but establishing a better complexity bound is a long-standing open problem in computational geometry [17].

Theorem 5. *There is a reduction from the square-root-sum problem to the permissive controller synthesis problem with* randomised *multi-strategies, for both* static *and* dynamic *penalties.*

4   MILP-Based Synthesis of Multi-strategies

We now consider practical methods for synthesising multi-strategies that are sound for a property ϕ and optimally permissive for some penalty scheme. Our methods use mixed integer linear programming (MILP), which optimises an objective function subject to linear constraints that mix both real and integer variables. A variety of efficient, off-the-shelf MILP solvers exists.

An important feature of the MILP solvers we use is that they work incrementally, producing a sequence of increasingly good solutions. Here, that means generating a series of sound multi-strategies that are increasingly permissive. In practice, when resources are constrained, it may be acceptable to stop early and accept a multi-strategy that is sound but not necessarily optimally permissive.

4.1 Deterministic Multi-strategies

We first consider synthesis of *deterministic* multi-strategies. Here, and in the rest of this section, we assume that the property ϕ is of the form $R^r_{\geqslant b}[\mathtt{C}]$. Upper bounds on expected rewards ($\phi = R^r_{\leqslant b}[\mathtt{C}]$) can be handled by negating rewards and converting to a lower bound. For the purposes of encoding into MILP, we rescale r and b such that $\sup_{\sigma,\pi} E^{\sigma,\pi}_{G,s}(r) < 1$ for all s, and rescale every (non-zero) penalty such that $\psi(s,a) \geqslant 1$ for all s and $a \in A(s)$.

Static Penalties. Fig. 2 shows an encoding into MILP of the problem of finding an optimally permissive deterministic multi-strategy for property $\phi = R^r_{\geqslant b}[\mathtt{C}]$ and a *static* penalty scheme (ψ, sta). The encoding uses 5 types of variables: $y_{s,a} \in \{0,1\}$, $x_s \in \mathbb{R}_{\geqslant 0}$, $\alpha_s \in \{0,1\}$, $\beta_{s,a,t} \in \{0,1\}$ and $\gamma_t \in [0,1]$, where $s,t \in S$ and $a \in A$. So the worst-case size of the MILP problem is $\mathcal{O}(|A|\cdot|S|^2\cdot\kappa)$, where κ stands for the longest encoding of a number used.

Variables $y_{s,a}$ encode a multi-strategy θ: $y_{s,a}=1$ iff θ allows action a in s (constraint (2) enforces at least one action per state). Variables x_s represent the worst-case expected total reward (for r) from state s, under any controller strategy complying with θ and under any environment strategy. This is captured by constraints (3)–(4) (which amounts to minimising the reward in an MDP). Constraint (1) imposes the required bound of b on the reward from $\bar{s}$.

The objective function minimises the static penalty (the sum of all local penalties) minus the expected reward in the initial state. The latter acts as a tie-breaker between solutions with equal penalties (but, thanks to rescaling, is always dominated by the penalties and therefore does not affect optimality).

As an additional technicality, we need to ensure that the values of x_s are the *least* solution of the defining inequalities, to deal with the possibility of zero reward loops [24]. To achieve this, we use an approach similar to the one taken in [28]. It is sufficient to ensure that $x_s = 0$ whenever the minimum expected reward from s achievable under θ is 0, which is the case if and only if, starting from s, it is possible to avoid ever taking an action with positive reward.

In our encoding, $\alpha_s = 1$ if x_s is positive (constraint (5)). The binary variables $\beta_{s,a,t} = 1$ represent, for each such s and each action a allowed in s, a choice of successor $t \in supp(\delta(s,a))$ (constraint (6)). The variables γ_s then represent a ranking function: if $r(s,a) = 0$, then $\gamma_s > \gamma_{t(s,a)}$ (constraint (8)). If a positive reward could be avoided starting from s, there would in particular be an infinite sequence $s_0, a_1, s_1, \ldots$ with $s_0 = s$ and, for all i, $s_{i+1} = t(s_i, a_i)$ and $r(s_i, a_i) = 0$, and therefore $\gamma_{s_i} > \gamma_{s_{i+1}}$. Since S is finite, this sequence would have to enter a loop, leading to a contradiction.

Dynamic Penalties. Next, we show how to compute an optimally permissive sound multi-strategy for a *dynamic* penalty scheme (ψ, dyn). This case is more

Minimise: $-x_{\bar{s}} + \sum_{s \in S_\Diamond} \sum_{a \in A(s)} (1 - y_{s,a}) \cdot \psi(s,a)$ subject to:

$$x_{\bar{s}} \geqslant b \tag{1}$$

$$1 \leqslant \sum_{a \in A(s)} y_{s,a} \qquad \text{for all } s \in S_\Diamond \tag{2}$$

$$x_s \leqslant \sum_{t \in S} \delta(s,a)(t) \cdot x_t + r(s,a) + (1 - y_{s,a}) \qquad \text{for all } s \in S_\Diamond, a \in A(s) \tag{3}$$

$$x_s \leqslant \sum_{t \in S} \delta(s,a)(t) \cdot x_t \qquad \text{for all } s \in S_\Box, a \in A(s) \tag{4}$$

$$x_s \leqslant \alpha_s \qquad \text{for all } s \in S \tag{5}$$

$$y_{s,a} = (1 - \alpha_s) + \sum_{t \in supp(\delta(s,a))} \beta_{s,a,t} \qquad \text{for all } s \in S, a \in A(s) \tag{6}$$

$$y_{s,a} = 1 \qquad \text{for all } s \in S_\Box, a \in A(s) \tag{7}$$

$$\gamma_t < \gamma_s + (1 - \beta_{s,a,t}) + r(s,a) \qquad \text{for all } (s,a,t) \in supp(\delta) \tag{8}$$

Fig. 2. MILP encoding for deterministic multi-strategies with static penalties

Minimise: $z_{\bar{s}}$ subject to (1), ..., (7) and:

$$\ell_s = \sum_{a \in A(s)} \psi(s,a) \cdot (1 - y_{s,a}) \qquad \text{for all } s \in S_\Diamond \tag{9}$$

$$z_s \geqslant \sum_{t \in S} \delta(s,a)(t) \cdot z_t + \ell_s - c \cdot (1 - y_{s,a}) \qquad \text{for all } s \in S_\Diamond, a \in A(s) \tag{10}$$

$$z_s \geqslant \sum_{t \in S} \delta(s,a)(t) \cdot z_t \qquad \text{for all } s \in S_\Box, a \in A(s) \tag{11}$$

Fig. 3. MILP encoding for deterministic multi-strategies with dynamic penalties

subtle since the optimal penalty can be infinite. Hence, our solution proceeds in two steps as follows. Initially, we determine if there is *some* sound multi-strategy. For this, we just need to check for the existence of a sound strategy, using standard algorithms for solution of stochastic games [12,15].

If there is no sound multi-strategy, we are done. If there *is*, we use the MILP problem in Fig. 3 to determine the penalty for an optimally permissive sound multi-strategy. This MILP encoding extends the one in Fig. 2 for static penalties, adding variables ℓ_s and z_s, representing the local and the expected penalty in state s, and three extra sets of constraints. Equations (9) and (10) define the expected penalty in controller states, which is the sum of penalties for all disabled actions and those in the successor states, multiplied by their transition probability. The behaviour of environment states is captured by Equation (11), where we only maximise the penalty, without incurring any penalty locally.

The constant c in (10) is chosen to be no lower than any *finite* penalty achievable by a deterministic multi-strategy, a possible value being $\sum_{i=0}^{\infty} (1 - p^{|S|})^i \cdot p^{|S|} \cdot i \cdot |S| \cdot pen_{\max}$, where p is the smallest non-zero probability assigned by δ, and $pen_{\max}$ is the maximal local penalty over all states. If the MILP problem has a solution, this is the optimal dynamic penalty over all sound multi-strategies. If not, no deterministic sound multi-strategy has finite penalty and the optimal penalty is ∞ (recall that we established there is *some* sound multi-strategy).

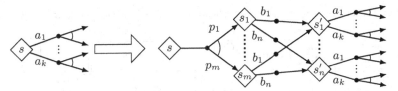

Fig. 4. Transformed game for approximating randomised multi-strategies (Section 4.2)

In practice, we might choose a lower value of c than the one above, resulting in a multi-strategy that is sound, but possibly not optimally permissive.

4.2 Approximating Randomised Multi-strategies

As shown in Section 3, randomised multi-strategies can outperform deterministic ones. The MILP encodings in Fig.s 2 and 3, though, cannot be adapted to the randomised case, since this would need non-linear constraints.

Instead, in this section, we propose an *approximation* which finds the optimal randomised multi-strategy θ in which each probability $\theta(s, B)$ is a multiple of $\frac{1}{M}$ for a given *granularity* M. Any such multi-strategy can then be simulated by a deterministic one on a transformed game, allowing synthesis to be carried out using the MILP-based methods described in the previous section.

The transformed game is illustrated in Fig. 4. For each controller state s, we add two layers of states: *gadgets* s_j' (for $1 \leqslant j \leqslant n$) representing the subsets $B \subseteq A(s)$ with $\theta(s, B) > 0$, and *selectors* s_i (for $1 \leqslant i \leqslant m$), which distribute probability among the gadgets. The s_i are reached from s via a transition using fixed probabilities $p_1, \ldots, p_m$ which need to be chosen appropriately (see below). For efficiency, we want to minimise the number of gadgets n and selectors m for each state s. We now present several results used to achieve this.

First, note that, if $|A(s)| = k$, a randomised multi-strategy chooses probabilities for all $n = 2^k - 1$ non-empty subsets of $A(s)$. Below, we show that it suffices to consider randomised multi-strategies whose support in each state has just two subsets, allowing us to reduce the number of gadgets from $n = 2^k - 1$ to $n = 2$, resulting in a smaller MILP problem to solve for multi-strategy synthesis.

Theorem 6. *1. For a (static or dynamic) penalty scheme (ψ, t) and any sound multi-strategy θ we can construct another sound multi-strategy θ' such that $pen_t(\psi, \theta) \geqslant pen_t(\psi, \theta')$ and $|supp(\theta'(s))| \leqslant 2$ for any $s \in S_\Diamond$.*
2. Furthermore, for static penalties, we can construct θ' such that, for each state $s \in S_\Diamond$, if $supp(\theta'(s)) = \{B_1, B_2\}$, then either $B_1 \subseteq B_2$ or $B_1 \subseteq B_2$.

Part 2 of Theorem 6 states that, for static penalties, we can further reduce the possible multi-strategies that we need to consider. This, however, does not extend to dynamic penalties (see [13]).

Lastly, we define the probabilities $p_1, \ldots, p_m$ on the transitions to selectors in Fig. 4. We let $m = \lfloor 1 + \log_2 M \rfloor$ and $p_i = \frac{l_i}{M}$, where $l_1 \ldots, l_m \in \mathbb{N}$ are defined recursively as follows: $l_1 = \lceil \frac{M}{2} \rceil$ and $l_i = \lceil \frac{M - (l_1 + \cdots + l_{i-1})}{2} \rceil$ for $2 \leqslant i \leqslant m$. Assuming $n = 2$, as discussed above, this allows us to encode any probability distribution $(\frac{l}{M}, \frac{M-l}{M})$ between two subsets B_1 and B_2.

Table 1. Experimental results for synthesising optimal deterministic multi-strategies

Name [param.s]	Param. values	States	Ctrl. states	Property	Penalty	Time (s)
cloud	5	8,841	2,177	$P_{\geqslant 0.9999}[\,F\ deployed\,]$	0.001	9.08
[vm]	6	34,953	8,705	$P_{\geqslant 0.999}[\,F\ deployed\,]$	0.01	72.44
android	1, 48	2,305	997		0.0009	0.58
[r, s]	2, 48	9,100	3,718	$R^{time}_{\leqslant 10000}[\,C\,]$	0.0011	10.64
	3, 48	23,137	9,025		0.0013	17.34
mdsm	3	62,245	9,173	$P_{\leqslant 0.1}[\,F\ deviated\,]$	52	50.97
[N]	3	62,245	9,173	$P_{\leqslant 0.01}[\,F\ deviated\,]$	186	15.84
investor	5,10	10,868	3,344	$R^{profit}_{\geqslant 4.98}[\,C\,]$	1	3.32
[vinit, vmax]	10, 15	21,593	6,644	$R^{profit}_{\geqslant 8.99}[\,C\,]$	1	18.99
team-form	3	12,476	2,023	$P_{\geqslant 0.9999}[\,F\ done_1\,]$	0.8980	0.12
[N]	4	96,666	13,793		0.704	2.26
cdmsn [N]	3	1240	604	$P_{\geqslant 0.9999}[\,F\ prefer_1\,]$	2	0.46

The following result states that, by varying the granularity M, we can get arbitrarily close to the optimal penalty for a randomised multi-strategy and, for the case of static penalties, defines a suitable choice of M.

Theorem 7. *Let θ be a sound multi-strategy. For any $\varepsilon > 0$, there is an M and a sound multi-strategy θ' of granularity M satisfying $pen_t(\psi, \theta') - pen_t(\psi, \theta) \leqslant \varepsilon$. Moreover, for static penalties it suffices to take $M = \lceil \sum_{s \in S, a \in A(s)} \frac{\psi(s,a)}{\varepsilon} \rceil$.*

5   Experimental Results

We have implemented our techniques within PRISM-games [9], an extension of the PRISM model checker for performing model checking and strategy synthesis on stochastic games. PRISM-games can thus already be used for (classical) controller synthesis problems on stochastic games. To this, we add the ability to synthesise multi-strategies using the MILP-based method described in Section 4. Our implementation currently uses CPLEX to solve MILP problems. It also supports SCIP and lp_solve, but in our experiments (run on a PC with a 1.7GHz i7 Core processor and 4GB RAM) these were slower in all cases.

We investigated the applicability and performance of our approach on a variety of case studies, some of which are existing benchmark examples and some of which were developed for this work. These are described in detail below and the files used can be found online [29].

Deterministic Multi-strategy Synthesis. We first discuss the generation of optimal *deterministic* multi-strategies, the results of which are summarised in Table 1. In each row, we first give details of the model: the case study, any parameters used, the number of states ($|S|$) and of controller states ($|S_\Diamond|$). Then, we show the property ϕ used, the penalty value of the optimal multi-strategy and the time to generate it. Below, we give further details for each case study, illustrating the variety of ways that permissive controller synthesis can be used.

cloud: We adapt a PRISM model from [6] to synthesise deployments of services across virtual machines (VMs) in a cloud infrastructure. Our property ϕ specifies that, with high probability, services are deployed to a preferred subset of VMs, and we then assign unit (dynamic) penalties to all actions corresponding to deployment on this subset. The resulting multi-strategy has very low expected penalty (see Table 1) indicating that the goal ϕ can be achieved whilst the controller experiences reduced flexibility only on executions with low probability.

android: We apply permissive controller synthesis to a model created for run-time control of an Android application that provides real-time stock monitoring (see [29] for details). We extend the application to use multiple data sources and synthesise a multi-strategy which specifies an efficient runtime selection of data sources (ϕ bounds the total expected response time). We use static penalties, assigning higher values to actions that select the two most efficient data sources at each time point and synthesise a multi-strategy that always provides a choice of at least two sources (in case one becomes unavailable), while preserving ϕ.

mdsm: Microgrid demand-side management (MDSM) is a randomised scheme for managing local energy usage. A stochastic game analysis [8] previously showed it is beneficial for users to selfishly deviate from the protocol, by ignoring a random back-off mechanism designed to reduce load at busy times. We synthesise a multi-strategy for a (potentially selfish) user, with the goal (ϕ) of bounding the probability of deviation (at either 0.1 or 0.01). The resulting multi-strategy could be used to modify the protocol, restricting the behaviour of this user to reduce selfish behaviour. To make the multi-strategy as permissive as possible, restrictions are only introduced where necessary to ensure ϕ. We also guide where restrictions are made by assigning (static) penalties at certain times of the day.

investor: This example [22] synthesises strategies for a futures market investor, who chooses when to reserve shares, operating in a (malicious) market which can periodically ban him from investing. We generate a multi-strategy that achieves 90% of the maximum expected profit (obtainable by a single strategy) and assign (static) unit penalties to all actions, showing that, after an immediate share purchase, the investor can choose his actions freely and still meet the 90% target.

team-form: This example [10] synthesises strategies for forming teams of agents in order to complete a set of collaborative tasks. Our goal (ϕ) is to guarantee that a particular task is completed with high probability (0.9999). We use (dynamic) unit penalties on all actions of the first agent and synthesise a multi-strategy representing several possibilities for this agent while still achieving the goal.

cdmsn: Lastly, we apply permissive controller synthesis to a model of a protocol for collective decision making in sensor networks (CDMSN) [8]. We synthesise strategies for nodes in the network such that consensus is achieved with high probability (0.9999). We use (static) penalties inversely proportional to the energy associated with each action a node can perform to ensure that the multi-strategy favours more efficient solutions.

Analysis. Unsurprisingly, permissive controller synthesis is slightly more costly to execute than (classical) controller synthesis. But we successfully synthesised

Table 2. Experimental results for approximating optimal randomised multi-strategies

Name[†]	Par-am.s	States	Ctrl. states	Property	Pen. (det.)	Pen. (randomised)		
						$M{=}100$	$M{=}200$	$M{=}300$
android	1,1	49	10	$P_{\geqslant 0.9999}[\mathbf{F}\ done]$	1.01	0.91	0.905	0.903
	1,10	481	112	$P_{\geqslant 0.999}[\mathbf{F}\ done]$	19.13	18.14*	17.73*	17.58*
cloud	5	8,841	2,177	$P_{\geqslant 0.9999}[\mathbf{F}\ deployed]$	1	0.91	0.905	0.906*
investor	5,10	10,868	3,344	$R^{profit}_{\geqslant 4.98}[\mathbf{C}]$	1	1*	1*	0.996*
team-form	3	12,476	2,023	$P_{\geqslant 0.9999}[\mathbf{F}\ done_1]$	264	263.96*	263.95*	263.94*

[†] See Table 1 for parameter names.
* Sound but possibly non-optimal multi-strategy obtained after 5 minute MILP time-out.

deterministic multi-strategies for a wide range of models and properties, with model sizes ranging up to approximately 100,000 states. The performance and scalability of our method is affected (as usual) by the state space size. But, in particular, it is affected by the number of actions in controller states, since these result in integer MILP variables, which are the most expensive part of the solution. Performance is also sensitive to the penalty scheme used: for example, states with all penalties equal to zero can be dealt with more efficiently.

Randomised Multi-strategy Synthesis. Finally, Table 2 presents results for approximating optimal *randomised* multi-strategies on several models from Table 1. We show the (static) penalty values for the generated multi-strategies for 3 different levels of precision (i.e. granularities M; see Section 4.2) and compare them to those of the deterministic multi-strategies for the same models.

The MILP encodings for randomised multi-strategies are larger than deterministic ones and thus slower to solve, so we impose a time-out of 5 minutes. We are able to generate a sound multi-strategy for all the examples; in some cases it is optimally permissive, in others it is not (denoted by a * in Table 2). As would be expected, we generally observe smaller penalties with increasing values of M. In the instance where this is not true (*cloud*, $M{=}300$), we attribute this to the size of the MILP problem, which grows with M. For all examples, we built randomised multi-strategies with smaller penalties than the deterministic ones.

6   Conclusions

We have presented a framework for permissive controller synthesis on stochastic two-player games, based on generation of multi-strategies that guarantee a specified objective and are optimally permissive with respect to a penalty function. We proved several key properties, developed MILP-based synthesis methods and evaluated them on a set of case studies. Topics for future work include synthesis for more expressive temporal logics and using history-dependent multi-strategies.

Acknowledgements. The authors are part supported by ERC Advanced Grant VERIWARE and EPSRC projects EP/K038575/1 and EP/F001096/1.

References

1. Behrmann, G., Cougnard, A., David, A., Fleury, E., Larsen, K.G., Lime, D.: UPPAAL-tiga: Time for playing games! In: Damm, W., Hermanns, H. (eds.) CAV 2007. LNCS, vol. 4590, pp. 121–125. Springer, Heidelberg (2007)
2. Bernet, J., Janin, D., Walukiewicz, I.: Permissive strategies: from parity games to safety games. ITA 36(3), 261–275 (2002)
3. Bouyer, P., Duflot, M., Markey, N., Renault, G.: Measuring permissivity in finite games. In: Bravetti, M., Zavattaro, G. (eds.) CONCUR 2009. LNCS, vol. 5710, pp. 196–210. Springer, Heidelberg (2009)
4. Bouyer, P., Markey, N., Olschewski, J., Ummels, M.: Measuring permissiveness in parity games: Mean-payoff parity games revisited. In: Bultan, T., Hsiung, P.-A. (eds.) ATVA 2011. LNCS, vol. 6996, pp. 135–149. Springer, Heidelberg (2011)
5. Calinescu, R., Ghezzi, C., Kwiatkowska, M., Mirandola, R.: Self-adaptive software needs quantitative verification at runtime. CACM 55(9), 69–77 (2012)
6. Calinescu, R., Johnson, K., Kikuchi, S.: Compositional reverification of probabilistic safety properties for large-scale complex IT systems. In: LSCITS (2012)
7. Canny, J.: Some algebraic and geometric computations in PSPACE. In: Proc. STOC 1988, pp. 460–467. ACM, New York (1988)
8. Chen, T., Forejt, V., Kwiatkowska, M., Parker, D., Simaitis, A.: Automatic verification of competitive stochastic systems. In: Flanagan, C., König, B. (eds.) TACAS 2012. LNCS, vol. 7214, pp. 315–330. Springer, Heidelberg (2012)
9. Chen, T., Forejt, V., Kwiatkowska, M., Parker, D., Simaitis, A.: PRISM-games: A model checker for stochastic multi-player games. In: Piterman, N., Smolka, S.A. (eds.) TACAS 2013. LNCS, vol. 7795, pp. 185–191. Springer, Heidelberg (2013)
10. Chen, T., Kwiatkowska, M., Parker, D., Simaitis, A.: Verifying team formation protocols with probabilistic model checking. In: Leite, J., Torroni, P., Ågotnes, T., Boella, G., van der Torre, L. (eds.) CLIMA XII 2011. LNCS, vol. 6814, pp. 190–207. Springer, Heidelberg (2011)
11. Chen, T., Kwiatkowska, M., Simaitis, A., Wiltsche, C.: Synthesis for multi-objective stochastic games: An application to autonomous urban driving. In: Joshi, K., Siegle, M., Stoelinga, M., D'Argenio, P.R. (eds.) QEST 2013. LNCS, vol. 8054, pp. 322–337. Springer, Heidelberg (2013)
12. Condon, A.: On algorithms for simple stochastic games. In: Advances in Computational Complexity Theory. DIMACS Series, vol. 13, pp. 51–73 (1993)
13. Draeger, K., Forejt, V., Kwiatkowska, M., Parker, D., Ujma, M.: Permissive controller synthesis for probabilistic systems. Technical Report CS-RR-14-01, Department of Computer Science, University of Oxford (2014)
14. Etessami, K., Kwiatkowska, M., Vardi, M., Yannakakis, M.: Multi-objective model checking of Markov decision processes. LMCS 4(4), 1–21 (2008)
15. Filar, J., Vrieze, K.: Competitive Markov Decision Processes. Springer (1997)
16. Forejt, V., Kwiatkowska, M., Norman, G., Parker, D., Qu, H.: Quantitative multi-objective verification for probabilistic systems. In: Abdulla, P.A., Leino, K.R.M. (eds.) TACAS 2011. LNCS, vol. 6605, pp. 112–127. Springer, Heidelberg (2011)
17. Garey, M.R., Graham, R.L., Johnson, D.S.: Some np-complete geometric problems. In: STOC 1976, pp. 10–22. ACM, New York (1976)
18. Hansson, H., Jonsson, B.: A logic for reasoning about time and reliability. Formal Aspects of Computing 6(5), 512–535 (1994)

19. Kemeny, J., Snell, J., Knapp, A.: Denumerable Markov Chains. Springer (1976)
20. Kumar, R., Garg, V.: Control of stochastic discrete event systems modeled by probabilistic languages. IEEE Trans. Automatic Control 46(4), 593–606 (2001)
21. Lahijanian, M., Wasniewski, J., Andersson, S., Belta, C.: Motion planning and control from temporal logic specifications with probabilistic satisfaction guarantees. In: Proc. ICRA 2010, pp. 3227–3232 (2010)
22. McIver, A., Morgan, C.: Results on the quantitative mu-calculus qMu. ACM Transactions on Computational Logic 8(1) (2007)
23. Ozay, N., Topcu, U., Murray, R., Wongpiromsarn, T.: Distributed synthesis of control protocols for smart camera networks. In: Proc. ICCPS 2011 (2011)
24. Puterman, M.: Markov Decision Processes: Discrete Stochastic Dynamic Programming. John Wiley and Sons (1994)
25. Schrijver, A.: Theory of Linear and Integer Programming. John Wiley & Sons (1998)
26. Shankar, N.: A tool bus for anytime verification. In: Usable Verification (2010)
27. Steel, G.: Formal analysis of PIN block attacks. TCS 367(1-2), 257–270 (2006)
28. Wimmer, R., Jansen, N., Ábrahám, E., Becker, B., Katoen, J.-P.: Minimal critical subsystems for discrete-time Markov models. In: Flanagan, C., König, B. (eds.) TACAS 2012. LNCS, vol. 7214, pp. 299–314. Springer, Heidelberg (2012); Extended version available as technical report SFB/TR 14 AVACS 88
29. http://www.prismmodelchecker.org/files/tacas14pcs/

Precise Approximations of the Probability Distribution of a Markov Process in Time: An Application to Probabilistic Invariance

Sadegh Esmaeil Zadeh Soudjani[1] and Alessandro Abate[2,1]

[1] Delft Center for Systems & Control, TU Delft, The Netherlands
[2] Department of Computer Science, University of Oxford, UK
{S.EsmaeilZadehSoudjani,A.Abate}@tudelft.nl

Abstract. The goal of this work is to formally abstract a Markov process evolving over a general state space as a finite-state Markov chain, with the objective of precisely approximating the state probability distribution of the Markov process in time. The approach uses a partition of the state space and is based on the computation of the average transition probability between partition sets. In the case of unbounded state spaces, a procedure for precisely truncating the state space within a compact set is provided, together with an error bound that depends on the asymptotic properties of the transition kernel of the Markov process. In the case of compact state spaces, the work provides error bounds that depend on the diameters of the partitions, and as such the errors can be tuned. The method is applied to the problem of computing probabilistic invariance of the model under study, and the result is compared to an alternative approach in the literature.

1 Introduction

Verification techniques and tools for deterministic, discrete time, finite-state systems have been available for many years [9]. Formal methods in the stochastic context is typically limited to discrete state structures, either in continuous or in discrete time [3, 12]. Stochastic processes evolving over continuous (uncountable) spaces are often related to undecidable problems (the exception being when they admit analytical solutions). It is thus of interest to resort to formal approximation techniques that allow solving corresponding problems over finite discretizations of the original models. In order to relate the approximate solutions to the original problems, it is of interest to come up with precise bounds on the error introduced by the approximations. The use of formal approximations techniques for such complex models can be looked at from the perspective of the research on abstraction techniques, which are of wide use in formal verification.

Successful numerical schemes based on Markov chain approximations of stochastic systems in continuous time have been introduced in the literature, e.g. [10]. However, the finite abstractions are only related to the original models asymptotically (at the limit), with no explicit error bounds. This approach has

E. Ábrahám and K. Havelund (Eds.): TACAS 2014, LNCS 8413, pp. 547–561, 2014.
© Springer-Verlag Berlin Heidelberg 2014

been applied to the approximate study of probabilistic reachability or safety of stochastic hybrid models in [8, 15]. In [1] a technique has been introduced to instead provide formal abstractions of discrete-time, continuous-space Markov models [2], with the objective of investigating their probabilistic invariance (safety) by employing probabilistic model checking over a finite Markov chain. In view of scalability, the approach has been improved and optimized in [7].

In this work we show that the approach in [1, 7] can be successfully employed to approximately compute the statistics in time of a stochastic process over a continuous state space. This additionally leads to an alternative method for probabilistic safety analysis of the process. We first provide a forward recursion for the approximate computation of the state distribution of a Markov process in time. The computation of the state distribution is based on a state-space partitioning procedure, and on the abstraction of the Markov process as a finite-state Markov chain. An upper bound on the error related to the approximation is formally derived. Based on the information from the state distribution, we show how the method can be used to approximately compute probabilistic invariance (safety) for discrete-time stochastic systems over general state spaces.

Probabilistic safety is the dual problem to probabilistic reachability. Over deterministic models reachability and safety have been vastly studied in the literature, and computational algorithms and tools have been developed based on both forward and backward reachability for these systems. Similarly, for the probabilistic models under study, we compare the presented approach (based on forward computations) with the existing approaches in the literature [1, 5–7] (which hinge on backward computations), particularly in terms of the introduced error.

The article is structured as follows. Section 2 introduces the model under study and discusses some structural assumptions needed for the abstraction procedure. The procedure comprises two separate parts: Section 3 describes the truncation of the dynamics of the model, whereas Section 4 details the abstraction of the dynamics (approximation of the transition kernel) – both parts formally assess the associated approximation error. Section 5 discusses the application of the procedure to the computation of probabilistic invariance, and compares it against an alternative approach in the literature.

2   Model, Preliminaries, and Goal of This Work

We consider a discrete time Markov process $\mathcal{M}$ defined over a general state space, which is characterized by a pair $(\mathcal{S}, T_s)$, where $\mathcal{S}$ is the continuous state space that we assume endowed with a metric and Borel measurable. We denote by $(\mathcal{S}, \mathcal{B}(\mathcal{S}), \mathcal{P})$ the probability structure on $\mathcal{S}$, with $\mathcal{B}(\mathcal{S})$ being the associated sigma algebra and $\mathcal{P}$ a probability measure to be characterized shortly. T_s is a conditional stochastic kernel that assigns to each point $s \in \mathcal{S}$ a probability measure $T_s(\cdot|s)$, so that for any measurable set $A \in \mathcal{B}(\mathcal{S})$, $\mathcal{P}(s(1) \in A|s(0) = s) = \int_A T_s(d\bar{s}|s)$. We assume that the stochastic kernel T_s admits a density function t_s, namely $T_s(d\bar{s}|s) = t_s(\bar{s}|s)d\bar{s}$.

Suppose that the initial state of the Markov process $\mathcal{M}$ is random and distributed according to the density function $\pi_0 : \mathcal{S} \to \mathbb{R}^{\geq 0}$. The state distribution of $\mathcal{M}$ at time $t \in \mathbb{N} \doteq \{1, 2, 3, \ldots\}$ is characterized by a density function $\pi_t : \mathcal{S} \to \mathbb{R}^{\geq 0}$, which fully describes the statistics of the process at t and is in particular such that, for all $A \in \mathcal{B}(\mathcal{S})$,

$$\mathbb{P}(s(t) \in A) = \int_A \pi_t(s)ds,$$

where the symbol $\mathbb{P}$ is loosely used to indicate the probability associated to events over the product space $\mathcal{S}^{t+1}$ with elements $\mathbf{s} = [s(0), s(1), \ldots, s(t)]$, whereas the bold typeset is constantly used in the sequel to indicate vectors.

The state density functions $\pi_t(\cdot)$ can be computed recursively, as follows:

$$\pi_{t+1}(\bar{s}) = \int_{\mathcal{S}} t_s(\bar{s}|s)\pi_t(s)ds \quad \forall \bar{s} \in \mathcal{S}. \tag{1}$$

In practice the forward recursion in (1) rarely yields a closed form for the density function $\pi_{t+1}(\cdot)$. A special instance where this is the case is represented by a linear dynamical system perturbed by Gaussian process noise: due to the closure property of the Gaussian distribution with respect to addition and multiplication by a constant, it is possible to explicitly write recursive formulas for the mean and the variance of the distribution, and thus express in a closed form the distribution in time of the solution of the model. In more general cases, it is necessary to numerically (hence, approximately) compute the density function of the model in time.

This article provides a numerical approximation of the density function of $\mathcal{M}$ as the probability mass function (pmf) of a finite-state Markov chain $\mathcal{M}_f$ in time. The Markov chain $\mathcal{M}_f$ is obtained as an abstraction of the concrete Markov process $\mathcal{M}$. The abstraction is associated with a guaranteed and tunable error bound, and algorithmically it leverages a state-space partitioning procedure. The procedure is comprised of two steps:

1. since the state space $\mathcal{S}$ is generally unbounded, it is first properly truncated;
2. subsequently, a partition of the truncated dynamics is introduced.

Section 3 discusses the error generated by the state-space truncation, whereas Section 4 describes the construction of the Markov chain by state-space partitioning. We employ the following example throughout the article as a running case study.

Example 1. Consider the one-dimensional stochastic dynamical system

$$s(t + 1) = as(t) + b + \sigma w(t),$$

where the parameters $a, \sigma > 0$, whereas $b \in \mathbb{R}$, and such that $w(\cdot)$ is a process comprised of independent, identically distributed random variables with a standard normal distribution. The initial state of the process is selected uniformly in the bounded interval $[\beta_0, \gamma_0] \subset \mathbb{R}$. The solution of the model is a Markov process, evolving over the state space $\mathcal{S} = \mathbb{R}$, and fully characterized by the conditional density function

$$t_s(\bar{s}|s) = \phi_\sigma(\bar{s} - as - b), \quad \phi_\sigma(u) = \frac{1}{\sigma\sqrt{2\pi}}e^{-u^2/2\sigma^2}. \qquad \square$$

We raise the following assumptions in order to be able to later relate the state density function of $\mathcal{M}$ to the probability mass function of $\mathcal{M}_f$.

Assumption 1. *For given sets $\Gamma \subset \mathcal{S}^2$ and $\Lambda_0 \subset \mathcal{S}$, there exist positive constants ϵ and ε_0, such that $t_s(\bar{s}|s)$ and $\pi_0(s)$ satisfy the following conditions:*

$$t_s(\bar{s}|s) \leq \epsilon \quad \forall (s, \bar{s}) \in \mathcal{S}^2 \backslash \Gamma, \text{ and } \pi_0(s) \leq \varepsilon_0 \quad \forall s \in \mathcal{S} \backslash \Lambda_0. \tag{2}$$

Assumption 2. *The density functions $\pi_0(s)$ and $t_s(\bar{s}|s)$ are (globally) Lipschitz continuous, namely there exist finite constants λ_0, λ_f, such that the following Lipschitz continuity conditions hold:*

$$|\pi_0(s) - \pi_0(s')| \leq \lambda_0 \|s - s'\| \quad \forall s, s' \in \Lambda_0, \tag{3}$$

$$|t_s(\bar{s}|s) - t_s(\bar{s}'|s)| \leq \lambda_f \|\bar{s} - \bar{s}'\| \quad \forall s, \bar{s}, \bar{s}' \in \mathcal{S}. \tag{4}$$

Moreover, there exists a finite constant M_f such that

$$M_f = \sup \left\{ \int_\mathcal{S} t_s(\bar{s}|s)ds \middle| \bar{s} \in \mathcal{S} \right\}. \tag{5}$$

The Lipschitz constants λ_0, λ_f are effectively computed by taking partial derivatives of the density functions $\pi_0(\cdot), t_s(\cdot|s)$ and maximizing its norm. The sets Λ_0 and Γ will be used to truncate the support of density functions $\pi_0(\cdot)$ and $t_s(\cdot|\cdot)$, respectively. Assumption 1 enables the precise study of the behavior of density functions $\pi_t(\cdot)$ over the truncated part of the state space. Further, the Lipschitz continuity conditions in Assumption 2 are essential to derive error bounds related to the abstraction of the Markov process over the truncated state space. In order to compute these error bounds, we assign the infinity norm to the space of bounded measurable functions over the state space $\mathcal{S}$, namely

$$\|f(s)\|_\infty = \sup_{s \in \mathcal{S}} |f(s)| \quad \forall f : \mathcal{S} \to \mathbb{R}.$$

In the sequel the function $\mathbb{I}_A(\cdot)$ denotes the indicator function of a set $A \subseteq \mathcal{S}$, namely $\mathbb{I}_A(s) = 1$, if $s \in A$; else $\mathbb{I}_A(s) = 0$.

Example 1 (Continued). Select the interval $\Lambda_0 = [\beta_0, \gamma_0]$ and define the set Γ by the linear inequality

$$\Gamma = \{(s, \bar{s}) \in \mathbb{R}^2 | |\bar{s} - as - b| \leq \alpha\sigma\}.$$

The initial density function π_0 of the process can be represented by the function

$$\psi_0(s) = \mathbb{I}_{[\beta_0, \gamma_0]}(s)/(\gamma_0 - \beta_0).$$

Then Assumption 1 holds with $\epsilon = \phi_1(\alpha)/\sigma$ and $\varepsilon_0 = 0$. The constant M_f in Assumption 2 is equal to $1/a$. Lipschitz continuity, as per (3) and (4), holds for constants $\lambda_0 = 0$ and $\lambda_f = 1/(\sigma^2\sqrt{2\pi e})$. $\qquad \square$

3 State-Space Truncation Procedure, with Error Quantification

We truncate the support of the density functions π_0, t_s to the sets Λ_0, Γ respectively, and recursively compute support sets Λ_t, as in (7) that are associated to the density functions π_t. Then we employ the quantities ϵ, ε_0 in Assumption 1 to compute error bounds ε_t, as in (6), on the value of the density functions π_t outside the sets Λ_t. Finally we truncate the unbounded state space to $\Upsilon = \cup_{t=0}^N \Lambda_t$.

As intuitive, the error related to the spatial truncation depends on the behavior of the conditional density function t_s over the eliminated regions of the state space. Suppose that sets Γ, Λ_0 are selected such that Assumption 1 is satisfied with constants ϵ, ε_0: then Theorem 2 provides an upper bound on the error obtained from evaluating the density functions in time $\pi_t(\cdot)$ over the truncated regions of the state space.

Theorem 1. *Under Assumption 1 the functions π_t satisfy the bound*

$$0 \le \pi_t(s) \le \varepsilon_t \quad \forall s \in \mathcal{S} \backslash \Lambda_t,$$

where the quantities $\{\varepsilon_t\}_{t=0}^N$ are defined recursively by

$$\varepsilon_{t+1} = \epsilon + M_f \varepsilon_t, \tag{6}$$

whereas the support sets $\{\Lambda_t\}_{t=0}^N$ are computed as

$$\Lambda_{t+1} = \Pi_{\bar{s}} \left(\Gamma \cap (\Lambda_t \times \mathcal{S}) \right), \tag{7}$$

where $\Pi_{\bar{s}}$ denotes the projection map along the second set of coordinates[1].

Remark 1. Notice that if the shape of the sets Γ and Λ_0 is computationally manageable (e.g., polytopes) then it is possible to implement the computation of the recursion in (7) by available software tools, such as the MPT toolbox [11].

Further, notice that if for some t_0, $\Lambda_{t_0+1} \supset \Lambda_{t_0}$, then for all $t \ge t_0$, $\Lambda_{t+1} \supset \Lambda_t$. Similarly, we have that

- if for some t_0, $\Lambda_{t_0+1} \subset \Lambda_{t_0}$, then for all $t \ge t_0$, $\Lambda_{t+1} \subset \Lambda_t$.
- if for some t_0, $\Lambda_{t_0+1} = \Lambda_{t_0}$, then for all $t \ge t_0$, $\Lambda_t = \Lambda_{t_0}$.

To clarify the role of Γ in the computation of Λ_t, we emphasize that $\Lambda_{t+1} = \cup_{s \in \Lambda_t} \Xi(s)$, where Ξ depends only on Γ and is defined by the set-valued map

$$\Xi : \mathcal{S} \to 2^{\mathcal{S}}, \quad \Xi(s) = \{\bar{s} \in \mathcal{S} | (s, \bar{s}) \in \Gamma\}.$$

Figure 1 provides a visual illustration of the recursion in (7).   □

Let us introduce a quantity $\kappa(t, M_f)$, which plays a role in the solution of (6) and will be frequently used shortly:

$$\kappa(t, M_f) = \begin{cases} \frac{1-M_f^t}{1-M_f}, & M_f \ne 1 \\ t, & M_f = 1. \end{cases} \tag{8}$$

---

[1] Recall that both Γ and $\Lambda \times \mathcal{S}$ are defined over $\mathcal{S}^2 = \mathcal{S} \times \mathcal{S}$.

The following theorem provides a truncation procedure, valid over a finite time horizon $\{0, 1, \ldots, N\}$, which reduces the state space $\mathcal{S}$ to the set $\Upsilon = \bigcup_{t=0}^{N} \Lambda_t$. The theorem also formally quantifies the associated truncation error.

Theorem 2. *Suppose that the state space of the process $\mathcal{M}$ has been truncated to the set $\Upsilon = \bigcup_{t=0}^{N} \Lambda_t$. Let us introduce the following recursion to compute functions $\mu_t : \mathcal{S} \to \mathbb{R}^{\geq 0}$ as an approximation of the density functions π_t:*

$$\mu_{t+1}(\bar{s}) = \mathbb{I}_\Upsilon(\bar{s}) \int_{\mathcal{S}} t_s(\bar{s}|s)\mu_t(s)ds, \quad \mu_0(s) = \mathbb{I}_{\Lambda_0}(s)\pi_0(s) \quad \forall \bar{s} \in \mathcal{S}. \quad (9)$$

Then the introduced approximation error is $\|\pi_t - \mu_t\|_\infty \leq \varepsilon_t$, for all $t \leq N$.

To recapitulate, Theorem 2 leads to the following procedure to approximate the density functions π_t of $\mathcal{M}$ over an unbounded state space $\mathcal{S}$:

1. truncate π_0 in such a way that μ_0 has a bounded support Λ_0;
2. truncate the conditional density function $t_s(\cdot|s)$ over a bounded set for all $s \in \mathcal{S}$, then quantify $\Gamma \subset \mathcal{S}^2$ as the support of the truncated density function;
3. leverage the recursion in (7) to compute the support sets Λ_t;
4. use the recursion in (9) to compute the approximate density functions μ_t over the set $\Upsilon = \cup_{t=0}^{N}\Lambda_t$. Note that the recursion in (9) is effectively computed over the set Υ, since $\mu_t(s) = 0$ for all $s \in \mathcal{S}\backslash\Upsilon$.

Note that we could as well deal with the support of $\mu_t(\cdot)$ over the time-varying sets Λ_t by adapting recursion (9) with $\mathbb{I}_{\Lambda_{t+1}}$ instead of $\mathbb{I}_\Upsilon$. While employing the (larger) set Υ may lead to a memory increase at each stage, it will considerably simplify the computations of the state-space partitioning and the abstraction as a Markov chain: indeed, employing time-varying sets Λ_t would render the partitioning procedure also time-dependent, and the obtained Markov chain would be time-inhomogeneous. We opt to work directly with Υ to avoid these difficulties.

Example 1 (Continued). We can easily obtain a closed form for the sets $\Lambda_t = [\beta_t, \gamma_t]$, via

$$\beta_{t+1} = a\beta_t + b - \alpha\sigma, \quad \gamma_{t+1} = a\gamma_t + b + \alpha\sigma.$$

The set Υ is the union of intervals $[\beta_t, \gamma_t]$. The error of the state-space truncation over set Υ is

$$\|\pi_t - \mu_t\|_\infty \leq \varepsilon_t = \kappa(t, M_f)\frac{\phi_1(\alpha)}{\sigma}, \quad M_f = \frac{1}{a}.$$

$\square$

4   State-Space Partitioning Procedure, with Error Quantification

In this section we assume that the sets Γ, Λ_0 have been properly selected so that $\Upsilon = \cup_{t=0}^{N}\Lambda_t$ is bounded. In order to formally abstract process $\mathcal{M}$ as a finite

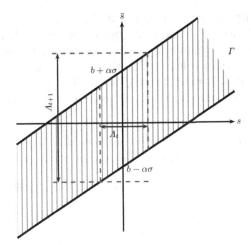

Fig. 1. Graphical representation of the recursion in (7) for Λ_t

Markov chain $\mathcal{M}_f$ and to approximate its state density functions, we select a finite partition of the bounded set Υ as $\Upsilon = \cup_{i=1}^{n}\mathcal{A}_i$, where the sets $\mathcal{A}_i$ have non-trivial measure. We then complete the partition over the whole state space $\mathcal{S} = \cup_{i=1}^{n+1}\mathcal{A}_i$ by considering the set $\mathcal{A}_{n+1} = \mathcal{S}\backslash\Upsilon$. This results in a finite Markov chain $\mathcal{M}_f$ with $n+1$ discrete abstract states in the set $\mathbb{N}_{n+1}\doteq\{1, 2, \cdots, n, n+1\}$, and characterized by the transition probability matrix $P = [P_{ij}] \in \mathbb{R}^{(n+1)^2}$, where the probability of jumping from any pair of states i to j (P_{ij}) is computed as

$$P_{ij} = \tfrac{1}{\mathcal{L}(\mathcal{A}_i)} \int_{\mathcal{A}_j} \int_{\mathcal{A}_i} t_s(\bar{s}|s)dsd\bar{s} \quad \forall i \in \mathbb{N}_n,$$
$$P_{(n+1)j} = \delta_{(n+1)j}, \tag{10}$$

for all $j \in \mathbb{N}_{n+1}$, and where $\delta_{(n+1)j}$ is the Kronecker delta function (the abstract state $n + 1$ of $\mathcal{M}_f$ is absorbing), and $\mathcal{L}(\cdot)$ denotes the Lebesgue measure of a set. The quantities in (10) are well-defined since the set Υ is bounded and the measures $\mathcal{L}(\mathcal{A}_i), i \in \mathbb{N}_n$, are finite and non-trivial.

Notice that matrix P for the Markov chain $\mathcal{M}_f$ is stochastic, namely

$$\sum_{j=1}^{n+1} P_{ij} = \sum_{j=1}^{n+1} \frac{1}{\mathcal{L}(\mathcal{A}_i)} \int_{\mathcal{A}_j} \int_{\mathcal{A}_i} t_s(\bar{s}|s)dsd\bar{s} = \frac{1}{\mathcal{L}(\mathcal{A}_i)} \int_{\mathcal{A}_i} \left(\sum_{j=1}^{n+1} \int_{\mathcal{A}_j} t_s(\bar{s}|s)d\bar{s} \right) ds$$

$$= \frac{1}{\mathcal{L}(\mathcal{A}_i)} \int_{\mathcal{A}_i} \int_{\mathcal{S}} t_s(\bar{s}|s)d\bar{s}ds = \frac{1}{\mathcal{L}(\mathcal{A}_i)} \int_{\mathcal{A}_i} ds = 1.$$

The initial distribution of $\mathcal{M}_f$ is the pmf $\mathbf{p_0} = [p_0(1), p_0(2), \ldots, p_0(n+1)]$, and it is obtained from π_0 as $p_0(i) = \int_{\mathcal{A}_i} \pi_0(s)ds, \forall i \in \mathbb{N}_{n+1}$. Then the pmf associated to the state distribution of $\mathcal{M}_f$ at time t can be computed as $\mathbf{p_t} = \mathbf{p_0}P^t$.

It is intuitive that the discrete pmf $\mathbf{p_t}$ of the Markov chain $\mathcal{M}_f$ approximates the continuous density function π_t of the Markov process $\mathcal{M}$. In the rest of the section we show how to formalize this relationship: $\mathbf{p_t}$ is used to construct an approximation function, denoted by ψ_t, of the density function π_t. Theorem 3 shows that ψ_t is a piece-wise constant approximation (with values that are the entries of the pmf $\mathbf{p_t}$ normalized by the Lebesgue measure of the associated partition set) of the original density function π_t. Moreover, under the continuity assumption in (4) (ref. Lemma 1) we can establish the Lipschitz continuity of π_t, which enables the quantification in Theorem 3 of the error of its piece-wise constant approximation.

Lemma 1. *Suppose that the inequality in (4) holds. Then the state density functions $\pi_t(\cdot)$ are globally Lipschitz continuous with constant λ_f for all $t \in \mathbb{N}$:*

$$|\pi_t(s) - \pi_t(s')| \leq \lambda_f \|s - s'\| \quad \forall s, s' \in \mathcal{S}.$$

Theorem 3. *Under Assumptions 1 and 2, the functions $\pi_t(\cdot)$ can be approximated by piece-wise constant functions $\psi_t(\cdot)$, defined as*

$$\psi_t(s) = \sum_{i=1}^{n} \frac{p_t(i)}{\mathcal{L}(\mathcal{A}_i)} \mathbb{I}_{\mathcal{A}_i}(s) \quad \forall t \in \mathbb{N}, \tag{11}$$

where $\mathbb{I}_B(\cdot)$ is the indicator function of a set $B \subset \mathcal{S}$. The approximation error is upper-bounded by the quantity

$$\|\pi_t - \psi_t\|_\infty \leq \varepsilon_t + E_t \quad \forall t \in \mathbb{N}, \tag{12}$$

where E_t can be recursively computed as

$$E_{t+1} = M_f E_t + \lambda_f \delta, \quad E_0 = \lambda_0 \delta, \tag{13}$$

and δ is an upper bound on the diameters of the partition sets $\{\mathcal{A}_i\}_{i=1}^{n}$, namely $\delta = \sup\{\|s - s'\|, \ s, s' \in \mathcal{A}_i, \ i \in \mathbb{N}_n\}$.

Note that the functions ψ_t are defined over the whole state space $\mathcal{S}$, but (11) implies that they are equal to zero outside the set Υ.

Corollary 1. *The recursion in (13) admits the explicit solution*

$$E_t = [\kappa(t, M_f)\lambda_f + M_f^t \lambda_0] \delta,$$

where $\kappa(t, M_f)$ is introduced in (8).

Underlying Theorem 3 is the fact that $\psi_t(\cdot)$ are in general sub-stochastic density functions:

$$\int_{\mathcal{S}} \psi_t(s)ds = \int_{\mathcal{S}} \sum_{i=1}^{n} \frac{p_t(i)}{\mathcal{L}(\mathcal{A}_i)} \mathbb{I}_{\mathcal{A}_i}(s)ds = \sum_{i=1}^{n} \frac{p_t(i)}{\mathcal{L}(\mathcal{A}_i)} \int_{\mathcal{S}} \mathbb{I}_{\mathcal{A}_i}(s)ds$$

$$= \sum_{i=1}^{n} \frac{p_t(i)}{\mathcal{L}(\mathcal{A}_i)} \mathcal{L}(\mathcal{A}_i) = \sum_{i=1}^{n} p_t(i) = 1 - p_t(n+1) \leq 1.$$

This is clearly due to the fact that we are operating on the dynamics of $\mathcal{M}$ truncated over the set Υ. It is thus intuitive that the approximation procedure and the derived error bounds are also valid for the case of sub-stochastic density functions, namely

$$\int_{\mathcal{S}} t_s(\bar{s}|s)d\bar{s} \leq 1 \quad \forall s \in \mathcal{S}, \quad \int_{\mathcal{S}} \pi_0(s)ds \leq 1,$$

the only difference being that the obtained Markov chain $\mathcal{M}_f$ is as well sub-stochastic.

Further, whenever the Lipschitz continuity requirement on the initial density function, as per (3) in Assumption 2, does not hold, (for instance, this is the case when the initial state of the process is deterministic) we can relax this continuity assumption on the initial distribution of the process by starting the discrete computation from the time step $t = 1$. In this case we define the pmf $\mathbf{p_1} = [p_1(1), p_1(2), \dots, p_1(n+1)]$, where

$$p_1(i) = \int_{\mathcal{A}_i} \int_{\mathcal{S}} t_s(\bar{s}|s)\pi_0(s)dsd\bar{s} \quad \forall i \in \mathbb{N}_{n+1},$$

and derive $\mathbf{p_t} = \mathbf{p_1}P^{t-1}$ for all $t \in \mathbb{N}$. Theorem 3 follows along similar lines, except for eqn. (13), where the initial error is set to $E_0 = 0$ and the time-dependent terms E_t can be derived as $E_t = \kappa(t, M_f)\lambda_f\delta$.

It is important to emphasize the computability of the derived errors and the fact that they can be tuned. Further, in order to attain abstractions that are practically useful, it imperative to seek improvements on the derived error bounds: in particular, the approximation errors can be computed locally (under corresponding local Lipschitz continuity assumptions), following the procedures discussed in [7].

Example 1 (Continued). The error of proposed Markov chain abstraction can be expressed as

$$\|\pi_t - \psi_t\|_\infty \leq \kappa(t, M_f)\left[\frac{\delta}{\sigma^2\sqrt{2\pi e}} + \frac{\phi_1(\alpha)}{\sigma}\right], \quad M_f = \frac{1}{a}.$$

The error can be tuned in two distinct ways:

1. by selecting larger values for α, which on the one hand leads to a less conservative truncation, but on the other requires the partition of a larger interval;
2. by reducing partitions diameter δ, which of course results in a larger cardinality of the partition sets.

Let us select values $b = 0, \beta_0 = 0, \gamma_0 = 1, \sigma = 0.1$, and time horizon $N = 5$. For $a = 1.2$ we need to partition the interval $\Upsilon = [-0.75\alpha, 2.49 + 0.75\alpha]$, which results in the error $\|\pi_t - \psi_t\|_\infty \leq 86.8\delta + 35.9\phi_1(\alpha)$ for all $t \leq N$. For $a = 0.8$ we need to partition the smaller interval $\Upsilon = [-0.34\alpha, 0.33 + 0.34\alpha]$, which results in the error $\|\pi_t - \psi_t\|_\infty \leq 198.6\delta + 82.1\phi_1(\alpha)$ for all $t \leq N$. In the case of $a = 1.2$, we partition a larger interval and obtain a smaller error, while for $a = 0.8$ we partition a smaller interval with correspondingly a larger error. It is obvious that the parameters δ, α can be chosen properly to ensure that a certain error precision is met. This simple model admits a solution in closed form, and its state density functions can be obtained as the convolution of a uniform distribution (the contribution of initial state) and a zero-mean Gaussian distribution with time-dependent variance (the contributions of the process noise). Figure 2 displays the original and the approximated state density functions for the set of parameters $\alpha = 2.4, \delta = 0.05$. $\Box$

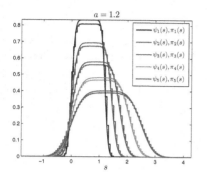
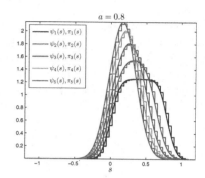

Fig. 2. Piece-wise constant approximation of the state density function $\psi_t(\cdot)$, compared to the actual function $\pi_t(\cdot)$ (derived analytically) for $a = 1.2$ (left) and $a = 0.8$ (right)

5   Application of the Formal Approximation Procedure to the Probabilistic Invariance Problem

The problem of probabilistic invariance (safety) for general Markov processes has been theoretically characterized in [2] and further investigated computationally in [1, 4–6]. With reference to a discrete-time Markov process $\mathcal{M}$ over a continuous state space $\mathcal{S}$, and a safe set $\mathcal{A} \in \mathcal{B}(\mathcal{S})$, the goal is to quantify the probability

$$p_s^N(\mathcal{A}) = \mathbb{P}\{s(t) \in \mathcal{A}, \text{ for all } t \in [0, N] | s(0) = s\}.$$

More generally, it is of interest to quantify the probability $p_{\pi_0}^N(\mathcal{A})$, where the initial condition of the process $s(0)$ is a random variable characterized by the density function $\pi_0(\cdot)$. We present a forward computation of probabilistic invariance by application of the approximation procedure above in Section 5.1, then review results on backward computation [1, 4–6] in Section 5.2. Section 5.3 compares the two approaches.

5.1   Forward Computation of Probabilistic Invariance

The approach for approximating the density function of a process in time can be easily employed for the approximate computation of probabilistic invariance. Define sub-density functions $W_t : \mathcal{S} \to \mathbb{R}^{\geq 0}$, characterized by

$$W_{t+1}(\bar{s}) = \mathbb{I}_A(\bar{s}) \int_S W_t(s) t_s(\bar{s}|s) ds, \quad W_0(\bar{s}) = \mathbb{I}_A(\bar{s}) \pi_0(\bar{s}) \quad \forall \bar{s} \in S. \quad (14)$$

Then the solution of the problem is obtained as $p_{\pi_0}^N(A) = \int_S W_N(s) ds$. A comparison of the recursions in (14) and in (9) reveals how probabilistic invariance can be computed as a special case of the approximation procedure. In applying the procedure, the only difference consists in replacing set Υ by A, and in restricting Assumption 2 to hold over the safe set (the solution over the complement of this set is trivially known) – in this case the error related to the truncation of the state space can be disregarded. The procedure consists in partitioning the safe set, in constructing the Markov chain $\mathcal{M}_f$ as per (10), and in computing $\psi_t(\cdot)$ as an approximation of $W_t(\cdot)$ based on (11). The error of this approximation is $\|W_t - \psi_t\|_\infty \le E_t$, which results in the following:

$$\left| p_{\pi_0}^N(A) - \int_A \psi_t(s) ds \right| \le E_N \mathcal{L}(A) = \kappa(N, M_f) \lambda_f \delta \mathcal{L}(A) \doteq E_f.$$

Note that these sub-density functions satisfy the inequalities

$$1 \ge \int_S W_0(s) ds \ge \int_S W_1(s) ds \ge \cdots \ge \int_S W_N(s) ds \ge 0.$$

5.2   Backward Computation of Probabilistic Invariance

The contributions in [1, 4–6] have characterized specifications in PCTL with a formulation based on backward recursions. In particular, the computation of probabilistic invariance is obtained via the value functions $V_t : S \to [0, 1]$, which are characterized as

$$V_t(s) = \mathbb{I}_A(s) \int_S V_{t+1}(\bar{s}) t_s(\bar{s}|s) d\bar{s}, \quad V_N(s) = \mathbb{I}_A(s) \quad \forall s \in S. \quad (15)$$

The desired probabilistic invariance is expressed as $p_{\pi_0}^N(A) = \int_S V_0(s) \pi_0(s) ds$. The value functions always map the state space to the interval $[0, 1]$ and they are non-increasing, $V_t(s) \le V_{t+1}(s)$ for any fixed $s \in S$. [1, 4–6] discuss efficient algorithms for the approximate computation of the quantity $p_{\pi_0}^N(A)$, relying on different assumptions on the model under study. The easiest and most straightforward procedure is based on the following assumption [1].

Assumption 3. *The conditional density function of the process is globally Lipschitz continuous within the safe set with respect to the conditional state. Namely, there exists a finite constant λ_b, such that*

$$|t(\bar{s}|s) - t(\bar{s}|s')| \le \lambda_b \|s - s'\| \quad \forall s, s', \bar{s} \in A.$$

A finite constant M_b is introduced as $M_b = \sup_{s \in A} \int_A t_s(\bar{s}|s) d\bar{s} \le 1$.

The procedure introduces a partition of the safe set $A = \cup_{i=1}^n A_i$ and extends it to $S = \cup_{i=1}^{n+1} A_i$, with $A_{n+1} = S \backslash A$. Then it selects arbitrary representative points $s_i \in \mathcal{A}_i$ and constructs a finite-state Markov chain $\mathcal{M}_b$ over the finite state space $\{s_1, s_2, \ldots, s_{n+1}\}$, endowed with transition probabilities

$$P(s_i, s_j) = \int_{\mathcal{A}_j} t_s(\bar{s}|s_i)d\bar{s}, \quad P(s_{n+1}, s_j) = \delta_{(n+1)j}, \tag{16}$$

for all $i \in \mathbb{N}_n, j \in \mathbb{N}_{n+1}$. The error of such an approximation is [5]:

$$E_b = \kappa(N, M_b)\lambda_b \delta \mathcal{L}(\mathcal{A}),$$

where δ is the max partitions diameter, $\mathcal{L}(\mathcal{A})$ is the Lebesgue measure of set $\mathcal{A}$.

5.3   Comparison of the Two Approaches

We first compare the two constructed Markov chains. The Markov chain in the forward approach $\mathcal{M}_f$ is a special case of Markov chain of backward approach $\mathcal{M}_b$, where the representative points can be selected intelligently to determine the average probability of jumping from one partition set to another. More specifically, the quantities (10) are a special case of those in (16) (based on mean value theorem for integration). We claim that this leads to a less conservative (smaller) error bound for the approximation.

The forward computation is in general more informative than the backward computation since it provides not only the solution of the safety problem in time, but also the state distribution over the safe set. Further the forward approach may provide some insight to the solution of the infinite-horizon safety problem [16, 17], for a given initial distribution. Finally, the forward approach can be used to approximate the solution of safety problem over unbounded safe sets, while boundedness of the safe set is required in all the results in the literature that are based on backward computations.

Next, we compare errors and related assumptions. The error computations rely on different assumptions: the Lipschitz continuity of the conditional density function with respect to the current or to the next states, respectively. Further, the constants M_f and M_b are generally different and play an important role in the error. M_b represents the maximum probability of remaining inside the safe set, while M_f is an indication of the maximum concentration at one point over a single time-step of the process evolution. M_b is always less than or equal to one, while M_f could be any finite positive number.

Example 1 (Continued) The constants λ_f, M_f and λ_b, M_b for the one dimensional dynamical system of Example 1 are

$$\lambda_f = \frac{1}{\sigma^2\sqrt{2\pi e}}, \quad \lambda_b = a\lambda_f, \quad M_f = \frac{1}{a}, \quad M_b \leq 1.$$

If $0 < a < 1$ the system trajectories converge to an equilibrium point (in expected value). In this case the system state gets higher chances of being in the neighborhood of the equilibrium in time and the backward recursion provides a better error bound. If $a > 1$ the system trajectories tend to diverge with time. In this case the forward recursion provides a much better error bound, compared to the backward recursion.

For the numerical simulation we select a safety set $\mathcal{A} = [0,1]$, a noise level $\sigma = 0.1$, and a time horizon $N = 10$. The solution of the safety problem for the two cases $a = 1.2$ and $a = 0.8$ is plotted in Figure 3. We have computed constants $\lambda_f = 24.20, M_b = 1$ in both cases, while $\lambda_b = 29.03, M_f = 0.83$ for the first case, and $\lambda_b = 19.36, M_f = 1.25$ for the second case. We have selected the center of the partition sets (distributed uniformly over the set $\mathcal{A}$) as representative points for Markov chain $\mathcal{M}_b$. In order to compare the two approaches, we have assumed the same computational effort (related to the same partition size of $\delta = 0.7 \times 10^{-4}$), and have obtained an error $E_f = 0.008, E_b = 0.020$ for $a = 1.2$ and $E_f = 0.056, E_b = 0.014$ for $a = 0.8$. The simulations show that the forward approach works better for $a = 1.2$, while the backward approach is better suitable for $a = 0.8$. Note that the approximate solutions provided by the two approaches are very close: the difference of the transition probabilities computed via the Markov chains $\mathcal{M}_f, \mathcal{M}_b$ are in the order of 10^{-8}, and the difference in the approximate solutions (black curve in Figure 3) is in the order of 10^{-6}. This has been due to the selection of very fine partition sets that have resulted in small abstraction errors. $\qquad\square$

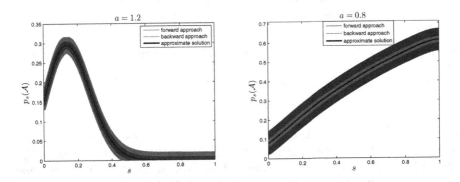

Fig. 3. Approximate solution of the probabilistic invariance problem (black line), together with error intervals of forward (red band) and backward (blue band) approaches, for $a = 1.2$ (left) and $a = 0.8$ (right)

Remark 2. Over deterministic models, [13] compares forward and backward reachability analysis and provides insights on their differences: the claim is that for systems with significant contraction, forward reachability is more effective than backward reachability because of numerical stability issues. On the other hand, for the probabilistic models under study, the result indicates that under Lipschitz continuity of the transition kernel the backward approach is more effective in systems with convergence in the state distribution. If we treat deterministic systems as special (limiting) instances of stochastic systems, our result is not contradicting with [13] since the Lipschitz continuity assumption on the transition kernels of probabilistic models does not hold over deterministic ones. $\qquad\square$

Motivated by the previous case study we study how convergence properties of a Markov process are related to the constant M_f.

Theorem 4. *Assume that the initial density function $\pi_0(s)$ is bounded and that the constant M_f is finite and $M_f < 1$. If the state space is unbounded, the sequence of density functions $\{\pi_t(s)|t \geq 0\}$ uniformly exponentially converges to zero. The sequence of probabilities $\mathbb{P}\{s(t) \in \mathcal{A}\}$ and the corresponding solution of the safety problem for any compact safe set $\mathcal{A}$ exponentially converge to zero.*

Theorem 4 indicates that under the invoked assumptions the probability "spreads out" over the unbounded state space as time progresses. Moreover, the theorem ensures the absence of absorbing sets [16, 17], which are indeed known to characterize the solution of infinite-horizon properties. Example 2 studies the relationship between constant M_f and the stability of linear stochastic difference equations.

Example 2. Consider the stochastic linear difference equations

$$x(t+1) = Ax(t) + w(t), \quad x(\cdot), w(\cdot) \in \mathbb{R}^n,$$

where $w(\cdot)$ are i.i.d. random vectors with known distributions. For such systems $M_f = 1/|\det A|$, then the condition $M_f < 1$ implies instability of the system in expected value. Equivalently, mean-stability of the system implies $M_f \geq 1$. Note that for this class of systems $M_f > 1$ does not generally imply stability, since $\det A$ is only the product of the eigenvalues of the system.   □

The Lipschitz constants λ_f and λ_b have a different nature. Example 3 clarifies this point.

Example 3. Consider the dynamical system

$$s(t+1) = f(s(t), w(t)),$$

where $w(\cdot)$ are i.i.d. with known distribution $t_w(\cdot)$. Suppose that the vector field $f : \mathbb{R}^n \times \mathbb{R}^n \to \mathbb{R}^n$ is continuously differentiable and that the matrix $\frac{\partial f}{\partial w}$ is invertible. Then the *implicit function theorem* guarantees the existence and uniqueness of a function $g : \mathbb{R}^n \times \mathbb{R}^n \to \mathbb{R}^n$ such that $w(t) = g(s(t+1), s(t))$. The conditional density function of the system in this case is [14]:

$$t_s(\bar{s}|s) = \left|\det\left[\frac{\partial g}{\partial \bar{s}}(\bar{s}, s)\right]\right| t_w(g(\bar{s}, s)).$$

The Lipschitz constants λ_f, λ_b are specified by the dependence of function $g(\bar{s}, s)$ from the variables $\bar{s}, s$, respectively. As a special case the invertability of $\frac{\partial f}{\partial w}$ is guaranteed for systems with additive process noise, namely $f(s, w) = f_a(s) + w$. Then $g(\bar{s}, s) = \bar{s} - f_a(s)$, λ_f is the Lipschitz constant of $t_w(\cdot)$, while λ_b is the multiplication of Lipschitz constant of $t_w(\cdot)$ and of $f_a(\cdot)$.   □

References

1. Abate, A., Katoen, J.-P., Lygeros, J., Prandini, M.: Approximate model checking of stochastic hybrid systems. European Journal of Control 6, 624–641 (2010)
2. Abate, A., Prandini, M., Lygeros, J., Sastry, S.: Probabilistic reachability and safety for controlled discrete time stochastic hybrid systems. Automatica 44(11), 2724–2734 (2008)

3. Baier, C., Katoen, J.-P., Hermanns, H.: Approximate symbolic model checking of continuous-time Markov chains (Extended abstract). In: Baeten, J.C.M., Mauw, S. (eds.) CONCUR 1999. LNCS, vol. 1664, pp. 146–162. Springer, Heidelberg (1999)
4. Esmaeil Zadeh Soudjani, S., Abate, A.: Adaptive gridding for abstraction and verification of stochastic hybrid systems. In: Proceedings of the 8th International Conference on Quantitative Evaluation of Systems, Aachen, DE, pp. 59–69 (September 2011)
5. Esmaeil Zadeh Soudjani, S., Abate, A.: Higher-Order Approximations for Verification of Stochastic Hybrid Systems. In: Chakraborty, S., Mukund, M. (eds.) ATVA 2012. LNCS, vol. 7561, pp. 416–434. Springer, Heidelberg (2012)
6. Esmaeil Zadeh Soudjani, S., Abate, A.: Probabilistic invariance of mixed deterministic-stochastic dynamical systems. In: ACM Proceedings of the 15th International Conference on Hybrid Systems: Computation and Control, Beijing, PRC, pp. 207–216 (April 2012)
7. Esmaeil Zadeh Soudjani, S., Abate, A.: Adaptive and sequential gridding procedures for the abstraction and verification of stochastic processes. SIAM Journal on Applied Dynamical Systems 12(2), 921–956 (2013)
8. Koutsoukos, X., Riley, D.: Computational methods for reachability analysis of stochastic hybrid systems. In: Hespanha, J.P., Tiwari, A. (eds.) HSCC 2006. LNCS, vol. 3927, pp. 377–391. Springer, Heidelberg (2006)
9. Kurshan, R.P.: Computer-Aided Verification of Coordinating Processes: The Automata-Theoretic Approach. Princeton Series in Computer Science. Princeton University Press (1994)
10. Kushner, H.J., Dupuis, P.G.: Numerical Methods for Stochastic Control Problems in Continuous Time. Springer, New York (2001)
11. Kvasnica, M., Grieder, P., Baotić, M.: Multi-parametric toolbox, MPT (2004)
12. Kwiatkowska, M., Norman, G., Segala, R., Sproston, J.: Verifying quantitative properties of continuous probabilistic timed automata. In: Palamidessi, C. (ed.) CONCUR 2000. LNCS, vol. 1877, pp. 123–137. Springer, Heidelberg (2000)
13. Mitchell, I.M.: Comparing forward and backward reachability as tools for safety analysis. In: Bemporad, A., Bicchi, A., Buttazzo, G. (eds.) HSCC 2007. LNCS, vol. 4416, pp. 428–443. Springer, Heidelberg (2007)
14. Papoulis, A.: Probability, Random Variables, and Stochastic Processes, 3rd edn. Mcgraw-hill (1991)
15. Prandini, M., Hu, J.: Stochastic reachability: Theory and numerical approximation. In: Cassandras, C.G., Lygeros, J. (eds.) Stochastic Hybrid Systems. Automation and Control Engineering Series, vol. 24, pp. 107–138. Taylor & Francis Group/CRC Press (2006)
16. Tkachev, I., Abate, A.: On infinite-horizon probabilistic properties and stochastic bisimulation functions. In: Proceedings of the 50th IEEE Conference on Decision and Control and European Control Conference, Orlando, FL, pp. 526–531 (December 2011)
17. Tkachev, I., Abate, A.: Characterization and computation of infinite-horizon specifications over markov processes. Theoretical Computer Science 515, 1–18 (2014)

SACO: Static Analyzer for Concurrent Objects

Elvira Albert[1], Puri Arenas[1], Antonio Flores-Montoya[2], Samir Genaim[1],
Miguel Gómez-Zamalloa[1], Enrique Martin-Martin[1],
German Puebla[3], and Guillermo Román-Díez[3]

[1] Complutense University of Madrid (UCM), Spain
[2] Technische Universität Darmstadt (TUD), Germany
[3] Technical University of Madrid (UPM), Spain

Abstract. We present the main concepts, usage and implementation of
SACO, a static analyzer for concurrent objects. Interestingly, SACO is
able to infer both *liveness* (namely termination and resource boundedness) and *safety* properties (namely deadlock freedom) of programs based
on concurrent objects. The system integrates auxiliary analyses such as
points-to and *may-happen-in-parallel*, which are essential for increasing
the accuracy of the aforementioned more complex properties. SACO provides accurate information about the dependencies which may introduce
deadlocks, loops whose termination is not guaranteed, and upper bounds
on the resource consumption of methods.

1 Introduction

With the trend of parallel systems, and the emergence of multi-core computing, the construction of tools that help analyzing and verifying the behaviour
of concurrent programs has become fundamental. Concurrent programs contain
several processes that work together to perform a task and communicate with
each other. Communication can be programmed using shared variables or message passing. When shared variables are used, one process writes into a variable
that is read by another; when message passing is used, one process sends a message that is received by another. Shared memory communication is typically
implemented using low-level concurrency and synchronization primitives These
programs are in general more difficult to write, debug and analyze, while its main
advantage is efficiency. The message passing model uses higher-level concurrency
constructs that help in producing concurrent applications in a less error-prone
way and also more modularly. Message passing is the essence of actors [1], the
concurrency model used in *concurrent objects* [9], in Erlang, and in Scala.

This paper presents the SACO system, a *S*tatic *A*nalyzer for *C*oncurrent
*O*bjects. Essentially, each concurrent object is a monitor and allows at most
one *active* task to execute within the object. Scheduling among the tasks of
an object is cooperative, or non-preemptive, such that the active task has to
release the object lock explicitly (using the **await** instruction). Each object has
an unbounded set of pending tasks. When the lock of an object is free, any task
in the set of pending tasks can grab the lock and start executing. When the
result of a call is required by the caller to continue executing, the caller and the

E. Ábrahám and K. Havelund (Eds.): TACAS 2014, LNCS 8413, pp. 562–567, 2014.
© Springer-Verlag Berlin Heidelberg 2014

callee methods can be synchronized by means of *future variables*, which act as proxies for results initially unknown, as their computations are still incomplete.

The figure below overviews the main components of SACO, whose distinguishing feature is that it infers both *liveness* and *safety* properties.

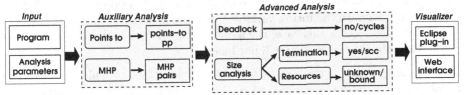

SACO receives as input a program and a selection of the analysis parameters. Then it performs two auxiliary analyses: points-to and may-happen-in-parallel (MHP), which are used for inferring the more complex properties in the next phase. As regards to liveness, we infer termination as well as resource boundedness, i.e., find upper bounds on the resource consumption of methods. Both analyses require the inference of *size relations*, which are gathered in a previous step. Regarding *safety*, we infer deadlock freedom, i.e., there is no state in which a non-empty set of tasks cannot progress because all tasks are waiting for the termination of other tasks in the set, or otherwise we show the tasks involved in a potential deadlock set. Finally, SACO can be used from a command line interface, a web interface, and an Eclipse plugin. It can be downloaded and/or used online from its website **http://costa.ls.fi.upm.es/saco**.

2   Auxiliary Analyses

We describe the auxiliary analyses used in SACO by means of the example below:

```
 1 class PrettyPrinter{          15 void insertCoin(){          29 //main method
 2  void showIncome(Int n){...}   16  coins=coins+1;             30 main(Int n){
 3  void showCoin(){...}          17 }                           31  PrettyPrinter p;
 4 }//end class                   18 Int retrieveCoins(){        32  VendingMachine v;
 5 class VendingMachine{          19  Fut⟨void⟩ f;               33  Fut⟨Int⟩ f;
 6  Int coins;                    20  Int total=0;               34  p=new PrettyPrinter();
 7  PrettyPrinter out;            21  while (coins>0){           35  v=new VendingMachine(0,p);
 8  void insertCoins(Int n){      22   coins=coins−1;            36  v ! insertCoins(n);
 9   Fut⟨void⟩ f;                 23   f=out ! showCoin();       37  f=v ! retrieveCoins();
10   while (n>0){                 24   await f?;                 38  await f?;
11    n=n−1;                      25   total=total+1; }          39  Int total=f.get;
12    f=this ! insertCoin();      26  return total;              40  p!showIncome(total);
13    await f?; }                 27 }                           41 }
14 }                              28 }//end class
```

We have a class PrettyPrinter to display some information and a class VendingMachine with methods to insert a number of coins and to retrieve all coins. The main method is executing on the object This, which is the initial object, and receives as parameter the number of coins to be inserted. Besides This, two other concurrent objects are created at Line 34 (L34 for short) and L35. Objects can be seen as buffers in which tasks are posted and that execute in parallel. In particular, two tasks are posted at L36 and L37 on object v. insertCoins executes asynchronously on v. However, the **await** at L38 synchronizes the execution of This with the completion of the task retrieveCoins in v by means of the future variable f. Namely, at the **await**, if the task spawned at L37 has not finished, the processor is released and any available task on the This object could take it. The result of the execution of retrieveCoins is obtained by means of the blocking **get** instruction which *blocks* the execution of This until the future variable f is ready. In general, the use of **get** can introduce deadlocks. In this case, the **await** at L38 ensures that retrieveCoins has finished and thus the execution will not block.

Points-to Analysis. Inferring the set of memory locations to which a reference variable *may* point-to is a classical analysis in object-oriented languages. In SACO we follow Milonava et al. [11] and abstract objects by the *sequence of allocation sites* of all objects that lead to its creation. E.g., if we create an object o_1 at program point pp_1, and afterwards call a method of o_1 that creates an object o_2 at program point pp_2, then the abstract representation of o_2 is $pp_1.pp_2$. In order to ensure termination of the inference process, the analysis is parametrized by k, the maximal length of these sequences. In the example, for any $k \geq 2$, assuming that the allocation site of the This object is ϵ, the points-to analysis abstracts v and out to $\epsilon.35$ and $\epsilon.34$, respectively. For $k = 1$, they would be abstracted to 35 and 34. As variables can be reused, the information that the analysis gives is specified at the program point level. Basically, the analysis results are defined by a function $\mathcal{P}(o_p, pp, v)$ which for a given (abstract) object o_p, a program point pp and a variable v, it returns the set of abstract objects to which v may point to. For instance, $\mathcal{P}(\epsilon, 36, v) = 35$ should be read as: when executing This and instruction L36 is reached, variable v points to an object whose allocation site is 35. Besides, we can trivially use the analysis results to find out to which task a future variable f is pointing to. I.e., $\mathcal{P}(o_p, pp, f) = o.m$ where o is an abstract object and m a method name, e.g., $\mathcal{P}(\epsilon, 37, f) = 35.\text{retrieveCoins}$. Points-to analysis allows making any analysis object-sensitive [11]. In addition, in SACO we use it: (1) in the resource analysis in order to know to which object the cost must be attributed, and (2) in the deadlock analysis, where the abstraction of future variables above is used to spot dependencies among tasks.

May-Happen-in-Parallel. An MHP analysis [10,3] provides a safe approximation of the set of pairs of statements that can execute in parallel across several objects, or in an interleaved way within an object. MHP allows ensuring absence of data races, i.e., that several objects access the same data in parallel and at least one of them modifies such data. Also, it is crucial for improving the accuracy of deadlock, termination and resource analysis. The MHP analysis implemented in SACO [3] can be understood as a function $\mathcal{MHP}(o_p, pp)$ which returns the set of program points that may happen in parallel with pp when executing in the abstract object o_p. A remarkable feature of our analysis is that it performs a local analysis of methods followed by a composition of the local results, and it has a polynomial complexity. In our example, SACO infers that the execution of showIncome (L2) cannot happen in parallel with any instruction in retrieveCoins (L18–L27), since retrieveCoins must be finished in the **await** at L38. Similarly, it also reveals that showCoin (L3) cannot happen in parallel with showIncome. On the other hand, SACO detects that the **await** (L24) and the assignment (L16) may happen in parallel. This could be a problem for the termination of retrieveCoins, as the shared variable coins that controls the loop may be modified in parallel, but our termination analysis can overcome this difficulty. Since the result of the MHP analysis refines the control-flow, we could also consider applying the MHP and points-to analyses continuously to refine the results of each other. In SACO we apply them only once.

3 Advanced Analyses

Termination Analysis. The main challenge is in handling *shared-memory* concurrent programs. When execution interleaves from one task to another, the shared-memory may be modified by the interleaved task. The modifications can affect the behavior of the program and change its termination behavior and its resource consumption. Inspired by the rely-guarantee principle used for compositional verification and analysis [12,5] of thread-based concurrent programs, SACO incorporates a novel termination analysis for concurrent objects [4] which assumes a *property* on the global state in order to prove termination of a loop and, then, proves that this property holds. The property to prove is the *finiteness* of the shared-data involved in the termination proof, i.e., proving that such shared-memory is updated a finite number of times. Our analysis is based on a circular style of reasoning since the finiteness assumptions are proved by proving termination of the loops in which that shared-memory is modified. Crucial for accuracy is the use of the information inferred by the MHP analysis which allows us to restrict the set of program points on which the property has to be proved to those that may actually interleave its execution with the considered loop.

Consider the function retrieveCoins from Sec. 2. At the **await** (L24) the value of the shared variable coins may change, since other tasks may take the object's lock and modify coins. In order to prove termination, the analysis first assumes that coins is updated a finite number of times. Under this assumption the loop is terminating because eventually the value of coins will stop being updated by other tasks, and then it will decrease at each iteration of the loop. The second step is to prove that the assumption holds, i.e., that the instructions updating coins are executed a finite number of times. The only update instruction that may happen in parallel with the **await** is in insertCoin (L16), which is called from insertCoins and this from main. Since these three functions are terminating (their termination can be proved without any assumption), the assumption holds and therefore retrieveCoins terminates. Similarly, the analysis can prove the termination of the other functions, thus proving the whole program terminating.

Resource Analysis. SACO can measure different types of costs (e.g., number of execution steps, memory created, etc.) [2]. In the output, it returns upper bounds on the worst-case cost of executing the concurrent program. The results of our termination analysis provide useful information for cost: if the program is terminating then the size of all data is bounded (we use x^+ to refer to the maximal value for x). Thus, we can give cost bounds in terms of the maximum and/or minimum values that the involved data can reach. Still, we need novel techniques to infer upper bounds on the number of iterations of loops whose execution might interleave with instructions that update the shared memory. SACO incorporates a novel approach which is based on the combination of *local* ranking functions (i.e., ranking functions obtained by ignoring the concurrent interleaving behaviors) with upper bounds on the *number of visits* to the instructions which update the shared memory. As in termination, the function $\mathcal{MHP}$ is used to restrict the set of points whose visits have to be counted to those that indeed may interleave.

Consider again the loop inside retrieveCoins. Ignoring concurrent interleavings, a local ranking function $RF =$ coins is easily computed. In order to obtain an upper bound on the number of iterations considering interleavings, we need to calculate the number of visits to L16, the only instruction that updates coins and MHP with the **await** in L24. We need to add the number of visits to L16 for every path of calls reaching it, in this case main–insertCoins–insertCoin only. By applying the analysis recursively we obtain that L16 is visited n times. Combining the local ranking function and the number of visits to L16 we obtain that an upper bound on the number of iterations of the loop in retrieveCoins is $coin^+ * n$.

Finally, we use the results of points-to analysis to infer the cost at the level of the distributed components (i.e., the objects). Namely, we give an upper bound of the form $c(\epsilon)^*(\ldots)+c(35)^*(coin^+ * n\ldots)+ c(34)^*(\ldots)$ which distinguishes the cost attributed to each abstract object o by means of its associated marker $c(o)$.

Deadlock Analysis. The combination of non-blocking (**await**) and blocking (**get**) mechanisms to access futures may give rise to complex deadlock situations. SACO provides a rigorous formal analysis which ensures deadlock freedom, as described in [6]. Similarly to other deadlock analyses, our analysis is based on constructing a *dependency graph* which, if acyclic, guarantees that the program is deadlock free. In order to construct the dependency graph, we use points-to analysis to identify the set of objects and tasks created along any execution. Given this information, the construction of the graph is done by a traversal of the program in which we analyze **await** and **get** instructions in order to detect possible deadlock situations. However, without further *temporal* information, our dependency graphs would be extremely imprecise. The

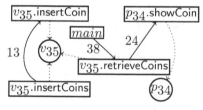

crux of our analysis is the use of the MHP analysis which allows us to label the dependency graph with the program points of the synchronization instructions that introduce the dependencies and, thus, that may potentially induce deadlocks. In a post-process, we discard *unfeasible* cycles in which the synchronization instructions involved in the circular dependency cannot happen in parallel. The dependency graph for our example is shown above. Circular nodes represent objects and squares tasks. Solid edges are tagged with the program point that generated them (**await** or **get** instructions). Dotted edges go from each task to their objects indicating ownership. In our example, there are no cycles in the graph. Thus, the program is deadlock free.

4 Related Tools and Conclusions

We have presented a powerful static analyzer for an actor-based concurrency model, which is lately regaining much attention due to its adoption in Erlang, Scala and concurrent objects (e.g., there are libraries in Java implementing concurrent objects). As regards to related tools, there is another tool [7] which performs deadlock analysis of concurrent objects but, unlike SACO, it does not rely on MHP and points-to analyses. We refer to [3,6] for detailed descriptions on the false positives that our tool can give. Regarding termination, we only know of the TERMINATOR tool [8] for thread-based concurrency. As far as we know, there are no other cost analyzers for imperative concurrent programs.

Acknowledgments. This work was funded partially by the EU project FP7-ICT-610582 ENVISAGE: Engineering Virtualized Services (http://www.envisage-project.eu) and by the Spanish projects TIN2008-05624 and TIN2012-38137.

References

1. Agha, G.A.: Actors: A Model of Concurrent Computation in Distributed Systems. MIT Press, Cambridge (1986)
2. Albert, E., Arenas, P., Genaim, S., Gómez-Zamalloa, M., Puebla, G.: Cost Analysis of Concurrent OO Programs. In: Yang, H. (ed.) APLAS 2011. LNCS, vol. 7078, pp. 238–254. Springer, Heidelberg (2011)
3. Albert, E., Flores-Montoya, A.E., Genaim, S.: Analysis of May-Happen-in-Parallel in Concurrent Objects. In: Giese, H., Rosu, G. (eds.) FMOODS/FORTE 2012. LNCS, vol. 7273, pp. 35–51. Springer, Heidelberg (2012)
4. Albert, E., Flores-Montoya, A., Genaim, S., Martin-Martin, E.: Termination and Cost Analysis of Loops with Concurrent Interleavings. In: Van Hung, D., Ogawa, M. (eds.) ATVA 2013. LNCS, vol. 8172, pp. 349–364. Springer, Heidelberg (2013)
5. Cook, B., Podelski, A., Rybalchenko, A.: Proving Thread Termination. In: PLDI 2007, pp. 320–330. ACM (2007)
6. Flores-Montoya, A.E., Albert, E., Genaim, S.: May-Happen-in-Parallel Based Deadlock Analysis for Concurrent Objects. In: Beyer, D., Boreale, M. (eds.) FMOODS/-FORTE 2013. LNCS, vol. 7892, pp. 273–288. Springer, Heidelberg (2013)
7. Giachino, E., Laneve, C.: Analysis of Deadlocks in Object Groups. In: Bruni, R., Dingel, J. (eds.) FMOODS/FORTE 2011. LNCS, vol. 6722, pp. 168–182. Springer, Heidelberg (2011)
8. http://research.microsoft.com/enus/um/cambridge/projects/terminator/
9. Johnsen, E.B., Hähnle, R., Schäfer, J., Schlatte, R., Steffen, M.: ABS: A Core Language for Abstract Behavioral Specification. In: Aichernig, B.K., de Boer, F.S., Bonsangue, M.M. (eds.) FMCO 2011. LNCS, vol. 6957, pp. 142–164. Springer, Heidelberg (2011)
10. Lee, J.K., Palsberg, J.: Featherweight X10: A Core Calculus for Async-Finish Parallelism. In: PPoPP 2010, pp. 25–36. ACM (2010)
11. Milanova, A., Rountev, A., Ryder, B.G.: Parameterized Object Sensitivity for Points-to Analysis for Java. ACM Trans. Softw. Eng. Methodol. 14, 1–41 (2005)
12. Popeea, C., Rybalchenko, A.: Compositional Termination Proofs for Multi-threaded Programs. In: Flanagan, C., König, B. (eds.) TACAS 2012. LNCS, vol. 7214, pp. 237–251. Springer, Heidelberg (2012)

VeriMAP: A Tool for Verifying Programs through Transformations

Emanuele De Angelis[1,*], Fabio Fioravanti[1],
Alberto Pettorossi[2], and Maurizio Proietti[3]

[1] DEC, University 'G. D'Annunzio', Pescara, Italy
{emanuele.deangelis,fioravanti}@unich.it
[2] DICII, University of Rome Tor Vergata, Rome, Italy
pettorossi@disp.uniroma2.it
[3] IASI-CNR, Rome, Italy
maurizio.proietti@iasi.cnr.it

Abstract. We present VeriMAP, a tool for the verification of C programs based on the transformation of constraint logic programs, also called constrained Horn clauses. VeriMAP makes use of Constraint Logic Programming (CLP) as a metalanguage for representing: (i) the operational semantics of the C language, (ii) the program, and (iii) the property to be verified. Satisfiability preserving transformations of the CLP representations are then applied for generating verification conditions and checking their satisfiability. VeriMAP has an interface with various solvers for reasoning about constraints that express the properties of the data (in particular, integers and arrays). Experimental results show that VeriMAP is competitive with respect to state-of-the-art tools for program verification.

1 The Transformational Approach to Verification

Program verification techniques based on *Constraint Logic Programming* (CLP), or equivalently *constrained Horn clauses* (CHC), have gained increasing popularity during the last years [2,4,8,17]. Indeed, CLP has been shown to be a powerful, flexible metalanguage for specifying the program syntax, the operational semantics, and the proof rules for many different programming languages and program properties. Moreover, the use of the CLP-based techniques allows one to enhance the reasoning capabilities provided by Horn clause logic by taking advantage of the many special purpose solvers that are available for various data domains, such as integers, arrays, and other data structures.

Several verification tools, such as ARMC [18], Duality [15], ELDARICA [12], HSF [7], TRACER [13], μZ [11], implement reasoning techniques within CLP (or CHC) by following approaches based on *interpolants, satisfiability modulo theories, counterexample-guided abstraction refinement*, and *symbolic execution* of CLP programs.

Our tool for program verification, called VeriMAP, is based on *transformation* techniques for CLP programs [3,4,19]. The current version of the VeriMAP can

---

* Supported by the National Group of Computing Science (GNCS-INDAM).

E. Ábrahám and K. Havelund (Eds.): TACAS 2014, LNCS 8413, pp. 568–574, 2014.

be used for verifying safety properties of C programs that manipulate integers and arrays. We assume that: (i) a safety property of a program P is defined by a pair $\langle \varphi_{init}, \varphi_{error} \rangle$ of formulas, and (ii) safety holds iff no execution of P starting from an initial configuration that satisfies φ_{init}, terminates in a final configuration that satisfies φ_{error}.

From the CLP representation of the given C program and of the property, VeriMAP generates a set of *verification conditions* (VC's) in the form of CLP clauses. The VC generation is performed by a transformation that consists in specializing (with respect to the given C program and property) a CLP program that defines the operational semantics of the C language and the proof rules for verifying safety. Then, the CLP program made out of the generated VC's is transformed by applying unfold/fold transformation rules [5]. This transformation 'propagates' the constraints occurring in the CLP clauses and derives equisatisfiable, easier to analyze VC's. During constraint propagation VeriMAP makes use of constraint solvers for linear (integer or rational) arithmetic and array formulas. In a subsequent phase the transformed VC's are processed by a *lightweight analyzer* that basically consists in a bounded unfolding of the clauses. Since safety is in general undecidable, the analyzer may not be able to detect the satisfiability or the unsatisfiability of the VC's and, if this is the case, the verification process continues by iterating the transformation and the propagation of the constraints in the VC's.

The main advantage of the transformational approach to program verification over other approaches is that it allows one to construct highly parametric, configurable verification tools. In fact, one could modify VeriMAP so as to deal with other programming languages, different language features, and different properties to be proved. This modification can be done by reconfiguring the individual modules of the tool, and in particular, (i) by replacing the CLP clauses that define the language semantics and proof rules, (ii) by designing a suitable strategy for specializing the language semantics and proof rules so as to automatically generate the VC's for any given program and property, (iii) by designing suitable strategies for transforming the VC's by plugging-in different constraint solvers and *replacement rules* (which are clause rewriting rules) depending on the theories of the data structures that are used, (iv) by replacing the lightweight analyzer currently used in VeriMAP by other, more precise analyzers available for CLP programs. These module reconfigurations may require considerable effort (and this is particularly true for the design of the strategies of Point (iii)), but then, by composing the different module versions we get, we will have at our disposal a rich variety of powerful verification procedures.

Another interesting feature of the transformational approach is that at each step of the transformation, we get a set of VC's which is equisatisfiable with respect to the initial set. This feature allows us both (i) to compose together various verification strategies, each one being expressed by a sequence of transformations, and (ii) to use VeriMAP as a front-end for other verifiers (such as those we have mentioned above) that can take as input VC's in the form of CLP clauses. Finally, the use of satisfiability preserving transformations eases the task of guaranteeing that VeriMAP computes sound results, as the soundness of the transformation rules can be proved once and for all, before performing any verification using VeriMAP.

2   The VeriMAP Tool: Architecture and Usage

Architecture. The VeriMAP tool consists of three modules (see Figure 1). (1) A *C-to-CLP Translator* (*C2CLP*) that constructs a CLP encoding of the C program and of the property given as input. *C2CLP* first translates the given C program into CIL, the C Intermediate Language of [16]. (2) A *Verification Conditions Generator* (*VCG*) that generates a CLP program representing the VC's for the given program and property. The *VCG* module takes as input also the CLP representations of the operational semantics of CIL and of the proof rules for establishing safety. (3) An *Iterated Verifier* (*IV*) that attempts to determine whether or not the VC's are satisfiable by iteratively applying unfold/fold transformations to the input VC's, and analyzing the derived VC's.

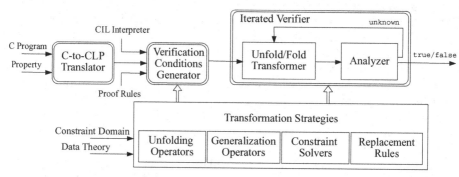

Fig. 1. The VeriMAP architecture

The *C2CLP* module is based on a modified version of the CIL tool [16]. This module first parses and type-checks the input C program, annotated with the property to be verified, and then transforms it into an equivalent program written in CIL that uses a reduced set of language constructs. During this transformation, in particular, commands that use *while*'s and *for*'s are translated into equivalent commands that use *if-then-else*'s and *goto*'s. This transformation step simplifies the subsequent processing steps. Finally, *C2CLP* generates as output the CLP encoding of the program and of the property by running a custom implementation of the CIL visitor pattern [16]. In particular, for each program command, *C2CLP* generates a CLP fact of the form at(L, C), where C and L represent the command and its label, respectively. *C2CLP* also constructs the clauses for the predicates phiInit and phiError representing the formulas φ_{init} and φ_{error} that specify the safety property.

The *VCG* module generates the VC's for the given program and property by applying a program specialization technique based on equivalence preserving unfold/fold transformations of CLP programs [5]. Similarly to what has been proposed in [17], the *VCG* module specializes the interpreter and the proof rules with respect to the CLP representation of the program and safety property generated by *C2CLP* (that is, the clauses defining at, phiInit, and phiError). The output of the specialization process is the CLP representation of the VC's. This specialization process is said to 'remove the interpreter' in the sense that it removes every reference to the predicates used in the CLP definition of the interpreter in favour of new predicates corresponding to (a subset of) the 'program points' of the original C program. Indeed, the structure of the call-graph of the CLP program generated by the *VCG* module corresponds to that of the control-flow graph of the C program.

The *IV* module consists of two submodules: (i) the *Unfold/Fold Transformer*, and (ii) the *Analyzer*. The *Unfold/Fold Transformer* propagates the constraints occurring in the definition of phiInit and phiError through the input VC's thereby deriving a new, equisatisfiable set of VC's. The *Analyzer* checks the satisfiability of the VC's by performing a lightweight analysis. The output of this analysis is either (i) true, if the VC's are satisfiable, and hence the program is safe, or (ii) false, if the VC's are unsatisfiable, and hence the program is unsafe (and a counterexample may be extracted), or (iii) unknown, if the lightweight analysis is unable to determine whether or not the VC's are satisfiable. In this last case the verification continues by iterating the propagation of constraints by invoking again the *Unfold/Fold Transformer* submodule. At each iteration, the *IV* module can also apply a *Reversal* transformation [4], with the effect of reversing the direction of the constraint propagation (either from phiInit to phiError or vice versa, from phiError to phiInit).

The *VCG* and *IV* modules are realized by using MAP [14], a transformation engine for CLP programs (written in SICStus Prolog), with suitable concrete versions of *Transformation Strategies*. There are various versions of the transformation strategies which, as indicated in [4], are defined in terms of: (i) *Unfolding Operators*, which guide the symbolic evaluation of the VC's, by controlling the expansion of the symbolic execution trees, (ii) *Generalization Operators* [6], which guarantee termination of the *Unfold/Fold Transformer* and are used (together with widening and convex-hull operations) for the automatic discovery loop invariants, (iii) *Constraint Solvers*, which check satisfiability and entailment within the Constraint Domain at hand (for example, the integers or the rationals), and (iv) *Replacement Rules*, which guide the application of the axioms and the properties of the Data Theory under consideration (like, for example, the theory of arrays), and their interaction with the Constraint Domain.

Usage. VeriMAP can be downloaded from http://map.uniroma2.it/VeriMAP and can be run by executing the following command: ./VeriMAP program.c, where program.c is the C program annotated with the property to be verified. VeriMAP has options for applying custom transformation strategies and for exiting after the execution of the *C2CLP* or *VCG* modules, or after the execution of a given number of iterations of the *IV* module.

3   Experimental Evaluation

We have experimentally evaluated VeriMAP on several benchmark sets. The first benchmark set for our experiments consisted of 216 safety verification problems of C programs acting on integers (179 of which are safe, and the remaining 37 are unsafe). None of these programs deal with arrays. Most problems have been taken from the TACAS 2013 Software Verification Competition [1] and from the benchmark sets of other tools used in software model checking, like DAGGER [9], TRACER [13] and InvGen [10]. The size of the input programs ranges from a dozen to about five hundred lines of code.

In Table 1 we summarize the verification results obtained by VeriMAP and the following three state-of-the-art CLP-based software model checkers for C programs: (i) ARMC [18], (ii) HSF(C) [7], and (iii) TRACER [13] using the strongest postcondition (*SPost*) and the weakest precondition (*WPre*) options.

Table 1. Verification results using VeriMAP, ARMC, HSF(C), and TRACER. Time is in seconds. The time limit for timeout is five minutes. (∗) These errors are due to incorrect parsing, or excessive memory requirements, or similar other causes.

	VeriMAP	ARMC	HSF(C)	TRACER	
				SPost	*WPre*
correct answers	185	138	160	91	103
safe problems	154	112	138	74	85
unsafe problems	31	26	22	17	18
incorrect answers	0	9	4	13	14
missed bugs	0	1	1	0	0
false alarms	0	8	3	13	14
errors (∗)	0	18	0	20	22
timeout	31	51	52	92	77
total time	10717.34	15788.21	15770.33	27757.46	23259.19
average time	57.93	114.41	98.56	305.03	225.82

The results of the experiments show that our approach is competitive with state-of-the-art verifiers. Besides the above benchmark set, we have used VeriMAP on a small benchmark set of verification problems of C programs acting on integers and arrays. These problems include programs for computing the maximum elements of arrays and programs for performing array initialization, array copy, and array search. Also for this benchmark, the results we have obtained show that our transformational approach is effective and quite efficient in practice.

All experiments have been performed on an Intel Core Duo E7300 2.66Ghz processor with 4GB of memory running GNU/Linux, using a time limit of five minutes. The source code of all the verification problems we have considered is available at http://map.uniroma2.it/VeriMAP.

4 Future Work

The current version of VeriMAP deals with safety properties of a subset of the C language where, in particular, pointers and recursive procedures do not occur. Moreover, the user is only allowed to configure the transformation strategies by choosing among some available submodules for unfolding, generalization, constraint solving, and replacement rules (see Figure 1). Future work will be devoted to make VeriMAP a more flexible tool so that the user may configure other parameters, such as: (i) the programming language and its semantics, (ii) the class of properties and their proof rules (thus generalizing an idea proposed in [8]), and (iii) the theory of the data types in use, including those for dynamic data structures, such as lists and heaps.

References

1. Beyer, D.: Second Competition on Software Verification (SV-COMP 2013). In: Piterman, N., Smolka, S.A. (eds.) TACAS 2013. LNCS, vol. 7795, pp. 594–609. Springer, Heidelberg (2013)
2. Bjørner, N., McMillan, K., Rybalchenko, A.: On solving universally quantified Horn clauses. In: Logozzo, F., Fähndrich, M. (eds.) SAS 2013. LNCS, vol. 7935, pp. 105–125. Springer, Heidelberg (2013)
3. De Angelis, E., Fioravanti, F., Pettorossi, A., Proietti, M.: Verification of imperative programs by constraint logic program transformation. In: SAIRP 2013, Electronic Proceedings in Theoretical Computer Science, vol. 129, pp. 186–210 (2013)
4. De Angelis, E., Fioravanti, F., Pettorossi, A., Proietti, M.: Verifying Programs via Iterated Specialization. In: PEPM 2013, pp. 43–52. ACM (2013)
5. Fioravanti, F., Pettorossi, A., Proietti, M.: Transformation rules for locally stratified constraint logic programs. In: Bruynooghe, M., Lau, K.-K. (eds.) Program Development in Computational Logic. LNCS, vol. 3049, pp. 291–339. Springer, Heidelberg (2004)
6. Fioravanti, F., Pettorossi, A., Proietti, M., Senni, V.: Generalization strategies for the verification of infinite state systems. Theory and Practice of Logic Programming 13(2), 175–199 (2013)
7. Grebenshchikov, S., Gupta, A., Lopes, N.P., Popeea, C., Rybalchenko, A.: HSF(C): A software verifier based on Horn clauses. In: Flanagan, C., König, B. (eds.) TACAS 2012. LNCS, vol. 7214, pp. 549–551. Springer, Heidelberg (2012)
8. Grebenshchikov, S., Lopes, N.P., Popeea, C., Rybalchenko, A.: Synthesizing software verifiers from proof rules. In: PLDI 2012, pp. 405–416. ACM (2012)
9. Gulavani, B.S., Chakraborty, S., Nori, A.V., Rajamani, S.K.: Automatically refining abstract interpretations. In: Ramakrishnan, C.R., Rehof, J. (eds.) TACAS 2008. LNCS, vol. 4963, pp. 443–458. Springer, Heidelberg (2008)
10. Gupta, A., Rybalchenko, A.: InvGen: An efficient invariant generator. In: Bouajjani, A., Maler, O. (eds.) CAV 2009. LNCS, vol. 5643, pp. 634–640. Springer, Heidelberg (2009)
11. Hoder, K., Bjørner, N., de Moura, L.: μZ– An efficient engine for fixed points with constraints. In: Gopalakrishnan, G., Qadeer, S. (eds.) CAV 2011. LNCS, vol. 6806, pp. 457–462. Springer, Heidelberg (2011)

12. Hojjat, H., Konečný, F., Garnier, F., Iosif, R., Kuncak, V., Rümmer, P.: A verification toolkit for numerical transition systems. In: Giannakopoulou, D., Méry, D. (eds.) FM 2012. LNCS, vol. 7436, pp. 247–251. Springer, Heidelberg (2012)
13. Jaffar, J., Murali, V., Navas, J.A., Santosa, A.E.: TRACER: A symbolic execution tool for verification. In: Madhusudan, P., Seshia, S.A. (eds.) CAV 2012. LNCS, vol. 7358, pp. 758–766. Springer, Heidelberg (2012)
14. The MAP system, http://www.iasi.cnr.it/~proietti/system.html
15. McMillan, K.L., Rybalchenko, A.: Solving constrained Horn clauses using interpolation. MSR Technical Report 2013-6, Microsoft Report (2013)
16. Necula, G.C., McPeak, S., Rahul, S.P., Weimer, W.: CIL: Intermediate language and tools for analysis and transformation of C programs. In: Horspool, R.N. (ed.) CC 2002. LNCS, vol. 2304, pp. 209–265. Springer, Heidelberg (2002)
17. Peralta, J.C., Gallagher, J.P., Saglam, H.: Analysis of imperative programs through analysis of Constraint Logic Programs. In: Levi, G. (ed.) SAS 1998. LNCS, vol. 1503, pp. 246–261. Springer, Heidelberg (1998)
18. Podelski, A., Rybalchenko, A.: ARMC: The logical choice for software model checking with abstraction refinement. In: Hanus, M. (ed.) PADL 2007. LNCS, vol. 4354, pp. 245–259. Springer, Heidelberg (2007)
19. De Angelis, E., Fioravanti, F., Pettorossi, A., Proietti, M.: Verifying Array Programs by Transforming Verification Conditions. In: McMillan, K.L., Rival, X. (eds.) VMCAI 2014. LNCS, vol. 8318, pp. 182–202. Springer, Heidelberg (2014)

CIF 3: Model-Based Engineering of Supervisory Controllers

D.A. van Beek, W.J. Fokkink, D. Hendriks, A. Hofkamp,
J. Markovski, J.M. van de Mortel-Fronczak,
and M.A. Reniers

Manufacturing Networks Group
Eindhoven University of Technology, Eindhoven, The Netherlands

Abstract. The engineering of supervisory controllers for large and complex cyber-physical systems requires dedicated engineering support. The Compositional Interchange Format language and toolset have been developed for this purpose. We highlight a model-based engineering framework for the engineering of supervisory controllers and explain how the CIF language and accompanying tools can be used for typical activities in that framework such as modeling, supervisory control synthesis, simulation-based validation, verification, and visualization, real-time testing, and code generation. We mention a number of case studies for which this approach was used in the recent past. We discuss future developments on the level of language and tools as well as research results that may be integrated in the longer term.

1 Introduction

A supervisory controller coordinates the behavior of a (cyber-physical) system from discrete-event observations of its state. Based on such observations the supervisory controller decides on the activities that the uncontrolled system can safely perform or on the activities that (are more likely to) lead to acceptable system behavior. Engineering of supervisory controllers is a challenging task in practice, amongst others because of the high complexity of the uncontrolled system.

In model-based engineering, models are used in the design process, instead of directly implementing a solution. The Compositional Interchange Format (CIF) is an automata-based modeling language that supports the entire model-based engineering development process of supervisory controllers, including modeling, supervisory controller synthesis (deriving a controller from its requirements), simulation-based validation, verification, and visualization, real-time testing, and code generation. CIF 3 is a substantially enhanced new version of CIF, after CIF 1 [BRRS08] and CIF 2 [NBR12]. It has been improved based on feedback from industry, as well as new theoretical advances. The various versions of CIF have been developed in European projects HYCON, HYCON2, Multiform, and C4C. CIF is actively being developed by the Manufacturing Networks Group[1] of the

---

[1] Until recently the group was named Systems Engineering Group.

E. Ábrahám and K. Havelund (Eds.): TACAS 2014, LNCS 8413, pp. 575–580, 2014.

Mechanical Engineering department, at the Eindhoven University of Technology (TU/e) [BHSR13]. The CIF tooling (see `cif.se.wtb.tue.nl`) is available under the MIT open source license (see `opensource.org/licenses/MIT`).

In Section 2, we introduce a simplified version of the framework for model-based engineering of supervisory controllers. In Section 3, we outline the role CIF and its related tools play in this framework. The most prominent features of CIF and its tools are highlighted there. In Section 4, we briefly discuss some industrial cases where the framework and tooling have been applied. Finally, in Section 5, we present a number of enhancements that are being considered for future addition to the CIF language and its tool set.

2   Model-Based Engineering of Supervisory Controllers

Fig. 1 depicts an overview of model-based engineering of supervisory controllers. Our starting point is a model (*uncontrolled hybrid plant*) of the uncontrolled system. The goal is to obtain a *supervisory controller* either by supervisory controller synthesis or by design. A *hybrid observer* forms an interface between the plant model and its supervisory controller. The first purpose of the observer is to interface the variable-based continuous world of the plant to the event-based world of the discrete-event controller. Its second purpose is the generation of additional events, from the state observed at the hybrid plant. They can be interpreted as *virtual sensors* by the controller, abstracting away timed behavior. Examples are a timeout, or an event that signals that a certain combination of values of physical quantities has occurred.

Fig. 2 depicts the workflow of the simplified framework for model-based engineering of supervisory controllers. First, the modeler manually designs an uncontrolled hybrid plant model, and a hybrid observer model. Next, from these two models, an abstraction of the uncontrolled system (*uncontrolled discrete-event plant*) is manually created.

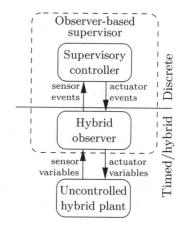

Fig. 1. Overview of model-based engineering of supervisory controllers

From the uncontrolled discrete-event plant and discrete-event *control requirements*, a discrete-event supervisory controller is synthesized (generated). This controller is safe by construction. To also ensure that all relevant behavior is present, additional liveness verification can be performed on the supervisory controller and the uncontrolled discrete-event plant. For timed verification, the uncontrolled hybrid plant and hybrid observer can be used instead of the uncontrolled discrete-event plant. The automated synthesis and verification enable the designer to perform rapid iterative corrections and improvements of the

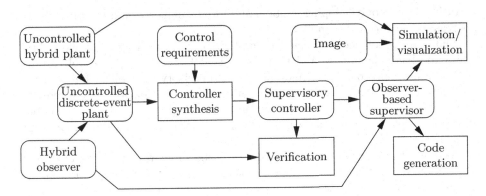

Fig. 2. Workflow for model-based engineering of supervisory controllers

plant model and the control requirements. The supervisory controller is combined with the hybrid observer, resulting in the actual controller (*observer-based supervisor*). This model is used for model-based validation, by means of real-time interactive simulation and visualization, based on a user-supplied *image* of the system. This brings a higher confidence that the models fulfill expected properties. The mentioned simulation-based visualization can also be used for validating the other models, such as the discrete-event and hybrid plant models.

As a final step, actual real-time control code is generated, for the implementation of the controller.

3   The Role of the CIF Language and Tools

The CIF language (see [BHSR13]) is based on networks of hybrid automata with invariants, and non-linear and/or discontinuous differential algebraic equations. The abilitiy of CIF to model large-scale systems is due to the orthogonal combination of parametrized process definition and instantiation (reuse, hierarchy), grouping of arbitrary components in sub-scopes, and an import mechanism. Components (automata) in a CIF model can interact in several different ways: multi-party synchronization via shared events, allowing communication via shared data; monitor automata to provide the functionality of nonblocking input events as defined in input-output automata [LSV01]; shared variables (local write, global read). Furthermore, CIF supports urgent events (events that must happen as soon as they are enabled by all synchronizing automata), a rich set of data types and expressions (e.g. lists, sets, dictionaries, tuples), functions, stochastic distributions, conditional updates, and multi-assignments.

CIF is well suited to model plants and supervisors in the application domain of cyber-physical systems (the blocks *uncontrolled hybrid plant, uncontrolled discrete-event plant, hybrid observer*, and *control requirements* in Fig. 2) as collections of automata using both discrete events and continuous-time behavior (see the cases mentioned in Section 4) in the same style as hybrid automata [ACH+95, Hen00, AGH+00, LSV01]. Developing a CIF model for the uncontrolled hybrid plant is an iterative process of developing a model and using simulation and visualization to increase confidence in the model.

The main difference between CIF and the other currently available hybrid automata-based languages and toolsets, is that CIF covers the complete integrated tool chain for the development of supervisory controllers for complex cyber-physical systems. For the specification of CIF models for plants, requirements, observers, etc, an Eclipse-based (`eclipse.org`) textual editor is available, which features syntax highlighting, and continuous background syntax and type checking.

An important feature of the CIF toolset is the simulator. It can be employed to validate each of the CIF models mentioned before in isolation. Additionally it may be used to validate the controller when put in the context of the uncontrolled hybrid plant (as indicated in Fig. 2). Based on a CIF model, the simulator generates code for high-performance visual simulation. The simulator allows interactive exploration of the behavior of the controlled system, by using the interactive visualization-based simulation mentioned in the previous section. This requires user-supplied SVG vector images (`w3.org/TR/SVG11`). The simulator is highly configurable and versatile, allowing for automatic testing of various use cases, and the production of various forms of output.

To support event-based supervisory controller synthesis, CIF features plant and requirement automata, marker predicates [CL07], as well as controllable and uncontrollable events. Furthermore, the tools include efficient implementations of the traditional event-based supervisory controller synthesis algorithms as presented in [WR87, CL07].

For verification, a transformation of CIF models to Uppaal [NRS+11] is available. Compositionality has been a central concern when designing CIF, because a compositional semantics facilitates property-preserving model transformations and compositional verification techniques. Currently, over twenty transformations for various purposes are available ([BHSR13]), some via CIF 2.

Interoperability with other languages and tools is achieved by means of model transformations, external functions, and co-simulation via the Matlab/Simulink S-function interface [The05]. Programmable Logic Controller (PLC) code generation conforming to the IEC 61131-3 standard [JT10] is also available, allowing for implementation of CIF controllers in actual systems.

4   Applications

CIF has been used in an industrial context for a number of years now. We mention some of the more prominent applications.

- Development of a coordinator for maintenance procedures for a high-tech Océ printer [MJB+10]
- Improving evolvability of a patient communication control system using state-based supervisory control synthesis [TBR12]
- Application of supervisory control theory to theme park vehicles [FMSR12]
- Supervisory control of MRI subsystems [Geu12]
- Design of a supervisory controller for a Philips MRI-scanner [Dij13]

– Design and real-time implementation of a supervisory controller for baggage handling [Kam13]

Although these projects showed different parts of the suggested model-based engineering framework, together they demonstrate all mentioned activities.

Currently, a project on control and performance analysis of wafer flow in wafer handlers is carried out at ASML, and a project on design and implementation of a certified controller with multiple control levels for a baggage handling system is carried out for Vanderlande Industries. Also in these projects supervisory controller synthesis and verification are considered.

5   Future Developments

CIF is constantly being improved and extended. A planned extension of CIF is the addition of point-to-point communication by means of channels. Our experience with industrial cases has shown that these are well suited to model physical movements of objects. The channels will be fully integrated into the language. For instance, supervisors will be able to prohibit channel communications.

For verification, we intend to support a larger class of CIF models for the transformation to Uppaal. We will develop model transformations to other model checking tools as experimented with in [MR12a]. For performance analysis we are considering model transformations to MRMC and/or PRISM [MR12b, MER13].

The Manufacturing Networks Group also works on extensions of supervisory control theory, such as the domain of plant models to which synthesis may be applied, and the expressivity of the logic for requirements. See [HFR13] for a first publication of this line of research. As soon as such extensions reach an acceptable level of maturity, they are incorporated in the CIF tooling.

Acknowledgments. The research leading to these results has received funding from the EU FP7 Programme under grant agreements no. FP7-ICT-223844 (C4C), no. FP7-ICT-224249 (MULTIFORM), and the Network of Excellence HYCON (IST-2002-2.3.2.5). The research leading to these results has received funding from the European Union Seventh Framework Programme [FP7/2007-2013] under grant agreement no. 257462 HYCON2 Network of excellence.

References

[ACH+95]   Alur, R., Courcoubetis, C., Halbwachs, N., Henzinger, T.A., Ho, P.-H., Nicollin, X., Olivero, A., Sifakis, J., Yovine, S.: The algorithmic analysis of hybrid systems. Theoretical Computer Science 138(1), 3–34 (1995)

[AGH+00]   Alur, R., Grosu, R., Hur, Y., Kumar, V., Lee, I.: Modular specification of hybrid systems in CHARON. In: Lynch, N.A., Krogh, B.H. (eds.) HSCC 2000. LNCS, vol. 1790, pp. 6–19. Springer, Heidelberg (2000)

[BHSR13]   van Beek, D.A., Hendriks, D., Swartjes, L., Reniers, M.A.: Report on the extensions of the CIF and transformation algorithms. Technical Report HYCON Deliverable D6.2.4 (2013)

[BRRS08] van Beek, D.A., Reniers, M.A., Rooda, J.E., Schiffelers, R.R.H.: Concrete syntax and semantics of the Compositional Interchange Format for hybrid systems. In: IFAC World Congress 2008, pp. 7979–7986, IFAC (2008)

[CL07]   Cassandras, C.G., Lafortune, S.: Introduction to Discrete Event Systems, 2nd edn. Springer (2007)

[Dij13]   van Dijk, D.: Supervisory control of a Philips MRI-scanner. Master's thesis, Eindhoven University of Technology (2013)

[FMSR12] Forschelen, S.T.J., van de Mortel-Fronczak, J.M., Su, R., Rooda, J.E.: Application of supervisory control theory to theme park vehicles. Discrete Event Dynamic Systems 22(4), 511–540 (2012)

[Geu12]   Geurts, J.W.P.: Supervisory control of MRI subsystems. Master's thesis, Eindhoven University of Technology (2012)

[Hen00]   Henzinger, T.A.: The theory of hybrid automata. In: Verification of Digital and Hybrid Systems. NATO ASI Series F: Computer and Systems Science, vol. 170, pp. 265–292. Springer (2000)

[HFR13]   van Hulst, A., Fokkink, W.J., Reniers, M.A.: Maximal synthesis for Hennessy-Milner Logic. In: ACSD 2013, pp. 1–10. IEEE (2013)

[JT10]   John, K.H., Tiegelkamp, M.: IEC 61131-3: Programming Industrial Automation Systems, 2nd edn. Springer (2010)

[Kam13]   Kamphuis, R.H.J.: Design and real-time implementation of a supervisory controller for baggage handling at Veghel Airport. Master's thesis, Eindhoven University of Technology (2013)

[LSV01]   Lynch, N., Segala, R., Vaandrager, F.: Hybrid I/O automata revisited. In: Di Benedetto, M.D., Sangiovanni-Vincentelli, A.L. (eds.) HSCC 2001. LNCS, vol. 2034, pp. 403–417. Springer, Heidelberg (2001)

[MER13]   Markovski, J., Estens Musa, E.S., Reniers, M.A.: Extending a synthesis-centric model-based systems engineering framework with stochastic model checking. ENTCS 296, 163–181 (2013)

[MJB⁺10] Markovski, J., Jacobs, K.G.M., van Beek, D.A., Somers, L.J.A.M., Rooda, J.E.: Coordination of resources using generalized state-based requirements. In: WODES 2010, pp. 300–305. IFAC (2010)

[MR12a]   Markovski, J., Reniers, M.A.: An integrated state- and event-based framework for verifying liveness in supervised systems. In: ICARCV 2012, pp. 246–251. IEEE (2012)

[MR12b]   Markovski, J., Reniers, M.A.: Verifying performance of supervised plants. In: ACSD 2012, pp. 52–61. IEEE (2012)

[NBR12]   Nadales Agut, D.E., van Beek, D.A., Rooda, J.E.: Syntax and semantics of the compositional interchange format for hybrid systems. Journal of Logic and Algebraic Programming 82(1), 1–52 (2012)

[NRS⁺11] Nadales Agut, D.E., Reniers, M.A., Schiffelers, R.R.H., Jørgensen, K.Y., van Beek, D.A.: A semantic-preserving transformation from the Compositional Interchange Format to UPPAAL. In: IFAC World Congress 2011, pp. 12496–12502, IFAC (2011)

[TBR12]   Theunissen, R.J.M., van Beek, D.A., Rooda, J.E.: Improving evolvability of a patient communication control system using state-based supervisory control synthesis. Advanced Engineering Informatics 26(3), 502–515 (2012)

[The05]   The MathWorks, Inc. Writing S-functions, version 6 (2005), http://www.mathworks.com

[WR87]   Wonham, W.M., Ramadge, P.J.: On the supremal controllable sublanguage of a given language. SIAM Journal on Control and Optimization 25(3), 637–659 (1987)

EDD: A Declarative Debugger
for Sequential Erlang Programs*

Rafael Caballero[1], Enrique Martin-Martin[1],
Adrian Riesco[1], and Salvador Tamarit[2]

[1] Universidad Complutense de Madrid, Madrid, Spain
rafa@sip.ucm.es, emartinm@fdi.ucm.es, ariesco@fdi.ucm.es
[2] Babel Research Group, Universitat Politécnica de Madrid, Madrid, Spain
stamarit@fi.upm.es

Abstract. Declarative debuggers are semi-automatic debugging tools
that abstract the execution details to focus on the program semantics.
This paper presents a tool implementing this approach for the sequential
subset of Erlang, a functional language with dynamic typing and strict
evaluation. Given an erroneous computation, it first detects an erroneous
function (either a "named" function or a lambda-abstraction), and then
continues the process to identify the fragment of the function responsible
for the error. Among its features it includes support for exceptions, predefined and built-in functions, higher-order functions, and trusting and
undo commands.

1 Introduction

Declarative debugging, also known as algorithmic debugging, is a well-known
technique that only requires from the user knowledge about the *intended behavior* of the program, that is, the expected results of the program computations,
abstracting the execution details and hence presenting a *declarative* approach. It
has been successfully applied in logic [5], functional [6], and object-oriented [4]
programming languages. In [3,2] we presented a declarative debugger for sequential Erlang. These works gave rise to EDD, the Erlang Declarative Debugger
presented in this paper. EDD has been developed in Erlang. EDD, its documentation, and several examples are available at https://github.com/tamarit/edd
(check the README.md file for installing the tool).

As usual in declarative debugging the tool is started by the user when an
unexpected result, called the *error symptom*, is found. The debugger then builds
internally the so-called *debugging tree*, whose nodes correspond to the auxiliary
computations needed to obtain the error symptom. Then the user is questioned

---

* Research supported by EU project FP7-ICT-610582 ENVISAGE, Spanish
projects *StrongSoft* (TIN2012-39391-C04-04), *DOVES* (TIN2008-05624), and *VI-
VAC* (TIN2012-38137), and Comunidad de Madrid *PROMETIDOS* (S2009/
TIC-1465). Salvador Tamarit was partially supported by research project POLCA,
Programming Large Scale Heterogeneous Infrastructures (610686), funded by the
European Union, STREP FP7.

E. Ábrahám and K. Havelund (Eds.): TACAS 2014, LNCS 8413, pp. 581–586, 2014.

about the validity of some tree nodes until the error is found. In our proposal, the debugger first concentrates in the function calls occurred during the computation. The goal is to find a function call that returned an *invalid* result, but such that all the function calls occurring in the function body returned a *valid* result. The associated node is called a *buggy node*. We prove in [3] that such function is a *wrong function*, and that every program producing an error symptom[1] contains at least one wrong function. An important novelty of our debugger w.r.t. similar tools is that it allows using *zoom debugging* to detect an erroneous fragment of code inside the wrong function. At this stage the user is required to answer questions about the validity of certain variable matchings, or about the branch that should be selected in a `case/if` statement for a given context. The theoretical results in [2] ensure that this code is indeed erroneous, and that a wrong function always contains an erroneous statement.

The rest of the paper is organized as follows: Section 2 introduces Erlang and EDD. Section 3 describes the questions that can be asked by the tool and the errors that can be detected. Section 4 concludes and presents the future work.

2   Erlang and EDD

In this section we introduce some pieces of Erlang [1] which are relevant for our presentation. At the same time we introduce the basic features of our tool. Erlang is a concurrent language with a sequential subset that is a functional language with dynamic typing and strict evaluation. Programs are structured using modules, which contain functions defined by collections of clauses.

Example 1. Obtain the square of a number X without using products. This is possible defining $Y = X - 1$ and considering $X^2 = (Y + 1)^2 = Y^2 + Y + Y + 1$.

```
-module(mathops).
-export([square/1]).
square(0) -> 0;
square(X) when X>0 -> Y=X-1, DoubleY=X+X, square(Y)+DoubleY+1.
```

Observe that variables start with an uppercase letter or underscore. In order to evaluate a function call Erlang scans sequentially the function clauses until a match is found. Then, the variables occurring in the head are bound. In our example the second clause of the function **square** is erroneous: the underlined subterm X+X should be Y+Y. Using this program we check that `mathops:square(3)` is unexpectedly evaluated to **15**. Then, we can start EDD, obtaining the debugging session in Fig. 1, where the user answers are boxed. Section 3.1 explains all the possible answers to the debugger questions. Here we only use 'n' (standing for 'no'), indicating that the result is invalid, and 'y' (standing for 'yes'), indicating that it is valid. After two questions the debugger detects that the tree node containing the call `mathops:square(1)` is buggy (it produces and invalid result while its only child `mathops:square(0)` returns a valid result). Consequently,

---

[1] Note that, if the module has multiple errors that compensate each other, there is no error symptom and hence declarative debugging cannot be applied.

```
> edd:dd("mathops:square(3)").
mathops:square(1) = 3?  [n]
mathops:square(0) = 0?  [y]
Call to a function that contains an error:
mathops:square(1) = 3
Please, revise the second clause:
square(X) when X > 0 -> Y=X-1, DoubleY=X+X, square(Y)+DoubleY+1.
Continue the debugging session inside this function?  [y]
In the function square(1) matching with second clause succeed.
Is this correct?  [y]
Given the context:   X = 1
the following variable is assigned: DoubleY = 2?  [n]
This is the reason for the error:
Variable DoubleY is badly assigned 2 in the expression:
DoubleY = X + X (line 4).
```

Fig. 1. EDD session corresponding to the call `mathops:square(3)`

the tool points out the second clause of `square` as wrong. Next, the user is asked if zoom debugging must be used. The user agrees with inspecting the code associated to the buggy node function call. The debugger proceeds asking about the validity of the chosen function clause, which is right (the second one), and about the validity of the value for `DoubleY`, which is incorrect (it should be 0 since X=1 implies Y=0). The session finishes pointing to this incorrect matching as the source of the error. Observe that an incorrect matching is not always associated to wrong code, because it could depend on a previous value that contains an incorrect result. However, the correctness results in [3] ensure that only matchings with real errors are displayed as errors by our tool. Note in this session the improvement with respect to the trace, the standard debugging facility for Erlang programs. While the trace shows every computation step, our tool focuses first on function calls, simplifying and shortening the debugging process.

The next example shows that Erlang allows more sophisticated expressions in the function bodies, including `case` or `if` expressions.

Example 2. Select the appropriate food taking into account different preferences.

```
-module(meal).
-export([food/1]).
food(Preferences) ->
    case Preferences of
        {vegetarian,ovo_vegetarian} -> omelette;
        {vegetarian,_lacto_vegetarian} -> yogurt;
        {vegetarian,vegan} -> salad;
        _Else -> fish
    end.
```

Now we can evaluate the expression `meal:food({vegetarian,vegan})` and we obtain the unexpected result `yogurt`. This time the first phase of the debugger is not helpful: it points readily to the only clause of `food`. In order to obtain more precise information we use zoom debugging, and the debugger asks:

```
For the case expression:
(... omitted for the sake of space ... )
Is there anything incorrect?
1.- The context:  Preferences = {vegetarian,vegan}
2.- The argument value: {vegetarian,vegan}.
3.- Enter in the second clause.
4.- The bindings:  _lacto_vegetarian = vegan
5.- The final value: yogurt.
6.- Nothing.
[1/2/3/4/5/6]?  3
```

This question asks for anything invalid in the evaluation of the **case** expressions with respect to its intended meaning. It is important to mention that in the case of something wrong the answer must be the first wrong item. In our case the context and the **case** argument are correct, but we did not expect to use the second branch/clause but the third. Therefore we answer 3 indicating that this is the first error in the list. The next question is:

```
Which clause did you expect to be selected [1/2/3/4]?  3
```

As explained above, we expected to use the third clause for this context. Then the debugger stops indicating the error:

```
This is the reason for the error:
The pattern of the second clause of case expression:
case Preferences of {vegetarian, _lacto_vegetarian} -> yogurt end
```

Indeed there is an erroneous underscore in **_lacto_vegetarian**. It converts the constant into an anonymous variable, and thus the branch was incorrectly selected. The debugger has found the error, indicating that the second branch is wrong and that in particular the pattern definition is incorrectly defined. Note that, with a trace-debugger, programmers proceed instruction by instruction checking whether the bindings, the branches selected in **case/if** expressions or inner function calls are correct. Our tool fulfills a similar task, although it discards inner function calls—they were checked in the previous phase. Moreover, the navigation strategy automatically guides the session without the participation of the user by choosing breakpoints and steps, finally pointing out the piece of code causing the bug. Therefore, it provides a simpler and clearer way of finding bugs in concrete functions, although the complexity is similar.

3   Using the Tool

3.1   User Answers

The possible answers to the debugging questions during the first phase are:

- *yes (y)/ no (n)*: the statement is valid/invalid.
- *trusted (t)*: the user knows that the function or λ-abstraction used in the evaluation is correct, so further questions about it are not necessary. In this case all the calls to this function are marked as valid.

- *inadmissible (i)*: the question does not apply because the arguments should not take these values. The statement is marked as valid.
- *don't know (d)*: the answer is unknown. The statement is marked as unknown, and might be asked again if it is required for finding the buggy node.
- *switch strategy (s)*: changes the navigation strategy. The navigation strategies provided by the tool are explained below.
- *undo (u)*: reverts to the previous question.
- *abort (a)*: finishes the debugging session.

In the case of zoom debugging, the answer *trusted* has not any sense and it is never available, while the answers *yes, no,* and *inadmissible* cannot be used in some situations, for instance in compound questions about `case/if` expressions. The rest of answers are always available.

The tool includes a memoization feature that stores the answers *yes, no, trusted,* and *inadmissible,* preventing the system from asking the same question twice. It is worth noting that *don't know* is used to ease the interaction with the debugger but it may introduce incompleteness; if the debugger reaches a deadlock due to these answers it presents two alternatives to the user: either answering some of the discarded questions to find the buggy node or showing the possible buggy code, depending on the answers to the nodes marked as unknown.

3.2   Strategies

As indicated in the introduction, the statements are represented in suitable debugging trees, which represents the structure of the wrong computation. The system can internally utilize two different navigation strategies [7,8], *Divide & Query* and *Top Down Heaviest First,* in order to choose the next node and therefore the next question presented to the user. Top Down selects as next node the largest child of the current node, while Divide & Query selects the node whose subtree is closer to half the size of the whole tree. In this way, Top Down sessions usually presents more questions to the user, but they are presented in a logical order, while Divide & Query leads to shorter sessions of unrelated questions.

3.3   Detected Errors

Next we summarize the different types of errors detected by our debugger. As we have seen, the first phase always ends with a wrong function. The errors found during the zoom debugging phase are:

Wrong case argument, which indicates that the argument of a specific `case` statement has not been coded as the user expected.

Wrong pattern, which indicates that a pattern in the function arguments or in a `case/if` branch is wrong.

Wrong guard, which indicates that a guard in either a function clause or in a `case/if` branch is wrong.

Wrong binding, which indicates that a variable binding is incorrect.

4   Concluding Remarks and Ongoing Work

EDD is a declarative debugger for sequential Erlang. Program errors are found by asking questions about the intended behavior of some parts of the program being debugged, until the bug is found. Regarding usability, EDD provides several features that make it a useful tool for debugging real programs, such as support for built-in functions and external libraries, anonymous (lambda) functions, higher-order values, *don't know* and *undo* answers, memoization, and trusting mechanisms, among others. See [2,3] for details.

We have used this tool to debug several programs developed by others. This gives us confidence in its robustness, but also illustrates an important point of declarative debugging: it does not require the person in charge of debugging to know the details of the implementation; it only requires to know the intended behavior of the functions, which is much easier and more intuitive, hence allowing a simpler form of debugging than other approaches, like tracing or breakpoints.

As future work we plan to extend this proposal to include the concurrent features of Erlang. This extension requires first to extend our calculus with these features. Then, we must identify the errors that can be detected in this new framework, define the debugging tree, and adapt the tool to work with these modifications.

References

1. Armstrong, J., Williams, M., Wikstrom, C., Virding, R.: Concurrent Programming in Erlang, 2nd edn. Prentice-Hall (1996)
2. Caballero, R., Martin-Martin, E., Riesco, A., Tamarit, S.: A zoom-declarative debugger for sequential Erlang programs. Submitted to the JLAP
3. Caballero, R., Martin-Martin, E., Riesco, A., Tamarit, S.: A declarative debugger for sequential Erlang programs. In: Veanes, M., Viganò, L. (eds.) TAP 2013. LNCS, vol. 7942, pp. 96–114. Springer, Heidelberg (2013)
4. Insa, D., Silva, J.: An algorithmic debugger for Java. In: Lanza, M., Marcus, A. (eds.) Proc. of ICSM 2010, pp. 1–6. IEEE Computer Society (2010)
5. Naish, L.: Declarative diagnosis of missing answers. New Generation Computing 10(3), 255–286 (1992)
6. Nilsson, H.: How to look busy while being as lazy as ever: the implementation of a lazy functional debugger. Journal of Functional Programming 11(6), 629–671 (2001)
7. Silva, J.: A comparative study of algorithmic debugging strategies. In: Puebla, G. (ed.) LOPSTR 2006. LNCS, vol. 4407, pp. 143–159. Springer, Heidelberg (2007)
8. Silva, J.: A survey on algorithmic debugging strategies. Advances in Engineering Software 42(11), 976–991 (2011)

APTE: An Algorithm
for Proving Trace Equivalence

Vincent Cheval

School of Computer Science, University of Birmingham, UK

Abstract. This paper presents APTE, a new tool for automatically proving the security of cryptographic protocols. It focuses on proving trace equivalence between processes, which is crucial for specifying privacy type properties such as anonymity and unlinkability.

The tool can handle protocols expressed in a calculus similar to the applied-pi calculus, which allows us to capture most existing protocols that rely on classical cryptographic primitives. In particular, APTE handles private channels and else branches in protocols with bounded number of sessions. Unlike most equivalence verifier tools, APTE is guaranteed to terminate.

Moreover, APTE is the only tool that extends the usual notion of trace equivalence by considering "side-channel" information leaked to the attacker such as the length of messages and the execution times. We illustrate APTE on different case studies which allowed us to automatically (re)-discover attacks on protocols such as the *Private Authentication* protocol or the protocols of the electronic passports.

1 Introduction

Cryptographic protocols are small distributed programs specifically designed to ensure the security of our communications on public channels like Internet. It is therefore essential to verify and prove the correctness of these cryptographic protocols. Symbolic models have proved their usefulness for verifying cryptographic protocols. However, the many sources of unboundedness in modelling of the capabilities of an attacker makes it extremely difficult to verify the security properties of a cryptographic protocol by hand. Thus, developing automatic verification tools of security protocols is a necessity. Since the 1980s, many tools have been developed to automatically verify cryptographic protocols (e.g. SCYTHER [10], PROVERIF [3], AVISPA [13] and others) but they mainly focus on *trace properties* such as authentication and secrecy, which typically specify that a protocol cannot reach a bad state. However, many interesting security properties such as anonymity, unlinkability, privacy, cannot be expressed as a trace property but require the notion of *equivalence property*. Intuitively, these properties specify the indistinguishability of some instances of the protocols. We focus here on the notion of *trace equivalence* which is well-suited for the analysis of security protocols.

E. Ábrahám and K. Havelund (Eds.): TACAS 2014, LNCS 8413, pp. 587–592, 2014.

Existing Tools. To our knowledge, there are only three tools that can handle equivalence properties: PROVERIF [3], SPEC [12] and AKISS [9]. The tool PROVERIF originally was designed to prove trace properties but it can also check some equivalence properties (so-called diff-equivalence) [4] that are usually too strong to model a real intruder since they consider that the intruder has complete knowledge of the internal states of all the honest protocols executed. Note that this is the only tool that can handle an unbounded number of sessions of a protocol with a large class of cryptographic primitives in practice. However, the downside of PROVERIF is that it may not terminate and it may also return a false-negative. More recently, the tool AKISS [9] was developed in order to decide the trace equivalence of bounded processes that do not contain non-trivial else branching. This tool was proved to be sound and complete and accepts a large class of primitives but the algorithm was only conjectured to terminate. At last, the tool SPEC [12] is based on a decision procedure for open-bisimulation for bounded processes. The scope is however limited: open-bisimulation coincides with trace equivalence only for determinate processes and the procedure also assumes a fixed set of primitives (symmetric encryption and pairing), and a pattern based message passing, hence, in particular, no non-trivial else branching.

Hence, some interesting protocols cannot be handle by these tools. It is particularly the case for the Private Authentication protocol [2], or the protocols of the electronic passport [1] since they rely on a conditional with a non-trivial else branch to be properly modelled. Moreover, even though recent work [6] led to a new release of ProVerif that can deal with the Private Authentication protocol, ProVerif is still not able to handle the protocols of the electronic passport and yields a false positive due to the too strong equivalence that it proves.

At last none of the existing tools take into account the fact that an attacker can always observe the length of a message, even though it can leak information on private data. For example, in most of existing encryption schemes, the length of ciphertext depends on the length of its plaintext. Thus the ciphertext $\{m\}_k$ corresponding to the encryption of a message m by the key k can always be distinguished from the ciphertext $\{m, m\}_k$ corresponding to the encryption of the message m repeated twice by the key k. This is simply due to the fact that $\{m, m\}_k$ is longer than $\{m\}_k$. However, these two messages would be considered as indistinguishable in all previous mentioned tools.

2   Trace Equivalence

Our tool is based on a symbolic model where the messages exchanged over the network are represented by *terms*. They are built from a set of variables and names by applying function symbols modelling the cryptographic primitives. For example, the symbol function senc (resp. sdec) represents the symmetric encryption (resp. decryption) primitive and the term $\mathsf{senc}(m, k)$ models the encryption of a message m by a key k. The behaviour of each primitive is modelled by a *rewriting system*. As such, a term $\mathsf{sdec}(\mathsf{senc}(m, k), k)$ will be rewritten m to model the fact that decrypting a ciphertext by the key that was used to encrypt indeed yields the plain text. Moreover, to take into account the length of messages, we associate to each cryptographic primitive f a length function $\ell_f : \mathbb{N}^n \to \mathbb{N}$ where n is the arity of f. Intuitively, a length function represents the length of the outcome of a cryptographic primitive depending on the length of his inputs. For example, the length function for the pairing could be the function $\ell_{\langle\rangle}(x, y) = x + y + 1$. The length function $\ell_{\mathsf{senc}}(x, y) = x$ for the symmetric encryption would imply that the length of a ciphertext is always the size of its plaintext. Typically, each encryption scheme would have a specific length function that depends on the characteristics of the encryption scheme.

Equivalence of sequence of terms. By interacting with a protocol, an attacker may obtain a sequence of messages, meaning that not only he knows each message but also the order in which he obtained them. Properties like anonymity rely on the notion of indistinguishability between two sequences of messages. This is called *static equivalence* and denoted by $\sim$. For example, consider the two sequences of messages $\Phi_m = [k; \mathsf{senc}(m, k)]$ and $\Phi_n = [k; \mathsf{senc}(n, k)]$ where m, n are two random numbers. The two sequences Φ_n and Φ_m are indistinguishable. Indeed, even if the attacker can decrypt the second message using the first message, *i.e.* k, he obtains in both cases two random numbers and so does not gain any particular informations. However, the two sequences $[k; \mathsf{senc}(m, k); m]$ and $[k; \mathsf{senc}(m, k); n]$ are distinguishable since the attacker can compare the plain text of the ciphertext with the third message he obtained.

When the attacker can also compare the size of message, the equivalence is called *length static equivalence* and denoted $\sim_\ell$.

Processes. Participants in the protocol are modelled as processes whose grammar is as follows:

$$P \mid Q \qquad P + Q \qquad \mathsf{new}\ k; P \qquad \mathsf{out}(u, v); P \qquad \mathsf{in}(u, x); P$$
$$\mathsf{if}\ u = v\ \mathsf{then}\ P\ \mathsf{else}\ Q \qquad \mathsf{let}\ x = u\ \mathsf{in}\ P$$

where P, Q are processes, u, v are terms and x is a variable. The nil process is denoted 0. The process $P + Q$ represents the non-deterministic choice between P and Q. The process $\mathsf{new}\ k$ is the creation of a fresh name. The process $\mathsf{out}(u, v)$ represents the emission of the message v into the channel u. Similarly, $\mathsf{in}(u, x)$ is the process that receives a message on the channel u and binds it to x. Typically, an attacker can interact with the process by emitting or receiving messages from honest participants through public channels. Hence we represent possible interactions of the attacker with P by the notion of *trace*, that is a pair (s, Φ) where s is the sequence of actions that the attacker performs and Φ is the sequence of messages that the attacker receives from the honest participants. A process is said to be determinate when the execution of the process is deterministic. For example, a process containing the choice operator is not determinate.

Definition 1 ((length) trace equivalence). *Let P and Q be two processes. The processes P and Q are trace equivalence if for all traces (s, Φ) of P there exists a trace (s', Φ') of Q such that $s = s'$ and $\Phi \sim \Phi'$ (and conversely).*

Moreover, we say that P and Q are in length trace equivalence when the length static equivalence $\sim_\ell$ is used to compare the sequence of messages Φ and Φ', i.e. $\Phi \sim_\ell \Phi'$.

Intuitively, this definition indicates that whatever the actions the attacker performs on P, the same actions can be performed on Q and the sequences of messages obtained in both cases are indistinguishable, and conversely.

3   The Tool APTE

We present the tool APTE that decides the trace equivalence for bounded of (possibly non-determinate, possibly with non-trivial else branches) processes that use standard primitives, namely signature, pairing, symmetric and asymmetric encryptions and any one-way functions such as hash, mac, etc. Moreover, by specifying the linear length functions of each cryptographic primitives, a user can also use APTE to decide the length trace equivalence between processes. When the trace equivalence or length trace equivalence between two processes is not satisfied, APTE provides a witness of the non-equivalence, *i.e.* it displays the actions that the attacker has to perform for him to distinguish the two processes. Note that, even though it is not the main purpose, APTE can also be used to verify reachability properties on a protocol.

Theoretical foundations. APTE relies on symbolic traces, that is a finite representation of infinitely many traces, to decide the equivalence. In particular from each symbolic trace of the two processes is extracted two sets of *constraint systems*. The two processes are then equivalent if and only if all pairs of sets of constant systems are symbolically equivalent. The algorithm used in APTE to decide the symbolic equivalence between sets of constraint systems was proved to be complete, sound and to always terminate in [7,5]. It relies on a set of rules on constraint systems that simplify the sets of constraint systems given as input to render the decision trivial. The extension to length trace equivalence between processes was presented and proved in [8].

Implementation details. The tool is implemented in Ocaml[1] and the source code has about 12Klocs. The source code is highly modular: each mathematical notion used in the algorithm is implemented in a separate module. To facilitate any new extension and optimisation of the tool, the data structures are always hidden in the modules, *i.e.* we only use abstract types (sometimes called opaque types) in the interface files. The format of the comments in the interface files is the one of Ocamldoc that generates a LaTex file with the documented interfaces.

Availability. APTE is an open source software and is distributed under GNU General Public Licence 3.0. It can be downloaded at `http://projects.lsv.ens-cachan.fr/APTE/` where a mailing list, some relevant examples and also a list of publications related or using APTE is available.

---

[1] `http://caml.inria.fr`

Anonymity on PrA	Status	Execution time
Original	satisfy trace equivalence but length attack	0.01 sec
Fix (one session)	safe	0.08 sec
Fix (two sessions)	safe	> 2 days

Unlinkability on BAC	Status	Execution time
French	attack	0.09 sec
UK	safe ?	> 2 days

Unkinkability on PaA	Status	Execution time
Original	length attack	0.08 sec
Fix	safe	2.8 sec

Others	Status	Execution time
Anonymity on PaA	safe	3.2 sec
Needham-Shroeder	attack	0.01 sec
Needham-Shroeder-Love	safe	0.4 sec

These results were obtained by using APTE on a 2.9 Ghz Intel Core i7, 8 GB DDR3.

Fig. 1. Experimental results

Upcoming features. Nowadays, all computers are equipped with a multi-core processor and sometimes with several processors, thus we are currently working on a distributed version of APTE that will take advantage of such multi-core processors and clusters. Moreover, we would like to include new cryptographic primitives such as XOR, blind signature and re-encryption used in very interesting protocols *e.g.* Caveat Coercitor [11].

4 Experimental Results

We use APTE on several case studies found in the literature. The figure 1 summarises the results. In particular, we focused on the Private Authentication (PrA) protocol [2] and the protocols of the electronic passport (a description of the protocols can be found in [5]). The two key results that we obtained using APTE are a new attack on the anonymity of the Private Authentication protocol and a new attack on the unlinkability of the Passive Authentication protocol (PaA) of the electronic passport. Both attacks rely on the attacker being able to observe the length of messages. In both cases, we propose possible fixes and show their security with APTE for few sessions of the protocols. Observe that execution times for the trace equivalence and length trace equivalence are very similar. However, depending on how many sessions you consider, the execution time varies greatly. For example, in the case of the Private Authentication protocol, one sessions is computed in less than a second whereas two sessions take more than two days. Using APTE, we also rediscovered an existing attack on the unlinkability of the Basic Access Control protocol (BAC) used in the French electronic passport. Note that proving the unlinkability of the BAC protocol for the UK passport took too much time and so we stopped the execution after two days. We applied APTE to prove the anonymity of the Passive Authentication protocol. At last, since all reachability properties can be expressed by an equivalence, APTE is also able to find the very classical attack on the secrecy of the Needham-Schroeder protocol and prove the secrecy on the Needham-Schroeder-Love protocol.

References

1. Machine readable travel document. Technical Report 9303, International Civil Aviation Organization (2008)
2. Abadi, M., Fournet, C.: Private authentication. Theoretical Computer Science 322(3), 427–476 (2004)
3. Blanchet, B.: An Efficient Cryptographic Protocol Verifier Based on Prolog Rules. In: 14th Computer Security Foundations Workshop, CSFW 2001 (2001)
4. Blanchet, B., Abadi, M., Fournet, C.: Automated verification of selected equivalences for security protocols. Journal of Logic and Algebraic Programming 75(1), 3–51 (2008)
5. Cheval, V.: Automatic verification of cryptographic protocols: privacy-type properties. Phd thesis. ENS Cachan, France (2012)
6. Cheval, V., Blanchet, B.: Proving more observational equivalences with ProVerif. In: Basin, D., Mitchell, J.C. (eds.) POST 2013. LNCS, vol. 7796, pp. 226–246. Springer, Heidelberg (2013)
7. Cheval, V., Comon-Lundh, H., Delaune, S.: Trace equivalence decision: Negative tests and non-determinism. In: 18th ACM Conference on Computer and Communications Security, CCS 2011 (2011)
8. Cheval, V., Cortier, V., Plet, A.: Lengths may break privacy – or how to check for equivalences with length. In: Sharygina, N., Veith, H. (eds.) CAV 2013. LNCS, vol. 8044, pp. 708–723. Springer, Heidelberg (2013)
9. Ciobâcă, Ş.: Automated Verification of Security Protocols with Applications to Electronic Voting. Thèse de doctorat, Laboratoire Spécification et Vérification. ENS Cachan, France (December 2011)
10. Cremers, C.J.F.: Unbounded verification, falsification, and characterization of security protocols by pattern refinement. In: CCS 2008: Proceedings of the 15th ACM Conference on Computer and Communications Security, pp. 119–128. ACM, New York (2008)
11. Grewal, G., Ryan, M., Bursuc, S., Ryan, P.: Caveat coercitor: Coercion-evidence in electronic voting. In: IEEE Symposium on Security and Privacy, pp. 367–381. IEEE Computer Society (2013)
12. Tiu, A., Dawson, J.: Automating open bisimulation checking for the spi calculus. In: Proc. 23rd IEEE Computer Security Foundations Symposium (CSF 2010), pp. 307–321. IEEE Computer Society Press (2010)
13. Viganò, L.: Automated security protocol analysis with the avispa tool. In: Proceedings of the XXI Mathematical Foundations of Programming Semantics (MFPS 2005). ENTCS, vol. 155, pp. 61–86. Elsevier (2006)

The Modest Toolset: An Integrated Environment for Quantitative Modelling and Verification*

Arnd Hartmanns and Holger Hermanns

Saarland University – Computer Science, Saarbrücken, Germany

Abstract Probabilities, real-time behaviour and continuous dynamics are the key ingredients of quantitative models enabling formal studies of non-functional properties such as dependability and performance. The MODEST TOOLSET is based on networks of stochastic hybrid automata (SHA) as an overarching semantic foundation. Many existing automata-based formalisms are special cases of SHA. The toolset aims to facilitate reuse of modelling expertise via MODEST, a high-level compositional modelling language; to allow reuse of existing models by providing import and export facilities for existing languages; and to permit reuse of existing tools by integrating them in a unified modelling and analysis environment.

1 Introduction

Our reliance on complex safety-critical or economically vital systems such as fly-by-wire controllers, networked industrial automation systems or "smart" power grids increases at an ever-accelerating pace. The necessity to study the reliability and performance of these systems is evident. Over the last two decades, significant progress has been made in the area of formal methods to allow the construction of mathematically precise models of such systems and automatically evaluate properties of interest on the models. Classically, model checking has been used to study functional correctness properties such as safety or liveness. However, since a correct system implementation may still be prohibitively slow or energy-consuming, performance requirements need to be considered as well. The desire to evaluate both *qualitative* as well as *quantitative* properties fostered the development of integrative approaches that combine probabilities, real-time aspects or costs with formal verification techniques [1].

The MODEST TOOLSET is an integrated collection of tools for the creation and analysis of formally specified behavioural models with quantitative aspects. It constitutes the second generation [8] of tools revolving around the MODEST modelling language [7]. By now, it has become a versatile and extensible toolset based on the rich semantic foundation of networks of stochastic hybrid automata (SHA), supporting multiple input languages and multiple analysis backends.

---

* This work is supported by the Transregional Collaborative Research Centre SFB/TR 14 AVACS, the NWO-DFG bilateral project ROCKS, and the 7th EU Framework Programme under grant agreements 295261 (MEALS) and 318490 (SENSATION).

E. Ábrahám and K. Havelund (Eds.): TACAS 2014, LNCS 8413, pp. 593–598, 2014.

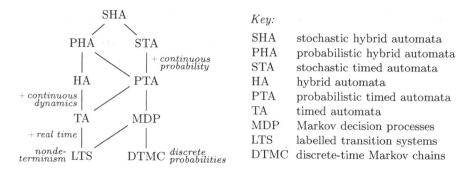

Fig. 1. Submodels of stochastic hybrid automata

The MODEST TOOLSET's aim is to incorporate the state of the art in research on the analysis of stochastic hybrid systems and special cases thereof, such as probabilistic real-time systems. In particular, it goes beyond the usual "research prototype" by providing a single, stable, easy-to-install and easy-to-use package.

In this paper, we illustrate how SHA provide a unified formalism for quantitative modelling that subsumes a wide variety of well-known automata-based models (Section 2); we highlight the MODEST TOOLSET's approach to modelling and model reuse through its support of three very different input languages (Section 3); we give an overview of the available analysis backends for different specialisations of SHA (Section 4); and we provide some background on technical aspects of the toolset and its cross-platform user interface (Section 5).

Related work. Two tools have substantially inspired the design of the MODEST TOOLSET: MÖBIUS [9] is a prominent multiple-formalism, multiple-solution tool. Focussing on performance and dependability evaluation, its input formalisms include Petri nets, Markov chains and stochastic process algebras. CADP [11], in contrast, is a tool suite for explicit-state system verification, comprising about fifty interoperable components, supporting various input languages and analysis approaches. The MODEST TOOLSET has so far focused on reusing existing tools on the analysis side whereas MÖBIUS and CADP rely on their own implementations.

2 A Common Semantic Foundation

The MODEST TOOLSET is built around a single overarching semantic model: networks of stochastic hybrid automata (SHA), i.e. sets of automata that run asynchronously and can communicate via shared actions and global variables. While action labels are used for synchronisation, a state-based approach is used for verification, i.e. the valuations of the global variables act as atomic propositions observable in properties. SHA combine three key modelling concepts:

Continuous dynamics To represent continuous processes, such as physical laws or chemical reactions, the evolution of general continuous variables over

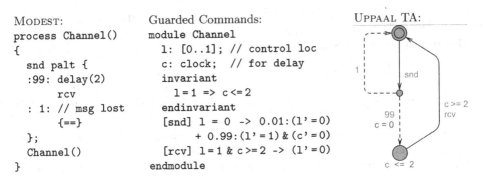

Fig. 2. Modelling a channel with loss probability 0.01 and transmission delay 2

time can be described using differential (in)equations. Continuous variables with constant derivative 1 are used as clocks to model real-time systems.

Nondeterminism To model concurrency (via an interleaving semantics) or the absence of knowledge over some choice, to abstract from details, and to represent the influence of an unknown environment, nondeterministic choices can be used. The number of choices may be finite or (countably or uncountably) infinite. The latter can be used to model nondeterministic delays.

Probability Probabilistic choices represent the case where an outcome is uncertain, but the probabilities of the outcomes are known. Such choices may be inherent to the system under study, e.g. in a randomised algorithm, or they may represent external influences such as failure rates where statistical data is available. Again, these choices may be discrete ("probabilistic") or continuous ("stochastic"), and they can be used to represent random delays.

On the syntactic representation of a SHA, each of these aspects is easy to identify. By restricting the occurrence of certain aspects, various well-known automata models appear as special cases of SHA as shown in Fig. 1. Additionally, sampling from the exponential distribution can be combined with clocks to obtain exponentially-distributed delays, allowing models based on continuous-time Markov chains to be represented as SHA, too.

3 Input Languages for Every Taste

As of the current version 2.0, the MODEST TOOLSET can process models specified in three very different input languages:

MODEST is a high-level textual modelling language. It is inspired by process algebras, but has an expressive programming language-like syntax that leads to concise models. MODEST was originally introduced with a STA semantics [7] and has recently been extended to allow the modelling of SHA [12].

Guarded Commands Probabilistic guarded commands are a low-level textual modelling language. Easy to learn with few key language constructs, it can be seen as the "assembly language" of quantitative modelling. It is the language

Fig. 3. Schematic overview of the MODEST TOOLSET's components

of the PRISM [17] model checker, so its support within the MODEST TOOLSET allows the reuse of many existing PRISM models.

UPPAAL TA UPPAAL is built upon a graphical interface to model (probabilistic) timed automata [3]. A textual language is used for expressions and to specify the composition of components. The MODEST TOOLSET can import and export UPPAAL TA models. It supports a useful subset of the language's advanced features such as parameterised templates and C-style functions.

Fig. 2 shows a comparison of the three languages for a small example PTA model. Through the use of the intermediate networks-of-SHA representation, models can be freely converted between the input languages.

4   Multiple Analysis Backends

A prime goal of the MODEST TOOLSET is to facilitate the reuse of existing analysis tools for specific subsets of SHA where possible in order to concentrate development effort on key areas where current tool support is still lacking or non-existent. The following analysis backends are part of version 2.0 of the toolset:

prohver   Computes upper bounds on max. probabilities of probabilistic safety properties in **SHA** [12]. Relies on a modified PHAVER [10] for a HA analysis.

mcpta   Performs model checking of **PTA** using PRISM for the probabilistic analysis; supports probabilistic and expected-time/expected-reward reachability properties in unbounded, time- and cost-bounded variants [14].

mctau   Connects to UPPAAL for model checking of **TA** [4], for which it is more efficient than mcpta. Automatically overapproximates probabilistic choices with nondeterminism for PTA, providing a quick first check of such models.

modes   Performs statistical model checking and simulation of **STA** with an emphasis on the sound handling of nondeterministic models [5,6,16]. Its trace generation facilities are useful for model debugging and visualisation.

Fig. 3 gives a schematic overview of the input languages and analysis backends that form the MODEST TOOLSET.

5   An Integrated Toolset

As presented in the previous sections, the MODEST TOOLSET consists of several components and concepts. Several of its analysis backends have been developed independently and presented separately before. However, it is their combination

Fig. 4. The mime graphical user interface for modelling (left) and analysis (right)

and integration that give rise to the advance in utility that the toolset presents. This integration is visible in the main interfaces of the toolset:

mime is the toolset's graphical **user interface**. It provides a modern editor for the supported textual input languages and gives full access to the analysis backends and their configuration. mime is cross-platform, based on web technologies such as HTML5, Javascript and the WebSocket protocol. Fig. 4 shows two screenshots of the mime interface. For scripting and automation scenarios, all backends are also available as standalone command-line tools.

The toolset itself is built around a small set of object-oriented **programming interfaces** for input components, SHA-to-SHA model conversions, model restrictions (to enforce certain subsets of SHA) and analysis backends. Adding a new input language, for example, can be accomplished by implementing the IInputFormalism interface and providing a semantics in terms of networks of SHA; for mime support, syntax highlighting information can be included.

The MODEST TOOLSET is implemented in C#. This allows the same binary distribution to run on 32- and 64-bit Windows, Mac OS and Linux machines. Libraries with a C interface are easy to use from C#. modes uses the runtime bytecode generation facilities in the standard Reflection.Emit namespace to generate fast simulation code for the specific model at hand.

6 Conclusion

We have presented the MODEST TOOLSET, version 2.0, highlighting how it facilitates reuse of modelling expertise via MODEST, a high-level compositional modelling language, while allowing reuse of existing models by providing import and export facilities for existing languages; and how it permits reuse of existing tools by integrating them in a unified modelling and analysis environment.

The toolset and the MODEST language have been used on several case studies, most notably to analyse safety properties of a wireless bicycle brake [2] and to evaluate stability, availability and fairness characteristics of power microgeneration control algorithms [15]. For a more extensive list of case studies, we refer the interested reader to [13].

The MODEST TOOLSET, including example models, is available for download on its website, which also provides documentation, a list of relevant publications and the description of several case studies, at www.modestchecker.net.

Planned improvements and extensions include distributed simulation and graphical automata modelling. We are very open for collaborations on case studies, new input languages and connecting to more analysis backends.

References

1. Baier, C., Haverkort, B.R., Hermanns, H., Katoen, J.P.: Performance evaluation and model checking join forces. Commun. ACM 53(9), 76–85 (2010)
2. Baró Graf, H., Hermanns, H., Kulshrestha, J., Peter, J., Vahldiek, A., Vasudevan, A.: A verified wireless safety critical hard real-time design. In: WoWMoM. IEEE (2011)
3. Behrmann, G., David, A., Larsen, K.G.: A tutorial on UPPAAL. In: Bernardo, M., Corradini, F. (eds.) SFM-RT 2004. LNCS, vol. 3185, pp. 200–236. Springer, Heidelberg (2004)
4. Bogdoll, J., David, A., Hartmanns, A., Hermanns, H.: mctau: Bridging the gap between modest and UPPAAL. In: Donaldson, A., Parker, D. (eds.) SPIN 2012. LNCS, vol. 7385, pp. 227–233. Springer, Heidelberg (2012)
5. Bogdoll, J., Ferrer Fioriti, L.M., Hartmanns, A., Hermanns, H.: Partial order methods for statistical model checking and simulation. In: Bruni, R., Dingel, J. (eds.) FMOODS/FORTE 2011. LNCS, vol. 6722, pp. 59–74. Springer, Heidelberg (2011)
6. Bogdoll, J., Hartmanns, A., Hermanns, H.: Simulation and statistical model checking for Modestly nondeterministic models. In: Schmitt, J.B. (ed.) MMB/DFT 2012. LNCS, vol. 7201, pp. 249–252. Springer, Heidelberg (2012)
7. Bohnenkamp, H.C., D'Argenio, P.R., Hermanns, H., Katoen, J.P.: MoDeST: A compositional modeling formalism for hard and softly timed systems. IEEE Trans. Software Eng. 32(10), 812–830 (2006)
8. Bohnenkamp, H.C., Hermanns, H., Katoen, J.-P.: MOTOR: The MODEST Tool Environment. In: Grumberg, O., Huth, M. (eds.) TACAS 2007. LNCS, vol. 4424, pp. 500–504. Springer, Heidelberg (2007)
9. Courtney, T., Gaonkar, S., Keefe, K., Rozier, E., Sanders, W.H.: Möbius 2.3: An extensible tool for dependability, security, and performance evaluation of large and complex system models. In: DSN, pp. 353–358. IEEE (2009)
10. Frehse, G.: PHAVer: Algorithmic verification of hybrid systems past HyTech. In: Morari, M., Thiele, L. (eds.) HSCC 2005. LNCS, vol. 3414, pp. 258–273. Springer, Heidelberg (2005)
11. Garavel, H., Lang, F., Mateescu, R., Serwe, W.: Cadp 2011: a toolbox for the construction and analysis of distributed processes. STTT 15(2), 89–107 (2013)
12. Hahn, E.M., Hartmanns, A., Hermanns, H., Katoen, J.P.: A compositional modelling and analysis framework for stochastic hybrid systems. Formal Methods in System Design 43(2), 191–232 (2013)
13. Hartmanns, A.: Modest - a unified language for quantitative models. In: FDL, pp. 44–51. IEEE (2012)
14. Hartmanns, A., Hermanns, H.: A Modest approach to checking probabilistic timed automata. In: QEST, pp. 187–196. IEEE Computer Society (2009)
15. Hartmanns, A., Hermanns, H., Berrang, P.: A comparative analysis of decentralized power grid stabilization strategies. In: Winter Simulation Conference (2012)
16. Hartmanns, A., Timmer, M.: On-the-fly confluence detection for statistical model checking. In: Brat, G., Rungta, N., Venet, A. (eds.) NFM 2013. LNCS, vol. 7871, pp. 337–351. Springer, Heidelberg (2013)
17. Kwiatkowska, M., Norman, G., Parker, D.: PRISM 4.0: Verification of probabilistic real-time systems. In: Gopalakrishnan, G., Qadeer, S. (eds.) CAV 2011. LNCS, vol. 6806, pp. 585–591. Springer, Heidelberg (2011)

Bounds2: A Tool for Compositional Multi-parametrised Verification

Antti Siirtola

Helsinki Institute for Information Technology HIIT
Department of Computer Science and Engineering, Aalto University

Abstract. Bounds2 is a two-part tool for parametrised verification. The instance generator inputs a parametrised system implementation and specification, computes cut-offs for the values of the parameters and outputs the specification and implementation instances up to the cut-offs. After that, the outputted instances are verified by using an instance checker. Bounds2 is unique since it lends support to compositional reasoning through three refinement-based notions of correctness and allows for parametrising not only the number of processes but also the size of data types as well as the structure of a system. Bounds2 provides a sound and complete approach to parametrised verification under explicit assumptions checked automatically by the tool. The decidable fragment covers, e.g., mutual exclusion properties of systems with shared resources.

1 Introduction

Modern software systems are not only multithreaded but also object-oriented and component-based. Such systems have several natural parameters, such as the number of processes and the number of data objects. Moreover, some components, like external libraries and subsystems concurrently under construction, may only be available in the interface specification form. That is why there is an evident need for verification techniques that can handle multi-parametrised systems in a compositional way.

Bounds2 is a tool that enables parametrised verification by establishing upper bounds, i.e., *cut-offs*, for the values of parameters such that if there is a bug in an implementation instance with a parameter value greater than the cut-off, then there is an analogous bug in an implementation instance where the values of the parameters are within the cut-offs. When using Bounds2, implementations and specifications are composed of labelled transitions systems (LTSs) with explicit input and output events by using parallel composition and hiding. We can also use several kinds of parameters: *types* represent the sets of the identifiers of replicated components or the sets of data values of an arbitrary size, *typed variables* refer to the identities of individual components or data values and *relation symbols* represent binary relations over replicated processes. Correctness is understood either as a refinement, which can be trace inclusion [1] or alternating simulation [2], or the compatibility of the components of the implementation [2]. Hence, Bounds2 enables compositional reasoning, too.

E. Ábrahám and K. Havelund (Eds.): TACAS 2014, LNCS 8413, pp. 599–604, 2014.

The tool consists of two parts. The instance generator determines cut-offs for the types, computes the allowed parameter values up to the cut-offs and outputs the corresponding finite state verification tasks. It can also apply a limited form of abstraction if the cut-offs cannot be determined without. After that, the outputted instances are verified by an instance checker specific to the notion of correctness. Trace refinement and compatibility checkers exploit the refinement checker FDR2 [1] to verify the instances, the alternating simulation checker makes use of the MIO Workbench [3] refinement checker, too. Bounds2 is publicly available at [4].

2   The Description Language

To get a grasp of the CSP-based (Communicating Sequential Processes [1]) formalism used by Bounds2, consider an arbitrary number of processes competing for an access to an arbitrary number of shared variables that store values of a parametric type. Each variable should be written to in a mutually exclusive way, so the interface of the shared variables is formalised as follows:

```
1  type P     type V     type D
2  var p:P     var v:V     var d:D
3  chan writebeg : P,V,D         chan writeend : P,V,D
4  plts VarIF =
5     lts
6        I = []p,d: ?writebeg(p,v,d) -> W(p,d)
7        W(p,d) = writeend(p,v,d) -> I
8     from I
9  plts VarsIF = ||v: VarIF
```

Types P and V represent the set of the identifiers of processes and variables, respectively, and D denotes the domain of the shared variables. Variables p, v and d are used to refer to an individual process, a shared variable and a value of a shared variable, respectively. The event writebeg(p,v,d) (writeend(p,v,d)) denotes that the process p starts (is finished with) writing the value d to the shared variable v. The input events are marked by ?, the other events are outputs. A parametrised LTS (PLTS) VarIF captures the interface of a shared variable v: only one process can access v at a time. As we let v to range over all identifiers of shared variables and compose the instances of VarIF in parallel, we obtain the PLTS VarsIF which captures the joint interface of all the shared variables.

Suppose that we also have an implementation VarImpl of the variable interface, the interface PrIF of a process p and the alphabet PrAlph of PrIF without the write events. In order to check that (a) all the variable and process interfaces are compatible, i.e., they can co-operate in some environment such that whenever an output is sent, it is matched by an input, (b) the implementation of the variable refines its interface and (c) no two process access the variable simultaneously, we specify the following parametrised verification tasks:

```
10 compatibility: verify (||p: PrIF) || VarsIF
```

```
11 alternating simulation: verify VarImpl against VarIF
12 trace refinement: verify (||p: PrIF) \ ((_)p: PrAlph) against VarsIF
```

We can also define binary relations over parametric types. For example, in order to specify a total order TO in which the processes access the shared variables we could write as follows:

```
relv TO : P,P    var p1 : P    var p2 : P    var p3 : P
vc irrefl = \/p1: ! p1 TO p1
vc asymm = \/p1,p2: ! (p1 TO p2 & p2 TO p1)
vc trans = \/p1,p2,p3: p1 TO p2 & p2 TO p3 -> p1 TO p3
vc total = \/p1,p2: !p1 = p2 -> p1 TO p2 | p2 TO p1
trace refinement: verify (||p1,p2: [p1 TO p2] Pr2IF) \ ((_)p: PrAlph)
                  against VarsIF when (irrefl & asymm & trans & total)
```

In this case, we need also a PLTS Pr2IF which describes the behaviour of the process interface from the viewpoint of two processes p1 and p2 such that p1 comes before p2 in the total order.

Once we have proved that a system implementation refines its interface specification, we can use the specification, which is usually much smaller, in place of the system implementation in further verification efforts. This is possible since the input formalism of Bounds2 is compositional.

3   Novel Features

The first version of Bounds was introduced in [5] and it featured the support for process types, relation symbols and trace refinement (tref). The novelties of Bounds2 introduced here are fourfold.

Sound and/or complete verification. The input language of Bounds2 is Turing complete in its full generality, but there are explicit conditions under which cut-offs can be computed. The main restriction is that each type must classify either as a data type or a process type, but not both. In the above example, V is thought as a process type since v is only used in the replicated parallel compositions (line 9) and D is considered a data type since d only occurs in the replicated choices (line 6). The variable p is used both in a replicated choice and a replicated parallel composition (lines 6,10,12), but sometimes, like in this case, Bounds2 can convert replicated choices into replicated parallel compositions, which means that P is classified as a process type. Depending on the notion of correctness, there are also limitations on non-determinism, hiding and the use of relation symbols. The decidable fragment covers, e.g., the mutual exclusion properties of concurrent systems with shared resources [6–8], and if any of the assumptions is removed, parametrised verification becomes undecidable [6–8].

All the conditions are checked automatically by the tool. If any of them is violated, the user is asked to provide a cut-off manually. In this case, verification is not sound but we can still detect bugs. Sometimes, the tool can perform an over-approximating conversion of replicated choices to replicated parallel compositions. In this case, the verification is sound but false negatives are possible. The exact and over-approximating conversions as well as the possibility to enter a cut-off manually are novel features of Bounds2.

More expressive input language. The main novelty of Bounds2 is a more expressive input language with a larger decidable fragment. This is enabled by the introduction of a replicated choice (data types), the classification of events into inputs and outputs, and two new notions of correctness: compatibility (comp) and alternating simulation (altsim) [2]. A replicated choice adds to expressiveness, since it allows us to express components with a parametrised state space. Earlier, it was only possible to parametrise the number of concurrent components. Distinguishing between input and output events allows us to consider the compatibility of PLTSs representing software interfaces and gives rise to another refinement, the alternating simulation, which is a natural notion of the correctness of software interfaces. However, the support for the alternating simulation is currently not as good as for two other notions of correctness, since the back end alternating simulation checker, MIO Workbench, can only handle relatively small models. The theoretical background of the extensions is described in [7, 8].

Faster operation. Bounds2 determines structural cut-offs for types based on the results in [7, 8]. After that, the tool computes the allowed values for all parameters up to the cut-offs by using a search-tree-based enumeration algorithm described in [5]. Since the values of relation symbols are defined in the universal fragment of first order logic, this is basically equivalent to computing the model class of a first order formula up to the cut-offs.

For the recent version of the tool, we have implemented a version of the search algorithm which is parallelised according to the exploratory partitioning scheme [9]. Initially, computation proceeds sequentially in a breadth-first search manner but when the search tree becomes wide enough (several times wider than the number of processor cores available), the subtrees are processed in parallel. This way, we can ensure that the work load is distributed evenly between threads, since some subtrees are much bigger than the others. Once the values of the parameters up to the cut-offs are computed, Bounds2 generates and outputs the corresponding instances of the system specification and implementation. Also this phase is parallelised in Bounds2 by using the input partitioning scheme [9].

Additionally, the internal data structures are optimised. Previously, all states and events were stored as a string which was highly inefficient. In Bounds2, the strings are first converted into integers for faster analysis and finally back into strings when the instances are outputted.

Improved reduction. The cut-offs computed earlier are rough structural ones. They are fast and easy to compute but they are often far from optimal, especially in the case of data types. Therefore, Bounds2 tries to improve the cut-offs further by analysing the instances up to the structural cut-offs. Basically, the tool discards instances that can be obtained as a composition of smaller ones as described in [7, 8]. Also this additional reduction is sound and complete and it is an important enhancement over Bounds1, because the discarded instances are always the biggest ones which are the most expensive to verify.

4   Experimental Results

We have made several case studies with Bounds2 and compared its performance against Bounds1 [5]. We have not compared Bounds2 with other parametrised verification tools, since most of them are targeted to low level software with finite data [10–14] whereas our focus is on higher level applications which are not only multithreaded but also object-oriented and component-based. The comparison with other tools would be difficult anyway, since the tools solve a different decidable fragment and we are not aware of any other tools for parametrised refinement checking.

For each system, the table below lists the number of types (typ), relation symbols (rel) and variables (var) used in the model, the notion of correctness (corr) and the structural cut-offs for types. For both versions of Bounds, the number of instances outputted and the running times of the instance generator (t_G) and the instance checker (t_C) are reported. For Bounds2, the former running times are given with a single core (t_{G1}) and six cores (t_{G6}) being used. We can see that the cut-offs provided by the tool are often very small and compared with Bounds1, the new version not only has a broader application domain but also operates faster and produces less instances that need to be checked. We can also see that the bottleneck in the verification chain is typically not Bounds2 but the back end finite state verification tool. The experiments were made on a six-core AMD Phenom II with 8GB of memory running Ubuntu 12.04 LTS.

system	typ	rel	var	corr	cut-offs	Bounds1 out	t_G	t_C	Bounds2 out	t_{G1}	t_{G6}	t_C
HCP	2	0	0	tref	2,9	not supported			4	0.15s	<0.1s	0.3s
cache_consistency	2	0	0	tref	1,13	not supported			5	15s	6s	9s
tokenring	1	1	2	tref	4	3	<0.1s	0.2s	3	<0.1s	<0.1s	0.2s
twotoken	1	2	2	tref	5	30	32s	5s	30	32s	8s	5s
miniSRS_comp	2	0	0	comp	2,1	not supported			2	<0.1s	<0.1s	0.15s
SRS	2	1	0	tref	2,3	14	0.4s	1m35s	6	0.1s	<0.1s	1m4s
SRSwithData	3	1	0	tref	2,3,1	not supported			5	0.1s	0.1s	1m4s
res_io	2	0	1	altsim	2,1	not supported			2	<0.1s	<0.1s	5.7s
peterson_io	2	0	1	altsim	2,1	not supported			1	<0.1s	<0.1s	11s
taDOM2+	2	2	0	tref	2,3	28	11s	>12h	14	6.5s	1.7s	6h36m

5   Conclusions

Bounds2 is a cut-off-based tool for parametrised verification. The cut-offs provided by the tool are often as good as we can intuitively hope for, which is necessary for practical parametrised verification. The distinctive feature of the tool is sound and complete verification with the support for compositional reasoning and the possibility to parametrise both the number of processes and the size of data types as well as the structure of the system. We believe that the tool will be useful in the analysis of multithreaded, component-based, object-oriented software systems, which involve both process and data parameters and where some components may only be available in the interface specification form. Hence, Bounds2 nicely complements other parametrised verification tools most of which are targeted for low level software acting on finite data.

Acknowledgements. We would like to thankfully acknowledge the funding from the SARANA project in the SAFIR 2014 program and the Academy of Finland project 139402.

References

1. Roscoe, A.W.: Understanding Concurrent Systems. Springer (2010)
2. De Alfaro, L., Henzinger, T.: Interface automata. ACM SIGSOFT Software Engineering Notes 26(5), 109–120 (2001)
3. Bauer, S.S., Mayer, P., Schroeder, A., Hennicker, R.: On weak modal compatibility, refinement, and the MIO workbench. In: Esparza, J., Majumdar, R. (eds.) TACAS 2010. LNCS, vol. 6015, pp. 175–189. Springer, Heidelberg (2010)
4. Siirtola, A.: Bounds website, http://www.cs.hut.fi/u/siirtoa1/bounds
5. Siirtola, A.: Bounds: from parameterised to finite-state verification. In: Caillaud, B., Carmona, J., Hiraishi, K. (eds.) ACSD 2011, pp. 31–35. IEEE (2011)
6. Siirtola, A.: Algorithmic Multiparameterised Verification of Safety Properties. Process Algebraic Approach. PhD thesis, University of Oulu (2010)
7. Siirtola, A., Heljanko, K.: Parametrised compositional verification with multiple process and data types. In: Carmona, J., Lazarescu, M.T., Pietkiewicz-Koutny, M. (eds.) ACSD 2013, pp. 67–76. IEEE (2013)
8. Siirtola, A.: Parametrised interface automata (unpublished draft) (2013), http://www.cs.hut.fi/u/siirtoa1/papers/pia_paper.pdf
9. Grama, A., Gupta, A., Karypis, G., Kumar, V.: Introduction to Parallel Computing. Addison Wesley (2003)
10. Delzanno, G., Raskin, J.-F., Van Begin, L.: Towards the automated verification of multithreaded Java programs. In: Katoen, J.-P., Stevens, P. (eds.) TACAS 2002. LNCS, vol. 2280, pp. 173–187. Springer, Heidelberg (2002)
11. Ghilardi, S., Ranise, S.: Backward reachability of array-based systems by SMT solving: termination and invariant synthesis. Log. Meth. Comput. Sci. 6(4) (2010)
12. Kaiser, A., Kroening, D., Wahl, T.: Dynamic cutoff detection in parameterized concurrent programs. In: Touili, T., Cook, B., Jackson, P. (eds.) CAV 2010. LNCS, vol. 6174, pp. 645–659. Springer, Heidelberg (2010)
13. La Torre, S., Madhusudan, P., Parlato, G.: Model-checking parameterized concurrent programs using linear interfaces. In: Touili, T., Cook, B., Jackson, P. (eds.) CAV 2010. LNCS, vol. 6174, pp. 629–644. Springer, Heidelberg (2010)
14. Yang, Q., Li, M.: A cut-off approach for bounded verification of parameterized systems. In: Kramer, J., Bishop, J., Devanbu, P.T., Uchitel, S. (eds.) ICSE 2010, pp. 345–354. ACM (2010)

On the Correctness
of a Branch Displacement Algorithm[*]

Jaap Boender[1] and Claudio Sacerdoti Coen[2]

[1] Foundations of Computing Group
Department of Computer Science
School of Science and Technology
Middlesex University, London, UK
J.Boender@mdx.ac.uk
[2] Dipartimento di Scienze dell'Informazione,
Università degli Studi di Bologna, Italy
sacerdot@cs.unibo.it

Abstract. The branch displacement problem is a well-known problem in assembler design. It revolves around the feature, present in several processor families, of having different instructions, of different sizes, for jumps of different displacements. The problem, which is provably NP-hard, is then to select the instructions such that one ends up with the smallest possible program.

During our research with the CerCo project on formally verifying a C compiler, we have implemented and proven correct an algorithm for this problem. In this paper, we discuss the problem, possible solutions, our specific solutions and the proofs.

Keywords: formal verification, interactive theorem proving, assembler, branch displacement optimisation.

1 Introduction

The problem of branch displacement optimisation, also known as jump encoding, is a well-known problem in assembler design [3]. Its origin lies in the fact that in many architecture sets, the encoding (and therefore size) of some instructions depends on the distance to their operand (the instruction 'span'). The branch displacement optimisation problem consists of encoding these span-dependent instructions in such a way that the resulting program is as small as possible.

This problem is the subject of the present paper. After introducing the problem in more detail, we will discuss the solutions used by other compilers, present the algorithm we use in the CerCo assembler, and discuss its verification, that is the proofs of termination and correctness using the Matita proof assistant [1].

---

[*] Research supported by the CerCo project, within the Future and Emerging Technologies (FET) programme of the Seventh Framework Programme for Research of the European Commission, under FET-Open grant number 243881.

E. Ábrahám and K. Havelund (Eds.): TACAS 2014, LNCS 8413, pp. 605–619, 2014.

Formulating the final statement of correctness and finding the loop invariants have been non-trivial tasks and are, indeed, the main contribution of this paper. It has required considerable care and fine-tuning to formulate not only the minimal statement required for the ulterior proof of correctness of the assembler, but also the minimal set of invariants needed for the proof of correctness of the algorithm.

The research presented in this paper has been executed within the CerCo project which aims at formally verifying a C compiler with cost annotations. The target architecture for this project is the MCS-51, whose instruction set contains span-dependent instructions. Furthermore, its maximum addressable memory size is very small (64 Kb), which makes it important to generate programs that are as small as possible. With this optimisation, however, comes increased complexity and hence increased possibility for error. We must make sure that the branch instructions are encoded correctly, otherwise the assembled program will behave unpredictably.

All Matita files related to this development can be found on the CerCo website, http://cerco.cs.unibo.it. The specific part that contains the branch displacement algorithm is in the ASM subdirectory, in the files PolicyFront.ma, PolicyStep.ma and Policy.ma.

2   The Branch Displacement Optimisation Problem

In most modern instruction sets that have them, the only span-dependent instructions are branch instructions. Taking the ubiquitous x86-64 instruction set as an example, we find that it contains eleven different forms of the unconditional branch instruction, all with different ranges, instruction sizes and semantics (only six are valid in 64-bit mode, for example). Some examples are shown in Figure 1 (see also [4]).

Instruction	Size (bytes)	Displacement range
Short jump	2	-128 to 127 bytes
Relative near jump	5	-2^{32} to $2^{32} - 1$ bytes
Absolute near jump	6	one segment (64-bit address)
Far jump	8	entire memory (indirect jump)

Fig. 1. List of x86 branch instructions

The chosen target architecture of the CerCo project is the Intel MCS-51, which features three types of branch instructions (or jump instructions; the two terms are used interchangeably), as shown in Figure 2.

Conditional branch instructions are only available in short form, which means that a conditional branch outside the short address range has to be encoded using three branch instructions (for instructions whose logical negation is available, it can be done with two branch instructions, but for some instructions this is not the case). The call instruction is only available in absolute and long forms.

Instruction	Size (bytes)	Execution time (cycles)	Displacement range
SJMP ('short jump')	2	2	-128 to 127 bytes
AJMP ('absolute jump')	2	2	one segment (11-bit address)
LJMP ('long jump')	3	3	entire memory

Fig. 2. List of MCS-51 branch instructions

Note that even though the MCS-51 architecture is much less advanced and much simpler than the x86-64 architecture, the basic types of branch instruction remain the same: a short jump with a limited range, an intra-segment jump and a jump that can reach the entire available memory.

Generally, in code fed to the assembler as input, the only difference between branch instructions is semantics, not span. This means that a distinction is made between an unconditional branch and the several kinds of conditional branch, but not between their short, absolute or long variants.

The algorithm used by the assembler to encode these branch instructions into the different machine instructions is known as the *branch displacement algorithm*. The optimisation problem consists of finding as small an encoding as possible, thus minimising program length and execution time.

Similar problems, e.g. the branch displacement optimisation problem for other architectures, are known to be NP-complete [7,9], which could make finding an optimal solution very time-consuming.

The canonical solution, as shown by Szymanski [9] or more recently by Dickson [2] for the x86 instruction set, is to use a fixed point algorithm that starts with the shortest possible encoding (all branch instruction encoded as short jumps, which is likely not a correct solution) and then iterates over the source to re-encode those branch instructions whose target is outside their range.

Adding Absolute Jumps

In both papers mentioned above, the encoding of a jump is only dependent on the distance between the jump and its target: below a certain value a short jump can be used; above this value the jump must be encoded as a long jump.

Here, termination of the smallest fixed point algorithm is easy to prove. All branch instructions start out encoded as short jumps, which means that the distance between any branch instruction and its target is as short as possible (all the intervening jumps are short). If, in this situation, there is a branch instruction b whose span is not within the range for a short jump, we can be sure that we can never reach a situation where the span of j is so small that it can be encoded as a short jump. This argument continues to hold throughout the subsequent iterations of the algorithm: short jumps can change into long jumps, but not *vice versa*, as spans only increase. Hence, the algorithm either terminates early when a fixed point is reached or when all short jumps have been changed into long jumps.

```
                              L₀: jmp X
                              X:  ...
                                  ...
                              L₁: ...
                              % Start of new segment if
                              % jmp X is encoded as short
      jmp X                       ...
         ...                   jmp L₁
  L₀: ...                         ...
  % Start of new segment if    jmp L₁
  % jmp X is encoded as short      ...
         ...                   jmp L₁
      jmp L₀                      ...
```

(a) Example of a program where a long
jump becomes absolute

(b) Example of a program where the
fixed-point algorithm is not optimal

Also, we can be certain that we have reached an optimal solution: a short
jump is only changed into a long jump if it is absolutely necessary.

However, neither of these claims (termination nor optimality) hold when we
add the absolute jump. With absolute jumps, the encoding of a branch instruction
no longer depends only on the distance between the branch instruction
and its target. An absolute jump is possible when instruction and target are in
the same segment (for the MCS-51, this means that the first 5 bytes of their
addresses have to be equal). It is therefore entirely possible for two branch instructions
with the same span to be encoded in different ways (absolute if the
branch instruction and its target are in the same segment, long if this is not the
case).

This invalidates our earlier termination argument: a branch instruction, once
encoded as a long jump, can be re-encoded during a later iteration as an absolute
jump. Consider the program shown in Figure 3a. At the start of the first iteration,
both the branch to X and the branch to L_0 are encoded as small jumps. Let us
assume that in this case, the placement of L_0 and the branch to it are such that
L_0 is just outside the segment that contains this branch. Let us also assume
that the distance between L_0 and the branch to it is too large for the branch
instruction to be encoded as a short jump.

All this means that in the second iteration, the branch to L_0 will be encoded as
a long jump. If we assume that the branch to X is encoded as a long jump as well,
the size of the branch instruction will increase and L_0 will be 'propelled' into the
same segment as its branch instruction, because every subsequent instruction
will move one byte forward. Hence, in the third iteration, the branch to L_0 can
be encoded as an absolute jump. At first glance, there is nothing that prevents
us from constructing a configuration where two branch instructions interact in
such a way as to iterate indefinitely between long and absolute encodings.

This situation mirrors the explanation by Szymanski [9] of why the branch displacement
optimisation problem is NP-complete. In this explanation, a condition

for NP-completeness is the fact that programs be allowed to contain *pathological* jumps. These are branch instructions that can normally not be encoded as a short(er) jump, but gain this property when some other branch instructions are encoded as a long(er) jump. This is exactly what happens in Figure 3a. By encoding the first branch instruction as a long jump, another branch instruction switches from long to absolute (which is shorter).

In addition, our previous optimality argument no longer holds. Consider the program shown in Figure 3b. Suppose that the distance between L_0 and L_1 is such that if jmp X is encoded as a short jump, there is a segment border just after L_1. Let us also assume that all three branches to L_1 are in the same segment, but far enough away from L_1 that they cannot be encoded as short jumps.

Then, if jmp X were to be encoded as a short jump, which is clearly possible, all of the branches to L_1 would have to be encoded as long jumps. However, if jmp X were to be encoded as a long jump, and therefore increase in size, L_1 would be 'propelled' across the segment border, so that the three branches to L_1 could be encoded as absolute jumps. Depending on the relative sizes of long and absolute jumps, this solution might actually be smaller than the one reached by the smallest fixed point algorithm.

3   Our Algorithm

3.1   Design Decisions

Given the NP-completeness of the problem, finding optimal solutions (using, for example, a constraint solver) can potentially be very costly.

The SDCC compiler [8], which has a backend targeting the MCS-51 instruction set, simply encodes every branch instruction as a long jump without taking the distance into account. While certainly correct (the long jump can reach any destination in memory) and a very fast solution to compute, it results in a less than optimal solution in terms of output size and execution time.

On the other hand, the gcc compiler suite, while compiling C on the x86 architecture, uses a greatest fix point algorithm. In other words, it starts with all branch instructions encoded as the largest jumps available, and then tries to reduce the size of branch instructions as much as possible.

Such an algorithm has the advantage that any intermediate result it returns is correct: the solution where every branch instruction is encoded as a large jump is always possible, and the algorithm only reduces those branch instructions whose destination address is in range for a shorter jump. The algorithm can thus be stopped after a determined number of steps without sacrificing correctness.

The result, however, is not necessarily optimal. Even if the algorithm is run until it terminates naturally, the fixed point reached is the *greatest* fixed point, not the least fixed point. Furthermore, gcc (at least for the x86 architecture) only uses short and long jumps. This makes the algorithm more efficient, as shown in the previous section, but also results in a less optimal solution.

In the CerCo assembler, we opted at first for a least fixed point algorithm, taking absolute jumps into account.

Here, we ran into a problem with proving termination, as explained in the previous section: if we only take short and long jumps into account, the jump encoding can only switch from short to long, but never in the other direction. When we add absolute jumps, however, it is theoretically possible for a branch instruction to switch from absolute to long and back, as previously explained. Proving termination then becomes difficult, because there is nothing that precludes a branch instruction from oscillating back and forth between absolute and long jumps indefinitely.

To keep the algorithm in the same complexity class and more easily prove termination, we decided to explicitly enforce the 'branch instructions must always grow longer' requirement: if a branch instruction is encoded as a long jump in one iteration, it will also be encoded as a long jump in all the following iterations. Therefore the encoding of any branch instruction can change at most two times: once from short to absolute (or long), and once from absolute to long.

There is one complicating factor. Suppose that a branch instruction is encoded in step n as an absolute jump, but in step $n + 1$ it is determined that (because of changes elsewhere) it can now be encoded as a short jump. Due to the requirement that the branch instructions must always grow longer, the branch encoding will be encoded as an absolute jump in step $n + 1$ as well.

This is not necessarily correct. A branch instruction that can be encoded as a short jump cannot always also be encoded as an absolute jump, as a short jump can bridge segments, whereas an absolute jump cannot. Therefore, in this situation we have decided to encode the branch instruction as a long jump, which is always correct.

The resulting algorithm, therefore, will not return the least fixed point, as it might have too many long jumps. However, it is still better than the algorithms from SDCC and gcc, since even in the worst case, it will still return a smaller or equal solution.

Experimenting with our algorithm on the test suite of C programs included with gcc 2.3.3 has shown that on average, about 25 percent of jumps are encoded as short or absolute jumps by the algorithm. As not all instructions are jumps, this does not make for a large reduction in size, but it can make for a reduction in execution time: if jumps are executed multiple times, for example in loops, the fact that short jumps take less cycles to execute than long jumps can have great effect.

As for complexity, there are at most $2n$ iterations, where n is the number of branch instructions. Practical tests within the CerCo project on small to medium pieces of code have shown that in almost all cases, a fixed point is reached in 3 passes. Only in one case did the algorithm need 4. This is not surprising: after all, the difference between short/absolute and long jumps is only one byte (three for conditional jumps). For a change from short/absolute to long to have an effect on other jumps is therefore relatively uncommon, which explains why a fixed point is reached so quickly.

3.2   The Algorithm in Detail

The branch displacement algorithm forms part of the translation from pseudo-code to assembler. More specifically, it is used by the function that translates pseudo-addresses (natural numbers indicating the position of the instruction in the program) to actual addresses in memory. Note that in pseudocode, all instructions are of size 1.

Our original intention was to have two different functions, one function `policy` : $\mathbb{N} \to \{\texttt{short\_jump}, \texttt{absolute\_jump}, \texttt{long\_jump}\}$ to associate jumps to their intended encoding, and a function σ : $\mathbb{N} \to \texttt{Word}$ to associate pseudo-addresses to machine addresses. σ would use `policy` to determine the size of jump instructions. This turned out to be suboptimal from the algorithmic point of view and impossible to prove correct.

From the algorithmic point of view, in order to create the `policy` function, we must necessarily have a translation from pseudo-addresses to machine addresses (i.e. a σ function): in order to judge the distance between a jump and its destination, we must know their memory locations. Conversely, in order to create the σ function, we need to have the `policy` function, otherwise we do not know the sizes of the jump instructions in the program.

Much the same problem appears when we try to prove the algorithm correct: the correctness of `policy` depends on the correctness of σ, and the correctness of σ depends on the correctness of `policy`.

We solved this problem by integrating the `policy` and σ algorithms. We now have a function σ : $\mathbb{N} \to \texttt{Word} \times \texttt{bool}$ which associates a pseudo-address to a machine address. The boolean denotes a forced long jump; as noted in the previous section, if during the fixed point computation an absolute jump changes to be potentially re-encoded as a short jump, the result is actually a long jump. It might therefore be the case that jumps are encoded as long jumps without this actually being necessary, and this information needs to be passed to the code generating function.

The assembler function encodes the jumps by checking the distance between source and destination according to σ, so it could select an absolute jump in a situation where there should be a long jump. The boolean is there to prevent this from happening by indicating the locations where a long jump should be encoded, even if a shorter jump is possible. This has no effect on correctness, since a long jump is applicable in any situation.

The algorithm, shown in Figure 4, works by folding the function F over the entire program, thus gradually constructing *sigma*. This constitutes one step in the fixed point calculation; successive steps repeat the fold until a fixed point is reached. We have abstracted away the case where an instruction is not a jump, since the size of these instructions is constant.

Parameters of the function F are:

- a function *labels* that associates a label to its pseudo-address;
- *old_sigma*, the σ function returned by the previous iteration of the fixed point calculation;
- *instr*, the instruction currently under consideration;

function F(*labels*,*old_sigma*,*instr*,*ppc*,*acc*)
  ⟨*added*, *pc*, *sigma*⟩ ← *acc*
  if *instr* is a backward jump to *j* **then**
    length ← jump_size(*pc*, *sigma*₁(*labels*(*j*)))   ▷ compute jump distance
  else if *instr* is a forward jump to *j* **then**
    length ← jump_size(*pc*, *old_sigma*₁(*labels*(*j*)) + *added*)
  end if
  old_length ← old_sigma₁(*ppc*)
  new_length ← max(*old_length*, *length*)   ▷ length must never decrease
  old_size ← old_sigma₂(*ppc*)
  new_size ← instruction_size(*instr*, *new_length*)   ▷ compute size in bytes
  new_added ← *added* + (*new_size* − *old_size*)   ▷ keep track of total added bytes
  new_sigma ← *old_sigma*
  *new_sigma*₁(*ppc* + 1) ← *pc* + *new_size*
  *new_sigma*₂(*ppc*) ← *new_length*   ▷ update σ
return ⟨*new_added*, *pc* + *new_size*, *new_sigma*⟩
end function

Fig. 4. The heart of the algorithm

– *ppc*, the pseudo-address of *instr*;
– *acc*, the fold accumulator, which contains *added* (the number of bytes added to the program size with respect to the previous iteration), *pc* (the highest memory address reached so far), and of course *sigma*, the σ function under construction.

The first two are parameters that remain the same through one iteration, the final three are standard parameters for a fold function (including *ppc*, which is simply the number of instructions of the program already processed).

The σ functions used by F are not of the same type as the final σ function: they are of type $\sigma : \mathbb{N} \to \mathbb{N} \times \{\texttt{short\_jump}, \texttt{absolute\_jump}, \texttt{long\_jump}\}$; a function that associates a pseudo-address with a memory address and a jump length. We do this to ease the comparison of jump lengths between iterations. In the algorithm, we use the notation $sigma_1(x)$ to denote the memory address corresponding to x, and $sigma_2(x)$ for the jump length corresponding to x.

Note that the σ function used for label lookup varies depending on whether the label is behind our current position or ahead of it. For backward branches, where the label is behind our current position, we can use *sigma* for lookup, since its memory address is already known. However, for forward branches, the memory address of the address of the label is not yet known, so we must use *old_sigma*.

We cannot use *old_sigma* without change: it might be the case that we have already increased the size of some branch instructions before, making the program longer and moving every instruction forward. We must compensate for this by adding the size increase of the program to the label's memory address according to *old_sigma*, so that branch instruction spans do not get compromised.

`sigma_policy_specification` $\equiv \lambda program.\lambda sigma.$

$sigma\ 0 = 0\ \wedge$

let $instr\_list \equiv code\ program$ **in**

$\forall ppc.ppc < |instr\_list| \rightarrow$

let $pc \equiv sigma\ ppc$ **in**

let $instruction \equiv$ `fetch_pseudo_instruction` $instr\_list\ ppc$ **in**

let $next\_pc \equiv sigma\ (ppc + 1)$ **in**

$next\_pc = pc +$ `instruction_size` $sigma\ ppc\ instruction\ \wedge$

$(pc +$ `instruction_size` $sigma\ ppc\ instruction < 2^{16}\ \vee$

$(\forall ppc'.ppc' < |instr\_list| \rightarrow ppc < ppc' \rightarrow$

let $instruction' \equiv$ `fetch_pseudo_instruction` $instr\_list\ ppc'$ **in**

`instruction_size` $sigma\ ppc'\ instruction' = 0)\ \wedge$

$pc +$ `instruction_size` $sigma\ ppc\ instruction = 2^{16})$

Fig. 5. Main correctness statement

4 The Proof

In this section, we present the correctness proof for the algorithm in more detail. The main correctness statement is shown, slightly simplified, in Figure 5. Informally, this means that when fetching a pseudo-instruction at ppc, the translation by σ of $ppc + 1$ is the same as $\sigma(ppc)$ plus the size of the instruction at ppc. That is, an instruction is placed consecutively after the previous one, and there are no overlaps. The rest of the statement deals with memory size: either the next instruction fits within memory ($next\_pc < 2^{16}$) or it ends exactly at the limit memory, in which case it must be the last translated instruction in the program (enforced by specfiying that the size of all subsequent instructions is 0: there may be comments or cost annotations that are not translated).

Finally, we enforce that the program starts at address 0, i.e. $\sigma(0) = 0$. It may seem strange that we do not explicitly include a safety property stating that every jump instruction is of the right type with respect to its target (akin to the lemma from Figure 7), but this is not necessary. The distance is recalculated according to the instruction addresses from σ, which implicitly expresses safety.

Since our computation is a least fixed point computation, we must prove termination in order to prove correctness: if the algorithm is halted after a number of steps without reaching a fixed point, the solution is not guaranteed to be correct. More specifically, branch instructions might be encoded which do not coincide with the span between their location and their destination.

Proof of termination rests on the fact that the encoding of branch instructions can only grow larger, which means that we must reach a fixed point after at most $2n$ iterations, with n the number of branch instructions in the program. This worst case is reached if at every iteration, we change the encoding of exactly one branch instruction; since the encoding of any branch instruction can change first from short to absolute, and then to long, there can be at most $2n$ changes.

4.1   Fold Invariants

In this section, we present the invariants that hold during the fold of F over the program. These will be used later on to prove the properties of the iteration. During the fixed point computation, the σ function is implemented as a trie for ease of access; computing $\sigma(x)$ is achieved by looking up the value of x in the trie. Actually, during the fold, the value we pass along is a pair $\mathbb{N} \times$ ppc_pc_map. The first component is the number of bytes added to the program so far with respect to the previous iteration, and the second component, ppc_pc_map, is the actual σ trie (which we'll call *strie* to avoid confusion).

out_of_program_none $\equiv \lambda prefix.\lambda strie.$

$\forall i.i < 2^{16} \rightarrow (i > |prefix| \leftrightarrow$ lookup_opt i (snd *strie*) = None)

The first invariant states that any pseudo-address not yet examined is not present in the lookup trie.

not_jump_default $\equiv \lambda prefix.\lambda strie.\forall i.i < |prefix| \rightarrow$

$\neg$is_jump (nth i $prefix$) $\rightarrow$ lookup i (snd *strie*) = short_jump

This invariant states that when we try to look up the jump length of a pseudo-address where there is no branch instruction, we will get the default value, a short jump.

jump_increase $\equiv \lambda pc.\lambda op.\lambda p.\forall i.i < |prefix| \rightarrow$

let $oj \equiv$ lookup i (snd op) in

let $j \equiv$ lookup i (snd p) in jmpleq oj j

This invariant states that between iterations (with op being the previous iteration, and p the current one), jump lengths either remain equal or increase. It is needed for proving termination. We now proceed with the safety lemmas. The lemma in Figure 6 is a temporary formulation of the main property sigma_policy_specification. Its main difference from the final version is that it uses instruction_size_jmplen to compute the instruction size. This function uses j to compute the span of branch instructions (i.e. it uses the σ under construction), instead of looking at the distance between source and destination.

sigma_compact_unsafe $\equiv \lambda prefix.\lambda strie.\forall n.n < |prefix| \rightarrow$

match lookup_opt n (snd *strie*) with

None $\Rightarrow$ False

Some $\langle pc, j \rangle \Rightarrow$

match lookup_opt $(n + 1)$ (snd *strie*) with

None $\Rightarrow$ False

Some $\langle pc_1, j_1 \rangle \Rightarrow pc_1 = pc+$

instruction_size_jmplen j (nth n $prefix$)

Fig. 6. Temporary safety property

sigma_safe $\equiv$ $\lambda prefix.\lambda labels.\lambda old\_strie.\lambda strie.\forall i.i < |prefix| \rightarrow$

    $\forall dest\_label.$is_jump_to (nth i prefix) $dest\_label \rightarrow$

    let $paddr \equiv$ lookup $labels$ $dest\_label$ in

    let $\langle j, src, dest \rangle \equiv$ if $paddr \leq i$ then

        let $\langle \_, j \rangle \equiv$ lookup i (snd $strie$) in

        let $\langle pc\_plus\_jl, \_ \rangle \equiv$ lookup $(i+1)$ (snd $strie$) in

        let $\langle addr, \_ \rangle \equiv$ lookup $paddr$ (snd $strie$) in

        $\langle j, pc\_plus\_jl, addr \rangle$

    else

        let $\langle \_, j \rangle \equiv$ lookup i (snd $strie$) in

        let $\langle pc\_plus\_jl, \_ \rangle \equiv$ lookup $(i+1)$ (snd old_strie) in

        let $\langle addr, \_ \rangle \equiv$ lookup $paddr$ (snd old_strie) in

        $\langle j, pc\_plus\_jl, addr \rangle$ in

    match j with

        short_jump $\Rightarrow$ short_jump_valid src $dest$

        absolute_jump $\Rightarrow$ absolute_jump_valid src $dest$

        long_jump $\Rightarrow$ True

Fig. 7. Safety property

This is because σ is still under construction; we will prove below that after the final iteration, sigma_compact_unsafe is equivalent to the main property in Figure 7 which holds at the end of the computation. We compute the distance using the memory address of the instruction plus its size. This follows the behaviour of the MCS-51 microprocessor, which increases the program counter directly after fetching, and only then executes the branch instruction (by changing the program counter again).

There are also some simple, properties to make sure that our policy remains consistent, and to keep track of whether the fixed point has been reached. We do not include them here in detail. Two of these properties give the values of σ for the start and end of the program; $\sigma(0) = 0$ and $\sigma(n)$, where n is the number of instructions up until now, is equal to the maximum memory address so far. There are also two properties that deal with what happens when the previous iteration does not change with respect to the current one. *added* is a variable that keeps track of the number of bytes we have added to the program size by changing the encoding of branch instructions. If *added* is 0, the program has not changed and vice versa.

We need to use two different formulations, because the fact that *added* is 0 does not guarantee that no branch instructions have changed. For instance, it is possible that we have replaced a short jump with an absolute jump, which does not change the size of the branch instruction. Therefore policy_pc_equal states that $old\_sigma_1(x) = sigma_1(x)$, whereas policy_jump_equal states that

$old\_sigma_2(x) = sigma_2(x)$. This formulation is sufficient to prove termination and compactness.

Proving these invariants is simple, usually by induction on the prefix length.

4.2 Iteration Invariants

These are invariants that hold after the completion of an iteration. The main difference between these invariants and the fold invariants is that after the completion of the fold, we check whether the program size does not supersede 64 Kb, the maximum memory size the MCS-51 can address. The type of an iteration therefore becomes an option type: None in case the program becomes larger than 64 Kb, or Some σ otherwise. We also no longer pass along the number of bytes added to the program size, but a boolean that indicates whether we have changed something during the iteration or not.

If the iteration returns None, which means that it has become too large for memory, there is an invariant that states that the previous iteration cannot have every branch instruction encoded as a long jump. This is needed later in the proof of termination. If the iteration returns Some σ, the fold invariants are retained without change.

Instead of using sigma_compact_unsafe, we can now use the proper invariant:

sigma_compact $\equiv \lambda program.\lambda sigma.$

$\qquad \forall n.n < |program| \rightarrow$

$\qquad$ **match** lookup_opt n (snd $sigma$) **with**

$\qquad\qquad$ None $\Rightarrow$ False

$\qquad\qquad$ Some $\langle pc, j \rangle \Rightarrow$

$\qquad\qquad$ **match** lookup_opt $(n + 1)$ (snd $sigma$) **with**

$\qquad\qquad\qquad$ None $\Rightarrow$ False

$\qquad\qquad\qquad$ Some$\langle pc1, j1 \rangle \Rightarrow$

$\qquad\qquad\qquad\qquad pc1 = pc +$ instruction_size n (nth n $program$)

This is almost the same invariant as sigma_compact_unsafe, but differs in that it computes the sizes of branch instructions by looking at the distance between position and destination using σ. In actual use, the invariant is qualified: σ is compact if there have been no changes (i.e. the boolean passed along is true). This is to reflect the fact that we are doing a least fixed point computation: the result is only correct when we have reached the fixed point.

There is another, trivial, invariant in case the iteration returns Some σ: it must hold that fst $sigma < 2^{16}$. We need this invariant to make sure that addresses do not overflow.

The proof of nec_plus_ultra goes as follows: if we return None, then the program size must be greater than 64 Kb. However, since the previous iteration did not return None (because otherwise we would terminate immediately), the program size in the previous iteration must have been smaller than 64 Kb.

Suppose that all the branch instructions in the previous iteration are encoded as long jumps. This means that all branch instructions in this iteration are long jumps as well, and therefore that both iterations are equal in the encoding of their branch instructions. Per the invariant, this means that *added* = 0, and therefore that all addresses in both iterations are equal. But if all addresses are equal, the program sizes must be equal too, which means that the program size in the current iteration must be smaller than 64 Kb. This contradicts the earlier hypothesis, hence not all branch instructions in the previous iteration are encoded as long jumps.

The proof of `sigma_compact` follows from `sigma_compact_unsafe` and the fact that we have reached a fixed point, i.e. the previous iteration and the current iteration are the same. This means that the results of `instruction_size_jmplen` and `instruction_size` are the same.

4.3   Final Properties

These are the invariants that hold after $2n$ iterations, where n is the program size (we use the program size for convenience; we could also use the number of branch instructions, but this is more complex). Here, we only need `out_of_program_none`, `sigma_compact` and the fact that $\sigma(0) = 0$.

Termination can now be proved using the fact that there is a $k \leq 2n$, with n the length of the program, such that iteration k is equal to iteration $k+1$. There are two possibilities: either there is a $k < 2n$ such that this property holds, or every iteration up to $2n$ is different. In the latter case, since the only changes between the iterations can be from shorter jumps to longer jumps, in iteration $2n$ every branch instruction must be encoded as a long jump. In this case, iteration $2n$ is equal to iteration $2n + 1$ and the fixed point is reached.

5   Conclusion

In the previous sections we have discussed the branch displacement optimisation problem, presented an optimised solution, and discussed the proof of termination and correctness for this algorithm, as formalised in Matita.

The algorithm we have presented is fast and correct, but not optimal; a true optimal solution would need techniques like constraint solvers. While outside the scope of the present research, it would be interesting to see if enough heuristics could be found to make such a solution practical for implementing in an existing compiler; this would be especially useful for embedded systems, where it is important to have as small a solution as possible.

In itself the algorithm is already useful, as it results in a smaller solution than the simple 'every branch instruction is long' used up until now—and with only 64 Kb of memory, every byte counts. It also results in a smaller solution than the greatest fixed point algorithm that gcc uses. It does this without sacrificing speed or correctness.

The certification of an assembler that relies on the branch displacement algorithm described in this paper was presented in [6]. The assembler computes the σ map as described in this paper and then works in two passes. In the first pass it builds a map from instruction labels to addresses in the assembly code. In the second pass it iterates over the code, translating every pseudo jump at address src to a label l associated to the assembly instruction at address dst to a jump of the size dictated by (σ src) to (σ dst). In case of conditional jumps, the translated jump may be implemented with a series of instructions.

The proof of correctness abstracts over the algorithm used and only relies on sigma_policy_specification (page 5). It is a variation of a standard 1-to-many forward simulation proof [5]. The relation R between states just maps every code address ppc stored in registers or memory to (σ ppc). To identify the code addresses, an additional data structure is always kept together with the source state and is updated by the semantics. The semantics is preserved only for those programs whose source code operations (f ppc_1 ... ppc_n) applied to code addresses $ppc_1 ... ppc_n$ are such that (f (σ ppc_1) ... (σ ppc_n) = f ppc_1 ppc_n)). For example, an injective σ preserves a binary equality test f for code addresses, but not pointer subtraction.

The main lemma (fetching simulation), which relies on sigma_policy_specification and is established by structural induction over the source code, says that fetching an assembly instruction at position ppc is equal to fetching the translation of the instruction at position (σ ppc), and that the new incremented program counter is at the beginning of the next instruction (compactness). The only exception is when the instruction fetched is placed at the end of code memory and is followed only by dead code. Execution simulation is trivial because of the restriction over well behaved programs w.r.t. sigma. The condition σ $0 = 0$ is necessary because the hardware model prescribes that the first instruction to be executed will be at address 0. For the details see [6].

Instead of verifying the algorithm directly, another solution to the problem would be to run an optimisation algorithm, and then verify the safety of the result using a verified validator. Such a validator would be easier to verify than the algorithm itself and it would also be efficient, requiring only a linear pass over the source code to test the specification. However, it is surely also interesting to formally prove that the assembler never rejects programs that should be accepted, i.e. that the algorithm itself is correct. This is the topic of the current paper.

5.1   Related Work

As far as we are aware, this is the first formal discussion of the branch displacement optimisation algorithm.

The CompCert project is another verified compiler project. Their backend [5] generates assembly code for (amongst others) subsets of the PowerPC and x86 (32-bit) architectures. At the assembly code stage, there is no distinction between the span-dependent jump instructions, so a branch displacement optimisation algorithm is not needed.

References

1. Asperti, A., Sacerdoti Coen, C., Tassi, E., Zacchiroli, S.: User interaction with the Matita proof assistant. Automated Reasoning 39, 109–139 (2007)
2. Dickson, N.G.: A simple, linear-time algorithm for x86 jump encoding. CoRR abs/0812.4973 (2008)
3. Hyde, R.: Branch displacement optimisation (2006), http://groups.google.com/group/alt.lang.asm/msg/d31192d442accad3
4. Intel: Intel 64 and IA-32 Architectures Developer's Manual, http://www.intel.com/content/www/us/en/processors/architectures-software-developer-manuals.html
5. Leroy, X.: A formally verified compiler back-end. Journal of Automated Reasoning 43, 363–446 (2009), http://dx.doi.org/10.1007/s10817-009-9155-4, doi: 10.1007/s10817-009-9155-4
6. Mulligan, D.P., Sacerdoti Coen, C.: On the correctness of an optimising assembler for the intel MCS-51 microprocessor. In: Hawblitzel, C., Miller, D. (eds.) CPP 2012. LNCS, vol. 7679, pp. 43–59. Springer, Heidelberg (2012), http://dx.doi.org/10.1007/978-3-642-35308-6_7
7. Robertson, E.L.: Code generation and storage allocation for machines with span-dependent instructions. ACM Trans. Program. Lang. Syst. 1(1), 71–83 (1979), http://doi.acm.org/10.1145/357062.357067
8. Small device C compiler 3.1.0 (2011), http://sdcc.sourceforge.net/
9. Szymanski, T.G.: Assembling code for machines with span-dependent instructions. Commun. ACM 21(4), 300–308 (1978), http://doi.acm.org/10.1145/359460.359474

Analyzing the Next Generation Airborne Collision Avoidance System

Christian von Essen[1,*] and Dimitra Giannakopoulou[2,*]

[1] Verimag, Grenoble, France
christian.vonessen@imag.fr
[2] NASA Ames Research Center
Moffett Field, CA, USA
dimitra.giannakopoulou@nasa.gov

Abstract. The next generation airborne collision avoidance system, ACAS X, departs from the traditional deterministic model on which the current system, TCAS, is based. To increase robustness, ACAS X relies on probabilistic models to represent the various sources of uncertainty. The work reported in this paper identifies verification challenges for ACAS X, and studies the applicability of probabilistic verification and synthesis techniques in addressing these challenges. Due to shortcomings of off-the-shelf probabilistic analysis tools, we developed a framework that is designed to handle systems with similar characteristics as ACAS X. We describe the application of our framework to ACAS X, and the results and recommendations that our analysis produced.

Keywords: Markov decision processes, probabilistic verification, probabilistic synthesis, aircraft collision avoidance.

1 Introduction

The current onboard collision avoidance standard, TCAS [7], has been successful in preventing mid-air collisions. However, its deterministic logic limits robustness in the presence of unanticipated pilot responses, as exposed by the collision of two aircraft in 2002 over Überlingen, Germany [4]. To increase robustness, Lincoln Laboratory has been developing a new system, ACAS X, which uses probabilistic models to represent uncertainty. Simulation studies with recorded radar data have confirmed that this novel approach leads to a significant improvement in safety and operational performance. The Federal Aviation Administration (FAA) has formed a team of organizations to mature the system, aiming to make ACAS X the next international standard for collision avoidance.

The adoption of a completely new algorithmic approach to a safety-critical system naturally poses a significant challenge for verification and certification.

---

* The first author performed this work while employed by SGT Inc. as an intern at the NASA Ames Research Center. This work was funded under the System-wide Safety Analysis Technologies Project of the Aviation Safety Program, NASA ARMD.

E. Ábrahám and K. Havelund (Eds.): TACAS 2014, LNCS 8413, pp. 620–635, 2014.
© Springer-Verlag Berlin Heidelberg 2014

Our goal in this work is to study the applicability of formal probabilistic verification and synthesis techniques, which go beyond simulation studies [8,5]. Our study was driven by tasks defined in collaboration with the ACAS X team to be complementary to their verification efforts. During the course of our work, we identified shortcomings of existing tools, which lead us to develop a framework customized for ACAS X (or similar systems). In our framework, models are expressed in a traditional programming language for increased expressiveness, and verification and synthesis algorithms are designed for scalability and efficiency.

The contributions of this work can be summarized as follows: 1) Development of a faithful model for synthesis of the ACAS X controller, based on the Lincoln Laboratory publications [6]; 2) Development of customized verification and synthesis algorithms for efficient handling of ACAS X (and like) systems; 3) Identification of design and verification challenges for ACAS X as related to probabilistic verification and synthesis; 4) Results obtained from the application of our framework to ACAS X and recommendations for the ACAS X effort.

The results of our work will serve as input for the certification of ACAS X. Due to access restrictions, we analyze a previous version of the system [6], but are currently working with the ACAS X team to extend our work to the current version. We believe that ACAS X presents researchers in probabilistic verification and synthesis with a unique opportunity to focus on a relevant, safety-critical case study. For this reason, we are preparing a public release of our models and framework, to encourage other members of the community to build on our work.

The remainder of this paper is organized as follows. Section 2 describes the ACAS X system as designed and deployed by the ACAS X team. In addition to these techniques, our work implements and applies formal verification and synthesis approaches, described in Sections 3 and 4. We discuss implementation details in Section 5, with Section 6 concluding the paper.

2   The ACAS X System

Model Description. Similarly to the current standard TCAS, ACAS X [6] uses several sources to estimate the current state of the plane on which it is deployed, and the planes in its vicinity. If it detects the possibility of an imminent collision (less than 40 seconds away), it produces vertical maneuver advisories (to climb or descend) in order to avoid the collision. Both TCAS and ACAS X operate at a frequency of one state update and advisory per second.

The ACAS X model consists of two airplanes on collision course. Loss of Horizontal Separation, from now on denoted as LHS, describes the situation where two airplanes are in the exact same location when their height difference is ignored. A Near Mid-Air Collision (NMAC) occurs when the two airplanes are within 100 ft of each other when LHS occurs. We refer to the plane equipped with ACAS X as *our* plane (often referred to as ownship in the literature), and the other plane as *intruder* (similarly to [6]).

The model has 5 parameters: (1) $h \in [-1000, 1000]$ ft, the height difference between the two planes, (2) $dh_0, dh_1 \in [-2500, 2500]$ ft / min, our and the intruder's climbing rates (3) adv the advisory produced by ACAS X one second ago (4) ps the pilot state. Pilot state and advisories can take the following values — note that the pilot can either follow the advisory (i.e., ps = adv) or perform random maneuvers (i.e., ps = COC), since studies have shown that pilots may not react immediately or at all to an advisory:

- COC stands for "clear of conflict" — the pilot is free to choose how to control the plane.
- CLI1500 / DES1500 stand for "climb / descend with 1500 ft / min", respectively; they advise the pilot to change the climbing rate with $\frac{1}{4}g$ until reaching a climbing rate of 1500 ft / min / -1500 ft / min, respectively.
- Advisories SCLI1500 / SDES1500 and SCLI2500 / SDES2500 are similar but employ an acceleration of $\frac{1}{3}g$. Moreover, SCLI2500 / SDES2500 target a final climbing rate of 2500 ft / min / -2500 ft / min, respectively.

In describing the dynamics of the system, we use $X \sim P$ to denote that X is sampled according to probability distribution P. Moreover, $N(\mu, \sigma)$ denotes a normal distribution with mean μ and standard deviation σ. Lastly, we denote by $\{p_1 : e_1, p_2 : e_2, \ldots\}$ the distribution in which e_i has probability p_i. Given a state $(dh_0, dh_1, h, \text{adv}, \text{ps})$ and an advisory a, the dynamics of the system are given by the following equations, which together describe a continuous probability distribution $\delta_c(dh_0', dh_1', h', \text{adv}', \text{ps}' \mid dh_0, dh_1, h, \text{adv}, \text{ps}, a)$, where the primed versions of variables (e.g., dh_0') characterize the next state. In these equations, function f returns the appropriate acceleration in ft$/s^2$ if the desired climbing rate has not been reached yet, and 0 otherwise.

$$\text{adv}' = a; \quad dh_1' \sim dh_1 + 60N(0,3); \quad h' = h + ((dh_0 + dh_0')/2 - (dh_1 + dh_1')/2)/60$$

$$\text{ps}' \sim \begin{cases} \{1 : a\} & \text{if } a = \text{COC} \vee a = \text{ps} \\ \{\frac{1}{6} : a, \frac{5}{6} : \text{COC}\} & \text{if } a \in \{\text{CLI1500, DES1500}\} \wedge a \neq \text{ps} \\ \{\frac{1}{5} : a, \frac{4}{5} : \text{COC}\} & \text{if } a \in \{\text{SCLI*, SDES*}\} \wedge a \neq \text{ps} \end{cases}$$

$$dh_0' \sim dh_0 + \begin{cases} 60N(0,3) & \text{if } \text{ps}' = \text{COC} \\ \{1 : \text{f}(dh_0, \text{ps}')\} & \text{otherwise} \end{cases}$$

Model Discretization. Similarly to [6], we generate an ACAS X controller by analyzing a Markov Decision Process (MDP) obtained through discretization of the above model. In our implementation, the number of discrete values that replace each continuous parameter is configurable by a *resolution* vector $(r_{dh_0}, r_{dh_1}, r_h)$, where r_{dh_0}, r_{dh_1}, r_h define the number of points below and above 0 used to discretise dh_0, dh_1, h, respectively. Formally, the set of discretization points is defined as $D_{r_{dh_0}, r_{dh_1}, r_h} = \{-2500, -2500 + 2500/r_{dh_0}, \ldots, 2500\} \times \{-2500, -2500 + 2500/r_{dh_1}, \ldots, 2500\} \times \{-1000, -1000 + 1000/r_h, \ldots, 1000\}$. The resolution of the controller defined in [6] is $(10, 10, 10)$.

The following two techniques are then employed in [6] to calculate the transition distribution over $D_{r_{dh_0}, r_{dh_1}, r_h}$. Instead of sampling from the continuous normal distribution $(N(0,3), N(0,3))$ for equations dh_0' and dh_1', we sample from the distribution $\{\frac{1}{6} : (0, \sigma), \frac{1}{6} : (0, -\sigma), \frac{1}{3} : (0, 0), \frac{1}{6} : (\sigma, 0), \frac{1}{6} : (-\sigma, 0)\}$, where

$\sigma = 3\sqrt{3}$. This is called sigma point sampling. After having modified the equations with sigma point sampling, we obtain a discrete probability distribution $\delta'(dh'_0, dh'_1, h, \mathrm{adv}', \mathrm{ps}' \mid dh_0, dh_1, h, \mathrm{adv}, \mathrm{ps}, a)$.

Secondly, linear interpolation matches the points of δ' to the discretization points in $D_{r_{dh_0}, r_{dh_1}, r_h}$. Let Δ_{dh_0} be the distance between two discretization points of the climbing rate of our plane, and let Δ_{dh_1} and Δ_h be defined analogously. We define function ι to capture how "close" a point (dh_0, dh_1, h) is to a discretization point (dh'_0, dh'_1, h') immediately surrounding it as

$$\iota((dh_0, dh_1, h), (dh'_0, dh'_1, h')) = (1 - \frac{|dh_0 - dh'_0|}{\Delta_{dh_0}})(1 - \frac{|dh_1 - dh'_1|}{\Delta_{dh_1}})(1 - \frac{|h - h'|}{\Delta_h}),$$

and 0 for all other points. Based on these, we define the transition relation as $\delta(s^d \mid s, a) = \sum_{s'} \delta'(s' \mid s, a)\,\iota(s', s^d)$.

Controller Generation. In order to generate a controller, each ACAS X advisory receives a cost/reward, where costs are rewards with negative values. Reward COC is associated with switching from any alerting state to COC; Alert is a cost associated with switching from COC to either CLI1500 or DES1500; Reversal is a cost associated with switching from any climbing to any descending advisory, or vice versa; Strengthening is a cost associated with switching from any climb/descent advisory with goal 1500 ft / min to SCLI2500/SDES2500, respectively; NMAC is a cost associated with the occurrence of an NMAC.

We henceforth refer to the costs/rewards as "weights", thus describing the fact that they capture the relative importance of different quality criteria of the controller. Let $c(s, a)$ be the sum of costs and rewards ACAS X receives for selecting advisory a in state s (for example, if a in state s activates an alert, then $c(s, a) = \mathrm{Alert}$). Moreover let $\mathbb{E}_{\delta(s'|s,a)}[\alpha(s')]$ describe the expected value of some function α under the probability distribution over the successor states s' of s when selecting action a. We then calculate a table equivalent to the family of functions $T_t(s, a) := c(s, a) + \mathbb{E}_{\delta(s'|s,a)}[\min_{a' \in A(s')} T_{t-1}(s', a')], 1 \leq t \leq 40$, where $A(s)$ stands for the set of advisories admissible in s. Further, $T_0(s, a) = \mathrm{NMAC}$ if s models an NMAC, and 0 otherwise. Essentially, for each state and each advisory the table stores the expected accumulated cost.

Controller Deployment. The generated controller is deployed as look-up table $T_t(s, a)$ described previously. Linear interpolation is used to determine the advisory for a state s in the continuous world at time t until loss of horizontal separation by: $\arg\min_{a \in A(s)} \sum_{s' \in D_{r_{dh_0}, r_{dh_1}, r_h}} \iota(s, s')T_t(s', a)$.

Figure 1(a) illustrates a part of the interpolated strategy generated according to [6]. In the figures, note that LHS occurs at time 0, located on the left hand side of the plots, so time in the plots flows from right to left. Thorough examination of such plots is part of the validation of ACAS X but goes beyond the scope of this paper. Our framework can easily generate such plots, though.

We would like to point out two features of the generated controller. Firstly, if the airplanes start out on the same height, then the controller waits for a long time until giving an advisory, as witnessed by the black space between the two "tails" on the right. This is because it is very unlikely that the two planes will

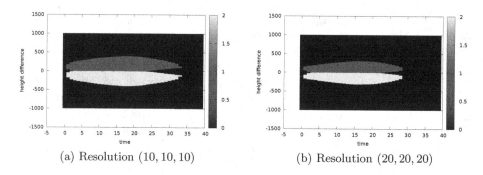

(a) Resolution $(10, 10, 10)$ (b) Resolution $(20, 20, 20)$

Fig. 1. Two controllers generated with the same weight in different resolutions. x-axis shows time until LHS, y-axis height difference. Parameters dh_0 and dh_1 are zero throughout, and adv = ps = COC. Color indicates selected advisory: black (0) for COC, red (1) for CLI1500, yellow (2) for DES1500.

remain on the same height for a long time (due to their random movement), and it is therefore better to wait until the intruder either starts climbing and or descending and go in the opposite direction. Secondly, notice the "mouth" shape close to time 0 and around height difference 0. In this collision situation, ACAS X is not giving any advisory, although one would intuitively expect that *some* advisory would be more informative to the pilot than COC, which may be misleading. This is an artifact of the costs used for synthesis, and we describe a technique that identifies situations like these in Section 3.

3 Verification

To complement the ACAS X work that primarily uses simulation, we apply formal analysis techniques to evaluate the ACAS X controller. Simulation-based techniques are studied and discussed in Section 4, where we explore the design-space of controllers and compare different generated controllers among themselves. In this section, we evaluate the ACAS X controller 1) in terms of the quality criteria used for its generation, and 2) through model checking of PCTL [3] properties, which are ideal for probabilistic models such as ACAS X's. For evaluation, we use models discretized at different resolutions, and could even use different model characteristics and parameters (although we do not do the latter in the experiments presented here).

The type of analysis that we perform provides a value $v(s)$ for each state of the discretized model. To easily compare results of analyses with each other and with simulations, we define a probability distribution $I(s)$ over the states of the model as follows (similarly to [6]). The only states we consider are those at 40 seconds from LHS, and in which ps = adv = COC. Over those states, we first define a continuous distribution over $(dh_0, dh_1, h) \in \mathbb{R}^3$ by sampling dh_0 and dh_1 uniformly from $[-1000, 1000]$ ft / min, denoted as $dh_0 \sim U(-1000, 1000)$ and $dh_1 \sim U(-1000, 1000)$. To make a collision likely, and therefore to provoke the controller into action, h is sampled from $40((dh_1 - dh_0)/60) + N(0, 25)$.

To define an analogous distribution of $D_{r_{dh_0}, r_{dh_1}, r_h}$, we assign probability masses to all three parameters so as to soak up the probability of the space around them. That is, the probability of picking sample point dh_0 is defined as: $P(dh_0 - \Delta_{dh_0}/2 \le H_0 \le dh_0 + \Delta_{dh_0}/2)$, with $H_0 \sim U(-1000, 1000)$. Note that $\Delta_{dh_0}, \Delta_{dh_1}$ and Δ_h are defined as in Section 2. We define the discretized probability of dh_1 analogously. The discretized probability of h is defined as: $P(h - \Delta_h/2 \le H \le h + \Delta_h/2)$, where $H \sim 40((dh_1 - dh_0)/60) + N(0, 25)$, i.e., the probability distribution of h depends on dh_0 and dh_1. We then use I to calculate the expected value $\mathbb{E}_{I(s)}[v(s)]$.

3.1   Influence of Resolution on Controller Evaluation

Our first step in evaluating the ACAS X controller involves calculating its performance in evaluation models of different resolutions for the two climbing rates and the height difference: $(10, 10, 20), \dots, (10, 10, 50), (20, 20, 10) \dots (50, 50, 10)$ and $(20, 20, 20) \dots (50, 50, 50)$.

For each of these resolutions, Figure 2 presents the evolution of the probability of seeing an NMAC versus the resolution. The three lines represent the three groups of increasing resolutions. Line "Height" represents resolutions $(10, 10, n)$, while line "Climbing Rate" represents the resolutions $(n, n, 10)$ and line "All" represents the resolutions (n, n, n), for $n \in \{10, 20, 30, 40, 50\}$.

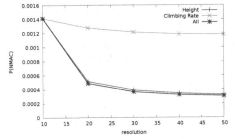

Fig. 2. P(NMAC) of baseline controller in various resolutions

These plots indicate that the probability of NMAC drops as we increase resolution. This in turn indicates (though does not guarantee) that a coarse resolution provides a conservative estimate for the quality criteria of the controller. Lines "Height" and "Climbing Rate" indicate that increasing the resolution of the height difference has a stronger influence on the quality of the analysis than the resolution of the climbing rate. This observation is reinforced by comparing lines "Height" and "All". The difference between these two lines is small, despite the fact that an n-fold increase in resolution of the climbing rate leads to an n^2-fold increase in state space.

3.2   PCTL Model Checking

The PCTL model checking engine that we have developed enables users to: (1) vary the resolution of the model to get more precise results, and (2) analyse non-trivial properties expressed in the PCTL formal property language. In contrast to simulation, PCTL model checking allows an exhaustive search of the state space and can thus uncover scenarios that simulations might easily miss. This is important given the low probability of some of the properties we want to check. **Property 1: Near Mid-Air Collision.** Studies the probability of a near

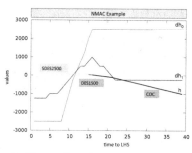 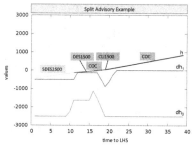

Fig. 3. Trace plots for properties 1 and 3. x-axis displays time to LHS, y-axis displays values of (dh_0, dh_1, h). The color of line h depicts the advisory, tagged above the line.

mid-air collision, formally $P_{=?}[\text{F NMAC}]$. During analysis, we observed that the most likely cases of this undesirable scenario stem from late reactions from the pilot. We therefore decided to instead concentrate on NMACs that occur despite immediate reactions to advisories by the pilot. We formulate this as $P_{=?}(\text{F NMAC} \mid \text{G adv} = \text{ps})$, i.e., what is the probability of reaching an NMAC state although the pilot always reacts immediately.

The highest probability over all initial states that we encounter with the conditional probability formula is $2.30 \cdot 10^{-8}$, as opposed to $6.92 \cdot 10^{-4}$ with the original formula. This confirms that the vast majority of NMACs happen because the pilot does not react fast enough or at all. To understand the NMACs that occur despite the fact that the pilot reacts to advisories, we analyzed some traces that are most likely to fulfill $P_{=?}(\text{F NMAC} \mid \text{G adv} = \text{ps})$. Figure 3 depicts such a scenario: initially, our airplane is 1000ft below the intruder and we are climbing with 2500 ft / min. The intruder, on the other hand, starts out with a climbing rate of -250 ft / min. Until 22 seconds to LHS, the two airplanes maintain their course, and therefore the height difference shrinks. If both planes were to continue to maintain their course, then our plane would be well above the intruder at time 0 to LHS, so ACAS X does not alert.

At this point, climbing rate of the intruder starts increasing, and the vertical distance becomes -150 ft. The height difference levels off as a result of the intruder's increase in climbing rate from now on. ACAS X signals the DES1500 advisory seven seconds later, and SDES2500 one second after that. As a result, our airplane starts descending steeply until it reaches -2500 ft / min. At the point of the first alarm, the vertical distance is 50 ft, i.e., our plane is slightly above the intruder. Unfortunately, the climbing rate of the intruder starts decreasing at exactly the same point and from that point on, the two climbing rates are not different enough to carry our plane outside of the danger zone and we end up with a vertical distance of 100 ft, and hence an NMAC.

Traces like these capture exactly the type of unforeseen behaviour that led to the Überlingen accident [4], and probabilistic model checking can detect cases like these easily. We consider it encouraging that the most likely case of collision requires relatively complex behaviour of the intruder (first increasing the climbing rate, then decreasing it, at exactly the right point in time).

Property 2: No advisory despite collision. Studies the probability of issuing no advisory although a future NMAC is likely, formally $P_{=?}[F(P_{=1}[X\ COC] \land P_{>0.1}[F\ NMAC])]$. This formula was motivated by our previous observation of Figure 1(a) in Section 2, according to which there is an area where ACAS X issues no advisory although an NMAC is imminent. Figure 4 shows the probability of the formula for all states in which $dh_0 = dh_1 = 0\ ft\ /\ min$ and $adv = ps = COC$. This probability is 1 until about 12 seconds away if the height difference between the planes is less than a 100 ft. Model checking the formula, however, reveals that among all initial states, the highest probability is 0.3%, so getting into such a situation is improbable.

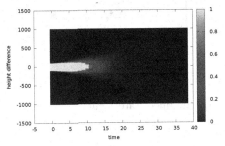

Fig. 4. Probability of fulfilling property 2. Plot parameters as in Figure 1(a); color depicts probability

Property 3: Split Advisory. Studies the probability of issuing an alert, switching it off, and then switching an alert on again (a *split advisory*), formally $P_{=?}[F(\neg COC \land P_{=1}[X\ COC] \land P_{>0}[F\ \neg COC])]$. Even though during controller generation ACAS X penalizes reversals, these costs only reflect immediate changes in controller advisories. Split advisories are also undesirable, but are harder to capture during controller generation. The PCTL property described above can however be used to study how likely such situations are. Analysis of the model checking results revealed that a main cause for such situations is the pilot not following the advisory. We therefore refined the property similarly to Property 1, by checking cases where split advisories occur under the condition that the pilot always reacts immediately to advisories.

Figure 3 depicts a split advisory scenario under the refined property. Initially (at 40 seconds to LHS), our plane is 830 ft above the intruder and descending with 2500 ft / min, while the intruder is in level flight. The vertical distance is therefore decreasing. Around 19 seconds into the scenario, the intruder starts descending, and soon after, ACAS X advises CLI1500 and maintains this advisory for 2 seconds, before switching it off again. Accordingly, the rate of descent of our plane gradually reduces to 1500 ft / min. The advisory is then switched off, as the intruder stops descending, effectively moving out of the way of our plane. ACAS X switches to COC but, a second later, gives advisories DES1500, followed by SDES2500, as the intruder's rate of descent increases again.

Let us further analyze this generated scenario. The first climb advisory aimed at avoiding a collision that would be likely if our plane continued to descend at the same rate. It could not force the pilot to increase the rate of descend further, since 2500 ft / min already is the maximum. Therefore, climbing was the only possibility. Then the intruder stopped descending, which reduced the probability of colliding with our current climbing rate. This may have caused ACAS X to shut the advisory off. Shortly before ACAS X switched the advisory back on, the

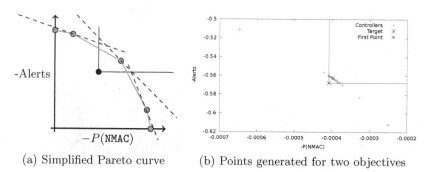

(a) Simplified Pareto curve   (b) Points generated for two objectives

Fig. 5. Fictional and actual Pareto fronts

difference in climbing rates was 1000 ft / min, and the height difference was -30 ft. Since we were about 15 seconds away from LHS, this amounted to a decreased vertical distance of about 260 ft. ACAS X decided to increase the vertical distance by increasing the rate of descent.

It would be interesting to study whether the cost function of ACAS X may encourage such cases of split advisories. Given that (Alert + COC < Reversal), it is possible that ACAS X decided to gain a small reward for selecting COC after the first advisory, and additionally avoid the cost of a reversal that would be incurred if the advisory was switched directly from a climb to a descend.

4   ACAS X Design Challenges

The generation of the ACAS X controller depends on two major design issues that have so far been unexplored: the selection of weights, and the discretization resolution. As reported in [6], the weights were selected based on an intuition of the relative importance of the different quality criteria. In this section, we study more systematic techniques for selecting controller weights, and investigate how discretization resolution influences the generated controller.

4.1   Generating Controller Weights

Our goal is to systematically explore deterministic controllers whose performances exceed requirements on NMAC, Alert, etc., provided by domain or certification experts. We refer to these requirements as "targeted performance", or simply "target". Central to achieving this goal is an existing result, which states that the performance of all controllers that can be generated by weights form a convex Pareto front [2]. The Pareto front is n-dimensional, where n is the number of costs/rewards. The performances of all possible controllers (even controllers using randomization and memory) lie on the inside of the Pareto front.

For example, Figure 5(a) illustrates a two-dimensional Pareto front. The performance of all deterministic controllers (green dots in the plot), lie on the vertices of the Pareto front. The targeted performance is depicted as a black dot in Figure 5(a). The box with a lower left corner at this target and extending to infinity in all dimensions, defines the section of the Pareto front in which we are interested. To find this section, we modified an algorithm presented in [9].

While the details of the approach are beyond the scope of this paper, the idea can be summarized as follows. Initially, the optimal controller for each dimension is generated, i.e., the controller with the lowest P(NMAC), the controller with the lowest expected number of Alerts (i.e., zero), etc. We add the performance of these controllers to the approximation of the Pareto front. These points, illustrated as the two green dots on the axes in Figure 5(a), reflect the performance of the corresponding controller in terms of the selected quality attributes.

We then keep adding points to the Pareto front in the following way. We calculate the convex hull of the points generated so far. This hull defines a set of n-dimensional faces (lines, in our picture), that connect the points. Further, the hull defines a lower bound for new points (the Pareto front is convex, so missing points must lie on or above the hull). In the picture, the lines connecting the green dots form the hull. The generated points also define an upper bound on the space of controller performances, illustrated by the dashed lines in the figure. The direction (normal) of the dashed line (separating hyperplane) is given by the weights we used to generate the point. If there are any more points we can generate, then these points exist between the hull and the upper bound.

Since we want to find new points in the box defined by the target, we pick new weights so as to refine the face (by lowering the upper bound or breaking up the face) above which there is a point that 1) lies inside the upper bound 2) lies above the target 3) is maximally far away from the face (as defined by the Euclidean distance). We continue until we either prove that the target lies outside the upper point (which means that no controller fulfilling the minimal requirement exists) or until we have found enough points above the target.

Figure 5(b) presents a subset of the points generated by this approach on Alert and NMAC exclusively. The target point and the box it defines are plotted in black, and the points generated are plotted in red. The algorithm first generated 8 points outside the box. The first point generated within the target box (the 9th overall) is depicted in blue. We generated 10 more points after we found it. We note that all subsequent 10 points that are generated also lie within the box. The same effect has been observed for three dimensions. We conclude that this algorithm is good at approximating the interesting part of the Pareto front (that inside the box) once it finds the first point that meets the target specifications.

We have checked this algorithm against various targets, and it always either finds a controller meeting the requirement, or proves that no such controller exists. Note that finding a controller in the box is an NP-complete problem (easy adaptation of proof from [1]). In the worst case, the algorithm has to generate all points of the Pareto front of the model, of which there are exponentially many. However, as the next section shows, little more than 100 points suffice to find a controller meeting the requirement for various resolutions.

We believe that this technique can be very helpful as the controller model ACAS X evolves. Each evolution (be it a change in discretization or a change in parameters), necessitates tuning weights anew (as witnessed by the first experiment in the next section). Our approach allows to semi-automatically select these weights by presenting domain experts with the trade-offs. They can then select a controller they deem sufficient, or select an area for further refinement.

4.2   Discretization Resolution

To study the effects of discretization resolution on the quality of the obtained controller, we designed a number of experiments described in this section. We will from now on refer to the controller presented in [6] as the "baseline" controller.

Experiment 1. This experiment aims to analyze the performance of controllers generated at resolutions $(20, 20, 20)$, $(30, 30, 30)$, $(40, 40, 40)$ and $(50, 50, 50)$, using the weights of the baseline controller. Our expectation was that a higher resolution would lead to a better performance, at least in terms of P(NMAC). However, the experiments showed that the controllers we generate by this method do not necessarily perform better in all the quality attributes. Instead, higher resolution controllers have a significantly higher P(NMAC) and significantly fewer alerts than the baseline controller in the same resolutions.

The reason becomes clear when we consider the controller plots in Figure 1(a) and Figure 1(b). The area in which an alert is signalled by the controller is significantly smaller in Figure 1(b) when compared to Figure 1(a). To understand the reason for this effect, we analyzed the controllers using the techniques from Section 3. It turns out that controllers in higher resolutions indeed perform better in the sense of having a higher expected reward than the baseline controller. Intuitively, the controllers use the additional information they receive from a higher resolution to improve the score they receive. To this end, the controllers improve their score by reducing the expected number of alerts, at the cost of a higher P(NMAC).

This experiment made it clear to us that weights may balance out the quality attributes of a controller differently, when different resolutions are considered. As a consequence, we believe that it is more meaningful to systematically explore the design space of controllers based on specific target quality attributes, as presented in Section 4.1. One could then compute weights based on these target values, and within the resolution where the generation will occur.

Experiment 2. Given the first experiment, we decided to study whether it is possible to generate controllers that are better than the baseline controller in all quality attributes, in higher resolutions. To generate a controller that performs better than the baseline controller in a given resolution $R = (r_h, r_{dh_0}, r_{dh_1})$, we first evaluate the performance of the baseline controller in resolution R. The result is a vector $v = ($NMAC, Alert, Strengthening, Reversal, NMAC$)$, which summarizes the performance of the baseline controller when model checked in resolution R (see Section 3 for more details). We then use the technique described above to approximate the Pareto front above v. From the generated controllers that meet the specification, we then pick the one with the lowest P(NMAC).

Figure 6(a) illustrates the obtained results. The bars show, for resolution factor n the performance of the baseline controller when checked against resolutions

$(n, n, 10)$ (Climbing Rate), $(10, 10, n)$ (Height) and (n, n, n) (All) respectively. It can be seen that we were almost unable to decrease P(NMAC) using the climbing rate alone. The relative performance of these controllers is consistently around 99.5%. When we increase the resolution of the height, then we get a relative performance of about 85%. Finally, when increasing the resolution of both we see a relative performance of about 83%. As witnessed in Section 3, the discretization of height seems to have the biggest influence on controller quality. Interestingly, the relative performance does not improve as we increase the resolution.

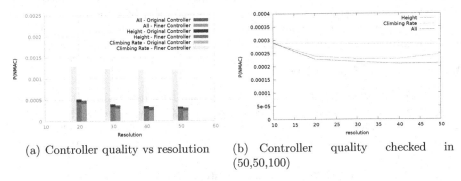

(a) Controller quality vs resolution

(b) Controller quality checked in $(50,50,100)$

Fig. 6. Plots for Experiment 3

To further judge the quality of the generated controllers, we checked them against resolution $(50, 50, 100)$ and present the results in Figure 6(b). On the x-axis, we have the controller resolution, while on the y-axis we have the probability of a Near Mid-Air Collision. As before, "Height" stands for the controllers of resolution $(10, 10, n)$, "Climbing Rate" for the controllers of resolution $(n, n, 10)$ and "All" for the controllers of resolution (n, n, n). This experiment confirms that increasing the resolution of the height difference between the two planes has the most impact up to and including $(10, 10, 30)$, after which we notice no further improvement. In contrast to this, we notice further improvements in category "All". Our experiments indicate that the best ratio of resolution for the three parameters is $(n, n, 3 \cdot n)$.

Experiment 3. Let $v_R(c)$ denote the quality vector of a controller c in resolution R (i.e., the vector of P(NMAC), P(Alert), etc). We organized this experiment to study if $\forall c_1, c_2, R_1, R_2 : v_{R_1}(c_1) \geq v_{R_1}(c_2) \wedge R_2 > R_1 \implies v_{R_2}(c_1) \geq v_{R_2}(c_2)$ holds. To this end, we compared the performance of the controller we generated in resolution $(20, 20, 20)$ to the baseline controller in resolutions $(20, 20, 20)$ and $(50, 50, 100)$, and present the results in the following table. Note that the higher resolution controller performs better than the baseline in all dimensions in resolution $(20, 20, 20)$; specifically, it is very close to the target performance in everything but NMAC, where it is notably better.

This attests to the efficacy of our Pareto front algorithm. When comparing this to the analysis results in resolution $(50, 50, 100)$, we observe that while the higher resolution controller and the baseline controller are still very close in all

	NMAC	Alert	Strengthening	Reversal	COC
$(10, 10, 10)$ in $(20, 20, 20)$	$-4.850 \cdot 10^{-4}$	-0.6310	-0.083	-0.019	0.629
$(20, 20, 20)$ in $(20, 20, 20)$	$-4.186 \cdot 10^{-4}$	-0.6306	-0.081	-0.019	0.631
$(10, 10, 10)$ in $(50, 50, 100)$	$-2.897 \cdot 10^{-4}$	-0.6245	-0.078	-0.020	0.622
$(20, 20, 20)$ in $(50, 50, 100)$	$-2.313 \cdot 10^{-4}$	-0.6308	-0.078	-0.019	0.630

characteristics except NMAC, the higher resolution controller is no longer strictly better in all dimensions. For example, it uses slightly more alerts and slightly more reversals. This is offset by the fact that the P(NMAC) of the higher resolution controller is still significantly better than that of the baseline controller. To summarize, the general tendencies of the relation of controllers when checked in higher resolutions are the same, but the exact relations are not preserved.

4.3   Bayesian Model Checking

In this section, we evaluate the generated controllers using simulation (where discretization is not required), and compare the results with model checking. To this aim, we implemented a parallel Bayesian model checking engine [10], which simulates the system based on the dynamic equations of Section 2. We used the same initial distribution as [6], described in Section 3. In [6], the authors also report on the use of a Bayesian network instead of the dynamic equations.

This approach allows us to run simulations, and state "given the traces observed, the probability that property φ holds lies in interval $[a, b]$ with confidence c. The level of confidence and the size of the interval are configurable. In the following, we use this framework to estimate the probability that an NMAC happens when using the baseline controller, and compare the results to Experiment 2. Our analysis reports that the probability of NMAC lies in range $[2.48 \cdot 10^{-4}, 2.58 \cdot 10^{-4}]$ with probability 95%. We needed to generate 38,796,000 samples to get this level of confidence for the given interval size.

We additionally applied this simulation technique to controllers of resolution $(10, 10, 10), \ldots, (10, 10, 50)$ generated previously. The following table presents the probability of seeing an NMAC for each of them.

Resolution	10	20	30	40	50
$P(\text{NMAC}) \cdot 10^4$	[2.51, 2.61]	[2.17, 2.27]	[2.08, 2.18]	[2.12, 2.22]	[2.27, 2.37]

We conclude that the trend follows that depicted in Figure 6(a): improvements in performance are significant until we reach resolution $(10, 10, 30)$, at which point they taper off. We were unable to perform this analysis on controllers with resolution larger than $(20, 20, 20)$ because we could not fit the whole table into memory at once. For $(20, 20, 20)$, though, we receive $P(\text{NMAC}) \in [2.06 \cdot 10^{-4}, 2.16 \cdot 10^{-4}]$, i.e., a number very close to that of the controller generated for $(10, 10, 30)$.

5   Implementation

We originally used existing probabilistic model checking tools for ACAS X but encountered several limitations. First, we could not express the linear interpolation needed in the controller evaluation. Second, we not only require capabilities for the specification of a model, but also for loading generated controllers for subsequent verification. Last but not least, for our mupliple experiments involving increasing resolution, the state spaces we generate grow prohibitively large, and there is a considerable slow-down that could benefit from parallelization, which is unavailable in current releases of existing tools.

More specifically, the size of the controller has $40 \cdot ((2r_{dh_0} + 1) \cdot (2r_{dh_1} + 1) \cdot (2r_h + 1) \cdot 13)$ states in resolution $(r_{dh_0}, r_{dh_1}, r_h)$. So, for example, the model from [6] has $4,815,720$ states overall. A controller with resolution $(50, 50, 50)$ has $535,756,520$ states. We wrote a simplified version of the model in [6] for PRISM [8] (without linear interpolation, but with sigma point sampling). While PRISM succeeded in loading the model as a BDD model, analyzing it was not possible (we aborted conversion to the hybrid representation after $10\,\mathrm{min}$).

These problems motivated us to create our own framework that takes advantage of two key insights into the ACAS X model. Firstly, if we want to calculate the values of any property in this model at time t, then we only need to keep the value of time $t - 1$ in memory. This alone leads to a reduction of memory consumption to 2.5%. Secondly, since we need to calculate value iteration steps only a relatively small number of times for each state, it is possible to avoid storing the transition matrix in memory and generate the values on-demand.

In addition, we parallelized value iteration, and the speed-up obtained in experiments using up to 12 cores was almost linear (1.94 for 2 cores, 3.37 for 4 cores, 4.67 for 6 cores, 6.47 for 8 cores, 7.54 for 10 cores, 8.93 for 12 cores). Parallelization proved essential for our experiments involving increasing discretization resolution; generating the Pareto fronts for all cases took about 2 days, as opposed to more than a month.

6   Conclusions and Future Work

ACAS X is a safety-critical system that the FAA plans on introducing as the new standard for collision avoidance. The system that will be deployed is the look-up table that is generated by the techniques described in [6]. It is therefore reasonable that a large number of the verification efforts would focus on the verification of the generated controller in operation. However, we believe that it is meaningful to take advantage of the existence of models for additional formal analysis both of the controller itself, and of the design choices.

Our experiments related to the effects of resolution on controller generation were particularly interesting. For example, we observed that height discretization is more effective that climbing rate alone, when exploring the space of controllers better than a particular target. We therefore recommend increasing height resolution first, when there is an upper bound in controller size that does not allow for uniform discretization of all variables. In the future, we intend to carry out more experiments in this domain in order to give more precise recommendations.

Some of the results that we obtained were also unexpected: the fact that a higher resolution may balance the weights of quality attributes differently and therefore result in a drop in performance of NMAC; or the fact that the relative performance of two controllers may change when moving to higher resolutions.

This cautions us, in exploring the space of controllers, to ultimately evaluate their relative performance in simulation. However, the Pareto-front-based techniques for controller generation provide a systematic way of generating and comparing controllers that can complement designer intuition.

PCTL model checking also proves valuable in studying properties of generated controllers. However, more useful than the model checking itself, is the capability to visualize its results and generate traces that help with understanding of the model checking results. We therefore found that latter aspect of our tools most helpful, together with a simulator that we built, which allows to interactively explore generated controllers. In the future, we plan to connect the simulator to the model checker, to allow replay of the generated traces.

The techniques and tools that we developed are general, and the customization for memory savings is applicable to problems that have a similar nature; for example, it could be used in the domain of car collision avoidance systems, which is important as we move towards self-driving cars. Our work on analysis of ACAS X will continue beyond this paper. Our plans for future work include the modeling of a reasonably adversarial pilot for the intruder plane, and alternative representations of the look-up table for verification and deployment. Moreover, we plan to study a version of ACAS X that is targeted to unmanned vehicles, as well as experiment with the evaluation of generated controllers in the context of hybrid verification tools, which the ACAS X team has expertise in.

Acknowledgement. We thank Guillaume Brat, and members of the ACAS X team Ryan Gardner, Mykel Kochenderfer and Yanni Kouskoulas, for valuable discussions and feedback.

References

1. Chatterjee, K.: Markov decision processes with multiple long-run average objectives. In: Arvind, V., Prasad, S. (eds.) FSTTCS 2007. LNCS, vol. 4855, pp. 473–484. Springer, Heidelberg (2007)
2. Forejt, V., Kwiatkowska, M., Parker, D.: Pareto curves for probabilistic model checking. In: Chakraborty, S., Mukund, M. (eds.) ATVA 2012. LNCS, vol. 7561, pp. 317–332. Springer, Heidelberg (2012)
3. Hansson, H., Jonsson, B.: A logic for reasoning about time and reliability. Formal Aspects of Computing 6, 102–111 (1994)
4. Johnson, C.: Final report: review of the BFU Überlingen accident report. Contract C/1.369/HQ/SS/04 to Eurocontrol (2004), http://www.dcs.gla.ac.uk/~johnson/Eurocontrol/Ueberlingen/Ueberlingen_Final_Report.PDF
5. Katoen, J.-P., Zapreev, I.S., Hahn, E.M., Hermanns, H., Jansen, D.N.: The ins and outs of the probabilistic model checker MRMC. Perform. Eval. 68(2) (2011)
6. Kochenderfer, M.J., Chryssanthacopoulos, J.P.: Robust airborne collision avoidance through dynamic programming. Project Report ATC-371, Massachusetts Institute of Technology, Lincoln Laboratory (2011)

7. Kuchar, J., Drumm, A.C.: The traffic alert and collision avoidance system. Lincoln Laboratory Journal 16(2), 277 (2007)
8. Kwiatkowska, M., Norman, G., Parker, D.: PRISM 4.0: Verification of probabilistic real-time systems. In: Gopalakrishnan, G., Qadeer, S. (eds.) CAV 2011. LNCS, vol. 6806, pp. 585–591. Springer, Heidelberg (2011)
9. Rennen, G., van Dam, E.R., den Hertog, D.: Enhancement of sandwich algorithms for approximating higher-dimensional convex Pareto sets. INFORMS Journal on Computing 23(4), 493–517 (2011)
10. Zuliani, P., Platzer, A., Clarke, E.M.: Bayesian statistical model checking with application to Stateflow/Simulink verification. Formal Methods in System Design 43(2), 338–367 (2013)

Environment-Model Based Testing
of Control Systems: Case Studies *

Erwan Jahier[1], Simplice Djoko-Djoko[1], Chaouki Maiza[1], and Eric Lafont[2]

[1] VERIMAG-CNRS, Grenoble, France
[2] ATOS-WORLDGRID, Grenoble, France

Abstract. A reactive system reacts to an environment it tries to control. Lurette is a black-box testing tool for such closed-loop systems. It focuses on environment modeling using Lutin, a language designed to perform guided random exploration of the System Under Test (SUT) environment, taking into account the feedback. The test decision is automated using Lustre oracles resulting from the formalisation of functional requirements.

In this article, we report on experimentations conducted with Lurette on two industrial case studies. One deals with a dynamic system which simulates the behavior of the temperature and the pressure of a fluid in a pipe. The other one reports on how Lurette can be used to automate the processing of an existing test booklet of a Supervisory Control and Data Acquisition (SCADA) library module.

Keywords: Reactive systems, Control-command, Dynamic systems, SCADA, Test Booklets, Black-box testing, Requirements engineering, Synchronous Languages.

1 Introduction

Lurette is a black-box testing tool for reactive systems that automates the tests decision and the stimulation of the System Under Test (SUT). Lurette is based on two synchronous languages: Lustre [1], to specify test oracles, and Lutin [2], to model reactive environments. Lurette does not require to analyze the code, thus it can deal with any kind of reactive systems, as the experimentations reported below illustrate.

The COMON project* gathered three industrial companies that conceive control-command systems of nuclear plants. *Corys Tess* designs plant simulators used in particular for training operators. *Atos Worldgrid* designs software and hardware of computerized control rooms. *Rolls-Royce* designs the software and hardware of classified automatisms in charge of the plant security. The goal for this consortium was to take advantage of the partners complementarity to set up a development framework based on early simulations, model refinements, continuous integration, and automatic testing. During the project, the consortium has crafted a case study representative of each of the partners activity [3]. They also wanted to experiment on their own designs the Lurette languages and methodology. This article presents those experimentations.

We first recall Lurette principles in Section 2, and briefly present enough of the Lustre and the Lutin languages to be able to understand the examples. Section 3 presents

---

* This work was supported by the COMON Minalogic project [2009-2012] funded by the french government (DGCIS/FUI), *la Metro*, and the city Grenoble – http://comon. minalogic.net/

E. Ábrahám and K. Havelund (Eds.): TACAS 2014, LNCS 8413, pp. 636–650, 2014.

the Corys case study and demonstrates the use of Lurette on a library object used to simulate the behavior of the temperature and the pressure of a fluid in a pipe. Section 4 presents the Atos case study that illustrates how Lurette can be used to automate the run of existing test plans designed for a Supervisory Control and Data Acquisition (SCADA) library object. We discuss related work and conclude in Sections 5 and 6.

2 Black-Box Testing of Reactive Systems Using Lustre and Lutin

Test of Reactive Systems. A *reactive system* is an combination of hardware or software (or both) that (1) acquires inputs (`set_inputs`), (2) performs a computation step (`step`), (3) and provides outputs (`get_outputs`). Testing a reactive system consists in writing or generating scripts that call the `set_inputs` and the `step` functions in turn. Such test scripts can be done offline, but a reactive system is meant to react to stimuli coming from its environment (e.g., from sensors), and to control it (e.g., using actuators). Thus a realistic test sequence should use `get_outputs` to provide input vectors that take into account the SUT inputs/outputs sequence history (i.e., its trace).

Stimulation. The environment is also a reactive system that executes in closed-loop with the SUT. It can be very versatile or underspecified. This motivated the design of Lutin [2], a language to program stochastic reactive systems and environment models.

Oracles. The test decision is deterministic and can be automated by formalizing the SUT expected properties via predicate over traces. A Lurette oracle is a program that returns as first output a Boolean that formalizes some requirements. Lurette reports a property violation each time one oracle returns false. As oracles for reactive systems often involve time, a language where time is a first-class concept like Lustre [1] is a legitimate choice. Moreover, Lustre can formalise any safety property [4].

Coverage. To decide when to stop generating tests, we use a notion of *requirements coverage*. Consider the requirement "`stable(X,30)` $\Rightarrow$ `stable(Y,5)`" where the "`stable(V,n)`" predicate states if a variable V was stable during the last n seconds; it is always satisfied if X is never stable. But from a coverage point of view, it is more interesting to generate input sequences where X is stable. That is an example where random simulations are not sufficient and a language to program some guided scenarios is useful. Note also that if X is a SUT input, covering this requirement is easy. If X is an output, it is more complicated as it requests to drive the SUT, which sometimes require a deep expertise on its internals (but it is always the case when designing tests).

Lurette. Lurette handles the test harness, by reading test parameters, executing all the reactive systems in turn (SUT, environment, oracles), computing requirements coverage, and displaying a test report[1]. It does not impose the use of Lustre or Lutin. The reaction steps can be either time-triggered, event-triggered, or both. In the experimentations we report in this article, the SUT was time-triggered. More detailed presentations of Lurette can be found in [3,5]. We now present a few Lustre and Lutin programs to illustrate their main characteristics. We use those examples in the forthcoming sections.

---

[1] cf http://www-verimag.imag.fr/lurette.html for tools, manuals, and tutorials.

Lustre. Lustre allows defining reactive programs via sets of data-flow equations that are virtually executed in parallel. Equations are structured into nodes. Nodes transform input sequences into output sequences. The Lustre node `r_edge` below processes one Boolean input sequence, and computes one Boolean output sequence.

```
node r_edge(x:bool)returns(r:bool);
let
   r = x -> x and not pre(x);
tel
```

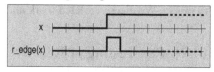

This node defines its output with one equation and four operators (i.e., predefined nodes). The memory operator "`pre`" gives access to the previous value in a sequence: if x holds the sequences $(x_1,x_2,...)$, then `pre(x)` holds $(\perp,x_1,x_2,...)$, where $\perp$ denotes an undefined value. The arrow operator "`->`" modifies the value of the first element of a sequence: if x holds $(x_1,x_2,x_3,...)$, then `init->x` holds $(init,x_2,x_3,...)$. This operator is useful for sequences that are undefined at their first instant, such as `pre(x)`. The "`and`" and "`not`" operators are the logical conjunction and negation lifted over sequences. Hence, `r_edge(x)` is equal to x at the first instant, and then is true if and only if x is true at the current instant and false at the previous one. This node detects rising edges.

Lutin. Lutin is a probabilistic extension of Lustre with an explicit control structure based on regular operators: sequence (`fby`, for "followed by"), Kleene star (`loop`), and choice (`|`). At each step, the Lutin interpreter (1) computes the set of reachable constraints, which depends on the current control-state; (2) removes from it unsatisfiable constraints, which depends on the current data-state (input and memories); (3) draws a constraint among the satisfiable ones (control-level non-determinism); (4) draws a point in the solution set of the constraint (data-level non-determinism). This chosen point defines the output for the current reaction. The solver of the current Lutin interpreter uses Binary Decision Diagrams (BDD) and convex polyhedron libraries [6]. It is thus able to deal with any combination of logical operators and linear constraints. Let us first illustrate the Lutin syntax and semantics with a program using equality constraints.

```
node sn_gen() returns (sn:int) =
loop[10,20] sn=1 fby
loop[20,30] sn=2
```

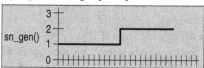

This node generates an integer finite sequence, without using any input. It first uses an atomic constraint that binds sn to 1, during between (uniformly) 10 and 20 reaction steps. Then it uses sn=2 during between 20 and 30 steps, and then stops. A constraint can actually have any number of solutions, as in the `x_gen` node below.

```
node x_gen(i:real) returns (x:real) = loop { 0<x and x<i }
```

At each step, the elected constraint is simplified by constant propagation of inputs and memories values, and solved. Here, when i is negative, the constraint is not satisfiable and the program stops. Otherwise, one solution is drawn in the solution set `]0;i[`.

Lutin also has a notion of typed macro, which is useful to structure constraints.

```
let abs(z: real):real = if z < 0.0 then -z else z
let zone1(x,y:real):bool = abs(x+3.0*y) < 3.0 and abs(20.0*x-y+2.0)<5.0
let zone4(x,y:real):bool = abs(x-y+6.0) < 3.0 and abs(-5.0*x+y-2.0)<7.0
```

The first macro defines the absolute value of any real. The next ones define two zones where a couple of real values (x,y) evolve. We present below a last example (used later) that illustrates how to use Lutin to guide the random exploration of the environment.

```
node x_y_gen() returns (x,y:real) =
  loop { {|3: zone1(x,y) |1: zone4(x,y)} fby loop~50:5 x=pre x and y=pre y }
```

For the first reaction, a point is drawn in zone1 with a probability of 3/(3+1)=0.75 or in zone4 with a probability of 1/(3+1)=0.25. Then x and y keep their previous values for 50 steps in average, with a standard deviation of 5. This process then starts again thanks to the outer loop. Preventing the environment outputs to change at each reaction produces better coverage for requirements guarded by stability conditions (which is common in control-command applications). More generally, a too chaotic environment might set the SUT into degraded modes, which would prevent the test of nominal modes. Lutin also has constructs to execute in parallel nodes (run) or constraints (&>), as well as exceptions [2].

3   Automatic Testing of an Alices Library Object

In this section we report on a case study provided by Corys, a 300 persons company that develops and commercializes the Alices workbench. Alices is a data-flow graphical programming language tool for modeling, simulating and analyzing dynamic systems in the domain of energy and transportation. Simulators of energy production plants implemented in Alices are typically used to train operators.

3.1   The SUT: The Node_Liquid_SPL Alices Object

Corys asked us to test one of their most frequently used library object, which is named Node_Liquid_SPL. This object simulates the behavior of the temperature and the pressure of a fluid in a pipe transporting homogeneous liquids through hydraulic networks. It is defined using mass and energy conservation equations:

$$\frac{dM}{dt} = \sum_i Q_{mi} \qquad \frac{dh}{dt} = \frac{\sum_i Q_{ei} - h \sum_i Q_{mi}}{M}$$

where $\sum_i Q_{mi}$ and $\sum_i Q_{ei}$ are respectively the sum of the mass flow (kg/s) and the sum of the powers arriving in the node; M and h are the mass (kg) and the mass enthalpy (J/kg) of the system; t is the time. The SUT is made of this object connected to two pipes, themselves connected to two objects (load loss) that models the fluid mass flow and transported power. The resulting equations are discretized and solved using the Newton-Raphson method. Table 1 describes the SUT input/output variables. We have shortened some variable names for the sake of readability.

---

[2] cf http://www-verimag.imag.fr/Lutin.html for more information.

Table 1. Description of the SUT input/output variables

Name	Producer	Meaning	Unit
Pin	Env.	Limit condition for input pressure	Pa
Pout	Env.	Limit condition for output pressure	Pa
Tin	Env.	Limit condition for input temperature	°c
Tout	Env.	Limit condition for output temperature	°c
T_amb	Env.	Temperature of the ambiant env	°c
Qe_amb	SUT	Power exchanged with the ambiant env	W
Qe1	SUT	Power exchanged with the first pipe	W
Qe2	SUT	Power exchanged with the second pipe	W
Qm1	SUT	Mass flow exchanged with the first pipe	kg/s
Qm2	SUT	Mass flow exchanged with the second pipe	kg/s
M	SUT	Mass of the system	kg
h	SUT	Mass enthalpy of the system	J/kg
T	SUT	Temperature of the system	°c

3.2 The SUT Environment

The input variables to stimulate this node are the limit conditions for the pressure (Pin and Pout), the temperature (Tin and Tout), and the ambient temperature (T_amb). The admissible values for those inputs are part of the object documentation, which states that pressure values vary within [10000.0, 190.0e5], and temperature values vary within [5.0, 365.0]. Moreover, Corys wanted to test this node in average conditions, and therefore required that the stimuli generator satisfies the following constraints:

- temperature and pressure cannot vary more than 10% between two instants;
- orders change only when mass and temperature values are stable (i.e., they do not change of more than 1% between two steps).

To stimulate the SUT, we therefore designed a Lutin program that is a direct formalization of the preceding constraints. We use the limit_der macro, which can be used both to test if an input varies more than a given percentage (limit_der(1.0,M) to test if M varies less than 1%), or to constraint the derivative of some output (limit_der(10.0,Pin) to constraint Pin to vary less than 10%).

```
let limit_der(pc:real; x:real ref):bool = abs(x-pre x) < abs(pc/100.0*pre x)
node liquid_spl_env(M, T: real) returns (
   Pin, Pout: real [10000.0; 190.0e5]; Tin,Tout,Tamb: real [5.0; 365.0];
) =
   -- a few aliases to make it more readable
let inputs_are_stable = limit_der(1.0,M) and limit_der(1.0,T) in
let dont_change = -- outputs keep their previous values
   Pin  = pre Pin  and Tin  = pre Tin  and
   Pout = pre Pout and Tout = pre Tout and Tamb = pre Tamb in
let change = -- outputs do not vary more than 10%
   limit_der(10.0,Pin) and limit_der(10.0,Pout) and
   limit_der(10.0,Tin) and limit_der(10.0,Tout) and limit_der(10.0,Tamb)
in -- a simple scenario
   true -- the first instant
   fby loop {if inputs_are_stable then change else dont_change}
```

The main node `liquid_spl_env` has two real inputs (produced by the SUT), and five real outputs. At the first instant, the only constraints on output variables are the ones mentioned in their declarations; a random value is drawn in their respective interval domains. For example, `Tamb` is drawn between 5 and 365. Then, for the remaining instants, variables keep their previous values if one of the environment input (`M` or `T`) varies more than 1%; otherwise they vary at random, but without exceeding 10%. One could of course imagine scenarios that are more complex. However, it hasn't been necessary to cover the expected properties we present in the following.

Note the feedback loop: the SUT reacts to its environment, which itself reacts to the SUT by testing the stability of `M` and `T`. This is typical of what offline test vectors generators cannot do when they ignore the reactive nature of the SUT.

3.3 The Oracles

In order to automate the test decision, we need to formalize the SUT expected properties. Actually, such requirements were not explicitly written in the object documentation. Hence we asked to the Corys engineer responsible for the Alices library to write down how he expects this object to behave. He came up with the following requirements.

1. **if** the sum of powers (coming from `Qe1`, `Qe2`, and `Qe_amb` sensors), **and** the sum of incoming mass flows (coming from `Qm1` and `Qm2` sensors) are positive, **then** the mass **and** the temperature of the node increase;
2. **if** the sum of powers `Qe`, **and** the sum of flows mass `Qm` are negative, **then** the mass and temperature of the node decrease;
3. **if** the sum of powers is zero, **and** the sum of mass flow rate `Qm` is positive, **then** the mass increases;
4. **if** the sum of `Qe` is zero, **and** the sum of mass flow rate `Qm` is negative, **then** the mass decreases;
5. **if** the sum of mass flows `Qm` is zero, **and** the sum of powers `Qe` is negative, **then** the temperature decreases;
6. **if** the sum of mass flows `Qm` is zero, **and** the sum of powers `Qe` is positive, **then** the temperature increases.

A possible Lustre formalization of the first requirement is:

```
Qe = Qe1+Qe2+Qe_amb;
Qm = Qm1+Qm2;
ok1 = (Qe >= 0.0 and Qm >= 0.0) => (increase(M, 0.0) and increase(T, 0.0));
```

where `increase` is defined like that:

```
node increase(x: real; threshold: real) returns (y: bool);
let y = true -> (x-pre(x) >= threshold); tel
```

When we run Lurette with the SUT, the environment, and the oracles we described, all oracles are violated after a few steps. After several discussions with the person who wrote down the requirements, we ended up in Lurette runs that worked fine for hours. We now sum-up the fixes we needed to perform.

First Problem. We have formalized the sentence "the sum of powers (coming from `Qe1`, `Qe2`, and `Qe_amb` sensors)", and "the sum of mass flows (coming from `Qm1` and `Qm2`") as `Qe=Qe1+Qe2+Qe_amb` and `Qm=Qm1+Qm2`. However, the node connectors are oriented: the first pipe flows in, whereas the second pipe flows out. Hence the correct interpretation leads to the following definitions: `Qe=Qe1-Qe2+Qe_amb` and `Qm=Qm1-Qm2`.

Second Problem. We have performed a bad interpretation of "are positive/negative" in the requirements. Indeed, when one compares to 0 a sum of values that are computed up to a certain precision (0.1 for flow mass, and 100 for powers), one has to specify some tolerance levels. Hence, for example, the second property should be rewritten as: "if `Qe<=-Tol_Qe` and `Qm<=-Tol_Qm` then the mass and temperature of the node decrease", where `Tol_Qe=300` (three times the precision of power sensors) and `Tol_Qm=0.2` (two times the precision of flow mass sensors).

Third Problem. In properties 5 and 6, the statements "the sum of powers `Qe` is positive" should take into account the mass enthalpy of the node (`Qe-h.Qm` instead of just `Qe`).

Fourth Problem. At this stage, the requirements fixes we have performed allow running simulations that last several minutes without violating oracles. After more steps (around 1000 steps in average), property 5 is violated. This time, the problem was more subtle and required a deeper investigation to the Corys engineer. His conclusion was that the convergence criteria (thresholds parametrizing the differential equation solver) in this simulation were too small. By setting a convergence criterion of 1 (versus 0.1) for the power, and of 1000 (versus 100) for the flow mass, no oracle is violated, even if we run the simulation for hours. Since the convergence criterion implies the precision of sensors computations, we need to modify again the values of `Tol_Qm` and `Tol_P`. Those new convergence criteria are actually the ones that are typically used in Alices for modeling pipes in power plants, which explain why this problem was (probably) never triggered before by Alices users.

Table 2. Summary of requirements fixes. Version 2 arises from the fixing of the first three problems. Version 3 arises from the fixing of the fourth problem.

Name	Unit	Meaning	Version 1	Version 2	Version 3	Involved Req.
Qm	kg/s	Sum of mass flow	Qm1+Qm2	Qm1-Qm2	ditto	all
Qe	W	Sum of powers	Qe1+Qe2+Qe_amb	Qe1-Qe2+Qe_amb	ditto	all
P	W	Node power	Qe	Qe-h.Qm	ditto	all
Tol_Qm	kg	Mass tolerance	0	0.2	2	3,4
Tol_P	W	Power tolerance	0	300	3000	1,2,5,6

3.4   Discussion and Lessons Learned from This First Experiment

The first three problems were due to a lack of precision when formulating requirements. One could argue that a specialist in physical systems simulators design would have interpreted such requirements correctly in the first place. Still, undoubtedly, the less a requirement is subject to a bad interpretation, the better it is. This experiment stresses out that Lurette can be seen as an engineering tool that helps to write consistent and precise requirements. The fourth problem was much more interesting for the Corys engineers and revealed a real feature of this very frequently used object that behaves unexpectedly when used with an unusual convergence criterion.

The principal lesson of this experimentation is that writing executable requirements is not that difficult and can be very effective. Indeed, the experiment was conducted by an engineer that was ignorant about Lustre, Lutin, Alices, and dynamic systems modeling. Still, he was able to pinpoint four issues in less than one week of work with a few interactions with the Alices libraries supervisor.

We performed a similar study during the COMON project on voters designed in Scade by Rolls-Royce. Their voters were much simpler, with no internal state. Hence their formalization into Lustre oracles ended up into something equivalent to the Scade implementation. We believe that using oracles in this context is still useful, as it amounts to have two teams implementing the same specification, which is a classical strategy to gain confidence in software implementations. In such cases, Lutin stimulators can still be useful to compare thoroughly two implementations. In the particular case of Rolls-Royce voters, it was not necessary as we were able to prove their equivalence by state exploration (using the Lesar model-checker [7]). This illustrates the synergy we can have between formal-based testing and formal verification.

4   Timed Test Plans Automation

4.1   Test Plans: A Standard Practice in Industry

A standard practice in industry is to base test campaigns on *test plans*. The test plans of our three partners in the COMON project were actually very similar, and were made of a three columns table: one for the time (physical or logical); one for the stimulation, that specifies what the tester should do to perform the test; and one last column that specifies what the tester should observe in reaction to its stimulations. Corys developed in collaboration with EDF and AREVA a tool (I&C Simulation) to automate the play of such test plans, both for the stimulation and the decision parts. This tool processes scripts, where one can ask to set a variable to a particular value at a specific time; and then one can check that another variable take a specific value at another specific time.

One problem with such test plans, being automated or not, is that they are overly deterministic, both at the data and at the temporal levels. In the case studies we addressed so far with Lurette, the strategy was different as it consisted in writing high-level constraints both for generating several stochastic scenarios (Lutin), and for checking several traces (Lustre). This allows covering much more cases with the same specifications.

Nevertheless, engineers are used to write test plans, and several years of know-how are associated to their design. This is why we find interesting to report how Lutin and Lustre could be used to implement test plans, and to show how easy it can be to add a little bit of data and temporal looseness.

In this section, we present a test plan provided by Atos, targeting a generic library object. This plan was extracted from an existing test campaign conducted some years ago. We first demonstrate how to automate the play of this test plan in a very faithful and deterministic manner, as it could have been done with the I&C Simulation tool of Corys for example. Then we demonstrate the benefits of our languages to relax and generalize the constraints on both the stimulation and the observation part, which leads to tests that cover more cases, and are easier to maintain.

4.2   The SUT: A SCADA Generic Object

A SCADA (Supervisory Control and Data Acquisition [8]) is a remote management system for large-scale processing in many real time telemetry and remote control industrial installations (manufacturing, food processing, energy). It typically handles in real-time thousands of data (e.g., coming from sensors), and presents a relevant synthesis in graphical form to operators so they can monitor and control the system. Atos develops and commercialises several SCADA dedicated to the supervisory and control of power generating plants (nuclear, fuel, gas).

The purpose of the generic object we want to test is to monitor the operating area of a pair of numeric values (which typically comes from the physical process) and to raise alarms when dreaded events occur. The space where the monitored point evolves in is divided into several operating domains (nominal, degraded, etc.), and into several zones. When the point enters in a *forbidden zone*, an alarm should be raised; when it remains in an *accumulating zone* too long, another alarm should be raised; in an *authorized zone*, there is nothing to check. The zones shapes differ for each domain. The system chooses a domain, depending on various criteria on the evolution of the operating point. The operator can ask to favor some domain, and he can force it (i.e., ask more categorically). The number and the shape of domains (that can overlap) and zones are parameters of the generic object.

The SUT is such a parametrized object, with four domains and five zones; zone 2 is forbidden; zones 3 and 5 are accumulating; zones 1 and 4 are authorized. The SUT environment is made of two integers (X and Y) that hold the monitored point coordinates, and three Boolean inputs per domain so that the operator can ask to choose a domain (dd1 to dd4), force a domain (fd1 to fd4), or un-force it (ud1 to ud4).

The Test Plan CRT_019_S04. The existing test campaign we based our work on consisted in 21 test plans. The CRT_019_S04 is one of them, and is shown in Table 3. This test plan is split into seven logical steps, and four stages. At each step, the operator sets the values of variables mentioned in the action column, and checks (visually) that the system behaves as specified in the expected result column.

The Atos I/O Stimulator. In order to ease the test of their SCADA objects, Atos developed an in-house tool called the Input/Output stimulator. This tool processes scripts, and is basically able to (1) set SCADA internal variable values; (2) display messages; (3) suspend the script until the operator presses a key (WAIT). This stimulator is used to ease the play of test plans by automating the run of the action column, and to limit the intervention of the operator to a few key presses. In the CRT_019_S04 plan, each of the four stages actually corresponds to a WAIT statement in the corresponding I/O stimulator script. The tester does the expected results checking.

4.3   Implementing Automated Test Plans with Lutin and Lustre

The first step to implement with Lurette an automated version of this test plan was to connect our languages APIs to the Atos SCADA. To do that, we re-used the infrastructure that was set up for the I/O stimulator. We also added a layer in charge of interfacing an event-triggered workbench (SCADA) with time-triggered programs (Lutin/Lustre). From

Table 3. The CRT_019_S04 test plan

step nb	Action	Expected result / Comment
1	Launch stage 1 which elects domain 1 and sets X,Y to (25,40) (in zone 1)	Check the image display
2	Launch stage 2 which sets X,Y to (40,28) in the forbidden zone 2	Check the operating point (position, color) Check the alarm raised in the alarm function Write down the timestamp
3	Launch stage 3, which elects domain 2 instead of domain 1	Check that the alarm above remains at the timestamp of step 2 X,Y remains in the forbidden zone 2
4	Force domain 3	Check that the alarm above remains at the timestamp of step 2 X,Y remains in the forbidden zone 2
5	Force domain 4	The alarm above disappear X,Y is now in an authorized zone 4
6	Unforce domain 4	The alarm is raised at the current timestamp domain 2 is elected X,Y is back in the forbidden zone 2
7	Launch stage 4 which sets X,Y to (-9,25) in the authorized zone 4	The alarm disappears X,Y in the authorized zone 4

Lurette to SCADA, we generate an event each time a variable value changes (up to a given threshold). From SCADA to Lurette, we perform a periodic sampling of the variable values. This sampling is done at 1 hertz, to avoid data race problems and to remain deterministic and reproducible: indeed, 1 second is enough for the SUT to address all events resulting from the change of all interface variables. Note that it would have been easy and interesting to test what happens at higher rates.

The « Expected result » column of Table 3 in Lustre. In order to detect bad behaviors, we formalize the observation column of the CRT_019_S04 test plan with a Lustre oracle that monitors the following inputs: the step number ($sn \in [1,7]$) ; the current zone ($czone \in [1,5]$); the alarm of zone 2 (A2); the elected domain (d_elec); the current timestamp (ts_c); and the timestamp of alarm A2 (ts_a2). Here again, we have shortened variable names for the sake of readability.

```
node crt019_s04(sn:int; czone:int; A2:bool; d_elec,ts_c,ts_a2:int)
returns(ok : bool);
var ok1,ok2,ok3,ok4,ok5,ok6,ok7:bool; lts_a2:int;
let
  lts_a2 = 0 -> if r_edge(A2) then ts_c else pre(lts_a2);
  ok1 = (sn=1 => (czone=1));
  ok2 = (sn=2 => (czone=2 and A2));
  ok3 = (sn=3 => (czone=2 and A2 and ts_a2=lts_a2));
  ok4 = (sn=4 => (czone=2 and A2 and ts_a2=lts_a2));
  ok5 = (sn=5 => (czone=4 and not A2));
  ok6 = (sn=6 => (czone=2 and d_elec=2 and ts_a2=ts_c));
  ok7 = (sn=7 => (czone=4 and not A2));
  ok  = ok1 and ok2 and ok3 and ok4 and ok5 and ok6 and ok7;
tel
```

The local variables ok1 to ok7 encode the seven steps of the third column. In order to « write down the timestamp » at step 2, we define a local variable lts_a2 as follows: initially set to 0, it then takes the value of the current timestamp ts_c when A2 is raised (r_edge(A2)), and keeps its previous value otherwise (pre(lts_a2)). To encode the expected result of steps 3 and 4, we compare the timestamp of the A2 provided in input ts_a2 with its counterpart computed locally lts_a2.

The « action » column of Table 3 in Lutin. We first present a completely deterministic Lutin program that mimics the behavior of an operator that processes this test plan. Then we show how slight modifications of this program can lead to a stimuli generator that covers much more cases. Let us first define a few Boolean macros to enhance the programs readability. The tfff macro below binds its first parameter to true, and all the other ones to false.

```
let tfff(x,y,z,t:bool):bool = x and not y and not z and not t
```

Similarly, we define ftff, which binds its second parameter to true; f7 and f8 bind all their parameters to false. The integer input sn is used to choose the instant at which we change the step. It can be controlled by a physical operator or by another Lutin node that sequentially assigns values from 1 to 7 (similar to the sn_gen node of Section 2). The fourteen outputs of this node controls the domain to display (display domain i if ddi is true), to force (force domain i if fdi is true), or to un-force (un-force domain i if udi is true).

```
node crt019_s04(sn:int) returns
(X, Y: real; dd1,dd2,dd3,dd4, fd1,fd2,fd3,fd4, ud1,ud2,ud3,ud4: bool) =
loop {
    sn=1 and X=25.0 and Y=40.0 and tfff(dd1,dd2,dd3,dd4) and
    f8(fd1,fd2,fd3,fd4,ud1,ud2,ud3,ud4)
```

As long as the sn input is equal to 1, the outputs of the crt019_s04 node satisfy the constraint above that states that only the first domain should be displayed, and no domain is forced or unforced. X and Y are set in the authorized zone 1. When sn becomes equal to 2, the control passes to the constraint below, which is the same as the previous one except that the point is set somewhere in zone 2.

```
} fby loop {
    sn=2 and X=40.0 and Y=28.0 and tfff(dd1,dd2,dd3,dd4) and
    f8(fd1,fd2,fd3,fd4,ud1,ud2,ud3,ud4)
} fby loop {
    sn=3 and X=40.0 and Y=28.0 and ftff(dd1,dd2,dd3,dd4) and
    f8(fd1,fd2,fd3,fd4,ud1,ud2,ud3,ud4)
} fby loop {
    sn=4 and X=40.0 and Y=28.0 and ftff(dd1,dd2,dd3,dd4) and
    fd3 and f7(fd1,fd2,    fd4,ud1,ud2,ud3,ud4)
} fby loop {
    sn=5 and X=40.0 and Y=28.0 and ftff(dd1,dd2,dd3,dd4) and
    fd4 and f7(fd1,fd2,fd3,    ud1,ud2,ud3,ud4)
} fby loop {
    sn=6 and X=40.0 and Y=28.0 and ftff(dd1,dd2,dd3,dd4) and
    ud4 and f7(fd1,fd2,fd3,fd4,ud1,ud2,ud3   )
} fby loop {
    sn = 7 and X=-9.0 and Y=25.0 and ftff(dd1,dd2,dd3,dd4) and
    f8(fd1,fd2,fd3,fd4,ud1,ud2,ud3,ud4)
}
```

This Lutin program, once run with the oracle of Section 4.3, allows test automation. However, it suffers from the same flaw as its original non-automated counterpart: it can be tedious to maintain. Indeed, if for some reason, the shape of zone 1 is changed, the chosen point (25,40) might no longer be part of zone 1. Choosing pseudo-randomly any point in zone 1 using the Lutin constraint solver makes the plan more robust to software evolution. Moreover, with the same effort, it covers much more cases. In the same spirit, we can further loosen this plan by replacing "choose a point in the authorized zone 1" by "choose a point in any authorized zone" (cf the x_y_gen node of Section 2). In step 3, 4, and 5, we could also toss the choice of the domain to be forced. Actually, by loosening this plan in this way, we obtain a plan that covers more cases than the twenty other plans of the test campaign!

4.4 Discussion and Lessons Learned from This Second Experiment

The original test plan was not deterministic, since the time between each step change was controlled by a physical tester. However, this non-determinism is easy to simulate with Lutin, for example using the sn generator (sn_gen) presented in Section 2. The advantage of the Lutin non-determinism over the human one is its reproducible nature. Indeed, one just needs to store the seed used by the Lutin pseudo-random engine to be able to replay the exact same simulation.

This test plan does not illustrate the feedback capability of Lurette. However, plans where the tester should perform some specific actions depending on some behavior of the SUT are very common.

We have shown a way to use Lurette and its associated languages to automate the run of an existing test plan, designed to be exercised by a human operator. The initial set-up for automated plans seems to require more effort, as each variable behavior has to be described precisely at each step, while the original plan was more allusive. But the Lurette version has four major advantages: (1) it can be run automatically, (2) each run is reproducible, (3) it covers (much!) more cases, and (4) it is more robust to software (or specification) evolutions.

The two last points are the most important. Indeed, Atos experimented with completely automated test scripts, but gave up as they were too difficult to maintain. One reason was that their scripts were too sensitive to minor time or data values changes. The use of languages with a clean semantics with respect to time and parallelism eases the writing of more abstract and general properties that can serve as oracles for several test scenarios. The concision and the robustness arguments hold both for the oracles and the stimulators, and from the data and the temporal points of view.

In previous experimentations ([3,5] and Section 3), the methodology was to derive oracles and stimulators from informal requirements. The initial stimulator is made of very general constraints. Then, to increase oracles coverage, Lutin scenarios are designed. During the COMON project, we also experimented with this methodology on the SCADA object, and the coverage was actually comparable. This "direct formalization approach" is more modular, as some variables sets can be defined separately, whereas with test plans, one needs to describe all variables at the same time. Moreover, it allows writing specific scenarios only when it is necessary, as some oracles are covered in the first place using simple constraints on the environment. Once all the easy cases are explored at random with a minimal effort, it remains the difficult work that consists in driving the SUT to set it in some configurations that exhibit interesting cases. This is a work of SUT experts. Leveraging testers from the tedious and systematic part, and letting them focus on interesting parts using high-level languages could restore the interest in testing, which often has a poor reputation. Writing Lutin programs is a creative activity, and generalising its use could ease to relocate test teams.

5 Related Work

Automating the test decision with executable oracles is a simple and helpful idea used by many others. The real distinction between Lurette and other tools lies in the way SUT inputs are generated. In the following, we group approaches according to the input generation techniques: source-based, model-based, or environment-model based. We found no work dealing with automated testing of SCADA systems. For dynamical systems workbenches (such as Alices), the literature is quite abundant, and mostly concerns Simulink [9]. Hence we focus here on works targeting Simulink, and refer to the related work section of [3] for a broader and complementary positioning of Lurette in the test of reactive systems.

Source Code Based Testing (White-Box). The White-box testing approach consists in trying to increase structural coverage by analysing the SUT source using techniques coming from formal verification such as model-checking [10], constraint solving, or search-based exploration [11,12]. Such approaches are completely automated, but can be confronted to the same limitations as formal verification with respect to state space explosion. Several industrial tools use white-box techniques to test Simulink designs, e.g., Safety Test Builder [13], or Design Verifier [14].

Model-Based Testing (Grey-Box). A very popular approach in the literature [15,16] consists in viewing the SUT as a black-box, and designing a more or less detailed model of it. This model should be faithful enough to provide valuable insights, and small enough to be analyzable. The model structure is sometimes used to define coverage criteria. The model is used both for the test decision and the stimuli generation. T-VEC [17,18] and Reactis Tester [19] are an industrial tools using this approach to generate tests offline. With Lurette, we also use a model of the SUT, but this model is only used for oracles. The input generation is developed by exploration of environment models. A way to combine this approach with Lurette would be to use such models of the SUT to generate Lutin scenarios to guide the SUT to specific states and increase coverage.

Environment Model Based Testing (Black-Box). While the white-box approach intends to increase structural coverage, the main goal of black-box testing is to increase (functional) requirements coverage [20]. Time Partition Testing (TPT) is an industrial black-box tool distributed by Piketec [21]. As Lurette, TPT have its own formalism to model the environment and automate the SUT stimulation [22,23]. It is a graphical formalism based on hierarchical hybrid automata that is able to react online on the SUT outputs. The major difference with Lutin is that those automata are deterministic. It uses python oracles to automate the test decision, although Lustre is arguably better for specifying high-level timed properties.

Another way to explore the environment state space, which has been experimented on Simulink programs [24,25], is to perform heuristic search (evolutionary algorithms, simulated annealing [26]). The idea is to associate to each SUT input a set of possible parametrized generators (ramp, sinus, impulse, spline). The search algorithms generate input sequences playing with several parameters, such as the number of steps each generator is used, their order, or the amplitude of the signal. A fitness function estimates the distance of the trace to the requirements. Then, another trace is generated with other parameters, until an optimal solution is found. A limitation of their generators is that they are not able to react to SUT outputs. More generally, for systems that have a complex internal state, it can be very difficult to drive it in some specific operating mode; to do that, the knowledge of the expert is mandatory (and being able to react to SUT outputs too). Instead of guiding a random exploration via heuristics, Lurette proposal consists in asking experts to write programs that performs a guided random exploration of the SUT input state space. A way to combine both approaches could be to let some evolutionary algorithms choose some parameters of Lutin programs, such as choice point weights or variable bounds.

6 Conclusion

The main lesson of the first experimentation is that writing executable requirements is not that difficult and allows to write precise and consistent requirements. This study gave new insights to Corys engineers on one of their most frequently used object.

The second experimentation demonstrates a way to automate the execution of timed test plans. Test plans are commonly used in industry, and automating their process aroused a big interest within our industrial partners. Lutin and Lustre allows improving their use by permitting the design of more abstract test plans that are more robust to temporal and data changes. One noteworthy outcome of this study is that the resulting randomized and automated test plan actually covers more than the 21 test plans of the original test suite.

There is a synergy between automated oracles and automated stimulus generation. Indeed, generating thousands of simulation traces would be useless without automatic test decision. Conversely, designing executable requirements to automate the decision of a few scenarios generated manually might not be worth the effort.

This work also demonstrates that synchronous languages are not only useful for designing critical systems (as the success of Scade gives evidence of), but can also be used to validate dynamic systems models (Alices) or event-based asynchronous systems (SCADA). The language-based approach of Lurette allows performing several kinds of test (unit, integration, system, non-regression) on various domains [3,5].

From an industrial use perspective, a general-purpose library and specialized domain-based ones are still to be done. That situation may progress in the near future, as the interest expressed in Lurette by the three industrial partners of the COMON project is one of the reasons that convinced people to establish in 2013 the Argosim company. Argosim is developing the Stimulus tool based on the Lurette principles [27].

References

1. Halbwachs, N., Caspi, P., Raymond, P., Pilaud, D.: The synchronous dataflow programming language Lustre. Proceedings of the IEEE 79(9), 1305–1320 (1991)
2. Raymond, P., Roux, Y., Jahier, E.: Lutin: a language for specifying and executing reactive scenarios. EURASIP Journal on Embedded Systems (2008)

3. Jahier, E., Halbwachs, N., Raymond, P.: Engineering functional requirements of reactive systems using synchronous languages. In: International Symposium on Industrial Embedded Systems, SIES 2013, Porto, Portugal (2013)

4. Halbwachs, N., Fernandez, J.C., Bouajjanni, A.: An executable temporal logic to express safety properties and its connection with the language lustre. In: ISLIP 1993, Quebec (1993)

5. Jahier, E., Raymond, P., Baufreton, P.: Case studies with lurette v2. Software Tools for Technology Transfer 8(6), 517–530 (2006)

6. Jahier, E., Raymond, P.: Generating random values using binary decision diagrams and convex polyhedra. In: CSTVA, Nantes, France (2006)

7. Raymond, P.: Synchronous program verification with lustre/lesar. In: Modeling and Verification of Real-Time Systems. ISTE/Wiley (2008)

8. Bailey, D., Wright, E.: Practical SCADA for industry. Elsevier (2003)

9. The Mathworks: Simulink/stateflow, http://www.mathworks.com

10. Hamon, G., de Moura, L., Rushby, J.: Generating efficient test sets with a model checker. In: Software Engineering and Formal Methods, pp. 261–270 (2004)

11. Satpathy, M., Yeolekar, A., Ramesh, S.: Randomized directed testing (redirect) for simulink/stateflow models. In: Proceedings of the 8th ACM International Conference on Embedded Software, EMSOFT 2008, pp. 217–226. ACM, New York (2008)

12. Zhan, Y., Clark, J.A.: A search-based framework for automatic testing of MATLAB/Simulink models. Journal of Systems and Software 81(2), 262–285 (2008)

13. TNI Software: Safety Test Builder, http://www.geensoft.com/fr/article/safetytestbuilder/

14. The Mathworks: Design verifier, http://www.mathworks.com/products

15. Broy, M., Jonsson, B., Katoen, J.-P., Leucker, M., Pretschner, A. (eds.): Model-Based Testing of Reactive Systems. LNCS, vol. 3472. Springer, Heidelberg (2005)

16. Zander, J., Schieferdecker, I., Mosterman, P.J.: 1. In: A Taxonomy of Model-based Testing for Embedded Systems from Multiple Industry Domains, pp. 3–22. CRC Press (2011)

17. T-VEC: T-vec tester, http://www.t-vec.com

18. Blackburn, M., Busser, R., Nauman, A., Knickerbocker, R., Kasuda, R.: Mars polar lander fault identification using model-based testing. In: 8th IEEE International Conference on Engineering of Complex Computer Systems, pp. 163–169 (2002)

19. Reactive Systems: Testing and validation of simulink models with reactis white paper

20. Cu, C., Jeppu, Y., Hariram, S., Murthy, N., Apte, P.: A new input-output based model coverage paradigm for control blocks. In: 2011 IEEE Aerospace Conference, pp. 1–12 (2011)

21. Piketec: Tpt, http://www.piketec.com

22. Lehmann, E.: Time partition testing: A method for testing dynamic functional behaviour. In: Proceedings of TEST 2000, London, Great Britain (2000)

23. Bringmann, E., Kramer, A.: Model-based testing of automotive systems. In: 2008 1st International Conference on Software Testing, Verification, and Validation, pp. 485–493 (2008)

24. Vos, T.E., Lindlar, F.F., Wilmes, B., Windisch, A., Baars, A.I., Kruse, P.M., Gross, H., Wegener, J.: Evolutionary functional black-box testing in an industrial setting. Software Quality Control 21(2), 259–288 (2013)

25. Baresel, A., Pohlheim, H., Sadeghipour, S.: Structural and functional sequence test of dynamic and state-based software with evolutionary algorithms. In: Cantú-Paz, E., et al. (eds.) GECCO 2003. LNCS, vol. 2724, pp. 2428–2441. Springer, Heidelberg (2003)

26. McMinn, P.: Search-based software test data generation: a survey: Research articles. Softw. Test. Verif. Reliab. 14(2), 105–156 (2004)

27. Argosim: Stimulus, http://www.argosim.com

Author Index